THE OFFICIAL®
PRICE GUIDE TO

BY
RUTH M. POLLARD

SEVENTH EDITION
THE HOUSE OF COLLECTIBLES, WESTMINSTER, MD 21157

Published by: The House of Collectibles
               P.O. Box 149
               Westminster, Maryland 21157
               Phone: (301) 583-6959

Distributed by Ballantine Books, a division of Random House, Inc., New York and simultaneously in Canada by Random House of Canada Limited, Toronto.

Manufactured in the United States of America

Library of Congress Catalog Card Number: 84-643009
ISBN: 0-87637-296-5
10 9 8 7 6 5 4 3 2 1

TABLE OF CONTENTS

ACKNOWLEDGMENTS

I wish to express my deepest thanks to all the wonderful artists and publishers who submitted material and photos in order that we might bring to you a current book full of information. There are so many in the business that space will not allow the listing of all the individual names. However, I do thank each and every one, especially Ron Faner, Cynthia Bogart, Sandra Giangiulio, and Lena Y. Liu for providing the cover photographs. Also my thanks go to the wonderful network of dealers who are supporting this project. A very special thanks to Mr. and Mrs. John Rudisill, The Alt Print Haus, and Sandy Verdin, Icart vendor, for their valuable assistance in special categories.

PICTURE COPYRIGHTS

ATTENTION ARTISTS

All artists, including those listed in the guide and those who want to be included, are encouraged to send their current address and their galleries' addresses to The House of Collectibles. Before the next edition of the OFFICIAL PRICE GUIDE TO COLLECTOR PRINTS is issued, the House of Collectibles will contact each artist for their information.

Artists should send their addresses to The House of Collectibles, Attn Prints, P.O. Box 149, Westminster, MD 21157.

NOTE TO READERS

MARKET REVIEW

This past year has seen an increasing interest in Americana and country prints on the collector print market. Such artists as P. Buckley Moss and Charles Wysocki are enjoying continuing success in this field. The old prints of Norman Rockwell and Currier & Ives are best-sellers, too.

However, no time in our history has ever captured the American spirit as much as the Old West. Western art is increasingly popular and has taken an esteemed place beside wildlife art on the current market. Last year, The Cowboy Artists of America held an exhibition at the Phoenix Art Museum in Arizona. This prestigious art show attracted the attention of artists, critics, and art patrons from all over the globe. Over 100 oils, sketches, watercolors, and bronzes were displayed by the artists who make up this fine organization. This highly respected art event lasted one month and was considered an international success.

Earlier this year, Bev Doolittle was selected "Western Artist of the Year," and Guy Coheleach "Wildlife Artist of the Year" at the annual Wildlife and Western Art Exhibition, now in its fifth year. This Minneapolis show, sponsored by the National Wildlife and Western Art Collectors Society, featured over 175 artists with attendance reaching well over 15,000. Other artists featured included David Maass, Olaf Wieghorst, Owen Gromme, and Robert Abbett.

In other events, The Leigh Yawkey Woodson Art Museum was the sight for the "Birds in Art" exhibit recently. This traveling exhibition included over 130 original artworks depicting gamebirds, waterfowl, and other birds in their natural environment. This exhibition also featured a salute to the 50th Anniversary of Roger Tory Peterson's field guide.

A party was held recently in New York to raise money for children's cancer treatment programs. The event, hosted by columnist Sylvia Porter, industrial tycoon Armand Hammer, and singer Perry Como, raised over $30,000 and marked the opening of artist Bob Timberlake's fifth one-man show there.

Furthermore, an astounding 82,000 people were in attendance at an art exposition held in Texas recently. Show management reported that a record $30 million worth of art was sold. This show also brought an increase in the exhibitors and countries featured.

Exhibitions and expositions are not the only things boosting the print market these days. Four of Frame House Gallery's artists have been a source of collector attention recently.

Charles Harper was recently commissioned to do a painting to promote "Water Awareness" in Kentucky. This painting, to be distributed as a poster, will be used to coax citizen groups into "adopting" a local body of water.

Artist Jim Harrison was commissioned by Women Involved in Rural Electrification (WIRE) to do a painting commemorating their 50th Anniversary, while Ray Harm won the Appalachian Gold Medallion from the University of Charleston. Harm was chosen because of his close relationship with the region and because he depicted their unique culture in "a profound and compelling way." He is the first artist to receive this award.

In addition, Dave Chapple was commissioned by the National Wild Turkey Foundation to paint the "First of State" Wild Turkey stamp and print for California.

Last year, the work of wildlife artist John Ruthven was presented to representatives of the Soviet government. This year, John Ruthven presented his opaque watercolor "Wild Boar" to Crown Prince Henri of Luxembourg.

There have also been new releases from almost every artist represented in this book, including Nancy Taylor Stonington, Maynard Reece, and M.C. Poulsen. Every artist represented here is an outstanding, award-winning master of his craft. An investment in any of the works listed here should be looked upon as a wise choice.

PRINTMAKING PROCESSES

Following is a brief description of the three common forms of printmaking. These include original lithograph, offset lithograph, and serigraph.

Original lithographs are made from hand drawn stones or plates. With the stone method, the artist does not engrave the stone, but rather paints on it like a canvas. The artist must reverse his drawing so when it is transferred to the paper it will be viewed in the proper perspective. For illustrating, the artist can use several items from crayons to brushes.

After the drawing is finished, a solution of gum arabic, water, and nitric acid is used to act as a protection against any air or dust particles. Since the stone must be kept wet during printing, the solution also prevents any alterations of the drawing.

The plate process is very similar to the stone method. Using pencils, pens, or brushes, the artist draws on the plate. The images on the plates are transferred to aluminum plates, which are then wetted with a solution to retard drying. Next the plates are rolled with ink. The non-image areas of the plate reject the ink while the image areas accept it. To hold the plates in the correct position, registration pins are used. Pressure created by the roller forces the ink against the paper and an image is made.

Color lithographs are difficult because a stone or plate must be made for each color used. Then, the stones or plates must register perfectly on the paper to have the color fall in the correct place. Therefore, the artist and lithographer must work closely together to obtain the correct color and ultimately the finished print.

An **offset lithograph** is a photomechanical reproduction of the original work. By using filters over a camera lens, particulars colors are separated. The result is a halftone negative. When this method first began, only four basic colors were used to print. Today, it is common to use ten or more halftones to reproduce the artist's work. Through this advancement, it is difficult to tell the original painting from the print.

Each halftone is transferred to a metal plate. The plates are put on a printing press with a rubber-blanketed roller. Each time the paper is fed through the press the registration of each color must be perfect to obtain the finished print. Reproductions vary from 500 to 5,000. The plates are destroyed in a limited edition series.

Serigraph or silk screening is a method of printing using a squeegie. The squeegie forces the ink through a screen in which a stencil forms the area where the ink is to go. A different screen or set of stencils is used for each color. With each screen, one can print solid colors but not graduated values.

Prints can be made on all types of surfaces including paper, cardboard, glass, or metal.

Old prints are works of art made before photomechanical reproduction began. They were reproduced by hand printing and were hand colored.

Some famous artists of old prints include Nathaniel Currier and James Ives, John James Audubon, and Louis Icart.

Determining values is complicated. Several factors are used to compile prices including authenticity, subject, condition, size, artist's workmanship, printing technique, quality of material, and the artist himself.

This book includes some of the more popular artists among old print collectors.

PAPER RESTORATION SPECIALISTS

American Association of
Conservators and Restorers
1250 E. Ridgewood Ave.
Ridgewood, NJ 07450

Mr. Arthur Beale
The Center For Conservation and
Technical Studies
Fogg Art Museum
Harvard University
Cambridge, MA 02138

Ms. Brigitte Boyadjian
43 Fern Street
Lexington, MA 02173

Brooklyn Museum
Brooklyn, NY 11238

Art Institute of Chicago
Chicago, IL 60603

Conservation Center of the Institute
of Fine Arts
New York University
1 East 78th Street
New York, NY 10028

Ms. Christa M. Gaehde
55 Falmouth Road
Arlington, MA 02174

Ms. Mary Todd Glaser
73 E. Linden Avenue
Englewood, NJ 07631

Graphic Conversation Company
325 W. Huron, Room 408
Chicago, IL 60610

Mr. Robert A. Hauser
Busyhaus
P.O. Box 422
North Andover, MA 01845

Mrs. Florence Hodes
145 Central Park West
New York, NY 10023

Mrs. Carolyn Horton
430 W. 22nd Street
New York, NY 10011

Murray Lebwohl Studio, Inc.
1212 I Street
Alexandria, VA 22307

Ms. Edith MacKennan
11 Rosalind Road
Poughkeepsie, NY 12601

Museum of Modern Art
11 W. 53rd Street
New York, NY 10019

National Gallery of Art
Washington, DC 20565

Ms. Wynne H. Phelan
3721 Ella Lee Lane
Houston, TX 77027

Pennsylvania Academy of Fine Arts
Philadelphia, PA 19102

John Pofelski
190 South Wood Dale Road
Wood Dale, IL 60191

Ms. Shirley J. Riddick
6561 Hil-Mar Drive, #203
Forestville, MD 20028

Ms. Marilyn Weidner
612 Spruce Street
Philadelphia, PA 19106

GLOSSARY

ALBUM A portfolio or series of prints.

ANNOTE Marked, designated, numbered.

AQUATINT A process used in etching or engraving to obtain effects similar to a wash.

ARTIST A painter, engraver, sculptor, etc. who creates an original artwork. The word "Painter" is often misused for a person who has created a work of art.

ARTIST PROOF A term used in printmaking processes meaning the plate which the artist must approve before the final prints are reproduced.

AVANT LA LETTRE Dedications, descriptions, lettering. Frequently added after the print has been finished and proofed. Proofs made before **Avant La Lettre** are quite rare and usually command high prices.

BLEED When the picture image extends beyond the margin of the paper or the paper's edge so there is no border.

BRUSH STROKED A clear plastic material which has the consistency of regular paint and is brushed on a picture and allowed to dry. This creates an illusion of being an original rather than a photomechanically reproduced print.

BURIN A needle used in engraving, especially used on copper.

CATALOG OF PRINTS The graphic work of an artist, cataloged and numbered with notes for easy identification of the prints. Normally contains title, date, edition, and description of various works which exist at that time.

CANCELLED PLATE A metal plate which has been defaced or destroyed. In offset lithography, the plates are cancelled to insure a limited edition.

CHROMOLITH A highly refined photomechanical reproductive process whereby an exact reproduction of a picture is produced. Tone, line, and color are reproduced not by the reduction of an original to a pattern of dots, but by taking a negative directly from the original in such a way that a reproductive plate can be made that precisely incorporates all of the continuous tones of the original. (Not to be confused with **Chromolithography**.)

CHROMOLITHOGRAPHY Printing lithographs in color from several plates.

COLLECTION An accumulation of a number of pieces of art.

COLLECTOR'S MARK It is the custom of some collectors and most museums to place a mark or monogram on the back of a print identifying it as part of a collection.

COLLOTYPE A process for making very high quality photomechanical reproductions. Normally used for printing on a soft finish or handmade paper. Reproduces with great fidelity the most delicate gradations of tone. Contains no dot process as does offset lithographs.

COLOR SEPARATION A term used in photomechanical reproduction which refers to the number of different plates used in separating colors from the original painting.

COMMISSION An order placed with an artist for an original work of art.

CONDITION Referred to as the preservation of a print. Faultless or mint means no marks, no creases, no finger marks, or absolutely perfect. Nice means very few or very slight markings with no creases. Poor means print has had careless handling with dominant creases and marks plainly visible.

CONDITIONS OF SALE Means terms set down in writing between print owner and gallery.

COPY Facsimile of another piece.

COLOUR The proper term for a lithograph printed from various plates in color.

DECKLE EDGE An irregular, untrimmed edge of paper.

DRY MOUNT Means to glue a picture to a stiff board or cardboard by means of a dry adhesive. Never recommended for a fine print or reproduction. Should be used only as a last resort to salvage a badly damaged print.

DRY STAMP Used by publishers to verify the genuineness of prints.

EDITION Number produced from a plate. Edition number does not usually include any artist's proofs pulled from the plate. There are regular and special editions.

ENGRAVING Design is cut into plate by means of a **"burin."** A type of intaglio.

EPREUVE A proof. There are artist's, trial, state, and printer's proofs.

ETAT If this appears on a print it means a proof was pulled at some stage prior to completion for the artist to determine if he is attaining the desired effect or to detect any errors and correct them prior to the final printing.

ETCHING The process of producing pictures by printing from a metal surface which has been etched. The artist draws the design into the acid-resistant wax. The plate is then placed in an acid solution which "burns" the design into the plate where the wax has been removed. The wax is then removed, ink is applied to the plate, and a print is pulled.

FILLET A small divider used in the rabbet of a frame to hold a print away from the glass to protect it from damage due to moisture condensation. This term is sometimes used to describe the thin area of a second color mat used by many framers.

FOXING A term used to describe damage found on prints. It is characterized by small dark stains, sometimes with a darker center, which resemble iron rust (but which are usually a species of mold) appearing anywhere on the picture.

GRAPHIC A nondescript term; used when referring to an original print.

HORS DE COMMERCE Means a print outside or apart from. Not for sale.

ILLUSTRATION A term used for drawings or original works of art.

IMAGE SIZE Means size of the picture area only, not the size of paper.

IMPRESSIONS The number of times a picture has been printed from a plate.

INK A colored liquid material used for printing.

INTAGLIO One of four techniques of original printmaking where the image is sunk below the surface of the print.

JAPON A Japanese paper.

JAUNIE Means yellowing of the paper, often occurs with age.

LITHOGRAPH There are two types of lithographs. An original lithograph is produced by an artist drawing directly on a stone or plate. Offset lithographs are produced by a photo-mechanical method.

MAT A cardboard material, used as decorative trim when framing.

MEZZOTINT A type of intaglio where a metal plate is entirely and evenly pitted and rough-ened with tiny holes. The holes are then burnished flat in all areas but where the artist wants the plate to hold ink. It is then inked and printed.

NUMBERED A process used to show the limit of an edition. The number is usually placed over the size of the edition, for example, 1/100. This indicates it is print number one of an edition of one hundred. In an etching or engraving the earlier numbers pulled are normally much sharper in appearance.

PAINTER One who applies a solution of pigment to a surface.

PEINTRE-GRAVEUR French term for a painter or sculptor who produces original graphic works.

PLATE A piece of stone or metal used in lithography.

PLATE SIGNED Means the artist has signed the plate upon which he has placed his design and the signature is printed along with the design. Usually no hand signed sig-nature by the artist appears on a plate signed print.

PLATE SIZE Actual size of the printing plate, the size of the image on the printed picture; not the paper size.

RABBET The inner portion of the frame material used to secure the print or painting and the glass or mats.

RAGBOARD A hundred percent rag content cardboard or mat board. It is completely free of any harmful substances which might damage or alter a picture. Used as backing and protection for fine picture framing and storage.

RAG PAPER A paper used in the printing process of lithography. It is a combination of cotton, rag, and wood pulp. It is manufactured in twenty-five, fifty, and one hundred per-cent rag.

RELIEF PROCESS The lines or surfaces which are raised in comparison to the surround-ing areas.

REMARQUE French term for a small sketch often made outside the actual area of the drawing or picture. It is normally done in pencil.

REPRODUCTION A picture, replica, or copy of an original art work produced by various methods. A facsimile.

RESTRIKE A print pulled from a plate after the original edition is issued. Restrikes are not part of an edition but constitute a legitimate print if unsigned and not represented as an original print of the artist. If the plate was not defaced it is very difficult to tell the restrike from the original.

SECONDARY MARKET VALUE It is the value of a print as determined by its being bought, sold, and traded by collectors and dealers after the edition is exhausted or sold out by the publisher or distributor.

SERIGRAPH (SILK SCREEN) A stencil method of producing an original print.

SIGNATURE The writing of an artist's name on the plate itself or on the print.

STEEL ENGRAVING A picture made from engraving a design on a steel plate or steel-faced copper plate. Very fine lines and subtle tones are possible in steel engravings and the plate can withstand a large printing.

STONE A concentration of mineral matter. In lithography, porous limestone from Solnhofen, Bavaria is used.

TRIAL PROOF Impression taken while the artwork is in progress.

VIGNETTE Term describing the fading of a background into the blank area surrounding the image.

WOODCUT This process begins with the artist drawing on a block of wood. Ink is then applied to the surface. A sheet of paper is placed over the block and passed through a press. When the paper is removed, the design has been imprinted on it.

WOOD ENGRAVING A variation of woodcut. Instead of a block the plate is cut from a cross-section of a tree and the work is done on the end grain. Engraving tools may be used. It is printed like engraving.

ZINCOGRAPHY A chemical printing process using a zinc plate.

BEGINNING A COLLECTION

A beginning print collector must become an investigator. First, he must examine the artist's style and subject material to determine if it is enjoyable to him. He must find out how often the artist releases limited edition prints and how many are in the editions. The collector must ask himself if that particular artist's prints are affordable.

Then, he must do some footwork. Visiting galleries or talking with an artist who is visiting a gallery is recommended. Many artists are happy to answer questions about their background and techniques. Most artists or galleries supply brochures and catalogs to interested collectors.

When a collector has found an affordable artist whose style and subject matter he enjoys, then he has almost started a collection. When he buys his first print, the investigation is over and the collection begins.

CARE, STORAGE, AND DISPLAY

After purchasing a print, care must be taken so it will remain in mint condition. Damage could result through handling, exposure to environmental extremes such as unfavorable temperatures and humidity, and restoration completed by an unqualified individual.

There are several ways to keep a print in good condition. There are binders made specifically for storing prints. Many contain ten acetate sheets with an inside paper cover enabling you to show several prints in one binder. Usually galleries stock this item.

Many galleries also have shrink wrap machines. This machine takes a print and wraps it in clear plastic, which is shrunk with heat to the print size.

Museum mounting is preferred when framing a print. Prints are usually produced on 100% rag paper. Rag paper is susceptible to mat bleed which means the color of the inner mat transfers to the print. Prints issued with a 50% or more rag content need two-ply ragboard placed on top and behind the print. When displaying a print, use a regular picture hook. Usually, professional framers will attach one to the back of the picture. When storing a framed print, the picture should not be exposed to extreme temperatures, which results in condensation between the glass and the print.

INVESTING AND SELLING

Three things should be considered when buying a print. Primarily, the print should appeal to the purchaser. The print edition and artist popularity should also be considered. For example, a popular artist's limited edition of 500 prints should sell out within a short period of time. Therefore, any person interested in the sold-out print would have to purchase it from a secondary market. What a person is willing to pay or has paid is how secondary market prices are determined.

There are a number of ways for a collector to sell his "sold-out" prints. Throughout the U.S. there are a number of galleries dealing in the secondary market. There is a ten to twenty-five percent fee for this service. Several periodicals accept ads from collectors who want to sell their prints themselves. There are many auction houses dealing with prints including Bernet, Christie's, and Phillips. Usually auction houses charge a ten percent fee to the buyer and seller.

PUBLISHERS' AND DISTRIBUTORS' CODES

At the end of each listing in the Contemporary Prints section are the initials for the publisher or distributor of each artist's print. Below is the list of initials with the company name and address following.

AB—ALFONS BACH, 201 Sandpiper Dr., Palm Beach, FL 33480

A & C—ALLISON & COMPANY, Limited editions, P.O. Box 32265, San Antonio, TX 78216

AIAC—AMERICAN INDIAN ARTS COLLECTION, Route 2 Box 311A, Shawnee, OK 74801*

AIAI—AMERICAN IMAGES N' ART, INC., P.O. Box 874, Mary Esther, FL 32569

ALI—ARTS LIMITED INC., 626 Sunset Rd., San Antonio, TX 78216

AMF—AMERICAN MASTERS FOUNDATION, 10688 Haddington, Suite 1200, Houston, TX 77043

ARI—ART RECOLLECTIONS, INC., 704 N. Glebe Rd., Suite 212, Arlington, VA 22203

AG—ATLAS GALLERY, 4168 N. Harlem Ave., Norridge, IL 60634

BBS—BRAD BENNETT STUDIOS, 405 65th St., Kenosha, WI 53140

BCS—BOB CARNEY STUDIOS, 245 New Sawyer Brown, Nashville, TN 37221

BDP—BURTON DYE PRINTS, 302 W. Vine St., Murfreesboro, TN 37130

BG—BURGER GALLERIES, 238 Airport Road, Whispering Pines, NC 28389

BGII—BERNARD GALLERIES, 1410 S. Coast Highway, Laguna Beach, CA 92651

BI—BERGSMA COLLECTIBLES, 1756 Iowa St., Bellingham, WA 98226

BJAD—B & J ART DESIGNS, P.O. Box 67, Georgetown, TX 78626

BM—BERNARD MARTIN, C-70 Lake, Lotawana, MO 64063

CAP—COMMODORE ART PUBLISHING, 10404 Patterson Ave., Suite 206, Richmond, VA 23233

CB—CUMBERLAND BEND PUBLISHING CO., *American Trust Bldg.,* 305 Union St., Nashville, TN 37201

CBW—CHARLES BANKS WILSON, 100½ North Main, Miami, OK 74354

CDR—CHARLES D. ROGERS, 11051 N. Clermont Dr., Thornton, CO 80233

CF—CHESTER FIELDS, E. 14210 22nd Ct., Veradale, WA 99037

CFAC—CIRCLE FINE ARTS CORP., 232 E. Ohio St., Chicago, IL 60611

CFRC—C. FORD RILEY & COMPANY, 3578 St. Johns Ave., Jacksonville, FL 33205

CG—COURT GALLERIES, 1235 Jerry Lane, Cincinnati, OH 45208

CGAL—CONNOISSEUR'S GALLERY OF ART, LTD., P.O. Box 94354, Schaumburg, IL 60194

CHWA—COTTAGE HILL WILDLIFE ART, no current address available.*

CII—CONTEMPLATIVE INVESTMENTS, INC., 2067 Range Rd., Clearwater, FL 33575

CIL—COLLECTORS INTERNATIONAL LTD., 67 Putnam St., Mount Vernon, NY 10550

CS—COUNTRYSIDE STUDIO, Box 88, Cottontown, TN 37048

CSH—CARDWELL S. HIGGINS STUDIO, 1511 Garfield St., Hollywood, FL 33020

DRN—D. R. NUTE FINE ARTS, 912 Coldbranch Dr., Columbia, SC 29204

DS—DEVINS STUDIO, Rt. 4, Box 42E, Mary Esther, FL 32569

DVS—DONALD VOORHEES STUDIO, 10 Ocean Blvd., Atlantic Highlands, NJ 07716

EDTW—EDGE OF THE WILD, Spring Creek Drive, Bonita Springs, FL 33923

EEI—ELEANOR ETTINGER, INC., 155 Sixth Avenue, New York, NY 10013

EEL—EAGLE EDITIONS, LTD., P.O. Box 1830, Sedona, AZ 86336

EHC—EDNA HIBEL CORP., P.O. Box 9967, Riviera Beach, FL 33404

EJ—EDNA B. JOHNSON, 913 Pinson St., Forney, TX 75126

EJB—EJB EDITIONS, P.O. Box 31, 8833 Lake Hill Dr., Lorton, VA 22079

EW—ED WARD, 296 Homecrest Avenue, Trenton, NJ 08638

EWGI—EDWARD WESTON GRAPHICS, INC., 19355 Business Center #3, Northridge, CA 91324

FFFA—FOXFIRE FINE ARTS INC., 2730 N. Graham, Charlotte, NC 28206

FFI—FRIEND FIELD, INC., P.O. Box 219, Locust Valley, NY 11560

FHG—FRAME HOUSE GALLERY, INC., 110 East Market Street, Louisville, KY 40202

FI—FELICIE, INC., 141 East 56th St., New York, NY 10022*

FOP—FOXMAN'S OIL PAINTINGS, LTD., 3350 Church St., Evanston, IL 60203

FP—FENTON'S PRESS, 20 East Concho, San Angelo, TX 76903

GB—GEORGE BOUTWELL, 3913 Ave. C., Austin, TX 78751

GBSL—*GRAPHICS BUYING SERVICE, LTD.,* 225 W. Hubbard, Chicago, IL 60610

GCWAPC—*GARY CARTER WESTERN ART PRINT CO.,* Box 241, Star Route, West Yellowstone, MN 59758

GHL—*GALLERY HOUSE,* 905 Alsworth, Winnsboro, LA 71295

GI—*GRAPHICS INTERNATIONAL,* P.O. Box 13292, Suite E, Oakland, CA 94661

GPL—*GRANSTAFF PRINTS LTD.,* Route 2, Princeton, KY 42445

GRG—*GEORGE RODRIGUE GALLERY,* 1206 Jefferson St., Lafayette, LA 70501

GSP—*GREY STONE PRESS,* 207 Louise Ave., Nashville, TN 37203

GU—*GIROUARD UNLIMITED,* P.O. Box 391, Ormond Beach, FL 32074

GW—*GREENWICH WORKSHOP (The),* 30 Lindeman Dr., Trumbull, CT 06611

HC—*HERB CHIDLEY,* 240 N. Bothwell, Palatine, IL 60067

HG—*HANCOCK GALLERY,* 6151 Estero Blvd., Fort Myers, FL 33931

HH—*HADLEY HOUSE,* 14200 23rd Ave. North, Plymouth, MN 55441 (formerly WB-The Wooden Bird)

HHSI—*HAMPTON HOUSE STUDIOS, INC.,* Route 1 Box 169, McDonald, TN 37353

HP—*HAMMER PUBLISHING CO.,* 33 West 57th St., New York, NY 10019

HRG—*HAROLD RIGSBY GRAPHICS,* P.O. Box 769, Glasgow, KY

HUI—*HANG UPS INC.,* 1319 West Katella Ave., Orange, CA 92667

IA—*IVAN ANDERSON,* 1060 Flamingo Rd., Laguna Beach, CA 92651

IGL—*IMPERIAL GRAPHICS, LTD.,* 10693 John Ayers Drive, Fairfax, VA 22032

IS—*IRENE SPENCER,* 1202 Star View Dr., Vista, CA 92083

IV—*ICART VENDOR GRAPHICS,* 8568 W. Pico Blvd., Los Angeles, CA 90048

JARP—*JAR PUBLISHERS,* now a division of the Edna Hibel Corp. (see EHC)

JGA—*J GETS ART,* P.O. Box 97, Blackwood Terrace, NJ 08096

JTAC—*JEROME TIGER ART CO.,* P.O. Box C, Muskogee, OK 74401

JTJ—*J T J IMAGES,* 10240 S. W. Nimbus, Suite L-11, Portland, OR 97223

KMS—*KATHRYN MILLER STUDIOS,* 122 East Oglethorpe Avenue, Savannah, GA 31401

KNC—*KALAMAZOO NATURE CENTER,* 7000 N. Westnedge, Kalamazoo, MI 49007

LAG—*LAPHAM'S ART GALLERY,* Rt. 17 South, Myrtle Beach, SC 29577

LBA—*LENORE BÉRAN ART,* 7332 Camellia Ave., No. Hollywood, CA 91605

LC—*LEGEND'S CORPORATION,* 9960 York Alpha Dr., North Royalton, OH 44133

LDS—*LILLIE DAWSON STUDIOS,* 1231 Ohio Ave., P.O. Box 274, Dunbar, WV 25064

LE—*LAUREL ENTERPRISES,* 1188 Laurel Lane, Phoenixville, PA 19460

LG—*LANDMARK GALLERIES,* Route 5, Box 103, Mooresville, NC 28115

LLG—*LINDAR GRAPHICS,* Box 57, Brinklow, MD 20862

LLS—*LENA LIU'S STUDIO,* 10693 John Ayers Drive, Fairfax, VA 22032

MCP—*M.C. POULSEN,* 2019 Kerper Blvd., Cody, WY 82414

MEI—*McCALLA ENTERPRISES, INC.,* HC 32 Box 218, Groom Creek Route, Prescott, AZ 86301

MHASA—*MICKEY HACKETT A.S.A.,* 1901 Woodfield Rd., Louisville, KY 40220

MLC—*MEREDITH LONG & COMPANY,* 2323 San Felipe, Houston, TX 77019

MM—*MIDWEST MARKETING,* P.O. Box 137, Sullivan, IL 61951

MMFC—*MASTERPIECE MOULDING & FINE ART CORP.,* P.O. Box 926, Morganton, NC 28655

MMGI—*ART SPECTRUM,* a Div. of Mitch Morse Gallery Inc., no longer representing artist listing, please note GBSL

MP—*MOSS PORTFOLIO (The),* 1055 Thomas Jefferson St., N. W., Washington, DC 20007

MPPI—*MILL POND PRESS, INC.,* 208 South Nassau Street, Venice, FL 33595

MS—*MALONE STUDIOS,* 2331 Pikewood Dr., Germantown, TN 38138

NAI—*NATIVE AMERICAN IMAGES,* P.O. Box 746, Austin, TX 78767

NC—*NORTHWOODS CRAFTSMAN,* 4144 Briar Ridge Lane, Colgate, WI 53017

NFC—*NAPLES FEDERAL,* 5801 Pelican Bay Blvd., P.O. Box 413004, Naples, FL 33941

NHFA—*NATURAL HERITAGE FINE ART,* P.O. Box 207, Carey, ID 83320

NHI—*NATURE HOUSE, INC.,* Purple Martin Junction, Griggsville, IL 62340

NWA—*NORTHWOODS WILDLIFE ART,* changed name to Wilderness Art (see WA)

NWAEI—*NATIONAL WILDLIFE ART EXCHANGE, INC.,* P.O. Drawer 3385, 1601 20th St., Vero Beach, FL 32960

NWGI—*NATIONAL WILDLIFE GALLERIES,* 12995 Cleveland Ave., Suite 130, Fort Myers, FL 33907

PLG—*PHILIP LASZ GALLERY,* P.O. Box 6284, Rockford, IL 61125

P&O—*PEMBERTON & OAKES,* 133 East Carillo St., Santa Barbara, CA 93101

PP—*PETERSEN PRINTS,* 6725 Sunset Blvd., Los Angeles, CA 90028

PSGI—*PAUL SAWYIER GALLERIES, INC.,* Route 3 U.S. 60E, Frankfort, KY 40601

QFA—*QUEST FINE ARTS,* Suite #120, Box 8999, Venice, FL 33595

RAF—*RUSSELL A. FINK,* 9843 Gunston Road, P.O. Box 250, Lorton, VA 22079

RDS—*RAY DAVENPORT STUDIOS,* 274 Keels Rd., Sumter, SC 29154

RG—*RAINTREE GRAPHICS,* 50 Music Square West, United Artists Tower, Suite 100, Nashville, TN 37203

RGF—*ROBERT G. FRANKOWIAK,* 4972 S. 20th St., Milwaukee, WI 53221

RI—*REMARQUE, INC.,* 514-16 N. Wrenn St., High Point, NC 27262

RIC—*RECO INTERNATIONAL CORP.,* P.O. Box 951, Port Washington, NY 11050

RO—*ROMAN, INC.,* 4850 N. Harlem Ave., Harwood Heights, IL 60656

RS—*ROZEMA STUDIO,* 226 Plymouth, N.E., Grand Rapids, MI 49503

RTG—*RICHARD THOMPSON GALLERY,* 80 Maiden Lane, San Francisco, CA 94108

SAG—*SEVEN ARTS GALLERY PUBLISHING,* P.O. Drawer H, Maryville, TN 37803

SB—*SCHMID BROS., INC.,* 55 Pacella Park Dr., Randolph, MA 02368

SCG—*SALT CREEK GRAPHICS,* P.O. Box 39, 3333 West Yellowstone, Casper, WY 82601

SEL—*SPORTSMAN'S EDGE, LTD.,* 136 East 74th Street, New York, NY 10021

SFA—*SOUDERS FINE ART, LTD.,* 4941 Stanley St., Forth Worth, TX 76115

SFAC—*SHENANDOAH FINE ARTS CO.,* P.O. Box 606, Stephens City, VA 22655

SG—*STONINGTON GALLERIES,* P.O. Box 2237, Ketchum, ID 23340

SGL—*SWAN GRAPHICS, LTD.,* P.O. Box 15185, Chattanooga, TN 37415

SHL—*SOMERSET HOUSE LIMITED,* Suite 900, 10688 Haddington, Houston, TX 77043

SIAG—*SEA ISLAND ART GALLERY,* 52 Sweetbriar Rd., Greenville, SC 29615

SLA—*STREAMSIDE LIMITED ART,* 736 Wooster Pike, Terrace Park, OH 45174

SP—*SAGE PRESS,* Cody, Wyoming 82414 . . . prints available through M. C. Poulsen, 2019 Kerper Blvd., Cody, WY 82414

SRS—*SPRING RIVER STUDIO,* R.R.1, Box 211-D, Miami, OK 74354

SRWA—*STEEP ROCK WILDLIFE ART,* P.O. Box 107, Bridgewater, CT 06752

SS—*STEARNS & ASSOCIATES,* Rd. 2, Box 320, Chestertown, MD 21620

SSWASI—*SALT SPRINGS ART STUDIOS, INC.,* 405 St. Johns Ave., Palatha, FL 32077

TAP—*TEXAS ART PRESS,* 1400 Main St., Dallas, TX 75202

TD—*TOP DRAWER,* 209 West Third St., Winston-Salem, NC 27101

THC—*THE HERITAGE COMPANY,* Box 1027, Lexington, NC 27292

TOT—*TAHMELS OF TAHLEQUAH,* P.O. Box 1123, Tahlequah, OK 74465

TRAD—*TRADITIONS,* 2109 Woodmere Drive, Knoxville, TN 37920

TWS—*THE WALDRON STUDIO,* RR #15, Box 544, Bedford, IN 47421

UG—*UNIQUE GRAPHICS,* 1024 50th Place South, Birmingham, AL 35222

VA—*VOYAGEUR ART,* P.O. Box 21321, Minneapolis, MN 55421

VFA—*VICTORIA'S FINE ARTS,* P.O. Box 3823, Longview, TX 75606

VFL—*VANITY FAIR LTD.,* prints now available thru Clive A. Burden, Inc., P.O. Box 2792, Naples, FL 33939

VOS—*THE VAN ORDER STUDIO,* P.O. Box 402, Boulder Junction, WI 54512

VSL—*VAGUE SHADOWS LIMITED,* Box 116, Staten Island, NY 10309

WA—*WILDERNESS ART,* P.O. Box 1297, Manistique, MI 49854

WANC INC.—*WILDLIFE ART OF NORTH CAROLINA,* P.O. Box 712, Rocky Mount, NC 27801

WAEL—*WORLD ART EDITIONS LTD.,* 67 Putnam St., Mt. Vernon, NY 10550, name changed to Collectors International, Ltd.

WB—*THE WOODEN BIRD,* 8600 Kennedy Memorial Dr., St. Bonifacius, MN 55375

WEI—*WINDBERG ENTERPRISES, INC.,* 2032 Centimeter Circle, Austin, TX 78758

WG—*WINDEMERE GALLERIES,* 932 Medina Rd., Wayzata, MN 55391

WII—*WILDLIFE INTERNATIONALE, INC.,* 6290 Old U.S. 68, Georgetown, OH 45121

WNG—*WREN'S NEST GALLERY,* 507B North Church St., Jacksonville, AL 36265

WOA—*WILDLIFE OF AMERICA,* P.O. Box 556, Minneapolis, MN 55440

WP—*WATERMARK PRESS,* P.O. Box 145, Glen Morgan, WV 25847

WSI—*WILDERNESS STUDIO, INC.,* 6800 S. Cloverdale Rd., Boise, ID 83709

WWAM—*WORLD WILDLIFE ART MUSEUM,* P.O. Box 1000, Monument, CO 80132

WWI—*WILD WINGS, INC.,* Lake City, MN 55041

*no longer in business

Recommended Reading . . .

The Official Price Guide to Collector Prints is designed for the novice as well as the seasoned collector. Information on price trends, industry development, investing, and collecting techniques such as care and repair, storage, or building a collection is written in a way a beginning hobbyist will understand yet gives specific details and helpful hints the hard-core collector will find useful.

This guide also offers up-to-date prices for both rare and common collectibles that are available in the current secondary market. This guide will give any collector confidence when determining what articles to purchase at what price. With the knowledge gained from this guide, a collector will move from flea market to auction house with ease knowing which items are "hot" and which articles are definitely overpriced.

As your interest in collecting grows, you may want to start a reference library of your favorite areas. For the collector who needs more extensive coverage of the collectibles market, The House of Collectibles publishes a complete line of comprehensive companion guides which are itemized at the back of this book. They contain full coverage on buying, selling, and caring of valuable articles, plus listings with thousands of prices for rare, unusual, and common antiques and collectibles.

$10.95-7th Edition, 672 pp., Order #470-4

The House of Collectibles recommends **The Official Price Guide to Collector Plates,** seventh edition, as the companion to this guide.

- **Over 18,400 current collector values** reflect the current trends in today's market. The most complete listing of all U.S. and Foreign plate manufacturers and distributors in print!
- **WHAT IS A COLLECTOR PLATE?** Follow the production of limited edition plates from concept to finished product. Decals, color separation and offset lithography are intelligently discussed and provide insight to the dealer as well as the collector.
- **BACKSTAMP REFERENCE GUIDE** — A pictorial variety of the hallmarks, representing the major plate manufacturers, is arranged alphabetically by manufacturer for easy identification.
- **MARKET REVIEW** — Examines the trends and events of last year's collector plate market. Find out which new artists' plates offer the best investment potential and collector enjoyment.
- **EVERY KNOWN COLLECTOR PLATE, FROM 1895 TO DATE** — Whether it is silver, pewter, porcelain, wood or glass, each plate is described in specific detail. Each plate description includes title and series, the original release date, designing artist, production methods used, quantities issued, original issue price and the current value.

Available from your local dealer or order direct from:
THE HOUSE OF COLLECTIBLES, *see order blank*

RECOMMENDED READING

A COMPLETE COURSE OF LITHOGRAPHY; by Alois Senefelder
AMERICAN ART & ANTIQUES; One Worth Avenue, Marion, Ohio 43302
AMERICAN ARTIST; One Astor Plaza, New York, NY 10036
AMERICAN ART REVIEW; P.O. Box 65007, Los Angeles, CA 90065
ANTIQUE JOURNAL; P.O. Box 1046, Dubuque, IA 52001
ANTIQUES MAGAZINE; Stright Enterprises Inc., 551 Fifth Avenue, New York, NY
    10017
ANTIQUE TRADER; P.O. Box 1050, Dubuque, IA 52001
ART BUSINESS NEWS; 2135 Summer St., P.O. Box 3837, Stamford, CT 06905
ART IN AMERICA; 150 East 58th St., New York, NY 10022
ART INVESTMENT REPORT; Wall Street Transcript, 120 Wall St., New York, NY
    10005
AUDUBON MAGAZINE; 950 Third Avenue, New York, NY 10022
COLLECTOR'S NEWS; Box 156, Grundy Center, IA 50638
COLLECTOR'S EDITIONS; A Quarterly . . . Acquire Publishing Co., 170 Fifth Ave.,
    New York, NY 10010
CURRIER & IVES PRINTS; An Illustrated Checklist; Frederick A. Conningham, revised
    edition updated by Colin Simkin, Copyright Mary Barton Conningham 1970, Crown
    Publishers, One Park Avenue, New York, NY 10016
DUCK STAMP DATA; Bureau of Sport Fisheries and Wildlife, U.S. Government
    Printing Office, Washington, DC 20402 (Further information available under Federal
    Duck Stamp listing).
PLATE COLLECTOR; 100 N. Edward Gray, P.O. Box 1729, San Marcos, TX 78667.
PRINT COLLECTOR'S NEWSLETTER; 205 East 78th Street, New York, NY 10021
PRINT TRADER; 6762 79th Street, Middle Village, NY 11379
PRINTS; P.O. Box 1468, Alton, IL 62002

HOW TO USE THIS BOOK

The artist sections in this book are divided into three parts. These are Old Prints, Contemporary Prints, and Federal and State Duck Stamp Prints.

The Old Prints section is made up of early American artists' prints which are highly collectible. Audubon, Currier And Ives, Louis Icart, Maxfield Parrish, Mark Catesby, and Vanity Fair are included in this section.

The Contemporary Prints section is alphabetized by artist name. The information in the listings under each artist follows this format: title, issue date, edition number, if the print is signed and numbered, size, and publisher. Any missing information means it was unavailable. Although most prints are produced photomechanically, when available it is stated whether the print is a lithograph or etching.

Issue Price is the price of the print upon its release on the market to dealers. Current Price is the current selling price. Sold Out means the publisher or distributor is sold out, however, there still may be prints available through the dealer network.

Explanation and key to codes in the listings are as follows:

s/a—signed and dated
s/n—signed and numbered
s/o—signed only
i/n—initialed and numbered
i/o—initialed only
n/o—numbered only
N/A—information not available
Cl. Out—closed out edition
sw/seal—signed with seal
D.U. Print—Ducks Unlimited Print

rem.—remarqued print*
u/s—unsigned
s/s—with state seal
litho—original lithograph
etch—original etching
pub—publisher
distr.—distributor
*remarqued copies are currently worth $85.00 to $100.00 more than the regular print in an edition

Also upon occasion you will find the word "embossed" in a listing which means that the publisher or artist has embossed the paper with a trademark to ensure its authenticity.

OLD PRINTS

JOHN JAMES AUDUBON
(1785-1851)

John James Audubon is a name synonymous with pictures of birds. His "Birds of America" are recognized everywhere.

Audubon was born in Haiti, but grew up in France. He came to America around 1803 and settled in Louisiana. Audubon turned to ornithology and to painting all of the known birds of North America. Between 1826 and 1842 he traveled throughout the United States and Canada, working and gathering material for his art, and at the same time selling subscriptions for the finished project. He roamed through most of the forests and swamps of America to create his original paintings for this tremendous and monumental task.

Because it was a tremendous job, Audubon had a difficult time finding engravers. He turned to Englishman William Lizars who completed the first ten plates but could not finish the project because of labor problems. Audubon took his plates to R. Havell in London. Although Havell died in 1832, his son completed the work.

In all there were 435 plates in the completed work called *"The Birds of America"*. They originally sold for $1,000.00 per set. It is believed that fewer than 200 sets were actually bound into volumes. There are a varying number of loose prints because several of the original subscribers defaulted and then additional persons subscribed during the eleven years it was in the making.

These prints are called the double-elephant-folio-size (approximately 25½" x 38"). All birds are life-size in the prints. All prints are aquatint engravings, hand printed and hand-colored by the Havells on Whatman watermarked paper. These are considered an excellent investment in the art field.

THE ORIGINAL EDITION
ENGRAVED BY HAVELL AND SON

PLATE NUMBER	SUBJECT	CURRENT RETAIL PRICE	PLATE NUMBER	SUBJECT	CURRENT RETAIL PRICE
☐ 1	Turkey Cock	24,200.00	☐ 25	Song Sparrow	1,320.00
☐ 2	Yellow-billed Cuckoo	2,310.00	☐ 26	Carolina Parrot	23,100.00
☐ 3	Prothonotary Warbler	935.00	☐ 27	Red-headed Woodpecker	2,640.00
☐ 4	Purple Finch	715.00	☐ 28	Solitary Flycatcher	990.00
☐ 5	Bonaparte's Flycatcher	990.00	☐ 29	Towhe Bunting	2,420.00
☐ 6	Hen Turkey	20,900.00	☐ 30	Vigor's Warbler	1,650.00
☐ 7	Purple Grackle	2,530.00	☐ 31	White-headed Eagle	6,600.00
☐ 8	White-throated Sparrow	1,870.00	☐ 32	Black-billed Cuckoo	5,500.00
☐ 9	Selby's Flycatcher	1,650.00	☐ 33	American Goldfinch	2,860.00
☐ 10	Brown Titlark	660.00	☐ 34	Worm-eating Warbler	1,430.00
☐ 11	Bird of Washington	3,300.00	☐ 35	Children's Warbler	1,045.00
☐ 12	Baltimore Oriole	5,225.00	☐ 36	Stanley Hawk	3,300.00
☐ 13	Snow Bird	1,100.00	☐ 37	Gold-winged Woodpecker	4,400.00
☐ 14	Prairie Warbler	1,760.00	☐ 38	Kentucky Warbler	1,210.00
☐ 15	Blue Yellow-backed Warbler	2,090.00	☐ 39	Crested Titmouse	1,650.00
☐ 16	Great Footed Hawk	2,530.00	☐ 40	American Redstart	1,650.00
☐ 17	Carolina Turtle Dove	13,200.00	☐ 41	Ruffed Grouse	13,200.00
☐ 18	Bewick's Wren	880.00	☐ 42	Orchard's Oriole	2,640.00
☐ 19	Louisiana Water Thrush	1,100.00	☐ 43	Cedar Warwing	4,070.00
☐ 20	Blue-winged Yellow Warbler	2,200.00	☐ 44	Summer Tanager	3,520.00
☐ 21	Mockingbird	11,000.00	☐ 45	Traul's Flycatcher	1,100.00
☐ 22	Purple Martin	2,860.00	☐ 46	Barred Owl	5,500.00
☐ 23	Maryland Yellow Throat	1,760.00	☐ 47	Ruby-throated Hummingbird	11,000.00
☐ 24	Roscoe's Yellow Throat	1,320.00	☐ 48	Cerulean Warbler	1,320.00

PLATE NUMBER	SUBJECT	CURRENT RETAIL PRICE
☐ 49	Blue Green Warbler	1,045.00
☐ 50	Magnolia Warbler	1,045.00
☐ 51	Red-tailed Hawk	3,410.00
☐ 52	Chuck Will's Widow	2,750.00
☐ 53	Painted Bunting	2,310.00
☐ 54	Rice Bird	1,760.00
☐ 55	Cuvier's Wren	1,870.00
☐ 56	Red-shouldered Hawk	8,800.00
☐ 57	Loggerhead Shrike	1,920.00
☐ 58	Hermit Thrush	1,430.00
☐ 59	Chestnut-sided Warbler	1,540.00
☐ 60	Carbonated Warbler	1,430.00
☐ 61	Great Horned Owl	9,350.00
☐ 62	Passenger Pigeon	7,700.00
☐ 63	White-eyed Flycatcher	1,210.00
☐ 64	Swamp Sparrow	1,100.00
☐ 65	Rathbone Warbler	2,860.00
☐ 66	Ivory-billed Woodpecker	17,600.00
☐ 67	Red-winged Starling	2,200.00
☐ 68	Cliff Sparrow	1,210.00
☐ 69	Bay-breasted Warbler	1,430.00
☐ 70	Henslow's Bunting	1,650.00
☐ 71	Winter Hawk	4,125.00
☐ 72	Swallow-tailed Hawk	2,970.00
☐ 73	Wood Thrush	1,210.00
☐ 74	Indigo Bunting	1,760.00
☐ 75	Le Petit Caporal	2,420.00
☐ 76	Virginia Partridge	19,250.00
☐ 77	Belted Kingfisher	4,950.00
☐ 78	Great Carolina Wren	1,540.00
☐ 79	Tyrant Flycatcher	1,540.00
☐ 80	Prairie Titlark	1,210.00
☐ 81	Fish Hawk	19,250.00
☐ 82	Whip-Poor-Will	3,960.00
☐ 83	House Wren	3,960.00
☐ 84	Blue Gray Flycatcher	1,320.00
☐ 85	Yellow-throated Warbler	1,100.00
☐ 86	Black Warrior	2,530.00
☐ 87	Florida Jay	4,125.00
☐ 88	Autumnal Warbler	1,045.00
☐ 89	Nashville Warbler	1,650.00
☐ 90	Black and White Creeper	1,100.00
☐ 91	Broad-winged Hawk	5,225.00
☐ 92	Pigeon Hawk	2,420.00
☐ 93	Sea Side Finch	4,620.00
☐ 94	Bay-winged Bunting	1,430.00
☐ 95	Blue-eyed Yellow Warbler	1,210.00
☐ 96	Columbia Jay	6,875.00
☐ 97	Little Screech Owl	7,700.00
☐ 98	White-bellied Swallow	825.00
☐ 99	Cow Pen Bird	770.00
☐ 100	Marsh Wren	1,320.00
☐ 101	Raven	2,750.00
☐ 102	Blue Jay	4,400.00
☐ 103	Canada Warbler	2,310.00
☐ 104	Chipping Sparrow	1,430.00
☐ 105	Red-breasted Nuthatch	1,320.00
☐ 106	Black Vulture	2,310.00
☐ 107	Canada Jay	4,675.00
☐ 108	Fox Colored Sparrow	1,540.00
☐ 109	Savannah Finch	2,310.00

PLATE NUMBER	SUBJECT	CURRENT RETAIL PRICE
☐ 110	Hooded Warbler	1,045.00
☐ 111	Pileated Woodpecker	14,300.00
☐ 112	Downy Woodpecker	3,300.00
☐ 113	Blue Bird	2,420.00
☐ 114	White-crowned Sparrow	1,100.00
☐ 115	Wood Pewee	1,210.00
☐ 116	Ferruginous Thrush	4,400.00
☐ 117	Mississippi Kite	3,300.00
☐ 118	Warbling Flycatcher	1,760.00
☐ 119	Yellow Throated Vireo	1,705.00
☐ 120	Pewee Flycatcher	1,540.00
☐ 121	Snowy Owl	24,200.00
☐ 122	Blue Grosbeak	2,860.00
☐ 123	Black and Yellow Warbler	2,475.00
☐ 124	Green Black-capped Flycatcher	1,430.00
☐ 125	Brown-headed Nuthatch	990.00
☐ 126	White-headed Eagle (young)	4,125.00
☐ 127	Rose-breasted Grosbeak	2,640.00
☐ 128	Cat Bird	2,310.00
☐ 129	Great Crested Flycatcher	1,100.00
☐ 130	Yellow-winged Sparrow	2,090.00
☐ 131	American Robin	7,150.00
☐ 132	Three-toed Woodpecker	1,760.00
☐ 133	Black Poll Warbler	1,430.00
☐ 134	Hemlock Warbler	1,430.00
☐ 135	Blackburnian Warbler	1,210.00
☐ 136	Meadow Lark	15,400.00
☐ 137	Yellow-breasted Chat	4,125.00
☐ 138	Connecticut Warbler	2,035.00
☐ 139	Field Sparrow	2,310.00
☐ 140	Pine-creeping Warbler	880.00
☐ 141	Goshawk	3,850.00
☐ 142	American Sparrow Hawk	4,400.00
☐ 143	Golden Crowned Thrush	1,100.00
☐ 144	Small Green Crested Flycatcher	1,320.00
☐ 145	Yellow Red Poll Warbler	2,420.00
☐ 146	Fish Crow	2,420.00
☐ 147	Night Hawk	3,960.00
☐ 148	Pine Swamp Warbler	1,320.00
☐ 149	Sharp-tailed Finch	2,420.00
☐ 150	Red-eyed Vireo	880.00
☐ 151	Turkey Buzzard	2,200.00
☐ 152	White Breasted Nuthatch	2,750.00
☐ 153	Yellow Rump Warbler	1,760.00
☐ 154	Tennessee Warbler	1,430.00
☐ 155	Black-throated Blue Warbler	1,760.00
☐ 156	American Crow	4,950.00
☐ 157	Rusty Grackle	990.00
☐ 158	American Swift	605.00
☐ 159	Cardinal Grosbeak	9,625.00
☐ 160	Black-capped Titmouse	1,430.00
☐ 161	Caracara Eagle	4,675.00
☐ 162	Zenaida Dove	4,125.00
☐ 163	Palm Warbler	1,430.00
☐ 164	Tawny Thrush	1,760.00
☐ 165	Bachman's Finch	1,870.00
☐ 166	Rough-legged Falcon	3,575.00
☐ 167	Key West Quail Dove	5,225.00
☐ 168	Fork-tailed Flycatcher	5,500.00

PLATE 203 HAVELL EDITION "Fresh Water Marsh Wren (King Rail)"

PLATE NUMBER	SUBJECT	CURRENT RETAIL PRICE
169	Mangrove Cuckoo	1,980.00
170	Gray Kingbird	1,540.00
171	Barn Owl	9,900.00
172	Pigeon	2,750.00
173	Barn Swallow	3,520.00
174	Olive Sided Flycatcher	1,045.00
175	Marsh Wren	1,760.00
176	Spotted Grouse	6,600.00
177	White-crowned Pigeon	6,325.00
178	Orange-crowned Warbler	660.00
179	Wood Wren	2,200.00
180	Pine Finch	1,210.00
181	Golden Eagle	5,225.00
182	Ground Dove	3,190.00
183	Golden-crested Wren	1,100.00
184	Mangrove Hummingbird	4,950.00
185	Bachman's Warbler	2,200.00
186	Pinnated Grouse	8,250.00
187	Boat-tailed Grackle	2,420.00
188	Tree Sparrow	990.00
189	Snow Bunting	1,320.00
190	Yellow-bellied Woodpecker	1,980.00
191	Willow Grouse	5,225.00
192	Great American Shrike	2,200.00
193	Lincoln Finch	2,640.00
194	Hudson's Bay Titmouse	1,100.00
195	Ruby-crowned Wren	990.00
196	Labrador Falcon	2,310.00
197	American Crossbill	1,760.00
198	Swanson's Warbler	1,320.00
199	Little Owl	2,310.00
200	Shore Lark	1,045.00
201	Canada Goose	19,800.00
202	Red-throated Diver	4,400.00
203	Fresh Water Marsh Wren	1,870.00
204	Salt Water Marsh Wren	1,980.00
205	Virginia Rail	2,090.00
206	Summer or Wood Duck	16,500.00
207	Booby Gannet	1,980.00
208	Esquimaux Curlew	715.00
209	Wilson's Plover	715.00
210	Least Bittern	2,860.00
211	Great Blue Heron	30,800.00
212	Common American Gull	2,090.00
213	Puffin	5,720.00
214	Razor Billed Auk	1,540.00
215	Phalarope	990.00
216	Wood Ibis	12,650.00
217	Louisiana Heron	13,750.00
218	Foolish Guillemot	2,090.00
219	Black Guillemot	1,870.00
220	Piping Plover	715.00
221	Mallard Duck	26,400.00
222	White Ibis	6,600.00
223	American Oyster Catcher	1,650.00
224	Kittiwake Gull	1,650.00
225	Kildeer Plover	1,320.00
226	Whooping Crane	17,050.00
227	Pin-tailed Duck	6,325.00
228	Green-winged Teal	6,050.00
229	Scaup Duck	3,050.00
230	Sanderling	660.00
231	Long-billed Curlew	18,700.00
232	Hooded Merganser	4,675.00
233	Sora Rail	1,650.00
234	Ring-necked Duck	2,475.00

PLATE 246 HAVELL EDITION "Eider Duck (American Eider)"

PLATE NUMBER	SUBJECT	CURRENT RETAIL PRICE
☐ 235	Sooty Tern	1,650.00
☐ 236	Night Heron	8,800.00
☐ 237	Great Esquimaux Curlew	3,520.00
☐ 238	Great Marbled Godwit	2,420.00
☐ 239	American Coot	2,530.00
☐ 240	Roseate Tern	2,530.00
☐ 241	Black Backed Gull	2,420.00
☐ 242	Snowy Heron	23,100.00
☐ 243	American Snipe	3,740.00
☐ 244	Common Gallinule	880.00
☐ 245	Thick-billed Murre	1,100.00
☐ 246	Eider Duck	21,450.00
☐ 247	Velvet Duck	2,090.00
☐ 248	American Pied Bill Dobchick	2,420.00
☐ 249	Tufted Auk	2,750.00
☐ 250	Arctic Tern	2,750.00
☐ 251	Brown Pelican	18,700.00
☐ 252	Florida Cormorant	4,400.00
☐ 253	Pomarine Jager	1,210.00
☐ 254	Wilson's Phalarope	1,100.00
☐ 255	Red Phalarope	1,210.00
☐ 256	Purple Egret	13,200.00
☐ 257	Double Crested Cormorant	1,980.00
☐ 258	Hudsonian Godwit	1,430.00
☐ 259	Horned Grebe	3,080.00
☐ 260	Fork-tail Petrel	1,210.00
☐ 261	Whooping Crane	14,850.00
☐ 262	Tropic Bird	5,775.00
☐ 263	Curlew Sandpiper	1,650.00
☐ 264	Fulmar Pertrel	1,320.00
☐ 265	Buff Breasted Sandpiper	1,100.00
☐ 266	Common Cormorant	4,125.00
☐ 267	Arctic Jager	1,540.00

PLATE NUMBER	SUBJECT	CURRENT RETAIL PRICE
☐ 268	American Woodcock	3,300.00
☐ 269	Greenshank	1,760.00
☐ 270	Stormy Petrel	825.00
☐ 271	Frigate Pelican	6,325.00
☐ 272	Richardson's Jager	1,100.00
☐ 273	Cayenne Tern	4,950.00
☐ 274	Semipalmated Snipe	1,870.00
☐ 275	Noddy Tern	1,540.00
☐ 276	King Duck	4,675.00
☐ 277	Hutchins's Goose	3,575.00
☐ 278	Schinz's Sandpiper	1,100.00
☐ 279	Sandwich Tern	1,870.00
☐ 280	Black Tern	770.00
☐ 281	Great White Heron	18,200.00
☐ 282	White-winged Silvery Gull	1,430.00
☐ 283	Wandering Shearwater	990.00
☐ 284	Purple Sandpiper	1,100.00
☐ 285	Fork-tailed Gull	1,100.00
☐ 286	White-fronted Goose	4,675.00
☐ 287	Ivory Gull	1,760.00
☐ 288	Yellow Shank	3,850.00
☐ 289	Solitary Sandpiper	1,540.00
☐ 290	Red-backed Sandpiper	1,320.00
☐ 291	Herring Gull	4,290.00
☐ 292	Crested Grebe	2,860.00
☐ 293	Large-billed Puffin	1,760.00
☐ 294	Pectoral Sandpiper	935.00
☐ 295	Manx Shearwater	990.00
☐ 296	Barnacle Goose	2,200.00
☐ 297	Harlequin Duck	2,310.00
☐ 298	Red-nicked Grebe	1,430.00
☐ 299	Dusky Petrel	1,100.00
☐ 300	Golden Plover	990.00

PLATE 308 HAVELL EDITION "Greater Yellow Legs"

PLATE NUMBER	SUBJECT	CURRENT RETAIL PRICE	PLATE NUMBER	SUBJECT	CURRENT RETAIL PRICE
☐ 301	Canvasback Duck	9,350.00	☐ 334	Black-bellied Plover	990.00
☐ 302	Black Duck	4,400.00	☐ 335	Red-breasted Snipe	990.00
☐ 303	Upland Sandpiper	1,540.00	☐ 336	Yellow Crowned Night Heron	11,550.00
☐ 304	Turnstone	880.00	☐ 337	American Bittern	5,500.00
☐ 305	Purple Gallinule	1,760.00	☐ 338	Bemaculated Duck	5,500.00
☐ 306	Common Loon	6,600.00	☐ 339	Little Auk	890.00
☐ 307	Little Blue Heron	15,950.00	☐ 340	Stormy Petrel	935.00
☐ 308	Greater Yellow Legs	2,090.00	☐ 341	Great Auk	4,950.00
☐ 309	Common Tern	2,560.00	☐ 342	Golden-eyed Duck	3,300.00
☐ 310	Spotted Sandpiper	1,320.00	☐ 343	Ruddy Duck	3,300.00
☐ 311	White Pelican	29,700.00	☐ 344	Long-legged Sandpiper	825.00
☐ 312	Old Squaw	4,510.00	☐ 345	American Widgeon	5,500.00
☐ 313	Blue-winged Teal	6,050.00	☐ 346	Black Throated Diver	10,450.00
☐ 314	Laughing Gull	1,100.00	☐ 347	Snew	1,430.00
☐ 315	Sandpiper	1,430.00	☐ 348	Gadwall Duck	3,300.00
☐ 316	Black-Bellied Darter	11,000.00	☐ 349	Least Water Hen	1,100.00
☐ 317	Surf Scoter	2,090.00	☐ 350	Rocky Mountain Plover	990.00
☐ 318	Avocet	3,300.00	☐ 351	Great Cinereous Owl	9,625.00
☐ 319	Lesser Tern	1,760.00	☐ 352	Black-winged Hawk	2,310.00
☐ 320	Little Sandpiper	1,760.00	☐ 353	Titmouse, Etc.	2,090.00
☐ 321	Roseate Spoonbill	26,400.00	☐ 354	Louisiana Tanager	3,190.00
☐ 322	Red-head Duck	6,600.00	☐ 355	MacGillivray's Finch	1,210.00
☐ 323	Black Skimmer	3,500.00	☐ 356	Marsh Hawk	3,850.00
☐ 324	Bonaparte's Gull	1,430.00	☐ 357	American Magpie	2,970.00
☐ 325	Bufflehead	3,850.00	☐ 358	Pine Grosbeak	1,100.00
☐ 326	Gannet	5,225.00	☐ 359	Arkansas Flycatcher	1,430.00
☐ 327	Shoveller Duck	7,700.00	☐ 360	Winter and Rock Wren	1,650.00
☐ 328	Blackneck Stilt	1,650.00	☐ 361	Long-tailed Grouse	2,200.00
☐ 329	Yellow Rail	1,325.00	☐ 362	Yellow-billed Magpie	2,420.00
☐ 330	Ring Plover	880.00	☐ 363	Bohemian Chatterer	1,210.00
☐ 331	Common Merganser	6,050.00	☐ 364	White-winged Grossbill	1,100.00
☐ 332	Labrador Duck	4,300.00	☐ 365	Lapland Longspur	990.00
☐ 333	Green Heron	6,600.00	☐ 366	Iceland Falcon	17,600.00

PLATE 401 HAVELL EDITION "Red Breasted Merganser"

PLATE NUMBER	SUBJECT	CURRENT RETAIL PRICE
☐ 367	Band-tailed Pigeon	5,500.00
☐ 368	Rock Grouse	3,300.00
☐ 369	Mountain Mockingbird	2,090.00
☐ 370	American Water Ouzel	990.00
☐ 371	Cock of the Plains	5,335.00
☐ 372	Common Buzzard	2,640.00
☐ 373	Evening Grosbeak	880.00
☐ 374	Sharp Shinned Hawk	1,210.00
☐ 375	Lesser Red Poll	1,320.00
☐ 376	Trumpeter Swan	6,600.00
☐ 377	Scolopaceys Courlan	2,200.00
☐ 378	Hawk Owl	1,870.00
☐ 379	Ruff-necked Hummingbird ...	5,500.00
☐ 380	Tengmalm's Owl	1,540.00
☐ 381	Snow Goose	4,400.00
☐ 382	Sharp-tailed Grouse	1,980.00
☐ 383	Long-eared Owl	1,870.00
☐ 384	Black-throated Bunting	1,320.00
☐ 385	Bank Swallow	825.00
☐ 386	Great American Egret	10,450.00
☐ 387	Glossy Ibis	7,700.00
☐ 388	Troopial (Orioles)	770.00
☐ 389	Red-cockaded Woodpecker ..	1,650.00
☐ 390	Prairie Finch	1,100.00
☐ 391	Brant Goose	2,310.00
☐ 392	Louisiana Hawk	2,750.00
☐ 393	Bluebirds and Warbler	1,540.00
☐ 394	Buntings and Finches	1,540.00
☐ 395	Audubon's Warbler	1,100.00
☐ 396	Burgomaster Gull	1,870.00
☐ 397	Scarlet Ibis	5,775.00
☐ 398	Lazuli Finch	1,100.00
☐ 399	Black-throated Warbler	880.00
☐ 400	Townsend's Finch	990.00
☐ 401	Red Breasted Merganser	6,050.00
☐ 402	Auks and Guillemots	1,540.00
☐ 403	Golden-eyed Duck	1,870.00
☐ 404	Eared Grebe	1,540.00
☐ 405	Semipalmated Sandpiper	1,100.00
☐ 406	Trumpeter Swan	24,200.00
☐ 407	Dusky Albatross	1,320.00
☐ 408	American Scoter Duck	1,980.00
☐ 409	Havell's Tern	2,420.00
☐ 410	Marsh Tern	1,650.00
☐ 411	Common American Swan ...	14,300.00
☐ 412	Violet Green Cormorant	1,320.00
☐ 413	California Partridge	2,640.00
☐ 414	Golden-winged Warbler	1,320.00
☐ 415	Brown Creeper	990.00
☐ 416	Hairy Woodpecker	4,950.00
☐ 417	Maria's Woodpecker	2,200.00
☐ 418	American Ptarmigan	1,320.00
☐ 419	Little Tawny Thrush	990.00
☐ 420	Prairie Starling	1,210.00
☐ 421	Brown Pelican	11,000.00
☐ 422	Rough-legged Falcon	4,950.00
☐ 423	Plumed Partridge	2,475.00
☐ 424	Lazuli Finch	770.00
☐ 425	Columbian Hummingbird	4,950.00
☐ 426	California Condor	4,400.00
☐ 427	White-legged Oyster Catcher	1,320.00
☐ 428	Townsend's Sandpiper	770.00
☐ 429	Western Duck	1,760.00
☐ 430	Slinder-billed Guillemot	1,375.00
☐ 431	American Flamingo	28,600.00
☐ 432	Burrowing Owl	1,870.00
☐ 433	Bullock's Oriole	660.00
☐ 434	Little Tyrant Pewee, 1, etc. ...	770.00
☐ 435	Columbian Water Ouzel	1,210.00

THE BIEN EDITION

The listing of prints that follows is not complete but represents all that could be located as available at publication.
Chromolithographs, in the original double elephant folio size, were done by Julius Bien in New York. There are 150 birds represented by 106 plates, with the smaller birds being printed two on a page. The Civil War halted the printing which was done in 1859 and 1860 and distribution of this edition of the Audubons. They are considered today to be the rarest of all editions.

PLATE NUMBER	SUBJECT	CURRENT RETAIL PRICE	PLATE NUMBER	SUBJECT	CURRENT RETAIL PRICE
	Full-size Plates:		☐ 124	Nuttall's Lesser Marsh Wren .	300.00
☐ 3	Black Vulture ....$	850.00	☐ 127	Carolina Titmouse	400.00
☐ 7	Red-tailed Hawk	1,500.00	☐ 128	Hudson's Bay Titmouse	400.00
☐ 14	White-headed Eagle	2,250.00	☐ 132	Amer. Golden-crested Wren .	350.00
☐ 16	Black Winged Hawk	1,500.00	☐ 133	Ruby-crowned Wren	350.00
☐ 18	Swallow-tailed Hawk	1,850.00	☐ 138	Mockingbird	2,500.00
☐ 19	Iceland Falcon	2,750.00	☐ 141	Ferruginous Thrush	1,850.00
☐ 20	Great Footed Hawk	1,750.00	☐ 144	Hermit Thrush	350.00
☐ 21	Pigeon Hawk	1,250.00	☐ 145	Wood Thrush	400.00
☐ 22	Sparrow Hawk	2,250.00	☐ 150	Prairie Titlark	350.00
☐ 34	Barn Owl	2,250.00	☐ 151	Brown Titlark	350.00
☐ 43	Night Hawk	1,250.00	☐ 156	American Crow	2,250.00
☐ 44	American Swift	350.00	☐ 159	Bay Winged Bunting	350.00
☐ 45	Purple Martin	1,500.00	☐ 163	Henslow's Bunting	350.00
☐ 46	White-bellied Sparrow	350.00	☐ 164	Field Sparrow	350.00
☐ 48	Republican or Cliff Swallow ..	350.00	☐ 165	Chipping Sparrow	350.00
☐ 48	Barn Swallow	350.00	☐ 172	Seaside Finch	400.00
☐ 53	Fork-Tailed Flycatcher	500.00	☐ 173	MacGillivray's Finch	350.00
☐ 54	Flycatcher	500.00	☐ 174	Sharp Tailed Finch	350.00
☐ 55	Pipiry Flycatcher	450.00	☐ 177	Lincoln Finch	350.00
☐ 56	Olive-sided Flycatcher	350.00	☐ 183	Pinnated Grouse	2,500.00
☐ 57	Great Crested Flycatcher	350.00	☐ 189	Song Sparrow	400.00
☐ 62	Small Green-crested		☐ 191	White Throated Sparrow	400.00
	Flycatcher	350.00	☐ 192	White-crowned Sparrow	350.00
☐ 63	Wood Pewee	350.00	☐ 195	Towhee Bunting	350.00
☐ 70	Blue Gray Flycatcher	350.00	☐ 196	Purple Finch	400.00
☐ 72	Hooded Warbler and Green .	400.00	☐ 199	Pine Grosbeak	350.00
☐ 71	Wilson's Warbler	350.00	☐ 200	Common Grosbill	1,250.00
☐ 72	Canada Warbler	400.00	☐ 205	Rose Breasted Grosbeak	1,750.00
☐ 73	Bonaparte Flycatcher	400.00	☐ 216	Red-winged Starling	1,850.00
☐ 74	Kentucky Warbler	400.00	☐ 217	Baltimore Oriole	2,750.00
☐ 75	Black Capped Flycatcher	400.00	☐ 219	Orchard Oriole	1,250.00
☐ 79	Yellow-throated Vireo	350.00	☐ 220	Boat-tailed Grackle	1,750.00
☐ 80	Bay Breasted Warbler	350.00	☐ 221	Purple Grackle	1,750.00
☐ 86	Cerulean Warbler	400.00	☐ 222	Rusty Grackle	1,250.00
☐ 87	Children's Warbler	400.00	☐ 225	American Crow	2,250.00
☐ 88	Blue eyed Yellow Warbler ...	350.00	☐ 226	Fish Crow	1,500.00
☐ 89	Rathbone Warbler	300.00	☐ 231	Blue Jays	1,700.00
☐ 90	Yellow Redpoll	400.00	☐ 239	Solitary Flycatcher	350.00
☐ 95	Black-throated Blue Warbler .	350.00	☐ 240	White-eyed Flycatcher	350.00
☐ 96	Black 'n Yellow Warbler	400.00	☐ 243	Red-eyed Vireo	350.00
☐ 104	Worm Eating Warbler	350.00	☐ 244	Yellow-breasted Chat	1,100.00
☐ 108	Bachman's Warbler	400.00	☐ 245	Boehemian Chatterer	400.00
☐ 109	Carbonated Warbler	400.00	☐ 246	Cedar Bird	450.00
☐ 113	Nashville Warbler	400.00	☐ 251	Mangrove Hummingbird	400.00
☐ 114	Black & White Creeper	400.00	☐ 251	Columbian Hummingbird	350.00
☐ 116	Winter Wren	400.00	☐ 253	Ruby-throated Hummingbird .	2,250.00
☐ 118	Bewick's Wren	350.00	☐ 255	Belted Kingfisher	1,500.00
☐ 119	Wood Wren	300.00	☐ 257	Pileated Woodpecker	1,950.00
☐ 120	House Wren	350.00	☐ 273	Gold-winged Woodpecker	1,500.00
☐ 123	Marsh Wren	400.00			

PLATE NUMBER	SUBJECT	CURRENT RETAIL PRICE	PLATE NUMBER	SUBJECT	CURRENT RETAIL PRICE
☐ 275	Yellow-billed Cuckoo	1,950.00	☐ 389	Crested Grebe	1,350.00
☐ 278	Carolina Parrot	3,000.00	☐ 391	Summer or Wood Duck	2,950.00
☐ 280	White-headed Pigeon	1,500.00	☐ 395	Canvasback Duck	2,950.00
☐ 287	Turkey Cock	7,500.00	☐ 396	Red-headed Duck	1,500.00
☐ 288	Fish Hawk or Osprey	2,500.00	☐ 397	Scaup Duck	900.00
☐ 289	Virginia Partridge	2,750.00	☐ 398	Tufted Duck	700.00
☐ 293	Ruffed Grouse	2,500.00	☐ 405	Eider Duck	1,750.00
☐ 294	Blue Grosbeak	1,950.00	☐ 414	Smew or White Num	1,100.00
☐ 296	Pinnated Grouse	1,750.00	☐ 428	Black Skimmer	850.00
☐ 308	Least Water Hen	350.00	☐ 423	Brown Pelican	2,950.00
☐ 309	Yellow-breasted Rail	350.00	☐ 434	Arctic Tern	500.00
☐ 330	Buff-breasted Sandpiper	350.00	☐ 465	Great Auk	1,550.00
☐ 331	Little Sandpiper	400.00	☐ 466	Razor-billed Auk	350.00
☐ 332	Red-backed Sandpiper	350.00	☐ 454	Puffin	400.00
☐ 332	Pectoral Sandpiper	350.00			
☐ 333	Curlew Sandpiper	325.00	**HALF-PAGE BIENS:**		
☐ 336	Semi-palmated Sandpiper	325.00	☐ 2	Yellow Billed Cuckoo	$300.00
☐ 342	Spotted Sandpiper	350.00	☐ 48	Barn Swallows	300.00
☐ 343	Solitary Sandpiper	350.00	☐ 54	Flycatchers	300.00
☐ 344	Yellow Shank	400.00	☐ 55	Pipiry Flycatcher	300.00
☐ 346	Green Shank	350.00	☐ 73	Bonaparte's Flycatcher	300.00
☐ 353	Great Marbled Godwit	350.00	☐ 80	Bay-breasted Warbler	300.00
☐ 357	Esquimaux Curlew	350.00	☐ 90	Redpoll Warbler	300.00
☐ 358	Glossy Ibis	1,950.00	☐ 109	Carbonated Warbler	300.00
☐ 363	Night Heron	1,950.00	☐ 113	Nashville Warbler	300.00
☐ 364	Yellow-crowned Heron	2,750.00	☐ 118	Bewick's Wren	300.00
☐ 367	Green Heron	1,500.00	☐ 133	Ruby-crowned Wren	300.00
☐ 368	Great White Heron	2,750.00	☐ 163	Henslow's Bunting	300.00
☐ 371	Redish Egret	2,500.00	☐ 172	Seaside Finch	300.00
☐ 372	Blue Crane	2,500.00	☐ 195	Towhee Bunting	300.00
☐ 375	American Flamingo	2,750.00	☐ 231	Blue Jays	300.00
☐ 380	White-fronted Goose	2,500.00	☐ 357	Esquimaux Curlew	300.00
☐ 385	Mallard Duck	2,950.00	☐ 388	Gadwall Duck	300.00
☐ 386	Dusky Duck	2,250.00	☐ 396	Red-headed Duck	300.00
☐ 388	Gadwall Duck	900.00	☐ 434	Arctic Tern	300.00

AUDUBON QUADRUPEDS

John James Audubon and Reverend John Bachman compiled this masterful work together, with Bachman doing the text. This series is known as the first comprehensive study with drawing of the quadruped of North America.

The prints were lithographed and colored by J. T. Bowen & Son of Philadelphia, the plates were issued in imperial folio size (21½″ x 27″) and later in the octavo (⅛″) size. Although these mammal prints have become quite valuable, they have never achieved the value of the bird prints.

PLATE NUMBER	SUBJECT	CURRENT RETAIL PRICE	PLATE NUMBER	SUBJECT	CURRENT RETAIL PRICE
☐ 1	Common American Wildcat	1,450.00	☐ 12	Northern Hare (Hare in winter coat)	900.00
☐ 2	Maryland Marmot	500.00	☐ 13	Musk-Rat	500.00
☐ 3	Townsend's Rocky Mountain Hare	500.00	☐ 14	Hudson's Bay Squirrel	1,100.00
☐ 4	Florida Rat	500.00	☐ 15	Oregon Flying Squirrel	1,100.00
☐ 5	Richardson's Columbian Squirrel	1,250.00	☐ 16	Canada Lynx	2,250.00
☐ 6	American Cross-Fox	1,750.00	☐ 17	Cat Squirrel	1,100.00
☐ 7	Carolina Gray Squirrel	900.00	☐ 18	Marsh Hare	600.00
☐ 8	Chipping Squirrel	1,450.00	☐ 19	Soft-Haired Squirrel	850.00
☐ 9	Parry's Marmot Squirrel	500.00	☐ 20	Townsend's Ground Squirrel	1,100.00
☐ 10	Common American Shrew Mole	500.00	☐ 21	Gray Fox	2,500.00
☐ 11	Northern Hare (Two hares)	1,100.00	☐ 22	Gray Rabbit	900.00
			☐ 23	Black Rat	900.00
			☐ 24	Four-Striped Ground Squirrel	1,100.00

PLATE NUMBER	SUBJECT	CURRENT RETAIL PRICE	PLATE NUMBER	SUBJECT	CURRENT RETAIL PRICE
☐ 25	Downy Squirrel	1,000.00	☐ 84	Franklin's Marmot-Squirrel ...	1,250.00
☐ 26	Wolverine	1,750.00	☐ 85	Jumping Mouse	350.00
☐ 27	Long-Haired Squirrel	1,100.00	☐ 86	Ocelot	3,250.00
☐ 28	Common Flying Squirrel	1,000.00	☐ 87	American Red Fox	1,850.00
☐ 29	Rocky Mountain Neotoma ...	550.00	☐ 88	Wormwood Hare	700.00
☐ 30	Cotton Rat	550.00	☐ 89	Say's Squirrel	900.00
☐ 31	Collared Peccary	1,500.00	☐ 90	Common Mouse	1,100.00
☐ 32	Polar Hare	900.00	☐ 91	Polar Bear	2,750.00
☐ 33	Mink	1,750.00	☐ 92	Texan Lynx	2,750.00
☐ 34	Black Squirrel	1,100.00	☐ 93	Black-Footed Ferret	1,250.00
☐ 35	Migratory Squirrel	1,100.00	☐ 94	Nuttall's Hare	700.00
☐ 36	Canada Porcupine	900.00	☐ 95	Orange Coloured Mouse	350.00
☐ 37	Swamp Hare	750.00	☐ 96	Cougar (Male)	2,750.00
☐ 38	Red-Bellied Squirrel	1,250.00	☐ 97	Cougar (Female and Half	
☐ 39	Leopard Spermophile	700.00		grown cub)	1,750.00
☐ 40	White-Footed Mouse	650.00	☐ 98	Ring-Tailed Bassaris	1,100.00
☐ 41	Pennant's Marten	1,650.00	☐ 99	Prairie Dog	550.00
☐ 42	Common American Skunk ...	1,500.00	☐ 100	Missouri Mouse	500.00
☐ 43	Hare Squirrel	1,100.00	☐ 101	Jaguar	3,250.00
☐ 44	Canada Pouched Rat	550.00	☐ 102	Large-Tailed Skunk	900.00
☐ 45	Wilson's Meadow Mouse	350.00	☐ 103	Hoary Marmot	900.00
☐ 46	American Beaver	1,650.00	☐ 104	Collies' Squirrel	900.00
☐ 47	American Badger	1,650.00	☐ 105	Columbia Pouched Rat	500.00
☐ 48	Douglass Squirrel	1,000.00	☐ 106	Columbian Black-Tailed Deer .	2,250.00
☐ 49	Douglasses Spermophile	550.00	☐ 107	Lewis' Marmot	500.00
☐ 50	Richardson's Spermophile ...	350.00	☐ 108	Bachman's Hare	500.00
☐ 51	Canada Otter	1,750.00	☐ 109	California Marmot-Squirrel ...	500.00
☐ 52	Swift Fox	1,950.00	☐ 110	Mole-Shaped Pouch Rat	500.00
☐ 53	Texas Skunk	1,100.00	☐ 111	Musk Ox	2,500.00
☐ 54	Brown, or Norway Rat	800.00	☐ 112	Californian Hare	1,000.00
☐ 55	Red-Tailed Squirrel	1,100.00	☐ 113	Esquimaux Dog	900.00
☐ 56	American Bison (Solitary		☐ 114	Say's Marmot Squirrel	1,100.00
	Male)	2,500.00	☐ 115	Yellow-Cheeked Meadow-	
☐ 57	American Bison (Male, female			Mouse	350.00
	and calf)	2,500.00	☐ 116	American Black or Silver Fox .	2,250.00
☐ 58	Orange-Bellied Squirrel	1,100.00	☐ 117	Dusky Squirrel	1,000.00
☐ 59	White Wease!	1,100.00	☐ 118	Long-Tailed Deer	950.00
☐ 60	Bridled Weasel	1,100.00	☐ 119	Hudson's Bay Lemming	500.00
☐ 61	Raccoon	1,500.00	☐ 120	Tawny Lemming-Back's	
☐ 62	American Elk	2,750.00		Lemming	500.00
☐ 63	Black-Tailed Hare	900.00	☐ 121	Arctic Fox	1,750.00
☐ 64	Little American Brown		☐ 122	Canada Otter	1,750.00
	Weasel	1,100.00	☐ 123	Sewellel	850.00
☐ 65	Little Harvest Mouse	850.00	☐ 124	Mexican Marmot-Squirrel	500.00
☐ 66	Virginia Opossum	1,100.00	☐ 125	American Marsh-Shrew	900.00
☐ 67	Black American Wolf	1,850.00	☐ 126	Caribou	2,250.00
☐ 68	Fox Squirrel	1,000.00	☐ 127	Cinnamon Bear	2,750.00
☐ 69	Common Star-Nose Mole	350.00	☐ 128	Rocky Mountain Goat	2,250.00
☐ 70	Say's Least Shrew	350.00	☐ 129	Northern Meadow-Mouse	350.00
☐ 71	Prairie Wolf	1,950.00	☐ 130	Pouched Jerboa Mouse	900.00
☐ 72	White American Wolf	1,850.00	☐ 131	Grizzly Bear	2,750.00
☐ 73	Rocky Mountain Sheep	2,250.00	☐ 132	Hare Indian Dog	1,100.00
☐ 74	Brewer's Shrew-Mole	350.00	☐ 133	Texan Hare	900.00
☐ 75	Carolina Shrew	350.00	☐ 134	Yellow-Bellied Marmot	850.00
☐ 76	Moose Deer	1,850.00	☐ 135	Richardson's Meadow-	
☐ 77	Prong-Horned Antelope	2,750.00		Mouse	350.00
☐ 78	Black-Tailed Deer	1,100.00	☐ 136	Common Deer	3,250.00
☐ 79	Annulated Marmot-Squirrel ...	500.00	☐ 137	Sea Otter	2,250.00
☐ 80	Leconte's Pine Mouse	350.00	☐ 138	Pine Marten	1,750.00
☐ 81	Common American Deer	3,250.00	☐ 139	Large-Tailed Spermophile ...	500.00
☐ 82	Red Texan Wolf	1,850.00	☐ 140	Little Nimble Weasel	1,100.00
☐ 83	Little Chief Hare	600.00	☐ 141	American Black Bear	2,250.00

PLATE NUMBER	SUBJECT	CURRENT RETAIL PRICE
☐ 142	Camas Rat	350.00
☐ 143	Severn River Flying Squirrel - Rocky Mountain Flying Squirrel	900.00
☐ 144	Townsend's Arvicola - Sharp-Nosed Arvicola	350.00
☐ 145	Townsend's Shrew Mole	700.00
☐ 146	Nine-Banded Armadillo	1,750.00

PLATE NUMBER	SUBJECT	CURRENT RETAIL PRICE
☐ 147	American Souslik - Oregon Meadow-Mouse, Texan Meadow-Mouse	350.00
☐ 148	Tawny Weasel	800.00
☐ 149	Fremont's Squirrel	700.00
☐ 150	Southern Pouched Rat - Dekay's Shrew - Long-Nosed Shrew - Silvery Shrew-Mole	350.00

THE AMSTERDAM AUDUBON EDITION

Done in Amsterdam, these prints are exact facsimiles of the Havell Edition prints. They are printed on rag paper and are limited to 250 copies of each print. Released in 1971, prints are 26½" x 39½" and are priced from $50.00 to $500.00.

THE OCTAVO EDITION

These small prints are modified reproductions of the Havell edition. They are one-eighth elephant folio size and bound into seven volumes. They are hand colored lithographs done by J. T. Bowen and Son of Philadelphia, and are considered original Audubon prints, as they were done under Audubon's personal supervision. Circa 1840, print size 7" x 10½", they are priced around $200.00-$300.00 each depending on condition of print.

AUDUBON PRINTS ON TEXTILE

These very rare bird prints on textile are attributed to John Potts. They appeared around 1830. Potts was an original subscriber to Audubon's "Birds of America." Size of these prints are 21½" x 27½" and they are considered extremely rare. Prices range in the area of $2,000.00 each.

MARK CATESBY

Mark Catesby was an English biologist who came to the Colonies as a collector of plant and animal specimens for a group of English patrons. Catesby, known as the *"Father of American Ornithology",* produced the first important work on American birds. Until the works of Alexander Wilson almost a half century later he remained the only artist to have painted any of them from first hand observation. He printed and hand colored most of the prints himself, which no single artist had done before him. Most of his work was done during the years of 1722 to 1726 in the southeastern coastal regions. His two-volume work "A Natural History of Carolina, Florida and the Bahama Islands" originally sold for less than $50.00. Today, a set in mint condition would command a price of around $60,000.00.

All of Catesby's paintings may be found in these two volumes.

PLATE NUMBER	SUBJECT	CURRENT RETAIL PRICE
☐ 1	White-Headed Eagle	625.00
☐ 2	Fishing Hawk	525.00
☐ 3	Pigeon Hawk	475.00
☐ 4	Swallow-Tail Hawk	575.00

PLATE NUMBER	SUBJECT	CURRENT RETAIL PRICE
☐ 5	Little Hawk	475.00
☐ 6	Turkey Buzzard	375.00
☐ 7	Little Owl	495.00
☐ 8	Goat Sucker	475.00

PLATE NUMBER	SUBJECT	CURRENT RETAIL PRICE
☐ 9	Cuckoo of Carolina	525.00
☐ 10	Parrot of Paradise	625.00
☐ 11	Parrot of Carolina	725.00
☐ 12	Purple Jackdow	475.00
☐ 13	Red-Wing Starling	525.00
☐ 14	Rice Bird	495.00
☐ 15	Crested Jay	600.00
☐ 16	Large White-Bellied Woodpecker	725.00
☐ 17	Gold-Winged Woodpecker	625.00
☐ 18	Red-Bellied Woodpecker	495.00
☐ 19	Red-Headed Woodpecker	625.00
☐ 20	Yellow-Bellied Woodpecker	475.00
☐ 21	Nuthatch	495.00
☐ 22	Passenger Pigeon	725.00
☐ 23	Carolina Turtle Dove	725.00
☐ 24	White Crowned Pigeon	600.00
☐ 25	Ground Dove	400.00
☐ 26	Mockingbird	575.00
☐ 27	Fox-Colored Thrush	600.00
☐ 28	Robin	525.00
☐ 29	Red-Legged Thrush	495.00
☐ 30	Little Thrush	525.00
☐ 31	Lark	495.00
☐ 32	Large Lark	625.00
☐ 33	Towhee Bird	525.00
☐ 34	Little Sparrow	495.00
☐ 35	Snow Bird	400.00
☐ 36	Bahama Sparrow	495.00
☐ 37	Red Bird	625.00
☐ 38	Blue Grosbeak	575.00
☐ 39	Purple Grosbeak	575.00
☐ 40	Purple Finch	475.00
☐ 41	Bahama Finch	495.00
☐ 42	American Goldfinch	525.00
☐ 43	Painted Finch	600.00
☐ 44	Blue Linnet	575.00
☐ 45	Chatterer	625.00
☐ 46	Blue Bird	675.00
☐ 47	Baltimore Bird	750.00
☐ 48	Orchard Oriole	625.00
☐ 49	Yellow-Breasted Chat	575.00
☐ 50	Purple Martin	575.00
☐ 51	Crested Flycatcher	525.00
☐ 52	Blackcap Flycatcher	575.00
☐ 53	Little Brown Flycatcher	495.00

PLATE NUMBER	SUBJECT	CURRENT RETAIL PRICE
☐ 54	Tyrant	495.00
☐ 55	Summer Red Bird	625.00
☐ 56	Crested Titmouse	595.00
☐ 57	Yellow Rump	450.00
☐ 58	Bahama Titmouse	495.00
☐ 59	Hooded Titmouse	495.00
☐ 60	Pine Creeper	475.00
☐ 61	Yellow-Throated Creeper	450.00
☐ 62	Yellow Titmouse	475.00
☐ 63	Finch Creeper	450.00
☐ 64	Hummingbird	575.00
☐ 65	Cat Bird	525.00
☐ 66	Red Start	495.00
☐ 67	Little Black Bullfinch	450.00
☐ 68	King Fisher	595.00
☐ 69	Soree or Rail	450.00
☐ 70	Plover	450.00
☐ 71	Turnstone	450.00
☐ 72	Flamingo	600.00
☐ 73	Bill of Flamingo	495.00
☐ 74	Whooping Crane	495.00
☐ 75	Blue Heron	725.00
☐ 76	Little White Heron	725.00
☐ 77	Brown Bittern	495.00
☐ 78	Crested Bittern	750.00
☐ 79	Small Bittern	725.00
☐ 80	Wood Pelican	675.00
☐ 81	White Curlew	750.00
☐ 82	Brown Curlew	750.00
☐ 83	Oyster Catcher	600.00
☐ 84	Great Booby	495.00
☐ 85	Booby	575.00
☐ 86	Noddy	465.00
☐ 87	Laughing Gull	595.00
☐ 88	Cut Water	595.00
☐ 89	Pied Bill Dopchick	450.00
☐ 90	Canada Goose	600.00
☐ 91	Hathera Duck	750.00
☐ 92	Round Crested Duck	650.00
☐ 93	Buffle-Head Duck	650.00
☐ 94	Blue-Wing Shoveler	600.00
☐ 95	Summer Duck	825.00
☐ 96	Little Brown Duck	575.00
☐ 97	Blue-Wing Teal	575.00
☐ 98	White-Face Teal	700.00

CURRIER AND IVES

Nathaniel Currier began his career in lithography in 1828. At that time, he was apprenticed at the age of 15, to Pendleton of Boston, one of the earliest American lithographic firms known. After five years, he left and engaged in various business ventures, one of which was with Stodart in New York. It was at this time in 1834 that the print *"Dartmouth College"* was published by Currier.

The venture with Stodart was short-lived, and, in 1835, Currier started his own firm at 1 Wall Street in New York. James Ives joined the firm in 1852 as a bookkeeper, after being recommended to Nathaniel Currier by his brother Charles, who also worked in the business. (Ives was married to Charles' sister-in-law.) The firm was located in New York City during its entire existence but occupied several locations over the years. The following chronology shows the addresses and the dates the business was located at each. This information is helpful to collectors interested in determining the dates of a print's publication which is not otherwise dated.

CHRONOLOGY

Currier & Stodart	1834	137 Broadway
N. Currier	1835	1 Wall Street
	1836-1837	148 Nassau Street
	1838-1856	152 Nassau Street & 2 Spruce Street
Currier & Ives	1857-1865	152 Nassau Street & 2 Spruce Street
	1866-1872	152 Nassau Street & 33 Spruce Street
	1872-1874	125 Nassau Street & 33 Spruce Street
	1874-1877	123 Nassau Street & 33 Spruce Street
	1877-1894	115 Nassau Street & 33 Spruce Street
	1894-1896	108 Fulton Street & 33 Spruce Street
	1896-1907	33 Spruce Street

Currier & Ives was the most prolific lithographic business of the time, and its output is estimated to be greater than all other lithographers combined. The prints have come to be recognized as practically our only source of colored pictures depicting American life during the middle and late 1800's. The credit for recognition of the significance and preservation of these works generally goes to the late Harry Peters. Without his efforts, this unique aspect of American life might well have vanished into obscurity. We are, however, fortunate to have not only this historical insight, but also a wide variety of subject matter fully depicting the life style, moral fiber, prejudices, and sentiments of the day. It is believed there were over 7,200 different titles published by Currier & Ives with subject matter ranging from hunting, fishing, whaling, and Mexican and Civil War events, to clipper ships, yachts, portraits, and many others covering a panorama of America.

Disaster propelled Currier and the firm into prominence. On January 13, 1840, the steamboat Lexington caught fire and was destroyed. Most of its 140 passengers and crew died. Three days later, an illustrated newspaper extra, *"The Extra Sun"*, was published. It contained a finely drawn picture of the holocaust by Currier. It was a publishing sensation and made Currier a national institution overnight. Also revealed was the sales potential for newsworthy pictures to an interested public. Currier was keen enough to recognize this fact and thereupon launched a business career which is unique in American history.

The firm was unique in its ability to combine artistic talent, skilled craftsmanship, appropriate technology, and merchandising acumen into a successful business enterprise. Well-known artists of the day including Maurer, Palmer, Tait, and Worth were a few who were employed at various times. Appropriate attention to detail is manifest in the work as examination of a clipper ship print or a country scene will attest. Only the finest materials were used: stones from Bavaria (where lithography was invented), lithographic crayons from France, and colors from Austria. The firm contributed to technology by inventing a lithographic crayon, reputed to be superior to any others available anywhere. It also produced a lithographic ink, which contained beef suet, goose grease, white wax, castile soap, gum mastic, shellac, and gas black. Innovative merchandising techniques were used. Mass distribution and low cost were the keys to success. Cost was important. Uncolored prints sold for as little as six cents each and even larger-colored folios sold for no more than three dollars. Anyone could afford a print at these prices. Prints were sold door-to-door by peddlers, in the streets by pushcart vendors, in geographically remote places through distributors, and even overseas through agents. Although an estimated ten million prints were sold, only a small percentage are in existence today.

The prints were published in various sizes but are commonly grouped into folio sizes which follow:

Very Small	Up to approximately 7″ x 9″
Small	Approximately 8.8″ x 12.8″
Medium	Approximately 9″ x 14″ to 14″ x 20″
Large	Anything over 14″ x 20″

The sizes pertain to the picture only, not to the margin around the picture. Often, print owners trimmed the margins of the pictures. Therefore, an uncut print is more valuable than a pared one.

Most of the prints were made in black and white and then handcolored. Although occasionally sold uncolored, usually a group of workers colored the prints by working from a professional artist's rendition. Because of this method, different colorings of the same print were found. Folio sizes very small, small, and medium were completed in this manner. However, the large folios were sometimes partially printed in color and then finished by hand, usually by only one artist.

Currier and Ives were successful men who worked well together. Currier retired in 1880 and died in 1888. Ives continued to run the business until his death in 1895. Although the sons of both men ran the business from 1895, it soon dissolved in 1907.

Currier and Ives prints are not only attractive and historically informative, but they represent a sound investment value. Studies indicate these prints have increased in value by 300 to 500 percent in the past twenty years. For example, the large folio "The Life of a Hunter-A Tight Fix" sold in 1928 for $3,000. Recently it sold at an auction for $7,500.

Currier and Ives prints are found in public and private collections. A large collection exists at the New York City Museum which holds over 2,885 of their prints. However, no known collection contains all of the prints because previously unknown titles are uncovered occasionally.

CURRIER & IVES: IS IT AN ORIGINAL PRINT?

© *Copyright 1978, Rudisill's Alt Print Haus*

During the years we have been collecting and dealing in Currier & Ives lithographs, the most frequent question we are asked concerning the prints is, *"How do I tell if it's a reproduction?"* The numerous books written about the Currier & Ives prints usually touch on this subject, but no one yet has pulled together in one place the various bits of information which can help a collector tell an original from a reproduction. This article is a summary of points of information we have gathered and which can be used effectively in the process of differentiating an original print from a reproduction. It should thus help the collector assure himself that he is buying an original print and, in some cases, the exact print he is seeking.

One note to make at the beginning is that it is always most desirable to examine a print in an unframed condition. Unfortunately, this is not practical at times for various reasons, such as the cumbersome nature of unframing in a shop, a dealer's understandable reluctance to "dismantle" his merchandise, and perhaps the implication such a request has to the dealer. However, this need not be a deterrent to a thorough examination of a print, as this article will make clear.

PRINT NOTATIONS

Currier & Ives prints have been reproduced at least since the turn of the century by reputable and unreputable persons using a variety of techniques. During this time, and continuing today, reputable firms have identified reproductions as such with a notation below the plate, such as, *"Reprinted from Lithographs by Currier & Ives"*, or *"Reproduction of Currier & Ives Lithograph."* Although these notations are obvious and would seem to serve to answer the question about authenticity, they are sometimes either overlooked or misunderstood. We are occasionally asked if such prints are originals and, of course, need only point out the notation and its significance.

AMERICAN HOMESTEAD WINTER by Currier and Ives

COLORING

For many years color printing techniques—including those used in making reproductions—have involved the use of thousands of tiny dots to obtain quality color prints. However, such techniques were not used by Currier & Ives and the detection of such dots in a print identifies it positively as a reproduction. Dot patterns can be discerned easily with the use of about an 8 to 9 power magnifying glass. Dots can even be detected by the unaided, but trained, eye of an expert.

Generally speaking, it will be found that colors on reproductions made by whatever means are not as vivid as, and lack the *"depth"* of, original prints. The differences are most striking when comparing an original in good condition with any reproduction, but less apparent when the comparison is between a good reproduction and an original which has deteriorated from age or lack of care.

It is well known that most of the small and medium folio prints done by Currier & Ives were printed in black and white and hand colored. The colors used were surprisingly consistent so that one becomes quickly accustomed to typical reds, greens, blues, browns, oranges and so on. Deviations from these *"normal"* colors become easily recognized after a little experience and become reasons for not buying a print.

Less well known is the fact that large folio prints were often colored by only one person, sometimes a struggling young artist trying to make a living until he was *"discovered"*. This practice resulted in less *"standardization"* in colors used and, thus, the color tests applied to small and medium folios are not equally applicable to large folios. In other words, a large folio should not be rejected on color test failure alone. A practiced eye or a reputable dealer are better tests to apply to the coloring of a large folio.

Very often Currier & Ives colorists applied a coating of gum arabic to certain portions of a print. Sometimes the application is referred to as *"sheen"*, because of the shiny appearance it gives to the area covered. The purpose in adding this coating was to give *"depth"*—a partial three-dimensional effect—to the print.

The practice of adding *"sheen"* to prints was not followed by those who reproduced prints. We have never seen *"sheen"* applied to a reproduction, even a good quality reproduction. Thus if one finds a print and notices *"sheen"* in certain areas, one has a good indication of authenticity.

A further word of caution is appropriate regarding color tests, especially on large folios. We were nearly hoodwinked on a couple of occasions because the colors looked *"right"*. However, careful examination revealed the prints failed other tests. These prints, it turned out, had been reproduced using photographic techniques, thus faithfully reproducing the original colors. The best protection against buying these prints is careful attention to the results of other tests or, again, a reputable dealer.

PAPER

As a rule, Currier & Ives used paper which was reasonably heavy—about midway between today's ordinary tablet paper and the school children's construction paper. We have measured the thickness of numerous prints and found the typical thickness to vary about a nominal thickness of ten-thousandths of an inch.

Many of the reproductions we have seen—both old and new—are printed on lighter weight paper and the thickness is about half that of the originals. The weight and stiffness often corresponds to good bond typing paper. Thus an examination of the paper a print is on, and, ideally, a comparison with any known original will be quite helpful in authenticating a print in question. The weight of two sheets of paper of the same length and width will be about proportional to the thickness of the papers. Based upon our measurements, an original print will be about twice as heavy as a reproduction. Although the absolute weights we are talking about are measured in ounces, it does not take many comparisons for a collector to develop a good sense of relative weight.

The tests of thickness and weight are valid and useful. However, there are exceptions in which the tests may fail and yet the print is, in fact, an original. The exceptions are some prints made in the late 1800's, not too many years before the firm of Currier & Ives closed its doors forever. The paper used in some cases in that era was lighter in weight, less stiff in composition, and had a smoother finish. An example of some of these prints is the small folio *"The Armoured Steel Cruiser New York"* dated 1893. In addition, Negro comic prints, done largely in the late 1870's and through the 1880's, many drawn by Thomas Worth, were often on this type of paper.

Another test which can be applied to paper is examination for water marks. Water marks here refers not to discoloration caused by the print having come in contact with water, but to the impression made in the paper to identify the manufacturer. Even though the use of water marks goes back hundreds of years, neither we nor other experts are aware of Currier & Ives having used such papers. This probably reflects the fact that water marked papers are typically higher quality, more expensive products, and that Currier & Ives were producing cheap prints for sale to a mass market. Cheap prints had to be made on inexpensive paper.

Examination for water marks cannot be done without removing a print from its frame. Proper examination requires strong backlighting to make the impression visible.

DEFINITION

The very techniques often used to make reproductions give clues to the fact that they are reproductions. These techniques result in clearly defined objects and figures and coloring is kept inside the outlines of those objects and figures. A print which looks *"too good"* for those reasons should be scrutinized closely.

A brief description of how Currier & Ives produced their prints will help the collector understand what he is looking for in figure and color definition. The original prints were mass produced using lithography and resulting in impressions in black and white and shades of gray. With the exception of some large folios which were done by young artists, coloring was added by an assembly line of women with a touch-up specialist at the end of the line. The intent was to be able to put attractive prints within the economic reach of almost everyone. Accordingly, costs had to be kept down and there was no time to allow precise applications of the colors within the outlines of the figures in print. On most originals, simple examination will reveal the evidence of hand-applied colors while most reproductions will show a sharper, more professional color definition.

COMPARISON

We were asked to make an appraisal some time ago, and in the process realized a simple lesson in determining originals and reproductions. The print in question was an old reproduction of a desirable railroad scene. The fact was obvious to us, but we had to convince the owner and a companion. Most of the points above were made and accepted for the most part, but some doubt seemed to linger. Nearing the end of our business conversation, we invited our customers to see our collection. During this "tour", the companion suddenly observed that, even without our points, it was obvious that the appraised print was a reproduction because a side-by-side comparison between it and almost any of our originals showed it to lack the depth, clarity, and general quality of an original. Thus a five minute personal observation did a more convincing job than had a half hour discourse. It taught us a lesson which we continue to use today—and which any collector can use for his edification.

PLATE SIZE

One test of a print is a check of the size of the plate against known dimensions for that print. Although incomplete, the best reference for this use is Conningham's *Currier & Ives Prints,* which was last updated in 1970. We had been told that the information in this book was accurate, usually to within ± ¹⁄₁₆ inch. Unfortunately, however, we have not been able to verify this degree of accuracy. Instead, we find that some dimensions stated with a precision of two decimal points are, in fact, incorrect by as much as ± ½ inch. As a result, we conclude that the test of plate size using this reference must be regarded as a rough one rather than a highly reliable one.

It is possible to reproduce any size print in any other size. As a result, with reproductions, one will often find large or medium folio originals reprinted in smaller sizes, but less frequently will small folio originals be found in larger sizes. In these cases, where gross differences are involved, a routine check with a book such as Conningham's is a very valuable and reliable way to detect a reprint. If one finds a print of incorrect size, the print is likely to be either a reproduction or an as yet undiscovered and unlisted subject. Because previously unknown titles are still being uncovered today, the latter occurrence is not impossible, but it is remote.

SUBJECT MATTER

It has been, and is today, possible to reproduce any print dealing with any subject matter. However, in practice it seems the tendency had been and still is to copy the more desirable Currier & Ives subjects. Thus one is more likely to see, say, a sailing ship, winter scene, or railroad print reproduced than, say, religious, juvenile, or portrait prints. This being the case, more careful scrutiny of the more desirable subjects is called for to authenticate their originality than is needed for less desirable subjects. This is not to say when one finds a desirable subject that he has probably found a reproduction. Rather, the message is, "Be on your toes".

To elaborate more specifically on subject matter, we have seen fine reproductions of many of the small folio Civil War battle prints. Some of the Negro comic prints have been reproduced. Reproductions of large folio prints of the American Country Life series (four prints) and railroad and clipper ship subjects are in circulation. Large and small folio prints of horses—especially trotters—have been reproduced.

Subjects which we have never seen unidentified reproductions of include portraits of men and women, juveniles, and religious portraits.

Some very specific information on reproductions is that the firm of Andres' Inc. published, in 1942, excellent large folio reprints of the 20 titles listed below. They advertised the prints with *"unframed plate size: 20 in. x 28 in."* Andres' Inc. was in New York, but had displays in Chicago at W. C. Owen, Inc. in the Merchandise Mart. Each print was offered in *"an antiquated mahogany or plain maple frame, 1½ in wide"*. They were also available in birdseye maple or mahogany at slightly higher cost.

ANDRES' INC. LARGE FOLIO REPRODUCTIONS

The Lightning Express Trains
Hudson Highlands
Clipper Ship "Sweepstakes"
Clipper Ship "Red Jacket"
Central Park Winter - Skating Pond
High Water on the Mississippi
Low Water on the Mississippi
Landscape Fruit and Flowers
Home to Thanksgiving
The Road Winter

The American National Game of Baseball
Seasons of Life: Childhood
Seasons of Life: Middle Age
American Winter Scenes: Morning
American Winter Scenes: Evening
New England Winter Scene
May Morning
The Old Grist Mill
American Express Train
Across the Continent

Although not all of these titles are exactly like the title on the original point, they do provide enough information to point out what prints to be wary of. For example, there is no Currier & Ives print called *May Morning*. However, in the series of four large folio *American Country Life* prints, one has a sub-title of *May Morning*. It was this print that Andres' offered.

TITLES

Some people—often beginning collectors—want to be sure that a print with a given title is contained in a reliable listing of known Currier & Ives prints. Its absence suggests the print may not be authentic. This, however, is not necessarily the case. Conningham's book is still the single most complete listing of Currier & Ives prints available today. It contains 6,896 titles. However, one collector has compiled a supplemental listing of 358 prints not in Conningham's book. Additionally, we have a listing of 26 prints not contained in either of these lists. In recent years, we have been finding about 10-12 prints a year with titles not contained in current listings.

Title vertification is a useful exercise to go through in trying to authenticate a print. However, lack of inclusion of a title in a listing of prints should not, in and of itself, be grounds for rejecting a print. This is especially true if the title varies only slightly from one listed.

THE BEST 50

In 1932, a number of Currier & Ives collectors got together and selected what they believed to be the Best 50 large folio prints published by Currier & Ives. A year later the process was repeated to determine a Best 50 list for small folio prints. (The latter list, although referred to as small folios, actually contains some medium folio prints.) Since that time these prints have enjoyed more popularity than many others and are prized possessions of serious and less serious collectors alike.

The Best 50 small folio list contains titles which appear on more than one Currier & Ives print. For example, *Noah's Ark* is one of the Best 50. Conningham's book lists five prints titled *Noah's Ark,* but with different subject compositions. Thus some collectors may be buying and paying a premium price for what they believe to be one of the Best 50, but, in fact, are obtaining the wrong print.

To help collectors buy what they want to buy, we have listed below the Best 50 small folios and Best 50 large folios and have identified each with the appropriate Conningham number. Those titles followed by an asterisk are known to appear on more than one composition.

SMALL FOLIO

			ISSUE PRICE	CURRENT PRICE
☐	1.	The Express Train - 1790*	750.00	1,000.00
☐	2.	American Railroad Scene - Snowbound - 187*	900.00	1,200.00
☐	3.	Beach Snipe Shooting - 445	900.00	1,100.00
☐	4.	Ice - boat Race on the Hudson - 3021	1,000.00	1,800.00
☐	5.	Central Park in Winter - 953	900.00	1,200.00
☐	6.	The Star of the Road - 5701	250.00	500.00
☐	7.	The High Bridge at Harlem, N.Y. - 2810*	250.00	400.00
☐	8.	Maple Sugaring, Early Spring in the Northern Woods - 3975	400.00	600.00
☐	9.	Shakers Near Lebanon - 5475	600.00	900.00
☐	10.	Winter Sports - Pickerel fishing - 6747	750.00	900.00
☐	11.	The American Clipper Ship Witch of the Wave - 115	600.00	800.00
☐	12.	Gold Mining in California - 2412	700.00	900.00
☐	13.	The Great International Boat Race - 2623	800.00	1,000.00
☐	14.	Wild Turkey Shooting - 6677	400.00	600.00
☐	15.	Perry's Victory on Lake Erie - 4754	400.00	550.00
☐	16.	Washington at Mount Vernon, 1797 - 6515	250.00	350.00
☐	17.	The Whale Fishery, "Laying On" - 6626	900.00	1,200.00
☐	18.	Chatham Square, New York - 1020	450.00	600.00
☐	19.	Water Rail Shooting - 6567*	500.00	650.00
☐	20.	The Sleigh Race - 5554*	500.00	800.00
☐	21.	Franklin's Experiment - 2128*	300.00	500.00
☐	22.	Washington Crossing the Delaware - 6523*	250.00	350.00
☐	23.	American Homestead Winter - 172	525.00	625.00
☐	24.	Washington Taking Leave of the Officers of His Army - 6547	250.00	350.00
☐	25.	Steamboat Knickerbocker - 5727	250.00	350.00
☐	26.	Kiss Me Quick! - 3349*	200.00	250.00
☐	27.	On the Mississippi Loading Cotton - 4607	250.00	350.00
☐	28.	Bound Down the River - 627	350.00	500.00
☐	29.	American Whalers Crushed in the Ice - 205	800.00	1,000.00
☐	30.	Dartmouth College - 1446*	1,000.00	1,300.00
☐	31.	Terrific Combat Between the Monitor, 2 Guns, and the Merrimac, 10 Guns - 5996*	350.00	500.00
☐	32.	General Francis Marion - 2250	200.00	300.00
☐	33.	Art of Making Money Plenty - 275	200.00	300.00
☐	34.	Hon. Abraham Lincoln - 2895*	150.00	250.00
☐	35.	Gen. George Washington (with cape) - 2261*	150.00	250.00
☐	36.	Black Bass Spearing - 543	1,100.00	1,300.00
☐	37.	Early Winter - 1652	1,500.00	2,000.00
☐	38.	Woodcock Shooting - 6773*	450.00	600.00
☐	39.	"Dutchman" and "Hiram Woodruff" - 1640	600.00	700.00
☐	40.	Great Conflagration at Pittsburgh, Pa. - 2581	500.00	600.00
☐	41.	Bear Hunting, Close Quarters - 446*	1,500.00	2,000.00
☐	42.	The Destruction of Tea at Boston Harbor - 1571	600.00	800.00
☐	43.	Cornwallis is Taken - 1258	250.00	400.00
☐	44.	Landing of the Pilgrims at Plymouth, 11th Dec., 1620 - 3435*	200.00	300.00
☐	45.	The Great Fight for the Championship - 2613	300.00	500.00
☐	46.	Benjamin Franklin - 499*	150.00	300.00
☐	47.	Noah's Ark - 4494*	150.00	200.00
☐	48.	Black Eyed Susan - 551*	125.00	150.00
☐	49.	The Bloomer Costume - 574*	150.00	175.00
☐	50.	The Clipper Yacht "America" - 1173*	700.00	1,000.00

LARGE FOLIO

☐	1.	Husking - 3008	4,000.00	8,500.00
☐	2.	American Forest Scene - Maple Sugaring - 157	3,000.00	4,500.00
☐	3.	Central Park Winter - The Skating Pond - 954	3,000.00	5,000.00
☐	4.	Home to Thanksgiving - 2882	7,000.00	8,000.00
☐	5.	Life of a Hunter - A Tight Fix - 3522	12,000.00	15,000.00

			ISSUE PRICE	CURRENT PRICE
☐	6.	Life on the Prairie - The Buffalo Hunt - 3527	5,500.00	6,000.00
☐	7.	The Lightning Express Trains Leaving the Junction - 3535*	5,000.00	6,500.00
☐	8.	Peytona and Fashion - 4763	7,000.00	8,000.00
☐	9.	The Rocky Mountains - Emigrants Crossing the Plains - 5196	7,500.00	10,000.00
☐	10.	Trolling for Blue Fish - 6158	3,000.00	4,000.00
☐	11.	Whale Fishery - The Sperm Whale in a Flurry - 6628*	7,000.00	8,000.00
☐	12.	Winter in the Country - The Old Grist Mill - 6738	5,500.00	7,000.00
☐	13.	American Farm Scenes No. 4 (Winter) - 136	2,000.00	4,000.00
☐	14.	American National Game of Baseball - 180	8,000.00	10,000.00
☐	15.	American Winter Sports - Trout Fishing on Chateaugay Lake - 210*	3,000.00	4,500.00
☐	16.	Mink Trapping - Prime - 4139	7,500.00	8,000.00
☐	17.	Preparing for Market - 4870*	1,500.00	3,000.00
☐	18.	Winter in the Country - Getting Ice - 6737	5,000.00	7,500.00
☐	19.	Across the Continent - Westward the Course of Empire Takes its Way - 33 ..	7,500.00	8,000.00
☐	20.	Life on the Prairie - The Trappers Defense - 3528	5,500.00	6,000.00
☐	21.	The Midnight Race on the Mississippi - 4116*	2,000.00	3,500.00
☐	22.	The Road - Winter - 5171	6,000.00	8,000.00
☐	23.	Summer Scenes in New York Harbor - 5876	2,000.00	3,000.00
☐	24.	Trotting Cracks at the Forge - 6169	2,000.00	3,500.00
☐	25.	View of San Francisco - 6409	4,000.00	6,000.00
☐	26.	Wreck of the Steamship "San Francisco" - 5492	3,500.00	4,500.00
☐	27.	Taking the Back Track "A Dangerous Neighborhood" - 5961	5,000.00	5,500.00
☐	28.	American Field Sports - Flush'd - 149	1,500.00	3,000.00
☐	29.	American Hunting Scenes - A Good Chance - 174	1,500.00	3,000.00
☐	30.	American Winter Scenes - Morning - 208	4,000.00	6,000.00
☐	31.	Autumn in New England - Cider Making - 322	2,500.00	3,500.00
☐	32.	Catching a Trout - "We Hab You Now, Sar" - 845	800.00	1,000.00
☐	33.	Clipper Ship "Nightingale" - 1159	5,500.00	7,000.00
☐	34.	The Life of a Fireman - The Race - 3519	2,000.00	4,000.00
☐	35.	Mac and Zachary Taylor - Horse Race - 3848	1,000.00	2,000.00
☐	36.	New England Winter Scene - 4420	3,500.00	5,000.00
☐	37.	Rail Shooting on the Delaware - 5054	3,500.00	5,000.00
☐	38.	Snowed Up - Ruffed Gouse - Winter - 5581	3,000.00	4,000.00
☐	39.	Surrender of General Burgoyne at Saratoga - 5907	3,000.00	3,500.00
☐	40.	Surrender of Cornwallis at Yorktown - 5906	3,000.00	3,500.00
☐	41.	Clipper Ship "Red Jacket" - 1165*	4,000.00	5,000.00
☐	42.	American Winter Sports - Deer Shooting on the Shattagee - 209	3,000.00	5,000.00
☐	43.	The Bark "Theoxana" - 371	1,500.00	2,500.00
☐	44.	The Cares of a Family - 814*	2,000.00	2,500.00
☐	45.	The Celebrated Horse Lexington - 887*	1,600.00	1,800.00
☐	46.	Grand Drive - Central Park - 2481	2,000.00	3,000.00
☐	47.	The Great Fire at Chicago - 2615	2,000.00	3,000.00
☐	48.	Landscape, Fruit and Flowers - 3440	1,500.00	2,500.00
☐	49.	The Life of a Fireman - The Metropolitan System - 3516	2,000.00	4,000.00
☐	50.	The Splendid Naval Triumph on the Mississippi - 5659	750.00	1,000.00

STATES AND RESTRIKES

The terms *"second state"* (or *"third state"*) and *"restrike"* are often used interchangeably when reference is made to prints which were made after the first impressions were taken from the stone plate. However, there is a distinction to be made between the terms.

"State" is properly used to refer to impressions taken during the development of a print. Thus an original print may have been made from a stone plate. The stone may then have been altered in some significant way (e.g. adding people to a scene) to insignificant way (e.g. changing a letter in the title) and a print made from the modified stone. The impression made is referred to as a "second state." If the plate were modified again, the print would be referred to as a *"third state"*, and so on. Obviously a *"second state"*, etc. print will closely resemble an original in quality. Collectors today appear to regard *"second state"*, etc. prints as being worth essentially the same as a *"pure"* original.

Restrikes are neither true originals nor true reproductions. They are considered collectible by some people and sometimes command attractive prices. Currier & Ives are believed to have produced restrikes of their own, but others who had access to some of the stone produced prints in the early 1900's. One such example is Joseph Koehler who bought some stones at auctions after Currier & Ives went out of business in 1907. He later published some Darktown comics and a large folio Lincoln portrait under his own name. Another example was a man named Max Williams who issued six restrikes of large folio clipper ships in 1915. The titles of these restrikes are listed below.

Clipper Ship Dreadnought off Tudkar Light   *Clipper Ship Ocean Express*
Clipper Ship Dreadnought off Sand Hook   *Clipper Ship Sweepstakes*
Clipper Ship Flying Cloud   *Clipper Ship Three Brothers*

Reputable dealers will represent *"second states"*, etc. and restrikes as such and this is yet another reason for doing business with these people.

MOUNTING

One sometimes finds prints which have been mounted. Mounting usually refers to placing a print onto a heavier piece of paper stock, often similar to mat board. However, it also is used to describe another practice, probably used as a form of preservation, which was to apply a linen backing to prints. The backing served to stiffen the paper and thus make it less susceptible to tearing or damage which might occur from inadvertent bending or rolling. This practice was especially effective on large folios.

If properly done, mounting or backing does not affect the appearance of the print and, in fact, provides a degree of protection against tearing of the paper. Nevertheless, some purists regard such prints as having been *"tampered with"* and regard them as being worth less than unmolested prints.

Mounted prints are almost impossible to detect except when they are unframed. If the collector is sensitive to this factor in buying prints, he should insist on examining the print out of its frame, especially if the surface looks *"too flat"*. Some undulations in the print surface—detectable even though framed—are proof that mounting has not taken place.

THE DEALER

A final important point for novices and serious collectors alike is to deal with reputable businessmen. As with any other business transactions, knowing from whom you are buying, and dealing with established and knowledgeable dealers, will practically assure against the purchase of undersirable merchandise. Of course, identifying such dealers may be an initial problem, but discreet inquiry can soon separate the wheat from the chaff. We have found that reputable people will answer questions no matter how trivial, admit to ignorance when it exists, refer you to others if they cannot help, allow complete examination of merchandise, agree to refund money if the purchaser is dissatisfied, and generally be helpful and cooperative. Less reputable dealers will show reluctance in one way or another to accommodate the wishes of the customers. We are reminded of a roadside sign often passed on trips we used to take. Its message sums up the point: "If you don't know furs, know your furrier".

It has not been our intention in this writing to condemn reproductions but to show how to recognize them. To the purist, reproductions are anathema. But they have their place in antique lore. More and more they are showing up in antique shops and have the redeeming features of being less expensive than originals, attractive in their own right, and probably represent an investment because we suspect their value will continue to increase with time as most other antiques are doing. However, one should not lose sight of the fact that today their value is primarily that of a pretty picture.

The information offered here is intended to help a purchaser make a sound buy. The elements of *"how to"* were added where appropriate, because the proper application of knowledge is, of course, what yields the desired results. Effectively used, this information will help a collector to avoid the financial loss and the personal embarrassment that come with owning a reproduction when the intent was to own an original.

LOUIS ICART

Louis Icart was born in the small southern French city of Toulouse. This city was the home of many famous French artists, the most famous being Henri de Toulouse-Lautrec. In this atmosphere Icart became aware of the fine arts. He began his sketching at the early age of six and by the age of fifteen was sketching designs for costumes. As a fashion artist he was quite successful.

While Icart was working for major design studios, women's fashions were undergoing a complete transition. Women were demanding less of the billowing skirts, high necklines, and lace and were desiring more of the clinging dresses. Because of his occupation, his first one-man show was not too successful as his critics associated his paintings with dress designing rather than artistic works.

With the outbreak of World War I, Icart went to the front as a soldier. Not completely abandoning his desire as an artist, he would sketch and etch on any available material. At the end of the war, with encouragement from friends, Icart began to make prints of the etchings he had made during this period. When they were published they became an immediate international success.

Icart's works demonstrate a mastery of dry point, line etching, aquatint, and their variations. Icart produced up to 500 prints each of over one thousand subjects. However, his works are scarce, because many have been lost or destroyed.

THE PRINTS

Most Icart prints are easily identified. Most bear his hallmark which is usually located near the edge of the print. The picture on the following page is his hallmark in actual size.

His signature is also easily identifiable, although subject to forgery and sometimes found on lithographic reproductions of his prints.

Earlier works will have his signature but may not bear the hallmark. Most will, however, bear the stamp of his gallery, an oval shape with the letters EM for "l'estampe moderne." It is possible to have an original Icart with no hallmark at all, but this is rare.

The prints are usually numbered in the traditional manner of a first number representing the number of the print then a slash mark followed by a second number. This second number represents the number of prints in the edition (excluding artist's proofs and hors commerce prints if they exist). For example 75/120 means the print is numbered seventy-five of an edition of one hundred and twenty prints.

Icart pulled two editions frequently, one for Europe and one for American distribution. Sometimes the number is preceded by the letter "A" for an American edition; as in the example A 75/120. All prints were not numbered.

The following is a listing of prints with current prices compiled from dealers' price lists across the country. These prices are for mint prints (perfect or near perfect), and of course, prices vary from one area of the country to another.

TITLE	PRICE RANGE	
☐ After The Raid	1,550.00	2,000.00
☐ Above the Wings	1,850.00	2,250.00
☐ Amazonia	4,500.00	5,000.00
☐ Angry Buddha	800.00	
☐ Apache Dancer	750.00	
☐ Arabian Nite (1926) (Masked nude rear)	850.00	

COURSING II *by Louis Icart*

TITLE	PRICE RANGE	
☐ Attic Room	1,100.00	
☐ Arrival (Woman entering doorway)	700.00	
☐ Autumn Leaves	750.00	850.00
☐ Backstage	750.00	
☐ Ballerina with roses	750.00	
☐ Bathing beauties	1,500.00	2,000.00
☐ Before the Raid	2,500.00	3,000.00
☐ Bird of Prey (Woman with eagle)	1,800.00	2,250.00
☐ Bird Seller	850.00	
☐ Black Fan	750.00	
☐ Birth of Venus	2,000.00	2,500.00
☐ Blue Book	750.00	
☐ Blue Buddha	750.00	
☐ Blue Broken Jug	750.00	
☐ Blue Parasol	750.00	
☐ Bo Peep	750.00	
☐ Bubbles	1,250.00	1,500.00
☐ Butterfly Falls	1,200.00	
☐ Carmen	750.00	
☐ Casanova	850.00	950.00
☐ Champs (Girls in buggy)	750.00	850.00
☐ Charm of Montmarte	750.00	
☐ Chestnut Vendor	750.00	850.00
☐ Clipped Wings	750.00	850.00
☐ Cinderella	850.00	
☐ Coach, The	750.00	
☐ Conchita	1,500.00	
☐ Courage France	2,000.00	2,500.00
☐ Coursing II	1,250.00	1,500.00
☐ Coursing III	1,500.00	2,000.00
☐ Cat with Paw in Fishbowl	750.00	
☐ Dame Rose	750.00	
☐ Dancer (Finale)	750.00	
☐ D'Artagnan	850.00	
☐ Date Tree	750.00	
☐ Dear Friends	1,100.00	1,250.00
☐ December	850.00	
☐ Defense of the Homeland	1,950.00	2,250.00

TITLE	PRICE RANGE	
☐ Descending Coach	700.00	
☐ Dollar	500.00	
☐ Don Juan	950.00	
☐ Dream Waltz	1,200.00	1,400.00
☐ Ecstasy	1,500.00	2,000.00
☐ Embrace	750.00	
☐ Eve (Nude) (Large Oval)	1,400.00	1,500.00
☐ Fair Dancer	750.00	
☐ Faust	900.00	1,000.00
☐ Favorites, The	950.00	
☐ Fashion Early	700.00	
☐ Feeding Time	750.00	850.00
☐ Finlandia	850.00	1,000.00
☐ Flower Vendor	750.00	
☐ Follies	3,000.00	4,000.00
☐ Forbidden Fruit	750.00	800.00
☐ Fountain, The	1,000.00	1,500.00
☐ Four Dears	950.00	
☐ Frou Frou	850.00	
☐ France de Foyer	1,800.00	2,000.00
☐ French Bus	900.00	
☐ French Doll	750.00	
☐ Gatsby 1920's	750.00	
☐ Gay Senorita	850.00	
☐ Gay Trio	1,850.00	2,000.00
☐ German Eagle	1,850.00	2,000.00
☐ Girl in Crinoline	800.00	
☐ Golden Veil	1,500.00	
☐ Goosed	700.00	
☐ Grande Eve	7,000.00	7,500.00
☐ Green Broken Jug	750.00	
☐ Guardian	900.00	
☐ Gust of Wind	1,250.00	
☐ Happy Birthday	1,200.00	1,500.00
☐ Hoop-La	900.00	
☐ Hortensia	750.00	850.00
☐ Human Grenade	2,000.00	2,500.00
☐ Illusion	5,000.00	7,500.00
☐ Inquest	900.00	
☐ Intimacy	750.00	
☐ Invitation	850.00	
☐ Jardinare (Woman lying at urn)	450.00	
☐ Joan of Arc	1,000.00	1,350.00
☐ Joy of Life	2,000.00	2,500.00
☐ Lady of the Camillas	850.00	900.00
☐ Lampshade	600.00	700.00
☐ Laughing	1,000.00	
☐ Laziness	1,200.00	
☐ Leda and the Swan	1,000.00	1,250.00
☐ Les Amis	1,250.00	
☐ Lillies	1,500.00	
☐ Lindberg	900.00	
☐ Love Birds	700.00	
☐ Love Letters	750.00	
☐ Lovers	800.00	
☐ Loves Awakening	900.00	
☐ Loves Blossom	2,250.00	2,500.00
☐ Madame Bovary	850.00	
☐ Mannequin	600.00	
☐ Manon	800.00	
☐ Mardi Gras	2,000.00	2,500.00
☐ Martini	1,850.00	2,000.00
☐ Masked	1,000.00	

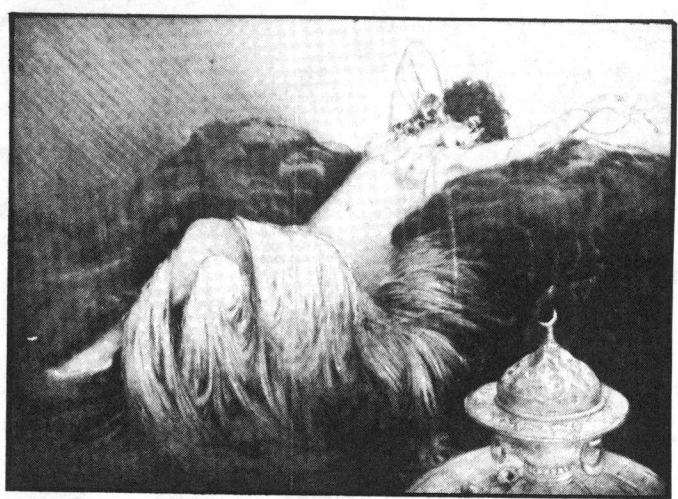

FUMEE - SMOKE *by Louis Icart*

TITLE	PRICE RANGE	
☐ Mealtime (Woman with puppies)	800.00	950.00
☐ Memories	1,800.00	2,200.00
☐ Melody Hour	7,000.00	9,000.00
☐ Milkmaid	700.00	
☐ Mimi looking out window	700.00	
☐ Miss America	1,000.00	1,200.00
☐ Miss Britain	1,500.00	2,000.00
☐ Miss California	1,000.00	1,200.00
☐ Miss France	1,500.00	
☐ Miss Liberty	1,500.00	1,800.00
☐ Mockery (The Red Screen)	750.00	
☐ Monkeyshines	850.00	
☐ Montmarte	750.00	
☐ Morning Cup	850.00	1,000.00
☐ Mother and child with soldier in background	2,000.00	2,250.00
☐ Musetta	750.00	850.00
☐ Mutt, The	700.00	
☐ Nijinsky	750.00	
☐ Nurse, The	750.00	
☐ One Beauty (Also known as "Dollar")	500.00	
☐ On the Beach	750.00	
☐ On the Green	750.00	
☐ Orange Seller	850.00	
☐ Orchids	1,500.00	2,000.00
☐ Parasol, The	1,000.00	1,250.00
☐ Paris (Two women overlooking Paris)	700.00	
☐ Paris Flowers	750.00	
☐ Peonies	750.00	
☐ Pierrot	750.00	
☐ Pink Alcove	750.00	
☐ Pink Slip	1,250.00	1,400.00
☐ Playful Pup	750.00	
☐ Poem	1,800.00	

TITLE	PRICE RANGE	
☐ Puppies	750.00	
☐ Rain	850.00	1,000.00
☐ Rainbow	1,800.00	2,000.00
☐ Recollections (Woman at desk)	750.00	850.00
☐ Red Alcove	750.00	
☐ Red Riding Hood	850.00	900.00
☐ Reflections Pool	1,500.00	1,800.00
☐ Repose	4,000.00	5,000.00
☐ Ritz, The	1,500.00	2,000.00
☐ Salome	750.00	
☐ Sappho	750.00	
☐ Scherazade	800.00	
☐ Seashell (Nude woman on shell)	1,500.00	2,000.00
☐ Secrets or Blue Book	750.00	
☐ Singing Lesson	850.00	
☐ Sleeping Beauty	950.00	1,250.00
☐ Smoke	1,350.00	1,500.00
☐ Speed (Woman and greyhound)	1,500.00	2,000.00
☐ Sofa	2,500.00	
☐ Spanish Dancer	850.00	
☐ Spilled Apples	750.00	
☐ Springtime	900.00	
☐ Summer Music	600.00	
☐ Swans	1,500.00	2,000.00
☐ Sweet Mystery	950.00	1,250.00
☐ Symphony in Blue	850.00	
☐ Symphony in White	1,200.00	1,500.00
☐ Tennis	900.00	1,000.00
☐ Three of Four Seasons	900.00	
☐ The Coach (There are several versions)	750.00	
☐ Tosca	850.00	950.00
☐ Thoroughbreds (Woman with horse, Rare)	3,500.00	4,000.00
☐ Treasure Chest	600.00	
☐ Trenches	2,250.00	2,500.00
☐ Two Beauties	5,000.00	5,500.00
☐ Unmasked	1,200.00	
☐ Venetian Nights	900.00	
☐ Venus (Companion to Eve)	1,500.00	
☐ Victory in the Skies	2,250.00	2,500.00
☐ Victory Wreath (Soldier holding woman holding wreath up in air, WWI)	2,250.00	2,500.00
☐ View of Montmarte	850.00	
☐ Voice of the Cannon - WWI	2,250.00	2,500.00
☐ Waltz Echoes	1,500.00	
☐ Waterfall	1,500.00	1,800.00
☐ White Lillies	1,500.00	2,000.00
☐ White Underwear	1,250.00	
☐ White Wings	900.00	
☐ Winsome	900.00	
☐ Wishing Well	600.00	
☐ Wisteria	900.00	1,200.00
☐ Woman descending coach and coachmen, arrival	600.00	
☐ Woman holding feeding dish, four cats	750.00	
☐ Woman holding little red cage	700.00	
☐ Woman in snow with statue	750.00	
☐ Woman on pillow eating grapes	700.00	
☐ Woman in boudoir with black cat	600.00	
☐ Woman stepping into coach and coachmen, departure	700.00	
☐ Wounded Dove	750.00	
☐ Young Mother	750.00	2,000.00
☐ Youth	2,500.00	
☐ Zest	1,400.00	1,500.00

MAXFIELD PARRISH

Born in 1870, Maxfield Parrish became a very successful illustrator and artist. In 1889, he studied at the Pennsylvania Academy of the Fine Arts. By the early 1900s, Parrish had drawn book and advertising illustrations, murals, and magazine covers. He experienced national acclaim until the early 1940s.

Although his popularity dwindled for the next twenty years, it soared again in the 1960s. He died in 1966. A popular collector's item is Parrish's Collier magazine covers.

For further information, contact The Illustrator Collector's News, P.O. Box 1958, Sequin, WA 98382.

ADS

	CURRENT RETAIL PRICE
☐ Article (Rape of the Rhine-Gold, 16 pages, 16 illustrations-scarce-1898)	30.00
☐ Colgate Ad (Violet Talc Ad back cover magazine). Dutch boy & girl pointing to talc can	25.00
☐ Colgate Ad (Violet Talc Ad). Dutch boy running away with talc & 4 Dutch maiden	30.00
☐ Colgate Ad. Shaving stick & Dutch boy shaving	30.00
☐ Fisk Tire Ad - King on throne, 8¼" x 12"	25.00
☐ Fisk Tire Ad - Knave riding on tire cover, 8½" x 12"	30.00
☐ Fisk Tire Ad - Fit For a King (king & 2 comical characters pulling tire apart on either side of king), 12" x 16", rare	25.00
☐ Ferry Seed Ad. Peter the Husbander (Woman on pumpkin & Peter in chair)	22.00
☐ Hires Ad (2 gnomes drinking Hires) 6" x 9½"	20.00
☐ Jello Ad (Polly Put the Kettle On) 7½" x 10½"	20.00

COLLIER COVERS

☐ April Showers (Youth holding umbrella in the rain) 1909	30.00
☐ Arithmetic (Child and schoolmaster among high letters) 1911	30.00
☐ Artist, The (Artist at painting-large blue sky) 1909	30.00
☐ Artist (Sitting in front of canvas) 1909	35.00
☐ Balloon Man, The (Gent in long scarf w/balloons) 1908	35.00
☐ Botanist 1908	30.00
☐ Boars Head, The (Gents having feast) 1905	40.00
☐ Buccaneer with Sword 1909	30.00
☐ Chef sitting between two giant lobsters 1910	35.00
☐ Comic Cop (little policeman holding billy club), scarce 1905	30.00
☐ Comical sign painter painting Colliers 1909	35.00
☐ Dramatic Numbers	75.00
☐ Discussion (two-gents having a conversation) 1909	30.00
☐ End, The (taking his final bow) . . . from Knave of Hearts 1929	35.00
☐ Fourth of July (Soldier w/large Sword) 1908	35.00
☐ Father Time	100.00
☐ Gardener, The (Gent standing with hoe and watering can) 1906	40.00
☐ Girl on sled going downhill in snow 1910	40.00
☐ Heralds, The (from the Knave of Hearts) 1929	40.00
☐ Idiot, The (comical gent in checkered gown reading book) 1910	40.00
☐ Independence (children carrying flags) 1905	30.00
☐ Jack Frost (Gnome painting leaves) 1936	40.00
☐ Lincolns Birthday (youth sitting on a rock looking into pool) 1906	40.00
☐ Little Girl in bed with hand in Christmas stocking 1906	35.00
☐ Lone Fisherman, The (Man fishing in large lake) 1909	35.00
☐ Man in top hat fishing from top of piling 1913	35.00
☐ Man with oxen walking through snow in the mountains 1906	35.00
☐ Manager, The (comical fellow bowing to viewer, from KOH-1929)	40.00
☐ Nature Lover, The (character in checker robe) 1911	30.00
☐ New Year, 1906 (Youth and Father Time)	35.00
☐ New Year, 1907 (Father Time shaking hands with youth)	40.00
☐ Nine little soldiers in a row, 1912	25.00
☐ Nude maiden sitting on a swing in trees, scarce. 1906	65.00
☐ Nude pastel surrounded by flowers, rare. 1911	50.00
☐ Oklahoma comes in (Indian and Cowboy holding a star) 1907	35.00

	CURRENT RETAIL PRICE
☐ Old Father Time winding clock, scarce. 1905	40.00
☐ Old King Cole (knaves carrying large platters to king) 1909	40.00
☐ Old King Cole (he called for his pipe & bowl) 1909	40.00
☐ Old King Cole (king with two sentries) 1913	35.00
☐ Page, The (from the Knave of Hearts)	40.00
☐ Philosopher, The (old man sitting, blue sky) 1912	35.00
☐ Prospector finding gold in desert, 1911	55.00
☐ School Days (Youth surrounded by high letters) 1908	85.00
☐ Scottish guard in uniform presenting arms. 1911	35.00
☐ Soldiers repeated all over cover. 1912	40.00
☐ Spring (Bare breasted maiden in field) scarce, 1905	65.00
☐ Summer	85.00
☐ Thanksgiving (man and children walking in snow) 1906	75.00
☐ Thanksgiving (Pioneer carrying musket and turkey) 1906	75.00
☐ Thanksgiving (Hobo sitting by fire) 1905	35.00
☐ Three Shepherds. 1904	35.00
☐ Tourists, The (Man standing in long coat) 1909	35.00
☐ Two chefs leaning over a pot of pudding. 1956	40.00
☐ Two comic chefs holding giant spoons, from kolt-1929	30.00
☐ Two comic guards, smile and frown, at attention. 1913	30.00
☐ Two figures facing each other with landscape in background. 1906	30.00
☐ Vaudeviller (comical fellow in checkered suit) 1908	40.00
☐ Wassail Bowl, The (Gent carrying large bowl), rare. 1909	55.00
☐ Young pirate sitting on lighted bomb, writing letter. 1909	35.00

MISCELLANEOUS COVERS

☐ Book news cover (maiden reading book), rare, 1897	37.50
☐ Century cover (nude sitting in forest), a prize cover, 1917	50.00
☐ Harpers Monthly cover (Three Cupids) 1901	50.00
☐ Harpers Weekly (Christmas issue-comical chief), scarce cover, 1908	40.00
☐ Ladies Home Journal cover (air castles, nude sitting) award cover, 1904	50.00
☐ Ladies Home Journal cover (Arizona . . . beautiful Arizona mountains sunlite with oranges) 1930	35.00
☐ Ladies Home Journal (Girl water skier) 1930	35.00
☐ Ladies Home Journal (Maiden with trees in background) 1896	55.00
☐ Ladies Home Journal (Princely character & maiden in garden with large urns) 1901	35.00
☐ Ladies Home Journal (A shower of fragrance) 1912	35.00
☐ Ladies Home Journal (Sweet nothings, maidens in window) 1921	35.00
☐ Life cover (Bookstuff No.) 1922	50.00
☐ Life cover (a dark futurist, self portrait) 1923	50.00
☐ Life cover (her window, knave on wall at night)	50.00
☐ Life cover (The masquerader, gent in checked costume)	50.00
☐ Life cover (Christmas cover, first for Life) 1899	60.00
☐ Life cover (St. Valentine) very rare	50.00
☐ Scribners cover (Christmas cover, 3 wise men) 1900	50.00

PRINTS

☐ Above the Balcony (knaves and maidens in garden)	35.00
☐ Air Castles (nude in bubbles)	125.00
☐ Aladdin in Cave of 40 Thieves, 12" x 16¼", on quality paper	85.00
☐ Aladdin and the Lamp, 10" x 12"	70.00
☐ Ancient Trees (large oak tree by lake)	95.00
☐ Argonauts, In Quest of the Golden Fleece, The	40.00
☐ Atlas (giant holding up sky)	70.00
☐ Arizona (landscape of mountain-rich blues) 11" x 13"	40.00
☐ Aucassin Seeks Nicolotte (knight on horse), Bookplate SM	18.00
☐ Autumn (Maiden standing on hilltop)	75.00
☐ Below the Balcony (Knaves and maidens in garden)	35.00
☐ Bookplate (John Cox-His Book)	20.00
☐ Brazen, The Boatman 10" x 12"	70.00
☐ Broadmoor, rare	750.00
☐ Brown & Bigelow Landscape (the village church) 24" x 27"	175.00

☐ Cadmus Showing the Dragons Teeth, 10″ x 12″	70.00
☐ Canyon (Maiden in canyon) 12″ x 5″	130.00
☐ Chef Serving King	50.00
☐ The Centaur	70.00
☐ Circes Palace (Maiden standing on porch)	70.00
☐ Cleopatra, rare, large	500.00
☐ Community Plate, 11″ x 13″, 1918	25.00
☐ Contentment, Large Edison Mazda Calendar, large	375.00
☐ Dawn (Maiden sitting on rock) Mazda print	42.00
☐ Daybreak (nude and maiden on porch), small size	125.00
☐ Daybreak, large size	200.00
☐ Dinkey Bird (nude on swing) 13½″ x 18″, 1904	125.00
☐ Djer-Kiss Ad (Maiden on swing in forest) 10½″ x 14″	40.00
☐ Dreaming (nude sitting under oak), medium size	225.00
☐ Dreaming, large size	400.00
☐ Dream Castle in the Sky, 9″ x 12″	35.00
☐ Duchess at Prayer, illustration for L'Allegro, 10″ x 15″, 1901	20.00
☐ Ecstasy (Maiden standing on rock), small size	125.00
☐ Ecstasy, Large Edison Mazda Calendar	500.00
☐ Enchantment (Maiden standing on stars at night) 9½″ x 20½″, large	400.00
☐ The End	45.00
☐ Errant Pan, The (Pan sitting by stream) 6″ x 8″, small	25.00
☐ Evening (Nude sitting on rock in lake)	135.00
☐ Evening (Nude sitting in lake), 13″ x 17″	80.00
☐ Fisherman and the Geni, The; 10″ x 12″	65.00
☐ Florentine Fete (Maidens in garden) 10″ x 16″	30.00
☐ Garden of Allah (3 maidens sitting in garden), medium size	125.00
☐ Garden of Allah, Large Edison Mazda Calendar	275.00
☐ Garden of Opportunity, The (Prince and princess)	325.00
☐ Garden of Opportunity Triptyk, 10″ x 13″	50.00
☐ Golden Hours (Maidens in forest) Large Edison Mazda Calendar	350.00
☐ Hilltop (youths sitting on mountain), medium size House of Art	200.00
☐ Hilltop, large size, House of Art	450.00
☐ Hilltop, small size	75.00
☐ His Christmas Dinner (Tramp having dinner)	50.00
☐ Interlude (Maidens sitting in garden playing lutes)	110.00
☐ Isola Bella Scene, 9″ x 10″	16.00
☐ Jason and His Teacher Chiron The Centeur, 1910	35.00
☐ King of the Black Isles (King on throne) 9″ x 11″	70.00
☐ King and Chancellor	40.00
☐ Kings Son, The (Arab in garden by fountain)	40.00
☐ Knaves and Maidens (conversing in garden)	50.00
☐ Knave and Frog	45.00
☐ Lady Violetta	65.00
☐ Lady Ursella	55.00
☐ Lamplighters, The (Mazda Calendar) 9″ x 13″, 1924	90.00
☐ Lampseller of Bagdad, The (Maiden on steps), Mazda Calendar	350.00
☐ Land of Make-Believe, The (Maiden to garden)	125.00
☐ Little Princess, The (Princess sitting by fountain)	18.00
☐ Lute Players, small size, House of Art	60.00
☐ Lute Players, large size, House of Art	400.00
☐ Milkmaid, The (Maiden walking in Mountain)	20.00
☐ Morning (Maiden sitting on rock) 13″ x 16″	120.00
☐ Night Call (Bare breasted girl in surf) 6″ x 8″	25.00
☐ October - 1900 (Woman in long gown holding fruit draped in her gown. Large orange moon behind her head) 18″ x 23″	25.00
☐ Old Romance (Nude sitting in pool) 6″ x 8″	45.00
☐ Old King Cole	375.00
☐ Pandora's Box (Maiden sitting by large box)	70.00
☐ The Page	110.00
☐ Pierrot (Clown with lute and gorgeous golds in water, sky glittering) 1912	110.00

GARDEN OF ALLAH *by Maxfield Parrish*

CURRENT
RETAIL PRICE

☐ Pool of the Vista D'Este (Nude boy lying down besides luminous pool) 7¼" x 10¾"	18.00
☐ Pied Piper, rare	375.00
☐ Pipe Night (Comical men with pipes and coffee urns sitting facing each other at table) 9" x 12½" ..	25.00
☐ Post standing by river in forest	25.00
☐ Potpourri (Nude in garden picking flowers)	40.00
☐ Primitive Man (Unique salesman's sample) 4¾" x 7½"	45.00
☐ Prince Godad (Pirates on boat)	70.00
☐ Prince, The (from Knave of Hearts) 10" x 12½", very rare	125.00
☐ Prosperina (Maiden in the sea) 10" x 12"	70.00
☐ Providing it By the Book (2 gents at table)	18.00
☐ Queen Gulnare (Maiden on porch) 10" x 12"	70.00
☐ Reluctant Dragon, rare	500.00
☐ Reveries (two maidens sitting by fountain)	35.00
☐ Reveries, Large Edison Mazda Calendar	200.00
☐ Rubiayat	375.00
☐ Sandman, The (Sandman with full moon) 6" x 7½"	40.00
☐ Scribners One of the Wise Men, 10" x 11½"	18.00
☐ Search for the Singing Tree	35.00
☐ Sea Nymphs, 12" x 14", 1914	45.00
☐ Seven Green Polls at Cintra, 6" x 8"	25.00
☐ Shepherd with Sheep, 8½" x 13½"	18.00
☐ Ship in Ocean, 11" x 13½"	35.00
☐ Sinbad and The Cyclops, 10" x 12"	35.00
☐ Sing a Song of Sixpence, 9" x 21"	425.00
☐ Six Ingredients	60.00
☐ Singing Tree, The; 10" x 12"	85.00
☐ Song of Sixpence	40.00
☐ Stars, House of Art, medium size (Nude sitting on Rock)	300.00
☐ Stars, House of Art, large size (Nude sitting on Rock)	525.00
☐ Story from Phoebus, 8" x 10", 1901	16.00
☐ Sugar Plum Tree	900.00
☐ Sunlit Valley (Scenic of river and mountains)	125.00
☐ Sunrise, Edison Mazda Calendar Top	125.00
☐ Sunrise, Edison Mazda Calendar, rare, large	500.00
☐ Swifts Ham Ad (Jack Sprat and wife)	40.00

VANITY FAIR

ORIGINAL LITHOGRAPHS

Vanity Fair was a periodical published in London from 1860 to 1914. In its own parlance it was a weekly show of political, social, literary, and financial ware, reaching the well-to-do and cultivated classes worldwide. Each issue featured a bound-in lithograph depicting an influential man or woman. The lithograph (either lifelike or satirical in nature) was usually accompanied by adjacent prose which extolled or lamented the virtures or vices of the personage being featured. Two of the most famous Vanity Fair artists were "Spy" (Leslie Ward) and "Ape" (Carlo Pelligrine).

From first publication, this feature of Vanity Fair enjoyed great interest and was widely collected among readers. Additional lithographs of the weekly featured subject were available upon request and payment to Vanity Fair. Most renderings were reproduced by stone lithography, thus severely limiting the quality of each issue.

Interest in Original Vanity Fair lithographs increased substantially after the demise of the publication because no new lithographs could be produced. The prints remaining at Vanity Fair were purchased by Paul B. Victorious, owner of a London rare book and print shop. During the war Victorious moved with his family to Charlottesville, Virginia where he lived quietly as the owner of a book, print, and framing shop. Largely untouched and uncatalogued, the collection remained in a warehouse until Victorious' death. The collection was offered for sale by executors. Following the purchase, Vanity Fair, Ltd. was founded and the next year was spent cataloging and cross indexing the entire collection. Vanity Fair, Ltd. represents the most comprehensive single collection known.

Original Vanity Fair lithographs are limited because the original plates no longer exist, the lithographs are relatively rare in number, and they appeal to a broad audience.

Original Vanity Fair lithographs were a true mirror of the society in which they were produced. They bring collectors a look at the manner, grace, and wit so treasured in the days of Queen Victoria.

ACCOUNTANT

CAPTION	YEAR	ARTIST	PRICE
☐ An undersheriff	1891	SPY	N/S

AMBASSADORS TO AND FROM ENGLAND

CAPTION	YEAR	ARTIST	PRICE
☐ One of the Most Precious	1870	APE	$14.00
☐ A Liberal and an Enemy	1871	APE	14.00
☐ He Might Have Been A King	1871	Unsigned	14.00
☐ The Most Interesting	1871	APE	14.00
☐ One of the Lambs	1871	APE	14.00
☐ The Spanish Minister	1871	Unsigned	14.00
☐ Diplomacy	1873	Unsigned	14.00
☐ Ill-Used	1874	APE	14.00
☐ Austria	1875	APE	14.00
☐ Russia	1875	APE	14.00
☐ Ther German Ambassador	1876	SPY	14.00
☐ Ambassador To The Porte	1877	SPY	14.00
☐ A Manipulation of Phrases	1877	SPY	14.00
☐ Odo	1877	SPY	14.00
☐ The Turkish Constitution	1877	SPY	14.00
☐ Diplomacy	1878	APE	14.00
☐ Promotion by Merit	1878	APE	14.00
☐ Siam	1879	SPY	14.00
☐ The Baron	1884	APE	14.00
☐ Justice! Justice!	1884	SPY	14.00
☐ The Russian Ambassador	1885	APE	14.00
☐ A Safe Ambassador	1886	APE	N/A
☐ Italy	1886	APE	14.00
☐ Count Paul Metternich	1895	SPY	14.00
☐ Austro-Hungary	1898	SPY	14.00
☐ Brazil	1898	SPY	14.00
☐ Portugal	1898	SPY	N/S
☐ French Ambassador	1899	GUTH	14.00
☐ Tokio	1901	SPY	14.00
☐ Berlin	1902	SPY	14.00
☐ The Italian Ambassador	1902	SPY	N/A
☐ Japan	1902	SPY	14.00
☐ Denmark in England	1903	SPY	N/S
☐ Russia in England	1903	SPY	14.00
☐ Washington	1903	SPY	14.00
☐ The Belgian Minister	1904	SPY	14.00
☐ Washington Post	1904	SPY	14.00
☐ Diplomacy	1907	SPY	14.00
☐ Marquis De Soveral	1907	K	14.00
☐ His Excellency The French Ambassador	1912	K	14.00

AMERICANS

CAPTION	YEAR	ARTIST	PRICE
☐ An Arbitrator	1872	Unsigned	20.00
☐ Captain, Tanner, Farmer	1872	Unsigned	24.00
☐ Consequential Damages	1872	Unsigned	N/A
☐ The Massive Grievance	1872	Unsigned	20.00
☐ The United States	1875	APE	20.00
☐ Uncle Sam	1880	SPY	N/A
☐ Barnum	1882	SPY	20.00
☐ President of the New York	1889	SPY	20.00
☐ The United States	1894	SPY	20.00
☐ USA	1897	SPY	20.00
☐ A Diplomatic Cousin	1899	SPY	20.00
☐ An American President	1899	FLAGG	20.00
☐ United States Embassy	1899	SPY	20.00

BARNUM

CAPTION	YEAR	ARTIST	PRICE
☐ U.S.A.	1902	FLAGG	24.00
☐ Mr. Alfred Gwynne Vanderbilt	1907	SPY	20.00
☐ The New President	1913	HESTER	N/A

ARTISTS

CAPTION	YEAR	ARTIST	PRICE
☐ Fairford Abbey	1898	SPY	18.00
☐ Max	1897	SIC	22.00
☐ The Queen's Sculptor	1881	SPY	22.00
☐ The Queen's Memorial	1905	SPY	18.00
☐ King Cole	1871	Unsigned	18.00
☐ Sensational Art	1877	SPY	22.00
☐ He Painted the Doctor	1892	SPY	18.00
☐ The Derby-Day	1873	SPY	22.00
☐ The Queen's Nephew	1884	GO	N/A
☐ An Able Artist	1871	APE	18.00
☐ An Art Critic	1871	Unsigned	N/A
☐ The Glorious East	1884	GO	22.00
☐ Posters	1912	STRICKLAND	18.00

U.S.A. — TEDDY ROOSEVELT

CAPTION	YEAR	ARTIST	PRICE
☐ Painter, Sculptor, Blacksmith	1884	FG	18.00
☐ The Pre-Raphaelite	1879	SPY	18.00
☐ He Paints Various Royalties	1913	RITCHIE	18.00
☐ Athlete and Sculptor	1883	Unsigned	18.00
☐ A Sacrifice To the Graces	1872	Unsigned	22.00
☐ A Sculptor	1877	SPY	22.00
☐ The Grosvenor Gallery	1883	Unsigned	18.00
☐ A Connoisseur	1899	N	18.00
☐ Phil	1895	SPY	22.00
☐ Great French Painter	1880	T	18.00
☐ Converted Pre-Raphaelite	1871	APE	22.00
☐ Artist & R.A.	1898	SPY	18.00
☐ Paris Exhibition	1878	SPY	18.00
☐ APE	1898	AFM	22.00
☐ P.R.A.	1897	SPY	18.00
☐ Val	1877	SPY	18.00

SPY

CAPTION	YEAR	ARTIST	PRICE
☐ He Thinks in Marble	1904	IMP	22.00
☐ A Great Realist	1909	MAX	22.00
☐ The Wallace Collection	1909	WHO	18.00
☐ Mr. Archibald Stuart-Wortley	1890	SPY	18.00
☐ Fifteen Churches	1879	SPY	N/A
☐ Ancient Painting	1879	APE	18.00
☐ Punch	1878	SPY	18.00
☐ The Graphics	1894	SPY	N/A
☐ Bronze Statuary	1892	SPY	18.00
☐ Historic Art	1873	SPY	18.00
☐ Spy	1889	PAL	22.00
☐ He Paints Portraits	1891	SPY	18.00
☐ A Symphony	1878	SPY	22.00
☐ Val	1877	SPY	18.00

AUTOMOBILE DEVOTEES

CAPTION	YEAR	ARTIST	PRICE
☐ Automobile	1899	GUTH	36.00
☐ Cabs	1903	SPY	N/A
☐ Steam	1907	SPY	24.00

CAPTION	YEAR	ARTIST	PRICE
☐ The Colonel	1909	ELF	N/A
☐ Frizzy	1909	HCO	N/A
☐ A Popular Secretary	1911	APE JR.	N/A
☐ Orangeman	1911	WHO	N/A
☐ The Deutsch Prize	1901	GEO. HUM	80.00
☐ The Air	1907	SPY	N/A
☐ Hastings and Aviation	1910	HLO	N/A
☐ All British	1911	RITCHIE	N/A
☐ Claudie	1911	TEC	36.00
☐ Flight	1912	WH	24.00

BANKERS AND FINANCIERS

CAPTION	YEAR	ARTIST	PRICE
☐ Winchester	1883	SPY	N/A
☐ Swansea Harbor	1909	WHO	N/A
☐ Go, Gas & Cold	1895	SPY	N/A
☐ South Herfordshire	1891	SPY	N/A
☐ Egyptian Finance	1899	SPY	N/A
☐ Dan	1908	SPY	N/A
☐ Colonial	1881	SPY	N/A
☐ A Man of Weight	1873	Unsigned	18.00
☐ Egypt	1902	SPY	N/A
☐ The Whip	1972	Unsigned	18.00
☐ Old Mother Hubbard	1884	SPY	18.00
☐ Piety and Banking	1876	APE	N/A
☐ St. John of Jerusalem	1883	T	18.00
☐ The Bank Holiday	1878	SPY	18.00
☐ C.M.	1909	SPY	N/A
☐ Whitechapel	1886	LIB	N/A
☐ Samuel Hope Morley	1905	SPY	N/A
☐ The Birbeck	1911	APE JR.	N/A
☐ The Wicked Baron	1909	SPY	18.00
☐ Barings	1888	LIB	N/A
☐ Barings	1898	SPY	N/A
☐ The Cape	1891	SPY	24.00
☐ Natty	1888	LIB	N/A
☐ Alfred	1884	SPY	N/A
☐ Alphonse	1894	GUTH	N/A
☐ Eros	1900	SPY	N/A
☐ Ferdy	1889	HAY	N/A
☐ Racing and Sporting	1884	SPY	24.00
☐ Baron Lionel	1877	APE	24.00
☐ The Winner of the Race	1871	APE	N/A
☐ The Aylesbury Division	1900	SPY	N/A
☐ The Bank of England	1895	SPY	18.00
☐ Hythie	1900	SPY	N/A
☐ Mr. Reuben Sassoon	1890	SPY	24.00
☐ Free Trade and Finance	1906	SPY	N/A
☐ Lloyd's Bank	1910	HCO	24.00
☐ Canada in London	1900	SPY	N/A
☐ Eastern Finance	1899	SPY	N/A
☐ Copper	1899	SPY	18.00
☐ Egyptian Finance	1878	APE	N/A

BOXERS

CAPTION	YEAR	ARTIST	PRICE
☐ A Good Lightweight	1877	SPY	N/A
☐ Hard Hitter	1896	SPY	50.00
☐ Peggy	1911	WH	24.00
☐ A Typical Englishman	1912	RITCHIE	24.00

BUSINESSMEN AND EMPIRE BUILDERS

CAPTION	YEAR	ARTIST	PRICE
☐ Burton Beer	1885	SPY	18.00
☐ The Ogre	1908	SPY	N/A
☐ C.P.R. in Europe	1910	ELF	18.00
☐ Falmouth	1910	HCO	18.00
☐ An Irish Landowner	1910	SPY	18.00
☐ Manchester	1875	APE	18.00
☐ The Commercial Traveller	1899	CLOISTER	18.00
☐ A Retired Financier	1876	JTJ	18.00
☐ The Lord Harry	1890	FC.G	18.00
☐ Telephones	1888	LIB	18.00
☐ A Master Craftsman	1912	WH	N/A
☐ Oil	1911	SPY	N/A
☐ Long John	1910	QUIP	18.00
☐ Burton	1908	SPY	18.00
☐ A Dandy	1909	SPY	N/A
☐ Prospectuses	1912	WH	18.00
☐ A Temperate Ulster Man	1887	APE	18.00
☐ Cardiff	1910	WHO	18.00
☐ Bexhill & Dunlop	1896	SPY	18.00
☐ Tea	1890	SPY	18.00
☐ Philip	1910	WHO	18.00
☐ Small Freeholds	1908	SPY	18.00
☐ Carberry Tower	1911	APE JR.	N/A
☐ Horace	1898	SPY	N/A
☐ A Well-Known Face	1911	HLO	N/A
☐ Not A Small Fry	1909	SPY	N/A
☐ The Furness Line	1908	SPY	18.00
☐ Housing	1912	RAY	18.00
☐ A Man of Business	1882	T	18.00
☐ Brummagem Varsity	1911	HLO	18.00
☐ Big Things in Oil	1912	WH	N/A
☐ Papworth	1896	SPY	18.00
☐ Malted Milk	1909	SPY	N/A
☐ West Marylebone	1893	SPY	18.00
☐ Endowed Lectures	1910	PRY	18.00
☐ Great Western	1908	SPy	18.00
☐ J	1895	SPY	18.00
☐ Collieries	1906	SPY	18.00
☐ Beggar General	1890	LIB	18.00
☐ King of Campsie	1910	HCO	N/A
☐ Prosperity	1876	JTJ	18.00
☐ Fair Trade	1882	SPY	18.00
☐ Arthur	1909	ELF	18.00
☐ McEwan & Co.	1902	SPY	18.00
☐ A Leading Figure in Cotton	1912	RITCHIE	18.00
☐ Bradford Goods	1890	SPY	18.00
☐ Metal	1892	SPY	N/A
☐ Tea Cum Rubber	1910	ELF	18.00
☐ The Heir of the Ages	1888	APE	18.00
☐ Peace	1887	SPY	N/A
☐ Bullion	1890	SPY	18.00
☐ Crystal Palace	1913	HIC	N/A
☐ Sir Horace, J.P.	1909	SPY	18.00
☐ Electric Traction	1909	SPY	N/A
☐ The Indian Rothschild	1879	SPY	N/A
☐ Self	1911	RITCHIE	18.00
☐ Beer & Budget & Brains	1909	SPY	N/A
☐ Head of the Greatest	1904	SPY	18.00
☐ Paper	1912	RAY	N/A
☐ Finance & Fruit	1909	SPY	N/A
☐ Glasgow	1883	Unsigned	18.00

CAPTION	YEAR	ARTIST	PRICE
☐ Glen	1910	HO	18.00
☐ Ludgate Hill	1894	SPY	18.00
☐ Herbs	1910	HCO	18.00
☐ Brightside D.V.	1909	SPY	18.00
☐ Sir Andrew Barclay	1890	LIB	18.00
☐ Philip	1910	WHO	18.00
☐ The King of Wales	1873	SPY	18.00
☐ A Squatter	1885	SPY	18.00
☐ He Has Engineered Nothing	1905	SPY	18.00

CHANCELLORS OF EXCHEQUER

CAPTION	YEAR	ARTIST	PRICE
☐ An Enemy to Democracy	1869	APE	14.00
☐ A Returned Colonist	1869	APE	14.00
☐ The Theory of Foreign	1869	Unknown	14.00
☐ He Does His Duty	1870	APE	14.00
☐ The Fat of the Land	1871	APE	14.00
☐ A Scagliola Appollo	1874	APE	14.00
☐ A Younger Son	1880	SPY	14.00
☐ Sugar Bounties	1885	APE	14.00
☐ East Worchestershire	1899	SPY	30.00
☐ A Retired Leader	1890	CLOISTER	14.00
☐ Winston	1900	SPY	N/A
☐ In the Winning Crew	1906	SPY	14.00
☐ Winnie	1911	NIBS	N/A

CLERGY

CAPTION	YEAR	ARTIST	PRICE
☐ The Chief Rabbi	1904	SPY	30.00
☐ Temple Reader	1892	SPY	14.00
☐ The Primate	1887	SPY	14.00
☐ The Head of the Dissenters	1872	Unsigned	14.00
☐ The Salvation Army	1882	SPY	14.00
☐ Prayers	1879	SPY	14.00
☐ Fearless But Intemperate	1904	SPY	14.00
☐ An Earnest and Liberal	1869	COICA	14.00
☐ The Apostle To The Genteel	1872	Unsigned	14.00
☐ St. Paul's	1886	LIB	14.00
☐ The Pentateuch	1874	APE	14.00
☐ Lay Episcopacy	1882	SPY	N/A
☐ The End of the World	1872	Unsigned	14.00
☐ Derry	1895	SPY	14.00
☐ A Wet Quacker	1882	SPY	14.00
☐ Swansea	1900	APE	14.00
☐ A Court Parson	1886	APE	N/A
☐ A Common Prayer Reformer	1871	APE	N/A
☐ He Had Decided	1905	SPY	14.00
☐ Revision	1885	SPY	N/A
☐ A Fashion Canon	1898	F.T.D.	14.00
☐ Chaplain to the Commons	1891	SPY	N/A
☐ Chester Square	1899	SPY	14.00
☐ Carlisle	1888	SPY	14.00
☐ Come to Jesus	1872	Unsigned	N/A
☐ The Revised Edition	1885	SPY	14.00
☐ An Apostle to Positivism	1886	APE	14.00
☐ The Parson, The Play	1888	APE	14.00
☐ St. Margaret's	1912	WH	14.00
☐ Domestic Chaplain	1907	AD	N/A
☐ Roses	1895	F.T.D.	14.00
☐ The Genial Dean	1912	WH	14.00
☐ London	1901	SPY	14.00

CAPTION	YEAR	ARTIST	PRICE
☐ One Who Has Grieved	1870	APE	14.00
☐ Greek	1876	SPY	14.00
☐ Kensington	1903	SPY	14.00
☐ An Angel of Peace	1912	STRICKLAND	14.00
☐ The Pope	1878	T.	14.00
☐ Lichfield	1897	STUFF	14.00
☐ Convocation	1884	SPY	N/A
☐ High Church	1876	SPY	N/A
☐ A Persecuted Bishop	1890	SPY	N/A
☐ Ecclesiastical History	1897	F.T.D.	N/A
☐ Father Ignatius	1887	APE	14.00
☐ Stonehenge 1911	1911	RITCHIE	14.00
☐ He Makes Religion A Tragedy	1870	APE	14.00
☐ The Next Pope	1871	APE	14.00
☐ The Noblest of English	1881	SPY	14.00
☐ Tracts For The Times	1877	SPY	14.00
☐ Not A Brawler	1869	APE	14.00
☐ Congressional Union	1884	APE	14.00
☐ If Eloquence Could Justify	1869	APE	14.00
☐ The Infallible	1870	Unsigned	14.00
☐ His Holiness Pius X	1903	LIB	N/A
☐ Wellington College	1902	SPY	14.00
☐ High Church	1875	APE	14.00
☐ D.V.	1872	Unsigned	N/A
☐ A Man Right Reverend	1906	SPY	14.00
☐ The Soldiers Bishop	1897	SPY	N/A
☐ An Erudite Dean	1905	SPY	N/A
☐ The Dean	1912	WH	N/A
☐ Liverpool	1881	APE	14.00
☐ Tolerance	1906	SPY	14.00
☐ A Great Marrier	1904	SPY	14.00
☐ The Sub-Dean	1911	APE JR.	14.00
☐ Southwell	1901	SPY	14.00
☐ No One Has Succeeded	1870	APE	14.00
☐ Philosophical Belief	1872	Unsigned	14.00
☐ I Felt Very Uncomfortable	1869	APE	N/A
☐ A Bishop	1906	Unsigned	N/A
☐ A Quaker	1886	SPY	14.00
☐ Rochester	1904	SPY	14.00
☐ Winton	1911	RAY	N/A
☐ Oxford University	1897	SPY	14.00
☐ He Has Displayed Ability	1869	Unsigned	14.00
☐ Just	1902	SPY	14.00
☐ Rochester	1885	SPY	N/A
☐ The Christian Martyr	1877	SPY	14.00
☐ A Most Perfect Preacher	1907	SPY	14.00
☐ A Modern Savonarola	1907	SPY	14.00
☐ Nolo Episcopari	1872	Unsigned	N/A
☐ St. Paul's Knightsbridge	1902	SPY	14.00
☐ I Have Much To Be Thankful For	1871	Unsigned	14.00
☐ Calcutta	1898	SPY	N/A
☐ The Old Dean	1876	SPY	18.00
☐ Westminister	1893	SPY	14.00
☐ Prayers	1874	APE	14.00
☐ The Chaplain	1909	SPY	14.00
☐ Truro	1885	SPY	14.00
☐ Prelate to the Garter	1901	SPY	14.00
☐ The Archbishop of Society	1871	APE	18.00
☐ From the Army	1891	SPY	18.00

CRICKETT

CAPTION	YEAR	ARTIST	PRICE
Bobby	1902	SPY	N/A
I Zingari	1895	SPY	N/A
Charlie	1910	ALS	N/A
Australian Cricket	1884	APE	N/A
An Artful Bowler	1904	SPY	N/A
In His Father's Steps	1904	SPY	N/A
The Champion Country	1913	OWL	N/A
Cricketing Christianity	1906	SPY	N/A
Cricket	1877	SPY	N/A
Kent	1881	SPY	N/A
Yorkshire Cricket	1892	SPY	N/A
Torn	1906	SPY	N/A
Yorkshire	1903	SPY	N/A
A Tested Centurion	1912	WH	N/A
Monkey	1891	STUFF	N/A
A Century Marker	1907	SPY	N/A
A Flannelled Fighter	1902	SPY	N/A
The Lobster	1902	SPY	N/A
The Croucher	1901	SPY	N/A
English Cricket	1884	APE	N/A
Repton, Oxford & Somerset	1903	SPY	N/A
Oxford Circuit	1880	SPY	N/A
Ranji	1897	SPY	N/A
W.W.	1888	LIB	N/A
The Demon Bowler	1878	SPY	N/A
Reggie	1906	SPY	N/A
A Big Hitter	1892	STUFF	N/A
Forty-Six Centuries In	1906	SPY	N/A
Plum	1903	SPY	N/A
Father	1907	SPY	N/A
Sammy	1892	STUFF	N/A
Hampshire	1898	CG	N/A

CRIMINALS

CAPTION	YEAR	ARTIST	PRICE
The Turf Frauds	1877	SPY	N/A
Richard Pigott	1889	SPY	N/A

DOCTORS AND SCIENTISTS

CAPTION	YEAR	ARTIST	PRICE
Astronomy	1875	PE	20.00
Wholemeal Bread	1911	RAY	20.00
Bones	1909	ELF	20.00
Physician To His Majesty's	1906	SPY	20.00
Orthodoxy	1902	SPY	20.00
Hospitals	1898	QUIZ	20.00
A Literary Oculist	1892	STUFF	20.00
He Has Devoted His Life	1888	SPY	N/A
Fashionable Surgery	1874	APE	20.00
Anti-Vivisection	1910	ELF	20.00
Alfred	1897	SPY	N/A
The Transit of Venus	1908	SPY	20.00
Mr. Frank Crisp	1890	SPY	20.00
The King's Oculist	1905	SPY	20.00
Ubi Crookes Ibi Lux	1903	SPY	20.00
His Lordship of London	1911	WH	20.00
Radium	1904	IMP	36.00
The Ear	1888	APE	20.00

	CAPTION	YEAR	ARTIST	PRICE
☐	Natural Selection	1871	Unsigned	N/A
☐	West Aberdeenshire	1895	SPY	20.00
☐	There is No Man Of	1870	APE	20.00
☐	The Ilkeston Division	1894	SPY	20.00
☐	A Master of the Knife	1907	SPY	20.00
☐	Electrical Energy	1910	HLO	20.00
☐	Chemistry & Optics	1891	SPY	20.00
☐	Surgical Diagnosis	1911	WH	20.00
☐	Physiological Physic	1875	APE	N/A
☐	Hydropathy	1876	SPY	20.00
☐	Steel	1912	WH	20.00
☐	How Much?	1904	SPY	N/A
☐	Mr. Johnathan Hutchinson	1890	SPY	20.00
☐	Spectroscopic Astronomy	1903	SPY	20.00
☐	The Chingford Pump	1913	HESTER	20.00
☐	A Great-Medicine Man	1871	APE	N/A
☐	Army Medical	1901	SPY	20.00
☐	Dr. Jim	1896	SPY	20.00
☐	Physic	1873	SPY	20.00
☐	Dietetics	1897	SPY	N/A
☐	The King's Physician	1903	SPY	20.00
☐	His Religion Is The Worship	1905	SPY	20.00
☐	Agricultural Science	1882	T.	20.00
☐	Horticulture	1899	SPY	20.00
☐	Agriculture	1883	SPY	20.00
☐	Astronomy	1878	SPY	20.00
☐	Gunshot Wounds	1896	SPY	20.00
☐	Disease of the Thoat	1887	APE	20.00
☐	In The Clouds	1904	SPY	20.00
☐	John Bull	1808	SPY	N/A
☐	A Faithful Friend	1870	APE	20.00
☐	Old Bones	1873	Unsigned	20.00
☐	Surgery	1876	SPY	N/A
☐	Hydrophobia	1887	T.	36.00
☐	The Prophet Of	1913	RITCHIE	20.00
☐	Chemistry	1875	APE	20.00
☐	Chests	1904	PY	20.00
☐	Astronomy	1883	SPY	20.00
☐	Lord Beaconsfield's Physician	1883	SPY	20.00
☐	Homeopathic Society	1872	Unsigned	20.00
☐	Chemistry	1908	SPY	20.00
☐	Argon	1899	FTD	20.00
☐	Petroleum	1908	SPY	20.00
☐	Rhys, K.C.	1913	OWL	20.00
☐	Brighton	1889	SPY	20.00
☐	Electricity	1908	SPY	20.00
☐	Oxford Physiology	1894	SPY	20.00
☐	Mens Sana	1912	RAY	20.00
☐	Laryngology	1902	SPY	24.00
☐	Science & Invention	1910	SPY	20.00
☐	Philosophy	1879	CG	20.00
☐	Rhinology	1902	SPY	20.00
☐	Medical Jurisprudence	1899	WAG	20.00
☐	A Great Surgeon	1910	ELF	20.00
☐	Cremation	1874	APE	20.00
☐	Freddie	1900	SPY	20.00
☐	The Scientific Use	1872	Unsigned	20.00
☐	Cellular Pathology	1893	SPY	N/A
☐	A Naturalist	1882	T.	20.00
☐	Philosophical Pathology	1892	SPY	20.00
☐	Dietetics	1900	SPY	20.00

EXPLORERS AND INVENTORS

CAPTION	YEAR	ARTIST	PRICE
☐ The Director	1874	APE	18.00
☐ He Walked Across Africa	1876	SPY	18.00
☐ Steel	1880	SPY	22.00
☐ Little Menlo	1889	APE	18.00
☐ A Traveller	1892	SPY	18.00
☐ Privy Councilor, Professor	1893	STUFF	18.00
☐ Odger	1895	SPY	18.00
☐ Westralia	1895	SPY	18.00
☐ Franz Josef Land	1897	SPY	22.00
☐ Natural Philosophy	1897	SPY	22.00
☐ A City Liberal	1909	SPY	N/A
☐ Birmingham University	1904	SPY	18.00
☐ Wires Without Wires	1905	SPY	36.00
☐ The South Pole	1909	KITE	36.00
☐ The Cutter of Continents	1913	AST	18.00
☐ The South Pole	1913	HESTER	36.00

FOX HUNTERS

CAPTION	YEAR	ARTIST	PRICE
☐ The Lord Annaly	1912	K	30.00
☐ The General	1881	SPY	30.00
☐ The Master Of	1906	SPY	30.00
☐ An MFH With a Sense	1905	SPY	30.00
☐ Long Burns	1900	CB	30.00
☐ To the Manner Born	1906	SPY	30.00
☐ The Quorn	1884	APE	30.00
☐ Alfred	1909	SPY	30.00
☐ The Huntsman	1884	SPY	N/A
☐ Billy	1906	SPY	30.00
☐ Serlby	1899	SPY	30.00
☐ Fox-Hunting	1883	SPY	N/A
☐ A Very Old Master	1896	SPY	30.00
☐ Belvoir	1899	CB	30.00
☐ A Masters' Meet	1895	SPY	N/A
☐ Kirby Gate	1901	CB	60.00
☐ A Fox-Hunting Constellation	1905	BEDE	N/A
☐ Blackmore Vale	1897	CG	30.00
☐ Cottesmore	1906	Unknown	30.00
☐ Mr. Hargreaves	1887	SPY	30.00
☐ Cattistock	1906	Unknown	30.00
☐ A Hard Rider	1904	SPY	30.00
☐ The Master Of The	1906	BEDE	30.00
☐ Bay	1883	T	30.00
☐ Tom	1885	PAT	30.00
☐ Otho	1902	CB	40.00
☐ Downing	1886	HAY	N/A
☐ An Old Master	1898	SPY	30.00
☐ Workshop Manor	1911	SPY	30.00
☐ Doggie	1884	APE	30.00
☐ The Sinner	1907	SPY	30.00
☐ A Leicestershire Man	1899	GAF	30.00
☐ Berks and Bucks	1903	AO	30.00
☐ A Father	1900	CB	30.00

FREEMASONS

CAPTION	YEAR	ARTIST	PRICE
☐ The Most Wonderful	1860	Unsigned	14.00
☐ Younger Son	1877	SPY	14.00

CAPTION	YEAR	ARTIST	PRICE
☐ The Foreign Office	1878	APE	14.00
☐ Suffolk	1881	SPY	N/A
☐ The Great Western	1882	SPY	N/A
☐ A Freemason	1885	APE	14.00
☐ The Lord Mayor	1887	SPY	N/A
☐ The Wimbledon Division	1898	SPY	14.00
☐ A New Lord Mayor	1889	SPY	N/A
☐ North Lancashire	1900	SPY	N/A
☐ The Lord Mayor	1902	SPY	14.00
☐ The Grand Secretary	1903	SPY	N/A
☐ The Pro Grand Master	1904	SPY	N/A
☐ Jimmy	1913	AST	N/A

GAME HUNTERS

CAPTION	YEAR	ARTIST	PRICE
☐ Pointers	1885	SPY	36.00
☐ Best Game Shot In	1890	SPY	N/A
☐ Letters to the Young	1893	SPY	36.00
☐ The Record Revolver Shot	1893	VA	36.00
☐ Big Game	1894	VA	36.00
☐ The New Forest	1897	SPY	36.00
☐ Drive Grouse	1905	SPY	36.00
☐ Rufford Abbey	1908	SPY	36.00
☐ Tracks and Triggers	1909	WHO	36.00

GOLFERS

CAPTION	YEAR	ARTIST	PRICE
☐ The Irish Secretary	1887	SPY	N/A
☐ Mr. Horace Hutchinson	1890	SPY	N/A
☐ Mr. John Ball, Jr.	1892	LIB	N/A
☐ Hoylake	1903	SPY	N/A
☐ Muir	1903	SPY	N/A
☐ A Celebrated Oarsman	1906	SPY	N/A
☐ John Henry	1906	SPY	N/A
☐ North Berwick	1906	SPY	N/A
☐ Jimmy	1907	SPY	N/A
☐ The Prince of Princes	1909	SPY	N/A
☐ Dialectics	1910	XIT	N/A
☐ Easton Hall	1911	SPY	N/A

HORSE TRAINERS

CAPTION	YEAR	ARTIST	PRICE
☐ Petrarch	1876	SPY	N/A
☐ Robert	1886	LIB	N/A
☐ Mr. John Porter	1889	LIB	16.00
☐ Punchestown	1889	KAY	N/A
☐ Baron Hirsch	1890	LIB	N/A
☐ Mr. Christopher W. Wilson	1891	SPY	16.00
☐ He Owns "Chancellor"	1893	SPY	N/A
☐ Whiskey & Horses	1907	SPY	N/A
☐ An Argentine Sportsman	1910	WHO	16.00
☐ John Porter	1910	XIT	16.00
☐ Lutteur	1910	HLO	16.00
☐ Sollie	1910	HCO	16.00

HORSES

CAPTION	YEAR	ARTIST	PRICE
☐ Newmarket 1885	1885	LIB	N/A
☐ Tattersall's 1887	1887	LIB	60.00

CAPTION	YEAR	ARTIST	PRICE
☐ Cyllene	1906	Percy Earl	N/A
☐ Santry	1907	F. Paton	N/A
☐ Bayardo	1909	Percy Earl	36.00
☐ Dean Swift	1909	Percy Earl	N/A
☐ Minoru	1909	Percy Earl	N/A
☐ Rock Sand	1910	Percy Earl	N/A
☐ Flying Fox	N/A	Percy Earl	N/A
☐ Lutteur III	N/A	Emil Adam	N/A
☐ Persimmon	N/A	Percy Earl	N/A
☐ Pretty Polly	N/A	Percy Earl	N/A
☐ Scepter & Maid of Corinth	N/A	Percy Earl	N/A
☐ St. Simon	N/A	Percy Earl	N/A
☐ Torpoint	N/A	Percy Earl	N/A

JOCKEYS

CAPTION	YEAR	ARTIST	PRICE
☐ The Favorite Jockey	1881	SPY	N/A
☐ Mr. Abington	1888	LIB	N/A
☐ Fred Barrett	1889	LIB	N/A
☐ George Barrett	1887	LIB	46.00
☐ Morny	1891	SPY	40.00
☐ Tom Cannon	1885	SPY	N/A
☐ Count Strickland	1893	HAY	N/A
☐ The Baby	1884	SPY	N/A
☐ Bernard	1906	SPY	40.00
☐ The Demon	1882	SPY	N/A
☐ He Rides for Lord Durham	1906	SPY	46.00
☐ The Winning Post	1888	LIB	60.00
☐ Top of the List	1906	SPY	40.00
☐ Wenty	1897	SPY	N/A
☐ A King's Jockey	1904	AO	N/A
☐ Sam Loates	1896	SPY	40.00
☐ Tom Loates	1890	SPY	40.00
☐ Otto Madden	1900	GDG	50.00
☐ Danny	1903	AO	50.00
☐ Skeets	1907	AO	40.00
☐ Johnny	1887	LIB	N/A
☐ Roddy	1891	SPY	40.00
☐ Johnny	1900	SPY	N/A
☐ Lester	1900	SPY	40.00
☐ Rick	1901	SPY	46.00
☐ An American Jockey	1899	GDG	N/A
☐ A Rising Star	1906	SPY	46.00
☐ Mr. George	1907	SPY	46.00
☐ J. E. Watts	1903	AO	50.00
☐ Johnny Watts	1887	SPY	N/A
☐ Fred Webb	1889	LIB	50.00
☐ Charlie Wood	1886	LIB	50.00
☐ James Woodburn	1890	SPY	50.00
☐ Frank Wooten	1909	SPY	46.00

LADIES

CAPTION	YEAR	ARTIST	PRICE
☐ H.R.N. The Princess	1882	CHARTRAN	N/A
☐ The Baroness Burdett-Coutts	1883	T	40.00
☐ The Countess Of Dalhousie	1883	T	N/A
☐ Gladys, Countess of Lonsdale	1883	CHARTRAN	40.00
☐ Her Grace The Duchess	1883	CHARTRAN	N/A
☐ The Marchioness of Waterford	1883	CHARTRAN	N/A
☐ H.I.M. The Empress	1884	GRIMM	N/A
☐ The Lady Florence Dixie	1884	T	N/A
☐ The Lady Holland	1884	T	N/A

CAPTION	YEAR	ARTIST	PRICE
☐ The Princess Royal	1884	NEMO	N/A
☐ Mrs. Weldon	1884	SPY	N/A
☐ The Marchioness of Tweeddale	1884	T	N/A
☐ Victory Mary of Teck	1893	WARD	40.00
☐ Cycling in Hyde Park	1896	HAL HURST	75.00
☐ Au Bois De Boulogne	1897	GUTH	N/A
☐ None	1906	WARD	40.00
☐ Lady Dorothy Nevill	1908	WHO	N/A
☐ Women's Suffrage	1910	SPY	N/A
☐ Her Majesty Queen Alexandra	1911	UNK	40.00
☐ The Lady Dorothy Nevill	1912	K	N/A
☐ Mrs. George Cornwallis West	1912	K	N/A

LEGAL

CAPTION	YEAR	ARTIST	PRICE
☐ Dick	1900	SPY	N/A
☐ Slim	1904	SPY	N/A
☐ A Judicial Judge	1897	SPY	N/A
☐ Contempt of Court	1873	VW	N/A
☐ A Popular Magistrate	1905	SPY	20.00
☐ The Court of Appeals	1875	APE	20.00
☐ The Lord Advocate	1886	SPY	20.00
☐ He Resisted Temptation	1870	Unsigned	56.00
☐ Good Form	1906	SPY	56.00
☐ Admiralty Jurisdiction	1893	SPY	N/A
☐ Lord Justice Barry	1889	LIB	20.00
☐ Under Sheriff	1891	SPY	20.00
☐ As Procureur General	1893	GUTH	56.00
☐ Billy	1910	PIP	N/A
☐ Northeast Bethnal Green	1897	SPY	20.00
☐ We Shall See	1898	SPY	N/A
☐ Worship Street	1907	SPY	20.00
☐ A Lord of Appeal	1881	SPY	20.00
☐ Bosey, Frederick	1901	SPY	56.00
☐ The Majesty of the Law	1870	APE	56.00
☐ Judicial Politeness	1892	SPY	56.00
☐ The Knight of the Malta	1879	SPY	20.00
☐ An Arbitrator	1892	SPY	20.00
☐ The Exchequer	1876	SPY	56.00
☐ A Man of Law and Broad Acres	1906	SPY	56.00
☐ Popular Judgment	1876	APE	N/A
☐ Birth, Behavior & Business	1881		20.00
☐ Justice to Dreyfus	1898	GUTH	20.00
☐ He Defended Abari	1889	SPY	N/A
☐ Holburn	1892	SPY	20.00
☐ Slow and Steady	1900	SPY	N/A
☐ Company Law	1900	SPY	N/A
☐ The Solicitor-General	1913	OWL	56.00
☐ Tommy	1900	SPY	N/A
☐ Divorce	1887	APE	N/A
☐ Chitty's Leader	1896	SPY	56.00
☐ City Justice	1880	SPY	N/A
☐ That Won't Do, You Know	1893	PY	56.00
☐ So Voluble An Advocate	1906	SPY	56.00
☐ An Amiable Judge	1898	SPY	N/A
☐ The New Judge	1888	SPY	N/A
☐ The Umpire	1885	SPY	N/A
☐ Sir Edward	1903	SPY	N/A
☐ Formerly of the Carlton	1876	SPY	56.00
☐ He Has Leathern Lungs	1891	STUFF	N/A
☐ The Lord Chief Justice	1869	APE	56.00
☐ The Silvered Voice	1909	SPY	56.00

CAPTION	YEAR	ARTIST	PRICE
☐ The Lord Chief Justice	1887	APE	56.00
☐ A Risen Barrister	1870	ATN	20.00
☐ Sir John Coleridge	1870	Unsigned	56.00
☐ Smith's Leading Case	1893	QUIZ	56.00
☐ Scotch Law	1873	SPY	20.00
☐ Guileless	1888	SPY	56.00
☐ North Norfolk	1893	SPY	20.00
☐ Fair Is Not Beautiful	1901	SPY	N/A
☐ Vicar General	1902	SPY	56.00
☐ South Bucks	1896	SPY	N/A
☐ Danky	1898	SPY	56.00
☐ Little Darling	1897	SPY	20.00
☐ 2nd Commissioner	1888	SPY	N/A
☐ Bargrave	1898	SPY	56.00
☐ The First of the Commoners	1870	ATN	56.00
☐ He Was An Ornament	1892	STUFF	56.00
☐ Public Prosecutions	1902	SPY	20.00
☐ His Father Invented Pickwick	1897	SPY	56.00
☐ Plausible	1902	SPY	56.00
☐ London Sessions	1891	SPY	56.00
☐ Law	1886	SPY	20.00
☐ George	1908	SPY	56.00
☐ Court Roll	1887	SPY	20.00
☐ A Good Judge	1911	APE JR.	56.00
☐ Powers	1900	FTD	56.00
☐ Stay Please	1887	SPY	N/A
☐ Hard Head	1888	APE	56.00
☐ North London	1908	SPY	20.00
☐ Specific Performance	1891	SPY	56.00
☐ Dublin University	1885	SPY	20.00
☐ The Solicitor General	1878	SPY	20.00
☐ Gill Brass	1891	SPY	56.00
☐ Barrister & Baronet	1872	Unsigned	20.00
☐ Lord Advocate	1874	APE	20.00
☐ Bells	1889	SPY	20.00
☐ Bench and Bar	1891	STUFF	N/A
☐ Heads of the Law	1902	SPY	75.00
☐ Purse, Pussy, Piety	1882	T	56.00
☐ Galvanic Electricity	1887	SPY	N/A
☐ Charley	1888	SPY	20.00
☐ From the Old Bailey	1890	SPY	N/A
☐ The Great Unmarrier	1888	SPY	N/A
☐ He Is A Smart Fellow	1893	SPY	20.00
☐ When He Who Has	1869	APE	56.00
☐ Lord Hatherton	1895	STUFF-G	20.00
☐ The Tichborne Case	1873	SPY	56.00
☐ Tim	1886	SPY	20.00
☐ Whitehaven	1896	SPY	N/A
☐ The New Recorder	1909	SPY	20.00
☐ The Irish Serjeant	1904	SPY	20.00
☐ The Solicitor General	1881	SPY	20.00
☐ Attorney General	1878	SPY	20.00
☐ The Autocrat	1886	SPY	N/A
☐ A Future Judge	1874	APE	56.00
☐ Tubby	1910	QUIP	20.00
☐ Hutchy	1911	APE JR.	56.00
☐ Divorce Court	1896	SPY	56.00
☐ Rufus	1904	SPY	56.00
☐ Nervous	1874	APE	56.00
☐ Oxford Circuit	1896	SPY	56.00
☐ He Believed in the Police	1899	SPY	20.00
☐ Ulsterman K. C.	1903	SPY	56.00
☐ The Lord Advocate	1888	SPY	20.00

CAPTION	YEAR	ARTIST	PRICE
☐ He Succeeded Lord Blackburn	1895	SPY	20.00
☐ Mr. Justice Manisty	1889	QUIZ	N/A
☐ Commercial Court	1896	SPY	N/A
☐ He Can Marshall Evidence	1892	SPY	56.00
☐ Parliamentary Practice	1871	APE	56.00
☐ Appeals	1876	SPY	56.00
☐ Judges the Claimant	1873	SPY	N/A
☐ An Irish Lawyer	1893	SPY	20.00
☐ Patents	1900	SPY	20.00
☐ For The Times	1899	SPY	56.00
☐ Lord Advocate	1896	SPY	20.00
☐ The Marlborough Street	1893	SPY	20.00
☐ The Claimant's Friend	1875	APE	56.00
☐ A Lawyer	1873	SPY	N/A
☐ The Speaker	1887	SPY	56.00
☐ A Judge & Peer	1869	UNK	N/A
☐ A Judicial Churchman	1898	SPY	56.00
☐ For the Crown	1886	SPY	56.00
☐ Jumbo	1885	SPY	56.00
☐ The President and the Law	1905	SPY	20.00
☐ Eton and Cambridge	1908	SPY	56.00
☐ Mr. Attorney	1895	SPY	N/A
☐ The New Judge	1897	FTD	56.00
☐ A Blunt Lord Justice	1901	SPY	56.00
☐ Mr. Solicitor	1893	STUFF	20.00
☐ The Solicitor General	1906	SPY	20.00
☐ Municipal Corporations	1886	SPY	N/A
☐ Bob	1891	STUFF	56.00
☐ Lord Beaconfield's Friend	1881	SPY	20.00
☐ A Splendid Advocate	1883	Unsigned	56.00
☐ A Son of His Father	1907	SPY	20.00
☐ Cross Examination	1890	QUIZ	N/A
☐ Workingham	1889	SPY	N/A
☐ Copyright	1911	APE JR.	56.00
☐ A Scot's Lawyer	1903	SPY	20.00
☐ Simple Simon	1911	WH	56.00
☐ The Serjeant	1886	SPY	20.00
☐ Equity	1897	SPY	56.00
☐ The Criminal Code	1885	SPY	56.00
☐ The New Judge	1879	SPY	20.00
☐ He Has Written	1893	SPY	20.00
☐ A Radical Lawyer	1902	SPY	N/A
☐ A Lawyer on the Bench	1902	SPY	56.00
☐ Director's Liability	1891	STUFF	56.00
☐ A Very Sound Judge	1907	SPY	N/A
☐ Law and Conscience	1883	Unsigned	N/A
☐ The Mandarin	1890	QUIZ	N/A
☐ A Rustic Judge	1899	CGD	20.00
☐ Benevolence On The Bench	1896	SPY	56.00
☐ Pridham	1910	ELF	56.00
☐ A Sporting Lawyer	1898	SPY	56.00
☐ He Declined Knighthood	1891	STUFF	56.00

LITERARY

CAPTION	YEAR	ARTIST	PRICE
☐ French Fiction	1880	T	20.00
☐ Waterloo	1883	T	20.00
☐ I Say The Critic	1871	Unsigned	24.00
☐ The Literary Mate	1894	SPY	20.00
☐ The Laureate	1896	SPY	24.00
☐ The Businessman	1913	OWL	24.00
☐ A Prophet	1885	APE	N/A

CAPTION	YEAR	ARTIST	PRICE
☐ Trafalgar Square	1888	SPY	20.00
☐ An Artist In Words	1908	GUTH	20.00
☐ Modern Poetry	1875	APE	24.00
☐ The Arabian Night	1885	APE	20.00
☐ The Manxman	1896	JRP	20.00
☐ The Diogenes of the Mod	1870	APE	20.00
☐ Free Libraries	1903	SPY	24.00
☐ Below the Mark	1908	SPY	N/A
☐ The Novelist	1872	Unsigned	20.00
☐ The Stickit Master	1897	FR	24.00
☐ He Wrote Sappho	1893	GUTH	24.00
☐ Chesterfield Letters	1874	APE	20.00
☐ Japan Society	1902	SPY	20.00
☐ He Discovered New America	1872	Unsigned	20.00
☐ Notes and Queries	1873	SPY	20.00
☐ Poetry	1877	SPY	24.00
☐ Trilby	1896	SPY	24.00
☐ French Fiction	1879	T	24.00
☐ Mr. Dooley	1905	SPY	20.00
☐ The Greatest Living Frenchman	1909	GUTH	20.00
☐ He Created Henry VIII	1872	Unsigned	N/A
☐ He Is Very Affluent	1906	RUTH	20.00
☐ Printed Books	1895	SPY	24.00
☐ Anything To Beat Grant	1872	Unsigned	N/A
☐ She	1887	SPY	24.00
☐ Tess	1892	SPY	24.00
☐ Unpath'd Waters	1913	OWL	24.00
☐ The Heathen Chinese	1879	SPY	20.00
☐ Anthony Hope	1895	SPY	20.00
☐ Anecdotes	1875	APE	20.00
☐ Silas Hocking	1906	SPY	20.00
☐ Tom Brown	1872	Unsigned	20.00
☐ A French Poet	1879	T	24.00
☐ The Master Builder	1901	SAPP	24.00
☐ Not an M.P.	1872	Unsigned	20.00
☐ The Apostle of the Flesh	1872	Unsigned	20.00
☐ Soldiers Three	1894	SPY	N/A
☐ The 18th Century	1882	SPY	20.00
☐ Spearmint	1906	SPY	N/A
☐ Pierre Loti	1895	GUTH	24.00
☐ Hosea Riglow	1880	T	20.00
☐ The Representative	1870	APE	20.00
☐ The Belgian Poet	1908	MAX	24.00
☐ Is Life Worth Living?	1882	SPY	20.00
☐ The Royal Literary Assistant	1877	SPY	20.00
☐ Four Feathers	1908	MAX	24.00
☐ The Novelist of Soc	1871	Unsigned	20.00
☐ Our First Novelist	1896	MAX	20.00
☐ A Feminine Philosopher	1873	SPY	20.00
☐ Esther Waters	1897	SIC	20.00
☐ Books	1874	APE	20.00
☐ A Puritan's Wife	1897	SPY	20.00
☐ The Earl and the Doctor	1888	APE	20.00
☐ As In A Looking Glass	1888	APE	20.00
☐ Lady Bountiful	1891	SPY	20.00
☐ Though It Is	1906	BULBO	20.00
☐ Impossible Romance	1873	Unsigned	20.00
☐ La Vie De Jesus	1879	T	20.00
☐ The Greatest	1910	GUTH	20.00
☐ The Realization	1872	Unsigned	24.00
☐ Thermidor	1891	RUTH	24.00
☐ G.B.S.	1911	RITCHIE	N/A
☐ Magnetic	1907	RUTH	24.00

CAPTION	YEAR	ARTIST	PRICE
☐ A Poet	1880	APE	20.00
☐ Self-Help	1882	SPY	20.00
☐ A Noble Writer	1874	APE	20.00
☐ Before Sunrise	1874	APE	20.00
☐ The Poet Laureate	1871	APE	24.00
☐ War and Peace	1901	SAPP	24.00
☐ The Competition Of	1873	SPY	20.00
☐ A Novelist	1872	SPY	24.00
☐ An Artist in Verbal	1913	HESTER	N/A
☐ Oscar	1884	APE	N/A
☐ A Child of the Ghetto	1897	SIC	20.00
☐ French Realism	1880	T	24.00

MILITARY AND NAVY

CAPTION	YEAR	ARTIST	PRICE
☐ Aberdeenshire	1902	SPY	N/A
☐ Adjutant-General to the Forces	1873	SPY	20.00
☐ Ossie	1896	SPY	20.00
☐ The Mite	1885	SPY	20.00
☐ Boy Scouts	1911	APE JR.	24.00
☐ Mafeking	1900	DRAWL	N/A
☐ An Old Coldstreamer	1883	T	20.00
☐ He Was Born a Serene Highness	1905	SPY	20.00
☐ Western Australia	1903	SPY	24.00
☐ Steam Reserve	1895	SPY	20.00
☐ Fighting Bull	1879	SPY	20.00
☐ Uncle Louis	1907	RYG	24.00
☐ La Revanche	1887	T	20.00
☐ BWAB	1886	APE	20.00
☐ Natal	1903	SPY	N/A
☐ He Sits For Colchester	1890	SPY	20.00
☐ Sir Sam	1887	APE	N/A
☐ Redrag	1900	SPY	N/A
☐ A Crimean Hero	1883	T	20.00
☐ The Auxiliary Forces	1875	APE	20.00
☐ A Radical General	1907	SPY	N/A
☐ Byngo	1892	STUFF	20.00
☐ Vice-Admiral Caillard	1905	GUTH	20.00
☐ 1st Life Guards	1906	SPY	20.00
☐ At Mafeking	1899	SPY	N/A
☐ Imperial Yeomanry	1900	SPY	20.00
☐ G.K.C.	1912	STRICKLAND	24.00
☐ 19th Hussars	1910	WHO	20.00
☐ Arms and Sport	1912	WH	20.00
☐ An Admiral of the Fleet	1903	SPY	20.00
☐ The Rule of the Road	1887	APE	20.00
☐ A Jingo	1881	T	N/A
☐ Adm. Sir John E. Commerell	1889	SPY	20.00
☐ Lord Congleton	1894	SPY	20.00
☐ Mount	1881	SPY	20.00
☐ Second in Zululand	1879	SPY	20.00
☐ Bisley Camp	1912	WH	N/A
☐ A Military Secretary	1903	SPY	20.00
☐ Irish Guards	1900	SPY	20.00
☐ Henry	1876	SPY	20.00
☐ The Kaid	1904	SPY	20.00
☐ The Premier Baron	1907	SPY	20.00
☐ De Wet	1902	EBN	N/A
☐ H.A.C.	1894	SPY	20.00
☐ Captain the Hon. Henry	1912	WH	20.00
☐ 40 H.P. in a Dinghy	1906	SPY	20.00
☐ Madras	1891	BINT	20.00

CAPTION	YEAR	ARTIST	PRICE
☐ North American and West Indies	1902	SPY	20.00
☐ Smartness	1883	SPY	20.00
☐ A General	1878	SPY	20.00
☐ An Old War Horse	1911	APE JR.	20.00
☐ Madagascar	1895	GUTH	20.00
☐ A Calvary Reformer	1902	SPY	20.00
☐ Brown	1891	SPY	20.00
☐ Nautical Freshness	1911	WHO	N/A
☐ The Adjutant General	1877	APE	20.00
☐ The Admiral	1878	SPY	20.00
☐ Major Esterhazy	1898	GUTH	20.00
☐ Croppy	1881	T	20.00
☐ The Star	1898	SPY	20.00
☐ The Queen's Landlord	1876	JTJ	20.00
☐ The Yellow Admiral	1891	SPY	N/A
☐ Uncle Bill	1912	RAY	20.00
☐ Jacky	1902	SPY	20.00
☐ Military Music	1905	SPY	20.00
☐ Shookey	1902	SPY	20.00
☐ An Equerry in Waiting	1895	SPY	20.00
☐ Swordmanship	1896	SPY	20.00
☐ Conspicuous & Cool	1879	SPY	N/A
☐ Keith	1880	SPY	N/A
☐ On 1 China Station	1894	PAT	20.00
☐ The Calvary Division	1900	GDG	24.00
☐ L'Admiral	1902	GUTH	20.00
☐ V.C.	1880	SPY	N/A
☐ Glick	1898	SPY	20.00
☐ The Constable of the Tower	1873	SPY	N/A
☐ Revolution	1878	T	20.00
☐ The Ever Victorious	1881	APE	20.00
☐ Bill	1880	APE	20.00
☐ Popular Members	1874	APE	20.00
☐ Keeper of the Crown Jewels	1906	SPY	N/A
☐ Charles II	1886	SPY	20.00
☐ Master of the Horse	1908	SPY	20.00
☐ General Sir Francis Grenfell, K.C.B.	1889	SPY	20.00
☐ A General Group	1900	SPY	60.00
☐ Rupert	1905	SPY	20.00
☐ Commander-in-Chief	1876	M	20.00
☐ Julian	1898	SPY	20.00
☐ He Will Be the Third Duke	1899	HADGE	20.00
☐ Mixed Forces	1901	SPY	20.00
☐ English Strategy	1887	APE	20.00
☐ The Soldiers Who Couldn't	1879	SPY	20.00
☐ The Retired List	1875	APE	20.00
☐ An Admiral	1875	APE	N/A
☐ Pompo	1901	SPY	N/A
☐ A Good Soldier	1884	SPY	20.00
☐ Naval Reserve	1883	SPY	20.00
☐ Hobart Pasha	1878	SPY	20.00
☐ The Beau Ideal	1877	SPY	20.00
☐ Lloyds	1883	Unsigned	20.00
☐ Our Youngest General	1899	SPY	40.00
☐ Patronage	1904	SPY	20.00
☐ Naval Ordnance	1906	SPY	20.00
☐ The Imperial Institute	1897	SPY	20.00
☐ The Father of the Rag	1885	APE	20.00
☐ Monty	1913	HESTER	20.00
☐ 6th Division	1901	SPY	20.00
☐ Commodore H.M. Yachts	1909	SPY	20.00
☐ Little Harry	1876	M	N/A
☐ '94'	1903	AO	20.00

CAPTION	YEAR	ARTIST	PRICE
☐ Lord Mark	1886	SPY	20.00
☐ A Sea Lord	1900	SPY	N/A
☐ The Court	1880	SPY	20.00
☐ Khartoum	1899	SPY	24.00
☐ I Regret To Report	1905	IMP	20.00
☐ H.M.S. Powerful	1900	SPY	20.00
☐ Rowdy	1906	SPY	N/A
☐ Cuthbert	1888	APE	20.00
☐ Colchester	1894	SPY	N/A
☐ Army, Court & Volunteers	1882	SPY	20.00
☐ The Victoria & Geneva Crosses	1876	SPY	20.00
☐ Tirah	1898	SPY	20.00
☐ The Vice-Commander	1876	SPY	20.00
☐ Balaklava	1881	APE	N/A
☐ A Keeper of the Tower	1907	SPY	N/A
☐ An Earnest African	1895	SPY	20.00
☐ Afghan Frontier B-417	1885	SPY	N/A
☐ Joe	1910	HCO	20.00
☐ Dan	1878	SPY	20.00
☐ 4th Division	1901	SPY	N/A
☐ Sir Hugh	1906	SPY	N/A
☐ Jim	1876	JTJ	20.00
☐ Rim	1880	SPY	N/A
☐ C.I.V.	1901	SPY	20.00
☐ R.M.C.	1902	SPY	20.00
☐ Handsome Fred	1878	APE	20.00
☐ Fred	1896	SPY	N/A
☐ Navy Control	1903	SPY	20.00
☐ The Home District	1892	SPY	20.00
☐ Admiral of the Fleet	1882	T	20.00
☐ Roley	1905	SPY	20.00
☐ Modern Strategy	1884	GO	20.00
☐ Oliver	1877	APE	20.00
☐ The Master General	1905	SPY	20.00
☐ Composite Regiment	1900	CLOISTER	20.00
☐ Chelsea Hospital	1903	SPY	20.00
☐ The Nitrate King	1889	SPY	20.00
☐ A Sub-Editor	1897	SPY	20.00
☐ Bully	1896	SPY	20.00
☐ Sam	1912	WH	N/A
☐ Soudan	1908	SPY	20.00
☐ A Soldier	1877	SPY	N/A
☐ Sailor, Politician	1875	APE	20.00
☐ The Swell of the Ocean	1876	SPY	N/A
☐ Order at Wimbledon	1880	APE	20.00
☐ Senior Equerry	1891	SPY	N/A
☐ Self-Reliant	1902	SPY	20.00
☐ Polly	1901	SPY	20.00
☐ Fresh from the Channel	1901	SPY	20.00
☐ Soldiers & Correspondent	1899	SPY	N/A
☐ The Royal Borough	1877	SPY	20.00
☐ Bobs	1880	WGR	24.00
☐ Bobs	1900	SPY	24.00
☐ Military Advice	1874	APE	20.00
☐ Guards	1875	APE	20.00
☐ Gunnery	1903	SPY	N/A
☐ China	1901	SPY	N/A
☐ Fortification	1877	APE	N/A
☐ Slatin	1899	SPY	N/A
☐ National Military Training	1909	SPY	N/A
☐ Dorren	1901	SPY	N/A
☐ War	1879	APE	N/A
☐ Aldershot	1878	APE	20.00

CAPTION	YEAR	ARTIST	PRICE
☐ Russian, Persian and Turkish	1902	SPY	20.00
☐ Dear Old Ben	1887	SPY	20.00
☐ Ahmed Khel	1887	APE	20.00
☐ He Is A Living Paradox	1870	APE	20.00
☐ He Was Made A Statesman	1870	APE	20.00
☐ Eddie	1899	SPY	20.00
☐ A Younger Son	1876	SPY	20.00
☐ Aldershot Cavalry	1897	SPY	20.00
☐ Upty	1888	APE	20.00
☐ Commanding 2nd Life Guards	1906	SPY	20.00
☐ The Hope of France	1870	Unsigned	20.00
☐ Home District	1902	SPY	20.00
☐ A Permanent Warrior	1901	SPY	20.00
☐ Bechuanaland	1886	APE	20.00
☐ Ladysmith	1900	SPY	N/A
☐ In His Military Capacity	1879	SPY	20.00
☐ The Prince	1878	APE	20.00
☐ In the Mahdi's Camp	1897	SPY	20.00
☐ The Man Who Won't Stop	1874	APE	N/A
☐ The Flying Column	1879	SPY	20.00
☐ Spanish Ironclads	1877	JTJ	20.00
☐ Alleno	1877	APE	20.00
☐ The Beggar's Friend	1870	Unsigned	14.00
☐ He Well Deserves His	1871	APE	14.00
☐ The Premier Marquess	1877	SPY	14.00
☐ The Squire	1877	APE	14.00
☐ The Great Man	1879	SPY	14.00
☐ Self-Conquest	1879	SPY	14.00
☐ Amiability	1881	SPY	14.00
☐ Our Little Duke	1881	SPY	14.00
☐ Brighton	1882	Unsigned	14.00
☐ Created in 1646	1882	SPY	14.00
☐ Lord Leicester's Nephew	1883	SPY	14.00
☐ Near the Rose	1886	SPY	14.00
☐ The Woolsack	1886	SPY	14.00
☐ Universal Knowledge	1887	APE	14.00
☐ In Vanity Fair	1890	VARIOUS	60.00
☐ Cobham Hall	1893	SPY	14.00
☐ Charlie Aylesford	1907	AO	14.00
☐ Dandy Dick	1913	AST	14.00
☐ Mr. Eadie	1913	HESTER	N/A

MUSIC

CAPTION	YEAR	ARTIST	PRICE
☐ Il Bacio	1885	APE	20.00
☐ Albert Hall	1894	SPY	24.00
☐ Sweet Sounds	1873	SPY	20.00
☐ Westminister Bridge	1904	SPY	20.00
☐ Royal English Opera	1891	SPY	N/A
☐ Orchestration	1872	Unsigned	20.00
☐ First Violin	1874	APE	32.00
☐ Ex Opera	1900	STUFF	20.00
☐ A Wandering Minstrel	1883	Unsigned	32.00
☐ Patience	1881	SPY	N/A
☐ Dan Godfrey	1888	SPY	20.00
☐ Emotional Music	1879	T	N/A
☐ Corney Grain	1885	SPY	20.00
☐ G	1891	SPY	20.00
☐ Impromptu	1908	SPY	24.00
☐ Opera Deluxe	1911	RAY	N/A
☐ A Londoner	1873	Unsigned	20.00
☐ Grand Opera	1898	SPY	20.00

CAPTION	YEAR	ARTIST	PRICE
☐ A Great Cellist	1897	CG	32.00
☐ The Last Of A Classic	1905	SPY	32.00
☐ Kubelik	1903	SPY	32.00
☐ A Great English Composer	1908	Unsigned	20.00
☐ The Abbe	1886	SPY	24.00
☐ English Tenor	1892	LIB	20.00
☐ Cotillion	1874	APE	20.00
☐ R.A.M.	1904	SPY	20.00
☐ Crystal Palace	1895	SPY	20.00
☐ The Intermezzo	1912	WH	20.00
☐ Cavalleria Rusticana	1893	LIB	20.00
☐ A Fine Baritone	1898	SPY	20.00
☐ Prayer & Praise	1875	APE	20.00
☐ Wagnerian Opera	1899	WAG	24.00
☐ Nikisch	1913	OWL	24.00
☐ Easy Execution	1899	SPY	N/A
☐ Patron's Fund	1909	ELF	N/A
☐ The English Tenor	1890	SPY	24.00
☐ Polish Tenor	1891	SPY	24.00
☐ Guildhall	1913	AST	N/A
☐ Opera in English	1913	AST	20.00
☐ Praise & Prayer	1875	APE	20.00
☐ Student & Singer	1902	SPY	20.00
☐ Sarasate	1889	APE	32.00
☐ The Minstrel Boy	1904	SPY	N/A
☐ Oxford Music	1891	SPY	20.00
☐ He Found Harmony	1905	SPY	20.00
☐ Eduard Strass	1895	EBN	32.00
☐ English Music	1874	APE	N/A
☐ For Ever and Ever	1885	APE	24.00
☐ Italian Music	1879	T.	N/A
☐ The Music of the Future	1877	SPY	N/A
☐ Queen's Hall	1907	SPY	24.00

NEWSPAPERMEN

CAPTION	YEAR	ARTIST	PRICE
☐ The Globe	1894	SPY	20.00
☐ New York Herald	1884	NEMO	20.00
☐ A Good Listener	1909	SPY	20.00
☐ The "Times" In Paris	1889	GUTH	20.00
☐ The Morning Post	1871	APE	20.00
☐ Algy	1898	SPY	20.00
☐ An Encyclopedia	1905	SPY	N/A
☐ Tommy	1889	SPY	N/A
☐ The Governing Classes	1873	Unsigned	20.00
☐ Punch	1881	APE	20.00
☐ An Art Critic	1893	SPY	20.00
☐ The Times	1879	SPY	20.00
☐ The Daily Times	1899	SPY	20.00
☐ The Pink 'Un'	1889	LIB	20.00
☐ The Pall Mall Gazette	1894	SPY	20.00
☐ Active	1878	APE	N/A
☐ The Echo	1885	APE	20.00
☐ The Fortnightly Review	1885	APE	20.00
☐ Thorough	1878	APE	20.00
☐ "? _____ !"	1911	RITCHIE	20.00
☐ He Created The Pall Mall	1880	APE	20.00
☐ Peace & War	1908	SPY	20.00
☐ The Pall Mall Magazine	1895	SPY	20.00
☐ The National Observer	1892	SPY	N/A
☐ The Birmingham Daily Post	1890	SPY	20.00
☐ The Standard	1874	APD	20.00

CAPTION	YEAR	ARTIST	PRICE
☐ The Daily Telegraph	1913	OWL	N/A
☐ The Sheffield Daily	1890	SPY	20.00
☐ The Daily Telegraph	1873	SPY	20.00
☐ Irish History	1885	SPY	20.00
☐ Financial News	1889	AJM	N/A
☐ South Africa	1906	SPY	20.00
☐ The Nonconformist	1871	APE	20.00
☐ The Fortnightly Review	1878	APE	20.00
☐ East Cambridgeshire	1894	SPY	20.00
☐ Tax Pay	1888	SPY	20.00
☐ The Times	1885	APE	20.00
☐ Joe's Stage Manager	1904	SPY	20.00
☐ The Saturday Review	1892	SPY	20.00
☐ New York Tribune	1902	SPY	20.00
☐ Telegrams	1872	Unsigned	N/A
☐ La Vouyoucratie	1870	Unsigned	20.00
☐ Our War Correspondence	1875	APE	20.00
☐ Journalism	1875	APE	20.00
☐ Three Editors	1894	SPY	20.00
☐ Newspapers	1872	Unsigned	20.00
☐ He Found Livingstone	1872	Unsigned	N/A
☐ Hoxton Division	1899	STUFF	20.00
☐ Common-Sense in Politics	1885	APE	20.00
☐ Punch	1876	SPY	20.00
☐ The Times	1881	SPY	20.00
☐ P.W.W.	1911	RITCHIE	20.00
☐ Diplomaticus	1911	RITCHIE	20.00
☐ The World	1878	SPY	20.00

ORIENTALS

CAPTION	YEAR	ARTIST	PRICE
☐ China	1877	SPY	20.00
☐ Chinese Customs	1894	IMP	20.00
☐ Li	1896	GUTH	20.00
☐ Emperor of Corea	1899	PRY	N/A
☐ China in London	1903	SPY	20.00

PHOTOGRAPHERS

CAPTION	YEAR	ARTIST	PRICE
☐ East Birmingham	1902	SPY	36.00
☐ A Self-Made African	1904	SPY	N/A
☐ Kinemacolor	1914	SPY	N/A

POLICEMEN

CAPTION	YEAR	ARTIST	PRICE
☐ The Police Champion	1872	Unsigned	18.00
☐ Police	1875	APE	18.00
☐ Force No. Remedy	1882	FURNISS	18.00
☐ Criminal Investigation	1883	SPY	18.00
☐ Parliamentary Police	1884	APE	24.00
☐ Bow Street	1886	SPY	18.00
☐ Bow Street	1890	SPY	18.00
☐ Metropolitan Police	1890	SPY	18.00
☐ Scotland Yard	1890	SPY	18.00
☐ Chief Magistrate	1891	SPY	18.00
☐ Explosives	1892	SPY	18.00
☐ Marlborough Street	1898	SPY	18.00
☐ A Model Magistrate	1900	WAG	18.00
☐ Maryleborn	1901	WAG	18.00
☐ Finger Prints	1905	SPY	24.00

CAPTION	YEAR	ARTIST	PRICE
☐ Bow Street	1905	SPY	18.00
☐ Scotland Yard	1908	SPY	18.00
☐ City Police	1911	RAY	18.00
☐ The Universal Puzzle Is	1913	OWL	18.00

POLITICIANS

CAPTION	YEAR	ARTIST	PRICE
☐ Promoted From A Viceroyalty	1869	APE	14.00
☐ The Tory Bloodhound	1875	APE	14.00
☐ The Past	1874	APE	14.00
☐ Three Dowagers	1880	T	14.00
☐ Johnnie	1910	WHO	14.00
☐ North Paddington	1891	SPY	14.00
☐ The Kent Gang	1885	APE	14.00
☐ Arnold	1894	SPY	14.00
☐ The Gatehead Giant	1893	SPY	14.00
☐ An Expert in Ceremony	1907	SPY	14.00
☐ Hungary in Effigy	1877	UNK	14.00
☐ St. Andrews District	1897	SPY	14.00
☐ A Practical Patriot	1880	SPY	14.00
☐ Dundee	1882	SPY	14.00
☐ The Heritage of Woe	1905	SPY	14.00
☐ Palmerston's Secretary	1883	SPY	14.00
☐ The Patriotic League	1882	SPY	14.00
☐ The Conciliator	1911	WH	30.00
☐ A Great Orator	1910	XIT	30.00
☐ Brains	1904	SPY	14.00
☐ The Seventh Duke	1879	SPY	14.00
☐ Mind and Morality	1869	APE	14.00
☐ Rhodes the Second	1908	SPY	14.00
☐ Baker Pasha	1878	APE	14.00
☐ Bal	1899	SPY	14.00
☐ Dialectics	1910	XIT	30.00
☐ A Chief Secretary	1896	SPY	14.00
☐ Burnley	1892	SPY	14.00
☐ J.B.	1890	SPY	14.00
☐ The Blocker	1913	COCK	14.00
☐ Isle of Wight	1910	SPY	14.00
☐ The Cape of Good Hope	1887	SPY	14.00
☐ Raby Castle	1898	GAF	14.00
☐ Barneu	1895	SPY	14.00
☐ A Young Man	1875	APE	14.00
☐ The Baroness's Husband	1881	SPY	14.00
☐ Mid Armagh	1898	SPY	14.00
☐ Australia	1902	SPY	14.00
☐ One Of Those	1886	SPY	14.00
☐ Beer	1871	APE	14.00
☐ Reciprocity	1879	APE	14.00
☐ Landed Estates In	1882	SPY	14.00
☐ Ancient Lineage	1874	APE	14.00
☐ Frome	1896	SPY	14.00
☐ A Relic	1873	Unsigned	14.00
☐ Montrose	1885	SPY	14.00
☐ West Hampshire	1895	SPY	14.00
☐ New South Wales	1899	SPY	14.00
☐ Whitby	1904	SPY	14.00
☐ Rousseau	1896	SPY	14.00
☐ Little Ben	1871	Unsigned	14.00
☐ Big Ben	1871	Unsigned	14.00
☐ The Little Rascal	1876	SPY	14.00
☐ Southwark	1876	SPY	14.00

CAPTION	YEAR	ARTIST	PRICE
☐ Batavian Grace	1870	APE	14.00
☐ Fred	1888	SPY	N/A
☐ None	1913	UNK	N/A
☐ Irish Obstruction	1877	SPY	14.00
☐ Her Majesty's Private Secretary	1900	SPY	14.00
☐ A Midland Imperialist	1908	SPY	14.00
☐ The Fisherman's Friend	1885	APE	14.00
☐ The Passive Resister's	1906	SPY	14.00
☐ South Longford	1894	SPY	14.00
☐ B	1881	T	14.00
☐ Buonparte B	1893	SPY	14.00
☐ Bobby	1877	SPY	14.00
☐ He Did Not Decline	1872	Unsigned	14.00
☐ Boycott	1881	SPY	N/A
☐ Iconoclast	1880	SPY	14.00
☐ North Cambridgeshire	1894	SPY	14.00
☐ Mr. Speaker	1872	Unsigned	14.00
☐ Ordnance	1884	SPY	14.00
☐ Lord Monk Bretton	1894	SPY	14.00
☐ The Private Secretary	1909	SPY	14.00
☐ The Apostle to Women	1877	SPY	14.00
☐ John Bright	1889	APE	14.00
☐ Will The Sentimental	1869	APE	14.00
☐ Theodore	1910	ELF	14.00
☐ War	1901	SPY	14.00
☐ Macclesfield	1888	SPY	14.00
☐ East Sussex	1898	SPY	14.00
☐ He Never Attacks Morality	1913	RITCHIE	N/A
☐ The Golden Pippin	1879	SPY	14.00
☐ The Earl of Brownlow	1913	WH	14.00
☐ He Has Gained Credit	1869	APE	14.00
☐ Portsmouth	1882	SPY	14.00
☐ Cornwall	1885	SPY	14.00
☐ A Safe Duke	1875	APE	14.00
☐ Hammersmith	1907	SPY	14.00
☐ A Superannuated	1870	APE	14.00
☐ North Northampshire	1887	APE	14.00
☐ Secretary for Scotland	1902	SPY	14.00
☐ York City	1901	SPY	14.00
☐ Home-Rule	1873	SPY	14.00
☐ When Birth Cannot Lead	1869	SPY	14.00
☐ Chelsea & The Colonies	1881	SPY	14.00
☐ Ottoman Public Debt	1897	SPY	14.00
☐ Indian Authority	1878	SPY	14.00
☐ The Rt. Hon. James	1909	SPY	14.00
☐ And Stratheden	1873	SPY	14.00
☐ The Earl of Camperdown	1895	SPY	14.00
☐ If The State Is Happy	1869	APE	14.00
☐ Bill	1893	SPY	14.00
☐ Mid-Herts	1909	ELF	14.00
☐ The Whole Life	1869	APE	14.00
☐ Small Holdings	1907	SPY	14.00
☐ I Never Ask Anyone	1912	WH	16.00
☐ Dublin University	1893	LIB	30.00
☐ Dublin University	1911	HESTER	30.00
☐ Oxfordshire	1884	SPY	N/A
☐ 'C'	1879	SPY	14.00
☐ A Cheery Paymaster	1906	SPY	14.00
☐ Amends	1874	APE	14.00
☐ Good Fellow	1886	SPY	14.00
☐ Heir Presumptive To	1895	SPY	14.00
☐ Chief of the Clans	1904	SPY	14.00

CAPTION	YEAR	ARTIST	PRICE
☐ Greenwich	1900	SPY	14.00
☐ Our Joe	1877	SPY	N/A
☐ The Colonies	1901	SPY	30.00
☐ War-Worn	1908	WHO	30.00
☐ The Great Imperialist	1914	AST	N/A
☐ The Deceased Wife's Sister	1884	SPY	14.00
☐ Isandula	1881	SPY	14.00
☐ It Is Hardly To Be	1870	Unsigned	14.00
☐ French Free Trade	1875	APE	14.00
☐ In A New Character	1889	LIB	30.00
☐ Conservative Whip	1904	SPY	N/A
☐ The Lord Chamberlain	1901	SPY	14.00
☐ To Say That He Is The Best	1869	APE	14.00
☐ Southwark	1880	SPY	14.00
☐ The Little Great Premier	1908	VANITAS	14.00
☐ Black Rod	1873	SPY	14.00
☐ Judicious Amelioration	1871	Unsigned	14.00
☐ North Ayrshire	1911	SPY	N/A
☐ Lanarkshire	1885	SPY	14.00
☐ 3 Acres and A Cow	1888	SPY	14.00
☐ Noisy Tom	1873	SPY	14.00
☐ A Good Fellow	1873	SPY	14.00
☐ The Constitutional Union	1892	SPY	14.00
☐ Sydney	1882	SPY	14.00
☐ The Pattern Private Secretary	1877	SPY	14.00
☐ A Liberal Whip	1883	SPY	14.00
☐ Customs	1876	SPY	14.00
☐ The City	1885	SPY	14.00
☐ The French Ambassador	1895	GUTH	14.00
☐ Proper Self-Sufficiency	1880	T	14.00
☐ Joe	1878	SPY	14.00
☐ Newcastle on Tyne	1872	Unsigned	14.00
☐ Cockie	1909	KITE	14.00
☐ The New Man	1874	APE	14.00
☐ Lowestoft	1888	SPY	N/A
☐ Persia and India	1892	SPY	14.00
☐ Il Marchese	1874	APE	14.00
☐ The Most Popular	1873	SPY	14.00
☐ Ipswich Senior	1892	SPY	14.00
☐ Hippy	1871	Unsigned	14.00
☐ Ivo	1904	SPY	14.00
☐ The Earl of Dartmouth	1895	STUFF	14.00
☐ Clever	1877	SPY	14.00
☐ Qualis Ab Inepto	1869	APE	14.00
☐ Intelligent Toryism	1880	APE	14.00
☐ Australia	1908	SPY	14.00
☐ M. Cecrais	1893	GUTH	14.00
☐ Currency	1872	Unsigned	14.00
☐ French Foreign Affairs	1899	GUTH	14.00
☐ A Catholic	1878	APE	14.00
☐ Education & Defense	1902	SPY	14.00
☐ Position	1874	APE	14.00
☐ A Far Advanced Radical	1871	Unsigned	14.00
☐ The Semi-Official Ambassador	1913	OWL	14.00
☐ The Plan of Campaign	1887	APE	14.00
☐ Ways and Means	1871	Unsigned	14.00
☐ A Most Discreet Under	1905	SPY	14.00
☐ East Roumelia	1879	SPY	14.00
☐ A Southern Scot	1896	SPY	14.00
☐ An Irish Wit	1871	APE	14.00
☐ At Rennes	1899	SPY	14.00
☐ Property	1870	APE	14.00
☐ Fetteresso	1883	Unsigned	14.00

CAPTION	YEAR	ARTIST	PRICE
☐ An Exceptional Irishman	1870	ATN	14.00
☐ Finsbury	1887	APE	14.00
☐ Duncannon	1904	SPY	N/A
☐ Sol	1897	SPY	N/A
☐ A Whipper	1875	APE	14.00
☐ South Warwickshire	1885	SPY	14.00
☐ Silk	1871	Unsigned	14.00
☐ The Devon and Somerset	1887	APE	N/A
☐ The German Attache	1898	SPY	N/A
☐ Canadian Finance	1909	WHO	N/A
☐ A Princess's Husband	1889	SPY	14.00
☐ Fulham	1900	SPY	N/A
☐ Knight of Kerry	1909	SPY	N/A
☐ A Message From the Queen	1873	SPY	14.00
☐ Bombay	1874	APE	14.00
☐ None	1906	UNK	N/A
☐ Calne	1878	SPY	14.00
☐ Barnie	1882	SPY	14.00
☐ Property and Principle	1878	APE	14.00
☐ East Sussex	1898	SPY	14.00
☐ Vive La Polgne!	1888	APE	14.00
☐ The Senator	1882	T	N/A
☐ The Friend of Pelissier	1883	SPY	14.00
☐ South Wilts	1880	APE	14.00
☐ Of Newe	1880	APE	14.00
☐ The Ex-Father of the House	1875	APE	14.00
☐ W.A.	1897	IMP	14.00
☐ If He Is Not An Advanced	1869	APE	14.00
☐ An Amateur Whip	1874	APE	14.00
☐ He Married Lady	1869	APE	14.00
☐ Sanitas	1881	T	14.00
☐ Mr. A. B. Forwood	1890	LIB	14.00
☐ The Fisherman's Friend	1907	SPY	N/A
☐ The Squire	1886	SPY	14.00
☐ The City	1881	T	14.00
☐ The Sanitary	1875	APE	14.00
☐ The Slave Trade	1873	SPY	14.00
☐ Army Reorganization	1873	Unsigned	14.00
☐ He Devoured France	1872	Unsigned	14.00
☐ Greece	1888	SPY	14.00
☐ A New Peer	1878	SPY	14.00
☐ The Russian Foreign Office	1884	NEMO	N/A
☐ Capital Punishment	1873	Unsigned	14.00
☐ St. Pancras	1887	APE	N/A
☐ His Father's Son	1882	SPY	N/A
☐ The Gladstone Memorial	1882	Unsigned	14.00
☐ Babble, Birth &	1880	T	N/A
☐ Swansea	1910	WHO	14.00
☐ Practical	1872	Unsigned	14.00
☐ A Man of Fashion and Politics	1870	APE	14.00
☐ Treasurer of the	1892	SPY	N/A
☐ Tory Organization	1880	SPY	14.00
☐ West St. Pancras	1893	SPY	14.00
☐ Leicester Square	1874	APE	14.00
☐ A Philosophic Liberal	1869	APE	14.00
☐ The Ablest Professor	1869	APE	14.00
☐ Walpole	1898	SPY	14.00
☐ East Sussex	1880	SPY	14.00
☐ A Private Secretary	1900	SPY	14.00
☐ A Chartered Administrator	1898	SPY	14.00
☐ A Privileged Person	1869	APE	14.00
☐ A Liberal Imperialist	1903	SPY	14.00
☐ The General Colour of the Sec'ty	1913	OWL	14.00

CAPTION	YEAR	ARTIST	PRICE
☐ Mixed Political Wares	1892	SPY	N/A
☐ The Fourth Party	1880	SPY	30.00
☐ The Cabinet Council, 1883	1883	T	30.00
☐ Collapse of The Conference	1913	MOUSE	30.00
☐ At Rennes (Dreyfus)	1899	GUTH	N/A
☐ Empire Makers & Breakers	1897	STUFF	60.00
☐ Lobby of the House of Commons	1886	LIB	60.00
☐ On the Terrace	1893	SPY	60.00
☐ The Lord Protect Us	1898	FURNISS	N/A
☐ Monty	1880	SPY	14.00
☐ Mr. Speaker	1896	SPY	14.00
☐ A Commissioner	1871	Unsigned	14.00
☐ Government Marked	1913	OWL	14.00
☐ A Hegelian Politician	1896	SPY	14.00
☐ A Legislator	1884	SPY	14.00
☐ Torquay	1882	SPY	14.00
☐ He Fell Off His Horse Into	1870	APE	14.00
☐ Southport Division	1903	SPY	14.00
☐ The Dowager	1877	SPY	14.00
☐ Bridegroom	1878	SPY	14.00
☐ Georgie	1879	SPY	N/A
☐ Premier Peer of Scotland	1873	Unsigned	14.00
☐ Hamlie	1881	SPY	14.00
☐ Foreign Policy	1875	APE	14.00
☐ Newcastle-Upon-Tyne	1893	SPY	14.00
☐ A Financial Secretary	1896	SPY	14.00
☐ Gentle and Liberal	1884	SPY	14.00
☐ Affaires Etrangeres	1896	GUTH	14.00
☐ Hansard	1884	APE	14.00
☐ The Lord Mayor	1886	APE	N/A
☐ Lulu	1895	SPY	N/A
☐ Queer Hardie	1906	SPY	N/A
☐ High Political Office	1874	APE	14.00
☐ Conservative	1872	Unsigned	14.00
☐ He Is Conservative	1895	SPY	14.00
☐ Leverton	1909	SPY	N/A
☐ The Sugar of Toryism	1885	APE	14.00
☐ The Last Generation	1871	APE	14.00
☐ His Ability and Industry	1869	APE	14.00
☐ The Right Hon. Marq.	1888	SPY	14.00
☐ Hereditary Whip	1881	T	14.00
☐ An Irish Property	1877	SPY	14.00
☐ He Has Kept His	1873	SPY	14.00
☐ A Loyal Irishman	1880	APE	14.00
☐ International Penny Postage	1887	SPY	14.00
☐ Council	1874	SPY	14.00
☐ Natal	1898	SPY	14.00
☐ Grimsby	1887	SPY	14.00
☐ Common Sense	1874	APE	14.00
☐ Colonial Government	1875	APE	14.00
☐ Home Rule	1879	SPY	14.00
☐ Croydon	1886	APE	14.00
☐ Of Muckross	1876	SPY	14.00
☐ Accrington	1892	SPY	14.00
☐ A Lord-In-Waiting	1910	WHO	14.00
☐ The Lord Chamberlain	1877	SPY	14.00
☐ Orangeman	1886	SPY	14.00
☐ A Reformed Radical	1883	SPY	14.00
☐ Board of Works	1873	SPY	14.00
☐ An Equerry	1899	SPY	14.00
☐ The Colonies	1887	APE	14.00
☐ Military Changes	1882	SPY	14.00
☐ The Princess's Private	1905	SPY	14.00

CAPTION	YEAR	ARTIST	PRICE
☐ First Conservative Whip	1903	SPY	14.00
☐ The Lord Chamberlain	1900	SPY	14.00
☐ The Eccentric Liberal	1872	Unsigned	14.00
☐ The Cool of the Evening	1870	APE	14.00
☐ A Young Viceroy	1892	SPY	14.00
☐ Manchester	1885	APE	14.00
☐ The Britisher's Best Friend	1911	SPY	14.00
☐ Dear Boy	1892	SPY	14.00
☐ Energetic Toryism	1881	SPY	14.00
☐ A Lancashire Lad	1895	SPY	14.00
☐ Rochester	1886	APE	14.00
☐ Fifth Earl	1882	SPY	14.00
☐ Lt. Col. Robert William	1913	WH	14.00
☐ Candidate for Chelsea	1880	SPY	14.00
☐ Why Man He Doth	1913	OWL	14.00
☐ Guiness Trust	1891	SPY	14.00
☐ A Great French Orator	1908	GUTH	N/A
☐ Ginx's Baby	1878	SPY	14.00
☐ The Colossus of Roads	1875	APE	14.00
☐ Marmaduke	1912	WH	N/A
☐ New South Wales	1890	SPY	14.00
☐ Jonesy	1912	WH	14.00
☐ Jack	1873	Unsigned	14.00
☐ Prosy Facts & Figures	1892	SPY	14.00
☐ Asia Minor	1878	APE	14.00
☐ The Lord Chamberlain	1881	SPY	14.00
☐ Devonshire	1886	SPY	14.00
☐ Denbigh Borough's	1888	SPY	14.00
☐ He Improves If Possible	1869	APE	14.00
☐ Charlie	1883	SPY	14.00
☐ The King	1886	SPY	14.00
☐ A Promising Apprentice	1870	APE	14.00
☐ Has Sat For Three	1884	SPY	14.00
☐ A Fine Old Tory	1881	SPY	14.00
☐ Black Rod	1877	APE	14.00
☐ Sir Francis Knollys	1891	SPY	14.00
☐ Knox	1913	WH	14.00
☐ Modest Assurance	1874	APE	14.00
☐ The Infant Samuel	1873	SPY	14.00
☐ Willie	1813	COCK	14.00
☐ Family	1874	APE	14.00
☐ Sir Frank Lascellos	1912	K	14.00
☐ Canada	1897	SPY	14.00
☐ The Opposition	1912	STRICKLAND	14.00
☐ The Prince's Cicerone	1905	SPY	14.00
☐ One of the Best	1871	APE	14.00
☐ Cirencester	1893	SPY	14.00
☐ Permissive Prohibition	1872	Unsigned	14.00
☐ He Combines the Love	1869	APE	14.00
☐ East St. Pancras	1907	SPY	14.00
☐ Our Army Critic	1907	SPY	14.00
☐ Sir Henry Austin Lee	1912	K	14.00
☐ A Yorkshire Solicitor	1872	Unsigned	14.00
☐ Aberdeen	1879	SPY	14.00
☐ My Dear George	1880	SPY	14.00
☐ The Cape High	1894	SPY	14.00
☐ The Only Man	1871	Unsigned	14.00
☐ West Essex	1894	SPY	14.00
☐ The London School Board	1896	FTD	14.00
☐ Local Taxation	1875	APE	14.00
☐ Mr. Speaker	1906	SPY	14.00
☐ Thanet	1900	SPY	N/A
☐ Westmoreland	1881	SPY	14.00

CAPTION	YEAR	ARTIST	PRICE
☐ Foreign Affairs	1891	SPY	14.00
☐ Toby M. P.	1905	SPY	14.00
☐ Now I Want to Know	1871	Unsigned	14.00
☐ A Man of Position	1871	APE	14.00
☐ Marshal of the Ceremonies	1875	APE	14.00
☐ The Vice-Empress	1876	SPY	14.00
☐ None	1906	UNK	N/A
☐ He Was Lord Salisbury's	1894	SPY	14.00
☐ The Member for	1896	SPY	14.00
☐ The Lord Mayor	1881	SPY	14.00
☐ Sir Anthony MacDonnell	1905	SPY	14.00
☐ Mac	1882	SPY	14.00
☐ An Elder Son	1876	SPY	14.00
☐ The Whitehead Torpedo	1892	SPY	14.00
☐ South Donegla	1902	SPY	14.00
☐ A Home Ruler	1872	Unsigned	14.00
☐ West Clare	1894	SPY	14.00
☐ Mhagthamma	1885	SPY	14.00
☐ North-West Suffolk	1898	SPY	14.00
☐ Diplomacy	1874	APE	14.00
☐ Kim	1882	SPY	14.00
☐ The Colonies	1878	SPY	14.00
☐ Lord Salisbury's Manners	1887	APE	14.00
☐ Let Arts and Commerce	1869	APE	14.00
☐ Cheap Fares	1891	SPY	14.00
☐ Goodwood	1896	SPY	14.00
☐ A Conservative Religionist	1871	APE	14.00
☐ Brighton	1883	T	14.00
☐ J'y suis, J'y reste	1879	T	14.00
☐ The Home Secretary	1887	SPY	14.00
☐ Wigtownshire	1893	SPY	14.00
☐ The Conservative Party	1901	SPY	14.00
☐ Steward	1876	SPY	14.00
☐ Yorkshire	1875	APE	14.00
☐ Philip	1879	SPY	14.00
☐ A Persevering Politician	1883	SPY	14.00
☐ High Commissioner	1897	SPY	14.00
☐ York	1885	APE	14.00
☐ The Painstaking Irishman	1871	APE	14.00
☐ A Working Conservative	1870	APE	14.00
☐ South Hants	1881	T	14.00
☐ Alfred	1878	SPY	14.00
☐ A Fifteenth Earl	1898	SPY	14.00
☐ Fred	1893	SPY	14.00
☐ Burials	1879	SPY	14.00
☐ Dissent	1872	Unsigned	14.00
☐ Peterborough	1893	SPY	14.00
☐ Ninety-One	1883	SPY	14.00
☐ Committee of Selection	1882	SPY	14.00
☐ Education and Arbitration	1871	Unsigned	14.00
☐ Birmingham	1875	APE	14.00
☐ The British Expedition	1878	SPY	14.00
☐ A Jesuit in Disguise	1870	APE	14.00
☐ Jim	1909	SPY	14.00
☐ An Imperialist	1908	SPY	N/A
☐ A Nice Little Fellow	1871	APE	14.00
☐ A Tory	1878	SPY	14.00
☐ By Birth A Man	1871	Unsigned	14.00
☐ The Lordship of Compton	1904	SPY	14.00
☐ British Rule in India	1876	SPY	14.00
☐ The Australian Commonwealth	1904	SPY	14.00
☐ The House of Percy	1884	SPY	14.00
☐ Colonial Self-Government	1892	SPY	14.00

CAPTION	YEAR	ARTIST	PRICE
☐ Roman Catholic Home Rule	1880	T	14.00
☐ The O'Donoghue	1880	SPY	14.00
☐ The Joker for Waterford	1875	PE	14.00
☐ An Irish Baronet	1872	Unsigned	14.00
☐ The Parliamentary Empire	1870	Unsigned	14.00
☐ A Parliamentary Title	1883	SPY	14.00
☐ The Smart Critic	1870	ATN	14.00
☐ Chairman of Committees	1905	SPY	14.00
☐ He Killed the Cat	1879	APE	14.00
☐ The Clerk Marshal	1875	APE	14.00
☐ Promotion by Marriage	1880	T	14.00
☐ He Was Chairman	1870	Unsigned	14.00
☐ Lincoln	1883	SPY	14.00
☐ Roger	1880	SPY	14.00
☐ He Refused Woolsack	1872	Unsigned	14.00
☐ The Member For Great Britain	1909	SPY	14.00
☐ Anti-Rent	1880	T	N/A
☐ The Turkish Alliance	1885	SPY	14.00
☐ Harry	1895	SPY	14.00
☐ The Foreign Office	1883	T	14.00
☐ A Professor Of Strong	1870	ATN	14.00
☐ Telegraphs	1871	Unsigned	14.00
☐ Slate	1882	SPY	14.00
☐ Cambridge Borough	1895	SPY	N/A
☐ Northumberland	1881	T	14.00
☐ Mansion House	1897	SPY	N/A
☐ Bethnal Green	1888	SPY	N/A
☐ Barnstaple	1887	SPY	14.00
☐ The Sailor's Champion	1873	Unsigned	14.00
☐ Wit & Wisdom	1908	SPY	14.00
☐ Hereditary Eloquence	1880	APE	14.00
☐ Good Works	1906	SPY	14.00
☐ The Privy Purse	1883	T	14.00
☐ Port	1878	SPY	14.00
☐ The Dasher	1894	SPY	14.00
☐ The Demon	1907	SPY	14.00
☐ The Manchester School	1877	SPY	14.00
☐ The Brains of Obstruction	1886	SPY	14.00
☐ Mouldy	1876	SPY	14.00
☐ To Abandon Conservative Ideals	1905	SPY	14.00
☐ Devonport	1882	SPY	14.00
☐ In Society and Member Of	1889	LIB	14.00
☐ Under-Secretary For 'War'	1901	SPY	N/A
☐ Order, Order	1875	APE	14.00
☐ Liverpool	1880	SPY	14.00
☐ Huddersfield	1884	SPY	14.00
☐ He Has Succeeded In	1870	APE	14.00
☐ M. F. H. of Herefordshire	1913	OWL	N/A
☐ South-East Essex	1896	SPY	14.00
☐ Our Eastern Policy	1873	SPY	14.00
☐ A Tenant Farmer	1875	APE	14.00
☐ The Lord Dictator	1875	APE	14.00
☐ The Nobleman of the Garden	1904	SPY	14.00
☐ Elisha	1892	SPY	N/A
☐ The Irish Petrel	1904	SPY	N/A
☐ Montgomery District	1907	SPY	14.00
☐ Loreburn	1913	OWL	14.00
☐ Property in Suffolk	1881	T	14.00
☐ Peace	1880	SPY	14.00
☐ Highly Respectable	1870	ATN	14.00
☐ Ex-Official	1881	APE	N/A
☐ East Cornwall	1882	SPY	14.00
☐ Admiralty	1907	SPY	N/A

CAPTION	YEAR	ARTIST	PRICE
☐ Diplomacy & Poetry	1897	SPY	14.00
☐ In Waiting	1876	SPY	14.00
☐ Tear 'Em	1874	APE	14.00
☐ The Clerk of Parliaments	1885	SPY	14.00
☐ The Kirk of Scotland	1881	T	14.00
☐ Borstal System	1910	SPY	14.00
☐ Westminister	1878	APE	14.00
☐ This Fell Sergeant	1873	Unsigned	14.00
☐ Loyal and Patriotic	1888	SPY	14.00
☐ He Was Once Offered	1871	Unsigned	14.00
☐ Foreign Policy	1879	SPY	14.00
☐ Foreign Affairs	1898	SPY	14.00
☐ A Soldier's Son	1889	SPY	14.00
☐ Peking	1903	SPY	14.00
☐ A New Lord Mayor	1890	SPY	14.00
☐ The Caucus	1892	STUFF	N/A
☐ The Safe Man	1874	APE	14.00
☐ East Sussex	1882	SPY	N/A
☐ Sheep	1883	SPY	N/A
☐ Pigs	1878	SPY	N/A
☐ Extinction, Distinction	1905	SPY	14.00
☐ Admiralty	1901	SPY	N/A
☐ Despatches	1884	SPY	14.00
☐ Albert's Seymour	1877	APE	14.00
☐ He is Not As Other Men	1869	APE	14.00
☐ The Yankee From Persia	1912	WH	N/A
☐ Shuttleworth	1904	SPY	N/A
☐ A Conservative Whip	1871	APE	14.00
☐ Manchester	1884	APE	14.00
☐ Straits Settlements	1892	KYO	14.00
☐ A Successful First Speech	1907	SPY	30.00
☐ No Surrender	1911	NIBS	N/A
☐ Sammy	1904	SPY	N/A
☐ First Lord of the Treasury	1887	SPY	14.00
☐ Proud and Sincere	1869	Unsigned	14.00
☐ An Old-Fashion Duke	1893	SPY	14.00
☐ Unlike Wilkes, Who Is	1912	RUTH	14.00
☐ Bradlaugh's Baby	1881	SPY	N/A
☐ The Messenger of Peace	1870	APE	14.00
☐ The Cape	1897	SPY	14.00
☐ White Dial	1883	SPY	14.00
☐ The Young Man	1879	SPY	14.00
☐ He Speaks With One Party	1869	APE	14.00
☐ Westhoughton	1894	SPY	14.00
☐ Pour Encourager Les Autres	1869	APE	14.00
☐ Two-and-Eighty	1884	SPY	14.00
☐ A Country Gentleman	1875	APE	N/A
☐ Suffolk	1875	APE	14.00
☐ Sheffield	1886	SPY	14.00
☐ East Dorsetshire	1892	SPY	N/A
☐ East and West	1912	RAY	14.00
☐ He Received the Royal	1869	Unsigned	14.00
☐ The Gull's Friend	1874	APE	14.00
☐ Our Mark	1912	WH	N/A
☐ The Blister	1888	SPY	14.00
☐ Lately Whipped	1874	APE	14.00
☐ Burra Dick	1881	SPY	14.00
☐ Dangerous Trades	1909	SPY	14.00
☐ Tom	1883	Unsigned	14.00
☐ Clapham	1900	SPY	N/A
☐ Baronet or Butcher	1871	APE	14.00
☐ Cheshire	1881	SPY	14.00

CAPTION	YEAR	ARTIST	PRICE
☐ Finsbury	1883	SPY	14.00
☐ A Man of the World	1876	SPY	14.00
☐ Lofty	1882	SPY	14.00
☐ The Norwood Division	1897	SPY	14.00
☐ The Lord Mayor	1908	SPY	14.00
☐ Sir Charles Tupper	1913	OWL	N/A
☐ A Late Whip	1894	SPY	14.00
☐ Oxford City	1899	SPY	14.00
☐ Bucks	1882	SPY	14.00
☐ He Was Considered An Able	1870	ATN	14.00
☐ He Advocated Free Trade	1872	Unsigned	14.00
☐ The Imperial Institute	1893	SPY	14.00
☐ Hook & Eye	1876	SPY	14.00
☐ Swansea, Sir H. H., M.P.	1886	SPY	14.00
☐ Always Pleasant	1870	SPY	14.00
☐ Earl Waldegrave	1912	WH	14.00
☐ E.D.	1909	QUIP	14.00
☐ The Hertford Property	1873	SPY	14.00
☐ He Defended Hyde Park	1872	Unsigned	14.00
☐ Whip	1886	LIB	14.00
☐ South Kensington	1897	SPY	14.00
☐ Hear! Hear! Hear!	1884	APE	14.00
☐ Orkney and Shetland	1909	WHO	14.00
☐ France at the Congress	1878	T	14.00
☐ The Lord Mayor	1872	Unsigned	14.00
☐ A Cynical Radical	1906	SPY	14.00
☐ The Treasury	1910	HLO	14.00
☐ The Iron Duke's Grandson	1885	APE	14.00
☐ Strathfieldseye	1903	SPY	N/A
☐ The Son of Waterloo	1872	Unsigned	14.00
☐ Madras	1893	BINT	14.00
☐ Algy	1892	SPY	14.00
☐ Denbigshire	1892	SPY	14.00
☐ An Eminent Christian	1869	APE	14.00
☐ The Richest Man in England	1870	APE	14.00
☐ The Great Believer	1871	APE	14.00
☐ Conservative Conversion	1875	APE	14.00
☐ Parliamentary Procedure	1895	SPY	N/A
☐ Bonnie Westmoreland	1889	HAY	14.00
☐ Liverpool	1880	SPY	14.00
☐ Chelsea	1901	SPY	14.00
☐ Wiggin	1892	TUFF	14.00
☐ The Champion of the Ladies	1909	HLO	14.00
☐ Montgomeryshire	1879	SPY	14.00
☐ Moray and Nairn	1909	HCO	14.00
☐ Birdseye	1893	SPY	14.00
☐ The Lash	1874	APE	14.00
☐ A Sticker	1908	SPY	14.00
☐ Consular Chaplains	1874	APE	14.00
☐ Our Sir George	1874	SPY	14.00
☐ Hanley	1896	SPY	14.00
☐ Tariff Reform	1908	SPY	14.00
☐ A Staffordshire Peer	1895	STUFF	14.00
☐ Dover and War	1900	SPY	14.00
☐ Aesthetics	1880	SPY	14.00
☐ Chester	1893	SPY	14.00
☐ Chester	1910	WHO	14.00
☐ Alick	1881	SPY	14.00
☐ Ayr Burghs	1910	HCO	14.00
☐ A Gentleman	1886	SPY	14.00
☐ Irish Loyalty	1887	APE	N/A

POLO

CAPTION	YEAR	ARTIST	PRICE
☐ Yeoman-Like Polo	1891	LIB	N/A
☐ Descended From Edward	1898	GAF	48.00
☐ I Say	1898	GAF	N/A
☐ Patiala	1900	MR	48.00
☐ Buck	1907	SPY	N/A

PRIME MINISTERS

CAPTION	YEAR	ARTIST	PRICE
☐ The Greatest Liberal	1869	APE	20.00
☐ He Educated The Tories	1869	SINGE	N/A
☐ He Is Too Honest	1869	APE	20.00
☐ It Is His Mission To	1869	APE	N/A
☐ Were He A Worse Man	1869	SINGE	N/A
☐ The Junior Ambassador	1878	APE	N/A
☐ The People's William	1879	SPY	24.00
☐ Power and Peace	1879	SPY	24.00
☐ The Grand Old Man	1887	SPY	N/A
☐ The Irish Secretary	1887	SPY	N/A
☐ East Fife	1891	SPY	20.00
☐ The Opposition	1899	SPY	N/A
☐ The Prime Minister	1900	SPY	20.00
☐ Little Bo-Peep	1901	SPY	20.00
☐ A Gentle Shepherd	1905	SPY	20.00
☐ Nonconformist Genius	1907	SPY	N/A

RAILWAY OFFICIALS

CAPTION	YEAR	ARTIST	PRICE
☐ Great Northern	1908	SPY	20.00
☐ Board of Trade	1880	SPY	20.00
☐ Cricket, Railways & Agriculture	1904	SPY	20.00
☐ Great Central	1907	SPY	20.00
☐ A Railroad Knight	1890	SPY	20.00
☐ North Western	1892	SPY	20.00
☐ L.C.D.R.	1900	SPY	N/A
☐ The Midland	1908	SPY	20.00
☐ A South Western Director	1896	SPY	20.00
☐ L. & N. W. R.	1894	SPY	N/A
☐ North Leeds	1899	SPY	20.00
☐ A Whip	1878	SPY	20.00
☐ A Railway Director	1894	SPY	20.00
☐ J.G.	1910	PRY	20.00
☐ South Western	1903	SPY	20.00
☐ Railway Trusts	1891	SPY	20.00
☐ A Railway Commissioner	1903	SPY	N/A
☐ Father Time	1888	LIB	N/A
☐ L. and N.W.	1912	WH	20.00
☐ London & South Western	1891	SPY	20.00
☐ The Canadian Pacific	1908	SPY	20.00
☐ Caledonian Railway	1895	SPY	20.00
☐ The Railway Interest	1875	APE	20.00
☐ G.W.R.	1902	SPY	20.00

RED ROBE JUDGES

CAPTION	YEAR	ARTIST	PRICE
☐ A Souvenir	1870	ATN	N/A
☐ The Lord Chief Baron	1871	Unsigned	N/A
☐ Gentle Manners	1887	SPY	N/A
☐ 3rd Commissioner	1888	SPY	N/A

CAPTION	YEAR	ARTIST	PRICE
☐ One of the Family	1890	QUIZ	N/A
☐ Mr. Justice Grantham	1890	SPY	N/A
☐ The Recorder	1903	SPY	N/A
☐ Judicial Light Weight	1907	SPY	N/A
☐ Lorry	1907	SPY	60.00
☐ Lord Chief Justice	1913	WH	N/A

ROWING

CAPTION	YEAR	ARTIST	PRICE
☐ Pembroke	1888	HAY	40.00
☐ Professional Champion	1889	SPY	30.00
☐ Wingfield Sculls	1889	SPY	N/A
☐ One of the Presidents	1890	SPY	N/A
☐ O.U.B.C.	1891	SPY	40.00
☐ Flea	1893	SPY	40.00
☐ Benjie	1894	SPY	50.00
☐ Fogg	1894	SPY	40.00
☐ O.U.B.C.	1895	SPY	40.00
☐ Rudy	1895	SPY	40.00
☐ Crumbo	1896	SPY	46.00
☐ Ducker	1897	SPY	N/A
☐ Tarka	1899	SPY	40.00
☐ C.U.B.C.	1900	SPY	N/A
☐ C.U.B.C.	1903	SPY	40.00
☐ Bush	1907	SPY	40.00
☐ Duggie	1907	SPY	N/A
☐ Ethel	1908	SPY	46.00
☐ Bill	1910	ELF	40.00
☐ A Good Stroke	1911	APE JR.	40.00
☐ The Light Blue Stroke	1912	WH	N/A
☐ Steered Three Winning Crews	1912	WH	N/A

ROYALTY

CAPTION	YEAR	ARTIST	PRICE
☐ Ote-Toi-De-La-Que	1869	COIDE	N/A
☐ Eddie	1888	HAY	N/A
☐ The Prince of Monaco	1900	SPY	N/A
☐ La Civilisation Russe	1869	COIDE	20.00
☐ H.R.H. Prince Alexander of Teck	1908	SPY	20.00
☐ My August Master	1884	NEMO	20.00
☐ A Born King	1893	Unsigned	20.00
☐ S. M. Alfonso XIII	1906	GUTH	N/A
☐ He Would Be A King	1872	Unsigned	20.00
☐ The Duke of Aosta	1903	LIB	20.00
☐ Ahmed Arabi The Egyptian	1883	FV	20.00
☐ God Bless the Duke	1869	APE	20.00
☐ Cuch Behar	1901	Unsigned	20.00
☐ The Gaekwar	1901	MR	20.00
☐ The Head of the Russels	1874	APE	20.00
☐ The Ablest Statesman	1870	Unsigned	20.00
☐ Plon-Plon	1879	T	20.00
☐ Le Prince Du Chic	1899	SPY	N/A
☐ Sarawak	1899	SPY	N/A
☐ Marlborough	1882	SPY	20.00
☐ The Bute	1910	WHO	20.00
☐ Legitimacy	1876	SPY	20.00
☐ M. Carnot, Pres.	1889	PAL	20.00
☐ The French Republic	1894	GUTH	20.00
☐ Restored	1882	SPY	N/A
☐ A Prince of Denmark	1902	SPY	N/A
☐ H.R.H. The Crown Prince Of	1895	SPY	N/A

CAPTION	YEAR	ARTIST	PRICE
☐ The Fourth Duke	1877	SPY	20.00
☐ A Future Commander	1876	SPY	20.00
☐ H.R.H.	1913	HESTER	N/A
☐ Prince Arthur	1913	OWL	20.00
☐ Our Soldier Prince	1890	SPY	20.00
☐ The Orleans Family	1884	NEMO	N/A
☐ The Duc D'Aumale	1891	GUTH	20.00
☐ (No Caption)	1878	SPY	24.00
☐ The Pacificator Of Europe	1910	XIT	24.00
☐ The Prince	1878	SPY	N/A
☐ His Majesty the King	1902	SPY	24.00
☐ The Eminently Respectable	1895	GUTH	20.00
☐ Greece	1876	SPY	20.00
☐ His Majesty the King	1911	APE JR.	24.00
☐ Prince Henry of Orleans	1897	GUTH	20.00
☐ Italy	1878	T	20.00
☐ She Has Throughout Her Life	1869	COIDE	20.00
☐ The Ex-Khedive	1881	T	20.00
☐ Johore	1891	KYO	20.00
☐ The Empire	1877	SPY	20.00
☐ Austria	1877	SUE	N/A
☐ An Indian Statesman	1876	SPY	N/A
☐ The Aga Khan	1904	SPY	20.00
☐ Oom Paul	1900	DRAWL	N/A
☐ The Student Prince	1877	SPY	20.00
☐ Un Roi Consitutionel	1869	COIDE	20.00
☐ The New French President	1899	GUTH	20.00
☐ Les Mangeoit Pour	1871	COIDE	20.00
☐ A Prince Royal	1895	SPY	20.00
☐ An Abyssinian General	1903	SPY	20.00
☐ Europe's Youngest	1909	NIBS	N/A
☐ Blenheim Palace	1898	SPY	20.00
☐ A Premier of France	1898	GUTH	20.00
☐ Abyssinia	1897	GLICK	20.00
☐ Michael	1908	SPY	20.00
☐ The Emperor	1891	PERY	20.00
☐ Persia	1903	SPY	20.00
☐ La Regime Parlementaire	1869	COIDE	N/A
☐ He Endowed Persia	1873	SPY	N/A
☐ A Living Monument To English	1870	ATN	20.00
☐ The Little Father	1897	GUTH	20.00
☐ L'er Conscrit Dé France	1890	GUTH	20.00
☐ Messieurs	1913	OWL	24.00
☐ Hereditary Grand Falconer	1873	Unsigned	N/A
☐ President No. 3	1880	APE	20.00
☐ The Premier Earl	1880	SPY	20.00
☐ Jodhpore	1887	SPY	20.00
☐ The Maharajah	1882	SPY	N/A
☐ Prince Soltykoff	1889	SPY	N/A
☐ Ex-President Steyn	1900	WAG	24.00
☐ Simple and Unassuming	1870	APE	N/A
☐ Frank	1902	SPY	N/A
☐ The Duke of Teck	1902	SPY	20.00
☐ The Most Popular	1870	ATN	20.00
☐ The Khedive	1883	FV	20.00
☐ Faute-De-Mieux-Premier	1872	Unsigned	20.00
☐ Il Re Galantoumo	1870	Unsigned	20.00
☐ Italia	1902	LIB	20.00
☐ Victor	1899	GUTH	20.00
☐ A Cimiez	1897	GUTH	24.00
☐ (Black & white reprint of above at death)	1901	GUTH	20.00
☐ H.R.H.	1911	NIBS	N/A
☐ The Prince	1873	Unsigned	24.00

CAPTION	YEAR	ARTIST	PRICE
☐ Our Sailor Prince	1890	SPY	20.00
☐ Fritz	1870	Unsigned	20.00
☐ Oh Child, Mayst Thou	1905	GUTH	20.00
☐ The Premier Marquess	1904	SPY	N/A

SCOTSMEN

CAPTION	YEAR	ARTIST	PRICE
☐ The Queen's Lord Steward	1894	SPY	20.00
☐ If Everywhere As	1870	APE	20.00
☐ Restless Peter	1908	SPY	20.00
☐ Scottish Horse	1905	SPY	20.00

SHIPPING OFFICIALS

CAPTION	YEAR	ARTIST	PRICE
☐ Plymouth	1888	SPY	20.00
☐ The Knight of the Cruise	1884	APE	20.00
☐ Union Steamship	1896	SPY	20.00
☐ Shipping	1890	SPY	20.00
☐ Cunarder	1904	SPY	20.00
☐ Jim	1909	SPY	20.00
☐ White Star	1894	LIB	20.00
☐ Docks and Harbours	1909	SPY	20.00
☐ He Built the Alabama	1873	SPY	20.00
☐ Shipping	1884	APE	20.00
☐ Harland & Wolff	1903	SPY	N/A
☐ Naval Construction	1875	APE	20.00
☐ Tariff Reform League	1910	WHO	20.00
☐ Iron Shipbuilding	1873	Unsigned	20.00
☐ Manchester Ship Canal	1910	ELF	20.00
☐ Pando	1887	APE	20.00
☐ Destroyers	1905	SPY	20.00
☐ Naval Construction	1910	SPY	20.00
☐ Hull	1885	APE	20.00

SPORTS, MISCELLANEOUS
BILLIARDS

CAPTION	YEAR	ARTIST	PRICE
☐ The French Republic	1879	T	30.00
☐ The Champion Roberts	1885	SPY	40.00
☐ He Might Be	1905	SPY	40.00

CARRIAGES

CAPTION	YEAR	ARTIST	PRICE
☐ A Military Difficulty	1870	ATN	20.00
☐ Charlie	1874	APE	20.00
☐ A Peninsular Veteran	1876	APE	20.00
☐ A Whip	1878	SPY	20.00
☐ A Great Officer	1881	SPY	N/A
☐ Old Times	1886	APE	N/A
☐ Coaching	1887	APE	N/A
☐ Four-In-Hand	1903	SPY	20.00

CHESS

CAPTION	YEAR	ARTIST	PRICE
☐ Chess	1888	APE	24.00

CURLING

CAPTION	YEAR	ARTIST	PRICE
☐ The King of Clubs	1909	ELF	N/A

DOG JUDGE

CAPTION	YEAR	ARTIST	PRICE
☐ A Judge	1901	CB	36.00

DUELLING

CAPTION	YEAR	ARTIST	PRICE
☐ A French Duellist	1879	T	24.00

FENCING

CAPTION	YEAR	ARTIST	PRICE
☐ He Insists That His Pen	1905	SPY	36.00
☐ Cold Steel	1903	JEST	36.00
☐ Henry	1880	APE	36.00

FISHING

CAPTION	YEAR	ARTIST	PRICE
☐ Mr. William Black	1891	SPY	30.00
☐ The Postmaster General	1907	SPY	40.00

GYMNAST

CAPTION	YEAR	ARTIST	PRICE
☐ Fred	1876	SPY	N/A

ICE-SKATING

CAPTION	YEAR	ARTIST	PRICE
☐ Old Wares	1900	SPY	N/A

MISCELLANEOUS

CAPTION	YEAR	ARTIST	PRICE
☐ A Real English Gentleman	1881	APE	N/A
☐ Mufti	1881	SPY	14.00
☐ Dolly	1889	HAY	14.00
☐ The Consul Market	1896	SPY	14.00
☐ The Warwickshire	1896	SPY	14.00
☐ Basutoland	1901	SPY	14.00
☐ Orleans	1903	CLOISTER	14.00
☐ Lord Barrington	1909	SPY	14.00
☐ His Grace The Duke	1912	WH	14.00

ROLLER-SKATING

CAPTION	YEAR	ARTIST	PRICE
☐ The Philanthropist	1874	APE	40.00

RUGBY

CAPTION	YEAR	ARTIST	PRICE
☐ Rugby Union	1890	SPY	N/A
☐ Rugby Union	1892	STUFF	N/A

SOCCER

CAPTION	YEAR	ARTIST	PRICE
☐ Soccer	1912	WH	N/A

SWIMMING

CAPTION	YEAR	ARTIST	PRICE
☐ Swam the Channel	1875	APE	24.00

SPORT RIDERS

CAPTION	YEAR	ARTIST	PRICE
☐ The Jockey Club	1882	SPY	20.00
☐ Bucks	1885	SPY	20.00
☐ A Hard Rider	1898	GAF	20.00
☐ Clocks	1883	SPY	20.00
☐ Science and Sport	1913	WH	20.00
☐ Born in the Scarlet	1883	SPY	20.00
☐ A Cunarder	1881	SPY	N/A
☐ A Good Sportsman	1896	SPY	20.00
☐ The Lord Mayor	1882	SPY	20.00
☐ A Liberal Peer	1882	SPY	20.00
☐ Taplow Court	1890	SPY	20.00
☐ Haute Ecole	1877	SPY	20.00
☐ Colonel William	1912	WH	N/A
☐ Wiltshire	1886	SPY	20.00
☐ Jim	1877	SPY	20.00
☐ A Coachman	1881	SPY	20.00
☐ A Father of the Belvoir	1990	CS	20.00

STOCK EXCHANGE OFFICIALS

CAPTION	YEAR	ARTIST	PRICE
☐ The Stock Exchange	1886	LIB	N/A
☐ Jack in the Box	1890	FC.G.	N/A
☐ Mr. F. Carruther Gould	1890	LIB	18.00
☐ Mr. James Coates	1890	SPY	N/A
☐ Pakky	1895	SPY	N/A
☐ Tommy Dodd	1901	SPY	N/A
☐ North Befordshire	1902	SPY	N/A
☐ The Official Assignee	1908	WHO	N/A

TEACHERS AND HEADMASTERS

CAPTION	YEAR	ARTIST	PRICE
☐ M'Tutor	1901	SPY	20.00
☐ All Souls	1901	SPY	20.00
☐ M.T.S.	1901	WAG	24.00
☐ Popular Astronomy	1905	SPY	20.00
☐ Marlborough College	1902	SPY	24.00
☐ St. John's Oxford	1893	SPY	20.00
☐ Fasti Etonenses	1903	SPY	20.00
☐ The Dean of Westminister	1888	SPY	20.00
☐ Merton College	1884	SPY	20.00
☐ O.B.	1888	HAY	N/A
☐ Winchester	1903	SPY	24.00
☐ The Master of Trinity	1889	HAY	24.00
☐ Trinity	1903	SPY	20.00
☐ Balliol	1895	SPY	20.00
☐ Walter D	1902	SPY	20.00
☐ Goody	1876	SPY	20.00
☐ Latin Literature	1894	SPY	24.00

CAPTION	YEAR	ARTIST	PRICE
☐ New Harrow	1912	STRICKLAND	24.00
☐ Corpus	1899	FTD	24.00
☐ Badger	1892	SPY	24.00
☐ Merchant Tailors	1874	APE	20.00
☐ The Head	1901	SPY	20.00
☐ Jacky	1892	SPY	20.00
☐ Ajax M.P.	1904	SPY	20.00
☐ Jimmy	1887	SPY	24.00
☐ A Sturdy Educationist	1911	WHO	N/A
☐ The Flea	1901	SPY	N/A
☐ ChristChurch	1875	APE	24.00
☐ Young Oxford	1880	SPY	20.00
☐ Haileybury	1901	SPY	20.00
☐ The School Master	1907	SPY	N/A
☐ Technical Education	1891	S. TEI	N/A
☐ Mike	1896	SPY	20.00
☐ Red Morgan	1889	HAY	24.00
☐ Black Morgan	1889	HAY	24.00
☐ The Science of Language	1875	APE	20.00
☐ The House	1894	SPY	24.00
☐ Oxford Modern History	1895	SPY	20.00
☐ A Professor	1884	SPY	N/A
☐ Westminister	1898	SPY	24.00
☐ The Shirt	1894	SPY	N/A
☐ Spooner	1898	SPY	20.00
☐ St. Paul's School	1901	SPY	24.00
☐ The Head	1885	SPY	24.00
☐ The Vice-Provost	1901	SPY	20.00
☐ Magdalen College, Oxford	1893	SPY	24.00
☐ Harrow	1899	GAF	24.00

TENNIS

CAPTION	YEAR	ARTIST	PRICE
☐ Tennis	1882	T	N/A
☐ Michael Michailovich	1894	WAG	N/A
☐ Thrice Champion	1904	SPY	N/A
☐ In His Lighter Moments	1912	WH	N/A
☐ Baby	1913	COCK	N/A

THEATRE

CAPTION	YEAR	ARTIST	PRICE
☐ Aubrey Tanqueray	1894	SPY	24.00
☐ The St. James's	1909	MAX	20.00
☐ Kismet	1911	RITCHIE	24.00
☐ Tony	1908	SPY	20.00
☐ B	1891	SPY	20.00
☐ The Modern Wiertz	1891	SPY	24.00
☐ Madame Sarah Bernhardt	1912	K	N/A
☐ Sarah Bernhardt	1879	T	N/A
☐ A Fellow Infinite	1905	SPY	24.00
☐ The Sensation Drama	1882	SPY	N/A
☐ A.B.	1896	SPY	20.00
☐ The Palace	1910	HCO	24.00
☐ Mr. Arthur Cecil	1889	SPY	20.00
☐ The Guv'nor	1910	HESTER	24.00
☐ Coquelin Aine	1893	GUTH	20.00
☐ Coquelin Aine	1898	GUTH	24.00
☐ Gerald	1907	SPY	24.00
☐ Gov'nor	1911	NIBS	24.00
☐ The Man on the Film	1913	AST	24.00
☐ Forbie	1895	SPY	20.00

CAPTION	YEAR	ARTIST	PRICE
☐ Mr. Forbes-Robertson	1913	RITCHIE	N/A
☐ Magic	1913	AST	24.00
☐ Amateur Theatricals	1886	SPY	N/A
☐ Sherlock Holmes	1907	SPY	N/A
☐ Goochie	1882	SPY	20.00
☐ The Pinafore	1888	SPY	20.00
☐ The Duffer	1905	SPY	20.00
☐ Mr. John Hare	1890	SPY	20.00
☐ Drury Lane	1889	SPY	24.00
☐ From Eton to the Stage	1892	SPY	24.00
☐ The Bells	1874	APE	24.00
☐ Mr. Laurence Irving	1912	WH	24.00
☐ Author-Manager	1892	SPY	24.00
☐ Hereditary Actor	1907	SPY	20.00
☐ Mr. W. H. Kendal	1893	SPY	20.00
☐ The Flying Stage	1912	RITCHIE	24.00
☐ Our Only Comedian	1875	APE	N/A
☐ Squirrel	1897	SPY	20.00
☐ Amateur Theatricals	1876	SPY	N/A
☐ Charley's Aunt	1893	SPY	N/A
☐ Examiner of Plays	1890	PAL	20.00
☐ Spencer	1878	SPY	N/A
☐ Cinematographs	1911	APE JR.	24.00
☐ Cyrano	1901	GUTH	24.00
☐ Othello	1875	APE	N/A
☐ Ficelle Dramatique	1890	T	24.00
☐ The Poet's Son	1879	APE	N/A
☐ The Coliseum	1911	APE JR.	20.00
☐ The Coliseum	1913	OWL	24.00
☐ The King's Jester	1912	WH	24.00
☐ Dorian Gray	1913	OWL	24.00
☐ Edward O'Connor Terry	1905	SPY	N/A
☐ A Spelling Bee	1876	SPY	20.00
☐ His Majesty's	1911	NIBS	24.00
☐ Mr. Herbert Beerbohm Tree	1890	SPY	24.00
☐ Leo	1905	SPY	20.00
☐ Romantic Drama	1904	IMP	24.00
☐ Le Doyen	1914	AST	24.00
☐ Modern Pantomime	1913	HESTER	N/A
☐ Through Every Passion	1910	ELF	24.00

TRACK

CAPTION	YEAR	ARTIST	PRICE
☐ The Champion	1884	APE	30.00
☐ Oxford Athletics	1894	SPY	N/A
☐ A.A.A.	1895	WAG	30.00
☐ Fitz	1896	SPY	30.00
☐ O.U.A.C.	1897	SPY	30.00

TRADE UNION OFFICIALS

CAPTION	YEAR	ARTIST	PRICE
☐ Social Revolution	1879	T	18.00
☐ The Working Man-Member	1884	SPY	18.00
☐ The Agricultural Labourer	1886	SPY	N/A
☐ Battersea	1892	SPY	18.00
☐ The Laborer is Worthy	1905	SPY	18.00
☐ Labour Men	1908	SPY	18.00

TURF DEVOTEES

CAPTION	YEAR	ARTIST	PRICE
☐ The Marquis	1888	LIB	20.00
☐ Bunny	1876	SPY	20.00
☐ Beer	1889	LIB	20.00
☐ The Head of the Pagets	1880	APE	20.00
☐ Fife	1882	SPY	20.00
☐ The Mate	1877	SPY	20.00
☐ Jed	1899	GAF	20.00
☐ Billy	1905	SPY	20.00
☐ Horses	1880	SPY	20.00
☐ Badminton	1893	SPY	20.00
☐ The Duke of Sport	1876	SPY	20.00
☐ The Jubilee Plunger	1887	SPY	20.00
☐ Starting	1890	LIB	20.00
☐ Master of the Horse	1874	APE	20.00
☐ Fred	1885	SPY	20.00
☐ Horsy	1884	SPY	20.00
☐ Shandy	1888	SPY	N/A
☐ A Turf Reformer	1874	APE	20.00
☐ Racing	1885	SPY	20.00
☐ Earlier	1881	APE	20.00
☐ Good Looks	1876	SPY	20.00
☐ Horses	1888	SPY	20.00
☐ Master of Her Majesty's	1872	Unsigned	20.00
☐ Covey	1881	APE	20.00
☐ Fairie	1910	SPY	20.00
☐ Topps	1912	WH	20.00
☐ Billy	1886	LIB	20.00
☐ The Gaffer	1908	SPY	20.00
☐ Vixcount Dangan	1889	SPY	20.00
☐ Matt	1886	LIB	20.00
☐ Old Warren	1894	SPY	20.00
☐ John	1885	SPY	20.00
☐ The Turf	1877	SPY	20.00
☐ Charlie	1878	SPY	20.00
☐ Coals	1887	SPY	20.00
☐ Official Handicapper	1889	LIB	20.00
☐ Bridgewater House	1887	APE	20.00
☐ Never Bets	1877	SPY	20.00
☐ The Lad	1883	SPY	20.00
☐ Racing & Politics	1881	SPY	20.00
☐ Cart Horses	1888	SPY	20.00
☐ Condition	1908	SPY	20.00
☐ Young Hopeful	1882	SPY	20.00
☐ On the Health	1896	SPY	60.00
☐ The French Tattersall	1913	OWL	N/A
☐ Melton	1886	SPY	20.00
☐ Havvy	1901	SPY	20.00
☐ The Purist of the Turf	1870	ATN	20.00
☐ Lord Hothfield	1889	SPY	20.00
☐ The New Steward	1890	SPY	20.00
☐ G.P.	1908	SPY	20.00
☐ Charley	1886	SPY	20.00
☐ Davie	1908	SPY	20.00
☐ Sir Robert Jardine	1890	SPY	20.00
☐ Willie	1909	ELF	20.00
☐ Freddy	1878	SPY	20.00
☐ Stanley House	1904	SPY	20.00
☐ George Fox	1878	SPY	20.00
☐ The Horse Has No Better Friend	1912	WH	20.00
☐ Horses	1886	SPY	20.00
☐ Billy	1892	SPY	20.00
☐ Mr. H. L. B. McCalmont	1889	SPY	20.00

CAPTION	YEAR	ARTIST	PRICE
☐ St. Bernards	1894	SPY	20.00
☐ Jem	1887	SPY	20.00
☐ The Universal Benefactor	1889	LIB	20.00
☐ Sir James Milner	1890	LIB	20.00
☐ Mr. Marcus Henry Miller	1890	LIB	20.00
☐ Scotland & Racing	1882	SPY	20.00
☐ Options	1908	ELF	20.00
☐ Kilkenny	1878	SPY	20.00
☐ Dandy	1888	SPY	20.00
☐ G.P.	1875	APE	20.00
☐ The Young Duke	1882	SPY	20.00
☐ Horse Race Management	1884	SPY	20.00
☐ Kemtoll	1903	CLOISTER	20.00
☐ Horseflesh	1876	SPY	20.00
☐ The Portly One	1907	SPY	20.00
☐ Rock	1883	SPY	20.00
☐ A Pupil	1888	LIB	20.00
☐ Newmarket	1904	SPY	20.00
☐ Horses	1876	SPY	20.00
☐ As Straight As A Reed	1870	ATN	20.00
☐ Sammy	1892	SPY	20.00
☐ The Turf	1880	SPY	20.00
☐ The Earl of Sefton	1894	LIB	20.00
☐ Charlie	1909	SPY	20.00
☐ Ralph	1898	STUFF	20.00
☐ Podge	1887	SPY	20.00
☐ He Invented The Conservative	1880	APE	20.00
☐ Charlie	1879	APE	20.00
☐ Suffield	1907	AO	20.00
☐ Dover	1887	LIB	20.00
☐ The Hatter	1904	SPY	20.00
☐ Tattersall's	1886	LIB	20.00
☐ Chippenham Park	1894	SPY	20.00
☐ J.O.S.	1907	SPY	20.00
☐ Versatility	1910	WHO	20.00
☐ He Patronises Literature	1906	SPY	20.00
☐ John	1909	SPY	20.00
☐ Peter	1905	SPY	20.00
☐ A Lucky Owner	1906	SPY	20.00
☐ The Badminton	1897	SPY	20.00
☐ The Match-Book	1901	SPY	20.00
☐ Mr. James Weatherby	1890	LIB	20.00
☐ The Affable Earl	1883	SPY	20.00
☐ Sandown Park	1891	SPY	20.00
☐ High Prices	1884	SPY	20.00
☐ Youth	1880	SPY	20.00
☐ Brokelsby	1896	SPY	20.00
☐ Arthur	1900	UNK	20.00

WAGERERS

CAPTION	YEAR	ARTIST	PRICE
☐ The Leviathan	1877	SPY	14.00
☐ Gang Forward	1879	SPY	14.00
☐ No Limit	1914	SPY	N/A

YACHTING DEVOTEES

CAPTION	YEAR	ARTIST	PRICE
☐ An Unexpected Earl	1873	Unsigned	20.00
☐ The Commodore	1873	Unsigned	20.00
☐ The Ocean Race	1874	APE	20.00
☐ Yachting	1874	APE	20.00

CAPTION	YEAR	ARTIST	PRICE
☐ Round the World	1877	APE	N/A
☐ Jour De Ma Vie	1879	SPY	20.00
☐ Ralph	1883	T	20.00
☐ The Regalia	1891	SPY	20.00
☐ At Cowes	1894	SPY	60.00
☐ Cambridge Registry	1894	SPY	N/A
☐ Saide, R.Y.S.	1894	SPY	N/A
☐ Vigilant	1894	SPY	20.00
☐ Derek	1895	SPY	N/A
☐ Ailsa	1896	MILLER	20.00
☐ Giralda	1896	SPY	20.00
☐ Knight of Kerry	1901	SPY	20.00
☐ Shamrock	1901	SPY	20.00
☐ Vice-Commodore	1906	SPY	20.00
☐ Tiggy	1907	SPY	20.00
☐ Fyvie	1909	SPY	20.00
☐ Tony	1910	ELF	20.00
☐ Istria	1913	OWL	20.00

CONTEMPORARY PRINTS

ROBERT ABBETT

THEMES: Sporting and wildlife art

MEDIUM: Oils, exclusively

STYLE: For this artist, the drawing stage of the work is vital. Abbett feels it is a learning process through which he comes to know about the subject

AWARDS: Salmagundi Club Medal (1973)

MEMBERSHIPS: American Artists Group, Society of Animal Artists

GALLERY/DISTRIBUTOR: Wild Wings, Inc.

COMMENTS: Selected to design several conservation stamps, including the first annual Trout Unlimited Stamp Print (1981), and the Wild Turkey, Ruffed Grouse Society, and American Sporting Dog Heritage Stamp Prints (1982)

WINNING POINT *by Robert Abbett*

	ISSUE PRICE	CURRENT PRICE
☐ **LUKE,** rel. 1973. ed. 500, s/n, 19″ x 24″, pub SEL	50.00	115.00
Remarqued print, ed. 50	125.00	300.00
☐ **BOBWHITES AND POINTER,** rel. 1974. ed. 1,000, s/n, 27″ x 18¾″, pub TGW	65.00	300.00
☐ **GRAY WATER - BLACK LAB,** rel. 1974. ed. 500, s/n, 17″ x 26″, pub SEL	60.00	200.00
☐ **WINDFALL,** rel. 1974. ed, 550, s/n, 18¼″ x 26¼″, pub SEL	55.00	400.00
☐ **FIRST SEASON,** rel. 1975. ed. 1,000, s/n, 30″ x 22½″, pub TGW	65.00	150.00
☐ **RINGNECK AND SETTER,** rel. 1975. ed. 1,000, s/n, 30″ x 22″, pub TGW	65.00	150.00
☐ **GERMAN SHORTHAIRED POINTER AND RUFFED GROUSE,** rel. 1976. ed. 1,000, s/n, 28¾″ x 22½″, pub TGW	65.00	Sold Out
☐ **NEW FIELDS,** rel. 1976. ed, 1,000, s/n, 29″ x 20½″, pub TGW	65.00	85.00
☐ **PARTNERS,** rel. 1976. ed. 500, s/n, 15½″ x 28⅝″, pub SEL	70.00	140.00
☐ **RINGNECK PHEASANT,** rel. 1976. ed. 1,000, s/n, 30″ x 17¼″, pub TGW	65.00	Sold Out
☐ **SETTER & WOODCOCK,** rel. 1976. ed. 500, s/n, 23″ x 18″, pub SEL	60.00	140.00
☐ **YANKEE DRUMMER,** rel. 1976. ed. 500, s/n, 17¼″ x 23″, pub SEL	70.00	85.00
☐ **CLOSE HONOR,** rel. 1977. ed. 1,000, s/n, 30″ x 21″, pub TGW	75.00	170.00
☐ **IRISH SETTER FAMILY,** rel. 1977. ed. 1,000, s/n, 34″ x 24″, pub TGW	75.00	150.00
☐ **SETTER & GROUSE,** rel. 1977. ed. 500, s/n, 18⅛″ x 27¼″, pub SEL	95.00	160.00
☐ **SPLIT RAIL BOBS,** rel. 1977. ed. 500, s/n, 18⅛″ x 27¼″, pub SEL	95.00	300.00
☐ **SPRINGTIME,** rel. 1977. ed. 1,000, s/n, 30″ x 21″, pub TGW	65.00	85.00
☐ **ENGLISH SETTER FAMILY,** rel. 1978. ed. 750, s/n, 17½″ x 27¼″, pub SEL	125.00	250.00
☐ **FISHING ON THE BITTERROOT,** rel. 1978. ed. 500, s/n, 18¼″ x 24″, pub SEL	125.00	325.00
☐ **HOLDING TIGHT,** rel. 1978. ed. 500, s/n, 18⅛″ x 27¼″, pub SEL	125.00	—
☐ **HUNTING THE EDGES,** rel. 1978. ed. 500, s/n, 18″ x 27″, pub SEL	125.00	—
☐ **LATE DAY WOODCOCKS,** rel. 1978. ed. 500, s/n, 18″ x 27″, pub SEL	125.00	—
☐ **HASTY EXIT,** rel. 1979. ed. 750, s/n, 18⅛″ x 27¼″, pub SEL	125.00	250.00
☐ **RIVERVIEW QUAIL,** rel. 1979. ed. 750, s/n, 18⅛″ x 27¼″, pub SEL	150.00	—
☐ **TRAINING AT HAWKEYE,** rel. 1979. ed. 750, s/n, 18⅛″ x 27¼″, pub SEL	125.00	—
☐ **WILD COVEY,** rel. 1979. ed. 750, s/n, 18⅛″ x 27¼″, pub SEL	125.00	—
☐ **BLACK LAB HEAD,** rel. 1980. ed. 500, s/n, 12″ x 15″, pub SEL	70.00	95.00
☐ **THE BUCKING STRAP,** rel. 1980. ed. 750, s/n, 19″ x 24″, pub SEL	125.00	—
☐ **ENGLISH SETTER HEAD,** rel. 1980. ed. 500, s/n, 12″ x 15″, pub SEL	70.00	—
☐ **GERMAN SHORTHAIR HEAD,** rel. 1980. ed. 500, s/n, 12″ x 15″, pub SEL	70.00	—
☐ **GOLDEN RETRIEVER HEAD,** rel. 1980. ed. 500, s/n, 12″ x 15″, pub SEL	70.00	—
☐ **LATE SUMMER—BEAVERKILL,** rel. 1980. ed. 750, s/n, 14″ x 20¾″, pub SEL	80.00	250.00
☐ **SECOND SEASON,** rel. 1980. ed. 750, s/n, 18⅛″ x 27¼″, pub SEL	150.00	325.00
☐ **SPRINGER SPANIEL HEAD,** rel. 1980. ed. 500, s/n, 12″ x 15″, pub SEL	70.00	—
☐ **YELLOW LAB HEAD,** rel. 1980. ed. 500, s/n, 12″ x 15″, pub SEL	75.00	—
☐ **BLACK LAB FAMILY,** rel. 1981. ed. 850, s/n, 18⅛″ x 27¼″, pub SEL	150.00	—
☐ **GERMAN SHEPHERD HEAD,** rel. 1981. ed. 500, s/n, 12″ x 15″, pub SEL	75.00	—
☐ **POINTER HEAD,** rel. 1981. ed. 500, s/n, 12″ x 15″, pub SEL	75.00	—
☐ **READY TO GO—GOLDEN RETRIEVER,** rel. 1981. ed. 750, s/n, 18½″ x 27¼″, pub SEL	150.00	—
☐ **BO AND DUKE,** rel. 1982. ed. 850, s/n, size not available, pub WWI	125.00	—
☐ **BRITTANY HEAD,** rel. 1982. ed. 750, s/n, size N/A, pub WWI	75.00	—
☐ **BROOMWEED COVEY RISE,** rel. 1982. ed. 850, s/n, size N/A, pub WWI	150.00	—
☐ **BULLDOGGIN;** rel. 1982. ed. 750, s/n litho, 27½″ x 17¾″, pub WWI	125.00	—
☐ **CROSSING AT SPLIT ROCK,** rel. 1982. ed. 750, s/n, size not available, pub WWI ...	125.00	—
☐ **WAITING AT HAWKEYE,** rel. 1982. ed. 750, s/n, size N/A, pub WWI	125.00	—
☐ **FENCEROW PHEASANTS,** rel. 1983. ed. 850, s/n, 16½″ x 25″, pub WWI	125.00	—
☐ **FIRST GO-ROUND . . . CUTTING HORSE,** rel. 1983. ed. 600, s/n, 12″ x 15″, pub WWI	125.00	—
☐ **GORDON SETTER HEAD,** rel. 1983. ed. 750, s/n, 12″ x 15″, pub WWI	75.00	—
☐ **HILLSIDE WOODCOCK,** rel. 1983. ed. 850, s/n, 16½″ x 25″, pub WWI	125.00	—
☐ **JANUARY THAW,** rel. 1983. ed. 850, s/n, 15″ x 20″, pub WWI	95.00	—
☐ **HUNTING AT HAWKEYE,** rel. 1983. ed. 850, s/n litho, 16½″ x 25″, pub WWI	125.00	—
☐ **LABRADOR RETRIEVER-BO,** rel. 1983. ed. 750, 12″ x 15″, pub WWI	75.00	—
☐ **WINNING POINT,** rel. 1983. ed. 950, s/n, 12″ x 15″, pub WWI	75.00	—
☐ **WOOD DUCKS,** rel. 1983. ed. 850, s/n, 15″ x 20″, pub WWI	95.00	—
☐ **AUTUMN POOLS,** rel. 1984. ed. 600, s/n, 11″ x 18″, pub WWI	60.00	—
☐ **AUTUMN POOLS,** rel. 1984. ed. unlimited, s/o, 11″ x 18″, pub WWI	45.00	—
☐ **OLD ROAD COVER,** rel. 1984. ed. 900, s/n litho, 16½″ x 25″, pub WWI	125.00	—
☐ **THIRD SEASON,** rel. 1984. ed. 850, s/n, 16½″ x 25″, pub WWI	125.00	—
☐ **BRITTANY HEAD II,** rel. 1985. ed. 750, s/n litho, 12″ x 15″, pub WWI	75.00	—
☐ **DUKE AND MIKE,** rel. 1985. ed. 650, s/n litho, 16½″ x 26″, pub WWI	125.00	←

HARRY ADAMSON

THEMES: Birds in flight
MEDIUM: Oils
BACKGROUND: Book illustrator at the Museum of Vertebrate Zoology
AWARDS: Ducks Unlimited Artist of the Year (1979)
GALLERY/DISTRIBUTOR: Wild Wings, Inc.

	ISSUE PRICE	CURRENT PRICE
☐ WINGING IN - PINTAILS, rel. 1971. ed. 450, s/n, 17" x 25", pub WWI	50.00	675.00
☐ WILD BOUNTY - BLACK DUCKS, rel. 1972. ed. 450, s/n, 17" x 25", pub WWI	50.00	800.00
ed. 75 remarque	125.00	900.00
☐ AUTUMNS ECHELON - CANADA GEESE, rel. 1973. ed. 480, s/n, 16" x 24", pub WWI	55.00	60.00
ed. 75 remarque	120.00	—
☐ OXBOW SORCERY - MALLARDS, rel. 1973. ed. 480, s/n, 16" x 24", pub WWI	55.00	675.00
ed. 75 remarque	125.00	775.00
☐ WHISPERING WINGS - PINTAILS, rel. 1973. ed. 600, s/n, 12" x 16" pub WWI	40.00	700.00
ed. 70 remarque	110.00	800.00
☐ ARCTIC CITADEL - DALL SHEEP, rel. 1974. ed. 580, s/n, 17½" x 25", pub WWI	55.00	700.00
☐ GREENHEAD EXODUS - MALLARDS, rel. 1974. ed. 580, s/n, 15½" x 25", pub WWI	60.00	250.00
ed. 50 remarque	145.00	350.00
☐ WINTER QUARTERS - WIGEON, rel. 1974. ed. 580, s/n, 16" x 24", pub WWI	55.00	75.00
ed. 75 remarque	125.00	175.00
☐ THE CONCLAVE - DESERT BIGHORNS, rel. 1975. ed. 580, s/n, 16½" x 24", pub WWI	70.00	85.00
☐ THE LOAFING BAR - MALLARDS, rel. 1975. ed. 580, s/n, 16½" x 25" pub WWI	70.00	350.00
ed. 50 remarque	150.00	450.00
☐ PINTAILS & THE SUTTER BUTTES, rel. 1975. ed. 580, s/n, 16" x 25", pub WWI	70.00	475.00
ed. 50 remarque	150.00	575.00
☐ EVENING FLOTILLA - CANVASBACKS, rel. 1976. ed. 600, s/n, 10½" x 16", pub WWI	52.50	60.00
ed. 50 remarque	150.00	160.00
☐ FLURRY OF BLACKS, rel. 1976. ed. 580, s/n, 16½" x 25", pub WWI	70.00	85.00
ed. 50 remarque	150.00	185.00
☐ WINDY RIDGE - QUAIL, rel. 1976. ed. 580, s/n, 16½" x 25", pub WWI	70.00	—
☐ JUGGLING ACT - GREEN WINGED TEAL, rel. 1977. ed. 580, s/n, 20" x 17", pub WWI	75.00	85.00
ed. 50 remarque	160.00	185.00
☐ PINTAILS TAKING FLIGHT, rel. 1977. ed. 580, s/n, 17¾" x 22½", pub WWI	75.00	170.00
ed. 50 remarque	160.00	370.00
☐ SWAMP MIST - MALLARDS, rel. 1977. ed. 580, s/n, 17¾" x 22½", pub WWI	75.00	300.00
ed. remarque	160.00	400.00
☐ WINGED ELEGANCE—PINTAILS, rel. 1977. ed. 580, s/n, 16½" x 25", pub WWI	75.00	85.00
ed. remarque	160.00	185.00
☐ AFTER THE STORM - PINTAILS, rel. 1978. ed. 850, s/n, 17½" x 23", pub WWI	85.00	—
ed. remarque	185.00	—
☐ EVENING SOLITUDE - BIG HORNS, rel. 1978. ed. 850, s/n, 25" x 17⅛", pub WWI	85.00	—
☐ THE RENDEZVOUS - MALLARDS, rel. 1979. ed. 850, s/n, 24¾" x 17⅛", pub WWI	85.00	—
ed. remarque	185.00	—
☐ AUTUMN TABLEAU - MALLARDS, rel. 1980. ed. 850, s/n, 16½" x 25", pub WWI	100.00	—
ed. remarque	200.00	—
☐ AVIAN ELITE - PINTAILS, rel. 1980. ed. 850, s/n, 25" x 16½", pub WWI	100.00	—
ed. remarque	200.00	—
☐ BROOMSEDGE COVER - BOBWHITE, rel. 1980. ed. 850, s/n, 16½" x 25", pub WWI	100.00	—
ed. remarque	200.00	—
☐ CORNER POCKET - PINTAIL AND CINNAMON TEAL, rel. 1980. ed. 850, s/n, 25" x 16½", pub WWI	100.00	—
ed. remarque	200.00	—

	ISSUE PRICE	CURRENT PRICE
☐ EMPTY BLIND AT SUTTER BUTTES, rel. 1980. ed. 650, s/n, 22″ x 17⅛″, pub WWI	100.00	—
ed. remarque	200.00	—
☐ GRYFALCON, rel. 1980. ed. 650, s/n, 22″ x 17⅝″ pub WWI	100.00	—
☐ JERSEY COAST - BLACK DUCKS, rel. 1980. ed. 850, s/n, 25″ x 16″, pub WWI	100.00	—
ed. 40 remarque	200.00	—
☐ WINTER IDYLL - MALLARDS, rel. 1980. ed. 850, s/n, 25″ x 16½″, pub WWI	100.00	—
ed. 40 remarque	200.00	—
☐ CALIFORNIA PINTAILS, rel. 1981, ed. 950, s/n, size N/A, pub WWI	125.00	—
☐ JOURNEY'S END - CANADA GEESE, rel. 1981. ed. 850, s/n, size N/A, pub WWI ...	125.00	—
☐ OCTOBER INTERLUDE - MALLARDS, rel. 1981. ed. 850, s/n, size N/A, pub WWI ..	125.00	—
☐ OVER THE MARSH - SNOW GEESE, rel. 1981. ed. 950, s/n, size N/A, pub WWI ...	125.00	—
☐ STARTLED - MALLARDS, rel. 1981. ed. 950, s/n, size N/A, pub WWI	125.00	—
☐ PULLING OUT - MALLARDS, rel. 1982. ed. 850, s/n, size N/A, pub WWI	100.00	—
☐ MORNING AT GHOST LAKE - MALLARDS, rel. 1982. ed. 850, s/n, 16½″ x 25½″, pub WWI..	125.00	—
☐ NOVEMBER FANTASY - WIGEON, rel. 1982. ed. 850. s/n, 16½″ x 25″, pub WWI ...	125.00	—
☐ CANADIAN GRANDEUR -STONE SHEEP, rel. 1983. ed. 950, s/n, 16½″ x 25″, pub WWI..	125.00	—
☐ HIGH BASTION - DALL SHEEP, rel. 1983. ed. 950. s/n, 18″ x 23″, pub WWI	125.00	—

MARGI ADEY

THEMES: Wildlife art

GALLERY/DISTRIBUTOR: Arts Limited Inc.

	ISSUE PRICE	CURRENT PRICE
☐ GREAT HORNED OWL, ed. 1,000, s/n, 16″ x 20″, pub ALI	50.00	—
☐ OCELOT, ed. 1,000, s/n, 16″ x 20″, pub ALI	50.00	—

J. J. ALEXANDER

THEMES: Varied

EDUCATION: Famous Artists School

GALLERY/DISTRIBUTION: Sawyier Collection, Inc., a subsidiary of Paul Sawyier Galleries, Inc.

	ISSUE PRICE	CURRENT PRICE
☐ MILLINERY SHOP, ed. 1000, s/n, 13½″ x 10″, pub SCI*	30.00	—
☐ NEIGHBORS, ed. 1000, s/n, 14⅞″ x 21⅛″, pub SCI*	30.00	—
☐ RALEIGH TAVERN, ed. 1000, s/n, 13⅛″ x 22½″, pub SCI*	45.00	—

*Represents the Sawyier Collection, Inc., and was formed as a subsidiary of Paul Sawyier Galleries, Inc.

NEIGHBORS by J. J. Alexander

AXEL AMUCHASTEGUI

THEMES: Wildlife art

MEDIUM: Watercolor

GALLERY/DISTRIBUTOR: Mill Pond Press, Inc.

COMMENTS: Author and Illustrator of a three-volume work titled *Birds of the World*

	ISSUE PRICE	CURRENT PRICE
☐ **JAGUAR RESTING,** rel. 1982. ed. 950, s/n, 31¾" x 24½", pub MPPI	245.00	—
☐ **NESTING - CANADA GOOSE,** rel. 1982. ed. 950, s/n, 31⅝" x 24", pub MPPI	265.00	—
☐ **CARDINAL,** rel. 1984. ed. 950, s/n, 15½" x 12", pub MPPI	60.00	—

NESTING - CANADA GOOSE *by Axel Amuchastegui*

BARNEY ANDERSON

THEMES: Wildlife art

MEDIUM: Pen and ink

STYLE: Anderson's technique is accomplished by making countless cross-hatchings with a needlepoint pen on fabric-like paper

GALLERY/DISTRIBUTOR: Wild Wings, Inc.

	ISSUE PRICE	CURRENT PRICE
☐ **BLUEBILLS,** rel. 1981. ed. 580, s/n, size N/A, pub WWI	40.00	—
☐ **MALLARDS,** rel. 1981. ed. 580, s/n, size N/A, pub WWI	40.00	—

IVAN ANDERSON

THEMES: People

STYLE: French Impressionist Method

AWARDS: Anderson is a winner of forty-three major design and art awards. Listed in Marquis *Who's Who in America* and *Who's Who in the World*

GALLERY/DISTRIBUTOR: Ivan Anderson

COMMENTS: Collectors and art critics compare Anderson's style to Renoir and Sorolla

	ISSUE PRICE	CURRENT PRICE
☐ **SECRETS,** rel. 1975. ed. 200, s/n, serigraph, 24″ x 20″, pub IA	60.00	1800.00
☐ **MOTHER AND CHILD,** rel. 1975. ed. 200, s/n, serigraph, 30″ x 23″, pub IA	60.00	295.00
☐ **BABY BROWN EYES,** rel. 1976. ed. 225, s/n, serigraph, 20″ x 24″, pub IA	60.00	295.00
☐ **BEACH BUDDIES,** rel. 1976. ed. 200, s/n, serigraph, 20″ x 24″, pub IA	60.00	325.00
☐ **BOY WITH STICK,** rel. 1976. ed. 200, s/n, serigraph, 30″ x 20″, pub IA	60.00	375.00
☐ **PINKIE,** rel. 1976. ed. 300, s/n, serigraph, 30″ x 24″, pub IA	60.00	150.00
☐ **BABY WITH BUTTERFLY,** rel. 1983. ed. 500, s/n, litho, 23″ x 18″, pub IA	50.00	75.00
☐ **BOY WITH YELLOW HAT,** rel. 1983. ed. 500, s/n, litho, 28″ x 22″, pub IA	50.00	75.00
☐ **DUCK WATCHERS,** rel. 1983. ed. 500, s/n, litho, 23″ x 25″, pub IA	75.00	125.00

SECRETS *by Ivan Anderson*

TONGUE RIVER COUNTRY *by Clyde Aspevig*

CLYDE ASPEVIG

THEMES: Landscape art

EDUCATION: Eastern Montana College

GALLERY/DISTRIBUTOR: Swan Graphics, Ltd.

	ISSUE PRICE	CURRENT PRICE
☐ **TONGUE RIVER COUNTRY,** rel. 1981. ed. N/A, s/n, 24″ x 16″, distr. SGL	75.00	—
☐ **PASSAGE,** rel. 1981. ed. N/A, s/n, 24″ x 16″, distr. SGL	65.00	—
☐ **THE VALLEY,** rel. 1981. ed. N/A, s/n, 25″ x 17″, distr. SGL	65.00	—
☐ **TONGUE RIVER COUNTRY,** rel. 1983. ed. 1,000, s/n, 26″ x 16″, distr. SGL	75.00	—

ALFONS BACH

THEMES: Varied

MEDIUM: Watercolor

BACKGROUND: Celebrated industrial designer who won medals, awards, citations, and had shows at the Metropolitan Museum in New York

MEMBERSHIPS: Past President of the Industrial Designers Society of America; *Who's Who in American Art*

GALLERY/DISTRIBUTOR: Alfons Bach

	ISSUE PRICE	CURRENT PRICE
☐ NEF DE LA CATHEDRALE DEMETZ, FRANCE, ed. 860, 18¾" x 22½"	200.00	—
☐ EGLISE SAINTE DEVOTE, MONTE CARLO, ed. 860, 18¾" x 22½"	200.00	—
☐ HARBOUR MENTON, FRANCE, ed. 860, 18¾" x 22½"	200.00	—
☐ AUGUST IN DEAUVILLE, FRANCE, ed. 860, 18¾" x 22½"	200.00	—
☐ IL DUOMO A MILAN, ITALY, ed. 860, 18¾" x 22½"	200.00	—
☐ LE PALAIS DE MONACO, MONTE CARLO, ed. 275, 18¾" x 22½"	200.00	—

These graphics were printed by Binocci, in Monte Carlo, Monaco.

	ISSUE PRICE	CURRENT PRICE
☐ NOTRE DAME, FRANCE, ed. 165, 27⅝" x 19¼"	250.00	—
☐ HARBOR OF CANNES, FRANCE, ed. 300, 27⅝" x 19¼"	250.00	—

These graphics were printed by Igis, in Milan, Italy.

FRISKY FILLY *by Wayne Baize*

WAYNE BAIZE

THEMES: Western art

BACKGROUND: Baize's artistic career began when he became a portrait painter in a Western goods store

GALLERY/DISTRIBUTOR: Fenton's Press

	ISSUE PRICE	CURRENT PRICE
☐ LAZY SUMMER DAYS, rel. 1974. ed. 2,500, s/o, 27″ x 15″, pub FHG	30.00	275.00
☐ LIMPIA CREEK CROSSING, rel. 1975. ed. 1,500, s/n, 28″ x 21½, pub FHG	40.00	1150.00
☐ WINTER STAGE, rel. 1976. ed. 1,000, s/n, 11½″ x 22″, pub FHG	30.00	275.00
☐ COWBOY CAMP, rel. 1977. ed. 500, s/n, 20″ x 28″, pub FHG	40.00	350.00
☐ HER GIFT, rel. 1977. ed. 500, s/n, 20″ x 28″, pub FHG	40.00	475.00
☐ HER PRIDE, rel. 1978. ed. 500, s/n, 28″ x 22″, pub FHG	50.00	550.00
☐ RANGE BABY, rel. 1978. ed. 500, s/n, 18″ x 24″, pub FHG	50.00	2500.00
☐ HER TENDER LOVING CARE, rel. 1979. ed. 750, s/n, 22″ x 28″, pub FHG	50.00	200.00
☐ THE GOAT KEEPER/WASHDAY, rel. 1979. ed. 750, s/n, 15″ x 18″, pub FHG	*40.00	—
*Sold as a pair.		
☐ THE HITCHHIKER, rel. 1979. ed. 750, s/n, 17″ x 30″, pub FHG	55.00	100.00
☐ THE NEW BORN, rel. 1979. ed. 750, s/n, 22″ x 28″, pub FHG	50.00	375.00
☐ THE WATERHOLE, rel. 1979. ed. 750, s/n, 26″ x 20″, pub FHG	55.00	100.00
☐ NATURE'S BLESSING, rel. 1981. ed. 1,000, s/n, 16½″ x 21½″, pub TAP	90.00	150.00
☐ SPRING, rel. 1981. ed. 1,000, s/n, 16¾″ x 21½″, pub TAP	60.00	350.00
☐ FIT TO BE HITCHED, rel. 1982. ed. 1,000, s/n, 16½″ x 21½″, pub TAP	90.00	—
☐ IN THE LEAD, rel. 1982. 1,000, s/n, 15¾″ x 25″, pub TAP	90.00	—
☐ WAITIN' UP, rel. 1982. ed. 1,000, s/n, 29″ x 14¾″, pub TAP	90.00	—
☐ A ROYAL BREED, rel. 1983. ed. 1,000, s/n, 16½″ x 21¼″, pub TAP	90.00	—
☐ FRISKY FILLY, rel. 1983. ed. 1,000, s/n, 12″ x 16″, pub TAP	80.00	—
☐ FROSTY MORN, rel. 1983. ed. 1,000, s/n, 12″ x 16″, pub TAP	80.00	—
☐ HIDING OUT, rel. 1983. ed. 1,000, s/n, 17″ x 22½″, pub TAP	90.00	—
☐ ON THE SHY SIDE, rel. 1984. ed. 500, s/n, size N/A, pub FP	125.00	200.00
☐ WHEN SUNSHINE PREVAILS OVER MIST, rel. 1984. ed. 500, s/n, size N/A, pub FP	125.00	250.00

RED FOX *by Don Balke*

DON BALKE

THEMES: Wildlife art

MEDIUM: Transparent and opaque watercolor

STYLE: Realism

MUSEUMS/COLLECTIONS: Many corporate and private collections

GALLERY/DISTRIBUTOR: Masterpiece Moulding and Fine Art Corp.

COMMENTS: The artist personally supervises every step of the printing process, and is present at the press for every proofing and the enire run. Each print is then inspected by him before it is signed and numbered

	ISSUE PRICE	CURRENT PRICE
BIRDS OF PREY SERIES		
☐ BARN OWL, rel. 1976. ed. 1,000, s/n, 20″ x 26″, distr. MMFC	40.00	—
☐ BALD EAGLE, rel. 1977. ed. 1,000, s/n, 27″ x 35½″, distr. MMFC	75.00	150.00
☐ OSPREY, rel. 1979. ed. 1,000, s/n, 23¼″ x 30¾″, distr. MMFC	55.00	Sold Out
☐ SNOWY OWL, rel. 1979. ed. 1,000, s/n, 22″ x 28″, distr. MMFC	55.00	Sold Out
FLEETWOOD SERIES		
☐ CANADA GOOSE, rel. 1979. ed. 1,000, s/n, 17½″ x 20½″, distr. MMFC	45.00	Sold Out
☐ THE INVESTIGATOR, rel. 1979. ed. 1,000, s/n, 19½″ x 20½″, distr. MMFC	45.00	Sold Out
HERITAGE SERIES		
☐ RUFFED GROUSE, rel. 1977. ed. 1,000, s/n, 20″ x 26″, distr. MMFC	45.00	—
☐ SUMMER BOBWHITES, rel. 1977. ed. 1,000, s/n, 23¾″ x 34½″, distr. MMFC	55.00	—
☐ WILD TURKEY, rel. 1977. ed. 1,000, s/n, 24″ x 34½″, distr. MMFC	60.00	120.00
☐ GRAY FOX, rel. 1978. ed. 1,000, s/n, 21¾″ x 33″, distr. MMFC	75.00	200.00
☐ TIMBER WOLVES, rel. 1978. ed. 1,000, s/n, 24″ x 32″, distr. MMFC	75.00	—
☐ COUGAR, rel. 1980. ed. 1,000, s/n, 24″ x 32″, distr. MMFC	75.00	—
☐ RED FOX FAMILY, rel. 1980. ed. 1,000, s/n, 27″ x 35½″, distr. MMFC	95.00	—
HOMESTEADING SERIES		
☐ AUTUMN DAY, rel. 1982. ed. 1,000, s/n, 18¾″ x 23″, distr. MMFC	75.00	—
☐ ESCAPE, rel. 1982. ed. 1,000, s/n, 14¾″ x 20″, distr. MMFC	75.00	—
☐ GOLD FINCHES, rel. 1982. ed. 1,000, s/n, 12″ x 15½″, distr. MMFC	65.00	—
☐ WILD TURKEY, rel. 1977. ed. 1,000, s/n, 24″ x 34½″, distr. MMFC	60.00	120.00
MASTERPIECE SERIES		
☐ BOBWHITE QUAIL, rel. 1976. ed. 1,000, s/n, 24″ x 32″, distr. MMFC	50.00	300.00
☐ RED FOX, rel. 1976. ed. 1,000, s/n, 24″ x 34½″, distr. MMFC	50.00	350.00
☐ WHITE-TAILED DEER, rel. 1976. ed. 1,000, s/n, 24″ x 32″, distr. MMFC	50.00	—
NATURE SERIES - (Black and White)		
☐ BARRED OWL, ed. 450, s/n, 11″ x 14″, distr. MMFC	6.00	60.00
☐ BOBWHITE QUAIL, ed. 450, s/n, 11″ x 14″, distr. MMFC	6.00	25.00
☐ CANADIAN LYNX, ed. 450, s/n, 11″ x 14″, distr. MMFC	6.00	15.00
☐ CARDINALS, ed. 450, s/n, 11″ x 14″, distr. MMFC	6.00	25.00
☐ GRAY SQUIRREL, ed. 450, s/n, 11″ x 14″, distr. MMFC	6.00	25.00
☐ MALLARDS, ed. 450, s/n, 11″ x 14″, distr. MMFC	6.00	60.00
☐ PHEASANT, ed. 450, s/n, 11″ x 14″, distr. MMFC	6.00	25.00
☐ RACCOONS, ed. 450, s/n, 11″ x 14″, distr. MMFC	6.00	60.00
☐ RED-TAILED HAWK, ed. 450, s/n, 11″ x 14″, distr. MMFC	6.00	25.00
☐ SMALL MOUTH BLACK BASS, ed. 450, s/n, 11″ x 14″, distr. MMFC	6.00	15.00
☐ WHITE-TAILED DEER, ed. 450, s/n, 11″ x 14″, distr. MMFC	6.00	25.00
NORTH AMERICAN SERIES		
☐ AMERICAN BADGER, rel. 1974. ed. 950, s/n, 22″ x 28″, distr. MMFC	35.00	—
☐ AMERICAN ROBIN, rel. 1974. ed. 950, s/n, 14″ x 18″, distr. MMFC	20.00	60.00
☐ BLACK-CAPPED CHICKADEE, rel. 1974. ed. 950, s/n, 14″ x 18″, distr. MMFC	20.00	—
☐ GRAY FOX, rel. 1974. ed. 950, s/n, 22″ x 28″, distr. MMFC	35.00	175.00
☐ RACCOON, rel. 1974. ed. 950, s/n, 18″ x 23″, distr. MMFC	25.00	115.00

	ISSUE PRICE	CURRENT PRICE
☐ RUFFED GROUSE, rel. 1974. ed. 950, s/n, 22″ x 28″, distr. MMFC	35.00	—
☐ BOBCAT KITTEN, rel. 1975. ed. 750, s/n, 10¾″ x 13⅝″, distr. MMFC	25.00	—
☐ BOBWHITES, rel. 1975. ed. 600, s/n, 20″ x 28″, distr. MMFC	45.00	200.00
☐ BROWN PELICAN, rel. 1975. ed. 600, s/n, 20″ x 28″, distr. MMFC	45.00	—
☐ CARDINALS, rel. 1975. ed. 950, s/n, 16⅝″ x 21″, distr. MMFC	35.00	225.00
☐ COUGAR CUB, rel. 1975. ed. 750, s/n, 10¾″ x 13⅝″, distr. MMFC	25.00	—
☐ GRAY SQUIRRELS, rel. 1975. ed. 950, s/n, 18″ x 23″, distr. MMFC	35.00	150.00
☐ HOMESTEADING, rel. 1975. ed. 750, s/n, 20″ x 28″, distr. MMFC	60.00	Sold Out
☐ MALLARDS, rel. 1975. ed. 950, s/n, 22″ x 28″, distr. MMFC	45.00	—
☐ RING-NECKED PHEASANT, rel. 1975. ed. 600, s/n, 24″ x 32″, distr. MMFC	45.00	210.00
☐ WHITE-TAILED FAWN, rel. 1975 (Plate 18). ed. 750, s/n, 15¾″ x 19¾″, distr. MMFC	30.00	—
☐ WHITE-TAILED FAWN, rel. 1975 (Plate 19). ed. 750, s/n, 15¾″ x 19¾″, distr. MMFC	30.00	—
NOTE: The two fawn prints could be sold as a pair	50.00	—
☐ WOOD DUCKS, rel. 1975. ed. 950, s/n, 22″ x 26″, distr. MMFC	45.00	145.00
☐ SHIPWRECK, rel. 1976. ed. 950, s/n, 20″ x 28″, distr. MMFC	50.00	125.00
SEA AND SHORE BIRD SERIES		
☐ SANDPIPERS, rel. 1978. ed. 1,000, s/n, 18″ x 23″, distr. MMFC	45.00	—
SONG BIRDS SERIES		
☐ RUBY THROATED HUMMINGBIRD, rel. 1980. ed. 1,000, s/n, 14″ x 19″, distr. MMFC	40.00	—
☐ RUFOUS HUMMINGBIRD, rel. 1980. ed. 1,000, s/n, 14″ x 19″, distr. MMFC	40.00	—
☐ CARDINALS IN SPRINGTIME, rel. 1982. ed. 1,000, s/n, 16″ x 19½″, distr. MMFC ...	65.00	—
VEIN MOUNTAIN SERIES		
☐ CARDINAL FAMILY, rel. 1978. ed. 1,000, s/n, 18″ x 23″, distr. MMFC	45.00	175.00
☐ CHIPMUNKS, rel. 1978. ed. 1,000, s/n, 17″ x 21″, dist. MMFC	40.00	—
☐ COTTONTAILS, rel. 1978. ed. 1,000, s/n, 18″ x 23″, dist. MMFC	45.00	—
☐ LITTLE BANDITS, rel. 1978. ed. 1,000, s/n, 18″ x 23″, dist. MMFC	45.00	175.00
☐ A PAIR OF QUAIL, rel. 1978. ed. 1,000, s/n, 17″ x 21″, dist. MMFC	40.00	—
☐ RED FOX PUP, rel. 1978. ed. 1,000, s/n, 17″ x 21″, dist. MMFC	40.00	175.00
☐ YOUNG SKUNKS, rel. 1978. ed. 1,000, s/n, 18″ x 23″, dist. MMFC	45.00	—
☐ BLUEBIRD FAMILY, rel. 1979. ed. 1,000, s/n, 18″ x 23″, dist. MMFC	45.00	140.00
☐ GRAY SQUIRREL FAMILY, rel. 1979. ed. 1,000, s/n, 18″ x 23″ dist. MMFC	45.00	175.00
☐ SCREECH OWL, rel. 1980. ed. 1,000, s/n, 17⅜″ x 23½″, distr. MMFC	55.00	—
☐ THE ENCOUNTER, rel. 1981. ed. 1,000, s/n, 22″ x 29″, distr. MMFC	110.00	—
☐ MORNING MIST, rel. 1983. ed. 1,000, s/n, 19¼″ x 26″, pub MMFC	60.00	—
☐ SUNSET ON THE LAKE, rel. 1983. ed. 1,000, s/n, 16″ x 19¾″, pub MMFC	55.00	—
☐ BUSYBODIES, rel. 1984. ed. 1,000, s/n, 16½″ x 17″, pub MMFC	55.00	—
☐ CURIOSITY, rel. 1984. ed. 1,000, s/n, 16½″ x 17″, pub MMFC	55.00	—
☐ GADWELL, rel. 1984. ed. 1,000, s/n, 14½″ x 17″, pub MMFC	45.00	—
☐ REDHEAD, rel. 1984. ed. 1,000, s/n, 14½″ x 17″, pub MMFC	45.00	—
☐ SCARLET TANAGER, rel. 1984. ed. 1,000, s/n, 12½″ x 14″, pub MMFC	35.00	—
☐ ORCHARD ORIOLE, rel. 1984. ed. 1,000, s/n, 12½″ x 14″, pub MMFC	35.00	—

JAMES BAMA

THEMES: Western art

EDUCATION: Art Student's League

BOOKS: *The Western Art of James Bama*, published in 1975

GALLERY/DISTRIBUTOR: Greenwich Workshop

COMMENTS: James Bama has done illustrations for *The Saturday Evening Post* and Bantam Books, painted portraits of the New York Giants and the Baseball Hall of Fame, and has made trips abroad to paint for the U.S. Air Force

SOUTHWEST INDIAN FATHER AND SON *by James Bama*

	ISSUE PRICE	CURRENT PRICE
☐ KEN HUNDER, WORKING COWBOY, rel. 1974. ed. 1,000, s/n, 21" x 24", pub GW ..	55.00	465.00
☐ SHOSHONE CHIEF, rel. 1974. ed. 1,000, s/n, 20" x 26", pub GW	65.00	545.00
☐ CHUCK WAGON IN THE SNOW, rel. 1975. ed. 1,000, s/n, 18½" x 16", pub GW	50.00	380.00
☐ SAGE GRINDER, rel. 1976. ed. 1,000, s/n, 20" x 24", pub GW	65.00	915.00
☐ A CROW INDIAN, rel. 1977. ed. 1,000, s/n, 22½" x 18", pub GW	65.00	240.00
☐ TIMBER JACK JOE, rel. 1977. ed. 1,000, s/n, 19" x 24", pub GW	65.00	485.00
☐ A MOUNTAIN UTE, rel. 1978. ed. 1,000, s/n, 19¼" x 24", pub GW	75.00	310.00
☐ CONTEMPORARY SIOUX INDIAN, rel. 1978. ed. 1,000, s/n, 32" x 22", pub GW	75.00	250.00
☐ MOUNTAIN MAN, rel. 1978. ed. 1,000, s/n, 19" x 24", pub GW	75.00	600.00
☐ ROOKIE BRONC RIDER, rel. 1978. ed. 1,000, s/n, 22" x 17½", pub GW	75.00	185.00
☐ HERITAGE, rel. 1979. ed. 1,500, s/n, 23½" x 23½", pub GW	75.00	225.00
☐ INDIAN AT CROW FAIR, rel. 1979. ed. 1,500, s/n, 17" x 22¼", pub GW	75.00	145.00
☐ LITTLE STAR, rel. 1979. ed. 1,500, s/n, 15" x 19", pub GW	80.00	535.00
☐ PRE-COLUMBIAN INDIAN WITH ATLATL, rel. 1979. ed. 1,500, s/n, 22" x 18", pub GW..	75.00	160.00
☐ KEN BLACKBIRD, AN ASSINIBOIN SIOUX, rel. 1980. ed. 1,500, s/n, 22" x 20½", pub GW..	95.00	160.00
☐ MOUNTAIN MAN 1820-1840 PERIOD, rel. 1980. ed. 1,500, s/n, 17½" x 24½", pub GW..	115.00	190.00
☐ MOUNTAIN MAN AND HIS FOX, rel. 1980. ed. 1,500, s/n, 21½" x 26", pub GW	90.00	435.00
☐ OLD SADDLE IN THE SNOW, rel. 1980. ed. 1,500, s/n, 21" x 15", pub GW	75.00	85.00
☐ OLD SOD HOUSE, rel. 1980. ed. 1,500, s/n, 23" x 13", pub GW	80.00	140.00

	ISSUE PRICE	CURRENT PRICE
☐ SHEEP SKULL IN DRIFT, rel. 1980. ed. 1,500, s/n, 20″ x 16″, pub GW	75.00	85.00
☐ YOUNG PLAINS INDIAN, rel. 1980. ed. 1,500, s/n, 25½″ x 26¼″, pub GW	125.00	420.00
☐ AT A MOUNTAIN MAN WEDDING, rel. 1981. ed. 1,500, s/n, 22″ x 22″, pub GW	145.00	200.00
☐ AT THE BURIAL OF GALLAGER AND BLIND BILL, rel. 1981. ed. 1,500, s/n, 26½″ x 21½″, pub GW	155.00	—
ed. 150, s/n, proceeds to Old Trail Town, Cody, Wyoming	135.00	175.00
☐ CROW INDIAN DANCER, rel. 1982. ed. 1,250, s/n, 22¾″ x 23½″, pub GW	150.00	—
☐ OLD ARAPAHO STORY-TELLER, rel. 1981. ed. 1,500, s/n, 22¼″ x 23¼″, pub GW .	135.00	—
☐ PORTRAIT OF A SIOUX, rel. 1981. ed. 1,500, s/n, 22½″ x 23″, pub GW	75.00	150.00
☐ WINTER TRAPPING, rel. 1981. ed. 1,500, s/n, 20″ x 24″, pub GW	215.00	—
☐ OLDEST LIVING CROW INDIAN, rel. 1982. ed. 1,500, s/n, 22″ x 26¼″, pub GW	150.00	—
☐ MOUNTAIN MAN WITH RIFLE, rel. 1982. ed. 1,250, s/n, 16″ x 25″, pub GW	135.00	165.00
☐ SIOUX INDIAN WITH EAGLE FEATHER, rel. 1982. ed. 1,500, s/n, 17¼″ x 21½″, pub GW..	135.00	175.00
☐ DON WALKER—BAREBACK RIDER, rel. 1983. ed. 1,250, s/n, 12½″ x 17″, pub GW	85.00	—
☐ THE DAVILLA BROTHERS—BRONC RIDERS, rel. 1983. ed. 1,250, s/n, 23″ x 19⅛″, pub GW..	145.00	—
☐ SOUTHWEST INDIAN FATHER AND SON, rel. 1983. ed. 1,250, s/n, 17½″ x 23½″, pub GW..	145.00	—

JOHN M. BARBER

THEMES: Marine art

EDUCATION: Virginia Commonwealth University

MEMBERSHIPS: Charter member of the American Society of Marine Artists, Chesapeake Foundation, Ducks Unlimited

GALLERY/DISTRIBUTOR: Commodore Art Publishing

COMMENTS: Mr. Barber has embarked upon a long-term project documenting, through his paintings, each of the remaining Chesapeake Bay Skipjacks

	ISSUE PRICE	CURRENT PRICE
☐ ATLANTIC SENTINEL, ed. 750, s/n, 18″ x 28″, dist. CAP	40.00	400.00
☐ AT THE NETS ed. 500, s/n, 15½″ x 11⅜″, dist. CAP	25.00	25.00
ed. 25, Artist Proofs	45.00	100.00
☐ BOAT SHED, ed. 750, s/n, 18″ x 28″, dist. CAP	40.00	250.00
☐ BUTLER'S BOAT YARD, ed. 500, s/n, 18″ x 28″, dist. CAP	40.00	250.00
☐ CAPT. WALTER'S WHARF, ed. 950, s/n, 18″ x 28″, dist. CAP	40.00	450.00
ed. 50, Artist Proofs, remarque	125.00	650.00
☐ CHESAPEAKE BAY SKIPJACK, ed. 750, s/n, 18″ x 28″, dist. CAP	40.00	500.00
☐ CHESAPEAKE OYSTER TONGERS, ed. 500, s/n, 15½″ x 11⅜″, dist. CAP	25.00	25.00
ed. 25, Artist Proofs	45.00	100.00
☐ DISTANT THUNDER, ed. 950, s/n, 24½″ x 13¾″, dist. CAP	75.00	75.00
ed. 50, Artist Proofs, remarque	225.00	450.00
☐ ELSWORTH, ed. 950, s/n, 18″ x 28″, dist. CAP	40.00	800.00
☐ GOOD DAYS CATCH, ed. 950, s/n, 17⅜″ x 26″, dist. CAP	55.00	110.00
ed. 50, Artist Proofs, remarque	175.00	350.00
☐ HAMPTON CREEK DERELICT, ed. 500, s/n, 18″ x 28″, dist. CAP	40.00	250.00
☐ MAGGIE LEE, ed. 950, s/n, 24½″ x 13¾″, dist. CAP	55.00	300.00
ed. 50, Artist Proofs, remarque	175.00	600.00
☐ MARTHA LEWIS, ed. 950, s/n, 18″ x 28″, dist. CAP	40.00	450.00
ed. 50, Artist Proofs, remarque	125.00	650.00
☐ MORNING AT BELL BUOY #12, ed. 500, s/n, 15½″ x 11⅜″, dist. CAP	25.00	25.00
ed. 25, Artist Proofs, remarque	45.00	100.00

	ISSUE PRICE	CURRENT PRICE
☐ **NELLIE CROCKETT OYSTER BOAT**, ed. 750, s/n, 18″ x 28″, dist. CAP	40.00	450.00
☐ **PARRAMORE ISLAND GUARDIAN**, ed. 250, s/n, 15″ x 25″, dist. CAP	250.00	500.00
☐ **SIGSBEE**, ed. 500, s/n, 15½″ x 11⅜″, dist. CAP	25.00	25.00
ed. 25, Artist Proofs, remarque	45.00	100.00
☐ **SIGSBEE**, ed. 950, s/n, 14⅛″ x 26″, dist. CAP	55.00	55.00
ed. 50, Artist Proofs, remarque	175.00	350.00
☐ **THE SKIPJACK 'LADY KATIE'**, ed. 950, s/n, 18″ x 28″, dist. CAP	40.00	400.00
ed. 50, Artist Proofs, remarque	125.00	600.00
☐ **SPRING PAINTING**, ed. 500, s/n, 18″ x 28″, dist. CAP	40.00	80.00
☐ **"WILD DUCK" ROUNDING HOOPER STRAIT LIGHTHOUSE**, ed. 500, s/n, 18″ x 28″, dist. CAP	40.00	1000.00
☐ **WILLIAM B. TENNISON**, ed. 950, s/n, 17⅜″ x 26″, dist. CAP	40.00	200.00
ed. 50, Artist Proofs, remarque	150.00	500.00
☐ **MORNING AT COVE POINT**, rel. 1984. ed. 950, s/n, litho, 24½″ x 13″, pub CAP	75.00	225.00
ed. 75, s/n, Artist Proofs, remarque	225.00	500.00
☐ **COMING SQUALL**, rel. 1984. ed. 950, s/n, litho, 17″ x 11″, pub CAP	50.00	130.00
ed. 75, s/n, Artist Proofs, remarque	175.00	250.00
☐ **BUYING OYSTERS AT DRUM POINT**, rel. 1984. ed. 950, s/n, litho, 24″ x 16″, pub CAP	100.00	100.00
ed. 75, s/n, Artist Proofs, remarque	275.00	275.00
☐ **MISTY MORNING**, rel. 1984. ed. 950, s/n, litho, 18″ x 12″, pub CAP	65.00	65.00
☐ **TRADEWINDS**, rel. 1984. ed. 950, s/n, litho, 18″ x 12″, pub CAP	65.00	65.00
☐ **GUARDIAN OF DIAMOND SHOALS**, rel. 1984. ed. 950, s/n, litho, 18″ x 12″, pub CAP	65.00	65.00
☐ **CHESAPEAKE MORNING** rel. 1985. ed. 1,450, litho, 24″ x 14″, pub Chesapeake Bay Foundation	130.00	—
☐ **BUY-BOATS ON JACKSON CREEK**, rel. 1985. ed. 950, litho, 17″ x 11″, pub CAP ...	65.00	—
☐ **NIGHT CROSSING**, rel. 1985. ed. 950, litho 30″ x 18″, pub CAP	95.00	—
☐ **GLOUCESTER POINT WATERMEN**, rel. 1985, ed. 950, litho, 22″ x 14″, pub CAP ...	75.00	—
☐ **WINDWARD START**, rel. 1985. ed. 950, litho, size N/A, pub CAP, but not available at this time	—	—

AL BARNES

THEMES: Varied

EDUCATION: Univeristy of Texas

GALLERY/DISTRIBUTOR: Meredith Long & Co.

	ISSUE PRICE	CURRENT PRICE
☐ **THE BLUE MARAUDER**, rel. 1982. ed. 600, s/n, 19½″ x 26½″, pub MLC	47.50	95.00

MILDRED BARRETT

THEMES: Children/flowers

MEDIUM: Watercolor

STYLE: Impressionism

EDUCATION: Art Student's League, National Academy of Fine Arts, Brooklyn Museum Art School

THE LOW FLYERS *by Larry Barton*

TIGER AT DAWN *by Robert Bateman*

MUSEUMS/COLLECTIONS: Permanent display at Bergdorf Goodman's Nina's Choice Gallery

GALLERY/DISTRIBUTOR: Felicie, Inc.

	ISSUE PRICE	CURRENT PRICE
☐ FLOWER CHILD, ed. 300, s/n, 36″ x 30″, original color silkscreen, pub FI	150.00	200.00
☐ FLOWER MARKET, ed. 300, s/n, 36″ x 30″, original color silkscreen, pub FI	150.00	200.00
☐ PARASOLS, ed. 300, s/n, 36″ x 30″, original color silkscreen, pub FI	150.00	200.00
☐ SPRING CHILDREN, ed. 300, s/n, 36″ x 30″, original color silkscreen, pub FI	150.00	200.00
☐ SWINGING, ed. 300, s/n, 36½″ x 30″, original color silkscreen, pub FI	200.00	—

LARRY BARTON

THEMES: Wildlife art

BACKGROUND: The artist started his career as a successful editorial cartoonist

GALLERY/DISTRIBUTOR: Petersen Prints

	ISSUE PRICE	CURRENT PRICE
☐ THE LOW FLYERS, ed. 800, s/n, 16″ x 24½″, pub. PP	75.00	—
remarque, s/n	165.00	—
☐ THE MORNING WATCH, ed. 800, s/n, 25″ x 17½″, pub. PP	75.00	—
remarque, s/n	165.00	—

ROBERT BATEMAN

THEMES: Wildlife art

SYTLE: Realism. The focus on environment is the essence of Bateman's paintings

GALLERY/DISTRIBUTOR: Mill Pond Press, Inc.

COMMENTS: His works have been exhibited worldwide and are featured in collections on three continents

	ISSUE PRICE	CURRENT PRICE
☐ BY THE TRACKS - KILLDEER, rel. 1978. ed. 950, s/n, 20″ x 27½″, pub MPPI	75.00	300.00
☐ CHEETAH WITH CUBS, rel. 1978. ed. 950, s/n, 21″ x 27½″, pub MPPI	95.00	135.00
☐ DOWNY WOODPECKER ON GOLDENROD GALL, rel. 1978. ed. 950, s/n, 21″ x 14″, pub MPPI	50.00	700.00
☐ LION CUBS, rel. 1978. ed. 950, s/n, 21″ x 28″, pub MPPI	125.00	150.00
☐ MAJESTY ON THE WING - BALD EAGLE, rel. 1978. ed. 950, s/n, 24″ x 36″, pub MPPI	150.00	2200.00
☐ WOLF PACK IN MOONLIGHT, rel. 1978. ed. 950, s/n, 21″ x 27½″, pub MPPI	95.00	1150.00

	ISSUE PRICE	CURRENT PRICE
☐ YOUNG BARN SWALLOW, rel. 1978. ed. 950, s/n, 27½" x 20½", pub MPPI	75.00	375.00
☐ AFTERNOON GLOW - SNOWY OWL, rel. 1979. ed. 950, s/n, 21½" x 27½", pub MPPI	125.00	275.00
☐ AMONG THE LEAVES - COTTONTAIL RABBIT, rel. 1979. ed. 950, s/n, 16" x 20", pub MPPI	75.00	625.00
☐ BULL MOOSE, rel. 1979. ed. 950, s/n, 23" x 29½", pub MPPI	125.00	650.00
☐ COUNTRY LANE - PHEASANT, rel. 1979. ed. 950, s/n, 19½" x 23", pub MPPI	85.00	200.00
☐ EVENING SNOWFALL - AMERICAN ELK, rel. 1979. ed. 950, s/n, 21½" x 31½", pub MPPI	150.00	600.00
☐ GOLDEN EAGLE, rel. 1979. ed. 950, s/n, 24½" x 37¼", pub MPPI	150.00	200.00
☐ GREAT BLUE HERON, rel. 1979. ed. 950, s/n, 22" x 28", pub MPPI	125.00	550.00
☐ HIGH COUNTRY - STONE SHEEP, rel. 1979. ed. 950, s/n, 22½" x 29", pub MPPI . . .	125.00	150.00
☐ KING OF THE REALM, rel. 1979. ed. 950, s/n, 20½" x 27½", pub MPPI	125.00	150.00
☐ MASTER OF THE HERD - AFRICAN BUFFALO, rel. 1979. ed. 950, s/n, 22½" x 31½", pub MPPI	150.00	425.00
☐ SURF AND SANDERLINGS, rel. 1979. ed. 950, s/n, 18" x 23", pub MPPI	65.00	160.00
☐ UP IN THE PINE - GREAT HORNED OWL, rel. 1979. ed. 950, s/n, 24½" x 35", pub MPPI	150.00	250.00
☐ WILY AND WARY - RED FOX, rel. 1979. ed. 950, s/n, 22½" x 28½", pub MPPI	125.00	600.00
☐ WINTER CARDINAL, rel. 1979. ed. 950, s/n, 20½" x 14⅛", pub MPPI	75.00	2800.00
☐ WINTER—SNOWSHOE HARE, rel. 1979. ed. 950, s/n, 18" x 25½", pub MPPI	95.00	450.00
☐ YELLOW-RUMPED WARBLER, rel. 1979. ed. 950, s/n, 14" x 18½", pub MPPI	50.00	300.00
☐ AFRICAN AMBER - LIONESS PAIR, rel. 1979. ed. 950, s/n, 24½" x 38", pub MPPI . .	175.00	250.00
☐ ANTARCTIC ELEMENTS, rel. 1980. ed. 950, s/n, 22¾ x 27", pub MPPI	125.00	150.00
☐ ARCTIC FAMILY - POLAR BEARS, rel. 1980. ed. 950, s/n, 22¼" x 30½", pub MPPI	150.00	550.00
☐ ASLEEP ON THE HEMLOCK - SCREECH OWL, rel. 1980. ed. 950, s/n, 25" x 17", pub MPPI	125.00	525.00
☐ AUTUMN OVERTURE - MOOSE, rel. 1980. ed. 950, s/n, 24½" x 36¼", pub MPPI . .	245.00	600.00
☐ BARN OWL IN THE CHURCHYARD, rel. 1980. ed. 950, s/n, 20" x 24", pub MPPI . . .	125.00	175.00
☐ BLUFFING BULL - AFRICAN ELEPHANT, rel. 1980. ed. 950, s/n, 22¾" x 26¾", pub MPPI	135.00	275.00
☐ BROWN PELICAN AND PILINGS, rel. 1980. ed. 950, s/n, 34½" x 25", pub MPPI . . .	165.00	500.00
☐ CHAPEL DOORS, rel. 1980. ed. 950, s/n, 29½" x 23", pub MPPI	135.00	150.00
☐ COYOTE IN WINTER SAGE, rel. 1980. ed. 950, s/n, 24½" x 34½", pub MPPI	245.00	1,300.00
☐ CURIOUS GLANCE - RED FOX, rel. 1980. ed. 950, s/n, 18¾" x 27½", pub MPPI . . .	135.00	550.00
☐ EVENING GROSBEAK, rel. 1980. ed. 950, s/n, 24⅛" x 19⅛", pub MPPI	125.00	350.00
☐ FALLEN WILLOW - SNOWY OWL, rel. 1980. ed. 950, s/n, 25" x 38", pub MPPI	200.00	275.00
☐ FLYING HIGH - GOLDEN EAGLE, rel. 1980. ed. 950, s/n, 31½" x 23¼", pub MPPI .	150.00	425.00
☐ HERON ON THE ROCKS, rel. 1980. ed. 950, s/n, 13½" x 22", pub MPPI	75.00	175.00
☐ KITTIWAKES GREETING, rel. 1980. ed. 950, s/n, 20" x 16", pub MPPI	75.00	225.00
☐ LEOPARD IN A SAUSAGE TREE, rel. 1980. ed. 950, s/n, 24¾" x 30¼", pub MPPI .	150.00	275.00
☐ LION AT TSAVO, rel. 1980. ed. 950, s/n, 21½" x 31½", pub MPPI	150.00	175.00
☐ MISCHIEF ON THE PROWL - RACCOON, rel. 1980. ed. 950, s/n, 14" x 23", pub MPPI	85.00	300.00
☐ MISTY COAST GULLS, rel. 1980. ed. 950, s/n, 23¼" x 29¼", pub MPPI	135.00	250.00
☐ ON THE ALERT - CHIPMUNK, rel. 1980. ed. 950, s/n, 12" x 16⅜", pub MPPI	60.00	400.00
☐ PRAIRIE EVENING-SHORTEARED OWL, rel. 1980. ed. 950, s/n, 23" x 31½", pub MPPI	150.00	175.00
☐ ROCKY WILDERNESS - COUGAR, rel. 1980. ed. 950, s/n, 24¾" x 31¼", pub MPPI	175.00	750.00
☐ SPRING CARDINAL, rel. 1980. ed. 950, s/n, 18" x 24½", pub MPPI	125.00	400.00
☐ SPRING THAW-KILLDEER, rel. 1980. ed. 950, s/n, 16½" x 22", pub MPPI	85.00	200.00
☐ THE AWESOME LAND - AMERICAN ELK, rel. 1980. ed. 950, s/n, 24½" x 38", pub MPPI	245.00	385.00
☐ VANTAGE POINT, rel. 1980. ed. 950, s/n, 24½" x 38", pub MPPI	245.00	550.00
☐ WHITE ENCOUNTER, rel. 1980. ed. 950, s/n, 24¾" x 31¾", pub MPPI	245.00	1500.00
☐ WHITE-FOOTED MOUSE IN WINTERGREEN, rel. 1980. ed. 950, s/n, 11¾" x 13¼", pub MPPI	60.00	300.00
☐ WINTER ELM - AMERICAN KESTREL, rel. 1980. ed. 950, s/n, 20" x 37½", pub MPPI	135.00	225.00
☐ WINTER - SNOWSHOE HARE, rel. 1980. ed. 950, s/n, 18" x 25½", pub MPPI	95.00	375.00
☐ WINTER SONG - CHICKADEES, rel. 1980. ed. 950, s/n, 17¼" x 14", pub MPPI	95.00	600.00

	ISSUE PRICE	CURRENT PRICE
☐ ARABI ROYAL FAMILY - MUTE SWANS, rel. 1981. ed. 950, s/n, 24⅝" x 37¼", pub MPPI	245.00	260.00
☐ BRIGHT DAY - ATLANTIC PUFFINS, rel. 1981. ed. 950, s/n, 22¾" x 25⅝", pub MPPI	175.00	195.00
☐ CANADA GEESE - NESTING, rel. 1981. ed. 950, s/n, 24" x 31", pub MPPI	295.00	1100.00
☐ CLEAR NIGHT - WOLVES, rel. 1981. ed. 950, s/n, 24⅝" x 32½", pub MPPI	245.00	1300.00
☐ COURTING PAIR - WHISTLING SWANS, rel. 1981. ed. 950, s/n, 22¾" x 29½", pub MPPI	245.00	450.00
☐ COURTSHIP DISPLAY - WILD TURKEY, rel. 1981. ed. 950, s/n, 24⅝" x 26¾", pub MPPI	175.00	200.00
☐ EDGE OF THE ICE - ERMINE, rel. 1981. ed. 950, s/n, 17¾" x 21½", pub MPPI	175.00	300.00
☐ EVENING LIGHT - WHITE GYRFALCON, rel. 1981. ed. 950, s/n, 24⅝" x 32½", pub MPPI	245.00	285.00
☐ GALLINULE FAMILY, rel. 1981. ed. 950, s/n, 20⅝" x 31½", pub MPPI	135.00	—
☐ GALLOPING HERD - GIRAFFES, rel. 1981. ed. 950, s/n, 29¾" x 24½", pub MPPI . .	175.00	225.00
☐ GENTOO PENGUINS & WHALE BONES, rel. 1981. ed. 950, s/n, 24½" x 37¼", pub MPPI	205.00	—
☐ GRAY SQUIRREL, rel. 1981. ed. 950, s/n, 21½" x 29¾", pub MPPI	180.00	500.00
☐ HIGH CAMP AT DUSK, rel. 1981. ed. 950, s/n, 24¼" x 38", pub MPPI	245.00	265.00
☐ IN FOR THE EVENING, rel. 1981. ed. 950, s/n, 21¼" x 25", pub MPPI	150.00	300.00
☐ KINGFISHER AND ASPEN, rel. 1981. ed. 950, s/n, 24½" x 29¼", pub MPPI	225.00	275.00
☐ LAST LOOK - BIGHORN SHEEP, rel. 1981. ed. 950, s/n, 24⅜" x 38", pub MPPI	195.00	—
☐ LAUGHING GULL & HORSESHOE CRAB, rel. 1981. ed. 950, s/n, 14½" x 22⅛", pub MPPI	125.00	150.00
☐ LITTLE BLUE HERON, rel. 1981. ed. 950, s/n, 19¼" x 12¾", pub MPPI	95.00	150.00
☐ MISTY MORNING - LOONS, rel. 1981. ed. 950, s/n, 20" x 27½", pub MPPI	150.00	750.00
☐ PAIR OF SKIMMERS, rel. 1981. ed. 950, s/n, 15⅜" x 27½", pub MPPI	150.00	175.00
☐ PIONEER MEMORIES - MAGPIE PAIR, rel. 1981. ed. 950, s/n, 18⅝" x 24½", pub MPPI	175.00	—
☐ RED-TAILED HAWK BY THE CLIFF, rel. 1981. ed. 950, s/n, 24½" x 34⅛", pub MPPI	245.00	400.00
☐ RED-WINGED BLACKBIRD AND RAIL FENCE, rel. 1981. ed. 950, s/n, 22¾" x 29½", pub MPPI	195.00	250.00
☐ ROUGH-LEGGED HAWK IN THE ELM, rel. 1981. ed. 950, s/n, 22¾" x 29½", pub MPPI	175.00	—
☐ ROYAL FAMILY - MUTE SWANS, rel. 1981. ed. 950, s/n, 24⅝" x 37½", pub MPPI . .	245.00	325.00
☐ SHEER DROP - MOUNTAIN GOATS, rel. 1981. ed. 950, s/n, 32" x 24½", pub MPPI .	245.00	400.00
☐ SWIFT FOX, rel. 1981. ed. 950, s/n, 15" x 24½", pub MPPI	175.00	325.00
☐ THE ARTIST AND HIS DOG, rel. 1981. ed. 950, s/n, 19¼" x 28½", pub MPPI	150.00	175.00
☐ THE OSPREY FAMILY, rel. 1981. ed. 950, s/n, 24½" x 34", pub MPPI	245.00	275.00
☐ THE SARAH E. WITH GULLS, rel. 1981. ed. 950, s/n, 30½" x 24½", pub MPPI	245.00	600.00
☐ WATCHFUL REPOSE - BLACK BEAR, rel. 1981. ed. 950, s/n, 24⅝" x 30", pub MPPI	245.00	275.00
☐ WHITE WORLD - DALL SHEEP, rel. 1981. ed. 950, s/n, 24⅝" x 28½", pub MPPI . . .	200.00	225.00
☐ WINTER MIST - GREAT HORNED OWL, rel. 1981. ed. 950, s/n, 38" x 24½", pub MPPI	245.00	375.00
☐ WINTER WREN, rel. 1981. ed. 950, s/n, 20⅝" x 20⅝", pub MPPI	135.00	225.00
☐ WRANGLER'S CAMPSITE - GRAY JAY, rel. 1981. ed. 950, s/n, 28½" x 20⅝", pub MPPI	195.00	260.00
☐ ABOVE THE RIVER - TRUMPETER SWANS, rel. 1982. ed. 950, s/n, 21⅛" x 32¼", pub MPPI	200.00	225.00
☐ ARTIC EVENING - WHITE WOLF, rel. 1982. ed. 950, s/n, 24⅝" x 20", pub MPPI	185.00	300.00
☐ ARTIC PORTRAIT - WHITE GYRFALCON, rel. 1982. ed. 950, s/n, 16¾" x 22¼", pub MPPI	175.00	225.00
☐ AT THE ROADSIDE - RED-TAILED HAWK, rel. 1982. ed. 950, s/n, 21⅝" x 29½", pub MPPI	185.00	300.00
☐ BAOBAB TREE AND IMPALA, rel. 1982. ed. 950, s/n, 30¼" x 24½", pub MPPI	245.00	—
☐ BARN SWALLOWS IN AUGUST, rel. 1982. ed. 950, s/n, 24½" x 34¾", pub MPPI . .	245.00	—
☐ CHEETAH PROFILE, rel. 1982. ed. 950, s/n, 24½" x 35", pub MPPI	245.00	265.00
☐ DIPPER BY THE WATERFALL, rel. 1982. ed. 950, s/n, 17¾" x 26¼", pub MPPI	165.00	185.00
☐ EDGE OF THE WOODS - WHITETAIL DEER, rel. 1982. ed. 950, s/n, 24½" x 35", pub MPPI	745.00	950.00

	ISSUE PRICE	CURRENT PRICE
☐ **FOX AT THE GRANARY,** rel. 1982. ed. 950, s/n, 20½" x 27¾", pub MPPI	165.00	—
☐ **FROSTY MORNING - BLUE JAY,** rel. 1982. ed. 950, s/n, 23¾" x 19¾", pub MPPI . .	185.00	800.00
☐ **GALLINULE FAMILY,** rel. 1982. ed. 950, s/n, 20⅝" x 31½", pub MPPI	135.00	—
☐ **GENTOO PENGUINS AND WHALE BONES,** rel. 1982. ed. 950, s/n, 24½" x 37¼", pub MPPI	205.00	—
☐ **GOLDEN CROWNED KINGLET AND RHODODEND,** rel. 1982. ed. 950, s/n, 16½" x 20⅛", pub MPPI	150.00	800.00
☐ **KINGFISHER IN WINTER,** rel. 1982. ed. 950, s/n, 28½" x 24½", pub AA, distr. MPPI	175.00	325.00
☐ **LEOPARD AMBUSH,** rel. 1982. ed. 950, s/n, 24½" x 32", pub MPPI	245.00	—
☐ **LIVELY PAIR - CHICKADEES,** rel. 1982. ed. 950, s/n, 14¾" x 18¾", pub MPPI	160.00	350.00
☐ **MEADOW'S EDGE - MALLARD,** rel. 1982. ed. 950, s/n, 20¼" x 27⅜", pub MPPI . . .	175.00	425.00
☐ **MERGANSER FAMILY IN HIDING,** rel. 1982. ed. 950, s/n, 21½" x 31½", pub MPPI .	200.00	300.00
☐ **PLEATED WOODPECKER ON BEECH TREE,** rel. 1982. ed. 950, s/n, 24½" x 18¼", pub MPPI	175.00	250.00
☐ **PIONEER MEMORIES - MAGPIE PAIR,** rel. 1982. ed. 950, s/n, 18⅝" x 24½", pub MPPI	175.00	225.00
☐ **POLAR BEAR PROFILE,** rel. 1982. ed. 950, s/n, 24½" x 35", pub MPPI	210.00	375.00
☐ **POLAR BEARS AT BAFFIN ISLAND,** rel. 1982. ed. 950, s/n, 31¾" x 24½", pub MPPI	245.00	300.00
☐ **QUEEN ANNE'S LACE AND AMERICAN GOLDFINCH,** rel. 1982. ed. 950, s/n, 16½" x 20¼", pub MPPI	150.00	650.00
☐ **READY FOR THE HUNT—SNOWY OWL,** rel. 1982. ed. 950, s/n, 24½" x 36", pub MPPI	245.00	300.00
☐ **RED SQUIRREL,** rel. 1982. ed. 950, s/n, 16⅜" x 22¼", pub MPPI	175.00	450.00
☐ **SPRING MARSH—PINTAIL PAIR,** rel. 1982. ed. 950, s/n, 22¾" x 29½", pub MPPI .	200.00	225.00
☐ **STILL MORNING—HERRING GULLS,** rel. 1982. ed. 950, s/n, 22" x 31¼", pub MPPI	200.00	225.00
☐ **WHITE-FOOTED MOUSE ON ASPEN,** rel. 1982. ed. 950, s/n, 13½" x 14⅜", pub MPPI	90.00	125.00
☐ **WHITE WORLD-DALL SHEEP,** rel. 1982. ed. 950, s/n, 24⅝" x 28⅛", pub MPPI · . . .	200.00	225.00
☐ **WILLET ON THE SHORE,** rel. 1982. ed. 950, s/n, 18" x 23", pub MPPI	125.00	—
☐ **CALL OF THE WILD—BALD EAGLE,** rel. 1983. ed. 950, s/n, 24½" x 31⅛", pub MPPI	200.00	225.00
☐ **EARLY SPRING—BLUEBIRD,** rel. 1983. ed. 950, s/n, 18⅞" x 29½", pub MPPI	185.00	200.00
☐ **GHOST OF THE NORTH—GREAT GRAY OWL,** rel. 1983. ed. 950, s/n, 24½" x 31½", pub MPPI	200.00	300.00
☐ **GREAT HORNED OWL IN WHITE PINE,** rel. 1983. ed. 950, s/n, 35" x 20⅝", pub MPPI	225.00	350.00
☐ **OSPREY IN THE RAIN,** rel. 1983. ed. 950, s/n, 19⅝" x 14", pub MPPI	110.00	245.00
☐ **PHEASANT IN CORNFIELD,** rel. 1983. ed. 950, s/n, 20" x 29", pub MPPI	200.00	250.00
☐ **RUBY-THROAT AND COLUMBINE,** rel. 1983. ed. 950, s/n, 16½" x 20¼", pub MPPI	150.00	700.00
☐ **TIGER PORTRAIT,** rel. 1983. ed. 950, s/n, 17¼" x 21", pub MPPI	130.00	160.00
☐ **WINTER BARN,** rel. 1983. ed. 950, s/n, 16" x 24", pub MPPI	170.00	200.00
☐ **WINTER LADY—CARDINAL,** rel. 1983. ed. 950, s/n, 16" x 19¾", pub MPPI	200.00	750.00
☐ **WOLVES ON THE TRAIL,** rel. 1983. ed. 950, s/n, 21⅛" x 31½", pub MPPI	225.00	450.00
☐ **WOODLAND DRUMMER—PUFFED GROUSE,** rel. 1983. ed. 950, s/n, 14" x 24", pub MPPI	185.00	200.00
☐ **YOUNG ELF OWL—OLD SAGUARD,** rel. 1983. ed. 950, s/n, 12" x 15½", pub MPPI	95.00	150.00
☐ **ACROSS THE SKY—SNOW GEESE,** rel. 1984. ed. 950, s/n, 24½" x 31", pub MPPI	220.00	275.00
☐ **ALONG THE RIDGE—GRIZZLY BEARS,** rel. 1984. ed. 950, s/n, 24" x 33¼", pub MPPI	200.00	250.00
☐ **AMERICAN GOLDFINCH—WINTER DRESS,** rel. 1984. ed. 950, s/n, 11¾" x 10¼", pub MPPI	75.00	95.00
☐ **BIG COUNTRY—PRONGHORN ANTELOPE,** rel. 1984. ed. 950, s/n, 18" x 29½", pub MPPI	185.00	—
☐ **DOWN FOR A DRINK—MOURNING DOVE,** rel. 1984. ed. 950, s/n, 13⅓" x 19¼", pub MPPI	135.00	150.00
☐ **REEDS,** rel. 1984. ed. 850, s/n, 19¾" x 29½", pub MPPI	185.00	200.00
☐ **SMALLWOOD,** rel. 1984. ed. 950, s/n, 21¾" x 29½", pub MPPI	200.00	—
☐ **STRETCHING—CANADA GOOSE,** rel. 1984. ed. 950, s/n, 31¼" x 24½", pub MPPI	225.00	550.00
☐ **TADPOLE TIME,** rel. 1984. ed. 950, s/n, 16½" x 22", pub MPPI . :	135.00	150.00
☐ **TIGER AT DAWN,** rel. 1984. ed. 950, s/n, 24½" x 35", pub MPPI	225.00	425.00

	ISSUE PRICE	CURRENT PRICE
☐ WINDOW INTO ONTARIO, rel. 1984. ed. 950, s/n, 21¾" x 37½", pub MPPI	265.00	350.00
☐ BEAVER POND REFLECTIONS, rel. 1985, ed. 950, s/n, 22" x 15⅞", pub MPPI	185.00	225.00
☐ GAMBEL'S QUAIL PAIR, rel. 1985, ed. 950, s/n, 12¹/₁₆" x 15⅜", pub MPPI	95.00	135.00
☐ IN THE MOUNTAINS, rel. 1985, ed. 950, s/n, 12⅛" x 15⅜", pub MPPI	95.00	—
☐ ORCA PROCESSION, rel. 1985, ed. 950, s/n, 24½" x 32¼", pub MPPI	245.00	850.00
☐ PEREGRINE FALCON & WHITE-THROATED SWIFTS, rel. 1985, ed. 950, s/n, 31¾" x 24½", pub MPPI	245.00	265.00
☐ SNOWY HEMLOCK—BARRED OWL, rel. 1985, ed. 950, s/n, 24½" x 31¾", pub MPPI	245.00	300.00
☐ STREAM BANK—JUNE, rel. 1985, ed. 950, s/n, 17⅜" x 24½", pub MPPI	160.00	—
☐ WEATHERED BRANCH—BALD EAGLE, rel. 1985. ed. 950, s/n, 12¼" x 15", pub MPPI	115.00	225.00
☐ WOOD BISON PORTRAIT, rel. 1985, ed. 950, s/n, 16" x 18¾", pub MPPI	165.00	200.00

TOM BEECHAM

THEMES: Wildlife art

EDUCATION: St. Louis School of Fine Arts at Washington University in Missouri

GALLERY/DISTRIBUTOR: Arts Limited, Inc.

COMMENTS: At school, the artist was hailed as "the finest natural talent to enter the school in twenty-five years"

THE OLD MILL RUN *by Tom Beecham*

	ISSUE PRICE	CURRENT PRICE
☐ **BRUSH ROYALTY,** rel. 1980. ed. 1,500, s/n, 32½" x 24⅛", pub ALI	60.00	—
☐ **THE AMERICAN LION,** rel. 1980. ed. 1,500, s/n, 29¾" x 25", pub ALI	60.00	—
☐ **THE OLD MILL RUN,** rel. 1980. ed. 1,500, s/n, 33½" x 24⅛", pub ALI	60.00	—

JOE BEELER

THEMES: Western art

EDUCATION: Kansas State Teachers College, Art Center School

AWARDS: Colt award; several medals of prestige from the Cowboy Artists of America

MEMBERSHIPS: Cowboy Artists of America

MUSEUMS/COLLECTIONS: Many of the country's leading museums have displayed the artist's works

GALLEY/DISTRIBUTOR: Frame House Gallery, Inc.

	ISSUE PRICE	CURRENT PRICE
☐ **DOG SOLDIER,** rel. 1976. ed. 1,000, s/n, 25" x 38", pub FHG	100.00	Sold Out
☐ **FINISHING OFF THE DAY,** rel. 1976. ed. 250, s/n, 21½" x 33", pub FHG	100.00	Sold Out
☐ **BIDDING FOR A BRIDE,** rel. 1977. ed. 250, s/n, 20¼" x 30", pub FHG	100.00	—

BRAD BENNETT

THEMES: America's cities and towns

MEDIUM: Watercolor

EDUCATION: University of Wisconsin

MEMBERSHIPS: Society of Illustrators

GALLERY/DISTRIBUTOR: Brad Bennett Studios

COMMENTS: The artist has the exclusive distinction of having his lithographs registered with the Library of Congress

	ISSUE PRICE	CURRENT PRICE
☐ **BIKE RACES,** rel. 1981. ed. 1,000, s/n, 10½" x 15", pub BBS	30.00	—
☐ **COHORAMA,** rel. 1981. ed. 1,000, s/n, 10½" x 15", pub BBS	30.00	—
☐ **EVOLUTION OF A SALTWATER PORT,** rel. 1981. ed. 1,000, s/n, 10½" x 15", pub BBS	30.00	—
☐ **FIRST SHIP OF THE SEASON,** rel. 1981. ed. 1,000, s/n, 10½" x 15", pub BBS	30.00	—
☐ **HARVEST TIME,** rel. 1981. ed. 1,000, s/n, 10½" x 15", pub BBS	30.00	—
☐ **KEMPER CENTER,** rel. 1981. ed. 1,000, s/n, 10½" x 15", pub BBS	30.00	—

	ISSUE PRICE	CURRENT PRICE
☐ MONUMENT, rel. 1981. ed. 1,000, s/n, 10½" x 15", pub BBS	30.00	—
☐ NORTHSHORE TROLLEY, rel. 1981. ed. 1,000, s/n, 10½" x 15", pub BBS	30.00	—
☐ PETRIFYING SPRINGS, rel. 1981. ed. 1,000, s/n, 10½" x 15", pub BBS	30.00	—
☐ STORMY HARBOR, rel. 1981. ed. 1,000, s/n, 10½" x 15", pub BBS	30.00	—
☐ WINTER CANNON, rel. 1981. ed. 1,000, s/n, 10½" x 15", pub BBS	30.00	—
☐ KENOSHA SERIES PORTFOLIO, rel. 1981. ed. 1,000, s/n, 10½" x 15", pub BBS, all twelve prints listed above with narratives and registered with the Library of Congress card catalog number #81-53106. Also includes a 13th print of artist's self-portrait	240.00	300.00
☐ ABSOLUTION, rel. 1982. ed. 1,000, s/n, 10½" x 15", pub BBS	30.00	—
☐ BAPTISM OF THE BEGGARS, rel. 1982. ed. 1,000, s/n, 10½" x 15", pub BBS	30.00	—
☐ DRESSING FOR BATTLE, rel. 1982. ed. 1,000, s/n, 10½" x 15", pub BBS	30.00	—
☐ HUMAN CHESS GAMES, rel. 1982. ed. 1,000, s/n, 10½" x 15", pub BBS	30.00	—
☐ KING RICHARD AND HIS COURT, rel. 1982. ed. 1,000, s/n, 10½" x 15", pub BBS ..	30.00	—
☐ THE JOUST, rel. 1982. ed. 1,000, s/n, 10½" x 15", pub BBS	30.00	—
☐ THE QUEEN'S DANCERS, rel. 1982. ed. 1,000, s/n, 10½" x 15", pub BBS	30.00	—
☐ THE SORCERER, rel. 1982. ed. 1,000, s/n, 10½" x 15", pub BBS	30.00	—
☐ TOOTHSOME WENCH, rel. 1982. ed. 1,000, s/n, 10½" x 15", pub BBS	30.00	—
☐ VILLAGE JESTERS, rel. 1982. ed. 1,000, s/n, 10½" x 15", pub BBS	30.00	—
☐ KING RICHARD'S FAIRE PORTFOLIO, rel. 1982. ed. 1,000, s/n, 16½" x 11½", pub BBS, all ten prints listed above with narratives and registered with the Library of Congress card catalog number #82-90452	250.00	300.00
☐ AZALEA TRAIL - BAYOU BEND, rel. 1983. ed. 1,000, s/n, 10½" x 15", pub BBS ...	30.00	—
☐ GREEN TUB CHURNING, rel. 1983. ed. 1,000, s/n, 10½" x 15", pub BBS	30.00	—
☐ HIGHWAYS AND SKYWAYS, rel. 1983. ed. 1,000, s/n, 10½" x 15", pub BBS	30.00	—
☐ HOUSTON FESTIVAL, rel. 1983. ed. 1,000, s/n, 10½" x 15", pub BBS	30.00	—
☐ HOUSTON SHIP CHANNEL, rel. 1983. ed. 1,000, s/n, 10½" x 15", pub BBS	30.00	—
☐ LET's RODEO, rel. 1983. ed. 1,000, s/n, 10½" x 15", pub BBS	30.00	—
☐ N.A.S.A, rel. 1983. ed. 1,000, s/n, 10½" x 15", pub BBS	30.00	—
☐ REFINERY, rel. 1983. ed. 1,000, s/n, 10½" x 15", pub BBS	30.00	—
☐ SAM HOUSTON, rel. 1983. ed. 1,000, s/n, 10½" x 15", pub BBS	30.00	—
☐ THE GALLERIA, rel. 1983. ed. 1,000, s/n, 10½" x 15", pub BBS	30.00	—
☐ TRAIL RIDERS, rel. 1983. ed. 1,000, s/n, 10½" x 15", pub BBS	30.00	—
☐ TRANQUILITY PARK, rel. 1983. ed. 1,000, s/n, 10½" x 15", pub BBS	30.00	—
☐ HOUSTON SERIES PORTFOLIO, rel. 1983. ed. 1,000, s/n, 10½" x 15", pub BBS, all twelve prints listed above with narratives and registered with the Library of Congress card catalog number #83-90043	—	—
☐ ART OF INSTITUTE OF CHICAGO, rel. 1983. ed. 1,000, s/n, litho, 10½" x 15", pub BBS	30.00	—
☐ BUCKINGHAM FOUNTAIN, rel. 1983. ed. 1,000, s/n, litho, 10½" x 15", pub BBS	30.00	—
☐ BURNHAM PARK, rel. 1983. ed. 1,000, s/n, litho, 10½" x 15", pub BBS	30.00	—
☐ CHICAGO MERCANTILE EXCHANGE, rel. 1983. ed. 1,000, s/n, litho, 10½" x 15", pub BBS	30.00	—
☐ CHINESE NEW YEAR, rel. 1983. ed. 1,000, s/n, litho, 10½" x 15", pub BBS	30.00	—
☐ LINCOLN PARK ZOO, rel. 1983. ed. 1,000, s/n, litho, 10½" x 15", pub BBS	30.00	—
☐ MACK RACE, rel. 1983. ed. 1,000, s/n, litho, 10½" x 15", pub BBS	30.00	—
☐ MICHIGAN AVENUE, rel. 1983. ed. 1,000, s/n, litho, 10½" x 15", pub BBS	30.00	—
☐ OAK STREET BEACH, rel. 1983. ed. 1,000, s/n, litho, 10½" x 15", pub BBS	30.00	—
☐ ST. PATRICK'S DAY PARADE, rel. 1983. ed. 1,000, s/n, litho, 10½" x 15", pub BBS .	30.00	—
☐ THE "EL", rel. 1983. ed. 1,000, s/n, litho, 10½" x 15", pub BBS	30.00	—
☐ WRIGLEY FIELD, rel. 1983. ed. 1,000, s/n, litho, 10½" x 15", pub BBS	30.00	—
☐ CHICAGO SERIES PORTFOLIO, rel. 1983. ed. 1,000, s/n, litho, 10½" x 15", pub BBS, all twelve prints listed above with narratives and registered with the Library of Congress, card catalog #83-62655	350.00	—
☐ ADARE COTTAGES, rel. 1984. ed. 500, s/n, litho, 14" x 20", pub BBS	85.00	—
☐ LOW TIDE AT DINGLE, rel. 1984. ed. 500, s/n, litho, 14" x 20", pub BBS	85.00	—
☐ THE CREAMERY, rel. 1984. ed. 500, s/n, litho, 14" x 20", pub BBS	85.00	—
☐ IRELAND SERIES PORTFOLIO, rel. 1984. ed. 500, s/n, litho, 14" x 20", pub BBS, all three listed above with narrative in portfolio	300.00	—
☐ BASCOM HALL, rel. 1984. ed. 1,000, s/n, litho, 14" x 20", pub BBS	75.00	—
☐ CAROLING TOWER, rel. 1984. ed. 1,000, s/n, litho, 14" x 20", pub BBS	75.00	—
☐ MEMORIAL UNION TERRACE, rel. 1984. ed. 1,000, s/n, litho, 14" x 20", pub BBS ..	75.00	—
☐ WISCONSIN CREW, rel. 1984. ed. 1,000, s/n, litho, 14" x 20", pub BBS	75.00	—

	ISSUE PRICE	CURRENT PRICE
☐ **WISCONSIN (UNIVERSITY OF) SERIES PORTFOLIO,** rel. 1984. ed. 1,000, s/n, litho, 14″ x 20″, pub BBS, all four prints listed above with accompanying narrative in portfolio	300.00	—
☐ **CHICAGO MERCANTILE EXCHANGE II,** rel. 1984. ed. 500, s/n, litho, 14″ x 20″, pub BBS	95.00	—
☐ **SPIEGEL,** rel. 1984. ed. 500, s/n, litho, 10½″ x 15″, pub BBS	45.00	—
☐ **WRIGLEY FIELD II,** rel. 1984. ed. 2,000, s/n, litho, 32″ x 23″, pub BBS	100.00	—

HERE, KITTY KITTY! *by Lenore Béran*

LENORE BÉRAN

THEMES: Varied

MEDIUM: Varied

STYLE: Her works range from fragile, almost ethereal oil wash paintings to bold, bronze sculpture

AWARDS: More than fifty first and second prizes in major competitions

GALLERY/DISTRIBUTOR: Lenore Béran Art

	ISSUE PRICE	CURRENT PRICE
☐ **FLUTIST DREAM,** rel. 1977. ed. 1,000, s/n, 22″ x 22″, pub JBFA	45.00	—
☐ **MEMORIES OF PAN,** rel. 1977. ed. 1,000, s/n, 22″ x 22″, pub JBFA	45.00	—
☐ **THE CALL OF THE PIPER,** rel. 1977. original lithograph, ed. 100, s/n, 21½″ x 30″, pub JBFA	150.00	—
ed. 10 Artist Proofs		

	ISSUE PRICE	CURRENT PRICE
☐ CIRCLE OF ENCHANTMENT, rel. 1978. ed. 500, s/n, 18″ x 18″, pub JBFA	50.00	—
☐ THE DREAM, rel. 1978. original lithograph w/embossing, ed. 100, s/n, 21½″ x 30″ pub JBFA, distr. GBS	200.00	—
ed. 10 Artist Proofs		
☐ FOR THE LOVE OF A MAIDEN, rel. 1980. original lithograph w/embossing, ed. 150, s/n, 27″ x 22″, pub LBA, distr. GBS	150.00	—
ed. 15 Artist Proofs		
☐ LESSONS FROM THE PAST, rel. 1980. original lithograph w/embossing, ed. 150, s/n, 22″ x 30″, pub LBA, distr. GBS	175.00	—
ed. 15 Artist Proofs		
☐ PREPARING FOR THE POW POW, rel. 1980. original lithograph w/embossing, ed. 150, s/n, 26½″ x 22″, pub LBA, distr. GBS	150.00	—
ed. 15 Artist Proofs		
☐ SACHIKO, rel. 1980. original lithograph w/hand coloring, ed. 50, s/n, 18″ x 26½″, pub LBA	175.00	—
ed. 5 Artist Proofs		
☐ SPRINGWATER AND THE KACHINA DOLL, rel. 1980. original lithograph w/embossing, ed. 150, s/n, 26″ x 22¼, pub LBS, distr. GBS	95.00	—
☐ THE GATHERING, rel. 1980. ed. 500, s/n, 21″ x 21″, pub LBA	50.00	—
50 remarques from the edition	95.00	—
☐ THE MESSAGE OF THE EAGLE, rel. 1980, original lithograph w/embossing, ed. 99, s/n, 30″ x 22″, pub LBA	175.00	—
ed. 10 Artist Proofs		
☐ VISION, rel. 1980. original lithograph w/embossing, ed. 99, s/n, 30″ x 22″, pub LBA ..	175.00	195.00
ed. 10 Artist Proofs		
☐ FUSION, rel. 1981. intaglio etching, ed. 42, s/n, 15″ x 16″, pub LBA	95.00	—
ed. 6 Artist Proofs		
☐ JAM SESSION, rel. 1981. intaglio etching, ed. 42, s/n, 15″ x 16″, pub LBA	95.00	—
ed. 6 Artist Proofs		
☐ UP, UP AND AWAY, rel. 1981. ed. 315, s/n, 25″ x 22″, pub LBA	60.00	—
☐ DANCE IN MY FANTASIES, rel. 1982. intaglio etching, ed. 44, s/n, 30″ x 22″, pub LBA	195.00	—
ed. 6 Artist Proofs		
☐ PEGASUS, rel. 1982. original embossing, ed. 99, s/n, 20″ x 22″, pub LBA	40.00	—
☐ UNICORN, rel. 1982, original embossing, ed. 99, s/n, 20″ x 22″, pub LBA	40.00	—
ed. 12 Artist Proofs		
☐ MOONDREAMS, rel. 1983. intaglio etching, ed. 99, s/n, 19″ x 22″, pub LBA	70.00	—
ed. 3 Artist Proofs		
☐ PIMA, rel. 1983. intaglio etching, ed. 22, s/n, 19″ x 15″, pub LBA	60.00	—
ed. 3 Artist Proofs		
☐ SERANADE, rel. 1983. intaglio etching, ed. 22, s/n, 19″ x 15″, pub LBA	60.00	—
ed. 3 Artist Proofs		
☐ HERE, KITTY KITTY!, rel. 1984. ed. 485, 16″ x 20″, pub LBA	39.00	—
ed. 50 Artist Proofs with remarques	80.00	—
☐ HORNS AND WINGS AND HOOVES, rel. 1984. intaglio etching, ed. 16, 14″ x 12″, pub LBA	75.00	—
ed. 2 Artist Proofs	80.00	—

JODY BERGSMA

THEMES: Big-eyed children and fantasy animals

MEDIUM: Watercolor

STYLE: Illustration

GALLERY/DISTRIBUTOR: Bergsma Collectibles

ANNOYED PIG by Jody Bergsma

	ISSUE PRICE	CURRENT PRICE
☐ **BOAT BOY I**, rel. 1979. ed. 1,000, s/o, 8″ x 10″, pub Bl	13.00	. 40.00
☐ **BUGGED FROG I**, rel. 1979. ed. 1,000, s/o, 8″ x 10″, pub Bl	13.00	40.00
☐ **DON'T HURRY I**, rel. 1979. ed. 1,000, s/o, 8″ x 10″, pub Bl	13.00	40.00
☐ **FLYING HORSE I**, rel. 1979. ed. 1,000, s/n, 12″ x 16″, pub Bl	23.00	150.00
☐ **HUGGING BEARS I**, rel. 1979. ed. 1,000, s/o, 8″ x 10″, pub Bl	13.00	60.00
☐ **PIG IN TUB I**, rel. 1979. ed. 1,000, s/n, 12″ x 16″ , pub Bl	8.00	140.00
☐ **UNICORN I**, rel 1979. ed. 1,000, s/n, 12″ x 16″, pub Bl	23.00	180.00
☐ **FRIENDS IN THE TUB I**, rel 1979. ed. 1,000, s/n, 12″ x 16″, pub Bl	23.00	80.00
☐ **FRIENDS WITH CLASS I**, rel. 1979. ed. 1,000, s/n, 12″ x 16″, pub Bl	23.00	200.00
☐ **MIXED FRIENDS**, rel. 1979. ed. 1,000, s/n, 12″ x 16″, pub Bl	23.00	80.00
☐ **ALONG CAME TODAY**, rel. 1980. ed. 2,500, s/o, 5″ x 7″, pub Bl	9.00	35.00
☐ **AMAZING ELF AND DUCK**, rel. 1980. ed, 2,500, s/o, 5″ x 7″, pub Bl	9.00	25.00
☐ **ANNOYED PIG**, rel. 1980. ed. 875, s/n, 12″ x 16″, pub Bl	9.00	120.00
☐ **BE YOURSELF, DRAGON AND STARCHILD**, rel. 1980. ed. 1,000, s/o, 8″ x 10″, pub Bl	4.00	40.00
☐ **BE YOURSELF, PIG AND TOAD**, rel. 1980. ed. 2,500, s/o, 5″ x 7″, pub Bl	2.00	25.00
☐ **BOAT CHILDREN I**, rel. 1980. ed. 2,500, s/o, 12″ x 16″, pub Bl	13.00	40.00
☐ **BOY, FROG, AND ELF UNDER TREE**, rel. 1980. ed. 1,000, s/n, 12″ x 16″, pub Bl ...	9.00	140.00
☐ **BOY IN THE MOUNTAIN**, rel. 1980. ed. 2,500, s/o, 8″ x 10″, pub Bl	5.00	60.00
☐ **BOY IN WOOD TUB**, rel. 1980. ed. 1,000, s/o, 8″ x 10″, pub Bl	14.00	50.00
☐ **CAT AND RAT**, rel. 1980. ed. 1,000, s/o, 8″ x 10″, pub Bl	14.00	40.00
☐ **COOKIE DOUGH**, rel. 1980. ed. 2,500, s/o, 5″ x 7″, pub Bl	9.00	25.00
☐ **ELF CHILDREN UNDER RAINBOW**, rel. 1980. ed. 2,500, s/o, 8″ x 10″, pub Bl	15.00	40.00
☐ **FLUSH I**, rel. 1980. ed. 2,500, s/o, 8″ x 10″, pub Bl	14.00	60.00
☐ **FREINDSHIP I**, rel. 1980. ed. 1,000, s/o, 8″ x 10″, pub Bl	14.00	60.00
☐ **GIRL WITH RAINBOW CATS I**, rel. 1980. ed. 1000, s/n, 12″ x 16″, pub Bl	24.00	150.00

	ISSUE PRICE	CURRENT PRICE
☐ GRANDMA AND GRANDPA I, rel. 1980. ed. 1,000, s/n, 12″ x 16″, pub Bl	14.00	50.00
☐ MOM'S HOLD I, rel. 1980. ed. 1,000, s/o, 8″ x 10″, pub Bl	14.00	60.00
☐ SISTERS I, rel. 1980. ed. 1,000, s/o, 8″ x 10″, pub Bl	14.00	50.00
☐ FLYING UNICORN FRIENDS, rel. 1980. ed. 875, s/n, 16″ x 20″, pub Bl	42.00	110.00
☐ FRIENDS WITH CLASS, PIG, OWL, AND TOAD, rel. 1980. ed. 1000, s/o, 8″ x 10″, pub Bl..	15.00	40.00
☐ HAPPINESS SHARED, LION AND LAMB, rel. 1980. ed. 2,500, s/o, 5″ x 7″ pub Bl ..	9.00	25.00
☐ HAPPINESS, UNICORN, TOAD AND MOUSE, rel. 1980. ed. 1,000, s/n, 8″ x 10″, pub Bl..	15.00	50.00
☐ HAPPY, FAT PIG, rel. 1980. ed. 875, s/n, 16″ x 20″, pub Bl	42.00	110.00
☐ HOT TUB, rel. 1980. ed. 2,500, s/o, 8″ x 10″, pub Bl	14.00	50.00
☐ IT'S RAINING WITH TURTLE AND TOAD, rel. 1980. ed. 1,000, s/o, 8″ x 10″, pub Bl	14.00	40.00
☐ JOURNEY, BOY IN OLD BOAT, rel. 1980. ed. 1,000, s/o, 8″ x 10″, pub Bl	15.00	60.00
☐ KANSAS TO OZ, rel. 1980. ed. 1,000, s/n, 8″ x 10″, pub Bl	14.00	40.00
☐ LOVING YOU, rel. 1980. ed. 2,500, s/o, 5″ x 7″ pub Bl	9.00	35.00
☐ MAGIC SHOES, rel. 1980. ed. 1,000, s/n, 12″ x 16″, pub Bl	9.00	110.00
☐ MAGIC, rel. 1980. ed. 1,000, s/o, 8″ x 10″, pub Bl	14.00	60.00
☐ MAMA CAT, rel. 1980. ed. 1,000, s/o, 8″ x 10″, pub Bl	15.00	50.00
☐ MR. LARK I, rel. 1980. ed. 1,000, s/n, 12″ x 16″, pub Bl	24.00	80.00
☐ NEVER DO TODAY, rel. 1980. ed. 2,500, s/o, 5″ x 7″, pub Bl	9.00	25.00
☐ RAINBOW ROAD I, rel. 1980. ed. 1,000, s/n, 12″ x 16″, pub Bl	24.00	80.00
☐ REALITY, rel. 1980. ed. 2,500, s/o, 8″ x 10″, pub Bl	14.00	30.00
☐ BUGGED FROG II, rel. 1980. ed. 1,000, s/n, 12″ x 16″, pub Bl	24.00	120.00
☐ FLYING HORSE II, rel. 1980. ed. 2,500, s/o, 12″ x 16″, pub Bl	24.00	120.00
☐ HUGGING BEARS II, rel. 1980. ed. 1,000, s/n, 12″ x 16″, pub Bl	24.00	180.00
☐ PARENT'S HOLD II, rel. 1980. ed. 2,500, s/n, 8″ x 10″, pub Bl	14.00	60.00
☐ UNICORN II, rel. 1980. ed. 2,500, s/o, 12″ x 16″, pub Bl	24.00	120.00
☐ THANKS FROG, rel. 1980. ed. 2,500, s/o, 5″ x 7″, pub Bl	9.00	25.00
☐ TURKEY, rel. 1980. ed. 2,500, s/o, 8″ x 10″, pub Bl	14.00	40.00
☐ UNICORN IN THE GARDEN, rel. 1980. ed. 2,500, s/o, 5″ x 7″, pub Bl	9.00	35.00
☐ I'M NOT PERFECT, rel. 1980. ed. 2,500, s/o, 5″ x 7″, pub Bl	9.00	25.00
☐ WET BATHROOM WITH TWO CHILDREN, rel. 1980. ed. 1,000, s/o, 8″ x 10″, pub Bl..	14.00	50.00
☐ FRIENDS/SISTERS IN SWING, rel. 1981. ed. 4,500, s/n, 12″ x 16″, pub Bl	11.00	120.00
☐ I WANT A COOKIE II, rel. 1981. ed. 7,500, s/o, 5″ x 7″, pub Bl	4.00	30.00
☐ MOM'S HOLD WITH BIRD, rel. 1981. ed. 4,500, s/n, 12″ x 16″, pub Bl	26.00	140.00
☐ SISTERS IN THE GARDEN, rel. 1981. ed. 7,500, s/o, 5″ x 7″, pub Bl	4.00	30.00
☐ THANKS GRANDMA, rel. 1981. ed. 7,500, s/o, 5″ x 7″, pub Bl	4.00	30.00
☐ TOGETHER, rel. 1981. ed. 7,500, s/o, 5″ x 7″, pub Bl	4.00	30.00
☐ FINDING A FRIEND, rel. 1981. ed. 7,500, s/o, 5″ x 7″, pub Bl	4.00	30.00
☐ COUNT ON ME, rel. 1981. ed. 7,500, s/o, 5″ x 7″, pub Bl	4.00	30.00
☐ WHAT FATHER MEANS TO ME, rel. 1981. ed. 7,500, s/o, 5″ x 7″, pub Bl	4.00	30.00
☐ SISTERS ARE FOREVER, rel. 1982. ed. 7,500, s/o, 5″ x 7″, pub Bl	4.00	30.00
☐ MOM'S HOLD WITH BUNNY, rel. 1982. ed. 7,500, 5″ x 7″, pub Bl	4.00	30.00
☐ LOVE IS THE PROMISE, rel. 1982. ed. 7,500, s/o, 5″ x 7″, pub Bl	4.00	30.00
☐ ROOTS AND WINGS AND RAINBOW, rel. 1982. ed. 7,500, s/o, 5″ x 7″, pub Bl	4.00	30.00
☐ BE YOURSELF, rel. 1980. ed. 2,500, s/o, 5″ x 7″, pub Bl	9.00	25.00
☐ BE YOURSELF, rel. 1980. ed. 1,000, s/o, 8″ x 10″, pub Bl	14.00	40.00
☐ ANGELS CHARGE, rel. 1981. ed. 7,500, s/o, 5″ x 7″, pub Bl	6.00	40.00
☐ COUNT ON ME, rel. 1981. ed. 7,500, s/o, 5″ x 7″, pub Bl	4.00	30.00
☐ FRIENDS ARE FLOWERS, rel. 1981. ed. 7,500, s/o, 5″ x 7″, pub Bl	4.00	30.00
☐ FUN TRYING, rel. 1981. ed. 7,500, s/o, 5″ x 7″, pub Bl	4.00	30.00
☐ HAPPY CHILDHOOD, rel. 1981. ed. 7,500, s/o, 5″ x 7″, pub Bl	6.00	40.00
☐ MOTHER & CHILD, rel. 1981. ed. 7,500, s/o, 5″ x 7″, pub Bl	6.00	50.00
☐ NO PLACE LIKE MOMS, rel. 1981. ed. 7,500, s/o, 5″ x 7″, pub Bl	4.00	30.00
☐ CLEANLINESS, rel. 1982. ed. 7,500, s/o, 5″ x 7″, pub Bl	4.00	35.00
☐ PARENTS HOLD, rel. 1982. ed. 7,500, s/o, 5″ x 7″, pub Bl	11.00	140.00
☐ JUST ONE YOU, rel. 1983. ed. 7,500, s/o, 5″ x 7″, pub Bl	4.00	30.00

EDWARD J. BIERLY

THEMES: Wildlife art

STYLE: Realism

BOOKS: The artist's work appears in the *Animal Life Encyclopedia* by Dr. Bernhard Grzimek

AWARDS: Federal Duck Stamp Competition (1956, 1963, 1970)

MEMBERSHIPS: Society of Animal Artists

MUSEUMS/COLLECTIONS: Numerous museums have exhibited his work worldwide

GALLERY/DISTRIBUTOR: EJB Editions

	ISSUE PRICE	CURRENT PRICE
☐ **AMERICAN MERGANSERS,** rel. 1956-7. Federal Duck Stamp Print, ed. 325, s/o, 10" x 11½", pub EJB	15.00	1,000.00
*ed. 125, s/o, 10" x 11½", rel. 1967, pub EJB	40.00	800.00
*2nd printing, etching plate now canceled		
☐ **AMERICAN BRANT,** rel. 1963-4. Federal Duck Stamp Print, ed. 550, s/o, 12½" x 14", pub EJB	20.00	1,000.00
*ed. 125, s/o, 12½" x 14", rel. 1967, pub EJB	40.00	800.00
*2nd printing, etching plate now canceled		
☐ **ROSS GEESE,** rel. 1970-71. Federal Duck Stamp Print, ed. 700, s/n, 13" x 15", pub EJB	60.00	2,500.00
ed. 300, remarqued, 13" x 15", rel. 1970, pub EJB	100.00	3,750.00
ed. 2,150, s/n, 13" x 15", rel. 1976. pub EJB	100.00	150.00
☐ **LIONS AT WANKIE (Lion and Lioness),** rel. 1968. ed. 500, s/n, 20¼" x 27½", dist. EJB	50.00	—
☐ **THE AFRICAN QUEEN (Lioness and Cubs),** rel. 1968. ed. 750, s/n, 23" x 27", dist. EJB	50.00	—
☐ **MOHINI & CUB (White Tigress and Cubs),** rel. 1971. ed. 1,000, s/n, 22¾" x 29½", dist. EJB *Commissioned for the Smithsonian "Save the Tiger Fund"	100.00	—
☐ **EMPEROR GEESE PITCHING,** rel. 1972. ed. 500, s/n, 19½" x 25½", pub SEL	50.00	—
☐ **GIANT PANDAS,** rel. 1972. ed. 500, s/n, 19¾" x 27¾", pub SEL	50.00	100.00
ed. 50, remarqued	125.00	250.00
☐ **THE SURVIVOR (Wolf),** rel. 1974. ed. 250, s/n, 21" x 27", dist. EJB	60.00	200.00
☐ **BREAKING THE TRAIL (Bison),** rel. 1976. ed. 375, s/n, 24" x 32", pub EJB	100.00	—
☐ **CHALBI STAMPEDE (Zebra),** rel. 1976. ed. 375, s/n, 24" x 32", pub EJB *Commissioned by the Buffalo Zoological Society.	100.00	—
☐ **SNOW LEOPARD,** rel. 1976. ed. 500, s/n, 24¾" x 35", dist. EJB	150.00	450.00
☐ **FLAGS UP (White-tailed deer),** rel. 1977. ed. 800, s/n, 21¾" x 29", pub PP, distr. EJB	60.00	120.00
☐ **READY FOX,** rel. 1977. ed. 800, s/n, 21" x 26¼", pub PP, distr. EJB	60.00	150.00
☐ **WINTER WOODS (White-tailed deer),** rel. 1977. ed. 600, s/n, 24" x 32", pub EJB	100.00	350.00
☐ **BENGAL SUNSET (Tiger),** rel. 1978. ed. 800, s/n, 22¾" x 26", pub PP, distr. EJB	60.00	—
☐ **FLORIDA BASS,** rel. 1978. ed. 950, s/n, 21" x 26½", pub EJB	45.00	—
☐ **LEOPARD'S POOL,** rel. 1978. ed. 800, s/n, 22¾" x 26", pub PP, distr. EJB	60.00	—
☐ **A CLOSE CALL (Red Fox and Ruffed Grouse),** rel. 1979. ed. 800, s/n, 22¾" x 29", pub PP, distr. EJB	60.00	—
☐ **GREATER KUDU,** rel. 1979. ed. 500, s/n, 22" x 30½", pub EJB	100.00	—
☐ **THE NIGHT HARVESTERS (Canada Geese),** rel. 1979. ed. 800, s/n, 23" x 27", pub PP, distr. EJB	60.00	—
☐ **CLOUDED LEOPARD,** rel. 1980. ed. 600, s/n, 24½" x 32½", pub EJB	100.00	—
☐ **FOUR FLUSHED (Grey Fox & Quail),** rel. 1980. ed. 950, s/n, 22¾" x 27", pub EJB	75.00	—
☐ **DEN MOTHER (Red Fox & Cubs),** rel. 1981. ed. 950, s/n, 22¼" x 25¼", pub EJB	85.00	—
☐ **HAPPY HOUR (White-tailed Deer & Fawns),** rel. 1981. ed. 950, s/n, 19¾" x 23½", pub EJB	75.00	—

	ISSUE PRICE	CURRENT PRICE
☐ **MASAI WARRIOR,** rel. 1981. ed. 500, s/n, 20¼″ x 27″, pub EJB	100.00	—
☐ **TRANQUILITY (Giraffes),** rel. 1981. ed. 500, s/n, 21¼″ x 28″, pub EJB	100.00	—
☐ **FLIGHT OF FREEDOM (Bald Eagle),** rel. 1981. ed. 950, s/n, 24″ x 28″, pub EJB	150.00	—
ed. 50 remarqued	300.00	Sold Out
☐ **THE CHALLENGE (White-Tailed Deer),** rel. 1982. ed. 1,500, s/n, 12″ x 14″, pub SGL 1982 Deer Unlimited Stamp Print, includes stamp.	130.00	—
☐ **BLUEBIRDS (Western, Eastern and Mountain),** rel. 1983. ed. 950, s/n, 15″ x 19½″, pub EJB	150.00	—
rel. 1983, ed. 3,000, I/o, 15″ x 19½″, pub EJB	75.00	—
Commissioned by Campfire, Inc. Sold only as a portfolio of three prints.		

RICHARD BISHOP

THEMES: Wildlife art

GALLERY/DISTRIBUTOR: Wild Wings, Inc.

	ISSUE PRICE	CURRENT PRICE
☐ **BLUE WINGS,** no information available, distr. WWI	35.00	250.00
☐ **FLOODED TIMBER - MALLARDS,** no information available, distr. WWI	40.00	400.00
☐ **GOOD CALLING - MALLARDS,** no information available, distr. WWI	60.00	400.00
☐ **IN THE BAG - MALLARDS,** no information available, distr. WWI	35.00	250.00
☐ **IN THE STOCKS - MALLARDS,** no information available, distr. WWI	60.00	300.00
☐ **OVERFLOW - MALLARDS,** no information available, distr. WWI	64.00	400.00
☐ **SAFE RETURN - MALLARDS,** no information available, distr. WWI	52.00	300.00

BEN BLACK

THEMES: Still life art

STYLE: Combination of resonant color, free-flowing texture, and disciplined pattern

EDUCATION: Massachusetts College of Art

AWARDS: Richard Minton Juror's Award, in the Annual Exhibition of Contemporary New England Artists

MUSEUMS/COLLECTIONS: His paintings are being exhibited internationally

GALLERY/DISTRIBUTOR: Eleanor Ettinger, Inc.

	ISSUE PRICE	CURRENT PRICE
☐ **BIRDS AND FAN,** rel. 1980. ed. 275, s/n, 26½″ x 20½″, pub EEI	200.00	225.00
☐ **LOVELY VICTORIANA,** rel. 1980. ed. 275, s/n, 24″ x 20″, pub EEI	200.00	225.00
☐ **MOMENT FOR THE CLOWN,** rel. 1980. ed. 275, s/n, 27″ x 19″, pub EEI	200.00	225.00
☐ **SWEET ALICE DOLLS,** rel. 1980. ed. 275, s/n, 24″ x 20″, pub EEI	200.00	225.00

ROBERT H. BLAIR

THEMES: Life in the Rocky Mountains in a past century

MEDIUM: Watercolor

AWARDS: Gold medal in watercolor at the first Western Artists of America exhibit in Reno, Nevada, 1979 and a similar medal at the Frank Tenney Johnson Memorial Show the following spring

GALLERY/DISTRIBUTOR: Wild Wings, Inc.

	ISSUE PRICE	CURRENT PRICE
☐ **SUCCESSFUL RAID,** rel. 1982. ed. 500, s/n, litho, 25¾" x 17¾", pub WWI	85.00	—
☐ **TURNING BACK AT RED LAKE HILL,** rel. 1982. ed. 500, s/n, litho, 26" x 17½", pub WWI...	85.00	—

CIRCLE OF ANTIQUITY *by Carolyn Blish*

CAROLYN BLISH

THEMES: Varied

MEDIUM: Watercolor

EDUCATION: Bradford Junior College; Studied with watercolorist Edgar A. Whitney

AWARDS: Numerous awards and honors throughout her career

MEMBERSHIPS: American Watercolor Society; Allied Artists of America

GALLERY/DISTRIBUTOR: Greenwich Workshop

	ISSUE PRICE	CURRENT PRICE
☐ BEACHED, rel. 1973. 1,500, s/n, 31" x 21", pub GW	65.00	125.00
☐ ROADSIDE DAISIES, rel. 1973. ed. 1,000, s/n, 34" x 24", pub GW	65.00	215.00
☐ SIMPLICITY, rel. 1973. ed. 1,500, s/n, 26" x 18¼", pub GW	45.00	105.00
☐ WONDERMENT, rel. 1973. ed. 1,000, s/n, 28" x 22", pub GW	45.00	250.00
☐ MISTY SEA, rel. 1975. ed. 1,000, s/n, 35" x 15½", pub GW	65.00	185.00
☐ SHORE BIRDS, rel. 1974. ed. 1,000, s/n, 26" x 18", pub GW	55.00	240.00
☐ SEASONS (Portfolio of 4 Prints), rel. 1975. ed. 1,000, s/n, 9" x 11", pub GW	60.00	95.00
☐ AFTER THE STORM, rel. 1976. ed. 1,000, s/n, 35" x 19", pub GW	65.00	105.00
☐ BLUEBELLS AND DAFFODILS, rel. 1976. ed. 1,000, s/n, 31" x 22½", pub GW	65.00	175.00
☐ DISCOVERY, rel. 1976. ed. 1,000, s/n, 31" x 18½", pub GW	65.00	170.00
☐ STORM'S EDGE, rel. 1977. ed. 1,000, s/n, 34" x 18", pub GW	65.00	115.00
☐ FLIGHT, rel. 1977. ed. 1,000, s/n, 40" x 26", pub GW	75.00	315.00
☐ THE HIGHEST DUNE, rel. 1977. ed. 1,500, s/n, 22" x 29", pub GW	55.00	145.00
☐ FLIGHT II, rel. 1978. ed. 1,500, s/n, 18" x 28", pub GW	65.00	185.00
☐ DAY DREAM, rel. 1978. ed. 1,500, s/n, 14½" x 22½", pub GW	65.00	150.00
☐ TIDE'S EDGE, rel. 1978. ed. 1,500, s/n, 34" x 17¼", pub GW	65.00	
☐ WASHDAY, rel. 1978. ed. 1,500, s/n, 32" x 22", pub GW	65.00	Sold Out
☐ WINDSURF, rel. 1978. ed. 1,500, s/n, 32" x 20", pub GW	65.00	Sold Out
☐ A CLOSER LOOK, rel. 1979. ed. 1,500, s/n, 21½" x 27", pub GW	65.00	—
☐ A QUIET PLACE, rel. 1979. ed. 1,500, s/n, 32" x 22", pub GW	65.00	Sold Out
☐ RAGGEDY ANN, rel. 1979. ed. 1,500, s/n, 18" x 20", pub GW	75.00	Sold Out
☐ BRIGHT ENCOUNTER, rel. 1980. ed. 1,500, s/n, 28" x 20", pub GW	75.00	Sold Out
☐ LAST LEAVES, rel. 1980. ed. 1,500, s/n, 32" x 21¾", pub GW	75.00	Sold Out
☐ REMEMBER A SWING, rel. 1980. ed. 1,500, s/n, 32" x 21½", pub GW	75.00	Sold Out
☐ MAKE A WISH, rel. 1982. ed. 1,000, s/n, 17⅝" x 22⅝", pub GW	125.00	—
☐ SAND TREASURES, rel. 1981. ed. 1,000, s/n, 28" x 22½", pub GW	125.00	—
☐ WIND BORNE, rel. 1981. ed. 1,500, s/n, 22½" x 29½", pub GW	85.00	—
☐ CIRCLE OF ANTIQUITY, rel. 1984. ed. 1,000, s/n, 10" x 18½", pub GW	95.00	—
☐ SLEEPY TIME PAL, rel. 1985. open edition, s/o, litho, 21⅞" x 18⅜", pub GW	50.00	—

CHRISTOPHER BLOSSOM

THEMES: Marine art

MEMBERSHIPS: Charter member of the American Society of Marine Artists

GALLERY/DISTRIBUTOR: Greenwich Workshop

COMMENTS: Christopher Blossom's sailing experience combined with careful research adds an air of authenticity to his work

	ISSUE PRICE	CURRENT PRICE
☐ **FIRST OUT,** rel. 1983. ed. 450, s/n, 31″ x 21″, pub GW	90.00	145.00
ed. 25, remarqued...	190.00	245.00
☐ **DECEMBER,MOONRISE,** rel. 1984. ed. 625, s/n, litho, 30¾″ x 22″, pub GW	135.00	150.00
ed. 25, remarqued	190.00	225.00
☐ **ALLERTON ON THE EAST RIVER,** rel. 1985. ed. 650, s/n, 30¾″ x 21¾″, pub GW .	145.00	—
☐ **TRANQUIL DAWN,** rel. 1985. ed. 650, s/n, litho, 2″ x 17¹³⁄₁₆″, pub GW	85.00	—

CYNTHIA BOGART

THEMES: Country landscapes, seascapes, events, children's subjects, (i.e. teddy bears, rocking horses)

MEDIUM: Acrylic on canvas on board

STYLE: Sophisticated Americana

GALLERY/DISTRIBUTOR: Friend Field, Inc.

COMMENTS: Cynthia Bogart has been receiving wide acclaim in her style and work nationally, as well as internationally. It is a mix of the American Primitive and the Realistic. She was a protégée of Harold Ransom Stevenson, who was a protégé of Norman Rockwell and famed illustrator Frank C. Riley

	ISSUE PRICE	CURRENT PRICE
☐ **A CHILD'S FANTASY,** rel. 1983. ed. 2,000, s/n, 20″ x 30″, pub FFI	22.50	80.00
☐ **SUNDAY PICNIC AT BERRY GROVE,** rel. 1983. ed. 2,000, s/n, 20″ x 26″, pub FFI ..	22.50	80.00
☐ **A CRANBERRY CONE FOURTH OF JULY,** rel. 1984. 16″ x 24″, pub FFI	25.00	36.00
☐ **A TWIN'S HOMECOMING,** rel. 1984. 15″ x 20″, pub FFI	25.00	36.00
☐ **HENRIETTA,** rel. 1984. 10″ x 14″, pub FFI	20.00	30.00
☐ **MOOTHILDA,** rel. 1984. 10″ x 14″, pub FFI	20.00	30.00
☐ **PIGNELOPE,** rel. 1984. 10″ x 14″, pub FFI	20.00	30.00
☐ **POLO, A DAY IN THE COUNTRY,** rel. 1984. 18″ x 24″, pub FFI	25.00	36.00
☐ **WOOLHEMINA,** rel. 1984. 10″ x 24″, pub FFI	20.00	30.00
☐ **TEDDA,** rel. 1985. 11″ x 16″, pub FFI	40.00	—
☐ **TEDDA BOY BLUE,** rel. 1985. 11″ x 16″, pub FFI	40.00	—

SEAN BOLLAR

THEMES: Wildlife art

BACKGROUND: Bollar worked as a marine research biologist, and a teacher of marine science

GALLERY/DISTRIBUTOR: Pandion Gallery, Ltd.

COMMENTS: Even when he portrays his subject at rest, the vibrant life and constant awareness upon which the survival of any wild cretaure depends is unmistakably conveyed

	ISSUE PRICE	CURRENT PRICE
☐ FLORIDA SCREECH OWL, rel. 1973. ed. 800, s/n, 16″ x 22″, pub PGL	25.00	180.00
ed. 1,200, s/o	15.00	105.00
☐ RED-SHOULDERED HAWK, rel. 1973. ed. 1,000, s/n, pub PGL	25.00	130.00
ed. 2,000, s/o	15.00	75.00
☐ FLORIDA PANTHER, rel. 1974. ed. 1,000, s/n, 16″ x 17″, pub PGL	25.00	160.00
ed. 2,000, s/o	15.00	80.00
☐ RED-HEADED WOODPECKER, rel. 1975. ed. 800, s/n, 12″ x 16″, pub PGL	24.00	30.00
ed. 1, 200, s/o	14.00	20.00
☐ JAGUAR PORTRAIT, rel. 1976. ed. 900, s/n, 16″ x 20″, pub PGL	45.00	55.00
ed. 1,000, s/o	35.00	45.00
☐ ROYAL BENGAL TIGER, rel. 1977. ed. 900, s/n, 19½″ x 25½″, pub PGL	60.00	75.00
ed. 1,000, s/o	50.00	60.00
☐ SQUIRREL TREEFROG, rel. 1977. ed. 900, s/n, 12″ x 16″, pub PGL	30.00	—
ed. 1,000, s/o	20.00	—
☐ BENGAL TIGER PORTRAIT, rel. 1979. ed. 900, s/n, 16″ x 20″, pub PGL	55.00	—

BRUCE BOMBERGER

THEMES: Varied

EDUCATION: Berkeley (CA) School of Arts and Crafts, Art Center School

GALLERY/DISTRIBUTOR: Eleanor Ettinger, Inc.

COMMENTS: Bomberger states: "I know many people like my pictures for the same reason that I create them—because they love the real places I'm depicting"

	ISSUE PRICE	CURRENT PRICE
☐ BASTILLE DAY, rel. 1977. ed. 250, s/n, litho, arches, 30″ x 24½″, pub EEI	150.00	1000.00
ed. 50, japon	175.00	1050.00
☐ BUTTER, EGGS & CHEESE, rel. 1977. ed. 250, s/n, litho, arches, 28″ x 22¾″, pub EEI	150.00	1,000.00
ed. 50 japon	175.00	1050.00
☐ RUE LE JOUR, rel. 1977. ed. 250, s/n, litho, arches, 28½″ x 23½″, pub EEI	175.00	400.00
ed. 50, japon	200.00	450.00
☐ ART DIRECTOR, rel. 1978. ed. 250, s/n, litho, arches, 31″ x 25″, pub EEI	200.00	800.00
ed. 50, japon	225.00	850.00
☐ BOOKSTALLS, rel. 1978. ed. 250, s/n, litho, arches, 27″ x 23″, pub EEI	250.00	400.00
ed. 50, japon	275.00	450.00
☐ ENGLISH PUBS PORTFOLIO, rel. 1978. ed. 250, s/n, litho, arches, 29″ x 24″, pub EEI	1,200.00	1,600.00
ed. 50, japon	1,400.00	1,800.00
☐ L'ESCARGOT, rel. 1978. ed. 250, s/n, litho, arches, 32″ x 27″, pub EEI	175.00	850.00
ed. 50, japon	200.00	950.00
☐ PONT ROYALE, rel. 1978. ed. 250, s/n, litho, arches, 27″ x 21½″, pub EEI	175.00	350.00
ed. 50, japon	200.00	400.00
☐ FLEA MARKET, rel. 1979. ed. 250, s/n, litho, arches, 34″ x 24″, pub EEI	275.00	350.00
ed. 50, japon	300.00	400.00
☐ GREENGROCER, rel. 1979. ed. 250, s/n, litho, arches, 29¼″ x 23¾″, pub EEI	250.00	350.00
ed. 50, japon	275.00	400.00
☐ SACRE COEUR, rel. 1979. ed. 250, s/n, litho, arches, 29¼″ x 24″, pub EEI	250.00	350.00
ed. 50, japon	275.00	400.00
☐ PARIS METRO, rel. 1980. ed. 250, s/n, litho, arches, 24″ x 34″, pub EEI	275.00	350.00
ed. 50, japon	300.00	400.00

RUE LE JOUR *by Bruce Bomberger*

HERB BOOTH

THEMES: Wildlife art

GALLERY/DISTRIBUTOR: Meredith Long & Company

	ISSUE PRICE	CURRENT PRICE
☐ **BLOWIN' IN,** rel. 1982. ed. 600, s/n, size NA, pub MLC	95.00	—
☐ **BREAK AWAY,** rel. 1982. ed. 600, s/n, size NA, pub MLC	85.00	95.00
☐ **BRUSHLAND BOB,** ed. 600, s/n, 22″ x 28½″, pub MLC	85.00	500.00
☐ **CALLIN 'EM IN,** rel. 1980. ed. 600, s/n, size NA, pub MLC	95.00	—
☐ **DOWN AND BACK,** ed. 600, s/n, 22″ x 28½″, pub MLC	85.00	85.00
☐ **GOOD SPORT,** ed. 600, s/o, 22″ x 28½″, pub MLC	60.00	85.00
☐ **HOME PLACE,** ed. 600, s/o, 22″ x 28½″, pub MLC	50.00	250.00
☐ **SEPTEMBER,** rel. 1980. ed. 600, s/n, 27″ x 20″, pub MLC	85.00	500.00
☐ **SPLIT COVEY,** ed. 600, s/o, 22″ x 28½″, pub MLC	60.00	85.00
☐ **THE THREE WISE MEN,** ed. 600, s/o, 22″ x 28½″, pub MLC	50.00	250.00

STAN BORACK

THEMES: Western art

GALLERY/DISTRIBUTOR: Sawyier Collection, Inc.

CALLIN' 'EM IN *by Herb Booth*

DAWN'S LIGHT *by Stan Borack*

		ISSUE PRICE	CURRENT PRICE
☐	**DAWN'S LIGHT,** rel. 1981. ed. 950, s/n, 18″ x 27″, pub SCI*	65.00	—
☐	**AWAITING THE SIGNAL,** rel. 1982. ed. 350, s/n, size NA, pub SCI*	65.00	—
	*Represents the Sawyier Collection, Inc., and was formed as a subsidiary of Paul Sawyier Galleries, Inc.		

WINTER AT THE PUEBLO *by James Boren*

JAMES BOREN

THEMES: Western art

EDUCATION: Kansas City Art Institute; Kansas City University

AWARDS: Texas State Artist (1976)

MEMBERSHIPS: Two-term president of the Cowboy Artists of America

GALLERY/DISTRIBUTOR: Texas Art Press; Mill Pond Press, Inc.

		ISSUE PRICE	CURRENT PRICE
☐	**RAINY DAY AT HILLSBORO,** rel. 1977. ed. 950, s/n, 20½″ x 27½″, pub MPPI	75.00	100.00
☐	**FIRST LIGHT OF A WINTER'S MORNING,** rel. 1978. ed. 2,250, s/n, 14″ x 22″, pub TAP	85.00	150.00
☐	**FIRST LIGHT OF A WINTER'S MORNING,** rel. 1979. ed. 2,250, s/n, 14″ x 22″, pub TAP	85.00	—
☐	**IN LATE APRIL,** rel. 1979. ed. 2,250, s/n, 16″ x 22″, pub TAP	85.00	—

	ISSUE PRICE	CURRENT PRICE
☐ REST STOP AT A WARM KITCHEN, rel. 1979. ed. 950, s/n, 21″ x 28¾″, pub MPPI	95.00	150.00
☐ A WET MORNING, rel. 1980. ed. 2,2,50, s/n, 14″ x 22″, pub TAP	100.00	—
☐ PRAYER MEETIN' TIME, rel. 1980. ed. 2,250, s/n, 20″ x 28″, pub TAP	100.00	—
☐ WINTER IN THE ROCKIES, rel. 1980. ed. 2,250, s/n, 21″ x 28″, pub TAP	100.00	—
☐ WINTER IN STEPHENVILLE, rel. 1980. ed. 2,250, s/n, 20½″ x 22″, pub TAP	100.00	—
☐ EARLY TEXAS OIL, rel. 1981. ed. 1,050, s/n, 17″ x 26½″, pub TAP	100.00	—
☐ EARLY TEXAS WINTER, rel. 1981. ed. 750, s/n, 16″ x 22″, pub TAP	100.00	—
☐ 'NEATH A WARM WINTER SUN, rel. 1981. ed. 950, s/n, 21¾″ x 32¼″, pub MPPI ..	150.00	—
☐ WINTER AT THE PUEBLO, rel. 1981. ed. 550, s/n, 23″ x 28¾″, pub MPPI	125.00	—
☐ LAZY DAY AT LUCKENBACH, rel. 1982. ed. 1,000, s/n, 20″ x 29″, pub TAP	100.00	—
☐ MENDING WALL, rel. 1982. ed. 1,250, s/n, 18¾″ x 25″, pub TAP	100.00	—
☐ AFTER THE SPRING STORM, rel. 1983. ed. 950. s/n, 17½″ x 23⅞″, pub MPPI	75.00	—

LITTLE BROWN CHURCH by Jodie Boren

JODIE BOREN

THEMES: Western art

EDUCATION: Art Institute in Kansas City

GALLERY/DISTRIBUTOR: Frame House Gallery, Inc.

COMMENTS: The artist states: "It is my desire to furnish the stage and the setting; you create the play"

	ISSUE PRICE	CURRENT PRICE
☐ **MAC'S TRADING POST,** rel. 1982. ed. 975, s/n, 24″ x 34″, pub FHG	75.00	—
☐ **MAIN STREET, DODGE CITY,** rel. 1982. ed. 975, s/n, 16″ x 32″, pub FHG	75.00	—
☐ **RETURNING HUNTER,** rel. 1982. ed. 975, s/n, 20″ x 25½″, pub FHG	75.00	—
☐ **THE LITTLE BROWN CHURCH,** rel. 1983. ed. 750, s/n, 18½″ x 20″, pub FHG	90.00	—
☐ **RENDEZVOUS WITH THE 707,** rel. 1983. ed. 750, s/n, 30″ x 18½″, pub FHG	90.00	—

JANUARY 14th by George Boutwell

GEORGE BOUTWELL

THEMES: Varied

MEDIUM: Watercolors

AWARDS: The artist has won many awards for his work

GALLERY/DISTRIBUTOR: George Boutwell

COMMENTS: The artist states: "I like people and I want those who view my work to feel relaxed and refreshed. I see beauty all around me and I try to share it"

	ISSUE PRICE	CURRENT PRICE
☐ FENCE LINE, rel. 1970. ed. 1,000, s/n, 5″ x 7″, offset litho, pub BGL	1.00	20.00
☐ GOLD MINER, rel. 1970. ed. 500, s/n, 15½″ x 13½″, offset litho, pub BGL	3.00	20.00
☐ MISSOURI PACIFIC RAILROAD, rel. 1970. ed. 500, s/n, 8″ x 20″, offset litho, pub BGL...	4.00	100.00
☐ RED-SHOULDERED HAWK, rel. 1970. ed. 500, s/n, 11¼″ x 12¾″, offset litho, pub BGL...	2.00	50.00
☐ ROADRUNNER, rel. 1970. ed. 500. s/n, 11¼″ x 10¼″, offset litho, pub BGL	2.00	60.00
☐ STEAM ENGINE, rel. 1971. ed. 25, signed on Plate and Hand Numbered Engravings, 11″ x 14″, pub BGL	90.00	500.00
☐ WILD TURKEYS, rel. 1971. ed. 25, signed on Plate and Hand Numbered Engraving, 11″ x 14″, pub BGL	90.00	500.00
☐ BRONC RIDER, rel. 1972. ed. 25, signed on Plate and Hand Numbered Engraving, 5″ x 7″, pub BGL	15.00	75.00
☐ MOUNTAIN CABIN, rel. 1972. ed. 25, signed on Plate and Hand Numbered Engraving, 5″ x 7″, pub BGL	15.00	75.00
☐ OWL, rel. 1972. ed. 25, signed on Plate and Hand Numbered Engraving, 8″ x 10″, pub. BGL..	40.00	200.00
☐ BREMOND HOUSE, rel. 1973. ed. 17, signed on Plate and Hand Numbered Engraving. 16″ x 20″, pub BGL	125.00	600.00
☐ BREMOND HOUSE, rel. 1973. ed. 1,000, s/n, 8½″ x 11″, offset litho, pub WPC ..... *Special Promotion Editions, used as Christmas Gifts and Sales Incentives.	*	40.00
☐ HOUGHTON HOUSE, rel. 1973. ed. 13, signed on Plate and Hand Numbered Engraving, 16″ x 20″, pub BGL	125.00	500.00
☐ HOUGHTON HOUSE, rel. 1973. ed. 1,000, s/n, 8½″ x 11″, offset litho, pub WPC .... *Special Promotion Editions, used as Christmas Gifts and Sales Incentives.	*	40.00
☐ ST. MARY'S CATHEDRAL, rel. 1973. ed. 14, signed on Plate and Hand Numbered Engraving, 16″ x 20″, pub BGL	125.00	500.00
☐ ST. MARY'S CATHEDRAL, rel. 1973. ed. 1,000, s/n, 8½″ x 11″, offset litho, pub WPC . *Special Promotion Editions, used as Christmas Gifts and Sales Incentives.	*	20.00
☐ SOUTHERN PACIFIC, rel. 1973. ed. 1,000, s/n, 4″ x 9″, offset litho, pub BGL .... *Special Promotion Editions, used as Christmas Gifts and Sales Incentives.	*	30.00
☐ ANTLER HOTEL, rel. 1974. ed. 7, s/n, 16″ x 20″, engraving, pub HLNB .... *Special Promotion Editions, used as Christmas Gifts and Sales Incentives.	*	200.00
☐ BIBLE HOUSE, rel. 1974. ed. s/n, 16″ x 20″, engraving, pub HLNB .... *Special Promotion Editions, used as Christmas Gifts and Sales Incentives.	*	150.00
☐ DRISKILL HOTEL, rel. 1974. ed. 17, signed on Plate and Hand Numbered Engraving, 16″ x 20″, pub BGL	150.00	600.00
☐ DRISKILL HOTEL, rel. 1974. ed. 1,000, s/n, 8½″ x 11″, offset litho, pub BGL .... *Special Promotion Editions, used as Christmas Gifts and Sales Incentives.	*	40.00
☐ FORT CROGAN, rel. 1974. ed. 76, s/n, 16″ x 20″, engraving, pub HLNB .... *Special Promotion Editions, used as Christmas Gifts and Sales Incentives.	*	175.00
☐ GRANITE MOUNTAIN, rel. 1974. ed. 76, s/n, 16″ x 20″, engraving, pub HLNB .... *Special Promotion Editions, used as Christmas Gifts and Sales Incentives.	*	175.00
☐ LBJ RANCH HOUSE, rel. 1974. ed. 76. s/n, 16″ x 20″, engraving, pub HLNB .... *Special Promotion Editions, used as Christmas Gifts and Sales Incentives.	*	200.00
☐ LITTLEFIELD HOUSE, rel. 1974. ed. 13, signed on Plate and Hand Numbered Engraving, 16″ x 20″, pub BGL	150.00	500.00
☐ LITTLEFIELD HOUSE, rel. 1974. ed. 1,000, s/n, 8½″ x 11″, offset litho, pub WPC ... *Special Promotion Editions, used as Christmas Gifts and Sales Incentives.	*	25.00
☐ LLANO HIGH SCHOOL, rel. 1974. ed. 76, s/n, 16″ x 20″, engraving, pub HLNB ..... *Special Promotion Editions, used as Christmas Gifts and Sales Incentives.	*	125.00
☐ MASON COURTHOUSE, rel. 1984. ed. 76, s/n, 16″ x 20″, engraving, pub HLNB ..... *Special Promotion Editions, used as Christmas Gifts and Sales Incentives.	*	150.00
☐ SOUTHWESTERN UNIVERSITY, rel. 1974. ed. 76. s/n, 16″ x 20″, engraving, pub HLNB.. *Special Promotion Editions, used as Christmas Gifts and Sales Incentives.	*	175.00
☐ TEXAS CAPITOL, rel. 1974. ed. 7. s/n, engraving, pub HLNB .... *Special Promotion Editions, used as Christmas Gifts and Sales Incentives.	*	250.00
☐ TEXAS GOVERNOR'S MANSION, rel. 1974. ed. 76, s/n, 16″ x 20″, engraving, pub HLNB.. *Special Promotion Editions, used as Christmas Gifts and Sales Incentives.	*	200.00

	ISSUE PRICE	CURRENT PRICE
☐ **WINDMILL,** rel. 1974. ed. 1,250, s/n, 4″ x 9″, offset litho, pub BGL	5.00	25.00
☐ **ARMADILLO,** rel. 1975. ed. 250, s/n, 7″ x 13″, offset litho, pub BGL	5.00	40.00
☐ **BOB WHITE,** rel. 1975. ed. 150, s/n, 8″ x 10″, offset litho, pub BGL	5.00	20.00
☐ **CANADA GOOSE,** rel. 1975. ed. 150. s/n, 7″ x 14″, offset litho, pub BGL	5.00	25.00
☐ **CASWELL HOUSE,** rel. 1975. ed. 6, signed on Plate and Hand Numbered Engraving, 16″ x 20″, pub BGL	150.00	500.00
☐ **CASWELL HOUSE,** rel. 1975. ed. 1,000, s/n, 8½″ x 11″, offset litho, pub WPC	*	20.00
*Special Promotion Editions, used as Christmas Gifts and Sales Incentives.		
☐ **DeWITT CLINTON RAILROAD,** rel. 1975. ed. 250, s/n, 10″ x 20″, offset litho, pub BGL	5.00	10.00
☐ **DONNAN HOUSE,** rel. 1975. ed. 5, signed on Plate and Hand Numbered Engraving, 16″ x 20″, pub BGL	150.00	500.00
☐ **DONNAN HOUSE,** rel. 1975. ed. 1,000, s/n, 8½″ x 11″, offset litho, pub WPC	*	15.00
☐ **ONE ROW PLANTER,** rel. 1975. ed. 1,750, s/n, 4″ x 6″, offset litho, pub BGL	*	10.00
*Special Promotion Editions, used as Christmas Gifts and Sales Incentives.		
☐ **PELICAN,** rel. 1975. ed. 150, s/n, 5″ x 12½″, offset litho, pub BGL	5.00	30.00
☐ **SQUIRREL,** rel. 1975. ed. 150. s/n, 8″ x 10″, offset litho, pub BGL	5.00	25.00
☐ **WILD TURKEYS,** rel. 1975. ed. 150, s/n, 12″ x 16″, offset litho, pub BGL	10.00	25.00
☐ **WINDMILL TANK,** rel. 1975. ed. 250, s/n, 9″ x 12″, offset litho, pub BGL	5.00	35.00
☐ **GAP GATE,** rel. 1975. ed. 1,000, s/n, 6″ x 9″, offset litho, pub BGL	2.00	20.00
☐ **GAIL TEXAS,** rel. 1975. ed. 1,000, s/n, 11″ x 16″, offset litho, pub BGL	10.00	60.00
☐ **THE ENCOUNTER,** rel. 1975. ed. 1,000, s/n, 19″ x 25″, offset litho, pub BGL	20.00	40.00
☐ **FREEDOM REGAINED,** rel. 1975. ed. 1,000, s/n, 11″ x 25″, offset litho, pub BGL	15.00	125.00
☐ **A PLAY OF LIGHT,** rel. 1975. ed. 1,000, s/n, 13″ x 17″, offset litho, pub BGL	15.00	25.00
☐ **BLACK PORCH ANNIE,** rel. 1976. ed. 750, s/n, 11″ x 16″, offset litho, pub BGL	15.00	250.00
☐ **BOUTWELL HOME,** rel. 1976. ed. 2,400, s/n, 8½″ x 11″, offset litho, pub BGL	10.00	30.00
☐ **CHRISTMAS EVE,** rel. 1976. ed. 750, s/n, 11″ x 25″, offset litho, pub BGL	20.00	40.00
☐ **HILL COUNTRY,** rel. 1976. ed. 750, s/n, 13″ x 17″, offset litho, pub BGL	20.00	40.00
☐ **MARTIN CABINESS HOUSE,** rel. 1976. ed. 4, signed on Plate and Hand Numbered Engraving, 16″ x 20″, pub BGL	150.00	500.00
☐ **MARTIN CABINESS HOUSE,** rel. 1976. ed. 1,000, s/n, 8½″ x 11″, offset litho, pub WPC	*	20.00
*Special Promotion Editions, used as Christmas Gifts and Sales Incentives.		
☐ **ST. EDWARDS UNIVERSITY,** rel. 1976. ed. 4, signed on Plate and Hand Numbered Engraving, 16″ x 20″, pub BGL	150.00	500.00
☐ **ST. EDWARDS UNIVERSITY,** rel. 1976. ed. 1,000, s/n, 8½″ x 11″, offset litho, pub WPC	*	25.00
*Special Promotion Editions, used as Christmas Gifts and Sales Incentives.		
☐ **I'VE CROSSED THAT BRIDGE BEFORE,** rel. 1977. ed. 500, s/n, 12″ x 17″, offset litho, pub BGL	20.00	80.00
☐ **MARTHA'S FANTASY,** rel. 1977. ed. 500, s/n, 13″ x 22″, offset litho, pub BGL	20.00	40.00
☐ **MY BACK YARD,** rel. 1977. ed. 310, pub BGL	10.00	30.00
☐ **NEIL COCHRAN HOUSE,** rel. 1977. ed. 2, signed on Plate and Hand Numbered Engraving, 16″ x 20″, pub BGL	150.00	500.00
☐ **NEIL COCHRAN HOUSE,** rel. 1977. ed. 1,000, s/n, 8½″ x 11″, offset litho, pub WPC	*	20.00
*Special Promotion Editions, used as Christmas Gifts and Sales Incentives.		
☐ **A NICE TREE,** rel. 1977. ed. 750, s/n, 19″ x 25″, offset litho, pub BGL	25.00	200.00
☐ **PRAIRIE DELL TEXAS,** rel. 1977. ed. 500, s/n, 13″ x 23″, offset litho, pub BGL	20.00	125.00
☐ **LAZY AFTERNOON,** rel. 1978. ed. 500, s/n, 17″ x 17″, offset litho, pub BGL	25.00	150.00
☐ **LUNCHLINE AT THE ANCHOR X,** rel. 1978. ed. 500, s/n, 9″ x 21″, offset litho, pub BGL	20.00	300.00
☐ **MEMORIES,** rel. 1978. ed. 500, s/n, 13″ x 16″, offset litho, pub BGL	20.00	60.00
☐ **MUDDY ROAD,** rel. 1978. ed. 4,400, s/n, 8½″ x 8½″, offset litho, pub BGL	10.00	40.00
☐ **TEXAS CLASSIC,** rel. 1978. ed. 500, s/n, 13″ x 25″, offset litho, pub BGL	25.00	300.00
☐ **A TRIBUTE TO TWO TREES,** rel. 1978. ed. 500, s/n, 17½″ x 23″, offset litho, pub BGL	25.00	250.00
☐ **THE BROWN LIZARD,** rel. 1979. ed. 500, s/n, 13″ x 17″, offset litho, pub BGL	25.00	125.00
☐ **A HERO THAT WOULDN'T DIE,** rel. 1979. ed. 500, s/n, 12″ x 16″, offset litho, pub BGL	25.00	150.00
☐ **PASSING BY,** rel. 1979. ed. 500, s/n, 19″ x 25″, offset litho, pub BGL	35.00	400.00
☐ **WEST TEXAS MORNING,** rel. 1979. ed. 500, s/n, 12″ x 25″, offset litho, pub BGL ...	25.00	70.00
☐ **WINGS OF IMAGINATION,** rel. 1979. ed. 6,700, s/n, 8½″ x 8½″, offset litho, pub BGL	*	20.00
*Special Promotion Editions, used as Christmas Gifts and Sales Incentives.		

	ISSUE PRICE	CURRENT PRICE
☐ BRIGHT COLORED BIRD, rel. 1980. ed. 7,600, s/n, 8½" x 5½", offset litho, pub BGL	*	10.00
*Special Promotion Editions, used as Christmas Gifts and Sales Incentives.		
☐ BRUSH COUNTRY, rel. 1980. ed. 500. s/n, 16" x 24", offset litho, pub BGL	35.00	250.00
☐ COUNTRY CANTINA, rel. 1980. ed. 500, s/n, 16" x 20", offset litho, pub BGL	35.00	400.00
☐ HIGHLIGHT OF THE DAY, rel. 1980. ed. 500, s/n, 16" x 20", offset litho, pub BGL ...	35.00	350.00
☐ McKINNEY FALLS, rel. 1980. ed. 500, s/n, 16" dia., offset litho, pub BGL	25.00	50.00
☐ THE LUCKY ONE, rel. 1981. ed. 9,300, s/n, size N/A, offset litho, pub BGL	*	10.00
*Special Promotion Editions, used as Christmas Gifts and Sales Incentives.		
☐ MUD ISLAND, rel. 1981. ed. 500, s/n, 12" x 24", offset litho, pub BGL	45.00	225.00
☐ MY FRONT YARD, rel. 1981. ed. 500, s/n, 12" x 16", offset litho, pub BGL	30.00	30.00
☐ TEXAS BLUE NORTHER, rel. 1981. ed. 500, s/n, 8½" x 24", offset litho, pub BGL ..	40.00	250.00
☐ EXOTIC BIRD, rel. 1982. ed. 10,600, s/n, offset litho, pub BGL	*	10.00
☐ HAVEN OF THORNS, rel. 1982. ed. 1,000, s/n, offset litho, pub GB	35.00	80.00
☐ IN THE NICK OF TIME, rel. 1982. ed. 500, s/n, offset litho, pub GB	45.00	100.00
☐ JANUARY 14th, rel. 1982. ed. 500, s/n, offset litho, pub GB	45.00	225.00
☐ PECAN STREET FESTIVAL POSTER, rel. 1982. ed. 1,000, s/n, size N/A, offset litho, pub BGL	25.00	35.00
☐ SHADY LANE, rel. 1982. ed. 500, s/n, offset litho, pub BGL	60.00	125.00
☐ WAITING FOR THE BUS, rel. 1982. ed. 500, s/n, 16" x 20", offset litho, pub BGL	45.00	80.00
☐ PRIDE OF THE OPEN RANGE, rel. 1983. ed. 500, s/n, offset litho, pub BGL	50.00	60.00
☐ STAR GAZERS, rel. 1983. ed. 500, s/n, offset litho, pub BGL	40.00	45.00
☐ A TIME FOR DECISION, rel. 1983. ed. 500, s/n, offset litho, pub BGL	40.00	150.00
☐ WHERE THEY PRAY FOR COTTON, rel. 1983. ed. 500, s/n, offset litho, pub BGL ...	50.00	60.00
☐ YEARS OF SERVICE, rel. 1983. ed. 500, s/n, offset litho, pub BGL	30.00	40.00
☐ PEACEFUL STREAM, rel. 1983. ed. 12,000, s/n, offset litho, pub BGL	—	10.00
☐ PALO DURO CROSSING, rel. 1984. ed. 500, s/n, offset litho, pub BGL	50.00	60.00
☐ LLANO GOLD, rel. 1984. ed. 500, s/n, litho, pub BGL	60.00	—
☐ CHASING THE RED BARON, rel. 1984. ed. 500, s/n, offset litho, pub GB	50.00	60.00
☐ MORNING VEIL, rel. 1984. ed. 500, s/n, offset litho, 9" x 24", pub GB	40.00	400.00
☐ SNOWBIRDS, rel. 1985. ed. 500, s/n, offset litho, 18" x 24", pub GB	75.00	75.00
☐ SNOWGEESE, rel. 1985. ed. 500, s/n, offset litho, 11" x 24", pub GB	50.00	50.00
☐ STARTING OUT RIGHT, rel. 1985. ed. 500, s/n, offset litho, 11" x 24", pub BG	50.00	50.00
☐ SIMPLE DAYDREAMS, rel. 1984. ed. 14,000, s/n, offset litho, 8" x 10", pub BG	10.00	—

*Represents prints used for special purposes; Christmas Gifts and Sales Incentives.
**Special Promotion Editons, due to demand they have become collectibles.

AMY BRACKENBURY

THEMES: Wildlife art

MEDIUM: Acrylic on canvas, oils

STYLE: Realism

EDUCATION: Amy Brackenburg studied art and painting at Colorado State University

GALLERY/DISTRIBUTOR: Mill Pond Press, Inc.

COMMENTS: The artist admires oriental art because of its feeling for composition, negative space, and simplicity

	ISSUE PRICE	CURRENT PRICE
☐ GREAT EXPECTATIONS, rel. 1983. ed. 950, 14½" x 12", pub MPPI	40.00	80.00
☐ UNDER THE RED TWIGS - COTTONTAILS, rel. 1983. ed. 950, 12" x 16", pub MPPI	40.00	80.00
☐ CATTAILS, rel. 1984. ed. 950, 19½" x 10½", pub MPPI	60.00	—

UNDER THE RED TWIGS - COTTONTAILS *by Amy Brackenbury*

	ISSUE PRICE	CURRENT PRICE
☐ **FIRST EXCURSION,** rel. 1984. ed. 950, 12″ x 14″, pub MPPI	40.00	—
☐ **GRIZZLY IN THE CHOKECHERRIES,** rel. 1984. ed. 950, 22″ x 17½″, pub MPPI	60.00	—
☐ **SLED DOGS,** rel. 1985. ed. 950, s/n, 13¼″ x 18½″, pub MPPI	50.00	—

CARL BRENDERS

THEMES: Wildlife illustration

MEDIUM: Watercolor, gouache

EDUCATION: Fine Arts Academy in Antwerp and Berchem

EXHIBITIONS: His art has been exhibited in the United States, France, Spain, Holland, and Belgium

GALLERY/DISTRIBUTOR: Mill Pond Press, Inc.

COMMENTS: Over the last decade, he has produced wildlife illustrations for more than twenty books in a series titled *The Secret Life of Animals*

	ISSUE PRICE	CURRENT PRICE
☐ **ON THE ALERT - RED FOX,** rel. 1984. ed. 950, 20″ x 21″, pub MPPI	95.00	—
☐ **PLAYFUL PAIR - CHIPMUNKS,** rel. 1984. ed. 950, 17½″ x 21″, pub MPPI	60.00	—
☐ **SILENT HUNTER - GREAT HORNED OWL,** rel. 1984. ed. 950, 20″ x 24″, pub MPPI .	95.00	—

MARGE BRICHLER

THEMES: Varied

MEDIUM: All mediums

EDUCATION: St. Louis Museum of Fine Art

GALLERY/DISTRIBUTOR: Arts Limited, Inc.

	ISSUE PRICE	CURRENT PRICE
☐ **THREE TO MAKE READY,** rel. 1980. ed. 1,500, s/n, 32½" x 25", pub ALI	60.00	—
☐ **FRANKIE MAE,** rel. 1981. ed. 1,500, s/n, 31⅜" x 25", pub ALI	60.00	—

STAN BROD

THEMES: Graphic art

BACKGROUND: A native of Cincinnati, Brad has contributed much to the city's visual appeal

MUSEUMS/COLLECTIONS: The artist has had his work exhibited internationally

GALLERY/DISTRIBUTOR: Frame House Gallery, Inc.

	ISSUE PRICE	CURRENT PRICE
☐ **CAT AND RAINBOW,** rel. 1978. ed. 750, s/n, 16" x 16", pub FHG	45.00	Sold Out
☐ **CIRCLE CAT,** rel. 1978. ed. 500, s/n, 15¼" x 19", pub FHG	45.00	Sold Out
☐ **OVAL OWL,** rel. 1978. ed. 750, s/n embossed, 17¾" x 13", pub FHG	45.00	Sold Out
☐ **SWAN LAKE,** rel. 1979. ed. 5,000, s/o, 8½" x 9⅜"	10.00	—

D. CROSBY BROWN

THEMES: Varied

GALLERY/DISTRIBUTOR: Frame House Gallery, Inc.

	ISSUE PRICE	CURRENT PRICE
☐ **PATCHES,** rel. 1978. ed. 750, s/n, 19¾" x 26½", pub FHG	50.00	—

TOM BROWNING

THEMES: Varied

GALLERY/DISTRIBUTOR: Wild Wings, Inc.

	ISSUE PRICE	CURRENT PRICE
☐ OLD WAYS, rel. 1982. ed. 600, s/n, litho, 15¾″ x 12¾″, pub WWI	50.00	—
☐ SANTA AND FRIENDS I, rel. 1982. ed. unlimited, 15″ x 12″, pub WWI	15.00	—
☐ SANTA AND FRIENDS II, rel. 1983. ed. unlimited, 15″ x 12″, pub WWI	15.00	—

LEE BRUBAKER

THEMES: Western art

EDUCATION: Art Center School of Los Angeles

GALLERY/DISTRIBUTOR: Sawyier Collection, Inc.

	ISSUE PRICE	CURRENT PRICE
☐ SHOWING OFF, ed. 1000, s/n, 18″ x 27¼″, pub SCI*	65.00	—
☐ SIOUX WAR PARTY, ed. 1000, s/n, 18″ x 27¼″, pub SCI*	65.00	—

*represents the Sawyier Collection Inc., and was formed as a subsidiary of Paul Sawyier Galleries, Inc.

RUTH BRUNNER-STROSSER

THEMES: Americana

GALLERY/DISTRIBUTOR: Frame House Gallery, Inc.

	ISSUE PRICE	CURRENT PRICE
☐ THE AMERICAN WAY, rel. 1982. ed. 975, s/n, 20″ x 24″, pub FHG	75.00	—
ed. 300 Exclusive First Day Issue		
☐ THE GOLDEN SPIKE, rel. 1982. ed. 975, s/n, 20″ x 24″, pub FHG	75.00	—
☐ WRIGHT FLIGHT, rel. 1982. ed. 975, s/n, 20″ x 24″, pub FHG	75.00	—
ed. 300, s/n, Exclusive First Day Issue		
☐ INDEPENDENCE DAY POSTER, rel. 1983, s/o, 26″ x 18″, pub FHG	25.00	—

AL BUELL

THEMES: Illustration, seascapes

MEDIUM: Acrylic and oils

PUBLICATIONS: Al Buell has been featured in *American Artist, Redbook,* and *National Geographic,* among others

MEMBERSHIPS: New York Society of Illustrators

GALLERY/DISTRIBUTOR: Mill Pond Press, Inc.

INDEPENDENCE DAY *by Ruth Brunner-Strosser*

COMMENTS: The artist's best known portrait is *Katharine Hepburn,* commissioned by Reader's Digest

	ISSUE PRICE	CURRENT PRICE
☐ JUST THE SEA AND ME, rel. 1982. ed. 950, s/n, 24″ x 19½″, pub MPPI	85.00	—
☐ DAYDREAMS, rel. 1983. ed. 950, s/n, 12″ x 14″, pub MPPI	40.00	—
☐ AN AFTERNOON BREEZE, rel. 1984. ed. 950, s/n, 22¾″ x 17½″, pub MPPI	85.00	—
☐ SUMMER DREAMS, rel. 1984. ed. 950, s/n, 24″ x 18¼″, pub MPPI	85.00	—

E. HOWARD BURGER

THEMES: Varied

GALLERY/DISTRIBUTOR: Burger Galleries

COMMENTS: The artist was commissioned by the 1982 World's Fair to create the World's Fair collector series of art

LADY WITH A HAT *by Al Buell*

DAY OF REST *by E. Howard Burger*

	ISSUE PRICE	CURRENT PRICE
☐ BACK HOME, rel. 1975. ed. 1000, s/n, 18″ x 20″, pub PSGI	30.00	250.00
ed. 25, remarqued	100.00	550.00
☐ BE THANKFUL, rel. 1975. ed. 1000, s/n, 16″ x 20″, pub PSGI	30.00	275.00
ed. 25, remarqued	100.00	450.00
☐ AUTUMN IN WALKER VALLEY, rel. 1976. ed. 1000, s/n, 17″ x 24¾″, pub PSGI	30.00	185.00
ed. 25, remarqued	100.00	275.00
☐ CHIEF DANIEL BOONE HORNBUCKLE, rel. 1976. ed. 1000, s/n, 16″ x 20″, pub PSGI	30.00	275.00
ed. 25, remarqued	100.00	400.00
☐ BRADY'S TENANT HOUSE, rel. 1977. ed. 1000. s/n. 17″ x 24¾″, pub PSGI	30.00	175.00
ed. 25, remarqued	100.00	275.00
☐ MELTON'S BARN & LAST DAYS (Pair), rel. 1977. ed. 2000, i/o, 11″ x 14″, pub PSGI	20.00	40.00
ed. 25, hand colored	60.00	650.00
☐ BENDABOUT, rel. 1978. ed. 1500, s/n, 16″ x 29¾″, pub PGSI	35.00	75.00
ed. 25, remarqued	100.00	225.00
☐ WHEN DAY IS DONE, rel. 1978. ed. 1000, s/n, 16″ x 20″, pub PSGI	55.00	350.00
ed. 25, remarqued	100.00	475.00
☐ WHERE IS THE MASTER, rel. 1978. ed. 1500, s/n, 16″ x 20″, pub PSGI	35.00	145.00
ed. 25, remarqued	100.00	250.00
☐ BLESS MOMMY & DADDY, rel. 1979. ed. 1000, s/n, 16″ x 20″, pub PSGI	55.00	135.00
ed. 25, remarqued	100.00	235.00
☐ THE LOOKOUT, rel. 1979. ed. 1000, s/n, 15½″ x 18½″, pub PSGI	55.00	95.00
ed. 25, remarqued	100.00	150.00
☐ YESTERDAY, rel. 1979. ed. 1000, s/n, 16″ x 20″, pub PSGI	55.00	70.00
ed. 25, remarqued	100.00	150.00
☐ CONCENTRATION, rel. 1980. ed. 1250, s/n, 16″ x 20″, pub PSGI	55.00	—
ed. 25, remarqued	100.00	—
☐ GRACE, rel. 1981. ed. 1,250, s/n, 16″ x 20″, pub PSGI	55.00	100.00
ed. 25, remarqued	100.00	200.00
☐ "OOPS", rel. 1981. ed. 1,250, s/n, 16″ x 20″, pub PSGI	55.00	95.00
ed. 25, remarqued	100.00	200.00
☐ A VIEW FROM THE PAST, rel. 1982. ed. 1,250, s/n, 16″ x 20″, pub BG	55.00	—
☐ GRANNY, rel. 1982. ed. 1,250, s/n, 126″ x 20″, pub BG	75.00	—
ed. 25, remarqued	100.00	175.00
☐ DAY OF REST, rel. 1983. ed. 1,000, s/n, 21″ x 32″, pub BG	75.00	—

LEE CABLE

THEMES: Wildlife art

AWARDS: Winner of the 1982-83 Florida Duck Stamp Contest, other honors

GALLERY/DISTRIBUTOR: Naples Federal Collection

COMMENTS: Cable, who once used a raccoon face as his trademark, has switched to hiding a paw print in his painting as an indicator of the painting's originality

	ISSUE PRICE	CURRENT PRICE
☐ DEER CREEK, ed. 550, pub NFC	95.00	150.00
☐ PRECARIOUS PERCH — GREEN HERON, rel. 1979. ed. 950, pub NFC	75.00	150.00
☐ SHADOWED STALKER - FLORIDA COUGAR, rel. 1980. ed. 950, pub NFC	75.00	150.00
☐ 1982 FLORIDA DUCK STAMP, rel. 1982. ed. 1,250, pub NFC	125.00	—

PAUL CALLE

THEMES: Western art

MEDIUM: Oil and pencil

MUSEUMS/COLLECTIONS: Phoenix Museum of Fine Arts, Pacific Northwest Indian Center, George Phippen Museum, NASA, and other public and private collections here and abroad

AWARDS: Official artist of the National Aeronautics and Space Administration's Fine Art Program, Franklin Mint Gold Medal for Distinguished Western Art

GALLERY/DISTRIBUTOR: Mill Pond Press, Inc.

COMMENTS: To Calle, Western art is not a romantic adventure but a realistic challenge, a personal commitment to portray America's past with the same sense of history that guided his hand in depicting our nation's space explorations

	ISSUE PRICE	CURRENT PRICE
☐ **PAUSE FOR A DRINK,** ed. 275, s/n, 30″ x 24″, pub ALI	50.00	—
ed. 25, Artist's proofs	50.00	Sold Out
☐ **THE LONELY WATCH,** ed. 275, s/n, 30″ x 24″, pub ALI	50.00	—
ed. 25, Artist's proofs	50.00	Sold Out
☐ **THE TRAIL BOSS,** ed. 275, s/n, 30″ x 24″, pub ALI	50.00	—
ed. 25, Artist's proofs	50.00	Sold Out
☐ **CARING FOR THE HERD,** rel. 1980. ed. 950, s/n, pencil, 22⅛″ x 29″, pub MPPI	110.00	125.00
☐ **CHIEF HIGH PIPE,** rel. 1980. ed. 950. s/n, pencil, 22¾″ x 29″, pub MPPI	75.00	150.00
☐ **CHIEF JOSEPH - MAN OF PEACE,** rel. 1980. ed. 950, s/n, pencil, 24½″ x 30¾″, pub MPPI	135.00	150.00
☐ **PRAYER TO THE GREAT MYSTERY,** rel. 1980. ed. 950, s/n, color, 24¾″ x 32¼″, pub MPPI	245.00	400.00
☐ **SIOUX CHIEF,** rel. 1980. ed. 950, s/n, pencil, 29⅜″ x 22″, pub MPPI	85.00	100.00
☐ **SOMETHING FOR THE POT,** rel. 1980. ed. 950, s/n, color, 24¾″ x 33¾″, pub MPPI	175.00	950.00
☐ **THE LANDMARK TREE,** rel. 1980. ed. 950, s/n, pencil, 24½″ x 30¾″, pub MPPI	125.00	240.00
☐ **THE WINTER HUNTER,** rel. 1980. ed. 950, s/n, pencil, 29½″ x 22″, pub MPPI	65.00	475.00
☐ **VIEW FROM THE HEIGHTS,** rel. 1980. ed. 950, s/n, color, 24⅝″ x 32½″, pub MPPI	245.00	400.00
☐ **WHEN SNOW CAME EARLY,** rel. 1980. ed. 950, s/n, pencil, 22⅛″ x 29″, pub MPPI	85.00	235.00
☐ **ALMOST HOME,** rel. 1981. ed. 950, s/n, color, 20¼″ x 25½″, pub MPPI	150.00	175.00
☐ **AND STILL MILES TO GO,** rel. 1981. ed. 950, s/n, color, 24⅝″ x 30″, pub MPPI	245.00	375.00
☐ **ANDREW AT THE FALLS,** rel. 1981. ed. 950, s/n, 24½″ x 32″, pencil, pub MPPI	150.00	175.00
☐ **CHIEF HIGH PIPE,** rel. 1981. ed. 950, s/n, color, 24⅝″ x 32¼″, pub MPPI	265.00	375.00
☐ **END OF A LONG DAY,** rel. 1981. ed. 950, s/n, pencil, 24¼″ x 31¾″, pub MPPI	150.00	175.00
☐ **FRIENDS,** rel. 1981. ed. 950, s/n, 18½″ x 22¼″, pub MPPI	150.00	—
☐ **FRESH TRACKS,** rel. 1981. ed. 950, s/n, pencil, 24½″ x 31¾″, pub MPPI	150.00	175.00
☐ **JUST OVER THE RIDGE,** rel. 1981. ed. 950, s/n, color, 24½″ x 38″, pub MPPI	245.00	325.00
☐ **ONE WITH THE LAND,** rel. 1981. ed. 950, s/n, color, 24⅝″ x 37″, pub MPPI	245.00	325.00
☐ **PAUSE AT THE LOWER FALLS,** rel. 1981. ed. 950, s/n, pencil 31¾″ x 20¼″, pub MPPI	110.00	150.00
☐ **TETON FRIENDS,** rel. 1981. ed. 950, s/n, pencil, 24½″ x 30¾″, pub MPPI	150.00	225.00
☐ **THE WINTER HUNTER,** rel. 1981. ed. 950, s/n, 36¼″ x 24½″, pub MPPI	245.00	550.00
☐ **EMERGING FROM THE WOODS,** rel. 1982. ed. 950, s/n, 23¼″ x 30¾″, pub MPPI	110.00	—
☐ **GENERATIONS IN THE VALLEY,** rel. 1982. ed. 950, s/n, 24½″ x 35½″, pub MPPI	245.00	—
☐ **RETURN TO CAMP,** rel. 1982. ed. 950, s/n, 24⅝″ x 37⅛″, pub MPPI	245.00	350.00
☐ **THE BREATH OF FRIENDSHIP,** rel. 1982. ed. 950, s/n, 24½″ x 32″, pub MPPI	225.00	—
☐ **TWO FROM THE FLOCK,** rel. 1982. ed. 950, s/n, 24½″ x 36½″, pub MPPI	245.00	400.00
☐ **FREE SPIRITS,** rel. 1983. ed. 950, s/n, 27″ x 24½″, pub MPPI	195.00	225.00
☐ **IN SEARCH OF BEAVER,** rel. 1983. ed. 950, s/n, 25½″ x 38½″, pub MPPI	225.00	325.00
☐ **STRAYS FROM THE FLYWAY,** rel. 1983. ed. 950, s/n, 22¾″ x 28¾″, pub MPPI	195.00	275.00

	ISSUE PRICE	CURRENT PRICE
☐ A BRACE FOR THE SPIT, rel. 1984. s/n, 16″ x 12⅛″, pub MPPI	110.00	125.00
☐ FATE OF THE LAKE MIGRANT, rel. 1984. s/n, 16″ x 12⅛″, pub MPPI	110.00	135.00
☐ WHEN TRAILS CROSS, rel. 1984. ed. 950, s/n, 24½″ x 32½″, pub MPPI	245.00	450.00
☐ THE STORYTELLER OF THE MOUNTAINS, rel. 1985. s/n, 24½″ x 34″, pub MPPI ..	225.00	—

JOHN CAMPBELL

THEMES: Varied

BACKGROUND: Founded the Art Students League of New Orleans

EDUCATION: Louisiana State University; Hans Wang Art School; Paris Conservatory of Fine Art

GALLERY/DISTRIBUTOR: Frame House Gallery, Inc.

COMMENTS: In 1953, the artist was invited to the White House to present his portrait of Dwight Eisenhower to the President

	ISSUE PRICE	CURRENT PRICE
☐ THE MARBLE PLAYERS, rel. 1974. ed. 1,500, s/n, 35″ x 24½″, pub FHG	45.00	95.00
☐ REFLECTIONS AND BLUEBONNETS, rel. 1974. ed. 1,500, s/n, 29″ x 24¼″, pub FHG	45.00	200.00
☐ MISTY MOUNTAIN, rel. 1977. ed. 800, s/n, 22″ x 32″, pub FHG	50.00	100.00
☐ SUMMER MORN, rel. 1977. ed. 800, s/n, 25″ x 20″, pub FHG	50.00	—

KEN CARLSON

THEMES: Wildlife art

MEDIUM: Oil, watercolor

STYLE: Realism

BOOKS: An unusual collection of Carlson's watercolor plates appears in the book *Birds of Western North America*

EDUCATION: Formal art training under the tutelage of the late Walker J. Wilwerding, Minneapolis Art Institute

AWARDS: National Wild Turkey Stamp Design Competition (1979-1980)

GALLERY/DISTRIBUTOR: Wild Wings, Inc.

	ISSUE PRICE	CURRENT PRICE
☐ PINTAILS, rel. 1974. ed. 580, s/n, 19½″ x 21″, pub WWI	60.00	75.00
ed. 50, remarque artist proof..	125.00	—
☐ BALD EAGLE, rel. 1975. ed. 580, s/n, 22″ x 17½″, pub WWI	60.00	75.00
ed. 50, remarque artist proof..	130.00	—

	ISSUE PRICE	CURRENT PRICE
☐ **WOODCOCK,** rel. 1976. ed. 600, s/n, 14½" x 17¾, pub WWI	50.00	100.00
ed. 50, remarque artist proof	130.00	—
☐ **SAND FLATS - PINTAILS,** rel. 1977. ed. 580, s/n, 15" x 26", pub WWI	65.00	75.00
☐ **DOMESTIC RABBITS,** rel. 1979. ed. 950, s/n, 13½" x 19", pub MPPI	50.00	—
☐ **MONARCH OF THE PLAINS - BISON,** rel. 1979. ed. 950, s/n, 18" x 29½", pub MPPI	95.00	—
☐ **PYGMY GOATS,** rel. 1979. ed. 950, s/n, 13½" x 19", pub MPPI	50.00	—
☐ **RAINBOW TROUT,** rel. 1979. ed. 300, s/n, size N/A, pub WWI	85.00	—
☐ **TETON WINTER - TRUMPETERS,** rel. 1979. ed. 850, s/n, 25" x 16⅝", pub WWI	75.00	—
☐ **WINTER RAMS,** rel. 1980. ed. 950, s/n, 22¾" x 28", pub MPPI	135.00	—
☐ **ARCTIC NOMADS,** rel. 1981. ed. 950, s/n, 20¾" x 28", pub MPPI	150.00	—
☐ **CATCHING A SCENT - RED FOX,** rel. 1981. ed. 550, s/n, 20" x 27½", pub MPPI ...	125.00	—
☐ **EVENING SHADOWS,** rel. 1981. ed. 950, s/n, 20" x 27½", pub MPPI	95.00	—
☐ **IN WINTER COAT - SNOWSHOE HARE,** rel. 1981. ed. 950, s/n, 14¾" x 24", pub MPPI	75.00	—
☐ **MASKED BANDIT - RACCOON,** rel. 1981. ed. 950, s/n, 24" x 14½", pub MPPI	75.00	—
☐ **WINGS OF NOBILITY - BALD EAGLE,** rel. 1981. ed. 950, s/n, 19⅞" x 29½", pub MPPI	95.00	—
☐ **OPENING DAY - MALLARDS,** rel. 1982. ed. 950, s/n, size unavailable pub MPPI	150.00	—
☐ **RIO GRANDE VIGIL - WHITETAIL DEER,** rel. 1982. ed. 950, s/n, 21½" x 32", pub MPPI	150.00	—
☐ **THREE RAMS,** rel. 1982. ed. 950. s/n, 16½" x 20", pub MPPI	65.00	—

MASKED BANDIT-RACCOON by Ken Carlson

BOB CARNEY

THEMES: Domestic animals

GALLERY/DISTRIBUTOR: Bob Carney Studios

	ISSUE PRICE	CURRENT PRICE
☐ PUPPY LOVE, ed. 1,250, signed/donated to National Ducks Unlimited, ed. 750, s/n, 16″ x 20″, pub BCS	50.00	—
☐ OPENING DAY, rel. 1976. ed. 980, s/n, 16″ x 20″, pub BCS	25.00	—
☐ DADDY'S MULE, rel. 1976. ed. 2,000, s/n, 16″ x 20″, pub BCS	25.00	100.00
☐ KENNEL COUSINS, rel. 1977. BLACK LABRADOR/YELLOW LABRADOR, ed. 1,500, s/n, 16″ x 20″, pub BCS .... *Priced for EACH PRINT	*20.00	—
**Priced as a SET	**35.00	—
☐ SMOKEY, rel. 1977. ed. 3,500, s/n, 16″ x 20″, pub BCS	20.00	—
☐ TENNESSEE-WALKER, rel. 1978. ed. 2,000, s/n, 16″ x 20″, pub BCS	30.00	—
☐ GRANDDADDY'S MULES, rel. 1979. ed. 2,000, s/n, 19″ x 23¾″, pub BCS	35.00	—
☐ POINT OF INDECISION, rel. 1979. ed. 1,200, s/n, 16″ x 20″, pub BCS	40.00	—
☐ MAMA'S MULE, rel. 1980. ed. 2,000, s/n, 16″ x 20″, pub BCS	35.00	—

CHARLES CARROLL

THEMES: Varied

GALLERY/DISTRIBUTOR: Frame House Gallery, Inc.

	ISSUE PRICE	CURRENT PRICE
☐ MORNING MISCHIEF, rel. 1978. ed. 950, s/n, 19″ x 15″, pub FHG	25.00	60.00

GARY CARTER

THEMES: Western art

EDUCATION: Art Center School of Design

MEMBERSHIPS: Cowboy Artists of America (current president)

GALLERY/DISTRIBUTOR: Gary Carter Western Art Print Co.

COMMENTS: Gary Carter, who father was an artist with the Disney Studios, remembers his father's comments: "If you want to starve, be an artist . . . if you want to eat well, become a chef"

	ISSUE PRICE	CURRENT PRICE
☐ GREENRIVER RENDEZVOUS, rel. 1975. ed. 1,000, s/n, litho, 20″ x 30″, pub GCWAPC	100.00	200.00
☐ "B" TROOP V/S DUSTCUTTERS, rel. 1978. ed. 250, s/n, litho, 12½″ x 17″, pub GCWAPC	70.00	100.00

	ISSUE PRICE	CURRENT PRICE
☐ CAMP MEAT, rel. 1981. ed. 1,000, s/n, litho, 18″ x 30″, pub GCWAPC	120.00	—
☐ THE BATTLE OF THE BIG HOLE, rel. 1981. ed. 1,000, s/n, litho, 22″ x 36″, pub GCWAPC	150.00	—
☐ WHEN STARVATION IS A FLINCH AWAY, rel. 1981. ed. 1,000, s/n, litho, 20″ x 30″, pub GCWAPC	120.00	400.00
☐ BRANDING AT THE HOME RANCH, rel. 1982. ed. 850, s/n, litho, 18″ x 30″, pub GCWAPC	150.00	—
☐ MANEUVERS, EYES LEFT, rel. 1982. ed. 850, s/n, litho, 17½″ x 35″, pub GCWAPC	120.00	—
☐ ROCHE JAUNE, rel. 1982. ed. 850, s/n, litho, 17″ x 35″, pub GCWAPC	120.00	—
☐ BEAR'S PAW ROPE CORRAL, rel. 1983. ed. 850, s/n, litho, 17½″ x 32″, pub GCWAPC	120.00	—
☐ PARTING OF THE BRIGADE, rel. 1983. ed. 850, s/n, litho, 16″ x 28″, pub GCWAPC .	100.00	—
☐ FOOFARRAW PARADE, rel. 1984. ed. 850, s/n, litho, 19¼″ x 31½″, pub GCWAPC .	120.00	—
☐ HIRING YOU WAS LIKE THREE GOOD MEN LEAVING, rel. 1984. ed. 850, s/n, litho, 14½″ x 32″, pub GCWAPC	120.00	—
☐ SHIPPING POINT, rel. 1984. ed. 850, s/n, litho, 19½″ x 32″, pub GCWAPC	120.00	—
☐ STEAM HEAT, rel. 1984. ed. 850, s/n, litho, 14½″ x 32″, pub GCWAPC	120.00	—
☐ HEREFORD HOTEL, rel. 1985. ed. 850, s/n, litho, 16″ x 32″, pub GCWAPC	120.00	—
☐ NO SECOND CHANCE, rel. 1985. ed. 850, s/n, litho, 17½″ x 35″, pub GCWAPC	120.00	—

JOHN L. CARTER

THEMES: Wildlife art

MEDIUM: Watercolors

AWARDS: First Place, Ducks Unlimited Midwest Art Show

GALLERY/DISTRIBUTOR: Petersen Prints

	ISSUE PRICE	CURRENT PRICE
☐ AN EARLY COVEY, ed. 800, s/n, 16″ x 22″, litho, pub PP	60.00	80.00
☐ RUFFS ON THE EDGE, ed. 450, s/n, 12¾″ x 25½″, litho, pub PP	50.00	80.00
☐ OLD CHANNEL WALDPORT GEESE, ed. 450, s/n, 17¾″ x 25½″, litho, pub PP ...	50.00	80.00
☐ BACKWATER WOODIES, ed. 800, s/n, 16″ x 22″, litho, pub PP	60.00	—
☐ MORNING FLIGHT, ed. 800, s/n, 18″ x 25″, litho, pub PP	60.00	—
☐ AUTUMN WINGS, ed. 800, s/n, 17″ x 23½″, litho, pub PP	60.00	—
☐ MALLARDS AND MASONS, ed. 800, s/n, 18½″ x 22″, litho, pub PP	60.00	—
☐ COVEY RISE, ed. 800, s/n, 18″ x 24″, litho, pub PP	60.00	—

DAVE CHAPPLE

THEMES: Birds

MEDIUM: Etching

STYLE: Realism

GALLERY/DISTRIBUTOR: Frame House Gallery, Inc.

MALLARDS by Dave Chapple

	ISSUE PRICE	CURRENT PRICE
☐ BACKWATER MALLARDS, rel. 1978. ed. 150, etching, pub EE	90.00	150.00
☐ BLACK DUCK, rel. 1978. ed. 150, etching, pub EE	90.00	150.00
☐ BLUEBILLS, rel. 1978. ed. 150, etching, pub EE	90.00	150.00
☐ BLUE-WINGED TEAL, rel. 1978. ed. 150, etching, pub EE	90.00	150.00
☐ CANADA GEESE, rel. 1978. ed. 150, etching, pub EE	90.00	200.00
☐ CANVASBACKS, rel. 1978. ed. 150, etching, pub EE	90.00	150.00
☐ IN TO FEED - CANADA GEESE, rel. 1978. ed. 150, etching, pub EE	90.00	150.00
☐ MALLARDS, rel. 1978. ed. 150, etching, pub EE	90.00	150.00
☐ NIGHT OWLS, rel. 1978. ed. 150, etching, pub EE	200.00	300.00
☐ OVER THE MARSH - PINTAILS, rel. 1978. ed. 150, etching, pub EE	90.00	150.00
☐ PINTAILS, rel. 1978. ed. 150, etching, pub EE	90.00	150.00
☐ SETTING DOWN - RED HEADS, rel. 1978. ed. 150, etching, pub EE	90.00	150.00
☐ WOOD DUCK, rel. 1978. ed. 150, etching, pub EE	90.00	200.00
☐ CANADA GOOSE, rel. 1979. ed. 150, etching, pub EE	200.00	400.00
☐ PEREGRINE FALCON, rel. 1979. ed. 150, etching, pub EE	200.00	750.00
☐ SPRINGER SPANIEL/PHEASANT, rel. 1979. ed. 150, etching, pub EE	200.00	750.00
☐ MALLARDS - COLOR, rel. 1980. ed. 150, etching, pub EE	200.00	250.00
☐ PINTAILS, rel. 1980. ed. 150, etching, pub EE	150.00	225.00
☐ CALIFORNIA QUAIL, rel. 1981. ed. 150, etching, pub EE	150.00	175.00
☐ GREEN-WINGED TEAL, rel. 1981. ed. 150, etching, pub EE	150.00	225.00
☐ PHEASANT, rel. 1981. ed. 150, etching, pub EE	150.00	250.00
☐ WOOD DUCK, rel. 1981. ed. 150, etching, pub EE	150.00	225.00

	ISSUE PRICE	CURRENT PRICE
☐ JUMPING-WOODDUCKS, rel. 1982. ed. 250, 18″ x 24″, hand-colored etching, pub EE	250.00	—
☐ AERIAL GRACE - SWALLOW, rel. 1983. ed. 250, s/n, 13″ x 15″, etching, pub FHG ..	95.00	—
☐ CARDINAL, rel. 1983. ed. 250, s/n, 18½″ x 15″, etching, pub FHG	150.00	250.00
☐ COVEY BREAK - BOBWHITE, rel. 1983. ed. 250, s/n, 19″ x 28″, etching, pub FHG ..	225.00	—
☐ HEDGEROW - PHEASANT, rel. 1983. ed. 250, s/n, 15″ x 18″, etching, pub FHG	150.00	250.00
☐ PEERING OUT, rel. 1983. ed. 250, s/n, 27″ x 22″, etching, pub FHG	225.00	—
☐ THE ARENA, rel. 1983. ed. 975. s/n, 25″ x 32″, litho, pub FHG	80.00	—
☐ THE LOOKOUT, rel. 1983. ed. 250, s/n, 15″ x 13″, etching, pub FHG	95.00	175.00
☐ TRANQUIL - WOODIES, rel. 1983. ed. 250, s/n, 18½″ x 15″, etching, pub FHG	120.00	225.00
☐ VALLEY QUAIL, rel. 1983. 240, s/n, 14¾″ x 18½″, etching, pub FHG	150.00	250.00
☐ AUTUMN MIST, rel. 1984. ed. 350, s/n, 27½″ x 22″, litho, pub FHG	150.00	275.00
☐ AUTUMN MIST I — WOODDUCKS, rel. 1984. ed. 1,500, s/n, exclusive	150.00	Sold Out
☐ AUTUMN MIST II — MALLARDS, rel. 1984. ed. 350, s/n, 27½″ x 22″, pub FHG	150.00	—
ed. 1,500, s/n, exclusive	150.00	Sold Out
☐ AUTUMN MIST III — CANADA GEESE, rel. 1984. ed. 350, s/n, 27½″ x 22″, pub FHG..	150.00	—
ed. 1,500, s/n, exclusive	150.00	—
☐ SILENT STALK - RED FOX, rel. 1984. ed. 250, s/n, 21½″ x 17½″, pub FHG	175.00	—
☐ FAMILY RETREAT, rel. 1984. ed. 250, s/n, etching, pub FHG	150.00	—
☐ PARTNERS FOR LIFE - CANADA GOOSE, rel. 1984. ed. 250, s/n, 21″ x 18″, etching, pub FHG	175.00	290.00
☐ PEREGRINE FALCON, rel. 1985. ed. 250, s/n, 20½″ x 18″, pub FHG	175.00	—
☐ GREAT BLUE HERON, rel. 1985. ed. 250, s/n, 23½″ x 14″, pub FHG	175.00	—
☐ BLUEBIRDS, rel. 1985. ed. 250, s/n, 16½″ x 14″, pub FHG	125.00	—
☐ ROBIN, rel. 1985. ed. 250, s/n, 16½″ x 14″, pub FHG	125.00	—
☐ REFLECTIONS, rel. 1985. ed. 250, s/n, 14¼″ x 16″, pub FHG	150.00	—

HERB CHIDLEY

THEMES: Wildlife art

GALLERY/DISTRIBUTOR: Herb Chidley

	ISSUE PRICE	CURRENT PRICE
☐ BOBWHITE QUAIL - AIRBORN, rel. 1977. ed. 575, s/n, 16½″ x 22″, pub HC	55.00	—
Remarqued	115.00	—
☐ SPECIAL DELIVERY - SPRINGER WITH PHEASANT, rel. 1977. ed. 575, s/n, 17″ x 20½″, pub HC	55.00	—
Remarqued	115.00	—
☐ TOUCHDOWN - MALLARDS, rel. 1977. ed. 575, s/n, 16½″ x 25″, pub HC	55.00	—
Remarqued	115.00	—

RAYMOND CHING

THEMES: Wildlife art

MEDIUM: Watercolor

BOOKS: *The Book of British Birds* and *The Bird Paintings* were illustrated by Raymond Ching

MUSEUMS/COLLECTIONS: Many of his paintings have been exhibited at the Tyron Gallery in London

GALLERY/DISTRIBUTOR: Russell A. Pink

	ISSUE PRICE	CURRENT PRICE
☐ **KESTREL,** rel. 1978. ed. 850, s/n, 23″ x 18⅝″, pub RAF	100.00	250.00
☐ **TREASURE CHEST,** rel. 1980. ed. 850, s/n, 24⅞″ x 18½″, pub RAF	100.00	250.00
☐ **SWALLOW,** rel. 1981. ed. 850, s/n, 26″ x 20″, distr. RAF	175.00	—
☐ **WINTER WREN,** rel. 1981. ed. 850, s/n, 11½″ x 14″, pub RAF	70.00	—
☐ **EARLY SNOW - MOURNING DOVES,** rel. 1982. ed. 850, s/n, 23¼″ x 17¼″, pub RAF	150.00	—
☐ **CANVASBACK,** rel. 1983. ed. 850, s/n, 17″ x 13″, pub RAF	80.00	—

EARLY SNOW - MOURNING DOVES *by Raymond Ching*

JOHN CHUMLEY
(1928-1984)

THEMES: Varied

MEDIUM: Tempera, watercolor

STYLE: Realism

EDUCATION: Pennsylvania Academy of Fine Arts

GALLERY/DISTRIBUTOR: Shenandoah Fine Arts Co.

	ISSUE PRICE	CURRENT PRICE
☐ **ABONI PARIS, VA,** ed. 1,000, s/n, 19½″ x 28″, pub SFAC	300.00	—
☐ **BABY RABBITS,** ed. 725, s/n, 14½″ x 17½″, pub SFAC	150.00	—
☐ **JOHN'S DOG,** s/n, 21″ x 26″, pub SFAC	500.00	Sold Out
☐ **MOUNTAIN CHURCH,** s/n, 15½″ x 25½″, pub SFAC	125.00	Sold Out
☐ **RENDEZVOUS,** ed. 2,000, numbered, 17½″ x 29″, pub SFAC	125.00	—
☐ **SATURDAY MORNING,** ed. 1,000, s/n, 16¾″ x 26″, pub SFAC	250.00	—
☐ **SKATERS,** ed. 1,000, s/n, 18″ x 26″, pub SFAC	300.00	—
☐ **THREE SWINGS,** ed. 1,000, s/n, 18½″ x 26″, pub SFAC	300.00	—
☐ **TRUMPET VINE,** ed. 1,000, s/n, pub SFAC	250.00	—

NESTING SWANS *by Robert Clark*

ROBERT CLARK

THEMES: Landscapes, Americana, still life

MEDIUM: Egg tempera

STYLE: Realism. Clark's paintings are distinguished by a glowing luminosity, a discriminating use of texture dramatically accented by light and dark

EDUCATION: Minneapolis School of Art, Walker Art Center School

GALLERY/DISTRIBUTOR: Mill Pond Press, Inc.

COMMENTS: The artist has been the subject of a documentary film produced by William P. Taylor

	ISSUE PRICE	CURRENT PRICE
☐ **AUGUST STILL LIFE,** rel. 1980. ed. 950, s/n, 23″ x 16″, pub MPPI	50.00	—
☐ **INDIAN SUMMER,** rel. 1980. ed. 950, s/n, 23″ x 16″, pub MPPI	50.00	—
☐ **NESTING SWAN,** rel. 1983. ed. 950, s/n, 17½″ x 23¼″, pub MPPI	85.00	—

MOMENT IN TIME *by Francois Cloutier*

FRANCOIS CLOUTIER

THEMES: Varied

AWARDS: The artist's dazzling creations have received top international awards

MUSEUMS/COLLECTIONS: His paintings can be found in many important private collections

GALLERY/DISTRIBUTOR: Edna Hibel Corporation

	ISSUE PRICE	CURRENT PRICE
☐ MOMENT IN TIME, ed. 500, s/n, 20⅛" x 37⅝", pub EHC	60.00	—
☐ MORNING RISE, ed. 500, s/n, 25" x 37¼", pub EHC	60.00	—
☐ THE PROPOSAL, ed. 500, s/n, 22¾" x 37¼", pub EHC	60.00	—

GUY COHELEACH

THEMES: Wildlife art

AWARDS: Conservationist of the Year (African Safari Club—1976)

GALLERY/DISTRIBUTOR: World Wildlife Art Museum

COMMENTS: Coheleach's *American Eagle* was chosen by the State Department for presentation to visiting heads of state, and another of his paintings hangs in the White House

	ISSUE PRICE	CURRENT PRICE
☐ LONG-EARED OWL, rel. 1967. ed. 400, s/n, 11" x 14"	30.00	950.00
Printed in New York prior to affiliation with Frame House Gallery. Not considered part of the Gallery collection. Highly valued by Coheleach collectors.		
☐ BALD EAGLE "Endangered Species", rel. 1968. ed. 1,000, s/n, 32" x 40"	75.00	650.00
Released through National Wildlife Federation		
☐ PURPLE GALLINULE, rel. 1968. ed. 19,500, s/o, 11¼" x 14¾", pub FHG	*	50.00
*Obtainable only with membership to National Audubon Society during 1968-69 Florida membership campaign.		
☐ GREAT BLUE HERON, rel. 1968. ed. 2,500, s/o, 22½" x 26½", pub FHG	40.00	75.00
ed. 500, s/n	50.00	100.00
☐ RED-TAILED HAWK, rel. 1968. ed. 3,500, s/o, 22" x 18", pub FHG	20.00	90.00
☐ GOLDEN EAGLE, rel. 1968. ed. 1,000, s/n, 28" x 35", pub FHG	75.00	400.00
☐ SNOWY EGRETS, rel. 1968. ed. 500, signed/numbered donated to National Audubon Society to raise money for Corkscrew Swamp Sanctuary	100.00	360.00
ed. 2,500, unsigned and unnumbered, 24" x 31", pub FHG	50.00	300.00
☐ BARN SWALLOW, rel. 1968. ed. 3,500, s/o, 18" x 22", pub FHG	20.00	35.00
☐ CARDINAL, rel. 1969. ed. 4,200, s/o, 18" x 22", pub FHG	20.00	85.00
Also offered as a free bonus to new membership during the 1969-70 Audubon Society membership campaign in North Carolina.		
☐ AMERICAN ELK, rel. 1968. ed. 3,500, s/o, 22" x 18", pub FHG	15.00	50.00
☐ GRIZZLY BEAR, rel. 1968. ed. 3,500, s/o, 22" x 18", pub FHG	15.00	50.00
☐ BLACK CRAPPIE, rel. 1968. ed. 3,500, s/o, 22" x 18", pub FHG	15.00	50.00
☐ STRIPED BASS, rel. 1968. ed. 3,500, s/o, 22" x 18", pub FHG	15.00	50.00
☐ GREAT HORNED OWL, rel. 1970. ed. 1,000 signed, numbered and imprinted with the college seal, printed exclusively for the alumni of Transylvania University, Lexington, Kentucky	65.00	275.00
ed. 2,000, s/o, 24" x 31", pub FHG	50.00	210.00
☐ KIRTLAND'S WARBLER, rel. 1970. ed. 5,000, s/o, 10" x 14", pub FHG	12.50	—
This print also offered as a free bonus during the 1970 Audubon Society membership campaign in Michigan, to new members.		
☐ WOOD THRUSH, rel. 1970. ed. 3,500, s/o, 12" x 16", pub FHG	15.00	35.00
☐ BLACK-CAPPED CHICKADEE, rel. 1970. ed. 3,500, s/o, 12" x 16", pub FHG	15.00	400.00
☐ LEOPARD, rel. 1970. ed. 650, s/n, 31½" x 25", pub FHG	75.00	525.00
☐ PEREGRINE FALCON, rel. 1970. ed. 3,500, s/o, 18" x 22", pub FHG	20.00	110.00
☐ SAW-WHET OWL, rel. 1969. ed. 5,000, s/o, 12¼" x 16½", pub FHG	10.00	135.00
☐ AMERICAN KESTREL, rel. 1971. ed. 5,000, s/o, 20" x 25", pub FHG	20.00	—
☐ SIBERIAN TIGER, rel. 1971. ed. 3,500, s/o, 20½" x 25", pub FHG	30.00	250.00
☐ ELEPHANT, rel. 1971. ed. 1,000, s/n, 31½" x 25", pub FHG	75.00	150.00
ed. 1,500, s/o	60.00	125.00

	ISSUE PRICE	CURRENT PRICE
☐ KILLDEER PLOVER, rel. 1971. ed. 5,000, s/o, 14" x 20", pub FHG	20.00	—
☐ IVORY-BILLED WOODPECKER, rel. 1971. ed. 1,000, s/n, 22" x 29¾", pub FHG	65.00	—
ed. 3,000, s/o	50.00	—
☐ AFRICAN LION, rel. 1971. ed. 5,000, s/o, 20½" x 25", pub FHG	30.00	90.00
☐ COMMON EGRET, rel. 1972. ed. 5,000, s/o, 30" x 23", pub FHG	35.00	—
☐ LEOPARD STARE, rel. 1972. ed. 1,000, s/n, 24" x 29", pub FHG	75.00	225.00
ed. 3,000, s/o	60.00	165.00
*ed. 1,000 donated to National Wildlife Federation to raise funds for conservation work	*60.00	140.00
☐ KOALA BEAR, rel. 1972. ed. 5,000, s/o, 12" x 16", pub FHG	15.00	125.00
☐ WAPITI STAG, rel. 1972. ed. 1,000, s/n, 22¾" x 29⅞", pub FHG	75.00	225.00
ed. 3,000, s/o	60.00	200.00
*ed. 1,500 signed special edition bearing the official seal of the Benevolent and Protective Order of Elks	*60.00	—
☐ BEWARE, rel. 1972. ed. 5,000, s/o, 23" x 19", pub FHG	*20.00	160.00
*500 donated to African Wildlife Leadership Foundation to raise funds for research and education projects.		
☐ GIANT PANDA, rel. 1972. ed. 5,000, s/o, 16" x 20", pub FHG	20.00	100.00
☐ SNOW LEOPARD, rel. 1972. ed. 1,000, s/n, 31⅝" x 25", pub FHG	75.00	475.00
ed. 3,000, s/o	60.00	380.00
*ed. 1,000 Fund for Animals, Inc.	*60.00	—
☐ THE CHASE, rel. 1973. ed. 5,000, s/o, 25¾" x 20½", pub FHG	35.00	165.00
☐ SNOWY OWL, rel. 1973. ed. 1,000, s/n, 34" x 24½", pub FHG	75.00	—
ed. 4,000, s/o	60.00	—
☐ WINTER CARDINALS, rel. 1973. ed. 5,000, s/o, 16" x 20", pub RHAI	20.00	90.00
☐ LEOPARD HEAD, rel. 1973. ed. 5,000, s/o, 16" x 20", pub RHAI	20.00	290.00
☐ JUNGLE JAGUAR, rel. 1973. ed. 5,000, s/o, 26" x 21", pub RHAI	40.00	220.00
☐ RED-SHAFTED FLICKER, rel. 1973. ed. 5,000, s/o, 16" x 20", pub RHAI	20.00	50.00
☐ CLOUDED LEOPARD, rel. 1973. ed. 5,000, s/o, 26", pub RHAI	40.00	125.00
☐ GOLDEN EAGLE, rel. 1974. ed. 5,000, s/o, 21" x 26", pub RHAI	40.00	90.00
☐ CATS OF THE AMERICAS, rel. 1974. Portfolio of six prints. ed. 5,000, i/o, 14½" x 18", pub RHAI	80.00	200.00
☐ SCREECH OWLS, rel. 1974. ed. 5,000, i/o, 16" x 20", pub RHAI	20.00	200.00
☐ FOX DEN, rel. 1974. ed. 1,000, s/n, 26" x 35", pub RHAI	100.00	300.00
ed. 500, s/o	80.00	225.00
ed. 500, s/o, donated to Fox Den Village	—	—
☐ IMPERIAL EAGLE, rel. 1974. ed. 5,000, i/o, 11" x 14", pub RHAI	10.00	50.00
☐ CHARGING ELEPHANT, rel. 1974. ed. 4,500, s/o, 26" x 19", pub RHAI	40.00	125.00
ed. 500 donated to Game Conservation International	80.00	125.00
☐ BLACK BEAR CUBS, rel. 1974. ed. 4,500, i/o, 16" x 20", pub RHAI	20.00	90.00
ed. 500 donated to the University of Tennessee	50.00	80.00
☐ CARIBOU, rel. 1974. ed. 3,000, s/o, 20¼" x 26", pub RHAI	40.00	135.00
☐ THE LOOKOUT, rel. 1974. ed. 1,000, s/n, 35" x 28", pub RHAI	100.00	425.00
ed. 1,000, s/o	80.00	350.00
☐ SHORT EARED OWL, rel. 1974. ed. 3,000, i/o, 16" x 20", pub RHAI	30.00	50.00
ed. 500 Obtainable only with membership to National Audubon Society	—	—
☐ JAGUAR HEAD, rel. 1975. ed. 3,500, i/o, 16" x 20", pub RHAI	30.00	150.00
☐ MUTE SWANS, rel. 1975. ed. 4,000, s/n, 25" x 19¾", pub RHAI	50.00	—
☐ LONG BILLED MARSHWREN, rel. 1975. ed. 4,000, i/o, 11" x 14", pub RHAI	20.00	40.00
☐ TIGER HEAD, rel. 1975. ed. 4,000, i/o, 16" x 20", pub RHAI	30.00	225.00
☐ BICENTENNIAL EAGLE, rel. 1975. ed. 1,000, s/n, 32⅞" x 25½", pub RHAI	100.00	170.00
ed. 2,000, s/o	80.00	150.00
☐ RACCOONS, rel. 1975. ed. 3,500, s/o, 20" x 26", pub RHAI	60.00	200.00
☐ CAPE BUFFALO, rel. 1975. ed. 2,000, s/o, 26" x 20¼", pub RHAI	60.00	Sold Out
☐ DUSK, rel. 1975. ed. 189, s/n, 15" x 18", stone lithograph, pub RHAI	150.00	470.00
☐ DAWN, rel. 1975. ed. 147, s/n, 15" x 18", stone lithograph, pub RHAI	200.00	510.00
☐ REFLECTIONS, rel. 1976. ed. 156, s/n, 15" x 11", stone lithograph, pub RHAI	200.00	250.00
☐ SCARLET TANAGER & WHIP-POOR-WILL, rel. 1976. ed. 5,000, i/o, 12" x 15", pub RHAI	20.00	Sold Out
☐ WILD TURKEY, rel. 1976. ed. 1,000, s/n, 25½" x 34", pub RHAI	100.00	Sold Out
ed. 1,500, s/o	80.00	Sold Out
ed. 500, s/o, donated National Foundation for Conservation & Environmental Officers	—	—

	ISSUE PRICE	CURRENT PRICE
☐ **GREAT WHITE SHARKS,** rel. 1976. ed. 4,000, i/o, 16″ x 20″, pub RHAI	30.00	45.00
☐ **YOUNG GREAT HORNED OWLS,** rel. 1976. ed. 5,000, s/o, 20″ x 26″, pub RHAI	50.00	90.00
☐ **SNOW LEOPARD HEAD,** rel. 1976. ed. 5,000, i/o, 16″ x 20″, pub RHAI	30.00	100.00
☐ **BLACK WATCH,** rel. 1976. ed. 1,000, s/n, 34″ x 25½″, pub RHAI	100.00	175.00
ed. 1,000, s/o	80.00	150.00
☐ **WOOD DUCKS,** rel. 1976. ed. 5,000, s/o, 26″ x 20″, pub RHAI	50.00	50.00
☐ **INDIAN ROLLERS,** rel. 1977. ed. 5,000, i/o, 16″ x 21″, pub RHAI	30.00	Sold Out
☐ **MOUNTAIN STALK,** rel. 1977. ed. 1,000, s/n, 32½″ x 25½″, pub RHAI	100.00	150.00
ed. 1,000, s/o	80.00	130.00
☐ **BOBCAT,** rel. 1977. ed. 3,500, s/o, 21″ x 26″, pub RHAI	60.00	Sold Out
☐ **WHITE TIGER HEAD,** rel. 1977. ed. 4,500, i/o, 16″ x 20″, pub RHAI	30.00	100.00
ed. 500, s/n, donated to New Paltz Peregrine Falcon Foundation	65.00	—
☐ **WHITE TAILED DEER,** rel. 1977. ed. 1,000, s/n, 25¼″ x 20¾″, pub RHAI	75.00	90.00
ed. 2,000, s/o	60.00	60.00
☐ **AT EASE,** rel. 1977. ed. 1,000, s/n, 32¾″ x 25½″, pub RHAI	100.00	170.00
ed. 1,000, s/o	80.00	150.00
☐ **KOALA BEAR,** rel. 1977. ed. 5,000, i/o, 16″ x 20″, pub RHAI	30.00	50.00
☐ **AUTUMN DUO,** rel. 1977. ed. 149, s/n, 18¼″ x 14¾″, stone lithograph, pub RHAI	200.00	260.00
☐ **LION HEAD,** rel. 1978. ed. 5,000, i/o, 16″ x 20″, pub RHAI	30.00	Sold Out
☐ **AMBUSH,** rel. 1978. ed. 1,000, s/n, 25½″ x 35″, pub RHAI	100.00	225.00
ed. 1,000, s/o	80.00	150.00
☐ **BOBWHITE,** rel. 1978. ed. 5,000, i/o, 16″ x 20″, pub RHAI	30.00	—
☐ **AFFIRMED,** rel. 1978. ed. 1,000, s/n, 20″ x 26″, pub RHAI	100.00	Sold Out
☐ **1978 BELMONT STAKES,** rel. 1978. ed. 1,000, s/n, 11″ x 14″, pub RHAI	*100.00	Sold Out
*Portfolio of four prints.		
☐ **PEREGRINE'S RETURN,** rel. 1978. ed. 1,000, s/n, 25½″ x 35″, pub RHAI	100.00	—
ed. 1,000, s/o	80.00	—
☐ **DOUBLE TROUBLE,** rel. 1978. ed. 221, s/n, 12″ x 20¾″, stone lithograph, pub RHAI	200.00	—
☐ **BABY SNOW LEOPARD** (Pair-Set), rel. 1978. ed. 4,000, i/o, 11″ x 14″, pub RHAI	40.00	—
☐ **SNOW LEOPARD (Mother and Cubs),** rel. 1978. ed. 2,000, s/o, 26″ x 20″, pub RHAI	60.00	125.00
☐ **SPOTTED OWL,** rel. 1979. ed. 2,000, s/o, 20″ x 26″, pub RHAI	60.00	75.00
☐ **BACHELOR PAIR,** rel. 1979. ed. 1,000, s/n, 30¼″ x 22¾″, pub RHAI	100.00	75.00
ed. 1,000, s/o	80.00	150.00
☐ **CHINESE LEOPARD HEAD,** rel. 1979. ed. 5,000, i/o, 16″ x 20″, pub RHAI	30.00	105.00
☐ **CANADIAN GEESE,** rel. 1979. ed. 3,000, s/o, 20″ x 26″, pub RHAI	60.00	—
☐ **BABY BUBO,** rel. 1979. ed. 168, s/n, 12¼″ x 20¾″, stone litho, pub RHAI	200.00	240.00
☐ **SIBERIAN CHASE,** rel. 1979. ed. 850, s/n, 15″ x 26″, pub RHAI	180.00	300.00
☐ **EARLY WARNING,** rel. 1979. ed. 5,000, i/o, 20″ x 16″, pub RHAI	30.00	—
☐ **COUGAR & CUBS,** rel. 1979. ed. 2,500, s/o, 20″ x 26″, pub RHAI	60.00	—
☐ **MALLARDS,** rel. 1979. ed. 3,000, s/o, 20″ x 26″, pub RHAI	60.00	—
☐ **PANDA & CUB,** rel. 1980. ed. 5,000, i/o, 16″ x 20″, pub RHAI	30.00	45.00
☐ **WHITE GYRFALCON,** rel. 1980. ed. 3,500, s/o, 20″ x 26″, pub RHAI	60.00	Sold Out
☐ **LIONESS HEAD,** rel. 1980. ed. 5,000, i/o, 16″ x 20″, pub RHAI	30.00	60.00
☐ **RACCOON MOTHER & CUB,** rel. 1980*. ed. 5,000, i/o, 11″ x 14″, pub RHAI	70.00	set —
*Sold as a Set with print "RACCOON".		
☐ **RACCOON,** rel. 1980*. ed. 5,000, s/o, 20″ x 24″, pub RHAI	70.00	set —
*Sold as a Set with print "RACCOON MOTHER & CUB".		
☐ **LEOPARD'S LAIR,** rel. 1980. ed. 4,000, s/o, 26″ x 15″, pub RHAI	60.00	—
☐ **BENGAL BRACE,** rel. 1980. ed. 1,000, s/n, 31⅝″ x 24½″, pub RHAI	100.00	125.00
ed. 1,000, s/o	80.00	100.00
☐ **ROCKY MOUNTAIN LION,** rel. 1980. ed. 1,500, s/n, 33½″ x 25″, pub RHAI	100.00	130.00
ed. 1,000, s/o	80.00	110.00
☐ **HAREE MOMENT,** rel. 1980. ed. 850, s/n, 26″ x 17¼″, pub RHAI	180.00	270.00
☐ **SIBERIAN TIGER HEAD,** rel. 1981. ed. 3,700, s/o, 20″ x 26″, pub RHAI	60.00	Sold Out
☐ **ROCKY MOUNTAIN CHASE,** rel. 1981. ed. 1,500, s/n, 26″ x 20″, pub RHAI	70.00	—
ed. 500, s/o	50.00	—
☐ **BABY SAW-WHET OWLS,** rel. 1981. ed. 5,000, i/o, 16″ x 20″, pub RHAI	30.00	—
☐ **WOLF PACK,** rel. 1981. ed. 1,500, s/n, 26″ x 20″, pub RHAI	70.00	—
ed. 500, s/o	50.00	—
☐ **CHEETAH HEAD,** rel. 1981. ed. 5,000, i/o, 16″ x 20″, pub RHAI	30.00	Sold Out

	ISSUE PRICE	CURRENT PRICE
☐ **LONG SHADOWS,** rel. 1981. ed. 850, s/n, 20″ x 15″, pub RHAI	180.00	Sold Out
☐ **STORM FLIGHT,** rel. 1981. ed. 850, s/n, 26″ x 15″, pub RHAI .... `	180.00	—
☐ **CLOUDED SIESTA,** rel. 1981. ed. 1,500, s/n, 25½″ x 34″, pub RHAI	100.00	—
ed. 1,500, s/o	80.00	—
☐ **MANCHURIAN CHASE,** rel. 1982. ed. 850, s/n, size not available, distr. WWAM	180.00	Sold Out
☐ **BARRIER BEACH CHASE,** rel. 1982. ed. 850, s/n, 15″ x 32″, distr. WWAM	180.00	—
☐ **BARRED OWL,** rel. 1982. ed. 1,000, s/n, 27″ x 32″, distr. WWAM	120.00	—
☐ **PRIMA HEAD,** rel. 1982. ed. 5,000, i/o, 16″ x 20″, distr. WWAM	30.00	—
☐ **BABY HARP SEALS,** rel. 1982. ed. 5,000, i/o, 16″ x 20″, distr. WWAM	30.00	—
☐ **WOLF HEAD,** rel. 1983. ed. 4,000, i/o, 16″ x 20″, distr. WWAM	35.00	—
☐ **BLACK JAGUAR,** rel. 1983. ed. 5,000, s/n, 20″ x 36″, distr. WWAM	150.00	—
☐ **SURVIVORS,** rel. 1983. ed. 950, s/n, 20″ x 26″, distr. WWAM	200.00	—
☐ **VANISHING GRANDEUR,** rel. 1984. ed. 999, s/n, 22½″ x 17″, pub HH	125.00	—
☐ **SHADY STALK,** rel. 1984. ed. 999, s/n, 16½″ x 22½″, pub HH	125.00	—
☐ **LYNX MOTHER AND KITTENS,** rel. 1984. ed. 4,000, s/n, 13¼″ x 20½″, pub HH	50.00	—
☐ **BRIGHTWATER'S CREEK,** rel. 1984. ed. 999, s/n, 14½″ x 29″, pub HH	125.00	—
ed. includes 99 A/P, 33 Hors Commerce & 5 printer's proofs		
☐ **NECK 'N NECK,** rel. 1984. ed. 4,000, s/n, 12″ x 21″, pub HH	50.00	—
ed. includes 400 artists proofs, 33 Hors Commerce & 5 printer's proofs		
☐ **BRAZILIAN NOON,** rel. 1984. ed. 999, s/n, 16½″ x 22″, pub HH	125.00	—
ed. includes 99 artists proofs, 33 Hors Commerce & 5 printer's proofs		

FARRELL R. COLLETT

THEMES: Wildlife, Western, and landscape art; portraiture

MEDIUM: All media

STYLE: Representational realism

AWARDS: Blue ribbons—Tulsa, Utah State Fair, etc.

MEMBERSHIPS: Society of Animal Artists; Ducks Unlimited; Utah Watercolor Society

GALLERY/DISTRIBUTOR: National Wildlife Galleries

COMMENTS: In 1982, the Weber State College Art Building was named for the artist

	ISSUE PRICE	CURRENT PRICE
☐ **THE JUNIPER BROWSER,** rel. 1981. ed. 450, offset litho, 12½″ x 14″, pub NWGI ...	40.00	—
☐ **THE LOOKOUT,** rel. 1981. ed. 450, offset litho, 14″ x 18″, pub NWGI	50.00	—
☐ **THE SORTIE,** rel. 1981. ed. 450, offset litho, 21″ x 27½″, pub NWGI	60.00	—

SIMON COMBES

THEMES: Wildlife art

BOOKS: *Cheetahs of Samburu* by Simon Combes, published in 1976

EXHIBITIONS: Nairobi (1979); World Wilderness Congress in Johannesburg (1977); Game Conservation International (1975, 1977, 1979)

GALLERY/DISTRIBUTOR: Greenwich Workshop

COMMENTS: The artist has spent most of his life in close communication with the wild animals of the African bush, a first-hand experience that makes him outstanding as a wildlife painter

	ISSUE PRICE	CURRENT PRICE
☐ **FACING THE WIND,** rel. 1980. ed. 1,500, s/n, 32" x 22", pub GW	75.00	—
☐ **INTERLUDE,** rel. 1980. ed. 1,500, s/n, 31" x 21½", pub GW	85.00	Sold Out
☐ **MANYARA AFTERNOON,** rel. 1980. ed. 1,500, s/n, 25¾" x 20⅛", pub GW	75.00	—
☐ **SERENGETI MONARCH,** rel. 1980. ed. 1,500, s/n, 28¼" x 22½", pub GW	85.00	—
☐ **THE SOLITARY HUNTER,** rel. 1980. ed. 1,500, s/n, 28½" x 22½", pub GW	75.00	90.00
☐ **ALERT,** rel. 1981. ed. 1,000, s/n, 30" x 21¼", pub GW	95.00	—
☐ **LEOPARD CUBS,** rel. 1981. ed. 1,000, s/n, 25½" x 20", pub GW	95.00	—
☐ **CHUI,** rel. 1983. ed. 275, s/n, 23¼" x 23¾", hand-drawn lithograph, pub GW	250.00	—
☐ **TENSION AT DAWN,** rel. 1985. ed. 825, s/n, 35" x 19½", pub WWI	125.00	—
☐ **TENSION AT DAWN (rem.),** rel. 1985. ed. 25, s/n, 35" x 19½", pub WWI	275.00	Sold Out

ART COOK

THEMES: Wildlife art

AWARDS: Federal Duck Stamp Design Competition (1972)

MEMBERSHIPS: National and International Wildlife Federations, Ducks Unlimited, National Audubon Society, Trout Unlimited

GALLERY/DISTRIBUTOR: Wild Wings, Inc.

	ISSUE PRICE	CURRENT PRICE
☐ **THE TRAVELER RESTS—ARCTIC TERN,** rel. 1974. ed. 450, s/n, 15" x 21", pub WWI	50.00	75.00
ed. 75 remarque artist proof	100.00	150.00

ROGER COOKE

THEMES: Western art

MEDIUM: Oils

EDUCATION: Portland State College; Art Center College of Design

GALLERY/DISTRIBUTOR: Greenwich Workshop

	ISSUE PRICE	CURRENT PRICE
☐ **GATHERING FOR THE HUCKLEBERRY FEAST,** rel. 1979. ed. 1,000, s/n, 27" x 22", pub GW...	75.00	Sold Out
☐ **PEACEFUL SUMMER,** rel. 1980. ed. 1,000, s/n, 31¼" x 21¾", pub GW	75.00	Sold Out

THE TRAVELER RESTS—ARCTIC TERN *by Art Cook*

ANN COOPER

THEMES: Varied

MUSEUMS/COLLECTIONS: Cooper's work has been exhibited nationwide

GALLERY/DISTRIBUTOR: Circle Fine Arts Corporation

	ISSUE PRICE	CURRENT PRICE
☐ **GOTHAM CITY,** rel. 1978. ed. 300, s/n, 30″ x 26″, pub FHG	125.00	—
☐ **PARTICULAR PARROTS,** ed. 275. s/n, 28″ x 24″, pub CFAC	125.00	—

WAYNE COOPER

THEMES: Varied

GALLERY/DISTRIBUTOR: Circle Fine Arts Corporation

	ISSUE PRICE	CURRENT PRICE
☐ **TUESDAY,** ed. 300, s/n, 30″ x 22″, litho, pub CFAC	—	400.00
☐ **BOSSY'S HOUSE,** ed. 300, s/n, 28″ x 18″, litho, pub CFAC	—	400.00

	ISSUE PRICE	CURRENT PRICE
☐ **BRUNCH,** ed. 300, s/n, 19″ x 26″, litho, pub CFAC	—	175.00
☐ **PAPA LEON,** ed. 300, s/n, 18″ x 26″, litho, pub CFAC	—	175.00
☐ **SEVEN SEAS,** ed. 300, s/n, 24″ x 34″, litho, pub CFAC	—	250.00
☐ **DECEMBER NINE,** ed. 300, s/n, 20″ x 27″, litho, pub CFAC	—	250.00
☐ **ENJOY,** ed. 300, s/n, 24″ x 34″, litho, pub CFAC	—	375.00
☐ **RED FORK,** ed. 260, s/n, 12″ x 17″, etching, pub CFAC	—	225.00
☐ **BLUE RIDGE,** ed. 300, s/n, 16″ x 22″, litho, pub CFAC	—	200.00
☐ **STEAM,** ed. 300, s/n, 20″ x 27″, litho, pub CFAC	—	250.00
☐ **WILLOW SLEW,** ed. 300, s/n, 24″ x 34″, litho, pub CFAC	—	250.00
☐ **COOPER'S RAINBOW,** ed. 300, s/n, 21″ x 29″, litho, pub CFAC	—	250.00
☐ **THE SECOND SNOW,** ed. 300, s/n, 21″ x 26″, litho, pub CFAC	—	175.00
☐ **EVENING MIST,** ed. 350, s/n, 21″ x 28″, litho, pub CFAC	—	175.00
☐ **BY THE SEA,** ed. 350, s/n, 24″ x 35″, litho, pub CFAC	—	175.00
☐ **NORTH,** ed. 300, s/n, 25″ x 28″, litho, pub CFAC	—	200.00
☐ **SPRING ROAD,** ed. 300, s/n, 21″ x 29″, litho, pub CFAC	—	200.00
ed. 35 on Rives Journal paper, litho, pub CFAC	—	225.00
☐ **ONE BULL,** ed. 350, s/n, 21″ x 24″, litho, pub CFAC	—	200.00
☐ **ABANDONED FARM,** ed. 5,000, s/n, 23″ x 29″, pub CFAC	—	135.00
☐ **WINTER MORN,** ed. 5,000, s/n, 23″ x 29″, pub CFAC	—	135.00
☐ **LONELY LIGHTHOUSE,** ed. 5,000, s/n, 23″ x 29″, pub CFAC	—	135.00
☐ **COUNTRY ROAD,** ed. 5,000, s/n, 23″ x 29″, pub CFAC	—	135.00
☐ **VANISHING IMAGES PORTFOLIO,** Deluxe 4 prints and special pages, ed. 100, s/n, 25″ x 35″, pub CFAC	—	875.00
☐ **TOBACCO ROAD,** ed. 300, s/n, 25″ x 35″, pub CFAC	—	350.00
☐ **WILL CREEK,** ed. 300, s/n, 25″ x 35″, pub CFAC	—	350.00
☐ **STONE VALLEY,** ed. 300, s/n, 25″ x 35″, pub CFAC	—	350.00
☐ **CROW HOLLOW,** ed. 300, s/n, 25″ x 35″, pub CFAC	—	350.00

MERV CORNING

THEMES: Varied

GALLERY/DISTRIBUTOR: Circle Fine Arts Corporation

	ISSUE PRICE	CURRENT PRICE
☐ **CAPTAIN EDDIE,** ed. 300, s/n, 22″ x 25″, litho, pub CFAC	—	300.00
☐ **THE RED BARON,** ed. 300, s/n, 23″ x 22″, litho, pub CFAC	—	325.00
☐ **FLYING FOOL,** ed. 300, s/n, 22″ x 25″, litho, pub CFAC	—	200.00
☐ **SET BACKS,** ed. 300, s/n, 22″ x 28″, litho, pub CFAC	—	175.00
☐ **OLD PRO,** ed. 300, s/n, 22″ x 28″, litho, pub CFAC	—	175.00
☐ **ON THE LINE,** ed. 300, s/n, 16″ x 20″, litho, pub CFAC	—	200.00
☐ **MARINE CORSAIR,** ed. 300, s/n, 24″ x 33″, litho, pub CFAC	—	750.00
☐ **BLACK FLIGHT,** ed. 300, s/n, 21″ x 26″, litho, pub CFAC	—	200.00
☐ **ARLINGTON HOUSE,** ed. 300, s/n, 22″ x 28″, litho, pub CFAC	—	850.00
☐ **SANTA MAGUERITA,** ed. 300, s/n, 31″ x 24″	—	700.00
ed. 30 on Rives Journal, litho, pub CFAC	—	750.00
☐ **GREEN RIVER,** ed. 300, s/n, 21″ x 28″	—	325.00
ed. 30 on Rives Journal, litho, pub CFAC	—	350.00
☐ **SUPER BOWL XI (OFASC - 1977),** ed. 600, s/n, 22″ x 28″, litho, pub CFAC	—	275.00
☐ **MIRAMAR HOUSE,** ed. 300, s/n, 24″ x 29″	—	325.00
ed. 60 on B F K Rives, litho, pub CFAC	—	350.00
☐ **CABINS,** ed. 300, s/n, 22″ x 28″	—	300.00
ed. 30 on Rives Journal, litho, pub CFAC	—	350.00
☐ **HIGH COUNTRY,** ed. 300, s/n, 22″ x 30″, litho, pub CFAC	—	275.00
☐ **MIRAMAR NOCTURN,** ed. 100, s/n, 24″ x 29″, litho, pub CFAC	—	400.00

	ISSUE PRICE	CURRENT PRICE
☐ OLD BALE MILL, ed. 300, s/n, 24″ x 30″, litho, pub CFAC	—	450.00
☐ JOYA, ed. 300, s/n, 22″ x 25″, litho, pub CFAC	—	375.00
☐ DOWN THE ROAD, ed. 300, s/n, 21″ x 24″, litho, pub CFAC	—	300.00
☐ SUPER BOWL XII (OFASC - 1978), ed. 950, s/n, 23″ x 26″, litho, pub CFAC	—	250.00
☐ CHAPERONE, ed. 300, s/n, 24″ x 29″, litho, pub CFAC	—	375.00
☐ PENSIVE, ed. 300, s/n, 21″ x 28″, litho, pub CFAC	—	250.00
☐ TOY SAILORS, ed. 300, s/n, size N/A, litho, pub CFAC	—	250.00
☐ MAN WITHOUT FEAR, ed. 300, s/n, 26″ x 24″, litho, pub CFAC	—	650.00
☐ LOST HILLS RANCH, ed. 300, s/n, 22″ x 30″, litho, pub CFAC	—	300.00
☐ FIGUEROA HOUSE, ed. 300, s/n, 26″ x 28″, litho, pub CFAC	—	525.00
☐ RAIN POOL, ed. 300, s/n, 21″ x 27″, pub CFAC	—	325.00
ed. 50 on BFK-Buff paper	—	375.00
☐ ANCIENT WARRIOR, ed. 300, s/n, 22″ x 27″, pub CFAC	—	525.00
ed. 50 on BFK-Buff paper	—	550.00
☐ SUPER BOWL XII/OFASC 1979, ed. 950, s/n, 26″ x 23″, pub CFAC	—	250.00
☐ SUPER BOWL XIV/OFASC 1980, ed. 950, s/n, 26″ x 23″, pub CFAC	—	275.00
☐ SUPER BOWL XV/OFASC 1981, ed. 950, s/n, 23″ x 26″, pub CFAC	—	225.00
☐ SUPER BOWL XVI/OFASC 1982, ed. 950, s/n, 23″ x 26″, pub CFAC	—	225.00
☐ THE GREAT AIRPLANES/1914-1918, 4 pc. suite consisting of Red Knight of Germany, Arizona Balloon Buster, Boy Legend, and King of the Air Fighters. ed. 300, s/n, 21″ x 26″, pub CFAC	—	1,200.00
Deluxe edition on buff paper, 8 pc. plus special pages	—	1,750.00

JOSEPH J. CORREALE, JR.

THEMES: Varied

AWARDS: Winner of many regional medals and awards, including the Cultural Arts Workshop's Gold Medal Quarterly

GALLERY/DISTRIBUTOR: Felicie, Inc.

	ISSUE PRICE	CURRENT PRICE
☐ AMERICAN AUTUMN, ed. 300, s/n, 24½″ x 34½″, original color lithograph, pub FI	200.00	—
☐ FROSTY SUN, ed. 300, s/n, 21½″ x 29½″, original color lithograph, pub FI	150.00	—
☐ LOW TIDE, ed. 300, s/n, 22¼″ x 30″, original color lithograph, pub FI	150.00	—
☐ PARIS MARKET, ed. 300, s/n, 24½″ x 35″, original color lithograph, pub FI	200.00	300.00
☐ PARIS STREET SWEEPER, ed. 300, s/n, 24½″ x 35″, original color lithograph, pub FI	200.00	300.00
☐ 74th & MADISON, ed. 300, s/n, 22¼″ x 30″, original color lithograph, pub FI	200.00	—
☐ TODAY'S SPECIAL, ed. 300, s/n, 29½″ x 21½″, original color lithograph, pub FI	150.00	—
☐ WHERE THE GULLS FLY, ed. 300, s/n, 22¼″ x 30″, original color lithograph, pub FI	150.00	200.00
☐ WINGAERSHEEK & BEYOND, ed. 300, s/n, 22¼″ x 30″, original color lithograph, pub FI	150.00	200.00

DINO COSTANZO

THEMES: Wildlife art

BACKGROUND: Volunteer in charge of cataloging bird egg collections at the Cincinnati Museum of Natural History

SCAUP AT REST *by Dino Costanzo*

EDUCATION: Miami University; University of Cincinnati

GALLERY/DISTRIBUTOR: Streamside Limited Art

COMMENTS: Actively pursuing his art studies, Costanzo is currently working as a freelance artist

	ISSUE PRICE	CURRENT PRICE
☐ **RACCOON,** rel. 1974. ed. 160, s/n, 12″ x 16″, pub SLA	6.00	200.00
☐ **BOBWHITE QUAIL,** rel. 1976, ed. 300, s/n, 12″ x 16″, pub SLA	6.00	130.00
☐ **FUZZY LITTLE BALL OF OWLET EYES,** rel. 1979. ed. 1,000, s/n, 17″ x 22″, pub SLA	20.00	—
☐ **BLUEGILL SUNFISH CHASING A BEETLE SPIN™,** rel. 1981. ed. 1,500, s/n, 14″ x 20″, pub SLA	30.00	—
ed. 200, s/n, special for Ducks Unlimited, 14″ x 20″	30.00	150.00
☐ **REFRESHING MORNING - CARDINAL,** rel. 1981. ed. 1,500, s/n, 14″ x 20″, pub SLA	30.00	—
☐ **SCAUP AT REST - LESSER SCAUP,** rel. 1981. ed. 1,200, s/n, 19″ x 26″, pub SLA . .	40.00	—
ed. 300, s/n, special for Ducks Unlimited, 18″ x 24″	40.00	150.00
ed. 200, s/n, special Ducks Unlimited Sponsor edition, 18″ x 24″	40.00	150.00
☐ **SILENT STARE IN STRIPES UNDER THE STARS - BENGAL TIGER,** rel. 1981. ed. 1,500, s/n, 27″ x 40″, pub SLA	60.00	—
☐ **TRANQUIL PAIR - TRUMPETER SWANS,** rel. 1981. ed. 1,500, s/n, 26″ x 31″, pub SLA	50.00	250.00
☐ **PHEASANTS IN THE SNOW - RINGED-NECK PHEASANTS,** rel. 1985. ed. 597, s/n, 11″ x 14″, pub SLA	30.00	—
☐ **SPRING'S ARRIVAL - BLUE-WINGED TEAL,** rel. 1985. ed. 597, s/n, 11″ x 13½″, pub SLA	30.00	—

JOHN P. COWAN

THEMES: Wildlife

EDUCATION: Art School of the Pratt Institute in New York

BOOKS: The artists paintings were used for the nationally distributed book, *The Golden Crescent*

AWARDS: Ducks Unlimited Artist (1977); two silver medals from the Houston Artists Guild

EXHIBITIONS: Columbia Museum, South Carolina

GALLERY/DISTRIBUTOR: Meredith Long & Co.

COMMENTS: Cowan's paintings have appeared on the cover of and center-fold of the *Ducks Unlimited Magazine*

	ISSUE PRICE	CURRENT PRICE
☐ AT HOME, rel. 1982. ed. 600, s/n, size N/A, distr. WWI	300.00	—
☐ BAD ANGLE, rel. 1982. ed. 600, s/n, size N/A, distr. WWI	85.00	500.00
☐ BAYLEAF BLIND, ed. 600, s/o, 22″ x 28½″, pub MLC	60.00	500.00
☐ BOAT BLIND, ed. 600, s/o, 22″ x 28½″, pub MLC	50.00	500.00
☐ CREEK BOTTOM, ed. 600, s/o, 22″ x 28½″, pub MLC	60.00	500.00
☐ DAMN LEVEE, rel. 1984. ed. 600, s/o, 22″ x 28½″, pub MLC	40.00	125.00.00
☐ DAWN FLIGHT, ed. 600, s/o, 22″ x 28½″, pub MLC	75.00	650.00
☐ DEEP RUN, ed. 600, s/o, 13″ x 17″, pub MLC	40.00	500.00
☐ EARLY LIMITS, ed. 600, s/o, 13″ x 17″, pub MLC	60.00	650.00
☐ FASTWATER, ed. 600, s/o, 22″ x 28½″, pub MLC	60.00	250.00
☐ FOX'S BLIND, ed. 600, s/n, size N/A, distr. WWI	85.00	650.00
☐ GETTIN' WELL, ed. 600, s/o, 13″ x 17″, pub MLC	25.00	750.00
☐ HEAVY COVER, ed. 600, s/o, 22″ x 28½″, pub MLC	60.00	1,000.00
☐ HOT TANK, ed. 600, s/o, 22″ x 28½″, pub MLC	60.00	1,000.00
☐ IN THE BROOMWEED - QUAIL, ed. 600, s/o, 22″ x 28½″, pub MLC	40.00	750.00
☐ LONGLEAF BOBS, ed. 600, s/o, 22″ x 28½″, pub MLC	60.00	500.00
☐ MAGIC MINUTES, rel. 1979. ed. 600, s/n, size N/A, distr. WWI	60.00	750.00
☐ MALLARDS HIGH, ed. 600, s/o, 22″ x 28½″, pub MLC	40.00	250.00
☐ MOVING OUT, ed. 600, s/o, 13″ x 17″, pub MLC	25.00	250.00
☐ NEW GUN, ed. 600, s/o, 22″ x 28½″, pub MLC	40.00	750.00
☐ NIGHT FEEDERS,/26.3x48.3ed. 600, s/o, 22″ x 28½″, pub MLC	40.00	700.00
☐ OFF BASE, ed. 600, s/o, 22″ x 28½″, pub MLC	40.00	750.00
☐ ONE MORE, rel. 1981. ed. 600, s/n, size N/A, distr. WWI	300.00	—
☐ PICKING UP PINTAILS, ed. 600, s/o, 22″ x 28½″, pub MLC	40.00	800.00
☐ PINE & PALMETTO, ed. 600, s/o, 22″ x 28½″, pub MLC	85.00	250.00
☐ PORTABLE BLIND, ed. 600, s/o, 22″ x 28½″, pub MLC	40.00	Sold Out
☐ QUAIL TREE, ed. 600, s/o, 22″ x 28½″, pub MLC	40.00	800.00
☐ SWEET WRECK, rel. 1981, ed. 600, s/n, size N/A, distr. WWI	95.00	650.00
☐ SUNKEN BLIND, ed. 600, s/o, 22″ x 28½″, pub MLC	85.00	650.00
☐ TEAL HUNT, ed. 600, s/o, 22″ x 28½″, pub MLC	60.00	500.00
☐ THE FLATS, ed. 600, s/o, 22″ x 28½″, pub MLC	60.00	500.00
☐ TIDEWATER BASS, ed. 600, s/o, 22″ x 28½″, pub MLC	40.00	Sold Out
☐ TOO SOON, ed. 600, s/o, 22″ x 28½″, pub MLC	60.00	650.00
☐ TWO DOWN, ed. 600, s/o, 22″ x 28½″, pub MLC	40.00	650.00

TIM COX

THEMES: Western art

EDUCATION: Brigham Young University, under the supervision of William Whitaker

GALLERY/DISTRIBUTOR: Texas Art Press

	ISSUE PRICE	CURRENT PRICE
☐ NO HELP FROM MOM, rel. 1979. ed. 2,250, s/n, 12″ x 18″, pub TAP	60.00	—
☐ BRANDING THE MAVERICK, rel. 1980. ed. 2,250, s/n, 13¾″ x 20⅛″, pub TAP	75.00	—
☐ FALL ALONG THE ANIMALS, rel. 1980. ed. 2,250, s/n, 13⅜″ x 20″, pub TAP	75.00	—
☐ JINGLIN' HORSES, rel. 1980. ed. 2,250, s/n, 13½″ x 20″, pub TAP	75.00	—
☐ MAKING THE CIRCLE, rel. 1980. ed. 2,250, s/n, 15⅞″ x 20⅛″, pub TAP	75.00	—
☐ AUTUMN MORNING RIDE, rel. 1982. ed. 1,000, s/n, 16″ x 24″, pub TAP	100.00	—
☐ COOLING THE SUMMER HEAT, rel. 1982. ed. 1,000, s/n, 16″ x 25″, pub TAP	100.00	—
☐ SPRING RANGE, rel. 1982. ed. 1,000, s/n, 16″ x 24″, pub TAP	100.00	—
☐ WINTER ROUNDUP, rel. 1982. ed. 1,000, s/n, 16″ x 23″, pub TAP	100.00	—

JERRY CRANDALL

THEMES: Western art

STYLE: Realism

MEMBERSHIPS: Listed in *Who's Who in the West, Who's Who in American Art, The International Who's Who of Contemporary Achievement, Contemporary Western Artists*

GALLERY/DISTRIBUTOR: Eagle Editions

COMMENTS: Because of his expertise on the American West, Crandall served as historical consultant for the early segments of the television series *Centennial* and also for the movie *The Mountain Men,* starring Charlton Heston. Articles in numerous publications have recently featured Jerry Crandall and his work. His art work can also be found in many public and private collections

	ISSUE PRICE	CURRENT PRICE
☐ SMOKE UP AHEAD, rel. 1977. ed. 450, s/n, 20″ x 30″, pub JH	60.00	450.00
☐ "I FOUND THE PASS", rel. 1979. ed. 500, s/n, 20″ x 30″, pub GI	60.00	350.00
☐ PURSUED, rel. 1979. ed. 525, s/n, 22″ x 27½″, pub GI	60.00	650.00
☐ ON TO TAOS, rel. 1980, ed. 560, s/n, 16½″ x 24″, pub GI	65.00	75.00
☐ SHRINE TO THE BUFFALO, rel. 1980. ed. 525, s/n, 21″ x 28″, pub GI	65.00	450.00
☐ CAUTION, rel. 1981. ed. 650, s/n, 11″ x 14″, pub GI	40.00	100.00
☐ NOT ALONE, rel. 1981. ed. 650, s/n, 20″ x 16″, pub GI	55.00	175.00
☐ COUREURS DES BOIS, rel. 1982. ed. 650, s/n, 20½″ x 27½″, pub GI	85.00	—
☐ SOLITUDE, rel. 1982. ed. 1,000, s/n, 19″ x 21″, pub GI	75.00	85.00
☐ AN EARLY SNOW, rel. 1983. ed. 750, s/n, 18¾″ x 28″, pub SGL	85.00	—
☐ AUTUMN IN THE BAYOU SALADE, rel. 1983. ed. 750, s/n, litho, 18″ x 24″, pub EEL	75.00	—
☐ TROUBLE ON CLEAR CREEK, rel. 1983. ed. 750, s/n, 18¾″ x 28″, pub EEL	85.00	—
☐ BUCKSKIN BILL, rel. 1984. ed. 750, s/n, litho, 22½″ x 18″, pub EEL	85.00	—
☐ I RECKON IT MIGHT BE FEBRUARY, rel. 1984. ed. 650, s/n, 14″ x 11″, litho, pub EEL	55.00	—
☐ WINTER'S CHILL, rel. 1984. ed. 650, s/n, 14″ x 11″, litho, pub EEL	55.00	—
☐ VISITING FIRST LADY, rel. 1985. ed. 650, s/n, litho, 15″ x 10″, pub EEL	55.00	—

VIVI CRANDALL

THEMES: Big game

MEDIUM: Acrylic

STYLE: Electrifying, almost photo realistic renderings of big game in action.

Vivi captures the movement and emotion of the big-game animal with remarkable accuracy

AWARDS: "Downhill Racer"-North American Sheep Foundation Print of the Year, 1984

MEMBERSHIPS: Children Unlimited ("Close Encounters" was a Fundraising print for this organization)

GALLERY/DISTRIBUTOR: National Wild Galleries, Inc.

	ISSUE PRICE	CURRENT PRICE
☐ **CLOSE ENCOUNTERS**, rel. 1982. ed. 780, s/n, 25″ x 12″, pub NWGI	90.00	—
☐ **CATWALK**, rel. 1983. ed. 670, s/n, 23½″ x 17½″, pub NWGI	95.00	175.00
☐ **DOWNHILL RACER**, rel. 1983. ed. 670, s/n, 18″ x 24″, pub NWGI	125.00	—
☐ **FLASHDANCE**, rel. 1983. ed. 670, s/n, 27″ x 22″, pub NWGI	85.00	—
☐ **FLAT OUT**, rel. 1983. ed. 670, s/n, 17″ x 27″, pub NWGI	125.00	—
☐ **REVEILLE**, rel. 1983. ed. 670, s/n, 18″ x 24″, pub NWGI	125.00	—
☐ **ROOKIES**, rel. 1985. ed. 670, s/n, 20½″ x 24″, pub NWGI	95.00	—

MALLARDS AT WINGMEAD by T. Phillip Crowe

T. PHILLIP CROWE

THEMES: Wildlife art

AWARDS: Often honored, Crowe has won numerous Diamond Awards, as well as an Addy Award in 1976

GALLERY/DISTRIBUTOR: Grey Stone Press

	ISSUE PRICE	CURRENT PRICE
☐ JANUARY MUD - Canvasback, ed. 300, s/n, 23″ x 17½″, litho, pub GSP	30.00	60.00
☐ BACKWATER WOOD DUCKS, ed. 1,000, s/n, 18¾″ x 22¼″, litho, pub GSP	40.00	—
2,000, s/o	25.00	—
☐ BEAVER CREEK RED - Red Fox, ed. 300, s/n, 24″ x 19″, litho, pub GSP	30.00	45.00
☐ BUCK COUNTRY - Deer, ed. 1,000, s/n, 29″ x 27⅞″	50.00	—
ed. 50, a/p, remarqued, litho, pub GSP	100.00	—
☐ REELFOOT WINTER GUESTS - Mergansers, ed. 300, s/n, 23½″ x 19″, litho, pub GSP	30.00	60.00
☐ TENNESSEE 1980-1981, Duck Stamp Print, rel. 1980. ed. 1,000, s/n, size N/A, pub GSP	100.00	200.00
ed. 250, remarque	250.00	—
☐ THE OUTLAWS, rel. 1980. ed. 2,000, s/n, size N/A, pub GSP	50.00	200.00
ed. 250, remarqued, artist proofs	100.00	N/A
☐ THE BANDITS, rel. 1981. ed. 2,000, s/n, 28″ x 29″, pub GSP	50.00	Sold Out
ed. 100, remarqued, artist proofs	100.00	Sold Out
☐ THE OLD MAN AND THE PUP, rel. 1981. ed. 2,000, s/n, 21½″ x 28½″, pub GSP ...	50.00	—
ed. 100, remarqued, artist proofs	100.00	—
☐ THE OLD TAYLOR PLACE, rel. 1981. ed. 1,000, s/n, 29½″ x 21¾″, pub GSP	65.00	—
ed. remarqued, artist proofs	125.00	—
☐ DECEMBER MORNING, rel. 1982. ed. 800, s/n, 29½″ x 20½″, pub GSP	75.00	—
ed. 100, remarqued, artist proofs	125.00	—
☐ NATIONAL RETRIEVER CLUB STAMP AND PRINT, rel. 1982. ed. N/A, 15″ x 15″, stamp and print, pub GSP	125.00	350.00
Watercolor remarques upon request	250.00	455.00
☐ THE DUKES OF HAZARD, rel. 1982. ed. 2,500, s/n, 29½″ x 20″, pub GSP	60.00	—
ed. 100, remarqued, artist proofs	110.00	—
☐ WHITETAILS, rel. 1982. ed. 1,500, s/n, 20½″ x 22″, pub GSP	75.00	—
ed. 100, remarqued, artist proofs	125.00	—
☐ MALLARDS AT WINGMEAD, rel. 1983. ed. 650, s/n, 19¾″ x 29″, pub GSP	75.00	—
remarqued, artist proofs	125.00	—
☐ BOBWHITES AT ROCKBEND SOUTH, rel. 1984. ed. 1,000, s/n, 22″ x 28″, pub GSP	75.00	—
ed. 100, remarqued, artist proofs	125.00	—
☐ GONE FISHING, rel. 1984. ed. 2,500, s/n, 26½″ x 17½″, pub GSP	60.00	—
ed. 100, remarqued, artist proofs	125.00	—
☐ I'VE BEEN THERE, rel. 1984. ed. 750, s/n, 29″ x 21½″, pub GSP	75.00	150.00
ed. 100, remarqued, artist proofs	150.00	—
☐ THE GOOSE HUNTERS, rel. 1984. ed. 2,500, s/n, 28″x 21½″, pub GSP	60.00	—
ed. 100, remarqued, artist proofs	125.00	—
☐ THE WOOD DUCKS, rel. 1984. ed. 2,000, s/n, 24″ x 18½″, pub GSP	40.00	—
ed. 100, remarqued, artist proofs	125.00	—
☐ 1985 NATIONAL RETRIEVER CLUB STAMP PRINT, rel. 1985. s/n, 13″ x 15″, pub GSP	130.00	—
Upon request, artist proof	255.00	—
☐ DESPERADOS, rel. 1985. ed. 2,000, s/n, 29″ x 22″, pub GSP	60.00	—
ed. 100, artist proof, 29″ x 22″, pub GSP	160.00	—
☐ LOUISIANA TURKEY STAMP PRINT, rel. 1985, s/n, 12″ x 14″	130.00	—
Artist proof, 12″ x 14″	255.00	—

DONALD V. CROWLEY

THEMES: Varied, with a concentration on Paiute and Apache Indian women and children

EDUCATION: Art Center College

MEMBERSHIPS: Society of Illustrators

GALLERY/DISTRIBUTOR: Greenwich Workshop

COMMENTS: He states: "I hope that through my work these very special people will see in themselves the beauty and dignity that I see in them"

HOPI BUTTERFLY *by Donald V. Crowley*

	ISSUE PRICE	CURRENT PRICE
☐ **THE STARQUILT,** rel. 1978. ed. 1,00, s/n, 19″ x 25½″, pub GW	65.00	325.00
☐ **DORENA,** rel. 1978. ed. 1,000, s/n, 23″ x 24″, pub GW	75.00	115.00
☐ **HUDSON'S BAY BLANKET,** rel. 1978. ed. 1,000, s/n, 20½″ x 17″, pub GW	75.00	110.00
☐ **DESERT SUNSET,** rel. 1979. ed. 1,500, s/n, 19″ x 25½″, pub GW	75.00	120.00
☐ **SECURITY BLANKET,** rel. 1979. ed. 1,500, s/n, 12½″ x 16½″, pub GW	65.00	85.00
☐ **ARIZONA MOUNTAIN MAN,** rel. 1979. ed. 1,500, s/n, 20″ x 21″, pub GW	65.00	130.00
☐ **APACHE IN WHITE,** rel. 1980. ed. 1,500, s/n, 19½″ x 32″, pub GW	85.00	200.00
☐ **BEAUTY AND THE BEAST,** rel. 1980. ed. 1,500, s/n, 19″ x 23½″, pub GW	85.00	Sold Out
☐ **THE LITTLEST APACHE,** rel. 1980. ed. 275, signed, titled and numbered, 19¹¹⁄₁₆″ x 26¾″, hand-drawn lithograph, pub GW	325.00	515.00
☐ **AFTERGLOW,** rel. 1981. ed. 1,500, s/n, 27″ x 22½″, pub GW	110.00	Sold Out
☐ **SHANNANDOAH,** rel. 1981. ed. 275, signed, titled and numbered, 20″ x 25″, hand-drawn lithograph, pub GW	325.00	365.00
☐ **THE HEIRLOOM,** rel. 1981. ed. 1,000, s/n, 21¾″ x 34¾″, pub GW	125.00	375.00
☐ **EAGLE FEATHERS,** rel. 1981. ed. 1,500, s/n, 24½″ x 21½″, pub GW	95.00	Sold Out
☐ **HOPI BUTTERFLY,** rel. 1982. ed. 275, signed, titled and numbered, 20″ x 25″, hand-drawn lithograph, pub GW	350.00	—

DONALD H. CURLEY

THEMES: Varied

GALLERY/DISTRIBUTOR: Mill Pond Press, Inc.

	ISSUE PRICE	CURRENT PRICE
☐ **HEADING BACK,** rel. 1984. ed. 950, 24″ x 19½″, pub MPPI	85.00	—

SATURDAY NIGHT *by Jim Daly*

JIM DALY

THEMES: Americana

MEDIUM: Acrylic

STYLE: Realism

AWARDS: Mill Pond Press Award (1981)

MUSEUMS/COLLECTIONS: Favell Museum

GALLERY/DISTRIBUTOR: Mill Pond Press, Inc.

	ISSUE PRICE	CURRENT PRICE
☐ SPRING FEVER, rel. 1982. ed. 950, s/n, 20¼" x 24", pub MPPI	85.00	—
☐ SATURDAY NIGHT, rel. 1983. ed. 950, s/n, 23½" x 17½", pub MPPI	85.00	—

ROBERT B. DANCE

THEMES: Varied

MEDIUM: Watercolors

STYLE: Realism (no opaque white or white used with color)

BOOKS: The artist is featured in *40 Watercolorists and How They Work*

EDUCATION: Philadelphia Museum College of Art

MUSEUMS/COLLECTIONS: Permanent print collection of the North Carolina Museum of Fine Art

GALLERY/DISTRIBUTOR: Remarque, Inc.

	ISSUE PRICE	CURRENT PRICE
☐ GEMEIN HAUS, rel. 1974, ed. 500, s/n, 22" x 28", pub RI	50.00	350.00
☐ FOLLOWING SUMMER, rel. 1975. ed. 500, s/n, 22" x 24", pub RI	50.00	150.00
☐ BLUE RIDGE BREAKDOWN, rel. 1976. ed. 500, s/n, 22" x 28", pub RI	60.00	125.00
☐ THE MARSHRIDERS, rel. 1976. ed. 500, s/n, 19" x 25" (portfolio of 2), pub RI	100.00	250.00
☐ HANDY'S WHEEL, rel. 1977. ed. 500, s/n, 20" x 9½", pub RI	75.00	75.00
☐ THE HOMEPLACE, rel. 1977. ed. 500, s/n, 23" x 32", pub RI	60.00	125.00
☐ THE RIG, rel. 1978. ed. 500, s/n, 17¼" x 17¼", pub RI	50.00	150.00
☐ CAPE LOOKOUT MORNING, rel. 1979. ed. 500, s/n, 16⅝" x 25", pub RI	75.00	175.00

KEVIN DANIEL

THEMES: Wildlife art

GALLERY/DISTRIBUTOR: Voyageur Art

	ISSUE PRICE	CURRENT PRICE
☐ A BREAK IN THE STORM, rel. 1984. ed. 580, s/n, 18" x 24", litho, pub VA	85.00	—
☐ A FRIEND IN THE MARSH, rel. 1976. ed. 750, s/n, size N/A, pub VA	60.00	220.00
☐ BACK ROAD GATHERING, rel. 1978. ed. 750, s/n, size N/A, pub VA	60.00	150.00
☐ BARNYARD TUSSLE, rel. 1981. ed. 580, s/n, 28" x 22½", litho, pub VA	85.00	—
☐ BEWILDERED, rel. 1982. ed. 580, s/n, 28" x 22", litho, pub VA	85.00	—
☐ BLUE HERONS, rel. 1982. ed. 580, s/n, 28" x 22", litho, artists proofs, pub VA	120.00	—
☐ CHICKADEE, rel. 1982. ed. 580, s/n, 20" x 15", litho, pub VA	50.00	—

A BREAK IN THE STORM by Kevin Daniel

	ISSUE PRICE	CURRENT PRICE
☐ DAYBREAK, rel. 1980. ed. 750, s/n, 18″ x 23″, litho, pub VA	60.00	200.00
☐ LOST DECOY, rel. 1984. ed. 580, s/n, 18″ x 22½″, litho, pub VA	85.00	—
☐ OUT ON A LIMB, rel. 1981. ed. 580, s/n, 28″ x 22″, litho, pub VA	85.00	—
☐ PINE RIDGE, rel. 1981. ed. 580, s/n, 18″ x 23″, litho, pub VA	85.00	150.00
☐ PRIDE OF THE LAKES, rel. 1983. ed. 580, s/n, 18″ x 27″, litho, pub VA	85.00	Sold Out
☐ RIVER'S EDGE, rel. 1980. ed. 750, s/n, size N/A, pub VA	60.00	150.00
☐ SAFE AND SOUND, rel. 1982. ed. 580, s/n, 20″ x 15″, litho, pub VA	50.00	—
☐ SILENT SENTINEL, rel. 1982. ed. 580, s/n, 24½″ x 16″, litho, pub VA	85.00	—
☐ SIMPLY CURIOUS, rel. 1981. ed. 580, s/n, size N/A, pub VA	85.00	250.00
☐ TOUCH OF ORANGE, rel. 1982. ed. 580, s/n, 15½″ x 20″, litho, pub VA	85.00	—
☐ TOUCH OF RED/TOUCH OF BLUE (Pair), rel. 1981. ed. 580, s/n, size N/A, pub VA ..	120.00	350.00
☐ WETLANDS AND WILDS, rel. 1980. ed. 750, s/n, size N/A, pub VA	60.00	170.00

PETER DARRO

THEMES: Wildlife art

BACKGROUND: Before finding artistic fulfillment in wildlife painting, his portraiture won him national fame

MEMBERSHIPS: Society of Animal Artists

MUSEUMS/COLLECTIONS: His works have been shown at the Cleveland Museum of Natural History, and are included in many prominent collections

GALLERY/DISTRIBUTOR: Connoisseur's Gallery of Art, Ltd.

	ISSUE PRICE	CURRENT PRICE
☐ **A LOT OF BULL,** ed. 950, s/n, 16″ x 24″, pub CGAL	139.00	160.00
ed. 12, Artist accented, s/n	450.00	500.00
☐ **THE SENTINEL,** ed. 950, s/n, 19″ x 24″, pub CGAL	139.00	160.00
ed. 12, Artist accented, s/n	450.00	500.00
☐ **INTREPID,** ed. 950, s/n, 19″ x 21″, pub CGAL	139.00	160.00
ed. 12, Artist accented, s/n	450.00	500.00
☐ **BEWARE,** ed. 950, s/n, 19″ x 21″, pub CGAL	139.00	160.00
ed. 12, Artist accented, s/n	450.00	500.00
☐ **MORNING, KUDU CALF,** ed. 950, s/n, 16½″ x 24″, pub CGAL	139.00	160.00
ed. 12, Artist accented, s/n	450.00	500.00
☐ **ON GUARD,** ed. 950, s/n, 12″ x 24″, pub CGAL	139.00	160.00
ed. 12, Artist accented, s/n	450.00	500.00
☐ **TRIPLE THREAT,** ed. 950, s/n, 10″ x 24″, pub CGAL	139.00	160.00
ed. 12, Artist accented, s/n	450.00	500.00
☐ **CURIOUS, ZEBRA FOAL,** ed. 950, s/n, 24½″ x 16½″, pub CGAL	139.00	160.00
ed. 12, Artist accented, s/n	450.00	500.00
☐ **HIS MAJESTY,** ed. 950, s/n, 21″ x 17½″, pub CGAL	139.00	160.00
ed. 12, Artist accented, s/n	450.00	500.00
☐ **MASILAND,** ed. 950, s/n, 18″ x 21″, pub CGAL	139.00	160.00
ed. 12, Artist accented, s/n	450.00	500.00
☐ **CHARGE,** ed. 950, s/n, 16½″ x 24″, pub CGAL	139.00	160.00
ed. 12, Artist accented, s/n	450.00	500.00
☐ **KING OF THE MOUNTAIN,** ed. 950, s/n, 24″ x 17″, pub CGAL	160.00	—
ed. 12, Artist accented, s/n	500.00	—
☐ **SUNNY AFTERNOON,** ed. 950, s/n, 24″ x 12″, pub CGAL	160.00	—
ed. 12, Artist accented, s/n	500.00	—
☐ **ON THE PROWL,** ed. 950, s/n, 24″ x 17″, pub CGAL	160.00	—
ed. 12, Artist accented, s/n	500.00	—
☐ **FROSTY MORNING,** ed. 950, s/n, 24″ x 17″, pub CGAL	160.00	—
ed. 12, Artist accented, s/n	500.00	—
☐ **ALASKAN PARADISE,** ed. 950, s/n, 24″ x 17″, pub CGAL	160.00	—
ed. 12, Artist accented, s/n	500.00	—
☐ **HUNTING BUDDIES,** ed. 950, s/n, 24⅝″ x 25″, pub CGAL	160.00	—
ed. 12, Artist accented, s/n	500.00	—
☐ **KILIMANJAROL,** ed. 950, s/n, 23″ x 15″, pub CGAL	160.00	—
☐ **ON THE PLAIN,** ed. 950, s/n, 23″ x 17″	160.00	—

RAY DAVENPORT

THEMES: Varied

STYLE: Meticulous brushwork and attention to fine detail; realism

EDUCATION: Pratt Institute

MEMBERSHIPS: Allied Artists of America, National Society of Painters, Guild of South Carolina Artists, etc.

GALLERY/DISTRIBUTOR: Ray Davenport Studios

	ISSUE PRICE	CURRENT PRICE
☐ **ANNA'S NEW DRESS,** rel. 1983. ed. 975, s/n, litho, 13″ x 16″, pub RDS	30.00	—
☐ **JERRY'S FRIENDS,** rel. 1983. ed. 975, s/n, litho, 16″ x 13″, pub RDS	30.00	—
☐ **STORY TIME,** rel. 1984. ed. 975, s/n, litho, 13″ x 16″, pub RDS	30.00	—
☐ **THE CANADIAN,** rel. 1984. ed. 34, s/n, original litho, 22″ x 16″, pub RDS	60.00	—
☐ **WELCOME II,** rel. 1984. ed. 200, s/n, embossment, 9½″ x 13″, pub RDS	20.00	—
☐ **BUTTERFLY,** rel. 1985. ed. 200, s/n, embossment, 3″ x 3″, pub RDS	7.00	—
☐ **PINTAIL,** rel. 1985. ed. 200, s/n, embossment, 9½″ x 13″, pub RDS	22.00	—
☐ **STEEPLECHASE,** rel. 1985. ed. 13, s/n, original litho, 17″ x 15″, pub RDS	40.00	—

STORY TIME *by Ray Davenport*

	ISSUE PRICE	CURRENT PRICE
☐ **TABBY,** rel. 1985. ed. 29, s/n, original litho, 8″ x 11½″, pub RDS	38.00	—
☐ **WOODEN BUCKET,** rel. 1985, ed. 33, s/n, hand colored original litho, 9½″ x 13″, pub RDS	35.00	—
☐ **WOOD DUCK,** rel. 1985. ed. 200, s/n, embossment, 3″ x 3″, pub RDS	7.00	—

LOWELL DAVIS

THEMES: Americana

GALLERY/DISTRIBUTOR: Schmid Brothers, Inc.

	ISSUE PRICE	CURRENT PRICE
☐ **PLUM TUCKERED OUT,** rel. 1981. ed. 900, s/n, 19″ x 21½″, pub SB	75.00	—
ed. 100, remarqued	100.00	—
☐ **DUKE'S MIXTURE,** rel. 1981. ed. 900, s/n, 13½″ x 17″, pub SB	75.00	—
ed. 100, remarqued	100.00	—
☐ **SURPRISE IN THE CELLAR,** rel. 1981. ed. 900, s/n, 19″ x 21½″, pub SB	75.00	—
ed. 100, remarqued	100.00	Sold Out
☐ **BIRTH OF BLOSSOM,** rel. 1982. ed. 400, s/n, 15″ x 18″, pub SB	125.00	—
ed. 50, remarqued	200.00	—
☐ **BUSTIN' WITH PRIDE,** rel. 1982. ed. 900, s/n, 13½″ x 17″, pub SB	75.00	—
ed. 100, remarqued	100.00	—
☐ **FOXFIRE FARM,** rel. 1982. ed. 800, s/n, 7″ x 23″, pub SB	125.00	—
ed. 100, remarqued	200.00	—
☐ **SUPPERTIME,** rel. 1982. ed. 400, s/n, 14″ x 18″, pub SB	125.00	—
ed. 50, remarqued	200.00	—

BIRTH OF BLOSSOM *by Lowell Davis*

RAY DAY

THEMES: Americana

MEDIUM: Watercolor

STYLE: "Vignette style." The image is allowed to "float" in the white space, allowing for no hard eges

GALLERY/DISTRIBUTOR: Masterpiece Moulding & Fine Art Corp.

	ISSUE PRICE	CURRENT PRICE
THE OLD ROAD SERIES		
☐ **MAIL POUCH BARN, PLATE I,** rel. 1973. ed. 500, s/n, 20″ x 24″, distr. MMFC	15.00	175.00
ed. 2,000, s/o	10.00	75.00
☐ **ROCK CITY BARN, PLATE II,** rel. 1974. ed. 500, s/n, 20″ x 24″, distr. MMFC	15.00	75.00
ed. 2,000, s/o	10.00	30.00
☐ **BURMA SHAVE COUNTRY, PLATE III,** rel. 1975. ed. 500, s/n, 16″ x 20″, distr.		
MMFC	15.00	35.00
ed. 2,000, s/o	10.00	—
☐ **COCA-COLA COUNTRY, PLATE IV,** rel. 1977. ed. 750, s/n, 18″ x 24″, distr. MMFC . .	20.00	175.00
ed. 1,250, s/o	15.00	50.00
☐ **COUNTRY GENERAL STORE, PLATE V,** rel. 1979. ed. 1,000. s/n, 16″ x 20″, distr.		
MMFC	25.00	70.00
☐ **THE OLD MILL, PLATE VI,** rel. 1980. ed. 1,000, s/n, 22″ x 17½″, distr. MMFC	25.00	90.00
☐ **AN OLD COVERED BRIDGE, PLATE VII,** rel. 1981. ed. 1,000, s/n, 17½″ x 22″, distr.		
MMFC	35.00	70.00

	ISSUE PRICE	CURRENT PRICE
☐ COUNTRY STATION, PLATE VIII, rel. 1981. ed. 1,000, s/n, 17½″ x 22″, distr. MMFC	35.00	—
☐ MAIL POUCH, MAIL POUCH, PLATE IX, rel. 1982. ed. 1,000, s/n, 16″ x 24″, distr. MMFC	35.00	50.00
☐ COUNTRY CHURCH, PLATE X, rel. 1982. ed. 1,000, s/n, 17½″ x 22″, distr. MMFC ..	35.00	—
☐ REEL REFRESHING, PLATE XI, rel. 1983. ed. 1,000, s/n, 22″ x 17″, distr. MMFC ...	35.00	—
THE COUNTRY COUSINS SERIES		
☐ POP'S CORN, PLATE I, rel. 1976. ed. 500, s/n, 12″ x 14″, distr. MMFC	10.00	45.00
ed. 500, s/o	7.50	45.00
☐ MOTHER'S BASKET, PLATE II, rel. 1976. ed. 500, s/n, 12″ x 14″, distr. MMFC	10.00	45.00
ed. 500, s/o	7.50	45.00
☐ STRAWBERRIES AND DAISIES, PLATE III, rel. 1978. ed. 1,000, s/n, 16″ x 20″, distr. MMFC	25.00	140.00
☐ EGGS IN THE BASKET, PLATE IV, rel. 1979. ed. 1,000, s/n, 14½″ x 18″, distr. MMFC	25.00	—
☐ PUMPKINS AND JUGS, PLATE V, rel. 1980. ed. 1,000, s/n, 15″ x 15″, distr. MMFC ..	30.00	50.00
☐ GERANIUMS, PLATE VI, rel. 1981. ed. 1,000, s/n, 14″ x 17½″, distr. MMFC	30.00	—
☐ THE COLLECTION, PLATE VII, rel. 1981. ed. 1,000, s/n, 15″ x 17″, distr. MMFC	30.00	—
☐ PEACHES ON THE PORCH, PLATE VIII, rel. 1982. ed. 1,000, s/n, 15″ x 18″, distr. MMFC	30.00	—
☐ HONEYSUCKLE AND ROSES, PLATE IX, rel. 1983. ed. 1,000, s/n, 12½″ x 17″, distr. MMFC	30.00	—
THE SEASONS SERIES		
☐ COUNTRY CHURCH IN AUTUMN, rel. 1983. ed. 1,000, s/n, 8½″ x 16″, pub MMFAC	20.00	—
☐ GREAT MILL IN WINTER, rel. 1983. ed. 1,000, s/n, 8½″ x 16″, pub MMFC	20.00	—
☐ COVERED BRIDGE IN SPRING, rel. 1984. ed. 1,000, s/n, 8½″ x 16″, pub MMFC ...	20.00	—
☐ FARMSTEAD IN SUMMER, rel. 1984. ed. 1,000, s/n, 8½″ x 16″, pub MMFC	20.00	—
THE OLD ROAD SERIES		
☐ COUNTRY SCHOOLHOUSE, rel. 1984. ed. 1,000, s/n, 17½″ x 22″, pub MMFC	40.00	—
☐ RUBY FALLS, rel. 1985. ed. 1,000, s/n, 17″ x 24″, pub MMFC	40.00	—
THE COUNTRY COUSINS SERIES		
☐ STRAWBERRY DAYS, rel. 1984. ed. 1,000, s/n, 11″ x 15″, pub MMFC	30.00	—
THE MED ART SERIES		
☐ ARTICLES OF ADMINISTRATION, rel. 1980. ed. 3,000, s/n, 20″ x 24″, pub MMFC ..	35.00	—
☐ COMMITMENT TO LIFE, rel. 1984. ed. 1,500, s/n, 20″ x 24″, pub MMFC	50.00	—

LINDA C. DEVINS

THEMES: Seascapes, rural America, still life

MEDIUM: Acrylics

STYLE: Representational realistic art

AWARDS: Received one of 100 Keys to the International Biographical Centre in Cambridge, England. Has received over 100 major awards in juried art shows throughout the United States

MEMBERSHIPS: International Platform Association, National League of American Penwomen, National Society of Painters in Casien & Acrylics

GALLERY/DISTRIBUTOR: Devins Studio and American Images 'N' Art, Inc.

	ISSUE PRICE	CURRENT PRICE
☐ DUNES, rel. 1980. ed. 950, s/n, litho, 5″ x 7″, pub DS	7.50	15.00
☐ MORNING DUNES, rel. 1980. ed. 950, s/n, litho, 8″ x 10″, pub DS	12.50	20.00
☐ BLUEBERRIES, rel. 1981. ed. 500, 7½″ x 10″, pub DS	12.50	—
☐ HAY RAKE II, rel. 1984. ed. 950, s/n, litho, 8″ x 10″, pub DS	15.00	—
☐ SAND ISLAND LIGHT, rel. 1984. ed. 950, s/n, litho, 8″ x 10″, pub DS	15.00	—
☐ SUMMERTIME, rel. 1984. ed. 950, s/n, litho, 8″ x 10″, pub DS	15.00	20.00
☐ TAD'S WAGON, rel. 1984. ed. 950, s/n, litho, 8″ x 10″, pub DS	15.00	—
☐ THE CANDY, rel. 1984. ed. 950, s/n, litho, 8″ x 10″, pub DS	12.50	—
☐ THE RED BARN, rel. 1984. ed. 950, s/n, litho, 8″ x 10″, pub DS	15.00	—
☐ WOLFE'S BARN, rel. 1985. ed. 950, s/n, litho, 21″ x 26½″, pub AIAI	85.00	—

LISETTE DeWINNE

THEMES: Varied

MEDIUM: Oils

STYLE: Figurative with an abstract effect created through the colorful backgrounds of gracefully conceived portraits

GALLERY/DISTRIBUTOR: Collectors International Ltd.

COMMENTS: The Royal Doulton Company chose DeWinne's work for a series of collector plates

	ISSUE PRICE	CURRENT PRICE
☐ GYPSY MOTHER, rel. 1978. ed. 175, s/n, 24″ x 30″, pub WAEL	125.00	325.00
☐ MIRELLE, rel. 1978. ed. 950, s/n, 24″ x 30″, pub WAEL	125.00	300.00
☐ MUSICIANS, rel. 1978. ed. 950, s/n, 24″ x 30″, pub WAEL	125.00	Sold Out
☐ TOM, rel. 1978. ed. 950, s/n, 20″ x 23″, pub WAEL	90.00	—
☐ VILLAGE CHILD, rel. 1978. ed. 175, s/n, 24″ x 30″, pub WAEL	125.00	Sold Out
☐ BRIGHTER DAY, rel. 1979. ed. 950, s/n, 24″ x 30″, pub WAEL	140.00	—
☐ DEBRA, rel. 1979. ed. 950, s/n, 20″ x 23″, pub WAEL	90.00	—
☐ SCARAMOUCHE, rel. 1979. ed. 325, s/n, 24″ x 30″, pub WAEL	100.00	—
☐ WE THREE, rel. 1979. ed. 950. s/n, 20″ x 23″, pub WAEL	140.00	—
☐ AT THE WINDOW, rel. 1982. ed. 300, s/n, size N/A, pub CIL	295.00	325.00
☐ GRETCHEN, rel. 1982. ed. 300, s/n, size N/A, pub CIL	295.00	325.00

GENE DIECKHONER

THEMES: Wildlife art

EDUCATION: Ohio University

MEMBERSHIPS: Western Artists of America, Wildlife Artists International, Game Coin International, etc.

GALLERY/DISTRIBUTOR: Eagle Editions

	ISSUE PRICE	CURRENT PRICE
☐ FIDDLER ON THE ROOF, rel. 1980. ed. 1,000, s/n, 12″ x 24″, litho, pub AM	40.00	75.00
☐ KOALAS, rel. 1982. ed. 950, s/n, 13½″ x 21″, litho, pub GD	40.00	75.00
☐ YELLOW BLOSSOMS, rel. 1982. ed. 500, s/n, litho, pub GD	40.00	75.00

KOALAS *by Gene Dieckhoner*

	ISSUE PRICE	CURRENT PRICE
☐ **ABOVE THE GROS VENTRE - GOLDEN EAGLE,** rel. 1984. ed. 550, s/n, litho, 14″ x 25″, pub EEL	85.00	—
☐ **BRIEF ENCOUNTER - RED FOX,** rel. 1985. ed. 500, s/n, litho, 7½″ x 11¼″, pub EEL	50.00	—

JIM DIETZ

THEMES: Varied

GALLERY/DISTRIBUTOR: Grey Stone Press

	ISSUE PRICE	CURRENT PRICE
☐ **THE OLD HAND,** rel. 1983. ed. 1,000, s/n, 21½″ x 28½″, pub GSP	75.00	—
☐ **EARLY MORNING OPS,** rel. 1983. ed. 1,000, s/n, 26″ x 18½″, pub GSP	75.00	—
☐ **DUEL AT ODDS,** rel. 1984. ed. 1,000, s/n, 26″ x 19″, pub GSP	75.00	—
☐ **SUNDAY AFTERNOON,** rel. 1985. ed. 1,000, s/n, 28″ x 22″, pub GSP	80.00	—

LARRY DODSON

THEMES: Landscape art

MUSEUMS/COLLECTIONS: There are nearly one hundred of the artist's original works in private collections throughout the South

GALLERY/DISTRIBUTOR: Swan Graphics, Ltd.

	ISSUE PRICE	CURRENT PRICE
☐ **SPRINGTIME IN ELIJAY,** rel. 1975. ed. 1,000, s/n, 18″ x 19″, pub SGL	20.00	175.00
ed. 100 artist proofs	40.00	250.00
☐ **CURING BARN,** rel. 1976. ed. 1,000, s/n, 16″ x 23″	20.00	100.00
ed. 100 artist proofs	40.00	150.00
☐ **MOUNTAIN VIEW ROAD,** rel. 1976. ed. 1,000, s/n, 22″ x 14″, pub SGL	25.00	150.00
ed. 100 artist proofs	50.00	200.00
☐ **MISTY SUMMER DAY,** rel. 1976. ed. 1,000, s/n, 24″ x 17″, pub SGL	30.00	150.00
ed. 100 artist proofs	50.00	200.00
☐ **SPRING AWAKENING,** rel. 1977. ed. 1,000, s/n, 23″ x 15″, pub SGL	30.00	250.00
ed. 100 artist proofs	50.00	250.00
☐ **APRIL MORNING,** rel. 1977. ed. 1,500, s/o, 22¼″ x 15½″, pub SGL	20.00	60.00
ed. 1,000, s/n	30.00	90.00
ed. 100 artist proofs	50.00	125.00
☐ **AUTUMN MIST,** rel. 1977. ed. 1,500, s/n, 24″ x 14¼″, pub SGL	20.00	60.00
ed. 1,000, s/n	30.00	75.00
ed. 100 artist proofs	50.00	125.00
☐ **WINTER REFLECTION,** rel. 1977. ed, 1,500, s/o, 22½″ x 17¾″, pub SGL	25.00	—
ed. 1,000, s/n	50.00	125.00
ed. 100 artist proofs	75.00	125.00
☐ **MOUNTAIN BREEZE,** rel. 1978. ed. 1,250, s/o, 22¼″ x 14¾″, pub SGL	25.00	50.00
ed. 1,500, s/n	35.00	75.00
ed. 100 artist proofs	50.00	100.00
☐ **LAUREL RIDGE,** rel. 1978. ed. 1,250, s/o, 22″ x 15¼″, pub SGL	25.00	—
ed. 1,500, s/n	35.00	—
ed. 100 artist proofs	50.00	—
☐ **TEA KETTLE/WATER PAIL** rel. 1978. ed. 3,000, s/o, 8″ x 8″, pub SGL	*15.00	—
ed. 100 artist proofs	25.00	—
*Sold as a pair		
☐ **YELLOW CREEK,** rel. 1978. ed. 1,250, s/o, 23″ x 15¼″, pub SGL	25.00	—
ed. 1,500, s/n	35.00	—
ed. 100 artist proofs	50.00	—
☐ **GOLDEN HARVEST,** rel. 1979. ed. 1,500, s/n, 22½″ x 17½″, pub SGL	45.00	—
ed. 100 artist proofs	75.00	—
☐ **SECLUDED TRAIL/TRAIL'S END,** rel. 1979. ed. 1,000, s/o, 9½″ x 12″, pub SGL	*30.00	—
ed. 100 artist proofs	50.00	—
*Sold as a pair		
☐ **PEACEFUL MEADOW,** rel. 1979. ed. 1,500, s/n, 23″ x 18½″, pub SGL	45.00	Sold Out
ed. 100 artist proofs	75.00	—
☐ **WINTER AT CHIMNEY TOPS,** rel. 1979. ed. 1,500, s/n, 23″ x 19¼″, pub SGL	45.00	—
ed. 100 artist proofs	75.00	—

BEV DOOLITTLE

THEMES: Wildlife and Western art

MEDIUM: Transparent watercolor

MUSEUMS/COLLECTIONS: Favell Museum of Western Art and Indian Artifacts, IBM Corporation Art Collection, private groups

AWARDS: 1985 Western Artist of the Year by the National Wildlife and Western Art Collectors Society

MEMBERSHIPS: National Watercolor Society

GALLERY/DISTRIBUTOR: Mill Pond Press, Inc.

COMMENTS: "I try to look beyond the obvious and create unique, meaningful paintings depicting our Western wilderness and its inhabitants"

LET MY SPIRIT SOAR *by Bev Doolittle*

	ISSUE PRICE	CURRENT PRICE
☐ **PINTOS,** rel. 1979. ed. 1,000, s/n, 21″ x 21″, pub GW	65.00	2,700.00
☐ **BUGGED BEAR,** rel. 1980. ed. 1,000, s/n, 19½″ x 19½″, pub GW	85.00	175.00
☐ **THE GOOD OMEN,** rel. 1980. ed. 1,000, s/n, 21⅛″ x 32½″, pub GW	85.00	900.00
☐ **WHO!?,** rel. 1980. ed. 1,000, s/n, 12″ x 28″, pub GW	75.00	165.00
☐ **SPIRIT OF THE GRIZZLY,** rel. 1981. ed. 1,500, s/n, 21″ x 31½″, pub GW	150.00	725.00
☐ **UNKNOWN PRESENCE,** rel. 1981. ed. 1,500, s/n, 31″ x 14¼″, pub GW	135.00	375.00
☐ **WOODLAND ENCOUNTER,** rel. 1981. ed. 1,500, s/n, 36″ x 20″, pub GW	145.00	3,000.00
☐ **EAGLES FLIGHT,** rel. 1982. ed. 1,500, s/n, 35½″ x 19½″, pub GW	185.00	900.00
☐ **CHRISTMAS DAY, GIVE OR TAKE A WEEK,** rel. 1983. s/n, 18½″ x 19″, pub GW ...	80.00	140.00
☐ **ESCAPE BY A HARE,** rel. 1983. ed. 1,500, s/n, 16½″ x 13¼″, pub GW	80.00	150.00
☐ **RUSHING WAR EAGLE,** rel. 1983. ed. 1,500, s/n, 28⅛″ x 20½″, pub GW	150.00	500.00
☐ **RUNS WITH THUNDER,** rel. 1983. ed. 1,500, s/n, 22¼″ x 33⅞″, pub GW	150.00	300.00
☐ **THE ART OF CAMOUFLAGE,** rel. 1983. ed. 2,000, s/n, 24″ x 30″, poster, pub GW ..	55.00	Sold Out
☐ **LET MY SPIRIT SOAR,** rel. 1984. ed. 1,500, s/n, 22¼″ x 28⅛″	195.00	350.00
☐ **THE FOREST HAS EYES,** rel. 1984. ed. 8,544, Personal Commission, s/n, litho, 39″ x 21½″, pub GW	175.00	365.00
☐ **WOLVES OF THE CROW,** rel. 1985. ed. 2,650, s/n, litho, 37″ x 16⅝″, pub GW	225.00	Sold Out

ANNE OPHELIA DOWDEN

THEMES: Botanical art

BACKGROUND: The artist is also a teacher, mural painter, and textile designer

EDUCATION: Carnegie Institute of Technology

GALLERY/DISTRIBUTOR: Frame House Gallery, Inc.

	ISSUE PRICE	CURRENT PRICE
☐ FLOWERING DOGWOOD, rel. 1969. ed. 5,000, s/o, 18″ x 23″, pub FHG	20.00	40.00
This print was also offered as a free bonus to new members during the 1969-70 Audubon Society membership campaign in North Carolina.		
☐ BUTTERFLY WEED, rel. 1970. ed. 5,000, s/o, 10″ x 14″, pub FHG		
This print was also offered as a free bonus to new members during the 1970 Audubon Society Membership campaign in Michigan.		
☐ GOLDENROD, rel. 1970. ed. 3,500, s/o, 18″ x 22″, pub FHG	20.00	25.00
☐ MUSHROOMS, (PORTFOLIO OF 6), rel. 1970. ed. 5,000, s/o, 6″ x 8″, pub FHG	20.00	75.00
One print signed by the artist constitutes signature for entire portfolio.		
☐ SPRING FLOWERS/AUTUMN FLOWERS, pair, rel. 1970. ed. 2,500, s/o, 11″ x 14″, pub FHG	20.00	85.00
☐ WILDFLOWERS OF THE PLAINS, rel. 1970. ed. 3,500, s/o, 18″ x 22″, pub FHG	20.00	40.00
☐ CRAB APPLE/APRICOT, pair, rel. 1971. ed. 2,500, s/o, 10″ x 13″, pub FHG	20.00	40.00
☐ FLAME AZALEA/PIEDMONT AZALEA, rel. 1971. ed. 2,500, s/o, 11″ x 15″, pub FHG	20.00	75.00
Of the above edition, 500 were with embossed seal printed exclusively for Callaway Gardens, Georgia.		
☐ PLUMLEAF AZALEA, rel. 1971. ed. 2,500, s/o, 16″ x 20″, pub FHG	20.00	40.00
Of the above edition, 500 were with embossed seal printed exclusively for Callaway Gardens, Georgia.		
☐ POMEGRANATE GRAPE, pair, rel. 1971. ed. 2,500, s/o, 10″ x 13″, pub FHG	20.00	40.00
☐ YELLOW BOUQUET, pair, rel. 1971. ed. 2,500, s/o, 11″ x 14″, pub FHG	20.00	85.00
☐ HYBRID TEA ROSES/OLD ROSES, pair, rel. 1972. ed. 1,500, s/o, 12″ x 18½″, pub FHG	20.00	50.00
☐ CAROLINA ROSE/CHEROKEE ROSE, pair, rel. 1973. ed. 1,500, s/o, 12″ x 16″, pub FHG	20.00	40.00
☐ HERBS, (PORTFOLIO OF 6), rel. 1973. ed. 5,000, s/o, 6″ x 9″, pub FHG	30.00	100.00
One print signed by the artist constitutes signature of portfolio.		
☐ AMERICAN BEAUTY ROSE, rel. 1974. ed. 3,000, s/o, 14″ x 12″, pub FHG	15.00	25.00
☐ BLACK-EYED SUSAN, rel. 1974. ed. 3,000, s/o, 14″ x 12″, pub FHG	15.00	60.00
☐ FLOWERING DOGWOOD, rel. 1974. ed. 3,000, s/o, 14″ x 12″, pub FHG	15.00	40.00
☐ GREAT LAUREL OR ROSE BAY, rel. 1974. ed. 3,000, s/o, 14″ x 12″, pub FHG	15.00	Sold Out
☐ HOLDEN RHODODENDRON, rel. 1974. ed. 2,000, s/o, 16″ x 20″, pub FHG	20.00	Sold Out
☐ FLOWERS OF THE FIELD/GARDEN OF HERBS, pair, rel. 1975. ed. 2,000, s/o, 22″ x 16″, pub FHG	45.00	Sold Out
☐ FOOD FOR LIFE, rel. 1975. ed. 2,000, s/o, 22″ x 30″, pub FHG	40.00	Sold Out
☐ PLANTS FOR THE TEMPLE/TREES OF THE LORD, pair, rel. 1975. ed. 2,000, s/o, 22″ x 16″, pub FHG	45.00	—
☐ PRAIRIE SUNFLOWER, rel. 1977. ed. 600, s/o, 20″ x 16″, pub FHG	35.00	60.00
☐ PRICKLY POPPY AND INDIAN PAINTBRUSH, rel. 1977. ed. 600, s/o, 20″ x 16″, pub FHG	35.00	60.00
☐ CHRISTMAS PLANTS, rel. 1978. ed. 2,000, s/o, 20″ x 16″, pub FHG	30.00	—
☐ MUSHROOMS FROM A DARK HUMID WOODS/MUSHROOMS FROM A SUNNY FOREST PATH, pair, rel. 1978. ed. 1,500, s/o, 14″ x 11″, pub FHG	35.00	50.00
☐ SQUASH BLOSSOM, rel. 1978. ed. 600, s/o, 16″ x 20″, pub FHG	40.00	—
☐ AUTUMN FOLIAGE, rel. 1978. ed. 2,000, s/o, 20″ x 16″, pub FHG	35.00	—
☐ CAMELLIA and FLOWERING QUINCE, rel. 1979. ed. 600, s/o, 16″ x 20″, pub FHG .	40.00	Sold Out
☐ PEPPERS/ARTICHOKE, pair, rel. 1979. ed. 1,000, s/o, 14″ x 11″, pub FHG	30.00	—
☐ MINIATURE BULB PAIR, pair, rel. 1980. ed. 1,500, i/o, 14″ x 11″, pub FHG	40.00	—

JACK DUMAS

THEMES: Wildlife art

BACKGROUND: He began his career as a professional artist working for Walt Disney Studios

EDUCATION: Cornish Art School; Seattle Academy of Arts

GALLERY/DISTRIBUTOR: Wild Wings, Inc.

	ISSUE PRICE	CURRENT PRICE
☐ **MAN TRACKS,** rel. 1982. ed. 850, s/n, 17½″ x 17½″, pub WWI	75.00	—

NOEL DUNN

THEMES: Wildlife art, primarily game birds

GALLERY/DISTRIBUTOR: Wild Wings, Inc.

	ISSUE PRICE	CURRENT PRICE
☐ **CROSSING THE TOTE ROAD - RUFFED GROUSE,** rel. 1981. ed. 500, s/n, size N/A, pub WWI	65.00	—
☐ **DOWNHILL FLUSH - CHUKAR,** rel. 1982. ed. 450, s/n, 17½″ x 24″, distr. WWI	75.00	—
☐ **STILLWATER MARSH SPRIG,** rel. 1982. ed. 450, s/n, size N/A, distr. WWI	75.00	—

TOM DUNNINGTON

THEMES: Birds

STYLE: Realism

EDUCATION: John Herron School of Art in Indianapolis; American Academy of Art in Chicago

GALLERY/DISTRIBUTOR: Cottage Hill Wildlife Art

	ISSUE PRICE	CURRENT PRICE
☐ **AMERICAN BALD EAGLE #1,** rel. 1971. ed. 4,700, s/o, 32″ x 23″, pub CHWA	30.00	60.00
ed. 200, s/n	100.00	225.00
ed. 100 Artist proofs		175.00
☐ **BALD EAGLE,** rel. 1972. ed. 4,700, s/o, 17″ x 23″, pub CHWA	40.00	60.00
ed. 200, s/n	70.00	140.00
ed. 100 Artist proofs		150.00
☐ **GOLDEN EAGLE,** rel. 1972. ed. 4,700, s/o, 23″ x 17″, pub CHWA	30.00	40.00
ed. 200, s/n	50.00	80.00
ed. 100 Artist proofs		125.00

	ISSUE PRICE	CURRENT PRICE
☐ GREAT PRAIRIE CHICKEN, rel. 1971. ed. 4,700, s/o, 17″ x 23″, pub CHWA	20.00	40.00
ed. 200, s/n	70.00	140.00
ed. 100 Artist proofs		150.00
☐ MASKED BOB WHITE, rel. 1973. ed. 4,700, s/o, 17″ x 23″, pub CHWA	20.00	40.00
ed. 200, s/n	50.00	75.00
ed. 100 Artist proofs		100.00
☐ PEREGRINE FALCON, rel. 1971. ed. 4,700, s/o, 23″ x 17″, pub CHWA	20.00	40.00
ed. 200, s/n	70.00	150.00
ed. 100 Artist proofs		175.00
☐ PILEATED WOODPECKER, rel. 1972. ed. 4,700, s/o, 17″ x 23″, pub CHWA	30.00	40.00
ed. 200, s/n	50.00	80.00
ed. 100 Artist proofs		125.00
☐ RED TAIL HAWK, rel. 1972. ed. 4,700, s/o, 17″ x 23″, pub CHWA	20.00	40.00
ed. 200, s/n	50.00	70.00
ed. 100 Artist proofs		100.00
☐ THE OSPREY, rel. 1972. ed. 4,700, s/o, 17″ x 23″	20.00	40.00
ed. 200, s/n	50.00	80.00
ed. 100 Artist proofs		125.00

GILBERT DURAN

THEMES: Wildlife art

MEDIUM: Watercolor

GALLERY/DISTRIBUTOR: Arts Limited Inc.

	ISSUE PRICE	CURRENT PRICE
☐ ALONE, ed. Open, s/o, 24″ x 31½″	45.00	—
ed. Open, unsigned	25.00	—
☐ BENGAL TIGER, ed. 1,500, s/n, 30″ x 24″	50.00	—
ed. 1,500, s/o	40.00	—
☐ BOB WHITE QUAIL, ed. 500, s/n, 37½″ x 24½″	100.00	Sold Out
ed. 1,500, s/o	25.00	Sold Out
☐ DANGER MOMENT, ed. 600, s/n, 28″ x 21½″	40.00	—
☐ INSTANT OF QUIETNESS, ed. 600, s/n, 28″ x 21½″	40.00	Sold Out
☐ JAGUAR, ed. 1,500, s/n, 30″ x 24″	50.00	—
ed. 1,500, s/o	40.00	—
☐ MORNING DRINK, ed. 600, s/n, 28″ x 21½″	40.00	Sold Out
☐ MOURNING DOVES, ed. 500, s/n, 24½″ x 37½″, pub ALI	100.00	Sold Out
ed. 1,500, n/o	25.00	Sold Out
☐ RIO TURKEY, ed. 1,500, s/n, 24″ x 30″	50.00	—
ed. 1,500, s/o	40.00	—
☐ SHORT STOP, ed. Open, s/o, 24″ x 31½″	45.00	—
ed. Open, unsigned	25.00	—
☐ THE LONELY ONE, ed. 600, s/n, 28″ x 21½″	40.00	—
☐ TURKEY, ed. 500, s/n, 37½″ x 24½″	100.00	Sold Out
ed. 1,500, n/o	25.00	Sold Out
☐ WHITETAIL DEER, ed. 1,500, s/n, 30″ x 24″	50.00	—
ed. 1,500, s/o	40.00	—
☐ WHITE WING DOVES, ed. 500, s/n, 24½″ x 37″, pub ALI	100.00	Sold Out
ed. 1,500, n/o	25.00	Sold Out
☐ WOOD DUCK, ed. 600, s/n, 28″ x 21½″	40.00	Sold Out

BURTON DYE

THEMES: Americana
MEDIUM: Oils
STYLE: Realism
EDUCATION: Watkins Institute
GALLERY/DISTRIBUTOR: Burton Dye Prints

FRESH STRAWBERRIES *by Burton Dye*

	ISSUE PRICE	CURRENT PRICE
☐ **FALLS MILL,** rel. 1975. ed. 1,000, s/n, 20″ x 26″, pub BDP	30.00	Sold Out
ed. 2,400, s/o	20.00	—
☐ **AUTUMN MEMORIES,** rel. 1976. ed. 1,000, s/n, 27½″ x 21½″, pub BDP	30.00	75.00
☐ **COUNTRY AFTERNOON,** rel. 1977. ed. 1,000, s/n, 15½″ x 22¾″, pub BDP	30.00	—
☐ **LAYNE'S GROCERY,** rel. 1977. ed. 1,000, s/n, 15″ x 21″, pub BDP	20.00	Sold Out
☐ **RUSTY BUCKET,** rel. 1978. ed. 3,000, s/o, 10½″ x 12½″, pub BDP	7.00	—
☐ **SUMMER DAY,** rel. 1978. ed. 1,000, s/n, 15″ x 22¾″, pub BDP	30.00	—
☐ **WILD DAISIES,** rel. 1978. ed. 3,000, s/o, 10½″ x 12½″, pub BDP	7.00	—
☐ **AFTERNOON SHADOWS,** rel. 1979. ed. 1,500, s/o, 14″ x 18″, pub BDP	15.00	—
☐ **AUNT MATTIE'S PLACE,** rel. 1980. ed. 500, s/n, 14½″ x 25½″, pub BDP	30.00	75.00
☐ **APPLE HARVEST,** rel. 1981. ed. 1,000, s/n, 18″ x 25″, pub BDP	35.00	—

	ISSUE PRICE	CURRENT PRICE
☐ **PEACEFUL STREAM,** rel. 1981. ed. 1,000, s/n, 13½″ x 17½″, pub BDP	20.00	—
☐ **SNOWDRIFTS,** rel. 1981. ed. 1,000, s/n, 13½″ x 17½″, pub BDP	20.00	—
☐ **MISTY MOUNTAIN TRAIL,** rel. 1982. ed. 1,000, s/n, 17″ x 22½″, pub BDP	30.00	—
☐ **BEACHED,** rel. 1983. ed. 1,000, s/n, 11½″ x 16″, pub BDP	25.00	—
☐ **CRIB WATCH,** rel. 1983. ed. 1,000, s/n, 18¾″ x 24½″, pub BDP	35.00	—
☐ **GULL TALK,** rel. 1983. ed. 1,000, s/n, 8½″ x 13″, pub BDP	20.00	—
☐ **LOW TIDE,** rel. 1983. ed. 1,000, s/n, 10¾″ x 21½″, pub BDP	35.00	—
☐ **MYSTIC PORT,** rel. 1983. ed. 1,000, s/n, 15″ x 23″, pub BDP	40.00	—
☐ **WINTER SOLITUDE,** rel. 1983. ed. 1,000, s/n, 19″ x 25″, pub BDP	40.00	—
☐ **BACK OFF,** rel. 1984. ed. 1,000, s/n, 11″ x 15″, pub BDP	25.00	—
☐ **FEEDING TIME,** rel. 1984. ed. 1,000, s/n, 16″ x 22″, pub BDP	40.00	—
☐ **FEEDING TIME,** rel. 1984. ed. 1,000, s/o, 16″ x 22″, pub BDP	35.00	—
☐ **ONCE A HOME,** rel. 1985. ed. 1,000, s/n, 13″ x 19″, pub BDP	35.00	—
☐ **TWO LATE FOR DINNER,** rel. 1985. ed. 1,500, s/n, 12″ x 14″, pub BDP	40.00	—

SHARING THE FAITH by Larry Dyke

LARRY DYKE

THEMES: Bible teachings

EDUCATION: Baylor University

GALLERY/DISTRIBUTOR: American Masters Foundation

COMMENTS: Dyke's philosophy that his artistic talent is a gift explains the most unique feature of his work—a scripture reference included with his signature

	ISSUE PRICE	CURRENT PRICE
☐ COLLECTOR'S SUITE, MATTHEW 11:28, GENESIS 46:32, HEBREWS 8:13, rel. 1979.		
ed. 1,000, s/n, size varies, pub AMF	48.00	110.00
ed. 1,800, s/o, released in 1980	35.00	75.00
☐ DANIEL 2:21 (Raccoon), rel. 1982. ed. 1,500, s/n, 16″ x 20″, pub AMF	70.00	105.00
ed. 2,500, s/o	45.00	65.00
☐ DEUTERONOMY 28:8 (Barn & Windmill), rel. 1980. ed. 1,000, s/n, 16″ x 20″, pub AMF..	55.00	250.00
ed. 1,800, s/o	37.50	150.00
☐ DEUTERONOMY 11:12, rel. 1983. ed. 1,600, s/n, 16″ x 21″, pub AMF	85.00	90.00
☐ EARLY ARRIVAL (Ephesians 5:8), rel. 1983. ed. 1,600, s/n, 16″ x 20″, pub AMF	75.00	100.00
☐ ECCLESIASTES 3:1 (Turkeys), rel. 1982. ed. 1,500, s/n, 18½″ x 23½″, pub AMF ...	70.00	130.00
☐ EZEKIEL 32:14 (Turkeys), rel. 1981. ed. 1,500, s/n, 15″ x 20″, pub AMF	65.00	125.00
ed. 2,500, s/o	40.00	65.00
☐ EZEKIEL 34:15 (White cows), rel. 1980. ed. 1,000, s/n, 14″ x 24″, pub AMF	55.00	105.00
ed. 1,800, s/o	37.50	85.00
☐ ISAIAH 40:3 (Stage coach), rel. 1978. ed. 1,000, s/n, 16″ x 20″, pub AMF	40.00	300.00
ed. 1,500, s/o	30.00	150.00
☐ ISAIAH 45:3 (Oil rig), rel. 1982. ed. 1,950, s/n, 18″ x 22½″, pub AMF	80.00	150.00
☐ ISAIAH 58:8 (Horizontal windmill), rel. 1978. ed. 1,000, s/n, 16″ x 20″, pub AMF ...	35.00	300.00
☐ JOB 39:8 (Elk), rel. 1982. ed. 1,500, s/n, 21″ x 27″, pub AMF	85.00	175.00
☐ JOHN 3:8 (Vertical windmill), rel. 1978. ed. 1,000, s/n, 16″ x 20″, pub AMF	30.00	700.00
☐ JOHN 8:32 (Mountain panorama), rel. 1982. ed. Time-Limited, 1,500, s/n, 16″ x 32″, pub AMF..	85.00	125.00
☐ JOHN 9:4 (Night scene), rel. 1979. ed. 1,000, s/n, 18″ x 24″, pub AMF	45.00	150.00
ed. 2,000, s/o, released in 1981	30.00	85.00
☐ JOHN 10:27 (Sheep & bluebonnets), rel. 1981, ed. 1,000, s/n, 16″ x 20″, pub AMF .	60.00	140.00
ed. 2,700, s/o	37.50	80.00
☐ JOSHUA 2:22 (Mountain man), rel. 1982. ed. 1,500, s/n, 18″ x 24″, pub AMF	70.00	105.00
ed. 2,500, s/o	45.00	60.00
☐ LAMENTATIONS 3:28 (Deer winter scene), rel. 1981. ed. 1,500, s/n, 18″ x 24″, pub AMF..	68.00	175.00
rel. 1982. ed. 2,500, s/o	45.00	120.00
☐ MAJESTIC MORNING (Amos 4:13), rel. 1984. ed. 1,600, s/n, 18″ x 22½″, pub AMF	85.00	95.00
☐ MATTHEW 6:30 (Horse pastoral), rel. 1981. ed. Time-Limited, s/n, 18″ x 24″, pub AMF..	40.00	90.00
☐ MATTHEW 9:37 (Corn patch), rel. 1981. ed. 1,000, s/n, 16″ x 20″, pub AMF	65.00	120.00
☐ MATTHEW 18:12 (Sheep at gate), rel. 1983. ed. 1,500, s/n, 16″ x 20″, pub AMF	75.00	140.00
☐ PROVERBS 8:25 (Horse), rel. 1979. ed. 1,000, s/n, 18″ x 24″, pub AMF	45.00	125.00
ed. 1,800, s/o, released in 1981	30.00	80.00
☐ PROVERBS 23:10 (Hereford cows), rel. 1981. ed. 1,000, sn, 18″ x 22½″, pub AMF .	60.00	175.00
ed. 2,200, so	37.50	110.00
☐ PSALM 27:4 (Mission), rel. 1978. ed. 1,000, s/n, 18″ x 24″, pub AMF	40.00	425.00
☐ PSALM 42:1 (Deer & stream), rel. 1980. ed. 1,000, s/n, 18″ x 24″, pub AMF	55.00	250.00
ed. 1,200, s/o	37.50	150.00
☐ PSALM 90:2 (Mountain & lake), rel. 1981. ed. 1,500, s/n, 18″ x 22½″, pub AMF	67.50	130.00
ed. 2,500, s/o	45.00	85.00
☐ PSALM 91:1 (Squirrel), rel. 1980. ed. 1,000, s/n, 12″ x 16″, pub AMF	45.00	75.00
ed. 2,200, s/o	30.00	50.00
☐ PSALM 113:3 (Bull), rel. 1979. ed. 1,000, s/n, 16″ x 20″, pub AMF	40.00	125.00
ed. 1,500, s/o, released in 1980	30.00	100.00
☐ PSALM 147:16 (Christmas print), rel. 1979. ed. 1,000, s/n, 16″ x 20″, pub AMF	45.00	125.00
ed. 1,200, s/o, released in 1980	30.00	95.00
☐ REVELATION 21:6 (Waterfall), rel. 1980. ed. 1,000, s/n, 20″ x 26½″, pub AMF	55.00	850.00
ed. 1,800, s/o	35.00	400.00

	ISSUE PRICE	CURRENT PRICE
☐ ROMANS 15:32 (Snow scene), rel. 1980. ed. 1,000, s/n, 16″ x 20″, pub AMF	57.50	100.00
☐ SHADY CREEK MILL (Job 40:22), rel. 1985. ed. 1,600, s/n, 18½″ x 20″, pub AMF ..	85.00	—
☐ SONG OF SOLOMON 2:17 (Deer & Cactus), rel. 1979. ed. 1,000, s/n, 18″ x 24″, pub AMF	45.00	135.00
ed. 1,800, s/o, released in 1980	30.00	90.00
☐ SHARING THE FAITH, rel. 1984. ed. N/A, s/n, pub AMF	85.00	150.00
☐ THE OFFERING (Mark 12:41-44), rel. 1985. ed. 3,000, s/n, 18″ x 24″, pub AMF	125.00	—
☐ TRANQUIL REFUGE (Jeremiah 48:40), rel. 1984. ed. 1,600, s/n, 16″ x 20″, pub AMF	80.00	90.00
☐ ZACHARIAH 14:7, rel. 1983. ed. 1,600, s/n, 18″ x 24″, pub AMF	85.00	100.00

EYVIND EARLE

THEMES: American countryside

BACKGROUND: Assistant background painter at Walt Disney Studios, worked on *Sleeping Beauty*

GALLERY/DISTRIBUTOR: Hammer Publishing Co.

	ISSUE PRICE	CURRENT PRICE
☐ BIG SUR, ed. 250, s/n, 26″ x 34″, serigraph, pub CFAC	—	550.00
☐ GREEN VALLEY, ed. 275, s/n, 30″ x 32″, serigraph, pub CFAC	—	500.00
☐ HIDDEN VALLEY, ed. 300, s/n, 25″ x 36″, serigraph, pub CFAC	—	500.00
☐ LANDSCAPE, ed. 250, s/n, 34″ x 45″, serigraph, pub CFAC	—	375.00

GAVIOTA PASS *by Eyvind Earle*

	ISSUE PRICE	CURRENT PRICE
☐ MIDNIGHT SNOW, ed. 250, s/n, 28″ x 34″, serigraph, pub CFAC	—	375.00
☐ PRECIPICE, ed. 275, s/n, 31″ x 36″, serigraph, pub CFAC	—	450.00
☐ RED BARN, ed. 300, s/n, 24″ x 47″, serigraph, pub CFAC	—	750.00
☐ RED POPPIES, ed. 250, s/n, 35″ x 46″, serigraph, pub CFAC	—	600.00
☐ SPRING SNOW, ed. 275, s/n, 30″ x 37″, serigraph, pub CFAC	—	375.00
☐ THE SEA BELOW, ed. 300, s/n, 25″ x 36″, serigraph, pub CFAC	—	375.00
☐ AUTUMN, rel. 1979. ed. 300, s/n, 28″ x 22″, serigraph, pub HP	—	Sold Out
☐ BLACK EVERGREEN FOREST, rel. 1979. ed. 300, s/n, 30″ x 40″, serigraph, pub HP	—	Sold Out
☐ BLUE PINE, rel. 1979. ed. 300, s/n, 28″ x 20″, serigraph, pub HP	—	550.00
☐ MOUNTAIN RISE, rel. 1979. ed. 300, s/n, 40″ x 20″, serigraph, pub HP	—	650.00
☐ SANTA YNEZ VALLEY rel. 1979. ed. 300, s/n, 20″ x 40″, serigraph, pub HP	—	Sold Out
☐ WINTER QUIET, rel. 1979. ed. 300, s/n, 24″ x 36″, serigraph, pub HP	—	Sold Out
☐ ENCHANTED COAST, rel. 1980. ed. 300, s/n, 40″ x 20″, serigraph, pub HP	—	Sold Out
☐ GOTHIC FOREST, rel. 1980. ed. 300, s/n, 24″ x 36″, serigraph, pub HP	—	Sold Out
☐ AWAKENING, rel. 1981. ed. 260, s/n, 30″ x 19″, serigraph, pub HP	—	400.00
☐ GIRL WITH RAVEN HAIR, rel. 1981. ed. 260, s/n 30″ x 20″, serigraph, pub HP	—	400.00
☐ SPRING, rel. 1981. ed. 280, s/n, 22″ x 28″, serigraph, pub HP	—	Sold Out
☐ SUMMER, rel. 1981. ed. 300, s/n, 22″ x 28½″, serigraph, pub HP	—	Sold Out
☐ VILLAGE, rel. 1981. ed. 300, s/n, 20½″ x 16½″, serigraph, pub HP	—	500.00
☐ WINTER, rel. 1981. ed. 300, s/n, 15″ x 30″, serigraph, pub HP	—	500.00
☐ AMERICAN BARNS, rel. 1982. ed. 85, s/n, 12″ x 30″, serigraph, pub HP	—	600.00
☐ AUTUMN LEAVES, rel. 1982. ed. 75, s/n, 12″ x 30″, serigraph, pub HP	—	600.00
☐ BLACK OAK, rel. 1982. ed. 40, s/n, 20″ x 16″, serigraph, pub HP	—	600.00
☐ BIG SUR AND BRANCH, rel. 1982. ed. 300, s/n, 10″ x 8″, serigraph, pub HP	—	250.00
☐ CALIFORNIA SUITE, a set of four prints, rel. 1982. ed. 100, s/n, 8″ x 10″, serigraph, pub HP	—	1,600.00
☐ EUCALYPTUS, rel. 1982. ed. 85, s/n, 22″ x 28″, serigraph, pub HP	—	Sold Out
☐ SEVEN WHITE HORSES, rel. 1982. 40, s/n, 20″ x 30″, serigraph, pub HP	—	Sold Out
☐ VALLEY, rel. 1982. ed. 300, s/n, 8″ x 10″, serigraph, pub HP	—	250.00
☐ WINTER BARNS, rel. 1982. ed. 85, s/n, 15″ x 30″, serigraph, pub HP	—	600.00
☐ WINTER BONZAI, rel. 1982. ed. 85, s/n, 28″ x 22″, serigraph, pub HP	—	Sold Out
☐ CARMEL HIGHLANDS, rel. 1983. ed. 85, s/n, 20″ x 16″, serigraph, pub HP	—	Sold Out
☐ CATTLE COUNTRY, rel. 1983. ed. 150, s/n, 20″ x 30″, serigraph, pub HP	—	650.00
☐ CENTRAL PARK, rel. 1983. ed. 200, s/n, 20″ x 30″, serigraph, pub HP	—	600.00
☐ GAVIOTA PASS, rel. 1983. ed. 300, s/n, 20″ x 30″, serigraph, pub HP	—	Sold Out
☐ GREEN VALLEY, rel. 1983. ed. 300, s/n, 20″ x 30″, serigraph, pub HP	—	—
☐ LAND OF THE MIDNIGHT SUN, rel. 1983. ed. 85, s/n, 26″ x 34″, serigraph, pub HP .	—	800.00
☐ MEDIEVAL PROMENADE, rel. 1983. ed. 85, s/n, 24″ x 34″, serigraph, pub HP	—	800.00
☐ MIDNIGHT BLUE, rel. 1983. ed. 80, s/n, 30″ x 20″, serigraph, pub HP	—	750.00
☐ WINTER BARNS SUITE, set of four prints, rel. 1983. ed. 100, s/n, 20″ x 16″, serigraph, pub HP	—	1,600.00

DON RICHARD ECKELBERRY

THEMES: Birds

BOOKS: His illustrations are featured in the *Audubon Bird Guides*

EDUCATION: Cleveland Institute of Art

GALLERY/DISTRIBUTOR: Frame House Gallery, Inc.

	ISSUE PRICE	CURRENT PRICE
☐ BARRED OWL, rel. 1968. ed. 1,000, 24″ x 31″, pub FHG	100.00	200.00
ed. 500, s/n, donated to National Audubon Society		
☐ CARIBBEAN HUMMINGBIRDS, pair, rel. 1968. ed. 5,000, i/o, 14½″ x 19″, pub FHG .	25.00	Sold Out
☐ FULVOUS TREE-DUCK, rel. 1968. ed. 1,000, i/n, 26″ x 23½″, canvas, pub FHG	35.00	50.00
ed. 1,000, i/o, canvas	25.00	40.00

	ISSUE PRICE	CURRENT PRICE
☐ **PALM TANAGER/GRAYISH SALTATOR,** pair, rel. 1968. ed. 2,000, i/o, 22″ x 26″, pub FHG	45.00	45.00
☐ **RED-BELLIED WOODPECKER,** rel. 1968. ed. 19,500, i/o, 14¾″ x 11¼″, pub FHG . . Obtainable only with membership to National Audubon Society during 1968-69 Florida membership campaign.	—	35.00
☐ **WHITE-EARED PUFFBIRD,** rel. 1969. ed. 5,000, s/o, 12″ x 16″, pub FHG	10.00	45.00
☐ **BLUE-GRAY TANAGER,** rel. 1970. ed. 2,500, i/o, 22″ x 26″, pub FHG	20.00	50.00
☐ **WOOD DUCKS,** rel. 1970. ed. 3,000, s/o, 21″ x 26″, pub FHG	20.00	30.00
☐ **BOBWHITE,** rel. 1971. ed. 5,000, i/o, 16″ x 20″, pub FHG	20.00	50.00
☐ **MALLARD DRAKES RISING,** rel. 1971. ed. 1,000, i/n, 25″ x 30″, pub FHG	65.00	Sold Out
ed. 1,500, i/o	50.00	Sold Out
☐ **SPRUCE GROUSE,** rel. 1971. ed. 2,000, i/o, 21″ x 26″, pub FHG	20.00	50.00
ed. 1,500, i/o, offered through Continental Magazine, Lincoln-Mercury Div., Ford Motor Co., to benefit National Wildlife Federation	20.00	50.00
☐ **"ALERT AND READY",** (White Gyrfalcon), rel. 1972. ed. 1,000, s/n, 23″ x 30½″, pub FHG	50.00	125.00
ed. 1,500, s/o	40.00	100.00
ed. 1,000 signed and bearing a special insignia for the Association of Graduates, U.S. Air Force Academy	40.00	100.00
☐ **BLACK DUCKS OVER THE MARSH,** rel. 1972. ed. 3,000, i/n, 31″ x 23½″, pub FHG	40.00	75.00
☐ **MOTTLED OWL,** rel. 1972. ed. 3,500, i/o, 18½″ x 23½″, pub FHG	20.00	50.00
☐ **WOODCOCK AND YOUNG,** rel. 1972. ed. 3,500, i/o, 18″ x 23½″, pub FHG	20.00	30.00
☐ **YELLOW-CROWNED NIGHT HERON/CAPPED HERON,** pair, rel. 1972. ed. 2,500, i/o, 10⅝″ x 22¼″, pub FHG	30.00	Sold Out
☐ **CARDINAL,** rel. 1973. ed. 5,000, i/o, 17″ x 22″, pub FHG	20.00	85.00
☐ **SKIMMERS,** rel. 1973. ed. 2,000, i/n, 42″ x 14¾″, pub FHG	50.00	80.00
☐ **TRUMPETER SWAN,** rel. 1973. ed. 2,500, i/o, 31″ x 24½″, pub FHG	50.00	Sold Out
☐ **WILD CANARY IN DAISIES,** rel. 1973. ed. 5,000, i/o, 19″ x 15½″, pub FHG	20.00	Sold Out
☐ **GREAT BLACK-BACKED GULL,** rel. 1974. ed. 2,000, i/o, 28″ x 22½″, pub FHG	40.00	Sold Out
☐ **MEADOWLARK,** rel. 1974. ed. 3,000, i/o, 18″ x 22½″, pub FHG	35.00	80.00
☐ **GOLDEN-OLIVE WOODPECKER,** rel. 1975. ed. 2,000, i/o, 22″ x 26″, pub FHG	30.00	Sold Out
☐ **WILD TURKEY,** rel. 1975. ed. 2,000, i/n, 20″ x 24″, pub FHG This limited edition print was released in the AMERICA'S WILDLIFE HERITAGE PORT- FOLIO, the portfolio consisting of six prints in all, each by a different Frame House Gallery artist.	50.00	—
☐ **CANVASBACK OVER THE BAY,** rel. 1976. ed. 750, i/n, 14½″ x 21″, pub FHG	50.00	Sold Out
☐ **RUFFED GROUSE,** rel. 1976. ed. 1,000, i/n, 18″ x 24″, pub FHG	100.00	50.00
☐ **CALIFORNIA QUAIL,** rel. 1977. ed. 1,000, i/n, 18″ x 24″, pub FHG	100.00	50.00
☐ **RING-NECK PHEASANT,** rel. 1977. ed. 500, i/n, 18″ x 24″, pub FHG	100.00	50.00
☐ **BLUE GROUSE,** rel. 1978. ed. 500, i/n, 18″ x 24″, pub FHG	100.00	50.00

KATALIN EHLING

THEMES: Southwestern art

EDUCATION: American Academy of Art

GALLERY/DISTRIBUTOR: Native American Images

	ISSUE PRICE	CURRENT PRICE
☐ **APACHE GIRL,** rel. 1980. ed. 100, s/n, stone litho, 30″ x 22″, pub NAI	400.00	—
☐ **PUEBLO EVENING,** rel. 1980. ed. 80, 27″ x 18″, pub NAI	600.00	—
☐ **PUEBLO SONG,** ed. 100, s/n, 22½″ x 30″, pub NWDHG	—	300.00
☐ **PUEBLO LULLABY,** rel. 1980. ed. 40, s/n, 30″ x 22″, litho, pub NAI	350.00	900.00
☐ **SUMMER'S MOON,** rel. 1981. ed. 100, s/n, 30″ x 22″, litho, pub NAI	300.00	—

	ISSUE PRICE	CURRENT PRICE
☐ WINTER'S MOON, rel. 1981. ed. 100, s/n, 30" x 22", litho, pub NAI	300.00	—
☐ NAVAJO FAMILY, rel. 1982. ed. 100, s/n, 22" x 30", litho, pub NAI	400.00	600.00
☐ NIGHT WALK, rel. 1982. ed. 100, s/n, 24" x 22", litho, pub NAI	250.00	450.00
☐ SUMMER STORM, rel. 1982. ed. 100, s/n, 30" x 22", litho, pub NAI	400.00	—

FLEA MARKET *by Stu Eichel*

STU EICHEL

THEMES: Varied

EDUCATION: The Society of Arts and Crafts; Pratt Institute

GALLERY/DISTRIBUTOR: Traditions

	ISSUE PRICE	CURRENT PRICE
☐ 51 YEARS SELLING ON BLOUNT AVE., rel. 1971. ed. 350, s/n, 16" x 20", pub TRAD	15.00	Sold Out
☐ COUNTRY STORE, rel. 1972. ed. 500, s/n, 20" x 16", pub TRAD	20.00	Sold Out
ed. 500, s/o	15.00	—
☐ AMERICAN, rel. 1973. ed. 500, s/n, 16" x 20", pub TRAD	20.00	Sold Out
ed. 500, s/o	15.00	—
☐ MARJORIE, rel. 1973. ed. 500, s/n, 16" x 20", pub TRAD	20.00	Sold Out
ed. 500, s/o	20.00	Sold Out
☐ SMOKY MTN. 110, rel. 1973. ed. 500, s/n, 20" x 16", pub TRAD	25.00	35.00
ed. 500, s/o	20.00	—
☐ TENNESSEE GOTHIC, ed. 500, s/n, 16" x 20", pub TRAD	25.00	—
ed. 500, s/o	15.00	35.00
☐ WE'VE BEEN MEANING TO DO SOMETHING ABOUT THE GARAGE, ed. 500, s/n, 20" x 16", pub TRAD	20.00	35.00
ed. 500, s/o	20.00	—

	ISSUE PRICE	CURRENT PRICE
☐ CALL HOME, rel. 1975. ed. 950, s/n, 16″ x 20″, pub TRAD	25.00	35.00
☐ THE MEETING PLACE, rel. 1973. ed. 500, s/n, 20″ x 16″, pub TRAD	25.00	Sold Out
ed. 500, s/o	20.00	—
☐ GRANDMA'S HOUSE, rel. 1974. ed. 950, s/n, 16″ x 20″, pub TRAD	20.00	Sold Out
ed. 500, s/o	20.00	—
☐ SATURDAY AFTERNOON, ed. 950, s/n, 16″ x 20″, pub TRAD	25.00	35.00
☐ SOMEWHERE TO WAIT, ed. 950, s/n, 16″ x 20″, pub TRAD	25.00	35.00
☐ LOW PRICES, ed. 950, s/n, 20″ x 16″, pub TRAD	25.00	35.00
☐ THE LAST ESSO STATION, ed. 950, s/n, 16″ x 10″, pub TRAD	25.00	35.00
☐ PORCH SITTIN', ed. 950, s/n, 20″ x 16″, pub TRAD	25.00	35.00
☐ BIG VALLEY GRIST MILL, rel. 1978. ed. 950, s/n, 20″ x 16″, pub TRAD	25.00	35.00
☐ JULIA'S GLASS SHOP, ed. 950, s/n, 20″ x 16″, pub TRAD	25.00	—
ed. 50, A/P	25.00	—
☐ THE U.S. MAIL, ed. 350, s/n, 20″ x 16″, pub TRAD	25.00	35.00
☐ FLEA MARKET, ed. 350, 20″ x 16″, pub TRAD	25.00	35.00
☐ BLOCKHEAD AND FRIENDS, ed. 350, 20″ x 16″, pub TRAD	25.00	35.00

JOSEF EIDENBERGER

THEMES: European and American scenes

MEDIUM: Pencil

EDUCATION: Graphic Academy of Art in Vienna

MUSEUMS/COLLECTIONS: Worldwide

GALLERY/DISTRIBUTOR: Graphics International

	ISSUE PRICE	CURRENT PRICE
☐ SAN FRANCISCO, GOLDEN GATE BRIDGE, (miniature), 5¼″ x 4¾″	—	220.00
☐ STANFORD UNIVERSITY, 9″ x 7¼″	—	100.00
☐ CARMEL MISSION, 12¼″ x 9½″	—	220.00
☐ SAN FRANCISCO, PANORAMA, 11¾″ x 15¾″	—	230.00
☐ PALACE GATE, AUSTRIA, VIENNA, 13″ x 8″	—	160.00
☐ ST. STEPHEN'S INTERIOR, VIENNA, 18″ x 12¾″	—	230.00
☐ ROOFTOPS OF VIENNA, 19½″ x 13″	—	240.00
☐ KARL'S CHURCH, VIENNA, 12¾″ x 10½″	—	160.00
☐ PARLIAMENT - RINGSTRASSE, 18¼″ x 12¼″	—	230.00
☐ CITY HALL - VIENNA, 16½″ x 12¼″	—	230.00
☐ SCHOENBRUNN CASTLE, 12″ x 8½″	—	130.00
☐ ST. STEPHEN'S SQUARE, VIENNA, 13¾″ x 10¾″	—	190.00
☐ TECHNOLOGICAL COLLEGE, 10¼″ x 9¾″	—	160.00
☐ SCHUBERT HOUSE, VIENNA, 9¾″ x 6¼″	—	70.00
☐ GENERAL VIEW, VIENNA, 9″ x 12½″	—	200.00
☐ BURGTHEATER, VIENNA, 11¾″ x 13½″	—	200.00
☐ FREYUNG SQUARE, VIENNA, 12½″ x 8¼″	—	130.00
☐ ST. STEPHAN'S INTERIOR, VIENNA, 19½″ x 14½″	—	200.00
☐ OPERA HOUSE, VIENNA, 13¾″ x 11″	—	160.00
☐ GRABEN, VIENNA, 16¼″ x 16″	—	230.00
☐ ST. STEPHAN - ROOFTOPS, AUSTRIA, 14″ x 9¾″	—	190.00
☐ UNIVERSITY OF VIENNA, 14½″ x 11″	—	190.00
☐ DACHSTEIN VIEW, AUSTRIA, 16¾″ x 12″	—	200.00
☐ CITY HALL, VIENNA, 4⅞″ x 3⅝″	—	90.00
☐ FIGARO HOUSE, VIENNA, 4⅞″ x 4⅛″	—	90.00

	ISSUE PRICE	CURRENT PRICE
☐ BELVEDERE PALACE, VIENNA, 4⅞" x 4⅛"	—	90.00
☐ PALACE GATE, VIENNA, 6" x 3¾"	—	90.00
☐ KARL'S CHURCH, VIENNA, 4⅞" x 4⅛"	—	90.00
☐ SCHOENBRUNN CASTLE, VIENNA, 4⅞" x 4⅛"	—	90.00
☐ OPERA HOUSE, VIENNA, 4⅞" x 4⅛"	—	90.00
☐ GENERAL VIEW, VIENNA, 4⅞" x 4⅛"	—	90.00
☐ GRAZ, KREBSENKELLER, AUSTRIA, 5" x 4¼"	—	90.00
☐ STALLBURGGASSE, VIENNA, 5¼" x 3¾"	—	90.00
☐ MARIA AM GESTADE CHURCH, VIENNA, 4¾" x 4⅛"	—	90.00
☐ RATTENBEG, MINATURE, AUSTRIA, 6¾" x 4¾"	—	90.00
☐ MARIA THERESIA STREET, INNSBRUCK, 7¼" x 5½"	—	100.00
☐ HEIBLING HOUSE, INNSBRUCK, 7¼" x 5½"	—	100.00
☐ CITY TOWER, INNSBRUCK, 7¼" x 5½"	—	100.00
☐ HERZOG-FRIEDRICH STREET, INNSBRUCK, 7¼" x 5½"	—	100.00
☐ UNDER THE ARCHES, INNSBRUCK, 7¼" x 5½"	—	100.00
☐ OTTOBURG CASTLE, INNSBRUCK, 7¼" x 5½"	—	100.00
☐ ARCHWAY, EPPAN, TYROL, INNSBRUCK, 7½" x 5¼"	—	80.00
☐ VILLANDERS, AUSTRIA, 7¾" x 5½"	—	90.00
☐ PUERSTEIN, CHAPEL, AUSTRIA, 7¼" x 5½"	—	80.00
☐ DUERNSTEIN, MONASTARY, AUSTRIA, 10¼" x 7¼"	—	100.00
☐ DUERSTERN, MONASTARY, FROM THE DANUBE, AUSTRIA, 10¾" x 9¾"	—	100.00
☐ KIRCHBERG, AUSTRIA, 10½" x 10¼"	—	100.00
☐ KLOSTERNEUBERG, AUSTRIA, 11" x 9¼"	—	190.00
☐ KREMS ON THE DANUBE, 10¾" x 9½"	—	130.00
☐ POTTENBRUNN CASTLE, AUSTRIA, 12" x 9¾"	—	180.00
☐ SEEBENSTEIN CASTLE, AUSTRIA, 15¾" x 19½"	—	200.00
☐ SEMMERING CHAPEL, AUSTRIA, 11½" x 7¼"	—	130.00
☐ WEISSENKIRCHEN, AUSTRIA, 10½" x 9¾"	—	130.00
☐ PERCHTOLDSDORF, AUSTRIA, 9¾" x 8¾"	—	130.00
☐ SCHALLABURG CASTLE, AUSTRIA, 13" x 9¼"	—	130.00
☐ ST. STEPHAN'S SQUARE, VIENNA (Old), 15½" x 11"	—	160.00
☐ MELK, MONASTARY, AUSTRIA, 17½" x 13¾"	—	230.00
☐ ROOFTOPS, LENTZ, AUSTRIA, 14¾" x 10¾"	—	230.00
☐ STEYR, AUSTRIA, 12½" x 9¾"	—	200.00
☐ GOSAU GLACIER, AUSTRIA, 11½" x 9¼"	—	130.00
☐ DACHSTEIN, AUSTRIA, 12¾" x 9¾"	—	130.00
☐ ST. WOLFGANG, AUSTRIA, 13¾" x 16¾"	—	200.00
☐ *SAN FRANCISCO, CALIFORNIA STREET, 13" x 9"	—	180.00
☐ SAN FRANCISCO, GOLDEN GATE BRIDGE, 14¼" x 9½"	—	180.00
☐ GRAZ, KREBSENKELLER, LANDHOUSE, AUSTRIA, 16½" x 12¼"	—	230.00
☐ MAUSOLEUM, GRAZ, AUSTRIA, 15" x 11¼"	—	180.00
☐ ROHRBACH MOUNTAIN, AUSTRIA, 13½" x 9¼"	—	190.00
☐ LINZ, OLD TOWN, AUSTRIA, 11¾" x 8¾"	—	130.00
☐ LINZ, HOFGASSE, AUSTRIA, 14½" x 9"	—	130.00
☐ LANDHAUS, AUSTRIA, 12¼" x 9¼"	—	130.00
☐ PFARRGASSE, AUSTRIA, 11½" x 9¼"	—	180.00
☐ HALSTATT, AUSTRIA, 12¾" x 9"	—	130.00
☐ STEYR, OLD COURTHOUSE, AUSTRIA, 15½" x 13"	—	180.00
☐ KRUMAU, AUSTRIA, 13¾" x 10½"	—	150.00
☐ DACHSTEIN, SOUTHWALL, AUSTRIA, 15½" x 20½"	—	200.00
☐ SALZBURG, CASTLE, AUSTRIA, 9½" x 7½"	—	160.00
☐ SALZBERG, MARGARETHEN CHURCH, AUSTRIA, 9½" x 6½"	—	160.00
☐ ST. FLORIAN, MONASTERY, AUSTRIA, 13¼" x 9"	—	200.00
☐ INNSBRUCK, GOLDEN ROOF, AUSTRIA, 10½" x 8¾"	—	130.00
☐ INNSBRUCK, MARIO THERESIA STREET, AUSTRIA, 17¼" x 13¾"	—	230.00
☐ CITY TOWER, INNSBRUCK, 14¼" x 10¼"	—	180.00
☐ HERZOG-FRIERICH STREET, INNSBRUCK, 14¼" x 10¼"	—	180.00
☐ STUBEN IN WINTER, AUSTRIA, 10¼" x 8"	—	130.00
☐ KITZBUEHEL, AUSTRIA, 12¼" x 9½"	—	160.00
☐ HOETTING, CHURCH, INNSBRUCK, 10½" x 8¾"	—	130.00
☐ FELDKIRCH MARKET, INNSBRUCK, 11¾" x 9¾"	—	160.00
☐ EPPAN, SOUTH TYROL, INNSBRUCK, 9½" x 6¾"	—	130.00

	ISSUE PRICE	CURRENT PRICE
☐ SALZBURG, GENERAL VIEW, AUSTRIA, 10" x 13"	—	180.00
☐ LANGKOFEL MOUNTAIN, AUSTRIA, 12½" x 15"	—	200.00
☐ MATTERHORN, SWITZERLAND, 15" x 11½"	—	200.00
☐ EISENSTADT, HAYDN HOUSE, INNSBRUCK, 11" x 8½"	—	130.00
☐ FORCHTENSTEIN, INNSBRUCK, 14½" x 11"	—	160.00
☐ KOTTINGBRUNN CASTLE, AUSTRIA, 11½" x 9¾"	—	190.00
☐ GOISERN, AUSTRIA, 10½" x 8¾"	—	190.00
☐ DUERNSTEIN, AUSTRIA, 8¾" x 6½"	—	190.00
☐ HOETTING, AUSTRIA (Small), 9½" x 7"	—	130.00
☐ DOLOMITES, WINTER, AUSTRIA, 10½" x 13¾"	—	200.00
☐ DOLOMITES, SUMMER, AUSTRIA, 10½" x 12"	—	200.00
☐ BAD GASTEIN, AUSTRIA, 10" x 13"	—	180.00
☐ KARL'S CHURCH, VIENNA (Large), 18½" x 15½"	—	200.00
☐ WEISSENKIRCHEN, AUSTRIA (LARGE), 14½" x 12½"	—	180.00
☐ ALT AUSSEE, AUSTRIA, 9" x 12¼"	—	130.00
☐ SALZBURG, ST. PETER'S GATE, AUSTRIA, 13¾" x 9¾"	—	180.00
☐ DELFT, SWITZERLAND (OVAL), 10½" x 7"	—	190.00
☐ ST. WOLFGANG, AUSTRIA (OVAL), 10½" x 7"	—	190.00
☐ POTTERY SHOP, AUSTRIA, 12¾" x 10¼"	—	180.00
☐ STUTTGART, GERMANY, 13¼" x 9¾"	—	200.00
☐ BONN, CITY HALL, 9¾" x 12¾"	—	200.00
☐ DURDSTADT, GERMANY, 12¾" x 10"	—	200.00
☐ BUEDINGEN, TOWN GATE, GERMANY, 13¼" x 10"	—	200.00
☐ DIEPHOLZ CASTLE, GERMANY, 13½" x 11¼"	—	210.00
☐ OLD TOWN DUESSELDORF, 14¾" x 12¾"	—	200.00
☐ HEIDELBERG, ROOFTOPS, 12½" x 9¾"	—	200.00
☐ KAUB ON THE RHINE, GERMANY, 12½" x 9½"	—	200.00
☐ MUNICH, GERMANY, 12¾" x 9½"	—	200.00
☐ NORTHSEA, GREETSIEL, 9¾" x 12¾"	—	200.00
☐ ULM ON THE DANUBE, 10" x 12¼"	—	200.00
☐ XANTEN, GERMANY, 13¾" x 10½"	—	200.00
☐ CASTLE DYCK, GERMANY, 10½" x 13¾"	—	200.00
☐ HAMBURG, HARBOR, GERMANY, 11¾" x 16¾"	—	200.00
☐ SAILBOAT HARBOR, HAMBURG, 12¼" x 10¼"	—	200.00
☐ HEIDELBERG, GERMANY, 12½" x 10"	—	200.00
☐ HEIDELBERG CASTLE COURTYARD, 13" x 9½"	—	200.00
☐ MAIKAMMER, GERMANY, 9½" x 13"	—	200.00
☐ NEUHARDINGSIEL, GERMANY, 10½" x 14½"	—	200.00
☐ OTTENDORF, GERMANY, 10¾" x 13¼"	—	200.00
☐ ROTHENBURG, PLOENLEIN, 12½" x 10½"	—	200.00
☐ ROEDER GATE, TORHENBURG, 12¼" x 10"	—	200.00
☐ BLACKSMITH SHOP, AUGSBURG, 12½" x 10"	—	200.00
☐ CASTLE BENRATH, GERMANY, 13¼" x 9½"	—	200.00
☐ BONN, BEETHOVEN HOUSE, GERMANY, 12¾" x 9½"	—	200.00
☐ DUISBERG, AROUND 1820, 13¾" x 9¾"	—	200.00
☐ CASTLE GEMEN, GERMANY, 9" x 13¼"	—	200.00
☐ MICHEL, HAMBURG, GERMANY, 13½" x 9½"	—	200.00
☐ COLOGNE, PROMENADE, 9½" x 13"	—	200.00
☐ KREUZNACH, GERMANY, 9" x 13"	—	200.00
☐ MARL, GERMANY, 9¼" x 13½"	—	200.00
☐ MICHELSTADT, GERMANY, 13½" x 9¾"	—	200.00
☐ DRESDEN, GERMANY, 11¼" x 15¼"	—	200.00
☐ DUISBERG, AROUND 1850, 11¾" x 14¾"	—	200.00
☐ DUSSELDORF, AROUND 1850, 12¼" x 16"	—	200.00
☐ HILDESHEIM, GERMANY, 13¼" x 10"	—	200.00
☐ COLOGNE, AROUND 1890, 9½" x 12½"	—	200.00
☐ COLOGNE, DEUTZER BRIDGE, 9½" x 14¼"	—	200.00
☐ ST. MARTIN'S 1820, COLOGNE, 9¾" x 13¾"	—	200.00
☐ ROTHENBURG, GERMANY, 13¼" x 10"	—	200.00
☐ TUEBINGER, GERMANY, 12½" x 10"	—	200.00
☐ ZONS, GERMANY, 13¾" x 10½"	—	200.00
☐ VENICE CANAL, ITALY, 14¾" x 11¾"	—	200.00

	ISSUE PRICE	CURRENT PRICE
☐ RIALTO BRIDGE, VIENNA, 9" x 7½"	—	130.00
☐ SAIL BOATS, VENICE, 14" x 13¼"	—	200.00
☐ NUREMBERG, GERMANY, 15" x 11½"	—	180.00
☐ MARKTBREIT, GERMANY, 10" x 17"	—	150.00
☐ ULM ON THE BLAU, GERMANY, 10" x 7½"	—	150.00
☐ REGENSBURG IN WINTER, GERMANY, 9¾" x 13½"	—	150.00
☐ PRAGUE, TYN CHURCH, VENICE, 12½" x 9"	—	140.00
☐ DIEPHOLZ CASTLE, GERMANY, 15¾" x 12½"	—	160.00
THE HERITAGE COLLECTION		
☐ PHILADELPHIA, INDEPENDENCE HALL, 20" x 24"	—	220.00
☐ MOUNT VERNON, 21" x 27"	—	220.00
☐ MONTICELLO, 21" x 27"	—	220.00
☐ HERMITAGE, 21" x 27"	—	220.00
SCENES FROM WILLIAMSBURG, VIRGINIA,		
☐ PUBLIC GOAL, 16" x 17"	—	180.00
☐ BURTON PARISH CHURCH, 19" x 22"	—	210.00
☐ THE CAPITOL, 19" x 22"	—	210.00
☐ WRENN BUILDING, 19" x 22"	—	210.00
☐ GOVERNOR'S PALACE, 19" x 22"	—	210.00
☐ CARTER'S GROVE PLANTATION, 19" x 22"	—	210.00
☐ WINTER, 16" x 17"	—	190.00
☐ HAWAIIAN SUNSET, 6¼" x 8"	—	150.00
☐ HAWAII, 8¾" x 11"	—	200.00
☐ SAN FRANCISCO FOG, 8" x 10¾"	—	180.00
☐ TRACKS IN THE SNOW, 4½" x 6¼"	—	100.00
☐ ST. OSWALD, 9" x 12⅛"	—	180.00
☐ ROTHENBURG, KLINGER GATE, pub Gl	—	180.00
☐ ROTHENBURG STILLER WINKEL, pub Gl	—	180.00
☐ IN HOLLAND, MINIATURE, pub Gl	—	90.00
☐ SPLIT PERISTYL, pub Gl	—	150.00
☐ IERMOSS, AUSTRIA	—	200.00
☐ DELFT, HORIZONTAL	—	200.00
☐ SCHERMERHORN, HOLLAND	—	200.00
☐ MOEDLING, AUSTRIA	—	180.00
☐ PRINZENSTEIN, OVAL	—	180.00
☐ OLD FARM IN AUSTRIA	—	180.00
☐ MUEHLVIERTEL, AUSTRIA	—	230.00
☐ DEFREGGEN VALLEY, AUSTRIA, OVAL	—	175.00
☐ WEISSENKIRCHEN, COURTYARD	—	140.00
☐ KARL'S CHURCH IN WINTER	—	200.00
☐ MARIA AM GESTADE, VIENNA	—	210.00
☐ WHARF	—	220.00
☐ SAN FRANCISCO FISHERMAN'S WHARF	—	220.00
☐ WATERFRONT	—	200.00
☐ UTAH STATE CAPITOL, SALT LAKE CITY	—	90.00
☐ IN WINTER, MINATURE	—	210.00
☐ YOSEMITE VALLEY	—	210.00
☐ YOSEMITE, EL CAPITAN	—	200.00
☐ SEASCAPE, CARMEL BY THE SEA	—	200.00
☐ GRAND CANYON	—	200.00
☐ GRAND CANYON, LARGE	—	200.00
☐ STAGE COACH	—	200.00
☐ NEW ORLEANS, BRULATOUR COURTYARD	—	200.00
☐ NEW ORLEANS, BRULATOUR COURTYARD, MINIATURE	—	200.00
☐ PIRATES ALLEY	—	200.00
☐ ACADEMY OF THE SACRED HEART, GRAND COTEU, LA	—	200.00
☐ SAN FRANCISCO, CALIFORNIA STREET, SMALL	—	100.00
☐ PIEDMONT, CALIFORNIA	—	210.00
☐ ROTHENBURG	—	210.00
☐ CASTLE TAUFERS	—	190.00
☐ SCHATTENBRUG CASTLE	—	180.00
☐ NEW ORLEANS, STREETCAR	—	230.00

	ISSUE PRICE	CURRENT PRICE
☐ NEW YORK, CENTRAL PARK	—	230.00
☐ DENVER	—	230.00
☐ LOUISIANA SWAMP	—	230.00
☐ AMERICAN OAK GROVE	—	240.00
☐ GOISERN	—	130.00
☐ NIEDERWALDKIRCHEN	—	170.00
☐ DROSENDORF	—	160.00
☐ ALPINE CABIN	—	100.00
☐ DIEX	—	170.00
☐ CASTLE HOCHOSTERWITZ	—	180.00
☐ MILLSTADT, OVAL	—	180.00
☐ SPITAL, DRAV	—	100.00
☐ MILLSTADT	—	150.00
☐ MAJORCA, SPAIN	—	200.00
☐ WILLIAMSBURG, GOVERNOR'S PALACE, VIEW #2	—	230.00
☐ SAN FRANCISCO VICTORIAN HOUSE	—	210.00
☐ ST. PETER	—	100.00
☐ THE REDWOODS	—	210.00
☐ MARIAZELL	—	100.00
☐ YELLOWSTONE CASTLE GEYSER	—	160.00
☐ VIENNA ROOFTOPS	—	100.00
☐ MILLSTATT MONASTERY	—	200.00

*All pieces are color etchings and contain no specific edition limits.

STAN EKMAN

PUBLICATIONS: Painting featured in *Saturday Evening Post, Colliers, American Weekly,* and *Coronet*

AWARDS: The artist has received many awards from the Chicago Art Directors Club and New York Art Directors Club

MEMBERSHIPS: He is a past member of the Illustrators Society of New York

GALLERY/DISTRIBUTOR: Mill Pond Press, Inc.

	ISSUE PRICE	CURRENT PRICE
☐ GONE FISHIN', rel. 1983. ed. 950, 12″ x 17″, pub MPPI	50.00	—

PETER ELLENSHAW

THEMES: Seascape/landscape

BACKGROUND: Mr. Ellenshaw is best known for his matte work in the motion picture industry. For Walt Disney Productions, the artist worked on the special effects background for "Treasure Island" and "20,000 Leagues Under The Sea" for which he won an Oscar

GALLERY/DISTRIBUTOR: Greenwich Workshop

WHERE FORCES MEET *by Peter Ellenshaw*

	ISSUE PRICE	CURRENT PRICE
☐ **CLIPPER SHIPS,** rel. 1977. ed. 100, pencil signed by artist, 24" x 36", black and white etching, pub HP	250.00	350.00
☐ **RIVULET,** rel. 1977. ed. 300, pencil signed by artist, 24" x 36", pub HP	500.00	600.00
☐ **ROAD TO COOMCALLEE,** rel. 1978. ed. 300, s/n, 24" x 36", pub HP .... ed. 50 Artist proofs	400.00	600.00
☐ **TIDE TURNING,** rel. 1978. ed. 300, s/n, 24" x 36", pub HP .... ed. 50 Artist proofs	400.00	750.00
☐ **KERRY SPRINGTIME,** rel. 1979. ed. 300, s/n, 24" x 36", pub HP	450.00	500.00
☐ **AFTERNOON TIDE,** rel. 1980. ed. 200, s/n, 24" x 20", pub HP	400.00	500.00
☐ **HYDE PARK,** rel. 1980. ed. 200, s/n, 24" x 20", pub HP	400.00	500.00
☐ **BOOKHILL FERRY,** rel. 1981. ed. 300, s/n, 20" x 30", pub HP	500.00	—
☐ **CRYSTAL STREAM,** rel. 1981. ed. 300, s/n, 20" x 30", pub HP	500.00	—
☐ **CALIFORNIA SANDS,** rel. 1982. ed. 300, s/n, 20" x 30", pub HP	500.00	—
☐ **MAYFLOWERS,** rel. 1982. ed. 300, s/n, 20" x 30½", pub HP	500.00	—
☐ **CRONANIY BURN,** rel. 1983. ed. 850, s/n, 16½" x 12½", pub GW	75.00	—
☐ **ERRIGAL MOUNTAIN,** rel. 1983. ed. 850, s/n, 16½" x 12½", pub GW	75.00	—
☐ **KNOCKSTOOKA FROM HOGS HEAD,** rel. 1983. ed. 850, s/n, 16½" x 11", pub GW...	75.00	—
☐ **WHERE FORCES MEET,** rel. 1984. ed. 650, s/n, 35" x 22¼", pub GW	145.00	—

RUSS ELLIOTT

THEMES: Varied

GALLERY/DISTRIBUTOR: Felicie, Inc.

	ISSUE PRICE	CURRENT PRICE
☐ CURACAO FLOWERS, ed. 300, s/n, 39½" x 30", original color silkscreen, pub FI ...	200.00	300.00
☐ LIONS & MONKEYS, ed. 300, s/n, 30½" x 43", original color silkscreen, pub FI	300.00	—
☐ MARKET, ed. 300, s/n, 36½" x 31", original color silkscreen, pub FI	200.00	300.00
☐ RED ZINNIAS, ed. 300, s/n, 36½" x 22½", original color silkscreen, pub FI	250.00	300.00
☐ TIGERS, ed. 300. s/n, 31" x 36", original color silkscreen, pub FI	250.00	300.00
☐ ZEBRAS, ed. 300, s/n, 31" x 36", original color silkscreen, pub FI	250.00	300.00

MONTE ELLIS

THEMES: Varied

GALLERY/DISTRIBUTOR: Nature House, Inc.

	ISSUE PRICE	CURRENT PRICE
☐ HIGH WATER SPRING, ed. 500, s/n, 38½" x 30", pub NHI	200.00	—
☐ MISTY RETURN, ed. 500, s/n, 30" x 40", pub NHI	200.00	—

RICHARD ELLIS

THEMES: Marine natural history

BOOKS: Ellis published a comprehensive nonfiction book on sharks, published by Grosset & Dunlap in 1977

GALLERY/DISTRIBUTOR: Sportsman's Edge, Ltd.

	ISSUE PRICE	CURRENT PRICE
☐ SPERM WHALE, rel. 1975. ed. 450, s/n, 22½" x 18", pub SEL	150.00	—
☐ TIGER SHARK, rel. 1975. ed. 450, s/n, 17¾" x 24½", pub SEL	150.00	—
☐ GREY NURSE SHARK, rel. 1977. ed. 975, s/n, 18¼" x 24", pub SEL	150.00	—

NITA ENGLE

THEMES: Landscapes

MEDIUM: Watercolor

STYLE: Realism. Engle is essentially a studio painter. She makes pencil sketches for composition and value in the field and supplements these with black and white photos

AWARDS: 1984 Artist of the Year *(American Artist)*

MEMBERSHIPS: American Watercolor Society

GALLERY/DISTRIBUTOR: Mill Pond Press, Inc.

QUIET WATERS by Nita Engle

	ISSUE PRICE	CURRENT PRICE
☐ **HOUSE BY THE SEA,** rel. 1981. ed. 950, s/n, 24″ x 18⅛″, pub MPPI	75.00	Sold Out
☐ **WILDERNESS MARSH,** rel. 1981. ed. 950, s/n, 16¾″ x 21¾″, pub MPPI	75.00	200.00
☐ **MORNING ON THE YELLOWDOG RIVER,** rel. 1983. ed. 950, s/n, 24″ x 17⅜″, pub MPPI	75.00	—
☐ **QUIET WATERS,** rel. 1983. ed. 950, s/n, 17½″ x 23¼″, pub MPPI	75.00	175.00
☐ **SUMMER RIVER,** rel. 1983. ed. 950, s/n, 17½″ x 23⅝″, pub MPPI	75.00	—
☐ **WILD OCTOBER,** rel. 1983. ed. 950, s/n, 17½″ x 22⅛″, pub MPPI	75.00	—
☐ **WINTER BROOK,** rel. 1983. ed. 950, s/n, 24″ x 17½″, pub MPPI	75.00	—
☐ **APRIL LIGHT,** rel. 1984. ed. 950, s/n, 18½″ x 24½″, pub MPPI	95.00	—
☐ **AUTUMN BLUEBERRIES,** rel. 1984. ed. 950, s/n, 16¾″ x 23½″, pub MPPI	75.00	—
☐ **EARLY SPRING IN THE CITY,** rel. 1984. ed. 950, s/n, 24″ x 18″, pub MPPI	95.00	—
☐ **EVENING HARBOR,** rel. 1984. ed. 950, s/n, 15¾″ x 24″, pub MPPI	75.00	—
☐ **ISLAND HOME,** rel. 1984. ed. 950, s/n, 16¼″ x 23¼″, pub MPPI	75.00	—
☐ **MARCH THAW,** rel. 1984. ed. 950, s/n, 18¾″ x 24½″, pub MPPI	95.00	—
☐ **MELTING INTO SPRING,** rel. 1984. ed. 950, s/n, 18¾″ x 24½″, pub MPPI	95.00	—
☐ **MIDDLE ISLAND POINT,** rel. 1984. ed. 950, s/n, 17½″ x 24″, pub MPPI	85.00	—
☐ **AUTUMN RIVER,** rel. 1985. ed. 950, s/n, 17½″ x 11¼″, pub MPPI	50.00	—
☐ **MORNING AT SEA,** rel. 1985. ed. 950, s/n, 24″ x 17¼″, pub MPPI	95.00	—
☐ **WILD ROSE MARCH,** rel. 1985. ed. 950, s/n, 24″ x 18½″, pub MPPI	95.00	—

HANS ERNI

THEMES: Varied

BOOKS: Erni has created original lithographs and etchings to illustrate more than 200 books from Sophocles to Sartre, and he has authored three books

BACKGROUND: In his native Switzerland, Erni ranks as the national artist

AWARDS: United Nations Peace Medal

MUSEUMS/COLLECTIONS: His work is widely exhibited throughout three continents

GALLERY/DISTRIBUTOR: Edna Hibel Corporation

COMMENTS: The most extensive collection of his works is housed in the Hans Erni Museum, part of Lucerne's vast Swiss Transport Museum, the largest in Europe

	ISSUE PRICE	CURRENT PRICE
ORIGINAL ETCHINGS		
☐ **FELIX AND POULO,** rel. 1974. ed. 40, s/n, 12½" x 13", 1 color, distr. EHC	450.00	495.00
☐ **MOTHER AND CHILD, GREEN,** rel. 1979. ed. 90, s/n, 13⅜" x 10", distr. EHC	450.00	495.00
☐ **MOTHER PLAYING WITH CHILD ON CHAIR,** rel. 1979. ed. 90, s/n, 13½" x 10¼", 3 colors, distr. EHC	450.00	495.00
☐ **PYGMALION,** rel. 1979. ed. 90, s/n, 8¾" x 8⅜", 3 colors, distr. EHC	295.00	350.00
☐ **ASKLEPIOS AND GIRL,** rel. 1980. ed. 90, s/n, 25¼" x 19¼", 1 color, distr. EHC	625.00	695.00
☐ **COUPLE ON CUSHION,** rel. 1980. ed. 90, s/n, 9" x 8¼", 4 colors, distr. EHC	450.00	495.00
☐ **COUPLE, RED BACKGROUND,** rel. 1980. ed. 90, s/n, 13" x 10¼", distr. EHC	450.00	495.00
☐ **READING SIBYLLE,** rel. 1980. ed. 60, s/n, 15" x 11", 1 color, distr. EHC	450.00	495.00
☐ **THE ARTIST AND HIS MODEL,** rel. 1980. ed. 90, s/n, 11½" x 8", 1 color, distr. EHC	450.00	495.00
☐ **THREE HORSES ON BLUE BACKGROUND,** rel. 1980. ed. 90, s/n, 25¼" x 19½", 3 colors, distr. EHC	625.00	695.00
ORIGINAL STONE LITHOGRAPHS		
☐ **CAPRICORN,** rel. 1974. ed. 150, s/n, 14" x 21½", distr. EHC	435.00	—
☐ **CAT ON A STOOL,** rel. 1974. ed. 200, s/n, 26½" x 19½", distr. EHC	450.00	495.00
☐ **GEMINI,** rel. 1974. ed. 150, s/n, 14" x 21½", distr. EHC	435.00	—
☐ **LIBRA,** rel. 1974. ed. 150, s/n, 14½" x 22", distr. EHC	435.00	—
☐ **LOVERS,** rel. 1974. ed. 150, s/n, 29" x 21", distr. EHC	750.00	850.00
☐ **TAURUS,** rel. 1974. ed. 150, s/n, 13¾" x 21½", distr. EHC	435.00	—
☐ **TIGER,** rel. 1974. ed. 150, s/n, 21" x 29", distr. EHC	625.00	695.00
☐ **FOUR IN DISCUSSION,** rel. 1975. ed. 150, s/n, 18¼" x 24¼", distr. EHC	495.00	550.00
☐ **FIVE PEOPLE DISCUSSING,** rel. 1976. ed. 150, s/n, 18⅜" x 24¾", 5 colors, distr. EHC	495.00	550.00
☐ **PASSIONATE ENGINEER,** rel. 1976. ed. 150, s/n, 18¾" x 25¼", distr. EHC	495.00	550.00
☐ **REFLECTING CONSTRUCTOR,** rel. 1976. ed. 150, s/n, 19" x 24¾", distr. EHC	495.00	550.00
☐ **THE ARCHITECTS,** rel. 1976. ed. 150, s/n, 18¾" x 23", 7 colors, distr. EHC	495.00	550.00
☐ **THE PLANNERS,** rel. 1976. ed. 150, s/n, 18¾" x 23", distr. EHC	495.00	550.00
☐ **TWO HORSES, GREEN/YELLOW,** rel. 1977. ed. 150, s/n, 21⅛" x 18⅞", 4 colors, distr. EHC	495.00	550.00
☐ **TWO HORSES, VIOLET/OCHRE,** rel. 1977. ed. 150, s/n, 21⅛" x 18⅞", 4 colors, distr. EHC	495.00	550.00
☐ **COUPLE WITH MIRROR,** rel. 1978. ed. 150, s/n, 23½" x 18⅞", distr. EHC	450.00	550.00
☐ **MOTHER AND CHILD ON GREY BACKGROUND,** rel. 1978. ed. 150, s/n, 21" x 16", distr. EHC	495.00	550.00
☐ **J. S. BACH,** rel. 1979. ed. 200, s/n, 21¼" x 17½", distr. EHC	495.00	550.00
☐ **ARTIST AND MODEL,** rel. 1980. ed. 150, s/n, 25¾" x 21¼", 4 colors, distr. EHC	495.00	550.00
☐ **CHEMIST,** rel. 1980. ed. 4,000, s/n, 26" x 19¼", 9 colors, distr. EHC	525.00	575.00
☐ **COUPLE IN FRONT OF MOON,** rel. 1980. ed. 150, s/n, 27" x 20⅜", 4 colors, distr. EHC	525.00	575.00
☐ **COUPLE SITTING ON FIG-BRANCH,** rel. 1980. ed. 150, s/n, 18" x 13", distr. EHC	450.00	495.00
☐ **CROUCHING COUPLE,** rel. 1980. ed. 150, s/n, 16⅝" x 21", distr. EHC	495.00	550.00
☐ **EUROPE,** rel. 1980. ed. 150, s/n, 28" x 20¾", distr. EHC	495.00	550.00
☐ **FATHER-CHILD,** rel. 1980. ed. 150, s/n, 17⅝" x 23½", 3 colors, distr. EHC	495.00	550.00
☐ **GIRL AND WINGED BULL,** rel. 1980. ed. 150, s/n, 23" x 16½", 4 colors, distr. EHC	525.00	575.00

	ISSUE PRICE	CURRENT PRICE
☐ **GIRL IN GREEN DRESS**, rel. 1980. ed. 150, s/n, 33¼" x 13¼", distr. EHC	595.00	650.00
☐ **GIRL IN PINK DRESS**, rel. 1980. ed. 150, s/n, 27¼" x 21", 4 colors, distr. EHC	750.00	850.00
☐ **GIRL LEADING HER HORSE**, rel. 1980. ed. 150, s/n, 23" x 19", distr. EHC	495.00	550.00
☐ **GIRL SITTING**, rel. 1980. ed. 150, s/n, 28½" x 20¼", distr. EHC	495.00	550.00
☐ **KYBERNETES**, rel. 1980. ed. 150, s/n, 30⅝" x 21⅝", 5 colors, distr. EHC	750.00	850.00
☐ **MATERNITY, GREEN/BEIGE**, rel. 1980. ed. 150, s/n, 23" x 18¾", 4 colors, distr. EHC	495.00	550.00
☐ **MOMENT OF INSTRUCTION**, rel. 1980. ed. 150, s/n, 29½" x 21¼", distr. EHC	750.00	850.00
☐ **MOTHER-CHILD**, rel. 1980. ed. 150, s/n, 18¼" x 23⅛", 3 colors, distr. EHC	495.00	550.00
☐ **MOTHER WITH CHILD, BLUE BACKGROUND**, rel. 1980. ed. 150, s/n, 25¼" x 19", 7 colors, distr. EHC	525.00	575.00
☐ **NIGHTLY DISCUSSION**, rel. 1980. ed. 150, s/n, 27" x 24¼", 6 colors, distr. EHC	495.00	550.00
☐ **PLAYING HORSES**, rel. 1980. ed. 150, s/n, 18½" x 24½", distr. EHC	495.00	550.00
☐ **REFLECTING MAN**, rel. 1980. ed. 150, s/n, 27½" x 21¼", distr. EHC	750.00	850.00
☐ **RIDING COUPLE**, rel. 1980. ed. 150, s/n, 16½" x 25¾", distr. EHC	495.00	550.00
☐ **RUNNERS**, rel. 1980. ed. 150, s/n, 27¾" x 19¾", 4 colors, distr. EHC	495.00	550.00
☐ **SEMINARY**, rel. 1980. ed. 150, s/n, 20½" x 30¼", distr. EHC	750.00	850.00
☐ **SIBYLLE, 1977**, rel. 1980. ed. 150, s/n, 22⅝" x 18½", distr. EHC	495.00	550.00
☐ **SITTING GIRL PLAYING WITH HER HAIR**, rel. 1980. ed. 150, s/n, 27½" x 21", 5 colors, distr. EHC	750.00	850.00
☐ **SOCRATES AND THE YOUTH**, rel. 1980. ed. 150, s/n, 27¾" x 28⅛", 7 colors, distr. EHC	750.00	850.00
☐ **STANDING GIRL, PLAYING WITH HER HAIR**, rel. 1980. ed. 150, s/n, 26" x 19½", distr. EHC	495.00	550.00
☐ **TECHNICIAN AND HIS SURROUNDING**, rel. 1980. ed. 150, s/n, 31" x 16⅝", distr. EHC	495.00	550.00
☐ **THE PROBLEM**, rel. 1980. ed. 150, s/n, 21⅝" x 17½", 4 colors, distr. EHC	495.00	500.00
☐ **THOUGHTS**, rel. 1980. ed. 150, s/n, 22" x 17¾", distr. EHC	495.00	550.00
☐ **THREE HORSES, GREEN/BROWN**, rel. 1980. ed. 150, s/n, 30⅞" x 21", 10 colors, distr. EHC	750.00	850.00
☐ **THREE HORSES IN THE MOONLIGHT**, rel. 1980. ed. 150, s/n, 28" x 20", distr. EHC	750.00	850.00
☐ **THREE HORSES IN THEIR STABLE**, rel. 1980. ed. 150, s/n, 22¾" x 18½", 5 colors, distr. EHC	750.00	850.00
☐ **TWO HORSES, 1978**, rel. 1980. ed. 150, s/n, 23⅝" x 19⅛", distr. EHC	525.00	575.00
☐ **TWO YOUNG COUPLES**, rel. 1980. ed. 150, s/n, 21" x 29¼", distr. EHC	495.00	550.00
☐ **COUPLE IN WINDOW**, rel. 1982. ed. 150, s/n, 20½" x 18½", distr. EHC	550.00	—
☐ **MOTHER PEELING POTATOES**, rel. 1982. ed. 150, s/n, 25" x 19", distr. EHC	550.00	—
☐ **THE FRAMEMAKER**, rel. 1982. ed. 150, s/n, 25¾" x 19", distr. EHC	550.00	—
☐ **THREE CONSTRUCTORS**, rel. 1982. ed. 150, s/n, 23½" x 17½", distr. EHC	550.00	—
☐ **COUPLE PLAYING CHESS**, rel. 1983. ed. 150, s/n, 18¼" x 24", distr. EHC	595.00	—
☐ **DREAMING MUSICIAN**, rel. 1983. ed. 150, s/n, 24¼" x 24", distr. EHC	625.00	—
☐ **PELEUS AND THETIS**, rel 1983. ed. 150, s/n, 25¼" x 20", distr. EHC	550.00	—
☐ **PYTHAGORAS**, rel. 1983. ed. 150, s/n, 26" x 18", distr. EHC	550.00	—
☐ **SAINT CHRISTOPHORUS**, rel. 1983. ed. 150, s/n, 16½" x 12⅝", distr. EHC	340.00	—
☐ **THE STALLION**, rel. 1983. ed. 150, s/n, 22¼" x 18¼", distr. EHC	695.00	—

ERTÉ

THEMES: Fashion illustration

BACKGROUND: The pseudonym Erté was created from the initials R. T. (for Romain de Tirtoff) when the artist first began his career

GALLERY/DISTRIBUTOR: Circle Fine Arts Corporation

	ISSUE PRICE	CURRENT PRICE
☐ **SPLENDOR**, ed. 260, serigraph, 34" x 26", pub CFA	—	2,700.00
☐ **WINTER RESORT NICE**, ed. 260, serigraph, 30" x 24", pub CFA	—	650.00
☐ **FASHIONS**, ed. 260, serigraph, 30" x 24", pub CFA	—	650.00

	ISSUE PRICE	CURRENT PRICE
☐ FURS, ed. 260, serigraph, 30″ x 24″, pub CFA	—	850.00
☐ TENNIS, ed. 260, serigraph, 30″ x 24″, pub CFA	—	400.00
☐ COMPACT VANITIES, ed. 260, serigraph, 30″ x 24″, pub CFA	—	850.00
☐ WINTER RESORTS, ed. 260, serigraph, 30″ x 24″, pub CFA	—	750.00
☐ LOVE, ed. 260, serigraph, 30″ x 24″, pub CFA	—	400.00
☐ THREE FACES, ed. 260, serigraph, 30″ x 24″, pub CFA	—	1,000.00
☐ BROWN BOOT, ed. 260, serigraph, 20″ x 17″, pub CFA	—	650.00
☐ MYSTIQUE, ed. 260, serigraph, 40″ x 26″, pub CFA	—	2,400.00
☐ BLACK ROSE, 260, serigraph, 25″ x 20″, pub CFA	—	1,500.00
☐ TOP HATS, ed. 260, serigraph, 24″ x 19″, pub CFA	—	3,100.00
☐ PRINTEMPS, ed. 260, serigraph, 29″ x 23″, pub CFA	—	600.00
☐ RENEE, ed. 260, litho, 17″ x 11″, pub CFA	—	325.00
☐ NICOLE, ed. 260, litho, 17″ x 11″, pub CFA	—	325.00
☐ YVETTE, ed. 260, litho, 17″ x 11″, pub CFA	—	325.00
☐ SIMONE, ed. 260, litho, 17″ x 11″, pub CFA	—	300.00
☐ ZSA ZSA, ed. 250, litho, 35″ x 21″, pub CFA	—	1,300.00
☐ PREMIER, ed. 300, litho, 16″ x 12″, pub CFA	—	465.00
☐ BON SOIR, ed. 300, litho 16″ x 12″, pub CFA	—	275.00
☐ ELEGANCE, ed. 300, litho, 16″ x 12″, pub CFA	—	275.00
☐ TRES CHIC, ed. 300, litho, 16″ x 12″, pub CFA	—	275.00
☐ THE KISS, ed. 300, litho/embossment, 12″ x 10″, pub CFA	—	850.00
☐ SUMMER AND WINTER, ed. 300, litho/embossment, 11″ x 12″, pub CFA	—	500.00
☐ THE VEIL, ed. 300, litho/embossment, 12″ x 9″, pub CFA	—	500.00
☐ EVENING CREATION, ed. 175, etching, 15″ x 11″, pub CFA	—	475.00
☐ FEATHERS, ed. 300, litho/embossment, 12″ x 9″, pub CFA	—	500.00
☐ DANCERS, ed. 300, litho/embossment, 6″ x 13″, pub CFA	—	850.00
☐ LA BELLE, ed. 300, litho, 15″ x 11″, pub CFA	—	475.00
☐ FICELLE, ed. 300, litho, 15″ x 11″, pub CFA	—	275.00
☐ MUFF, ed. 300, litho, 15″ x 11″, pub CFA	—	500.00
☐ FANTAISIE, ed. 300, litho, 15″ x 11″, pub CFA	—	375.00
☐ REFLECTIONS, ed. 300, serigraph, 26″ x 24″, pub CFA	—	850.00
☐ THE CURTAIN, ed. 300, serigraph/flocking, 26″ x 18″, pub CFA	—	925.00
☐ BROADWAY'S IN FASHION, ed. 300, serigraph/embossment, 24″ x 18″, pub CFA	—	900.00
☐ WINGS OF VICTORY, ed. 325, serigraph, 32″ x 24″, pub CFA	—	3,350.00
☐ SUMMER BREEZE, ed. 300, serigraph, 31″ x 23″, pub CFA	—	2,200.00
☐ FLAMES OF LOVE, ed. 300, serigraph, 37″ x 21″, pub CFA	—	1,300.00
☐ RIVIERA, ed. 300, serigraph, 24″ x 19″, pub CFA	—	800.00
☐ LES POUPEES RUSSES, ed. 300, serigraph, 31″ x 23″, pub CFA	—	1,250.00
☐ BAGDAD, ed. 300, litho, 16″ x 13″, pub CFA	—	375.00
☐ ZOBEIDE, ed. 300, litho, 16″ x 13″, pub CFA	—	400.00
☐ DINARZADE, ed. 300, litho, 16″ x 13″, pub CFA	—	375.00
☐ KING'S FAVORITE, ed. 300, litho, 26″ x 20″, pub CFA	—	750.00
☐ GABY DESLYS, ed. 300, litho, 26″ x 20″, pub CFA	—	900.00
☐ MANHATTAN MARY I, ed. 300, litho, 22″ x 18″, pub CFA	—	400.00
☐ LAFAYETTE, ed. 300, serigraph, 32″ x 24″, pub CFA	—	850.00
☐ AFTER THE RAIN, ed. 300, serigraph, 31″ x 23″, pub CFA	—	700.00
☐ SPRING FASHIONS, ed. 300, serigraph, 31″ x 23″, pub CFA	—	1,050.00
☐ BLOSSOM UMBRELLA, ed. 300, serigraph, 30″ x 23″, pub CFA	—	1,100.00
☐ THE GOLDEN CLOAK, ed. 300, litho, 25″ x 17″, pub CFA	—	600.00
☐ MANHATTAN MARY II, ed. 300, litho/serigraph, 24″ x 17″, pub CFA	—	350.00
☐ THE BLUE DRESS, ed. 300, litho, 25″ x 19″, pub CFA	—	350.00
☐ FALL, ed. 300, serigraph, 31″ x 24″, pub CFA	—	1,850.00
☐ HEAT, ed. 300, serigraph, 25″ x 19″, pub CFA	—	1,900.00
☐ THE CHASTE SUSANNA, ed. 300, serigraph, 24″ x 19″, pub CFA	—	1,500.00
☐ FIREFLIES, ed. 300, serigraph, 32″ x 24″, pub CFA	—	1,800.00
☐ THE FRENCH ROOSTER, ed. 300, serigraph, 31″ x 22″, pub CFA	—	2,250.00
☐ VINTAGE, ed. 300, serigraph, 31″ x 23″, pub CFA	—	2,600.00
☐ THE BATH OF THE MARQUISE, ed. 300, serigraph, 24″ x 18″, pub CFA	—	1,950.00
☐ LA TOILETTE, ed. 300, serigraph, 11″ x 14″, pub CFA	—	600.00
☐ THE WAVE, ed. 300, serigraph, 11″ x 13″, pub CFA	—	750.00
☐ THE RIVIERA, ed. 300, serigraph, 10″ x 15″, pub CFA	—	450.00
☐ NOON, ed. 300, serigraph, 14″ x 11″, pub CFA	—	600.00
☐ QUEEN OF SHEBA, ed. 300, serigraph, 30″ x 22″, pub CFA	—	1,700.00

	ISSUE PRICE	CURRENT PRICE
☐ MICHELLE, ed. 300, serigraph, 30″ x 22″, pub CFA	—	1,200.00
☐ MYSTERE, ed. 300, serigraph, 32″ x 24″, pub CFA	—	1,375.00
☐ PARESSEUSE, ed. 300, serigraph, 31″ x 23″, pub CFA	—	1,800.00
☐ RAIN, ed. 300, serigraph/embossment, 10″ x 20″, pub CFA	—	750.00
☐ LA MERVEILLEUSE, ed. 300, serigraph, 31″ x 23″, pub CFA	—	1,100.00
☐ WOMAN AND SATYR, ed. 300, serigraph, 32″ x 23″, pub CFA	—	2,400.00
☐ LOVERS AND IDOL, ed. 300, serigraph, 23″ x 17″, pub CFA	—	1,100.00
☐ SAMSON AND DELILAH, ed. 300, serigraph/embossment, 19″ x 24″, pub CFA ...,..	—	1,700.00
☐ CHARLESTON COUPLE, ed. 300, serigraph, 17″ x 15″, pub CFA	—	600.00
☐ TWIN SISTERS, ed. 300, serigraph/embossment, 40″ x 55″, pub CFA	—	2,700.00
☐ THE DUEL, ed. 300, serigraph, 31″ x 23″, pub CFA	—	1,750.00
☐ FOUR SEASONS FOLIO, four pcs., ed. 260, serigraph, 20″ x 14″, pub CFA	—	1,500.00
☐ WINTER or SUMMER .... each	—	400.00
☐ AUTUMN	—	450.00
☐ SPRING	—	500.00
☐ ALPHABET PORTFOLIO, 26 pcs., ed. 350, litho/serigraph, 26″ x 19″, pub CFA	—	21,000.00
☐ Pcs. C - H - I - J - N - O - U - V and X .... each	—	700.00
☐ Pc. Y	—	750.00
☐ Pcs. A - E - Q .... each	—	800.00
☐ Pc. S	—	850.00
☐ Pcs. K - W .... each	—	900.00
☐ Pcs. B - D .... each	—	1,000.00
☐ Pc. T	—	1,050.00
☐ Pcs. F - G - P .... each	—	1,100.00
☐ Pc. Z	—	1,350.00
☐ Pc. R	—	1,450.00
☐ Pc. M	—	1,900.00
☐ Pc. L	—	2,900.00
☐ TWENTIES REMEMBERED FOLIO, eight pcs., ed. 300, serigraph, 24″ x 20″ and 25″ x 22″, pub CFA	—	10,500.00
☐ BRIDE, 24″ x 20″	—	1,100.00
☐ AMOUREUSE	—	600.00
☐ LES JOLIES DAMES	—	1,200.00
☐ RAINBOW IN BLOSSOM	—	800.00
☐ BEAUTY OF THE BEAST, 25″ x 22″	—	3,000.00
☐ AUTUMN SONG	—	1,200.00
☐ FISHBOWL	—	900.00
☐ DREAM VOYAGE	—	2,000.00
☐ TWENTIES REMEMBERED AGAIN FOLIO, eight pcs., ed. 300, serigraph, 24″ x 19″, pub CFA	—	9,800.00
☐ SPRING OPENING	—	925.00
☐ LEGERETE	—	1,150.00
☐ SELECTION OF A HEART	—	1,250.00
☐ TEMPEST	—	2,000.00
☐ RUSSIAN FAIRYTALE	—	1,300.00
☐ EARTH'S DREAM	—	1,700.00
☐ MAKEUP	—	1,100.00
☐ FIRST DRESS	—	1,250.00
☐ SUITE, three pcs., ed. 300, litho, 20″ x 16″, pub CFA	—	1,800.00
☐ ROSE TURBAN	—	650.00
☐ YELLOW TURBAN	—	650.00
☐ THE MIRROR	—	700.00
☐ THE FOUR EMOTIONS FOLIO, four pcs., ed. 300, serigraph, 23″ x 18″, pub CFA ...	—	5,500.00
☐ NUMBERS PORTFOLIO, 10 pcs (Numberals 0 through 9), ed. 350, serigraph/embossment, 23″ x 17″, pub CFA	—	10,500.00
☐ Pcs. 0 - 1 .... each	—	900.00
☐ Pc. 2	—	950.00
☐ Pc. 3	—	800.00
☐ Pc. 4	—	1,700.00
☐ Pc. 5	—	1,800.00
☐ Pc. 6	—	1,100.00
☐ Pc. 7	—	1,000.00
☐ Pc. 8	—	1,300.00
☐ Pc. 9	—	1,500.00

TONY EUBANKS

THEMES: Varied

MEDIUM: Oil, mixed media

EDUCATION: North Texas State University, Art Center School

MUSEUMS/COLLECTIONS: Permanent display at the Library of Congress

GALLERY/DISTRIBUTOR: Wild Wings, Inc.

	ISSUE PRICE	CURRENT PRICE
☐ **THE BORROWED MARE,** rel. 1982. ed. 600, s/n, 17½″ x 26¼″, pub WWI	95.00	—
☐ **WESTCLIFFE FEEDS,** rel. 1982. ed. 600, s/n, litho, 24″ x 17¾″, pub WWI	95.00	—

CECIL EVERLEY

THEMES: Varied

MEDIUM: Silkscreen

GALLERY/DISTRIBUTOR: Felicie, Inc.

	ISSUE PRICE	CURRENT PRICE
☐ **VALLEY OF LUCERAM,** ed. 225, s/n, 26″ x 32″, original color silkscreen, pub FI	125.00	·
☐ **VILLEFRANCHE,** ed. 225, s/n, 26″ x 32″, original color silkscreen, pub FI	125.00	—

CARL EVERS

THEMES: Marine art

MEDIUM: Watercolor

COMMISSIONS: The artist has painted for the U.S. Naval Institute, for steamship and freightlines, for publications, and for private commissions

GALLERY/DISTRIBUTOR: Greenwich Workshop

	ISSUE PRICE	CURRENT PRICE
☐ **AMERICA'S CUP 1984,** rel. 1975. ed. 750, s/n, 30½″ x 22½″, pub GW	75.00	310.00
*ed. 250, s/n, with three signatures and remarque-like sketches of Ted Hood and Olin Stephens......................................	*200.00	400.00
☐ **APPROACHING THE HORN,** rel. 1975. ed. 1,000, s/n, 26″ x 19¼″, pub GW	65.00	170.00
☐ **USS CONSTITUTION,** rel. 1975. ed. 1,000, s/n, 30¼″ x 22″, pub GW	75.00	—
☐ **HURRICANE,** rel. 1976. ed. 1,000, s/n, 26″ x 18¾″, pub GW	65.00	135.00
☐ **SOUTH STREET, NEW YORK, 1879,** rel. 1976. ed. 1,000, s/n, 28¾″ x 18½″, pub GW..	65.00	Sold Out
☐ **AMERICA'S CUP 1870,** rel. 1977. ed. 1,000, s/n, 30″ x 19¼″, pub GW	65.00	Sold Out
☐ **THE PRIVATEERS,** rel. 1977. ed. 1,000, s/n, 30″ x 21″, pub GW	65.00	—

	ISSUE PRICE	CURRENT PRICE
☐ HEAVY SEAS, rel. 1979. ed. 1,000, s/n, 26″ x 19¼″, pub GW	65.00	—
☐ BATTLE OF THE MONITOR AND MERRIMACK, rel. 1980. ed. 1,000, s/n, 29″ x 21″, pub GW...	75.00	—
☐ FORCE TEN—SURVIVOR, rel. 1981. ed. 1,000, s/n, 30¼″ x 21″, pub GW	125.00	—
☐ LETTER OF MARQUE 1814, rel. 1981. ed. 500, s/n, 27″ x 19¼″, pub GW	110.00	—
☐ EAGLE AT SEA, rel. 1983. ed. 650, s/n, 28½″ x 21¼″, pub GW	135.00	—

BURR FAIRLAMB

THEMES: Varied

GALLERY/DISTRIBUTOR: Frame House Gallery, Inc.

	ISSUE PRICE	CURRENT PRICE
☐ CUTTING GARDEN, rel. 1980. ed. 700, s/n, 23½″ x 29½″, pub FHG	60.00	—

JOHN FALTER
(1910-1982)

THEMES: Americana

STYLE: Illustrations

AWARDS: Illustrators Hall of Fame

GALLERY/DISTRIBUTOR: Mill Pond Press, Inc.

COMMENTS: John Falter produced 185 covers for the *Saturday Evening Post.* Norman Rockwell called him "America's most gifted illustrator"

	ISSUE PRICE	CURRENT PRICE
☐ THE GUSHER, rel. 1981. ed. 950, s/n, 28½″ x 22¾″, pub MPPI	150.00	—

RON FANER

THEMES: Landscape and animals of the Southwest; Indian art

GALLERY/DISTRIBUTOR: Frame House Gallery, Inc.

	ISSUE PRICE	CURRENT PRICE
☐ KEEPER OF THE OWLS, rel. 1980. ed. 375, s/n, 26″ x 33⅓″, pub FHG	100.00	225.00
☐ THE DEER SLAYER, rel. 1980. ed. 375, s/n, 20″ x 23½″, pub FHG	100.00	175.00

THE GUSHER *by John Falter*

	ISSUE PRICE	CURRENT PRICE
☐ CUNNING AS THE FOX, SUDDEN AS THE RABBIT, rel. 1981. ed. 375, s/n, 24″ x 24″, pub FHG	125.00	—
☐ LITTLE SPARROW WOMAN, rel. 1981. ed. 375, s/n, 28″ x 24″, pub FHG	125.00	225.00
☐ NIGHT DREAMER, rel. 1981. ed. 375, s/n, 24″ x 24″, pub FHG	125.00	—
☐ THUNDER GOD AND THE CREATION OF BIRDS, rel. 1981. ed. 375, s/n, 31¼″ x 24½″, pub FHG	125.00	300.00
☐ BUTTERFLY KATCHINA, rel. 1982. ed. 375, s/n, 32¾″ x 24½″, pub FHG	150.00	—
☐ MORNING SONG, rel. 1982. ed. 375, s/n, 24″ x 24″, pub FHG	150.00	—
☐ SUNBIRD KATCHINA, rel. 1982. ed. 375, s/n, pub FHG	150.00	—
☐ WINTER WOLF, rel. 1982. ed. 375, s/n, 24″ x 24″, pub FHG	150.00	—
☐ BUFFALO DREAM, rel. 1983. ed. 375, s/n, 24½″ x 31½″, pub FHG	150.00	—
☐ SPIRIT WARRIOR, rel. 1983. ed. 375, s/n, 20″ x 37″, pub FHG	150.00	—
☐ THE RAVEN'S CALL, rel. 1983. ed. 375. s/n, 23″ x 32½″, pub FHG	150.00	—

BUTTERFLY KATCHINA *by Ron Faner*

IMOGENE FARNSWORTH

THEMES: Wildlife art

AWARDS: Printing Industry of America Award for four years

GALLERY/DISTRIBUTOR: Paul Sawyier Collection, Inc.

	ISSUE PRICE	CURRENT PRICE
☐ **BENGAL TIGER,** rel. 1973. ed. 1,000, s/n, 20″ x 24″, pub II	35.00	750.00
ed. 2,000, s/o	25.00	350.00
☐ **AFRICAN LION,** rel. 1974. ed. 1,000, s/n, 20″ x 24″, pub II	35.00	350.00
ed. 2,000, s/o	25.00	200.00
☐ **BROWN BEAR,** rel. 1974. ed. 1,000, s/n, 20″ x 24″, pub II	35.00	150.00
ed. 4,000, s/o	25.00	75.00
☐ **YOUNG ZEBRA,** rel. 1974. ed. 1,000, s/n, 20″ x 24″, pub II	35.00	100.00
ed. 2,000, s/o	25.00	40.00
☐ **GIRAFFES,** rel. 1975. ed. 1,000, s/n, 20″ x 24″, pub II	35.00	150.00
ed. 2,000, s/o	25.00	50.00

LION *by Imogene Farnsworth*

	ISSUE PRICE	CURRENT PRICE
☐ **TIGER,** rel. 1975. ed. 3,000, s/n, 20″ x 24″, pub II	35.00	350.00
☐ **AFRICAN LEOPARD,** rel. 1976. ed. 3,000, s/n, 20″ x 24″, pub II	45.00	350.00
☐ **AFRICAN LIONESS & CUB,** rel. 1976. ed. 3,000, s/n, 24″ x 20″, pub II	35.00	150.00
☐ **CHEETAH (Head),** rel. 1976. ed. 3,000, s/n, 16″ x 20″, pub II	35.00	75.00
☐ **THE STALK (Cheetah),** rel. 1976. ed. 3,000, s/n, 29¾″ x 16¾″, pub II	45.00	—
☐ **BENGAL TIGER CUBS,** rel. 1977. ed. 3,000, s/n, 22″ x 21½″, pub II	45.00	100.00
☐ **LION AND PUMA,** rel. 1975. (A & B), ed. 2,000, s/n, size not available, 24″, pub II	35.00	300.00
☐ **MELANISTIC LEOPARD,** rel. 1977. ed. 3,000, s/n, 26½″ x 21½″, pub II	50.00	150.00
☐ **PERSIAN LEOPARD & SIBERIAN TIGER,** rel. 1977. (A & B), ed. 3,000, s/n, 11½″ x 11½″, pub II	40.00	120.00
☐ **COUGAR,** rel. 1978. ed. 3,000, s/n, 20″ x 24″, pub II	50.00	—
☐ **JAGUAR,** rel. 1978. ed. 3,000, s/n, 22″ x 21½″, pub II	50.00	—
☐ **JAGUAR CUBS,** rel. 1978. ed. 3,000, s/n, 20″ x 22″, pub II	50.00	—
☐ **CHEETAH KITTENS,** rel. 1979. ed. 3,000, s/n, 20″ x 22″, pub II	50.00	—
☐ **THE FOX AND THE FROG,** rel. 1979. ed. 3,000, s/n, 20″ x 24″, pub II	45.00	—
☐ **THE RED-TAILED HAWK,** rel. 1979. ed. 3,000, s/n, 20″ x 24″, pub II	45.00	—
☐ **SNOW LEOPARDS,** rel. 1979. ed. 1,750, s/n, 18⅜″ x 22″, pub SCI*	55.00	—
☐ **WHITE BENGAL TIGER,** rel. 1979. ed. 1,750, s/n, 23″ x 19″, pub SCI*	55.00	300.00
☐ **LION,** rel. 1980. ed. 2,000, s/n, 19″ x 21″, pub SCI*	55.00	—
☐ **PERSIAN LEOPARD,** rel. 1980. ed. 1,750, s/n, 19″ x 21″, pub SCI*	55.00	—
☐ **CANEBRAKE,** rel. 1981. ed. 1,750, s/n, 18″ x 22½″, pub SCI*	55.00	—
☐ **ENCOUNTER,** rel. 1981. ed. 1,500, s/n, 16″ x 20″, pub SCI*	55.00	—
☐ **TIGER CUB AND BOBCAT KITTEN,** rel. 1981. ed. 2,500, s/n, 11″ x 12″, pub SCI* .... pair	40.00	—
☐ **BENGAL CUB/FOOTBALL,** rel. 1982. ed. 3,000, s/n, size N/A, pub SCI	25.00	—
☐ **PANTHER,** rel. 1982. ed. 1,500, s/n, size not available, pub SCI*	55.00	—

*Represents the Sawyier Collection, Inc., and was formed as a subsidiary of Paul Sawyier Galleries.

RALPH FASANELLA

THEMES: New York City

GALLERY/DISTRIBUTOR: Felicie, Inc.

	ISSUE PRICE	CURRENT PRICE
☐ **BASEBALL PARK,** ed. 250, s/n, 31″ x 43½″, original color silkscreen, pub FI	300.00	600.00
☐ **EMPIRE STATE,** ed. 300, s/n, 45″ x 28″, original color silkscreen, pub FI	400.00	600.00
☐ **FAMILY SUPPER,** ed. 250, s/n, 41½″ x 30¾″, original color silkscreen, pub FI	300.00	600.00
☐ **MAY DAY,** ed. 250, s/n, 31″ x 45″, original color silkscreen, pub FI	300.00	500.00
☐ **NEW YORK GOING TO WORK,** ed. 300, s/n, 31″ x 35⅝″, original color silkscreen, pub FI	400.00	—
☐ **NEW YORK SCENE,** ed. 250, s/n, 30″ x 42″, original color silkscreen, pub FI	300.00	1,000.00
☐ **SAN GENNARO,** ed. 300, s/n, 29″ x 32¾″, original color silkscreen, pub FI	300.00	400.00
☐ **STICKBALL,** ed. 300, s/n, 29¾″ x 30½″, original color silkscreen, pub FI	300.00	400.00

JAMES FAULKNER

THEMES: Wildlife art

STYLE: Realism

GALLERY/DISTRIBUTOR: Edna Hibel Corporation

	ISSUE PRICE	CURRENT PRICE
☐ **RED FOX,** ed. 500, s/n, 16″ x 20″, distr. EHC	40.00	—
☐ **OTTER PLAYGROUND,** ed. 500, s/n, 16″ x 20″, distr. EHC	40.00	—
☐ **SPRING SNOW,** ed. 500, s/n, 16″ x 20″, distr. EHC	40.00	—

FRED FELLOWS

THEMES: Contemporary Western art

AWARDS: Grumbacher Fine Arts Award, Printing Institute of America Award, etc.

GALLERY/DISTRIBUTOR: Salt Creek Graphics

COMMENTS: Fellows is one of three artists whose paintings were picked by Phillip Morris to use in worldwide advertising of *Marlboro*

	ISSUE PRICE	CURRENT PRICE
☐ **MORNING LIGHT ON THE SWAN,** rel. 1976. ed. 1,000, s/n, 26″ x 33″, pub FGH	100.00	—
☐ **THE WELCOME COMMITTEE,** rel. 1976. ed. 250, s/n, 20″ x 30″, pub FGH	100.00	—
☐ **HIS FIRST SNOW,** rel. 1977. ed. 250, s/n, 18″ x 26″, pub FGH	100.00	200.00
☐ **FIRST GLIMPSE OF THE ROCKIES,** rel. 1980. ed. 1,000, s/n, 21″ x 32″, pub SCG ..	115.00	57.50
☐ **SACRED TIMES,** rel. 1980. ed. 1,000, s/n, 30″ x 15″, pub SCG	115.00	57.50
☐ **A WILDERNESS HERITAGE,** rel. 1980. ed. 1,000, s/n, 18¼″ x 35″, pub SCG	100.00	50.00
☐ **WHEN IT PAYS TO BE MOUNTED,** rel. 1981. ed. 1,000, s/n, 16″ x 24″, pub SCG ...	115.00	Sold Out
☐ **BREAKING THE MORNING TRAIL,** rel. 1982. ed. 1,000, s/n, 17½″ x 30″, pub SCG .	125.00	Sold Out

OTTER PLAYGROUND *by James Faulkner*

MARIO FERNANDEZ

THEMES: Wildlife art

GALLERY/DISTRIBUTOR: Voyageur Art

	ISSUE PRICE	CURRENT PRICE
☐ **AMERICA! AMERICA!,** rel. 1982. ed. 580, s/n, 20″ x 24″, litho, pub VA	85.00	Sold Out
☐ **A WONDERING MOMENT,** rel. 1984. ed. 780, s/n, 12″ x 24″, litho, pub VA	85.00	Sold Out
☐ **CLIMBING LESSON,** rel. 1984. ed. 780, s/n, 16″ x 20″, litho, pub VA	80.00	—
☐ **CURIOUS PAIR,** rel. 1981. ed. 580, s/n, 20″ x 16″, litho, pub VA	65.00	—
☐ **FIRST DAY OUT,** rel. 1982. ed. 580, s/n, 8¼″ x 11″, litho, pub VA	45.00	—
☐ **FLOWERS OF THE WIND,** rel. 1984. ed. 780, s/n, 6″ x 6″, litho, pub VA	155.00	—
☐ **HARMONY,** rel. 1984. ed. 580, s/n, 17½″ x 26½″, litho, pub VA	90.00	—
☐ **HIDEOUT,** rel. 1982. ed. 580, s/n, 17½″ x 26½″, litho, pub VA	80.00	Sold Out
☐ **INTERLUDE,** rel. 1981. ed. 580, s/n, 8½″ x 6″, litho, pub VA	30.00	—
☐ **LOVING MAJESTY,** rel. 1981. ed. 580, s/n, 18″ x 18″, litho, pub VA	80.00	—
☐ **MORNING LIGHT,** rel. 1982. ed. 580, s/n, 17¼″ x 24″, litho, pub VA	85.00	Sold Out
☐ **PARTRIDGE IN A PEAR TREE,** rel 1981. s/n, 10″ x 12½″, litho, pub VA	35.00	Sold Out
☐ **RED ON A WINTER'S DAY,** rel. 1982. ed. 580, s/n, 11″ x 12″, litho, pub VA	35.00	Sold Out
☐ **RENDEZVOUS,** rel. 1983. ed. 580, s/n, 32½″ x 23″, litho, pub VA	90.00	Sold Out
☐ **RHAPSODY IN BLUE,** rel. 1983. ed. 580, s/n, 14″ x 18″, litho, pub VA	75.00	Sold Out
☐ **RINGNECK PHEASANTS,** rel. 1980. ed. 350, s/n, 25″ x 17″, litho, pub VA	50.00	—
☐ **SPIRIT OF THE ENTREPRENEUR** (Small), rel. 1982. ed. 500, s/n, 10½″ x 15½″, litho, pub VA	50.00	Sold Out
☐ **SPIRIT OF THE ENTREPRENEUR** (Large), rel. 1982. ed. 95, s/n, 29″ x 20″, litho, pub VA	175.00	Sold Out
☐ **SPRINGTIME AND ROBINS,** rel. 1983. ed. 580, s/n, 14″ x 18″, litho, pub VA	75.00	—

COURTSHIP FLIGHT *by Mario Fernandez*

	ISSUE PRICE	CURRENT PRICE
☐ THINKING BLUE, rel. 1983. ed. 580, s/n, 14″ x 18″, litho, pub VA	75.00	—
☐ THREE FRENCH HENS, rel. 1983. ed. 780, s/n, 10″ x 12½″, litho, pub VA	35.00	Sold Out
☐ TWO TURTLE DOVES, rel. 1983. ed. 780, s/n, 10″ x 12½″, litho, pub VA	35.00	Sold Out
☐ WINTER BRANCHES I, rel. 1983. ed. 780, s/n, 14″ x 19½″, litho, pub VA	75.00	Sold Out
☐ WINTER BRANCHES II, rel. 1983. ed. 780, s/n, 14″ x 19½″, litho, pub VA	75.00	Sold Out
☐ WINTER HOME, rel. 1982. ed. 580, s/n, 8″ x 11″, litho, pub VA	45.00	—

JUAN FERRANDIZ

THEMES: Varied

EDUCATION: Barcelona School of Arts

GALLERY/DISTRIBUTOR: Schmid Brothers, Inc.

	ISSUE PRICE	CURRENT PRICE
☐ MOST PRECIOUS GIFT, rel. 1980. ed. 475, s/n, 17″ x 27″, litho, pub SB	125.00	1,000.00
ed. 75 (#676-750), remarqued	225.00	2,600.00
☐ MY STAR, rel. 1980. ed. 750, s/n, 10½″ x 17″, pub SB	100.00	450.00
ed. 75 (#676-750), remarqued	175.00	1,600.00

HEART OF SEVEN COLORS *by Juan Ferrandiz*

	ISSUE PRICE	CURRENT PRICE
☐ HE SEEMS TO SLEEP, rel. 1981. ed. 450, s/n, 17¾″ x 10¾″, pub SB	150.00	450.00
ed. 25, a/p, remarqued	300.00	2,500.00
☐ HEART OF SEVEN COLORS, rel. 1981. ed. 750, s/n, 10¼″ x 14½″, pub SB	100.00	275.00
ed. 75 (#676-750), remarqued	175.00	1,600.00
☐ MIRROR OF THE SOUL, rel. 1982. ed. 225. s/n, 15¼″ x 10¾″, pub SB	150.00	225.00
ed. 35, a/p, remarqued	250.00	2,500.00
☐ OH SMALL CHILD, rel. 1982. ed. 375. s/n, 11″ x 15½″, pub SB	125.00	350.00
ed. 100, (#1-50, #426-475), remarqued	275.00	1,350.00
☐ ON THE THRESHOLD OF LIFE, rel. 1982. ed. 475, s/n, 13½″ x 19″, pub SB	150.00	300.00
ed. 50, (#426-475), remarqued	275.00	1,200.00
☐ RIDING THRU THE RAIN, rel. 1982. ed. 900, s/n, 16″ x 11″, pub SB	165.00	—
ed. 100, (#801-900), a/p, remarqued	300.00	895.00
☐ SPREADING THE WORD, rel. 1982. ed. 725, s/n, 9¾″ x 10½″, pub SB	125.00	—
ed. 50, (#1-50), 726-750, remarqued	225.00	1,075.00
☐ FRIENDSHIP, rel. 1982. ed. 475, s/n, pub SB	165.00	—
ed. 15 (#1-15), remarqued	1,200.00	2,200.00
☐ STAR IN THE TEAPOT, rel. 1984. ed. 410, s/n, pub SB	165.00	—
ed. 15, remarqued	1,200.00	2,000.00

KEITH FERRIS

THEMES: Aviation art

COMMISSIONS: A variety of U.S. Government commissions including two murals in the National Air and Space Museum, and almost every major defense contractor

MEMBERSHIPS: Life member of the Air Force Association

GALLERY/DISTRIBUTOR: Greenwich Workshop

COMMENTS: Today, the artist is involved in many fields including inventing, writing, lecturing, and flying, as well as painting

	ISSUE PRICE	CURRENT PRICE
☐ SUNRISE ENCOUNTER, rel. 1982. ed. 1,000, s/n, 23″ x 23½″, pub GW	145.00	—
☐ LITTLE WILLIE COMING HOME, rel. 1983. ed. 1,000, s/n, 37″ x 18¼″, pub GW	145.00	Sold Out

SUNRISE ENCOUNTER *by Keith Ferris*

CHESTER FIELDS

THEMES: Western art

GALLERY/DISTRIBUTOR: Chester Fields

	ISSUE PRICE	CURRENT PRICE
☐ **COUGAR COUNTRY,** rel. 1983. ed. 1,000, s/n, 21″ x 26¼″, pub Washington State Alumni Association will be marketing to their current and past alumni	100.00	—
ed. 100 Artist proofs, pub CF	200.00	—

WALDO BRIDGE *by Donny Finley*

DONNY FINLEY

THEMES: Americana

STYLE: Realism

AWARDS: Finley has won over 70 awards in national shows; *Who's Who in American Art*

GALLERY/DISTRIBUTOR: Grey Stone Press

	ISSUE PRICE	CURRENT PRICE
☐ **BACK PORCH,** ed. 1,000, s/n, 25½″ x 18⅜″, pub GSP	50.00	—
☐ **FRIED PIES,** ed. 1,000, s/n	40.00	—
ed. 2,000, s/o, 25½″ x 18½″, pub GSP	30.00	—
☐ **JIM DANDY,** ed. 1,000, s/n	40.00	—
ed. 2,000, s/o, 29″ x 21″, pub GSP	30.00	—
☐ **MIGHT RAIN,** ed. 1,000, s/n, 20½″ x 29½″, litho, pub GSP	30.00	150.00
☐ **PRINCE ALBERT,** ed. 1,000, s/n	40.00	—
ed. 2,000, s/o, 22″ x 27½″, pub GSP	30.00	—
☐ **MUSCADINE WINE,** rel. 1981. ed. 1,000, s/n, 17″ x 22¼″, pub GSP	50.00	—

	ISSUE PRICE	CURRENT PRICE
☐ **SPRING PASTURES,** rel. 1981. ed. 1,000, s/n, 29½" x 20½", pub GSP	60.00	—
☐ **A FEW DAISIES,** rel. 1982. ed. 1,000, s/n, 29" x 20½", pub GSP	60.00	—
☐ **PRINCE ALBERT,** rel. 1982. ed. 1,000, s/n, 22" x 27½", pub GSP	40.00	—
ed. 2,000, s/o	30.00	—
☐ **WALDO BRIDGE,** rel. 1982. ed. 1,000, s/n, 29½" x 16½", pub GSP	60.00	—

JAMES P. FISHER

THEMES: Wildlife art

EDUCATION: Howard Pyle School of Illustrators

AWARDS: Federal Duck Stamp Competition (1975)

GALLERY/DISTRIBUTOR: Wild Wings, Inc.

	ISSUE PRICE	CURRENT PRICE
☐ **1975-76 FEDERAL DUCK STAMP DESIGN (Canvasback Decoy),** ed. 3,150 with portion of edition remarqued	reg.	950.00
size 6½" x 9" plus margins, pub WWI	rem.	1,100.00
☐ **BLACK LABRADOR,** ed. 450, s/n, 19" x 14½" litho, pub SEL	55.00	—
☐ **MALLARD DECOY,** ed. 950, s/n, 6" x 9" litho, pub WWI	60.00	—
☐ **CANVASBACK DECOY,** ed. 950, s/n, 6" x 9" litho, pub WWI	25.00	150.00
☐ **YELLOW LABRADOR,** ed. 450, s/n, 19" x 14½" litho, pub SEL	55.00	—
☐ **WOOD DUCK DECOY,** ed. 450, s/n, 10½" x 15½" litho, pub SEL	50.00	—
☐ **PINTAIL DECOY,** ed. 450, s/n, 10½" x 15½" litho, pub SEL	60.00	—
☐ **AMERICAN GOLDENEYE,** ed. 450, s/n, 16" x 20" litho, pub WWI	60.00	—
☐ **MALLARD DECOY,** ed. 450, s/n, 16" x 20" litho, pub WWI	60.00	—
☐ **RED HEAD DECOY,** ed. 450, s/n, 15" x 11" litho, pub WWI	50.00	—
☐ **PRIMITIVE MALLARD,** ed. 450, s/n, 15" x 11" litho, pub WWI	50.00	—
☐ **CANVAS ON WIRE - CANADA GOOSE,** rel. 1978. ed. 450, s/n, 18½" x 16½", pub WWI	55.00	100.00
ed. 50, remarque artist proof	130.00	175.00
☐ **GREENHEAD DECOY,** rel. 1977. ed. 950, s/n, 6" x 9", pub WWI	25.00	150.00
☐ **1948 WARD BLACK DUCK,** rel. 1978. ed. 450, s/n, size not available, pub WWI	55.00	—

BART FORBES

THEMES: Western art

MEDIUM: Watercolor

EDUCATION: University of North Carolina; Art Center School

AWARDS: Over 40 Merit awards

MEMBERSHIPS: New York Society of Illustrators, American Institute of Graphic Arts

GALLERY/DISTRIBUTOR: Salt Creek Graphics

	ISSUE PRICE	CURRENT PRICE
☐ STURBRIDGE FARM, ed. 450, s/n, 25″ x 34″, litho, pub SCG	110.00	–
☐ SHAKER GIRL, ed. 150, s/n, 22″ x 30″, litho, pub SCG	150.00	250.00
☐ 1932, ed. 450, s/n, 18″ x 24″, litho, pub SCG	60.00	–
☐ PHOENIX, ed. 450, s/n, 18″ x 24″, litho, pub SCG	68.00	200.00
☐ SPRING, ed. 450, s/n, 18″ x 26″, litho, pub SCG	80.00	–
☐ SUMMER, ed. 450, s/n, 18″ x 26″, litho, pub SCG	65.00	300.00
☐ FALL, ed. 450, s/n, 18″ x 26″, litho, pub SCG	80.00	–
☐ WINTER, ed. 450, s/n, 18″ x 26″, litho, pub SCG	120.00	150.00
☐ BLUE GIRLS, ed. 700, s/n, 18″ x 24″, litho, pub SCG	120.00	–
☐ WINGS, ed. 700, s/n, 18″ x 24″, litho, pub SCG	86.00	–
☐ JAZZ SOLO, ed. 150, s/n, 24″ x 37″, litho, pub SCG	150.00	750.00
☐ DAY HERDER, ed. 50, s/n, 34″ x 44″, litho, pub SCG	450.00	600.00
☐ FORT WORTH, ed. 300, s/n, 26″ x 34″, litho, pub SCG	80.00	150.00
☐ WAR HAWK, ed. 300, s/n, 24″ x 34″, litho, pub SCG	150.00	250.00
☐ SEE EES TK, ed. 750, s/n, 22″ x 28″, litho, pub SCG	60.00	–
☐ SPIRIT WORLD, ed. 1,500, s/n, 22″ x 28″, litho, pub SCG	60.00	–
☐ TIM-HOO-LAUH, ed. 1,000, s/n, 22″ x 28″, litho, pub SCG	100.00	75.00
☐ OT-WAY, ed. 450, s/n, 22″ x 30″, litho, pub SCG	80.00	–
☐ TE-MY, ed. 450, s/n, 22″ x 30″, litho, pub SCG	80.00	–
☐ BRAVE, ed. 400, s/n, 24″ x 34″, litho, pub SCG	30.00	350.00
☐ WESTWARD, ed. 1,000, s/n, 22″ x 28″, litho, pub SCG	150.00	–
☐ IN-MUT-TOO-YAH-LAT-LAT, ed. 450, s/n, 22″ x 24″, litho, pub SCG	50.00	300.00
☐ OGLALLA SIOUX, ed. 150, s/n, 24″ x 34″, litho, pub SCG	40.00	750.00
☐ RED WING, ed. 150, s/n, 16″ x 20″, litho, pub SCG	80.00	200.00
☐ KIOWA, ed. 380, s/n, 20″ x 24″, litho, pub SCG	110.00	–
☐ HOO-HA-LA-KIN, ed. 380, s/n, 16″ x 20″, litho, pub SCG	80.00	–
☐ WAT-CHUM-YUSH, ed. 450, s/n, 22″ x 23″, litho, pub SCG	50.00	850.00
☐ WEP-TES, ed. 450, s/n, 18″ x 26″, litho, pub SCG	180.00	–
☐ JAZZ DUO, ed. 500, s/n, 24″ x 35″, litho, pub SCG	180.00	–
☐ HOLDING EAGLE, ed. 450, s/n, 22″ x 24″, litho, pub SCG	120.00	–
☐ WAR PONY, rel. 1980. ed. 450, s/n, 22″ x 24″, litho, pub SCG	120.00	–
☐ MOTHER & CHILD, rel. 1980. ed. 200, s/n, 27″ x 21″, pub SGC	120.00	350.00
☐ RANCH HAND, rel. 1980. ed. 250, s/n, 24″ x 36″, pub SCG	140.00	–
☐ SEA OTTER, rel. 1980. ed. 450, s/n, 21″ x 25″, pub SCG	150.00	–
☐ TRUMPETER SWAN, rel. 1980. ed. 450, s/n, 21″ x 23″, pub SCG	150.00	200.00
☐ BIG HORN SHEEP, rel. 1980. ed. 450, s/n, 23″ x 21″, pub SCG	150.00	180.00

STEVE FORBIS

THEMES: Indian art

STYLE: Subtle balance of light and delicate shading

GALLERY/DISTRIBUTOR: Native American Images

	ISSUE PRICE	CURRENT PRICE
☐ INNOCENCE, rel. 1979. ed. 80, s/n, 8″ x 10″, litho, pub NAI	125.00	425.00
☐ SCALPLOCK AND BLEEDING HEART, rel. 1979. ed. 80, s/n, 8″ x 11″, litho, pub NAI	110.00	175.00
☐ BUTTERFLY MAIDEN KACHINA, rel. 1979. ed. 65, s/n, 6″ x 8″, litho, pub NAI	80.00	80.00
☐ HOPI GIRL, rel. 1981. ed. 100, s/n, 9″ x 12″, litho, pub NAI	125.00	175.00
☐ BUFFALO, rel. 1981. ed. 60, s/n, 10″ x 7″, litho, pub NAI	115.00	150.00
☐ BUTTERFLIES, rel. 1982. ed. 25, s/n, 9″ x 12″, litho, pub NAI	150.00	200.00
☐ NEW BUCKSKINS, rel. 1982. ed. 150, s/n, 19″ x 24″, litho, pub NAI	400.00	1,200.00
☐ WAITING TO DANCE, rel. 1983. ed. 150, s/n, 14″ x 21″, litho, pub NAI	400.00	1,600.00
☐ SUNNY, rel. 1983. ed. 650, s/n, 13″ x 15″, offset print, pub NAI	60.00	–

IN HER IMAGE *by Steve Forbis*

	ISSUE PRICE	CURRENT PRICE
☐ **HOPI BUFFALO DANCERS,** rel. 1983. ed. 150, s/n, 15″ x 22″, litho, pub NAI	450.00	—
☐ **GRANDMOTHER'S PRIDE,** rel. 1983. ed. 25, s/n, 9″ x 12″, litho, pub NAI	150.00	200.00
☐ **CROW PARADE,** rel. 1984. ed. 650, s/n, 16″ x 20″, offset print, pub NAI	100.00	—
☐ **COOLER IN THE SHADE,** rel. 1984. ed. 150, s/n, 18″ x 24″, litho, pub NAI	600.00	—
☐ **MEDICINE SHIELD,** rel. 1984. ed. 100, s/n, 8½″ x 12″, litho, pub NAI	175.00	—
☐ **TESUQUE SNOWBIRD DANCER,** ed. 100, s/n, size not available, stone litho, pub NWDHG	300.00	1,200.00
☐ **PASSING TIME AT HUBBELL'S,** ed. 100, s/n, size not available, stone litho, pub NWDHG	300.00	4,500.00
☐ **BREAD DAY AT TAOS,** ed. 100, s/n, size not available, stone litho, pub NWDHG	260.00	500.00
☐ **DRESSED FOR THE FAIR,** ed. 80, s/n, 13″ x 8″, stone litho, pub NWDHG	125.00	200.00
☐ **SIOUX HEADDRESS,** ed. 80, s/n, 12″ x 8″, stone litho, pub NWDHG	125.00	375.00
☐ **A NEW LOOK AT THE OLD,** ed. 100, s/n, 14″ x 19½″, stone litho, pub NWDHG	300.00	500.00
☐ **IN HER IMAGE,** ed. 100, s/n, 18″ x 27″, stone litho, pub NAI	375.00	850.00
☐ **PRIDE OF TEXAS,** rel. 1985. ed. 90, s/n, 7″ x 9″, stone litho, pub NAI	125.00	—
☐ **SUMMER SUN,** rel. 1985. ed. 90, s/n, 15″ x 17″, stone litho, pub NAI	450.00	—

FALL FLIGHT *by Chris Forrest*

CHRISTOPHER P. FORREST

THEMES: Wildlife art

MEDIUM: Acrylics and oils

EDUCATION: Virginia Polytechnic Institute; North Carolina State University

MEMBERSHIPS: Society of Animal Artists

GALLERY/DISTRIBUTOR: Hang Ups, Inc.

	ISSUE PRICE	CURRENT PRICE
☐ ARAPAHO CREEK REDTAIL, rel. 1982. ed. 300, s/n, 22″ x 28″, litho, pub HUI	200.00	250.00
☐ EVENING'S VIGIL, rel. 1982. ed. 300, s/n, 21″ x 27″, litho, pub HUI	200.00	—
☐ FALL FLIGHT, rel. 1982. ed. 300, s/n, 22″ x 27″ litho, pub HUI	200.00	250.00
☐ FLYING WOODIE, rel. 1982. ed. 300, s/n, 22″ x 28″, litho, pub HUI	200.00	250.00
☐ GOLDEN EAGLE, rel. 1982. ed. 300, s/n, 21″ x 27″, litho, pub HUI	150.00	175.00
☐ INDIAN PAINTBRUSH, rel. 1982. ed. 300, s/n, 22″ x 27″, litho, pub HUI	200.00	225.00
☐ JOURNEY'S END, rel. 1982. ed. 300, s/n, 22″ x 27″, litho, pub HUI	200.00	Sold Out
☐ LONE TRAVELER, rel. 1982. ed. 300, s/n, 13″ x 19″, litho, pub HUI	125.00	125.00
☐ TIMBER LINE, rel. 1982. ed. 300, s/n, 22″ x 27″, litho, pub HUI	150.00	175.00
☐ DUSK DEPARTURE, rel. 1983. ed. 300, s/n, 22″ x 27″, litho, pub HUI	225.00	250.00
☐ HAPPY HOVERS, rel. 1983. ed. 300, s/n, 14″ x 20″, litho, pub HUI	150.00	150.00
☐ OCTOBER JOURNEY, rel. 1983. ed. 300, s/n, 21″ x 26″, litho, pub HUI	250.00	300.00
☐ PINE HAVEN, rel. 1983. ed. 300, s/n, 13″ x 19″, litho, pub HUI	125.00	125.00

	ISSUE PRICE	CURRENT PRICE
☐ **PINTAIL,** rel. 1983. ed. 300, s/n, 22″ x 27″, litho, pub HUI	225.00	250.00
☐ **SPRING STROLL,** rel. 1983. ed. 300, s/n, 22″ x 28″, litho, pub HUI	250.00	300.00
☐ **SPRING VISITORS,** rel. 1983. ed. 300, s/n, 14″ x 20″, litho, pub HUI	150.00	150.00
☐ **TWILIGHT WANDERS,** rel. 1983. ed. 300, s/n, 21″ x 27″, litho, pub HUI	250.00	300.00
☐ **WOODY'S REST,** rel. 1983. ed. 300, s/n, 21″ x 28″, litho, pub HUI	250.00	300.00

DON FORREST

THEMES: Wildlife art

GALLERY/DISTRIBUTOR: Russell A. Fink

	ISSUE PRICE	CURRENT PRICE
☐ **GOLDEN EAGLE,** ed. 500, s/n, 12″ x 16″, pub RAF	30.00	50.00
☐ **SPARROW HAWKS,** ed. 500, s/n, 12″ x 16″, pub RAF	30.00	50.00
☐ **SPRUCE GROUSE,** ed. 500, s/n, 12″ x 16″, pub RAF	30.00	50.00

UNO *by Charles Fracé*

CHARLES FRACÉ

THEMES: Wildlife art

EDUCATION: Philadelphia College of Art

AWARDS: Numerous honors, American Cultural Art Register, *Who's Who in American Art*, etc.

MEMBERSHIPS: National Audubon Society, Society of Animal Artists, National Wildlife Federation, and the Humane Society

GALLERY/DISTRIBUTOR: Frame House Gallery, Inc.

	ISSUE PRICE	CURRENT PRICE
☐ **AFRICAN LEOPARD,** rel. 1981. ed. 12,500, s/o, 16″ x 20″, pub AMF	25.00	70.00
☐ **AFRICAN LION,** rel. 1973. ed. 3,000, s/o, 23″ x 23½″, pub FHG	35.00	300.00
☐ **AMERICAN EAGLE (At Walking Dunes),** rel. 1980. ed. 2,000, s/n, 22½″ x 30″, pub FHG..	75.00	135.00
ed. 2,000, s/o	60.00	110.00
ed. 1,000 exclusive		
☐ **AMERICAN MONARCH,** rel. 1984. ed. 3,750, s/n, 22″ x 36″, pub AMF	120.00	225.00
☐ **A SUNNY SPOT,** rel. 1985. ed. 2,500, s/n, 18″ x 23″, pub AMF	110.00	—
ed. 2,500, s/o	70.00	—
☐ **NEW ARRIVAL,** rel. 1984. ed. 7,500, s/o, 16″ x 20″, pub AMF	25.00	
☐ **BANDIT,** rel. 1984. ed. 6,431, s/n, 18″ x 26″, pub AMF	90.00	125.00
☐ **BIGHORN COUNTRY,** rel. 1982. ed. 2,500, s/n, 25″ x 29″, pub AMF	75.00	200.00
☐ **BISON,** rel. 1975. ed. 2,000, s/n, 20″ x 24″, pub FHG	**50.00	100.00
**This limited edition print was released in the AMERICA'S WILDLIFE HERITAGE PORTFOLIO, which consists of six prints in all, each by a different Frame House Gallery artist.		
☐ **BLACK LEOPARD,** rel. 1978. ed. 3,000, s/o, 28″ x 24″, pub FHG	50.00	425.00
☐ **BOBCAT,** rel. 1977. ed. 3,000, s/o, 22″ x 18″, pub FHG	40.00	70.00
☐ **CANADA LYNX,** rel. 1977. ed. 3,000, s/o, 22″ x 24″, pub FHG	50.00	150.00
☐ **CAVALIER KING CHARLES SPANIELS,** rel. 1976. ed. 1,500, s/n, 20″ x 24″, pub FHG	35.00	80.00
☐ **CHEETAH,** rel. 1977. ed. 3,000, s/o, 20″ x 26″, pub FHG	50.00	90.00
☐ **CHEETAH KITTEN,** rel. 1974. ed. 5,000, s/o, 24″ x 22½″, pub FHG	40.00	350.00
☐ **CLOUDED LEOPARD,** rel. 1979. ed. 2,000, s/n, 23″ x 34″	65.00	110.00
ed. 2,000, s/o, pub FHG	50.00	100.00
☐ **CLOUDED LEOPARD CUB,** rel. 1979. ed. 2,000, s/n, 25″ x x 22″	75.00	100.00
ed. 3,000, s/o, pub FHG	60.00	125.00
☐ **COUGAR,** rel. 1978. ed. 1,000, s/n, 25½″ x 30″, pub FHG	90.00	675.00
ed. 4,000, s/o	75.00	675.00
☐ **COUGAR CUB,** rel. 1977. ed. 3,000, s/o, 18″ x 22″, pub FHG	50.00	175.00
☐ **DOUBLE TROUBLE,** rel. 1984. ed. 2,500, s/n, 19″ x 26″, pub AMF	90.00	225.00
ed. 2,500, s/o	60.00	175.00
☐ **ELEPHANTS AT KILLIMANJARO,** rel. 1976. ed. 1,000, s/n, 21″ x 30″, pub FHG	75.00	210.00
ed. 2,000, s/o	60.00	175.00
☐ **GIANT PANDA,** rel. 1973. ed. 5,000, s/o, 21″ x 24½″, pub FHG	45.00	200.00
☐ **GOLDEN EAGLE,** rel. 1973. ed. 1,000, s/n, 30″ x 25¾″, pub FHG	75.00	200.00
ed. 4,000, s/o	60.00	135.00
☐ **GREATER KUDU,** rel. 1977. ed. 3,000, s/o, 21½″ x 20″, pub FHG	50.00	65.00
☐ **GYRFALCON,** rel. 1976. ed. 2,000, s/o, 26″ x 20″, pub FHG	40.00	100.00
ed. 1,000, s/o with the Air Force Emblem	40.00	60.00
☐ **HARLAN'S HAWK,** rel. 1977. ed. 1,500, s/n, 20″ x 24″, pub FHG	60.00	100.00
☐ **HARP SEAL,** rel. 1980. ed. 2,000, s/n, 23″ x 24″	75.00	275.00
ed. 2,000, s/o, pub FHG	60.00	225.00
ed. 1,500, s/n, w/Roman Numerals exclusive for International Fund for Animal Welfare	100.00	320.00
☐ **HERRING GULL,** rel. 1974. ed. 5,000, s/o, 21¾″ x 26¾″, pub FHG	45.00	125.00
☐ **HIMALAYAN PRINCE,** rel. 1981. ed. 2,000, s/n, 23″ x 28″, pub AMF	75.00	300.00
ed. 3,000, s/o	60.00	200.00

	ISSUE PRICE	CURRENT PRICE
☐ IMPALA, rel. 1978. ed. 2,000, s/n, 25½" x 24", pub FHG	60.00	125.00
☐ JAGUAR, rel. 1981. ed. 2,000, s/n, 26¼" x 31⅛", pub FHG	75.00	325.00
ed. 2,000, s/o	60.00	275.00
☐ JAGUAR (Head Series), rel. 1982. ed. 12,500, s/n, 16" x 20", pub AMF	25.00	325.00
☐ KOALA BEAR, rel. 1979. ed. 2,000, s/n, 30" x 24"	65.00	220.00
ed. 2,000, s/o, pub FHG	50.00	190.00
ed. 1,000 exclusive for Australia		
☐ LEOPARD, rel. 1977. ed. 1,500, s/n, 20" x 25", pub FHG	75.00	250.00
ed. 1,000, s/n, remarqued	125.00	300.00
☐ LEOPARD CUB, rel. 1979. ed. 2,000, s/n, 22" x 28", pub FHG	65.00	300.00
ed. 2,000, s/o	50.00	190.00
☐ LION CUB, rel. 1975. ed. 4,000, s/o, 21½" x 18½", pub FHG	35.00	125.00
☐ LOFTY VIEW - RED-TAILED HAWK, rel. 1981. ed. 2,500, s/n, 24" x 32", pub AMF	75.00	100.00
☐ HIS MAJESTY (White-tail Deer), rel. 1982. ed. 2,500, s/n, 26" x 29", pub AMF	80.00	85.00
ed. 2,000, s/o	60.00	—
☐ MASAI GIRAFFES AT AMBOSELI, rel. 1976. ed. 3,000, s/o, 24" x 18", pub FHG	40.00	150.00
☐ MORRIS THE CAT, rel. 1976. ed. 5,000, s/o, 16" x 20", pub FHG	30.00	175.00
☐ NORTHERN GOSHAWK, rel. 1975. ed. 4,000, s/o, 25" x 27", pub FHG	50.00	475.00
☐ OCELOT KITTENS, rel. 1976. ed. 5,000, s/o, 18" x 20", pub FHG	35.00	160.00
☐ PALS, rel. 1985. ed. 2,500, s/n, 16" x 20", pub AMF	70.00	—
ed. 2,500, s/o	40.00	—
☐ POLAR BEAR, rel. 1980. ed. 2,000, s/n, 22" x 36", pub FHG	100.00	120.00
ed. 3,000, s/o	80.00	90.00
☐ PRONGHORN, rel. 1973. ed. 5,000, s/o, 22" x 27¼", pub FHG	50.00	90.00
☐ QUIET TIME IN SAMBURU, rel. 1985. ed. 2,500, s/n, 20" x 24", pub AMF	100.00	—
☐ RACCOON, rel. 1974. ed. 5,000, s/o, 24" x 28", pub FHG	50.00	250.00
☐ RACCOONS (3), rel. 1978. ed. 5,000, s/o, 24" x 30", pub FHG	50.00	425.00
☐ RED RASCAL, rel. 1983. ed. 2,500, s/n, 18" x 25½", pub AMF	80.00	350.00
☐ RED SHOULDERED HAWK, rel. 1975. ed. 2,000, s/n, 28" x 24", pub FHG	60.00	100.00
☐ ROYAL PRIDE, rel. 1982. ed. 2,500, s/n, 25" x 28", pub AMF	100.00	115.00
ed. 2,500, s/o	80.00	90.00
☐ SCREECH OWLS, rel. 1975. ed. 3,500, s/o, 17" x 16", pub FHG	20.00	70.00
☐ SIBERIAN LYNX CUB, rel. 1980. ed. 2,000, s/n, 22" x 25", pub FHG	75.00	150.00
ed. 2,000, s/o	60.00	120.00
☐ SIBERIAN TIGER, rel. 1979. ed. 2,000, s/n, 27" x 33"	100.00	175.00
ed. 3,000, s/o, pub FHG	80.00	155.00
☐ SNOW LEOPARD, rel. 1975. ed. 1,500, s/n, 21⅛" x 24⅞", pub FHG	75.00	975.00
ed. 1,000, s/n, remarqued	125.00	1,350.00
☐ SNOW LEOPARD HEAD, rel. 1979. ed. 5,000, s/o, 16" x 20", pub FHG	20.00	145.00
☐ SNOWY OWLS, rel. 1979. ed. 2,000, s/n, 23" x 29", pub FHG	65.00	95.00
☐ THE LIONS, rel. 1974. ed. 5,000, s/o, 30½" x 23½", pub FHG	40.00	225.00
☐ TIGER, rel. 1973. ed. 3,000, s/o, 23" x 23½", pub FHG	35.00	300.00
☐ TIGER CUB, rel. 1975. ed. 3,500, s/o, 15" x 18½", pub FHG	35.00	250.00
☐ UNO, rel. 1982. ed. 2,500, s/n, 27" x 22", pub AMF	75.00	90.00
ed. 2,500, s/o	65.00	75.00
ed. 100 exclusive to Columbus Ohio Zoo.		
☐ WHITE TIGER, rel. 1976. ed. 1,500, s/n, 26½" x 34", pub FHG	75.00	225.00
ed. 1,000, s/n, remarqued	125.00	300.00
☐ WHITE TIGER HEAD, rel. 1980. ed. 20,000, s/o, 16" x 30", pub FHG	25.00	50.00
☐ LONE HUNTER, rel. 1982. ed. 2,500, s/n, 22" x 32", pub AMF	100.00	—
ed. 2,000, s/o	80.00	—
☐ ZEBRA, rel. 1975. ed. 4,000, s/o, 39" x 22¼", pub FHG	60.00	100.00
☐ ZEBRA FOAL, rel. 1975. ed. 4,000, s/o, 15¼" x 19¼", pub FHG	35.00	125.00

THE FRANKLIN MINT

In 1973 The Franklin Mint embarked upon a program of limited edition art with each piece being offered through their Gallery of Art. In the years following most programs were offered in sets.

Inasmuch as their entire offering has been through the Gallery of Art rather than a dealer network it is virtually impossible to determine a collector value, as most dealers have neither seen the sets nor know their value and hesitate to offer a customer any secondary market price. This does not necessarily mean they have no value . . . it is just that not very many sets have been sold on the secondary. There have been a few sets sold through coin shops across the country because they deal exclusively in Franklin Mint material.

	ISSUE PRICE	CURRENT PRICE
☐ 1973 GOLD MEDAL AWARDS, ed. 4,333, each print individually signed/dated by the artist, series of ten prints, 22″ x 30″	500.00	—
APPOINTMENT IN TOWN by Donald Teague; SELLING THE WHITE STALLION by Melvin Warren; AT'EED YAZHI by Ray Swanson; DEATH TO LONG KNIVES by Joe Grandee; TRIBAL HUNT by John Clymer; THE RAIDERS by Frank McCarthy; TEXAS LONGHORN by Robert Summers; FOGGY MORNING by Joe Beeler; CALLING ON NEIGHBORS by Gordon Phillips; NOON CHUCK by James Reynolds		
☐ 1974 GOLD MEDAL AWARDS, ed. 2,908, each print individually signed/dated by the artist, series of twelve prints, 22″ x 30″	660.00	—
TUMBLEWEED SERENADE by Tom Lovell; PURSUIT AND ATTACK by Joe Grandee; NIGHT RIDER by Melvin Warren; MIST OF MORNING by Ralf Wall; WOOD GATHERER OF WALPI by Paul Calle; LAYING A HEEL TRAP by Bill Owen; DUSK ON THE SANTE FE HILLS by Robert Lougheed; THE SUPPLY WAGON by James Reynolds; WAITING TO GO TO THE POWWOW by Ray Swanson; THE GREAT HUNT by Buck McCain; CROSSING TRAILS by Gordon Phillips; THE NIGHT MAIL by Donald Teague		
☐ 1973 GALLERY OF AMERICAN ART by ten well known entertainers . . . Portfolio titled "Celebrity Art Prints". ed. 750, each print individually signed/numbered by artist, series of ten prints, 22″ x 28″	1,500.00	—
THIRD FLOOR by Henry Fonda; MEMORIES OF SUSSEX by Richard Chamberlain; NEW YORK by Tony Bennett; EVER ONWARD & UPWARD by Duke Ellington; MIGRANT WORKER'S CHILDREN by Dinah Shore; SUMMER CREATURE by Candice Bergen; THE CLOWN by Red Skelton; THE GAMBLERS by Elke Sommer; GABY by Peggy Lee; THE GULL by Kim Novak.		
☐ 1974-1977 FLOWERS OF AMERICA ART. This was a series of eighteen prints from original paintings by the internationally known artist Jeanne Holgate. Each painting portrayed two or more of America's state flowers grouped together as they would be in nature. ed. 2,992, s/n, 22″ x 28″	900.00	—
☐ 1974 BIRD ART PRINTS. Set consists of 5 prints, each portraying one of America's most beautiful birds, ed. 1,968, signed/dated by the artist, 27″ x 20″	300.00	—
GREAT BLUE HERON, LONG-EARED OWL, WOOD DUCK, BALTIMORE ORIOLE, RED-BELLIED WOODPECKER		
☐ 1974 GOLD MEDAL AWARDS, ed. 2,908, each print individually signed/dated by the artist, series of twelve prints, 22″ x 30″	600.00	—
BOILING TIME, VERMONT by Tom Nicholas; DUSK by Marion Brown; DAISIES by Phillip Jamison; HEADING HOME by Paul Rickert; CHARLIE'S WORLD by Mel Crawford; EVENING LIGHT by Paul Strisik; NANA'S BOY by Don Stone; RAINY TRYST by John Pike; WINTER IN CENTRAL PARK by Bogmoir Bogdanovic; WINDMILLS ON DON QUIXOTE by Donald Teague; MILKING TIME by Guy Fry; HARBOR SENTINEL by Rex Brandt.		
☐ 1974 AMERICA THE BEAUTIFUL ART PRINTS. Consisting of eight prints by eight distinguished landscape artists, each print is individually signed by the artist, ed. 2,985, 22″ x 30″	400.00	—
O BEAUTIFUL FOR SPACIOUS SKIES by Wilson Hurley; FOR AMBER WAVES OF GRAIN by Ray Hosford; FOR PURPLE MOUNTAIN MAJESTIES by Hall Diteman; ABOVE THE FRUITED PLAIN by John Chumley; AMERICA! AMERICA! by James Fetheroff; GOD SHED HIS GRACE ON THEE by Dean Fausett; AND CROWN THY GOOD WITH BROTHERHOOD by Robert Sticker; FROM SEA TO SHINING SEA by Alex Dzigurski.		
☐ 1975 BIG GAME ART PRINTS. Consists of ten prints of big game issued by the World Wildlife Fund—U.S. and produced by the Franklin Mint Gallery of Art. The collection was created exclusively for this collection by Gary Swanson, ed. 885, signed/dated by the artist, 22″ x 8″	500.00	—

	ISSUE PRICE	CURRENT PRICE

AFRICAN LION, NORTH AMERICAN ELK, GRIZZLY BEAR, GIRAFFES OF KILI-MANHARO, BENGAL TIGER, SHEEP, AFRICAN ELEPHANT, IMPALA, PERSIAN LEOPARD, ROCKY MOUNTAIN GOAT

☐ **1975 SHIPS OF AMERICA ETCHINGS,** Consists of four etchings by well known artist, Alan Jay Gaines, ed. 19,351, signed/dated by the artist, 27⅜" x 21¾" .... **300.00** —
THE SCHOONER 'WILLIAM L. WHITE', THE WHALER 'CHARLES W. MORGAN', THE RIVER STEAMBOAT 'ROBERT E. LEE', THE CLIPPER 'SEA WITCH'

☐ **1977 THE FRIGATE 'U.S.S. CONSTITUTION',** ed. 846 . . . special historic ship etching was issued during the holiday season .... **95.00** —

☐ **1976-77 AMERICAN BIRD ENGRAVINGS,** Consists of four engravings. Issued in commemoration of the 150th Anniversary of John James Audubon's Birds of America engravings. Commissioned by the National Audubon Society and drawn by one of our great wildlife artists, Albert Earl Gilbert, ed. 10,253, signed/dated by the artist, 24½" x 30⅞" **480.00** —
AMERICAN BALD EAGLE, BLUE JAY, SCREECH OWL, CARDINAL

☐ **1976-78 LOCOMOTIVE ETCHINGS,** Consists of four etchings by American artist Kathleen Cantin, ed. 4,872, signed/dated by the artist, 18" x 32¼" .... **360.00** —
THE GREAT LOCOMOTIVE CHASE, EAST MEETS WEST, ENGINE 999, THE TOM THUMB

☐ **1977 SEASCAPES,** Consists of four color lithographs by one of America's most respected seascape artist, Tom Nicholas, ed. 9,189, signed/dated by the artist, 24½" x 20½" .... **480.00** —
NEW ENGLAND LIGHTHOUSE, WINTER BEACH (Oregon Coast), ALONG THE GULF COAST (Gulf of Mexico), MONTEREY BEACH (California)

☐ **1977 OLD GEORGIA FARMHOUSE,** artist Butler Brown. Brown's portrayal of the images of his native Georgia are direct and plain spoken. His inspiration has come from the Georgia midlands where he was born to a farm family, ed. 4,989, signed/remarqued by the artist, 29" x 25½" .... **150.00** —

☐ **1979 LANDSCAPES OF AMERICA,** artist Butler Brown. This series will consist of four lithographs, with the artist signing and remarquing each edition. Edition size not available at this time because of recent issue; size of lithograph will be 25⅜" x 22⅜" .... **150.00** —
MILLPOND REFLECTIONS (number one of four)

☐ **1977-78 BIRD LITHOGRAPHS,** artist Larry Toschik. An accomplished outdoorsman who is widely regarded as one of America's most distinguished wildlife artists. Will consist of four prints when completed, ed. 4,579, signed/dated by the artist, 22⅝" x 28½" ..... **380.00** —
WILD CRY OF MORNING (Canada Geese) (number one of four)

☐ **1978-80 COWBOY COLOR LITHOGRAPHS,** artist Paul Calle. Each of the four lithographs in this series will portray a different moment in the life of the American Cowboy, ed. 2,467, signed/dated by the artist, 21½" x 25½" .... **380.00** —
54 YEARS A COWBOY, MILES TO GO (first two prints in the series)

☐ **1979-80 FLOWERS OF THE YEAR MINIATURES,** artist Davis Carroll. One of America's most renowned flower artists, he was commissioned by The American Horticultural Society to paint twelve new and original works of flower art . . . these to be issued in authentic limited edition lithographs. Each work to depict the favorite and most captivating flower that blooms during a single month in the gardens of the headquarters of the Society at River Farm. Edition size not available at this time, signed/dated by the artist, 8" x 9¼", consists of twelve lithographs .... **420.00** —

☐ **1979-80 CONQUEST OF SPACE COLOR LITHOGRAPH, AND STAMPS,** artist Paul Calle. Issued to commemorate the tenth anniversary of the first moon landing in 1969. Set will consist of fifteen stamps and color lithographs each providing a pictorial history of America's exploration of space. To preserve its mint condition each stamp is set into a transparent protective capsule with each lithograph specially commissioned to accompany the stamp. Edition size worldwide 15,000, 21¼" x 18", signed by the artist .. each **95.00** —
ECHO 1—COMMUNICATIONS FOR SPACE (1¢ stamp); PROJECT MERCURY (4¢ stamp); ROBERT H. GODDARD (8¢ stamp); APOLLO 8 (6¢ stamp); FIRST MAN ON THE MOON (10¢ stamp); U.S. IN SPACE—A DECADE OF ACHIEVEMENT (8¢ stamp); SKYLAB (10¢ stamp); PIONEER—JUPITER (10¢ stamp); MARINER 10 VENUS/MERCURY (10¢ stamp); APOLLO-SUYUZ SPACE TEST PROJECT (10¢ stamp); VIKING MISSION TO MARS (15¢ stamp); There are two in the set untitled as of this writing.

☐ **1979-80 MEL HUNTER LITHOGRAPHS,** This collection of four original color lithographs was created exclusively for this issue by well-known artist, Mel Hunter. In the great tradition of American realism, he has chosen to portray the world he knows best—the countryside surrounding his home and studio in Vermont. Edition size not available at this time, signed/dated by the artist, 24½" x 20¼" .... **480.00** —
CATHERINE'S FARM (first title of four)

BROWN TROUT *by Robert Frankowiak*

ROBERT G. FRANKOWIAK

THEMES: Wildlife art

BACKGROUND: Bob Frankowiak, Assistant Art Director of the Milwaukee Public Museum, has painted 36 diorama backgrounds depicting wildlife habitats of the United States, the Canadian Arctic, Central America, and Africa

GALLERY/DISTRIBUTOR: Northwoods Craftsman

	ISSUE PRICE	CURRENT PRICE
☐ **BRULE RIVER,** rel. 1976. ed. 300, s/n, 16″ x 20″, pub RGF, distr. NC	45.00	—
☐ **WOLF RIVER,** rel. 1976. ed. 300, s/n, 16″ x 20″, pub RGF, distr. NC	45.00	—
☐ **DEER CROSSING,** rel. 1977. ed. 300, s/n, 18″ x 24″, pub RGF, distr. NC	55.00	—
☐ **WOOD DUCKS,** rel. 1977. ed. 300, s/n, 18″ x 24″, pub RGF, distr. NC	55.00	—
☐ **BROWN TROUT,** rel. 1980. ed. 600, s/n, 12″ x 14″, pub NC	85.00	350.00
ed. 100 remarqued	160.00	600.00
1980 Wisconsin Trout Stamp print		
☐ **MUSKELLUNGE,** rel. 1980. ed. 600, s/n, 28″ x 22″, pub RGF, distr. NC	60.00	—
☐ **CARDINALS,** rel. 1981. ed. 500, s/n, 22″ x 16½″, pub RGF, distr. NC	45.00	—
☐ **PHEASANTS,** rel. 1981. ed. 500, s/n, 18⅞″ x 23″, pub RGF, distr. NC	45.00	—

ROD FREDERICK

THEMES: Wildlife art

STYLE: Realism

GALLERY/DISTRIBUTOR: Greenwich Workshop

	ISSUE PRICE	CURRENT PRICE
☐ **FIRST MOMENTS OF GOLD,** rel. 1984. ed. 825, s/n, 35″ x 22⅜″, pub GW	145.00	150.00
☐ **FIRST MOMENTS OF GOLD REMARQUED,** rel. 1984. ed. 25, s/n, 35″ x 22⅜″, pub GW..	295.00	Sold Out
☐ **FROM TIMBER'S EDGE,** rel. 1984. ed. 850, s/n, 31″ x 18½″, pub GW	125.00	170.00
☐ **MISTY MORNING SENTINEL,** rel. 1984. ed. 850, s/n, 24″ x 29½″, pub GW	125.00	160.00
☐ **HIGH SOCIETY,** rel. 1985. ed. 850, s/n, 8¾″ x 28¾″, pub GW	115.00	150.00
☐ **EARLY EVENING GATHERING,** rel. 1985. ed. 450, s/n, 18⅛″ x 45″, pub GW	350.00	Sold Out
☐ **LOS COLORES DE CHIAPAS,** rel. 1985. ed. 950, s/n, 7¹⁵⁄₁₆″ x 16¹⁄₁₆″, pub GW	85.00	Sold Out·

FROM TIMBER'S EDGE *by Rod Frederick*

KENNETH FREEMAN

THEMES: Western art

EDUCATION: Stanford University, American Academy of Art

GALLERY/DISTRIBUTOR: Connoisseur's Gallery of Art, Ltd.

	ISSUE PRICE	CURRENT PRICE
☐ **NUMBER 1 AT PRADO DE SOL.** ed. 950, s/n, 16″ x 23½″, pub CGAL	150.00	—
ed. 12, Artist accented, s/n	420.00	—
☐ **PREPPING FOR THE BRONCS,** ed. 950, s/n, 24″ x 18″, pub CGAL	150.00	—
ed. 12, Artist accented, s/n	420.00	—
☐ **LONESOME WAIT,** ed. 950, s/n, 18″ x 24″, pub CGAL	150.00	—
ed. 12, Artist accented, s/n	420.00	—

RED FOX *by Louis Frisino*

LOUIS FRISINO

THEMES: Wildlife art

EDUCATION: Maryland School for the Deaf; Maryland Institute of Art

AWARDS: Peabody Award, Maryland Duck Shamp Competition (1976-1977), and many other awards on the East Coast

GALLERY/DISTRIBUTOR: Russell A. Fink

	ISSUE PRICE	CURRENT PRICE
☐ **SINGLE MALLARD,** ed. 500, s/n, 11″ x 14″, litho, pub RAF	15.00	30.00
☐ **SINGLE WOOD MALLARD,** ed. 500, s/n, 11″ x 14″, litho, pub RAF	15.00	30.00
☐ **SINGLE GREEN WING,** ed. 500, s/n, 11″ x 14″, litho, pub RAF	15.00	30.00
☐ **SINGLE BLUE WING,** ed. 500, s/n, 11″ x 14″, litho, pub RAF	15.00	30.00
☐ **SINGLE CANADA GOOSE,** ed. 500, s/n, 11″ x 14″, litho, pub RAF	15.00	30.00
☐ **SINGLE CANVASBACK,** ed. 500, s/n, 11″x 14″, litho, pub RAF	15.00	30.00

	ISSUE PRICE	CURRENT PRICE
☐ REDHEADS - PAIR, ed. 500, s/n, 14″ x 18″, litho, pub RAF	30.00	60.00
☐ CANVASBACKS - PAIR, ed. 500, s/n, 14″ x 18″, litho, pub RAF	30.00	60.00
☐ WOOD DUCKS - PAIR, ed. 500, s/n, 14″ x 18″, litho, pub RAF	30.00	60.00
☐ CANADA GEESE - PAIR, ed. 500, s/n, 14″ x 18″, litho, pub RAF	30.00	60.00
☐ MALLARDS - PAIR, ed. 500, s/n, 14″ x 18″, litho, pub RAF	30.00	60.00
☐ PINTAILS - PAIR, ed. 500, s/n, 14″ X 18″, litho, pub RAF	30.00	60.00
☐ REBEL - GERMAN SHEPHERD, ed. 600, s/n, 14″ x 18″, litho, pub RAF	20.00	60.00
☐ BLACK LAB W/WOOD DUCK, ed. 500, s/n, 14″ x 18″, litho, pub RAF	30.00	100.00
☐ YELLOW LAB W/CANVASBACK, ed. 500, s/n, 14″ x 18″, litho, pub RAF	30.00	100.00
☐ RED FOX, ed. 950, s/n, 14″ x 18″, litho, distr. MM	—	35.00
☐ CHESAPEAKE W/GOOSE, ed. 500, s/n, 20″ x 24″, litho, distr. MM	—	50.00
☐ BLACK LAB W/CANVASBACK, ed. 550, s/n, 20″ x 24″, litho, distr. MM	—	100.00
☐ POINTER HEAD, ed. 1,000, s/n, 9⅜″ x 12½″, litho, distr. MM	—	20.00
☐ BRITTANY HEAD, ed. 1,000, s/n, 9⅜″ x 12½″, litho, distr. MM	—	20.00
☐ SPRINGER HEAD, ed. 1,000, s/n, 9⅜″ x 12½″, litho, distr. MM	—	20.00
☐ BEAGLE HEAD, ed. 1,000, s/n, 9⅜″ x 12½″, litho, distr. MM	—	20.00
☐ BLACK LAB W/PINTAIL, ed. 1,000, s/n, 18″ x 22″ litho, distr. MM	—	100.00
☐ GOLDEN RETRIEVER W/MALLARD, ed. 1,000, s/n, 18″ x 22″, litho, distr. MM	—	100.00
☐ BLUE BILLS ON WATER, ed. 550, s/n, 20″ x 25″, litho, distr. MM	—	25.00
☐ BLACK LAB HEAD, ed. 1,000, s/n, 9⅜″ x 12½″, litho, distr. MM	—	20.00
☐ YELLOW LAB HEAD, ed. 1,000, s/n, 9⅜″ x 12½″, litho, distr. MM	—	20.00

ON KATHLEEN'S COAT by *Jerry Gadamus*

	ISSUE PRICE	CURRENT PRICE
☐ GOLDEN RETRIEVER HEAD, ed. 1,000, s/n, 9⅜" x 12½", litho, distr. MM	—	20.00
☐ ENGLISH SETTER HEAD, ed. 1,000, s/n, 9⅜" x 12½", litho, distr. MM	—	20.00
☐ ON THE ALERT, ed. 950, s/n, 16" x 24", pub RAF	40.00	—
☐ RED FOX, ed. 950, s/n, 11¼" x 9", pub RAF	25.00	—

JERRY GADAMUS

THEMES: Wildlife art

STYLE: Gadamus paints wildlife with an airbrush

EDUCATION: University of Wisconsin at Stevens Point

GALLERY/DISTRIBUTOR: Northwoods Craftsman

	ISSUE PRICE	CURRENT PRICE
☐ FIRST DAY ON THE JOB, rel. 1980. ed. 600, s/n, 28" x 22", pub NC	60.00	500.00
☐ KINDERGARTNER, rel. 1980. ed. 600, s/n, 28" x 22", pub NC	60.00	—
☐ ABBY-ALIAS MUD, rel. 1981. ed. 600, s/n, 22" x 27¼", pub NC	75.00	—
☐ BRULE RIVER MORNING, rel. 1981. ed. 600, s/n, 35" x 24", pub NC	85.00	—
☐ FLAMING FENCE POST CARDINALS, rel. 1983. ed. 600, s/n, 20" x 24", pub NC ...	75.00	200.00
☐ KILLDEER EGGS, rel. 1983. ed. 600, s/n, 13⅛" x 25", pub NC	55.00	—
☐ ON KATHLEEN'S COAT, rel. 1984. ed. 600, s/n, 16" x 20", pub NC	75.00	—
☐ THE FOX CROSSING, rel. 1984. ed. 600, s/n, 16" x 20", pub NC	75.00	—
☐ GOLDEN RETRIEVER, rel. 1985. ed. 600, s/n, 23" x 17", pub NC	85.00	—
☐ ORCHARD BLUE, rel. 1985. ed. 600, s/n, 9½" x 13", pub NC	40.00	—

JOE GARCIA

THEMES: Wildlife art

MEDIUM: Watercolor

EDUCATION: Art Center College of Design in Los Angeles, California

GALLERY/DISTRIBUTOR: Wild Wings, Inc.

	ISSUE PRICE	CURRENT PRICE
☐ SERENITY—PAIR OF CANADAS, rel. 1983. ed. 950, s/n, litho, 13¼" x 17½", pub WWI	35.00	—
☐ LONE BULL SPRIG, rel. 1984. ed. 950, s/n, litho, 12½" x 16", pub WWI	40.00	—

JOSEPH GETSINGER

THEMES: Varied

GALLERY/DISTRIBUTOR: J. Getsinger Art

FALL *by Joseph Getsinger*

	ISSUE PRICE	CURRENT PRICE
☐ ANTIQUE SHOW, ed. 175, s/n, 10″ x 15″, etching, pub JGA	20.00	35.00
☐ ARTIST'S POSTER PRINT (Clown), ed. 1,900, s/n, 21″ x 28″, offset litho, pub JGA ..	25.00	35.00
☐ BARN, ed. 175, s/n, etching, pub JGA	20.00	35.00
☐ BARNEGAT LIGHTHOUSE, ed. 150, s/n, 24″ x 27″, etching, pub JGA	60.00	Sold Out
☐ BIRDWING, ed. 175, s/n, etching, pub JGA	45.00	85.00
☐ 1910 BUICK, ed. 150, s/n, 14″ x 17″, etching, pub JGA	35.00	50.00
☐ CENTER RING, ed. 285, s/n, 24″ x 29″, litho, pub JGA	50.00	135.00
☐ 28 CHEVROLET, ed. 175, s/n, 13″ x 16″, etching, pub JGA	40.00	45.00
☐ 29 CHRYSLER ROADSTER, ed. 100, s/n, 20″ x 24″, etching, pub JGA	60.00	Sold Out
☐ 1936 CORD, ed. 175, s/n, etching, pub JGA	40.00	60.00
☐ 53 CORVETTE, ed. 150, s/n, 10″ x 15″, etching, pub JGA	35.00	55.00
☐ DOG FIGHT, ed. 175, s/n, 17″ x 20″, etching, pub JGA	40.00	50.00
☐ DRIFTIN' ALONG, ed. 175, s/n, 11″ x 14″, etching, pub JGA	20.00	45.00
☐ FIRST INDY, ed. 100, s/n, 10″ x 15″, etching, pub JGA	30.00	Sold Out
☐ FIRST MOON, ed. 300, s/n, 8″ x 11″, litho, pub JGA	25.00	40.00
☐ FLYIN', ed. 10, s/n, 8″ x 8″, etching, pub JGA	10.00	30.00
☐ 1903 FORD, ed. 75, s/n, 16″ x 20″, etching, pub JGA	40.00	Sold Out
☐ FREE AS THE WIND, ed. 175, s/n, 20″ x 24″, etching, pub JGA	35.00	80.00
☐ GABLE, ed. 225, s/n, 17″ x 18″, litho, pub JGA	20.00	40.00
☐ HAPPY, ed. 175, s/n, 16″ x 19″, etching, pub JGA	40.00	65.00
☐ HERE'S LOOKIN AT YOU KID, ed. 75, s/n, 15″ x 16″, etching, pub JGA	35.00	Sold Out
☐ KIKI, ed. 175, s/n, 19″ x 21″, linoleum, pub JGA	45.00	80.00
☐ LES CHEVAUX, ed. 175, s/n, 26″ x 33″, litho, pub JGA	60.00	195.00
☐ LE CHEVAUX II, ed. 300, s/n, 16″ x 20″, litho, pub JGA	40.00	70.00
☐ LE CHEVAUX SUITE, 25 suites from an edition of 300. A five-piece suite including: Les Chevaux II, First Moon, Moondrift, Luna, and Whispers	175.00	350.00
☐ LET'S CLOWN AROUND, ed. 175. s/n, 17″ x 20″, etching, pub JGA	45.00	60.00
☐ LITTLE DOLPHINS, ed. 175, s/n, 11½″ x 13″, etching, pub JGA	20.00	30.00
☐ LONG ISLAND SOUND, ed. 150, s/n, 16″ x 17″, etching, pub JGA	50.00	75.00
☐ LOST FRONTIER, ed. 75, s/n, 14″ x 18″, etching, pub JGA	45.00	Sold Out
☐ MACAW, ed. 175, s/n, 14″ x 22″, etching, pub JGA	40.00	75.00
☐ MAIN STREET, ed. 200, s/n, 23″ x 29″, litho, pub JGA	70.00	100.00

Winter's Chill
by Jerry Crandall

Wood Ducks *by Larry K. Martin*

Chesapeake Schooner
by George C. Vail

First Out *by Christopher Blossom*

Lion Cubs
by Peter Skirka

Into The Wind *by Morten E. Solberg*

Hooded Mergansers *by Rod Lawrence*

Gilley's House
by Bob Timberlake

Largemouth Bass-Feeding Time *by Roger Preuss*

Edge of Winter, Grand Canyon *by Wilson Hurley*

Chance Encounter *by Paul Calle*

Clouded Leopard
by Edward J. Bierly

Heidi
by Edna Hibel

Reverie *by John McClelland*

Sunset - Canada Geese *by Owen J. Gromme*

'Tis Spring *by Richard Earl Thompson*

	ISSUE PRICE	CURRENT PRICE
☐ **MARE & FOAL,** ed. 175, s/n, 16″ x 19″, etching, pub JGA	40.00	80.00
☐ **MOONDRIFT,** ed. 200, s/n, 4″ x 8″, litho, pub JGA	17.50	25.00
☐ **MUSHROOMS,** ed. 175, s/n, 15″ x 17″, etching, pub JGA	30.00	Sold Out
☐ **NIGHTCALL,** ed. 2,000, s/n, 21″ x 26″, offset litho, pub JGA	25.00	40.00
☐ **OLD FORD PANEL,** ed. 100, s/n, 16″ x 18″, etching, pub JGA	35.00	Sold Out
☐ **1928 PACKARD,** ed. 175, s/n, 17″ x 20″, etching, pub JGA	50.00	95.00
☐ **PEGASUS,** ed. 75, s/n, 18″ x 22″, etching, pub JGA	35.00	Sold Out
☐ **RIDING,** ed. 150, s/n, 8″ x 11″, etching, pub JGA	15.00	Sold Out
☐ **31 ROLLS,** ed. 100, s/n, 14″ x 17″, etching, pub JGA	30.00	Sold Out
☐ **RUNNING FREE,** ed. 50, s/n, 8″ x 10″, etching, pub JGA	20.00	Sold Out
☐ **SAVE THE DOLPHINS,** ed. 175, s/n, 16″ x 19″, etching, pub JGA	30.00	45.00
☐ **SHORELINE,** ed. 1,900, s/n, 8½″ x 22″, offset litho, pub JGA	10.00	35.00
☐ **SPRING,** ed. 175, s/n, 16″ x 18″, etching, pub JGA	60.00	75.00
☐ **STUCK,** ed. 25, s/n, 24″ x 30″, litho, pub JGA	95.00	Sold Out
☐ **SUMMER,** ed. 175, s/n, 16″ x 18″, etching, pub JGA	60.00	75.00
☐ **THE ROSE,** ed. 75, s/n, 7″ x 10″, etching, pub JGA	15.00	Sold Out
☐ **TOPPY,** ed. 150, s/n, 17″ x 17″, etching, pub JGA	35.00	60.00
☐ **T-TOURING,** ed. 100, s/n, 14″ x 17″, etching, pub JGA	35.00	45.00
☐ **TUT & AYE,** ed. 285, s/n, 29″ x 34″, litho, foil embossed, pub JGA	150.00	250.00
☐ **WHISPERS,** ed. 300, s/n, 8″ x 11″, litho, pub JGA	25.00	40.00
☐ **WHITE CLOUD,** ed. 100, s/n, 17″ x 20″, etching, pub JGA	45.00	50.00
☐ **YOUNG NUDE,** ed.d 75, s/n, 12″ x 16″, etching, pub JGA	35.00	Sold Out
☐ **BACK FORTY (BARN),** rel. 1984. ed. 950, s/n, 11″ x 14″, offset litho, pub JGA	25.00	35.00
☐ **FALL (WITH CHILDREN),** rel. 1984. ed. 950, s/n, 18″ x 24″, offset litho, pub JGA	45.00	50.00
☐ **BILLY DANIELS (COMMEMORATIVE PRINT),** rel. 1985. ed. 500, s/n, litho, 10″ x 13″, pub JGA	10.00	—
☐ **FIRST IMPRESSIONS,** rel. 1985. ed. 2,000, s/n, litho, 18″ x 24″, pub JGA	45.00	—
☐ **SEA SHACK,** rel. 1985. ed. 2,000, s/n, 11″ x 14″, pub JGA	25.00	—

SANDRA GIANGIULIO

THEMES: Varied

MEDIUM: Watercolor

BACKGROUND: After a successful career as an actress/singer, she turned her talents to art

EDUCATION: College of Saint Teresa; Boston University; University of Miami

AWARDS: Windsor-Newton Watercolor Prize, Neographics Silver Medal Award (1982)

GALLERY/DISTRIBUTOR: Laurel Enterprises

	ISSUE PRICE	CURRENT PRICE
☐ **KIMBERTON POND,** rel. 1980. ed. 950, s/n, 21½″ x 15¼″, pub LE	60.00	—
☐ **STRAWBERRY TIN,** rel. 1980. ed. 950, s/n, 11″ x 14″ oval, pub LE	40.00	—
☐ **BETSY ROSS HOUSE** rel. 1981. ed. 600, s/n, 20″ x 13½″, pub LE	50.00	—
☐ **ENGLISH COWPARSLEY,** rel. 1982. ed. 600, s/n, 11″ x 14″ oval, pub LE	40.00	—
☐ **INDEPENDENCE HALL,** rel. 1981. ed. 600, s/n, 20″ x 13½″, pub LE	50.00	—
☐ **VICTORIAN PINK HOUSE,** rel. 1982. ed. 600, s/n, 21½″ x 16″, pub LE	60.00	—
☐ **FLOWER LADY OF PARIS,** rel. 1983. ed. 650, s/n, 22¼″ x 29½″, pub LE	90.00	—
☐ **PINK LADIES,** rel. 1983. ed. 750, s/n, 8″ x 10⅜″, pub LE	25.00	—
☐ **SPRINGTIME BY THE ART MUSEUM,** rel. 1983. ed. 750, s/n, 15¾″ x 26″, pub LE ..	70.00	—

	ISSUE PRICE	CURRENT PRICE
☐ **WILD BLACKBERRIES,** rel. 1983. ed. 750, s/n, 8″ x 10⅜″, pub LE	25.00	—
☐ **A TOUCH OF SPRING,** rel. 1984. ed. 650, s/n, 21⅞″ x 15¾″, pub LE	60.00	—
☐ **SHADES OF FALL,** rel. 1984. ed. 650, s/n, 20¾″ x 14″, pub LE	50.00	—
☐ **BOAT HOUSE ROW,** rel. 1985. ed. 550, s/n, 19¼″ x 31½″, pub LE	120.00	—

ALBERT EARL GILBERT

THEMES: Wildlife art

AWARDS: *Who's Who in American Art,* 1978-79 Federal Duck Stamp Competition

MEMBERSHIPS: Society of Animal Artists

MUSEUMS/COLLECTIONS: Carnegie Museum, American Museum of Natural History, etc.

	ISSUE PRICE	CURRENT PRICE
INTERNATIONAL WILDLIFE SERIES		
☐ **AMERICAN BALD EAGLES,** rel. 1973. ed. 1,000, s/n, 24″ x 20″, pub NWAEI*	65.00	
☐ **CARDINALS ON APPLE BLOSSOM,** rel. 1973. ed. 300, s/n, 20″ x 24″, pub NWAEI*	75.00	700.00
☐ **MOCKINGBIRDS ON ORANGE BLOSSOM,** rel. 1973. ed. 750, s/n, 20″ x 24″ pub NWAEI*	75.00	600.00
☐ **EASTERN BLUEBIRDS,** rel. 1973. ed. 1,500, s/n, 20″ x 24″, pub NWAEI*	60.00	
☐ **COUGAR,** rel. 1973. ed. 3,500, s/n, 24″ x 20″, pub NWAEI*	50.00	
☐ **CARDINALS IN THE SNOW,** rel. 1973. ed. 1,500, s/n, 20″ x 24″, pub NWAEI*	60.00	
THE DECORATOR SERIES		
☐ **WILD TURKEY,** rel. 1973. ed. 3,000, s/n, 16″ x 20″, pub NWAEI*	30.00	
☐ **HOODED MERGANSER 1978-79 Federal Duck Stamp Print,** rel. 1978. ed. 5,800, s/n, 13″ x 14⅞″, pub SRWA	100.00	200.00
ed. 1,350, s/n, remarqued in watercolor	375.00	675.00
ed. 300 Artists proofs		
☐ **SAW-WHET OWL,** rel. 1978, ed. 950, s/n, 16″ x 20″, pub SRWA	50.00	—
☐ **CHICKADEE ON HOLLY,** rel. 1978. ed. 950, s/n, 16″ x 20″, pub SRWA	50.00	—
☐ **AMAZON JUNGLE JAGUAR & CUB,** rel. 1978. ed. 750, s/n, 32″ x 40″, pub SRWA ..	150.00	—
☐ **AFRICAN LIONESS & CUBS,** rel. 1978. ed. 750, s/n, 32″ x 40″, pub SRWA	150.00	—

*These prints were published by National Wildlife Art Exchange of Florida. This company is no longer in business and because these prints are not actively bought and sold on the collector market at this time we hestitate to place any collector value on these issues.

H. COBB GILBERT

THEMES: Wildlife art

GALLERY/DISTRIBUTOR: Natural Heritage Fine Art

	ISSUE PRICE	CURRENT PRICE
☐ **FEMALE BELTED KINGFISHER,** rel. 1980. ed. 350, s/n, 12″ x 10″, pub NHFA	65.00	—
w/pencil remarque	130.00	—
w/color remarque	175.00	—
☐ **RED-BELLIED WOODPECKER,** rel. 1980. ed. 250, s/n, 12″ x 13″, pub NHFA	65.00	—
w/pencil remarque	130.00	—
w/color remarque	175.00	—

	ISSUE PRICE	CURRENT PRICE
☐ **COAST CANVASBACKS,** rel. 1980. ed. 250, s/n, 19″ x 26″, pub NHFA	65.00	—
w/pencil remarque	130.00	—
w/color remarque	175.00	—
☐ **WOOD DUCKS,** rel. 1981. ed. 500, s/n, 19″ x 24″, pub NHFA	85.00	—
w/pencil remarque	150.00	—
w/color remarque	195.00	—
☐ **RED-BREASTED MERGANSERS,** rel. 1981. ed. 350, s/n, 7″ x 10″, pub NHFA	45.00	—
w/pencil remarque	110.00	—
w/color remarque	155.00	—
☐ **ELK,** rel. 1982. ed. 1,500, s/n, 7″ x 10″, pub NHFA	125.00	—
w/stamp	130.50	—
w/pencil remarque	190.00	—
w/pencil remarque and stamp	195.50	—
w/color remarque	235.00	—
w/color remarque and stamp	240.50	—
☐ **HUNGARIAN PARTRIDGE,** rel. 1982. 1st in a Series (5) Idaho Upland Game Birds, ed. 500, s/n, 19″ x 23″, pub NHFA	75.00	—
w/pencil remarque	140.00	—
w/color remarque	185.00	—
☐ **BLACK DUCKS,** rel. 1983. ed. 750, s/n, 4″ x 5¾″, litho, pub NHFA	35.00	—
☐ **BALD EAGLE — SPIRIT OF FREEDOM,** rel. 1984. ed. to be determined, s/n, 20″ x 17″, litho, pub NHFA	195.00	—
☐ **BLUE-WINGED TEAL DRAKES,** rel. 1984. ed. 500, s/n, 7″ x 10″, litho, pub NHFA ...	55.00	—
☐ **MATCHED WITS,** rel. 1984. ed. 1,500, s/n, 7″ x 10″, litho, pub NHFA	125.00	—

MATCHED WITS *by H. Cobb Gilbert*

GRANT GILDERHUS

THEMES: Landscape art

MEDIUM: Watercolor

EDUCATION: Carthage College

GALLERY/DISTRIBUTOR: Northwoods Craftsman

	ISSUE PRICE	CURRENT PRICE
☐ OPENING DAY - LAKE EMMA, rel. 1979. ed. 400, s/n, 28¾" x 22¾", distr. NC	60.00	—
☐ EARLY MATES - PHEASANTS, rel. 1980. ed. 600, s/n, 29" x 22¾", distr. NC	80.00	—

LUNDA HOYLE GILL

THEMES: Varied

EDUCATION: Chouinard Art Institute, Art Students League, Academia de Belli Arti

GALLERY/DISTRIBUTOR: Hammer Publishing Co.

	ISSUE PRICE	CURRENT PRICE
☐ LUNDY IN THE SAND, rel. 1972. ed. 1,000, s/n, 31" x 23½", pub FHG	35.00	120.00
☐ LUNDY IN THE WHEAT, rel. 1973. ed. 1,500, s/n, 25" x 29", pub FHG	35.00	—
☐ LUNDY ON THE ROCK, rel. 1974, ed. 1,000, s/n, 20" x 33½", pub FHG	45.00	80.00
☐ GABRA NAB, rel. 1975. ed. 500, s/n, 18" x 22", pub FHG	50.00	—
☐ NATIVE OF THE NORTH, portfolio of three	1,200.00	Sold Out
☐ Individually, WISE KAKARUK, ed. 300, s/n, 20" x 16", pub HP	450.00	—
☐ SEWING MY MUKLUK'S, ed. 300, s/n, 20" x 23", pub HP	550.00	—
☐ MY LAND, ed. 300, s/n, 21" x 28", pub HP	650.00	—

WILLIAM GILLIES

THEMES: Dogs, sporting art

BACKGROUND: In 1961, he started The Portrait Group School of Painting

EDUCATION: University of Southern California, Art Center School; Chouinard Art Institute; Grand Central Art School

GALLERY/DISTRIBUTOR: Petersen Prints

	ISSUE PRICE	CURRENT PRICE
☐ COMING IN - BLACK LAB, rel. 1981. ed. 850, s/n, size not available, pub WWI	65.00	—
☐ MARK, rel. 1981. ed. 800, s/n, 18" x 24", pub PP	75.00	—
s/n, remarqued	165.00	—

BARBARA GIROUARD

THEMES: Varied

MEDIUM: Watercolor

EDUCATION: Florida State University

GALLERY/DISTRIBUTOR: Girouard Unlimited

	ISSUE PRICE	CURRENT PRICE
☐ **INDIANA WINTER,** rel. 1981. ed. 450, s/n, 22″ x 28″, pub GU	30.00	70.00
☐ **JUST RESTING,** rel. 1981. ed. 300, s/n, 17½″ x 23½″, pub GU	30.00	50.00
☐ **PONCE DE LEON INLET,** rel. 1981. ed. 300, s/n, 17½″ x 23½″, pub GU	30.00	50.00
☐ **THE WINDMILL,** rel. 1981. ed. 300, s/n, 17½″ x 23½″, pub GU	30.00	50.00

INDIANA WINTER *by Barbara Girouard*

ANDRE GISSON

THEMES: Varied

STYLE: Influenced by French Impressionism; stylistic trademark of color restraint, letting the great power of white tell his story

EDUCATION: Pratt Institute

GALLERY/DISTRIBUTOR: Eleanor Ettinger, Inc.

	ISSUE PRICE	CURRENT PRICE
☐ BREEZE AT TRURO, rel. 1977. ed. 250, s/n, 18″ x 15½″, litho, arches, pub EEI	125.00	200.00
☐ SHADOW, rel. 1978, ed. 250, s/n, 38″ x 28½″, litho, arches, pub EEI	200.00	450.00
☐ CAROUSEL, rel. 1979. ed. 250, s/n, 27½″ x 24″, litho, arches, pub EEI	150.00	300.00
ed. 50, japon	175.00	325.00
☐ PATH, rel. 1981. ed. 250, s/n, 34″ x 28½″, litho, arches, pub EEI	200.00	400.00

NANCY GLAZIER

THEMES: Wildlife art (of North America, primarily)

MUSEUMS/COLLECTIONS: Her works are featured in several collections

GALLERY/DISTRIBUTOR: Wild Wings, Inc.

	ISSUE PRICE	CURRENT PRICE
☐ THE AMERICANS, rel. 1981. ed. 600, s/n, size not available, pub WWI	100.00	250.00
☐ BEAUTY AND THE BEAST, rel. 1982. ed. 600, s/n, size not available, pub WWI	85.00	—
☐ ROYALTY, rel. 1982. ed. 600, s/n, size not available, pub WWI	85.00	—
☐ MORNING GLORY - MULE DEER, rel. 1983. ed. 600, s/n, 13″ x 16½″, pub WWI . . .	50.00	—
☐ THE MATRIARCH, rel. 1983. ed. 750, s/n, 17″ x 22½″, pub WWI	100.00	—
☐ WRITTEN ON THE WIND, rel. 1983. ed. 600, s/n, 20″ x 17″, pub WWI	65.00	—
☐ KING'S CROSSING—ELK, rel. 1984. ed. 600, s/n, litho, 16½″ x 25″, pub WWI	85.00	—
☐ LONG WINTER'S NAP—FOX, rel. 1985. ed. 600, s/n, litho, 15″ x 18″, pub WWI	65.00	—

MICHAEL GNATEK

THEMES: American Indians

MEDIUM: Pencil and colored pencil

GALLERY/DISTRIBUTOR: Wild Wings, Inc.

COMMENTS: Recently, he received international publicity with his illustration of "Jimmy - The Eight-Year-Old Heroin Addict," commissioned by *The Washington Post* to accompany Janet Cooke's fraudulent Pulitzer Prize winning story. This art was reprinted in *Time, Newsweek, U.S. News and World Report, The Saturday Evening Post,* and *Der Spiegel.*

	ISSUE PRICE	CURRENT PRICE
☐ SITTING BULL, rel. 1982. ed. 600, s/n, litho, 22½″ x 17¾″, pub WWI	75.00	—
☐ SUNDANCER, rel. 1983. ed. 600, s/n, litho, 22½″ x 17¾″, pub WWI	75.00	—
☐ PATTON AT BASTOGNE—DEC, 1944, rel. 1984. ed. 750, s/n, litho, 24½″ x 18″, pub WWI.	100.00	250.00

MORNING GLORY-MULE DEER *by Nancy Glazier*

FRANCIS GOLDEN

THEMES: Wildlife art

MEDIUM: Watercolor

BACKGROUND: The artist had a brief career as a muralist who worked with Salvador Dali

EDUCATION: Museum School of Fine Arts in Boston

GALLERY/DISTRIBUTOR: Wild Wings, Inc.

	ISSUE PRICE	CURRENT PRICE
☐ TROUT FISHING, ed. 750, s/n, 17″ x 25″, pub SEL	70.00	—
☐ CANADAS AND YOUNG, rel. 1980. ed. 850, s/n, size not available, pub WWI	65.00	—

TROUT FISHING *by Francis Golden*

BARBARA GOLDSTEIN

THEMES: Varied

EDUCATION: University of Texas; the Palacio de Bella Artes; Art Students League; Froman School of Art

GALLERY/DISTRIBUTOR: Arts Limited Inc.

	ISSUE PRICE	CURRENT PRICE
☐ **MORNING LACE,** rel. 1981. ed. 1,500 s/n, 32¼″ x 25″, pub ALI	60.00	—
☐ **WOODLAWN,** rel. 1981. ed. 1,500, s/n, 32½″ x 25″, pub ALI	60.00	—
☐ **HILL FLOWERS,** rel. 1982. ed. 1,500, s/n, 25½″ x 19″, pub ALI	60.00	—

BILL GRANSTAFF

THEMES: Varied

EDUCATION: Kansas City Art Institute; Chicago's American Academy of Art

AWARDS: *Who's Who in American Art*, The International Biography (Cambridge, England)

GALLERY/DISTRIBUTOR: Granstaff Prints, Ltd.

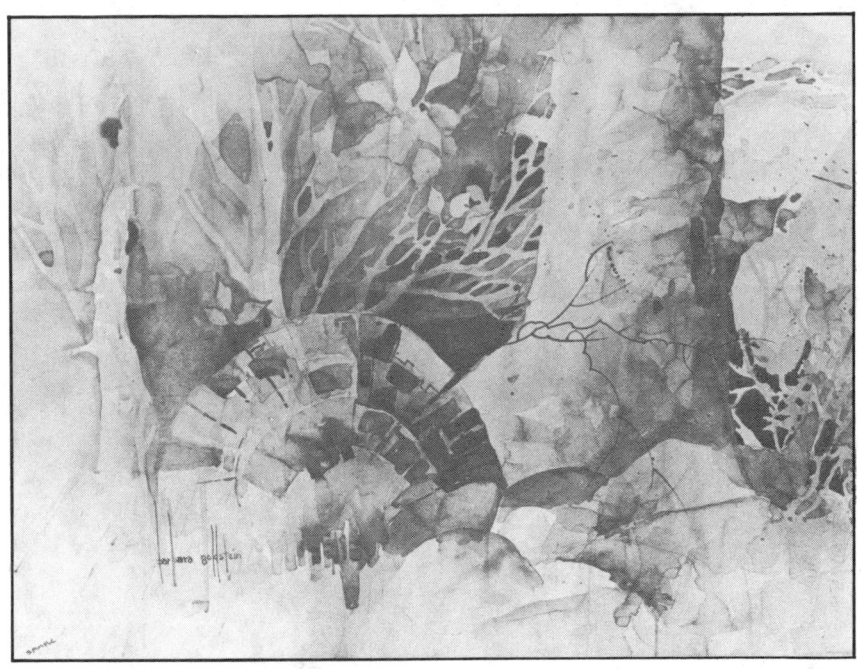

WOODLAWN *by Barbara Goldstein*

	ISSUE PRICE	CURRENT PRICE
MEMENTO SERIES		
☐ **AT EASE,** rel. 1973. ed. 200, s/n, 12″ x 16″, pub GPL	12.00	110.00
ed. 800, s/o	10.00	100.00
ed. 25 Artist proof	25.00	—
☐ **MONDAY MORN,** rel. 1973. ed. 200, s/n, 12″ x 16″, pub GPL	12.00	110.00
ed. 2,300, s/o	10.00	100.00
ed. 25 Artist proof	25.00	—
☐ **EASY AS PIE,** rel. 1974. ed. 300, s/n, 12″ x 16″, pub GPL	15.00	75.00
ed. 2,000, s/o	10.00	65.00
ed. 25 Artist proof	25.00	—
☐ **JOHNNY REB,** rel. 1974. ed. 200, s/n, 12″ x 16″, pub GPL	15.00	75.00
ed. 2,300, s/o	10.00	65.00
ed. 25 Artist proof	25.00	—
☐ **SUNDAY AFTERNOON,** rel. 1974. ed. 200, s/n, 12″ x 16″, pub GPL	12.00	110.00
ed. 2,300, s/o	10.00	100.00
ed. 25 Artist proof	25.00	—
☐ **BABY TALK,** rel. 1975. ed. 350, s/n, 12″ x 16″, pub GPL	15.00	85.00
ed. 1,400, s/o	10.00	65.00
ed. 26 Artist proof	25.00	—
☐ **SATURDAY NITE,** rel. 1975. ed. 250, s/n, 12″ x 16″, pub GPL	15.00	85.00
ed. 1,500, s/o	10.00	75.00
ed. 25 Artist proof	25.00	—
☐ **VANITY,** rel. 1975. ed. 500, s/n, 12″ x 16″, pub GPL	15.00	85.00
ed. 1,250, s/o	12.00	75.00
ed. 26 Artist proof	25.00	—

HOMEMAKER *by Bill Granstaff*

	ISSUE PRICE	CURRENT PRICE
☐ **CANDLES '76,** rel. 1976. ed. 500, s/n, 12″ x 16″, pub GPL	15.00	45.00
ed. 1,450, s/o	12.00	35.00
ed. 26 Artist proof	25.00	—
☐ **PLA' LIKE,** rel. 1976. ed. 500, s/n, 12″ x 16″, pub GPL	17.00	45.00
ed. 2,050, s/o	12.00	35.00
ed. 50 Artist proof	25.00	—
☐ **PLANTIN' TIME,** rel. 1976. ed. 500, s/n, 12″ x 16″, pub GPL	15.00	45.00
ed. 1,450, s/o	12.00	35.00
ed. 26 Artist proof	25.00	—
☐ **MADE FROM SCRATCH,** rel. 1977. ed. 500, s/n, 12″ x 16″, pub GPL	17.00	45.00
ed. 2,000, s/o	14.00	25.00
ed. 35 Artist proof	25.00	—
☐ **MILKIN' TIME,** rel. 1977. ed. 500, s/n, 12″ x 16″, pub GPL	17.00	35.00
ed. 2,000, s/o	14.00	25.00
ed. 35 Artist proof	25.00	—
☐ **VIOLETS,** rel. 1977. ed. 500, s/n, 12″ x 16″, pub GPL	17.00	75.00
ed. 1,565, s/o	12.00	65.00
ed. 35 Artist proof	25.00	—
☐ **BEGONIAS,** rel. 1978. ed. 500, s/n, 12″ x 16″, pub GPL	17.00	25.00
ed. 2,000, s/o	14.00	20.00
ed. 35 Artist proof	25.00	—
☐ **KEEP COOL,** rel. 1978. ed. 500, s/n, 12″ x 16″, pub GPL	17.00	25.00
ed. 2,000, s/o	15.00	20.00
ed. 35 Artist proof	25.00	—
☐ **TUESDAY MORN,** rel. 1978. ed. 500, s/n, 12″ x 16″, pub GPL	17.00	25.00
ed. 2,000, s/o	15.00	20.00
ed. 35 Artist proof	25.00	—

	ISSUE PRICE	CURRENT PRICE
☐ **PUTTIN' BY,** rel. 1979. ed. 500, s/n, 12″ x 16″, pub GPL	17.00	25.00
ed. 2,000, s/o	15.00	20.00
ed. 35 Artist proof	25.00	25.00
☐ **RAINED OUT,** rel. 1979. ed. 500, s/n, 12″ x 16″, pub GPL	17.00	25.00
ed. 2,000, s/o	15.00	20.00
ed. 35 Artist proof	25.00	20.00
☐ **DUCK DAYS,** rel. 1980. ed. 500, s/n, 12″ x 16″, pub GPL	30.00	—
ed. 1,000, s/o	25.00	—
ed. 100 Artist proof	35.00	—
☐ **GERANIUMS,** rel. 1980. ed. 500, s/n, 12″ x 16″, pub GPL	20.00	—
ed. 2,000, s/o	17.00	—
ed. 35 Artist proof	25.00	—
☐ **OUR DAILY BREAD,** rel. 1980. ed. 500, s/n, 12″ x 16″, pub GPL	20.00	Sold Out
ed. 1,500, s/o	17.00	Sold Out
ed. 35 Artist proof	25.00	Sold Out
☐ **SCHOOL DAYS,** rel. 1980. ed. 500, s/n, 12″ x 16″, pub GPL	25.00	—
ed. 1,500, s/o	20.00	—
ed. 35 Artist proof	35.00	—
☐ **SEW SEW,** rel. 1980. ed. 500, s/n, 12″ x 16″, pub GPL	17.00	Sold Out
ed. 1,500, s/o	15.00	Sold Out
ed. 35 Artist proof	25.00	Sold Out
☐ **SUGAR PLUM,** rel. 1980. ed. 500, s/n, 12″ x 16″, pub GPL	20.00	—
ed. 1,500, s/o	17.00	—
ed. 35 Artist proof	25.00	—
☐ **SUMMERTIME,** rel. 1980. ed. 500, s/n, 12″ x 16″, pub GPL	20.00	—
ed. 1,500, s/o	17.00	—
ed. 35 Artist proof	200.00	—
☐ **TOYLAND,** rel. 1982. ed. 500, s/n, pub GPL	20.00	—
ed. 1,000, s/o	25.00	—
ed. 100 Artist proof	30.00	—
☐ **HOMEMAKER,** rel. 1983. ed. 500, s/n, pub GPL	20.00	—
ed. Open, s/o	25.00	—
ed. 100 Artist proof	30.00	—
REGULAR SERIES		
☐ **OLD CITY HALL,** rel. 1971. ed. 150, s/m, 12″ x 16″, pub GPL	12.50	225.00
ed. 100, s/o	10.00	190.00
☐ **TOBACCO LAND,** rel. 1971. ed. 200, s/n, 16″ x 20″, pub GPL	12.50	200.00
ed. 300, s/o	10.00	190.00
☐ **OLD FIRE HALL,** rel. 1972. ed. 501, s/n, 12″ x 16″, pub GPL	12.00	75.00
RAILROAD SERIES		
☐ **SENTIMENTAL JOURNEY,** rel. 1973. ed. 200, s/n, 12″ x 16″, pub GPL	12.00	110.00
ed. 800, s/o	10.00	100.00
ed. 25 Artist proof	25.00	—
☐ **POWDERMAN,** rel. 1977. ed. 900, s/n, 17½″ x 23″, pub GPL	25.00	75.00
☐ **NUMBER PLEASE,** rel. 1984. ed. 500, s/n, litho, 12″ x 16″, pub GPL	25.00	—
ed. 2,000, s/o, litho, pub GPL	20.00	—
ed. 100, Artist proof, pub GPL	30.00	—
OTHER SERIES		
☐ **VIETNAM,** rel. 1985. ed. 500, s/n, litho, 16″ x 20″, pub GPL	35.00	—
ed. 250, s/o, 16″ x 20″, pub GPL	30.00	—
ed. 100, Artist proof, 16″ x 20″, pub GPL	40.00	—

LONE SURVIVOR *by Paul Grant*

PAUL GRANT

THEMES: Portraits, illustrations, wildlife art

MEDIUM: Watercolor

MEMBERSHIPS: Signature member of the Midwest Society since 1981

GALLERY/DISTRIBUTOR: Mill Pond Press, Inc.

COMMENTS: Grant has illustrated several books, including stories for the Reader's Digest Condensed Books

	ISSUE PRICE	CURRENT PRICE
☐ LONE SURVIVOR, rel. 1984. ed. 950, 19″ x 24″, pub MPPI	85.00	—
☐ MENACING MOON, rel. 1984. ed. 950, 19″ x 24″, pub MPPI	85.00	—

DON GRAY

THEMES: Pioneer

AWARDS: One Man Show at Eastern Oregon State College, 1981, presented with Distinguished Alumnus in the Arts award

GALLERY/DISTRIBUTOR: Wild Wings, Inc.

COMMENTS: Don Gray recently teamed up with writer Rick Steber and photographer Jerry Gildenmeister to produce *Rendezvous,* a book combining their respective talents to tell stories from Oregon's past. Their latest book, *Traces,* is a tribute to the last surviving pioneers who traveled the Oregon Trail

	ISSUE PRICE	CURRENT PRICE
☐ **SEASON OF THE FLY,** rel. 1981. ed. 750, s/n, litho, 26″ x 17¼″, pub WWI	95.00	—
☐ **THE JIGGER BOSS,** rel. 1982. ed. 750, s/n, litho, 17¾″ x 20″, pub WWI	95.00	—

JOHN GREEN

THEMES: Wildlife art

GALLERY/DISTRIBUTOR: Voyageur Art

PASSING THROUGH *by John Green*

	ISSUE PRICE	CURRENT PRICE
☐ **LAST PASS,** rel. 1981. ed. 550, 15″ x 21½″, litho, pub VA	50.00	—
☐ **PASSING THROUGH,** rel. 1981. ed. 580, 10½″ x 14″, litho, pub VA	35.00	—

QUINTEN GREGORY

THEMES: Northwest landscapes and wildlife art

MEDIUM: Oil and watercolor

STYLE: Gregory has his own unique style of lithography, which involves hand drawing on special vinyl plates

GALLERY/DISTRIBUTOR: Wilderness Studio, Inc.

	ISSUE PRICE	CURRENT PRICE
☐ ASPEN GROVE, rel. 1980. ed. 45, s/n, 14″ x 20″, pub WSI	70.00	90.00
☐ BUCKSKINS, rel. 1980. ed. 45, s/n, 14″ x 20″, pub WSI	70.00	—
☐ DOE AND FAWN, rel. 1980. ed. 100, s/n, 7″ x 9″, pub WSI	30.00	40.00
☐ DUCK HUNTER, rel. 1980. ed. 95, s/n, 7″ x 9″, pub WSI	30.00	—
☐ HEADIN HOME, rel. 1980. ed. 95, s/n, 7″ x 9″, pub WSI	30.00	—
☐ PRONGHORN, rel. 1980. ed. 95, s/n, 7″ x 9″, pub WSI	30.00	—
☐ FAWN, rel. 1980. ed. 95, s/n, 7″ x 9″, pub WSI	30.00	60.00
☐ STANLEY LAKE, rel. 1980. ed. 95, s/n, 20″ x 28″, pub WSI	150.00	350.00
☐ THE MILL, rel. 1980. ed. 45, s/n, 14″ x 20″, pub WSI	70.00	200.00
☐ WOOD DUCKS, rel. 1980. ed. 100, s/n, 7″ x 9″, pub WSI	30.00	—
☐ MT. HOOD, rel. 1981. ed. 125, s/n, 20″ x 28″, pub WSI	150.00	—
☐ OWYHEE CANYON, rel. 1981. ed. 95, s/n, 20″ x 28″, pub WSI	150.00	200.00
☐ SAWTOOTH MOUNTAIN FALL, rel. 1981. ed. 95, s/n, 20″ x 28″, pub WSI	150.00	250.00
☐ SAWTOOTH MOUNTAIN SHEEP CAMP, rel. 1981. ed. 95, s/n, 20″ x 28″, pub WSI	150.00	300.00
☐ SNAKE RIVER MALLARDS, rel. 1981. ed. 95, s/n, 20″ x 28″, pub WSI	150.00	200.00
☐ TETON WINTER MORNING, rel. 1981. ed. 95, s/n, 20″ x 28″, pub WSI	150.00	325.00
☐ SUN VALLEY, IDAHO, rel. 1982. ed. 140, s/n, 20″ x 28″, pub WSI	150.00	—
☐ WEST SIDE OF THE TETONS, rel. 1982. ed. 140, s/n, 20″ x 28″, pub WSI	150.00	—
☐ WINTER AT THE RANCH, rel. 1982. ed. 140, s/n, 20″ x 28″, pub WSI	150.00	—
☐ MT. RAINIER, rel. 1983. ed. 140, s/n, 20″ x 28″, pub WSI	150.00	—
☐ TROUT PLATE, rel. 1983. ed. 140, s/n, 20″ x 28″, pub WSI	175.00	—
☐ TETON SHEEP CAMP, rel. 1983. ed. 150, s/n, 20″ x 28″, pub WSI	195.00	—

GERRIT GREVE

THEMES: Varied

STYLE: His images fall somewhere between the representational and the abstract

GALLERY/DISTRIBUTOR: Eleanor Ettinger, Inc.

	ISSUE PRICE	CURRENT PRICE
☐ LA BOHEME, rel. 1981. ed. 350, 22″ x 28½″, litho, arches, pub EEI	275.00	300.00
ed. 50, japon	300.00	325.00
☐ ELEKTRA, rel. 1981. ed. 350, 22″ x 28½″, litho, arches, pub EEI	275.00	300.00
ed. 50, japon	300.00	325.00
☐ THOUGHTS, rel. 1981. ed. 350, 22″ x 28″, litho, arches, pub EEI	275.00	—
ed. 50, japon	300.00	—
☐ CAT & TOAD, rel. 1981. ed. 350, 33″ x 22″, litho, arches, pub EEI	275.00	—
☐ OLD INDIAN, rel. 1981. ed. 350, 22½″ x 28½″, litho, arches, pub EEI	275.00	—
ed. 50, japon	300.00	—

	ISSUE PRICE	CURRENT PRICE
☐ **INDIGO BUNTING,** rel. 1981. ed. 350, 22½" x 28½", litho, arches, pub EEI	275.00	—
ed. 50, japon	300.00	—
☐ **DESERT DREAM,** rel. 1981. ed. 350, 22½" x 28½", litho, arches, pub EEI	275.00	—
ed. 50, japon	300.00	—

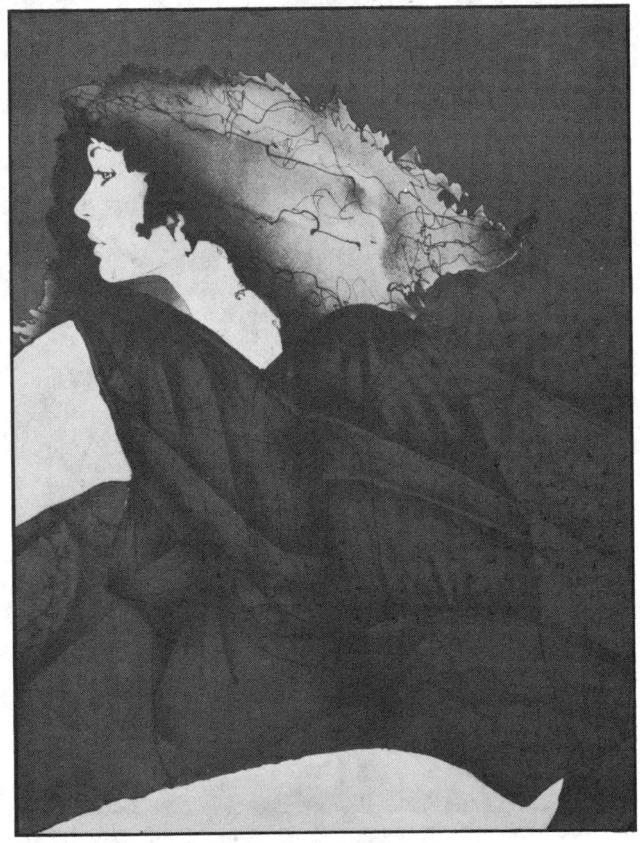

ELEKTRA *by Gerrit Greve*

DOUGLAS GRIER

THEMES: Varied

GALLERY/DISTRIBUTOR: Sea Island Art Gallery

	ISSUE PRICE	CURRENT PRICE
☐ **LEO,** rel. 1978. ed. 500, s/n, 14" x 20", pub RLB	25.00	—
☐ **PATH TO THE BEACH,** rel. 1978. ed. 500, s/n, 14" x 20", pub RLB	25.00	75.00
☐ **ROLLING DUNE,** rel. 1978. ed. 500, s/n, 14" x 20", pub RLB	25.00	—

	ISSUE PRICE	CURRENT PRICE
☐ **TIMELESS,** rel. 1978. ed. 500, s/n, 14″ x 20″, pub RLB	25.00	—
☐ **OAK ISLAND PLANTATION,** rel. 1979. ed. 500, s/n, 14″ x 20″, pub RLB	25.00	—
☐ **STILL IN SERVICE,** rel. 1979. ed. 1,400, s/n, 22½″ x 14¾″, pub RLB	25.00	—
Commissioned by the South Carolina District Civitan Organization.		
☐ **A MORNING'S TREASURES,** rel. 1980. ed. 1,000, s/n, 15″ x 30″, pub RLB	35.00	—
☐ **A NEW DAY,** rel. 1980. ed. 1,000, s/n, 15″ x 30″, pub SIAG	25.00	75.00
☐ **EBB TIDE,** rel. 1981. ed. 450, s/n, 11⅞″ x 21⅝″, pub SIAG	35.00	—
☐ **A QUIET MOMENT,** rel. 1981. ed. 450, s/n, 14¾″ x 22″, pub SIAG	35.00	—
☐ **LEFT ALONE,** rel. 1981. ed. 1,000, s/n, 17¼″ x 26½″, pub SIAG	25.00	—
Commissioned by the South Carolina District Civitan Organization.		

I'VE GROWN ACCUSTOMED TO YOUR PLACE *by Burt Groedel*

BURT GROEDEL

THEMES: Varied

MEDIUM: Varied

STYLE: Figurative graphics

EDUCATION: Art Students League, Manhattan's High School of Music and Art, Pratt Institute

GALLERY/DISTRIBUTOR: Eleanor Ettinger, Inc.

	ISSUE PRICE	CURRENT PRICE
☐ HER SERENE HIGHNESS, rel. 1980. ed. 300, 22″ x 28″, litho, arches, pub EEI	225.00	—
☐ EDIFICE COMPLEX, rel. 1980. ed. 300, 22″ x 28″, litho, arches, pub EEI	225.00	—
☐ LADY GO-DIVA, rel. 1980. ed. 300, 22″ x 28″, litho, arches, pub EEI	200.00	250.00
☐ LADY WORTHINGTON'S BIRD, rel. 1980. ed. 300, 22″ x 28″, litho, arches, pub EEI .	200.00	275.00
☐ TAKE ME TO YOUR LEDA, rel. 1980. ed. 300, 22″ x 28″, litho, arches, pub EEI	200.00	250.00
☐ I'VE GROWN ACCUSTOMED TO YOUR PLACE, rel. 1980. ed. 300, 22″ x 28″, litho, arches, pub EEI	200.00	350.00
☐ STILL LIFE FANTASY, rel. 1984. ed. 300, s/n, 22″ x 28″, pub EEI	225.00	—
☐ SEA FANTASY, rel. 1984. ed. 300, s/n, 22″ x 24″, pub EEI	225.00	—

OWEN J. GROMME

THEMES: Wildlife art

BOOKS: *Birds of Wisconsin*, published in 1963

AWARDS: Federal Duck Stamp Competition (1945), Master Wildlife Artist Award (1976), Ducks Unlimited Artist of the Year (1978); Honorary Doctorate from Marian College in Wisconsin

GALLERY/DISTRIBUTOR: Wild Wings, Inc.

COMMENTS: The artist has been acknowledged as one of the greatest living bird painters, equal, in fact, to Audubon, Wilson, and Fuertes

	ISSUE PRICE	CURRENT PRICE
☐ WINTERING QUAIL, rel. 1970. ed. 550, s/n, 17″ x 22½″, pub WWI	40.00	1,400.00
☐ BRITTANY ON POINT - WOODCOCK, rel. 1971. ed. 450, s/n, 17″ x 25″, pub WWI ..	50.00	900.00
☐ BACK TO COVER - PHEASANT, rel. 1971. ed. 450, s/n, 18″ x 24″, pub WWI	50.00	575.00
☐ LATE SEASON - CANVASBACKS, rel. 1972. ed. 450, s/n, 18″ x 24″, pub WWI	50.00	450.00
☐ SUNLIT GLADE - RUFFED GROUSE, rel. 1972. ed. 450, s/n, 18″ x 22½″, pub WWI..	50.00	1,200.00
☐ WINTERING GROSBEAKS, rel. 1973. ed. 600, s/n, 16″ x 22½″, pub WWI	45.00	700.00
☐ BLUE JAY, rel. 1973. ed. 800, s/o, 13¾″ x 10¾″, pub WWI	35.00	350.00
☐ STARTLED GROUSE - GOLDEN RETRIEVER, rel. 1973. ed. 480, s/n, 18″ x 22″, pub WWI	55.00	525.00
☐ OVER THE TRIANGLE - PINTAILS, rel. 1973. ed. 480, s/n, 18″ x 25″, pub WWI	55.00	120.00
☐ ISLAND LAKE - LOON, rel. 1973. ed. 580, s/n, 16½″ x 24¾″, pub WWI	55.00	1,200.00
☐ EXPECTATION, rel. 1973. ed. 580, s/n, 18″ x 22½″, pub WWI	55.00	1,200.00
☐ ENGLISH SETTER, rel. 1974. ed. 580, s/n, 22″ x 17¾″, pub WWI	55.00	575.00
☐ SACRED CRANES OVER HOKKAIDO, rel. 1974. ed. 600, s/n, 16″ x 26¼″, pub WWI	55.00	125.00
☐ TAMARACK LAKE - CANADA GEESE, rel. 1974. ed. 580, s/n, 16″ x 24″, pub WWI .	60.00	300.00
☐ PILEATED WOODPECKER, rel. 1974. ed. 580, s/n, 20″ x 15″, pub WWI	50.00	100.00
☐ CALIFORNIA QUAIL, rel. 1974. ed. 580, s/n, 17½″ x 23½″, pub WWI	60.00	125.00
☐ HEMLOCK HIDEAWAY - RUFFED GROUSE, rel. 1974. ed. 580, s/n, 16″ x 24″, pub WWI	60.00	750.00
☐ WHISTLING SWANS, rel. 1974. ed. 580, s/n, 17½″ x 23½″, pub WWI	60.00	1,000.00
☐ EDGE TO FIELD - POINTER, rel. 1974. ed. 580, s/n, 18″ x 24″, pub WWI	60.00	75.00
☐ DROPPING IN - MOURNING DOVES, rel. 1974. ed. 580, s/n, 16″ x 24″, pub WWI ...	60.00	125.00
☐ RASCAL'S REVENGE - GREAT HORNED OWL, rel. 1975. ed. 580, s/n, 17¾″ x 23¾″, pub WWI	60.00	300.00
☐ WINTER AFTERNOON - PHEASANT, ed. 580, s/n, 16″ x 24″, pub WWI	60.00	700.00
☐ SCURRING GREEN WINGS, rel. 1975. ed. 580, s/n, 16″ x 24″, pub WWI	60.00	170.00
☐ AMONG THE SHOCKS - PRAIRIE CHICKEN, rel. 1975. ed. 580, s/n, 16″ x 24″, pub WWI	60.00	400.00

	ISSUE PRICE	CURRENT PRICE
☐ MORNING FROST - RUFFED GROUSE, rel. 1975. ed. 580, s/n, 16¾" x 22½", pub WWI	60.00	600.00
☐ MID-DAY RETREAT - BOBWHITE, rel. 1975. ed. 580, s/n, 16¾" x 22½", pub WWI .	70.00	800.00
☐ OUR NATIONAL BIRD - BALD EAGLE, rel. 1976. ed. 580, s/n, 17¾" x 21", pub WWI	70.00	175.00
☐ PRAIRIE SHARP - TAILED GROUSE, rel. 1976. ed. 580, s/n, 16½" x 25", pub WWI	70.00	85.00
☐ EARLY AUTUMN - RUFFED GROUSE, rel. 1976. ed. 580, s/n, 16¾" x 22½", pub WWI	70.00	850.00
☐ EVENING STILLNESS - BARRED OWL, rel. 1976. ed. 580, s/n, 22" x 17⅝", pub WWI	60.00	325.00
☐ RAIL FENCE COVEY - BOBWHITES, rel. 1976. ed. 580, s/n, 16¾" x 22½", pub WWI	70.00	500.00
☐ KILLDEER, rel. 1976. ed. 800, s/o, 9" x 12", pub WWI	37.50	175.00
☐ BY THE ROADSIDE - RUFFED GROUSE, rel. 1976. ed. 580, s/n, 16¾" x 22½", pub WWI	70.00	425.00
☐ HOSTILE SKY - CANVASBACKS, rel. 1976. ed. 580, s/n, 17¼" x 25", pub WWI	70.00	200.00
☐ CARDINALS, rel. 1976. ed. 800, s/o, 14" x 10", pub WWI	40.00	400.00
☐ GROSBEAKS, rel. 1976. ed. 600, s/n, 22" x 17⅝", pub WWI	60.00	175.00
☐ CEDAR SHELTER - BOBWHITES, rel. 1976. ed. 580, s/n, 16¾" x 22½", pub WWI .	75.00	300.00
☐ EASING IN - CANADA GEESE, rel. 1976. ed. 580, s/n, 16½" x 25", pub WWI	75.00	250.00
☐ LABRADOR RETRIEVER, rel. 1977. ed. 580, s/n, 16½" x 25", pub WWI	75.00	375.00
☐ WINTER MORNING - RUFFED GROUSE, rel. 1977. ed. 580, s/n, 15" x 26", pub WWI	75.00	600.00
☐ SCOLDING BLUE JAY, rel. 1977. ed. 800, s/n, 13½" x 10", pub WWI	40.00	225.00
☐ CORNER COVEY - BOBWHITE, rel. 1977. ed. 580, s/n, 17½" x 25", pub WWI	75.00	200.00
☐ CEDAR CREEK - MALLARDS, rel. 1977. ed. 580, s/n, 17½" x 22", pub WWI	75.00	275.00
☐ WINTER WOODS - WHITETAIL DEER, rel. 1977. ed. 580, s/n, 17¾" x 23½", pub WWI	75.00	400.00
☐ DEPARTURE FROM LAKE KATHERINE, rel. 1978. ed. 850, s/n, 17¾" x 24¼", pub WWI	100.00	375.00
☐ EDGE OF THE THICKET - WOODCOCK, rel. 1978. ed. 850, s/n, 17¾" x 13¼", pub WWI	60.00	75.00
☐ FLUSHED FROM COVER - RINGNECKS, rel. 1978. ed. 850, s/n, 17¾" x 22¾", pub WWI	85.00	200.00
☐ GERMAN SHORT-HAIRED POINTER, rel. 1978. ed. 850, s/n, 16½" x 25", pub WWI	85.00	—
☐ HIGH COUNTRY - MULE DEER, rel. 1978. ed. 850, s/n, 17¾" x 23½", pub WWI ...	85.00	—
☐ SECLUDED POND - WOOD DUCKS, rel. 1978. ed. 850, /sn, 17¾" x 22½", pub WWI	85.00	200.00
☐ HUMMINGBIRD, rel. 1978. ed. 850, s/o, 10" x 13⅞", pub WWI	40.00	400.00
☐ GOLDFINCH, rel. 1978. ed. unlimited, 10" x 21½", pub WWI	40.00	—
☐ DUKE - AMERICAN WATER SPANIEL, rel. 1978. ed. 850, s/n, 17¾" x 22", pub WWI	75.00	85.00
☐ STAND OFF - FOX & GOOSE, rel. 1978. ed. 850, s/n, 17¾" x 22", pub WWI	85.00	—
☐ STARTLED TRIO - WHITETAIL DEER, rel. 1978. ed. 850, s/n, 16½" x 25", pub WWI	85.00	500.00
☐ WINTER SHADOWS - RUFFED GROUSE, rel. 1978. ed. 850, s/n, 17¾" x 22¾", pub WWI	85.00	200.00
☐ WINTERTIME - CARDINAL, rel. 1978. ed. 4,000, s/o, 13½" x 11¾", pub WWI	40.00	150.00
☐ WISCONSIN STATE DUCK STAMP DESIGN - 1978, ed. not available (see Duck stamp listings), pub WWI	100.00	325.00
☐ A TOUCH OF WHITE - PHEASANTS, rel. 1978. ed. 850, s/n, size not available, pub WWI	75.00	170.00
☐ AFRICAN ELEPHANTS, rel. 1978. ed. 850, s/n, 17½" x 25", pub WWI	75.00	85.00
☐ CHARGING RHINO - SEREGETI, rel. 1978. ed. 850, s/n, size not available, pub WWI	75.00	85.00
☐ CONFRONTATION - GAZELLE AND EAGLE, rel. 1978. ed. 850, s/n, size not available, pub WWI	75.00	85.00
☐ DOUBLE FLUSH - RUFFED GROUSE, rel. 1978. ed. 850, s/n, size not available, pub WWI	75.00	85.00
☐ EARLY SNOWFALL - WHITETAIL DEER, rel. 1978. ed. 850, s/n, size not available, pub WWI	75.00	500.00
☐ GOSHAWK AND RUFFED GROUSE, rel. 1978. ed. 850, s/n, size not available, pub WWI	75.00	85.00

	ISSUE PRICE	CURRENT PRICE
☐ HANGING LOOSE - LEOPARD, rel. 1978. ed. 850, s/n, size not available, pub WWI .	75.00	85.00
☐ MATES - SERENGETI LIONS, rel. 1978. ed. 850, s/n, size not available, pub WWI ..	75.00	85.00
☐ STORMY DAY -SERENGETI BUFFALO, rel. 1978. ed. 850, s/n, size not available, pub WWI	75.00	85.00
☐ SPRING BREAK UP - WHISTLING SWANS, rel. 1979. ed. 850, s/n, 25″ x 16½″, pub WWI.	85.00	100.00
☐ RETURN TO LAKE DE NEVEU, rel. 1979. ed. 850, s/n, 25″ x 16½″, pub WWI	100.00	—
☐ GOSHAWK AND YOUNG, rel. 1979. ed. 850, s/n, 22″ x 17¾″, pub WWI	100.00	—
☐ EYES OF THE NIGHT - GREAT HORNED OWL, rel. 1979. ed. 850, s/n, 21⅜″ x 17¾″, pub WWI	100.00	—
☐ MORNING HAZE - WOOD DUCKS, rel. 1979. ed. 850, s/n, 16½″ x 25″, pub WWI . . .	100.00	—
☐ AUTUMN SPECTACLE - WOOD DUCKS, rel. 1979. ed. 850, s/n, 25″ x 16½″, pub WWI.	100.00	—
☐ ROBIN, rel. 1979. ed. 850, s/n, 13½″ x 10⅛″, pub WWI	50.00	130.00
☐ SHARPTAILS ON THE RISE, rel. 1979. ed. 850, s/n, 23½″ x 17¾″, pub WWI	100.00	—
☐ MALLARDS AT SUNSET, rel. 1979. ed. 850, s/n, 25″ x 16½″, pub WWI	100.00	—
☐ SOUTHERN PINES - WILD TURKEYS, rel. 1980. ed. 850, s/n, 17½″ x 23″, pub WWI	100.00	—
☐ EARLY SPRING DRUMMER - RUFFED GROUSE, rel. 1980. ed. 850, s/n, 22″ x 17⅝″, pub WWI	125.00	250.00
☐ A PAIR OF CANADAS, rel. 1980. ed. 850, s/n, 16″ x 20″, pub WWI	100.00	300.00
☐ BARN OWL, rel. 1980. ed. 850, s/n, 17⅝″ x 22″, pub WWI	100.00	—
☐ BLUE JAY AND CARDINAL, rel. 1980. ed. 850, s/n, size not available, pub WWI	100.00	—
☐ BLUE JAYS HARASSING SCREECH OWL, rel. 1980. ed. 850, s/n, 17⅝″ x 22″, pub WWI	100.00	—
☐ BUCKING THE STORM - CANVASBACKS, rel. 1980. ed. 850, s/n, 16½″ x 25″, pub WWI	100.00	—
☐ DAY'S END - MIXED BAG, rel. 1980. ed. 850, s/n, 22″ x 17¾″, pub WWI	100.00	—
☐ EVENING GROSBEAKS, rel. 1980. ed. 850, s/n, size not available, pub WWI	75.00	85.00
☐ EVICTING THE INTRUDER, rel. 1980. ed. 850, s/n, 17⅝″ x 23½″, pub WWI	100.00	—
☐ EXPLODING FROM COVER - RUFFED GROUSE, rel. 1980. ed. 850, s/n, size not available, pub WWI	100.00	200.00
☐ FROSTY MORNING - WHISTLING SWANS, rel. 1980. ed. 850, s/n, size not available, pub WWI	100.00	200.00
☐ HEN MALLARD BROOD, rel. 1980. ed. 850, s/n, 17¾″ x 23½″, pub WWI	100.00	—
☐ KINGFISHER, rel. 1980. ed. 850, s/n, 13½″ x 10¾″, pub WWI	50.00	—
☐ MALLARDS AND BLACK DUCKS, rel. 1980. ed. 850, s/n, 17½″ x 23½″, pub WWI .	100.00	—
☐ POLAR BEAR - HUDSON'S BAY, rel. 1980. ed. 850, s/n, 11⅛″ x 15⅝″, pub WWI . .	50.00	—
☐ SNOWY OWL, rel. 1980. ed. 850, s/n, 22″ x 17⅝″, pub WWI	100.00	500.00
☐ TRIO OF BOBWHITES, rel. 1980. ed. 850, s/n, 17½″ x 20½″, pub WWI	100.00	—
☐ YELLOWHEADED BLACKBIRD, rel. 1980. ed. 850, s/n, 14″ x 10⅞″, pub WWI	50.00	—
☐ AUTUMN LEAVES - RUFFED GROUSE, rel. 1981. ed. 950, s/n, 19¼″ x 27½″, pub WWI	225.00	325.00
☐ BLUE WING TEAL, rel. 1981. ed. 850, s/n, 17½″ x 22″, pub WWI	125.00	—
☐ CANVASBACKS, rel. 1981. ed. 850, s/n, 16½″ x 25″, pub WWI	125.00	—
☐ CARDINALS IN SNOW, rel. 1981. ed. 800, s/n, size not available, pub WWI	100.00	500.00
☐ CONNER'S DITCH - HORICON MARSH, rel. 1981. ed. 850, s/n, 17¾″ x 23½″, pub WWI.	125.00	—
☐ INDIAN SUMMER - RUFFED GROUSE, rel. 1981. ed. 950, s/n, 20½″ x 27¼″, pub WWI.	225.00	—
☐ PHEASANTS, rel. 1981. ed. 850, s/n, 17¾″ x 23¾″, pub WWI	125.00	250.00
☐ PURPLE MARTINS, rel. 1981. ed. 850, s/n, 13¾″ x 10¼″, pub WWI	50.00	—
☐ RED HEADED WOODPECKER, rel. 1981. ed. 850, s/n, 13½″ x 10½″, pub WWI	50.00	—
☐ RUFFED GROUSE IN WINTER, rel. 1981. ed. 950, s/n, 20½″ x 27¼″, pub WWI	200.00	1,000.00
☐ SKY PIRACY - EAGLE & OSPREY, rel. 1981. ed. 950, s/n, 27½″ x 20⅝″, pub WWI .	225.00	—
☐ CHANGING OF THE GUARD - COMMON LOON, rel. 1982. ed. 950, s/n, 18″ x 27″, pub WWI.	225.00	—
☐ EGRETS BELOW THE BRIDGE, rel. 1982. ed. 980, s/n, size not available, pub WWI	175.00	—
☐ HUNTING IN THE WEST - CANADA GEESE, rel. 1982. ed. 950, s/n, 17½″ x 23½″, pub WWI.	100.00	—
☐ INDIGO BUNTING, rel. 1982. ed. 850, s/n, 11½″ x 9⅝″, pub WWI	40.00	200.00
☐ JUMPING BLACKS AND MALLARDS, rel. 1982. ed. 950, s/n, 16½″ x 25″, pub WWI	150.00	—

	ISSUE PRICE	CURRENT PRICE
☐ LATE SUMMER - MEADOWLARK, rel. 1982. ed. 950, s/n, 15¾" x 11½", pub WWI .	50.00	—
☐ CEDAR WAXWINGS IN SUMMER, rel. 1982. ed. 850, s/n, litho, 20" x 16", pub WWI .	85.00	—
☐ RED SQUIRREL AND BLUE JAY, rel. 1982. ed. 850, s/n, 16" x 20", pub WWI	85.00	—
☐ RUFFED GROUSE - HOLLYBERRIES, rel. 1982. ed. 850, s/n, size not available, pub WWI..	350.00	500.00
☐ SPRING'S EARLY ARRIVALS, rel. 1982. ed. 950, s/n, 15½" x 19½", pub WWI	85.00	—
☐ WHISTLING SWANS - BEYOND THE TEMPEST, rel. 1982. ed. 950, s/n, 16½" x 21¾", pub WWI	100.00	—
☐ ON THE ALERT - RED FOX, rel. 1983. ed. 850, s/n, 13¼" x 17½", pub WWI	75.00	—
☐ WHITETAILS IN SUMMER, rel. 1983. ed. 900, s/n, 16½" x 25", pub WWI	125.00	—
☐ EARLY SPRING GOBBLERS, rel. 1984. ed. 850, s/n, 16½" x 25", pub WWI	100.00	—
☐ CHICKADEES, rel. 1984. ed. 850, s/n, litho, 13½" x 10½", pub WWI	60.00	200.00
☐ GETTING EVEN - GREAT HORNED OWL AND CROWS, rel. 1984. ed. 850, s/n, 23" x 18", pub WWI..	100.00	—
☐ GREAT BLUE HERON, rel. 1984. ed. 850, s/n, litho, 24" x 18", pub WWI	125.00	—
☐ HUMMINGBIRD AND TRUMPET FLOWER, rel. 1984. ed. 850, s/n, 11½" x 9½", pub WWI	50.00	100.00
☐ MOVING TO COVER - BOBWHITES, rel. 1984. ed. limited, s/n, 17½" x 22", pub WWI	125.00	—
☐ PRAIRIE CHICKENS IN WINTER, rel. 1984. ed. 850, s/n, 16½" x 25", pub WWI	100.00	—
☐ PURPLE FINCHES, rel. 1984. ed. 850, s/n, 15½" x 11½", pub WWI	50.00	100.00
☐ SUNSET - CANADA GEESE, rel. 1984. ed. 850, s/n, 17½" x 22", pub WWI	125.00	—
☐ WINTERTIME FAVORITE - CHICKADEE, rel. 1984. ed. 850, s/n, 13½" x 10½", pub WWI	60.00	150.00
☐ BALTIMORE ORIOLES AT NEST, rel. 1985. ed. 850, s/n, litho, 14" x 18", pub WWI ..	75.00	—
☐ BLUEBIRD FAMILY, rel. 1985. ed. 850, s/n, litho, 14" x 11", pub WWI	50.00	—
☐ RAINBOW TROUT - THE ONE THAT GOT AWAY, rel. 1985. ed. 850, s/n, litho, 16" X 20", pub WWI	85.00	—
☐ RIVER VALLEY GOBBLER, rel. 1985. ed. 850, s/n, litho, 17½" X 22", pub WWI	100.00	—
☐ SANDHILL CRANES & YOUNG, rel. 1985. ed. 850, s/n, litho, 15½" X 25", pub WWI	100.00	—
☐ UPLAND PLOVER - SANDPIPER, rel. 1985. ed. 850, s/n, litho, 20" X 16", pub WWI .	85.00	—
☐ WINTERTIME - SNOWY OWL, rel. 1985. ed. 850, s/n, litho, 24" X 18", pub WWI	125.00	—
☐ YELLOW BILLED CUCKOO, rel. 1985. ed. 850, s/n, litho, 20" X 16", pub WWI	85.00	—

EARL GUSTAVESON

THEMES: Wildlife art

MEDIUM: Acrylic

EDUCATION: University of Wisconsin

MEMBERSHIPS: Ducks Unlimited, National Wildlife Association

GALLERY/DISTRIBUTOR: Northwoods Craftsman

	ISSUE PRICE	CURRENT PRICE
☐ MALLARDS, rel. 1979. ed. 600, s/n, 26" x 22", pub NC	60.00	—
☐ WOOD DUCKS, rel. 1979. ed. 600, s/n, 22" x 28", pub NC	60.00	—
☐ A FINE PAIR, rel. 1979. ed. 600, s/n, 16" x 20", pub NC	35.00	—
☐ NO HUNTING, rel. 1979. ed. 600, s/n, 16" x 20", pub NC	35.00	—

RON GUTHRIE

THEMES: Varied

BACKGROUND: Guthrie is head designer for Roper Corporation

GALLERY/DISTRIBUTOR: Connoisseur's Gallery of Art, Ltd.

	ISSUE PRICE	CURRENT PRICE
☐ HARD DOWN, WIND BEFORE RAIN, ed. 300, s/n, 17″ x 24″, pub CGAL	200.00	220.00
ed. 12, Artist accented/signed	260.00	290.00
ed. 38, s/o, Artist proofs	200.00	220.00
ed. 600 general print	55.00	60.00
☐ THE HIGHLANDS, UPPER PENINSULA, ed. 950, s/n, 24½″ x 16½″, pub CGAL	90.00	100.00
ed. 12, Artist accented/signed	260.00	290.00
☐ MICHIGAN STONE, ed. 950, s/n, 15″ x 24″, pub CGAL	90.00	100.00
ed. 12, Artist accented/signed	260.00	290.00
☐ REEF THE MAIN, DOUSE NUMBER ONE, ed. 950, s/n, 23″ x 18″, pub CGAL	90.00	100.00
ed. 12, Artist accented/signed	260.00	290.00
☐ PRAIRIE IRON, ed. 950, s/n, 16″ x 24″, pub CGAL	90.00	100.00
ed. 12, Artist accented/signed	260.00	290.00
☐ GIRARD STATION, ed. 950, s/n, 22″ x 17″, pub CGAL	90.00	100.00
ed. 12, Artist accented/signed	260.00	290.00
☐ PASSAGES, ed. 950, s/n, 24½″ x 17½″, pub CGAL	90.00	100.00
ed. 12, Artist accented/signed	260.00	290.00
☐ FIELD HANDS, ed. 950, s/n, 17″ x 24½″, pub CGAL	90.00	100.00
ed. 12, Artist accented/signed	260.00	290.00
☐ SEASON'S OUT, ed. 950, s/n, 23″ x 18″, pub CGAL	90.00	100.00
ed. 12, Artist accented/signed	260.00	290.00
☐ RESURRECTION 1951, ed. 950, s/n, 16½″ x 25½″, pub CGAL	90.00	100.00
ed. 12, Artist accented/signed	260.00	290.00
☐ BURNING OFF, ed. 950, s/n, 23″ x 17″, pub CGAL	90.00	100.00
ed. 12, Artist accented/signed	260.00	290.00
☐ PRAIRIE STATION, ed. 950, s/n, 16″ x 24½″, pub CGAL	90.00	100.00
ed. 12, Artist accented/signed	260.00	290.00
☐ NORTH MANITOU ISLAND, SOUTH POINT, ed. 950, s/n, 24″ x 18″, pub CGAL	90.00	100.00
ed. 12, Artist accented/signed	260.00	290.00
☐ DUNE WAGON, ed. 950, s/n, 24″ x 18″, pub CGAL	90.00	100.00
ed. 12, Artist accented/signed	260.00	290.00

MICKEY HACKETT

THEMES: Nature prints and poster art

MEDIUM: Watercolor

AWARDS: The artist has won numerous awards for landscapes, abstracts, etc.

MEMBERSHIPS: American Society of Artists (A.S.A.), Kentucky Watercolor Society, etc.

GALLERY/DISTRIBUTOR: Mickey Hackett A.S.A.

	ISSUE PRICE	CURRENT PRICE
☐ **BLUE FROST,** rel. 1982. ed. 1,500, limited edition, s/n, 18″ x 24″, pub MHASA	20.00	—
☐ **OLD FISHING SHACK,** rel. 1982. ed. 1,500, limited edition, s/n, 18″ x 24″, pub MHASA	20.00	—
☐ **CASTERS' COVE,** rel. 1983. ed. 1,500, limited edition, s/n, 18″ x 24″, pub MHASA ..	20.00	—
☐ **DAY'S END,** rel. 1983. 1,500, limited edition, s/n, 18″ x 24″, pub MHASA	20.00	—
☐ **FOREST GREENS,** rel. 1983. ed. 1,500, limited edition, s/n, 18″ x 24″, pub MHASA .	20.00	—
☐ **OLD SYCAMORE,** rel. 1983. ed. 1,500, limited edition, s/n, 18″ x 24″, pub MHASA ..	20.00	—
☐ **THE WHITE HOUSE,** rel. 1983. 1,500, limited edition, s/n, 18″ x 24″, pub MHASA ...	20.00	—
☐ **AUTUMN GOLD,** rel. 1984. ed. 1,500, limited edition, s/n, 18″ x 24″, pub MHASA	20.00	—
☐ **NOW THAT'S A CALICO CAT,** rel. 1984. ed. poster, limited edition, s/n, 28″ x 18″, pub MHASA	30.00	—

JAN HAGARA

THEMES: Wild-eyed, storybook children

MEDIUM: Watercolor

STYLE: Hagara's children are created totally from real children put into old-style surroundings

GALLERY/DISTRIBUTOR: B & J Art Designs

ABBY by Jan Hagara

	ISSUE PRICE	CURRENT PRICE
☐ **HATTIE & THE JUMEAU DOLL,** rel. 1977. ed. 2,000, s/o, 11″ x 14″, pub BJAD	8.00	25.00
Of this edition 250 s/n	25.00	50.00
☐ **JASON & THE RABBITT,** rel. 1977. ed. 2,000, s/o, 11″ x 14″, pub BJAD	8.00	25.00
Of this edition 250 s/n	25.00	50.00
☐ **LAURIE AND THE POUTY DOLL,** rel. 1977. ed. 2,000, s/o, 11″ x 14″, pub BJAD	8.00	25.00
Of this edition 250 s/n	25.00	50.00
☐ **MARC & THE TOYBOX,** rel. 1977. ed. 2,000, s/o, 11″ x 14″, pub BJAD	8.00	25.00
Of this edition 250 s/n	25.00	50.00
☐ **FLOWERS IN THE CAN,** rel. 1977. ed. 2,000, s/o, 16″ x 20″, pub BJAD	12.00	35.00
Of this edition 250 s/n	30.00	—
☐ **SPRING AND LANCE,** rel. 1977. ed. 2,000, s/o, 16″ x 20″, pub BJAD	12.00	50.00
Of this edition 250 s/n	30.00	55.00
☐ **JODY AND THE TOY HORSE,** ed. 2,000, s/n, 16″ x 20″, pub BJAD	45.00	—
☐ **JENNY AND THE BYELO DOLL,** ed. 2,000 s/o, 16″ x 20″, pub BJAD	45.00	120.00
☐ **OLIVIA,** rel. 1978. ed. 600, s/n, 18″ x 22″, pub BJAD	55.00	750.00
☐ **LISA,** rel. 1978. ed. 1,200, s/n, 7″ x 9″, pub BJAD	20.00	35.00
☐ **JUMEAU DOLL,** rel. 1978. ed. 1,200, s/n, 7″ x 9″, pub CGAL	20.00	—
Above two prints sold as a companion pair.		
☐ **LISA AND THE JUMEAU DOLL,** rel. 1978. ed. 900, s/o, 8″ x 8″, pub CGAL	20.00	—
☐ **DAISIES FROM MARY BETH,** rel. 1978. ed. 900, s/o, 8″ x 8″, pub BJAD	20.00	100.00
☐ **JIMMY,** rel. 1979. ed. 750, s/n, 16″ x 20″, pub BJAD	45.00	200.00
☐ **BETSY AND HER DREAMBABY,** rel. 1979. ed. 750, s/n, 16″ x 20″, pub BJAD	45.00	400.00
☐ **ADRIANNE AND THE BYELO DOLL,** rel. 1979. ed. 450, s/n, 16″ x 20″, pub BJAD ..	65.00	700.00
☐ **LYDIA AND THE SHIRLEY TEMPLE DOLL,** ed. 650, s/n, 16″ x 20″, pub BJAD	65.00	85.00
☐ **MELANIE AND THE SCARLET O'HARA DOLL,** rel. 1980. ed. 900, s/n, 16″ x 20″, pub BJAD ..	85.00	Sold Out
☐ **LITTLE SHARICE,** ed. 850, s/n, 16″ x 20″, pub BJAD	85.00	—
☐ **STORYTIME,** ed. 450, s/n, 23″ x 28″, pub BJAD	125.00	250.00
☐ **DAISIES FROM JIMMY,** rel. 1979. ed. 900, s/o, 8″ x 8″, pub BJAD	20.00	—
☐ **DAISIES FROM MEG,** rel. 1980. ed. 900, s/o, 8″ x 8″, pub BJAD	20.00	35.00
☐ **DAISIES FROM MOMMY,** rel. 1981. ed. 900, s/o, 8″ x 8″, pub BJAD	20.00	—
☐ **CARA AND THE DREAMBABY,** rel. 1979. ed. 900, s/n, 12″ x 12″, pub BJAD	30.00	40.00
☐ **NATALIE,** rel. 1980. ed. 900, s/n, 12″ x 12″, pub BJAD	30.00	—
☐ **SHARICE,** rel. 1981. ed. 1,000, s/o, 8″ x 10″, pub BJAD	18.00	30.00
☐ **PARRY,** rel. 1981. ed. 1,000, s/o, 8″ x 10″, pub BJAD	18.00	30.00
☐ **WENDY,** rel. 1981. ed. 1,000, s/o, 8″ x 10″, pub BJAD	18.00	60.00
☐ **ADELL,** rel. 1982. ed. 2,000, s/o, size N/A, pub BJAD	15.00	—
☐ **ALLEGRA,** rel. 1982. ed. 1,000, s/o, size N/A, pub BJAD	25.00	—
☐ **CAROL,** rel. 1982. ed. 2,000, s/o, size N/A, pub BJAD	25.00	—
☐ **TODD,** rel. 1982. ed. 2,000, s/o, size N/A, pub BJAD	25.00	—
☐ **CRISTINA,** rel. 1982. ed. 2,000, s/o, size N/A, pub BJAD	25.00	—
☐ **IN LINE,** rel. 1982. ed. 1,000, s/n, size N/A, pub BJAD	65.00	300.00
☐ **JESSICA,** rel. 1982. ed. 2,000, s/o, size N/A, pub BJAD	15.00	—
☐ **MANDY,** rel. 1982. ed. 500, s/o, size N/A, pub BJAD	60.00	200.00
☐ **HEARTY SAILOR,** rel. 1982. ed. 500, s/n, size N/A, pub BJAD	30.00	—
☐ **SHANNON'S VALENTINE,** rel. 1982. ed. 500, s/n, size N/A, pub BJAD	30.00	—
☐ **MOTHER AND CHILD,** rel. 1982. ed. 2,000, s/o, size N/A, pub BJAD	45.00	—
☐ **ABBY,** rel. 1983. ed. 2,000, s/n, 16″ x 20″, litho, pub BJAD	47.50	—
☐ **BECKY,** rel. 1983. ed. 2,000, size N/A, pub BJAD	27.50	—
☐ **CHRIS,** rel. 1983. ed. 2,000, s/o, size N/A, pub BJAD	27.50	—
☐ **DAISIES IN BALL JAR,** rel. 1983. ed. 500, s/o, size N/A, pub BJAD	20.00	—
☐ **JENNIFER,** rel. 1983. ed. 700, s/n, 18″ x 24″, litho, pub BJAD	60.00	—
☐ **LAUREL,** rel. 1984. ed. 1,200, s/o, size N/a, pub BJAD	60.00	—
☐ **PAIGE,** rel. 1983. ed. 2,000, s/n, 16″ x 20″, litho, pub BJAD	47.50	—
☐ **AMY,** rel. 1985. ed. 2,000, s/n, litho, 8″ x 10″, pub BJAD	20.00	—
☐ **ASHLEY,** rel. 1985. ed. 2,000, s/n, litho, 8″ x 10″, pub BJAD	20.00	—
☐ **BILLY AND BRENNA,** rel. 1985. ed. 2,000, s/n, litho, 16″ x 20″, pub BJAD	47.50	—
☐ **CYNTHIA,** rel. 1985. ed. 600, s/n, litho, 13¼″ x 11¼″, pub BJAD	50.00	—
☐ **GOLDIE,** rel. 1985. ed. 1,200, s/n, litho, 14″ x 20″, pub BJAD	47.50	—
☐ **LARRY,** rel. 1985. ed. 2,000, s/n, litho, 11″ x 14″, pub BJAD	30.00	—
☐ **LESLEY,** rel. 1985. ed. 2,000, s/n, litho, 11″ x 14″, pub BJAD	30.00	—
☐ **NOEL,** rel. 1985. ed. 2,000, s/n, litho, 11″ x 14″, pub BJAD	30.00	—
☐ **SARA MAE,** rel. 1985. ed. 2,000, s/n, litho, 8″ x 10″, pub BJAD	20.00	—

MIXED DOUBLE - PHEASANT AND BOBWHITE *by David Hagerbaumer*

DAVID HAGERBAUMER

THEMES: Wildlife art

EDUCATION: San Diego State University

GALLERY/DISTRIBUTOR: Hager

	ISSUE PRICE	CURRENT PRICE
☐ OCTOBER EVENING-PINTAILS, rel. 1963. ed. 400, s/n, 18″ x 27″	47.50	1200.00
☐ PLACID MARSH-BLACK DUCKS, rel. 1964. ed. 400, s/n, 17½″ x 27″	47.50	1200.00
☐ WOODLOT COVEY-BOBWHITE QUAIL, rel. 1965. ed. 400, s/n, 17½″ x 27″	47.50	1200.00
☐ FOGGY MORNING-MALLARDS, rel. 1965. ed. 400, s/n, 17½″ x 27″	47.50	1200.00
☐ PORTFOLIO OF FOUR PRINTS, rel. 1967. (Canvasbacks, Pintails, Canada Geese, Mallards). ed. 400, s/n, 12″ x 15½″	80.00	1000.00
☐ GREEN WING FLURRY - GREEN WING TEAL, rel. 1969. ed. 600, s/n, 19½″ x 27″ .	47.50	450.00
☐ AUTUMN RUFFS-RUFFED GROUSE, rel. 1969. ed. 600, s/n, 19½″ x 27″	47.50	500.00
☐ THE NARROWS-WOOD DUCK, rel. 1971. ed. 450, s/n, 17″ x 23″	47.50	400.00
☐ DOUBLE RISE-WOODCOCK, rel. 1971. ed. 450, s/n, 17″ x 23″	47.50	400.00
☐ SHANTY, THE, rel. 1972. (PENCIL, w/text), ed. 450, s/n, 12½″ x 16½″	25.00	75.00
☐ THRU THE PINE-MOURNING DOVES, rel. 1972. ed. 450, s/n, 17″ x 23″	50.00	400.00
☐ HILL COUNTRY GOBBLERS-TURKEY, rel. 1972. ed. 450, s/n, 12½″ x 16½″	50.00	400.00

	ISSUE PRICE	CURRENT PRICE
☐ GATHERING STORM-PINTAILS, rel. 1972. ed. 450, s/n, 13″ x 17″	50.00	350.00
☐ OVER THE RIDGE-PHEASANTS, rel. 1973. ed. 450, s/n, 17″ x 23″	60.00	450.00
☐ MINUS TIDE-CANVASBACK, rel. 1973. ed. 450, s/n, 17″ x 23″	60.00	250.00
☐ TIMBER POTHOLE-MALLARDS & WIDGEON, rel. 1973. Historical Series #1 w/illustrated text. ed. 350, s/n, 17″ x 23″	80.00	400.00
☐ HOG RANCH POINT-BLACK BRANT, rel. 1974. ed. 350, s/n, 19″ x 31″, (rel. w/text) .	80.00	125.00
☐ SINK BOX GUNNING-CANVASBACKS, rel. 1974. Historical Series #2 w/illustrated text. ed. 350, s/n, 17″ x 23″	80.00	125.00
☐ TWIN ISLAND MARCH-BLUE WING TEAL, rel. 1974. ed. 450, s/n, 17″ x 23″	60.00	100.00
☐ THE OLD DUCK CAMP-MALLARD, rel. 1974. ed. 450, s/n, 17″ x 23″	60.00	250.00
☐ GREAT BASIN MARSH-BUFFLEHEADS AND TULE DECOYS, rel. 1975. Historical Series #3 w/illustrated text. ed. 350, s/n, 17″ x 23″	80.00	200.00
☐ HICKORY GROVE-BOBWHITE QUAIL, rel. 1975. ed. 450, s/n, 17″ x 23″	60.00	250.00
☐ AFTERNOON SQUALL-CANADA GEESE, rel. 1975. ed. 450, s/n, 17″ x 23″	60.00	200.00
☐ TAMARACK POND-BLACK DUCKS, rel. 1976. ed. 450, s/n, 17″ x 23″	65.00	150.00
☐ FIRST SNOW-RUFFED GROUSE, rel. 1976. ed. 450, s/n, 17″ x 23″	65.00	350.00
☐ SOUTH BOTTOMS-PINTAILS, rel. 1976. Historical Series #4 w/illustrated text. ed. 350, s/n, 17″ x 23″	80.00	200.00
☐ MIXED DOUBLE-WOODCOCK & GROUSE, rel. 1977. ed. 450, s/n, 17″ x 23″	65.00	450.00
☐ MARSHY LAKE-WOOD DUCKS, rel. 1977. ed. 450, s/n, 17″ x 23″	65.00	175.00
☐ ARMISTICE DAY STORM-MALLARDS, rel. 1977. Historical Series #5 w/illustrated text. ed. 350, s/n, 17″ x 23″	85.00	250.00
☐ MIDDLE FORK-WIGEON, TEAL & SPRIG, rel. 1978. ed. 450, s/n, 17″ x 23″	75.00	125.00
☐ BEAR CREEK BOTTOMS-PHEASANTS, rel. 1978. ed. 450, s/n, 17″ x 23″	75.00	175.00
☐ BEECH GROVE-PASSENGER PIGEON, rel. 1978. Historical Series #6 w/illustrated text. ed. 350, s/n, 17″ x 23″	95.00	—
☐ SPRING HILL - BOBWHITE QUAIL, rel. 1979. ed. 380, s/n, size not available	125.00	200.00
☐ APPROACHING SPRING - WILD TURKEY, rel. 1979. ed. 450, s/n, 17″ x 23″	75.00	150.00
☐ INDIAN SUMMER - GREEN-WINGED TEAL, rel. 1979. ed. 450, s/n, 17″ x 23″	75.00	100.00
☐ LAST LEAVES OF AUTUMN - RUFFED GROUSE, rel. 1979. ed. 850, s/n, 17″ x 23″ .	95.00	—
☐ THE BOTTOMS - PINTAILS, rel. 1980. ed. 450, s/n, 17″ x 23″	95.00	—
☐ EVENING FLIGHT - MOURNING DOVES, rel. 1980. ed. 450, s/n, 17″ x 23″	95.00	—
☐ MIXED DOUBLE - MALLARD & BLACK DUCK, rel. 1980. ed. 450, s/n, 17″ x 23″ ...	95.00	—
☐ FRANK'S PLACE - GREEN-WINGED TEAL, rel. 1980. ed. 2,000, s/n, size not available, produced by Frank Williams for Ducks Unlimited	—	125.00
☐ AUTUMN SPLENDOR - MALLARD, rel. 1980. ed. 450, s/n, 17″ x 23″	100.00	—
☐ MIXED DOUBLE - PHEASANT & BOBWHITE, rel. 1981. ed. 450, s/n, 17″ x 23″	125.00	—
☐ OVAL - MALLARD, rel. 1981. ed. 450, s/n, 6½″ x 9″	35.00	120.00
☐ OVAL - PHEASANT, rel. 1981. ed. 450, s/n, 6½″ x 9″	35.00	120.00
☐ RUFFED GROUSE SOCIETY #3, rel. 1981. ed. 1,780, s/n, size not available, produced by Ruffed Grouse Society	125.00	130.00
☐ WINTER NOBILITY - WILD TURKEY, rel. 1981. ed. 950, s/n, size not available, produced by the National Wild Turkey Federation	125.00	—
ed. 100, s/n	1000.00	—
☐ AUTUMN GRANDEUR - PHEASANTS, rel. 1981. ed. 380 (50 were a/p) s/n, size not available	250.00	—
☐ MIXED DOUBLE - WOODCOCK & GROUSE, rel. 1981. ed. 90, s/n, size not available, etching...	125.00	—
☐ PINTAILS, rel. 1981. ed. 90, s/n, size not available, etching	125.00	—
☐ WOODCOCK, rel. 1981. ed. 90, s/n, size not available, etching	125.00	—
☐ FENCE ROW COVEY - BOBWHITES, rel. 1981. ed. 90, s/n, size not available, etching	150.00	—
☐ RUFFED GROUSE, rel. 1981. ed. 90, s/n, size not available, etching	125.00	—
☐ PHEASANTS, rel. 1981. ed. 90, s/n, size not available, etching	125.00	—
☐ VALLEY QUAIL, rel. 1981. ed. 90, s/n, size not available, etching	125.00	—
☐ JUMPING MALLARDS, rel. 1981. ed. 90, s/n, size not available, etching	125.00	—
☐ OVAL - GREEN-WINGED TEAL, rel. 1982. ed. 450, s/n, size not available, etching ..	40.00	—
☐ OVAL - RUFFED GROUSE, rel. 1982. ed. 450, s/n, 6½″ x 9″	40.00	120.00
☐ HARD ROCK FARM - BOBWHITE, rel. 1982. ed. 850, s/n, 17″ x 23″	95.00	—
☐ INDIAN SUMMER - RUFFED GROUSE, rel. 1982. ed. 450, s/n, 17″ x 23″	150.00	—
☐ OVAL - LOON, rel. 1982. ed. 450, s/n, 6½″ x 9″	40.00	—
☐ WOODCOCK, BOBWHITE & GROUSE TRIPTYCH, rel. 1982. ed. 450, s/n, no further information available	60.00	—

	ISSUE PRICE	CURRENT PRICE
☐ THE TRAMMEL HOLE, rel. 1982. ed. 850, s/n, 11″ x 15″, pub WWI	75.00	—
☐ WOOD DUCK OVAL, rel. 1982. ed. 450, s/n, 7″ x 9″, pub HAGER	40.00	—
☐ BOBWHITE QUAIL OVAL, rel. 1983. ed. 450, s/n, 7″ x 9″, pub HAGER	40.00	—
☐ IN EARLY - MALLARDS AND TEAL, rel. 1983. ed. 850, s/n, 16½″ x 23½″, pub WWI	125.00	—
☐ MALLARD, BLACK DUCK PINTAIL TRIPTYCH, rel. 1983. ed. 450, s/n, size not available, pub HAGER	60.00	—
☐ PINTAIL OVAL, rel. 1983. ed. 450, s/n, 7″ x 9″, pub HAGER	40.00	—
☐ MALLARD II OVAL, rel. 1984. ed. 450,, s/n, 7″ x 9″, pub HAGER	40.00	.
☐ PHEASANT II OVAL, rel. 1984. ed. 450,, s/n, 7″ x 9″, pub HAGER	40.00	—
☐ SWAN OVAL, rel. 1984. ed. 450, s/n, 7″ x 9″, pub HAGER	40.00	—

EARLY MORNING HAVEN by Betty Gene Haile

BETTY GENE HAILE

THEMES: Landscape art

MEDIUM: Watercolor

EDUCATION: University of Texas; McHay Art Institute; Trinity University

MEMBERSHIPS: Southwestern Watercolor Society, Texas Watercolor Society, Kentucky Watercolor Society, etc.

GALLERY/DISTRIBUTOR: Arts Limited Inc.

	ISSUE PRICE	CURRENT PRICE
☐ **EARLY MORNING HAVEN,** rel. 1980. ed. 1,500, s/n, 28″ x 22″, pub ALI	60.00	—

THE RAVEN *by Ben Hampton*

BEN HAMPTON

THEMES: Varied

BACKGROUND: Official artist for the United States Pavilion at the 1982 World's Fair

GALLERY/DISTRIBUTOR: Hampton House Studios, Inc.

	ISSUE PRICE	CURRENT PRICE
☐ **MONUMENT TO AN ERA,** rel. 1972. ed. 1,000, s/n, 25¾″ x 19″, pub HHSI	22.00	1,450.00
☐ **WINTER REFUGE,** rel. 1972. ed. 1,500, s/n, 13″ x 26″, pub HHSI	20.00	450.00
☐ **THE GOOD EARTH,** rel. 1973. ed. 987, s/n, 24″ x 15½″, pub HHSI	22.00	525.00
☐ **CLAUDE'S CREEK,** rel. 1973. ed. 992, s/n, 13″ x 26″, pub HHSI	22.00	300.00
☐ **PONDERING QUAIL,** rel. 1973. ed. 1,000, s/n, 17½″ x 17½″, pub HHSI	30.00	550.00
☐ **THE STUMP,** rel. 1973. ed. 1,000, s/n, 14¼″ x 20″, pub HHSI	25.00	375.00
☐ **SAND MOUNTAIN CABIN,** rel. 1973. ed. 1,000, s/n, 16½″ x 20″, pub HHSI	25.00	550.00
☐ **DAD,** rel. 1973. ed. 1,500, s/n, 16½″ x 20″, pub HHSI	20.00	175.00
☐ **APPALACHIAN SPRING,** rel. 1974. ed. 1,000, s/n, 18″ x 24″, pub HHSI	30.00	725.00
ed. 2,500, s/o	20.00	500.00

	ISSUE PRICE	CURRENT PRICE
☐ GENTLE MIST, rel. 1974. ed. 1,000, s/n, 14½″ x 21¾″, pub HHSI	30.00	175.00
ed. 2,500, s/o	20.00	135.00
☐ AUTUMN WATCH, rel. 1974. ed. 1,000, s/n, 14¼″ x 21¾″, pub HHSI	30.00	175.00
ed. 2,500 s/o	20.00	125.00
☐ SUNDAY MORNING, rel. 1974. ed. 1,000, s/n, 10¾″ x 22″, pub HHSI	30.00	300.00
ed. 2,500, s/o	20.00	250.00
☐ BRIDGEPORT FERRY, rel. 1974. ed. 1,000, s/n, 14½″ x 21¾″, pub HHSI	30.00	275.00
ed. 2,500, s/o	20.00	250.00
☐ CAROLINA HAZE, rel. 1975. ed. 1,500, s/n, 14¼″ x 25″, pub HHSI	30.00	400.00
ed. 2,500, s/o	20.00	325.00
☐ CRIB HOUSE & CREEK HOUSE, rel. 1976. ed. 1,500, s/n, 11¾″ x 18″, pub HHSI	45.00	200.00
ed. 2,500, s/o	30.00	175.00
☐ NANCY WARD, rel. 1976. ed. 5,000, s/o, 21½″ x 20″	25.00	700.00
☐ SORGHUM MILL, rel. 1976. ed. 1,500, s/n, 13″ x 26″, pub HHSI	35.00	200.00
ed. 3,500, s/o	25.00	150.00
☐ REFLECTING SYCAMORES, rel. 1977. ed. 1,500, s/n, 13″ x 26″, pub HHSI	35.00	200.00
ed. 3,500 s/o	25.00	150.00
☐ WINTER SOUTH, rel. 1977. SOLD AS A PAIR - North Carolina "Mile in the Sky", Tennessee "Era of the Past", ed. 1,500, s/n, 18″ x 11″, pub HHSI	60.00	200.00
ed. 6,500, s/o	45.00	150.00
☐ STANDING PROUD, rel. 1978. ed. 1,500, s/n, 21½″ x 20″, pub HHSI	35.00	225.00
ed. 6,500, s/o	25.00	175.00
☐ CASTLE OF CHILLON, rel. 1978. ed. 1,500, s/n, 13″ x 26″, pub HHSI	45.00	150.00
ed. 6,500, s/o	30.00	75.00
☐ SEA OF GALILEE, rel. 1978. ed. 1,500, s/n, 13″ x 26″, pub HHSI	45.00	150.00
ed. 6,500, s/o	30.00	75.00
☐ APPALACHIAN SPRING, rel. 1974. ed. 1,000, s/n, 18″ x 24″, pub HHSI	30.00	150.00
ed. 2,500, s/o	20.00	100.00
☐ FAREWELL SUMMERS, rel. 1979. ed. 1,500, s/n, 23″ x 25¾″, pub HHSI	55.00	225.00
ed. 5,000, s/o	40.00	175.00
☐ HIGH SPLENDOR, rel. 1979. ed. 1,500, s/n, 21½″ x 20″, pub HHSI	40.00	150.00
ed. 6,500, s/o	30.00	125.00
☐ NANCY WARD HERITAGE SERIES, rel. 1979. Set of three - CHOTA ARTIFACTS, POINT LOOKOUT, THE INN. ed. 8,000, i/o, pub HHSI	30.00	65.00
☐ RAMBLING ROSE, rel. 1980. ed. 1,500, s/n, 20″ x 26″, pub HHSI	55.00	250.00
ed. 3,500, s/o	40.00	175.00
Photo etching of RAMBLING ROSE		
ed. 500, s/n, 13″ x 15″, hand coloured by artist	200.00	—
☐ STEPPING STONES, rel. 1980. ed. 1,500, s/n, 20″ x 26″, pub HHSI	55.00	350.00
ed. 3,500, s/o	40.00	250.00
☐ SPRING PLACE, rel. 1980. ed. 1,500, s/n, 17¾″ x 24″, pub HHSI	55.00	125.00
ed. 3,500, s/o	40.00	65.00
☐ THE BLACKSMITH SHOP, rel. 1981. ed. 1,500, s/n, 16″ x 24″, pub HHSI	65.00	150.00
ed. 4,500, s/o	45.00	110.00
☐ FIVE KILLER HERITAGE SERIES, rel. 1981. Set of three - CATHERINE'S BASKET, BIG BEND, FORT MARR. ed. 8,000, i/o, pub HHSI	40.00	60.00
☐ HISKYTEEHEE (Five Killer), rel. 1981. ed. 1,500, s/n, 21½″ x 20″, pub HHSI	65.00	250.00
ed. 4,000, s/o	40.00	225.00
☐ SHALLOW FORD, rel. 1982. ed. 1,500, s/n, 16″ x 24″, pub HHSI	65.00	150.00
ed. 4,500, s/o	45.00	110.00
☐ SWINGING BRIDGE, rel. 1982. ed. 1,500, s/n, 20″ x 23″, pub HHSI	65.00	250.00
ed. 4,500, s/o	45.00	200.00
☐ THOUGHTS OF SPRING, rel. 1982. ed. 1,500, s/n, size not available, pub HHSI	65.00	100.00
ed. 4,500, s/o	40.00	50.00
☐ PLUM THICKET, rel. 1983. ed. 1,500, s/n, 18″ x 21¼″, pub HHSI	65.00	175.00
ed. 4,500, s/o	45.00	125.00
☐ THE RAVEN, Nancy Ward's Brother, rel. 1983. ed. 1,500, s/n, 20″ x 21½″, pub HHSI	65.00	160.00
ed. 4,500, s/o	45.00	110.00
ed. 250, a/p	100.00	—
☐ APPALACHIAN TRAIL, rel. 1984. ed. 1,500, s/n, size N/A, pub HHSI	75.00	110.00
ed. 4,500, s/o	50.00	—
ed. 250, a/p	110.00	150.00

	ISSUE PRICE	CURRENT PRICE
☐ BLUE RIDGE, rel. 1984. ed. 1,500, s/n, size N/a, pub HHSI	75.00	110.00
ed. 4,500, s/o	50.00	60.00
ed. 250 a/p	110.00	150.00
☐ MOODY CHICKAMAUGA, rel. 1984. ed. 1,500, s/n, 13" x 27⅓", pub HHSI	65.00	100.00
ed. 1,500, s/o	45.00	60.00
☐ SUNRISE SERVICE, rel. 1984. ed. 1,500, s/n, 16⅜" x 22", pub HHSI	75.00	150.00
ed. 4,500, s/o	50.00	100.00
ed. 250, Artist proof	110.00	200.00
☐ WISTERIA, rel. 1985. ed. 1,500, s/n, 16" x 21¼", pub HHSI	75.00	—
ed. 4,500, s/o	50.00	—
ed. 250 Artist proof	110.00	—

W. HAROLD HANCOCK

THEMES: Varied

GALLERY/DISTRIBUTOR: Hancock Gallery

	ISSUE PRICE	CURRENT PRICE
☐ FOUR SEASONS OF BROWN COUNTY, INDIANA, rel. 1964. ed. 350, s/n, 12½" x 18", pub HG	30.00	400.00
☐ FOUR WILDLIFE SERIES, rel. 1973, consisting of Raccoons, Pheasants, Deer, Wild Turkey. ed. 1,200, s/n, 11½" x 15", pub HG	30.00	160.00
☐ EMMETT WITH WALL STREET JOURNAL, rel. 1974. ed. 999, s/n, 18" x 24", pub HG	25.00	160.00
☐ CUMBERLAND FALLS KENTUCKY, rel. 1976. ed. 500, s/n, 20" x 26", pub HG	10.00	120.00
☐ WESTERN SERIES, rel. 1976, consisting of Lake Tahoe, Virginia City, Genoa, Carson River. ed. 1,200, s/n, 14" x 18", pub HG	30.00	160.00
☐ FOUR CLOWNS, rel. 1981, consisting of Red Skelton, Indiana Farmer, Emmett Kelly, Happy. ed. 1,000, s/n, 12" x 16", pub HG	50.00	120.00
☐ BALLOONS, rel. 1981. ed. 99, s/n, 22" x 28", serigraph, pub HG	85.00	190.00
☐ SAILS, rel. 1981. ed. 99, s/n, 22" x 28", serigraph, pub HG	85.00	190.00
☐ BIRD SERIES, rel. 1981, consisting of White Egret, Blue Heron, Pelicans, Sandpipers, ed. 1,000, s/n, 13½" x 21", pub HG	35.00	65.00
☐ 4 FAMOUS PARKE COUNTY COVERED BRIDGES, rel. 1981. ed. 1,000, s/n, 8" x 11", pub HG	20.00	60.00
☐ NEW FOUR SEASONS, rel. 1982. ed. 1,000, s/n, 12" x 16", pub HG	30.00	100.00
☐ WINTER SHADOWS, rel. 1983. ed. 750, s/n, 15" x 30", pub HG	85.00	145.00

ENOCH KELLY HANEY

THEMES: Indian Art, primarily Seminole Indian

AWARDS: Kelly has received several national awards

MEMBERSHIPS: He is one of the Masters of the Five Civilized Tribes

GALLERY/DISTRIBUTOR: American Indian Arts Collection

INDIGNITY OF THE FLAG OF TRUCE by *Enoch Kelly Haney*

	ISSUE PRICE	CURRENT PRICE
☐ SPIRIT OF OSCEOLA, ed. 1,500, s/n, size unknown, pub AIAC	40.00	175.00
☐ MEKUSUKEY BICENTENNIAL OWL, ed. 500, s/n, 25⅜″ x 32″, pub AIAC	200.00	1500.00
☐ BROKEN PROMISES, ed. 1,000, s/n, 12″ x 22″, pub AIAC	30.00	100.00
☐ APSAROKE WARRIOR, ed. 2,000, s/n, 18″ x 24″, pub AIAC	30.00	—
☐ MARK OF THE KNIFE, ed. 1,000, s/n, 22½″ x 38½″, pub AIAC	100.00	—
☐ INDIGNITY OF THE FLAG OF TRUCE, ed. 1,500, s/n, 19″ x 34″, pub AIAC	75.00	300.00
☐ MINIATURE SET (three prints). FLIGHT OF THE OWL, 5″ x 7″ SACRED FEATHERS, 5″ x 7″ AMERICAN INDIAN CHIEF, 5″ x 7″ ed. 2,000, s/n, pub AIAC	30.00	—
☐ RED-TAILED HAWK, ed. 500, s/n, size unknown, pub AIAC	150.00	500.00
☐ AMERICAN BALD EAGLE, ed. 500, s/n, size unknown, pub AIAC	200.00	650.00
☐ THE WOLF, GREAT GRANDPA, ed. 500, s/n, size unknown, pub AIAC	200.00	500.00
☐ SEMINOLE LIFESTYLE, ed. 2,000, s/n, 15½″ x 21½″, pub AIAC	30.00	—
☐ FREEDOM'S END, ed. 250, s/n, size unknown, pub AIAC	150.00	1200.00
☐ SIOUX RAINMAKER, ed. 1,500, s/n, size unknown, pub NWDHG	100.00	150.00
☐ WAR CHIEF, ed. 1,500, s/n, size unknown, pub NWDHG	40.00	90.00
☐ SYMBOLS OF INDIAN THEOLOGY, ed. 1,000, s/n, size unknown, pub AIAC	30.00	—
☐ OWL TRANSFORMATION, ed. 650, s/n, 18⅝″ x 23¼″, pub AIAC	100.00	—
☐ HAWK WARRIOR, ed. 1,000, s/n, 16″ x 20″, pub AIAC	40.00	—
☐ FLUTE PLAYER, ed. 750, s/n, 20″ x 25½″	100.00	250.00

DERK HANSEN

THEMES: Western and wildlife art

GALLERY/DISTRIBUTOR: Voyageur Art

	ISSUE PRICE	CURRENT PRICE
☐ JOURNEY ON THE WING, rel. 1978. ed. 550, s/n, 16″ x 23″, litho, pub VA	40.00	—
☐ THE DUKE, rel. 1979. ed. 550, s/n, 11″ x 14″, litho pub VA	25.00	—
☐ THE PRINCE, rel. 1979. ed. 550, s/n, 11″ x 14″, litho, pub VA	25.00	—
☐ WEARY TRAVELERS, rel. 1979. ed. 550, s/n, 16″ x 23″, litho, pub VA	40.00	—
☐ EARLY SNOW, rel. 1980. ed. 580, s/n, 15½″ x 24″, litho, pub VA	60.00	—
☐ LONG SHOT, rel. 1980. ed. 950, s/n, 18″ x 24″, litho, pub VA	50.00	—
☐ PAUSE FROM THE JOURNEY, rel. 1983. ed. 580, s/n, litho, pub VA	75.00	—

LAST OF THE FREE *by Derk Hansen*

H. HARGROVE

THEMES: Americana

BACKGROUND: In his first job after he migrated to the U.S., Hargrove worked as a wine chemist. There he decorated the winery room with paintings. Since visitors were impressed with the paintings he decided to become a professional artist

GALLERY/DISTRIBUTOR: International Gallery; Foxman's Oil Paintings, Ltd.

FIRST SNOW *by H. Hargrove*

CANADA GEESE *by Ray Harm*

	ISSUE PRICE	CURRENT PRICE
☐ **FIRST SNOW,** rel. 1982. ed. 770, s/n, pub AG or IG	150.00	750.00
ed. 20, Artist proof	—	—
☐ **TAKING IT EASY,** rel. 1982. ed. 770, s/n, pub AG or IG	170.00	350.00
ed. 20, Artist proof	—	—
☐ **WINDROWING,** rel. 1982. ed. 770, s/n, pub AG or IG	170.00	475.00
ed. 20, Artist proof	—	—
☐ **GENERAL STORE, U.S.A.,** rel. 1983. ed. 770, s/n, pub AG or IG	225.00	650.00
ed. 20, Artist proof	—	—
☐ **THE CIDER MAKER,** rel. 1983. ed. 770, s/n, pub AG or IG	200.00	475.00
ed. 20, Artist proof	—	—
☐ **CHRISTMAS,** rel. 1984. ed. 750, s/n, 20 a/p, s/n, serigraph, 20″ x 24″, pub FOP	275.00	475.00
☐ **COUNTRY CHURCH,** rel. 1985. ed. 750, s/n, 20 a/p, s/n, serigraph, 20″ x 24″, pub FOP	275.00	350.00
☐ **FARM AND FEED STORE,** rel. 1985. ed. 750, s/n, 20 a/p, s/n, serigraph, 20″ x 24″, pub FOP	275.00	350.00
☐ **GLORIOUS FOURTH,** rel. 1985. ed. 750, s/n, 20 a/p, s/n, serigraph, 20″ x 24″, pub FOP	275.00	450.00
☐ **GRANDMA'S KITCHEN,** rel. 1984. ed. 750, s/n, 20 a/p, s/n, serigraph, 20″ x 24″, pub FOP	250.00	600.00
☐ **McDONALD'S BARN,** rel. 1984. ed. 750, s/n, 20 a/p, s/n, serigraph, 20″ x 24″, pub FOP	250.00	375.00
☐ **THANKSGIVING,** rel. 1984. ed. 750, s/n, 20 a/p, s/n, serigraph, 20″ x 24″, pub FOP	275.00	425.00
☐ **VILLAGE SMITHY,** rel. 1983. ed. 750, s/n, 20 a/p, s/n, serigraph, 20″ x 24″, pub FOP	225.00	350.00

RAY HARM

THEMES: Wildlife art

BACKGROUND: Founder of Frame House Gallery, Inc.

EDUCATION: Cooper School of Art

AWARDS: Honorary doctorates from three colleges and numerous other accolades

GALLERY/DISTRIBUTOR: Frame House Gallery, Inc.

	ISSUE PRICE	CURRENT PRICE
☐ **AFRICAN SKETCHBOOK,** rel. 1973. ed. 10,000, s/o, 11″ x 15″, pub FHG	50.00	—
☐ **AMERICAN BISON,** rel. 1978. ed. 1,000, s/n, 24″ x 30″, pub FHG	60.00	Sold Out
ed. 1,200, s/o Exclusive - the U.S. Field Artillery Association is using a portion of the edition to raise funds for atmospheric control equipment for the building housing the Ft. Sill Museum's Conservation Laboratory.		
800 will bear the inscription "Monarch of the Plains" and the Field Artillery Museum's seal	75.00	Sold Out
400 will bear a First Day of Issue seal and the Field Artillery Museum seal	100.00	Sold Out
☐ **AMERICAN BUTTERFLIES,** rel. 1966. ed. 5,000, s/o, 22⅜″ x 17″, pub FHG	10.00	75.00
☐ **AMERICAN EAGLE,** rel. 1971. ed. 3,500, s/o, 24″ x 32″, pub FHG	60.00	200.00
ed. 500, s/n	75.00	300.00
ed. 1,000 (West Point Edition), signed and bearing a United States Military Academy shield. Sold exclusively to cadets and members of their families, military personnel and personnel closely affiliated with the Academy. Proceeds of sale donated to U.S.M.A. to further fine arts activities	—	325.00
☐ **AMERICAN GOLDFINCH,** rel. 1966. ed. 5,000, s/o, 16″ x 20″, pub FHG	10.00	50.00
☐ **AMERICAN KESTREL,** rel. 1982. ed. 1,000, s/n, 21″ x 23¾″, pub FHG	60.00	—
☐ **AMERICAN REDSTART,** rel. 1974. ed. 7,500, s/o, 12″ x 15″, pub FHG	20.00	40.00
☐ **BALD EAGLE,** rel. 1975. ed. 2,000, s/n, 20″ x 24″, pub FHG	50.00	—

	ISSUE PRICE	CURRENT PRICE
☐ BALD EAGLE (FAMILY), rel. 1963. ed. 1,000, s/o, 23″ x 29″, pub FHG	30.00	500.00
☐ BALD EAGLE (WINGS SPREAD), rel. 1968. ed. 500, s/n, 30½″ x 22½″, pub FHG ..	60.00	350.00
ed. 2,500, s/o	55.00	250.00
☐ BALD EAGLE, rel. 1983. ed. 1,000, s/n, 23½″ x 33½″, pub FHG	75.00	—
ed. 100, s/n	—	—
☐ BALTIMORE ORIOLE, rel. 1963. ed. 5,000, s/o, 16″ x 20″, pub FHG	10.00	100.00
☐ BALTIMORE ORIOLE, rel. 1982. ed. 1,000, s/n, 20″ x 16″, pub FHG	60.00	—
☐ BARN SWALLOW, rel. 1974. ed. 5,000, s/o, 16″ x 20″, pub FHG	20.00	50.00
☐ BARRED OWL, rel. 1980. ed. 1,000, s/n, 24″ x 20″, pub FHG	60.00	Sold Out
ed. 850, s/n, Exclusive for Oklahoma Christian College Children's Hospital Fund, Louisville, KY.		
☐ BELTED KINGFISHER, rel. 1966. ed. 5,000, s/o, 16″ x 20″, pub FHG	10.00	50.00
☐ BIGHORN SHEEP, rel. 1976. ed. 1,000, s/n, 22″ x 28″, pub FHG	50.00	Sold Out
ed. 3,000, s/o	40.00	Sold Out
ed. 500, s/o, exclusive for the Rocky Mountain Nature Association.		
☐ BLACK BEAR, rel. 1973. ed. 1,000, s/n, 21″ x 27″, pub FHG	85.00	150.00
ed. 500, s/o	70.00	130.00
ed. 500, s/o, donated to Pikeville College, Pikeville, Kentucky	—	Sold Out
☐ BLACK-BILLED MAGPIE, rel. 1976. ed. 5,000, s/o, 20″ x 16″, pub FHG	30.00	Sold Out
☐ BLACK-CAPPED CHICKADEE, rel. 1979. ed. 3,000, s/o, 20″ x 16″, pub FHG	40.00	—
☐ BLACK-THROATED WARBLER, rel. 1974. ed. 7,500, s/o, 15″ x 12″, pub FHG	20.00	40.00
☐ BLUEBIRD, rel. 1981. ed. 1,000, s/n, 24″ x 20″, pub FHG	60.00	100.00
ed. 300, s/n, Exclusive	60.00	Sold Out
☐ BLUEBIRD, rel. 1982. ed. 5,000, s/o, 15″ x 8″, pub FHG	25.00	—
☐ BLUE JAY, rel. 1982. ed. 5,000, s/o, 16″ x 20″, pub FHG	10.00	75.00
☐ BLUE JAY/AMERICAN ROBIN (Pair), rel. 1981. ed. 1,000, s/n, 17″ x 14″, pub FHG .	75.00	125.00
☐ BLUE-WINGED TEAL, rel. 1984. ed. 1,000, 24″ x 16″, pub FHG	90.00	—
☐ BOBCAT (KENTUCKY WILDCAT), rel. 1966. ed. 1,500, 22½″ x 27½″, pub FHG		
*900 prints of this edition were titled "Kentucky Wildcat" and furnished to the University of Kentucky Alumni Association for a fund-raising drive. Of this number - 400 were signed and numbered	*35.00	350.00
500 were signed only	*30.00	200.00
**600 prints of the edition were titled "Bobcat"		
100 were signed and numbered	**35.00	350.00
500 were signed only	**30.00	300.00
☐ BOBCAT (KITTENS), rel. 1981. ed. 1,000, s/n, 29½″ x 23½″, pub FHG	60.00	—
☐ BOBWHITE, rel. 1963. ed. 5,000, s/o, 16″ x 20″, pub FHG	20.00	300.00
☐ BOBWHITE COVEY CIRCLE, rel. 1982. ed. 1,000, s/n, 28″ x 23″, pub FHG	60.00	175.00
☐ BRIDLED TITMOUSE, rel. 1975. ed. 5,000, s/o, 15″ x 12″, pub FHG	20.00	30.00
☐ BROWN THRASHER, rel. 1964. ed. 5,000, s/o, 16″ x 20″, pub FHG	10.00	60.00
☐ CACTUS WREN, rel. 1979. ed. 750, s/n, 20″ x 16″, pub FHG	40.00	—
ed. 250, s/n, Exclusive for Arizona Nature Conservancy	—	Sold Out
☐ CALIFORNIA GROUND SQUIRREL, rel. 1969. ed. 5,000, s/o, 16″ x 20″, pub FHG ..	20.00	40.00
☐ CALIFORNIA QUAIL, rel. 1973. ed. 5,000, s/o, 16″ x 20″, pub FHG	20.00	125.00
☐ CAPE BUFFALO, rel. 1976. ed. 1,000, s/n, 19½″ x 29½″, pub FHG	75.00	Sold Out
ed. 2,500, s/o	60.00	—
☐ CANADA GOOSE, rel. 1968. ed. 3,000, 31″ x 24″, pub FHG	—	—
*2,500 unsigned and unnumbered	*50.00	125.00
**500 signed and numbered donated to National Audubon Society to raise money for Corkscrew Swamp Sanctuary	**100.00	250.00
☐ CANADA GOOSE, rel. 1983. ed. 1,000, s/n, 23½″ x 33½″, pub FHG	75.00	—
☐ CARDINAL, rel. 1979. ed. 5,000, s/o, 14″ x 11″, pub FHG	20.00	30.00
☐ CARDINAL (DOGWOOD), rel. 1963. ed. 5,000, s/o, 20″ x 16″, pub FHG	10.00	300.00
☐ CARDINAL (DOGWOOD), rel. 1983. ed. 1,000, s/n, 24″ x 20″, pub FHG	75.00	—
ed. 550, s/n	—	—
☐ CARDINAL (SUNFLOWER), rel. 1969. ed. 5,000, s/o, 16″ x 20″, pub FHG	20.00	100.00
☐ CARDINAL (WITH YOUNG), rel. 1975. ed. 5,000, s/o, 26″ x 22″, pub FHG	40.00	125.00
☐ CAROLINA WREN, rel. 1970. ed. 5,000, s/o, 16″ x 20″, pub FHG	20.00	50.00
☐ CEDAR WAXWING, rel. 1968. ed. 5,000, s/o, 16″ x 20″, pub FHG	20.00	50.00
☐ CHEETAH, rel. 1975. ed. 1,000, s/n, 22½″ x 30″, pub FHG	75.00	100.00
ed. 2,500, s/o	60.00	Sold Out

	ISSUE PRICE	CURRENT PRICE
☐ CHIPMUNK, rel. 1979. ed. 1,500, s/n, 18" x 28", pub FHG	45.00	70.00
☐ COTTONTAIL RABBIT, rel. 1979. ed. 2,000, s/o, 16" x 20", pub FHG	40.00	110.00
☐ COUGAR, rel. 1977. ed. 3,000, s/o, 20" x 16", pub FHG	40.00	90.00
☐ DOWNY WOODPECKER, rel. 1967. ed. 5,000, s/o, 16" x 20", pub FHG	20.00	50.00
☐ DOWNY WOODPECKER, rel. 1982. ed. 1,000, s/n, 24" x 20", pub FHG	65.00	—
☐ EAGLE AND OSPREY, rel. 1964. ed. 500, s/n, 43¼" x 30¼", pub FHG	75.00	2000.00
☐ EASTERN BLUEBIRD, rel. 1966. ed. 5,000, s/o, 16" x 20", pub FHG	10.00	100.00
☐ EASTERN BOBWHITE, rel. 1966. ed. 5,000, s/o, 16" x 20", pub FHG	10.00	200.00
☐ EASTERN BOBWHITE, rel. 1980. ed. 1,000, s/n, 24" x 20", pub FHG	50.00	80.00
☐ ELF OWL, rel. 1977. ed. 3,500, s/o, 15" x 12", pub FHG	20.00	35.00
☐ EVENING GROSBEAK, rel. 1973. ed. 5,000, s/o, 16" x 20", pub FHG	20.00	40.00
☐ FEEDER GROUP, rel. 1963. ed. 5,000, s/o, 16" x 20", pub FHG	10.00	60.00
☐ THE FLEDGLINGS, rel. 1983. ed. 1,000, s/n, 17" x 30", pub FHG	75.00	—
☐ FLICKER, rel. 1966. ed. 5,000, s/o, 16" x 20", pub FHG	10.00	60.00
☐ FOX SQUIRREL, rel. 1985. ed. 2,000, s/n, 28" x 20", pub FHG	40.00	—
☐ GAMBEL'S QUAIL, rel. 1979. ed. 3,000, s/o, 16" x 20", pub FHG	40.00	40.00
☐ GOLDEN EAGLE, rel. 1977. ed. 5,000, s/o, 16" x 20", pub FHG	60.00	120.00
ed. 2,000, signed only, The General Creighton W. Abrams Commemorative Golden Eagle, First Day Issue, The Patton Museum, Fort Knox, Kentucky.		
☐ GOLDFINCH, rel. 1978. ed. 3,000, s/n, 15" x 12", pub FHG	20.00	—
☐ GRAY FOX, rel. 1980. ed. 1,500, s/n, 26" x 22", pub FHG	50.00	Sold Out
☐ GRAY SQUIRREL, ed. 1,500, s/n, 27½" x 23", pub FHG	60.00	100.00
☐ GREAT HORNED OWL, rel. 1972. ed. 1,000, s/n, 21" x 27", pub FHG	75.00	135.00
ed. 3,000, s/o	60.00	115.00
*ed. 1,000 signed and bearing a distinctive seal, donated to Kentucky Bankers Assn. to raise funds for Trooper Island, Kentucky State Police summer camp project for underprivileged boys	*100.00	Sold Out
☐ GREAT HORNED OWL, rel. 1981. ed. 1,000, s/n, 24" x 20", pub FHG	60.00	—
☐ HOUSE WREN, rel. 1963. ed. 5,000, s/o, 16" x 20", pub FHG	10.00	50.00
☐ HUMMINGBIRDS AND CARDINAL FLOWERS, rel. 1968. ed. 7,500, 9" x 12", pub FHG Donated to Kentucky Chapter, The Nature Conservancy to raise funds for the preservation of Murphy's Pond, Kentucky's last Cypress Swamp (1968-69); and to the Alabama Conservancy for a 1971 membership campaign.		
☐ IMPALA, rel. 1973. ed. 5,000, s/o, 18" x 24", pub FHG	45.00	90.00
☐ INDIGO BUNTING, rel. 1966. ed. 5,000, s/o, 16" x 20", pub FHG	10.00	40.00
☐ KENTUCKY 1985 "FIRST OF STATE" DUCK STAMP PRINT, rel. 1985. ed. limited to orders placed by 8/31/85, 12" x 14", print and stamp, pub FHG	140.25	—
Print, stamp, and medallion	305.25	—
Print, stamp, medallion, pencil remarque	405.25	—
Print, stamp, medallion, color remarque	555.25	—
☐ KENTUCKY WARBLER, rel. 1972. ed. 5,000, s/o, 16" x 20", pub FHG	20.00	40.00
☐ KESTREL (SPARROW HAWK), rel. 1967. ed. 5,000, s/o, 16" x 20", pub FHG	20.00	40.00
☐ LATE SUMMER AND FALL WILD FLOWERS, rel. 1978. ed. 5,000, signed one print in each set 14½" x 7½", pub FHG	30.00	—
☐ LAZULI BUNTING, rel. 1972. ed. 7,500, s/o, 12" x15", pub FHG	15.00	35.00
☐ LITTLE BLUE HERON, rel. 1967. ed. 5,000, s/o, 16" x 20", pub FHG	10.00	40.00
☐ MAGPIE, rel. 1974. ed. 5,000, s/n, 16" x 20", pub FHG	20.00	—
☐ MALLARD DUCK, rel. 1971. ed. 5,000, s/o, 16" x 20", pub FHG	20.00	50.00
☐ MEADOWLARK, rel. 1969. ed. 5,000, s/o, 16" x 20", pub FHG	20.00	75.00
☐ MOCKINGBIRD, rel. 1963. ed. 5,000, s/o, 16" x 20", pub FHG	10.00	90.00
☐ MOCKINGBIRDS, rel. 1980. ed. 1,000, s/n, 24" x 20", pub FHG	60.00	120.00
☐ MOUNTAIN CHICKADEE, rel. 1975. ed. 5,000, s/o, 15" x 12", pub FHG	20.00	40.00
☐ MOUNTAIN LION, rel. 1972. ed. 1,000, s/n, 31" x 24½", pub FHG	75.00	100.00
ed. 4,000, s/o	60.00	90.00
☐ MOUNTAIN QUAIL, rel. 1975. ed. 5,000, s/o, 16" x 20", pub FHG	30.00	45.00
☐ MOURNING DOVE, rel. 1970. ed. 5,000, s/o, 16" x 20", pub FHG	20.00	50.00
☐ OVENBIRD, rel. 1972. ed. 7,500, s/o, 12" x 15", pub FHG	15.00	25.00
☐ PAINTED BUNTING, rel. 1963. ed. 5,000, s/o, 20" x 16", pub FHG	10.00	45.00
☐ PELICANS, rel. 1967, ed. 500, s/n, 30½" x 22½", pub FHG	60.00	130.00
ed. 4,500, s/o	50.00	110.00
☐ PEREGRINE FALCON, rel. 1980. ed. 5,000, s/o, 16½" x 14", pub FHG	25.00	—

	ISSUE PRICE	CURRENT PRICE
☐ PHAINOPEPLA, rel. 1974. ed. 5,000, s/o, 12″ x 15″, pub FHG	20.00	Sold Out
☐ PILEATED WOODPECKER, rel. 1966. ed. 5,000, s/o, 16″ x 20″, pub FHG	10.00	95.00
☐ PILEATED WOODPECKER, rel. 1984. ed. 1,000, s/n, 30″ x 17″, pub FHG	75.00	—
☐ PINTAIL, rel. 1978. ed. 3,000, s/o, 20″ x 16″, pub FHG	40.00	—
☐ PURPLE FINCH, rel. 1978. ed. 3,000, s/n, 15″ x 12″, pub FHG	20.00	—
☐ PURPLE MARTIN, rel. 1973. ed. 5,000, s/o, 16″ x 20″, pub FHG	20.00	40.00
☐ PYRRHLOXIA, rel. 1974. ed. 5,000, s/o, 12″ x 15″, pub FHG	20.00	Sold Out
☐ RACCOON (FAMILY), rel. 1968. ed. 500, s/n, 22″ x 28″, pub FHG	75.00	325.00
ed. 4,500, s/o...	60.00	250.00
☐ RACCOON, rel. 1976. ed. 5,000, s/o, 20″x 18″, pub FHG	35.00	100.00
☐ RACCOON, rel. 1982. ed. 1,500, s/n, 24″ x 20″, pub FHG	65.00	120.00
ed. 500, Exclusive - Louisville Zoological Gardens.		
☐ RACCOON FAMILY, rel. 1984. ed. 1,000, s/n, 20″ x 16″, pub FHG	75.00	—
☐ RED FOX, rel. 1973. ed. 1,000, s/n, 20″ x 24″, pub FHG	75.00	160.00
ed. 4,000, s/o..	60.00	125.00
☐ REDHEADED WOODPECKER, rel. 1979. ed. 2,000, s/o, 20″ x 16″, pub FHG	45.00	—
☐ RED-TAILED HAWK, rel. 1981. ed. 1,000, s/n, 28″ x 12″, pub FHG	60.00	—
ed. 100, s/n, Exclusive, St. Lukes Hospital, Fort Thomas Kentucky.		
☐ RED-WINGED BLACKBIRD, rel. 1967. ed. 5,000, s/o, 16″ x 20″, pub FHG	20.00	50.00
☐ RED-WINGED BLACKBIRD, rel. 1983. ed. 1,000, s/n, 26″ x 13″, pub FHG	75.00	—
☐ RETICULATED GIRAFFE, rel. 1973. ed. 1,000, s/n, 20″ x 28″, pub FHG	65.00	140.00
ed. 4,000, s/o..	50.00	110.00
☐ RING-NECKED PHEASANT, rel. 1965. ed. 500, s/n, 29¼″ x 21″, pub FHG	35.00	300.00
ed. 750, s/o..	30.00	250.00
☐ RING-NECKED PHEASANT, rel. 1979. ed. 1,500, s/n, 22″ x 30″, pub FHG	50.00	—
☐ ROADRUNNER, rel. 1969. ed. 5,000, s/o, 20″ x 16″, pub FHG	20.00	40.00
☐ ROBIN, rel. 1963. ed. 5,000, s/o, 16″ x 20″, pub FHG	10.00	125.00
☐ ROSE-BREASTED GROSBEAK, rel. 1971. ed. 5,000, s/o, 16″ x 20″, pub FHG	20.00	50.00
☐ RUFFED GROUSE, rel. 1972. ed. 5,000, s/o, 16″ x 20″, pub FHG	20.00	75.00
☐ RUFFED GROUSE, rel. 1983. ed. 1,000, s/n, 24″ x 20″, pub FHG	75.00	—
ed. 100, s/n	—	—
☐ RUFOUS-SIDED TOWHEE, rel. 1969. ed. 5,000, s/o, 16″ x 20″, pub FHG	20.00	60.00
☐ RUFOUS-SIDED TOWHEE, rel. 1984. ed. 1,000, s/n, 20″ x 16″, pub FHG	75.00	—
☐ SAW-WHET OWL, rel. 1977. ed. 3,500, s/o, 12″ x 15″, pub FHG	20.00	50.00
☐ SCALED QUAIL, rel. 1977. ed. 3,000, s/o, 16″ x 20″, pub FHG	40.00	—
☐ SCARLET TANAGER, rel. 1963. ed. 5,000, s/o, 16″ x 20″, pub FHG	10.00	90.00
☐ SCREECH OWL, rel. 1967. ed. 12,500, Free bonus print available only with membership in National Audubon Society during 1967-68 Kentucky membership campaign	—	35.00
☐ SCREECH OWLS, rel. 1975. ed. 5,000, s/o, 16″ x 20″, pub FHG	20.00	75.00
☐ SEA OTTER, rel. 1981. ed. 1,000, s/n, 14″ x 24″, pub FHG	60.00	120.00
ed. 300, s/n, Exclusive - Friends of the Sea Otter Society	—	Sold Out
☐ SPRING WARBLERS, rel. 1968. ed. 5,000, s/o, 16″ x 20″, pub FHG	35.00	75.00
Sold only as a pair		
☐ SPRING WILDFLOWERS, rel. 1964. ed. 5,000, s/o, 7″ x 16½″, pub FHG	10.00	75.00
Set of six, artist's signature on one print of set constitutes signature of entire set.		
☐ STRIPED SKUNK, rel. 1977. ed. 3,000, s/o, 16″ x 20″, pub FHG	40.00	—
☐ SUMMER FEEDER, rel. 1985. ed. 2,000, s/n, 28″ x 16″, pub FHG	40.00	—
☐ SUMMER TANAGER, rel. 1963. ed. 5,000, s/o, 16″ x 20″, pub FHG	10.00	50.00
☐ SUMMER WILDFLOWERS, rel. 1967. ed. 10,000, s/o, 7″ x 16½″, pub FHG	10.00	75.00
Set of six, artist's signature on one print of set constitutes signature of entire set.		
☐ THE FLEDGLINGS, rel. 1983. ed. 1,000, s/n, 17″ x 30″, lithograph, pub FHG	75.00	—
☐ TRUMPETER SWAN, rel. 1979. ed. 2,000, s/n, 22″ x 26″, pub FHG	45.00	—
☐ TUFTED TITMOUSE, rel. 1974. ed. 5,000, s/o, 16″ x 20″, pub FHG	20.00	30.00
☐ UPLAND BIRDS, rel. 1967. ed. 500, s/n, 30″ x 22¼″, pub FHG	60.00	100.00
4,500, s/o	50.00	85.00
☐ VERMILION FLYCATCHER, rel. 1972. ed. 7,500, s/o, 12″ x 15″, pub FHG	15.00	35.00
☐ WESTERN TANAGER, rel. 1977. ed. 3,000, s/o, 16″ x 20″, pub FHG	40.00	—
☐ WHITE-BREASTED NUTHATCH, rel. 1975. ed. 5,000, s/o, 19″ x 23½″, pub FHG ...	30.00	Sold Out
☐ WHITE-TAILED FAWNS, rel. 1980. ed. 1,000, s/n, 30″ x 23″, pub FHG	60.00	120.00
ed. 500, s/n, Exclusive - Bernheim Forest, Clermont Kentucky.		
☐ WHITE-THROATED SPARROW, rel. 1972. ed. 7,500, s/o, 12″ x 15″, pub FHG	15.00	35.00

	ISSUE PRICE	CURRENT PRICE
☐ **WHITE-TAILED DEER,** rel. 1980. ed. 500, s/n, 22″ x 28″, pub FHG	75.00	125.00
4,500, s/o	60.00	90.00
☐ **WILDCAT,** rel. 1979. ed. 5,000, s/o, 11″ x 14″, pub FHG	20.00	—
☐ **WILD TURKEY,** rel. 1970. ed. 500, s/n, 20″ x 25″, pub FHG	60.00	125.00
ed. 4,500, s/o	45.00	100.00
☐ **WINTER FEEDER,** rel. 1984. ed. 2,000, s/n, 28″ x 16″, pub FHG	40.00	—
☐ **WINTER FEEDER,** rel. 1985. ed. 2,000, s/n, 28″ x 16″, pub FHG	40.00	—
☐ **WOOD DUCK,** rel. 1966. ed. 500, s/n, 22½″ x 27½″, pub FHG	35.00	180.00
ed. 2,000, s/o	30.00	150.00
☐ **WOOD THRUSH,** rel. 1970. ed. 5,000, s/o, 16″ x 20″, pub FHG	20.00	50.00
☐ **YELLOW-BILLED CUCKOO,** rel. 1971. ed. 5,000, s/o, 16″ x 20″, pub FHG	20.00	65.00
☐ **YELLOW-BREASTED CHAT,** rel. 1973. ed. 7,500, s/o, 12″ x 15″, pub FHG	15.00	35.00
☐ **YELLOW-HEADED BLACKBIRD,** rel. 1973. ed. 5,000, s/o, 16″ x 20″, pub FHG	20.00	40.00
☐ **YELLOW-THROAT,** rel. 1973. ed. 7,500, s/o, 12″ x 15″, pub FHG	15.00	35.00

BRETT HARPER

THEMES: Fruits and flowers

MEDIUM: Silkscreen

STYLE: The artist draws and develops his prints from ink drawings

EDUCATION: Brown University

GALLERY/DISTRIBUTOR: Frame House Gallery, Inc.

	ISSUE PRICE	CURRENT PRICE
☐ **CONSIDER THE LILLIES,** rel. 1975. ed. 250, s/n, 12⅞″ x 20″, pub FHG	20.00	Sold Out
☐ **PETUNIA POWER,** rel. 1975. ed. 250, s/n, 13″ x 18½″, pub FHG	20.00	40.00
☐ **ZINNIA,** rel. 1975. ed. 250, s/n, 13″ x 19½″, pub FHG	20.00	40.00
☐ **BITTERSWEET,** rel. 1976. ed. 500, s/n, 15⅞″ x 19⅞, pub FHG	20.00	75.00
☐ **EUCALYPTUS,** rel. 1976. ed. 500, s/n, 24″ x 16″, pub FHG	20.00	75.00
☐ **MELLOW YELLOW,** rel. 1976. ed. 250, s/n, 19⅜″ x 13⅜″, pub FHG	20.00	100.00
☐ **TULIPS,** rel. 1976. ed. 250, s/n, 19¾″ x 15″, pub FHG	20.00	40.00
☐ **AMARYLLIS,** rel. 1977. ed. 500, s/n, 20″ x 15½″, pub FHG	25.00	Sold Out
☐ **COUNTRY PICKIN'S,** rel. 1977. ed. 500, s/n, 24″ x 20″, pub FHG	20.00	45.00
☐ **MUSHROOMS,** rel. 1977. ed. 500, s/n, 12″ x 12″, pub FHG	25.00	Sold Out
☐ **SENTINEL,** rel. 1977. ed. 500, s/n, 18½″ x 10″, pub FHG	25.00	Sold Out
☐ **ANCIENT SYMBOLS,** rel. 1978. ed. 500, s/n, 17⅜″ x 12¾″, pub FHG	25.00	Sold Out
☐ **BEACHCOMBERS' DREAM,** rel. 1978. ed. 300, s/n, 17½″ x 21″, pub FHG	40.00	Sold Out
☐ **COLLECTIBLES,** rel. 1978. ed. 500, s/n, 14″ x 15¾″, pub FHG	25.00	Sold Out
☐ **HANGING FERN,** rel. 1978. ed. 750, s/n, 30″ x 22″, pub FHG	25.00	Sold Out
☐ **HOBBY HORSE,** rel. 1978. ed. 500, s/n, 14¾″ x 22¼″, pub FHG	—	Sold Out
☐ **MUSICAL INSTRUMENTS,** rel. 1978. ed. 500, s/n, 20½″ x 18½″, pub FHG	25.00	Sold Out
☐ **FINDINGS FROM THE FIELD,** rel. 1979. ed. 750, s/n, 23″ x 17″, pub FHG	25.00	Sold Out
☐ **FIREWORKS FROM THE EARTH,** rel. 1979. ed. 750, s/n, 26″ x 19″, pub FHG	30.00	Sold Out
☐ **OCTOBER GATHERINGS,** rel. 1979. ed. 750, s/n, 18″ x 21″, pub FHG	25.00	Sold Out
☐ **POTTED PLANTS,** rel. 1979. ed. 750, s/n, 16″ x 20″, pub FHG	25.00	Sold Out

GREEN CUISINE *by Charles Harper*

CHARLES HARPER

THEMES: Varied

STYLE: Charles Harper's technique deals with simple suggestions of shape and design based on the fundamentals of nature

BOOKS: Harper has illustrated a number of books for *Golden Press* on birds, animals, and biology, as well as other publications

EDUCATION: Cincinnati Art Academy

GALLERY/DISTRIBUTOR: Frame House Gallery, Inc.

	ISSUE PRICE	CURRENT PRICE
☐ HOUSE WRENS, rel. 1968. ed. 500, s/n, 20″ x 15″, serigraph, pub FHG	20.00	175.00
☐ LADYBUG, rel. 1968. ed. 500, s/n, 15¼″ x 20½″, serigraph, pub FHG	20.00	250.00
☐ PORTFOLIO FOUR PRINTS, rel. 1968. ed. 500, s/n, 15½″ x 20½″, serigraph, pub FHG.......................	60.00	200.00
☐ ANHINGA, rel. 1969. ed. 500, s/n, 50″ x 24″, litho on canvas, pub FHG	50.00	225.00
☐ HUNGRY EYES, rel. 1969. ed. 500, s/n, 12⅝″ x 20½″, serigraph, pub FHG	20.00	400.00
☐ WATER STRIDER, rel. 1969. ed. 500, s/n, 50¼″ x 24″, serigraph, pub FHG	40.00	400.00
☐ BOBWHITE FAMILY, rel. 1970. ed. 750, s/n, 9½″ x 24¾″, serigraph, pub FHG	30.00	125.00
☐ BURROWING OWL, rel. 1970. ed. 500, s/n, 20″ x 11″, serigraph, pub FHG	30.00	75.00
☐ CARDINAL (ON CORN), rel. 1970. ed. 500, s/n, 15¼″ x 20½″, serigraph, pub FHG	30.00	350.00
☐ CRAYFISH MOLTING, rel. 1970. ed. 750, s/n, 13¼″ x 17¼″, serigraph, pub FHG ...	30.00	125.00
☐ PILEATED WOODPECKER, rel. 1970. ed. 750, s/n, 15¼″ x 20½″, serigraph, pub FHG	30.00	125.00
☐ BEAR IN THE BIRCHES, rel. 1971. ed. 1,500, s/n, 23″ x 22⅝″, serigraph, pub FHG .	35.00	425.00
☐ BEETLE BATTLE, rel. 1971. ed. 750, s/n, 15¼″ x 20½″, serigraph, pub FHG	30.00	90.00
☐ BLUE JAY BATHING, rel. 1971. ed. 1,500, s/n, 18¾″ x 24¼″, serigraph, pub FHG ..	30.00	60.00
☐ LADYBUG LOVERS, rel. 1971. ed. 1,500, s/n, 16¼″ x 17½″, serigraph, pub FHG ...	30.00	60.00
☐ PUFFIN, rel. 1971. ed. 750, s/n, 15¼″ x 20½″, serigraph, pub FHG	30.00	125.00
☐ RED-BELLIED WOODPECKER, rel. 1971. ed. 1,500, s/n, 21⅜″ x 15¾″, serigraph, pub FHG.....................	30.00	75.00
☐ BOX TURTLE, rel. 1972. ed. 1,500, s/n, 9⅛″ x 22⅝″, serigraph, pub FHG	30.00	75.00
☐ CHIPMUNK, rel. 1972. ed. 1,500, s/n, 17¼″ x 13″, serigraph, pub FHG	30.00	60.00
☐ FAMILY OWLBUM, rel. 1972. ed. 1,500, s/n, 11⅜″ x 11⅞″, serigraph, pub FHG	30.00	80.00
☐ LADYBUG, rel. 1972. ed. 10,000, s/o, 12½″ x 12″, litho, pub FHG	6.00	30.00
☐ PELICAN IN A DOWNPOUR, rel. 1972. ed. 1,500, s/n, 16½″ x 21½″, serigraph, pub FHG.....................	30.00	325.00
☐ YELLOW-BELLIED SAPSUCKER, rel. 1972. ed. 1,500, s/n, 16½″ x 16¾″, serigraph, pub FHG....................	30.00	80.00
☐ ROUND ROBIN, rel. 1973. ed. 1,500, s/n, 15″ x 20″, serigraph, pub FHG	30.00	60.00

	ISSUE PRICE	CURRENT PRICE
☐ THE LAST SUNFLOWER SEED, rel. 1973. ed. 1,500, s/n, 16½" x 21⅝", serigraph, pub FHG	30.00	200.00
☐ WATERMELON MOON, rel. 1973. ed. 1,500, s/n, 15½" x 19⅞", serigraph, pub FHG	30.00	300.00
☐ WEDDING FEAST, rel. 1973. ed. 1,500, s/n, 17½" x 17", serigraph, pub FHG	30.00	85.00
☐ WOOD DUCK, rel. 1973. ed. 1,500, s/n, 21⅞" x 12", serigraph, pub FHG	30.00	175.00
☐ BIRDS OF A FEATHER, rel. 1974. ed. 2,000, s/n, 23½" x 31", serigraph, pub FHG . .	50.00	100.00
☐ COOL CARDINAL, rel. 1974. ed. 2,000, s/n, 21" x 8½", serigraph, pub FHG	30.00	350.00
☐ CROW IN THE SNOW, rel. 1974. ed. 1,500, s/n, 23½" x 23", serigraph, pub FHG . . .	35.00	150.00
☐ FINE FEATHER, rel. 1974. ed. 1,500, s/n, 23½" x 10", serigraph, pub FHG	30.00	100.00
☐ PAINTED BUNTING, rel. 1974. ed. 1,500, s/n, 19½" x 17", serigraph, pub FHG	30.00	120.00
☐ TALL TAIL, rel. 1974. ed. 2,000, s/n,21" x 12⅞", serigraph, pub FHG	30.00	85.00
☐ BIRDWATCHER, rel. 1975. ed. 2,000, s/n, 16½" x 13", serigraph, pub FHG	40.00	250.00
☐ BLUEBIRDS IN THE BLUE GRASS, rel. 1975. ed. 2,000, s/n, 23½" x 23", serigraph, pub FHG	45.00	75.00
☐ PFWHOOOOOOO, rel. 1975. ed. 2,000, s/n, 20½" x 15", serigraph, pub FHG	40.00	120.00
☐ WHITECOAT, rel. 1975. ed. 2,000, s/n, 13" x 12½", serigraph, pub FHG	30.00	175.00
☐ CLAWS, rel. 1976. ed. 2,000, s/n, 23½" x 16", serigraph, pub FHG	40.00	85.00
☐ CORNPRONE, rel. 1976. ed. 2,500, sn, 18¼" x 16½", serigraph, pub FHG	40.00	135.00
☐ DEVOTION IN THE OCEAN, rel. 1976. ed. 2,000, s/n, 17⅞" x 13¼", serigraph, pub FHG	40.00	75.00
☐ LOVE FROM ABOVE, rel. 1976. ed. 2,000, s/n, 31½" x 9¼", serigraph, pub FHG . . .	40.00	325.00
☐ SKIMMERSCAPE, rel. 1976. ed. 2,000, s/n, 24½" x 17½", serigraph, pub FHG	40.00	90.00
☐ BRRRTHDAY, rel. 1977. ed. 2,500, s/n, 21" x 16", serigraph, pub FHG	40.00	70.00
☐ CATNIP, rel. 1977. ed. 2,500, s/n, 17¾" x 15¼", serigraph, pub FHG	50.00	100.00
☐ DOLFUN, rel. 1977. ed. 2,500, s/n, 20" x 15", serigraph, pub FHG	50.00	75.00
☐ DOWN UNDER, DOWN UNDER, rel. 1977. ed. 2,500, s/n, 23" x 14", serigraph, pub FHG	40.00	50.00
☐ PHANCY PHEATHERS, rel. 1977. ed. 2,500, s/n, 30" x 11¼", serigraph, pub FHG . .	50.00	120.00
☐ SEEING RED, rel. 1977. ed. 2,500, s/n, 17" x 23", serigraph, pub FHG	40.00	125.00
☐ SKIPPING SCHOOL, rel. 1977. ed. 2,500, s/n, 22¼" x 20¾" serigraph, pub FHG50 .	50.00	75.00
☐ BITTERN SUITE, rel. 1978. ed. 2,500, s/n, 19½" x 14¼", serigraph, pub FHG	50.00	90.00
☐ CRAWLING TALL, rel. 1978. ed. 2,500, s/n, 19" x 18¼", serigraph, pub FHG	50.00	90.00
☐ FROG EAT FROG, rel. 1978. ed. 2,500, s/n, 18" x 18", serigraph, pub FHG	50.00	90.00
☐ HARE'S BREADTH, rel 1978. ed. 2,500, s/n, 24" x 19", serigraph, pub FHG	50.00	90.00
☐ LOVEY DOVEY, rel. 1978. ed. 2,500, s/n, 18" x 18", serigraph, pub FHG	50.00	80.00
☐ RACCROBOAT, rel. 1978. ed. 10,000, s/o, 16" x 11½", litho, pub FHG	10.00	—
☐ BUZZ OFF YOU TURKEY, rel. 1979. ed. 2,500, s/n, 12¾" x 27", serigraph, pub FHG	55.00	Sold Out
☐ COOL CARNIVORE, rel. 1979. ed. 2,500, s/n, 24" x 24", serigraph, pub FHG	50.00	Sold Out
☐ DREAM TEAM, rel. 1979. ed. 5,000, s/o, 10" x 14", serigraph, pub FHG	20.00	110.00
☐ FURRED FEEDER, rel. 1979. ed. 2,500, s/n, 30" x 11¼", serigraph, pub FHG	50.00	Sold Out
☐ KOALA KOALA, rel. 1979. ed. 5,000, s/o, 11" x 14", serigraph, pub FHG	20.00	—
☐ SERENGETI SPAGHETTI, rel. 1979. ed. 2,500, s/n, 21½" x 28", serigraph, pub FHG	55.00	90.00
☐ HEXIT, rel. 1980. ed. 1,500, s/n, 20" x 20", serigraph, pub FHG	60.00	100.00
☐ JUMBRELLA, rel. 1980. ed. 1,500, s/n, 16" x 24", serigraph, pub FHG	60.00	100.00
☐ POTLUCK, rel. 1980. ed. 1,500, s/n, 26" x 10⅛", serigraph, pub FHG	60.00	110.00
☐ REDBIRDS AND REDBUDS, rel. 1980. ed. 1,500, s/n, 19¼" x 18¾", serigraph, pub FHG	60.00	100.00
☐ LAST APHID, rel. 1981. ed. 1,500, s/n, 20" x 20", serigraph, pub FHG	60.00	—
☐ RACC AN' RUIN, rel. 1981. ed. 1,500, s/n, 16" x 20", serigraph, pub FHG	60.00	—
☐ RACCPACK, rel. 1981. ed. 2,000, s/n, 19½" x 13", serigraph, pub FHG	35.00	115.00
☐ ROMANCE ON THE RICHTER SCALE, rel. 1981. ed. 1,500, s/n, 20" x 16", serigraph, pub FHG	60.00	—
☐ ARMADITTO, rel. 1982. ed. 1,500, s/n, 17" x 17", serigraph, pub FHG	60.00	—
☐ PELICAN PANTRY, rel. 1982. ed. 1,500, s/n, 18" x 18", serigraph, pub FHG	60.00	—
☐ PRICKLY PAIR, rel. 1982. ed. 1,500, s/n, 16" x 16", serigraph, pub FHG	60.00	—
☐ TERN, STONES AND TURNSTONES, rel. 1982. ed. 1,500, s/n, 16" x 22", serigraph, pub FHG	60.00	—
☐ CONFISKATION, rel. 1983. ed. 1,000, s/n, 17" x 13½", serigraph, pub FHG	90.00	—
☐ FOXSIMILES, rel. 1983. ed. 1,500, s/n, 21¾" x 18", serigraph, pub FHG	60.00	—
☐ QUAILSAFE, rel. 1983. ed. 1,000, s/n, 22" x 16", serigraph, pub FHG	90.00	—
☐ RACCSNACK, rel. 1983. ed. 1,000, s/n, 30" x 12", serigraph, pub FHG	90.00	—
☐ SQUIRREL IN A SQUALL, rel. 1983. ed. 1,000, s/n, 16" x 16", serigraph, pub FHG . .	90.00	—

	ISSUE PRICE	CURRENT PRICE
☐ **PIER GROUP,** rel. 1984. ed. 1,000, s/n, 20″ x 18″, serigraph, pub FHG	90.00	—
☐ **BLACKBEARY JAM,** rel. 1984. ed. 1,000, s/n, 20″ x 22½″, serigraph, pub FHG	90.00	—
☐ **BARK EYES,** rel. 1985. ed. 1,000, s/n, 22″ x 22″, pub FHG	90.00	—
☐ **GREEN CUISINE,** rel. 1985. ed. 1,000, s/n, 10½″ x 28″, pub FHG	90.00	—
☐ **RACCOONNAISSANCE,** rel. 1985. ed. 1,000, s/n, 18″ x 28″, pub FHG	90.00	—
☐ **VOWLENTINE,** rel. 1985. ed. 1,000, s/n, 9″ x 9″, pub FHG	45.00	—
☐ **WINGDING,** rel. 1985. ed. 1,000, s/n, 20″ X 15″, pub FHG	90.00	—

EDIE HARPER

THEMES: Varied

EDUCATION: Art Academy in Cincinnati

GALLERY/DISTRIBUTOR: Frame House Gallery, Inc.

	ISSUE PRICE	CURRENT PRICE
☐ **IN THE GARDEN,** rel. 1975. ed. 250, s/n, 16½″ x 14½″, serigraph, pub FHG	20.00	90.00
☐ **JONAH,** rel. 1975. ed. 250, s/n, 29″ x 21½″, serigraph, pub FHG	20.00	250.00
☐ **NOAZARK,** rel. 1975. ed. 250, s/n, 15¾″ x 16¼″, serigraph, pub FHG	20.00	300.00
☐ **DAN'S DEN,** rel. 1976. ed. 750, s/n, 20″ x 8½″, serigraph, pub FHG	30.00	150.00
☐ **LITTLE DAVID,** rel. 1978. ed. 750, s/n, 16½″ x 15¾″, serigraph, pub FHG	35.00	60.00
☐ **SOLOMON SEZ,** rel. 1976. ed. 750, s/n, 14½″ x 7″, serigraph, pub FHG	20.00	40.00
☐ **SONRISE,** rel. 1976. ed. 750, s/n, 17½″ x 15″, serigraph, pub FHG	30.00	45.00
☐ **UP, UP AND AWAY,** rel. 1976. ed. 1,000, s/n, 20″ x 24″, serigraph, pub FHG	40.00	Sold Out
☐ **PENNY CANDY,** rel. 1977. ed. 750, s/n, 14½″ x 12″, serigraph, pub FHG	35.00	Sold Out
☐ **THE DISCIPLES,** rel. 1977. ed. 750, s/n, 20″ x 20″, serigraph, pub FHG	35.00	60.00
☐ **TREE HOUSE,** rel. 1977. ed. 750, s/n, 21″ x 9⅜″, serigraph, pub FHG	35.00	60.00
☐ **ADAM and MS. EVE,** rel. 1978. ed. 750, s/n, 20″ x 16″, serigraph, pub FHG	35.00	Sold Out
☐ **NET PROPHET,** rel. 1976. ed. 750, s/n, 12″ x 20″, serigraph, pub FHG	30.00	90.00
☐ **SAMSON AND DELILAH,** rel. 1978. ed. 750, s/n, 13″ x 18¾″, serigraph, pub FHG ..	35.00	75.00
☐ **SUNDAY SCHOOL OUTING,** rel. 1978. ed. 750, s/n, 12¾″ x 17″, serigraph, pub FHG	35.00	Sold Out
☐ **FAMILY PORTRAIT,** rel. 1979. ed. 750, s/n, 15″ x 15″, serigraph, pub FHG	40.00	—
☐ **HERE HE COMES!,** rel. 1979. ed. 750, s/n, serigraph, pub FHG	35.00	—
☐ **POW,** rel. 1979. ed. 750, s/n, 15½″ x 18″, serigraph, pub FHG	35.00	—
☐ **WOW,** rel. 1979. ed. 750, s/n, 20″ x 13″, serigraph, pub FHG	35.00	—
☐ **LOT'S LOT,** rel. 1980. ed. 375, s/n, 15″ x 15″, serigraph, pub FHG	40.00	—
☐ **PEEPKIN,** rel. 1980. ed. 375, s/n, 12″ x 20″, serigraph, pub FHG	40.00	70.00
☐ **SPRING CREEPER,** rel. 1980. ed. 375, s/n, 12″ x 20″, serigraph, pub FHG	40.00	70.00
☐ **FISHFUL THINKING,** rel. 1981. ed. 375, s/n, 12⅝″ x 13¼″, serigraph, pub FHG	40.00	70.00
☐ **SANDPEEPER,** rel. 1981. ed. 375, s/n, 12″ x 20″, serigraph, pub FHG	40.00	—
☐ **WINTER WATCH,** rel. 1981. ed. 375, s/n, 12″ x 20″, serigraph, pub FHG	40.00	—
☐ **BASKIT,** rel. 1982. ed. 375, s/n, 15″ x 19″, serigraph, pub FHG	45.00	—
☐ **CLEOPETRA,** rel. 1982. ed. 375, s/n, 16″ x 16″, serigraph, pub FHG	40.00	—
☐ **SLEEPYTIMETOM,** rel. 1982. ed. 375, s/n, 13⅞″ x 20″, serigraph, pub FHG	40.00	—
☐ **SUMMER WATCH,** rel. 1982. ed. 375, s/n, 14″ x 19″, serigraph, pub FHG	45.00	—
☐ **MAGNIFICAT,** rel. 1983. ed. 375, s/n, 24″ x 11½″, serigraph, pub FHG	60.00	—
☐ **KITTEN 'N KNITTIN',** rel. 1984. ed. 375, s/n, 15″ x 16″, serigraph, pub FHG	60.00	—
☐ **NINE TAILS,** rel. 1984. ed. 375, s/n, 28″ x 13″, serigraph, pub FHG	60.00	—
☐ **CAT AND HOUSE,** rel. 1985. ed. 375, s/n, 19″ x 15″, pub FHG	65.00	—

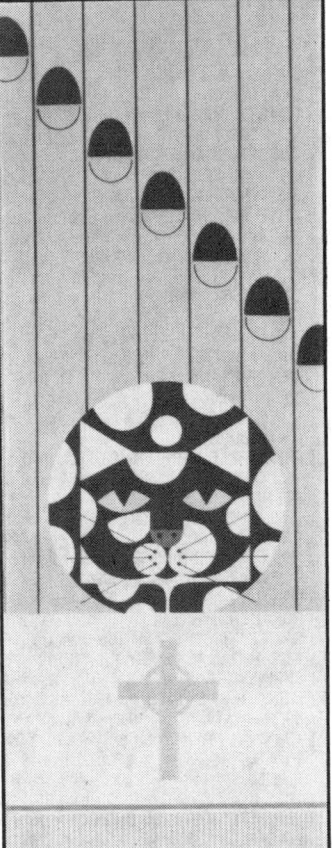

MAGNIFICAT *by Edie Harper*

JIM HARRISON

THEMES: Americana

STYLE: Harrison prefers to be known as a "mood" painter, stating that he is really concerned with the "spirit" of a place rather than the object itself

EDUCATION: University of South Carolina

GALLERY/DISTRIBUTOR: Frame House Gallery, Inc.

	ISSUE PRICE	CURRENT PRICE
☐ **ABANDONED BOAT,** rel. 1974. ed. 1,000, s/n, 13¾" x 17½", pub JH	25.00	50.00
☐ **AMERICAN BYWAYS,** rel. 1975. ed. 1,500, s/n, 28" x 22", pub FHG	40.00	225.00
☐ **BRUSH AND BUCKET,** rel. 1981. ed. 300, s/n, 18¼" x 26¼", pub FHG	300.00	—
ed. 50, Artist proof	350.00	—

	ISSUE PRICE	CURRENT PRICE
☐ BULL OF THE WOODS, rel. 1982. ed. 1,500, s/n, 18″ x 21½″, pub FHG	75.00	125.00
☐ BURMA SHAVE, rel. 1977. ed. 1,500, s/n, 13″ x 21½″, pub FHG	50.00	185.00
☐ CLABBER GIRL, rel. 1979. ed. 1,500, s/n, 23″ x 30″, pub FHG	75.00	200.00
☐ COASTAL MARSHES, rel. 1973. ed. 1,000, s/n, 16½″ x 28″, pub JH	30.00	125.00
☐ 666 COLD TABLETS, rel. 1978. ed. 1,500, s/n, 22″ x 28″, pub FHG	50.00	150.00
☐ COMMUNITY CHURCH, rel. 1977. ed. 1,500, s/n, 12″ x 20″, pub FHG	50.00	90.00
☐ COUNTRY SEASONIN', rel. 1975. ed. 1,500, s/n, 14¾″ x 17¾″, pub FHG	40.00	225.00
☐ DISAPPEARING AMERICA, rel. 1975. ed. 1,500, s/n, 33″ x 18½″, pub FHG	40.00	900.00
☐ DR. PEPPER, rel. 1977. ed. 1,500, s/n, 14¾″ x 12″, pub FHG	50.00	175.00
☐ FALLOW AND FORGOTTEN, rel. 1977. ed. 1,500, s/n, 16″ x 24‴, pub FHG	50.00	85.00
☐ FILLIN' STATION, rel. 1984. ed. 1,500, s/n, 18″ x 28″, pub FHG	80.00	—
☐ FRESH GRITS, rel. 1983. ed. 1,500, s/n, 17¾″ x 30″, pub FHG	80.00	175.00
☐ GOLD DUST TWINS, rel. 1977. ed. 1,500, s/n, 24″ x 15½″, pub FHG	55.00	75.00
☐ GOODY'S, rel. 1979. ed. 1,500, s/n, 18¾″ x 33″, pub FHG	50.00	100.00
☐ HOUSE AND BARN, pair, rel. 1981. ed. 1,500, s/n, 12″ x 14″, pub FHG	50.00	80.00
☐ LUCKY STRIKE, rel. 1979. ed. 1,500, s/n, 12″ x 32″, pub FHG	50.00	150.00
☐ MEMORIES I, rel. 1984. ed. 750, s/n, 21½″ x 29½″, pub FHG	90.00	—
remarqued...	135.00	—
☐ MEMORIES II, rel. 1985. ed. 750, s/n, 24″ x 21¼″, pub FHG	90.00	—
remarqued...	135.00	—
☐ MOUNTAIN BRIDGE, rel. 1983. ed. 1,500, s/n, 19¾″ x 30″, pub FHG	80.00	—
☐ OLD DUTCH CLEANSER, rel. 1981. ed. 1,500, s/n, 20″ x 34″, pub FHG	75.00	100.00
☐ PEANUTS and PEPSI, pair, rel. 1980. ed. 1,500, s/n, 15″ x 18″, pub FHG	60.00	160.00
☐ PHILIP MORRIS, rel. 1978. ed. 1,500, s/n, 17″ x 26″, pub FHG	50.00	185.00
☐ RAILROAD CROSSING, rel. 1982. ed. 1,500, s/n, 18″ x 32″, pub FHG	75.00	115.00
☐ RED COVERED BRIDGE, rel. 1978. ed. 1,500, s/n, 16½″ x 30″, pub FHG	50.00	130.00
☐ RED GOOSE SHOES, rel. 1985. ed. 1,500, s/n, 25½″ x 20½″, pub FHG	90.00	—
☐ RURAL AMERICANA, rel. 1974. ed. 1,500, s/n, 23½″ x 15″, pub FHG	40.00	250.00
☐ RURAL DELIVERY, rel. 1976. ed. 1,500, s/n, 16½″ x 23″, pub FHG	40.00	250.00
☐ SAND DUNES/INLET MARSH (Pair), rel. 1985. ed. 1,500, s/n, 16″ x 19¼″, pub FHG	75.00	—
☐ 7-UP AND BLACK-EYED SUSANS, rel. 1981. ed. 1,500, s/n, 20″ x 24″, pub FHG ...	75.00	100.00
☐ SHRINE CIRCUS, rel. 1983. ed. 1,500, s/n, 21″ x 27″, pub FHG	80.00	—
☐ SIGNS OF THE TIMES, rel. 1984. ed. 3,000, s/o, 22″ x 18″, pub FHG	45.00	—
☐ SPRING CLOUDS, rel. 1985. ed. 1,500, s/n, 21½″ x 31½″, pub FHG	90.00	—
☐ TONIC & LINIMENT, pair, rel. 1980. ed. 1,500, s/n, 10⅜″ x 25″, pub FHG	85.00	125.00
☐ TOOLS, rel. 1978. ed. 300, s/n, serigraph, 19″ x 27″, pub FHG	275.00	400.00
ed. 50, Artist proof	325.00	450.00
☐ TUBE ROSE SNUFF, rel. 1980. ed. 1,500, s/n, 18″ x 23½″, pub FHG	60.00	100.00
☐ UNPAINTED COVERED BRIDGE, rel. 1980. ed. 1,500, s/n, 16¼″ x 24″, pub FHG ...	60.00	100.00
☐ WINDMILL, rel. 1982. ed. 1,500, s/n, 22¼″ x 20½″, pub FHG	75.00	Sold Out
☐ WOODPILE, rel. 1978. ed. 1,500, s/n, 18″ x 18¾″, pub FHG	*75.00	90.00
*Package includes one color work drawing/two black & white sketches.		
☐ YESTERYEAR, rel. 1976. ed. 1,500, s/n, 12″ x 20¾″, pub FHG	50.00	120.00

JERRY HARSTON

THEMES: Western art

MEDIUM: Acrylic and oil

EDUCATION: University of Utah

AWARDS: Gold and silver awards from the Salt Lake City Art Director's Club and others

GALLERY/DISTRIBUTOR: Salt Creek Graphics

	ISSUE PRICE	CURRENT PRICE
☐ **UTE BRAVE,** ed. 750, s/n, 24″ x 34″, litho, pub SGC	80.00	—
☐ **WA-TA-LO,** rel. 1980. ed. 450, s/n, 22″ x 30″, litho, pub SGC	88.00	—

GORDON AND IRISH SETTERS by Ernest H. Hart

ERNEST H. HART

THEMES: Dogs

BOOKS: The artist has written over twenty books on dogs and pets

GALLERY/DISTRIBUTOR: Nature House, Inc.

	ISSUE PRICE	CURRENT PRICE
☐ **ENGLISH POINTERS,** ed. 2,500, s/n, 22″ x 28″, pub NHI	60.00	—
☐ **ENGLISH SETTER,** ed. 2,500, s/n, 22″ x 28″, pub NHI	60.00	—
☐ **GERMAN SHORT HAIRED POINTERS,** ed. 2,500, s/n, 22″ x 28″, pub NHI	60.00	—
☐ **GORDON AND IRISH SETTERS,** ed. 2,500, s/n, 22″ x 28″, pub NHI	60.00	—
☐ **SPRINGER SPANIELS,** ed. 2,500, s/n, 22″ x 28″, pub NHI	60.00	—
☐ **YELLOW AND BLACK LABS,** ed. 2,500, s/n, 22″ x 28″, pub NHI	60.00	—

ON THE STREETS OF NEW ORLEANS by G. Harvey

G. HARVEY

THEMES: Western art

AWARDS: New Master's Award from the American Arts Professional League's Grand National Competition

MUSEUMS/COLLECTIONS: Life Membership in Grand Central Galleries in New York

GALLERY/DISTRIBUTOR: Texas Art Press (now handled by SHL)

	ISSUE PRICE	CURRENT PRICE
☐ CAREFREE COWHANDS, ed. 500, s/n, 31" x 25½", pub ALI	50.00	—
ed. 1,000, s/o	40.00	—
☐ POKER PALS, ed. 500, s/n, 31" x 25½", pub ALI	50.00	—
ed. 1,000, s/o	40.00	—
☐ THE DRIFTING COWHAND, rel. 1974. ed. 2,000, s/o, 29½" x 24¾", pub FHG	60.00	200.00
☐ CROSSING THE CANYON, rel. 1975. ed. 2,000, s/n, 33" x 23½", pub FHG	50.00	300.00
☐ LEAVIN' THE LINE SHACK, rel. 1975. ed. 2,000, s/n, 23" x 28½", pub FHG	50.00	250.00
☐ BOSS' NEW RIG, rel. 1976. ed. 1,500, s/n, 20" x 26", pub FHG	50.00	100.00
☐ BOOMTOWN DRIFTERS, rel. 1978. ed. 2,250, s/n, size not available, pub TAP	100.00	600.00
☐ CHANGING OF THE RANGELAND, rel. 1978. ed. 250, s/n, size not available, pub TAP	150.00	1,500.00
☐ ALONG THE CANYON WALL, rel. 1979. ed. 2,250, s/n, 17" x 20½", pub TAP	100.00	—
☐ COURTING DAYS, rel. 1979. ed. 2,250, s/n, 14½" x 21½", pub TAP	100.00	—
☐ GRAMPA'S NEIGHBORS, rel. 1979. ed. 2,250, s/n, 17" x 21½", pub TAP	100.00	—
☐ IN THE LAND OF THE BLACKFEET, rel. 1979. ed. 2,250, s/n, 22" x 14½", pub TAP	100.00	—
☐ IN THE LAND OF THE ROCKIES, rel. 1979. ed. 1,000, s/n, 27" x 21½", pub TAP	125.00	—
☐ IN THE LAND OF THE WALKING RAIN, rel. 1979. ed. 1,000, s/n, 14½" x 22", pub TAP	100.00	—
☐ LIGHTS ALONG THE AVENUE, rel. 1979. ed. 2,250, s/n, 14½" x 22", pub TAP	100.00	—

	ISSUE PRICE	CURRENT PRICE
☐ RANCHING - PUMP JACK STYLE, rel. 1979. ed. 1,000, s/n, 18" x 27", pub TAP	150.00	—
☐ RIDING THE SALT RIVER CANYON, rel. 1979. ed. 1,000, s/n, 16" x 20", pub TAP ..	100.00	—
☐ RIDING WITH GRAMPA, rel. 1979. ed. 1,000, s/n, 20" x 27", pub TAP	150.00	200.00
☐ SATURDAY NIGHT POKER PALACE, rel. 1979. ed. 1,000, s/n, 16" x 22", pub TAP ..	125.00	—
☐ SPRING PALETTE, rel. 1979. ed. 1,000, s/n, 21" x 18", pub TAP	150.00	—
☐ SPRING VIEWS, rel. 1979. ed. 2,250, s/n, 16½" x 21⅞", pub TAP	100.00	—
☐ TAKING TEXAS NORTH, rel. 1979. ed. 2,250, s/n, 14½" x 21⅞", pub TAP	100.00	—
☐ TEXAS - FROM HIDE AND HORN, rel. 1979. ed. 1,000, s/n, 17" x 27", pub TAP	90.00	—
☐ THE COMING HOME, rel. 1979. ed. 1,000, s/n, 17½" x 22", pub TAP	100.00	—
☐ THE EARLY RUN, rel. 1979. ed. 1,000, s/n, 17½" x 22", pub TAP	125.00	225.00
☐ THE GOOD LORD WILLIN AND THE CREEK DON'T RISE, rel. 1979. ed. 1,000, s/n, 15½" x 27", pub TAP	125.00	—
☐ THE KATY DEPOT, rel. 1979. ed. 2,250, s/n, 14½" x 21⅞", pub TAP	100.00	—
☐ THE NEW FILLY, rel. 1979. ed. 2,250, s/n, 21½" x 17", pub TAP	100.00	—
☐ THE SILENT HUNTER, rel. 1979. ed. 1,000, s/n, 22" x 17½", pub TAP	100.00	—
☐ TIMES REMEMBERED, rel. 1979. ed. 2,250, s/n, 13⅛" x 22", pub TAP	100.00	—
☐ WHEN BANKERS WORE BOOTS, rel. 1979. ed. 1,000, s/n, 14½" x 22", pub TAP ..	75.00	200.00
☐ WHEN THE LONESOMES SET IN, rel. 1979. ed. 2,250, s/n, 14⅛" x 22", pub TAP ..	100.00	—
☐ WINTER'S EVE, rel. 1979. ed. 2,250, s/n, 14½" x 22", pub TAP	100.00	—
☐ BOOMTOWN DRIFTERS, rel. 1980. ed. 2,250, s/n, 19⅝" x 28", pub TAP	100.00	600.00
☐ BORDER PATROL, rel. 1980. ed. 2,250, s/n, 26½" x 22⅛", pub TAP	100.00	—
☐ DALLAS, rel. 1980. ed. 1,200, s/n, size not available, pub TAP	150.00	450.00
☐ MAN AMONG NATURE, rel. 1980. ed. 2,250, s/n, 26½" x 22", pub TAP	100.00	—
☐ THE NEW STALLION, rel. 1980. ed. 2,250, s/n, 20" x 28", pub TAP	100.00	—
☐ WHEN SNOW MELTS INTO MUSIC, rel. 1980. ed. 2,250, s/n, 28½" x 20⅞", pub TAP	100.00	—
☐ WHERE EAGLES SOAR, rel. 1980. ed. 2,250, s/n, 28" x 19½", pub TAP	100.00	—
☐ COWTOWN, rel. 1981. ed. 1,000, s/n, 17¾" x 27½", pub TAP	150.00	400.00
☐ OIL PATCH, rel. 1981. ed. 1,000, s/n, 22¼" x 30¾", pub TAP	150.00	550.00
☐ SUPPLIES FOR THE MISSION, rel. 1981. ed. 1,000, s/n, 17¾" x 26½", pub TAP ...	150.00	—
☐ TWENTIETH CENTURY RANCHING, rel. 1981. ed. 1,000, s/n, size not available, pub TAP	150.00	400.00
☐ WALL STREET, rel. 1981. ed. 1,000, s/n, size not available, pub TAP	150.00	400.00
☐ WITH NO INTENTION OF CHANGING, rel. 1981. ed. 1,000, s/n, size not available, pub TAP	150.00	450.00
☐ BOOT TOP DEEP, rel. 1982. ed. 1,000, s/n, 19½" x 26", pub TAP	150.00	Sold Out
☐ THE COWBOY'S CHRISTMAS BALL, rel. 1981. ed. 1,000, s/n, 27" x 18", pub TAP ..	150.00	Sold Out
☐ INDEPENDENT OILMEN, rel. 1982. ed. 1,000, s/n, 19½" x 26", pub TAP	150.00	Sold Out
☐ ON THE STREETS OF NEW ORLEANS, rel. 1982. ed. 1,000, s/n, 15¾" x 26½", pub TAP	150.00	225.00
☐ THE PLAZA, NEW YORK, rel. 1982. ed. 1,000, s/n, 19½" x 26", pub TAP	150.00	Sold Out
☐ A NEW LEASE, rel. 1985. ed. 1,250, s/n, 18" x 27", pub SHL	150.00	—
Artist proof	175.00	—

DONALD M. HEDIN

THEMES: Western art

MEDIUM: Acrylic on Masonite, prepared with a gesso ground

EDUCATION: Pratt Institute

MEMBERSHIPS: American Watercolor Society, Society of Illustrators

GALLERY/DISTRIBUTOR: Mill Pond Press, Inc.

	ISSUE PRICE	CURRENT PRICE
☐ A LETTER COMES TO POVERTY BAR, rel. 1981. ed. 550, s/n, 26¾" x 19¾", pub MPPI	120.00	—
☐ THE WELLS FARGO GUARD, rel. 1981. ed. 450, s/n, 26¾" x 19½", pub MPPI	85.00	—

THE WELLS FARGO GUARD *by Donald M. Hedin*

PETER HELCK

THEMES: Automobile racing

BOOKS: *The Checkered Flag* and *Great Auto Races*

EDUCATION: Art Students League

GALLERY/DISTRIBUTOR: Greenwich Workshop

	ISSUE PRICE	CURRENT PRICE
☐ **SAFE ON THE R.R. SIDING,** rel. 1983. ed. 475, s/n, 35½″ x 19¼″, pub GW	165.00	—
ed. 25, signed, numbered, and remarqued	285.00	—

SAFE ON THE R.R. SIDING *by Peter Helck*

DR. WILLIAM HEMMERDINGER

THEMES: Varied

MEDIUM: Watercolor

EDUCATION: Art Center College of Design; University of California; Claremont Graduate School

MUSEUMS/COLLECTIONS: National Academy of Design; Whitney Museum of American Art, etc.

GALLERY/DISTRIBUTOR: Connoisseur's Gallery of Art, Ltd.

	ISSUE PRICE	CURRENT PRICE
☐ **SUNMAID RAISIN,** General run, 18½″ x 8½″, pub CGAL	13.00	—
ed. 12, Artist accented, s/n	100.00	—
☐ **SAKAI RANCH,** General run, 18″ x 8½″	13.00	—
ed. 12, Artist accented, s/n	100.00	—

BOB HENLEY

THEMES: Animals

STYLE: He creates his subjects on gessoed Masonite with no preliminary sketches, using an oil lift or pickup technique. He finishes pieces with multiple color glazes

AWARDS: Best of Show, President's Award, People's Choice Award in many juried exhibitions

GALLERY/DISTRIBUTOR: Remarque, Inc.

	ISSUE PRICE	CURRENT PRICE
☐ FOREST SECRET, rel. 1981. ed. 950, s/n, 22" x 16½", pub RI	50.00	50.00

TOM HENNESSEY

THEMES: Sporting art

AWARDS: Massachusetts Waterfowl Stamp Competition

MEMBERSHIPS: Ducks Unlimited

GALLERY/DISTRIBUTOR: Petersen Gallery

	ISSUE PRICE	CURRENT PRICE
☐ LAST CHANCE, rel. 1973. ed. 400, 23½" x 15½", remarque by request, pub Savage Arms Co.	—	200.00
☐ PAYDAY, rel. 1977. ed. 200, 15" x 24", remarque by request, pub T. Hennessey	—	80.00
☐ SALMON POOL, rel. 1977. ed. 100, 15" x 24", remarque by request, pub T. Hennessey	—	250.00
☐ SILVER IN THE SUN, rel. 1977. ed. 100, 11" x 15", remarque, pub Atlantic Salmon Association of Montreal	—	150.00
☐ EVENING SALMON, rel. 1978. ed. 100, 11" x 15", pub Atlantic Salmon Association of Montreal	—	150.00
☐ SENTINELS AT SUN-UP, rel. 1978. ed. 800, 16" x 22½", signed/numbered, pub Petersen Gallery	—	60.00
☐ PINE CORNER COVERY, rel. 1978. ed. 800, s/n, 16" x 22½", pub Petersen Gallery	—	60.00

EDNA HIBEL

THEMES: Varied portraiture

BACKGROUND: The Hibel Museum of Art opened in Palm Beach, Florida in Janaury, 1977

EDUCATION: Boston Museum School of Arts

AWARDS: Presidential Award from the National Academy, Arts with the Handicapped (1985); Peter Paul Rubens Medal; citation from Pope John Paul II; honored by the United Nations, etc.

MUSEUMS/COLLECTIONS: Miss Hibel has been exhibited in hundreds of museums and galleries on four continents

GALLERY/DISTRIBUTOR: Edna Hibel Corporation

	ISSUE PRICE	CURRENT PRICE
☐ MOTHER & 4 CHILDREN, ed. 60, s/n, 38¾" x 25½", litho, pub JARP	150.00	1,090.00
☐ RACHEL & CHILD, ed. 90, s/n, 20" x 27", litho, pub JARP	90.00	1,000.00
☐ PORTUGAL, ed. 52, s/n, 24" x 32", litho, pub JARP	200.00	1,000.00
☐ BRETON WOMAN, ed. 172, s/n, 17" x 21¼", litho, pub JARP	75.00	325.00
☐ THREE MUSICIANS, ed. 65, s/n, 24" x 34", litho, pub JARP	150.00	1,000.00
☐ OBI, ed. 116, s/n, 25½" x 37¼", litho, pub JARP	225.00	2,000.00
☐ MOTHER & 2 CHILDREN (Cain & Abel), ed. 125, s/n, 24" x 36", litho, pub JARP	150.00	2,100.00
☐ JULIANA, ed. 51, s/n, 14½" x 21⅛", litho, pub JARP	85.00	1,400.00
☐ THE MOTHER, ed. 82, s/n, 10" x 13", litho, pub JARP	85.00	1,400.00
☐ MOTHER & BABY, ed. 235, s/n, 9⅛" x 13½", litho, pub JARP	60.00	500.00
☐ PICCOLO PLAYER, one color. ed. 59, s/n, 10¾" x 15⅛, litho, pub JARP	75.00	650.00
☐ PICCOLO PLAYER, multi-color, ed. 99, s/n, 10¾" x 15", litho, pub JARP	110.00	650.00
☐ SINGLE NUDE, ed. 69, s/n, 9" x 12½", litho, pub JARP	80.00	650.00
☐ TORAH, one color. ed. 135, s/n, 11" x 14¼", litho, pub JARP	65.00	1,200.00
☐ TORAH, two color. ed. 47, s/n, 11" x 14¼", litho, pub JARP	90.00	1,200.00
☐ RUTH (Unique only), 5" x 8¾", litho, pub JARP	60.00	450.00
☐ YASUKO (Unique only), 5¾" x 8", litho, pub JARP	60.00	450.00
☐ DAVID AND BATHSHEBA (Unique only), 6" x 8⅞", litho, pub JARP	60.00	450.00
☐ LOUISE (Unique only), 5" x 7", litho, pub JARP	60.00	450.00
☐ PEASANT WOMAN SMILING, ed. 45, s/n, 11¼" x 13", litho, pub JARP	60.00	550.00
☐ NEW PEASANT WOMAN, ed. 146, s/n, 11" x 13½", litho, pub JARP	75.00	450.00
☐ PEASANT MAN, ed. 120, s/n, 14" x 15", litho, pub JARP	60.00	600.00
☐ PORTUGUESE FISHERMAN, ed. 120, s/n, 13½" x 15¼", litho, pub JARP	75.00	650.00
☐ BOUQUET, one color. ed. 101, s/n, 12¾" x 19⅛", litho, pub JARP	85.00	600.00
☐ BOUQUET, three & four color. A-K sections, 12¾" x 19⅛, litho, pub JARP	125.00	600.00
☐ THREE VASES, small. ed. 50, s/n, 11" x 14", litho, pub JARP	75.00	595.00
☐ GIRL WITH JUG, ed. 120, s/n, 14" x 20", litho, pub JARP	75.00	650.00
☐ VIOLINIST, two color. ed. 72, s/n, 14" x 18¼", litho, pub JARP	90.00	1,100.00
☐ VIOLINIST, one color. ed. 42, s/n, 14" x 18¼", litho, pub JARP	70.00	1,100.00
☐ SAMI, one color. ed. 116, s/n, 8¾" x 9¾", litho, pub JARP	75.00	1,800.00
☐ SAMI THINKING, ed. 60, s/n, 10⅛" x 12¾", litho, pub JARP	75.00	3,000.00
☐ LOVERS, ed. 170, s/n, 9½" x 12⅝", litho, pub JARP	60.00	700.00
☐ MAN & WOMAN, ed. 75, s/n, 14½" x 22¼", litho, pub JARP	95.00	375.00
☐ BAREFOOT CELLIST, ed. 97, s/n, 14½" x 24¼", litho, pub JARP	75.00	700.00
☐ BERET, ed. 68. s/n, 7¼" x 9¾", litho, pub JARP	75.00	595.00
☐ ELEPHANT, ed. 143, s/n, 15¼" x 11¼", litho, pub JARP	75.00	375.00
☐ DUTCH GIRL, three color. ed. 90, s/n, 14" x 18", litho, pub JARP	80.00	500.00
☐ DUTCH GIRL, one color. ed. 24, s/n, 14" x 18", litho, pub JARP	60.00	400.00
☐ MOTHER & 2 CHILDREN, one color. ed. 120, s/n, 21¾" x 27", litho, pub JARP	125.00	950.00
☐ JANET, ed. 98, s/n, 14½" x 11", litho, pub JARP	90.00	950.00
☐ NEW BABY, Regular edition, three color. ed. 100, s/n, 9" x 12¾"	80.00	600.00
Special edition, three color. ed. 58, s/n, 9" x 12¾"	80.00	600.00
A/E edition, two color. ed. 50, s/n, 9" x 12¾"	80.00	600.00
lithos, all pub JARP		
☐ PLAYING MOTHER & CHILD, one color. ed. 60, s/n, 11¾" x 14"	75.00	850.00
Experimental edition, two color. ed. 15, s/n, 11¾" x 14"	75.00	850.00
lithos, pub JARP		
☐ FLUTIST, ed. 100, s/n, 11½" x 15½", litho, pub JARP	50.00	500.00
☐ LOIRE VALLEY, one color. ed. 49, s/n, 8¾" x 20⅜", litho, pub JARP	75.00	700.00
☐ SHIZUE. Regular edition, ed. 45, s/n, 9½" x 13"; A/E edition, ed. 50, s/n, 9½" x 13", litho, pub JARP	60.00	1,000.00

	ISSUE PRICE	CURRENT PRICE
☐ **THREE NUDES,** ed. 87, s/n, 8½″ x 12¼″, litho, pub JARP	70.00	385.00
☐ **CELLIST,** one color. **A/E edition,** 9⅝″ x 15″	75.00	600.00
Regular edition, two color, s/n, 9⅝″ x 15″	70.00	600.00
lithos, pub JARP		
☐ **PROFILE,** ed. 75, s/n, 7″ x 8¼″, litho, pub JARP	65.00	600.00
☐ **PAULINE,** edition on silk only, 7″ x 10⅞″	—	3,600.00
☐ **BEGGAR,** black/white. ed. 70, s/n, 27¾″ x 38¼″, litho, pub JARP	150.00	1,800.00
☐ **BEGGAR,** three color. ed. 63, s/n, 27¾″ x 38¼″, litho, pub JARP	250.00	2,800.00
☐ **BRETON GIRL,** one color. ed. 140, s/n, 11″ x 14″	75.00	800.00
two color, ed. 72, s/n, 11″ x 14″	75.00	800.00
lithos, pub JARP		
☐ **BEARDED MAN,** ed. 100, s/n, 13″ x 15¾″, litho, pub JARP	75.00	650.00
☐ **FLOWER VENDOR,** ed. 63, s/n, 16″ x 22, litho, pub JARP	125.00	495.00
☐ **JAPANESE GIRL HEAD** (Unique only). s/n, 10″ x 10″, litho, pub JARP	90.00	600.00
☐ **FIELDS OF ITALY,** ed. 93, s/n, 22½″ x 15″, litho, pub JARP	110.00	950.00
☐ **BETH,** ed. 207, s/n, 9½″ x 10⅜″, litho, pub JARP	75.00	1,050.00
☐ **TWO FLOWER GIRLS,** edition on silk only, 25″ x 40″	—	6,000
☐ **BYRON** (Border). ed. 76, s/n, 12½″ x 14½″	75.00	550.00
(No Border), ed. 9, 10¾″ x 12¾″	75.00	550.00
lithos, pub JARP		
☐ **BYRON'S SISTER,** two color. ed. 57, s/n, 11¾″ x 13¾″, litho, pub JARP	75.00	550.00
☐ **BYRON'S SISTER,** one color. ed. 9, s/n, 11¾″ x 13¾″, litho, pub JARP	75.00	550.00
☐ **TWO FARMERS,** ed. 43, s/n, 9½″ x 13¾″, litho, pub JARP	60.00	465.00
☐ **MOTHER & CHILD,** one color. ed. 77, s/n, 12½″ x 20″	75.00	495.00
two color, ed. n/a, 12½″ x 20″	75.00	495.00
lithos, pub JARP		
☐ **PORTUGUESE MOTHER & CHILD,** ed. n/a, 11½″ x 16″, litho, pub JARP	75.00	700.00
☐ **PRINCESS,** two color. ed. 29, s/n, 13½″ x 18″	75.00	700.00
A/E edition, one color. ed. 49, s/n, 13⅝″ x 18½″	75.00	700.00
lithos, pub JARP		
☐ **VENICE,** one color. ed. n/a, 15¼″ x 20¾″, uniques or A/P	—	540.00
Uniques or A/P w/pastel pencil or Oil Paint	—	630.00
pub JARP		
☐ **PEASANT WOMAN,** one color, Experimental edition, 12¾″ x 15″, A/P	—	1,400.00
☐ **REBECCA,** two color. ed. n/a, 24″ x 36″, uniques or A/P	—	1,400.00
Uniques or A/P w/pastel pencil or Oil Paint	—	1,600.00
☐ **BABY LLAMA,** ed. n/a, 12½″ x 17½″	75.00	1,100.00
☐ **MAN WITH WHEELBARROW,** ed. 27, s/n, 16¼″ x 14″, litho, pub JARP	75.00	385.00
☐ **BRITTANY,** ed. 75, s/n, 13½″ x 20⅜″, litho, pub JARP	90.00	385.00
☐ **MOTHER & 3 CHILDREN,** ed. 25, s/n, 24″ x 35½″, litho, pub JARP	150.00	1,295.00
☐ **FOUR NUDES & 2 CATS,** ed. 8, 22½″ x 30½″, litho, pub JARP	125.00	560.00
☐ **TWO NUDES** (Left Side). A/P only, 18″ x 24″, litho, pub JARP	75.00	560.00
☐ **TWO NUDES,** 1, 2, 3 color. ed. A/P's only, 18″ x 24″, litho, pub JARP	75.00	560.00
☐ **JIMMY BUDDHA,** ed. 25, 15¼″ x 23⅛″, litho, pub JARP	90.00	800.00
☐ **ESAU, SARAH & BROS,** ed. 45, 16″ x 21¼″, litho, pub JARP	90.00	850.00
☐ **GYPSY VIOLINIST,** one color. ed. 30, 14″ x 18″	75.00	500.00
two & three color	95.00	500.00
ed. 103, 14″ x 18″	110.00	610.00
lithos, pub JARP		
☐ **THREE GRACES,** ed. 140, 11″ x 15″, litho, pub JARP	75.00	500.00
☐ **BETTY'S FIELDS LANDSCAPE,** one color. ed. 33, 14″ x 22″	90.00	550.00
two color, ed. 73, 14″ x 22″	75.00	550.00
lithos, pub JARP		
☐ **THREE MUSES & VASE,** ed. 40, 14″ x 22″, litho, pub JARP	90.00	500.00
☐ **VASES OF FLOWERS** (Lg. Floral). ed. 36 on japon, 22″ x 31″, litho, pub JARP	175.00	1,200.00
☐ **VASES OF FLOWERS** (Lg. Floral). ed. 40, 25¼″ x 35¾″, litho, pub JARP	175.00	1,200.00
☐ **ONE FARMER WOMAN,** ed. 46, 6½″ x 11½″	60.00	385.00
Keystone ed. 9, 6½″ x 11½″	60.00	385.00
lithos, pub JARP		
☐ **PROVENCE LANDSCAPE,** ed. 48, 14″ x 19¼″, litho, pub JARP	85.00	650.00
☐ **WENDY,** no edition, silks only - 11″ x 19″	N/A	4,500.00

	ISSUE PRICE	CURRENT PRICE
☐ **GERRY,** no edition, silks only - 16" x 20"	N/A	4,500.00
☐ **SANTE FE GARDENS,** no edition, silks only, 12½" x 17½"	N/A	3,300.00
☐ **WENDY W/FLOWERS,** ed. 118, 24" x 36", litho, pub JARP	175.00	950.00
☐ **RUTH & CHILD,** line drawing. ed. 33, 14" x 15"	75.00	800.00
one color, ed. 109, 20" x 27"	85.00	800.00
two color, ed. 95, 20" x 27"	95.00	850.00
three color, ed. 95, 20" x 27", pub JARP	95.00	850.00
☐ **SARAH & CHILDREN,** ed. 185, 24" x 36"	150.00	1,600.00
Special edition 7, 24" x 36"	150.00	1,600.00
☐ **SARAH & CHILDREN,** (½ Stone). ed. 57, 20" x 24", litho, pub JARP	150.00	650.00
☐ **JAPANESE MOTHER & CHILD,** ed. 107. 11⅝" x 14⅝"	85.00	700.00
A/E ed. 45, 11⅝" x 14⅝", litho, pub JARP	85.00	700.00
☐ **LOVERS OF FLORENCE,** one color. rel. 1975. ed. 11, 24" x 30½"	90.00	800.00
six colors, ed. 140, 27" x 34", litho, pub JARP	175.00	950.00
☐ **ROCKPORT,** rel. 1975. ed. 50, 16" x 24", litho, pub JARP	110.00	1,200.00
☐ **LUTE PLAYER,** rel. 1975. two color. ed. 19, 19½" x 37½"	110.00	800.00
four color, ed. 110, 29½" x 37½"	200.00	900.00
☐ **GAIL & CAT** - long, rel. 1975. ed. 25, 16" x 25½"	95.00	550.00
☐ **GAIL & CAT** - short. ed. 19, 18¼" x 19", litho, pub JARP	95.00	550.00
☐ **WENDY W/VEIL,** rel. 1974. ed. 140, 12" x 16¼", litho, pub JARP	85.00	600.00
☐ **SAMI PAINTING,** rel. 1974. no edition, silks only	N/A	6,000.00
☐ **GREEK DANCERS,** rel. 1974. ed. 137, 16½" x 21", litho, pub JARP	125.00	950.00
☐ **JERUSALEM SCENE,** rel. 1974. no edition, unique - A/P only 9" x 20"	—	825.00
☐ **3 VASES,** rel. 1974. no edition, silks only, 30" x 40" both pub by JARP	—	4,500.00
☐ **MOTHER & 3 CHILDREN** (horiz.), rel. 1974. ed. 132, 26" x 36½", litho, pub JARP	200.00	1,000.00
☐ **SAMI THE ARTIST,** rel. 1974. ed. 148, 14¼" x 18", litho, pub JARP	125.00	1,000.00
☐ **OLD MAN HEAD,** rel. 1974. ed. 98, 10¾" x 13", litho, pub JARP	90.00	500.00
☐ **GIRL W/KERCHIEF (Caroline),** rel. 1974. ed. 115, released in one color, two, three color, 12¼" x 18", litho, pub JARP	110.00	1,500.00
☐ **JEANNE,** rel. 1974. ed. 85, 12¼" x 16½", litho, pub JARP	85.00	600.00
☐ **BOY W/DONKEY,** rel. 1974. one, two color, ed. 82, 21½" x 27½", litho, pub JARP	110.00	700.00
☐ **FAMILY (Mother, Father & 4 Children),** rel. 1974. ed. 150, 27¾" x 39", litho, pub JARP	150.00	1,200.00
☐ **MOTHER & TWO BOYS,** rel. 1974. ed. 150, 22¾" x 32½", litho, pub JARP	125.00	1,200.00
☐ **SAMI DANCING,** rel. 1974. ed. 110, 22" x 30", litho, pub JARP	135.00	1,250.00
☐ **NEW SMALL MOTHER & BABY,** rel. 1974. ed. 149, 7½" x 10¼", litho, pub JARP	90.00	500.00
☐ **JAN,** rel. 1974. ed. 139, 10" x 14", (a portion on wood veneer)	85.00	900.00
(a portion was litho) pub JARP	85.00	900.00
☐ **NEW DANCERS,** (on wood veneer) rel. 1974. ed. 10, 12½" x 23", pub JARP	90.00	900.00
☐ **BANGKOK,** six color, rel. 1974. ed. 109, 24" x 33"	175.00	900.00 ·
one color, ed. 23, 14" x 20", litho, pub JARP	90.00	450.00
☐ **LA TURBIE,** ed. 158, 20" x 31", litho, pub JARP	175.00	550.00
☐ **VENICE,** rel. 1974. ed. 56, 16½" x 25½", litho, pub JARP	175.00	700.00
☐ **HEDDI,** rel. 1974. ed. 290, 16½" x 25½", litho, pub JARP	135.00	600.00
☐ **SINGLE VASE & FLOWERS,** ed. 250, edition consists of 3 color & 4 color, 9" x 17", litho, pub JARP	95.00	600.00
☐ **MEXICAN MOTHER & BABY,** rel. 1974. ed. 250, editions consist of 3 color & 4 color, 10¾" x 16", litho, pub JARP	95.00	650.00
☐ **MAN W/TURBAN,** rel. 1974. ed. 145, 15¾" x 21", one color	90.00	450.00
two color, same size, litho, pub JARP	110.00	500.00
☐ **PETER,** rel. 1974. ed. 250, three color, 10¾" x 14"	95.00	600.00
ed. 250, four color same size	95.00	650.00
☐ **ISABEL,** rel. 1974. ed. 250, three color & four color, 10⅛" x 15½", litho, pub JARP	95.00	600.00
☐ **CHINESE MOTHER & BABY,** rel. 1974. ed. 225, one color, 27" x 37"	175.00	1,200.00
two color, 27" x 37"	175.00	1,200.00
three & four color, 27" x 37"	195.00	1,200.00
four color, 24" x 36" on rice paper	215.00	1,200.00
☐ **HEDDI & CHILDREN,** rel. 1974. ed. 200, 24" x 35", litho, pub JARP	150.00	1,250.00
☐ **SANDY (Kissing Baby),** rel. 1974. ed. 140, edition in one color & two color, litho, pub JARP	75.00	1,250.00

	ISSUE PRICE	CURRENT PRICE
☐ **LINDA & SON,** rel. 1975. ed. 140, one & two color, 14″ x 19″, ed. 30, one color only .	85.00	800.00
☐ **VILLAGE FIELD,** rel. 1975. ed. 125, issued in one color & two color, 7½″ x 16½″, litho, pub JARP	75.00	400.00
☐ **DEBBIE & BABY,** rel. 1975. ed. 165, 17½″ x 23½″, wood veneer & one color	85.00	800.00
two color & three color, pub JARP	110.00	850.00
☐ **BABS W/FLOWERS,** rel. 1975. ed. 150, 27″ x 37″, litho, pub JARP	175.00	1,000.00
☐ **HONG KONG HARBOR,** rel. 1975. ed. 195. 10¼″ x 14½″, one color	75.00	300.00
three color, litho, pub JARP	95.00	350.00
☐ **MARY-ANN,** rel. 1975. ed. 195, 8″ x 11¾″, one color	75.00	600.00
three color, litho, pub JARP	95.00	540.00
☐ **JOSHUA,** rel. 1975. ed. 195, 7¾″ x 9¾″, one color	75.00	450.00
three color, litho, pub JARP	90.00	425.00
☐ **NEW SAMI,** rel. 1975. ed. 195, 7½″ x 9″, one color	75.00	650.00
three color, litho, pub JARP	90.00	700.00
☐ **ALBERTO,** rel. 1975. ed. 195, 9″ x 10″, one color	75.00	400.00
three color, litho, pub JARP	90.00	400.00
☐ **ELEANOR,** rel. 1975. ed. 195, 9″ x 9″, one color	75.00	450.00
three color, litho, pub JARP	90.00	450.00
☐ **RUTH-ANN (Mother & 3 Children),** rel. 1975. ed. 250, 26½″ x 34″, one color	150.00	950.00
three color, litho, pub JARP	215.00	1,020.00
☐ **JAPANESE BOY,** rel. 1975. ed. 250, 9″ x 14″, two, three color	115.00	550.00
three, four color, litho, pub JARP	125.00	550.00
☐ **JAPANESE GIRL,** rel. 1975. ed. 250, 9″ x 12″, two, three color	115.00	550.00
three, four color, litho, pub JARP	125.00	550.00
☐ **YOU BE KING,** rel. 1975. ed. 98, 25″ x 33½″, one color	150.00	750.00
two color	185.00	750.00
three or four color, litho, pub JARP	215.00	750.00
☐ **SWISS MAN,** rel. 1976. ed. 300, 20¼″ x 24″, one color	85.00	225.00
eight color, litho, pub JARP	150.00	375.00
☐ **SWISS WOMAN,** rel. 1976. ed. 300, 20¼″ x 24″, one color	85.00	225.00
eight color, litho, pub JARP	150.00	375.00
☐ **ELSA & BABY,** rel. 1976. ed. 300, 16½″ x 24″, one color	85.00	3,500.00
eight color, litho, pub JARP	150.00	3,500.00
☐ **3 VASES,** rel. 1976. ed. 290, 23½″ x 36″, litho, pub JARP	250.00	1,400.00
☐ **OLD MAN HEAD,** rel. 1976. ed. 50, 10″ x 13″, etching, pub JARP	80.00	395.00
☐ **GREEK GIRL,** rel. 1976. ed. 50, 10″ x 13″, etching, pub JARP	70.00	395.00
☐ **DUTCH GIRL & BOY,** rel. 1976. ed. 50, 10″ x 13″, etching, pub JARP	70.00	395.00
☐ **MOTHER & BABY,** rel. 1976. ed. 50, 9½″ x 12″, etching, pub JARP	60.00	550.00
☐ **PICCOLO PLAYER,** rel. 1976. ed. 50, 10½″ x 11½″, etching, pub JARP	60.00	395.00
☐ **TORSO,** rel. 1970. ed. 50, 2½″ x 2½″, etching, pub JARP	50.00	450.00
☐ **GREEK FIELD,** rel. 1975. ed. 135, 22″ x 30″, litho, pub JARP	125.00	500.00
☐ **SAMI NO. 9,** rel. 1976. ed. 250, 17½″ x 25½″	125.00	1,100.00
ed. 45, same size but on silk, pub JARP	175.00	1,250.00
☐ **CHRIS,** rel. 1975. ed. 150, 13″ x 18¼″, litho, pub JARP	85.00	800.00
☐ **CHRYSTAL,** rel. 1975. ed. 120, 12¾″ x 17⅝″, one color	85.00	700.00
three color	100.00	800.00
four color, litho, pub JARP	110.00	800.00
☐ **GUATEMALA SCENE,** rel. 1976. ed. 295, 13″ x 24⅛″, one color	95.00	550.00
nine color, litho, pub JARP	145.00	650.00
☐ **VIOLIN & FLUTE PLAYER,** rel. 1976. ed. 290, 15½″ x 18″, litho, pub JARP	90.00	800.00
☐ **LITTLE LOVERS,** rel. 1976. ed. 280, 5¼″ x 9″, litho, pub JARP	75.00	600.00
☐ **GIRL'S HEAD,** rel. 1976. ed. 280, 10¾″ x 13½″, litho, pub JARP	75.00	600.00
☐ **CHRISTA IN PIG TAILS,** rel. 1976. ed. 55, 13¼″ x 17⅛″, one color	85.00	800.00
four color, pub JARP	95.00	800.00
☐ **MAYAN WATER CARRIER,** rel. 1976. ed. 300, 11″ x 21¾″, one color	95.00	700.00
nine color, litho, pub JARP	145.00	650.00
☐ **MAYAN WATER CARRIER W/CHILD,** rel. 1976. ed. 300, 11″ x 21¾″	95.00	600.00
nine color, litho, pub JARP	145.00	650.00
☐ **JAPANESE DOLL,** rel. 1976. ed. 28, 7½″ x 11¼″, one color	85.00	2,000.00
ed. 52, same size, twelve colors + gold on silk	160.00	2,200.00
ed. 280, 9″ x 12″, twelve colors + gold on silk, pub JARP	160.00	2,200.00
☐ **KIKUE (Japon),** rel. 1976. ed. 150, 11¾″ x 21½″	150.00	1,700.00

	ISSUE PRICE	CURRENT PRICE
☐ KIKUE (Silk), rel. 1976. ed. 145, 11¾" x 21½", pub JARP	195.00	2,200.00
☐ SWITZERLAND, rel. 1976. ed. 270, 24" x 37", litho, pub JARP	350.00	1,400.00
☐ MOTHER & 4 CHILDREN, rel. 1975. ed. 300, 27¼" x 39¼", litho, pub JARP	250.00	1,200.00
☐ MAYAN WEAVER (Japon), rel. 1975. ed. 175, 9" x 11¾"	115.00	700.00
☐ MAYAN WEAVER (Silk), rel. 1975. ed. 105, 9" x 11¾", pub JARP	165.00	750.00
☐ MAYAN PRINCESS, rel. 1975. ed. 300, 26½" x 40¼", litho, pub JARP	250.00	695.00
☐ JULIET & BABY (Japon), rel. 1976. ed. 285, 8½" x 11", pub JARP	115.00	1,200.00
☐ COUPLE IN FIELDS, rel. 1976. ed. 290, 10" x 13", litho, pub JARP	70.00	195.00
☐ FARM WOMAN W/BASKET, rel. 1976. ed. 290, 8" x 10½", litho, pub JARP	70.00	195.00
☐ MOTHER & DAUGHTER, rel. 1976. ed. 290, 7½" x 11", litho, pub JARP	70.00	195.00
☐ FISHERMAN, rel. 1976. ed. 290, 7" x 12¾", litho, pub JARP	70.00	195.00
☐ VENICE, rel. 1976. ed. 290, 11" x 11", litho, pub JARP	70.00	195.00
☐ SMALL BRETON WOMAN W/CHILD, rel. 1976. ed. 290, 9½" x 10½", litho, pub JARP	70.00	195.00
☐ THREE WOMEN IN FIELDS, rel. 1976. ed. 290, 12½" x 16", litho, pub JARP	75.00	195.00
☐ TWO DUTCH GIRLS, rel. 1976. ed. 300, 13" x 17¼", litho, pub JARP	85.00	420.00
☐ 4 MUSICIANS, rel. 1976. ed. 300, 13" x 17", litho, pub JARP	85.00	550.00
☐ 2 DANCERS, rel. 1976. ed. 300, 7" x 9½", litho, pub JARP	75.00	395.00
☐ SAMPAN (On Silk), rel. 1976. ed. 209, 9" x 12", nine colors + gold	250.00	700.00
☐ SAMPAN (On Japon), ed. 32, 9" x 12", nine colors + gold, pub JARP	225.00	700.00
☐ SAMPAN, ed. 234, 9" x 12", pub JARP	195.00	700.00
☐ MAYAN TWIN BOY, rel. 1976. ed. 290, 15¾" x 26", pub JARP	150.00	750.00
☐ MAYAN TWIN GIRL, rel. 1976. ed. N/A, 9" x 15"	100.00	700.00
☐ MARCH OF DIMES MOTHER & BABY, rel. 1976. ed. 190, 7" x 12½", litho, pub JARP	75.00	900.00
☐ RENAISSANCE GIRL, rel. 1976. ed. 300, 9¾" x 10", litho, pub JARP	125.00 w/Bk	900.00 w/Bk
☐ RENAISSANCE BOY, rel. 1976. ed. 300, 9" x 12", pub JARP	125.00 w/Bk	900.00
☐ MARGO & CHILD, One print only; stone unfinished, no edition		
☐ MOTHER & BABY, Broken stone	—	—
☐ JAPANESE FAMILY, rel. 1976. ed. 290, 19½" x 26½", litho, pub JARP	165.00	295.00
☐ ULLA, rel. 1976. ed. 295, 13½" x 19¾", litho, pub JARP	150.00	325.00
☐ ELLIE & CHILD, rel. 1976. ed. 295, 12" x 18¼", litho, pub JARP	150.00	1,000.00
☐ SERINA & CHILD (Japon), rel. 1976. ed. 252, 23½" x 30½"	250.00	1,200.00
☐ SERINA & CHILD (Silk), rel. 1976. ed. 35, 23½" x 30½"	350.00	1,200.00
☐ SERINA & CHILD (Paper), rel. 1976. ed. 10, 23½" x 30½", all pub by JARP	175.00	1,200.00
☐ INGRID & CHILD, rel. 1976. ed. 276, 25½" x 37¼", litho, pub JARP	295.00	900.00
☐ SOPHIA & CHILDREN, rel. 1976. ed. 296, 28" x 39"	325.00	2,500.00
☐ ROMANCE (Japon), rel. 1977. ed. 375, 8½" x 10¼", pub JARP	125.00	250.00
☐ SMALL M & B, rel. 1977. ed. 250, 7" x 8¼", litho, pub JARP	125.00	450.00
☐ MAYAN MAN, rel. 1977. ed. 295, 28½" x 41¼", litho, pub JARP	350.00	1,600.00
☐ NEW SINGLE NUDE, rel. 1977. ed. 250, 9" x 14", nine color	150.00	295.00
two color on silk, 9" x 14"	150.00	325.00
two color, 9" x 14", pub JARP	125.00	295.00
☐ MAYAN MOTHER & BABY, rel. 1977. ed. 250, 7¼" x 10½", litho, pub JARP	125.00	700.00
☐ MARGARET & CHILD, rel. 1977. ed. 250, (In Hibel Lithographs, Only), 7½" x 10¼", litho, pub JARP	125.00 w/Bk	650.00
☐ LORRIE & CHILD, rel. 1977. ed. 250, (In Hibel Lithographs, Only), 8" x 10½", litho, pub JARP	125.00 w/Bk	650.00
☐ PEARL & CHILD, rel. 1977. ed. 250, 7" x 9¼", litho, pub JARP	125.00	650.00
☐ JENNIE, rel. 1977. ed. 398, 9" x 12", litho, pub JARP	300.00	2,000.00
☐ MUSEUM SUITE, rel. 1977. ed. 375, consists of the following litho: Tamiko, 9" x 12", 16 colors; Friesland, 20" x 10¾", 11 colors; Martha & Iris, 9" x 12", 14 colors; Klassina, 8½" x 11¾", 21 colors; Okasan to Kodoma, 9" x 12", 16 colors; Piazza San Marco, 11¾" x 17¾", 15 colors, pub JARP	1,900.00	8,900.00
☐ GIRL WITH EARRING, rel. 1977. ed. 375, 6" x 8", in Progressions w/Museum Suite only, pub JARP	—	150.00
☐ GIRL WITH PAINTBRUSH, rel. 1977. ed. 375, 6" x 8", in Progression book, litho, pub JARP	70.00 w/Bk	200.00 w/Bk
☐ BOY WITH CHICKEN, rel. 1977. ed. 375, 7½" x 11", white gold on Japanese rice paper, pub JARP	300.00	475.00
☐ COLETTE & CHILD, rel. 1977. ed. 275, 14½" x 20", litho, pub JARP	195.00	1,400.00
☐ SHOFAR, rel. 1977. ed. 275, 11" x 14", litho, pub JARP	135.00	700.00

	ISSUE PRICE	CURRENT PRICE
☐ **YOUNG RABBI,** rel. 1977. ed. 299, 10″ x 14″, one color	100.00	700.00
two color, 10″ x 14″, litho, pub JARP	100.00	700.00
☐ **LILLIAN & CHILD,** rel. 1977. ed. 150 (I-Japon), 10″ x 13½″		
ed. 152 (II-Japon), smae size, litho, pub JARP	100.00	750.00
☐ **SUZANNA & CHILD,** ed. 290, 14″ x 17¼″, litho, pub JARP	125.00	700.00
☐ **KRISTINA & CHILD,** rel. 1977. ed. 290, 22″ x 30″, eleven colors	265.00	1,200.00
ed. 25, 22″ x 30″, one color Sec. II	145.00	1,200.00
ed. 25, 22″ x 30″, one color Sec. III, litho, all pub by JARP	145.00	1,200.00
☐ **DORIS & CHILDREN,** rel. 1977. ed. 295, 19″ x 24″, litho, pub JARP	275.00	900.00
☐ **FIELDS NEAR CHARTRES,** rel. 1977. ed. 295, 15″ x 21, litho, pub JARP	295.00	450.00
☐ **PARISIAN FLOWER VENDOR,** rel. 1977. ed. 295, 10″ x 14″, litho, pub JARP	165.00	375.00
☐ **MOTHER & CHILD (Children's Hospital),** rel. 1977. ed. 295, 16″ x 20″, litho, pub JARP	195.00	1,000.00
☐ **DUTCH LANDSCAPE,** rel. 1977. ed. 295 on Japon, except 13 on silk; litho on Japon	175.00	325.00
on silk, pub JARP	—	2,500.00
☐ **LARGE MOTHER & TWO CHILDREN,** rel. 1978. ed. 295, 30 were proofs, 7 silks, litho on Rives paper	450.00	800.00
proofs	570.00	725.00
silk, pub JARP	N/A	
☐ **WEDDING OF DAVID AND BATHSHEBA,** rel. 1978. ed. 385, 15″ x 18½″, litho, twelve color + gold, pub JARP	500.00	1,400.00
☐ **WHO IS RICH?,** rel. 1978. ed. N/A, 15″ x 19¾″, litho on Japon, pub JARP	135.00	700.00
☐ **ISRAELI RABBI,** rel. 1978. ed. N/A, litho ten color + gold, pub JARP	450.00	575.00
☐ **AKKO,** rel. 1978. ed. 294, 18″ x 24″, litho, pub JARP	325.00	375.00
☐ **LARGE SINGLE VASE OF FLOWERS,** rel. 1978. ed. 297, 26″ x 36″, litho, pub JARP	375.00	750.00
☐ **JERUSALEM SCENE,** rel. 1978. ed. 298, 30″ x 40″, 18 color + gold, litho, pub JARP	500.00	900.00
☐ **WOMAN W/CHILDREN,** rel. 1978. ed. 296, 30″ x 40″, litho, pub JARP	500.00	850.00
☐ **JAPANESE WOMAN,** rel. 1978. ed. 282, 10″ x 23½″, Torinoko	235.00	900.00
on silk, litho, pub JARP	295.00	900.00
☐ **INDIAN BOWL OF FLOWERS,** rel. 1978. ed. 285, 14″ x 30¼″, litho, pub JARP	375.00	600.00
☐ **ANGELINA,** rel. 1978. ed. 295, 12″ x 14″, two color on Rives	135.00	650.00
one color on Rives, litho, pub JARP	135.00	650.00
☐ **GRECIAN MOTHER & BABY,** rel. 1978. ed. 425, 18½″ x 25″, one color	165.00	700.00
ten color, litho, pub JARP	245.00	700.00
☐ **BOY W/HORN,** rel. 1978. ed. 380, 10¾″ x 14½″, litho, pub JARP	245.00	395.00
☐ **SAMI #11,** rel. 1978. ed. 320, 14½″ x 18½″, one color	195.00	325.00
eleven color, litho, pub JARP	325.00	385.00
☐ **MORNING BOWL OF FLOWERS,** rel. 1978. ed. 350, 17″ x 23″, litho, pub JARP	245.00	450.00
☐ **FELICIA,** rel. 1978. ed. 148, 21″ x 30¾″, litho, sixteen color + two gold, pub JARP	900.00	2,500.00
☐ **ANDREA & CHILD,** rel. 1978. ed. 420, 16¼″ x 22½″, one color	165.00	600.00
seven colors, same size, litho, pub JARP	245.00	700.00
☐ **LENORE,** rel. 1978. ed. N/A, 7½″ x 9½″, six color + gold porcelain, pub JARP	600.00	1,400.00
☐ **DAVID SUITE,** rel. 1978. ed. 375 consisting of seven lithographs (one on porcelain)	3,600.00	5,800.00
☐ **MADCHEN,** rel. 1978. ed. on porcelain, 7¼″ x 9½″, six colors + one gold, pub JARP	600.00	1,200.00
☐ **FAMILY - HORIZONTAL,** rel. 1978. ed. 340, s/n, 28″ x 39″, litho, 2 colors, pub JARP	300.00	700.00
☐ **THREE BALLERINAS,** rel. 1978. ed. 305, s/n, 17½″ x 14½″, litho, 9 colors, pub JARP	210.00	475.00
☐ **BARONESS JOHANNA,** rel. 1978. ed. 310, s/n, 15¼″ x 12¼″, litho, 2 colors, pub JARP	135.00	550.00
☐ **MOTHER AND TWO CHILDREN,** rel. 1978. ed. 319, s/n, 27½″ x 22″, litho, 13 colors, pub JARP	245.00	800.00
☐ **RITA AND CHILD,** rel. 1978. ed. 365, s/n, 24″ x 18″, litho, 10 colors, pub JARP	245.00	700.00
☐ **GREEK FARMERS,** rel. 1978. ed. 310, s/n, 24″ x 19″, litho, 8 colors, pub JARP	265.00	400.00
☐ **GIRL WITH LILLIES,** rel. 1978. ed. 375, s/n, 24¾″ x 20¼″, litho, 11 colors, pub JARP	275.00	800.00
☐ **LARGE FLORAL,** rel. 1978. ed. 295, s/n, 30″ x 40″, litho, 15 colors, pub JARP	525.00	1,000.00
☐ **GIRL WITH HAT,** rel. 1978. ed. 310, s/n, 14″ x 12½″, litho, 6 colors, pub JARP	250.00	1,500.00

	ISSUE PRICE	CURRENT PRICE
☐ **MONICA AND CHILD,** rel. 1978. ed. 398, s/n, 24¾" x 20½", litho, 8 colors, pub JARP	245.00	800.00
☐ **TRIO,** rel. 1979. ed. 360, s/n, 21" x 30¼", litho, 9 colors, pub JARP	395.00	475.00
☐ **MOTHER & TWO CHILDREN,** rel. 1979. ed. 265, s/n, 17" x 13½", litho, 2 colors, on Rives	145.00	650.00
on Japon, pub JARP	175.00	650.00
☐ **TERRE,** rel. 1979. ed. 315, s/n, 12" x 9", pub JARP	135.00	650.00
☐ **IN MY GARDEN/RAIN THAT FALLS,** rel. 1979. ed. 375, s/n, 25" x 17¾", pub JARP .	*1,050.00 w/book	1,150.00
☐ **SWAYING GRASSES/SNOWMAN,** rel. 1979. ed. 375, s/n, 25" x 17¾", pub JARP ...	*1,050.00 w/book	1,150.00
*One set of the above prints was included with the purchase of the book titled "Sundial Ticking"		
☐ **DAVID THE SHEPHERD,** rel. 1979. ed. 150, s/n, 41" x 30", litho, 8 colors + gold, pub JARP	1,650.00	1,875.00
☐ **MARIA & CHILDREN,** rel. 1979. ed. 352, s/n, 11" x 9½", litho, 3 colors, pub JARP ..	135.00	500.00
☐ **SONDRA,** rel. 1979. ed. 314, s/n, 20¾" x 16½", litho, 2 colors on Japon	325.00	750.00
10 colors on Rives	295.00	900.00
2 colors on Rives, Barcham, pub JARP	295.00	750.00
☐ **DAVID BATHSHEBA & SOLOMON,** rel. 1979. ed. 371, s/n, 18" x 16", litho, 10 colors + gold, pub JARP	500.00	1,050.00
☐ **AKIKO & CHILDREN,** rel. 1979. ed. 335, s/n, 29¾" x 22", litho, 12 colors + gold ...	450.00	1,600.00
litho, 3 colors on Rives, pub JARP	450.00	1,400.00
☐ **MIRIAM & CHILDREN,** rel. 1979. ed. 359, s/n, 38½" x 27", litho, 8 colors on Rives ..	495.00	1,350.00
3 colors on Rives, pub JARP	295.00	1,100.00
☐ **INGA,** rel. 1979. ed. 374, s/n, 10" x 8½", pub JARP	135.00	265.00
☐ **ANNA,** rel. 1979. ed. 310, s/n, 16" x 11", pub JARP	150.00	400.00
☐ **FRANCESCA,** rel. 1979. ed. 335, s/n, 14⅝" x 12", litho, 6 colors, pub JARP	195.00	600.00
☐ **PIERRE,** rel. 1979. ed. 335, s/n, 13½" x 12", litho, 6 colors, pub JARP	195.00	600.00
☐ **MAN WITH HOE,** rel. 1979. ed. 350, s/n, 38⅝" x 27½", litho, 7 colors, pub JARP ...	495.00	700.00
☐ **YOUNG MANCHU,** rel. 1979. ed. 350, s/n, 17¼" x 12", litho, 7 colors plus gold background	335.00	850.00
litho, 11¾" x 9" on Japon	295.00	850.00
litho, 17⅜" x 12", silk background + gold	375.00	850.00
litho, 11¾" x 9", silk background only	350.00	900.00
7 colors plus gold on Bavarian Porcelain	850.00	1,600.00
total edition pub JARP		
☐ **PETRA MIT KINDER,** rel. 1979. ed. 320, s/n, 29¾" x 22", pub JARP	345.00	2,500.00
☐ **VICTORIA,** rel. 1979. ed. 310, s/n, 17" x 10¾", litho, 3 colors, pub JARP	165.00	500.00
☐ **VICTORIA,** rel. 1979. ed. 9¼" x 6½", pub JARP	*	
*This litho was not offered for sale		
Gift - Collectors Society Meeting, Monaco, July 13, 1979.		
☐ **NIWA-NO-CHO,** rel. 1979. ed. 300, s/n, 12" x 9", litho, 11 colors + gold on Rives ...	375.00	900.00
same as above on silk, pub JARP	395.00	900.00
☐ **KRISTA & CHILD,** rel. 1979. ed. 400, s/n, 13" x 10½", 7 colors + gold on Bavarian Porcelain, pub JARP	850.00	1,250.00
☐ **INTERNATIONAL YEAR OF THE CHILD SUITE,** rel. 1979. ed. 420, s/n, 11⅞" x 9⅝", CHILD OF SWEDEN, 7 colors + 2 golds; CHILD OF ITALY, 8 colors + 1 gold; CHILD OF THAILAND, 8 colors + 2 golds; CHILD OF PORTUGAL, 7 colors, pub JARP	900.00	3,000.00
☐ **RENOIR'S GARDEN,** rel. 1980. ed. 330, s/n, 22½" x 19", pub JARP	350.00	500.00
☐ **VICKIE & CHILDREN,** rel. 1980. ed. 395, s/n, 20½" x 15½", pub JARP	245.00	600.00
☐ **MICHELLE & NINA,** rel. 1980. ed. 280, s/n, 11¾" x 8¾", pub JARP	195.00	275.00
☐ **SAMUEL THE KINGMAKER,** rel. 1980. ed. 338, s/n, 23" x 20½", pub JARP	275.00	750.00
☐ **NORA,** rel. 1980. ed. 394, s/n, 13" x 12¼", pub JARP	175.00	400.00
☐ **MILDRED,** rel. 1980. ed. 383, s/n, 10¼" x 5¼", pub JARP	135.00	300.00
☐ **DELORES,** rel. 1980. ed. 383, s/n, 10¼" x 5¼", pub JARP	135.00	300.00
☐ **HARU,** rel. 1980. ed. 397, s/n, 10¼" x 5¼", pub JARP	50.00	195.00
☐ **UME,** rel. 1980. ed. 390, S/N, 10¼" x 5¼", pub JARP	135.00	195.00
☐ **JOSEPH,** rel. 1980. ed. 335, s/n, 19" x 14", pub JARP	495.00	900.00
☐ **FLOWER SONG,** rel. 1980. ed. 289, s/n, 22" x 16", pub JARP	375.00	900.00
☐ **THAI PRINCESS,** rel. 1980. ed. 395, s/n, 12¼" x 9½", pub JARP	375.00	900.00
hand applied gold on Rives	495.00	1,000.00

	ISSUE PRICE	CURRENT PRICE
☐ GUATEMALA MOTHER & BABY, rel. 1980. ed. 325, s/n, 10″ x 8″, pub JARP	295.00	350.00
☐ PAMELA, rel. 1980. ed. 395, s/n, 11″ x 9″, pub JARP	295.00	375.00
☐ PRINTEMPS, rel. 1980. ed. 420, s/n, 15¾″ x 10″, pub JARP	250.00	300.00
☐ ALICIA, rel. 1980. ed. 400, s/n, 16½″ x 15″, pub JARP	275.00	600.00
☐ TINA, rel. 1980. ed. 200, s/n, 24″ x 19¾″, pub JARP	750.00	1,200.00
☐ CAROL & JENNIE, rel. 1980. ed. 428, s/n, 21″ x 14″, pub JARP	275.00	650.00
☐ MATTHEW, rel. 1980. ed. 392, s/n, 16″ x 15″, pub JARP	450.00	525.00
☐ CHERYLL & WENDY, rel. 1980. ed. 100, s/n, 24″ x 19¼″, pub JARP	3,900.00	8,000.00
☐ OF WISDOM, rel. 1980. ed. 385, s/n, consists of FAMILY, 16½″ x 8½″, CHILDHOOD, 17″ x 10½″, AGE OF BEAUTY, 17″ x 10½″, AGE OF WISDOM, 16½″ x 8½″, pub JARP	1,200.00	2,400.00
☐ JAPANESE GIRLS, rel. 1980. ed. 390, 26″ x 38¼″, pub EHC	675.00	750.00
☐ GINA AND CHILD, rel. 1980. ed. 396, 21″ x 16″, pub EHC	395.00	450.00
☐ THE COMMANDMENT, rel. 1980. ed. 394, s/n, 14¾″ x 18¾″, pub EHC	250.00	295.00
☐ HOPE, rel. 1980. ed. 396, 14¼″ x 14¼″, pub EHC	400.00	550.00
☐ CHO CHO SAN, rel. 1980. ed. 396, s/n, 29½″ x 9¾″, pub EHC		
Series I & II Barcham	450.00	650.00
Series III, IV Torinoko	450.00	700.00
Series V, VI, VII & VIII Silk	500.00	900.00
☐ LEONA & BABY, rel. 1980. ed. 396, two colors, s/n, 29″ x 19″, pub EHC	425.00	500.00
six colors, II, III Rives	475.00	550.00
☐ KOW LOON PEACH TREES, rel. 1980. ed. 340, s/n, 27½″ x 39½″, pub EHC	650.00	675.00
☐ ETERNAL LOVE, rel. 1980. ed. 399, s/n, one color, 9¾″ x 5¼″, pub EHC	295.00	475.00
ten colors + gold on rives	475.00	650.00
ten colors + gold on Bavarian porcelain	850.00	900.00
☐ THAI FAMILY, rel. 1981. ed. 340, s/n, 13 colors, 16¼″ x 10¾″, pub EHC	225.00	235.00
☐ HADASSAH - THE GENERATIONS, rel. 1981. ed. 408, 8 colors + gold, 21½″ x 17″, pub EHC	475.00	475.00
☐ LA LECHE - NURSING MOTHER, rel. 1981. ed. 379, 7 colors + gold, 20½″ x 16″, pub EHC	395.00	395.00
☐ VINEYARD, rel. 1981. ed. 396, s/n, 17½″ x 13½″, I Rives, pub EHC	425.00	475.00
☐ THE FIO, rel. 1981. eleven colors + gold colors, ed. 354, s/n, 17⅝″ x 11⅝″, I thru VIII on Rives, pub EHC	445.00	—
eleven colors + gold, IX on Bavarian Porcelain	1,400.00	—
☐ THE FIRST COUPLE, rel. 1981. ed. 404, s/n, pub EHC	—	—
☐ one color on Rives	225.00	400.00
☐ eight colors + gold on Rives	425.00	450.00
☐ MARILYN & CHILDREN, rel. 1981. ed. 318, s/n, 25″ x 36″, pub EHC	695.00	750.00
☐ THE LITTLE EMPEROR, rel. 1981. ed. 275, s/n, 41½″ x 27½″, pub EHC	1,000.00	1,650.00
☐ THAI DANCERS, rel. 1981. ed. 395, s/n, 12″ x 18½″, pub EHC		
I, II, III on Silk	475.00	750.00
IV, V, VI Torinoko	475.00	500.00
VII, VIII, IX on Rives	425.00	600.00
X on Bavarian Porcelain	1,200.00	1,200.00
☐ YASMIN, rel. 1981. ed. 319, s/n, 8¾″ x 16¼″, pub EHC	225.00	250.00
☐ NINA, rel. 1981. ed. 269, s/n, 8¾″ x 16¼″, pub EHC	225.00	250.00
☐ MIKA, rel. 1981. ed. 295, s/n, seven colors + gold, 7½″ x 9¾″, on Rives	325.00	375.00
	w/book	w/book
ed. 100 on Bavarian Porcelain	750.00	1,000.00
	w/book	
☐ LITTLE EMPRESS, rel. 1981. ed. 319, s/n, II thru XVII, 41½″ x 27⅜″, pub EHC	1,000.00	1,250.00
one color I on Rives	500.00	650.00
☐ MAGDA, rel. 1981. ed. 252, s/n, 17″ x 12⅛″, pub EHC	195.00	195.00
☐ PRELUDE, rel. 1981. ed. 312, s/n, 9½″ x 4½″, two colors, I Hibel watermark	295.00	295.00
four colors + gold, II Hibel watermark	295.00	295.00
four colors, III Hibel watermark	265.00	265.00
☐ PIROUETTE, rel. 1981. ed. 142, s/n, 12″ x 9″, one color on Silk, pub EHC	195.00	195.00
two colors, 14¾″ x 10⅞″ on Japon	195.00	195.00
two colors, 14¾″ x 10⅞″ on Rives	195.00	195.00
☐ PAS DE DEUX, rel. 1981. ed. 256, s/n, 11⅜″ x 11⅝″, I thru IV on Rives	195.00	195.00
100 on Bavarian Porcelain	195.00	195.00

	ISSUE PRICE	CURRENT PRICE
☐ ABRAHAM, rel. 1981. ed. 306. s/n, 25⅝" x 20¾", pub EHC	375.00	375.00
three colors, VII Torinoko	295.00	295.00
two colors, VIII Torinoko, pub EHC	275.00	275.00
☐ HENRI, rel. 1981. ed. 314, five colors, 16½" x 8¾", pub EHC	235.00	235.00
one color, II on Rives	175.00	175.00
five colors, III Hibel watermark, 14¼" x 8"	265.00	265.00
☐ RENATA, rel. 1981. ed. 314, s/n, 16½" x 8¾", four colors, I on Rives	235.00	235.00
one color, 13¼" x 8⅜", III Hibel watermark, pub EHC	175.00	175.00
four colors, 16½" x 8¾", pub EHC	265.00	265.00
☐ INFANTA, rel. 1981. ed. 315, s/n, 8 colors + gold, 21" x 14⅜", I, II, III on Rives	445.00	675.00
one color, 18½" x 11⅞", IV on Japon, pub EHC	210.00	325.00
☐ CORA AND JULIE, rel. 1981. ed. 210, s/n, 6⅛" x 4", pub EHC	110.00	175.00
☐ DAWN, rel. 1981. ed. 205, s/n, 6½" x 4½", pub EHC	110.00	110.00
☐ JACKLIN AND CHILD, rel. 1981. ed. 197, s/n, 5½" x 3⅝", pub EHC	110.00	250.00
☐ JAPANESE DANCERS, rel. 1981. ed. 206, s/n, 5⅞" x 4⅛", pub EHC	110.00	110.00
☐ AURIE, rel. 1981. five colors, ed. 317, s/n, 16¼" x 14", V, VI on Rives	320.00	320.00
five colors, III, IV on japon	350.00	350.00
one color, 12¾" x 8½", I on japon	220.00	220.00
one color, 12¼" x 8½" on Rives, pub EHC	200.00	200.00
☐ SUSAN AND CHILDREN, rel. 1981. seven colors, ed. 397, s/n, 15¼" x 11¼", II, III on Rives	335.00	375.00
one color, 12" x 9", I on silk	265.00	395.00
seven colors, 12" x 9", IV on Bavarian Porcelain, pub EHC	795.00	850.00
☐ GLORIA, rel. 1981. one color, ed. 288, 10¾" x 10¾", I, II on Rives	195.00	250.00
two colors, 14¾" x 11" on japon	215.00	350.00
two colors, 14¾" x 11", IV on Rives, pub EHC	195.00	350.00
☐ ROBERTA & ROBERTO, rel. 1981. ed. 344, s/n, 6¾" x 6", pub EHC	155.00	175.00
☐ TREE OF LIFE, rel. 1981. eight colors + gold, ed. 350, s/n, 11½" x 17½", I thru IV on Rives, pub EHC	395.00	425.00
eight colors + gold, VI on Bavarian Porcelain	1,400.00	1,500.00
☐ KIMI-NO, rel. 1981. eleven colors + gold colors, ed. 354, s/n, 17⅞" x 11⅝" thru VIII on Rives, pub EHC	445.00	725.00
eleven colors + gold, IX on Bavarian Porcelain	1,400.00	1,500.00
☐ MAID OF KEZAR, rel. 1981. ed. 385, s/n, 9⅞" x 13¾", found in Fay Berg's Cookbook, pub EHC	225.00	235.00
☐ JOELLE, rel. 1982. ten colors, ed. 348, 14⅛" x 12", I thru III on Rives, pub EHC	295.00	750.00
three colors, IV on Rives	265.00	750.00
two colors, V on Rives	225.00	750.00
☐ KELLY, rel. 1982. nine colors, ed. 347, 14¼" x 12", I thru III on Rives, pub EHC	320.00	750.00
two colors, IV on Rives	225.00	750.00
☐ TRUDY, rel. 1982. five colors, ed. 305, s/n, 14¾" x 12", I thru VI on Rives, pub EHC .	265.00	265.00
two colors, VI-VIII on Rives	225.00	225.00
☐ TUSCAN FIELDS, rel. 1982, eight colors, ed. 394, s/n, 18" x 18¾", I thru VI on Rives, pub EHC	375.00	375.00
eight colors, VII thru XII on japon	395.00	395.00
☐ THE FAMILY SUITE 1982, rel. 1982. ed. 396, s/n, consisting of SOWING, nine colors, 12½" x 9" RIPENING, eight colors + gold, 9" x 12½" HARVESTING, nine colors + gold, 12½" x 9" THROUGH THE GENERATIONS, two colors, 9" x 12½", pub EHC	800.00	1,080.00
☐ PORTRAIT OF A FAMILY, rel. 1982. ed. 330, s/n, 40½" x 28¾", pub EHC	750.00	750.00
☐ LITTLE RAJAH AND THE UNICORNS, rel. 1982. ed. 319, s/n, 41¾" x 29½", pub EHC	1,000.00	1,000.00
☐ KATRINA & CHILDREN, rel. 1982. ed. 329, s/n, 29" x 19½", pub EHC	345.00	600.00
☐ ZORINA, rel. 1982. ed. 329, s/n, 21" x 13¾", pub EHC	295.00	350.00
☐ TONI, rel. 1982. ed. 313, s/n, 16⅜" x 8⅝", pub EHC	235.00	295.00
☐ JANUARY, rel. 1982. ed. 319, s/n, 15½" x 13¼", pub EHC	295.00	350.00
☐ RENA AND RACHEL, rel. 1982. ed. 329, s/n, 15½" x 13¼", pub EHC	345.00	400.00
☐ NARO-SAN, rel. 1982. ed. 322, s/n, 24" x 17¾", pub EHC	275.00	400.00
☐ BETTINA AND CHILDREN, rel. 1982. ed. 300, s/n, 31½" x 18¼", pub EHC	310.00	650.00
☐ HELVA, rel. 1982. ed. 214, s/n, 16⅜" x 8⅝", pub EHC	235.00	235.00

	ISSUE PRICE	CURRENT PRICE
☐ WILLA AND CHILD, rel. 1982. ed. 361, s/n, 8″ x 6¾″, pub EHC	195.00	195.00
☐ LYDIA, rel. 1982. ed. 298, s/n, 12½″ x 11″ pub EHC	195.00	325.00
☐ FAMILY OF THE MOUNTAIN LAKE, rel. 1982. ed. 305, s/n, 35″ x 24″, pub EHC	395.00	895.00
☐ FLORA, rel. 1982. ed. 302, s/n, 30½″ x 22″, pub EHC	425.00	425.00
☐ LOTTE AND HER CHILDREN, rel. 1983. ed. 358, s/n, 37″ x 27″, pub EHC	695.00	695.00
☐ SONJA AND DIANA, rel. 1983. ed. 230, s/n, 15″ x 10″, pub EHC	215.00	215.00
☐ NICOLE WITH BABY, rel. 1983. ed. 297, s/n, 16″ x 11″, pub EHC	250.00	250.00
☐ ROSA AND CHILD, rel. 1983. ed. 310, s/n, 13″ x 18″, pub EHC	175.00	175.00
☐ BECCA, rel. 1983. ed. 410, s/n, 12″ x 14½″, pub EHC	165.00	165.00
☐ OLD FRIENDS, rel. 1983. ed. 300, s/n, 17½″ x 12″, pub EHC	215.00	215.00
☐ VALERIE AND CHILDREN, rel. 1983. ed. 400, s/n, 13″ x 21¼″, pub EHC	295.00	295.00
☐ MICHAEL'S FAMILY, rel. 1983. ed. 398, s/n, 36″ x 26″, pub EHC	495.00	495.00
☐ FAMILY ON THE TAKAIDO ROAD, rel. 1983. ed. 395, s/n, 35″ x 25″, pub EHC	550.00	675.00
☐ NATURE STUDY, rel. 1983. ed. 330, s/n, 5⅞″ x 5½″, pub EHC	100.00	100.00
☐ SOLO, rel. 1983. ed. 340, s/n, 6″ x 6¼″, pub EHC	100.00	100.00
☐ MEDITATION, rel. 1983. ed. 345, s/n, 3¾″ x 5½″, pub EHC	100.00	100.00
☐ TEMPLE VISIT, rel. 1983. ed. 345, s/n, 6¼″ x 5⅜″, pub EHC	100.00	100.00
☐ AMANDA, rel. 1983. ed. 340, s/n, 6″ x 5⅞″, pub EHC	100.00	100.00
☐ SWIFT RIDER, rel. 1983. ed. 330, s/n, 6⅞″ x 7⅛″, pub EHC	100.00	100.00
☐ ORIENTAL DAYDREAM, rel. 1983. ed. 382, s/n, 16″ x 13½″, pub EHC	275.00	275.00
☐ PRIMA, rel. 1983. ed. 186, s/n, 17″ x 10½″, pub EHC	165.00	175.00
☐ CHINESE VASES, rel. 1983. ed. 366, s/n, 29½″ x 41½″, pub EHC	595.00	595.00
☐ NAVA AND CHILDREN, rel. 1983. ed. 385, s/n, 30″ x 20¼″, pub EHC	385.00	385.00
☐ ANTHONY, rel. 1984. ed. 313, s/n, 11″ x 9″, pub EHC	175.00	—
☐ THE CARESS, rel. 1984. ed. 430, s/n, 23⅜″ x 17⅛″, pub EHC	425.00	—
☐ DARENE AND CHILD, rel. 1984. ed. 331, s/n, 16″ x 13″, pub EHC	225.00	—
☐ SANDY AND CHILDREN, rel. 1984. ed. 419, s/n, 18¼″ x 25⅞″, pub EHC	465.00	—
☐ JAPANESE ROSE, rel. 1984. ed. 295, s/n, 29″ x 9⅞″, pub EHC	295.00	—
☐ SHEILA AND CHILD, rel. 1984. ed. 209, s/n, 9″ x 5½″, pub EHC	160.00	—
☐ THE GLEANERS, rel. 1984. ed. 209, s/n, 7¼″ x 12¾″, pub EHC	160.00	—
☐ NATASHA AND CHILDREN, rel. 1984. ed. 308, s/n, 16″ x 13″, pub EHC	175.00	—
☐ GERARD, rel. 1984. ed. 200, s/n, 12¼″ x 9⅞″, pub EHC	325.00	—
☐ CLAIRE, rel. 1984. ed. 206, s/n, 18⅞″ x 14⅝″, pub EHC	395.00	—
☐ WENDY WITH HAT, rel. 1984. ed. 308, s/n, 18″ x 12″, pub EHC	495.00	—
☐ WILLIE AND TWO QUAN XINS, rel. 1984. ed. 289, s/n, 10⅛″ x 16″, pub EHC	365.00	—
☐ APRIL'S CHILD, rel. 1984. ed. 393, s/n, 10″ x 15″, pub EHC	395.00	—
☐ MAI CHOY, rel. 1984. ed. 349, s/n, 24″ x 10″, pub EHC	195.00	—
☐ CHILD OF THE EAST, rel. 1984. ed. 277, s/n, 17¾″ x 13″, pub EHC	325.00	—
☐ HEIDI, rel. 1984. ed. 304, s/n, 16″ x 10½″, pub EHC	325.00	—
☐ JENNIFER AND CHILDREN, rel. 1984. ed. 318, s/n, 24″ x 18″, pub EHC	410.00	—
☐ TONETTE, rel. 1984. ed. 319, 17½″ x 11″, pub EHC	300.00	—
☐ ARIELLE AND AMY, rel. 1985. ed. 275, s/n, size N/A, pub EHC	325.00	—
☐ BEVERLY AND CHILD, rel. 1985. ed. 216, s/n, size N/A, pub EHC	160.00	—
☐ BOY WITH TURBAN, rel. 1985. ed. 348, s/n, size N/A, pub EHC	325.00	—
☐ CELESTE, rel. 1985. ed. 256, s/n, size N/A, pub EHC	175.00	—
☐ DES FLEURS ROUGES, rel. 1985. ed. 298, s/n, size N/A, pub EHC	245.00	—
☐ DREAM SKETCHBOOK, rel. 1985. ed. 298, s/n, size N/A, pub EHC	195.00	—
☐ FAMILY IN THE FIELD, rel. 1985. ed. 376, s/n, size N/A, pub EHC	420.00	—
☐ FIELDS NEAR GRENOBLE, rel. 1985. ed. 313, s/n, size N/A, pub EHC	495.00	—
☐ MRS. HSU, rel. 1985. ed. 399, s/n, size N/A, pub EHC	350.00	—
☐ SARAH AND JOSHUA, rel. 1985. ed. 343, s/n, size N/A, pub EHC	475.00	—
☐ SETSU, rel. 1985. ed. 337, s/n, size N/A, pub EHC	450.00	—

The above listing represents the entire edition of Edna Hibel original lithographs. Recently The Edna Hibel Corporation introduced a line of limited edition reproductions each representing a photo-mechanical reproduction of an original lithograph and each was issued in an edition of 1,000 prints.

The following is a listing of these prints. Prices shown are for framed prints. With each print three different framings were available, therefore, prices may vary depending on the type framing the collector selected.

	FRAMED PRICE RANGE	
☐ **ESTHER,** ed. 1,000, s/o, 35½" x 23¾", pub EHC	195.00	325.00
☐ **MEXICAN BEGGAR,** ed. 1,000, s/n, 39¼" x 28", pub EHC	295.00	420.00
☐ **LAMB OF KNOSSOS,** ed. 1,000, s/n, 35¾" x 25¾", pub EHC	195.00	315.00
☐ **JOSEPH,** ed. 1,000, s/n, 47" x 27", pub EHC	295.00	345.00
☐ **CANALE IN VENICE,** ed. 1,000, s/n, 29¾" x 17¾", pub EHC	180.00	265.00
☐ **TOMO,** ed. 1,000, s/n, 30" x 18", pub EHC	155.00	235.00
☐ **BALLERINAS,** ed. 1,000, s/n, 40" x 25", pub EHC		295.00
☐ **PATTY,** ed. 1,000, s/n, 22" x 19", pub EHC	175.00	185.00
☐ **BLACK BERET,** ed. 1,000, s/n, 18" x 31", pub EHC	165.00	195.00
☐ **RED BERRIES,** ed. 1,000, s/n, 17½" x 29½", pub EHC	155.00	265.00
☐ **JENNIE,** ed. 1,000, s/n, 9" x 14", pub EHC	100.00	130.00
☐ **SHIZUE,** ed. 1,000, s/n, 28½" x 19¼", pub EHC	250.00	450.00
☐ **ULLA & CHILD,** ed. 1,000, s/n, 9¼" x 21¼", pub EHC	110.00	135.00
☐ **A TALL ROSE,** ed. 1,000, s/n, 30" x 9¾", pub EHC	135.00	210.00
☐ **LOVERS OF FLORENCE,** ed. 1,000, s/n, 15" x 22½", on satin	150.00	210.00
☐ ed. 1,000, s/n, on paper, pub EHC	95.00	160.00
☐ **THE BLUE VASE,** ed. 1,000, s/n, 25" x 13½", pub EHC	155.00	220.00
☐ **REHEARSAL,** ed. 1,000, s/n, 16" x 12½", pub EHC	115.00	180.00
☐ **THE GOLDEN HORN,** ed. 1,000, s/n, 24" x 19", pub EHC	125.00	140.00
☐ **THE FLAUTIST,** ed. 1,000, s/n, 12" x 15", on satin	150.00	180.00
☐ ed. 1,000, s/n, 12" x 15", on paper, pub EHC	115.00	170.00
☐ **LIEVE FROM BELGIUM,** ed. 1,000, s/n, 34" x 16½", pub EHC	145.00	275.00
☐ **VANESSA AND CHILDREN,** ed. 1,000, s/n, 18¾" x 14½", pub EHC	145.00	270.00
☐ **MONIQUE,** ed. 1,000, s/n, 9¼" x 10¼", pub EHC	125.00	160.00
☐ **ORIENTAL CHILD,** ed. 1,000, s/n, 10¼" x 9¼", pub EHC	135.00	195.00
☐ **MARGARET AND NICKI,** ed. 1,000, s/n, 18" x 10¼", pub EHC	150.00	185.00
☐ **DUET,** ed. 1,000, s/n, 15¼" x 20¼", pub EHC	195.00	225.00
☐ **FLOWER GIRL,** ed. 1,000, s/n, 20" x 11", pub EHC	130.00	225.00
☐ **VOLLRNDAM,** ed. 1,000, s/n, 12¼" x 18¼", pub EHC	135.00	195.00
☐ **KLASINA FROM FRIESLAND,** ed. 1,000, s/n, 10¼" x 8¼", pub EHC	130.00	150.00
☐ **GRANDMOTHER,** ed. 1,000, s/n, 12" x 9¾", pub EHC	135.00	150.00
☐ **MOTHER AND TWO CHILDREN,** ed. 1,000, s/n, 14¾" x 12", pub EHC	125.00	165.00
☐ **MARIANNE AND DANIELLE,** ed. 1,000, s/n, 12¼" x 11", pub EHC	140.00	185.00
☐ **HEIDI,** ed. 1,000, s/n, 12¼" x 8¼", pub EHC	115.00	140.00
☐ **PATRICIA AND BABY,** ed. 1,000, s/n, 9¼" x 10¼", pub EHC	110.00	125.00
☐ **FRENCH FIELDS,** ed. 1,000, s/n, 23¼" x 30¼", pub EHC	185.00	210.00
☐ **FLOWERS,** ed. 1,000, s/n, 20¼" x 24", pub EHC	170.00	180.00
☐ **GRAPE PICKERS OF ALSACE,** ed. 1,000, s/n, 10¼" x 14¼", pub EHC	135.00	175.00
☐ **VIVIAN AND CHILD,** ed. 1,000, s/n, 21" x 15¾", pub EHC	165.00	525.00
☐ **BEATRICE AND BABY,** ed. 1,000, s/n, 30" x 23½", pub EHC	160.00	260.00
☐ **HANNA AND HER TWO CHILDREN,** ed. 1,000, s/n, 30¼" x 36", pub EHC	235.00	350.00
☐ **STEPHANIE AND CHILD,** ed. 1,000, s/n, 37" x 28", pub EHC	435.00	750.00
☐ **MICHIO,** ed. 1,000, s/n, 23½" x 17½", pub EHC	165.00	225.00
☐ **GREECE,** ed. 1,000, s/n, 23½" x 47", pub EHC	325.00	385.00
☐ **LINDA AND ELIZABETH,** ed. 1,000, s/n, 21½" x 19½", pub EHC	185.00	195.00
☐ **REJOICE,** ed. 2,000, n/o, 9⅛" x 19¼", pub EHC	90.00	120.00
☐ **MOTHER AND TWO CHILDREN,** ed. 2,000, n/o, 9⅛" x 6¼", pub EHC	75.00	95.00
☐ **FOUR VASES OF FLOWERS,** ed. 2,000, n/o, 10¾" x 7⅞", pub EHC	75.00	85.00
☐ **VASES OF FLOWERS,** ed. 2,000, n/o, 10¾" x 7⅞", pub EHC	95.00	100.00
☐ **BLUE VASES OF FLOWERS,** ed. 2,000, n/o, 12⅜" x 6⅞", pub EHC	75.00	95.00
☐ **RED HEAD,** ed. 2,000, s/o, 9½" x 6⅝", pub EHC	75.00	120.00

CARDWELL S. HIGGINS

THEMES: Varied

BACKGROUND: Mr. Higgins was most well known for his painting of the famous World War II U.S.O. poster, showing a soldier, a U.S.O. volunteer, and a sailor

EDUCATION: National Academy of Design, Art Students League

GALLERY/DISTRIBUTOR: Cardwell S. Higgins Studio

	ISSUE PRICE	CURRENT PRICE
☐ **SIAMESE DANCERS,** rel. 1980. ed. 500, s/n, 19½″ x 14¼″, pub CSH	50.00	—
☐ **DRAGON LADY,** rel. 1980. ed. 500, s/n, 19½″ x 14¼″, pub CSH	50.00	—
☐ **THE CIRCLE OF LIFE,** rel. 1980. ed. 500, s/n, 19½″ x 16½″, pub CSH	50.00	*200.00
☐ **SLAVES OF DESIRE,** rel. 1980. ed. 500, s/n, 19½″ x 16″, pub CSH	50.00	—
☐ **A DELIGHTFUL PAGE IN THE RECORD OF MY EXISTENCE,** rel. 1980. ed. 500, s/n, 19½″ x 13″, pub CSH	50.00	—
☐ **THE ELEMENTS INVOLVED,** rel. 1980. ed. 500, s/n, 19½″ x 13″, pub CSH	50.00	—

*Note: Bid and sold price for the Circle of Life Print at public television Channel 2 art auction, 1980

DRAGON LADY *by Cardwell S. Higgins*

ROBYN HINDMAN

THEMES: Landscapes, seascapes

MEDIUM: Serigraphs

STYLE: Contemporary

GALLERY/DISTRIBUTOR: Unique Graphics

	ISSUE PRICE	CURRENT PRICE
☐ **FLIGHT,** rel. 1984. ed. 300, s/n, 23″ x 29″, pub UG	60.00	—
☐ **METAMORPHOSIS I,** 1984. ed. 300, s/n, 23″ x 29″, pub UG	50.00	—
☐ **METAMORPHOSIS II,** 1984. ed. 300, s/n, 23″ x 29″, pub UG	50.00	—
☐ **TENNESSEE MOON,** 1984. ed. 300, s/n, 23″ x 29″, pub UG	70.00	—
☐ **OF THE SILVERY MOON,** 1985. ed. 300, s/n, 23″ x 29″, pub UG	70.00	—
☐ **TILL TOMORROW,** 1985. ed. 250, s/n, 11″ x 29″, pub UG	35.00	—

SOFTLY IN THE EAR OF THE WARRIOR by Jack Hines

JACK HINES

THEMES: Western art

MEDIUM: An excellent draftsman with a flawless technique, Hines fits media to the subject

GALLERY/DISTRIBUTOR: Mill Pond Press, Inc.

COMMENTS: The artist is involved in the contemporary "Buckskinning" movement of America (dedicated to preserving and recruiting the mountain man tradition)

	ISSUE PRICE	CURRENT PRICE
☐ MEMORIES OF A MAN, rel. 1979. ed. 950, s/n, 24½" x 20", pub MPPI	65.00	—
☐ THE FALLEN SHIELD, rel. 1979. ed. 950, s/n, 29½" x 19", pub MPPI	95.00	—
☐ THE TASTE OF THE WARRIOR SPIRIT, rel. 1979. ed. 950, s/n, 20½" x 27½", pub MPPI	75.00	—
☐ WHEN THE EAGLE SPOKE, rel. 1979. ed. 950, s/n, 24½" x 20", pub MPPI	65.00	135.00
☐ ETERNITY IS IN THE MOUNTAINS, rel. 1980. ed. 950, s/n, 20½" x 27½", pub MPPI	75.00	—
☐ SOFTLY IN THE EAR OF THE WARRIOR, rel. 1980. ed. 950, s/n, 25½" x 20", pub MPPI	70.00	—
☐ THE ECHOES SOUND SOFTLY, rel. 1980. ed. 950, s/n, 25½" x 20", pub MPPI	70.00	—
☐ WHILE YOUNG HANDS LEARN, rel. 1980. ed. 950, s/n, 25½" x 19¾", pub MPPI ..	75.00	—
☐ EVENING ENCOUNTER AT INDEPENDENCE ROCK, rel. 1981. ed. 950, s/n, 20" x 30", pub SCG	80.00	—
☐ FORT LARAMIE . . . GATHERING OF THE TRIBES . . . 1851, rel. 1981. ed. 950, s/n, 20" x 30", pub SCG	80.00	—
☐ THE PERILS OF JEDIDIAH SMITH, rel. 1981. ed. 1,350, s/n, 20" x 30", pub SCG ...	50.00	Sold Out
☐ FIRST DAY IN CAMP, rel. 1982. ed. 1,000, s/n, 13" x 26⅝", pub SCG	45.00	—
☐ PORTUGEE PHILLIP'S RIDE . . . 1866, rel. 1982. ed. 500, s/n, 20" x 30", pub SCG .	85.00	—
☐ RIDIN' TO GREENUP, rel. 1982. ed. 950, s/n, 17⅛" x 22⅞", pub MPPI	85.00	—

WILLIAM HOLLYWOOD

THEMES: Wildlife art

MEDIUM: Oil

EDUCATION: Belfast College of Art

MEMBERSHIPS: Society of Animal Artists

MUSEUMS/COLLECTIONS: His paintings are in private collections in Ireland, the United States, and Great Britain

GALLERY/DISTRIBUTOR: Sportsman's Edge, Ltd.

	ISSUE PRICE	CURRENT PRICE
☐ OCTOBER SHOW-WOODCOCK, rel. 1979. ed. 500, s/n, 19½" x 27½", pub SEL ...	125.00	—
☐ PINTAILS ON A QUIET INLET, rel. 1976. ed. 510, s/n, 16" x 24", pub SEL	95.00	—
☐ PHEASANT, rel. 1969. ed. 500, s/n, 19¼" x 15¼", pub SEL	95.00	—

	ISSUE PRICE	CURRENT PRICE
☐ RISING MALLARDS, rel. 1979. ed. 500, s/n, 18½" x 27¼", pub SEL	125.00	—
☐ GREENWING TEAL, rel. 1980. ed. 750, s/n, 18⅛" x 27¼", pub SEL	150.00	—
☐ WINTERTIME—PHEASANTS, rel. 1980. ed. 750, s/n, 18⅛" x 27¼", pub SEL	150.00	—

RANCE HOOD

THEMES: Indian art

AWARDS: Three Grand awards at the Indian Art Exhibit at the American Indian Exhibition, etc.

MEMBERSHIPS: Oklahoma Indian Arts and Crafts Cooperative

GALLERY/DISTRIBUTOR: Native American Images

	ISSUE PRICE	CURRENT PRICE
☐ WAR CHIEF, ed. 1,500, s/n, 18½" x 17", pub NWDHG	20.00	250.00
☐ WAR ON THE PLAIN, ed. 1,500, s/n, 28" x 23½", pub NWDHG	40.00	800.00
remarqued	100.00	800.00
☐ SIOUX RAINMAKERS, ed. 1,500, s/n, pub NAI	100.00	800.00

WINTERTIME - PHEASANTS *by William Hollywood*

FRANCES HOOK

THEMES: Men, women, and children

EDUCATION: Pennsylvania Museum School of Art

MUSEUMS/COLLECTIONS: All Mrs. Hook's collectibles and much of her earlier work are showcased in the Frances Hook Museum, Mishicot, Wisconsin

GALLERY/DISTRIBUTOR: Roman, Inc.

	ISSUE PRICE	CURRENT PRICE
☐ THE CARPENTER, rel. 1981. ed. 3,800, s/n, 20″ x 24″, pub RO	100.00	450.00
ed. 1,500, remarques	100.00	1,450.00
☐ LITTLE CHILDREN, COME TO ME, rel. 1982. ed. 1,950, s/n, 16″ x 20″, pub RO	50.00	150.00
ed. 50, remarques	100.00	300.00
☐ BOUQUET, rel. 1982. ed. 1,150, s/n, 29″ x 22″, pub RO	70.00	Sold Out
☐ FROLICKING, rel. 1982. ed. 1,150, s/n, 22″ x 26″, pub RO	60.00	—
☐ GATHERING, rel. 1982. ed. 1,150, s/n, 22″ x 26″, pub RO	60.00	—

THE CARPENTER *by Frances Hook*

	ISSUE PRICE	CURRENT PRICE
☐ **POSING,** rel. 1982. ed. 1,150, s/n, 28″ x 22″, pub RO	70.00	—
☐ **POULETS,** rel. 1982. ed. 1,150, s/n, 20½″ x 25″, pub RO	60.00	—
☐ **SURPRISE,** rel. 1982. ed. 1,150, s/n, 18″ x 22″, pub RO	50.00	—

CLAUDE HOWELL

MEDIUM: Silkscreen

GALLERY/DISTRIBUTOR: Foxfire Fine Arts Inc.

	ISSUE PRICE	CURRENT PRICE
☐ **SUNNY DAY,** rel. 1976, ed. 300, s/n, 22″ x 27″, pub FFFA	100.00	580.00
☐ **LATE AFTERNOON,** rel. 1977. ed. 300, s/n, 22″ x 27″, pub FFFA	100.00	375.00
☐ **NOONDAY GLARE,** rel. 1978. ed. 300, s/n, 21″ x 28″, pub FFFA	100.00	375.00
☐ **NORTHEASTER,** rel. 1979. ed. 300, s/n, 21″ x 28″, pub FFFA	100.00	375.00
matched set of above four	400.00	1,500.00
☐ **BALKAN SKETCHBOOK,** ed. 500, s/n, 6″ x 9″, 120 page hardcover book of sketches by the artist, pub FFFA	25.00	—

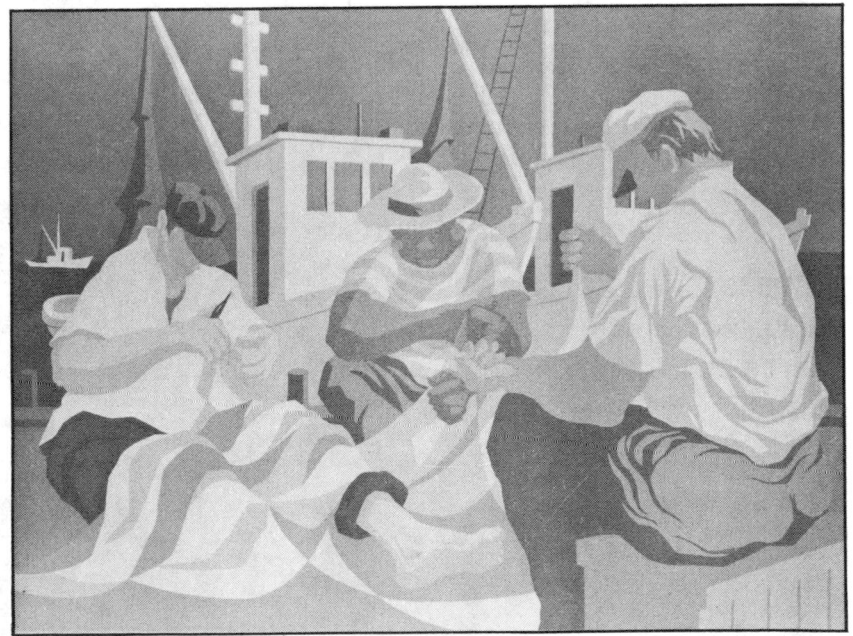

SUNNY DAY *by Claude Howell*

JIM HOWLE

THEMES: Contemporary American clowns

MEDIUM: Oil

STYLE: Realism

GALLERY/DISTRIBUTOR: Quest Fine Arts

COMMENTS: The artist was a professional clown with Ringling Brothers Barnum & Bailey Circus from 1968 to 1974, and the official circus artist in 1975. Jim was a featured artist at the 1982 World's Fair Fine Arts Pavilion in Knoxville, TN. Several pieces have been catalogued by the National Portrait Gallery of the Smithsonian Institution

	ISSUE PRICE	CURRENT PRICE
☐ **EMMETT KELLY,** rel. 1980. ed. 500, s/n, litho, 18″ x 24″, pub QFA	875.00	—
☐ **LOU JACOBS,** rel. 1980. ed. 500, s/n, litho, 18″ x 24″, pub QFA	450.00	—
☐ **THE MIME,** rel. 1980. ed. 500, s/n, litho. 17″ x 23″, pub QFA	950.00	—
☐ **AL ROSS,** rel. 1981. ed. 500, s/n, litho, 17″ x 23″, pub QFA	375.00	—
☐ **MAGIC OF THE MAKE-UP,** rel. 1981. ed. 500, s/n, litho, 17″ x23″, pub QFA	225.00	—
☐ **THE PIERROT,** rel. 1981. ed. 500, s/n, litho, 17″ x 23″″, pub QFA	525.00	—
☐ **NATALIE,** rel. 1982. ed. 500, s/n, litho, 17″ x 23″, pub QFA	75.00	—
☐ **SANDY KAYE,** rel. 1982. ed. 500, s/n, litho, 17″ x 23″, pub QFA	225.00	—
☐ **WAYNE SIDLEY,** rel. 1982. ed. 500, s/n, litho, 17″ x 23″, pub QFA	150.00	—
☐ **BERNIE,** rel. 1983. ed. 500, s/n, litho, 17″ x 23″, pub QFA	75.00	—
☐ **JEFF,** rel. 1983. ed. 500, s/n, litho, 17″ x 23″, pub QFA	75.00	—
☐ **RED SKELTON,** rel. 1983. ed. 500, s/n, litho, 17″ x 23″, pub QFA	425.00	—
☐ **LOU AND HIS DOG (Autographed special edition)** rel. 1984. ed. 100, s/n, litho, 17″ x 23″, pub QFA	175.00	—
☐ **LOU AND HIS DOG,** rel. 1984. ed. 250, s/n, litho, 17″ x 23″, pub QFA	125.00	—
☐ **THE TOYMAKER,** rel. 1984. ed. 500, s/n, litho, 17″ x 23″, pub QFA	75.00	—

MARTHA HUDSON

THEMES: Landscape

MEDIUM: Watercolor

GALLERY/DISTRIBUTOR: Wildlife Art of North Carolina, Inc.

COMMENTS: The artist is committed to capturing the character of her environment and sharing it with others

	ISSUE PRICE	CURRENT PRICE
☐ **JUST BROWSING,** rel. 1983. ed. 1,000, s/n, 26″ x 35″, pub WA INC.	60.00	—
☐ **SWANORAMA,** rel. 1983. ed. 1,000, s/n, 22″ x 39″, pub WA INC.	60.00	—

ALLEN HUGHES, M.D.

THEMES: Sporting art

MEDIUM: Watercolor

EDUCATION: Southwestern College in Memphis

AWARDS: He has won ten "Best of Show" ribbons at the Midwest Wildlife Art Show in Kansas City, etc.

GALLERY/DISTRIBUTOR: Swan Graphics, Ltd.

	ISSUE PRICE	CURRENT PRICE
☐ RETURNING WOODIES, rel. 1974. ed. 750, s/n, 18½″ x 23½″, pub SGL	65.00	100.00
s/n, remarqued	100.00	150.00
☐ FLOODED TIMBER MALLARDS, rel. 1976. ed. 500, s/n, 16″ x 20″, pub SGL	50.00	375.00
s/n, remarqued	75.00	425.00
☐ CYPRESS SWAMP WOODIES, rel. 1976. ed. 1,250, s/n, 16″ x 20″, pub SGL	*	
ed. 100 Artist proofs	75.00	300.00
Artist proof remarqued . . . ., . .	100.00	375.00
*Were donated to Ducks Unlimited.		
☐ MISSISSIPPI WATERFOWL STAMP, rel. 1977. ed. 500, s/n, 6½″ x 9″, pub SGL	65.00	500.00
ed. 100 Artist proofs remarqued	100.00	550.00
☐ DRIFTING IN, rel. 1977. ed. 750, s/n, 23¾″ x 18¾″, pub SGL	65.00	150.00
Artist proof remarqued	100.00	175.00
☐ STARTLED, rel. 1978. ed. 750, s/n, 23″ x 17½″, pub SGL	65.00	250.00
ed. 5 Artist proofs	100.00	275.00
A portion of the edition s/n remarqued	125.00	200.00
☐ RESTING PLACE, rel. 1978. ed. 950, s/n, 22½″ x 17″, pub SGL	65.00	—
s/n remarqued	100.00	—
ed. 50 Artist proofs	100.00	—
Artist proofs remarqued	125.00	—
☐ THE HUSTLERS, rel. 1979. ed. 750, s/n, 22″ x 18¾″, pub SGL	65.00	150.00
s/n remarqued	100.00	200.00
ed. 50 Artist proofs	100.00	250.00
Artist proof remarqued	125.00	275.00
☐ THE CHALLENGE, rel. 1978. ed. 500, s/n, 23″ x 18½″, pub SGL	65.00	250.00
50 Artist proofs	100.00	300.00
Artist proof remarqued	125.00	350.00
☐ EARLY ARRIVALS, rel. 1979. ed. 1,650, s/n, 16″ x 20″, pub SGL	—	—
*Were donated to Ducks Unlimited, ed. 100 Artist proofs	100.00	200.00
Artist proof remarqued	150.00	275.00
☐ SPRING FEVER, rel. 1979. ed. 500, s/n, 16″ x 20″, pub SGL	65.00	200.00
s/n remarqued	100.00	275.00
ed. 50 Artist proofs	100.00	275.00
Artist proof remarqued	150.00	300.00
☐ HEADING SOUTH, rel. 1979. ed. 750, s/n, 23″ x 18″, pub SGL	65.00	—
s/n remarqued	100.00	—
ed. 50 Artist proofs	100.00	—
Artist proof remarqued	150.00	—
☐ THE OLD HOMEPLACE, rel. 1980. ed. 750, s/n, 23½″ x 18½″, pub SGL	65.00	—
s/n remarqued	100.00	—
ed. 50 Artist proofs	100.00	—
Artist proof remarqued	150.00	—
☐ WINTERS CALLING, rel. 1980. ed. 500, s/n, 23″ x 17¼″, pub SGL	75.00	—
s/n remarqued	125.00	—
☐ ATLANTIC FLYWAY, rel. 1981. ed. 500, s/n, 23″ x 17″, pub SGL	75.00	—
s/n remarqued	125.00	—
☐ THROUGH THE TIMBER, rel. 1981. ed. 750, s/n, 23″ x 18″, pub SGL	75.00	—
s/n remarqued	150.00	—
☐ GOING FOR COVER, rel. 1981. ed. 750, s/n, 23″ x 15½″, pub SGL	75.00	—
s/n remarqued	150.00	—

	ISSUE PRICE	CURRENT PRICE
☐ **SETTLING IN,** rel. 1980. ed. 2,250, s/n, 16″ x 20″, pub SGL	100.00	—
Donated to Ducks Unlimited.		
☐ **QUAIL CONSERVATION STAMP PRINT,** rel. 1982. ed. 1,500, s/n, 6½″ x 9″, pub SGL	130.00	—
☐ **OFF THE ROOST,** rel. 1983. ed. 750, s/n, 19″ x 16″, pub SGL	75.00	—
☐ **MORNING FLIGHT,** rel. 1983. ed. 450, s/n, 20″ x 15″, pub SGL	75.00	—
☐ **1984-85 TENNESSEE WATERFOWL STAMP PRINT,** rel. 1984. ed. 1,250, s/n, pub SGL	131.50	—

GOING FOR COVER by *Allen Hughes*

MEL HUNTER

THEMES: Varied

STYLE: Realism, varied

GALLERY/DISTRIBUTOR: Circle Fine Arts Corporation

	ISSUE PRICE	CURRENT PRICE
☐ **JANUARY NIGHT,** rel. 1979. ed. 290, s/n, 17½″ x 23″, Mylar Litho, pub MPPI	125.00	—
☐ **UP AT THE JASPER PLACE,** rel. 1979. ed. 290, s/n, 17½″ x 23″, Mylar litho, pub MPPI	125.00	—
☐ **HORSE FOLIO,** 10 Pieces. ed. 500, s/n, litho, 30″ x 22″ or 23″ or 24″, pub CFAC	—	1,000.00*
The folio contains lithos of Appaloosa, Standard Bred Arabian, Hunter-Jumper, Thoroughbred, Pinto, Tennessee Walker, Morgan, Saddlebred, and Quarter Horse.		
*Each print may be purchased individually, between $125.00 and $150.00.		
☐ **ALONE TOGETHER,** ed. 200, s/n, litho, 22″ x 19″, pub CFAC	—	175.00
ed. 35, s/n, litho, Rines BFK . . . . , ...	—	225.00

JANUARY NIGHT *by Mel Hunter*

	ISSUE PRICE	CURRENT PRICE
☐ U. S. OPEN GOLF/OF ASC-1977, ed. 600, s/n, litho, 22″ x 28″, pub CFAC	—	200.00
☐ STAG HOUND IN FULL GALE, ed. 300, s/n, litho, 22″ x 25″, pub CFAC	—	175.00
☐ THE RAVEN AHEAD OFF TIMOR, ed. 300, s/n, litho, 22″ x 25″, pub CFAC	—	175.00
☐ CHALLENGE OFF CHILE, ed. 300, s/n, litho, 26″ x 19″, pub CFAC	—	250.00
☐ DREADNAUGHT, ed. 300, s/n, litho, 24″ x 31″, pub CFAC	—	225.00
☐ SNOW GEESE OVER CANADIAN ROCKIES, ed. 300, s/n, litho, 20″ x 30″, pub CFAC	—	350.00
☐ NIGHT WINDS, ed. 300, s/n, litho, 19″ x 29″, pub CFAC	—	350.00
☐ SNOWIES NESTING, ed. 300, s/n, litho, 22″ x 32″, pub CFAC	—	225.00
☐ LIGHT AT EMERALD POINT, ed. 300, s/n, litho, 22″ x 36″, pub CFAC	—	300.00
☐ DAWN MEADOW, ed. 300, s/n, litho, 22″ x 30″, pub CFAC	—	175.00
☐ DOLL HOUSE, ed. 300, s/n, litho, 22″ x 30″, pub CFAC	—	175.00
☐ PATRIARCH, ed. 300, s/n, litho, 23″ x 30″, pub CFAC	—	175.00
☐ PAINTED LADY, ed. 300, s/n, litho, 28″ x 19″, pub CFAC	—	175.00

PETER HURD

THEMES: Western art

GALLERY/DISTRIBUTOR: Circle Fine Arts Corporation

	ISSUE PRICE	CURRENT PRICE
☐ APACHE PLUME, ed. 250, s/n, 15″ x 19″, serigraph, pub CFAC	—	275.00
☐ A WATERING AT SUNDOWN, ed. 250, s/n, 26″ x 30″, serigraph, pub CFAC	—	1,000.00
☐ A PRACTICE GAME, ed. 250, s/n, 32″ x 43″, serigraph, pub CFAC	—	450.00

	ISSUE PRICE	CURRENT PRICE
☐ A RACE WITH RAIN, ed. 250, s/n, 32″ x 45″, serigraph, pub CFAC	—	450.00
☐ SUNSET THROUGH DUST, ed. 250, s/n, 24″ x 36″, serigraph, pub CFAC	—	450.00
☐ DUSTY SUN, ed. 250, s/n, 16″ x 20″	—	325.00
ed. 25 on Japon, litho, pub CFAC	—	350.00
☐ FENCE RIDER, ed. 250, s/n, 11″ x 12″	—	275.00
ed. 25 on Japon, litho, pub CFAC	—	325.00
☐ A FAR AWAY PLACE, ed. 260, s/n, 23″ x 33″, litho, pub CFAC	—	450.00
☐ NIGHT VISITOR, ed. 260, s/n, 24″ x 20″	—	550.00
ed. 25 on Japon, litho, pub CFAC	—	600.00
☐ A RANCH AT DAWN, ed. 250, s/n, 15″ x 15″	—	275.00
ed. 25 on Japon, litho, pub CFAC	—	325.00
☐ DAY'S END, ed. 260, s/n, 26″ x 26″, serigraph, pub CFAC	—	550.00
☐ WINDMILL TROUBLE, ed. 260, s/n, 19″ x 25″	—	300.00
ed. 25 on Japon, litho, pub CFAC	—	325.00
☐ A SURGING CUMULUS, ed. 280, s/n, 25″ x 19″	—	300.00
ed. 25 on Japon, litho, pub CFAC	—	375.00
☐ DOMINIQUEZ WELL, ed. 260, s/n, 14″ x 16″	—	300.00
ed. 25 on Japon, litho, pub CFAC	—	350.00
☐ SHOWER ON THE PRAIRIE, ed. 260, s/n, 20″ x 29″	—	350.00
ed. 25 on Japon, litho, pub CFAC	—	400.00
☐ THE DAY IT RAINED, ed. 260, s/n, 22″ x 29″	—	350.00
ed. 35 on Japon, litho, pub CFAC	—	375.00
☐ WESTWARD INTO NIGHT, ed. 275, s/n, litho, 22″ x 34″, pub CFA	—	300.00

WILSON HURLEY

THEMES: Landscape art

EDUCATION: George Washington University; West Point

AWARDS: Prix de West Cowboy Hall of Fame Purchase Award (1984)

GALLERY/DISTRIBUTOR: Greenwich Workshop

COMMENTS: The artist is called the "Landscapist of Grandeur"

	ISSUE PRICE	CURRENT PRICE
☐ EDGE OF WINTER GRAND CANYON, ed. 475, s/n, 35¼″ x 23¾″, pub GW	245.00	—
☐ COLUMBIA AT 30 SECONDS, rel. 1982. ed. 850, s/n, 23¼″ x 26″, pub GW	150.00	—

JERRY INGRAM

THEMES: Indian art

STYLE: The natural balance and composition of his work reflect a special sensitivity that reveals a new dimension to even familiar subjects

EDUCATION: Institute of American Indian Arts; Oklahoma State Tech

AWARDS: Top awards at the Heard Museum in Phoenix, the Scottsdale National Competition, etc.

GALLERY/DISTRIBUTOR: Native American Images

WAR HONORS *by Jerry Ingram*

	ISSUE PRICE	CURRENT PRICE
☐ **PROUD WARRIOR,** edition and size not available, pub NWDHG	300.00	900.00
☐ **BLACKFOOT MEDICINE,** edition and size not available, pub NWDHG	300.00	600.00
☐ **BLACKFOOT CHIEFS,** ed. 950, s/n, 14″ x 19″, pub NWDHG	60.00	—
☐ **OUR BATTLES ARE MANY,** ed. 650, s/n, 14″ x 18″, pub NWDHG	50.00	75.00
☐ **ELK WOMAN,** ed. 100, s/n, 22″ x 30″, stone litho, pub NWDHG	300.00	—
☐ **WAR HONORS,** ed. 90, s/n, 20″ x 30″, stone litho, pub NAI	400.00	—

PHILIP JAMISON

THEMES: Varied

EDUCATION: Philadelphia College of Art

AWARDS: National Academy of Design; Gold Medal of Honor from Allied Arts of America, etc.

MEMBERSHIPS: American Watercolor Society

MUSEUMS/COLLECTIONS: Metropolitan Museum of Art in New York City, the Boston Museum of Art, etc.

SUMMER BOUQUET by Philip Jamison

GALLERY/DISTRIBUTOR: Mill Pond Press, Inc.

	ISSUE PRICE	CURRENT PRICE
☐ RAILROAD CROSSING, rel. 1980. ed. 950, s/n, 20″ x 32½″, pub MPPI	75.00	—
☐ SUMMER BOUQUET, rel. 1980. ed. 950, s/n, 22″ x 25½″, pub MPPI	65.00	—

JEAN JANSEM

THEMES: Varied

GALLERY/DISTRIBUTOR: Felicie, Inc.

	ISSUE PRICE	CURRENT PRICE
☐ ARLEQUIN AU FOND ROUGE, ed. 120, s/n, 29½″ x 21″, original color litho, pub FI .	260.00	—
☐ ARLEQUIN AU FOND GRIS, ed. 20, a/p, 29½″ x 21″, Japon, original color litho, pub FI	300.00	—
☐ GRAND ECART A LA TUNIQUE, ed. 120, s/n, 22″ x 30″, original color litho, pub FI .	260.00	—
☐ DANSEUSE SE CHAUSSANT, ed. 120, s/n, 25½″ x 19¾″, original color litho, pub FI	200.00	—
☐ CLOWN, ed. 120, s/n, 30″ x 20″, original color litho, pub FI	260.00	280.00
☐ MOTHER AND CHILD, ed. 120, s/n, 30″ x 20″, original color litho, pub FI	300.00	—

CHARLEN JEFFERY

THEMES: Varied

MEDIUM: Varied

STYLE: Ranges from realism to impressionism

EDUCATION: Seattle Pacific University

GALLERY/DISTRIBUTOR: Swan Graphics, Ltd.

	ISSUE PRICE	CURRENT PRICE
☐ LORD OF THE TUNDRA, rel. 1980. ed. 750, s/n, 23″ x 17″, pub SGL	65.00	175.00
s/n remarqued	175.00	250.00
☐ EVENING WATCH, rel. 1980. ed. 750, s/n, 22″ x 17″, pub SGL	65.00	150.00
s/n remarqued	125.00	250.00
☐ IN TRAINING, rel. 1980. ed. 750, s/n, 23″ x 16½″, pub SGL	65.00	350.00
s/n remarqued	125.00	—
☐ WAIT FOR ME MOM, rel. 1981. ed. 750, s/n, 23″ x 19″, pub SGL	75.00	400.00
s/n remarqued	125.00	450.00

EVENING WATCH *by Charlen Jeffery*

	ISSUE PRICE	CURRENT PRICE
☐ CHECKING THE LINE, rel. 1981. ed. 750, s/n, 23″ x 17″, pub SGL	75.00	—
s/n remarqued	125.00	—
☐ SEPTEMBER IN ALASKA, rel. 1981. ed. 750, s/n, 23″ x 17″, pub SGL	75.00	—
s/n remarqued	125.00	—
☐ JOHN OLIVER CABIN, rel. 1982. ed. 1,000, s/n, 11″ x 14″, pub SGL	25.00	—
☐ CADES COVE, rel. 1982. ed. 1,000, s/n, 11″ x 14″, pub SGL	25.00	—
☐ NEWFOUND GAP, rel. 1982. ed. 1,000, s/n, 11″ x 14″, pub SGL	25.00	—
☐ SMOKY MOUNTAIN POSTER, rel. 1982. ed. 750, s/n, 23″ x 17″, pub SGL	20.00	—
☐ LUNCH BREAK, rel. 1982. ed. 750, s/n, 23″ x 17″, pub SGL	75.00	—
s/n remarqued	125.00	—
☐ EVENING CATCH, rel. 1982. ed. 750, s/n, 11″ x 15″, pub SGL	75.00	—
s/n remarqued	125.00	—
☐ ON GUARD, rel. 1983. ed. 750, s/n, 23″ x 19″	75.00	—
s/n remarqued	150.00	—
☐ 1983 GAME CONSERVATION STAMP PRINT, rel. 1983. ed. 950, s/n, 6½″ x 9″	130.00	—
s/n remarqued	255.00	—
☐ PUFFIN, rel. 1983. ed. 750, s/n, 11″ x 13″	35.00	—
☐ SEAGULL, rel. 1983. ed. 750, s/n, 11″ x 13″, pub SGL	35.00	—

EDNA B. JOHNSON

MEDIUM: Oil

EDUCATION: North Texas College

GALLERY/DISTRIBUTOR: Edna B. Johnson

	ISSUE PRICE	CURRENT PRICE
☐ THE QUAIL HUNT, rel. 1982. ed. 1,000, s/n, 18″ x 24″, pub Wilson Engraving, distr. EJ..	30.00	35.00
☐ ALTHEAS, rel. 1982. ed. 1,000, s/n, 19½″ x 24″, pub Wilson Engraving, distr. EJ	30.00	35.00

RAY "PADRE" JOHNSON

THEMES: Western art

GALLERY/DISTRIBUTOR: Voyageur Art

	ISSUE PRICE	CURRENT PRICE
☐ ANNIE OAKLEY, rel. 1981. ed. 250, s/n, 19″ x 15″, litho, pub VA	45.00	—
☐ BULLDOG, rel. 1980. ed. 250, s/n, 16¼″ x 22″, litho, pub VA	45.00	—
☐ EARLY MORNING CIRCLE, rel. 1981. ed. 780, s/n, 18″ x 22½″, litho, pub VA	75.00	—
☐ FABRIC OF HIS LIFE, rel. 1982. ed. 1,500, s/n, 19¾″ x 22¼″, litho, pub VA	80.00	—
☐ FIVE CARD STUD, rel. 1981. ed. 580, s/n, litho, pub VA	75.00	—
☐ GHOST RIDERS, rel. 1983. ed. 580, s/n, 20″ x 26″, litho, pub VA	80.00	—
☐ INDIAN JOE, rel. 1980. ed. 225, s/n, 18″ x 14, litho, pub VA	45.00	—
☐ MAJESTIC AND FREE, rel. 1982. ed. 580, s/n, 18″ x 23″, litho, pub VA	75.00	—
☐ OLD LEATHER, DENIM AND DREAMS, rel. 1982. ed. 580, s/n, 23″ x 25½″, litho, pub VA...	75.00	—
☐ SUNDOWN AT DIAMOND BAR, rel. 1982. ed. 780, s/n, 30″ x 23½″, litho, pub VA ...	75.00	—

THE QUAIL HUNT *by Edna B. Johnson*

RUSSELL JOHNSON

THEMES: Wildlife art

STYLE: Subtlety of color and imaginative use of background landscapes

GALLERY/DISTRIBUTOR: Petersen Prints

	ISSUE PRICE	CURRENT PRICE
☐ EARLY ARRIVALS, ed. 800, s/n, 18″ x 24″, litho, pub PP	60.00	120.00
☐ THE UPPER POND, ed. 800, s/n, 16″ x 24″, litho, pub PP	60.00	—
☐ "UP TO MISCHIEF", ed. 800, s/n, 21½″ x 16″, pub PP	75.00	—
remarqued, signed, and numbered	165.00	—
☐ "MORNING", ed. 800, s/n, 18″ x 24″, pub PP	75.00	—
remarqued, signed, and numbered	165.00	—
☐ "LAST YEAR'S BLIND—THIS YEAR'S MALLARDS", ed. 800, s/n, 16″ x 24″, pub PP	75.00	—
remarqued, signed, and numbered	165.00	—
☐ "OPEN WATER REFUGE", ed. 800, s/n, 16″ x 24″, pub PP	75.00	—
remarqued, signed, and numbered	165.00	—
☐ "AMERICAN CLASSICS", ed. 800, s/n, 16″ x 24″, pub PP	75.00	—
remarqued, signed, and numbered	165.00	—
☐ TEAL TIME, ed. 800, s/n, 16″ x 24″, pub PP	75.00	—
remarqued, signed, and numbered	165.00	—

EARLY MORNING CIRCLE *by Ray "Padre" Johnson*

AFTERNOON BATH *by Vicki D. Jones*

GLENDA JONES

THEMES: Still life, landscape, and people

MEDIUM: Watercolor

STYLE: Realism

AWARDS: Many blue, red, and white awards and two "Best of Show" awards

MEMBERSHIPS: Monroe Art Association

GALLERY/DISTRIBUTOR: Gallery House

	ISSUE PRICE	CURRENT PRICE
☐ **LOUISIANA BAYOU,** rel. 1981. ed. 1,000, s/n, prints, 11" x 20", pub GHL	30.00	—
☐ **DOGWOOD,** rel. 1982. ed. 950, s/n, prints, 11" x 14", pub GHL	20.00	—
☐ **JO'S BOUQUET,** rel. 1982. ed. 950, s/n, prints, 16" x 20", pub GHL	30.00	—
☐ **MAGNOLIA I,** rel. 1982. ed. 950, s/n, prints, 16" x 23", pub GHL	40.00	—
☐ **PURPLE MAGNOLIA,** rel. 1982. ed. 950, s/n, prints, 11" x 14", pub GHL	20.00	—
☐ **SPRING BOUQUET,** rel. 1982. ed. 950, s/n, prints, 16" x 23", pub GHL	30.00	—
☐ **COUNTRY CATS,** rel. 1983. ed. 950, s/n, prints, 11" x 14", pub GHL	20.00	—
☐ **COUNTRY GOOSE,** rel. 1983. ed. 950, s/n, prints, 11" x 14", pub GHL	20.00	—
☐ **COUNTRY ROOSTER,** rel. 1983. ed. 950, s/n, prints, 11" x 14", pub GHL	20.00	—
☐ **LITTLE WOMEN,** rel. 1984. ed. 950, s/n, prints, 14" x 23", pub GHL	40.00	—
☐ **MAGNOLIA II,** rel. 1984. ed. 1,000, s/n, prints, 16" x 23", pub GHL	40.00	—
☐ **PINK CAMELLIA,** rel. 1984. ed. 1,000, s/n, prints, 8" x 10", pub GHL	16.00	—
☐ **RED CAMELLIA,** rel. 1984. ed. 1,000, s/n, prints 8" x 10", pub GHL	16.00	—
☐ **SUNDAY MORNING SUMMER,** rel. 1985. ed. 1,000, s/n, prints, 16" x 22", pub GHL	40.00	—
☐ **VIOLETS & OLD LACE,** rel. 1985. ed. 1,000, s/n, prints, 12" x 15", pub GHL	20.00	—

VICKI D. JONES

THEMES: Wildlife art

STYLE: Realism

EDUCATION: University of Nevada at Las Vegas; University of Texas

GALLERY/DISTRIBUTOR: Victoria's Fine Arts

	ISSUE PRICE	CURRENT PRICE
☐ **EARLY MALLARDS,** rel. 1982. ed. 475, s/n, 18" x 23", litho, pub VFA	60.00	—
☐ **IN THE 'TATER SHED,** rel. 1982. ed. 475, s/n, 14" x 19", litho, pub VFA	30.00	—
☐ **AFTERNOON BATH,** rel. 1983. ed. 290, s/n, 16" x 20", litho, pub VFA	75.00	—

MARSHALL WOODSIDE JOYCE

THEMES: Seascapes

PUBLICATION: Recently, *American Artist* selected the artist for an anthology entitled: *Twenty Landscape Artists and How They Work*

RISING TIDE *by Marshall Woodside Joyce*

AWARDS: Gold medal from the Franklin Mint, gold medal from the Rockport Art Society

GALLERY/DISTRIBUTOR: Mill Pond Press, Inc.

	ISSUE PRICE	CURRENT PRICE
☐ SEA GHOST, rel. 1979. ed. 950, s/n, 20″ x 24″, pub MPPI	85.00	125.00
☐ SEA MOSS GATHERER, rel. 1978. ed. 950, s/n, 20″ x 28″, pub MPPI	95.00	110.00
☐ RISING TIDE, rel. 1980. ed. 950, s/n, 20″ x 25″, pub MPPI	65.00	—
☐ THE SCULLER, rel. 1980. ed. 950, s/n, 21″ x 29″, pub MPPI	85.00	—

LYNN KAATZ

THEMES: Wildlife and landscape art

MEDIUM: Acrylic and watercolor

EDUCATION: Ohio State; School of Art in Cleveland

AWARDS: Ohio Ducks Unlimited Artist of the year; "Best of Show" at the Oklahoma Waterfowl Festival, and many other prestigious awards

GALLERY/DISTRIBUTOR: Voyageur Art

	ISSUE PRICE	CURRENT PRICE
☐ **CANVASBACKS,** rel. 1978. ed. 800, s/n, 19¼" x 29", litho, pub VA	85.00	—
☐ **THE LAB,** rel. 1979. ed. 250, s/n, 16½" x 25½", litho, pub VA	85.00	—
☐ **ALONE ON THE LAKE,** rel. 1980. ed. 800, s/n, 16½" x 26", litho, pub VA	85.00	—
☐ **LASTING MEMORIES,** rel. 1980. ed. 250, s/n, 16½" x 26", litho, pub VA	85.00	—
☐ **QUIET WATERS,** rel. 1981. ed. 450, s/n, 13" x 17½", litho, pub VA	70.00	—
☐ **PAIR OF KINGS,** rel. 1983. ed. 580, s/n, 13" x 17½", litho, pub VA	70.00	—
☐ **SUNSET POINT,** rel. 1983. ed. 580, s/n, 12" x 22", litho, pub VA	75.00	—

DIANA KAN

THEMES: Nature

EDUCATION: Art Students League

SHANGRI-LA by Diana Kan

AWARDS: She has received innumerable awards including eight from *The Pen and Brush,* four from the American Watercolor Society, etc.

MUSEUMS/COLLECTIONS: Metropolitan Museum of Art, The Philadelphia Museum of Art

GALLERY/DISTRIBUTOR: Greenwich Workshop

	ISSUE PRICE	CURRENT PRICE
☐ **FALLING WATERS,** rel. 1978. ed. 1,500, s/n, 40″ x 22″, pub FHG	50.00	—
☐ **RING AROUND THE ROSEY,** rel. 1978. ed. 750, s/n, 28″ x 22″, pub FHG	60.00	—
☐ **LOVE,** rel. 1979. ed. 5,000, s/o, 14″ x 14″, pub FHG	25.00	—
☐ **SHANGRI-LA,** rel. 1983. ed. 475, signed, numbered, and titled, 19⅛″ x 25¾″, pub GW	95.00	—

JOHN KELLY

THEMES: Marine art

EDUCATION: Art Center School

MUSEUMS/COLLECTIONS: Permanent display in Malibu's Courthouse; San Francisco's City Hall, and in Glasgow, Scotland

GALLERY/DISTRIBUTOR: Eleanor Ettinger, Inc.

COMMENTS: The artist's list of collectors includes James Caan, Robert Goulet, Jonathan Winters, Don Rickles, and Herb Alpert, among others

	ISSUE PRICE	CURRENT PRICE
☐ **TIVERTON,** rel. 1977. ed. 250, s/n, 26″ x 20″, litho, arches, pub EEI	100.00	300.00
ed. 25, japon	120.00	350.00
☐ **VIEW OF THE THAMES,** rel. 1977. ed. 250, s/n, 26″ x 20″, litho, arches, pub EEI	100.00	300.00
ed. 25, japon	120.00	350.00

MEL KESTER

THEMES: Americana

MEDIUM: He works in watercolor and tempera but seldom mixes opaque and transparent colors

GALLERY/DISTRIBUTOR: Foxfire Fine Arts, Inc.

	ISSUE PRICE	CURRENT PRICE
☐ **STABLE STILL LIFE,** ed. 583, s/n, 19″ x 16″, pub Omega Press	35.00	—
☐ **RHODODENDRON,** ed. 583, s/n, 20¾″ x 25″, pub Omega Press	40.00	—
☐ **THE SADDLEMAKER,** ed. 583, s/n, 20⅜″ x 24⅜″, pub Omega Press	35.00	—
☐ **ROCKING CHAIR,** ed. 583, s/n, 21″ x 27¾″, pub Omega Press	45.00	135.00

ROCKING CHAIR by *Mel Kester*

	ISSUE PRICE	CURRENT PRICE
☐ THE OLD PUSHCART, rel. 1975. ed. 850, s/n, 19½″ x 15½″, pub AGI	25.00	—
☐ BARN BEE, rel. 1975. ed. 850, s/n, 24¾″ x 21¾″, pub AGI	35.00	—
☐ OLD FRIENDS, rel. 1977. ed. 750, s/n, 16″ x 20″, pub FFFA	35.00	105.00
☐ ROAD HOME, rel. 1977. ed. 750, s/n, 20″ x 16″, pub FFFA	35.00	95.00
☐ SUZY-Q, rel. 1977. ed. 750, s/n, 24″ x 20″, pub FFFA	40.00	—
☐ ANOTHER MORNING, rel. 1977. ed. 750, s/n, 24″ x 20″, pub FFFA	40.00	—
☐ ROCK HOUSE, rel. 1978. ed. 500, s/n, 26″ x 20″, pub FFFA	25.00	—
☐ THE HAYLOFT, rel. 1978. ed. 750, s/n, 26″ x 20″, pub FFFA	40.00	75.00
☐ THE HOUSE DOWN THE ROAD, rel. 1978. ed. 750, s/n, 26″ x 20″, pub FFFA	40.00	—
☐ SUMMER PUMP, rel. 1980. ed. 1,500, s/n, 26″ x 20″, pub FFFA	45.00	·
☐ SUMMER HIDEAWAY & PEACEFUL VALLEY, rel. 1981. ed. 1,500, s/n, 12″ x 15″, pub FFFA	35.00	—

AUNT NETTIE'S PORCH *by M.V. "Cotton" Ketchie*

M. V. "COTTON" KETCHIE

THEMES: Varied

MEDIUM: Watercolor

BACKGROUND: Ketchie has always had a keen interest in art but never painted until nine years ago. He opened his own gallery in 1981

MUSEUMS/COLLECTIONS: His work is included in corporate and private collections nationwide

GALLERY/DISTRIBUTOR: Landmark Galleries

COMMENTS: The artist is gaining widespread recognition for the sensitive way he captures the "timeliness" of his subject

	ISSUE PRICE	CURRENT PRICE
☐ AUNT NETTIE'S PORCH, ed. 750, s/n, 16¼" x 22½", litho, pub LG	55.00	—
☐ AUTUMN'S NEST, ed. 750, s/n, 12" x 16", litho, pub LG	35.00	Sold Out
☐ CHURNING TIME, ed. 750, s/n, 16¼" x 22", litho, pub LG	55.00	—
☐ HOWARD'S CREEK MILL, ed. 500, s/n, 20½" x 26½", litho, pub LG	50.00	—
☐ NOVEMBER MORNING 1865, ed. 750, s/n, 17" x 20", litho, pub LG	50.00	—
☐ HATTERAS DORY, rel. 1985. ed. 750, s/n, litho, 11¼" x 14½", pub LG	35.00	—
☐ REHOBETH*, rel. 1985. ed. 250, s/n, litho, 16¾" x 18", pub LG	40.00	—
☐ WILLIAMSBURG WELLS (two prints in set), rel. 1985. ed. 750, s/n, litho, 11½" x 14½", pub LG	75.00	—
☐ WILLIAMSBURG VIGNETTE, rel. 1985. ed. 750, s/n, litho, 11½" x 14½", pub LG . . .	35.00	—

*Note: Rehobeth was printed especially for The Rehobeth United Methodist Church of Terrell, NC. All proceeds are going towards the church.

JAMES H. KILLEN

THEMES: Wildlife art

MEDIUM: Watercolor

AWARDS: President's Award (1980), Ducks Unlimited National Wildlife Art Show

MEMBERSHIPS: Ducks Unlimited, Rod and Gun, Sports Afield, National Wildlife and Turkey Call

GALLERY/DISTRIBUTOR: Petersen Prints

	ISSUE PRICE	CURRENT PRICE
☐ QUIET WOODS (Wild Turkey), ed. 800, s/n, 16" x 24", litho, pub PP	60.00	—
☐ WILDERNESS RETREAT, ed. 800, s/n, 16" x 24", litho, pub PP	60.00	Sold Out
☐ FEEDING TIME - MALLARDS, ed. 800, s/n, 17" x 23", litho, pub PP	60.00	—
☐ PITCHING-IN (Canvasbacks), ed. 800, s/n, 18" x 24", litho, pub PP	—	—
☐ THE HOMESTEADERS, ed. 800, s/n, 16" x 24", litho, pub PP	60.00	120.00
☐ A NOBLE PAIR, ed. 800, s/n, 16" x 24", litho, pub PP	60.00	Sold Out
☐ STARTLED, ed. 800, s/n, 16" x 24", pub PP	75.00	—
remarqued, s/n	165.00	—
☐ RUFFLED GROUSE, ed. 800, s/n, 16¼" x 25", pub PP	75.00	—
remarqued, s/n	165.00	—
☐ MUSKRAT BAY, ed. 800, s/n, 16" x 24½", pub PP	75.00	—
remarqued, s/n	165.00	—
☐ EARLY SNOW (Canada Goose), ed. 800, s/n, 16" x 24½", pub PP	60.00	—
remarqued, s/n	150.00	—
☐ AFTER THE SNOWFALL - MALLARDS, rel. 1980. ed. 850, s/n, size not available, pub PP	75.00	—
☐ ON THE HIGH PLAINS, rel. 1981. ed. 990, s/n, size not available, pub PP	75.00	—
☐ WINTER TRIO - WILD TURKEYS, rel. 1981. ed. 800, s/n, size not available, pub PP	75.00	—

DONG KINGMAN

THEMES: Chinese-American art

MEDIUM: Watercolor

BOOKS: *Dong Kingman's Watercolors,* published by Watson-Guptill, Inc.

STARTLED *by James H. Killen*

DRAGON DANCE *by Dong Kingman*

GALLERY/DISTRIBUTOR: Greenwich Workshop

COMMENTS: For the past 25 years, the artist has been traveling with the Thurman Hewitt Painting Workshop in the U.S. and abroad. He is also one of the founders of the Famous Artist Schools in Westport, Connecticut

	ISSUE PRICE	CURRENT PRICE
☐ **DRAGON DANCE,** rel. 1983. ed. 375, signed, titled and numbered, 28⅜″ x 24″, hand-drawn litho, pub GW	275.00	—

SHADOW BOXING *by Don Kloetzke*

DON KLOETZKE

THEMES: Wildlife art

MEDIUM: Oil

STYLE: Realism

AWARDS: "Best of Show" (1983) at the National Art Exhibition of Alaska Wildlife; Wildlife Artist of the Year (1982)

GALLERY/DISTRIBUTOR: Northwoods Craftsman

		ISSUE PRICE	CURRENT PRICE
☐ **SHADOW BOXING,** rel. 1983. ed. 600, s/n, 24″ x 20¼″, pub NC	....	95.00	—
☐ **OUT FOXED,** rel. 1983. ed. 600, s/n, 25″ x 18½″, pub NC	....	95.00	—
☐ **AUTUMN EXIT,** rel. 1984. ed. 600, s/n, 26″ x 13″, pub NC	....	85.00	—
☐ **ON THE ROAD AGAIN,** rel. 1984. ed. 600, s/n, 25″ x 16½″, pub NC	....	95.00	—
☐ **DEEP WOODS CARDINAL,** rel. 1985. ed. 600, s/n, 9½″ x 13″, pub NC	....	40.00	—
☐ **IN THE SHELTER,** rel. 1985. ed. 600, s/n, 25″ x 16½″, pub NC	....	95.00	—

TERRILL KNAACK

THEMES: Wildlife art

MEDIUM: Oil on canvas

STYLE: Realism

EDUCATION: University of Wisconsin

GALLERY/DISTRIBUTOR: Wild Wings, Inc.

COMMENTS: "One must study birds from the inside out in order to paint them well," states the artist, who is also a student of taxidermy

MORNING STILLNESS - LOON *by Terrill Knaack*

	ISSUE PRICE	CURRENT PRICE
☐ **MORNING STILLNESS - LOON,** rel. 1977. ed. 600, s/n, 16½" x 25", pub WWI	50.00	300.00
ed. 50 remarque, Artist proof	100.00	400.00
☐ **BLUE BIRD,** rel. 1978. ed. 850, s/n, 13⅜" x 10¾", pub WWI	40.00	45.00
☐ **OCTOBER DAY - BOBWHITE,** rel. 1978. ed. 850, s/n, 16½" x 25", pub WWI	60.00	—
ed. 50 remarque, Artist proof	130.00	—
☐ **CEDAR WAXWINGS,** rel. 1979. ed. 850, s/n, 10¾" x 13⅝", pub WWI..............	40.00	45.00
☐ **LAKE COUNTRY - LOON,** rel. 1979. ed. 850, s/n, 25" x 16½", pub WWI	75.00	300.00
☐ **CARDINALS,** rel. 1980. ed. 850, s/n, size not available, pub WWI	45.00	—
☐ **OVER THE SHOCKS—CANADA GEESE,** rel. 1980. ed. 850, s/n, litho, 16½" x 25", pub WWI..	75.00	—
☐ **WILDERNESS LAKE LOON FAMILY,** rel. 1984. ed. 600, s/n, litho, 16½" x 25", pub WWI	95.00	—

EVEL KNIEVEL

THEMES: Wildlife art, portraits

MEMBERSHIPS: The artist is an active conservationist

GALLERY/DISTRIBUTOR: Legend's Corporation

COMMENTS: The artist is best known for his daredevil stunts, but his art is critically acclaimed worldwide

	ISSUE PRICE	CURRENT PRICE
☐ **UPSIDE DOWN,** ed. 1,000, s/n, 11" x 14", pub LC	100.00	—
☐ **BIRDS FLY, WHY CAN'T I,** ed. 1,000, s/n, 11" x 14", pub LC	100.00	—
☐ **MASTER OF THE HIGH COUNTRY,** ed. 1,000, s/n, 16" x 20", pub LC	200.00	—
☐ **EAGLE AND PREY,** ed. 5,000, s/n, 16" x 20", pub LC	500.00	—
☐ **THE SCOUT,** ed. 3,000, s/n, 16" x 20", pub LC	350.00	—
☐ **FACING DECISION,** ed. 3,000, s/n, 16" x 20", pub LC	350.00	—
☐ **BEFORE THE STORM,** ed. 3,000, s/n, 16" x 20", pub LC	350.00	—
☐ **STANDING TALL,** ed. 2,500, s/n, 11" x 14", pub LC	150.00	—
☐ **PEACEFUL FLIGHT,** ed. 3,000, s/n, 16" x 20", pub LC	200.00	—
☐ **THE WISE ONE,** ed. 1,000, s/n, 16" x 20", pub LC	150.00	—
☐ **SPIRIT,** ed. 5,000, s/n, 11" x 14", pub LC	200.00	—
☐ **GENTLEMAN,** ed. 3,000, s/n, 11" x 14", pub LC	200.00	—
☐ **THE RED ROOSTER,** ed. 2,500, s/n, 11" x 14", pub LC	100.00	—
☐ **FIRE,** ed. 5,000, s/n, 16" x 20", pub LC	200.00	—
☐ **THE KING,** ed. 1,000, s/n, 16" x 20", pub LC	200.00	—
☐ **BEWARE,** ed. 1,000, s/n, 16" x 20", pub LC	200.00	—
☐ **BAMBI,** ed. 1,000, s/n, 11" x 14", pub LC	100.00	—
☐ **SNOW HAWK,** ed. 1,000, s/n, 11" x 14", pub LC	100.00	—
☐ **SERENITY,** ed. 1,000, s/n, 11" x 14", pub LC	100.00	—
☐ **HIGH COUNTRY,** ed. 1,000, s/n, 11" x 14", pub LC	100.00	—
☐ **SAGEBRUSH PRINCE,** ed. 1,000, s/n, 16" x 20", pub LC	200.00	—

HENRY KOEHLER

THEMES: Sporting art

MUSEUMS/COLLECTIONS: Famous collections of the Duchess of Windsor, William S. Paley, Edward Kennedy, etc.

GALLERY/DISTRIBUTOR: Circle Fine Arts Corp.

	ISSUE PRICE	CURRENT PRICE
☐ RACING COLOURS - PORTFOLIO OF FOUR, rel. 1972. ed. 1,500, s/n, 18″ x 22½″, pub FHG	75.00	225.00
☐ WARWICKSHIRE STEEPLE CHASE AWAITING START, rel. 1972. ed. 1,500, s/n, 33″ x 23½″, pub FHG	40.00	85.00
☐ RIVA RIDGE, rel. 1973. ed. 2,500, s/n, 33″ x 23½″, pub FHG	30.00	100.00
☐ SECRETARIAT, rel. 1974. ed. 4,500, s/o, 29″ x 21½″, pub FHG	40.00	160.00
☐ RED JOCKEY BELOW, ed. 300, s/n, 31″ x 23″, litho, pub CFAC	125.00	150.00
☐ CONSTELLATION BELOW, ed. 300, s/n, 35″ x24″, litho, pub CFAC	120.00	275.00
☐ FIVE ENGLISH JOCKEYS, ed. 300, s/n, 23″ x 31″, litho, pub CFAC	125.00	250.00

WILLIAM J. KOELPIN

THEMES: Wildlife art

STYLE: The artist regards himself to be "visual reporter" rather than a studio painter

OFF SEASON *by William J. Koelpin*

AWARDS: Wisconsin Duck Stamp Design (1983) and other honors

GALLERY/DISTRIBUTOR: Northwoods Craftsman

	ISSUE PRICE	CURRENT PRICE
☐ **THE POACHER**, rel. 1976. ed. 300, s/n, 24″ x 30″, dist. NC	60.00	2,600.00
☐ **THE BATTERY**, rel. 1977. ed. 580, s/n, 24″ x 36″, dist. NC	60.00	400.00
☐ **REFLECTIONS**, rel. 1977. ed. 580, s/n, 24″ x 30″, dist. NC	60.00	400.00
☐ **DAMN THE WIND**, rel. 1978. ed. 580, s/n, 18″ x 23½″, dist. NC	75.00	—
☐ **HARD TIMES**, rel. 1978. ed. 600, s/n, 18″ x 24″, dist. NC	45.00	—
☐ **PHEASANTS**, rel. 1978. ed. 400, 19″ x 24″, dist. NC	65.00	—
☐ **THE PLOVER GUN**, rel. 1978. ed. 600, s/n, 18″ x 24″, dist. NC	45.00	—
☐ **FLAMING SUMAC - CARDINALS**, rel. 1979. ed. 605, s/n, 14″ x 18″, dist. NC	50.00	—
remarqued print	125.00	—
☐ **OFF SEASON**, rel. 1979. ed. 600, s/n, 24″ x 30″, dist. NC	75.00	—
remarqued print	150.00	—
☐ **THE ENTHUSIAST**, rel. 1980. ed. 600, s/n, 27½″ x 22¼″, dist. NC	75.00	350.00
☐ **GOOD TIMES**, rel. 1980. ed. 600, s/n, 24″ x 30″, dist. NC	85.00	—
remarqued print	160.00	—
☐ **PRIMEVAL CEREMONY/GREATER PRAIRIE CHICKEN**, rel. 1980. ed. 400, s/n, 24″ x 30″, dist. NC	75.00	—
remarqued print	150.00	—
☐ **THOU SHALT NOT POACH**, rel. 1980. ed. 600, s/n, 24″ x 30″, dist. NC	85.00	550.00
☐ **BARK RIVER WOODIES**, rel. 1981. ed. 600, s/n, 24″ x 30″, dist. NC	100.00	—
☐ **ILLINOIS RIVER CLASSICS**, rel. 1981. ed. 600, s/n, 24″ x 20″, dist. NC	85.00	—
remarqued print	160.00	—
☐ **MAN'S BEST FRIEND**, rel. 1981. ed. 800, s/n, 24¼″ x 28¼″, dist. NC	100.00	250.00
remarqued print	200.00	—
☐ **JUMPING THE GUN**, rel. 1982. ed. 600, s/n, 20″ x 24″, dist. NC	75.00	—
☐ **PINTAILS**, 1982 Wisconsin Duck Stamp print, rel. 1982. ed. 2,300, s/n, 14″ x 12″, dist. NC	135.00	200.00

SPICE MARKET by James Kramer

JAMES KRAMER

THEMES: Western art

MEDIUM: Watercolor

EDUCATION: Cleveland Institute of Art; Ohio State University

MEMBERSHIPS: National Academy of Western Art

GALLERY/DISTRIBUTOR: Mill Pond Press, Inc.

	ISSUE PRICE	CURRENT PRICE
☐ SPICE MARKET, rel. 1982. d. 950, s/n, 16⅛" x 21¾", pub MPPI	75.00	—
☐ FLOWER MARKET, rel. 1982. d. 950, s/n, 16⅛" x 21¾", pub MPPI	75.00	—

MILDRED SANDS KRATZ

THEMES: American scenes

STYLE: Realism

AWARDS: Holds over 100 art awards with five Gold medals in national competition

GALLERY/DISTRIBUTOR: Wildlife Internationale, Inc.

REFLECTIONS *by Mildred Sands Kratz*

	ISSUE PRICE	CURRENT PRICE
☐ THREE ARCH BRIDGE, ed. 950, s/n, 23¼" x 17", pub WII	50.00	—
☐ VILLAGE WALK, ed. 950, s/n, 23¼" x 15½", pub WII	50.00	—
☐ BLUE WAGON, ed. 950, s/n, 26½" x 20", pub WII	75.00	—
☐ SILENT CLOISTERS, ed. 950, s/n, 18" x 29", pub WII	60.00	—
☐ REFLECTIONS, ed. 950, s/n, 18" x 29", pub WII	60.00	—
☐ IN PORT, ed. 950, s/n, 22" x 33", pub WII	125.00	—
☐ SILENT PARADE, ed. 950, s/n, 22" x 26", pub WII	125.00	—

DIETMAR KRUMREY

THEMES: Wildlife art

AWARDS: Michigan Ducks Unlimited Artist of the Year (1984-85); New Jersey Ducks Unlimited Artist (1985); Michigan Wildlife Artist of the Year (1985), etc.

GALLERY/DISTRIBUTOR: Wilderness Art

GOLDEN RETRIEVER by Dietmar Krumrey

	ISSUE PRICE	CURRENT PRICE
☐ RACCOONS, rel. 1973. ed. 172, s/o, 17″ x 23″, pub CHWA	20.00	60.00
ed. 100, Artist proofs	50.00	120.00
☐ RING-NECKED PHEASANT, rel. 1972. ed. 355, s/o, 23″ x 17″, pub CHWA	20.00	90.00
ed. 100, Artist proofs	50.00	180.00
☐ WOOD DUCK, rel. 1972. ed. 246, s/o, 23″ x 17″, pub CHWA	20.00	90.00
ed. 100, Artist proofs	50.00	180.00
☐ RUFFED GROUSE, rel. 1973. ed. 76, s/o, 17″ x 23″, pub CHWA	20.00	60.00
ed. 100, Artist proofs	50.00	120.00
☐ WOODCOCK, rel. 1973. ed. 46, s/o, 14″ x 11″, pub CHWA	12.00	40.00
ed. 100, Artist proofs	30.00	80.00
☐ GROUSE, rel. 1975. ed. 300, s/n, pub NWA	40.00	300.00
☐ WOODCOCK, rel. 1975. ed. 950, s/n, pub NWA	40.00	120.00
☐ BLUE GOOSE, rel. 1976. ed. 150, s/n, pub NWA	70.00	100.00
☐ BLUE JAYS, rel. 1976. ed. 300, s/n, pub NWA	25.00	150.00
☐ EASTERN CHIPMUNK, rel. 1976. ed. 300, s/n, pub NWA	25.00	80.00
ed. 100, Artist proofs	40.00	50.00
☐ EASTERN COTTONTAILS, rel. 1976. ed. 300, s/n, pub NWA	40.00	120.00
ed. 100, Artist proofs	60.00	—
☐ OTTERS, rel. 1977. ed. 300, s/n, pub NWA	60.00	—
☐ SCREECH OWL, rel. 1978. ed. 300, s/n, pub NWA	40.00	200.00
☐ BLUEBILLS, rel. 1978. ed. 300, s/n, pub NWA	50.00	200.00
☐ EASTERN COTTONTAILS, rel. 1978. ed. 100 A/P, pub Michigan Conservation Club	60.00	90.00
☐ GROSBEAKS, rel. 1979. ed. 300, s/n, pub NWA	40.00	60.00
☐ GROUSE, rel. 1979. ed. 220, s/n, pub NWA	60.00	100.00
ed. 100, Artist proofs	80.00	—
☐ CHICKADEES, rel. 1980. ed. 300, s/n, pub NWA	50.00	100.00
ed. 100, Artist proofs	80.00	90.00
☐ GOLDEN LABRADOR, rel. 1980. ed. 850, s/n, pub Artist Portfolio	60.00	—
ed. 50, s/n, Artist proofs	90.00	—
☐ GOLDEN RETRIEVER, rel. 1980. ed. 850, s/n, pub Artist Portfolio	60.00	—
ed. 50, s/n, Artist proofs	90.00	—
☐ GROUSE, rel. 1980. ed. 850, s/n, pub WA*	80.00	—
☐ NUTHATCHES, rel. 1980. ed. 300, s/n, pub WA	50.00	—
☐ TIMBERWOLF, rel. 1980. ed. 850, s/n, pub WA	80.00	—
☐ BLACK LABRADOR, rel. 1981. ed. 850, s/n, pub WWI	90.00	—
ed. 40, s/n, Artist proofs	90.00	—
☐ BLUE WINGED TEAL, rel. 1981. ed. 300, s/n, pub WA	60.00	—
☐ BRITTANY, rel. 1981. ed. 850, s/n, pub WWI	60.00	—
ed. 40, s/n, A/P	90.00	—

*Company name changed from Northwoods Wildlife Art to Wilderness Art.

	ISSUE PRICE	CURRENT PRICE
☐ ERMINE, rel. 1981. ed. 300, s/n, pub WA	40.00	—
☐ MALLARDS, rel. 1981. ed. 300, s/n, pub WA	80.00	100.00
☐ CARDINAL, rel. 1982. ed. 300, s/n, 9″ x 11″, pub WA	50.00	
☐ GROUSE WITH CHICKS, rel. 1982. ed. 200, s/n, 12″ x 14½″, pub WA, donation to Wildlife Unlimited of Dickinson County, Michigan	100.00	—
ed. 50, Artist proofs	100.00	—
☐ RIVER OTTER, rel. 1982. ed. 300, s/n, 10″ x 12″, pub WA	60.00	—
☐ SAWWHET OWL, rel. 1982. ed. 300, s/n, 10″ x 12″, pub WA	60.00	—
☐ SNOWSHOE HARE, rel. 1982. ed. 300, s/n, 7″ x 8″, pub WA	40.00	—
☐ MISCHIEVOUS TRIO—RACCOONS, rel. 1983. ed. 200, s/n, 14″ x 17½″, pub WA	80.00	—
ed. 50, Artist proofs	100.00	—

*The above print is a fundraising print for Delta County of Michigan Wildlife Unlimited Organization.

	ISSUE PRICE	CURRENT PRICE
☐ BRACING THE CHILL—RUDDY TURNSTONE, rel. 1984. ed. 300, s/n, 12″ x 15″, pub WA	60.00	
☐ LAST SNOW RUFFED GROUSE, rel. 1984. ed. 500, s/n, 16″ x 24″, pub WA	95.00	
ed. 50, Artist proofs		

*Above print published by Willow Creek of Oshkosh, WI.

	ISSUE PRICE	CURRENT PRICE
☐ MISTY MORNING HARBOR LAUGHING GULL, rel. 1984. ed. 300, s/n, 10″ x 14″, pub WA	50.00	—
☐ MORNING WATCH—CANADA GEESE, rel. 1984. ed. 300, s/n, 14″ x 18″, pub WA	80.00	—
☐ TRANQUIL WATERS—GREENWINGED TEAL, rel. 1984. ed. 450, s/n, 11½″ x 17½″, pub WA	80.00	—

BOB KUHN

THEMES: Wildlife art

BOOKS: *The Animal Art of Bob Kuhn—a Lifetime of Drawing and Painting*

EDUCATION: Pratt Institute

GALLERY/DISTRIBUTOR: Arts Limited Inc.

	ISSUE PRICE	CURRENT PRICE
☐ SOFT TOUCH, rel. 1972. ed. 1,500, s/n, 30″ x 24″, pub ALI	80.00	—
☐ SUNSHINE AND SHADOWS, ed. 500, s/n, 32″ x 22½″, pub ALI	70.00	Sold Out
☐ JAGUAR, ed. 1,000, s/o, 32¾″ x 23¼″, pub ALI	60.00	Sold Out
☐ HIGH SIESTA - LEOPARD, rel. 1978. ed. 500, s/n, 15⅞″ x 12⅛″, pub SEL	70.00	—
☐ DRINKING TIGER, rel. 1980. ed. 750, s/n, 15½″ x 30″, pub SEL	125.00	Sold Out
☐ SERENGETI MONARCHS, rel. 1981. ed. 750, s/n, 18⅛″ x 27¼″, pub ALI	150.00	Sold Out

BRAVE WARRIOR *by Mort Künstler*

MORT KÜNSTLER

THEMES: Old West Art

EDUCATION: Pratt Institute

GALLERY/DISTRIBUTOR: Collectors International Ltd.

	ISSUE PRICE	CURRENT PRICE
☐ HOLIDAY HOMECOMING, rel. 1976. ed. 1,000, s/n, 19" x 25", pub FHG	40.00	115.00
*A portion of the edition reserved for First Day of Issue, Connecticut Valley Railroad Museum, Essex, Connecticut		
☐ STROUD FARM, HUTCHINSON, KANSAS, 1917, rel. 1976. ed. 2,000, s/n, 22" x 28", pub FHG	25.00	200.00
☐ THIS WE'LL DEFEND, rel. 1976. ed. 5,000, s/o, pub FHG	35.00	Sold Out
☐ SILVER GHOST, AUTUMN LEAVES, rel. 1977. ed. 1,000, s/n, 22" x 28", pub FHG ..	40.00	—
☐ THAT WAS THE DAY, rel. 1977. ed. 1,000, s/n, 22" x 28", pub FHG	40.00	—
☐ TUCSON STAGE, rel. 1977. ed. 1,000, s/n, 20" x 26", pub FHG	50.00	—
☐ AAU/USA INDOOR TRACK & FIELD NATIONALS, rel. 1978. ed. 600, s/n, pub CFAC	165.00	—
☐ AMONGST THE SACRED ELDERBERRY, rel. 1978. ed. 1,000, s/n, 20" x 26", pub FHG	50.00	—
☐ EARLY SNOW, rel. 1978. ed. 300, s/n, 22" x 30", pub CFAC	165.00	275.00
☐ THE KANSAN, rel. 1978. ed. 300, s/n, 29" x 24", pub CFAC	110.00	200.00
☐ RUNNIN' LATE, rel. 1978. ed. 300, s/n, pub HPC	400.00	600.00
☐ APACHE RAIDING PARTY, rel. 1979. ed. 500, s/n, 22½" x 30", pub FHG	60.00	150.00
☐ BRAVE WARRIOR, rel. 1979. ed. 5,000, s/o, 22" x 18", pub FHG	25.00	—
☐ EARLY CROSSING, rel. 1979. ed. 500, s/n, 21" x 30", pub FHG	60.00	80.00
☐ STORM CLOUDS, rel. 1980. ed. 300, s/n, silkscreen, 34½" x 25½"	400.00	500.00
☐ TREATY TALK, rel. 1979. ed. 500, s/n, 24" x 30", pub FHG	65.00	Sold Out
☐ WAR CRY, rel. 1979. ed. 550, s/n, 18½" x 30"	70.00	—
ed. 150, s/n, remarqued, pub FHG	115.00	—
☐ BOUNDARY LINE, rel. 1980. ed. 750, s/n, 30" x 24", pub FHG	70.00	—
☐ LONELY NIGHT, rel. 1980. ed. 750, s/n, 23¼" x 28", pub FHG	70.00	—
☐ SURPRISE ATTACK, rel. 1980. ed. 750, s/n, 24" x 30", pub FHG	70.00	—
☐ GOING AFTER BIG BULL, rel. 1981. ed. 300, s/n, 24" x 30", pub HP	500.00	—
☐ HIS NEW BLUE COAT, rel. 1981. ed. 300, s/n, 32" x 23", pub HP	500.00	—
☐ CHEYENNE WINTER, rel. 1983. ed. 500, s/n, size N/A, pub CIL	295.00	325.00
☐ MORNING MIST, rel. 1983. ed. 500, s/n, size N/A, pub CIL	295.00	325.00

JIM LAMB

THEMES: Sporting art

GALLERY/DISTRIBUTOR: Gray Stone Press

	ISSUE PRICE	CURRENT PRICE
☐ RACE FOR THE WIRE, rel. 1983. ed. 1,000, s/n, 26" x 19½", pub GSP	80.00	—
☐ SWALE WINS THE DERBY, rel. 1984. ed. 1,000, s/n, 28" x 23", pub GSP	80.00	—
ed. 100, Artist proofs	250.00	—

STAYIN' HIGH *by Hayden Lambson*

HAYDEN LAMBSON

THEMES: Wildlife art

STYLE: Realism

EDUCATION: Brigham Young University; Mesa Community College

GALLERY/DISTRIBUTOR: Swan Graphics, Ltd.

	ISSUE PRICE	CURRENT PRICE
☐ **ON THE TRACK,** rel. 1980. ed. 750, s/n, 23″ x 25″, pub SGL	65.00	—
s/n, remarqued	125.00	—
☐ **DEBATING THE CLEARING,** rel. 1980. ed. 750, s/n, 23″ x 15″, pub SGL	65.00	—
s/n, remarqued	125.00	—
☐ **THE HIGHLANDERS,** rel. 1981. ed. 750, s/n, 15½″ x 20″, pub SGL	65.00	—
s/n, remarqued	125.00	—
☐ **STAYIN' HIGH,** rel. 1981. ed. 750, s/n, 16″ x 20″, pub SGL	65.00	—
s/n, remarqued	125.00	—
☐ **THE APPRENTICE,** rel. 1982. ed. 950, s/n, 24″ x 16″, pub SGL	50.00	—
s/n, remarqued	125.00	—

PAUL LANDRY

THEMES: Marine art; varied themes

MEDIUM: Oil wash, etchings

BOOKS: *On Drawing and Painting, On Technique and Procedure*, both written by the artist

EDUCATION: Nova Scotia College of Art; Art Students League

GALLERY/DISTRIBUTOR: Greenwich Workshop

	ISSUE PRICE	CURRENT PRICE
☐ **REGATTA,** rel. 1984. ed. 525, s/n, 21″ x 16″, pub GW	75.00	—
☐ **REGATTA (Remarqued),** rel. 1984. ed. 25, s/n, 21″ x 16″, pub GW	165.00	—
☐ **THE SKATERS,** rel. 1985. ed. 525, s/n, 21″ x 16″, pub GW	75.00	—
☐ **THE SKATERS (Remarqued),** rel. 1985. ed. 25, s/n, 21″ x 16″, pub GW	165.00	—

J. FENWICK LANSDOWNE

THEMES: Birds

BOOKS: The artist's most recent title is *Birds of the West Coast*

MUSEUMS/COLLECTIONS: His paintings hang in Buckingham Palace, London's Tyron Gallery, and the National Wildlife Federation Gallery

GALLERY/DISTRIBUTOR: Greenwich Workshop

	ISSUE PRICE	CURRENT PRICE
☐ **BALD EAGLE,** rel. 1972. ed. 1,500, s/n, 22″ x 28″, pub GW	100.00	—
ed. 1,000 s/o, prints bearing the seal of the Connecticut Audubon Society. Proceeds to their Educational Development Fund	—	—
☐ **BARN OWL,** rel. 1972. ed. 1,500, s/n, 22″ x 28″, pub GW	100.00	150.00
☐ **BARRED OWL,** rel. 1972. ed. 1,500, s/n, 22″ x 28″, pub GW	100.00	175.00
☐ **EASTERN MEADOWLARK,** rel. 1972. ed. 1,500, s/n, 20″ x 25″, pub GW	65.00	—
☐ **SCREECH OWL,** rel. 1972. ed. 850, s/n, 17½″ x 22″, pub GW	N/A	350.00
☐ **PINTAIL DUCKS,** rel. 1973. ed. 1,000, s/n, 24″ x 18″, pub GW	75.00	170.00
☐ **WOOD DUCKS,** rel. 1973. ed. 1,000, s/n, 18″ x 24″, pub GW	75.00	130.00
☐ **RUFFED GROUSE,** rel. 1976. ed. 1,000, s/n, 18″ x 24″, pub GW	75.00	125.00
☐ **KENTUCKY WARBLER,** rel. 1983. ed. 650, s/n, 13⁷/₁₆″ x 15¹⁵/₁₆″, pub GW	75.00	—
☐ **WILSON'S WARBLER,** rel. 1983. ed. 650, s/n, 13⁷/₁₆″ x 15¹⁵/₁₆″, pub GW	75.00	—

DICK LAPHAM

THEMES: Landscape and marine art

MEDIUM: Oil and mixed media

STYLE: Representative

AWARDS: Over 40 to date, including Purchase awards

GALLERY/DISTRIBUTOR: Lapham's Art Gallery

	ISSUE PRICE	CURRENT PRICE
☐ THE SENTRY, rel. 1978. ed. 500, s/n, 16″ x 20″, litho, pub LAG	20.00	100.00
☐ FOGGY OATS, rel. 1980. ed. 1,000, s/n, 21″ x 15½″, litho, pub LAG	30.00	—
☐ THE LORD'S MORNING, rel. 1980. ed. 1,000, s/n, 20½″ x 15½″, litho, pub LAG	40.00	—
☐ LOW COUNTRY TWILIGHT, rel. 1981. ed. 850, s/n, 18″ x 14″, litho, pub LAG	30.00	—
☐ SNOW BIRD, rel. 1981. ed. 850, s/n, 18″ x 14″, litho, pub LAG	30.00	—
☐ DESERTED AUTUMN, rel. 1982. ed. 850, s/n, 12″ x 24″, litho, pub LAG	35.00	—
☐ SEA OATS SERENADE, rel. 1982. ed. 850, s/n, 12″ x 24″, litho, pub LAG	35.00	—
☐ SEA SCAPE, rel. 1982. ed. 850, s/n, 20″ x 14″, litho, pub LAG	35.00	—
☐ FRAMED SOLITUDE, rel. 1984. ed. 850, s/n, 27½″ x 22″, litho, pub LAG	65.00	—

PHILIP LASZ

THEMES: Wildlife art

MEDIUM: Acrylic and oil

GALLERY/DISTRIBUTOR: Philip Lasz Gallery

	ISSUE PRICE	CURRENT PRICE
☐ ELEPHANT HERD ON THE MOVE, ed. 1,000, s/n, 34″ x 21″, pub PLG	60.00	—
☐ HIS MAJESTY, ed. 1,000, s/n, 34″ x 21″, pub PLG	60.00	—
☐ GREATER KUDU, ed. 1,000, s/n, 34″ x 21″, pub PLG	60.00	—
☐ PEACE BEFORE THE STORM, ed. 1,000, s/n, 34″ x 21″, pub PLG	60.00	—

ROD LAWRENCE

THEMES: Wildlife art

PUBLICATIONS: Rod's art has appeared on the covers of such magazines as *Michigan Out-Of-Doors, Michigan Sportsman,* and *Michigan Angling Report*

AWARDS: Michigan Wildlife Artist of the Year (1981), Waterfowl Artist of the Year (1979)

MEMBERSHIPS: He is an active member of many wildlife and conservation organizations

GALLERY/DISTRIBUTOR: Mill Pond Press, Inc.

COMMENTS: In 1981, the artist designed Michigan's Trout Stamp

	ISSUE PRICE	CURRENT PRICE
☐ MISTY MORNING - MERGANSERS, rel. 1983. ed. 950, 17½″ x 21″, pub MPPI	85.00	—
☐ PINTAILS, rel. 1984. ed. 950, size not available, pub MPPI	50.00	—

LE BA DANG

THEMES: Oriental art

EDUCATION: School of Fine Arts in Toulouse, France

GALLERY/DISTRIBUTOR: Circle Fine Arts Corp.

	ISSUE PRICE	CURRENT PRICE
☐ **LOLLIPOP TREE,** ed. 120, s/o, litho. 20″ x 26″, pub CFAC	—	225.00
☐ **ORANGE JUNKS,** ed. 120, s/o, litho, 20″ x 26″, pub CFAC	—	225.00
☐ **AFRIQUE,** ed. 180, s/o, litho, 19″ x 26″, pub CFAC	—	200.00
☐ **LESCHEVAUX ORANGES,** ed. 180, s/o, litho, 19″ x 26″, pub CFAC	—	225.00
☐ **REVE,** ed. 180, s/o, litho, 19″ x 26″, pub CFAC	—	150.00
☐ **JUNGLE,** ed. 180, s/o, litho, 19″ x 26″, pub CFAC	—	200.00
☐ **PAYSAGE AUX BARQUES,** ed. 225, s/o, litho, 21″ x 29″, pub CFAC	—	150.00
☐ **LALUNE ROUGE,** ed. 225, s/o, litho, 21″ x 29″, pub CFAC	—	150.00
☐ **LE LAC,** ed. 225, s/o, litho, 21″ x 29″, pub CFAC	—	150.00
☐ **LE CHEVAL,** ed. 225, s/o, litho, 21″ x 29″, pub CFAC	—	150.00
☐ **STALLIONS,** ed. 275, s/o, etching, 11″ x 15″, pub CFAC	—	150.00
☐ **ARBRE JAUNE,** ed. 275, s/o, etching, 11″ x 15″, pub CFAC	—	150.00
☐ **FIGURE DE LA LUNE,** ed. 275, s/o, etching, 11″ x 15″, pub CFAC	—	150.00
☐ **PASSAGE DE LA LUNE,** ed. 175, s/o, etching, 11″ x 15″, pub CFAC	—	150.00
☐ **FEMME NATIVE,** ed. 275, s/o, etching, 11″ x 15″, pub CFAC	—	150.00
☐ **TRAVAILLE DU MATIN,** ed. 275, s/o, etching, 11″ x 15″, pub CFAC	—	150.00
☐ **FORET,** ed. 175, s/o, etching, 11″ x 15″, pub CFAC	—	150.00
☐ **NUE,** ed. 175, s/o, etching, 11″ x 15″, pub CFAC	—	150.00
☐ **LE CHEVAL CAVALLIER,** ed. 175, s/o, etching, 11″ x 15″, pub CFAC	—	150.00
☐ **MUTHUSWAMY,** ed. 275, s/o, etching, 11″ x 15″, pub CFAC	—	150.00
☐ **GOLDEN ORB,** ed. 275, s/o, litho, 26″ x 38″, pub CFAC	—	1,000.00
☐ **TEMPEST,** ed. 275, s/o, litho, 27″ x 38″, pub CFAC	—	175.00
☐ **MOONSHADOW,** ed. 275, s/o, litho, 21″ x 30″, pub CFAC	—	175.00
☐ **IMAGINATIVE LANDSCAPE,** ed. 275, s/o, litho, 24″ x 34″, pub CFAC	—	175.00
☐ **TEN HORSE FOLIO,** ed. 275, s/o, litho, 21″ x 30″, pub CFAC	—	3,300.00
ed. 50 on Japon	—	4,000.00
☐ **FANTASIE SUITE,** ed. 200, s/o, remarqued litho, 21″ x 29″, pub CFAC	—	3,900.00
☐ **LES BARQUES A MINUIT,** ed. 200, s/o, remarqued litho, 21″ x 29″, pub CFAC	—	375.00
☐ **LA RIVIERE ORANGE,** ed. 200, s/o, remarqued litho. 21″ x 29″, pub CFAC	—	400.00
☐ **VERRE DES FLEURS,** ed. 200, s/o, remarqued litho, 21″ x 29″, pub CFAC	—	400.00
☐ **BOUQUET DES FLEURS,** ed. 200, s/o, remarqued litho, 21″ x 29″, pub CFAC	—	450.00
☐ **COMPOSITION AVEC LES FLEURS,** ed. 200, s/o, remarqued litho, 21″ x 29″, pub CFAC	—	450.00
☐ **COMPOSITION,** ed. 200, s/o, remarqued litho, 21″ x 29″, pub CFAC	—	425.00
☐ **POT DES FLEURS,** ed. 200, s/o, remarqued litho, 21″ x 29″, pub CFAC	—	400.00
☐ **LES BARQUES EN BLEU ET ROUGE,** ed. 200, s/o, remarqued litho, 21″ x 29″, pub CFAC	—	400.00
☐ **LE SOLEIL ORANGE,** ed. 200, s/o, remarqued litho, 21″ x 29″, pub CFAC	—	400.00
☐ **LA LUNE MYSTERIEUX,** ed. 200, s/o, remarqued litho, 21″ x 29″, pub CFAC	—	400.00
☐ **LA FEMME REPOSEE,** ed. 200, s/o, remarqued litho, 15″ x 22″, pub CFAC	—	325.00
☐ **PETITE NATURE MORTE AVEC UNE VERRE,** ed. 200, s/o, remarqued litho, 15″ x 22″, pub CFAC	—	350.00
☐ **LES FLEURS DE MINUIT,** ed. 200, s/o, remarqued litho, 15″ x 22″, pub CFAC	—	400.00
☐ **LA COLOMBE,** ed. 200, s/o, remarqued litho, 15″ x 22″, pub CFAC	—	400.00
☐ **LA BRANCHE MORTE,** ed. 200, s/o, remarqued litho, 25″ x 41″, pub CFAC	—	500.00
☐ **FANTASIE DU SOIR,** ed. 200, s/o, remarqued litho, 26″ x 39″, pub CFAC	—	500.00
☐ **NATURE PRAYS WITHOUT WORDS,** ed. 125, s/o, 22″ x 30″, pub EWG	—	* 1,800.00
*Portfolio of 16 original litho, ed. 125, on Arches paper with one on Japon Nacre	—	2,000.00
☐ **LES CHEVAUX SUITE,** ed. 125, s/n, 11″ x 15″, pub EWG	—	* 1,800.00
*Portfolio of 27 original mixed media, ed. 125 Deluxe edition with 7 additional	-	2,000.00
☐ **UNWRITTEN WORDS,** ed. 80, s/o, original color litho, 20″ x 26″, pub EWG	—	250.00
☐ **LE SOLEIL BLEU,** ed. 275, s/o, serigraph, 30″ x 22″, pub CFA	—	350.00
☐ **LA MONTAGNE,** ed. 175, s/o, serigraph, 30″ x 22″, pub CFA	—	350.00

	ISSUE PRICE	CURRENT PRICE
☐ **LE CHEVAL NOIR,** ed. 275, s/o, serigraph, 30″ x 22″, pub CFA	—	350.00
☐ **LE CHEVALIER SOLITAIRE,** ed. 275, s/o, serigraph, 30″ x 22″, pub CFA	—	375.00
☐ **LES VOILIERS,** ed. 275, s/o, serigraph, 30″ x 22″, pub CFA	—	350.00
☐ **LA BRANCHE SECHE,** ed. 275, s/o, serigraph, 31″ x 47″, pub CFA	—	550.00
☐ **LES MONTAGNES DOREES,** ed. 275, s/o, serigraph, 31″ x 47″, pub CFA	—	600.00
☐ **CHEVEL D'AMTAM,** ed. 275, s/o, serigraph, 31″ x 47″, pub CFA	—	650.00
☐ **LA CAVALIERE SOLITAIRE,** ed. 275, s/o, serigraph, 30″ x 22″, pub CFA	—	400.00
☐ **LE ROCHER, LA MERE ET L'ENFANT,** ed. 275, s/o, serigraph, 30″ x 22″, pub CFA .	—	350.00
☐ **LA MONTAGNE DE LA MERE ET L'ENFANT,** ed. 275, s/o, serigraph, 30″ x 22″, pub CFA	—	300.00
☐ **LE ROCHER DE LA GRANDE DAME,** ed. 275, s/o, serigraph, 30″ x 22″, pub CFA ..	—	325.00
☐ **LA MONTAGNE ENSOLEILLEE,** ed. 275, s/o, serigraph, 31″ x 31″, pub CFA	—	400.00
☐ **LE PRINTEMPS,** ed. 275, s/o, serigraph, 47″ x 21″, pub CFA	—	350.00
☐ **FLEURS,** ed. 300, s/o, serigraph, 64″ x 48″, pub CFA	—	1,000.00
☐ **PLEASURES,** ed. 275, s/o, serigraph, 11″ x 11″, pub CFA	—	125.00
☐ **DREAMS,** ed. 275, s/o, serigraph, 11″ x 11″, pub CFA	—	125.00
☐ **MYSTERIEUX,** ed. 275, s/o, serigraph, 11″ x 11″, pub CFA	—	125.00
☐ **IMAGINATION,** ed. 275, s/o, serigraph, 11″ x 11″, pub CFA	—	125.00
☐ **JOYEUX,** ed. 175, s/o, serigraph, 31″ x 16″, pub CFA	—	325.00
☐ **LE MONUMENT,** ed. 300, s/o, litho embossment, 24″ x 30″, pub CFA	—	400.00
☐ **LA PETITE CABANE DU PECHEUR,** ed. 300, s/o, litho embossment, 30″ x 22″, pub CFA	—	425.00
☐ **LE BOUT DU PASSAGE,** ed. 300, s/o, litho embossment, 30″ x 22″, pub CFA	—	400.00
☐ **L'AUTRE MONDE,** ed. 300, s/o, litho embossment, 34″ x 25″, pub CFA	—	425.00
☐ **LE PAPILLON,** ed. 300, s/o, litho embossment, 24″ x 17″, pub CFA	—	375.00
☐ **LA BARQUE SOLITAIRE II,** ed. 300, s/o, litho embossment, 30″ x 22″, pub CFA	—	375.00
☐ **LA DEMIE LUNE,** ed. 300, s/o, litho embossment, 34″ x 25″, pub CFA	—	400.00
☐ **LA BARQUE ET LA LUNE,** ed. 300, s/o, litho embossment, 25″ x 17″, pub CFA	—	375.00
☐ **LA BARQUE SOLITAIRE I,** ed. 300, s/o, litho embossment, 25″ x 17″, pub CFA	—	300.00
☐ **L'ABERRATION,** ed. 300, s/o, litho embossment, 25″ x 17″, pub CFA	—	300.00
☐ **LA LUNE ROUGE ET l'HIVER,** ed. 300, s/o, litho embossment, 24″ x 17″, pub CFA ..	—	325.00
☐ **LE PAYSAGE MELANCOLIQUE,** ed. 300, s/o, litho embossment, 24″ x 17″, pub CFA	—	325.00
☐ **LA COMEDIE HUMAINE #4,** ed. 300, s/o, litho embossment, 35″ x 13″, pub CFA ...	—	325.00
☐ **LA COMEDIE HUMAINE #3,** ed. 300, s/o, litho embossment, 35″ x 13″, pub CFA ...	—	325.00
☐ **LA COMEDIE HUMAINE #2,** ed. 300, s/o, litho embossment, 24″ x 24″, pub CFA ...	—	400.00
☐ **LA COMEDIE HUMAINE #1,** ed. 300, s/o, litho embossment, 24″ x 24″, pub CFA ...	—	325.00
☐ **LA COMEDIE HUMAINE #5,** ed. 300, s/o, litho embossment, 30″ x 23″, pub CFA ...	—	425.00
☐ **LA LUNE BLANC,** ed. 300, s/o, litho embossment, 30″ x 23″, pub CFA	—	525.00
☐ **CE N'EST PAS ENCORE L'HIVER,** ed. 250, s/o, etching embossment, 14″ x 10″, pub CFA	—	225.00
☐ **UNE PETITE CHANSON DANS L'ESPACE,** ed. 250, s/o, etching embossment, 14″ x 10″, pub CFA	—	225.00
☐ **UNE PETITE CHANSON,** ed. 250, s/o, etching embossment, 14″ x 10″, pub CFA	—	225.00
☐ **TRANQUILITE,** ed. 250, s/o, etching embossment, 14″ x 10″, pub CFA	—	225.00
☐ **CALME ET DIGNITE,** ed. 250, s/o, etching embossment, 21″ x 10″, pub CFA	—	350.00
☐ **LA VIE ET LE BONHEUR,** ed. 250, s/o, etching embossment, 32″ x 10″, pub CFA ...	—	350.00
☐ **LA NATURE PRIE SANS PAROLE,** ed. 250, s/o, etching embossment, 26″ x 20″, pub CFA	—	425.00
☐ **CALME ET BEAUTE,** ed. 250, s/o, etching embossment, 26″ x 20″, pub CFA	—	425.00

LEE LeBLANC

THEMES: Wildlife art

MEDIUM: Oil and watercolor

STYLE: LeBlanc depicts his subjects with exacting anatomical accuracy, while drawing on his illustrative experience for the colorful and imaginative backdrops which distinguish his work

BACKGROUND: An artist with *Twentieth Century Fox* and a Disney Studio animator, Lee LeBlanc worked in the motion picture industry for 25 years

EDUCATION: He attended art schools in New York, Philadelphia, and Los Angeles

AWARDS: Federal Duck Stamp Contest (1973), Ducks Unlimited Artist of the Year (1980), and other honors

GALLERY/DISTRIBUTOR: Petersen Prints

	ISSUE PRICE	CURRENT PRICE
☐ OBION RIVER MEMORY, ed. 800, s/n, 16″ x 24″, litho, pub PP	60.00	200.00
☐ HORSESHOE MEMORY - GEESE, ed. 800, s/n, 17½″ x 25″, litho, pub PP	60.00	120.00
☐ A LACASSINE MEMORY, ed. 800, s/n, 16″ x 25″, litho, pub PP	60.00	100.00
☐ A CACHE RIVER MEMORY, ed. 800, s/n, 16″ x 25″, pub PP	60.00	160.00
☐ A HATCHEE RIVER MEMORY, ed. 800, s/n, 16″ x 25″, pub PP	60.00	120.00
☐ McCULLUM'S FLOODED TIMBER, ed. 800, s/n, 16″ x 25″, litho, pub PP	60.00	120.00
☐ THE GATHERING, ed. 800, s/n, 16″ x 24″, pub PP	75.00	—
remarqued, s/n	165.00	—
☐ SYCAMORE AND BOBWHITES, ed. 800, s/n, 17″ x 25″, pub PP	75.00	—
remarqued, s/n	165.00	—
☐ WHITE TAILS, ed. 800, s/n, 15½″ x 25″, pub PP	75.00	—
remarqued, s/n	165.00	—
☐ WOOD DUCKS AND CYPRESS, ed. 800, s/n, 16″ x 26″, pub PP	75.00	—
remarqued, s/n	165.00	—
☐ ALONG THE BUFFALO, ed. 800, s/n, 16″ x 24″, pub PP	75.00	—
remarqued, s/n	165.00	—
☐ A NOBLE PAIR - WILD TURKEYS, rel. 1974. ed. 580, s/n, size not available, pub WWI	60.00	—
☐ A STATELY PAIR - MALLARDS, rel. 1974. ed. 580, s/n, size not available, pub WWI	60.00	300.00
☐ ARKANSAS MALLARDS, rel. 1974. ed. 400, s/n, size not available, pub WWI	45.00	150.00
☐ HONKERS AT HORICON, rel. 1974. ed. 400, s/n, size not available, pub WWI	45.00	120.00
☐ A HATCHEE RIVER MEMORY - WOOD DUCKS, rel. 1974. ed. 800, s/n, size not available, pub PP	60.00	120.0
☐ MID-MORNING MALLARDS, rel. 1984. ed. 800, s/n, 14½″ x 20½″, pub PP	45.00	—
☐ GREENHEAD GRANDEUR, rel. 1984. ed. 950, s/n, plate I, 27″ x 17″, pub PP (A suite of 3 prints) PLATE II and PLATE III, 12½″ x 17″	125.00	—

MARTHA BLAIR LEONE

THEMES: Country

STYLE: Primitivism with a sense of sophistication

EDUCATION: Rhode Island School of Design

GALLERY/DISTRIBUTOR: Mill Pond Press, Inc.

	ISSUE PRICE	CURRENT PRICE
☐ COUNTRY CROSSROADS, rel. 1981. ed. 950, s/n, 16½″ x 22¾″, pub MPPI	65.00	—
☐ SUNSHINE FAIR, rel. 1981. ed. 950, s/n, 19″ x 18⅜″, pub MPPI	75.00	—

MANES LICHTENBERG

THEMES: Varied

STYLE: Impressionism

EDUCATION: Art Students League, Academie de la Grande Chaimiere in Paris

AWARDS: He has been honored with numerous awards in exhibitions, both in the United States and Paris

GALLERY/DISTRIBUTOR: Eleanor Ettinger, Inc.

	ISSUE PRICE	CURRENT PRICE
☐ **CONNECTICUT SHORE,** rel. 1980. ed. 300, s/n, litho, arches, 23″ x 28″, pub EEI ...	250.00	—
☐ **DOVE COTE,** rel. 1980, ed. 300, s/n, litho, arches, 25″ x 20″, pub EEI	250.00	—
☐ **MARCHE AUX FLEURS, PARIS,** rel. 1980. ed. 300, s/n, litho, arches, 23″ x 28″, pub EEI	250.00	—

MAGGIE LINN

THEMES: Wildlife art

BACKGROUND: Maggie spent her early years in the Far East. Her childhood in China has been the major influence on her art. Art was a key ingredient of survival for her during a perilous escape from war-torn China, and four years of hardship as a refugee in India

AWARDS: Has twice received awards from the American Watercolor Society

MEMBERSHIPS: American Watercolor Society

GALLERY/DISTRIBUTOR: Mill Pond Press, Inc.

COMMENTS: Upon her days as a refugee, Ms. Linn reflects, "Art gave me an identity. It helped me survive, and it gave me a tool with which to communicate"

	ISSUE PRICE	CURRENT PRICE
☐ **CHICKADEE AND SUNFLOWERS,** rel. 1983. ed. 950, 17½″ x 11″, pub MPPI	45.00	—
☐ **EARLY ARRIVALS,** rel. 1983. ed. 950, 18″ x 14″, pub MPPI	50.00	—

LENA Y. LIU

THEMES: Oriental art

EDUCATION: The artist studies in oriental art began at a very early age. She was with the Li-Shui studio under Professor Sun Chia-Chin for three years, and then, under Professor Huang Chun-Pi for five years before coming to study in the United States. Lena graduated from the School of Architecture & Design at the State University of N.Y./Buffalo in 1974, and later went to the graduate school at U.C.L.A. Since 1977, she has devoted full time to painting

AWARDS: She has won numerous awards at national shows and exhibits. Her works are represented in many public and private collections throughout the United States, as well as in Europe and the Far East

GALLERY/DISTRIBUTOR: Lena Liu's Studio

	ISSUE PRICE	CURRENT PRICE
☐ THE DREAMER, rel. 1984. s/n, 18″ x 24″, pub LLS	65.00	—
☐ KINGFISHER & LOTUS, rel. 1984. s/n, 16″ x 20″, pub LLS	45.00	—
☐ HUMMINGBIRDS & HIBISCUS, rel. 1984, s/n, 16″ x 20″, pub LLS	45.00	—
☐ BUTTERFLY & MORNING GLORIES, rel. 1984. s/n, 12″ x 15″, pub LLS	35.00	—
☐ BUTTERFLY & HIBISCUS, rel. 1984. s/n, 12″ x 15″, pub LLS	35.00	—
☐ MAUVE VEILTAIL, rel. 1984. s/n, 12″ x 15″ pub LLS	35.00	—
☐ PEACH VEILTAIL, rel. 1984. s/n, 12″ x 15″, pub LLS	35.00	—
☐ SPRING FAIRY, rel. 1984. s/n, 16″ x 20″, pub LLS	35.00	—
☐ KINGFISHER, rel. 1984. s/n, 16″ x 20″, pub LLS	35.00	—
☐ LILY POND, rel. 1984. s/n, 16″ x 20″, pub LLS	35.00	—
☐ THREE LITTLE DEER, rel. 1984. s/n, 16″ x 20″, pub LLS	35.00	—
☐ BLUE PEACOCK, rel. 1984. s/n, 18″ x 24″, pub LLS	65.00	—
☐ WHITE PEACOCK, rel. 1984. s/n, 18″ x 20″, pub LLS	65.00	—
☐ IRIS, rel. 1984. s/n, 16″ x 20″, pub LLS	45.00	—
☐ ORCHID, rel. 1984. s/n, 16″ x 20″, pub LLS	45.00	—
☐ AT PEACE, rel. 1984. s/n, 10″ x 26″, pub LLS	45.00	—
☐ AIMING HIGH, rel. 1984. s/n, 20″ x 26″, pub LLS	65.00	—
☐ FLYING FREE, rel. 1984. s/n, 10″ x 26″, pub LLS	45.00	—
☐ WATERFALL I, rel. 1984. s/n, 18″ x 24″, pub LLS	55.00	—
☐ WATERFALL II, rel. 1984. s/n, 18″ x 24″, pub LLS	55.00	—
☐ SPRING, rel. 1984. s/n, 12″ x 15″, pub LLS	35.00	—
☐ SUMMER, rel. 1984. s/n, 12″ x 15″, pub LLS	35.00	—
☐ FALL, rel. 1984. s/n, 12″ x 15	35.00	—
☐ WINTER, rel. 1984. s/n, 12″ x 15″, pub LLS	35.00	—
☐ FREE FLIGHT 1 (RUST BUTTERFLY), rel. 1985. s/n, 19″ x 26″, pub LLS	60.00	—
☐ FREE FLIGHT 2 (PINK BUTTERFLY), rel. 1985. s/n, 19″ x 26″, pub LLS	60.00	—
☐ CARDINAL (SPRING), rel. 1985. s/n, 8″ x 20″, pub LLS	35.00	—
☐ BLUEBIRDS (SUMMER), rel. 1985. s/n, 8″ x 20″, pub LLS	35.00	—
☐ WOODPECKER (FALL), rel. 1985. s/n, 8″ x 20″, pub LLS	35.00	—
☐ CHICKADEES (WINTER), rel. 1985. s/n, 8″ x 20″, pub LLS	35.00	—
☐ HUMMINGBIRD & COLUMBINE, rel. 1985. s/n, 8″ x 20″, pub LLS	35.00	—
☐ HUMMINGBIRDS & TRUMPET VINE,, rel. 1985. s/n, 8″ x 20″, pub LLS	35.00	—
☐ OPERA LADY, rel. 1985. 950, s/n, 23″ x 31½″, pub LLS	195.00	—

DAVID G. LOCKHART

THEMES: Varied

MEDIUM: Watercolor and oil

GALLERY/DISTRIBUTOR: Wild Wings, Inc.

	ISSUE PRICE	CURRENT PRICE
☐ COVEY POINT - QUAIL, rel. 1973. ed. 480, s/n, 17″ x 23½″, pub WWI	40.00	—
☐ PUDDLE JUMPERS, rel. 1978. ed. 490, s/n, size not available, pub WWI	65.00	—
☐ AUTUMN CALM - BLACK DUCKS, rel. 1980. ed. 850, s/n, size not available, pub WWI	70.00	—
☐ DOVE CLUB AT WEBER'S, rel. 1980, ed. 600, s/n, 14″ x 21″, pub WWI	50.00	—

ART LONG

THEMES: Wildlife art

MEDIUM: Oil, watercolor, and acrylic

STYLE: Realism

GALLERY/DISTRIBUTOR: Northwoods Craftsman

	ISSUE PRICE	CURRENT PRICE
☐ WINTERY AFTERNOON - RUFFED GROUSE, rel. 1979. ed. 300, s/n, 28¼″ x 22½″, distr. NC	50.00	400.00
☐ EAGLE WITH NORTHERN PIKE, rel. 1980. ed. 480, s/n, 17¼″ x 21½″, distr. NC	35.00	—
☐ FIGHTING MUSKY, rel. 1980. ed. 480, s/n, 24¼″ x 20″, distr. NC	45.00	—
☐ QUIET POND - WOOD DUCKS, rel. 1980. ed. 350, s/n, 27¼″ x 19½″, distr. NC	50.00	—
☐ LOONS AT DUSK, rel. 1981. ed. 150, s/n, 29″ x 23″, distr. NC	100.00	200.00
☐ MAJESTIC MOUNTAINS - ELK, rel. 1981. ed. 500, s/n, 28″ x 21″, distr. NC	60.00	—
☐ NEW YEARS DAY, rel. 1981. ed. 500, s/n, 37″ x 25½″, distr. NC	85.00	—
☐ BACKYARD BUDDY - BARRED OWL, rel. 1982. ed. 500, s/n, 11¾″ x 15¾″, distr. NC	30.00	—
☐ SPIRIT OF THE NORTH - LOON, rel. 1982. ed. 480, s/n, 17¼″ x 21¼″, distr. NC	40.00	—
☐ SPRINGTIME SPLENDOR, rel. 1983. ed. 480, s/n, 29″ x 23″, distr. NC	60.00	—
☐ STONY BROOK - GREAT BLUE HERON, rel. 1983. ed. 480, s/n, 17⅛″ x 21¼″, distr. NC	80.00	—
☐ UNDER THE BALSAM, rel. 1983. ed. 480, s/n, 29″ x 23″, distr. NC	40.00	—

ROBERT LONG

THEMES: Varied

MEDIUM: Transparent watercolor and oil

STYLE: Realism

MEMBERSHIPS: Midwest Watercolor Society

MUSEUMS/COLLECTIONS: His paintings hang in selected galleries throughout the United States

GALLERY/DISTRIBUTOR: Seven Arts Gallery Publishing

COMMENTS: The artist's decision to paint had its roots in a quotation from philosopher Will James: "The best use of life is to spend it for something which will outlast it"

	ISSUE PRICE	CURRENT PRICE
☐ A HERITAGE PASSING, rel. 1975. ed. 1,000, s/n, litho, pub SAG	25.00	—
ed. 1,000, s/o	15.00	—
☐ NATURE'S LATTICEWORK, rel. 1975. ed. 250, s/n, litho, pub SAG	25.00	—
ed. 250	15.00	—
☐ RETIREMENT, rel. 1978. ed. 1,150, s/n, litho, pub SAG	25.00	—
ed. 100, s/n, remarqued in watercolor	50.00	145.00
☐ HUB, rel. 1979. ed. 750, s/n, litho, pub SAG	40.00	—
ed. 100, s/n, remarqued in watercolor	75.00	160.00

BLACK GINGER AND HOMEMADE SIN *by Robert Long*

	ISSUE	CURRENT
☐ **AUTUMN'S SUBTLE BEAUTY**, rel. 1982. ed. 550, s/n, litho, pub SAG	65.00	—
ed. 300, s/n, remarqued in watercolor	100.00	150.00
☐ **BLACK GINGER AND HOMEMADE SIN**, rel. 1983. ed. 950, s/n, litho, pub SAG	42.50*	—
ed. 50, s/n, remarqued in watercolor	95.00	175.00
☐ **NUZZLIN'**, rel. 1983. ed. 950, s/n, litho, pub SAG	42.50*	—
ed. 50, s/n, remarqued in watercolor	95.00	185.00
☐ **SOMEONE'S PRINCE**, rel. 1983. ed. 950, s/n, litho, pub SAG	85.00	—
ed. 300, s/n, remarqued in watercolor	150.00	220.00

*Unremarqued prints of "Nuzzlin'" and "Black Ginger and Homemade Sin" sold as a pair.

TED LONG

THEMES: Western art

BACKGROUND: Long's career, prior to becoming a full-time artist, included being a movie director and a television art director

GALLERY/DISTRIBUTOR: Guildhall, Inc.

	ISSUE PRICE	CURRENT PRICE
☐ **IN SEARCH OF BEAVER**, ed. 500, s/n, 21" x 17", distr. GI	65.00	—

ROBERT LOUGHEED

THEMES: Wildlife art

BOOKS: Illustrated *Mustang* and *San Domingo* by Marguerite Henry

BACKGROUND: As a commercial artist, his most memorable work is the "Flying Red Horse" of Mobil Oil, and the steeplechase horses of Texaco

EDUCATION: Ontario College of Arts; École des Beaux Arts in Montreal

MEMBERSHIPS: Society of Animal Artists; National Academy of Western Art; Cowboy Artists of America

MUSEUMS/COLLECTIONS: National Cowboy Hall of Fame

GALLERY/DISTRIBUTOR: Mill Pond Press, Inc.

	ISSUE PRICE	CURRENT PRICE
☐ IN THE QUIET OF WINTER, rel. 1977. ed. 950, s/n, 18″ x 30″, pub MPPI	85.00	—
☐ DUST TRAIL OF THE BELL REMUDA, ed. 800, s/n, 16½″ x 33″, pub PP	125.00	—
☐ OPEN RANGE ENCOUNTER, rel. 1980. ed. 1,000, s/n, 20½″ x 35″, pub SCG	150.00	Sold Out
☐ SUNSET IN THE HIGH COUNTRY, rel. 1980. ed. 1,000, s/n, 18″ x 36″, pub SCG	115.00	—
☐ NAVAJO TAPESTRY, rel. 1982. ed. 950, s/n, 19¼″ x 32½″, pub MPPI	115.00	—

RICHARD LOUNSBURY

THEMES: Landscapes, florals, geometrics, music

MEDIUM: Serigraphs

STYLE: Contemporary

AWARDS: Sylvania Award "Toys for Tots", Christmas, 1978

GALLERY/DISTRIBUTOR: Unique Graphics

	ISSUE PRICE	CURRENT PRICE
☐ ON BLUEGERRY HILL, rel. 1980. ed. 500, s/n, 23″ x 29″, pub UG	60.00	Sold Out
☐ DIMENSION, rel. 1980. ed. 300, s/n, 23″ x 29″, pub UG	70.00	110.00
☐ MOONSCAPE, rel. 1981. ed. 250, s/n, 23″ x 29″, pub UG	70.00	Sold Out
☐ MOONGLOW, rel. 1982. ed. 250, s/n, 10″ x 26″, pub UG	35.00	45.00
☐ BIRD OF PARADISE, rel. 1983. ed. 250, s/n, 23″ x 29″, pub UG	70.00	120.00
☐ OPUS II, rel. 1983. ed. 250, s/n, 23″ x 29″, pub UG	70.00	120.00
☐ BEYOND THE BEACH, rel. 1984. ed. 250, s/n, 23″ x 29″, pub UG	70.00	120.00
☐ BLUE VASE WITH FLOWERS, rel. 1984. ed. 250, s/n, 23″ x 29″, pub UG	70.00	—
☐ VIEW FROM ROSWELL, rel. 1985. ed. 250, s/n, 23″ x 29″, pub UG	70.00	—
☐ VIEW FROM ANTIGUA, rel. 1985. ed. 250, s/n, 23″ x 29″, pub UG	70.00	—
☐ MORNING MIST, rel. 1985. ed. 250, s/n, 11″ x 29″, pub UG	40.00	—
☐ SILENT PLANET, rel. 1985. ed. 250, s/n, 25″ x 40″, pub UG	80.00	—

RONALD J. LOUGUE

THEMES: Wildlife art

STYLE: Realism

EDUCATION: Lousiana State University

AWARDS: Winner of World Championship Wildfowl Painting Competition (1984); Ohio Duck Stamp Contest (1985); Indiana Duck Stamp Contest (1986)

GALLERY/DISTRIBUTOR: National Wildlife Galleries, Inc.

	ISSUE PRICE	CURRENT PRICE
☐ **BOBWHITES,** rel. 1978. ed. 750, s/n, photo offset litho, 16″ x 20″, pub NWGI	35.00	—
☐ **CARDINALS AND MAGNOLIA,** rel. 1978. ed. 750, s/n, photo offset litho, 16″ x 20″, pub NWGI........	35.00	Sold Out
☐ **GREAT HORNED OWL,** rel. 1978. ed. 750, s/n, photo offset litho, 18″ x 24″, pub NWGI........	35.00	Sold Out
☐ **MALLARDS,** rel. 1979. ed. 1,000, s/n, photo offset litho, 16″ x 20″, pub NWGI	35.00	Sold Out
☐ **RED TAILED HAWK,** rel. 1979. ed. 1,000, s/n, photo offset litho, 18″ x 24″, pub NWGI........	35.00	Sold Out
☐ **WOOD DUCKS,** rel. 1979. ed. 1,000, s/n, photo offset litho, 16″ x 20″, pub NWGI	35.00	Sold Out
☐ **BROKEN COVEY,** rel. 1980. ed. 1,000, s/n, photo offset litho, 18″ x 24″, pub NWGI ..	40.00	Sold Out
☐ **FOX SQUIRREL,** rel. 1980. ed. 1,000, s/n, photo offset litho, 16″ x 20″, pub NWGI ...	40.00	Sold Out

CHARLES LOVATO

THEMES: Indian art

STYLE: Abstract

AWARDS: Avery Memorial Award and many other prestigious honors

GALLERY/DISTRIBUTOR: Native American Images

	ISSUE PRICE	CURRENT PRICE
☐ **LIFE'S INTRACACIES,** rel. 1978. ed. 100, s/n, stone litho, 30″ x 22″, pub NAI	2,800.00	—
☐ **SILHOUETTES IN HARMONY,** rel. 1979. ed. 100, s/n, stone litho, 22″ x 15″, pub NAI........	500.00	—
☐ **OF BEAUTY & WOMEN,** rel. 1979. ed. 100, s/n, stone litho, 15″ x 22″, pub NAI	500.00	—
☐ **SILENT DEEP,** rel. 1979. ed. 50, s/n, stone litho, 22″ x 15″, pub NAI	500.00	—
☐ **FLIGHT OF THE CENTURIES,** rel. 1980. ed. 100, s/n, stone litho, 21″ x 15″, pub NAI........	250.00	—
☐ **THEN THERE IS MAN,** rel. 1980. ed. 65, s/n, stone litho, 22″ x 30″, pub NAI	600.00	—
☐ **SENTRIES OF TIME,** rel. 1981. STATE I-50, STATE II-50, s/n, stone litho, 25″ x 30″, pub NAI........	400.00	—
☐ **FERTILITY,** 1981. pub NAI	180.00	—
☐ **MEMORIES OF THUNDER, ECHOES OF DUST,** rel. 1981. ed. 100, s/n, stone litho, 16″ x 20″, pub NAI	400.00	—
☐ **SUNRISE, A GIFT,** rel. 1982. ed. 125, s/n, stone litho, 18″ x 30″, pub NAI	400.00	—
☐ **FACE OF THE EARTH,** rel. 1983. ed. 110, s/n, stone litho, 14″ x 16″, pub NAI	250.00	—

SUGAR IN THE COFFEE *by Tom Lovell*

TOM LOVELL

THEMES: Contemporary Western art

MEMBERSHIPS: Cowboy Artists of America, National Academy of Western Art, Society of Illustrators Hall of Fame

GALLERY/DISTRIBUTOR: Greenwich Workshop

	ISSUE PRICE	CURRENT PRICE
☐ CARSON'S BOATYARD, rel. 1981. ed. 1,000, s/n, 27″ x 18½″, pub GW	150.00	—
☐ THE DECEIVER, rel. 1981. ed. 1,000, s/n, 30″ x 18½″, pub GW	150.00	—
☐ FIRES ON THE OREGON TRAIL, rel. 1981. ed. 1,000, s/n, 22″ x 26½″, pub GW	150.00	—
☐ INVITATION TO TRADE, rel. 1982. ed. 1,000, s/n, 22″ x 29″, pub GW	150.00	—
☐ THE WHEELSOAKERS, rel. 1982. ed. 1,000, s/n, 30¼″ x 19¾″, pub GW	150.00	—
☐ SUGAR IN THE COFFEE, rel. 1983. ed. 650, s/n, 30½″ x 18⅝″, pub GW	165.00	—
☐ WALKING COYOTE AND THE BUFFALO ORPHANS, rel. 1983. ed. 650, s/n, 22½″ x 28″, pub GW	165.00	—
☐ WINTER HOLIDAY, rel. 1984. ed. 850, s/n, 21¼″ x 15¾″, pub GW	95.00	—
☐ CHIRICAHUA SCOUT, rel. 1985. ed. 650, s/n, 13⁷⁄₁₆″ x 15¹¹⁄₁₆″, pub GW	90.00	—

RICHARD LUCE

THEMES: Western art

STYLE: Realism

GALLERY/DISTRIBUTOR: Frame House Gallery, Inc.

PRAYER TO THE FOUR WINDS *by Richard Luce*

	ISSUE PRICE	CURRENT PRICE
☐ A TRAPPER'S WEALTH, rel. 1981. ed. 975, s/n, 24″ x 34½″, pub FHG	80.00	130.00
☐ EAGLE COUNTRY, rel. 1981. ed. 975, s/n, 22″ x 30″, pub FHG	80.00	160.00
☐ QUIET PAUSE, rel. 1981. ed. 975, s/n, 22″ x 30″, pub FHG	65.00	200.00
☐ THE SCOUTS, rel. 1981. ed. 975, s/n, 24″ x 36¾″, pub FHG	80.00	130.00
☐ BREAKING THE SKYLINE, rel. 1982. ed. 975, s/n, 21″ x 35″, pub FHG	80.00	130.00
☐ DOWNWIND, rel. 1982. ed. 975. s/n, 20″ x 38″, pub FHG	80.00	—
☐ LAST CROSSING, rel. 1982. ed. 975, s/n, 24″ x 34″, pub FHG	80.00	—
☐ PRIMING THE PIECE, rel. 1982. ed. 975, s/n, 32″ x 24″, pub FHG	80.00	130.00
☐ PRAYER TO THE FOUR WINDS, rel. 1983. ed. 975, s/n, 24″ x 26½″, pub FHG	80.00	—
☐ THE TROPHY, rel. 1983. ed. 975, s/n, 22″ x 32″, pub FHG	80.00	—
☐ MID-SUMMER JOURNEY, rel. 1984. ed. 875, s/n, 21″ x 36″, pub FHG	95.00	—
ed. 100, remarqued	140.00	Sold Out
☐ TWILIGHT FORMATION, rel. 1984. ed. 400, sn, 23¼″ x 33½″, pub FHG	95.00	—
ed. 100, remarqued	140.00	Sold Out
☐ WHEN PELTS WERE PRIME, rel. 1984. ed. 400, s/n, 22″ x 30″, pub FHG	80.00	—
ed. 100, remarqued	125.00	Sold Out

GARY LUCY

THEMES: Wildlife art
GALLERY/DISTRIBUTOR: Voyageur Art

	ISSUE PRICE	CURRENT PRICE
☐ **MERRIAM'S WILD TURKEY,** rel. 1980. ed. 750, s/n, size not available, pub WWI	45.00	—
☐ **DOE AND FAWNS,** rel. 1984. ed. 780, s/n, 22½″ x 17″, litho, pub VA	80.00	—

DOE AND FAWNS *by Gary Lucy*

STEPHEN E. LYMAN

THEMES: Wildlife art
STYLE: Realism. The artist has a penchant for detail
GALLERY/DISTRIBUTOR: Greenwich Workshop

	ISSUE PRICE	CURRENT PRICE
☐ **EARLY WINTER IN THE MOUNTAINS,** rel. 1983. ed. 850, s/n, 30½″ x 18¾″, pub GW...	95.00	—
☐ **END OF THE RIDGE,** rel. 1983. ed. 850, s/n, 30½″ x 19⅜″, pub GW	95.00	115.00
☐ **THE PASS,** rel. 1983. ed. 850, s/n, 30½″ x 16⅞″, pub GW	95.00	—
☐ **FREE FLIGHT,** rel. 1984. ed. 850, s/n, 13¹¹⁄₁₆″ x 14¹³⁄₁₆″, pub GW	70.00	—

EARLY WINTER IN THE MOUNTAINS *by Steve Lyman*

	ISSUE PRICE	CURRENT PRICE
☐ **NOISY NEIGHBORS,** rel. 1984. ed. 650, s/n, 30½" x 19½", pub GW	95.00	—
ed. 25 remarqued. rel. 1984. s/n, 30½" x 19½", pub GW	215.00	—
☐ **AHWANEE,** rel. 1985. ed. 450, s/n, 44" x 20½", pub GW	325.00	—

DAVID MAASS

THEMES: Wildlife art

AWARDS: Federal Duck Stamp Competition (1974); Ducks Unlimited Artist of the Year (1974); Conservationist of the Year, etc.

GALLERY/DISTRIBUTOR: Wild Wings, Inc.

COMMENTS: A true conservationist, Maass has donated a number of original paintings and more than 1,000 limited edition prints to Ducks Unlimited chapters nationwide

	ISSUE PRICE	CURRENT PRICE
☐ **MISTY MORNING - WOODCOCK,** rel. 1972. ed. 450, s/n, 20" x 17", pub WWI	50.00	1,250.00
ed. 100 remarqued	125.00	1,350.00
☐ **BACK BAY - MALLARDS,** rel. 1973. ed. 600, s/n, 11" x 15½", pub WWI	40.00	750.00
ed. 100 remarqued	110.00	850.00
☐ **MISTY MORNING - RUFFED GROUSE,** rel. 1973. ed. 580, s/n, 20" x 17", pub WWI .	55.00	1,300.00
ed. 190 remarqued	135.00	1,400.00
☐ **BREAKING IN BLUEBILLS,** rel. 1973. ed. 480, s/n, 16" x 25", pub WWI	55.00	725.00
ed. 131 remarqued	125.00	875.00
☐ **AMONG THE PINES - QUAIL,** rel. 1973. ed. 600, s/n, 11" x 16", pub WWI	40.00	500.00
ed. 100 remarqued	110.00	600.00
☐ **MISTY MORNING - WOOD DUCKS,** rel. 1974. ed. 580, s/n, 30" x 17", pub WWI	55.00	1,200.00
ed. 161 remarqued	125.00	1,300.00

CANVASBACKS ON THE DELTA MARSH *by David Maass*

	ISSUE PRICE	CURRENT PRICE
☐ BREAKING WEATHER - CANADA GEESE, rel. 1973. ed. 580, s/n, 16″ x 25″, pub WWI	55.00	800.00
ed. 111 remarqued	125.00	900.00
☐ ON THE MOVE - CANVASBACKS, rel. 1974. ed. 580, s/n, 16″ x 25″, pub WWI	60.00	550.00
ed. 100 remarqued	145.00	650.00
☐ RIVER FLATS - PINTAILS, rel. 1974. ed. 580, s/n, 16″ x 25″, pub WWI	60.00	475.00
ed. 70 remarqued	145.00	650.00
☐ RIDGE LINE - RUFFED GROUSE, rel. 1974. ed. 580, s/n, 15½″ x 25″, pub WWI	70.00	775.00
ed. 101 remarqued	150.00	875.00
☐ AUTUMN BIRCH - WOODCOCK, rel. 1974. ed. 580, s/n, 16″ x 25″, pub WWI	70.00	850.00
ed. 64 remarqued	150.00	950.00
☐ RED HEAD BAY, rel. 1975. ed. 580, s/n, 16½″ x 25″, pub WWI	70.00	400.00
ed. 75 remarqued	150.00	550.00
☐ DUSK IN THE BAY - CANADA GEESE, rel. 1975. ed. 600, s/n, 11″ x 15″, pub WWI	50.00	350.00
ed. 75 remarqued	145.00	450.00
☐ MISTY MORNING - MALLARDS, rel. 1975. ed. 580, s/n, 20″ x 17″, pub WWI	85.00	750.00
ed. 156 remarqued	175.00	850.00
☐ TWISTING THROUGH - BLUE WING TEAL, rel. 1975. ed. 580, s/n, 16½″ x 25″, pub WWI	70.00	275.00
ed. 75 remarqued	150.00	375.00
☐ MISTY MORNING - QUAIL, rel. 1975. ed. 580, s/n, 20″ x 17″, pub WWI	85.00	750.00
ed. 154 remarqued	175.00	850.00
☐ WINTER WINDS - BLUEBILLS, rel. 1976. ed. 580, s/n, 16¼″ x 25″, pub WWI	70.00	250.00
ed. 75 remarqued	150.00	350.00
☐ OVER THE POND - RUFFED GROUSE, rel. 1976. ed. 600, s/n, 11″ x 16″, pub WWI	52.50	200.00
ed. 75 remarqued	150.00	300.00
☐ HASTY DEPARTURE - RUFFED GROUSE, rel. 1976. ed. 580, s/n, 16½″ x 25″, pub WWI	70.00	600.00
ed. 75 remarqued	150.00	700.00
☐ MISTY MORNING - GREEN WINGS, rel. 1976. ed. 580, s/n, 20″ x 17″, pub WWI	85.00	600.00
ed. 75 remarqued	175.00	600.00

	ISSUE PRICE	CURRENT PRICE
☐ **PLACID BACKWATERS - WOODDUCKS,** rel. 1976. ed. 580, s/n, 16½" x 25", pub WWI	70.00	350.00
ed. 75 remarqued	150.00	450.00
☐ **SWEEPING THE NARROWS - CANVASBACKS,** rel. 1976. ed. 580, s/n, 16½" x 25", pub WWI	70.00	300.00
ed. 75 remarqued	150.00	400.00
☐ **WESTERN MARSH - PINTAILS,** rel. 1976. ed. 580, s/n, 16½" x 25", pub WWI	70.00	140.00
ed. 75 remarqued	150.00	220.00
☐ **RIVERS EDGE - MALLARDS,** rel. 1977. ed. 580, s/n, 16½" x 25", pub WWI	75.00	350.00
ed. 75 remarqued	160.00	450.00
☐ **INTO THE SHALLOWS - CANADA GEESE,** rel. 1977. ed. 580, s/n, 15½" x 25", pub WWI	75.00	150.00
ed. 75 remarqued	160.00	250.00
☐ **COVEY BREAK - QUAIL,** rel. 1977. ed. 580, s/n, 16½" x 25", pub WWI	75.00	225.00
ed. 75 remarqued	160.00	325.00
☐ **AUTUMN MARSH - MALLARDS,** rel. 1977. ed. 580, s/n, 16½" x 25", pub WWI	75.00	425.00
remarqued	160.00	525.00
☐ **BACK COUNTRY - RUFFS,** rel. 1977. ed. 580, s/n, 16½" x 25", pub WWI	75.00	150.00
remarqued	160.00	250.00
☐ **AUTUMN DAY - RUFFED GROUSE,** rel. 1977. ed. 850, s/n, 24" x 20", pub WWI	100.00	700.00
remarqued	185.00	800.00
☐ **EARLY ARRIVALS - MALLARDS,** rel. 1977. ed. 850, s/n, 11" x 16½", pub WWI	55.00	150.00
remarqued	115.00	275.00
☐ **DECEMBER SQUALL - PHEASANT,** rel. 1978. ed. 850, s/n, 16½" x 25", pub WWI	75.00	85.00
remarqued	160.00	185.00
☐ **CAUTIOUS TRIO - TURKEY,** rel. 1978. ed. 850, s/n, 16½" x 25", pub WWI	75.00	85.00
remarqued	160.00	185.00
☐ **FIRST PASS - MALLARDS,** rel. 1978. ed. 850, s/n, 16½" x 25", pub WWI	85.00	200.00
remarqued	185.00	300.00
☐ **NEW SNOW - RUFFED GROUSE,** rel. 1978. ed. 850, s/n, 16½" x 15⅛", pub WWI	85.00	225.00
remarqued	185.00	325.00
☐ **SWINGING THE CHANNEL - CANVASBACKS,** rel. 1978. ed. 850, s/n, 16½" x 25", pub WWI	85.00	100.00
remarqued	185.00	200.00
☐ **WOODLAND REPOSE - RUFFED GROUSE,** rel. 1978. ed. 850, s/n, 16½" x 25", pub WWI	100.00	650.00
remarqued	200.00	750.00
☐ **WORKING THE BAY - BLUEBILLS,** rel. 1978. ed. 850, s/n, 16½" x 25", pub WWI	85.00	200.00
remarqued	185.00	300.00
☐ **DEADWOOD CORNER - MALLARDS,** rel. 1978. ed. 850, s/n, 25" x 16½", pub WWI	85.00	175.00
ed. 25 Artist proofs remarqued	185.00	275.00
☐ **MARSHLAND - CANADA GEESE,** rel. 1978. ed. 850, s/n, 25" x 16½", pub WWI	75.00	150.00
ed. 25 Artist proofs remarqued	160.00	250.00
☐ **AUTUMN DAY - WOODCOCK,** rel. 1979. ed. 850, s/n, 20" x 24", pub WWI	100.00	150.00
ed. 25 Artist proofs remarqued	200.00	250.00
☐ **REELFOOT VISITORS AT MIDDLEFORK CLUB,** rel. 1979. ed. 850, s/n, 25" x 16¼", pub WWI	100.00	—
ed. 30 Artist proofs remarqued	200.00	—
☐ **GROUSE COVER,** rel. 1979. ed. 850, s/n, 25" x 16½", pub WWI	100.00	200.00
ed. 30 Artist proofs remarqued	200.00	300.00
☐ **HEAVY WEATHER - REDHEADS,** rel. 1979. ed. 850, s/n, 25" x 16½", pub WWI	100.00	—
ed. 30 Artist proofs remarqued	200.00	—
☐ **PINTAILS IN AUTUMN,** rel. 1979, ed. 950, s/n, 15⅝" x 11⅛", pub WWI	50.00	65.00
☐ **MALLARDS IN AUTUMN,** rel. 1980. ed. 950, s/n, 15⅝" x 11⅛", pub WWI	50.00	130.00
☐ **COMING IN - CANADA GEESE,** rel. 1969. ed. 400, s/n, size not available, pub WWI	50.00	700.00
☐ **MALLARDS,** rel. 1972. ed. 600, s/n, size not available, pub WWI	60.00	700.00
Artists proofs, remarqued	N/A	800.00
☐ **QUAIL,** rel. 1971. ed. 600, s/n, size not available, pub WWI	60.00	700.00
Artists proofs, remarqued	N/A	800.00
☐ **ABANDONED ORCHARD - BUFFED GROUSE,** rel. 1980. ed. 850, s/n, pub WWI	125.00	250.00
Artists proofs, remarqued	N/A	350.00

	ISSUE PRICE	CURRENT PRICE
☐ AFTER THE RAIN - BOBWHITE, rel. 1980. ed. 850, s/n, 16″ x 25″, pub WWI	100.00	400.00
Artists proofs, remarqued	200.00	500.00
☐ CANVASBACKS IN AUTUMN, rel. 1980. ed. 950, s/n, 16″ x 11″, pub WWI	50.00	65.00
☐ INTO QUIET WATERS - MALLARDS, rel. 1980. ed. 850, s/n, 25″ x 18″, pub WWI ...	100.00	—
remarqued...............................	200.00	—
☐ NORTH SHORE - GOLDENEYES, rel. 1980. ed. 850, s/n, 25″ x 17″, pub WWI	100.00	—
remarqued...............................	200.00	—
☐ RUFFED GROUSE IN AUTUMN, rel. 1980. ed. 950, s/n, 16″ x 11″, pub WWI	50.00	130.00
☐ TWO AWAY - WOODCOCK, rel. 1980. ed. 850, s/n, 15″ x 18″, pub WWI	85.00	170.00
remarqued...............................	185.00	370.00
☐ BACKWATER HIDEAWAY - WOOD DUCKS, rel. 1981. ed. 950, s/n, 16½″ x 25″, pub WWI...............................	150.00	—
☐ EARLY WINTER MORNING - BOBWHITE, rel. 1981. ed. 850, s/n, size not available, pub WWI.............................	150.00	550.00
remarqued...............................	275.00	675.00
☐ FARM POND - GREEN WINGED TEAL, rel. 1981. ed. 850, s/n, 16½″ x 25″, pub WWI...............................	125.00	—
☐ JIMMY'S POINT - DELTA MARSH BLUEBILLS, rel. 1981. ed. 950, s/n, 16½″ x 25″, pub WWI...............................	125.00	—
☐ LOW CEILING - CANADA GEESE, rel. 1981. ed. 850, s/n, 16½″ x 25″, pub WWI ...	100.00	200.00
☐ SUNLIT MARSH - MALLARDS, rel. 1981. ed. 950, s/n, 16½″ x 25″, pub WWI	125.00	250.00
☐ TIMBER'S EDGE - RUFFED GROUSE, rel. 1981. ed. 950, s/n, 16½″ x 25″, pub WWI...............................	150.00	—
☐ WILD WINGS LOGO - GREENWING TEAL, rel. 1981. ed. 950, s/n, 16½″ x 25″, pub WWI...............................	75.00	100.00
☐ EARLY WINTER MORNING - RUFFED GROUSE, rel. 1982. ed. 950, s/n, size not available, pub WWI	550.00	—
☐ SASKATCHEWAN GREENHEADS, rel. 1982. ed. 950, s/n, 16½″ x 25″, pub WWI ...	125.00	—
☐ THUNDERING OUT - RUFFED GROUSE, rel. 1982. ed. 900, s/n, size not available, pub WWI...............................	300.00	—
☐ WINDSWEPT MARSH - CANVASBACK, rel. 1982. ed. 950, s/n, 16½″ x 25″, pub WWI...............................	150.00	—
☐ CANVASBACKS ON THE DELTA MARSH, rel. 1983. ed. 1,000, s/n, 10″ x 15″, pub WWI...............................	45.00	—
☐ EARLY WINTER MORNING - PHEASANTS, rel. 1983. ed. 950, s/n, size not available, pub WWI.............................	250.00	—
☐ HILLSIDE FLUSH - RUFFED GROUSE, rel. 1983. ed. 950, s/n, 16½″ x 25″, pub WWI...............................	125.00	—
☐ INTO THE COVE - CANADA GEESE, rel. 1983. ed. 950, s/n, 16½″ x 26½″, pub WWI...............................	125.00	—
☐ CANVASBACKS ON THE DELTA MARSH, rel. 1984. ed. 750, s/n, 16½″ x 25″, pub WWI...............................	125.00	—
☐ CANVASBACKS ON THE DELTA MARSH, rel. 1984. ed. 200, s/n, 19½″ x 28″, pub WWI...............................	275.00	—
☐ EDGE OF THE MARSH - PINTAILS, rel. 1984. ed. 950, s/n, 17½″ x 23″, pub WWI ..	125.00	—
☐ ON THE MOVE - MALLARDS, rel. 1984. ed. 1,500, s/n, 12″ x 16″, pub WWI	50.00	—
☐ SHELTERED HIDEAWAY - WOOD DUCKS, rel. 1984. ed. 950, s/n, 21″ x 19″, pub WWI...............................	125.00	—
☐ WOODLOT FLUSH - RUFFED GROUSE, rel. 1984. ed. 1,500, s/n, 12″ x 16″, pub WWI...............................	50.00	—
☐ ABANDONED ORCHARD - WOODCOCK, rel. 1985. ed. 850, s/n, litho, 17″ x 25″, pub WWI...............................	125.00	—
☐ EARLY WINTER MORNING - TURKEY, rel. 1985. ed. 950, s/n, litho, 21″ x 17½″, pub WWI...............................	150.00	—
☐ LOW CEILING - SNOWS AND BLUES, rel. 1985. ed. 850, s/n, litho, 15½″ x 21″, pub WWI...............................	100.00	—
☐ SWINGING IN - MALLARDS, rel. 1985. ed. 650, s/n, litho, 16½″ x 25″, pub WWI ...	125.00	—
☐ WILLOW POINT - REDHEADS, rel. 1985. ed. 950, s/n, litho, 17¾″ x 15″, pub WWI ..	85.00	—

MIDDAY MOONLIGHT by Fred Machetanz

FRED MACHETANZ

THEMES: Alaska's people, animals, and seasons

BOOKS: A book of his paintings, *The Alaskan Paintings of Fred Machetanz*, was published in 1977

AWARDS: "Distinguished Associate of Art" (University of Alaska, 1963); Alaska Hall of Fame (1966); Honorary Doctorate in Fine Arts (University of Alaska, 1973); Alaskan of the Year (1977)

GALLERY/DISTRIBUTOR: Mill Pond Press, Inc.

	ISSUE PRICE	CURRENT PRICE
☐ **FACE TO FACE,** rel. 1978. ed. 950, s/n, 36″ x 24″, pub MPPI	150.00	1,500.00
☐ **HUNTER'S DAWN,** rel. 1978. ed. 950, s/n, 22″ x 25″, pub MPPI	125.00	500.00
☐ **INTO THE HOME STRETCH,** rel. 1978. ed. 950, s/n, 25″ x 37½″, pub MPPI	175.00	700.00
☐ **BEGINNINGS,** rel. 1979. ed. 950, s/n, 23″ x 27″, pub MPPI	175.00	425.00
☐ **DECISION ON THE ICE FIELD,** rel. 1979. ed. 950, s/n, 22½″ x 32½″, pub MPPI	150.00	425.00
☐ **PICK OF THE LITTER,** rel. 1979. ed. 950, s/n, 22¾″ x 27″, pub MPPI	165.00	450.00
☐ **REACHING THE CAMPSITE,** rel. 1979. ed. 950, s/n, 25″ x 37½″, pub MPPI	200.00	400.00
☐ **KING OF THE MOUNTAIN,** rel. 1980. ed. 950, s/n, 25″ x 29″, pub MPPI	200.00	300.00

	ISSUE PRICE	CURRENT PRICE
☐ NELCHINA TRAIL, rel. 1980. ed. 950, s/n, 24½" x 30", pub MPPI	245.00	375.00
☐ SOURDOUGH, rel. 1980. ed. 950, s/n, 24½" x 30", pub MPPI	245.00	400.00
☐ WHEN THREE'S A CROWD, rel. 1980. ed. 950, s/n, 24¾" x 35", pub MPPI	225.00	400.00
☐ GOLDEN YEARS, rel. 1981. ed. 950, s/n, 24½" x 35½", pub MPPI	245.00	350.00
☐ MIDDAY MOONLIGHT, rel. 1981. ed. 950, s/n, 23" x 27", pub MPPI	265.00	400.00
☐ WHAT EVERY HUNTER FEARS, rel. 1981. ed. 950, s/n, 24½" x 30", pub MPPI	245.00	375.00
☐ WHERE MEN & DOGS SEEM SMALL, rel. 1981. ed. 950, s/n, 29¾" x 24½", pub MPPI	N/A	Sold Out
☐ WINTER HARVEST, rel. 1981. ed. 950, s/n, 24½" x 37½", pub MPPI	265.00	300.00
☐ MIGHTY HUNTER, rel. 1982. ed. 950, s/n, 24⅝" x 35¼", pub MPPI	265.00	400.00
☐ MOOSE TRACKS, rel. 1982. ed. 950, s/n, 24⅝" x 31", pub MPPI	265.00	300.00
☐ MOONLIT STAKEOUT, rel. 1982. ed. 950, s/n, 24½" x 37¾", pub MPPI	265.00	400.00
☐ THE TENDER ARCTIC, rel. 1982. ed. 950, s/n, 24½" x 37¾", pub MPPI	265.00	475.00
☐ NANOOK, rel. 1983. ed. 950, s/n, 24½" x 37", pub MPPI	295.00	—
☐ THEY'VE OPENED THE NORTH COUNTRY, rel. 1983. ed. 950, s/n, 24⅝" x 30⅝", pub MPPI	245.00	350.00
☐ MANY MILES TOGETHER, rel. 1984. ed. 950, s/n, 24½" x 29½", pub MPPI	245.00	350.00
☐ MIDNIGHT WATCH, rel. 1984. ed. 950, s/n, 19" x 32", pub MPPI	250.00	—
☐ SMOKE DREAMS, rel. 1984. ed. 950, s/n, 24⅝" x 31", pub MPPI	250.00	—
☐ THE HERITAGE OF ALASKA, rel. 1984. ed. 950, s/n, 37" x 24½", pub MPPI	400.00	800.00

ALDERSON MAGEE

THEMES: Wildlife art

MEDIUM: Scratchboard engraving

AWARDS: *Who's Who in American Art*; Federal Duck Stamp Print Competition (1976-77)

GALLERY/DISTRIBUTOR: Wild Wings, Inc.

	ISSUE PRICE	CURRENT PRICE
☐ COACHMAN'S CONQUEST - BROOK TROUT, rel. 1975. ed. 450, s/n, 7⅞" x 9⅞", pub SEL	45.00	400.00
☐ FIRST HATCHED - CANADA GEESE, rel. 1978. ed. 580, s/n, 10" x 8", pub WWI	75.00	85.00
☐ PROFESSOR PRIZE - RAINBOW TROUT, rel. 1978. ed. 580, s/n, 8" x 10", pub WWI	75.00	100.00
☐ JUMPING MALLARD, rel. 1976. ed. 600, s/n, 16" x 20", pub WWI	100.00	125.00
☐ BOBCAT, rel. 1982. ed. 600, s/n, 16" x 20", pub WWI	85.00	—
☐ BALD EAGLE, rel. 1983. ed. 600, s/n, 16" x 20", pub WWI	95.00	—

MaGo (MAURIZIO GORACCI)

THEMES: Varied

STYLE: MaGo says he combines impressionism and super-realism in his paintings

GALLERY/DISTRIBUTOR: World Art Editions, Ltd.

AZURE IN GOLD - BLUE JAY *by Don Malick*

COMMENTS: It is not surprising that he is called a "Renaissance Painter," for his canvases reflect the legacy of Leonardo da Vinci in his quest for the "ultimate truth"

	ISSUE PRICE	CURRENT PRICE
☐ **DEPOSITION,** rel. 1981. ed. 300, s/n, 20″ x 23″, pub WAEL	295.00	325.00
☐ **SIPARIO,** rel. 1981. ed. 300, s/n, 20″ x 23″, pub WAEL	295.00	325.00
☐ **BEDTIME STORY,** rel. 1982. ed. 300, s/n, 17½″ x 22″, pub WAEL	295.00	325.00
☐ **GOODNIGHT KISS,** rel. 1982. ed. 300, s/n, 17½″ x 22″, pub WAEL	295.00	325.00
☐ **BLOSSOMS,** rel. 1984. ed. 550, s/n, 15½″ x 20½″, litho, pub WAEL	150.00	—
☐ **NOCTURNE,** rel. 1984. ed. 550, s/n, 12″ x 16″, litho, pub WAEL	100.00	—

DONALD MALICK

THEMES: Birds

BOOKS: Illustrated a major portion of *The Birds of Colorado* in 1962

AWARDS: Silver Medal from the Academy of Science, Philadelphia (1980)

MEMBERSHIPS: Society of Animal Artists

GALLERY/DISTRIBUTOR: Mill Pond Press, Inc.

COMMENTS: Malick's work has been exhibited widely, and many private and public collections are pleased to own some of his paintings

	ISSUE PRICE	CURRENT PRICE
☐ AZURE IN GOLD - BLUE JAY, rel. 1983. ed. 950, 16¾" x 12", pub MPPI	60.00	—

BETTY MALONE

EDUCATION: Harding University and Memphis State University

MEMBERSHIPS: Germantown Art League; Tennessee Watercolor Society; American League of Penwomen

GALLERY/DISTRIBUTOR: Malone Studios

	ISSUE PRICE	CURRENT PRICE
☐ NARY A NIBBLE, rel. 1975. ed. 1,250, s/n, 16" x 20", pub SG	30.00	—
☐ CURIOSITY, rel. 1976. ed. 1,250, s/n, 16" x 20", pub SG	30.00	—
☐ GATEWAY TO A LEGEND, rel. 1978. ed. 500, s/n, 16" x 20", pub SG	30.00	60.00
ed. 4,500, s/o	20.00	—
☐ THE WAY HOME, rel. 1979. ed. 1,250, s/n, 18½" x 24", pub SG	40.00	—
☐ PLAYING UNDER THE HOUSE, rel. 1980. ed. 750, s/n, 16" x 20", pub MS	30.00	—

CAROLYN MARSHALL

MEDIUM: Marshall's work ranges from pen and ink drawing to oil and acrylics

STYLE: Marshall's work ranges from realism to abstraction

EDUCATION: Newcomb College of Tulane University; Art Students League; Columbia University; University of Texas

GALLERY/DISTRIBUTOR: Herb Chidley

	ISSUE PRICE	CURRENT PRICE
☐ SAILING SHIP "A", ed. 950, s/o, 16" x 20", pub HC	10.00	—
black and white, hand colored	25.00	—
☐ SAILING SHIP "B", ed. 950, s/o, 16" x 20", pub HC	10.00	—
black and white, hand colored	25.00	—
☐ SAILING SHIP "C", ed. 950, s/o, 16" x 20", pub HC	10.00	—
black and white, hand colored	25.00	—
☐ SAILING SHIP "D", ed. 950, s/o, 16" x 20", pub HC	10.00	—
black and white, hand colored	25.00	—
☐ SUNFISH, ed. 950, s/o, 12" x 16", pub HC	9.00	—
black and white, hand colored	20.00	—

	ISSUE PRICE	CURRENT PRICE
☐ **SNIPE,** ed. 950, s/o, 12″ x 16″, pub HC	9.00	—
black and white, hand colored	20.00	—
☐ **HOBIE 16,** ed. 950, s/o, 12″ x 16″, pub HC	9.00	—
black and white, hand colored	20.00	—
☐ **LIGHTING,** ed. 950, s/o, 12″ x 16″, pub HC	9.00	—
black and white, hand colored	20.00	—
☐ **SAILING YACHT,** ed. 950, s/o, 17″ x 23″, pub HC	44.00	—

OVER THE CATTAILS *by Bernard Martin*

BERNARD MARTIN

THEMES: Wildlife art

BOOKS: The artist has written and illustrated hundreds of nature features and has illustrated over forty books

GALLERY/DISTRIBUTOR: Bernard Martin

	ISSUE PRICE	CURRENT PRICE
☐ **SPRING IS THE ROBIN,** rel. 1972. ed. 1,500, s/n, 14″ x 16½″, pub BM	20.00	60.00
☐ **EASTERN BLUEBIRD,** rel. 1974. ed. 500, s/n, 16″ x 18⅜″, pub BM	20.00	200.00
☐ **RING-NECKED PHEASANT,** rel. 1974. ed. 500, s/o, 17″ x 19″, pub BM	25.00	60.00
☐ **CARDINAL,** rel. 1975. ed. 500, s/n, 16″ x 18⅜″, pub BM	20.00	200.00
☐ **MALLARDS & PINTAILS,** rel. 1975. ed. 500, s/n, 16″ x 18⅜″, pub BM	20.00	60.00
☐ **BALTIMORE ORIOLE,** rel. 1976. ed. 350, s/n, 16″ x 18⅜″, pub BM	20.00	100.00
☐ **BOBWHITE,** rel. 1976. ed. 350, s/n, 16″ x 18⅜″, pub BM	20.00	60.00
☐ **GOLDFINCH,** rel. 1977. ed. 350, s/n, 16″ x 18⅜″, pub BM	25.00	100.00

	ISSUE PRICE	CURRENT PRICE
☐ CANADA GOOSE, rel. 1977. ed. 350, s/n, 16″ x 18⅜″, pub BM	25.00	100.00
☐ OZARKS GOBBLER, rel. 1977. ed. 500, s/n, 18″ x 24″, pub BM	35.00	75.00
☐ BLUE JAY, rel. 1978. ed. 350, s/n, 16″ x 18⅜″, pub BM	25.00	60.00
☐ CARDINAL FAMILY, rel. 1980. ed. 500, s/n, 16″ x 18⅜″, pub BM	30.00	150.00
☐ MALLARDS, rel. 1980. ed. 500, s/n, 16″ x 18⅜″, pub BM	30.00	—
☐ SPORTSMAN'S SET, rel. 1972. ed. 350, s/n, 16″ x 18⅜″, pub BM	30.00	60.00
☐ STRANGER ON THE TRAIL, rel. 1980. ed. 350, s/n, 19½″ x 28″, pub BM	40.00	60.00
☐ WOOD DUCK, rel. 1978. ed. 350, s/n, 16″ x 18⅜″, pub BM	25.00	200.00
☐ MEADOWLARK, rel. 1979. ed. 500, s/n, 16″ x 18⅜″, pub BM	30.00	60.00
☐ GREEN-WINGED TEAL, rel. 1979. ed. 500, s/n, 16″ x 18⅜″, pub BM	30.00	60.00
☐ SUNDAY MORNING BLUEBIRDS, rel. 1981. ed. 500, s/n, 16″ x 18⅜″, pub BM	35.00	150.00
☐ STONY POINT COVEY, rel. 1981. ed. 500, s/n, 16″ x 18⅜″, pub BM	35.00	60.00
☐ ROOST TREE, rel. 1981. ed. 350, s/n, 16″ x 18⅜″, pub BM	40.00	60.00
☐ MORNING GLORY WRENS, rel. 1982. ed. 500, s/n, 16″ x 18⅜″, pub BM	35.00	35.00
☐ OVER THE CATTAILS, rel. 1982. ed. 1,850, s/n, 18″ x 25″, pub BM	40.00	40.00
☐ BALD EAGLE, rel. 1983. ed. 350, 15¼″ x 19¼″, pub BM	35.00	—
☐ CHICKADEES, rel. 1983. ed. 350, s/n, litho, 11¾″ x 13½″, pub BM	30.00	—
☐ LIGHTHOUSE EYRIE, rel. 1985. ed. 50, Artist proofs, 19¾ x 17″, pub BM	70.00	—
☐ SNOWBOUND COVEY, rel. 1985. ed. 500, 18 x 24″, pub BM	55.00	—
☐ SPRING FLEDGLING, rel. 1985. ed. 500, s/n, litho, 15″ x 18″, pub BM	45.00	—
☐ WINTER REDBIRD, rel. 1985. ed. 500, 10½″ x 12½″, pub BM	35.00	—

LARRY K. MARTIN

THEMES: Wildlife and human subjects

BOOKS: Included in Goldblatt's "Artists of the Century" and numerous other books and periodicals

AWARDS: Meritorious Service Award of the National Audubon Society; winner Alabama Waterfowl Stamp (1985)

GALLERY/DISTRIBUTOR: Wren's Nest Gallery

	ISSUE PRICE	CURRENT PRICE
☐ IN PURSUIT (Bass), rel. 1978. ed. 1,150, s/n, 20″ x 27″, pub TCG	30.00	40.00
ed. 100 remarqued	60.00	125.00
☐ INTRUDER (Squirrel & Jay), rel. 1978. ed. 1,150, s/n, 20″ x 27″, pub TCG	30.00	40.00
ed. 100 remarqued	60.00	125.00
☐ DE N'OVO SERIES		
This set consists of six prints, was sold in singles, pairs, or sets of six BLUEBIRDS, BARN OWLS, PINTAILS, MALLARD, BOBWHITE QUAIL, GREAT BLUE HERON; rel. 1979. ed. 1,000, s/n, 8″ x 10″, pub WNG	20.00 ea.	—
	34.00 pr.	—
	105.00 seven	—
remarqued prints available at	50.00	150.00
☐ WINTER WHITETAILS, rel. 1979. ed. 950, s/n, 18″ x 24″, pub WNG	45.00	65.00
ed. 100 remarqued	100.00	200.00
BI-LEVEL SERIES		
☐ BUFFLEHEADS, RUDDY DUCKS, rel. 1980. ed. 950, s/n, 12″ x 16″, pub WNG	36.00	Sold Out
	60.00 pr.	Sold Out
ed. 25 remarqued	90.00	175.00
☐ MALLARDS, rel. 1982. ed. 950, s/n, 12″ x 19″, pub WNG	50.00	Sold Out
☐ PINTAILS, rel. 1983. ed. 950, s/n, 22″ x 19″, pub WNG	50.00	Sold Out
ed. 12 remarqued	90.00 pr.	Sold Out
	175.00	300.00

	ISSUE PRICE	CURRENT PRICE
☐ **BARN OWLS,** rel. 1980. ed. 950, s/n, 25″ x 22″, pub WNG	55.00	65.00
ed. 25 remarqued	110.00	200.00
☐ **AFRICAN ELEPHANTS,** rel. 1981. ed. open, 18″ x 12″, pub WNG	10.00	—
ed. 2,000, s/o	12.00	—
ed. 50, s/n	45.00	Sold Out
☐ **BIGHORN RAM,** rel. 1981. ed. open, 16″ x 12″, pub WNG	8.00	—
ed. 2,000, s/o	10.00	—
ed. 50, s/n	—	Sold Out
☐ **CHIPMUNKS,** rel. 1981. ed. open, 16″ x 18″, pub WNG	8.00	—
ed. 2,000, s/o	10.00	—
ed. 50, s/n	—	Sold Out
☐ **KEEPERS OF THE MILL,** rel. 1981. ed. open, 22″ x 19″, pub WNG	15.00	—
ed. 2,000, s/o	20.00	—
ed. 100, s/n	45.00	Sold Out
☐ **MANDARIN DUCKS,** rel. 1981. ed. 950, s/n, 30″ x 22″, pub WNG	60.00	75.00
ed. 25 remarqued	110.00	200.00
☐ **MR. VICTOR CHADWICK, AMERICAN HOBO,** rel. 1981. ed. open, 16″ x 25″, pub WNG	16.00	—
ed. 2,000, s/o	20.00	—
ed. 50, s/n	45.00	Sold Out
☐ **PARKER ISLAND RACCOONS,** rel. 1981****. ed. open, 14″ x 11″, pub WNG	8.00	—
ed. 2,000, s/o	10.00	—
ed. 50, s/n	—	Sold Out
****1,000 prints donated for "Save Parker Island" fund.		
☐ **SCREECH OWLS,** rel. 1981****. ed. open, 11″ x 14″, pub WNG	8.00	—
ed. 2,000, s/o	10.00	—
ed. 50, s/n	—	Sold Out
****500 prints donated for fund raising by Wildlife Rescue Service, Birmingham, Alabama.		
☐ **WHITETAIL DOE,** rel. 1981. ed. open, 8″ x 10″, pub WNG	5.00	—
ed. 2,000, s/o	7.00	—
ed. 50, s/n	—	Sold Out
☐ **WHITETAIL MATURE BUCK,** rel. 1981. ed. open, 8″ x 10″, pub WNG	5.00	—
ed. 2,000, s/o	7	—
ed. 50, s/n	—	Sold Out
☐ **WHITETAIL YOUNG BUCK,** rel. 1981. ed. open, 8″ x 10″, pub WNG	5.00	—
ed. 2,000, s/o	7.00	—
ed. 50, s/n	—	Sold Out
☐ **WINTER RACCOONS,** rel. 1981. ed. open, 11″ x 14″, pub WNG	8.00	—
ed. 2,000, s/o	10.00	—
ed. 50, s/n	25.00	Sold Out
☐ **YOUNG COTTONTAIL,** rel. 1981. ed. open, 10″ x 8″, pub WNG	5.00	8.00
ed. 2,000, s/o	10.00	—
ed. 50, s/n	—	Sold Out
☐ **EVERGREEN BOUGH, BALD EAGLES,** rel. 1982. ed. 950, s/n, 32″ x 25½″, pub WNG	80.00	—
ed. 12 remarqued	200.00	Sold Out
☐ **AMERICA'S GOAT MAN, MR. CHES MCCARTNEY,** rel. 1983. ed. open, 18″ x 25″, pub WNG	—	—
ed. 2,000, s/o	20.00	—
ed. 100, s/n	45.00	Sold Out
☐ **JUVENILE GRAY SQUIRREL,** rel. 1983. ed. open, 15″ x 12″, pub WNG	10.00	—
ed. 2,000, s/o	12.00	—
ed. 50, s/n	—	Sold Out
☐ **SUE ALSTON GUARDIAN ANGEL OF HAMPTON,** rel. 1983. ed. open, 24″ x 19″, pub WNG	—	—
ed. 2,000, s/o	20.00	—
ed. 100, s/n	45.00	Sold Out
☐ **TRUMPETER SWANS,** rel. 1983. ed. 950, s/n, 9″ x 8″, pub WNG	26.00	26.00
ed. 12 remarqued	175.00	Sold Out
☐ **YOUNG KILLDEER,** rel. 1983. ed. open, 10″ x 8″, pub WNG	5.00	—
ed. 2,000, s/o	12.00	—
ed. 50, s/n	—	Sold Out

	ISSUE PRICE	CURRENT PRICE
☐ **BARNSTORMER—MR. BOB STROOP,** rel. 1984. ed. 2,000, s/o, 14″ x 18″, pub WNG	20.00	—
ed. 180, s/n, 14″ x 18″, pub WNG	55.00	—
☐ **EGRET IN FLIGHT,** rel. 1984. ed. 950, s/n, 16″ x 20″, pub WNG	65.00	—
☐ **GENTLE FLORA—AND SOME PINDLY WINDLY,** rel. 1984. ed. 2,000, s/o, 20″ x 25″, pub WNG	20.00	—
ed. 180, s/n, 20″ x 25″, pub WNG	55.00	—
☐ **REMINISCING,** rel. 1984. ed. 2,000, s/o, 14″ x 17″, pub WNG	18.00	—
ed. 180, s/n, 14″ x 17″, pub WNG	45.00	—
☐ **T'ANKS DA LAWD—SUE ALSTON,** rel. 1984. ed. 2,000, s/o, 14″ x 18″, pub WNG . .	18.00	—
ed. 180, s/n, 14″ x 18″, pub WNG	45.00	—

JAMIE by Francisco Masseria

FRANCISCO J. J. C. MASSERIA

THEMES: Children

STYLE: Masseria does not use models. His subjects are the product of his imagination, of his idealized perception of children and the deeply felt religious mysticism that guides his brush

GALLERY/DISTRIBUTOR: World Art Editions, Ltd.

	ISSUE PRICE	CURRENT PRICE
☐ EDUARDO, rel. 1980. ed. 300, s/n, size N/A, pub WAEL	275.00	2,700.00
☐ FIRST KISS, rel. 1980. ed. 300, s/n, size N/A, pub WAEL	375.00	1,600.00
☐ NINA, rel. 1980. ed. 300, s/n, size N/A, pub WAEL	325.00	1,850.00
☐ ROSANNA, rel. 1980. ed. 300, s/n, size N/A, pub WAEL	275.00	3,200.00
☐ ELEANOR, rel. 1981. ed. 300, s/n, size N/A, pub WAEL	375.00	900.00
☐ ELISA WITH FLOWER, rel. 1981. ed. 300, s/n, size N/A, pub WAEL	325.00	1,300.00
☐ FIRST FLOWER, rel. 1981. ed. 300, s/n, size N/A, pub WAEL	325.00	1,600.00
☐ JESSICA, rel. 1981. ed. 300, s/n, size N/A, pub WAEL	375.00	1,650.00
☐ JULIE, rel. 1981. ed. 300, s/n, size N/A, pub WAEL	375.00	950.00
☐ SELENE, rel. 1981. ed. 300, s/n, size N/A, pub WAEL	325.00	1,300.00
☐ SOLANGE, rel. 1980. ed. 300, s/n, size N/A, pub WAEL	325.00	950.00
☐ SUSAN SEWING, rel. 1981. ed. 300, s/n, size N/A, pub WAEL	375.00	2,300.00
☐ AMY, rel. 1982. ed. 300, s/n, size N/A	425.00	525.00
☐ JAMIE, rel. 1982. ed. 300, s/n, 18″ x 22″, pub WAEL	425.00	550.00
☐ JILL, rel. 1982. ed. 300, s/n, 18″ x 22″, pub WAEL	425.00	500.00
☐ JODIE, rel. 1982. ed. 300, s/n, 18″ x 22″, pub WAEL	425.00	500.00
☐ JUDITH, rel. 1980. ed. 300, s/n, size N/A	425.00	525.00
☐ ROBIN, rel. 1982. ed. 300, s/n, 18″ x 22″, pub WAEL	425.00	575.00
☐ YASMIN, rel. 1982. ed. 300, s/n, size N/A	425.00	525.00
☐ YVETTE, rel. 1982. ed. 300, s/n, size N/A	425.00	525.00
☐ ANTONIO, rel. 1983. ed. 300, s/n, size N/A	450.00	1,100.00
☐ CHRISTOPHER, rel. 1983. ed. 300, s/n, size N/A, pub CIL	450.00	525.00
☐ MEMOIRS, rel. 1983. ed. 300, s/n, 20″ x 24″, pub CIL	450.00	500.00
☐ TARA, rel. 1983. ed. 300, s/n, size N/A	450.00	1,100.00
☐ CHRISTOPHER, ed. 300, s/n, size N/A, pub WAEL	450.00	500.00
☐ MEMOIRS, ed. 300, s/n, size N/A, pub WAEL	450.00	525.00
☐ REGINA, (On Porcelain), ed. 950, size N/A, pub WAEL	395.00	495.00
☐ PETER, (On Porcelain), ed. 950, size N/A, pub WAEL	395.00	495.00
☐ TO CATCH A BUTTERFLY, (On Porcelain), ed. 950, s/n, size N/A, pub WAEL	395.00	495.00
☐ MARGARITA, (On Porcelain), ed. 950, s/n, size N/A, pub WAEL	395.00	495.00
☐ BETTINA, ed. 250, s/n, size N/A, pub WAEL	550.00	700.00
☐ VINCENTE, ed. 360, s/n, size N/A, pub WAEL	550.00	700.00
☐ JORGITO, rel. 1985. ed. 300, s/n, 18″ x 22″, pub WAEL	500.00	—
☐ CHRISTINA, rel. 1985. ed. 300, s/n, 18″ x 22″, pub WAEL	500.00	—

IKKI MATSUMOTO

THEMES: Varied

BOOKS: Illustrated the book *Animal Rides,* collaborated with Charles Harper on *Zoo It Yourself*

EDUCATION: John Herron Art Institute in Indianapolis, Cincinnati Art Academy

GALLERY/DISTRIBUTOR: Frame House Gallery, Inc.

	ISSUE PRICE	CURRENT PRICE
☐ BLUEBIRD IN RED BERRIES, ed. 200, s/n	30.00	—
☐ BLUE HERON, ed. 50, s/n	N/A	150.00
☐ BUTTERFLY, ed. 200, s/n	20.00	Sold Out
☐ GO FLY A KITE, ed. 130, s/n	N/A	100.00
☐ FISHY, ed. 200, s/n	30.00	Sold Out
☐ FLY ON THE MOON, ed. 200, s/n	20.00	Sold Out
☐ LITTLE GIRL BLUE, ed. 200, s/n	40.00	Sold Out
☐ MAILMAN OF AUTUMN, ed. 200, s/n	20.00	Sold Out
☐ PELICAN, ed. 100, s/n	N/A	100.00
☐ RAINBOW DROPS, ed. 150, s/n	N/A	125.00
☐ SANDPIPERS, ed. 100, s/n	N/A	1,100.00
☐ STRANGER ON THE BEACH, ed. 130, s/n	N/A	100.00
☐ BUTTERFLY TREE, rel. 1977. ed. 250, s/n, 22″ x 22″, pub FHG	40.00	250.00
☐ POPPY FIELD, rel. 1977. ed. 750, s/n, 26½″ x 22″, pub FHG	40.00	75.00
☐ UP, UP BUTTERFLY, rel. 1977. ed. 750, s/n, 26½″ x 20″, pub FHG	40.00	85.00
☐ ANHINGA, rel. 1978. ed. 750, s/n, 30″ x 21″, pub FHG	75.00	120.00
☐ COMMON EGRET, rel. 1978. ed. 750, s/n, 30″ x 24″, pub FHG	75.00	120.00
☐ FLY BY NIGHT, rel. 1978. ed. 750, s/n, 25″ x 20″, pub FHG	50.00	65.00
☐ GREAT BLUE HERON, rel. 1978. ed. 750, s/n, 21″ x 30″, pub FHG	75.00	150.00
☐ SAND CASTLE, rel. 1978. ed. 750, s/n, 20″ x 28″, pub FHG	40.00	Sold Out
☐ OVER THE BUTTERFLY HILLS, rel. 1979, ed. 750, s/n, 22½″ x 22″, pub FHG	55.00	—
☐ PELICAN, rel. 1979. ed. 750, s/n, 30″ x 33″, pub FHG	75.00	150.00
☐ SWANS, rel. 1979. ed. 750, s/n, 15″ x 30″, pub FHG	55.00	—
☐ YOU'LL NEVER MAKE IT OVER THE ATLANTIC WITH THAT THING/AHH, YOU CAN'T LIVE ON SEASHELLS ALONE, pair, rel. 1979. ed. 2,500, s/o, 12¼″ x 12¾″, pub FHG	20.00	—
☐ BAMBOO TIGER, rel. 1980. ed. 750, s/n, 20″ x 30″, pub FHG	80.00	—
☐ BLUE AND GOLD MACAW, rel. 1980. ed. 750, s/n, 30″ x 18″, pub FHG	80.00	—
☐ TOUCANS, rel. 1980. ed. 750, s/n, 17″ x 30″, pub FHG	80.00	—

PATSY McAULEY

THEMES: Wildlife art

GALLERY/DISTRIBUTOR: Wildlife Art of North Carolina

	ISSUE PRICE	CURRENT PRICE
☐ EASTERN COTTONTAIL AND DANDELIONS, rel. 1982. ed. 1,000, s/n, 16″ x 20″, pub WA INC.	60.00	—
☐ WOODDUCKS AND WILD GINGER, rel. 1983. ed. 1,000, s/n, 16″ x 22″, pub WA INC.	60.00	—

ARTHUR McCALL

THEMES: Western art

MEDIUM: Acrylic and oil

GALLERY/DISTRIBUTOR: Arts Limited, Inc.

	ISSUE PRICE	CURRENT PRICE
☐ SANDY CREEK QUAIL, rel. 1981. ed. 1,500, s/n, 23⅛″ x 31¾″, pub ALI	60.00	—

IRISH McCALLA

THEMES: Western art

MEDIUM: Watercolor

EDUCATION: Studied with Fritz Willis, Carlo Buonora, and Grace Harvey

AWARDS: "Blossom Soft" tied for first place in *Plate Collector Magazine*'s "Litho of the Year" award; Special Artist award (Women Artists of the American West)

MEMBERSHIPS: Women Artists of the American West

MUSEUMS/COLLECTIONS: Federal Bank's Collection of American Artists; Bell Telephone Company; L.A. Museum of Science, etc.

GALLERY/DISTRIBUTOR: McCalla Enterprises, Inc.

COMMENTS: At age seventeen, Irish McCalla decided to be an actress. She had the starring role of "Sheena, Queen of the Jungle" television series

	ISSUE PRICE	CURRENT PRICE
☐ MAIL ORDER BRIDE, ed. 500, s/n, size not available, pub MEI	75.00	150.00
ed. 25, Artist proofs	75.00	150.00
☐ HIGH COUNTRY CABIN, ed. 750, s/n, 14″ x 25″, pub MEI	55.00	—
ed. 50, Artist proofs	55.00	75.00
☐ WHO BE YA CALLIN A RUNT, ed. 900, s/n, 14¾″ x 19½″, pub MEI	35.00	—
ed. 50, Artist proofs	35.00	45.00
ed. 45, remarqued	125.00	—
☐ PLENTY MUCH FIREWATER, ed. 900, s/n, 14¾″ x 19½″, pub MEI	35.00	—
ed. 50, Artist proofs	35.00	45.00
ed. 45, remarqued	125.00	—
☐ MOUNTAIN MEN, (rel. as a pair). ed. 950, s/n, size N/A, pub MEI	65.00	—
ed. 45, remarqued	125.00	175.00
ed. 50, singly	35.00	—
☐ FIRST LIGHT OF DAWN, ed. 350, s/n, size N/A, pub MEI	35.00	60.00
available on canvas	95.00	—
ed. 25, Artist proofs	60.00	80.00
☐ THE LETTER, ed. 500, s/n, size N/A, pub MEI	95.00	—
☐ BRIGHT LEAF, ed. 2,000, s/n, 16″ x 20″, pub MEI	24.50	—
☐ LITTLE BIG CHIEF, ed. 1,500, s/n, 16″ x 20″, pub MEI	24.50	—
☐ BRIDAL BLANKET, ed. 100, s/n, 16″ x 20″, pub MEI	125.00	145.00
☐ BRIDAL BLANKET, ed. 100, s/n, on canvas, size N/A, pub MEI	125.00	145.00
☐ SOME LAND OF HIS OWN, rel. 1985. ed. 150, s/n, print on canvas, 20″ x 30″, pub MEI	175.00	—

D. MICHAEL McCARTHY

THEMES: Landscape art

MEDIUM: Watercolor

STYLE: Emphasis on color and light

GALLERY/DISTRIBUTOR: Greenwich Workshop

COMMENTS: McCarthy states, "What I seek to do in my painting is to capture people's imagination, not their attention. To make people truly feel the sensation of nature in my painting is a deeply felt conviction"

	ISSUE PRICE	CURRENT PRICE
☐ **THE MOUNTAIN OF THE HOLY CROSS,** rel. 1981. ed. 500, s/n, 22½" x 29½", pub GW	125.00	140.00
☐ **MT. ROBSON,** rel. 1983. ed. 100, s/n, 25" x 19⅝", stone litho pulled at the Tamarind Institute, pub GW	225.00	—
☐ **THE GRAND TETONS,** rel. 1983. ed. 650, s/n, 25" x 19⅝", pub GW	125.00	—
☐ **SPIRIT OF THE CASCADES,** rel. 1984. ed. 650, s/n, 23¾" x 29½"	125.00	—

THE GRAND TETONS *by D. Michael McCarthy*

FRANK C. McCARTHY

THEMES: Old West

BACKGROUND: His formal education was acquired at Pratt Institute and the Art Student's League. A successful career in commercial art and illustration followed, including book covers and advertising art

BOOKS: *The Western Paintings of Frank C. McCarthy* (Ballantine Books, 1974)

MEMBERSHIPS: Cowboy Artists of America

THE SAVAGE TAUNT *by Frank C. McCarthy*

GALLERY/DISTRIBUTOR: Greenwich Workshop

COMMENTS: Viewing a McCarthy painting of the Old West is like walking in on an Indian raid or chasing bandits, or riding with the cavalry in two columns

	ISSUE PRICE	CURRENT PRICE
☐ **LONE SENTINEL,** rel. 1974. ed. 1,000, s/n, 20" x 25½", pub GW	55.00	1,525.00
☐ **LONG COLUMN,** rel. 1974. ed. 1,000, s/n, 30½" x 21½", pub GW	75.00	975.00
☐ **THE HUNT,** rel. 1974. ed. 1,000, s/n, 30½" x 19½", pub GW	75.00	700.00
☐ **THE NIGHT THEY NEEDED A GOOD RIBBON MAN,** rel. 1974. ed. 1,000, s/n, 24" x 27", pub GW	65.00	495.00
☐ **RETURNING RAIDERS,** rel. 1975. ed. 1,000, s/n, 30" x 17¼", pub GW	75.00	500.00
☐ **SMOKE WAS THEIR ALLY,** rel. 1975. ed. 1,000, s/n, 26" x 18¾", pub GW	75.00	400.00
☐ **THE SURVIVOR,** rel. 1975. ed. 1,000, s/n, 26" x 20", pub GW	65.00	460.00
☐ **WAITING FOR THE ESCORT,** rel. 1975. ed. 1,000, s/n, 30½" x 21½", pub GW	75.00	335.00
☐ **PACKING IN,** rel. 1976. ed. 1,000, s/n, 18" x 22½", pub GW	65.00	350.00
☐ **SIOUX WARRIORS,** rel. 1976. ed. 650, s/n, 20" x 16", pub GW	55.00	445.00
☐ **THE HOSTILES,** rel. 1976. ed. 1,000, s/n, 30½" x 21½", pub GW	75.00	685.00
☐ **THE WARRIOR,** rel. 1976. ed. 650, s/n, 20" x 20½", pub GW	55.00	500.00
☐ **AN OLD-TIME MOUNTAIN MAN,** rel. 1977. ed. 1,000, s/n, 16" x 19¼", pub GW	65.00	365.00
☐ **COMANCHE MOON,** rel. 1977. ed. 1,000, s/n, 30½" x 20½", pub GW	75.00	355.00

	ISSUE PRICE	CURRENT PRICE
☐ DISTANT THUNDER, rel. 1977. ed. 500, s/n, 30″ x 22″, pub GW	75.00	675.00
*ed. 1,000 prints bearing the embossed Old Trooper seal. Proceeds to ongoing restoration of the United States Cavalry Museum, Ft. Riley, Kansas	75.00	675.00
☐ DUST-STAINED POSSE, rel. 1977. ed. 1,000, s/n, 30″ x 22″, pub GW	75.00	695.00
☐ ROBE SIGNAL, rel. 1977. ed. 850, s/n, 18″ x 23″, pub GW	60.00	445.00
☐ THE BEAVER MEN, rel. 1977. ed. 1,000, s/n, 26½″ x 18½″, pub GW	75.00	440.00
☐ BEFORE THE NORTHER, rel. 1978. ed. 1,000, s/n, 30″ x 18″, pub GW	90.00	540.00
☐ NIGHT CROSSING, rel. 1978. ed. 1,000, s/n, 22″ x 13″, pub GW	75.00	300.00
☐ SINGLE FILE, rel. 1978. ed. 1,000, s/n, 13″ x 22″, pub GW	75.00	380.00
☐ THE FORDING, rel. 1978. ed. 1,000, s/n, 30″ x 16½″, pub GW	75.00	440.00
☐ TO BATTLE, rel. 1978. ed. 1,000, s/n, 30½″ x 21″, pub GW	75.00	360.00
☐ IN THE PASS, rel. 1979. ed. 1,500, s/n, 30″ x 21″, pub GW	90.00	275.00
☐ ON THE WARPATH, rel. 1979. ed. 1,000, s/n, 20″ x 15½″, pub GW	75.00	250.00
☐ RETREAT TO HIGHER GROUND, rel. 1979. ed. 1,000, s/n, 32″ x 22″, pub GW	*90.00	325.00
*ed. 1,000, s/n, bearing the embossed Old Trooper seal proceeds to U.S. Cavalry Museum Ft. Riley, Kansas		—
☐ THE AMBUSH, rel. 1979. ed. 1,000, s/n, 40″ x 21½″, pub GW	125.00	330.00
☐ THE LONER, rel. 1979. ed. 1,000, s/n, 25½″ x 21″, pub GW	75.00	425.00
☐ THE PRAYER, rel. 1979. ed. 1,500, s/n, 33½″ x 20¾″, pub GW	90.00	650.00
☐ A TIME OF DECISION, rel. 1980. ed. 1,000, s/n, 32″ x 22″, pub GW	125.00	290.00
ed. 150, s/n, proceeds to the Red Rock Volunteer Ambulance Service of Sedona, Arizona......................	125.00	Sold Out
☐ BEFORE THE CHARGE, rel. 1980. ed. 1,000, s/n, 31″ x 21½″, pub GW	115.00	255.00
☐ BURNING THE WAY STATION, rel. 1980. ed. 1,000, s/n, 32″ x 22″, pub GW	125.00	375.00
☐ FORBIDDEN LAND, rel. 1980. ed. 1,000, s/n, 32″ x 32″, pub GW	125.00	325.00
☐ ROAR OF THE NORTHER, rel. 1980. ed. 1,000, s/n, 16″ x 20¼″, pub GW	90.00	300.00
☐ SNOW MOON, rel. 1980. ed. 1,000, s/n, 32″ x 22″, pub GW	115.00	525.00
☐ THE TROOPER, rel. 1980. ed. 1,000, s/n, 16″ x 20¼″, pub GW	90.00	275.00
☐ HEADED NORTH, rel. 1981. ed. 1,000, s/n, 32½″ x 19½″, pub GW	150.00	260.00
☐ RACE WITH THE HOSTILES, rel. 1981. ed. 1,000, s/n, 15″ x 26¾″, pub GW	135.00	220.00
☐ SURROUNDED, rel. 1981. ed. 1,000, s/n, 30″ x 21½″, pub GW	150.00	265.00
☐ THE COUP, rel. 1981. ed. 1,000, s/n, 24½″ x 19¾″, pub GW	125.00	360.00
☐ UNDER HOSTILE FIRE, rel. 1981. ed. 1,000, s/n, 30″ x 21½″, pub GW	150.00	335.00
☐ ALERT, rel. 1982. ed. 1,000, s/n, 23″ x 11″, pub GW	135.00	185.00
☐ APACHE SCOUT, rel. 1982. ed. 1,000, s/n, 29½″ x 19¾″, pub GW	165.00	290.00
☐ ATTACK ON THE WAGON TRAIN, rel. 1982. ed. 1,000, s/n, 31¾″ x 22¹¹⁄₁₆″, pub GW.................	150.00	230.00
ed. 400, s/n, donated to Arizona Kidney Foundation	—	—
☐ THE CHALLENGE, rel. 1982. ed. 1,000, s/n, 26″ x 18⅞″, pub GW	175.00	275.00
☐ THE WARRIORS, rel. 1982. ed. 1,000, s/n, 32″ x 18″, pub GW	150.00	215.00
☐ WHIRLING, HE RACED TO MEET THE CHALLENGE, rel. 1982. ed. 1,000, s/n, 26″ x 18⅞″, pub GW	175.00	280.00
☐ BLACKFOOT RAIDERS, rel. 1983. ed. 1,000, s/n, 13⁵⁄₁₈″ x 15¹⁵⁄₁₈, pub GW	90.00	170.00
☐ IN THE LAND OF THE SPARROW HAWK PEOPLE, rel. 1983. ed. 1,000, s/n, 30″ x 16¾″, pub GW	165.00	185.00
☐ MOONLIT TRAIL, rel. 1983. ed. 1,000, s/n, 16½″ x 10¾″, pub GW	90.00	185.00
☐ OUT OF THE MIST THEY CAME, rel. 1983. ed. 1,000, s/n, 21″ x 20⅜″, pub GW ...	165.00	250.00
☐ UNDER ATTACK, rel. 1983. ed. *, s/n, 35″ x 18¼″, pub GW	125.00	190.00
*This is a Personal Commission print and edition size will be determined by number of orders received by September 30, 1983.		
☐ ALONG THE WEST FORK, rel. 1984. ed. 1,000, s/n, 17″ x 21½″, pub GW	175.00	205.00
☐ THE DECOYS, rel. 1984. ed. 450, s/n, 44″ x 25¾″, pub GW	325.00	475.00
☐ THE SAVAGE TAUNT, rel. 1984. ed. 1,000, s/n, 21″ x 30½″, pub GW	225.00	325.00
☐ WATCHING THE WAGONS, rel. 1984. ed. 1,400, s/n, 30¾″ x 20⅛″, pub GW	175.00	245.00
☐ CHARGING THE CHALLENGER, rel. 1985. ed. 1,000, s/n, 12½″ x 23″, pub GW	150.00	Sold Out
☐ SCOUTING THE LONG KNIVES, rel. 1985. ed. 1,400, s/n, 16⅝″ x 36″, pub GW	175.00	Sold Out
☐ THE FIREBOAT, rel. 1985. ed. 1,000, s/n, 34½″ x 22¾″, pub GW	175.00	Sold Out
☐ THE LONG KNIVES, rel. 1985. ed. 1,000, s/n, 30½″ x 21¹¹⁄₁₆″, pub GW	175.00	Sold Out

JAMES McCLELLAND

THEMES: Wildlife art

BOOKS: His paintings of each hummingbird species found in America appear in the book, *Hummingbirds of North America*

EDUCATION: Andrews University in Michigan

AWARDS: Nebraska Habitat Stamp Competition; numerous "Best of Show" awards

GALLERY/DISTRIBUTOR: Wild Wings, Inc.

	ISSUE PRICE	CURRENT PRICE
☐ CHICKADEE FAMILY, rel. 1981. ed. 600, s/n, size not available, pub WWI	65.00	—
☐ CARDINAL FAMILY, rel. 1983. ed. 600, s/n, 17″ x 13½″, pub WWI	45.00	—

JOHN McCLELLAND

THEMES: Portraiture

MEDIUM: Watercolor

EDUCATION: Auburn University; Grand Central School of Art; Art Career School; studied with Jerry Farnsworth

MEMBERSHIPS: Fairfield Watercolor Group; Silvermine Guild of Artists

MUSEUMS/COLLECTIONS: National Museum of Sports

GALLERY/DISTRIBUTOR: Reco International Corp.

COMMENTS: The artist is also an award-winning plate artist

	ISSUE PRICE	CURRENT PRICE
☐ OLIVIA, rel. 1979. ed. 300, s/n, 28″ x 22″, pub RIC	175.00	—
ed. 30, Artist proofs	175.00	—
☐ SWEET DREAMS, rel. 1979. ed. 300, s/n, 27½″ x 20½″, pub RIC	145.00	—
ed. 60, Artist proofs	145.00	—
☐ JUST FOR YOU, rel. 1979. ed. 300, s/n, 27½″ x 20½″, pub RIC	155.00	—
ed. 60, Artist proofs	155.00	—
☐ REVERIE, rel. 1982. ed. 300, s/n, 23″ x 19¾″, pub RIC	110.00	—
ed. 30, Artist proofs	110.00	—
☐ I LOVE TAMMY, rel. 1984. ed. 500, s/n, 25½″ x 21″, pub RIC	75.00	—
ed. 50, Artist proofs	75.00	—

GEESE AT GADDY'S POND *by Ralph McDonald*

RALPH J. McDONALD

THEMES: Wildlife art

STYLE: Realism

AWARDS: Ducks Unlimited Artist of the Year (1981-82); Tennessee's "Wildlife Artist and Sculptor" (1979); many "Best of Show" awards

GALLERY/DISTRIBUTOR: Countryside Studio

	ISSUE PRICE	CURRENT PRICE
☐ A VIEW FROM THE BUSH, ed. 1,500, s/n, 24" x 31", pub CS	45.00	250.00
ed. 500, s/n, donated to Tennessee Lions Club-District 12-1		—
☐ AMERICAN BALD EAGLE, ed. 1,776, s/n, 23½" x 29½", pub AGI	40.00	600.00
☐ AMERICAN INDIAN, ed. 1,776, s/n, pub AGI	30.00	225.00
☐ AMERICAN WILD TURKEY, ed. 1,776, s/n, 20½" x 26½", pub AGI	40.00	250.00
☐ AMERICAN WHITETAIL DEER, ed. 1,776, s/n, pub AGI	40.00	150.00

	ISSUE PRICE	CURRENT PRICE
☐ AUTUMN RUST, rel. 1980. ed. 950, s/n, size unavailable, pub CS	80.00	225.00
☐ BEAVER DAM MALLARDS, rel. 1977. ed. 800, s/n, 16″ x 21″, pub PPC	60.00	450.00
☐ BEAVER DAM WOOD DUCKS, rel. 1983. ed. 950, s/n, size unavailable, pub CS	95.00	145.00
☐ BICENTENNIAL SET, rel. 1980. ed. five prints, pub CS	180.00	1,000.00
☐ BLACK WATER MALLARDS, rel. 1983. ed. 1,000, s/n, size unavailable, pub CS	50.00	75.00
☐ BLUEBIRD, ed. 5,000, s/o, 16″ x 20″, pub AGI	20.00	150.00
☐ BOBCAT, ed. 1,000, s/n, 20½″ x 26½″, pub AGI	40.00	90.00
☐ BOBWHITE QUAIL, ed. 1,000, s/n, 20½″ x 26½″, pub AGI	35.00	250.00
☐ BOBWHITE QUAIL (In Snow), rel. 1978. ed. 5,000, size unavailable, pub AGI	12.50	50.00
☐ CAHABA 'COON, ed. 2,000, s/n, 21″ x 24″, pub CS	35.00	150.00
☐ CAMP BRYAN WHITETAIL, ed. 600, s/n/remarqued, 24″ x 31″, pub CS	125.00	350.00
s/n only	75.00	250.00
☐ CANADAS AT CAIRO, rel. 1977. ed. 1,250, s/n, pub CS	55.00	100.00
☐ CARDINAL, ed. 5,000, s/o, 16″ x 20″, pub AGI	20.00	100.00
☐ CAROLINA WREN, ed. 2,750, s/o, 12″ x 16″, pub AGI	15.00	80.00
☐ CHAIRMAN OF THE BOARD, ed. 4,000, s/o, 16″ x 20″, pub AGI	20.00	200.00
☐ CHIPMUNK, ed. 2,750, s/o, 12″ x 16″, pub AGI	15.00	60.00
☐ COUGAR, rel. 1981. ed. 500, s/n, size unavailable, pub CS	95.00	150.00
☐ EASTERN COTTONTAIL, ed. 1,000, s/n, 18″ x 24″, pub AGI	30.00	200.00
ed. 2,000, s/o	20.00	100.00
☐ THE FOUR SEASONS PORTFOLIO, ed. 2,000, s/n, 10″ x 12″, pub CS	*45.00	150.00
*This portfolio consists of four prints.		
☐ FRONTIERSMAN, ed. 1,776, s/n, pub AGI	30.00	175.00
☐ GEESE AT GADDY'S POND, rel. 1980. ed. 850, s/n, size unavailable, pub CS	80.00	150.00
☐ GOLDEN DAYS, rel. 1982. ed. 950, s/n, size unavailable, pub CS	80.00	100.00
☐ GREEN TIMBER GREENHEADS, rel. 1978. ed. 1,250, s/n, 18½″ x 26½″, pub CS	55.00	200.00
☐ LARGEMOUGH BASS, ed. 3,500, s/n, 18″ x 24″, pub AGI	25.00	175.00
☐ MAJESTIC SILENCE (Deer Stamp), rel. 1980. ed. 1,000, s/n, size unavailable, pub CS	100.00	400.00
☐ MALLARDS, ed. 1,000, s/n, 20″ x 26½″, pub AGI	40.00	95.00
ed. 2,000, s/o	30.00	70.00
☐ MISSISSIPPI FLYWAY, Set of Four, rel. 1977-78. ed. 1,250, s/n, size unavailable, pub CS	220.00	600.00
☐ MOCKINGBIRD, ed. 500, s/n, 22″ x 28″, pub AGI	25.00	1,000.00
ed. 2,000, signed and bearing a seal	25.00	500.00
☐ PINTAILS AND PIROGUES, rel. 1978. ed. 1,250, s/n, size unavailable, pub CS	55.00	200.00
☐ RACCOONS, ed. 1,000, s/n, 20″ x 28″, pub AGI	35.00	300.00
ed. 2,000, s/o	25.00	250.00
☐ SAGE GROUSE, ed. 2,500, s/n, 12½″ x 16″, pub AGI	15.00	150.00
☐ SENTINEL, ed. 1,000, s/n, 20″ x 24½″, pub AGI	40.00	400.00
Released through Ducks Unlimited, 1974. ed. 1,000, s/o	30.00	250.00
☐ SMALLMOUTH BASS, ed. 2,000, s/n, 18″ x 24″, pub AGI	25.00	50.00
☐ SOUTH CAROLINA WHITETAIL DEER, ed. 1,000, s/n, 20½″ x 26½″, pub AGI	25.00	150.00
ed. 2,000, signed and bearing a seal with the signature of the Governor	25.00	60.00
☐ SOUTHERN BOUND, rel. 1982. ed. 500, s/n, size unavailable, pub CS	80.00	95.00
☐ STRIPED BASS, ed. 1,000, s/n, 20½″ x 26½″, pub AGI	25.00	50.00
ed. 2,000, signed and bearing a seal with South Carolina Governor's signature	25.00	—
☐ TENNESSEE BOBWHITE QUAIL, ed. 3,000, signed and bearing a seal, 20½″ x 26½″	35.00	—
Commissioned by Tennessee Wildlife Resources Agency, pub AGI		
☐ THE BAYOU GUIDE, ed. 1,000, s/n, 26½″ x 20½″	**60.00	—
**This print commissioned by Ducks Unlimited is now being offered to the general public through Countryside Studio.		
☐ THE BETHEL COLLEGE WILDCAT, rel. 1978. ed. 1,500, s/n, 18″ x 22″, pub CS	**—	—
**Commissioned by Bethel College, McKenzie, Tennesse special fund-raising edition.		
☐ THE BIG WHEEL, rel. 1980. ed. 1,500, s/n, size unavailable, pub CS	60.00	150.00
☐ THE CHAMPION, rel. 1978. ed. 1,500, s/n, size unavailable, pub CS	65.00	95.00
☐ THE DAVIDSON WILDCAT, ed. 1,750, s/n, 20″ x 26″, pub CS	**37.50	—
**This print was commissioned by the Booster Club of Davidson College, North Carolina, for use in raising funds for the school's athletic program.		
☐ THE HARVESTER, rel. 1980. ed. 1,500, s/n, size unavailable, pub CS	60.00	150.00
☐ THE JUDGE, ed. 2,000, s/n, 16″ x 29″, pub CS	30.00	150.00
☐ THE REFUGE, rel. 1978. ed. 1,500, s/n, size unavailable, pub CS	35.00	90.00

	ISSUE PRICE	CURRENT PRICE
☐ THE STATESMAN, rel. 1980. ed. 850, s/n, size unavailable, pub CS	80.00	350.00
☐ UNCLE JOHNNY'S COVEY, rel. 1977. ed. 1,250, s/n, size unavailable, pub CS	55.00	300.00
☐ WALKER'S POND BLACK DUCKS, rel. 1980. ed. 850, s/n, size unavailable, pub PPC	75.00	250.00
☐ WALKER'S POND MALLARDS, rel. 1982. ed. 850, s/n, size unavailable, pub PPC ..	95.00	350.00
☐ WALKER'S POND PINTAIL, rel. 1984. ed. 980, s/n, size unavailable, pub CS	125.00	175.00
☐ WALKER'S POND TEAL, rel. 1981. ed. 850, s/n, size unavailable, pub PPC	80.00	300.00
☐ WALKER'S POND (WOOD DUCKS), rel. 1976. ed. 800, s/n, 16″ x 24¼″, pub PPC ..	60.00	1,500.00
☐ WHISTLING SWAN, ed. 1,000, s/n, 19″ x 24″, pub AGI	30.00	75.00
ed. 1,000, s/o	20.00	50.00
☐ WHITETAIL AND DESCENDING CANVASBACK, ed. 2,500, s/n, 18″ x 24″, pub AGI .	25.00	300.00
☐ WOODIES AT WALNUT LOG, rel. 1978. ed. 1,250, s/n, 19″ x 23½″, pub CS	55.00	225.00
☐ COUNTRY CARDINALS, rel. 1983. ed. 1,000, s/n, 22½″ x 28″, pub CS	85.00	—
☐ HIS WORLD, rel. 1983. ed. 850, oil, s/n, 28″ x 21″, pub CS	95.00	—
☐ MY LAB, rel. 1983. ed. 850, s/n, 24″ x 29¼″, pub CS	125.00	Sold Out
☐ DAD & ME, rel. 1984. ed. 980, s/n, 20¾″ x 25¼″, pub CS	80.00	—
☐ GOLDEN DAYS, rel. 1984. ed. 950, s/n, 31″ x 24½″, pub CS	125.00	—
☐ MISSING DECOY, rel. 1984. ed. 1,500, s/n, 23″ x 28″, pub CS	80.00	—
☐ WILD RIVER, rel. 1984. ed. 950, s/n, 27⅜″ x 20¼″, pub CS	70.00	—
☐ BLACK WATER WOODDUCKS, rel. 1985. ed. 2,000, s/n, 22″ x 17¼″, pub CS	50.00	—
☐ MR. BIG EYE, rel. 1985. ed. 3,000, s/n, 17″ x 20″, pub CS	40.00	—
☐ TWELVE POINT FEVER, rel. 1985. ed. 580, s/n, 23¾″ x 29½″, pub CS	95.00	—

CLAY McGAUGHY

THEMES: Wildlife art

BOOKS: Featured in *The Cowboy in Art* by Ed Ainsworth

EDUCATION: University of Texas

MEMBERSHIPS: Society of Animal Artists

GALLERY/DISTRIBUTOR: Arts Limited, Inc.

	ISSUE PRICE	CURRENT PRICE
☐ BACHELOR, rel. 1970. ed. 500, s/n, 34″ x 27″, pub ALI	50.00	300.00
ed. 1,000, s/o	40.00	150.00
☐ BIRDS OF A FEATHER, rel. 1970. ed. 500, s/n, 34″ x 27″, pub ALI	50.00	300.00
ed. 1,000, s/o	40.00	150.00
☐ FOLLOW THE LEADER, rel. 1970. ed. 500, s/n, 34″ x 27″, pub ALI	50.00	300.00
ed. 1,000, s/o	40.00	50.00
☐ INTRUDER, rel. 1970. ed. 500, s/n, 34″ x 27″, pub ALI	50.00	300.00
ed. 1,000, s/o	40.00	150.00
☐ AT HOME, rel. 1971. ed. 500, s/n, 34″ x 27″, pub ALI	50.00	300.00
ed. 1,000, s/o	40.00	50.00
☐ CHECKIN' IN, rel. 1971. ed. 500, s/n, 34″ x 27″, pub ALI	50.00	300.00
ed. 1,000, s/o	40.00	150.00
☐ SHOW OFF, rel. 1971. ed. 500, s/n, 34″ x 27″, pub ALI	50.00	60.00
ed. 1,000, s/o	40.00	50.00
☐ ANTELOPE, rel. 1972. ed. 1,500, s/o, 12¼″ x 10¼″, pub ALI	10.00	—
☐ BLUE QUAIL, rel. 1972. ed. 1,500, s/o, 12¼″ x 10¼″, pub ALI	10.00	—
☐ BOBWHITE QUAIL, rel. 1972. ed. 1,500, s/o, 12¼″ x 10¼″, pub ALI	10.00	—
☐ LOAFERS, rel. 1972. ed. 500, s/n, 34″ x 27″, pub ALI	50.00	300.00
ed. 1,000, s/o	40.00	150.00

	ISSUE PRICE	CURRENT PRICE
☐ **SEA GULL,** rel. 1972. ed. 1,500, s/o, 12¼" x 10¼", pub ALI	10.00	—
☐ **THE ARISTOCRAT,** rel. 1972. ed. 500, s/n, 34" x 27", pub ALI	50.00	60.00
ed. 1,000, s/o	40.00	50.00
☐ **TIME TO MOVE,** rel. 1972. ed. 500, s/n, 34" x 27", pub ALI	50.00	60.00
ed. 1,000, s/o	40.00	50.00
☐ **COMMOTION,** rel. 1974. ed. 500, s/n, 16" x 20", pub ALI	35.00	—
ed. 1,000, s/o	30.00	—
☐ **HIDE AND SEEK,** rel. 1974. ed. 500, s/n, 16" x 20", pub ALI	35.00	—
ed. 1,000, s/o	30.00	—
☐ **ONE SHOT,** rel. 1975. ed. 500, s/n, 34" x 27", pub ALI	75.00	300.00
ed. 1,000, s/o	65.00	—
☐ **TRY AGAIN,** rel. 1975. ed. 500, s/n, 34" x 27", pub ALI	75.00	—
ed. 1,000, s/o	65.00	—
☐ **THE RACE,** rel. 1976. ed. 500, s/n, 34" x 27", pub ALI	75.00	300.00
ed. 1,000, s/o	65.00	—
☐ **FIRST CAST,** rel. 1980. ed. 1,500, s/n, 31" x 25", pub ALI	60.00	—
☐ **RIVAL,** rel. 1980. ed. 1,500, s/n, 31" x 25", pub ALI	60.00	—
☐ **SHORT CUT,** rel. 1980. ed. 1,500, s/n, 31" 25", pub ALI	60.00	—
☐ **FEATHERLIGHT,** rel. 1981. ed. 1,500, s/n, 31" x 25", pub ALI	75.00	—
☐ **NICE COUPLE,** rel. 1981. ed. 1,500, s/n, 31" x 22½", pub ALI	75.00	—

BALTIMORE *by Paul McGehee*

PAUL McGEHEE

THEMES: Varied

MEMBERSHIPS: Charter member of the American Society of Marine Artists;
Salmagundi Club; Steamship Historical Society

MUSEUMS/COLLECTIONS: Numerous corporate and private collections in the United States and Canada

GALLERY/DISTRIBUTOR: Art Recollections, Inc.

	ISSUE PRICE	CURRENT PRICE
☐ THE ABANDONED WORKBOAT, rel. 1983. s/o, 9¼" x 16⅝", pub ARI	15.00	–
☐ ANNAPOLIS, rel. 1983. ed. 1,500, s/n, 20" x 30", pub ARI	100.00	–
ed. 300, s/n, remarqued	200.00	–
☐ BALTIMORE, rel. 1980. ed. 750, s/n, 18¾" x 30", pub ARI	100.00	450.00
ed. 200, s/n, remarqued	150.00	600.00
ed. 95, Artist proofs, signed, remarqued	200.00	400.00
☐ BAY COUNTRY LANDING, rel. 1979. ed. 850, s/n, 19" x 30½", pub ARI	100.00	–
ed. 100, s/n, remarqued	150.00	500.00
ed. 95, Artist proofs, signed, remarqued	200.00	400.00
☐ CHESAPEAKE BAY CRAB BOAT, rel. 1983. s/o, 9¼" x 16⅝", pub ARI	15.00	–
☐ CHESAPEAKE BAY HARBOR, rel. 1979. ed. 850, s/n, 19" x 30½", pub ARI	100.00	–
ed. 100, s/n, remarqued	150.00	500.00
ed. 95, Artist proofs, signed, remarqued	200.00	400.00
☐ THE CITY DOCK, ANNAPOLIS, MD., rel. 1983. s/o, 9¼" x 16⅝", pub ARI	15.00	–
☐ COLOGNE ON THE RHINE, rel. 1984. ed. 1,700', s/n, 20" x 32", pub ARI	100.00	–
ed. 300, s/n, remarqued	200.00	–
☐ DOWN THE BAY, rel. 1979. ed. 850, s/n, 19" x 30½", pub ARI	100.00	–
ed. 100, s/n, remarqued	150.00	500.00
ed. 95, Artist proofs, signed, remarqued	200.00	400.00
☐ EASTERN SHORE MALLARDS, rel. 1982. ed. 750, s/n, 18¾" x 25", pub ARI	100.00	–
ed. 200, s/n, remarqued	150.00	–
☐ END OF THE LINE, rel. 1979. s/o, 16" x 24", pub ARI	35.00	–
signed, remarqued	85.00	–
☐ FAITHFUL COMPANION, rel. 1984. ed. 650, s/n, 20" x 30", pub ARI	100.00	–
ed. 300, s/n, remarqued	200.00	–
☐ FIRST SNOW, rel. 1984. ed. 1,700, s/n, 26" x 21½", pub ARI	100.00	–
ed. 300, s/n, remarqued	200.00	–
☐ THE GATEWAY TO THE NEW WORLD, rel. 1985. ed. 1,700, s/n, 20" x 32", pub ARI..	100.00	–
ed. 300, s/n, remarqued	200.00	–
☐ GEORGETOWN, rel. 1980. ed. 750, s/n, 20" x 24", pub ARI	80.00	–
ed. 200, s/n, remarqued	130.00	–
☐ HARVESTING THE CHESAPEAKE, rel. 1984. ed. 650, s/n, 15" x 30", pub ARI	100.00	–
ed. 300, s/n, remarqued	200.00	–
☐ THE HILTON INN, ANNAPOLIS, MD., rel. 1983. s/o, 9¼" x 16⅝", pub ARI	15.00	–
☐ IN TROPICAL WATERS, rel. 1980. ed. 750, s/n, 18¾" x 30", pub ARI	100.00	–
ed. 200, s/n, remarqued	150.00	–
☐ JACKSONVILLE, rel. 1985. ed. 1,700, s/n, 20" x 32", pub ARI	100.00	–
ed. 300, s/n, remarqued	200.00	–
☐ LIBERTY, rel. 1985. s/o, 24" x 18", pub ARI	50.00	–
☐ LIFTING FOG, rel. 1983. ed. 1,700, s/n, 20" x 30", pub ARI	100.00	–
ed. 300, s/n, remarqued	200.00	–
☐ MALLARDS AT TILGHMAN ISLAND, rel. 1980. ed. 750, s/n, 16" x 20", pub ARI	60.00	–
ed. 200, s/n, remarqued	110.00	–
☐ THE MELON BOAT, rel. 1980. ed. 750, s/n, 24" x 18", pub ARI	80.00	–
ed. 200, s/n, remarqued	130.00	–
☐ NANTUCKET, rel. 1982. ed. 750, s/n, 18¾" x 30", pub ARI	100.00	–
ed. 200, s/n, remarqued	150.00	–
☐ NEW YORK, rel. 1982. ed. 4,700, s/n, 18½" x 33", pub ARI	100.00	–
ed. 300, s/n, remarqued	200.00	–
☐ THE "PRIDE OF BALTIMORE", rel. 1983. s/o, 9¼" x 16⅝", pub ARI	15.00	–
☐ REMARQUE COLLECTORS PRINT, rel. 1984. s/o, 11" x 16", pub ARI	20.00	–
☐ THE ROAD HOME, rel. 1980. ed. 750, s/n, 24" x 20", pub ARI	100.00	–
ed. 200, s/n, remarqued	150.00	–
☐ SKIPJACKS OF THE CHESAPEAKE BAY, rel. 1983. s/o, 9¼" x 16⅝", pub ARI	15.00	–

	ISSUE PRICE	CURRENT PRICE
☐ **SKIPJACKS IN TANGIER SOUND,** rel. 1979. ed. 850, s/n, 17″ x 20½″, pub ARI	80.00	—
ed. 100, s/n, remarqued	130.00	300.00
ed. 95, Artist proofs, signed, remarqued	180.00	200.00
☐ **THE STATE HOUSE FROM EAST ST., ANNAPOLIS,** rel. 1983. s/o, 9¼″ x 16⅝″, pub ARI........	15.00	—
☐ **STORMY PASSAGE,** rel. 1980. ed. 750, s/n, 19″ x 25½″, pub ARI	100.00	—
ed. 200, s/n, remarqued	150.00	—
☐ **SUNDAY MORNING,** rel. 1980. ed. 750, s/n, 16″ x 20″, pub ARI	60.00	—
ed. 200, s/n, remarqued	110.00	—
☐ **THOMAS POINT LIGHTHOUSE,** rel. 1983. s/o, 9¼″ x 16″, pub ARI	15.00	—
☐ **WINTER IN HEIDELBERG,** rel. 1980. ed. 750, s/n, 19″ x 25½″, pub ARI	100.00	—
ed. 200, s/n, remarqued	150.00	—

BOB McGINNIS

THEMES: Varied

BACKGROUND: The artist started his career in commercial art. He worked on national magazines and movie productions as well

GALLERY/DISTRIBUTOR: Greenwich Workshop

	ISSUE PRICE	CURRENT PRICE
☐ **WINTER WHEAT,** rel. 1976. ed. 850, s/n, 28″ x 16¼″, pub GW	60.00	65.00
☐ **SLEEPY HOLLOW,** rel. 1977. ed. 1,000, s/n, 25″ x 17½″, pub GW	60.00	—
☐ **STEER HORN LANTERN,** rel. 1980. ed. 1,000, s/n, 28″ x 18¼″, pub GW	75.00	—
☐ **MEMORIES,** rel. 1980. ed. 1,000, s/n, 32″ x 18″, pub GW	75.00	—
☐ **ETHAN,** rel. 1980. ed. 1,000, s/n, 22″ x 28½″, pub GW	90.00	420.00
☐ **SILENT AND STILL,** rel. 1981. ed. 1,000, s/n, 32″ x 18½″, pub GW	95.00	—

NANCY McGOWAN

GALLERY/DISTRIBUTOR: Arts Limited, Inc.

	ISSUE PRICE	CURRENT PRICE
☐ **THE SENTINEL,** rel. 1973. ed. 500, s/n, 14″ x 18″, pub ALI	20.00	Sold Out
ed. 2,500, s/o	15.00	—
☐ **FIRST SPRING,** rel. 1973. ed. 500, s/n, 14″ x 18″, pub ALI	20.00	—
ed. 2,500, s/o	15.00	—

R. BROWNELL McGREW

THEMES: Native Americans

GALLERY/DISTRIBUTOR: Mill Pond Press, Inc.

COMMENTS: McGrew paints the Navajo and Hopi Indians from the inside out, which is why imitations of his paintings resemble the originals only as strips of colored paper resemble rainbows. Others paint Indian subjects—McGrew paints his friends

	ISSUE PRICE	CURRENT PRICE
☐ **TIME TO TALK,** rel. 1984. ed. 700, s/n, 24½" x 37½", pub MPPI	200.00	—

CANADA GEESE AND GOSLINGS *by George McLean*

GEORGE McLEAN

THEMES: Wildlife art

BOOKS: McLean's place in the contemporary art world has been exposed in a major book, *Paintings from the Wild*

GALLERY/DISTRIBUTOR: Mill Pond Press, Inc.

	ISSUE PRICE	CURRENT PRICE
☐ **CANADA GEESE AND GOSLINGS,** rel. 1982. ed. 950, s/n, 14⅝" x 24", pub MPPI ..	95.00	—
☐ **CHARLES IN THE GRASS,** rel. 1982. ed. 950, s/n, 14" x 20", pub MPPI	125.00	—
☐ **RED-TAILED HAWK MANTLING,** rel. 1982. ed. 950, s/n, 19⅛" x 38", pub MPPI	245.00	260.00
☐ **RED-WINGED BLACK BIRD AND CATTAILS,** rel. 1982. ed. 950, s/n, 24" x 17¼", pub MPPI	90.00	—
☐ **SILENT WATCH - GREAT HORNED OWL,** rel. 1982. ed. 950, s/n, 24" x 17³⁄₁₆", pub MPPI	90.00	—
☐ **YELLOW LABRADOR RETRIEVER,** rel. 1982. ed. 950, s/n, 22" x 38", pub MPPI	175.00	—

RODGER McPHAIL

THEMES: Wildlife art

GALLERY/DISTRIBUTOR: Russell A. Fink

	ISSUE PRICE	CURRENT PRICE
☐ FIRST LIGHT-WOOD DUCKS, ed. 850, s/n, 17″ x 24¾″, distr. RAF	80.00	
☐ COVEY RISE, ed. 850, s/n, 13¾″ x 17″, distr. RAF	80.00	—

WILLIAM N. McPHEETERS

THEMES: Americana

MEDIUM: Watercolor and pencil

STYLE: The artist mixes imagery and realism together for a unique effect

AWARDS: His numerous awards include two from the New York Society of Illustrators

GALLERY/DISTRIBUTOR: Grey Stone Press

	ISSUE PRICE	CURRENT PRICE
☐ MR. CAGLES SHOP, ed. 2,500, s/n, 29″ x 23″, litho, pub GSP	20.00	—
☐ CATCHING BAIT, ed. 1,000, s/n, 19″ x 23½″, litho, pub GSP	25.00	—
ed. 1,500, s/o	20.00	—
☐ THE SEWING BASKET, ed. 1,000, signed & dated 1976, 12″ x 15″, pub GSP	10.00	—
☐ COMMON SENSE, ed. 1,000, signed & dated, 12″ x 15″, pub GSP	10.00	—
☐ WISDOM, ed. 850, s/n, 27⅞″ x 22⅞″, pub GSP	15.00	150.00
☐ MOTHER EARTH, ed. 1,000, s/n, 21″ x 24″, pub GSP	20.00	100.00

MARGARET MEE

THEMES: Flowers

STYLE: Realism

BOOKS: *Flowers of the Brazilian Forests* by Margaret Mee

BACKGROUND: Born in Buckinghamshire, England, she does her scientific work deep in the Amazon jungle

GALLERY/DISTRIBUTOR: Frame House Gallery, Inc.

	ISSUE PRICE	CURRENT PRICE
☐ FAM. BIGNONIACEAE, rel. 1976. ed. 1,000, s/n, 23″ x 17″, pub FHG	35.00	Sold Out
☐ GUSTAVIA, rel. 1976. ed. 1,000, s/n, 23″ x 17″, pub FHG	35.00	Sold Out

JAMES A. MEGER

THEMES: Wildlife art

EDUCATION: St. John's University; University of Minnesota

AWARDS: He has received numerous awards and honors throughout his career

GALLERY/DISTRIBUTOR: Voyageur Art

	ISSUE PRICE	CURRENT PRICE
☐ **FIRST BORN,** rel. 1983. ed. 500, s/n, 10″ x 15″, litho, pub VA	85.00	—
☐ **RISKY BUSINESS,** rel. 1983. ed. 580, s/n, 15″ x 20″, litho, pub VA	75.00	—
☐ **WILDSIDE - CANVASBACKS,** rel. 1983. ed. 100, s/n, 21¼″ x 25¼″, litho, pub VA	100.00	—
☐ **BREAKAWAY,** rel. 1984. ed. 580, s/n, 20″ x 15″, litho, pub VA	85.00	—

STANLEY MELTZOFF

THEMES: Marine art (focusing on the fish of the sea)

BACKGROUND: Meltzoff is an undersea diver and is proud to hold the spearfishing records for striped bass and bluefish

AWARDS: Award of Merit (1980) from the Society of Animal Artists

BELOW ON THE FLATS · BONE AND PERMIT FISH *by Stanley Meltzoff*

MEMBERSHIPS: Society of Animal Artists, Society of Illustrators

GALLERY/DISTRIBUTOR: Stanley Meltzoff's work is distributed through several sources, including Wild Wings, Inc.

	ISSUE PRICE	CURRENT PRICE
☐ *DOUBLE HEADER #1-BLUE MARLIN, rel. 1981. ed. 750, s/n, 19¾″ x 27″	125.00	—
☐ BELOW ON THE FLATS-BONE AND PERMIT FISH, rel. 1981. ed. 750, s/n, 10¾″ x 27¼″	85.00	—

	ISSUE PRICE	CURRENT PRICE
☐ **SHINING SAILFISH AND BALLYHOO,** rel. 1981. ed. 750, s/n, 18½" x 27¼"	125.00	—
☐ **BABY BONES IN A CONCH,** rel. 1982. ed. 750, s/n, 13" x 10"	60.00	—

Stanley Meltzoff prints are distributed through several sources. Please note sources listing under SEL and WWI.

GREATER SCAUPS *by Sallie Middleton*

SALLIE MIDDLETON

THEMES: Wildlife art

MEDIUM: Translucent watercolor

STYLE: Realism

EDUCATION: Vesper George School (Boston)

GALLERY/DISTRIBUTOR: Foxfire Fine Arts Inc.

	ISSUE PRICE	CURRENT PRICE
SPECIAL MINIATURE EDITIONS (DUCK STAMP ENTRIES)		
☐ REDHEAD LANDING, rel. 1977. ed. 985, s/n, 8″ x 10″	25.00	85.00
☐ AMERICAN GOLDENEYE, rel. 1979. ed. 985, s/n, 8″ x 10″	25.00	85.00
ed. 250, s/o, exclusive for Nature Society, Asheville, North Carolina.		
☐ BLUE WINGED TEAL, rel. 1981. ed. 1,500, s/n, 9″ x 10″	25.00	70.00
☐ MATCHED NUMBER SET OF ALL THREE DUCK MINIATURES	75.00	300.00
WILDFLOWER SERIES		
☐ WILD ROSE AND VIOLET, pair, Plates I & II, rel. 1975. ed. 1,00, s/n, 12″ x 9″	35.00	85.00
☐ GENTIAN AND FOAMFLOWER, pair, Plates III & IV, rel. 1976. ed. 1,500, s/n, 12″ x 9″ .	45.00	75.00
☐ BLOODROOT AND WILD IRIS, pair, Plates V & VI, rel. 1977. ed. 1,500, s/n, 12″ x 9″ . .	45.00	75.00
☐ BUTTERCUPS AND BIRDFOOT VIOLETS, pair, Plates VII & VIII, rel. 1981. ed. 1,500,		
s/n, 12″ x 9″	50.00	80.00
☐ MATCHED NUMBER SET OF ALL FOUR WILDFLOWER PAIRS	175.00	300.00
☐ SCARLET TANAGER, rel. 1981. ed. 2,500, s/n, 20½″ x 26¼″	75.00	—
☐ THE OTTER AND THE TEAL, rel. 1982. ed. 1,500, s/n, 20½″ x 26½″	75.00	—
☐ A CAT CALLED BOB, rel. 1982. ed. 1,500, s/n, 20″ x 26½″	75.00	—
☐ YOUNG GRAY SQUIRRELS, rel. 1983. ed. 1,500, s/n, 15½″ x 19½″	50.00	—
☐ WARBLER IN SPRING, rel. 1983. ed. 1,500, s/n, 24½″ x 18½″	50.00	—
☐ SCREECH OWL, rel. 1983. ed. 1,500, s/n, 18½″ x 24½″	75.00	—
☐ MALLARD, rel. 1970. ed. 1,000, s/n, 22″ x 27½″	35.00	375.00
ed. 1,500, s/o	25.00	340.00
☐ GREAT HORNED OWL, rel. 1970. ed. 1,000, s/n, 25½″ x 22″	35.00	375.00
ed. 1,500, s/o	25.00	300.00
☐ RACCOON, rel. 1971. ed. 1,000, s/n, 25″ x 21½″	35.00	275.00
ed. 1,500, s/o	25.00	200.00
☐ MOURNING DOVES, rel. 1971. ed. 1,000, s/n, 20″ x 25″	35.00	150.00
ed. 1,500, s/o	25.00	110.00
☐ ROBIN AND SPARROW, rel. 1971. ed. 1,000, s/n, 17¼″ x 25½″	50.00	300.00
☐ CHIPMUNKS IN AUGUST, rel. 1971. ed. 1,000, s/n, 21½″ x 26½″	50.00	375.00
☐ CARDINALS IN WINTER, rel. 1971. ed. 1,000, s/n, 26¼″ x 22″	35.00	300.00
ed. 1,500, s/o	25.00	225.00
☐ TURTLE, rel. 1971. ed. 1,000, s/n, 19″ x 23½″	35.00	175.00
ed. 1,500, s/o	25.00	125.00
☐ YELLOW SHAFTER FLICKER, rel. 1972. ed. 1,000, s/n, 19½″ x 28½″	35.00	425.00
ed. 1,500, s/o	25.00	375.00
☐ RABBIT (Single), rel. 1972. ed. 1,000, s/n, 14″ x 19¼″	35.00	125.00
ed. 1,500, s/o	25.00	100.00
☐ PILEATED WOODPECKER, rel. 1973. ed. 1,000, s/n, 18″ x 25″	35.00	125.00
ed. 1,500, s/o	25.00	75.00
☐ EASTERN COTTONTAILS (Rabbits in Rhododendron), rel. 1973. ed. 1,000, s/n,		
18½″ x 26″	50.00	300.00
☐ BLUE JAY, rel. 1973. ed. 1,000, s/n, 18½″ x 24″	35.00	275.00
ed. 1,500, s/o	25.00	200.00
☐ PURPLE FINCHES, rel. 1973. ed. 1,000, s/n, 20″ x 16″	35.00	60.00
ed. 1,500, s/o	25.00	—
☐ BOBWHITE QUAIL, rel. 1973. ed. 1,000, s/n, 26¼″ x 20½″	50.00	250.00
☐ BARN OWL, rel. 1974. ed. 2,000, s/n, 16½″ x 24″	40.00	225.00
☐ CHIPMUNK IN THE SNOW, rel. 1974. ed. 2,000, s/n, 25″ x 18″	40.00	175.00
☐ RUFFED GROUSE, rel. 1974. ed. 2,000, s/n, 21½″ x 25″	40.00	80.00
☐ WOODCHUCK, rel. 1975. ed. 2,000, s/n, 23″ x 25″	40.00	100.00
☐ REDHEADED DUCK, rel. 1975. ed. 2,000, s/n, 22″ x 25½″	40.00	110.00
☐ CHAMELEON AND OPOSSUM, pair, rel. 1975. ed. 1,000, s/n, 9½″ x 9½″	35.00	60.00
☐ INDIGO BUNTING, rel. 1976. ed. 2,000, s/n, 17″ x 22″	40.00	275.00
☐ WILLET, rel. 1976. ed. 750, s/n, 21″ x 28½″	75.00	200.00
☐ TULIP POPLAR, rel. 1976. ed. 1,776, s/n, 24″ x 20″	40.00	60.00
ed. (200 bearing pencil remarque by the artist)	75.00	100.00
☐ YOUNG RABBITS IN CLOVER, rel. 1976. ed. 2,000, s/n, 16″ x 20″	40.00	485.00
☐ YOUNG RED FOX, rel. 1977. ed. 1,500, s/n, 26″ x 21″	75.00	450.00
☐ CHICKADEE, rel. 1977. ed. 1,500, s/n, 20″ x 24″	45.00	275.00
☐ RUBY THROATED HUMMINGBIRD, rel. 1977. ed. 1,500, s/n, 25″ x 21″	50.00	125.00
☐ WOOD DUCKS, rel. 1978. ed. 1,500, s/n, 20½″ x 26½″	125.00	475.00

	ISSUE PRICE	CURRENT PRICE
☐ **BUTTERFLIES I AND II,** rel. 1984. ed. 1,500, s/n, 13″ x 20″, litho, pub FFFA	50.00	—
☐ **GREATER SCAUPS,** rel. 1984. ed. 1,500, s/n, 18½″ x 24″, litho, pub FFFA	75.00	—
☐ **OVEN BIRDS,** rel. 1984. ed. 1,500, s/n, 18½″ x 24½″, litho, pub FFFA	50.00	—
☐ **CATBIRDS,** rel. 1984. ed. 1,500, s/n, litho, 18″ x 24½″, pub FFFA	65.00	—
☐ **BUTTERFLIES IN AUTUMN,** rel. 1985. ed. 1,500, s/n, litho, 16½″ x 24″, pub FFFA	45.00	—
☐ **BUTTERFLIES IN SUMMER,** rel. 1985. ed. 1,500, s/n, litho, 16½″ x 24″, pub FFFA . . .	45.00	—
☐ **MERLIN,** rel. 1985. ed. 1,500, s/n, litho, 18″ x 24″, pub FFFA	75.00	—
☐ **BLUEBIRDS,** rel. 1986. ed. 1,500, s/n, litho, 18″ x 24″, pub FFFA	TBA	—

LJUBOMIR MILINKOV

THEMES: Scenes of Yugoslavia

GALLERY/DISTRIBUTOR: Eleanor Ettinger, Inc.

	ISSUE PRICE	CURRENT PRICE
☐ **COUNTRYSIDE,** rel. 1981. ed. 300, s/n, 24″ x 28½″, litho, arches, pub EEI	300.00	—
☐ **SPRING BLOSSOM,** rel. 1981. ed. 300, s/n, 24″ x 28½″, litho, arches, pub EEI	300.00	—
☐ **MY MUSTANG,** rel. 1982. ed. 300, s/n, 10¼″ x 12½″, litho, arches, pub EEI	100.00	—
☐ **BUSY, BUSY,** rel. 1982. ed. 300, s/n, 12½″ x 10¼″, litho, arches, pub EEI	100.00	—
☐ **HAPPY DAY,** rel. 1982. ed. 300, s/n, 10¼″ x 12½″, litho, arches, pub EEI	100.00	—
☐ **FLOWER PICKING,** rel. 1982. ed. 300, s/n, 12½″ x 10¼″, litho, arches, pub EEI	100.00	—

SUGAR BUSH *by Gerhard C. F. Miller*

GERHARD C. F. MILLER

THEMES: Landscape art

MEDIUM: Watercolor

BOOKS: *Residue* (book of poetry), published in 1944

MUSEUMS/COLLECTIONS: Metropolitan Museum; National Academy

GALLERY/DISTRIBUTOR: Court Galleries

COMMENTS: In preparation of a book on European castles, the artist has been spending some time in Europe

	ISSUE PRICE	CURRENT PRICE
☐ BELGIAN BARN, ed. 500, s/n, litho, 21½" x 27½", pub CG	85.00	—
☐ BOAT HOIST, ed. 500, s/n, 21½" x 27½", pub CG	60.00	100.00
☐ THE CHAPEL, ed. 375, s/n, 21½" x 27½", pub CG	60.00	300.00
☐ JANUARY SHADOWS, ed. 500, s/n, 21½" x 27½", pub CG	60.00	100.00
☐ MARSHMARIGOLDS, ed. 500, s/n, 21½" x 27½", pub CG	75.00	125.00
☐ OLD PINE STUMP, ed. 500, s/n, 21½" x 27½", pub CG	75.00	100.00
☐ OLSON'S BUGGY, ed. 500, s/n, 21½" x 27½", pub CG	85.00	100.00
☐ RETURN TO NATURE, ed. 500, s/n, 21½" x 27½", pub CG	50.00	125.00
☐ RETURN OF THE CROWS, ed. 500, s/n, 21½" x 27½", pub CG	50.00	125.00
☐ THE SEEDLING, ed. 500, s/n, 21½" x 27½", pub CG	85.00	85.00
☐ SMOKE HOUSE, ed. 500, s/n, 21½" x 27½", pub CG	50.00	75.00
☐ STABLE DOOR, ed. 500, s/n, 21½" x 27½", pub CG	50.00	125.00
☐ SUGAR BUSH, ed. 500, s/n, 21½" x 27½", pub CG	60.00	100.00
☐ SUGAR MAPLE, ed. 500, s/n, 21½" x 27½", pub CG	60.00	100.00
☐ THE VETERAN, ed. 190, s/n, 21½" x 27½", pub CG	50.00	600.00
☐ WILD GRAPES, ed. 500, s/n, 21½" x 27½", pub CG	50.00	125.00

KATHRYN MILLER

THEMES: Landscape art, wildlife art

MEDIUM: Oil, watercolor, etchings

STYLE: Varied

EDUCATION: University of North Carolina; Savannah College of Art and Design

AWARDS: Award of Distinction; Most Popular Artist (St. Simon's Island Gascoigne Promenade)

GALLERY/DISTRIBUTOR: Kathryn Miller Studios

	ISSUE PRICE	CURRENT PRICE
☐ GOLDEN SEA OATS, rel. 1974. ed. 1,500, s/n, 24" x 36", pub KMS	30.00	—
☐ RIVER SHACK, rel. 1974. ed. 2,000, s/n, 20" x 24", pub KMS	25.00	—
☐ COUNTRY HERITAGE, rel. 1975. ed. 950, s/n, 20" x 24", pub KMS	30.00	—
☐ RUSTIC CHARM, rel. 1975. ed. 950, s/n, 16" x 20", pub KMS	20.00	—
☐ SUMMER MARSHES, rel. 1975. ed. 950, s/n, 20" x 24", pub KMS	30.00	100.00

SOUTHERN BEAUTY *by Kathryn Miller*

	ISSUE PRICE	CURRENT PRICE
☐ **MOSS CREEK,** rel. 1977. ed. 950, s/n, 20″ x 24″, pub KMS	30.00	—
☐ **SANDY SHORES,** rel. 1977. ed. 950, s/n, 20″ x 24″, pub KMS	30.00	100.00
☐ **SOUTHERN BEAUTY,** rel. 1978. ed. 950, s/n, 20″ x 24″, pub KMS	20.00	—
☐ **SUMMERTIME,** rel. 1978. ed. 950, s/n, 20″ x 24″, pub KMS	30.00	100.00
☐ **DAUFUSKIE ISLAND,** rel. 1979. ed. 950, s/n, 22″ x 28″, pub KMS	50.00	—
☐ **SOUTHERN LANDSCAPE,** rel. 1979. ed. 950, s/n, 22″ x 28″, pub KMS	50.00	—
☐ **LAND OF THE TREMBLING EARTH,** rel. 1980. ed. 950, s/n, 22″ x 28″, pub KMS	50.00	—
☐ **LOW COUNTRY HAVEN,** rel. 1980. ed. 950, s/n, 22″ x 28″, pub KMS	50.00	—
☐ **NIGHTTIME SHELLS,** rel. 1980. ed. 950, s/n, etching, 22″ x 28″, pub KMS	20.00	—
☐ **SUNRISE,** rel. 1980. ed. 950, s/n, 22″ x 28″, pub KMS	30.00	—
☐ **BABY BIRDS,** ed. 200, s/n, etching, 8″ x 10″, pub KMS	20.00	—
☐ **THE BEACHCOMBERS,** ed. 200, s/n, etching, 8″ x 10″, pub KMS	20.00	—
☐ **BLUE HERON,** ed. 200, s/n, etching, 8″ x 10″, pub KMS	20.00	—
☐ **BUTTERFLIES,** ed. 200, s/n, etching, 8″ x 10″, pub KMS	20.00	—
☐ **THE CANADIANS,** ed. 200, s/n, etching, 12″ x 16″, pub KMS	60.00	—
☐ **COASTAL SCENES,** ed. 200, s/n, etching, 11″ x 14″, pub KMS	50.00	—
☐ **COCKATOO,** ed. 200, s/n, etching, 14″ x 11″, pub KMS	50.00	—
☐ **COUNTRY BARN,** ed. 200, s/n, etching, 11″ x 14″, pub KMS	40.00	—
☐ **THE EGRETS,** ed. 200, s/n, etching, 11″ x 15″, pub KMS	60.00	—
☐ **GEORGIA BACKWATER,** ed. 50, s/n, etching, 14″ x 15″, pub KMS	60.00	—
☐ **GERANIUMS,** ed. 100, s/n, etching, 8″ x 10″, pub KMS	30.00	—

	ISSUE PRICE	CURRENT PRICE
☐ GOOD MORNING WORLD, ed. 100, s/n, etching, 8″ x 10″, pub KMS	30.00	—
☐ GREEN FROG, ed. 200, s/n, etching, 8″ x 10″, pub KMS	20.00	—
☐ HANGIN′ OUT, ed. 200, s/n, etching, 8″ x 10″, pub KMS	20.00	—
☐ HIGH SOCIETY, ed. 200, s/n, etching, 18″ x 11″, pub KMS	60.00	—
☐ HUMMINGBIRD, ed. 200, s/n, etching, 8″ x 10″, pub KMS	20.00	—
☐ KINGFISHER, ed. 200, s/n, etching, 11″ x 14″, pub KMS	40.00	—
☐ LIFT OFF, ed. 200, s/n, etching, 14″ x 11″, pub KMS	50.00	—
☐ LOWCOUNTRY CRABBER, ed. 50, s/n, etching, 8″ x 10″, pub KMS	20.00	Sold Out
☐ MALLARD, ed. 200, s/n, etching, 8″ x 10″, pub KMS	20.00	—
☐ MARKET PLACE, ed. 50, s/n, etching, 8″ x 10″, pub KMS	20.00	—
☐ PELICAN, ed. 200, s/n, etching, 8″ x 10″, pub KMS	20.00	—
☐ POSSUM TIME, ed. 200, s/n, etching, 11″ x 15″, pub KMS	60.00	—
☐ PREENING HERON, ed. 200, s/n, etching, 15″ x 11″, pub KMS	60.00	—
☐ PRELUDE TO SPRING, ed. 200, s/n, etching, 11″ x 14″, pub KMS	40.00	—
☐ SAVANNAH GARDEN, ed. 50, s/n, etching, 14″ x 15″, pub KMS	60.00	—
☐ SEA TREASURES, ed. 200, s/n, etching, 11″ x 14″, pub KMS	40.00	—
☐ SHELL MEDLEY, ed. 200, s/n, etching, 12″ x 16″, pub KMS	60.00	—
☐ SQUIRREL AND ACORNS, ed. 200, s/n, etching, 8″ x 10″, pub KMS	20.00	—
☐ SUN DOWN, ed. 50, s/n, etching, 14″ x 15″, pub KMS	40.00	Sold Out
☐ SUN DOWN, SECOND STATE, ed. 200, s/n, etching, 14″ x 15″, pub KMS	60.00	—
☐ TRITON′S TRUMPET, ed. 200, s/n, etching, 11″ x 14″, pub KMS	40.00	—
☐ THE UNICORN, ed. 200, s/n, etching, 11″ x 14″, pub KMS	60.00	—
☐ UP AND AWAY, ed. 200, s/n, etching, 11″ x 16″, pub KMS	60.00	—
☐ WATER LILY, ed. 200, s/n, etching, 11″ x 14″, pub KMS	50.00	—
☐ WINTER MILL, ed. 200, s/n, etching, 11″ x 14″, pub KMS	40.00	—
☐ WOOD DUCK, ed. 200, s/n, etching, 11″ x 14″, pub KMS	50.00	—
☐ CATS! rel. 1985. ed. 200, s/n, etching, 10″ x 10″, pub KMS	60.00	—
☐ CRUISING, rel. 1985. ed. 200, s/n, etching, 6″ x 7″, pub KMS	30.00	—
☐ DRAGON, rel. 1985. ed. 200, s/n, etching, 12″ x 21″, pub KMS	80.00	—
☐ DUCKS AND DAISIES, rel. 1985. ed. 200, s/n, etching, 9″ x 17″, pub KMS	60.00	—
☐ FAT CAT, rel. 1985. ed. 200, s/n, etching, 2″ x 4″, pub KMS	10.00	—
☐ GREAT BLUE, rel. 1985. ed. 200, s/n, etching, 12″ x 8″, pub KMS	60.00	—
☐ MOTHER HEN, rel. 1985. ed. 200, s/n, etching, 5″ x 4″, pub KMS	20.00	—
☐ THE HEN PARTY, rel. 1985. ed. 200, s/n, etching, 11″ x 22″, pub KMS	60.00	—
☐ TRIO OF HUMMERS, rel. 1985. ed. 200, s/n, etching, 7″ x 7″, pub KMS	30.00	—
☐ PELICAN BAY, rel. 1985. ed. 200, s/n, etching, 13″ x 10″, pub KMS	60.00	—
☐ PELICAN FLIGHT, rel. 1985. ed. 200, s/n, etching, 13″ x 10″, pub KMS	60.00	—
☐ ROOSTER AND CHICKS, rel. 1985. ed. 200, s/n, etching, 6″ x 4″, pub KMS	30.00	—
☐ SUNSET, rel. 1985. ed. 950, s/n, etching, 20″ x 24″, pub KMS	50.00	—

ROSEMARY MILLETTE

THEMES: Wildlife art

STYLE: Realism

AWARDS: Her work has captured many awards and other recognitions, the most recent being "Best Big Game Animal," "Best Small Animal," and "Best Bird of Prey" at the 1984 National Wildlife Art Show held in Kansas City. This year she appeared at the show as a Featured Artist and was honored with "Best of Show" awards for the Bird of Prey and Non-game Waterbird categories. She has won the South Dakota Pheasant Stamp Competition in both 1983 and 1985, along with winning the 1985—1986 South Carolina Duck Stamp Contest

GALLERY/DISTRIBUTOR: Wild Wings, Inc.

	ISSUE PRICE	CURRENT PRICE
☐ ABANDONED HOMESTEAD—PHEASANTS, rel. 1984. ed. 580, s/n, litho, 16″ x 24″, pub WWI	85.00	170.00
☐ DAPPLED SUNLIGHT—RACCOONS, rel. 1984. ed. 580, s/n, litho, 16″ x 20¼″, pub WWI	75.00	—
☐ HOMESTEAD REVISITED, rel. 1985. ed. 580, s/n, litho, 16″ x 24″, pub WWI	95.00	—

1983 WISCONSIN SALMON *by Chuck Mitchell*

CHUCK MITCHELL

THEMES: Wildlife art

BOOKS: The artist has extensively illustrated for *Encyclopedia Brittanica* and *Comptons Encyclopedia*

AWARDS: The artist has received awards from the Chicago Artists Guild and the Society of Illustrators of New York

GALLERY/DISTRIBUTOR: Northwoods Craftsman

	ISSUE PRICE	CURRENT PRICE
☐ LAKE TROUT, rel. 1983. 1983 Wisconsin Great Lakes Salmon & Trout Stamp Print. ed. 600, s/n, 14″ x 12″, pub NC	135.00	—
ed. 150 remarqued	250.00	—

FAWN WITH GOLDFINCH *by Harry J. Moeller*

HARRY J. MOELLER

THEMES: Nature and wildlife

MEDIUM: Opaque and transparent watercolor

STYLE: Realism

BOOKS: *Woodland Portraits* by Ideal Publishing

MUSEUMS/COLLECTIONS: He has exhibits throughout the United States and Europe

GALLERY/DISTRIBUTOR: Northwoods Craftsman

	ISSUE PRICE	CURRENT PRICE
☐ **BALD EAGLE,** rel. 1969. ed. 1,000, s/n, 18″ x 24″, dist. NC	30.00	—
☐ **MASTER'S PRIDE,** rel. 1970. ed. 1,000, s/n, 18″ x 24″, dist. NC	30.00	—
☐ **RING-NECKED PHEASANT,** rel. 1970. ed. 1,000, s/n, 18″ x 24″, dist. NC	30.00	—
☐ **FAWN WITH GOLDFINCH,** rel. 1979. ed. 600, s/n, 22″ x 28″, pub. NC	60.00	—
☐ **RACCOON WITH CHIPMUNK,** rel. 1979. ed. 600 s/n, 22″ x 28″, pub. NC	60.00	—
☐ **MOOSE,** rel. 1980. ed. 600, s/n, 30″ x 24″, pub NC	70.00	—
☐ **WARLORDS,** rel. 1980. ed. 600, s/n, 24″ x 30″, pub NC	70.00	—
☐ **WATERFOWL FLIGHTFOLIO,** rel. 1980. ed. 600, s/n, 9″ x 12″, pub NC (Portfolio of four prints).	75.00	—
☐ **GREAT EXPECTATIONS,** rel. 1981. ed. 600, s/n, 22″ x 28″, pub NC	75.00	—
☐ **RUFFED GROUSE,** rel. 1981. ed. 600, s/n, 28″ x 21″, pub NC	75.00	—

WILMA MOHNER-LANGHAMER

THEMES: Castles, flowers, and delicate landscapes of the medieval period

GALLERY/DISTRIBUTOR: Grey Stone Press

THE FLOWER BALLOON *by Wilma Mohner-Langhamer*

	ISSUE PRICE	CURRENT PRICE
☐ CASTLE SAUMUR-MEDIEVAL GRAPE HARVEST, ed. 950, s/n, 20″ x 24″, pub GSP	65.00	—
ed. 50, Artist proofs	85.00	—
☐ FLOWERS-MEDIEVAL SCENE IN TUSCANY, ed. 950, s/n, 20″ x 24″, pub GSP	75.00	—
ed. 50 Artist proofs	95.00	—
☐ HARVEST DANCE-MEDIEVAL SCENE ON THE RHINE, ed. 950, s/n, 20″ x 24″, pub GSP...	65.00	—
☐ PALAIS LINDENHOF WITH PANHARD 1902, rel. 1984. ed. 1,000, s/n, 20″ x 16½″, pub GSP...	75.00	—
☐ THE FAIR, ed. 1,000, s/n, 28½″ x 22½″, pub GSP	75.00	—
☐ WINTER DAY-MEDIEVAL SCENE, ed. 950, s/n, 20″ x 16″, pub GSP	45.00	—

BOB MOLINE

THEMES: Western art

BOOKS: *XIT—The American Cowboy; Colt Pistols; Bob Moline—A Cowboy and His Art*

AWARDS: Rand Stephen Award (1978); Gold Award from the Texas Ranger Hall of Fame (1980)

GALLERY/DISTRIBUTOR: Frame House Gallery, Inc.

	ISSUE PRICE	CURRENT PRICE
☐ DAY'S END, rel. 1981. ed. 975, s/n, 24″ x 30″, pub FHG	75.00	—
☐ TALLY GATE, rel. 1981. ed. 975, s/n, 22″ x 29″, pub FHG	75.00	—
☐ FUR TRAPPER, rel. 1982. ed. 975, s/n, 28″ x 22″, pub FHG	75.00	—

BURTON E. MOORE, JR.

THEMES: Wildlife art

MEMBERSHIPS: Ducks Unlimited, the National Rifle Association, National Audubon Society

GALLERY/DISTRIBUTOR: Mill Pond Press, Inc.

COMMENTS: The artist has completed a series of hen and drake illustrations for a film produced by the South Carolina Wildlife and Marine Resources Department

	ISSUE PRICE	CURRENT PRICE
☐ LEE DUDLEY-CANVASBACK, rel. 1979. ed. 950, s/n, 24″ x 19″, pub MPPI	65.00	130.00
☐ HARRY SHOURDES REDHEAD, rel. 1979. ed. 950, s/n, 24″ x 19″, pub MPPI	65.00	115.00
☐ WARD BROTHERS CANADAS, rel. 1979. ed. 950, s/n, 27½″ x 23″, pub MPPI	85.00	115.00
☐ WARD BROTHERS CANVASBACKS, rel. 1980. ed. 950, s/n, 27¼″ x 23″, pub MPPI...	85.00	—

	ISSUE PRICE	CURRENT PRICE
☐ **JOSEPH LINCOLN PINTAIL ON THE SANTEE,** rel. 1981. ed. 950, s/n 28¾" x 22¾", pub MPPI	85.00	—
☐ **THE WAITING,** rel. 1981. ed. 950, s/n, 27½" x 22¾", pub MPPI	85.00	100.00
☐ **THE WIND CALLED HIS NAME,** rel. 1981. ed. 950, s/n, 27½" x 22¾", pub MPPI	85.00	135.00
☐ **GOLDEN DAWN,** rel. 1982. ed. 950, s/n, 27½" x 22¾", pub MPPI	85.00	150.00
☐ **BECKY,** rel. 1983. ed. 950, s/n, 22" x 17½", pub MPPI	75.00	—

GOLDEN DAWN by Burton E. Moore, Jr.

CHARLEYN MOORE

THEMES: Wildlife art

MEDIUM: Pastels

GALLERY/DISTRIBUTOR: Swan Graphics, Ltd.

	ISSUE PRICE	CURRENT PRICE
☐ AFRICAN LION, rel. 1976. ed. 2,000, numbered only, 20″ x 24″, pub SGL	40.00	—
☐ COUGAR CUB, rel. 1976. ed. 2,000, s/n, 20″ x 24″, pub SGL	50.00	—
☐ SIBERIAN TIGER, rel. 1976. ed. 2,000, s/n, 20″ x 24″, pub SGL	50.00	—
☐ BANDIT (RACCOON), rel. 1977. ed. 2,000, s/n, 20″ x 24″, pub SGL	50.00	—
☐ KOALA, rel. 1978. ed. 1,000, s/n, 16″ x 20″, pub SGL	40.00	—
☐ MOTHERLY LOVE (JAGUAR & CUB), rel. 1978. ed. 1,000, s/n, 20″ x 24″, pub SGL .	60.00	—
☐ TROUBLES/CUDDLES, rel. 1979. ed. 2,000, s/n, 14″ x 16″, pub SGL	45.00	—
Priced as a Pair.		

TARA MOORE

THEMES: Wildlife art

MEDIUM: Oil and acrylic

GALLERY/DISTRIBUTOR: Wild Wings, Inc.

	ISSUE PRICE	CURRENT PRICE
☐ IN TROUBLE AGAIN, rel. 1977. ed. 300, s/n, size not available, distr. WWI	65.00	500.00
☐ LAB PUPS AND WATERBUG, rel. 1979. ed. 850, s/n, 20″ x 17″, distr. WWI	65.00	500.00
remarqued...	N/A	450.00
☐ CHOW TIME, rel. 1979. ed. 600, s/n, 15″ x 20″, distr. WWI	65.00	450.00
remarqued...	N/A	550.00
☐ BOX LUNCH, rel. 1980. ed. 850, s/n, 15″ x 20″, distr. WWI	65.00	250.00
remarqued...	N/A	350.00
☐ FIRST ADVENTURE, rel. 1980. ed. 850, s/n, 21″ x 17″, distr. WWI	65.00	200.00
remarqued...	N/A	300.00
☐ FLIGHT OF THE BUMBLEBEE, rel. 1980. ed. 840, s/n, 20″ x 22″, distr. WWI	65.00	125.00
remarqued...	N/A	N/A
☐ FLOUR CHILD, rel. 1980. ed. 850, s/n, size not available, distr. WWI	65.00	200.00
☐ ARCTIC SPRING, rel. 1981. ed. 850, s/n, size not available, pub WWI	65.00	—
☐ PAINT JOB, rel. 1981. ed. 850, s/n, size not available, dist. WWI	65.00	—
☐ PRIDE OF THE SHORE, rel. 1977. ed. 300, s/n, size not available, distr. WWI	75.00	—
☐ SOMETHING'S FISHY, rel. 1981. ed. 850, s/n, size not available, pub WWI	65.00	100.00
☐ THREE'S A CROWD, rel. 1981. ed. 850, s/n, size not available, pub WWI	65.00	65.00
☐ BEACH BOYS, rel. 1983. ed. 600, s/n, litho, 16½″ x 21½″, pub WWI	75.00	—
☐ BEACH PARTY, rel. 1984. ed. 600, s/n, litho, 16″ x 20″, pub WWI	65.00	—
☐ PUPPY LOVE, rel. 1984. ed. 600, s/n, litho, 16″ x 20″, pub WWI	65.00	—

WAYLAND MOORE

THEMES: Sporting art

BACKGROUND: In 1967, his work in editorial cartoons won him a Pulitzer Prize

EDUCATION: Ringling School of Art

MEMBERSHIPS: New York Society of Illustrators

GALLERY/DISTRIBUTOR: Felicie, Inc.

COMMENTS: Mr. Moore serves as a graphaics director for the Atlanta Braves, combining his career interests in art with his leisure time love for sports

	ISSUE PRICE	CURRENT PRICE
☐ AMERICA'S CHAMPION, rel. 1977. ed. 500, s/n, 40⅞" x 29¾", original color silkscreen, pub FI	200.00	800.00
☐ BALLOON, rel. 1976. ed. 300, s/n, 42" x 30", original color silkscreen, pub FI	250.00	1,200.00
☐ BALLOONING, rel. 1979. ed. 300, s/n, 42½" x 30", original color silkscreen, pub FI	375.00	800.00
☐ BASEBALL, rel. 1979. ed. 300, s/n, 30½" x 24", original color silkscreen, pub FI	250.00	350.00
☐ BICYCLE, rel. 1978. ed. 300, s/n, 27" x 42", original color silkscreen, pub FI	250.00	350.00
☐ BLUE GRASS, rel. 1978. ed. 300, s/n, 25½" x 36", original color silkscreen, pub FI	250.00	—
☐ BRICKYARD START, rel. 1977. ed. 300, s/n, 27" x 36", original color silkscreen, pub FI	200.00	800.00
☐ CENTER COURT, rel. 1978. ed. 300, s/n, 30½" x 42", original color silkscreen, pub FI	300.00	400.00
☐ CHURCHILL DOWNS, rel. 1979. ed. 300, s/n, 31½" x 40", original color silkscreen, pub FI	350.00	450.00
☐ DOWNHILL, rel. 1979. ed. 300, s/n, 36½" x 28", original color silkscreen, pub FI	325.00	500.00
☐ THE EIGHTH FURLONG, rel. 1976. ed. 300, s/n, 28¾" x 40¾", original color silkscreen, pub FI	200.00	800.00
☐ FLYING ICE, rel. 1979. ed. 300, s/n, 30" x 42", original color silkscreen, pub FI	350.00	450.00
☐ FOOTBALL, rel. 1978. ed. 300, s/n, 27" x 22", original color litho, pub FI	150.00	250.00
☐ FRENCH SEAPORT, rel. 1979. ed. 300, s/n, 18½" x 30", original color silkscreen, pub FI	325.00	425.00
☐ GIRAFFE, rel. 1978. ed. 300, s/n, 44½" x 23¼", original color silkscreen, pub FI	250.00	600.00
☐ GOAL POST, rel. 1979. ed. 300, s/n, 38" x 28", original color silkscreen, pub FI	350.00	450.00
☐ GOLF, rel. 1978. ed. 300, s/n, 28¾" x 36", original color silkscreen, pub FI	300.00	600.00
☐ HOCKEY, rel. 1977. ed. 300, s/n, 25" x 32", original color silkscreen, pub FI	250.00	800.00
☐ IN THE PIT, rel. 1977. ed. 300, s/n, 22" x 30", original color litho, pub FI	150.00	250.00
☐ JOCKEY, rel. 1976. ed. 300, s/n, 42" x 24", original color silkscreen, pub FI	200.00	400.00
☐ JUMPERS, rel. 1976. ed. 300, s/n, 36" x 36", original color silkscreen, pub FI	250.00	500.00
☐ LEOPARD'S HEAD, rel. 1977. ed. 300, s/n, 43" x 30", original color silkscreen, pub FI	250.00	450.00
☐ LIFT OFF, rel. 1980. ed. 300, s/n, 36½" x 26", original color silkscreen, pub FI	475.00	—
☐ LION, rel. 1979. ed. 300, s/n, 22" x 29¾", original color litho, pub FI	200.00	300.00
☐ LIONS, rel. 1978. ed. 300, s/n, 28¾" x 36½", original color silkscreen, pub FI	200.00	1,200.00
☐ MARATHON, rel. 1979. ed. 300, s/n, 26" x 36", original color silkscreen, pub FI	300.00	500.00
☐ MARDI GRAS, rel. 1977. ed. 300, s/n, 29½" x 40¾", original color silkscreen, pub FI	350.00	500.00
☐ MOTO-X, rel. 1976. ed. 300, s/n, 28¾" x 40¾", original color silkscreen, pub FI	200.00	350.00
☐ OLD PARISIAN, rel. 1979. ed. 300, s/n, 42½" x 30", original color silkscreen, pub FI	325.00	425.00
☐ PARTNERS, rel. 1979. ed. 300, s/n, 35½" x 29", original color silkscreen, pub FI	350.00	450.00
☐ PILE UP, rel. 1977. ed. 300, s/n, 35" x 29", original color silkscreen, pub FI	250.00	400.00
☐ RACQUETBALL (M. HOGAN), rel. 1979. ed. 300, s/n, 30" x 41", original color silkscreen, pub FI	375.00	—
(Signed by W. Moore and M. Hogan)		
☐ REGATTA, rel. 1978. ed. 300, s/n, 28½" x 21½", original color litho, pub FI	150.00	250.00
☐ RODEO, rel. 1978. ed. 300, s/n, 32" x 28½", original color silkscreen, pub FI	250.00	350.00
☐ ROUGH SEAS, rel. 1976. ed. 300, s/n, 42¼" x 30", original color silkscreen, pub FI	200.00	1,200.00
☐ SAND TRAP, rel. 1976. ed. 300, s/n, 46½" x 30", original color silkscreen, pub FI	200.00	600.00
☐ SCHOONER, rel. 1977. ed. 300, s/n, 27¼" x 36", original color silkscreen, pub FI	150.00	500.00
☐ SEA BREEZE, rel. 1977. ed. 300, s/n, 39¾" x 31¼", original color silkscreen, pub FI	350.00	800.00
☐ SKIER, rel. 1977. ed. 300, s/n, 23½" x 29", original color silkscreen, pub FI	200.00	450.00
☐ SOCCER, rel. 1978. ed. 300, s/n, 36" x 30", original color silkscreen, pub FI	300.00	400.00
☐ SPINMAKER, rel. 1979. ed. 300, s/n, 41" x 29¾", original color silkscreen, pub FI	375.00	800.00
☐ STORMY WEATHER, rel. 1979. ed. 300, s/n, 42¼" x 30", original color silkscreen, pub FI	375.00	600.00
☐ THE TALL SHIP, rel. 1976. ed. 100, s/n, 20¼" x 15", original etching, pub FI	80.00	300.00
☐ TROTTERS, rel. 1978. ed. 300, s/n, 29½" x 41½", original color silkscreen, pub FI	300.00	400.00

	ISSUE PRICE	CURRENT PRICE
☐ UNDEFEATED, rel. 1977. ed. 300, s/n, 28″ x 34″, original color silkscreen, pub FI	250.00	800.00
☐ WASH ART LITHO, rel. 1977. ed. 100, s/n, 15¾″ x 19½″, original litho, pub FI	80.00	100.00
☐ WHITE WATER CANOE, rel. 1977. ed. 300, s/n, 29½″ x 35″, original color silkscreen, pub FI	200.00	300.00
☐ WINDSURFER, rel. 1979. ed. 300, s/n, 36¼″ x 29¾″, original color silkscreen, pub FI	475.00	—
☐ WINNING VOLLEY, rel. 1976. ed. 300, s/n, 24″ x 18″, original color silkscreen, pub FI	200.00	350.00
☐ CIRCUS SUITE, rel. 1977. ed. 300, s/n, consists of 3 silkscreens .... CIRCUS CLOWNS, 31″ x 29⅛″; CIRCUS TIGERS, 29½″ x 40½″; THE BIG TOP, 29¾″ x 41⅝″	700.00	1,000.00
☐ NEW ORLEANS SUITE, rel. 1977. ed. 250, s/n, consists of 4 lithos .... NATCHEZ, 20″ x 15″, SLAVE EXCHANGE, 20⅜″ x 14⅞″; HAPPY MARDI GRAS, 21¼″ x 14¾″; SUGARFOOT, 20¼″ x 14½″	400.00	—
☐ PARIS SUITE, rel. 1977. ed. 250, s/n, consists of 4 lithos .... PARIS KIOSK, 23¼″ x 16¼″; LE PONT ALEXANDRE, 17″ x 23¼″; PLACE DES VOSGES, 23¼″ x 16¼″; VERSAILLES, 23¼″ x 16¼″	320.00	400.00
☐ SAN FRANCISCO SUITE, rel. 1977. ed. 250, s/n, consists of 4 lithos .... CHINATOWN, 17″ x 12″; CABLE CAR I, 13¾″ x 17″; CABLE CAR II, 13¾″ x 17″; GOLDEN GATE, 23¼″ x 16″	320.00	40.00
☐ STOCK EXCHANGE SUITE, rel. 1979. ed. 300, s/n, consists of 2 pieces .... BULL AND BEAR, 30½″ x 24″, original color silkscreen; WALL STREET, 24½″ x 35″, original color litho.	500.00	600.00

1984 FEDERAL DUCK STAMP *by William C. Morris*

WILLIAM C. MORRIS

THEMES: Wildlife art

BACKGROUND: The artist first received attention with his two paintings depicting the University of Alabama's Football Team and Coach Bryant

AWARDS: Alabama Waterfowl Competition (1984-85); Federal Duck Stamp (1984-85)

GALLERY/DISTRIBUTOR: Voyageur Art

	ISSUE PRICE	CURRENT PRICE
☐ WEATHERED REFLECTIONS, rel. 1980. ed. 1,000, s/n, 29″ x 21″, litho, pub VA	30.00	—
☐ WOODDUCKS, rel. 1980. ed. 950, s/n, 21½″ x 14½″, litho, pub VA	80.00	—
☐ PINTAILS, rel. 1982. ed. 950, s/n, 21½″ x 14″, litho, pub VA	40.00	—
☐ 1984 ALABAMA DUCK STAMP PRINT, rel. 1984. ed. 1,500, s/n, 12″ x 14″, litho, pub VA...	110.00	—
☐ 1984 FEDERAL DUCK STAMP PRINT, rel. 1984. s/n, 12″ x 14″, litho, pub VA	135.00	—

GARY MOSS

THEMES: Wildlife art

MEDIUM: Oil and watercolor

STYLE: Realism

BACKGROUND: He was a Marine Corps combat artist in Vietnam

EDUCATION: Minneapolis College of Art and Design

AWARDS: Combat Artist of the Year (1970)

GALLERY/DISTRIBUTOR: Wild Wings, Inc.

	ISSUE PRICE	CURRENT PRICE
☐ FAMILY OF SWANS, rel. 1978. ed. 850, s/n, 16½″ x 25″, pub WWI	75.00	—
ed. remarque artist proof	160.00	—
☐ TRIO OF CANADAS, rel. 1978. ed. 850, s/n, 17½″ x 23¾″, pub WWI	250.00	Sold Out
ed. remarque	160.00	Sold Out
☐ CANADAS ON THE COAST, rel. 1979. ed. 850, s/n, 23⅝″ x 17¾″, pub WWI	350.00	—
☐ SNOWS AND BLUES ON THE COAST, rel. 1980. ed. 850, s/n, 24″ x 18″, pub WWI .	75.00	—
☐ TRIO OF CANVASBACKS, rel. 1980. ed. 580, s/n, 23″ x 18″, pub WWI	85.00	—
☐ LAST OF THE SEASON - GOLDENEYES, rel. 1981. ed. 580, s/n, size not available, pub WWI..	75.00	—
☐ REFLECTIONS - PINTAILS, rel. 1981. ed. 580, s/n, size not available, distr. WWI	150.00	—
☐ ROOSTER TRAIL - RING NECKED PHEASANT, rel. 1981. ed. 580, s/n, size not available, distr. WWI	75.00	—
☐ PINE REFUGE - RUFFED GROUSE, rel. 1982. ed. 580, s/n, litho, 15¼″ x 25″, pub WWI..	85.00	—
☐ PRAIRIE LAKES - WHISTLING SWANS, rel. 1982. ed. 580, s/n, litho, 16″ x 22″, pub WWI..	85.00	—
☐ WATCHFUL TRIO - WILD TURKEYS, rel. 1982. ed. 580, s/n, litho, 16½″ x 22″, pub WWI..	85.00	—

THE LONG WINTER *by Gary Moss*

	ISSUE PRICE	CURRENT PRICE
☐ **WATCHFUL TRIO - WILD TURKEYS,** rel. 1982. ed. 580, s/n, size not available, distr. WWI	85.00	—
☐ **LONG WINTER - CANADA GEESE,** rel. 1983. ed. 580, s/n, litho, 16″ x 24″, pub WWI	85.00	—
☐ **ON THE PROWL - RUFFED GROUSE,** rel. 1983. ed. 580, s/n, litho, 17″ x 24″, pub WWI	85.00	—
☐ **LONG SHADOWS - RING NECKED PHEASANTS,** rel. 1984. ed. 950, s/n, litho, 17″ x 25¼″, pub WWI	70.00	—
☐ **FOG BOUND—SNOWS/BLUES,** rel. 1985. ed. 850, s/n, litho, 15″ x 22½″, pub WWI	90.00	—

P. BUCKLEY MOSS

THEMES: Symbolic landscapes and figures

MEDIUM: Watercolor

STYLE: A hybrid of abstract and realism

BACKGROUND: When she was ten years old, a serious automobile accident kept her out of school for a year, giving her unlimited time for drawing and painting

EDUCATION: Cooper Union

GALLERY/DISTRIBUTOR: Moss Portfolio (distributor)

HOMEWARD BOUND *by P. Buckley Moss*

	ISSUE PRICE	CURRENT PRICE
☐ **A WELCOME,** rel. 1982. ed. 1,000, s/n, 13¾″ x 10″, pub MP	45.00	Sold Out
☐ **ADAM,** rel. 1983. ed. 1,000, s/n, 9″ x 6″, pub MP	20.00	Sold Out
☐ **ALL IN THE TREE,** rel. 1982. ed. 1,000, s/n, 22″ x 15″, pub MP	80.00	100.00
☐ **ALONG THE CANAL,** rel. 1982. ed. 1,000, s/n, 12½″ x 16¾″, pub MP	80.00	Sold Out
☐ **AMY,** rel. 1983. ed. 1,000, s/n, 9″ x 6″, pub MP	20.00	Sold Out
☐ **APPLE DAY,** rel. 1983. ed. 1,000, s/n, 18″ x 18″, pub MP	80.00	Sold Out
☐ **APPLE GIRL,** rel. 1982. ed. 1,000, s/n, 10″ x 9″, pub MP	30.00	Sold Out
☐ **APPLE HARVEST,** rel. 1979. ed. 1,000, s/n, 21″ x 16″, pub MP	75.00	Sold Out
☐ **APPLE PICKER,** rel. 1978. ed. 1,000, s/n, 10″ x 8″, pub MP	35.00	Sold Out
☐ **AUTUMN RIDE,** rel. 1982. ed. 1,000, s/n, 18″ x 18″, pub MP	80.00	Sold Out
☐ **AUTUMN TRIPTYCH,** rel. 1984. ed. 1,000, s/n, 18½″ x 27″, pub MP	150.00	—
☐ **AWAKE O'EARTH,** rel. 1979. ed. 1,000, s/n, 11″ x 13″, pub MP	50.00	—
☐ **BALLOON BOY,** rel. 1984. ed. 1,000, s/n, 6½″ x 4½″, pub MP	20.00	—
☐ **BALLOON GIRL,** rel. 1984. ed. 1,000, s/n, 6½″ x 4½″, pub MP	20.00	—
☐ **BALLOON RIDE,** rel. 1982. ed. 1,000, s/n, 18″ x 17″, pub MP	100.00	—
☐ **BARELIMBED REFLECTIONS,** rel. 1978. ed. 1,000, s/n, 8″ x 10″, pub MP	25.00	Sold Out
☐ **BECKY,** rel. 1983. ed. 1,000, s/n, 10″ x 8″, pub MP	20.00	Sold Out
☐ **BECKY AND TOM,** rel. 1978. ed. 1,000, s/n, 11″ x 8″, pub MP	10.00	Sold Out
☐ **BEHOLD,** rel. 1979. ed. 1,000, s/n, 16″ x 11″, pub MP	35.00	—
☐ **BEST FRIENDS,** rel. 1985. ed. 1,000, s/n, 14″ x 19″, pub MP	70.00	—
☐ **BETROTHED,** rel. 1982. ed. 1,000, s/n, 24″ x 19½″, pub MP	150.00	—
☐ **BILLY,** rel. 1985. ed. 1,000, s/n, 9½″ x 8¾″, pub MP	25.00	—
☐ **BIRD BOY,** rel. 1982. ed. 1,000, s/n, 19″ x 16″, pub MP	110.00	—
☐ **BLACK CAT,** rel. 1981. ed. 1,000, s/n, 17″ x 14″, pub MP	50.00	—

	ISSUE PRICE	CURRENT PRICE
☐ BLACK CAT ON A PINK CUSHION, rel. 1982. ed. 1,000, s/n, 8″ x 8″, pub MP	40.00	—
☐ BLESSED ASSURANCE, rel. 1979. ed. 1,000, s/n, 16″ x 12″, pub MP	40.00	—
☐ BLESSING, THE, rel. 1984. ed. 7,230, s/n, 12″ x 12″, pub MP	—	Sold Out
☐ BLUE BALLOON, rel. 1982. ed. 1,000, s/n, 17″ x 11″, pub MP	60.00	—
☐ BLUE BOUQUET, rel. 1981. ed. 1,000, s/n, 5″ x 9″, pub MP	16.00	—
☐ BLUE BOY, rel. 1983. ed. 1,000, s/n, 11½″ x 14″, pub MP	40.00	—
☐ BLUE CRUCIFIXION, THE, rel. 1985. ed. 1,000, s/n, 18″ x 20⅜″, pub MP	150.00	—
☐ BLUE PLATE, rel. 1984. ed. 1,000, s/n, 19″ x 24½″, pub MP	125.00	—
☐ BLUE SHOES, rel. 1982. ed. 1,000, s/n, 9″ x 9″, pub MP	35.00	—
☐ BLUE WINTER, rel. 1982. ed. 1,000, s/n, 22″ x 17″, pub MP	100.00	—
☐ BOATS, rel. 1985. ed. 1,000, s/n, 9¾″ x 11¾″, pub MP	60.00	—
☐ BROTHERS, rel. 1983. ed. 1,000, s/n, 8″ x 7½″, pub MP	35.00	—
☐ BROTHERS FOUR, rel. 1984. ed. 1,000, s/n, 10¼″ x 8¾″, pub MP	50.00	—
☐ BROWER HOMESTEAD, rel. 1984. ed. 1,000, s/n, 19½″ x 19½″, pub MP	100.00	—
☐ BROWN BEAUTY, rel. 1985. ed. 1,000, s/n, 11½″ x 11½″, pub MP	50.00	—
☐ CAMEO GEESE, rel. 1982. ed. 1,000, s/n, 12″ x 12″, pub MP	40.00	Sold Out
☐ CANADA GEESE, rel. 1978. ed. 1,000, s/n, 9″ x 26″, pub MP	60.00	Sold Out
☐ CAPITOL SKATERS, rel. 1980. ed. 1,000, s/n, 22″ x 18″, pub MP	60.00	—
☐ CARRIE, rel. 1983. ed. 1,000, s/n, 11¼″ x 9¼″, pub MP	30.00	—
☐ CATHY, rel. 1985. ed. 1,000, s/n, 8″ x 8⅛″, pub MP	—	Sold Out
☐ CENTRAL PARK, rel. 1981. ed. 1,000, s/n, 18″ x 19″, pub MP	80.00	Sold Out
☐ CHERISHED, rel. 1983. ed. 1,000, s/n, 8½″ x 9″, pub MP	35.00	Sold Out
☐ CHICKEN FARMERS, rel. 1983. ed. 1,000, s/n, 12″ x 12″, pub MP	40.00	Sold Out
☐ CHILDREN'S MUSEUM CAROUSEL, THE, rel. 1985. ed. 1,000, s/n, 12¾″ x 13¼″, pub MP	80.00	—
☐ CHRIS, rel. 1982. ed. 1,000, s/n, 7″ x 10″, pub MP	25.00	—
☐ CHRISTMAS CAROL, rel. 1983. ed. 1,000, s/n, 12″ x 12″, pub MP	—	Sold Out
☐ COLONIAL SLEIGHRIDE, rel. 1983. ed. 1,000, s/n, 12½″ x 28″, pub MP	125.00	Sold Out
☐ THE COLT, rel. 1983. ed. 1,000, s/n, 27¼″ x 18¼″, pub MP	90.00	—
☐ COUNTRY CHURCH, rel. 1983. ed. 1,000, s/n, 16″ x 20″, pub MP	80.00	—
☐ CRAZY QUILT, rel. 1984. ed. 1,000, s/n, 10″ x 10″, pub MP	50.00	Sold Out
☐ CUBIST CRUCIFIX, rel. 1985. ed. 1,000, s/n, 12⅛″ x 8⅞″, pub MP	80.00	—
☐ DAILY CHORES, rel. 1978. ed. 1,000, s/n, 10″ x 8″, pub MP	16.00	Sold Out
☐ DANIEL, rel. 1982. ed. 1,000, s/n, 8″ x 10″, pub MP	20.00	Sold Out
☐ DANIELLE, rel. 1984. ed. 1,000, s/n, 10″ x 9½″, pub MP	50.00	—
☐ DASHING AWAY, rel. 1982. ed. 1,000, s/n, 12½″ x 28″, pub MP	100.00	Sold Out
☐ DEAR LORD, large, rel. 1979. ed. 1,000, s/n, 22″ x 26″, pub MP	30.00	Sold Out
☐ DEAR LORD, small, rel. 1978. ed. 1,000, s/n, 11″ x 9″, pub MP	35.00	Sold Out
☐ DEVOTION, rel. 1983. ed. 1,000, s/n, 12″ x 9½″, pub MP	50.00	—
☐ DIANA, rel. 1985. ed. 1,000, s/n, 9½″ x 9¼″, pub MP	25.00	—
☐ DONKEY BOY, rel. 1982. ed. 1,000, s/n, 10½″ x 9″, pub MP	40.00	—
☐ EARLY LIGHT, rel. 1982. ed. 1,000, s/n, 14″ x 18″, pub MP	80.00	—
☐ EBONY'S JET, rel. 1982. ed. 1,000, s/n, 18″ x 27″, pub MP	150.00	—
☐ EMILY, rel. 1984. ed. 1,000, s/n, 8⅜″ x 10½″, pub MP	—	Sold Out
☐ ENGAGEMENT, THE, rel. 1984. ed. 1,000, s/n, 7″ x 7″, pub MP	40.00	Sold Out
☐ EQUUS BLUE, rel. 1981. ed. 1,000, s/n, 18″ x 24″, litho, pub MP	300.00	—
☐ ERIN, rel. 1985. ed. 1,000, s/n, 9¾″ x 8¾″, pub MP	25.00	—
☐ EVENING GUESTS, rel. 1983. ed. 1,000, s/n, 18″ x 18″, pub MP	60.00	Sold Out
☐ EVENING HOUR, THE, rel. 1984. ed. 1,000, s/n, 16″ x 10¾″, pub MP	70.00	—
☐ EVENING RUN, rel. 1978. ed. 1,000, s/n, 7″ x 24″, pub MP	55.00	Sold Out
☐ EVENING WELCOME, rel. 1983. ed. 1,000, s/n, 11″ x 9″, pub MP	—	Sold Out
☐ EVERY BLESSING, rel. 1979. ed. 1,000, s/n, 10″ x 17″, pub MP	50.00	—
☐ FAMILY HEIRLOOM, rel. 1985. ed. 1,000, s/n, 15″ x 15½″, pub MP	80.00	—
☐ FAMILY OUTING, rel. 1978. ed. 1,000, s/n, 17″ x 18″, pub MP	65.00	Sold Out
☐ FAMILY, THE, rel. 1983. ed. 1,000, s/n, 19″ x 22″, pub MP	—	Sold Out
☐ FANEUIL HALL, rel. 1979. ed. 1,000, s/n, 12″ x 12″, pub MP	40.00	Sold Out
☐ FAWN, rel. 1983. ed. 1,000, s/n, 12″ x 12″, pub MP	40.00	—
☐ FINISHING TOUCHES, rel. 1983. ed. 1,000, s/n, 16″ x 16″, pub MP	60.00	—
☐ FIRST BORN, rel. 1984. ed. 1,000, s/n, 9″ x 9¼″, pub MP	50.00	—
☐ FIRST LOVE, rel. 1983. ed. 1,000, s/n, 16″ x 18″, pub MP	60.00	—
☐ FIVE ON A PONY, rel. 1981. ed. 1,000, s/n, 12″ x 12″, pub MP	40.00	—

	ISSUE PRICE	CURRENT PRICE
☐ FLAG BOY, rel. 1978. ed. 1,000, s/n, 9″ x 6″, pub MP	16.00	Sold Out
☐ FLAG GIRL, rel. 1978. ed. 1,000, s/n, 9″ x 6″, pub MP	16.00	Sold Out
☐ FLOWER GIRL, rel. 1982. ed. 1,000, s/n, 10″ x 8″, pub MP	20.00	Sold Out
☐ FLYNN MANSION, rel. 1984. ed. 1,000, s/n, 23″ x 18½″, pub MP	200.00	—
☐ FOUR LITTLE GIRLS, rel. 1978. ed. 1,000, s/n, 8″ x 10″, pub MP	30.00	Sold Out
☐ FRANKFURT OLD TOWN HALLS, rel. 1984. ed. 1,000, s/n, 14″ x 14″, pub MP	60.00	—
☐ FREE SPIRIT, rel. 1978. ed. 1,000, s/n, 14″ x 37″, pub MP	110.00	—
☐ FRENCH MARKET, rel. 1984. ed. 1,000, s/n, 12¾″ x 14″, pub MP	60.00	—
☐ FRENCH QUARTER, large, rel. 1981. ed. 1,000, s/n, 20″ x 20″, pub MP	75.00	—
☐ FRENCH QUARTER, small, rel. 1981. ed. 1,000, s/n, 8″ x 8″, pub MP	25.00	—
☐ FRESH BOUQUET, rel. 1978. ed. 1,000, s/n, 11″ x 8″, pub MP	30.00	Sold Out
☐ FRIENDLY STEED, rel. 1978. ed. 1,000, s/n, 10″ x 16″, pub MP	50.00	Sold Out
☐ FRIENDS, rel. 1978. ed. 1,000, s/n, 12″ x 10″, pub MP	35.00	Sold Out
☐ FROSTY FROLIC, rel. 1978. ed. 1,000, s/n, 22″ x 22″, pub MP	75.00	Sold Out
☐ FROSTY RIDE, rel. 1984. ed. 1,000, s/n, 14½″ x 17″, pub MP	—	Sold Out
☐ FRUIT OF THE VALLEY, rel. 1982. ed. 1,000, s/n, 15″ x 16″, pub MP	80.00	Sold Out
☐ FRUITS OF THE VINE I, rel. 1978. ed. 1,000, s/n, 29″ x 15″, pub MP	80.00	100.00
☐ FRUITS OF THE VINE II, rel. 1978. ed. 1,000, s/n, 29″ x 15″, pub MP	80.00	100.00
☐ GAGGLE OF GEESE, rel. 1982. ed. 1,000, s/n, 11⅛″ x 28″, pub MP	—	Sold Out
☐ GAGGLE OF GEESE, rel. 1982. ed. 99, s/n, silk screen, 13″ x 40″, pub MP	—	Sold Out
☐ GENTLE DAY, rel. 1982. ed. 1,000, s/n, 28″ x 10″, pub MP	75.00	100.00
☐ GENTLE HANDS, rel. 1979. ed. 1,000, s/n, 15½″ x 13″, pub MP	50.00	—
☐ GINGER, rel. 1983. ed. 1,000, s/n, 11″ x 8″, pub MP	40.00	—
☐ GINNY, rel. 1981. ed. 2,000, s/n, 6″ x 4″, pub MP	16.00	—
☐ GINNY AND CHRIS WITH LAMBS, rel. 1978. ed. 1,000, s/n, 9″ x 7″, pub MP	35.00	Sold Out
☐ GIRLS IN GREEN, rel. 1983. ed. 1,000, s/n, 14″ x 11″, pub MP	40.00	—
☐ GOLDEN AUTUMN, rel. 1983. ed. 1,000, s/n, 19″ x 19½″, pub MP	—	Sold Out
☐ GOLDEN WINTER, rel. 1978. ed. 1,000, s/n, 37″ x 37″, pub MP	150.00	Sold Out
☐ GOLDEN JOY, rel. 1985. ed. 1,000, s/n, 23¼″ x 19″, pub MP	150.00	—
☐ GOOD COMPANIONS, rel. 1983. ed. 1,000, s/n, 9½″ x 12″, pub MP	40.00	—
☐ GOOD SHEPHERD, rel. 1978. ed. 1,000, s/n, 12″ x 6″, pub MP	20.00	—
☐ GOSSIP, rel. 1978. ed. 1,000, s/n, 9″ x 12″, pub MP	45.00	Sold Out
☐ GOVERNOR'S PLACE, rel. 1983. ed. 1,000, s/n, 15″ x 15″, pub MP	50.00	Sold Out
☐ GRACEFUL LADY, rel. 1984. ed. 1,000, s/n, 18″ x 8⅛″, pub MP	50.00	—
☐ GRANDMA'S BED, rel. 1984. ed. 1,000, s/n, 12½″ x 13″, pub MP	—	Sold Out
☐ GRANDMOTHER, rel. 1981. ed. 1,000, s/n, 15″ x 16″, pub MP	60.00	—
☐ GRANDPA'S HOUSE, rel. 1982. ed. 1,000, s/n, 12″ x 12″, pub MP	40.00	Sold Out
☐ GRANNY'S FAVORITE, rel. 1981. ed. 1,000, s/n, 11″ x 8″, pub MP	40.00	Sold Out
☐ GRANNY'S GIRL, rel. 1983. ed. 1,000, s/n, 14″ x 12″, pub MP	50.00	—
☐ GRANNY'S LESSON, rel. 1981. ed. 1,000, s/n, 8″ x 27″, pub MP	35.00	—
☐ GREEN APPLES, rel. 1984. ed. 1,000, s/n, 10¼″ x 8¾″, pub MP	50.00	—
☐ HAIL, rel. 1983. ed. 1,000, s/n, 9″ x 5½″, pub MP	20.00	—
☐ HAIL THE DAY, SOLACE, rel. 1979. ed. 1,000, s/n, 22″ x 22″, pub MP	75.00	Sold Out
☐ HAND IN HAND, rel. 1982. ed. 1,000, s/n, 10″ x 10″, pub MP	40.00	Sold Out
☐ HAPPY DAY, rel. 1979. ed. 1,000, s/n, 13″ x 9″, pub MP	25.00	—
☐ HARK, rel. 1979. ed. 1,000, s/n, 14″ x 10″, pub MP	40.00	Sold Out
☐ HAYRIDE, rel. 1982. ed. 1,000, s/n, 19″ x 16″, pub MP	50.00	Sold Out
☐ HEARTLAND, THE, rel. 1985. ed. 1,000, s/n, 12½″ x 18″, pub MP	80.00	—
☐ HEATHER, rel. 1985. ed. 1,000, s/n, 9″ x 9″, pub MP	25.00	—
☐ HE LIVES, rel. 1979. ed. 1,000, s/n, 22″ x 5″, pub MP	25.00	Sold Out
☐ HELPERS, rel. 1978. ed. 1,000, s/n, 9″ x 14″, pub MP	35.00	Sold Out
☐ HER HIGHNESS, rel. 1982. ed. 1,000, s/n, 12″ x 10″, pub MP	50.00	—
☐ HIGHLAND FLING, rel. 1982. ed. 1,000, s/n, 7½″ x 4¼″, pub MP	25.00	—
☐ HITCHING A RIDE, rel. 1984. ed. 1,000, s/n, 14″ x 14″, pub MP	—	Sold Out
☐ HOMEWARD BOUND, rel. 1984. ed. 1,000, s/n, 15″ x 15″, pub MP	—	Sold Out
☐ HOUSE BY THE PARK, rel. 1982. ed. 1,000, s/n, 16″ x 12″, pub MP	80.00	—
☐ HOW CALM THE MORN, rel. 1979. ed. 1,000, s/n, 15″ x 30″, pub MP	75.00	Sold Out
☐ HOW GENTLE, rel. 1978. ed. 1,000, s/n, 7″ x 8″, pub MP	20.00	—
☐ HUNGRY BABY BIRD, rel. 1978. ed. 1,000, s/n, 9″ x 5″, pub MP	15.00	Sold Out
☐ HURRAH!, rel. 1982. ed. 1,000, s/n, 8″ x 7″, pub MP	20.00	Sold Out
☐ ICE CREAM PARLOR, rel. 1982. ed. 1,000, s/n, 17″ x 13″, pub MP	80.00	—

	ISSUE PRICE	CURRENT PRICE
☐ **IMPERIAL MAJESTY,** rel. 1985. ed. 99, s/n, silk screen, 32″ x 22⅜, pub MP	600.00	—
☐ **INDUSTRIAL REVOLUTION BUILDINGS,** large, rel. 1980. ed. 1,000, s/n, 12″ x 12″, pub MP	70.00	—
☐ **INDUSTRIAL REVOLUTION BUILDINGS,** small, rel. 1980. ed. 1,000, s/n, 8″ x 8″, pub MP	50.00	—
☐ **INNER HARBOR,** rel. 1983. ed. 1,000, s/n, 12″ x 12″, pub MP	50.00	—
☐ **JAKE,** rel. 1985. ed. 1,000, s/n, 10½″ x 7½″, pub MP	25.00	—
☐ **JEFF,** rel. 1985. ed. 1,000, s/n, 10⅝″ x 6¾″, pub MP	25.00	—
☐ **JEFFERSON SKATERS,** rel. 1980. ed. 1,000, s/n, 16″ x 13″, pub MP	60.00	—
☐ **JEFFERSON SPRINGTIME,** rel. 1984. ed. 1,000, s/n, 10″ x 15 1/16″, pub MP	60.00	—
☐ **JOE,** rel. 1984. ed. 1,000, s/n, 11″ x 7¾″, pub MP	30.00	—
☐ **JOHN,** rel. 1981. ed. 2,000, s/n, 6″ x 6″, pub MP	16.00	—
☐ **JOHN AND MARY,** rel. 1981. ed. 1,000, s/n, 36″ x 36″, pub MP	200.00	—
☐ **JOY,** rel. 1979. ed. 1,000, s/n, 6″ x 5″, pub MP	16.00	Sold Out
☐ **JULY FOUR,** rel. 1982. ed. 1,000, s/n, 9″ x 12″, pub MP	40.00	—
☐ **LANDSCAPE GEESE, blue,** rel. 1981. ed. 75, s/n, 56″ x 36″, pub MP	500.00	—
☐ **LANDSCAPE GEESE, gold,** rel. 1981. ed. 24, s/n, 56″ x 36″, pub MP	500.00	—
☐ **LESSON IN PATIENCE,** rel. 1978. ed. 1,000, s/n, 22″ x 27″, pub MP	120.00	—
☐ **LILLY AND LIZ,** rel. 1982. ed. 1,000, s/n, 10½″ x 8″, pub MP	40.00	—
☐ **LISA AND TIGER,** rel. 1982. ed. 1,000, s/n, 9″ x 8″, pub MP	30.00	—
☐ **LITTLE APPLES IN A ROW,** rel. 1978. ed. 1,000, s/n, 10″ x 38″, pub MP	80.00	100.00
☐ **LITTLE FELLOW,** rel. 1978. ed. 1,000, s/n, 20″ x 12″, pub MP	57.00	Sold Out
☐ **LITTLE GIRL BLUE,** rel. 1981. ed. 1,000, s/n, 7½″ x 5″, pub MP	16.00	Sold Out
☐ **LITTLE GIRL'S PRAYER,** rel. 1982. ed. 1,000, s/n, 22″ x 7″, pub MP	35.00	Sold Out
☐ **LORDS OF THE REALM,** rel. 1981. ed. 1,000, s/n, 20″ x 20″, pub MP	80.00	Sold Out
☐ **LORDS OF THE VALLEY,** rel. 1983. ed. 1,000, s/n, 19½″ x 28″, pub MP	175.00	Sold Out
☐ **LOUISA,** rel. 1983. ed. 1,000, s/n, 8″ x 6″, pub MP	20.00	—
☐ **LOVE,** rel. 1979. ed. 1,000, s/n, 6″ x 5″, pub MP	10.00	Sold Out
☐ **MARKET PLACE, CHIPPING CAMDEN,** rel. 1982. ed. 1,000, s/n, 10″ x 10″, pub MP	50.00	—
☐ **MARY'S LAMB,** large, rel. 1979. ed. 1,0000, s/n, 22″ x 22″, pub MP	75.00	Sold Out
☐ **MARY'S LAMB,** small, rel. 1978. ed. 1,000, s/n, 22″ x 22″, pub MP	40.00	Sold Out
☐ **MARY AND MAGNOLIA,** rel. 1978. ed. 1,000, s/n, 11″ x 8″, pub MP	15.00	Sold Out
☐ **MATTHEW,** rel. 1984. ed. 1,000, s/n, 10¾″ x 6½″, pub MP	30.00	—
☐ **MIKE AND JESSIE,** rel. 1984. ed. 1,000, s/n, 14″ x 14″, pub MP	—	Sold Out
☐ **MILK LAD,** rel. 1978. ed. 1,000, s/n, 10″ x 8″, pub MP	—	Sold Out
☐ **MILK MAID,** rel. 1978. ed. 1,000, s/n, 10″ x 8″, pub MP	—	Sold Out
☐ **MOLLY,** rel. 1984. ed. 1,000, s/n, 11¼″ x 8″, pub MP	30.00	—
☐ **MOMMA APPLE, blue,** rel. 1978. ed. 1,000, s/n, 11″ x 4¾″, pub MP	—	Sold Out
☐ **MOMMA APPLE, gold,** rel. 1978. ed. 1,000, s/n, 11″ x 4¾″, pub MP	—	Sold Out
☐ **MONARCH,** rel. 1983. ed. 1,000, s/n, 11⅝″ x 9″, pub MP	35.00	—
☐ **MOONLIT SKATERS I,** rel. 1978. ed. 1,000, s/n, 22½″ x 28½″, pub MP	—	Sold Out
☐ **MOONLIT SKATERS II,** rel. 1978. ed. 2,000, s/n, 11″ x 11″, pub MP	40.00	—
☐ **MORNING SONG,** rel. 1982. ed. 1,000, s/n, 7″ x 10″, pub MP	20.00	—
☐ **MOTHERS TO BE,** rel. 1982. ed. 1,000, s/n, 8¾″ x 8¼″, pub MP	35.00	—
☐ **MOUNTAIN REFLECTIONS,** rel. 1981. ed. 1,000, s/n, 17⅞″ x 21⅞″, pub MP	70.00	—
☐ **MUFFET BOY I,** rel. 1978. ed. 1,000, s/n, 4¼″ x 5″, pub MP	—	Sold Out
☐ **MUFFET BOY II,** rel. 1981. ed. 2,000, s/n, 8⅝″ x 5¼″, pub MP	16.00	—
☐ **MUFFET GIRL I,** rel. 1978. ed. 1,000, s/n, 4¼″ x 5″, pub MP	—	Sold Out
☐ **MUFFET GIRL II,** rel. 1981. ed. 2,000, s/n, 8⅝″ x 5″, pub MP	16.00	—
☐ **MY BOY,** rel. 1985. ed. 1,000, s/n, 12″ x 12″, pub MP	60.00	—
☐ **MY GIRLS,** rel. 1983. ed. 1,000, s/n, 13″ x 16¼″, pub MP	60.00	—
☐ **MY HANDS TO THEE,** rel. 1981. ed. 2,000, s/n, 28″ x 10¼″, pub MP	75.00	100.00
☐ **MY PLACE,** rel. 1982. ed. 1,000, s/n, 8″ x 8″, pub MP	—	Sold Out
☐ **MY SISTERS,** rel. 1982. ed. 1,000, s/n, 8″ x 8 3/16″, pub MP	40.00	—
☐ **NANCY,** rel. 1985. ed. 1,000, s/n, 11″ x 10½″, pub MP	—	Sold Out
☐ **NEIGHBORS,** rel. 1978. ed. 1,000, s/n, 17¾″ x 29″, pub MP	100.00	—
☐ **NEVER ALONE,** rel. 1979. ed. 1,000, s/n, 10½″ x 9″, pub MP	35.00	—
☐ **NEWBORN, THE,** rel. 1984. ed. 1,000, s/n, 10½″ x 12¼″, pub MP	—	Sold Out
☐ **NINE MENNONITE GIRLS,** rel. 1981. ed. 1,000, s/n, 10″ x 16″, pub MP	—	Sold Out
☐ **NO HANDS,** rel. 1982. ed. 1,000, s/n, 12″ x 9¾″, pub MP	40.00	—
☐ **NOBLE FILLY,** rel. 1985. ed. 1,000, s/n, 12¾″ x 14¾″, pub MP	60.00	—

	ISSUE PRICE	CURRENT PRICE
☐ NOTRE DAME, rel. 1983. ed. 1,000, s/n, 18½" x 24", pub MP	90.00	—
☐ NURSES, THE, rel. 1985. ed. 1,000, s/n, 13½" x 13½", pub MP	70.00	—
☐ O GENTLE FRIEND, rel. 1979. ed. 1,000, s/n, 14" x 14", pub MP	—	Sold Out
☐ OCEAN, rel. 1981. ed. 1,000, s/n, 19" x 20", pub MP	80.00	—
☐ OCEAN FANTASY, rel. 1984. ed. 1,000, s/n, 15" x 15", pub MP	70.00	—
☐ OH LIFE, rel. 1979. ed. 1,000, s/n, 16¾" x 13½", pub MP	40.00	—
☐ OHIO STAR, rel. 1984. ed. 1,000, s/n, 10⅞" x 15½", pub MP	—	Sold Out
☐ OLD MILL HOUSE, THE, rel. 1983. ed. 1,000, s/n, 11½" x 28", pub MP	125.00	—
☐ OLD STONE CHURCH, THE, rel. 1984. ed. 1,000, s/n, 18½" x 19½", pub MP	150.00	—
☐ ON THE CANAL, rel. 1980. ed. 1,000, s/n, 16" x 22½", pub MP	—	Sold Out
☐ ON THE SWING, rel. 1982. ed. 1,000, s/n, 17" x 8", pub MP	—	Sold Out
☐ ON THE WALL, rel. 1981. ed. 1,000, s/n, 9⅜" x 11⅜", pub MP	40.00	—
☐ ORCHARD GIRL, rel. 1983. ed. 1,000, s/n, 11½" x 9½", pub MP	40.00	—
☐ ORCHARD HELPERS, rel. 1978. ed. 1,000, s/n, 23" x 29", pub MP	75.00	Sold Out
☐ OUR BIG BROTHER, rel. 1983. ed. 1,000, s/n, 8½" x 5⅞", pub MP	35.00	—
☐ OUR GIRLS, rel. 1985. ed. 1,000, s/n, 13" x 14", pub MP	60.00	—
☐ OUR LITTLE BROTHER, rel. 1982, rel. 14" x 10", pub MP	50.00	Sold Out
☐ OUR LITTLE SISTER, rel. 1982. ed. 1,000, s/n, 12" x 12", pub MP	50.00	Sold Out
☐ PALS, rel. 1982. ed. 1,000, s/n, 8" x 6½", pub MP	25.00	—
☐ PARADE, THE, rel. 1984. ed. 1,000, s/n, 10" x 24¾", pub MP	80.00	—
☐ PATTI, rel. 1982. ed. 1,000, s/n, 11" x 14", pub MP	60.00	—
☐ PAVILLION AT WOLFBORO, rel. 1979. ed. 1,000, s/n, 13" x 10", pub MP	40.00	—
☐ PEACH HARVEST, rel. 1980. ed. 300, s/n, litho, 22" x 13", pub MP	150.00	Sold Out
☐ PERFECT PET, rel. 1978. ed. 1,000, s/n, 9" x 5", pub MP	15.00	Sold Out
☐ PETER, rel. 1982. ed. 1,000, s/n, 4¾" x 10½", pub MP	20.00	—
☐ PIE MAKERS, THE, rel. 1985. ed. 1,000, s/n, 15¾" x 15", pub MP	—	Sold Out
☐ PINK BALLERINA, rel. 1982. ed. 1,000, s/n, 10" x 6", pub MP	25.00	—
☐ PLAYMATES, rel. 1985. ed. 1,000, s/n, 15⅛" x 15½", pub MP	—	70.00
☐ PLEASE GOD, rel. 1982. ed. 1,000, s/n, 11" x 11", pub MP	50.00	Sold Out
☐ PLEASE!, rel. 1982. ed. 1,000, s/n, 9" x 9", pub MP	35.00	Sold Out
☐ PLEASE MA'AM, rel. 1985. ed. 1,000, s/n, 9¾" x 12½", pub MP	50.00	—
☐ PONTE VECCHIO, FLORENCE, rel. 1982. ed. 1,000, s/n, 16" x 22", pub MP	90.00	—
☐ PONTE VECCHIO REMEMBERED, rel. 1984. ed. 1,000, s/n, 14" x 14", pub MP	60.00	—
☐ POPPA APPLE, blue, rel. 1978. ed. 1,000, s/n, 11" x 5", pub MP	10.00	Sold Out
☐ POPPA APPLE, gold, rel. 1978. ed. 1,000, s/n, 11" x 5", pub MP	15.00	Sold Out
☐ PRINCELY PAIR, rel. 1984. ed. 1,000, s/n, 14" x 14", pub MP	—	Sold Out
☐ PROMISED, rel. 1979. ed. 1,000, s/n, 10" x 12", pub MP	40.00	—
☐ PUBLIC GARDENS AND BEACON STREET, BOSTON, rel. 1979. ed. 1,000, s/n, 11" x 9", pub MP	50.00	Sold Out
☐ PUMPKIN KIDS, rel. 1985. ed. 1,000, s/n, 13" x 13", pub MP	60.00	—
☐ QUEEN "B", rel. 1985. ed. 1,000, s/n, 9" x 7³⁄₁₆", pub MP	50.00	—
☐ THE QUILT, rel. 1982. ed. 1,000, s/n, 20" x 20", pub MP	90.00	—
☐ QUILTING BEE, rel. 1978. ed. 1,000, s/n, 16" x 17", pub MP	55.00	Sold Out
☐ QUILTING DREAMS, rel. 1981. ed. 1,000, s/n, 10" x 18", pub MP	40.00	—
☐ QUILTING LADIES, rel. 1978. ed. 1,000, s/n, 7" x 10", pub MP	40.00	Sold Out
☐ QUINTET, rel. 1984. ed. 1,000, s/n, 9" x 13¼", pub MP	50.00	—
☐ RACHEL AND JACOB, rel. 1978. ed. 1,000, s/n, 30" x 37", pub MP	150.00	Sold Out
☐ RED BIKE, rel. 1983. ed. 1,000, s/n, 10" x 10", pub MP	35.00	Sold Out
☐ RED HOUSE, rel. 1983. ed. 1,000, s/n, 18" x 18", pub MP	100.00	Sold Out
☐ RED WAGON, rel. 1984. ed. 1,000, s/n, 12½" x 12½", pub MP	—	Sold Out
☐ REJOICE, rel. 1979. ed. 1,000, s/n, 9" x 6", pub MP	16.00	—
☐ RELUCTANT BALLERINA, rel. 1978. ed. 1,000, s/n, 9" x 5", pub MP	15.00	Sold Out
☐ RHAPSODY, rel. 1984. ed. 1,000, s/n, 11" x 13¼", pub MP	50.00	—
☐ RING AROUND A ROSIE, rel. 1980. ed. 1,000, s/n, 8" x 17", pub MP	40.00	Sold Out
☐ ROANOKE, FARMERS' MARKET, rel. 1985. ed. 1,000, s/n, 12⅞" x 13¼", pub MP	80.00	—
☐ ROBBIE, rel. 1985. ed. 1,000, s/n, 7⅛" x 8⅛", pub MP	20.00	—
☐ ROCKING, rel. 1982. ed. 1,000, s/n, 18" x 9", pub MP	40.00	Sold Out
☐ ROTHENBURG, rel. 1983. ed. 1,000, s/n, 9½" x 11½", pub MP	40.00	Sold Out
☐ ROTHENBURG II, rel. 1983. ed. 1,000, s/n, 16" x 16", pub MP	80.00	—
☐ ROYAL STREET, rel. 1982. ed. 1,000, s/n, 14" x 10", pub MP	500.00	—
☐ SAM, rel. 1981. ed. 1,000, s/n, 8" x 5", pub MP	16.00	Sold Out

	ISSUE PRICE	CURRENT PRICE
☐ SARAH, rel. 1981. ed. 1,000, s/n, 8″ x 5″, pub MP	16.00	Sold Out
☐ SCHOOL YARD, THE, rel. 1984. ed. 1,000, s/n, 13⁷⁄₁₆″ x 13⁷⁄₁₆″, pub MP	60.00	—
☐ SEASON'S OVER, rel. 1978. ed. 1,000, s/n, 6″ x 16″, pub MP	35.00	Sold Out
☐ SECRET, THE, rel. 1984. ed. 1,000, s/n, 10¾″ x 11¼″, pub MP	50.00	—
☐ SENATORS, THE, rel. 1985. ed. 1,000, s/n, 16¹⁄₁₆″ x 37″, pub MP	275.00	—
☐ SENTINELS, THE, rel. 1985. ed. 1,000, s/n, 13″ x 18⅛″, pub MP	65.00	—
☐ SERENTITY IN BLACK & WHITE, rel. 1978. ed. 1,000, s/n, 29″ x 22″, pub MP	120.00	Sold Out
☐ SHENANDOAH HARVEST, rel. 1982. ed. 1,000, s/n, 18″ x 14″, pub MP	60.00	Sold Out
☐ SHENANDOAH SILHOUETTE, ed. 1,000, s/n, 10″ x 8″, pub MP	25.00	Sold Out
☐ SHOWALTER'S FARM, rel. 1978. ed. 1,000, s/n, 14″ x 24″, pub MP	75.00	Sold Out
☐ SISTERS, rel. 1978. ed. 1,000, s/n, 12″ x 6″, pub MP	20.00	Sold Out
☐ SISTERS FOUR, rel. 1983. ed. 1,000, s/n, 14″ x 14″, pub MP	—	Sold Out
☐ SISTERS TWO, rel. 1984. ed. 1,000, s/n, 10″ x 19½″, pub MP	60.00	—
☐ SKATING AWAY I, rel. 1978. ed. 1,000, s/n, 16″ x 30″, pub MP	70.00	Sold Out
☐ SKATING DUET, rel. 1982. ed. 1,000, s/n, 9¼″ x 7½″, pub MP	40.00	—
☐ SKATING JOY, rel. 1981. ed. 1,000, s/n, 36″ x 36″, pub MP	200.00	300.00
☐ SKATING LESSON, rel. 1978. ed. 1,000, s/n, 14″ x 20″, pub MP	150.00	Sold Out
☐ SKATING PARTY, rel. 1985. ed. 1,000, s/n, 13¾″ x 27½″, pub MP	200.00	—
☐ SLEEPY JANE, rel. 1985. ed. 1,000, s/n, 12⅛″ x 10¼″, pub MP	—	55.00
☐ SLEIGH RIDE, rel. 1982. ed. 1,000, s/n, 13″ x 10″, pub MP	50.00	Sold Out
☐ SNOW GOOSE, rel. 1982. ed. 1,000, s/n, 14″ x 20″, pub MP	50.00	Sold Out
☐ SNOWY BIRCHES, rel. 1978. ed. 1,000, s/n, 15″ x 18″, pub MP	60.00	Sold Out
☐ SOLITARY SKATER, rel. 1978. ed. 1,000, s/n, 10″ x 8″, pub MP	35.00	Sold Out
☐ SOLITARY SKATER II, rel. 1981. ed. 1,000, s/n, 9″ x 11″, pub MP	35.00	Sold Out
☐ SOLO, rel. 1981. ed. 1,000, s/n, 9″ x 6″, pub MP	15.00	Sold Out
☐ SPIRIT OF EQUUS, rel. 1978. ed. 1,000, s/n, 18″ x 36″, pub MP	100.00	—
☐ SPRING BOUQUET, rel. 1983. ed. 1,000, s/n, 11″ x 9″, pub MP	40.00	—
☐ SPRING LOVE, rel. 1981. ed. 2,000, s/n, 11″ x 9″, pub MP	25.00	—
☐ SPRING SHEPHERDS, rel. 1983. ed. 1,000, s/n, 11½″ x 9½″, pub MP	40.00	—
☐ STACK OF BOYS, rel. 1983. ed. 1,000, s/n, 15″ x 7½″, pub MP	30.00	—
☐ STACK OF GIRLS, rel. 1978. ed. 1,000, s/n, 16″ x 8″, pub MP	25.00	50.00
☐ STATE HOUSE, THE, rel. 1984. ed. 1,000, s/n, 12″ x 12″, pub MP	50.00	—
☐ STILL LIFE MINIATURE, THE, rel. 1984. ed. 1,000, s/n, 7″ x 6″, pub MP	30.00	—
☐ ST. MARKS IN THE RAIN, rel. 1984. ed. 1,000, s/n, 13½″ x 11¾″, pub MP	60.00	—
☐ STORY TIME, rel. 1984. ed. 1,000, s/n, 13″ x 13″, pub MP	60.00	—
☐ STREET BY THE PARK, rel. 1980. ed. 300, s/n, litho, 16″ x 22″, pub MP	200.00	300.00
☐ STREET BY THE PARK II, rel. 1981. ed. 1,000, s/n, 20″ x 28″, pub MP	125.00	250.00
☐ SUGAR VALLEY FARM, rel. 1978. ed. 1,000, s/n, 22″ x 30″, pub MP	80.00	—
☐ SUMMER LOVE, rel. 1983. ed. 1,000, s/n, 14″ x 12″, pub MP	—	Sold Out
☐ SUMMER'S BLESSING, rel. 1985. ed. 1,000, s/n, 10½″ x 12½″, pub MP	—	60.00
☐ SUNDAY MORNING, rel. 1981. ed. 1,000, s/n, 15″ x 16″, pub MP	60.00	Sold Out
☐ SUNDAY'S APPLES, rel. 1983. ed. 1,000, s/n, 10″ x 10½″, pub MP	—	Sold Out
☐ SUNDAY'S PRAYER, rel. 1984. ed. 1,000, s/n, 9⅜″ x 10″, pub MP	—	Sold Out
☐ SUNDAY'S RIDE, rel. 1981. ed. 1,000, s/n, 14″ x 17″, pub MP	60.00	Sold Out
☐ SUZIE, rel. 1983. ed. 1,000, s/n, 7″ x 7″, pub MP	25.00	—
☐ SWAN HOUSE, rel. 1984. ed. 1,000, s/n, 17¾″ x 15″, pub MP	80.00	—
☐ SWEET PROMISES, rel. 1979. ed. 1,000, s/n, 11″ x 12″, pub MP	40.00	—
☐ TAKING TURNS, rel. 1982. ed. 1,000, s/n, 14″ x 14″, pub MP	50.00	Sold Out
☐ TARRY NOT, rel. 1979. ed. 1,000, s/n, 10″ x 10″, pub MP	35.00	Sold Out
☐ TENDER SHEPHERD, rel. 1983. ed. 1,000, s/n, 14¼″ x 14¼″, pub MP	—	Sold Out
☐ TENDING HER FLOCK, rel. 1978. ed. 1,000, s/n, 21″ x 28″, pub MP	80.00	—
☐ TERRACE HILL, rel. 1983. ed. 1,000, s/n, 20″ x 16″, pub MP	110.00	—
☐ THREE SISTERS, rel. 1985. ed. 1,000, s/n, 14″ x 16″, pub MP	—	Sold Out
☐ TIMOTHY, rel. 1983. ed. 1,000, s/n, 10½″ x 8½″, pub MP	30.00	—
☐ 'TIS GRACE, rel. 1979. ed. 1,000, s/n, 7″ x 10″, pub MP	20.00	Sold Out
☐ 'TIS NIGHT, rel. 1979. ed. 1,000, s/n, 16″ x 9″, pub MP	50.00	—
☐ TO GRANDMOTHER'S HOUSE WE GO, rel. 1984. ed. 1,000, s/n, 14¼″ x 20″, pub MP	80.00	—
☐ TO LOVE, rel. 1981. ed. unlimited, s/o, 14″ x 4″, pub MP	10.00	—
☐ TO WALK, small, rel. 1981. ed. unlimited, s/o, 14″ x 4″, pub MP	10.00	—
☐ TO WALK, large, rel. 1981. ed. unlimited, s/o, 15″ x 5″, silk screen, pub MP	20.00	—
☐ TOGETHER, rel. 1981. ed. 99, s/n, silk screen, 30″ x 30″, pub MP	450.00	Sold Out

	ISSUE PRICE	CURRENT PRICE
☐ TOGETHER ON SUNDAY, rel. 1983. ed. 99, s/n, silk screen, 30″ x 24″, pub MP	—	Sold Out
☐ TOGETHER IN THE PARK, rel. 1982. ed. 1,000, s/n, 10″ x 14″, pub MP	80.00	Sold Out
☐ TREE HOUSE, rel. 1982. ed. 1,000, s/n, 15″ x 18″, pub MP	80.00	—
☐ TWO LITTLE HANDS, ed. 1,000, s/n, 11″ x 8″, pub MP	35.00	Sold Out
☐ TWO ON A BARREL, rel. 1982. ed. 1,000, s/n, 8½″ x 5½″, pub MP	25.00	Sold Out
☐ TWO ON A SWING, rel. 1982. ed. 1,000, s/n, 18½″ x 10″, pub MP	50.00	Sold Out
☐ VALLEY FARM, rel. 1980. ed. 1,000, s/n, 15″ x 16″, pub MP	60.00	—
☐ VALLEY VISITORS, rel. 1982. ed. 1,000, s/n, 47″ x 15″, pub MP	250.00	—
☐ VALLEY WEDDING, rel. 1985. ed. 1,000, s/n, 14¹⁄₁₆″ x 37″, pub MP	275.00	—
☐ VALLEY WINTER, rel. 1980. ed. 1,000, s/n, 48″ x 32″, pub MP	300.00	400.00
☐ VICTORIAN LEGACY, rel. 1984. ed. 1,000, s/n, 19½″ x 20½″, pub MP	150.00	—
☐ VIEW FROM ROOM 48, rel. 1982. ed. 1,000, s/n, 16″ x 22″, pub MP	90.00	—
☐ WAITING FOR TOM, rel. 1981. ed. 1,000, s/n, 8″ x 6″, pub MP	40.00	Sold Out
☐ WAYSIDE INN, rel. 1980. ed. 1,000, s/n, 15″ x 15″, pub MP	65.00	Sold Out
☐ WEDDING, rel. 1982. ed. 1,000, s/n, 16″ x 16″, pub MP	80.00	Sold Out
☐ WEDDING II, rel. 1982. ed. 1,000, s/n, 21″ x 19″, pub MP	90.00	Sold Out
☐ WEDDING III, rel. 1983. ed. 1,000, s/n, 22½″ x 18″, pub MP	90.00	—
☐ WEDDING DAY, rel. 1982. ed. 1,000, s/n, 19″ x 28″, pub MP	160.00	—
☐ WEDDING RIDE, THE, rel. 1984. ed. 1,000, s/n, 18¾″ x 20¾″, pub MP	—	Sold Out
☐ WEDDING RING, rel. 1984. ed. 1,000, s/n, 13¾″ x 18″, pub MP	75.00	—
☐ WHITE CHURCH, THE, rel. 1983. ed. 1,000, s/n, 10″ x 15″, pub MP	80.00	—
☐ WHITE RABBIT, rel. 1983. ed. 1,000, s/n, 11″ x 11″, pub MP	30.00	—
☐ WINFIELD FARM, rel. 1978. ed. 1,000, s/n, 13″ x 33″, pub MP	100.00	—
☐ WINFIELD FARM II, rel. 1981. ed. 1,000, s/n, 12″ x 20″, pub MP	100.00	—
☐ WINTER AT THE MILL, rel. 1981. ed. 1,000, s/n, 20″ x 20″, pub MP	80.00	Sold Out
☐ WINTER CAMEO, rel. 1978. s/n, 12″ x 12″, pub MP	30.00	Sold Out
☐ WINTER DUET, rel. 1982. ed. 1,000, s/n, 28″ x 11″, pub MP	60.00	Sold Out
☐ WINTER RIDE, rel. 1983. ed. 1,000, s/n, 14¾″ x 17¾″, pub MP	—	Sold Out
☐ WINTER SERENTIY, rel. 1984. ed. 1,000, s/n, 10¼″ x 10¼″, pub MP	40.00	—
☐ WINTER SILHOUETTE, rel. 1981. ed. 99, s/n, 28″ x 20″, litho, pub MP	300.00	—
☐ WINTER SKATER, rel. 1983. ed. 1,000, s/n, 11″ x 9½″, pub MP	40.00	—
☐ WINTER VISITOR, rel. 1978. ed. 1,000, s/n, 26″ x 14″, pub MP	80.00	Sold Out
☐ WINTER'S DAY, rel. 1983. ed. 1,000, s/n, 9″ x 9″, pub MP	50.00	Sold Out
☐ WINTER'S GLIMPSE, rel. 1982. ed. 1,000, s/n, 12″ x 12″, pub MP	40.00	Sold Out
☐ WINTER'S GLORY, rel. 1984. ed. 1,000, s/n, 24½″ x 18½″, pub MP	200.00	—
☐ WINTER'S HOUSE, rel. 1980. ed. 300, s/n, 29″ x 21″, litho, pub MP	250.00	350.00
☐ WINTER'S JOY, rel. 1982. ed. 99, 18″ x 22″, silk screen, pub MP	500.00	—
☐ WINTER'S MAJESTY, rel. 1982. ed. 1,000, s/n, 32″ x 48″, pub MP	300.00	400.00
☐ WINTER'S TRAVELERS, rel. 1985. ed. 1,000, s/n, 17″ x 11½″, pub MP	60.00	—
☐ WOMAN TALK, rel. 1979. ed. 1,000, s/n, 11″ x 10″, pub MP	35.00	Sold Out
☐ WORKDAY'S O'ER, rel. 1978. ed. 1,000, s/n, 25″ x 27″, pub MP	110.00	Sold Out
☐ YELLOW FRUIT, rel. 1984. ed. 1,000, s/n, 15¾″ x 25½″, pub MP	125.00	—
☐ YORKIE, rel. 1983. ed. 1,000, s/n, 11″ x 8″, pub MP	35.00	—
☐ YOUNG NEIGHBORS, rel. 1982. ed. 1,000, s/n, 7″ x 7″, pub MP	30.00	Sold Out

RIE MUÑOZ

THEMES: Wildlife art

AWARDS: Nominated as outstanding Alaskan artist by the Anchorage Fine Arts Museum Association (1977)

GALLERY/DISTRIBUTOR: Mill Pond Press, Inc.

COMMENTS: Alaska became the artist's home in 1950. She has explored and sketched as much of its magnificent territory and wildlife as possible in the past 35 years

CROW IN A MOUNTAIN ASH TREE *by Rie Muñoz*

	ISSUE PRICE	CURRENT PRICE
☐ BELUGA WHALE AND CALF, rel. 1978. ed. 950, s/n, 14″ x 22″, pub MPPI	25.00	75.00
☐ CROW IN A MOUNTAIN ASH TREE, rel. 1978. ed. 950, s/n, 15″ x 22″, pub MPPI ...	30.00	—
☐ RAFT OF DUCKS, rel. 1978. ed. 950, s/n, 14″ x 22″, pub MPPI	30.00	Sold Out
☐ RIBBON SEALS, rel. 1978. ed. 950, s/n, 11″ x 14″, pub MPPI	20.00	—
☐ CANNERY WORKER, rel. 1979. ed. 350, s/n, 18¼″ x 21¾″, pub MPPI	50.00	Sold Out
☐ SEINER, rel. 1979. ed. 350, s/n, 18¼″ x 21¾″, pub MPPI	50.00	Sold Out

MARTIN R. MURK

THEMES: Wildlife art

EDUCATION: Layton School of Art

AWARDS: Federal Duck Stamp Competition (1977); Wisconsin Trout Stamp (1979); Wisconsin Duck Stamp (1980)

GALLERY/DISTRIBUTOR: Northwoods Craftsman

	ISSUE PRICE	CURRENT PRICE
☐ 1979 WISCONSIN TROUT STAMP PRINT, rel. 1979. ed. 500, s/n, 14″ x 12″, dist. NC	75.00	450.00
ed. 100 remarqued	225.00	900.00
☐ 1982 TIMBERWOLF PRESERVATION SOCIETY STAMP PRINT, rel. 1982. ed. N/A, s/n, 14¾″ x 12″, distr. NC	125.00	—

FRANK C. MURPHY

THEMES: Cattle

BACKGROUND: For over 25 years, his work for the American Angus Association has achieved worldwide recognition

EDUCATION: Iowa State University

GALLERY/DISTRIBUTOR: Arts Limited, Inc.

	ISSUE PRICE	CURRENT PRICE
☐ BRUSH POPPER, rel. 1982. ed. 1,500, s/n, 22″ x 28″, pub ALI	75.00	—

SUSAN NEELON

THEMES: Portraits of children

MEDIUM: Oil and watercolor

BACKGROUND: Susan Neelon's interest in art developed out of a need to communicate with her hearing-impaired sister

GALLERY/DISTRIBUTOR: McCalla Enterprises, Inc.

	ISSUE PRICE	CURRENT PRICE
☐ PAPER ROSES, ed. 1,450, s/n, 11″ x 14″, pub MEI	19.50	—
ed. 50 Artist proofs	19.50	—
☐ CAN I KEEP HIM? ed. 700, s/n, 12″ x 16″, pub MEI	29.50	—
ed. 50, Artist proofs	29.50	Sold Out

LEROY NEIMAN

THEMES: Sporting art

GALLERY/DISTRIBUTOR: Circle Fine Arts Corp.

	ISSUE PRICE	CURRENT PRICE
☐ DEUCE, ed. 275, s/n, 26″ x 32″, serigraph, pub CFAC	—	1,500.00
☐ SAILING, ed. 275, s/n, 20″ x 24″, serigraph, pub CFAC	—	900.00
☐ CHIPPING ON, ed. 275, s/n, 26″ x 32″, serigraph, pub CFAC	—	900.00
☐ MATCHPOINT, ed. 300, s/n, 36″ x 48″, serigraph, pub CFAC	—	2,200.00
☐ TIGER, ed. 300, s/n, 36″ x 48″, serigraph, pub CFAC	—	2,800.00
☐ TENNIS PLAYER, ed. 300, s/n, 18″ x 18″, serigraph, pub CFAC	—	900.00
☐ POOL ROOM, ed. 350, s/n, 23″ x 26″, serigraph, pub CFAC	—	850.00
☐ THE RACE, ed. 300, s/n, 17″ x 25″, serigraph, pub CFAC	—	500.00
☐ IN THE STRETCH, ed. 250, s/n, 26″ x 34″, serigraph, pub CFAC	—	600.00
☐ STOCK MARKET, ed. 300, s/n, 30″ x 42″, serigraph, pub CFAC	—	4,000.00

	ISSUE PRICE	CURRENT PRICE
☐ **JOCKEY**, ed. 300, s/n, 22″ x 26″, serigraph, pub CFAC	—	800.00
☐ **CASINO**, ed. 300, s/n, 26″ x 32″, serigraph, pub CFAC	—	1,000.00
☐ **PADDOCK**, ed. 300, s/n, 30″ x 30″, serigraph, pub CFAC	—	800.00
☐ **PUNCHINELLO**, ed. 250, s/n, 21″ x 30″, serigraph, pub CFAC	—	300.00
☐ **PIERROT**, ed. 250, s/n, 20″ x 26″, serigraph, pub CFAC	—	350.00
☐ **SLIDING HOME**, ed. 300, s/n, 24″ x 36″, serigraph, pub CFAC	—	750.00
☐ **SKIER**, ed. 300, s/n, 18″ x 26″, serigraph, pub CFAC	—	600.00
☐ **FOUR ACES**, ed. 300, s/n, 27″ x 36″, serigraph, pub CFAC	—	600.00
☐ **SLALOM**, ed. 300, s/n, 26″ x 32″, serigraph, pub CFAC	—	700.00
☐ **LEOPARD**, ed. 300, s/n, 38″ x 50″, serigraph, pub CFAC	—	4,200.00
☐ **AL CAPONE**, ed. 300, s/n, 30″ x 40″, serigraph, pub CFAC	—	500.00
☐ **PIERROT THE JUGGLER**, ed. 200, s/n, 21″ x 30″, litho, pub CFAC	—	350.00
☐ **HARLEQUIN**, ed. 200, s/n, 18″ x 20″, litho, pub CFAC	—	325.00
☐ **HARLEQUIN WITH SWORD**, ed. 250, s/n, 19″ x 29″, litho, pub CFAC	—	300.00
☐ **HOCKEY PLAYER**, ed. 300, s/n, 30″ x 40″, serigraph, pub CFAC	—	1,800.00
☐ **PUNCHINELLO WITH TEXT**, ed. 200, s/n, 24″ x 30″, litho, pub CFAC	—	200.00
☐ **HARLEQUIN WITH TEXT**, ed. 200, s/n, 24″ x 30″, litho, pub CFAC	—	250.00
☐ **TEE SHOT**, ed. 300, s/n, 24″ x 30″, serigraph, pub CFAC	—	1,000.00
☐ **END AROUND**, ed. 300, s/n, 24″ x 30″, serigraph, pub CFAC	—	750.00
☐ **LION PRIDE**, ed. 300, s/n, 36″ x 48″, serigraph, pub CFAC	—	3,500.00
☐ **MARATHON**, ed. 300, s/n, 26″ x 34″, serigraph, pub CFAC	—	750.00
☐ **SCRAMBLE**, ed. 300, s/n, 27″ x 33″, serigraph, pub CFAC	—	750.00
☐ **DOWNHILL**, ed. 300, s/n, 17″ x 32″, serigraph, pub CFAC	—	750.00
☐ **INNSBRUCK**, ed. 300, s/n, 16″ x 32″, serigraph, pub CFAC	—	1,500.00
☐ **DOUBLES**, ed. 300, s/n, 36″ x 48″, serigraph, pub CFAC	—	900.00
☐ **TROTTERS**, ed. 300, s/n, 36″ x 48″, serigraph, pub CFAC	—	700.00
☐ **GOAL**, ed. 300, s/n, 24″ x 30″, serigraph, pub CFAC	—	3,500.00
☐ **ROULETTE**, ed. 40, s/n, 50″ x 60″, serigraph, pub CFAC	—	800.00
☐ **BACKHAND**, ed. 300, s/n, 24″ x 31″, serigraph, pub CFAC	—	900.00
☐ **SLAPSHOT**, ed. 300, s/n, 30″ x 35″, serigraph, pub CFAC	—	800.00
☐ **FOX HUNT**, ed. 300, s/n, 30″ x 26″, serigraph, pub CFAC	—	1,000.00
☐ **SMASH**, ed. 300, s/n, 26″ x 26″, serigraph, pub CFAC	—	1,200.00
☐ **OCELOT**, ed. 250, s/n, 30″ x 39″, serigraph, pub CFAC	—	1,100.00
☐ **SUDDEN DEATH**, ed. 250, s/n, 31″ x 30″, serigraph, pub CFAC	—	700.00
☐ **HOMMAGE TO BOUCHER**, ed. 250, s/n, 26″ x 40″, serigraph, pub CFAC	—	900.00
☐ **12 METER YACHT RACE**, ed. 250, s/n, 19″ x 30″, serigraph, pub CFAC	—	1,600.00
☐ **BASEBALL PLAYER FOLIO**, ed. 150, s/n, 15″ x 16″ consisting of ten etchings: Batting Practice, Wind Up, Awaiting The Decision, Warm Up Swings, Next At Bat, The Pitch, The Argument, The Umps, Sliding Home, The Hit, pub CFAC		
☐ **SKIING FOLIO**, ed. 150, s/n, 15″ x 16″ consisting of ten etchings: Single Skier, Between Trees, Top of The Crest, Two Racers, Break, Jump, Village In The Valley, House On The Slopes, Pine Trail, Three Skiers, pub CFAC	—	1,600.00
☐ **HOCKEY FOLIO**, ed. 150, s/n, 15″ x 16″ consisting of ten etchings: Face Off No. 20, Score No. 22, Fight, Fight With Policeman, Study of No. 4, 1 Against 1 (Straight Shot) 1 Against 1 (Goalie On Ice), Goalie Down, Goal No. 5, High Stick, pub CFAC	—	1,600.00
☐ **ALI-FRAZIER FOLIO**, ed. 150, s/n, 15″ x 20″ consisting of fifteen etchings: Study of Ali, Ali Down, The Introduction, Frazier's Corner, Ali's Corner, The Winner, After The Fight, Study of Frazier and Ali, Rounds 1 and 2, Rounds 3 and 4, Rounds 5 and 6, Rounds 7 through 9, Rounds 10 and 11, Rounds 12 through 14, Round 15, pub CFAC	—	2,500.00
☐ **POLAR BEARS** (new release 1979), ed. 300, s/n, 38″ x 28″, serigraph, pub CFAC	—	300.00

GARY NIBLETT

THEMES: Western art

BACKGROUND: He worked as an animation artist for Hanna-Barbera for nine years

EDUCATION: Eastern New Mexico University, Art Center School

AWARDS: Cowboy Artists of America

GALLERY/DISTRIBUTOR: Mill Pond Press, Inc.

	ISSUE PRICE	CURRENT PRICE
☐ A DISTANT LIGHT, rel. 1979. ed. 2,250, s/n, 16″ x 22″, pub TAP	100.00	—
☐ CONFIRMING THE COUNT, rel. 1979. ed. 2,250, s/n, 15½″ x 22″, pub TAP	100.00	—
☐ SANGRE DE CRISTO AUTUMN, rel. 1979. ed. 2,250, s/n, 16″ x 22″, pub TAP	100.00	—
☐ WINTER SUPPLIES, rel. 1979. ed. 2,250, s/n, 14½″ x 22″, pub TAP	100.00	—
☐ COOL WATER, rel. 1980. ed. 2,250, s/n, 22⅛″ x 28⅛″, pub TAP	100.00	—
☐ NIGHT VISITOR, rel. 1980. ed. 2,250, s/n, 18⅛″ x 28⅛″, pub TAP	100.00	—
☐ SUNDAY FLOWERS, rel. 1980. ed. 2,250, s/n, 21″ x 28⅛″, pub TAP	100.00	—
☐ THE RABBIT HUNTERS, rel. 1980. ed. 2,250, s/n, 18½″ x 28″, pub TAP	100.00	—
☐ WINTER IN THE VERMEJO, rel. 1980. ed. 2,250, s/n, 22½″ x 27½″, pub TAP	100.00	—
☐ BITTER COLD, rel. 1982. ed. 950, s/n, 22¾″ x 29½″, pub MPPI	135.00	—
☐ RAIN OR SHINE, rel. 1981. ed. 950, s/n, 23″ x 32¼″, pub MPPI	150.00	—
☐ RABBIT STEW, rel. 1982. ed. 950, s/n, 19½″ x 24″, pub MPPI	95.00	—

DOG CREEK MILL by Ward H. Nichols

WARD H. NICHOLS

THEMES: Americana, varied

STYLE: Interpretive realism, a modern form of trompe l'oeil

AWARDS: *Who's Who In American Art; The International Who's Who in Art and Antiques,* and other listings

GALLERY/DISTRIBUTOR: Top Drawer

	ISSUE PRICE	CURRENT PRICE
☐ BY-PASSED, rel. 1974. ed. 500, s/n, 22″ x 28″, pub RI	40.00	150.00
☐ EARLY LIGHT, rel. 1975. ed. 500, s/n, 22″ x 28″, pub RI	40.00	150.00
☐ ADAMS PORCH, rel. 1976. ed. 500, s/n, 17″ x 33″, pub RI	40.00	150.00
☐ SUPPER TIME, rel. 1976. ed. 500, s/n, 22¼″ x 32½″, pub RI	50.00	600.00
☐ MICHAEL'S SHIRT, rel. 1976. ed. 500, s/n, 22″ x 28″, pub RI	30.00	30.00
☐ CASTAWAY, rel. 1976. ed. 500, s/n, 22″ x 28″, pub RI	50.00	225.00
☐ THE LEGACY, rel. 1977. ed. 500, s/n, 22″ x 28″, pub RI	50.00	175.00
☐ THE OLD WELL, rel. 1977. ed. 500, s/n, 20″ x 24″, pub RI	50.00	250.00
☐ BUTLER'S MILL, rel. 1977. ed. 750, s/n, 19½″ x 32½″, pub RI	50.00	175.00
☐ MEMORABILIA, rel. 1978. ed. 750, s/n, 18½″ x 28½″, pub RI	50.00	175.00
☐ FARM PORTRAIT, rel. 1978. ed. 750, s/n, 12½″ x 28½″, pub RI	50.00	175.00
☐ SNOWFALL IN ROCKFORD, rel. 1978. ed. 750, s/n, 18″ x 27½″, pub RI	50.00	200.00
☐ STEEL, STEAM & SMOKE, rel. 1978. ed. U/L, s/n, (portfolio of 4), 11″ x 18″ and 11″ x 11″, pub RI	30.00	30.00
☐ AMERICAN TYPE 4-4-0, rel. 1979. ed. 750, s/n, 17″ x 25¾″, pub RI	75.00	75.00
☐ HAY RAKE, rel. 1979. ed. 500, s/n, 17″ x 17″, pub RI	50.00	50.00
☐ SHENANDOAH FARM, rel. 1979. ed. 750, s/n, 16″ x 24″, pub RI	75.00	75.00
☐ A COUNTRY WALK, rel. 1980. ed. 750, s/n, 28″ x 19½″, pub RI	75.00	75.00
☐ MILKING TIME, rel. 1980. ed. 750, s/n, 15½″ x 28″, pub RI	75.00	225.00
☐ THE SURVIVOR, rel. 1980. ed. U/L, s/o, 8½″ x 22″, pub RI	20.00	20.00
☐ STILL LIFE WITH BUTTERFLIES, rel. 1981. ed. 750, s/n, 13¼″ x 22″, pub RI	75.00	75.00
☐ TOOLS OF FREEDOM, rel. 1981. ed. 2,000, s/n, 15¾″ x 25″, pub for PICA, Scholarship Fund..	75.00	75.00
☐ BEE YARD, rel. 1981. ed. 2,000, s/n, 17″ x 22″, pub for Southern States Beekeepers project	75.00	75.00
☐ IVEY MOORE RIFLE, rel. 1981. ed. 850, s/n, 17″ x 31″, pub RI	85.00	85.00
☐ THE 610, rel. 1981. ed. U/L, s/o, 8½″ x 29″, pub RI	20.00	20.00
☐ GUTENBERG CREATION, rel. 1982. ed. 2,000, s/n, 18″ x 25″, pub for PICA, Scholarship Fund..	150.00	105.00
☐ DOG CREEK MILL, rel. 1984. ed. 750, s/n, 11⅝″ x 29⅜″, pub TD	85.00	85.00
☐ QUIET REFLECTIONS, rel. 1984. ed. 750, s/n, 12¾″ x 26″, pub TD	85.00	85.00
☐ QUIET SUNDAY, rel. 1983. ed. 750, s/n, 14⅜″ x 28″, pub TD	85.00	125.00
☐ WHITE ACCENT, rel. 1984. ed. 750, s/n, 17¼″ x 27″, pub TD	95.00	95.00

ROBERT NIPP

THEMES: Wildlife art

EDUCATION: Ringling School of Art; Memphis Academy of Arts

GALLERY/DISTRIBUTOR: Raintree Graphics

COMMENTS: Nipp's paintings are regarded by many as an authentic record and preservattion of our natural heritage

	ISSUE PRICE	CURRENT PRICE
☐ THE RED FOX, ed. 2,500, s/n, 22½″ x 28¾″, pub RG	20.00	Sold Out
☐ TENNESSEE BLACK BEARS, ed. 2,500, s/n, 28″ x 22¾″, pub RG	20.00	Sold Out
☐ EASTERN COTTONTAILS, ed. 1,000, s/n, 18″ x 23″, pub RG	25.00	—
ed. 1,500, s/o	20.00	—
☐ INNOCENCE, ed. 1,000, s/n, 18″ x 22″, pub RG	30.00	—
☐ BULL CANS, ed. 500, s/n, 29″ x 23″, pub RG	40.00	—
ed. 1.500. s/o	25.00	—

BLUE WINGS OVER YUCATAN *by Robert Nipp*

	ISSUE PRICE	CURRENT PRICE
☐ BOBWHITE QUAIL, rel. 1977. ed. 500, s/n, 16″ x 20″, pub RG	30.00	—
ed. 1,000, s/o	20.00	—
☐ RACCOON FAMILY, rel. 1977. ed. 500, s/n, 18½″ x 25″, pub RG	40.00	—
ed. 1,000 s/o	25.00	—
☐ DAWN FLIGHT, rel. 1977. ed. 500, s/n, 18″ x 23″, pub RG	40.00	—
ed. 1,000, s/o	25.00	—
☐ FLAGS UP, rel. 1978. ed. 500, s/n, 24″ x 18″, pub RG	40.00	—
ed. 1,000, s/o	25.00	—
☐ THE INTRUDER, ed. 500, s/n, 18½″ x 25½″, pub RG	20.00	—
☐ SNOWY EGRET, ed. 400, s/n, 11″ x 17″, pub RG	20.00	—
☐ THE WOOD DUCK, ed. 650, s/n, 21½″ x 27¾″, pub RG	**100.00	Sold Out

**This print was proclaimed Tennessee's first Natural Areas Commemorative Edition. This edition was to help raise funds for the Save Radnor Lake Preservation Fund.

☐ BICENTENNIAL EDITION		
THE AMERICAN BALD EAGLE, THE AMERICAN WILD TURKEY		

This series was commissioned by American Advertisers for special promotional distribution by them.

	ISSUE PRICE	CURRENT PRICE
ed. 1,000 sets, signed and dated by artist, 12″ x 15″	10.00	—
☐ OLE BRIGHT EYES, ed. 500, s/n, 13″ x 16″, pub RG	30.00	—
ed. 1,000, s/o	15.00	—
☐ BLUE WINGS OVER YUCATAN, ed. 580, s/n, 19″ x 24″, pub RG	40.00	—
☐ CHESAPEAKE GOLD, ed. 580, s/n, 19″ x 25″, pub RG	40.00	—
☐ BORDER WHITE WINGS, ed. 580, s/n, 19″ x 24″, pub RG	40.00	—
☐ MOURNING AT MOMOTOMBO, ed. 580, s/n, 19″ x 24″, pub RG	40.00	—

THE WHITE HOUSE *by Cherrie Nute*

CHERRIE NUTE

THEMES: Varied

MEDIUM: Acrylic on canvas

GALLERY/DISTRIBUTOR: D. R. Nute Fine Arts

	ISSUE PRICE	CURRENT PRICE
☐ GOVERNOR'S MANSION, rel. 1975. ed. 1,000, s/n, 25½" x 22", pub FFFA, distr. DRN	25.00	165.00
☐ TIGER, rel. 1977 (through Clemson University Athletic Dept.). ed. 1,500, s/n, 24½" x 35½", pub FFFA, distr. DRN	35.00	40.00
☐ THE BATTERY, rel. 1980. ed. 950, s/n, 26¼" x 20", pub FFFA, distr. DRN	—	400.00
☐ RAINBOW ROW, rel. 1981. ed. 950, s/n, 26¼" x 20", pub FFFA, distr. DRN	40.00	275.00
☐ CHURCH STREET, rel. 1982. ed. 950, s/n, 26¼" x 20", pub FFFA, distr. DRN	45.00	150.00
☐ SHEM CREEK, rel. 1982. ed. 950, s/n, 22" x 17", pub FFFA, distr. DRN	40.00	125.00
☐ MEETING STREET, rel. 1983. ed. 950, s/n, 26¼" x 20", pub FFFA, distr. DRN	50.00	—
☐ PAWLEY'S ISLAND, rel. 1983. ed. 950, s/n, 26¼" x 20", pub FFFA, distr. DRN	50.00	—
☐ THE MARKET, rel. 1983. ed. 950, s/n, 22" x 17", pub FFFA, distr. DRN	45.00	—
☐ SOUTH BATTERY, rel. 1984. ed. 950, s/n, 26¼" x 20", pub FFFAI, distr. DRN	50.00	—
☐ THE WHITE HOUSE, rel. 1984. ed. 950, s/n, 26¼" x 20", pub FFFA, distr. DRN	100.00	—

TIM O'KANE

THEMES: Wildlife art

EDUCATION: O'Kane has a degree in painting and printmaking from Virginia Commonwealth University

STYLE: The artist paints poetic images with razor-sharp details and disciplined draftsmanship

AWARDS: Many regional awards

GALLERY/DISTRIBUTOR: Greenwich Workshop

	ISSUE PRICE	CURRENT PRICE
☐ SAFFRON, rel. 1974. ed. 1,500, s/n, 26" x 18", pub GW	35.00	—
ed. 500, s/n	45.00	85.00

ROBERT A. OLSON

THEMES: Classical, romantic realist

EDUCATION: Minneapolis College of Art and Design, continued study at exclusive New York and Paris workshops

STYLE: His style is comparable to that of the Old Masters. He uses a fresh approach to a classical feeling, with a contemporary eye for subject and mood

AWARDS: His abilities have also earned him the accolades of his peers. He has won several coveted Society of Illustrators Awards, a New York Desi Award, world-renowned New York Art Directors Awards, the Publication and Design Award, the Anaheim Collectors Society "Best of Show" Award, and "Print" Design Awards

MEMBERSHIPS: Oasis Art Studio founding member

GALLERY/DISTRIBUTOR: Windemere Galleries

COMMENTS: Lofty achievements for a young artist, and testimony that whether viewed in a collection, home or professional environment, the works of Robert A. Olson capture the emotion and imagination, as well as the eye

	ISSUE PRICE	CURRENT PRICE
☐ PIANO MOODS, rel. 1983. ed. 750, s/n, 25" x 25½", pub WG	145.00	245.00
Artist proofs, rel. 1983. ed. 75, s/n, 29" x 25½", pub WG	145.00	245.00
☐ YOUNG FLUTISTS, rel. 1984. ed. 750, s/n, 25" x 25½", pub WG	145.00	—
Artists proofs, rel. 1984. ed. 75, s/n, 25" x 25½", pub WG	145.00	—
☐ TWILIGHT REFRAIN, rel. 1985. ed. 750, s/n, 25" x 25½", pub WG	145.00	—
Artists proofs, rel. 1985. ed. 75, s/n, 25" x 25½", pub WG	145.00	—

SCREECH OWL *by John P. O'Neill*

JOHN P. O'NEILL

THEMES: American and tropical birds

MEDIUM: Watercolor and gouache

STYLE: Realism

BOOKS: *The New Encyclopedia Britannica* carries more than twenty of his drawings, and he has illustrated numerous articles, scientific reports, and books

GALLERY/DISTRIBUTOR: Mill Pond Press, Inc.

COMMENTS: The artist is also an internationally recognized ornithologist. Dr. O'Neill is presently curator of Higher Vertebrates at the Louisiana State University Museum of Zoology in Baton Rouge

	ISSUE PRICE	CURRENT PRICE
☐ **SCREECH OWL,** rel. 1978. ed. 950, s/n, 21½″ x 16″, pub MPPI	45.00	—
☐ **PYGMY OWL,** rel. 1978. ed. 950, s/n, 20¼″ x 15″, pub MPPI	40.00	—

BILL OWEN

THEMES: Western art

AWARDS: Gold Medal for distinguished Western art, presented by The Franklin Mint, the Silver Medal, etc.

GALLERY/DISTRIBUTOR: Salt Creek Graphics

	ISSUE PRICE	CURRENT PRICE
☐ **SPRING WATER,** rel. 1976. ed. 1,000, s/n, 23½" x 33", pub FHG	100.00	—
☐ **THE LAST ONE,** rel. 1976. ed. 250, s/n, 21½" x 39", pub FHG	100.00	Sold Out
☐ **SINCE SUNUP,** rel. 1977. ed. 250, s/n, 22" x 30", pub FHG	100.00	—
☐ **CO BAR AT WUPATKI,** rel. 1979. ed. 2,250, s/n, 21½" x 17", pub TAP	100.00	—
☐ **HOLDING UP FOR THE DRAGS,** rel. 1980. ed. 1,000, s/n, 20" x 30", pub SCG	115.00	57.50
☐ **NO PLACE FOR A GUNSEL,** rel. 1980. ed. 1,000, s/n, 22" x 30", pub SCG	115.00	57.50
☐ **RIMFIRED,** rel. 1980. ed. 1,000, s/n, 21" x 28", pub SCG	115.00	57.50
☐ **A LITTLE ENCOURAGEMENT,** rel. 1981. ed. 1,000, s/n, 16" x 24", pub SCG	115.00	Sold Out
☐ **MAKING A CUT AT WILD BILL,** rel. 1981. ed. 1,000, s/n, 18" x 36", pub SCG	115.00	57.50

FRANK S. PANABAKER

THEMES: Landscape art (done on location)

EDUCATION: He studied with McGillivary Knowles, R.C.A.; Ontario College of Art; Grand Central School of Art; Art Students League

MEMBERSHIPS: Salmagundi Club; Royal Canadian Academy; National Gallery of Ottawa

GALLERY/DISTRIBUTOR: Mill Pond Press, Inc.

	ISSUE PRICE	CURRENT PRICE
☐ **MAPLE SUGARING,** rel. 1980. ed. 950, s/n, 20" x 24¾", pub MPPI	75.00	—
☐ **NORTHWEST WINDS,** rel. 1980. ed. 950, s/n, 20" x 24¾", pub MPPI	75.00	—
☐ **WINDY ISLAND,** rel. 1980. ed. 950, s/n, 15¾" x 18¼", pub MPPI	60.00	—
☐ **WINTER IN THE WOODS,** rel. 1980. ed. 950, s/n, 19¾" x 24", pub MPPI	75.00	—
☐ **A WINTER FARM,** rel. 1981. ed. 950, s/n, 15¾" x 18¼", pub MPPI	60.00	—
☐ **FRESH SNOW,** rel. 1981. ed. 950, s/n, 19¾" x 23⅛", pub MPPI	75.00	—
☐ **GOLDEN OCTOBER,** rel. 1981. ed. 950, s/n, 20" x 24½", pub MPPI	75.00	—
☐ **CHICKADEES IN AUTUMN,** rel. 1984. ed. 950, s/n, 18⅝" x 14⅞", pub MPPI	95.00	—
☐ **FACE OF THE NORTH,** rel. 1984. ed. 950, s/n, 21¼" x 17¼", pub MPPI	95.00	—
☐ **GRAY WOLF PORTRAIT,** rel. 1984. ed. 950, s/n, 17½" x 24", pub MPPI	115.00	—
☐ **WHEN PATHS CROSS,** rel. 1984. ed. 950, s/n, 27" x 21", pub MPPI	185.00	200.00

DINO PARAVANO

THEMES: African wildlife

EDUCATION: Johannesburg School of Art

FRESH SNOW *by Frank Panabaker*

MEMBERSHIPS: African Wildlife Society

GALLERY/DISTRIBUTOR: Sportsman's Edge, Ltd.

	ISSUE PRICE	CURRENT PRICE
☐ **REGAL DOMAN,** rel. 1979. ed. 950, s/n, 23″ x 35″, pub SEL	110.00	—
☐ **SPRINGBOK,** rel. 1979. ed. 950, s/n, 19¼″ x 29″, pub SEL	90.00	—

RON S. PARKER

THEMES: Wildlife art

MEDIUM: Watercolor

GALLERY/DISTRIBUTOR: Mill Pond Press, Inc.

SNOW ON THE PINE - CHICKADEE by Ron Parker

	ISSUE PRICE	CURRENT PRICE
☐ **RACCOON PAIR,** rel. 1982. ed. 950, s/n, 21⅝" x 17¼", pub MPPI	95.00	175.00
☐ **RAIDING THE CACHE,** rel. 1982. ed. 950, s/n, 19⅝" x 15¾", pub MPPI	95.00	—
☐ **SNOW ON THE PINE - CHICKADEES,** rel. 1982. 950, s/n, 21½" x 17½", pub MPPI	95.00	150.00
☐ **SPRING MIST - GRAY WOLF,** rel. 1982. ed. 950, s/n, 22⅞" x 31½", pub MPPI	155.00	250.00
☐ **WEATHERED WOOD - BLUEBIRDS,** rel. 1982. ed. 950, s/n, 17¾" x 14¾", pub MPPI	75.00	125.00
☐ **FAT AND SASSY - ROBIN,** rel. 1983. ed. 950, s/n, 17½" x 21¼", pub MPPI	95.00	—
☐ **MALLARD FAMILY,** rel. 1983. ed. 950, s/n, 17½" x 21½", pub MPPI	95.00	—
☐ **MOUNTAIN BLOOMS - GROUND SQUIRREL,** rel. 1983. ed. 950, s/n, 15" x 12", pub MPPI	50.00	—
☐ **RED SQUIRREL,** rel. 1983. ed. 950, s/n, 12" x 14⅝", pub MPPI	65.00	—
☐ **RIVERSIDE PAUSE - RIVER OTTER,** rel. 1983. ed. 950, s/n, 22¾" x 17½", pub MPPI	95.00	—
☐ **SILENT STEPS,** rel. 1984. ed. 950, s/n, 29" x 22¾", pub MPPI	145.00	—
☐ **WHEN PATHS CROSS,** rel. 1984. ed. 950, s/n, 24½" x 30", pub MPPI	185.00	250.00

NOAH'S ARK by *Peter Parnall*

PETER PARNALL

THEMES: Animals

BOOKS: Parnall has illustrated over eighty books

BACKGROUND: Parnall's talent for design led him from being a veterinarian to the life of an editorial and advertising art director in New York City

AWARDS: Has been the recipient of many awards from the American Institute of Graphic Arts

GALLERY/DISTRIBUTOR: Greenwich Workshop

COMMENTS: The artist's renderings portray the animal's essential nature

	ISSUE PRICE	CURRENT PRICE
☐ **FOX,** rel. 1972. ed. 1,500, s/n, 28″ x 21″, pub GW	60.00	150.00
☐ **HORSEHEAD,** rel. 1972. ed. 1,500, s/n, 28″ x 20″, pub GW	60.00	Sold Out
☐ **PIGMY OWL,** rel. 1972. ed. 1,500, s/n, 22″ x 17″, pub GW	30.00	190.00
☐ **RICHARDSON'S OWL,** rel. 1972. ed. 1,500, s/n, 22″ x 17″, pub GW	30.00	215.00
☐ **GOSHAWK,** rel. 1973. ed. 1,500, s/n, 17″ x 22″, pub GW	35.00	110.00
☐ **OSPREY,** rel. 1973. ed. 1,500, s/n, 26″ x 18″, pub GW	45.00	180.00
☐ **SHORT-EARED OWL,** rel. 1973. ed. 1,500, s/n, 22″ x 17″, pub GW	30.00	185.00
☐ **YOUNG SAW-WHET OWLS,** rel. 1973. ed. 1,500, s/n, 22″ x 17″, pub GW	30.00	290.00
☐ **BEE,** rel. 1974. ed. 1,000, s/n, 14″ x 14″, pub GW	45.00	365.00
☐ **BUFFALO SUN,** rel. 1974. ed. 1,000, s/n, 31″ x 17″, pub GW	45.00	390.00
☐ **SANCTUARY,** rel. 1974. ed. 1,000, s/n, 17″ x 22″, pub GW	45.00	135.00
☐ **COYOTE PUPS,** rel. 1975. ed. 1,000, s/n, 26″ x 19″, pub GW	50.00	225.00

	ISSUE PRICE	CURRENT PRICE
☐ **FROG,** rel. 1975. ed. 1,000, s/n, 14" × 14", pub GW	45.00	225.00
☐ **GOLDFINCH,** rel. 1975. ed. 1,000, s/n,14" x 14", pub GW	45.00	185.00
☐ **PEREGRINE FALCON,** rel. 1975. ed. 500, s/n, 29" x 17", pub GW	45.00	115.00
ed. 1,000, s/n, for Cornell Laboratory of Ornithology	*55.00	—
*Includes one year membership to Laboratory. Proceeds to their ongoing Ornithological Study Programs.		
☐ **ELF OWL,** rel. 1976. ed. 1,000, s/n, 22" x 17", pub GW	35.00	160.00
☐ **HONEYCOMB,** rel. 1976. ed. 1,000, s/n, 22½" x 14¾", pub GW	55.00	—
☐ **RACCOON,** rel. 1976. ed. 1,000, s/n, 20" x 29¾", pub GW	50.00	140.00
☐ **RIVER OTTER,** rel. 1976. ed. 1,000, s/n, 29" x 17", pub GW	50.00	160.00
☐ **SEA OTTERS,** rel. 1976. ed. 1,000, s/n, 31" x 17", pub GW	50.00	475.00
☐ **SPERM WHALE,** rel. 1976. ed. 1,000, s/n, 31" x 17", pub GW	50.00	550.00
☐ **ADELIE PENGUINS,** rel. 1977. ed. 1,000, s/n, 18" x 26", pub GW	50.00	100.00
☐ **BLUE WHALE,** rel. 1977. ed. 1,500, s/n, 30½" x 20½", pub GW	55.00	205.00
☐ **BUTTERFLY,** rel. 1977. ed. 1,500, s/n, 14" x 14", pub GW	45.00	190.00
☐ **HARBOR SEAL,** rel. 1977. ed. 1,000, s/n, 30" x 17", pub GW	55.00	165.00
☐ **ROADRUNNER,** rel. 1977. ed. 1,000, s/n, 30" x 17", pub GW	55.00	85.00
☐ **CALIFORNIA QUAIL,** rel. 1978. ed. 1,500, s/n, 30" x 15½", pub GW	60.00	90.00
☐ **CHICKADEES,** rel. 1978. ed. 1,500, s/n, 18" x 26", pub GW	55.00	115.00
☐ **DEAD-END MOLE,** rel. 1978. ed. 1,500, s/n, 14" x 14", pub GW	45.00	100.00
☐ **HUMPBACK WHALE,** rel. 1978. ed. 1,500, s/n, 14¼" x 21", pub GW	55.00	185.00
☐ **SNOWY OWL,** rel. 1978. ed. 1,500, s/n, 28" x 20", pub GW	60.00	80.00
☐ **BARN OWL,** rel. 1979. ed. 1,500, s/n, 17" x 20¼", pub GW	60.00	115.00
☐ **BISON,** rel. 1979. ed. 1,500, s/n, 33" x 16¾", pub GW	65.00	115.00
☐ **HARP SEAL,** rel. 1979. ed. 1,500, sn, 30" x 17", pub GW	55.00	105.00
☐ **RIGHT WHALE,** rel. 1979. ed. 2,000, s/n, 22" x 14½", pub GW	60.00	90.00
500 of edition were sold through Center for Environmental Education, Washington, D.C.; net proceeds to the Whale Protection Fund	60.00	105.00
☐ **GREAT HORNED OWL,** rel. 1980. ed. 1,500, s/n, 17" x 20½", pub GW	60.00	100.00
☐ **LADYBUGS,** rel. 1980. ed. 1,500, s/n, 14" x 14", pub GW	60.00	100.00
150 sold through the Ohio Historical Society, Columbus, Ohio; net proceeds to their ongoing Natural History programs.		
☐ **ORCA,** rel. 1980. ed. 1,500, s/n, 18¼" x 25", pub GW	85.00	130.00
☐ **PELICAN,** rel. 1980. ed. 1,500, s/n, 17½" x 27", pub GW	70.00	95.00
☐ **THE ALARM,** rel. 1980. ed. 350, signed, titled and numbered, 30½" x 23¼", hand-drawn litho, pub GW	195.00	—
☐ **AFRICAN SUN,** rel. 1981. ed. 1,000, s/n, 29" x 19½", pub GW	125.00	—
☐ **BOTTLENOSE PORPOISE,** rel. 1981. ed. 1,000, s/n, 31" x 17", pub GW	125.00	—
☐ **MARSH HARBOR COONS,** rel. 1981. ed. 1,500, s/n, 22" x 26½", pub GW	95.00	—
☐ **OWL'S NEST,** rel. 1981. ed. 1,000, s/n, 30" x 19", pub GW	95.00	—
☐ **POLAR BEAR,** rel. 1981. ed. 1,500, s/n, 31" x 18¼", pub GW	95.00	—
☐ **ELEPHANTS,** rel. 1982. ed. 1,000, s/n, 19" x 19½", pub GW	125.00	—
☐ **HORNED OWL SUN,** rel. 1982. ed. 1,250, s/n, 20⅝" x 21⅛", pub GW	95.00	—
☐ **RECESS,** rel. 1982. ed. 1,000, s/n, 31" x 14", serigraph, pub GW	125.00	—
☐ **MONUMENT VALLEY SUN,** rel. 1983. ed. 1,000, s/n, 23" x 13½", pub GW	95.00	—
☐ **NOAH'S ARK,** rel. 1983. ed. 2,500, s/n, 30⅝" x 18¼", pub GW	60.00	—

GREGORY PERILLO

THEMES: Western art, wildlife art

MEDIUM: Oil

EDUCATION: Pratt Institute; School of Visual Arts; Art Students League and artist William Robinson Leigh

AWARDS: *Who's Who in Western Art*; Artist of the Year by the National Association of Limited Edition Dealers; Silver Chalice Award

GALLERY/DISTRIBUTOR: Vague Shadows Limited

HOOFBEATS by Gregory Perillo

	ISSUE PRICE	CURRENT PRICE
☐ **MADRE,** rel. 1977. ed. 500, s/n, 22″ x 28″, pub VSL	125.00	300.00
☐ **MADONNA OF THE PLAINS,** rel. 1978. ed. 500, s/n, 22″ x 28″, pub VSL	125.00	250.00
☐ **SIOUX SCOUT and BUFFALO HUNT,** rel. 1978. ed. 500, s/n, 18″ x 22″, pub VSL	*75.00 Each	—
*To be sold as matched number sets	150.00 Set	300.00
☐ **SNOW PALS,** rel. 1978. ed. 500, s/n, 22″ x 28″, pub VSL	125.00	250.00
☐ **BABYSITTER,** rel. 1979. ed. 3,000, s/n, 16″ x 20″, pub VSL	45.00	—
☐ **PUPPIES,** rel. 1979. ed. 3,000, s/n, 16″ x 20″, pub VSL	45.00	—
☐ **LONESOME COWBOY,** rel. 1980. ed. 950, s/n, size not available, pub VSL	75.00	—
☐ **TENDER LOVE,** rel. 1980. ed. 950, s/n, size not available, pub VSL	75.00	—
☐ **CHIEF PONTIAC,** rel. 1981. ed. 950, s/n, size not available, pub VSL	75.00	—
☐ **PEACEABLE KINGDOM,** rel. 1981. ed. 950, s/n, 29″ x 23″, pub VSL	100.00	150.00
☐ **MARIA,** rel. 1981. ed. 550, s/n, size not available, pub VSL	150.00	—
☐ **TINKER,** rel. 1981. ed. 3,000, s/n, 24″ x 20″, pub VSL	45.00	—
☐ **HOOFBEATS,** rel. 1982. ed. 950, s/n, 29″ x 23″, pub VSL	75.00	—
☐ **INDIAN STYLE,** rel. 1982. ed. 950, s/n, size not available, pub VSL	75.00	—
☐ **OUT OF THE FOREST,** rel. 1984. Club Piece, s/n, litho, 24″ x 20″, pub VSL	50.00	—
☐ **CHIEF CRAZY HORSE,** rel. 1985. ed. 950, s/n, litho, 24″ x 30″, pub VSL	125.00	—
☐ **CHIEF SITTING BULL,** rel. 1985. ed. 500, s/n, litho, 20″ x 24″, pub VSL	125.00	—
☐ **MARIGOLD,** rel. 1985. ed. 500, s/n, litho, 20″ x 24″, pub VSL	125.00	—
☐ **SECRETARIAT,** rel. 1985. ed. 950, s/n, litho, 24″ x 24″, pub VSL	125.00	—
☐ **WHIRLAWAY,** rel. 1985. ed. 950, s/n, litho, 24″ x 24″, pub VSL	125.00	—

TOM PERKINSON

THEMES: Western landscape art

MEDIUM: The artist is well-versed in all media

EDUCATION: John Herron Art Institute; Oklahoma Baptist University; University of New Mexico

GALLERY/DISTRIBUTOR: Paul Sawyier Galleries, Inc.

	ISSUE PRICE	CURRENT PRICE
☐ CHANGING WEATHER, ed. 1,500, s/n, 10" x 15½", pub PSGI	35.00	—
☐ ORANGE SKY, ed. 1,000, s/n, 17½" x 24½", pub PSGI	80.00	—
☐ YELLOW HILLS, ed. 1,000, s/n, 19¼" x 22½", pub PSGI	80.00	—

ROGER TORY PETERSON

THEMES: Rare and exotic birds

STYLE: Realism

BOOKS: He has authored fourteen books including *Field Guide to the Birds*

EDUCATION: Art Students League; National Academy of Design

AWARDS: Has been awarded eleven honorary doctorates, numerous awards and medals, including the Presidential Medal of Freedom

MEMBERSHIPS: Special consultant to the Audubon Society

GALLERY/DISTRIBUTOR: Mill Pond Press, Inc.

	ISSUE PRICE	CURRENT PRICE
☐ BALTIMORE ORIOLE, rel. 1973. ed. 450, s/n, 18" x 18", pub MPPI	150.00	300.00
☐ CARDINAL, rel. 1973. ed. 450, s/n, 18" x 18", pub MPPI	150.00	600.00
☐ FLICKER, rel. 1973. ed. 450, s/n, 18" x 18", pub MPPI	150.00	300.00
☐ WOOD THRUSH, rel. 1973. ed. 450, s/n, 18" x 18", pub MPPI	150.00	400.00
☐ BALD EAGLE, rel. 1974. ed. 950, s/n, 31" x 22½", pub MPPI	150.00	450.00
☐ BARN SWALLOW, rel. 1974. ed. 750, s/n, 20" x 20", pub MPPI	150.00	200.00
☐ BOB-O-LINK, rel. 1974. ed. 750, s/n, 20" x 20", pub MPPI	150.00	200.00
☐ GREAT HORNED OWL, rel. 1974. ed. 950, s/n, 31" x 22½", pub MPPI	150.00	750.00
☐ BARN OWL, rel. 1975. ed. 950, s/n, 38" x 25", pub MPPI	225.00	275.00
☐ BOBWHITES, rel. 1975. ed. 950, s/n, 31" x 22½", pub MPPI	150.00	400.00
☐ FUR SEALS, rel. 1975. ed. 950, s/n, 11" x 14", pub MPPI	25.00	Sold Out
☐ JAYS - COLOR PLATE #30, rel. 1975. ed. 450, s/n, 21½" x 14", pub MPPI	150.00	—
☐ OWLS - COLOR PLATE #16, rel. 1975. ed. 950, s/n, 21½" x 14", pub MPPI	150.00	—
☐ RUFFED GROUSE, rel. 1975. ed. 950, s/n, 31" x 22½", pub MPPI	150.00	425.00
☐ SEA OTTERS, rel. 1975. ed. 950, s/n, 11" x 14", pub MPPI	25.00	100.00
☐ ADELIE PENGUINS, rel. 1976. ed. 950, s/n, 14" x 11", pub MPPI	35.00	Sold Out
☐ BLUE JAYS, rel. 1976. ed. 950, s/n, 22½" x 29", pub MPPI	150.00	285.00
☐ GOLDEN EAGLE, rel. 1976. ed. 950, s/n, 31" x 22½", pub MPPI	200.00	250.00
☐ QUAIL - COLOR PLATE #9, rel. 1976. ed. 950, s/n, 21½" x 14", pub MPPI	150.00	—

GREAT HORNED OWL *by Roger Tory Peterson*

	ISSUE PRICE	CURRENT PRICE
☐ **ROADRUNNER,** rel. 1976. ed. 950, s/n, 22½" x 31", pub MPPI	175.00	—
☐ **SNOWY OWL,** rel. 1976. ed. 950, s/n, 31" x 22½", pub MPPI	175.00	600.00
☐ **BLUEBIRD,** rel. 1977. ed. 950, s/n, 16¼" x 14", pub MPPI	75.00	200.00
☐ **PEREGRINE FALCON,** rel. 1977. ed. 950, s/n, 31" x 22½", pub MPPI	175.00	300.00
☐ **ROBIN,** rel. 1977. ed. 950, s/n, 19½" x 16½", pub MPPI	125.00	325.00
☐ **SCARLET TANAGER,** rel. 1977. ed. 950, s/n, 19½" x 16½", pub MPPI	125.00	200.00
☐ **SOOTY TERNS,** rel. 1977. ed. 450, s/n, 14" x 11", pub MPPI	50.00	85.00
☐ **WILD ORCHIDS AND TRILLIUMS,** rel. 1977. ed. 450, s/n, 21½" x 14", pub MPPI ...	75.00	—
☐ **WILLETS,** rel. 1977. ed. 450, s/n, 14" x 11", pub MPPI	50.00	85.00
☐ **MOCKINGBIRD,** rel. 1978. ed. 950, s/n, 19½" x 16½", pub MPPI	125.00	275.00
☐ **RING-NECKED PHEASANT,** rel. 1978. ed. 950, s/n, 25" x 35", pub MPPI	200.00	250.00
☐ **ROSE-BREASTED GROSBEAK,** rel. 1978. ed. 950, s/n, 19½" x 16½", pub MPPI ..	125.00	—
☐ **SHOWY WAYSIDE FLOWERS,** rel. 1978. ed. 450, s/n, 21½" x 14", pub MPPI	75.00	—
☐ **GYRFALCON,** rel. 1979. ed. 950, s/n, 33" x 25", pub MPPI	225.00	325.00
☐ **PUFFIN,** rel. 1979. ed. 950, s/n, 23" x 31½", pub MPPI	175.00	—
☐ **WILD TURKEYS,** rel. 1981. ed. 950, s/n, 24½" x 34¼", pub MPPI	195.00	—
☐ **ARCTIC GLOW - SNOWY OWL,** rel. 1983. ed. 950, s/n, 35¾" x 24½", pub MPPI ...	200.00	—

CARL PHELPS

THEMES: Wildlife art

GALLERY/DISTRIBUTOR: Grey Stone Press

	ISSUE PRICE	CURRENT PRICE
☐ BABY CHICKADEES, ed. 500, s/n, 20" x 14", pub GSP.	30.00	—
ed. 2,500, s/o	20.00	—
☐ BABY RABBIT, ed. 500, s/n, 14" x 18", pub GSP	30.00	—
ed. 2,500, s/o	20.00	—
☐ FOX CUBS, ed. 500, s/n, 16" x 22", pub GSP	30.00	—
ed. 2,500, s/o	20.00	—
☐ YOUNG COTTONTAILS, ed. 500, s/n, 18" x 15", pub GSP	30.00	—
ed. 2,500, s/o	20.00	—

WILLIAM S. PHILLIPS

THEMES: Aviation art

STYLE: Realism

MEMBERSHIPS: Air Force Art Program

MUSEUMS/COLLECTIONS: His works hang in numerous public and private collections throughout the world

GALLERY/DISTRIBUTOR: Greenwich Workshop

COMMENTS: Bill Phillips comments, "In my work, I hope to convey to the viewer the beauty and exhilaration of flight"

	ISSUE PRICE	CURRENT PRICE
☐ ADVANTAGE EAGLE, rel. 1982. ed. 1,000, s/n, 27½" x 22½", pub GW	135.00	—
☐ WELCOME HOME YANK, rel. 1982. ed. 1,000, s/n, 27½" x 22½", pub GW	135.00	140.00
☐ THE GIANT BEGINS TO STIR, rel. 1983. ed. 1,250 signed and numbered by the artist, Gen. James H. Doolittle, and 15 Aviators who participated in the Raid Over Tokyo, 29¼" x 23½", pub GW	185.00	350.00
☐ THOSE CLOUDS WON'T HELP YOU NOW, rel. 1983. ed. 625, s/n, by artist and counter-signed by Marine Corps Ace Marion E. Carl, 27½" x 22½", pub GW	135.00	—
☐ THOSE CLOUDS WON'T HELP YOU NOW, ed. 25, signed/numbered/countersigned and double remarqued, 27½" x 22½", pub GW	295.00	300.00
☐ HELLFIRE CORNER, rel. 1984. ed. 1,250, s/n, countersigned by British, German, Canadian, and American Air Aces of World War II, 29¼" x 23½", pub GW	185.00	205.00
ed. 25, remarque	335.00	410.00
☐ INTO THE TEETH OF THE TIGER, rel. 1984. ed. 1,000, s/n, countersigned by World War II Ace Don Lopez, 29¼" x 17⅛, pub GW	135.00	Sold Out
ed. 25, remarque	285.00	Sold Out
☐ LEST WE FORGET, rel. 1985. ed. 1,250, multiple images & signatures/n, 35¾" x 24", pub GW	195.00	—
☐ THE PHANTOMS AND THE WIZARD, rel. 1985. ed. 850, s/n, 35⅝" x 20½", pub GW	145.00	—

THE GIANT BEGINS TO STIR *by Bill Phillips*

DIANE PIERCE

THEMES: Wildlife art

STYLE: Realism

AWARDS: *Who's Who in American Women; The World's Who's Who in Women*; State Duck Stamp Contest (1979); Long Island Waterfowl Stamp Contest (1980)

MEMBERSHIP: Pierce belongs to and supports over 25 conservation organizations

MUSEUMS/COLLECTIONS: Over 500 of her paintings are in private collections internationally

GALLERY/DISTRIBUTOR: Edge of the Wild

COMMENTS: In 1981, the artist was sent to India to present a painting of Siberian Cranes to Prime Minister Indira Gandhi during the Conference on International Trade of Endangered Species

GOLDEN EAGLES WITH YOUNG *by Diane Pierce*

	ISSUE PRICE	CURRENT PRICE
SINGLE COLOR - Brown & White.		
☐ **SCRATCHBOARD OWLS*** - rel. 1973.		
Barn Owl, ed. 500, s/n, 14″ x 18″, pub EDTW	5.00	20.00
Great Horned Owl, ed. 500, s/n, 14″ x 18″, pub EDTW	5.00	20.00
Saw Whet Owl, ed. 500, s/n, 14″ x 18″, pub EDTW	5.00	25.00
Screech Owl, ed. 500, s/n, 14″ x 18″, pub EDTW	5.00	Sold Out
*50 of each donated to Charity.		
☐ **SCRATCHBOARD ANIMALS** - rel. 1975.		
Chipmunks, ed. 500, s/n, 11″ x 14″, pub ETDW	5.00	—
Cottontail, ed. 500, s/n, 10″ x 12″, pub ETDW	5.00	—
Deermice, ed. 500, s/n, 10″ x 12″, pub ETDW	5.00	—
Flying Squirrels, ed. 500, s/n, 11″ x 14″, pub ETDW	5.00	—
MULTI or FULL COLOR		
☐ **SERIES 1 - WILD INHERITORS.**		
Screech Owls, rel. 1973. ed. 200, s/n, 16″ x 20″, pub EDTW	40.00	Sold Out
American Kestrel, rel. 1974. ed. 200, s/n, 16″ x 20″, pub EDTW	40.00	280.00
Blue Jays with Young, rel. 1975. ed. 200, s/n, 16″ x 20″, pub EDTW	40.00	Sold Out
American Woodcock, rel. 1976. ed. 200, s/n, 16″ x 20″, pub EDTW	50.00	—
Cottontail with Young, rel. 1976. ed. 200, s/n, 16″ x 20″, pub EDTW	50.00	—
Remarqued prints of the Series	80.00	—
☐ **SERIES 2 - WOODLAND LEGACIES.**		
Cecropias, rel. 1974. ed. 300, s/n, 11″ x 12½″, pub EDTW	12.00	25.00
Goldfinches, rel. 1974. ed. 300, s/n, 11″ x 12½″, pub EDTW	12.00	Sold Out
Indigo Bunting, rel. 1974. ed. 300, s/n, 11″ x 12½″, pub EDTW	12.00	40.00
R-T Hummingbird, rel. 1974. ed. 300, s/n, 11″ x 12½″, pub EDTW	12.00	40.00
Summer Goldfinches, rel. 1979. ed. 300, s/n, 11½″ x 14″, pub EDTW	25.00	—
Remarqued prints in this Series - Additional cost	25.00	—

	ISSUE PRICE	CURRENT PRICE
☐ **SERIES 3 - WATERFOWL.**		
Before the North Wind - Cans, rel. 1977. ed. 750, s/n, 22″ x 28″, pub EDTW	50.00	Sold Out
Circling the Savannah - Snows, rel. 1977. ed. 750, s/n, 22″ x 28″, pub EDTW	50.00	60.00
Into the Cypress - Woodies, rel. 1977. ed. 750, s/n, 22″ x 28″, pub EDTW	50.00	60.00
Remarqued print in this series	90.00	—
Up from the Prairie - Sprigs, rel. 1977. ed. 750, s/n, 22″ x 28″, pub EDTW	50.00	60.00
Donated to National Wildlife Federation - 150 prints of each in this series		
☐ **SERIES 4**		
Golden Eagles with Young, rel. 1973. ed. 350, s/n, 22″ x 28″, pub EDTW	60.00	75.00
Remarqued...	110.00	—
25 prints donated to Cornell Laboratory of Ornithology.		
Mute Swan with Young, rel. 1976. ed. 450, s/n, 27½″ x 37½″, pub EDTW	85.00	—
Remarqued..	160.00	—
300 prints donated to Kellogg Sanctuary.		

AUTUMN BLACKCAPS *by John Pitcher*

JOHN PITCHER

THEMES: Birds/landscape (primarily Alaska)

MEDIUM: Watercolor, oil, mixed media

BOOKS: The artist has contributed scientific illustrations for *World Book Encyclopedia, A Guide to the Birds of Alaska,* and other fine publications.

GALLERY/DISTRIBUTOR: Mill Pond Press, Inc.

	ISSUE PRICE	CURRENT PRICE
☐ WHISTLING SWANS - FALL MIGRANTS, rel. 1978. ed. 950, s/n, 20″ x 28″, pub MPPI	85.00	—
☐ MORNING FLIGHT - BALD EAGLE, rel. 1982. ed. 950, s/n, 33¼″ x 24½″, pub MPPI	200.00	—
☐ AUTUMN BLACKCAPS CHICKADEES, rel. 1983. ed. 950, s/n, 11¾″ x 8½″, pub MPPI	40.00	—
☐ COASTAL PEREGRINES, rel. 1983. ed. 950, s/n, 24″ x 17½″, pub MPPI	85.00	—
☐ WINDY CARDINAL, rel. 1983. ed. 950, s/n, 11¾″ x 8½″, pub MPPI	40.00	—

RICHARD W. PLASSCHAERT

THEMES: Landscape and wildlife art

AWARDS: Federal Duck Stamp Print (1980)

GALLERY/DISTRIBUTOR: Watermark Press

	ISSUE PRICE	CURRENT PRICE
☐ DRUM SONG, rel. 1979. ed. 580, s/n, size not available, pub WP	55.00	275.00
☐ AUTUMN RETREAT - WOOD DUCKS, rel. 1980. ed. 580, s/n, size not available, pub WWI	75.00	300.00
☐ BROKEN COVEY - BOBWHITES, rel. 1980. ed. 580, s/n, size not available, pub WWI	100.00	—
☐ MOONAN MARSH - GREENWINGED TEAL, rel. 1980. ed. 580, s/n, size not available, pub WWI	75.00	175.00
☐ MOONAN MARSH - MALLARDS, rel. 1980. ed. 580, s/n, size not available, pub WWI	55.00	300.00
☐ SETTLING IN - CANADA GEESE, rel. 1980. ed. 580, s/n, size not available, pub WWI	60.00	150.00
☐ WINTER FLIGHT - PHEASANTS, rel. 1980. ed. 580, s/n, size not available, pub WWI	60.00	350.00
☐ GREAT BLUE HERON, rel. 1981. ed. 750, s/n, size not available, pub WP	45.00	Sold Out
☐ TRANQUIL AUTUMN DAYS - TURKEYS, rel. 1981. ed. 580, s/n, size not available, pub WWI	75.00	150.00
☐ WOODLOT FEEDING - RINGNECKED PHEASANTS, rel. 1981. ed. 750, s/n, size not available, pub WWI	100.00	200.00
☐ MOONAN MARSH - WOOD DUCKS, rel. 1982. ed. 580, s/n, size not available, pub WP	100.00	200.00
☐ OVER THE POINT - BLUEBILLS, rel. 1982. ed. 750, s/n, size not available, pub WP	100.00	Sold Out
☐ SECLUDED MARSH - MALLARDS, rel. 1982. ed. 750, s/n, size not available, pub WP	100.00	150.00

OGDEN PLEISSNER

THEMES: Wildlife art

MEDIUM: Oil and watercolor

STYLE: Realism

EDUCATION: Art Students League

AWARDS: National Academy of Design's Samuel F. B. Morse Medal of Honor (1959), Gold Medal of the American Watercolor Society (1956), Audubon Artists' Medal of Honor (1950), etc.

MEMBERSHIPS: National Academy of Design, American Watercolor Society, etc.

MUSEUM/COLLECTIONS: Metropolitan Museum of Art, Brooklyn Museum, etc.

GALLERY/DISTRIBUTOR: Wild Wings, Inc.

HEAD OF THE POOL *by Ogden Pleissner*

	ISSUE PRICE	CURRENT PRICE
☐ ATLANTIC SALMON FISHING, rel. 1939. ed. 300, pub Frost & Reed	—	1,200.00
☐ CASTING FOR SALMON, rel. 1949. ed. 300, pub Sportsman's Gallery & Bookshelf	—	1,200.00
☐ TROUT FISHING IN WYOMING, rel. 1949. ed. 250, pub Sportsman's Gallery & Bookshelf	—	1,200.00

	ISSUE PRICE	CURRENT PRICE
☐ BEAVERKILL BRIDGE, rel. 1953. ed. 221, pub Anglers Club	—	2,000.00
☐ DOWNS GULCH, rel. 1957. ed. 300, pub Anglers Club of New York	—	1,000.00
☐ LEAPING SEA TROUT, rel. 1957. ed. 300, pub Frost & Reed	—	1,200.00
☐ THE BRIDGE POOL, rel. 1957. ed. 300, pub Frost & Reed	—	1,200.00
☐ WEST DUNCAN, CLOVE VALLEY, rel. 1957. ed. 104, pub Clove Valley Club	—	1,500.00
☐ BLUE BOAT ON THE SAINT ANNE, rel. 1959. ed. 300, pub Anglers Club of New York	—	2,000.00
☐ DRIVEN GROUSE, GLANCIE BEAT, rel. 1959. ed. 300, pub Frost & Reed	—	1,750.00
☐ GRANDE RIVE, UPPER MALBRAIE, rel. 1959. ed. 300, pub Frost & Reed	—	1,500.00
☐ OCTOBER SNOW, rel. 1959. ed. 350, pub Anglers Club of New York	—	1,750.00
☐ RISING SALMON, rel. 1961. ed. 300, pub Sportsman's Gallery & Bookshelf	—	1,000.00
☐ GROUSE SHOOTING, (Unsigned), rel. 1967. ed. 400, pub Vance Hood	—	300.00
☐ JUNE TROUT FISHING, rel. 1967. ed. 350, pub Theodore Gordon Flyfishers	—	750.00
☐ LYE BROOK POOL, rel. 1971. ed. 400, pub American Museum of Flyfishing	—	450.00
☐ QUAIL HUNTERS, rel. 1973. ed. 425, pub Crossroads of Sport	225.00	500.00
☐ HILLSIDE ORCHARD, GROUSE SHOOTING, rel. 1975. ed. 275, pub Crossroads of Sport	275.00	800.00
☐ WOODCOCK COVER, rel. 1976. ed. 275, pub The Crossroads of Sport	275.00	750.00
☐ BATTENKILL AT BENEDICTS CROSSING, rel. 1978. ed. 290, pub Crossroads of Sport & Orvis Co.	275.00	600.00
☐ DAWN ON THE DUCK MARSH, rel. 1978. ed. 275, pub The Crossroads of Sport ...	285.00	400.00
☐ FISHING THE AUSABLE, HENDRICKSON POOL, rel. 1979. ed. 275, pub Trout Un-limited, Mich.	—	280.00
☐ HEAD OF THE POOL, rel. 1979. ed. 280, pub Crossroads and Orvis	285.00	500.00
☐ HENDRICKSON'S POOL, rel. 1980. ed. 275, pub Crossroads and Orvis	300.00	300.00
☐ CLOVE VALLEY, rel. 1982. ed. 156, s/n, size not available, distr. WWI	350.00	—
☐ DRY FLY FISHING FOR SALMON, rel. 1982. ed. 300, s/n, size not available, pub Theodore Gordon Flyfishers	300.00	300.00
☐ MARSH GUNNERS, rel. 1982. ed. 300, s/n, 16″ x 25″, distr. WWI	300.00	300.00

JOE POLSENO

THEMES: Birds

BOOKS: The artist has illustrated more than 100 books

BACKGROUND: Joe Polseno is a product of inner-city New York. As such, he spent many hours studying the bird paintings of Fuertes at New York's Museum of Natural History

GALLERY/DISTRIBUTOR: Greenwich Workshop

	ISSUE PRICE	CURRENT PRICE
☐ CANADA GEESE, rel. 1973. ed. 1,000, s/n, 24″ x 18″, pub GW	40.00	—
☐ GREEN-WINGED TEAL, rel. 1974. ed. 1,000, s/n, 16″ x 12″, pub GW	*40.00	—
*Portfolio of two prints		

M. C. POULSEN

THEMES: Contemporary Western art

EDUCATION: University of Arizona; apprenticed with an artist in Hawaii for over a year

COMPANIONS *by M.C. Poulsen*

MUSEUMS/COLLECTIONS: Many of his paintings hang in major corporate collections throughout the world

GALLERY/DISTRIBUTOR: M. C. Poulsen

	ISSUE PRICE	CURRENT PRICE
☐ **WRANGLER IN YELLOW SLICKER,** rel. 1979. ed. 250, s/n, 15½" x 23", pub SP* ...	55.00	650.00
☐ **FALES PACK TRAIN,** rel. 1981. ed. 250, s/n, 16½" x 21", pub EP	100.00	350.00
☐ **... AND THE HEARTS OF THE CHILDREN SHALL TURN TO THEIR FATHERS,** rel. 1982. ed. 250, s/n, 17½" x 20¼", by AW Subject of this painting was Ben Nighthorse. Prints were also signed by Ben Nighthorse	125.00	300.00
☐ **COMPANIONS,** rel. 1983. ed. 250, s/n, 20¼" x 15"	125.00	350.00
☐ **WORKIN' FOR THE BRAND,** rel. 1983. ed. 250, s/n, 17½" x 21"	100.00	125.00
☐ **CHUCK POULSEN - OUTFITTER,** rel. 1984. ed. 100, s/n, 10½" x 13½"	200.00	—
☐ **FRENCH LEAVE,** rel. 1984. ed. 1,000, s/n, 17" x 19½"	65.00	—

*M.C. Poulsen prints, although published by different companies, are available through the artist at 2019 Kerper Blvd., Cody, Wyoming 82414.

DON PRECHTEL

THEMES: Historical

AWARDS: A charter member of the prestigious Northwest Rendezvous Group, Mr. Prechtel has received much recognition and numerous honors for his work throughout the West, including the Western Art Association's Purchase Award in 1978 and the Judge's Award from the Pacific Northwest Indian Center, Spokane, Washington

GALLERY/DISTRIBUTOR: Wild Wings, Inc.

COMMENTS: The works of this fine artist, who is listed in *Who's Who in American Art,* are exhibited and sold in galleries in the West and Southwest and are owned by many private collectors

	ISSUE PRICE	CURRENT PRICE
☐ **RED RIVER,** rel. 1981. ed. 500, s/n, litho, 21¼" x 17¾", pub WWI	85.00	—
☐ **THE MISSOURI BREAKS TRADING CO.,** rel. 1981. ed. 500, s/n, litho, 26" x 17½", pub WWI..	85.00	—
☐ **TRACKING SNOW,** rel. 1981. ed. 500, s/n, litho, 17¾" x 23½", pub WWI	85.00	—
☐ **NATIVE SONS - BLACK HORSE CAVALRY,** rel. 1984. ed. 750, s/n, litho, 15¾" x 23¾", pub WWI	85.00	—

ROGER PREUSS

THEMES: Wildlife art

STYLE: Realism

BOOKS: *Where Wildlife Meets the World of "Real Art"* by Roger Preuss

AWARDS: He has 26 art awards to date and numerous honors and mentions

MEMBERSHIPS: Charter member of Wildlife Artists of the World

MUSEUMS/COLLECTIONS: Maytag, Michaels, and Ridder collections, among others

GALLERY/DISTRIBUTOR: Wildlife of America

COMMENTS: The artist is revered by colleagues as the chief spokesman, catalyst and pioneering proponent of the movement to help improve the status of superior wildlife art as recognized fine art

	ISSUE PRICE	CURRENT PRICE
☐ **AMERICAN GOLDENEYE,** rel. 1949. Federal Duck Stamp Print stone litho. ed. 250, s/o, 6⅝" x 9⅛", pub WOA	15.00	2,600.00
ed. 8, remarqued	40.00	3,200.00
☐ **SHOVELLERS,** rel. 1950. Ducks Unlimited issue. ed. N/A, 9½" x 7⅛", pub WOA	—	300.00
☐ **GREENHEADS,** rel. 1951. ed. 300, s/o, 11½" x 15½", pub WOA	15.00	890.00
☐ **SNOW GEESE WINGING SOUTH,** rel. 1951. ed. 4, s/in plate, 23" x 20", chromolith, pub WOA	30.00	3,900.00

	ISSUE PRICE	CURRENT PRICE
☐ GOLDENEYES AT LEECH LAKE, rel. 1952. ed. 400, s/o, 13½" x 18", pub WOA	20.00	750.00
☐ TEAL - UP AND AWAY, rel. 1952. ed. 350, s/o, 13½" x 18", pub WOA	20.00	800.00
☐ WOOD DUCKS - ALONG THE CREEK, rel. 1953. ed. 300, s/in plate, 8⅞" x 6¾", engraving, pub WOA	25.00	400.00
☐ WOODIES ON A SPRING MORN, rel. 1954. ed. 400, s/o, 11½" x 15½", pub WOA ..	25.00	1,075.00
☐ WILDERNESS YULETIDE, rel. 1955. ed. 60, s/o, 10" x 7", pub WOA	20.00	140.00
ed. 940, i/o	10.00	90.00
☐ FANTASY OF THE GOLDEN VALLEY, rel. 1956. ed. 940, i/o, 14" x 11", pub WOA ...	—	170.00
ed. 60, Artist proofs	—	200.00
☐ HERE THEY COME - BLUEBILLS, rel. 1957. ed. 940, s/in plate, 7" x 9½", pub WOA	20.00	140.00
ed. 60, i/o	—	175.00
☐ AMERICAN WIDGEON, rel. 1958, ed. 1,140, s/in plate, 38" x 48", pub WOA	15.00	130.00
ed. 60, i/o	—	150.00
☐ FAWNS IN SPRINGTIME, rel. 1958. ed. 1,000, s/o, 11½" x 15½", pub WOA	20.00	125.00
☐ RUFFED GROUSE AT SUNDOWN, rel. 1959. ed. 200, s/n, 11½" x 15½", pub WOA .	20.00	180.00
ed. 500, s/o	15.00	125.00
ed. 300, u/s	—	100.00
☐ WOOD DUCKS ON A SUMMER MARSH, rel. 1960. ed. 400, s/o, 13½" x 18", pub WOA	20.00	185.00
ed. 600, i/o	15.00	150.00
☐ FROM BEYOND THE NORTH WIND, rel. 1961. ed. 200, s/n, 11½" x 15½", pub WOA	20.00	210.00
ed. 300, s/o	15.00	175.00
ed. 20, Artist proofs, remarqued	N/A	310.00
☐ CANADA GEESE - FEEDING TIME, rel. 1962. ed. 200, s/n, 11½" x 15½", pub WOA	20.00	140.00
ed. 300, s/o	15.00	100.00
ed. 500, i/o	—	80.00
☐ KING OF THE WEST, rel. 1962. ed. 200, s/n, 11½" x 15½", pub WOA	20.00	140.00
ed. 300, s/o	15.00	90.00
ed. 500, i/o	—	75.00
☐ MONARCH OF THE WILDERNESS, rel. 1962. ed. 200, s/n, 11½" x 15½", pub WOA	20.00	125.00
ed. 300, s/o	15.00	85.00
ed. 500, u/s	—	75.00
☐ PHEASANTS IN SPRINGTIME, rel. 1962. ed. 200, n/o, 11½" x 15½", pub WOA	20.00	120.00
ed. 300, s/o	15.00	80.00
ed. 500, i/o	—	75.00
☐ CANVASBACKS AT DAWN, rel. 1963. ed. 200, s/n, 11½" x 15½", pub WOA	20.00	160.00
ed. 300, s/o	15.00	135.00
ed. 500, u/s	—	85.00
☐ NIGHT WATCH - RACCOONS, rel. 1964. ed. 200, s/n, 11½" x 15½", pub WOA	20.00	145.00
ed. 300, s/o	15.00	110.00
ed. 500, u/s	—	85.00
☐ SNOW GEESE, rel. 1964. ed. 100, s/o, 8½" x 7½", serigraph, pub WOA	25.00	900.00
☐ PHEASANTS IN AN AUTUMN MARSH, rel. 1964. ed. 200, s/n, 11½" x 15½", pub WOA	20.00	150.00
ed. 300, s/o	15.00	130.00
ed. 500, u/s	—	80.00
☐ THE FIRST FLUSH - BOBWHITE, rel. 1965. ed. 750, s/o, 11½" x 15½", pub WOA ..	30.00	75.00
ed. 200, s/n	50.00	90.00
ed. 60, watercolor remarqued Artist proofs	N/A	375.00
☐ THE WALLEYE, rel. 1965. ed. 200, s/n, 11½" x 15½", pub WOA	20.00	140.00
ed. 300, s/o	15.00	110.00
ed. 500, u/s	—	75.00
☐ TAKE A BOY HUNTING, rel. 1967. ed. 250, engraving signed in plate, 10" x 8", pub WOA	30.00	450.00
☐ COUGAR!, rel. 1968. ed. 740, s/o, 13" x 21", pub WOA	50.00	75.00
ed. 200, s/n	60.00	85.00
ed. 60, remarqued Artist proofs	175.00	475.00

	ISSUE PRICE	CURRENT PRICE
☐ LARGEMOUTH BASS - FEEDING TIME, rel. 1968. ed. 200, s/n, 11½" x 15½", pub WOA	50.00	120.00
ed. 740, s/o	40.00	85.00
ed. 60, Artist proofs	N/A	200.00
☐ STARTLED BLUE-WINGED TEAL, rel. 1968. ed. 200, s/n, 11½" x 15½", pub WOA	50.00	85.00
ed. 300, s/o	40.00	80.00
ed. 500, i/o	—	75.00
☐ SHARP-TAILED GROUSE, rel. 1968. ed. 200, s/n, 13" x 21", pub WOA	60.00	125.00
ed. 740, s/o	50.00	100.00
☐ CANADA GEESE AT SUNRISE, rel. 1969. ed. 400, s/o, 16⅛" x 20¼", pub WOA	25.00	1,075.00
ed. 20, Artist proofs	N/A	Sold Out
☐ WAITING FOR MOM, rel. 1970. ed. 400, s/n, 16½" x 21", pub WOA	30.00	1,150.00
ed. 20, Artist proofs	N/A	Sold Out
☐ THE INTRUDER - COTTONTAILS, rel. 1971. ed. 200, s/n, 11½" x 15½", pub WOA	50.00	85.00
ed. 300, s/o	40.00	75.00
ed. 500, i/o	—	65.00
☐ BLACK DUCKS AGAINST THE TWILIGHT, rel. 1974. ed. 560, s/n, 18½" x 23½", pub WOA	55.00	1,100.00
ed. 25, remarqued	150.00	1,400.00
☐ FOREST INDIAN - ALASKA, rel. 1975. ed. 100, n/o, 8" x 6½", pub WOA	125.00	875.00
☐ THE SNOW-WHITETAILS, rel. 1975. ed. 500, s/n, 11½" x 15½", pub WOA	40.00	75.00
☐ RUTTING TIME - MISTY MORNING WHITETAILS, rel. 1976. ed. 200, s/n, 11½" x 15½", pub WOA	50.00	180.00
ed. 740, s/o	40.00	130.00
ed. 60, Artist proofs	N/A	210.00
☐ FLAG UP - WHITETAIL BOUNDS OVER CREEK, rel. 1977. ed. 200, s/n, 11½" x 15½", pub WOA	50.00	120.00
ed. 740, s/o	40.00	75.00
ed. 60, Artist proofs	N/A	Sold Out
☐ IN THE MEADOW - WHITETAIL FAMILY, rel. 1977. ed. 200, s/n, 11½" x 15½", pub WOA	50.00	120.00
ed. 300, s/o	40.00	90.00
ed. 500, i/o	—	Sold Out
☐ WHITE-TAILED DEER AT TWILIGHT, rel. 1977. ed. 200, s/n, 11½" x 15½", pub WOA	50.00	85.00
ed. 300, s/o	40.00	75.00
ed. 500, i/o	—	Sold Out
☐ WHITETAILS FEEDING IN THE SNOW, rel. 1977. ed. 200, s/n, 11½" x 15½", pub WOA	50.00	90.00
ed. 300, s/o	40.00	80.00
ed. 500, i/o	—	Sold Out
☐ DOLINKA - INDIAN GIRL, rel. 1980. ed. 5, signed in plate, 20" x 16¼", pub WOA	275.00	1,010.00
☐ PHEASANTS IN AUTUMN HABITAT, rel. 1981. First of Issue, Pheasant Habitat Stamp Print. ed. 1,981, s/n, 6½" x 9½", pub WOA	125.00	365.00
☐ WILD TURKEY, rel. 1981. ed. 5, s/n, 11⅝" x 19½", chromolith, pub WOA	275.00	1,050.00
☐ THE WHITE-TAILED DEER, rel. 1982. ed. 450, s/n, 18¼" x 25½", pub WOA	70.00	100.00
ed. 25, remarqued	200.00	250.00
☐ FORMING THE V, rel. 1983. ed. 580, s/n, 18⅛" x 23", pub WOA	85.00	125.00
☐ OUT OF THE NORTH WIND - BLUEBILLS!, rel. 1983. ed. 580, s/n, 13¾" x 19¾", pub WOA	75.00	—
ed. 20, remarqued Artist proofs	175.00	—
☐ PIN OAK RETREAT, rel. 1984. ed. 680, s/n, 11½" x 15½", litho, pub WOA	75.00	—
☐ THE SON - WHITETAILS, rel. 1984. ed. 500, s/n, 11½" x 15½", pub WOA	60.00	75.00

ROBERT PUMMILL

THEMES: Western art

STYLE: Strong narrative element and dramatic light

EDUCATION: Art Center School

GALLERY/DISTRIBUTOR: Texas Art Press

	ISSUE PRICE	CURRENT PRICE
☐ A DRY MATCH, rel. 1979. ed. 2,250, s/n, 14″ x 22″, pub TAP	75.00	—
☐ A HOT MEAL AND A WARM FIRE, rel. 1979. ed. 2,250, s/n, 13½″ x 22″, pub TAP . .	75.00	—
☐ A MATTER OF RIGHT-A-WAY, rel. 1982. ed. 1,000, s/n, 18″ x 27″, pub TAP	100.00	—
☐ BACK TO TEXAS, rel. 1980. ed. 2,250, s/n, 12¾″ x 22″, pub TAP	85.00	—
☐ BRAZOS CROSSING, rel. 1980. ed. 2,250, s/n, 13¼″ x 22″, pub TAP	85.00	—
☐ END OF A HARD DAY, rel. 1980. ed. 2,250, s/n, 17″ x 22″, pub TAP	85.00	—
☐ MULES AND MODEL T'S, rel. 1983. ed. 1,000, s/n, 19½″ x 27¾″, pub TAP	100.00	—
☐ OIL TOWN DEPOT, rel. 1981. ed. 1,000, s/n, 18″ x 27″, pub TAP	100.00	—
☐ OVER THE TOP, rel. 1981. ed. 1,000, s/n, 25¾″ x 20½″, pub TAP	100.00	—
☐ RAWHIDE AND DUST, rel. 1979. ed. 2,250, s/n, 14½″ x 22″, pub TAP	75.00	—
☐ SHADOWS OF THE TETONS, rel. 1983. ed. 1,000, s/n, 16½″ x 27″, pub TAP	100.00	—
☐ TAKING THE POINT, rel. 1980. ed. 2,250, s/n, 13½″ x 22″, pub TAP	85.00	—
☐ TEAMWORK, rel. 1982. ed. 1,000, s/n, 20¾″ x 27¾″, pub TAP	100.00	—
☐ THE PROVIDER, rel. 1979. ed. 2,250, s/n, 13½″ x 22″, pub TAP	75.00	—
☐ THREE'S COMPANY, rel. 1980. ed. ed. 2,250, s/n, 13⅝″ x 22″, pub TAP	85.00	—
☐ WET WEATHER WANDERERS, rel. 1980. ed. 2,250, s/n, 14½″ x 22″, pub TAP	85.00	—

THOMAS QUINN

THEMES: Wildlife art

GALLERY/DISTRIBUTOR: Mill Pond Press, Inc.

	ISSUE PRICE	CURRENT PRICE
☐ ALERT PINTAILS AND KILLDEER, rel. 1984. ed. 950, s/n, 31½″ x 24″, pub MPPI . .	100.00	—
☐ RUNNING COTTONTAIL, rel. 1984. ed. 950, s/n, 18″ x 24″, pub MPPI	65.00	—

ROBERT R. REDDEN

THEMES: Wildlife art

STYLE: Realism

GALLERY/DISTRIBUTOR: Grey Stone Press

	ISSUE PRICE	CURRENT PRICE
☐ BLUE BIRD AFTERNOON, ed. 500, s/n, 18½″ x 24″, litho, pub GSP	30.00	60.00
☐ HONEY AGARIC/CAESAR'S MUSHROOM, ed. 2,500, s/n, 14″ x 18″, litho, pub GSP, (sold as a set only)	20.00	—

PINTAILS *by Tom Quinn*

	ISSUE PRICE	CURRENT PRICE
☐ MORNING WATCH (Blue Jay), ed. 500, s/n, 18½″ x 24″, litho, pub GSP	30.00	60.00
☐ PASSION FLOWER & CAROLINA WREN, ed. 1,000, s/n, 18″ x 22″, litho, pub GSP .	30.00	—
☐ THE FLUSH (Bobwhite), ed. 3,000; 1,000, s/n, 2,000, s/o	40.00	—
litho, pub GSP	30.00	—

MARK REECE

THEMES: Wildlife art

STYLE: Realism

EDUCATION: Bachelor of Science in Zoology from Iowa State University, and a Master of Science in Biology from Drake University

AWARDS: Winner of the 1975 Iowa Duck Stamp Design Contest

GALLERY/DISTRIBUTOR: Mill Pond Press, Inc.

HONKERS by Mark Reece

COMMENTS: Mark Reece is the son of the distinguished artist, Maynard Reece. He is currently attending medical school

	ISSUE PRICE	CURRENT PRICE
☐ **HONKERS - CANADA GEESE,** rel. 1977. ed. 950, s/n, 19½" x 22½", pub MPPI	60.00	—
☐ **QUAIL BREAK - BOBWHITES,** rel. 1978. ed. 950, s/n, 19½" x 22½", pub MPPI	60.00	—
☐ **LOONS,** rel. 1979. ed. 950, s/n, 16¾" x 22½", pub MPPI	60.00	85.00
☐ **DUCKLINGS - REDHEADS,** rel. 1980. ed. 950, s/n, 8" x 10", pub MPPI	20.00	40.00
☐ **MALLARDS,** rel. 1980. ed. 950, s/n, 13½" x 18¼", pub MPPI	40.00	—
☐ **RESTING UP - MALLARDS,** rel. 1980. ed. 950, s/n, 13½" x 18¼", pub MPPI	40.00	—
☐ **SNOOZING - MALLARDS,** rel. 1980. ed. 950, s/n, 8" x 10", pub MPPI	20.00	—

MAYNARD REECE

THEMES: Wildlife art

STYLE: Realism

BACKGROUND: In 1940, Reece was hired as an artist for the Iowa Department of History and Archives; he also served as an artist in the Signal Corps during World War II

AWARDS: Five-time winner of the Federal Duck Stamp Competition, Artist of the Year from Ducks Unlimited, and countless other awards

GALLERY/DISTRIBUTOR: Mill Pond Press, Inc.

COMMENTS: It is possible that more people possess a print from a Reece painting than from the work of any other wildlife artist

DARK SKY PHEASANT by Maynard Reece

	ISSUE PRICE	CURRENT PRICE
☐ **BOBWHITES,** rel. 1964. ed. 950, stone litho, 14″ x 18″	20.00	660.00
☐ **MALLARDS,** rel. 1964. ed. 250, stone litho, 14″ x 18″	20.00	660.00
☐ **MALLARDS - PITCHING IN,** rel. 1969. ed. 500, s/n, 25¾″ x 35½″, pub MPPI	40.00	610.00
☐ **EDGE OF THE HEDGEROW - BOBWHITES,** rel. 1970. ed. 1,000, s/n, 25″ x 29½″, pub MPPI	60.00	710.00
☐ **AGAINST THE WIND - CANVASBACKS,** rel. 1972. ed. 550, s/n, 23½″ x 29½″, pub MPPI	60.00	460.00
☐ **FEEDING TIME - CANADA GEESE,** rel. 1973. ed. 550, s/n, 24½″ x 30″, pub MPPI	75.00	410.00
☐ **LATER AFTERNOON - MALLARDS,** rel. 1973. ed. 450, s/n, 25″ x 31″, pub MPPI	150.00	160.00
☐ **MARSHLANDER MALLARDS,** rel. 1973. ed. 600, s/n, 17″ x 26″, pub MPPI	60.00	70.00
☐ **PHEASANT COUNTRY,** rel. 1973. ed. 550, s/n, 22¾″ x 28½″, pub MPPI	60.00	210.00
☐ **WOOD DUCKS,** rel. 1973. ed. 550, s/n, 25½″ x 32″, pub MPPI	125.00	210.00
☐ **A BURST OF COLOR - RING-NECKED PHEASANTS,** rel. 1974. ed. 950, s/n, 20″ x 26″, pub MPPI	75.00	185.00
☐ **COURTSHIP FLIGHT - PINTAILS,** rel. 1974. ed. 950, s/n, 15″ x 21″, pub MPPI	75.00	185.00
☐ **EARLY ARRIVALS - MALLARDS,** rel. 1974. ed. 950, s/n, 13″ x 18″, pub MPPI	50.00	135.00
☐ **FLOODED OAKS - MALLARDS,** rel. 1974. ed. 850, s/n, 23″ x 31½″, pub MPPI	150.00	310.00
☐ **MALLARDS - DROPPING IN,** rel. 1974. ed. 950, s/n, 20″ x 26″, pub MPPI	75.00	160.00
☐ **QUAIL COVER,** rel. 1974. ed. 750, s/n, 25″ x 30½″, pub MPPI	150.00	360.00
☐ **SNOW GEESE - BLUE GEESE,** rel. 1974. ed. 950, s/n, 23″ x 23½″, pub MPPI	150.00	185.00
☐ **SNOWY CREEK - MALLARDS,** rel. 1974. ed. 950, s/n, 20″ x 26″, pub MPPI	75.00	210.00

	ISSUE PRICE	CURRENT PRICE
☐ SOLITUDE - WHITETAIL DEER, rel. 1974. ed. 950, s/n, 20″ x 27½″, pub MPPI	85.00	160.00
☐ THE PASSING STORM-CANVASBACKS, rel. 1974. ed. 950, s/n, 13″ x 18″, pub MPPI	50.00	110.00
☐ THE SANDBAR - CANADA GEESE, rel. 1974. ed. 950, s/n, 13″ x 18″, pub MPPI ...	50.00	110.00
☐ WINGING SOUTH - CANADA GEESE, rel. 1974. ed. 750, s/n, 23″ x 31¼″, pub MPPI	150.00	285.00
☐ WOODED SECLUSION - TURKEY, rel. 1974. ed. 950, s/n, 20″ x 26″, pub MPPI	75.00	135.00
☐ AFTERNOON SHADOWS - BOBWHITES, rel. 1975. ed. 950, s/n, 20″ x 27½″, pub MPPI	100.00	360.00
☐ HAZY DAY - BOBWHITES, rel. 1975. ed. 950, s/n, 22½″ x 31″, pub MPPI	150.00	410.00
☐ AUTUMN TRIO - RING-NECKED PHEASANTS, rel. 1976. ed. 950, s/n, 20″ x 26″, pub MPPI	85.00	260.00
☐ CANADA GEESE - COMING IN, rel. 1976. ed. 950, s/n, 20″ x 25″, pub MPPI	85.00	185.00
☐ DARK SKY - MALLARDS, rel. 1976. ed. 950, s/n, 20″ x 26″, pub MPPI	85.00	685.00
☐ FLIGHT - CANADA GEESE, rel. 1976. ed. 950, s/n, 14″ x 20″, pub MPPI	50.00	110.00
☐ GENTOO PENGUINS, rel. 1976. ed. 260, hand-colored stone litho, 16″ x 20″, pub MPPI	125.00	185.00
☐ GOOD FETCH - LABRADOR RETRIEVER, rel. 1976. ed. 950, s/n, 22½″ x 31″, pub MPPI	150.00	210.00
☐ SHALLOW POND - MALLARDS, rel. 1976. ed. 950, s/n, 22″ x 29″, pub MPPI	125.00	135.00
☐ THE RAIL FENCE - BOBWHITES, rel. 1976. ed. 950, s/n, 20″ x 25″, pub MPPI	85.00	185.00
☐ THUNDERHEAD - CANADA GEESE, rel. 1976. ed. 260, stone litho, 20½″ x 17″, pub MPPI	125.00	310.00
☐ WEATHERED WOOD - BOBWHITES, rel. 1976. ed. 950, s/n, 14″ x 20″, pub MPPI ..	50.00	160.00
☐ COVEY RISE - BOBWHITE, rel. 1977. ed. 950, s/n, 25″ x 38″, pub MPPI	150.00	610.00
☐ DARK SHADOWS - WHITETAIL DEER, rel. 1977. ed. 950, s/n, 20″ x 26″, pub MPPI	85.00	135.00
☐ EASY LANDING - PINTAILS, rel. 1977. ed. 950, s/n, 21″ x 27½″, pub MPPI	95.00	210.00
☐ GRACEFUL PAIR - RING-NECKED PHEASANTS, rel. 1977. ed. 950, s/n, 14″ x 20″, pub MPPI	50.00	135.00
☐ JUMPING GREENWINGS - GREEN-WINGED TEAL, rel. 1977. ed. 950, s/n, 24½″ x 19½″, pub MPPI	85.00	160.00
☐ NINE TRAVELERS - CANADA GEESE, rel. 1977. ed. 950, s/n, 21″ x 27½″, pub MPPI	95.00	185.00
☐ QUIET POND - MALLARDS, rel. 1977. ed. 950, s/n, 20½″ x 27½″, pub MPPI	95.00	160.00
☐ RESTING - WOOD DUCKS, rel. 1977. ed. 950, s/n, 14″ x 20″, pub MPPI	50.00	110.00
☐ STICK POND - MALLARDS, rel. 1977. ed. 950, s/n, 22″ x 29″, pub MPPI	125.00	160.00
☐ THE BIRCH - RUFFED GROUSE, rel. 1977. ed. 950, s/n, 20½″ x 27½″, pub MPPI .	85.00	—
☐ THE SENTINEL - WHITETAIL DEER, rel. 1977. ed. 950, s/n, 23″ x 31″, pub MPPI ...	150.00	185.00
☐ THROUGH THE TREES - WOOD DUCKS, rel. 1977. ed. 950, s/n, 21″ x 27½″, pub MPPI	95.00	410.00
☐ CHINSTRAP PENGUINS, rel. 1978. ed. 950, s/n, 17½″ x 22″, pub MPPI	50.00	—
☐ CRESCENT LAKE - MALLARDS, rel. 1978. ed. 950, s/n, 22″ x 29″, pub MPPI	125.00	185.00
☐ DARK SKY - CANADA GEESE, rel. 1978. ed. 950, s/n, 25″ x 35″, pub MPPI	175.00	310.00
☐ NEW SNOW - WHITETAIL DEER, rel. 1978. ed. 950, s/n, 22″ x 29″, pub MPPI	95.00	120.00
☐ OAK FOREST - TURKEY, rel. 1978. ed. 950, s/n, 22″ x 29″, pub MPPI	125.00	225.00
☐ OVER THE POINT - LESSER SCAUPS, rel. 1978. ed. 950, s/n, 21″ x 29″, pub MPPI	125.00	145.00
☐ RENDEZVOUS - WHITE-FRONTED GEESE, rel. 1978. ed. 950, s/n, 20″ x 27″, pub MPPI	85.00	—
☐ ROUGH WATER - CANVASBACKS, rel. 1978. ed. 950, s/n, 22″ x 30″, pub MPPI	150.00	210.00
☐ WINTER COVEY - BOBWHITES, rel. 1978. ed. 950, s/n, 25″ x 38″, pub MPPI	225.00	660.00
☐ DARK SKY - BOBWHITES, rel. 1979. ed. 950, s/n, 25″ x 35″, pub MPPI	225.00	410.00
☐ PHEASANT COVER - RING-NECKED PHEASANTS, rel. 1979. ed. 950, s/n, 23½″ x 32″, pub MPPI	175.00	325.00
☐ QUAIL COUNTRY, rel. 1979. ed. 950, s/n, 25″ x 35″, pub MPPI	250.00	335.00
☐ REGAL FLIGHT - WHISTLING SWANS, rel. 1979. ed. 950, s/n, 29½″ x 27½″, pub MPPI	125.00	160.00
☐ RENDEZVOUS, rel. 1979. ed. 950, s/n, 20½″ x 27½″, pub MPPI	85.00	95.00
☐ SUNRISE - GREEN WINGED TEAL, rel. 1979. ed. 950, s/n, 23″ x 31½″, pub MPPI .	150.00	210.00
☐ THE MARSH, rel. 1979. ed. 950, s/n, 18″ x 23″, pub MPPI	75.00	110.00
☐ THE QUIET PLACE - CANADA GEESE, rel. 1979. ed. 950, s/n, 25″ x 38″, pub MPPI	175.00	235.00

	ISSUE PRICE	CURRENT PRICE
☐ THE VALLEY - PINTAILS, rel. 1979. ed. 950, s/n, 23″ x 31½″, pub MPPI	150.00	210.00
☐ WINDY DAY - MALLARDS, rel. 1979. ed. 950, s/n, 23″ x 31½″, pub MPPI	150.00	210.00
☐ ALONG THE SHORE - REDHEADS, rel. 1980. ed. 950, s/n, 23″ x 31½″, pub MPPI .	160.00	185.00
☐ COLD MORNING - MALLARDS, rel. 1980. ed. 950, s/n, 23⅝″ x 33½″, pub MPPI . . .	175.00	185.00
☐ DARK SKY - CANVASBACKS, rel. 1980. ed. 950, s/n, 24½″ x 37¼″, pub MPPI	195.00	235.00
☐ DIAMOND ISLAND - MALLARDS, rel. 1980. ed. 950, s/n, 22½″ x 38″, pub MPPI . . .	195.00	270.00
☐ LANDING - CANADA GEESE, rel. 1980. ed. 950, s/n, 22″ x 27½″, pub MPPI	125.00	135.00
☐ MOUNTAIN SNOW, rel. 1980. ed. 950, s/n, 22¾″ x 29″, pub MPPI	95.00	185.00
☐ POINTERS AND BOBWHITES, rel. 1980. ed. 950, s/n, 24⅝″ x 35″, pub MPPI	245.00	310.00
☐ QUAIL COUNTRY, rel. 1980. ed. 950, s/n, 24⅞″ x 35¼″, pub MPPI	250.00	260.00
☐ THE WILLOW - GREEN-WINGED TEAL, rel. 1980. ed. 950, s/n, 23″ x 31½″, pub MPPI	160.00	210.00
☐ TIMBER - WOOD DUCKS, rel. 1980. ed. 950, s/n, 23″ x 31½″, pub MPPI	160.00	210.00
☐ TUNDRA - BLACK BRANT, rel. 1980. ed. 950, s/n, 20½″ x 27½″, pub MPPI	85.00	110.00
☐ TWILIGHT - AMERICAN WIGEON, rel. 1980. ed. 950, s/n, 18″ x 23″, pub MPPI	75.00	135.00
☐ DARK SKY - RUFFED GROUSE, rel. 1981. ed. 950, s/n, 24⅝″ x 36″, pub MPPI	245.00	310.00
☐ DARK SKY - SNOW GEESE, rel. 1981. ed. 950, s/n, 21¾″ x 29½″, pub MPPI	175.00	185.00
☐ EARLY SPRING - MALLARDS, rel. 1981. ed. 950, s/n, 24⅝″ x 36″, pub MPPI	220.00	230.00
☐ ESCAPE - RING-NECKED PHEASANTS, rel. 1981. ed. 950, s/n, 23″ x 32¼″, pub MPPI	195.00	205.00
☐ FROSTY MORNING - CANADA GEESE, rel. 1981. ed. 950, s/n, 28½″ x 22¾″, pub MPPI	175.00	285.00
☐ OUT OF THE PINES - BOBWHITES, rel. 1981. ed. 950, s/n, 24⅝″ x 38″, pub MPPI .	245.00	310.00
☐ SHALLOW RIVER - AMERIGAN WIGEON, rel. 1981. ed. 950, s/n, 24⅝″ x 38″, pub MPPI	195.00	205.00
☐ SUNSET - CANADA GEESE, rel. 1981. ed. 950, s/n, 23″ x 32¼″, pub MPPI	195.00	205.00
☐ BASS AND OTHER SUNFISH, rel. 1982. ed. 950, s/n, 24″ x 18″, pub MPPI	10.00	15.00
☐ BREAKING AWAY - PINTAILS, rel. 1982. ed. 950, s/n, 21¾″ x 29½″, pub MPPI	150.00	160.00
☐ FLOODED TIMBER - MALLARDS, rel. 1982. ed. 450, no other information available .	150.00	820.00
☐ HEAVY SNOW - RUFFED GROUSE, rel. 1982. ed. 950, s/n, 20″ x 26¼″, pub MPPI .	150.00	160.00
☐ MINIATURE SERIES I - MALLARDS, rel. 1982. ed. 950, s/n, 12″ x 15⅞″, pub MPPI .	75.00	85.00
☐ MINIATURE SERIES II - WOOD DUCKS, rel. 1982. ed. 950, s/n, 12″ x 15⅞″, pub MPPI	75.00	85.00
☐ QUAIL COVEY - BOBWHITES, rel. 1982. ed. 950, s/n, 24½″ x 35¾″, pub MPPI	245.00	255.00
☐ STONY LAKE - MALLARDS, rel. 1982. ed. 950, s/n, 17⅞″ x 24″, pub MPPI	100.00	—
☐ THE SPLASH - SMALLMOUTH BASS, rel. 1982. ed. 950, s/n, 18¾″ x 24″, pub MPPI	95.00	—
☐ ALONG THE RIVER - TRUMPETER SWAN, rel. 1983. ed. 950, s/n, 12″ x 16″, pub MPPI	50.00	—
☐ COASTING DOWN - CANADA GEESE, rel. 1983. ed. 950, s/n, 8¼″ x 10″, pub MPPI	40.00	—
☐ DARK SKY - PHEASANTS, rel. 1983. ed. 950, s/n, 21¾″ x 29½″, pub MPPI	125.00	—
☐ PREENING - BLUE WINGED TEAL, rel. 1983. ed. 950, s/n, 18¾″ x 22½″, pub MPPI	115.00	—
☐ RUNNING BLUES, SCALED QUAIL, rel. 1983. ed. 950, s/n, 17⅞″ x 24″, pub MPPI .	100.00	—
☐ TRANQUIL MARSH - MALLARDS, rel. 1983. ed. 950, s/n, 11″ x 15″, pub MPPI	60.00	—
☐ DARK SKY - PINTAILS, rel. 1984. ed. 950, s/n, 21¾″ x 29½″, pub MPPI	125.00	—
☐ WETLAND HERITAGE - CANADA GEESE, rel. 1984. ed. 500, s/n, 17½″ x 24″, pub MPPI	—	—
1948-49 FEDERAL DUCK STAMP PRINT		
☐ BUFFLEHEAD - Stone Litho, 1st edition - 200, s/n, 13″ x 18″	15.00	1,100.00
2nd edition - 150, s/n, 13″ x 18″	15.00	950.00
3rd edition - 400, s/n, 13″ x 18″	60.00	700.00
Color Edition (reproduced from original watercolor), 350, s/n, 13″ x 18″	250.00	400.00
1951-52 FEDERAL DUCK STAMP PRINT		
☐ GADWALLS - Stone Litho, 1st edition - 250, s/n, 13″ x 18″	150.00	1,000.00
2nd edition - 400, s/n, 13″ x 18″	60.00	700.00
1959-60 FEDERAL DUCK STAMP PRINT		
☐ LABRADOR RETRIEVER - Stone Litho, 1st edition - 400, s/n, 13″ x 18″	60.00	1,200.00
2nd edition - 300, s/n, 13″ x 18″	60.00	1,000.00
3rd edition - 400, s/n, 13″ x 18″	60.00	950.00

	ISSUE PRICE	CURRENT PRICE
1969-70 FEDERAL DUCK STAMP PRINT		
☐ **WHITE-WINGED SCOTERS** - Stone Litho, 1st edition - 750, s/n, 13″ x 18″	60.00	850.00
1971-72 FEDERAL DUCK STAMP PRINT		
☐ **CINNAMON TEAL** - Litho, Hand-colored. 1st edition - 950, s/n, 13″ x 18″	75.00	4,500.00
1972 IOWA DUCK STAMP PRINT		
☐ **MALLARDS** - Reproduced from original watercolor. 1st edition - 500, s/n, 13″ x 17″ ..	60.00	3,500.00
1977 IOWA DUCK STAMP PRINT		
☐ **BLUEBILLS - LESSER SCAUP** - Reproduced from original watercolor. 1st edition - 950, s/n, 12½″ x 17″	80.00	700.00
1973 DUCKS UNLIMITED PRINT		
☐ **MARSHLANDER MALLARDS,** ed. 600, s/n, 23½″ x 32″	Auctioned	550.00
☐ **MALLARDS,** rel. 1969. ed. 1,500, s/n, 21¾″ x 26¼″	*N/A	N/A
*Distributed by Winnebago Industries		
☐ **CANADA GEESE,** rel. 1971. ed. 1,500, s/n, 21¾″ x 26¼″	*N/A	N/A
*Distributed by Winnebago Industries		

JOYCE HAGERBAUMER REED

THEMES: Wildlife art

EDUCATION: University of California at Los Angeles; University of California at Santa Barbara

GALLERY/DISTRIBUTOR: Wild Wings, Inc.

	ISSUE PRICE	CURRENT PRICE
☐ **BACKWATER TEAL,** rel. 1974. ed. 450, s/n, size not available, pub WWI	85.00	—
☐ **WINTERING DOVES,** rel. 1975. ed. 450, s/n, 16″ x 22″, pub WWI	60.00	—
☐ **QUIET MORNING - MALLARDS,** rel. 1981. ed. 850, s/n, size not available, pub WWI	60.00	—

CHUCK REN

THEMES: Western art

BACKGROUND: The artist painted the 1980 Super Bowl poster and program and has been commissioned by several major companies

EDUCATION: University of Arizona

GALLERY/DISTRIBUTOR: Grey Stone Press

	ISSUE PRICE	CURRENT PRICE
☐ **AFTER THE RIDE,** ed. 600, s/n, 18¾″ x 24½″, pub GSP	75.00	—
☐ **FIRST SNOW,** ed. 600, s/n, 27¾″ x 22½″, pub GSP	75.00	150.00
☐ **GRAND DAD'S WAGON,** ed. 600, s/n, 21″ x 25½″, pub GSP	75.00	—
☐ **THE CHAMPIONS,** ed. 600, s/n, 29½″ x 22½″, pub GSP	75.00	—
☐ **HOW THE WEST WAS WON,** rel. 1980. ed. 600, s/n, 18¾″ x 24½″, pub GSP	75.00	—

HOW THE WEST WAS WON *by Chuck Ren*

	ISSUE PRICE	CURRENT PRICE
☐ **THE MOUNTAIN MEN,** rel. 1981. ed. 600, s/n, 22″ x 24½″, pub GSP	75.00	150.00
ed. 100, remarqued Artist proofs	125.00	250.00
☐ **DOUBLE TROUBLE,** rel. 1982. ed. 600, s/n, 29″ x 21⅛″, pub GSP	75.00	—
ed. 10, remarqued Artist proofs	125.00	—
☐ **THE STRANGER,** rel. 1982. ed. 600, s/n, 29½″ x 22½″, pub GSP	75.00	—
☐ **THE HUNTERS,** rel. 1983. ed. 1,000, s/n, 28½″ x 22½″, pub GSP	75.00	—
ed. 100, remarqued	150.00	—
☐ **WOLFSMAN,** rel. 1983. ed. 600, s/n, 24½″ x 22″, pub GSP	75.00	—
ed. 100, remarqued	150.00	—
☐ **TO CATCH A THIEF,** rel. 1984. ed. 1,000, s/n, 29½″ x 17½″, pub GSP	75.00	—
Artist proofs, remarqued	150.00	—
☐ **THE MYSTIC WARRIOR,** rel. 1985. ed. 1,000, s/n, 29½″ x 21″, pub GSP	80.00	400.00

CHET RENESON

THEMES: Wildlife art

EDUCATION: University of Hartford Art School

GALLERY/DISTRIBUTOR: Wild Wings, Inc.

	ISSUE PRICE	CURRENT PRICE
☐ **SNOW SQUALL,** rel. 1972. ed. 400, s/n, 27″ x 17″, distr. WWI	—	400.00
☐ **OPENING DAY,** rel. 1974. ed. 400, s/n, 26″ x 16″, distr. WWI	—	400.00
☐ **WINTER GROUSE,** rel. 1974. ed. 400, s/n, 26″ x 16″, distr. WWI	—	125.00
☐ **CORN HUNTERS,** rel. 1976. ed. 400, s/n, 27″ x 17″, distr. WWI	—	150.00
☐ **ON THE FLATS,** rel. 1976. ed. 200, s/n, 16″ x 26″, pub SEL	75.00	400.00
Remarqued print	100.00	550.00
☐ **WINTER BROADBILLS,** rel. 1976. ed. 200, s/n, 26″ x 16″, distr. WWI	—	225.00
☐ **EARLY VISIT,** rel. 1977. ed. 580, s/n, 26″ x 16″, distr. WWI	—	350.00
☐ **AMBUSH,** rel. 1978. ed. 200, s/n, 26″ x 16″, distr. WWI	—	200.00
☐ **IN THE KEYS,** rel. 1978. ed. 300, s/n, 16½″ x 25⅛, pub SEL	75.00	175.00
Remarqued print	125.00	200.00
☐ **MATCHMAKERS,** rel. 1978. ed. 300, s/n, 26″ x 16″, distr. WWI	—	200.00
☐ **WILD FLOWERS,** rel. 1978. ed. 300, s/n, 26″ x 16″, distr. WWI	—	200.00
☐ **TEA TIME,** rel. 1979. ed. 400, s/n, 18″ x 27¼″, pub SEL	100.00	125.00
Remarqued print	150.00	175.00
☐ **WINTER MARSH,** rel. 1980. ed. 400, s/n, 26″ x 16″, distr. WWI	—	75.00
☐ **FLIGHT BIRDS,** rel. 1981. ed. 400, s/n, size not available, distr. WWI	—	150.00
☐ **GOOD LUCK WIND,** rel. 1981. ed. 200, s/n, 16″ x 11″, distr. WWI	—	125.00
☐ **OUT OF REACH,** rel. 1981. ed. 500, s/n, size not available, distr. WWI	—	150.00
☐ **PARTNERS,** rel. 1981. ed. 500, s/n, size not available, distr. WWI	—	40.00
☐ **WALKING THE RIFFLES,** rel. 1981. ed. 500, s/n, 16″ x 11″, distr. WWI	—	40.00
☐ **WELL HOOKED,** rel. 1981. ed. 500, s/n, size not available, distr. WWI	—	100.00
☐ **BAYGUNNERS,** rel. 1982. ed. 300, s/n, 29″ x 21″, distr. WWI	—	200.00
☐ **TROPHY FISH,** rel. 1982. ed. 400, s/n, size not available, distr. WWI	—	100.00
☐ **PARTRIDGE TREE,** rel. 1983. ed. 500, s/n, litho, 11″ x 16″, pub WWI	50.00	—
☐ **POTHOLE CREEK,** rel. 1983. ed. 500, s/n, litho, 11″ x 16″, pub WWI	50.00	—
☐ **SECRET POOL,** rel. 1983. ed. 500, s/n, litho, 11″ x 16″, pub WWI	50.00	—
☐ **CAUGHT IN THE OPEN,** rel. 1984. ed. 400, s/n, litho, 11″ x 15½″, pub WWI	50.00	—
☐ **EARLY SEASON,** rel. 1984. ed. 400, s/n, litho, 16½″ x 25½″, pub WWI	100.00	—
☐ **FIRST RUN,** rel. 1985. ed. 400, s/n, litho, 11″ x 16″, pub WWI	50.00	—
☐ **GOOD OLD DAYS,** rel. 1985. ed. 400, s/n, litho, 16″ x 25½″, pub WWI	100.00	—
☐ **ON POINT,** rel. 1984. ed. 400, s/n, litho, 16½″ x 25½″, pub WWI	100.00	—
☐ **SEASON'S BEST,** rel. 1985. ed. 400, s/n, litho, 11″ x 16″, pub WWI	60.00	—

JAMES REYNOLDS

THEMES: Contemporary Western art

GALLERY/DISTRIBUTOR: Mill Pond Press, Inc.

COMMENTS: Among the people who appreciate contemporary Western art, Jim Reynolds' name will appear at, or near, the top of everyone's choices of "the best"

COFFEE BREAK *by James Reynolds*

	ISSUE PRICE	CURRENT PRICE
☐ **THE GOOD LIFE,** rel. 1975. ed. 950, s/n, 23″ x 31½″, pub MPPI	150.00	400.00
☐ **BORN TOO EARLY,** rel. 1979. ed. 950, s/n, 23″ x 30½″, pub MPPI	150.00	225.00
☐ **EATIN' DUST,** rel. 1979. ed. 950, s/n, 21″ x 29″, pub MPPI	125.00	—
☐ **COFFEE BREAK,** rel. 1981. ed. 950, s/n, 23″ x 31⅛″, pub MPPI	175.00	—
☐ **SPRING CALVES,** rel. 1981. ed. 950, s/n, 23″ x 32¼″, pub MPPI	195.00	—
☐ **ANOTHER DAY,** rel. 1983. ed. 1,000, s/n, 17″ x 25½″, pub TAP	100.00	—
☐ **COLORADO COLD,** rel. 1983. ed. 1,000, s/n, 17″ x 25½″, pub TAP	100.00	—

ROBERT RICHERT

THEMES: Wildlife art

GALLERY/DISTRIBUTOR: Voyageur Art

	ISSUE PRICE	CURRENT PRICE
☐ **BIRD IN LEAVES,** rel. 1979. ed. 950, s/n, 13″ x 16″, litho, pub VA	40.00	—
☐ **CALIFORNIA DUCK STAMP 1982,** rel. 1982. ed. 950, s/n, litho, pub VA	125.00	—
☐ **CANVASBACKS,** rel. 1981. ed. 780, s/n, 13″ x 16″, litho, pub VA	30.00	—
☐ **CEDAR WAXWINGS,** rel. 1983. ed. unlimited, 11¼″ x 8½″, litho, pub VA	8.00	—
☐ **DUCK HEADS,** rel. 1983. ed. unlimited, s/n, 6″ x 8″, litho, pub VA	5.00	—
☐ **EAGLEHEAD,** rel. 1980. ed. 550, s/n, 17½″ x 15½″, litho, pub VA	40.00	—
☐ **LESSER SCAUP,** rel. 1981. ed. 780, s/n, 13″ x 16″, litho, pub VA	30.00	—

	ISSUE PRICE	CURRENT PRICE
☐ **REDHEAD,** rel. 1981. ed. 780, s/n, 13″ x 16″, litho, pub VA	30.00	—
☐ **RINGBILL,** rel. 1981. ed. 780, s/n, 13″ x 16″, litho, pub VA	30.00	—
☐ **RINGNECK PHEASANT,** rel. 1980. ed. 950, s/n, 13″ x 16″, litho, pub VA	30.00	—
☐ **WILSON WARBLER,** rel. 1983. ed. unlimited, 11″ x 7½″, litho, pub VA	8.00	—
☐ **WOODDUCKS ON LOG,** rel. 1980. ed. 950, s/n, 20″ x 24″, litho, pub VA	40.00	

1982 CALIFORNIA DUCK STAMP *by Robert Richert*

MICHAEL JAMES RIDDET

THEMES: Birds

STYLE: Realism

GALLERY/DISTRIBUTOR: Northwoods Craftsman

	ISSUE PRICE	CURRENT PRICE
☐ **AMERICAN GOLDFINCH,** rel. 1972. ed. 4,700, s/o, 11″ x 14″, pub CHWA	12.00	25.00
ed. 200, s/n	30.00	—
ed. 100 Artist proofs		
☐ **BLUE JAY,** rel. 1972. ed. 4,700, s/o, 11″ x 14″, pub CHWA	12.00	25.00
ed. 200, s/n	30.00	—
ed. 100 Artist proofs		
☐ **CARDINAL,** rel. 1972. ed. 4,700, s/o, 11″ x 14″, pub CHWA	12.00	25.00
ed. 200, s/n	30.00	—

1984 WISCONSIN DUCK STAMP *by Michael Riddet*

	ISSUE PRICE	CURRENT PRICE
☐ **EASTERN BLUEBIRD,** rel. 1972. ed. 4,700, s/o, 11″ x 14″, pub CHWA	12.00	25.00
ed. 200, s/n	30.00	—
ed. 100 Artist proofs		
☐ **EASTERN MEADOWLARK,** rel. 1972. ed. 4,700, s/o, 11″ x 14″, pub CHWA	12.00	25.00
ed. 200, s/n	30.00	—
ed. 100 Artist proofs		
☐ **ROBIN,** rel. 1972. ed. 4,700, s/o, 11″ x 14″, pub CHWA	12.00	25.00
ed. 200, s/n	30.00	—
ed. 100 Artist proofs		
☐ **WOOD THRUSH,** rel. 1972. ed. 4,700, s/o, 11″ x 14″, pub CHWA	12.00	25.00
ed. 200, s/n	30.00	—
ed. 100 Artist proofs		
☐ **WISCONSIN DUCK STAMP,** rel. 1984. ed. 1,500, s/n, 6½″ x 9″, pub NC	135.00	—
☐ **1984 WISCONSIN DUCK STAMP PRINT,** rel. 1984. ed. 1,500, s/n, 14″ x 12″, pub NC	135.00	—
Color remarqued, ed. 100	350.00	—
Pencil remarqued, ed. 200	250.00	—
☐ **SPRINGTIME SPLENDOR,** rel. 1985. ed. 600, s/n, 9½″ x 13″, pub NC	40.00	—

HAROLD RIGSBY

THEMES: Wildlife art

EDUCATION: Indiana University; Western Kentucky University; Louisville School of Art, etc.

GALLERY/DISTRIBUTOR: Harold Rigsby Graphics

RACCOON II *by Harold Rigsby*

	ISSUE PRICE	CURRENT PRICE
☐ *SIBERIAN TIGER, rel. 1978. ed. 500, s/n, pub HRG	20.00	325.00
*ed. 2,500, s/o	15.00	225.00
☐ *CHEETAH, rel. 1978. ed. 500, s/n, pub HRG	20.00	50.00
*ed. 1,500, s/o	15.00	15.00
☐ *AFRICAN LION, rel. 1978. ed. 500, s/n, pub HRG	20.00	100.00
*ed. 2,000, s/o	15.00	50.00
☐ *BOBCAT, rel. 1979. ed. 500, s/n, pub HRG	15.00	75.00
*ed. 750, s/o	10.00	50.00
☐ *RACCOON, rel. 1979. ed. 500, s/n, pub HRG	15.00	75.00
*ed. 750, s/o	10.00	50.00
☐ BENGAL TIGER, rel. 1979. ed. 500, s/n, pub HRG	20.00	20.00
*ed. 1,000, s/o	15.00	15.00
☐ *SNOW TIGER, rel. 1979. ed. 500, s/n, pub HRG	25.00	100.00
*ed. 1,000, s/o	20.00	50.00
☐ SNOW LEOPARD, rel. 1979. ed. 500, s/n, pub HRG	25.00	25.00
*ed. 1,000, s/o	20.00	20.00
☐ *TIGER CUB, rel. 1980. ed. 500, s/n, pub HRG	20.00	150.00
*ed. 1,000, s/o	15.00	75.00
☐ *WHITE TIGER CUB, rel. 1980. ed. 500, s/n, pub HRG	20.00	150.00
*ed. 1,000, s/o	15.00	75.00
☐ *GIRAFFE, rel. 1980. ed. 500, s/n, pub HRG	25.00	60.00
*ed. 1,000, s/o	20.00	20.00
☐ *KOALA, rel. 1980. ed. 500, s/n, pub HRG	25.00	50.00
*ed. 1,000, s/o	20.00	20.00
☐ *BENGAL TIGER II, rel. 1980. ed. 200, s/n, pub HRG	50.00	300.00
☐ *AFRICAN LION II, rel. 1980. ed. 200, s/n, pub HRG	50.00	200.00
☐ LEOPARD, rel. 1980. ed. 1,500, s/n, pub HRG	25.00	25.00

	ISSUE PRICE	CURRENT PRICE
☐ **RED FOX I,** rel. 1980. ed. 950, s/n, pub HRG	30.00	30.00
☐ **RED FOX II,** rel. 1980. ed. 950, s/n, pub HRG	30.00	30.00
☐ **AFRICAN LION CUB,** rel. 1981. ed. 950, s/n, pub HRG	30.00	30.00
☐ ***ZEBRA FOAL,** rel. 1981. ed. 500, s/n, pub HRG	50.00	250.00
☐ **GREAT HORNED OWL,** rel. 1981. ed. 950, s/n, pub HRG	20.00	20.00
☐ **BENGAL TIGER III,** rel. 1981. ed. 950, s/n, pub HRG	40.00	40.00
☐ ***COTTONTAIL RABBIT,** rel. 1981. ed. 950, s/n, pub HRG	15.00	45.00
☐ ***COUGAR,** rel. 1982. ed. 500, s/n, pub HRG	50.00	250.00
☐ **POLAR BEAR,** rel. 1982. ed. 500, s/n, pub HRG	32.50	32.50
☐ ***TIGER IV,** rel. 1982. ed. 950, s/n, pub HRG	20.00	50.00
☐ ***COUGAR II,** rel. 1982. ed. 950, s/n, pub HRG	20.00	20.00
☐ ***GREY SQUIRREL,** rel. 1982. ed. 950, s/n, pub HRG	15.00	25.00
☐ ***BABY HARP SEAL,** rel. 1983. ed. 950, s/n, pub HRG	25.00	150.00
☐ **LSU BENGAL TIGER,** rel. 1983. ed. 2,000, s/o, pub HRG	25.00	20.00
☐ **WHITE BENGAL TIGER,** rel. 1983. ed. 950, s/n, pub HRG	20.00	15.00
☐ **BALD EAGLE,** rel. 1983. ed. 950, s/n, pub HRG	15.00	20.00
☐ **PELICAN,** rel. 1983. ed. 950, s/n, pub HRG	20.00	20.00
☐ ***BENGAL TIGER CUB,** rel. 1983. ed. 500, s/n, pub HRG	50.00	200.00
☐ **WHITETAIL DEER FAWN,** rel. 1983. ed. 950, s/n, pub HRG	35.00	35.00
☐ **PANDA,** rel. 1983. ed. 950, s/n, pub HRG	35.00	35.00
☐ **RACCOON,** rel. 1984. ed. 950, s/n, pub HRG	25.00	25.00

*No longer available from publisher.

GREAT HORNED OWL AT CROSS CREEK *by C. Ford Riley*

C. FORD RILEY

THEMES: Birds

MEDIUM: Watercolor

STYLE: He layers colors, creating the multitude of shades and illusions in his work

MUSEUMS/COLLECTIONS: His work is in numerous private and public collections

GALLERY/DISTRIBUTOR: C. Ford Riley & Company

	ISSUE PRICE	CURRENT PRICE
☐ FALL WOODCOCK, rel. 1979. ed. 150, s/n, 30" x 22", pub CFRC	75.00	Sold Out
☐ ROSIE-BREASTED GROSBEAKS, rel. 1981. ed. 300, s/n, 30" x 22", pub CFRC	60.00	Sold Out
☐ PARULA WARBLERS ON A COOL FALL MORN, rel. 1982. ed. 800, s/n, 12" x 16", pub CFRC	30.00	—
☐ WOODCOCK AT McGIRTS CREEK, rel. 1982. ed. 500, s/n, 26" x 28", pub CFRC ...	100.00	—
☐ WOOD DUCKS AT McGIRTS CREEK, rel. 1982. ed. 500, s/n, 26" x 28", pub CFRC .	100.00	—
☐ YELLOW-BREASTED CHAT, rel. 1982. ed. 500, s/n, 30" x 22", pub FGA	100.00	—
☐ BLACK THROATED BLUE WARBLER, rel. 1983. ed. 500, s/n, 12" x 16", pub CFRC	42.00	—
☐ COOPERS HAWK WITH FALL LEAVES, rel. 1983. ed. 350, s/n, 30" x 22", pub CFRC	100.00	—
☐ MANDARIN CARDINALS WITH MAGNOLIAS, rel. 1983. ed. 350, s/n, 30" x 22", pub CFRC	100.00	Sold Out
☐ RED HEADED WOODPECKERS IN ST. JOHNS OAK, rel. 1983. ed. 300, s/n, 23" x 28", pub CFRC	100.00	Sold Out
☐ AMERICAN REDSTART, rel. 1984. ed. 500, s/n, 12" x 16", pub CFRC	42.00	—
☐ GREAT HORNED OWL AT CROSS CREEK, rel. 1984. ed. 350, s/n, 16" x 20", pub CFRC	75.00	—
☐ HOODED MERGANSERS AT MARSH LANDING, rel. 1984. ed. 150, s/n, 25" x 32", pub CFRC	100.00	Sold Out
☐ PAINTED BUNTINGS, rel. 1984. ed. 350, s/n, 30" x 22", pub CFRC	100.00	—
☐ THE CHALLENGE, rel. 1985. ed. 150, s/n, 26" x 34", pub CFRC	200.00	Sold Out

CHUCK RIPPER

THEMES: Wildlife art

GALLERY/DISTRIBUTOR: Russell A. Fink

	ISSUE PRICE	CURRENT PRICE
☐ BRIARPATCH COVEY, ed. 950, s/n, 16" x 24", pub RAF	40.00	—
☐ CARDINALS, ed. 950, s/n, 13" x 11", pub RAF	25.00	50.00
☐ EARLY FLIGHT - CANADA GEESE, ed. 950, s/n, 13" x 18", pub RAF	30.00	60.00
☐ MID-WINTER BOBWHITES, ed. 950, s/n, 16" x 23⅜", pub RAF	40.00	—

DELLA ROBERTS

THEMES: Varied

EDUCATION: Boston Museum of Fine Arts School; Randolph-Macon Woman's College

GALLERY/DISTRIBUTOR: Remarque Inc.

	ISSUE PRICE	CURRENT PRICE
☐ **ONE DAY,** rel. 1978. ed. 500, s/n, 17¾" x 15½", pub RI	40.00	40.00
☐ **SEA SHELLS,** rel. 1978. ed. 500, s/n, 9½" x 19", pub RI	50.00	50.00
☐ **GERANIUM AND SHELLS,** rel. 1979. ed. 500, s/n, 17¾" x 15½", pub RI	50.00	50.00
☐ **NARCISSI STUDY,** rel. 1981. ed. 750, s/n, 15¾" x 12½", pub RI	75.00	75.00

LINDA ROBERTS

THEMES: Snowscapes

MEDIUM: Watercolor

GALLERY/DISTRIBUTOR: Lindar Graphics

	ISSUE PRICE	CURRENT PRICE
☐ **FOUR PLAY,** rel. 1980. ed. 1,000, offset litho, 12" x 18", pub LLG	50.00	—
☐ **SOLITUDE,** rel. 1981. ed. 500, offset litho, 16½" x 21", pub LLG	80.00	—
☐ **STRATTON,** rel. 1981. ed. 750, offset litho, 14½" x 20¼", pub LLG	60.00	—
☐ **PARK CITY,** rel. 1982. ed. 1,000, offset litho, 15" x 21", pub LLG	50.00	—
☐ **JERRY FORD AMERICAN SKI CLASSIC,** rel. 1983. ed. 250, offset litho, 19" x 25¼", pub LLG	250.00	—
☐ **ANNAPOLIS ADRIFT,** rel. 1983. ed. 650, offset litho, 15¼" x 23¼", pub LLG	80.00	—
☐ **ECSTASY,** rel. 1983. ed. 1,000, offset litho, 15" x 21", pub LLG	50.00	—
☐ **1983 JERRY FORD GOLF,** rel. 1983. ed. 150, offset litho, 16" x 24", pub LLG	250.00	—
☐ **MOUNTAIN DAISIES,** rel. 1983. ed. 1,000, offset litho, 12½" x 21¾", pub LLG	60.00	—
☐ **IN THE AFTERGLOW,** rel. 1984. ed. 400, offset litho, 16¼" x 20⅝", pub LLG	100.00	—
☐ **RHYTHM II,** rel. 1984. ed. 1,000, offset litho, 12½" x 18", pub LLG	50.00	—

E. JOHN ROBINSON

THEMES: Marine art

MEDIUM: Oil

BOOKS: *Marine Painting in Oil; Seascape Painters' Problem Book*

EDUCATION: California College of Arts and Crafts, San Francisco State College

GALLERY/DISTRIBUTOR: Frame House Gallery, Inc.

	ISSUE PRICE	CURRENT PRICE
☐ **FROLIC,** rel. 1976. ed. 2,000, s/n, 22″ x 28″, pub FHG	30.00	60.00
☐ **FULL MOON,** rel. 1976. ed. 2,000, s/n, 22″ x 28″, pub FHG	30.00	60.00
☐ **BIG SUR COAST,** rel. 1977. ed. 800, s/n, 28″ x 22″, pub FHG	40.00	Sold Out
☐ **EVENTIDE,** rel. 1977. ed. 800, s/n, 16″ x 28″, pub FHG	40.00	80.00
☐ **PACIFIC NORTHWEST,** rel. 1977. ed. 800, s/n, 22″ x 28″, pub FHG	40.00	80.00
☐ **CHANCE OF RAIN,** rel. 1978. ed. 800, s/n, 16″ x 20″, pub FHG	30.00	Sold Out
☐ **KONA SURF,** rel. 1978. ed. 800, s/n, 16″ x 20″, pub FHG	30.00	Sold Out

NORMAN ROCKWELL

THEMES: Americana illustration

MEDIUM: Oil

BACKGROUND: Primary illustrator for *The Saturday Evening Post*

MUSEUMS/COLLECTIONS: The Old Corner House in Stockbridge houses the Rockwell Collection

GALLERY/DISTRIBUTOR: Circle Fine Arts Corp.

	ISSUE PRICE	CURRENT PRICE
☐ **A DAY IN THE LIFE OF A BOY,** rel. 1976. ed. 200, s/n, 19″ x 20″	1,000.00	6,000.00
ed. 25 on Japon, s/n, 19″ x 20″, litho, pub CFAC	1,050.00	6,250.00
☐ **A STUDY FOR THE DOCTOR'S OFFICE,** rel. 1976. ed. 200, s/n, 22″ x 25″, litho, pub CFAC	600.00	6,500.00
☐ **AMERICAN FAMILY FOLIO** (consisting of 5 prints). **Teacher's Pet, Fido's House, Two O'Clock Feeding, Debut, Save Me,** rel. 1976. ed. 200, s/n, 20″ x 26″, litho, pub CFAC	1,500.00	10,000.00
☐ **AT THE BARBER,** rel. 1976. ed. 200, s/n, 30″ x 22″, litho, pub CFAC	—	3,300.00
☐ **AVIARY,** rel. 1976. ed. 200, s/n, 20″ x 26″, litho, pub CFAC	200.00	3,300.00
☐ **BARBERSHOP QUARTET,** rel. 1976. ed. 200, s/n, 24″ x 30″, litho, pub CFAC	200.00	3,000.00
☐ **BLACKSMITH SHOP,** rel. 1976. ed. 200, s/n, 14″ x 30″, litho, pub CFAC	N/A	7,000.00
☐ **BOOKSELLER,** rel. 1976. ed. 200, s/n, 17″ x 23″	N/A	2,250.00
ed. 25 on Japon, s/n, 17″ x 23″, litho, pub CFAC	—	2,500.00
☐ **CHILDREN AT WINDOW,** rel. 1976. ed. 200, s/n, 20″ x 26″, litho, pub CFAC	350.00	1,700.00
☐ **CIRCUS,** rel. 1976. ed. 200, s/n, 20″ x 26″, litho, pub CFAC	N/A	1,750.00
☐ **COUNTY AGRICULTURAL AGENT,** rel. 1976. ed. 200, s/n, 24″ x 35″, collotype, pub CFAC	250.00	2,800.00
☐ **DISCOVERY,** rel. 1976. ed. 200, s/n, 28″ x 32″, collotype, pub CFAC	200.00	7,500.00
☐ **DOCTOR AND BOY,** rel. 1976. ed. 200, s/n, 20″ x 26″, litho, pub CFAC	N/A	2,000.00
☐ **DOCTOR AND DOLL,** rel. 1976. ed. 200, s/n, 29″ x 35″, collotype, pub CFAC	N/A	12,500.00
☐ **DRESSING UP,** rel. 1976. ed. 200, s/n, (in pencil), 20″ x 26″	300.00	2,800.00
ed. 60, s/n, (in ink), 20″ x 26″, litho, pub CFAC	350.00	3,500.00
☐ **FAMILY TREE,** rel. 1976. ed. 200, s/n, 25″ x 30″, litho, pub CFAC	N/A	4,500.00
☐ **FOOTBALL MASCOT,** rel. 1976. ed. 200, s/n, 20″ x 26″, litho, pub CFAC	N/A	1,800.00
☐ **FOUR SEASONS FOLIO** (consisting of 4 prints). **Winter, Spring, Summer, Autumn,** rel. 1976. ed. 200, s/n, 20″ x 21″	N/A	6,000.00
ed. 25 on Japon, s/n, 20″ x 21″, litho, pub CFAC	N/A	6,200.00
☐ **FREEDOM FROM FEAR,** rel. 1976. ed. 200, s/n, 29″ x 35″, collotype, pub CFAC	200.00	7,500.00
☐ **FREEDOM FROM WANT,** rel. 1976. ed. 200, s/n, 29″ x 35″, collotype, pub CFAC	200.00	7,500.00
☐ **FREEDOM OF RELIGION,** rel. 1976. ed. 200, s/n, 29″ x 35″, collotype, pub CFAC ...	200.00	7,500.00
☐ **FREEDOM OF SPEECH,** rel. 1976. ed. 200, s/n, 29″ x 35″, collotype, pub CFAC	200.00	7,500.00
☐ **GAIETY DANCE TEAM,** rel. 1976. ed. 200, s/n, 24″ x 30″, litho, pub CFAC	N/A	4,000.00

	ISSUE PRICE	CURRENT PRICE
☐ GIRL AT MIRROR, rel. 1976. ed. 200, s/n, 29″ x 35″, collotype, pub CFAC	N/A	8,500.00
☐ GOLDEN RULE, rel. 1976. ed. 200, s/n, 29″ x 35″, collotype, pub CFAC	N/A	3,500.00
☐ GOSSIPS, rel. 1976. ed. 200, s/n, 22″ x 25″	700.00	3,900.00
ed. 25 on Japon, s/n, 22″ x 25″, litho, pub CFAC	750.00	4,000.00
☐ HIGH DIVE, rel. 1976. ed. 200, s/n, 24″ x 30″, collotype, pub CFAC	500.00	2,000.00
☐ HUCK FINN FOLIO (consisting of 8 prints). Then Miss Watson, Jim Got Down on His Knees, Miss Mary Jane, My Hand Shook, Your Eyes is Lookin', The For Three Minutes, There Warn't No Harm, When I Lit My Candle, rel. 1976. ed. 200, s/n, 20″ x 26″, litho, pub CFAC	1,500.00	11,000.00
☐ ICHABOD CRANE, rel. 1976. ed. 200, s/n, 20″ x 26″, litho, pub CFAC	700.00	7,000.00
☐ JERRY, rel. 1976. ed. 200, s/n, 20″ x 26″, litho, pub CFAC	N/A	1,850.00
☐ LOBSTERMAN, rel. 1976. ed. 200, s/n, 29″ x 22″, litho, pub CFAC	—	4,100.00
☐ LINCOLN, rel. 1976. ed. 200, s/n, 20″ x 26″, litho, pub CFAC	600.00	12,500.00
☐ MARRIAGE LICENSE, rel. 1976. ed. 200, s/n, 28″ x 32″, collotype, pub CFAC	200.00	7,500.00
☐ MOVING DAY, rel. 1976. ed. 200, s/n, 24″ x 30″, collotype, pub CFAC	200.00	2,200.00
☐ MUSIC HATH CHARM, rel. 1976. ed. 200, s/n, 24″ x 30″, collotype, pub CFAC	300.00	5,000.00
☐ OUTWARD BOUND (Looking Out To Sea), rel. 1976. ed. 200, s/n, 29″ x 35″, collotype, pub CFAC	N/A	7,000.00
☐ PRESCRIPTION, rel. 1976. ed. 200, s/n, 24″ x 30″	800.00	6,000.00
ed. 25 on Japon, s/n, 24″ x 30″, litho, pub CFAC	850.00	6,200.00
☐ POOR RICHARD'S ALMANAC FOLIO (consisting of 7 prints). Ben Franklin's Philadelphia, The Drunkard, Ben's Belles, The Village Smithy, Ye Old Print Shoppe, The Golden Age, The Royal Crown, rel. 1976. ed. 200, s/n, 20″ x 26″, litho, pub CFAC ..	2,500.00	16,000.00
☐ PUPPIES, rel. 1976. ed. 200, s/n, 20″ x 26″, litho, pub CFAC	N/A	2,500.00
☐ RALEIGH THE DOG, rel. 1976. ed. 200, s/n, 29″ x 35″, collotype, pub CFAC	200.00	2,700.00
☐ ROCKET SHIP, rel. 1976. ed. 200, s/n, 20″ x 26″, litho, pub CFAC	N/A	1,750.00
☐ RUNAWAY, rel. 1976. ed. 200, s/n, 28″ x 32″, collotype, pub CFAC	200.00	4,800.00
☐ SAFE AND SOUND, rel. 1976. ed. 200, s/n, 17″ x 20″, litho, pub CFAC	N/A	1,900.00
☐ SATURDAY PEOPLE, rel. 1976. ed. 200, s/n, 24″ x 30″, collotype, pub CFAC	200.00	2,000.00
☐ SAYING GRACE, rel. 1976. ed. 200, s/n, 29″ x 35″, collotype, pub CFAC	N/A	7,500.00
☐ SCHOOL DAY FOLIO (consisting of 4 prints). Baseball, Golf, Studying, Cheering, rel. 1976. ed. 200, s/n, 20″ x 26″, litho, pub CFAC	1,800.00	8,000.00
☐ SEE AMERICA FIRST, rel. 1976. ed. 200, s/n, 17″ x 24″	700.00	5,000.00
ed. 25 on Japon, s/n, 17″ x 24″, litho, pub CFAC	750.00	5,250.00
☐ SETTLING IN. rel. 1976. ed. 200, s/n, 20″ x 26″, litho, pub CFAC	1,300.00	1,800.00
☐ SHUFFLETON'S BARBERSHOP, rel. 1976. ed. 200, s/n, 28″ x 35″, collotype, pub CFAC	N/A	7,500.00
☐ SPELLING BEE, rel. 1976. ed. 200, s/n, 14″ x 30″, litho, pub CFAC	200.00	7,000.00
☐ SPRING FLOWERS, rel. 1976. ed. 200, s/n, 27″ x 33″, collotype, pub CFAC	200.00	4,500.00
☐ SUMMER STOCK, rel. 1976. ed. 200, s/n, 21″ x 27″	600.00	4,200.00
ed. 25 on Japon, 21″ x 27″, litho, pub CFAC	650.00	4,500.00
☐ THE BRIDGE, rel. 1976. ed. 200, s/n, 20″ x 26″, litho, pub CFAC	N/A	2,200.00
☐ THE CRITIC, rel. 1976. ed. 200, s/n, 28″ x 32″, collotype, pub CFAC	200.00	3,750.00
☐ THE EXPECTED AND UNEXPECTED, rel. 1976. ed. 200, s/n, 17″ x 20″, litho, pub CFAC	500.00	2,500.00
☐ THE HOMECOMING, rel. 1976. ed. 200, s/n, 25″ x 30″, litho, pub CFAC	N/A	1,750.00
☐ THE HOUSE, rel. 1976. ed. 200, s/n, 20″ x 26″, litho, pub CFAC	N/A	1,850.00
☐ THE INVENTOR, rel. 1976. ed. 200, s/n, 19″ x 19″, litho, pub CFAC	N/A	3,000.00
☐ THE PROBLEM WE ALL LIVE WITH, rel. 1976. ed. 200, s/n, 31″ x 44″, collotype, pub CFAC	250.00	3,000.00
☐ THE SCHOOLHOUSE, rel. 1976. ed. 200, s/n, 15″ x 18″	350.00	1,650.00
ed. 25 on Japon, s/n, 15″ x 18″, litho, pub CFAC	400.00	1,750.00
☐ THE TEACHER, rel. 1976. ed. 200, s/n, 17″ x 23″	400.00	1,425.00
ed. 25 on Japon, s/n, 17″ x 23″, litho, pub CFAC	450.00	1,525.00
☐ THE TEXAN, rel. 1976. ed. 200, s/n, 24″ x 30″, collotype, pub CFAC	300.00	3,000.00
☐ TOM SAWYER FOLIO (consisting of 8 prints). Church, Smoking, Cat, Out The Window, White Washing, Grotton, Spanking, Medicine, rel. 1976. ed. 200, s/n, 20″ x 26″, litho, pub CFAC	3,000.00	16,000.00
☐ TOM SAWYER COLOR SUITE, rel. 1976. ed. 200, s/n, 20″ x 26″, combination of collotypes & lithos, pub CFAC	5,800.00	18,000.00
☐ TRUMPETER, rel. 1976. ed. 200, s/n, 21″ x 26″	N/A	2,900.00
ed. 25 on Japon, s/n, 21″ x 26″, litho, pub CFAC	N/A	2,900.00

	ISSUE PRICE	CURRENT PRICE
☐ WELCOME, rel. 1976. ed. 200, s/n, 20″ x 26″, litho, pub CFAC	N/A	1,600.00
☐ WET PAINT, rel. 1976. ed. 200, s/n, 24″ x 30″, collotype, pub CFAC	300.00	2,500.00
☐ WINDOW WASHER, rel. 1976. ed. 200, s/n, 20″ x 26″, litho, pub CFAC	250.00	1,800.00
☐ THREE FARMERS, rel. 1977. ed. 200, s/n, 20″ x 16″, litho, pub CFAC	275.00	1,500.00
☐ TICKETSELLER, rel. 1977. ed. 200, s/n, 21″ x 27″	800.00	2,200.00
ed. 25 on Japon, s/n, 21″ x 27″, litho, pub CFAC	850.00	2,500.00
☐ TOP OF THE WORLD, rel. 1977. ed. 200, s/n, 29″ x 35″, collotype, pub CFAC	200.00	2,100.00
☐ AMERICA MARCHES AHEAD, rel. 1976. ed. 260, s/n, 35″ x 20″, litho, pub EEI	350.00	2,300.00
☐ THREE BOYS FISHING, rel. 1978. ed. 260, s/n, 23″ x 33″, collotype, pub EEI	350.00	3,000.00
☐ COLONIAL SIGN PAINTER, rel. 1976. ed. 260, s/n, 35″ x 23″, litho, pub EEI	700.00	5,800.00
☐ THE RIVALS, rel. 1976. ed. 260, s/n, 20″ x 26″, litho, pub EEI	375.00	5,500.00
☐ APRIL FOOL, rel. 1976. ed. 260, s/n, 24″ x 26″, collotype, pub EEI	400.00	7,500.00
☐ BUTTERCUP, rel. 1976. ed. 260, s/n, 21″ x 24″, litho, pub EEI	450.00	5,500.00
ed. 25 on Japon, s/n	500.00	5,700.00
☐ PUPPY LOVE PORTFOLIO, rel. 1978. ed. 260, s/n, litho, pub EEI	1,500.00	15,000.00
☐ CHARWOMEN, rel. 1976. ed. 260, s/n, 25″ x 31″, collotype, pub EEI	600.00	7,000.00
☐ GILDING THE EAGLE, rel. 1978. ed. 260, s/n, 20″ x 26″, litho, pub EEI	600.00	3,800.00
ed. 25 on Japon	650.00	4,100.00
☐ BEN FRANKLIN, rel. 1978. ed. 260, s/n, 20″ x 26″, litho, pub EEI	1,100.00	4,200.00
ed. 25 on Japon	1,150.00	4,450.00
☐ CONVENTION, rel. 1978. ed. 260, s/n, 25″ x 31″, collotype, pub EEI	600.00	3,300.00
☐ THE SWING, rel. 1978. ed. 260, s/n, 20″ x 21″, litho, pub EEI	600.00	5,000.00
ed. 25 on Japon	650.00	5,300.00
☐ TOP HAT & TAILS, rel. 1978. ed. 260, s/n, 28″ x 34″, litho, pub EEI	1,000.00	8,000.00
☐ RACER, rel. 1978. ed. 260, s/n, 24″ x 29″, litho, pub EEI	600.00	2,300.00
ed. 25 on Japon	650.00	2,500.00
☐ FOOTBALL HERO, rel. 1978. ed. 260, s/n, litho, pub EEI	600.00	2,300.00
ed. 25 on Japon	650.00	2,500.00
☐ EXTRA GOOD BOYS & GIRLS, rel. 1978. ed. 260, s/n, 24″ x 31″, litho, pub EEI	900.00	6,000.00
ed. 25 on Japon	1,000.00	6,300.00
☐ SHE'S MY BABY, rel. 1978. ed. 260, s/n, 23″ x 31″, litho, pub EEI	600.00	2,700.00
ed. 25 on Japon	650.00	2,950.00
☐ YOUNG LINCOLN, rel. 1978. ed. 260, s/n, 19″ x 34″, litho, pub EEI	1,200.00	10,000.00
ed. 14 on Japon	1,500.00	10,500.00
☐ REJECTED SUITOR, rel. 1978. ed. 260, s/n, 21″ x 26″, litho, pub EEI	700.00	2,800.00
ed. 25 on Japon	750.00	3,050.00
☐ YOUNG SPOONERS, rel. 1978. ed. 260, s/n, 20″ x 24″, litho, pub EEI	700.00	6,300.00
	750.00	6,600.00
☐ SPORTS PORTFOLIO (consisting of 4 prints). **Basketball, Baseball, Golf, Football,** rel. 1978. ed. 260, s/n, litho, pub EEI	3,000.00	10,000.00
ed. 25 on Japon	3,200.00	11,000.00
☐ HAYSEED CRITIC, rel. 1978. ed. 260, s/n, 20″ x 26″, litho, pub EEI	700.00	3,600.00
ed. 25 on Japon	750.00	3,800.00
☐ BOY ON STILTS, rel. 1976. ed. 260, s/n, 24″ x 31″, litho, pub EEI	800.00	3,000.00
ed. 25 on Japon, rel. 1978	900.00	3,200.00
☐ BACK FROM CAMP, rel. 1978. ed. 260, s/n, 20″ x 26″, litho, pub EEI	800.00	2,800.00
ed. 25 on Japon	900.00	3,050.00
☐ DREAMS OF LONG AGO, rel. 1978. ed. 260, s/n, 20″ x 26″, litho, pub EEI	1,000.00	7,000.00
ed. 25 on Japon	1,100.00	7,250.00
☐ JESTER, rel. 1978. ed. 260, s/n, 20″ x 26″, litho, pub EEI	800.00	2,900.00
ed. 25 on Japon	900.00	3,150.00
☐ AFTER CHRISTMAS, rel. 1978. ed. 260, s/n, 20″ x 26″, litho, pub EEI	800.00	4,300.00
ed. 25 on Japon	900.00	4,500.00
☐ CAN'T WAIT, rel. 1978. ed. 260, s/n, 20″ x 26″, litho, pub EEI	800.00	4,200.00
ed. 25 on Japon	900.00	4,500.00
☐ CHILD'S SURPRISE, rel. 1978. ed. 260, s/n, 20″ x 26″, litho, pub EEI	1,000.00	4,200.00
ed. 25 on Japon	1,100.00	4,400.00
☐ VOYAGER, rel. 1978. ed. 260, s/n, 25″ x 32″, collotype, pub EEI	1,000.00	8,000.00
☐ THE WIND UP, rel. 1978. ed. 260, s/n, 23″ x 29″, litho, pub EEI	1,500.00	3,500.00
	1,700.00	3,750.00
☐ CATCHING THE BIG ONE, rel. 1978. ed. 260, s/n, 26″ x 34″, litho, pub EEI	1,000.00	3,300.00
ed. 25 on Japon	1,200.00	3,550.00

	ISSUE PRICE	CURRENT PRICE
☐ AFTER THE PROM, rel. 1978. ed. 260, s/n, 21″ x 27″, litho, pub EEI	1,500.00	4,400.00
ed. 25 on Japon	1,700.00	4,650.00
☐ HORSESHOE FORGING CONTEST, rel. 1978. ed. 260, s/n, 12″ x 25″, collotype, pub EEI...	3,500.00	10,000.00
☐ MUGGLETON STAGECOACH, rel. 1978. ed. 260, size not available, s/n, pub EEI ...	2,200.00	3,200.00
ed. 25 on Japon	2,400.00	3,400.00
☐ FIRST AIRPLANE RIDE, rel. 1980. ed. 260, s/n, 21″ x 26″, pub EEI	2,200.00	4,200.00
ed. 25 on Japon	2,400.00	4,400.00
☐ JAZZ IT UP, rel. 1980. ed. 260, s/n, 21″ x 28½″, pub EEI	2,200.00	3,200.00
ed. 25 on Japon	2,400.00	3,400.00
☐ SCHOOL WALK, rel. 1979. ed. 260, s/n, 25″ x 21″, pub EEI	2,000.00	4,200.00
ed. 25 on Japon	2,200.00	4,400.00
☐ LAW STUDENT, rel. 1980. ed. 260, s/n, 23¾″ x 32½″, litho, arches, pub EEI	3,200.00	5,200.00
ed. 25 on Japon	3,400.00	5,400.00
☐ TRIPLE SELF PORTRAIT, rel. 1979. ed. 260, s/n, 23½″ x 31½″, litho, arches, pub EEI...	5,000.00	13,000.00
ed. 25 on Japon	5,500.00	13,500.00
☐ SECRETS, rel. 1979. ed. 260, s/n, 21″ x 27″, litho, arches, pub EEI	2,000.00	4,000.00
ed. 25 on Japon	2,200.00	4,200.00
☐ CONNOISSEUR, rel. 1980. ed. 260, s/n, 24¼″ x 30¼″, collo, rives, pub EEI	6,000.00	10,000.00
☐ DREAMBOATS, rel. 1980. ed. 260, s/n, 24″ x 29¾″, litho, arches, pub EEI	2,000.00	4,000.00
ed. 25 on Japon	2,200.00	4,200.00
☐ STARSTRUCK, rel. 1980. ed. 260, s/n, 24″ x 29¾″, litho, arches, pub EEI	2,000.00	4,000.00
ed. 25 on Japon	2,200.00	4,200.00
☐ OUR HERITAGE, rel. 1980. ed. 260, s/n, 25″ x 33¼″, collo, rives, pub EEI	1,500.00	4,300.00
☐ UNDER SAIL, rel. 1981. ed. 260, s/n, 18½″ x 24¾″, litho, arches, pub EEI	2,000.00	2,600.00
ed. 25 on Japon	2,200.00	2,800.00
☐ FISHING, rel. 1981. ed. 260, s/n, 20½″ x 23″, litho, arches, pub EEI	1,900.00	3,000.00
ed. 25 on Japon	2,100.00	3,200.00
☐ JOHN KENNEDY, rel. 1982. ed. 260, s/n, 17″ x 23¼″, litho, arches, pub EEI	2,000.00	3,000.00
ed. 25 on Japon	2,200.00	3,400.00
☐ RUNAWAY, ed. 200, s/n, 26″ x 20″, litho, pub CFAC	—	2,500.00
☐ THE BIG DAY, ed. 200, s/n, 29″ x 21″, litho, pub CFAC	—	1,750.00
☐ THE BIG TOP, rel. 1982. ed. 200, s/n, 26″ x 20″, litho, pub CFAC	875.00	—

GEORGE RODRIGUE

THEMES: Louisiana themed art

BOOKS: *The Cajuns*

EDUCATION: Art Center of Design

AWARDS: *Who's Who in American Art; International Directory of Art; French Artist's Society*

MUSEUMS/COLLECTIONS: His works hang in museums and galleries worldwide

GALLERY/DISTRIBUTOR: George Rodrigue Gallery

	ISSUE PRICE	CURRENT PRICE
☐ AIOLI DINNER, ed. 300, s/n, 24″ x 32″, pub GRG	150.00	—
Artist proof	1,000.00	—
☐ BROUSSARD'S BARBER SHOP, ed. 300, s/n, 24″ x 32″, pub GRG	150.00	—
Artist proof	1,000.00	—

	ISSUE PRICE	CURRENT PRICE
☐ **BREAUX BRIDGE BAND,** ed. 300, s/n, 24″ x 32″, pub GRG	150.00	—
Artist proof	1,000.00	—
☐ **JOLIE BLONDE,** ed. 300, s/n, 16″ x 20″, pub GRG	150.00	Sold Out
☐ **MAMOU RIDING ACADEMY,** ed. 300, s/n, 24″ x 32″, pub GRG	150.00	—
Artist proof	1,000.00	—
☐ **RAYNE-BO RAMBLERS,** ed. 1,000, s/o, pub GRG	2,500.00	—
☐ **THE CLASS,** ed. 1,000, s/o, pub GRG	25.00	—
☐ **THE GOURMET CLUB,** ed. 300, s/n, 23¼″ x 28″, pub GRG	250.00	—
☐ **WISHING FOR LAFITTE'S GOLD,** ed. 150, s/n, 21½″ x 13½″, pub GRG	150.00	—

CHARLES D. ROGERS

THEMES: Wildlife art

MEDIUM: Watercolor

EDUCATION: Rocky Mountain School of Art

MUSEUMS/COLLECTIONS: Rogers' paintings are in both private and public collections

GALLERY/DISTRIBUTOR: Charles D. Rogers

COMMENTS: The artist feels that communication with other artists and the interchange of ideas is very important to the development of art today

	ISSUE PRICE	CURRENT PRICE
☐ **DEEP SNOW,** ed. 1,200, s/n, 19¾″ x 7¼″, pub CDR	25.00	40.00
ed. 50 Artist proofs with remarque, s/n	55.00	65.00
☐ **GRANDPA'S PLACE,** ed. 1,200, s/n, 19¾″ x 10″, pub CDR	25.00	40.00
ed. 50 Artist proofs with remarque, s/n	55.00	65.00
☐ **MARCH EVENING,** ed. 1,200, s/n, 19¾″ x 10″, pub CDR	25.00	40.00
ed. 50 Artist proofs with remarque, s/n	55.00	65.00
☐ **PASSING LEAVES,** ed. 750, s/n, 23½″ x 13½″, pub CDR	60.00	—
ed. 50 Artist proofs with remarque, s/n	90.00	100.00
☐ **WINTER STORAGE,** ed. 1,200, s/n, 19¾″ x 10″, pub CDR	25.00	40.00
ed. 50 Artist proofs with remarque, s/n	55.00	65.00
☐ **CACTUS WREN,** rel. 1979. ed. 750, s/n, 11″ x 14″, pub CDR	40.00	—
ed. 50 Artist proofs, remarqued		
☐ **BLACK CAPPED CHICKADEES,** rel. 1981. ed. 750, s/n, 13″ x 19″, pub CDR	40.00	—
ed. 50 Artist proofs, remarqued		
☐ **FANTASY,** rel. 1981. ed. unlimited, s/o, 6½″ x 9″, pub CDR	10.00	—
☐ **MADAME BUTTERFLY,** rel. 1981. ed. unlimited, s/o, 6½″ x 9″, pub CDR	10.00	—
☐ **SPRING'S PROMISE,** rel. 1981. ed. unlimited, s/o, 6½″ x 9″, pub CDR	10.00	—

RICHARD ROFLOW

THEMES: Portraiture, nature

EDUCATION: Cincinnati Art Academy

GALLERY/DISTRIBUTOR: Court Galleries

	ISSUE PRICE	CURRENT PRICE
☐ **SYCAMORE BARN,** ed. 500, s/n, litho, 16″ x 20″, pub CG	25.00	—
☐ **SYCAMORE CREEK,** ed. 500, s/n, litho, 16″ x 20″, pub CG	25.00	—

FALL SHORELINE *by Robert Ross*

E. ROBERT ROSS

THEMES: Landscape art

STYLE: A former student of Bateman, Ross is among a new breed of artists from the "Kodachrome" style of painting

GALLERY/DISTRIBUTOR: Mill Pond Press, Inc.

	ISSUE PRICE	CURRENT PRICE
☐ **AUTUMN POPLARS,** rel. 1980. ed. 950, s/n, 17½″ x 23¾″, pub MPPI	75.00	—
☐ **BLUE SHADOWS,** rel. 1981. ed. 550, s/n, 24¾″ x 24″, pub MPPI	95.00	—
☐ **FALL SHORELINE,** rel. 1980. ed. 950, s/n, 24″ x 17¼″, pub MPPI	75.00	—

	ISSUE PRICE	CURRENT PRICE
☐ **MORNING FROST,** rel. 1980. ed. 950, s/n, 20″ x 27½″, pub MPPI	75.00	—
☐ **NORTHERN SHORELINE,** rel. 1980. ed. 950, s/n, 18″ x 25¼″, pub MPPI	75.00	—
☐ **RIVER RAPIDS,** rel. 1981. ed. 550, s/n, 25½″ x 20″, pub MPPI	95.00	—

1981 WISCONSIN TROUT *by Tom Rost*

TOM ROST

THEMES: Wildlife art

EDUCATION: University of Wisconsin-Milwaukee School of Fine Art; Layton School of Art

GALLERY/DISTRIBUTOR: Northwoods Craftsman

	ISSUE PRICE	CURRENT PRICE
☐ **1978 WISCONSIN TROUT STAMP PRINT,** rel. 1978. ed. 600, s/n, 14″ x 17″, pub NC	60.00	300.00
ed. 100 remarqued	110.00	500.00
☐ **1981 WISCONSIN TROUT STAMP PRINT,** rel. 1981. ed. 500, s/n, 14″ x 12″, pub NC	100.00	250.00
ed. 100 remarqued	200.00	450.00

G. H. ROTHE

THEMES: Varied

MEDIUM: Mezzotint etchings

EDUCATION: Pforzheim Academy of Design

GALLERY/DISTRIBUTOR: Hammer Publishing Co.

	ISSUE PRICE	CURRENT PRICE
☐ **THE HEART,** rel. 1973. ed. 75, s/n, mezzotint, 35″ x 26″, pub HP	—	600.00
☐ **ALVIN WITH THE DUTCH,** rel. 1974. ed. 300, s/n, 43″ x 30½″, serigraph, pub HP	—	Sold Out
☐ **PAS DE TROIS,** rel. 1975. ed. 300, s/o, 37½″ x 24¾″, serigraph, pub HP	—	650.00
☐ **AMERICA'S PRIDE,** rel. 1976. ed. 150, s/n, 27″ x 26″, mezzotint, pub HP	—	Sold Out
☐ **GLASS ROSE,** rel. 1976. ed. 150, s/n, 23⅝″ x 25¾″, mezzotint, pub HP	—	Sold Out
☐ **MOLLUSK,** rel. 1976. ed. 150, s/n, 24″ x 36″, mezzotint, pub HP	—	Sold Out
☐ **ARISE AROSE,** rel. 1977. ed. 150, s/n, 32⅜″ x 23¾″, mezzotint, pub HP	—	Sold Out
☐ **BUTTERFLY,** rel. 1977. ed. 150, s/n, 23½″ x 23″¾″, mezzotint, pub HP	—	Sold Out
☐ **MINDSCAPE,** rel. 1977. ed. 150, s/n, 24″ x 36″, mezzotint, pub HP	—	Sold Out
☐ **PAS DE DEUX,** rel. 1977. ed. 150, s/n, 23½″ x 23½″, mezzotint, pub HP	—	800.00
☐ **THOROUGHBRED,** rel. 1977. ed. 150, s/n, 23¾″ x 17¾″, mezzotint, pub HP	—	Sold Out
☐ **THE WINDOW,** rel. 1977. ed. 150, s/n, 25⅝″ x 24″, pub HP	—	1,300.00
☐ **AUGUSTA,** rel. 1978. ed. 150, s/n, 21″ x 15″, mezzotint, pub HP	—	750.00
☐ **DON QUIXOTE,** rel. 1978. ed. 150, s/n, 27½″ x 22½″, mezzotint, pub HP	—	Sold Out
☐ **HOMECOMING,** rel. 1978. ed. 150, s/n, 15″ x 21″, mezzotint, pub HP	—	Sold Out
☐ **JOY,** rel. 1978. ed. 150, s/n, 21½″ x 9½″, mezzotint, pub HP	—	Sold Out
☐ **MORGANS,** rel. 1978. ed. 150, s/n, 8¾″ x 11½″, mezzotint, pub HP	—	550.00
☐ **MORNING,** rel. 1978. ed. 150, s/n, 8½″ x 21½″, mezzotint, pub HP	—	Sold Out
☐ **MYTH,** rel. 1978. ed. 200, s/n, 21″ x 17″, mezzotint, pub HP	—	Sold Out
☐ **NIGHT,** rel. 1978. ed. 150, s/n, 8½″ x 21½″, mezzotint, pub HP	—	Sold Out
☐ **SECRET PLACE,** rel. 1978. ed. 150, s/n, 14¾″ x 20¾″, mezzotint, pub HP	—	800.00
☐ **SPANISH ROSE,** rel. 1978. ed. 100, s/n, 7¾″ x 5¾″, mezzotint, pub HP	—	Sold Out
☐ **SUNDAY ROSES,** rel. 1978. ed. 100, s/n, 6″ x 8″, pub HP	—	Sold Out
☐ **ANCESTORS,** rel. 1979. ed. 150, s/n, 5¾″ x 3¾″, mezzotint, pub HP	—	400.00
☐ **COMPETITORS,** rel. 1979. ed. 150, s/n, 5¾″ x 8″, mezzotint, pub HP	—	Sold Out
☐ **CORAL CORRAL,** rel. 1979. ed. 150, s/n, 11½″ x 35¼″, mezzotint, pub HP	—	Sold Out
☐ **DANCE SUITE,** set of five mezzotints, rel. 1979. ed. 200, s/n, pub HP	—	Sold Out
☐ **ENDURANCE,** rel. 1979. ed. 150, s/n, 6″ x 7⅞″, mezzotint, pub HP	—	Sold Out
☐ **GLASSTOWN,** rel. 1979. ed. 99, s/n, 25½″ x 33¾″, mezzotint, pub HP	—	Sold Out
☐ **GRACE AND THE STALLION,** rel. 1979. ed. 150, s/n, 5½″ x 8″, pub HP	—	Sold Out
☐ **HERD,** rel. 1979. ed. 150, s/n, 8″ x 6″, mezzotint, pub HP	—	450.00
☐ **LANDMARK,** rel. 1979. ed. 150, s/o, 27½″ x 21¾″, mezzotint, pub EWG	—	750.00
☐ **MINIATURE SUITE,** set of five mezzotints, rel. 1979, s/n, pub HP	—	Sold Out
☐ **MOONDANCE II,** rel. 1979. ed. 100, s/n, 25⅞″ x 15⅞″, mezzotint, pub HP	—	Sold Out
☐ **PEACE,** rel. 1979. ed. 150, s/n, 9¾″ x 11¾″, mezzotint, pub HP	—	750.00
☐ **POET,** rel. 1979. ed. 150, s/n, 35¼″ x 23½″, mezzotint, pub HP	—	Sold Out
☐ **ROSESCAPE,** rel. 1979. ed. 200, s/n, 21¾″ x 27½″, mezzotint, pub HP	—	1,000.00
☐ **SOLITUDE,** rel. 1979. ed. 150, s/n, 20¾″ x 14¾″, mezzotint, pub HP	—	800.00
☐ **SONATA,** rel. 1979. ed. 200, s/n, 5¾″ x 4¾″, mezzotint, pub HP	—	Sold Out
☐ **STRENGTH,** rel. 1979. ed. 200, s/n, 27⅜″ x 16¼″, mezzotint, pub HP	—	Sold Out
☐ **BALLET PICTURE I,** rel. 1980. ed. 150, s/n, 35¼″ x 23¾″, mezzotint, pub HP	—	1,600.00
☐ **BALLET PICTURE II,** rel. 1980. ed. 150, s/n, 27½″ x 21⅝″, mezzotint, pub HP	—	1,400.00
☐ **FLOWER LIFE,** rel. 1980. ed. 150, s/n, 7⅞″ x 6″, mezzotint, pub HP	—	500.00
☐ **GROWTH,** rel. 1980. ed. 100, s/n, 15⅝″ x 21¾″, mezzotint, pub HP	—	800.00
☐ **PENSIVE MOTION,** rel. 1980. ed. 100, s/n, 19¾″ x 8″, mezzotint, pub HP	—	Sold Out
☐ **RED DRESS,** rel. 1980. ed. 200, s/n, 15¾″ x 15¾″, mezzotint, pub HP	—	Sold Out
☐ **THE FIGHT,** rel. 1980. ed. 150, s/n, 11¾″ x 9⅝″, mezzotint, pub HP	—	650.00
☐ **ALMANAC,** rel. 1981. ed. 150, s/n, 27½″ x 22″, mezzotint, pub HP	—	1,350.00
☐ **BABY BALLERINAS,** rel. 1981. ed. 150, s/n, 27½″ x 21½″, mezzotint, pub HP	—	Sold Out
☐ **BACHELORS,** rel. 1981. ed. 100, s/n, 13¾″ x 10¾″, mezzotint, pub HP	—	Sold Out

	ISSUE PRICE	CURRENT PRICE
☐ BOUGAINVILLEA, rel. 1981. ed. 150, s/n, 16" x 10¾", mezzotint, pub HP	–	Sold Out
☐ CHASE, rel. 1981. ed. 150, s/n, 23¾" x 35¼", mezzotint, pub HP	–	Sold Out
☐ DANCE FOR PLEASURE, rel. 1981. ed. 100, s/n, 5¾" x 4", mezzotint, pub HP	–	Sold Out
☐ DANCE PICTURE I, rel. 1981. ed. 150, s/n, 27½" x 21½", mezzotint, pub HP	–	1,300.00
☐ ENDEAVORS, rel. 1981. ed. 150, s/n, 22½" x 27½", mezzotint, pub HP	–	1,350.00
☐ EXPERIMENT, rel. 1981. ed. 150, s/n, 15¾" x 21¾", mezzotint, pub HP	–	Sold Out
☐ HARBOR AT NIGHT, rel. 1981. ed. 100, s/n, 10¾" x 13¾", mezzotint, pub HP	–	Sold Out
☐ JULIE, rel. 1981. ed. 100, s/n, 6¾" x 4", mezzotint, pub HP	–	325.00
☐ JUNCTION, rel. 1981. ed. 100, s/n, 10¾" x 16¾", mezzotint, pub HP	–	600.00
☐ MOSS LANDING, rel. 1981. ed. 100, s/n, 11" x 14", mezzotint, pub HP	–	600.00
☐ RHAPSODIC COMMITMENT, rel. 1981. ed. 150, s/n, 24½" x 17", mezzotint, pub HP ..	–	Sold Out
☐ SPRING ROSE, rel. 1981. ed. 100, s/n, 5⅞" x 7¾", mezzotint, pub HP	–	350.00
☐ TASSAJARA, rel. 1981. ed. 150, s/n, 13¾" x 10¾", mezzotint, pub HP	–	550.00
☐ WHARF, rel. 1981. ed. 150, s/n, 16½" x 25", mezzotint, pub HP	–	1,000.00
☐ WHILE THEY WERE RUNNING, rel. 1981. ed. 150, s/n, 23⅞" x 35¼", mezzotint, pub HP	–	Sold Out
☐ YOUTH, rel. 1981. ed. 150, s/n, 27½" x 22", mezzotint, pub HP	–	Sold Out
☐ BALL DANCE, rel. 1982. ed. 150, s/n, 27½" x 21½", mezzotint, pub HP	–	200.00
☐ BEECHLANE, rel. 1982. ed. 75, s/n, 6¾" x 4¾", mezzotint, pub HP	–	350.00
☐ COLTS, rel. 1982. ed. 150, s/n, 23¾" x 34¾", mezzotint, pub HP	–	1,800.00
☐ CURRENT, rel. 1982. ed. 150, s/n, 21¾" x 27½", mezzotint, pub HP	–	1,350.00
☐ DEPRIVED CONDITION, rel. 1982. ed. 96, s/n, 23⅝" x 17⅞", mezzotint, pub HP ...	–	1,000.00
☐ ELECTRON, rel. 1982. ed. 96, s/n, 12⅛" x 8¾", mezzotint, pub HP	–	550.00
☐ EMOTIONAL INTENSITY, rel. 1982. ed. 150, s/n, 27½" x 21¾", mezzotint, pub HP ..	–	Sold Out
☐ PATTERN, rel. 1982. ed. 96, s/n, 7" x 9¾", mezzotint, pub HP	–	450.00
☐ PENUEL, rel. 1982. ed. 96, s/n, 7" x 9¾", mezzotint, pub HP	–	475.00
☐ PENUEL II, rel. 1982. ed. 96, s/n, 6⅞" x 10", mezzotint, pub HP	–	475.00
☐ RECITAL, rel. 1982. ed. 200, s/n, 16⅞" x 24¾", mezzotint, pub HP	–	1,100.00
☐ RECURRENT, rel. 1982. ed. 96, s/n, 9¾" x 7", mezzotint, pub HP	–	350.00
☐ ROOTS IN LOVE, rel. 1982. ed. 96, s/n, 24½" x 16¾", mezzotint, pub HP	–	1,000.00
☐ RUNNERS, rel. 1982. ed. 150, s/n, 9" x 11⅝", mezzotint, pub HP	–	550.00
☐ SALINAS HILL, rel. 1982. ed. 96, s/n, 11¾" x 8⅞", mezzotint, pub HP	–	500.00
☐ SOLO OF GEMINI, rel. 1982. ed. 75, s/n, 12" x 9", mezzotint, pub HP	–	650.00
☐ TASSAJARA STAIRS, rel. 1982. ed. 96, s/n, 11¾" x 17⅞", mezzotint, pub HP	–	600.00
☐ TRADITIONAL STANDARD, rel. 1982. ed. 150, s/n, 15⅝" x 10¾", mezzotint, pub HP	–	500.00
☐ TRIO, rel. 1982. ed. 200, s/n, 16⅛" x 11⅛", mezzotint, pub HP	–	1,000.00
☐ BENRABBA, rel. 1983. ed. 150, s/n, 8½" x 12½", mezzotint, pub HP	–	600.00
☐ CONBRIO, rel. 1983. ed. 150, s/n, 16" x 11", mezzotint, pub HP	–	600.00
☐ CONQUISTADOR CIELO, rel. 1983. ed. 150, s/n, 23¾" x 35¾", mezzotint, pub HP .	–	Sold Out
☐ GRAPES, rel. 1983. ed. 150, s/n, 8½" x 12¼", mezzotint, pub HP	–	–
☐ SAN BONANCIAO, rel. 1983. ed. 150, s/n, 24" x 36", mezzotint, pub HP	–	1,200.00

PALADINE ROYE

THEMES: Indian art

BACKGROUND: Paladine, whose Indian name is Pon-Cee-Cee ("Watch Out For This One"), grew up on the windy plains of While Eagle, Oklahoma

GALLERY/DISTRIBUTOR: Native American Images

COMMENTS: Preserving the traditional customs and beliefs of his people is an overriding concern for the artist, and one senses this intensity in both the man and his work

	ISSUE PRICE	CURRENT PRICE
☐ WARMAKER'S DECISION, rel. 1978. ed. 450, s/n, 26″ x 21″, stone litho, pub NAI ...	50.00	300.00
☐ HUNTER'S SONG, rel. 1979. ed. 750, s/n, 31″ x 24″, stone litho, pub NAI	60.00	650.00
☐ NIGHT SOUNDS TRAVEL FAR, rel. 1980. ed. 950, s/n, 25″ x 31″, stone litho, pub NAI.............................	75.00	700.00
☐ WHERE FREEDOM ENDS, rel. 1981. ed. 1,500, s/n, 24″ x 18″, stone litho, pub NAI .	75.00	—
☐ BREAKING THE MORNING SILENCE, rel. 1982. ed. 950, s/n, 26″ x 20″, stone litho, pub NAI.............................	100.00	—
☐ IN A DREAM I SAW, rel. 1982. ed. 650, s/n, 20″ x 23″, stone litho, pub NAI	75.00	—
☐ THERE ARE MANY WAGONS, rel. 1982. ed. 950, s/n, 26″ x 20″, stone litho, pub NAI.............................	100.00	—
☐ MORNING CHAMPION, rel. 1983. ed. 650, s/n, 21″ x 32″, stone litho, pub NAI	150.00	—
☐ WHITE MEN HANG HORSE THIEVES, rel. 1983. ed. 150, s/n, 26″ x 21″, stone litho, pub NAI.............................	350.00	500.00
☐ COUNCIL OF THE MEDICINE MEN, rel. 1984. ed. 650, s/n, 18″ x 27″, stone litho, pub NAI.............................	150.00	—

HAL ROZEMA

THEMES: Aviation art

EDUCATION: Kendall Art School; Aquinas College; Slade University in London

MUSEUMS/COLLECTIONS: National Air and Space Museum; Battle Creek Art Center; Air Force Art Collection

GALLERY/DISTRIBUTOR: Rozema Studio

	ISSUE PRICE	CURRENT PRICE
☐ ASSAM DAWN FLIGHT, P 40 D Tomahawk Fighters, Flying Tigers, ed. 1,000, s/n, 21″ x 17″, pub RS	78.00	—
☐ AWACs REFUELING, ed. 1,000, s/n, 21″ x 17″, pub RS	78.00	—
☐ BLUE ANGELS, A4 (MOD) SKYHAWK, ed. 1,000, s/n, 21″ x 17″, pub RS	78.00	—
☐ CHRISTIAN EAGLE, ed. 1,000, s/n, 21″ x 17″, pub RS	78.00	—
☐ F5E (FM2) WILDCAT, 1939-40 VF41, ed. 1,000, s/n, 21″ x 17″, pub RS	78.00	—
☐ F5E TIGER II, ed. 1,000, s/n, 21″ x 17″, pub RS	78.00	—
☐ F14 TOMCAT, VF38, ed. 1,000, s/n, 21″ x 17″, pub RS	78.00	—
☐ F15 BITBURG EAGLE IN NATO COLORS IN FLIGHT OVER WEST GERMANY, ed. 1,000, s/n, 21″ x 17″, pub RS	78.00	—
☐ TALLY HO, ed. 1,000, s/n, 21″ x 17″, pub RS	78.00	—
☐ THE PICCARD BALLOON, XJ90 AT SUNSET, ed. 1,000, s/n, 21″ x 17″, pub RS	78.00	—
☐ THRESHOLD, Space Shuttle Columbia lifts off, ed. 1,000, s/n, 21″ x 17″, pub RS	78.00	—
☐ T-38 THUNDERBIRDS 1980, CALYPSO PASS, ed. 1,000, s/n, 21″ x 17″, pub RS ...	78.00	—

CLAIRE RUBY

THEMES: Flowers

STYLE: Impressionism

EDUCATION: Budapest Fine Arts Academy; Chicago Art Institute

PETUNIAS *by Claire Ruby*

GALLERY/DISTRIBUTOR: Richard Thompson Gallery

	ISSUE PRICE	CURRENT PRICE
☐ **BOUGAINVILLEAS,** rel. 1984. ed. 1,000, s/n, 22″ x 28″, litho, pub RTG	100.00	—
☐ **PETUNIAS,** rel. 1984. ed. 1,000, s/n, 22″ x 28″, litho, pub RTG	100.00	—
☐ **VIEW OF THE BAY,** rel. 1984. ed. 750, offset litho, s/n, 27″ x 35″, pub RTG	200.00	—

JOHN A. RUTHVEN

THEMES: Wildlife art

MEDIUM: Watercolor

STYLE: Realism

GALLERY/DISTRIBUTOR: Wildlife Internationale, Inc.

COMMENTS: Mr. Ruthven is a leader in conservation and protection of endangered species, and is also widely known as a lecturer and writer. He is often called "the 20th Century Audubon"

	ISSUE PRICE	CURRENT PRICE

AQUATINT SERIES

	ISSUE PRICE	CURRENT PRICE
☐ CAROLINA PARAQUET, ed. 500, s/n, 25″ x 36″, pub WII	300.00	1,500.00
☐ PASSENGER PIGEON, ed. 500, s/n, 25″ x 36″, pub WII	350.00	1,500.00
☐ IVORY BILLED WOODPECKER, ed. 500, s/n, 25″ x 36″, pub WII	350.00	800.00
☐ LABRADOR DUCK, ed. 500, s/n, 25″ x 36″, pub WII	350.00	600.00

SAFARI SERIES

	ISSUE PRICE	CURRENT PRICE
☐ BENGAL TIGER, ed. 5,000, s/n, 25″ x 33″, pub WII	65.00	700.00
☐ AFRICAN ELEPHANTS, ed. 5,000, s/n, 25″ x 33″, pub WII	65.00	100.00
☐ GIANT PANDAS, ed. 5,000, s/n, 25″ x 33″, pub WII	65.00	100.00
☐ BLACK MANED LION, ed. 5,000, s/n, 27″ x 35″, pub WII	65.00	100.00
☐ GRANT'S ZEBRA, ed. 5,000, s/n, 27″ x 34″, pub WII	75.00	100.00
☐ LEOPARD, ed. 3,500, s/n, 27″ x 35″, pub WII	75.00	100.00

NORTH AMERICAN SERIES

	ISSUE PRICE	CURRENT PRICE
☐ SNOWY OWL, ed. 1,000, s/n, 18″ x 24″, pub WII	50.00	500.00
☐ RUDDY DUCKS, ed. 1,000, s/n, 18″ x 24″, pub WII	50.00	425.00
☐ CANVASBACKS ON THE OHIO, ed. 1,000, s/n, 18″ x 24″, pub WII	50.00	450.00
☐ REDHEADED WOODPECKER, ed. 1,000, s/n, 18″ x 24″, pub WII	50.00	425.00
☐ WANDERING BRAVE, ed. 1,000, s/n, 25″ x 33″, pub WII	90.00	600.00
☐ N. Y. STATE BLUEBIRD, ed. 1,000, s/n, 18″ x 24″, pub WII	50.00	325.00
☐ WOOD DUCKS, ed. 1,000, s/n, 25″ x 31″, pub WII	90.00	475.00
☐ RED FOX FAMILY, ed. 1,000, s/n, 25″ x 33″, pub WII	90.00	1,050.00
☐ ROBINS, ed. 1,000, s/n, 18″ x 24″, pub WII	50.00	450.00
☐ ON THE HUNT, ed. 1,000, s/n, 25″ x 33″, pub WII	90.00	150.00

AMERICANA SERIES

	ISSUE PRICE	CURRENT PRICE
☐ ROADRUNNER, ed. 1,000, s/n, 20″ x 25″, pub WII	50.00	325.00
☐ HERRING GULLS, ed. 1,000, s/n, 20″ x 26½″, pub WII	50.00	375.00
☐ GREAT HORNED OWL, ed. 1,000, s/n, 22½″ x 30″, pub WII	90.00	400.00
☐ CANADA GEESE, ed. 1,000, s/n, 24″ x 31″, pub WII	95.00	225.00
☐ BOBWHITE QUAIL, ed. 1,000, s/n, 20½″ x 24″, pub WII	80.00	250.00

GEORGETOWN SERIES

	ISSUE PRICE	CURRENT PRICE
☐ CINNAMON TEAL, ed. 1,000, s/n, 12″ x 15″, pub WII	30.00	150.00
ed. 1,000, n/o	20.00	—
☐ FOX MASQUE I, ed. 1,000, s/n, 11″ x 11″, pub WII	30.00	150.00
☐ FOX MASQUE II, ed. 1,000, s/n, 11″ x 11″, pub WII	30.00	150.00
☐ HOODED MERGANSER, rel. 1979. ed. 1,000, s/n, 11″ x 10″, pub WII	50.00	125.00
☐ RUDDY DUCK, rel. 1979. ed. 1,000, s/n, 11″ x 10″, pub WII	50.00	—
☐ INDIGO BUNTING, rel. 1980. ed. 950, s/n, 11″ x 11″, mezzotint, pub WII	50.00	—

REGAL SERIES

	ISSUE PRICE	CURRENT PRICE
☐ BENGAL TIGER, ed. 1,000, s/n, 25″ x 36″, pub WII	80.00	1,800.00
☐ RED FOX, ed. 1,000, s/n, 25″ x 36″, pub WII	90.00	1,450.00

MASTERPIECE SERIES

	ISSUE PRICE	CURRENT PRICE
☐ GRAY FOX, ed. 950, s/n, 25″ x 33″, pub WII	125.00	1,400.00
☐ JAGUAR, ed. 950, s/n, 20″ x 24″, pub WII	65.00	400.00
☐ FLICKERS, ed. 950, s/n, 20″ x 24″, pub WII	65.00	150.00
☐ FLYING SNOW OWL, ed. 950, s/n, 33″ x 25″, pub WII	150.00	—
☐ GRAY FOX FAMILY, ed. 950, s/n, 33″ x 25″, pub WII	125.00	1,100.00

JOHN A. RUTHVEN SERIES

	ISSUE PRICE	CURRENT PRICE
☐ RUFFED GROUSE, Plate I and Plate II, ed. 99, s/n, 22½″ x 29¼″, pub WII *Sold only as matched pair	*750.00	1,850.00
☐ WOOD DUCK/MALLARD, Plate III & IV, ed. 99, s/n, 22½″ x 29¼″, pub WII *Sold only as matched pair	*750.00	1,600.00
☐ PHEASANTS, Plate V & VI, ed. 99, s/n, 22¼″ x 29¼″, pub WII *Sold only as matched pair	*850.00	1,500.00

INITIAL SERIES

	ISSUE PRICE	CURRENT PRICE
☐ BALD EAGLE, ed. 1,000, s/n, 18″ x 24″, pub WII	30.00	850.00
☐ PHEASANT, ed. 1,000, s/n, 18″ x 24″, pub WII	30.00	550.00
☐ CARDINALS, ed. 1,000, s/n, 18″ x 24″, pub WII	30.00	850.00
☐ QUAIL, ed. 1,000, s/n, 18″ x 24″, pub WII	30.00	550.00
☐ WILD TURKEY, ed. 1,000, s/n, 18″ x 24″, pub WII	30.00	475.00
☐ BLUEBIRD, ed. 1,000, s/n, 18″ x 24″, pub WII	30.00	600.00
☐ SCREECH OWL, ed. 1,000, s/n, 18″ x 24″, pub WII	30.00	700.00

	ISSUE PRICE	CURRENT PRICE
☐ WOOD DUCK, ed. 1,000, s/n, 18″ x 24″, pub WII	40.00	350.00
☐ RUFFED GROUSE, ed. 1,000, s/n, 18″ x 24″, pub WII	40.00	450.00
☐ MALLARD, ed. 1,000, s/n, 18″ x 24″, pub WII	50.00	400.00
COMMISSIONS		
☐ BARDSTOWN OF CALUMET FARMS, ed. 2,000, s/n, 22″ x 17″, pub WII	50.00	—
☐ BENGAL TIGER, ed. 1,000, s/n, 30″ x 40″, pub WII	*100.00	500.00
*Commissioned by Idaho State University.		
☐ DECOY (Labrador Retriever), ed. 950, s/n, 21″ x 24″, pub WII	125.00	700.00
250 of the edition used as a donation		
700 released by Wildlife International as a donation		
☐ EAGLE TO THE MOON, ed. 500, s/n, 30″ x 40″, pub WII	*150.00	1,800.00
*For the Neil A. Armstrong Air & Space Museum and the Ohio Historical Society.		
☐ EASTERN CHIPMUNK, ed. 750, s/n, 12″ x 19″, pub WII	50.00	300.00
☐ FRANCIS OF ASSISI, ed. 2,000, s/n, 20″ x 26″, pub WII	*60.00	—
*Commissioned by St. Francis College		
☐ GREAT AUK, ed. 200, s/n, 24″ x 33½″, pub WII	250.00	—
☐ KINGFISHER, ed. 250, s/n, size not known, pub WII	100.00	—
☐ KIRTLAND'S WARBLER, ed. 1,000, s/n, 18″ x 24″, pub WII	100.00	—
☐ KIT FOX, ed. 500, s/n, 25″ x 21″, pub WII	100.00	350.00
☐ OAKGROVE PINTAIL (Small), ed. 3,000, s/n, 16″ x 20″, pub WII	50.00	—
☐ OAKGROVE PINTAIL (Large), ed. 1,000, s/n, 30″ x 40″, pub WII	100.00	—
☐ PASSENGER PIGEON, rel. 1974. ed. 1,000, s/n, 25″ x 21″, pub WII	100.00	—
☐ NATURE CENTER CARDINAL, rel. 1970. ed. 1,000, s/n, 25″ x 21″, pub WII	50.00	450.00
☐ REDHEAD DUCKS (Aquatint Process), ed. 450, s/n, 15″ x 14″	*350.00	450.00
*1960 - 1961 Federal Duck Stamp		
☐ WHITE TIGERS, ed. 1,000, s/n, size not known, pub WII	150.00	350.00
KNOB CREEK SERIES		
☐ WHITE-TAILED DEER, ed. 750, s/n, 25″ x 32″, pub WII	150.00	400.00
☐ BOBWHITE QUAIL, ed. 750, s/n, 18″ x 24″, pub WII	75.00	250.00
☐ ALGONQUIN, ed. 750, s/n, 18″ x 24″, pub WII	75.00	125.00
☐ EASTERN WILD TURKEY, ed. 750, s/n, 18″ x 24″, pub WII	75.00	300.00
☐ HOODED MERGANSERS, ed. 750, s/n, 18″ x 24″, pub WII	75.00	125.00
☐ TERNS, ed. 750, s/n, 30″ x 40″, pub WII	150.00	350.00
WILLIAMSBURG SERIES		
☐ THE CARDINALS OF WILLIAMSBURG, ed. 1,000, s/n, 16″ x 20″, pub WII	*50.00	—
☐ THE MOCKINGBIRDS OF WILLIAMSBURG, ed. 1,000, s/n, 16″ x 20″, pub WII	*50.00	—
☐ THE BLUE JAYS OF WILLIAMSBURG, ed. 1,000, s/n, 16″ x 20″, pub WII	*50.00	—
*Sold only through Craft House, Williamsburg, VA and Williamsburg Shops in Fine Stores throughout the U.S.A.		
PATRIOT SERIES		
☐ SHAWNEE INDIAN, ed. 3,000, numbered only, 16″ x 20″, pub WII	22.50	—
☐ MOURNING DOVE, ed. 3,000, numbered only, 16″ x 20″, pub WII	22.50	—
☐ MEADOW LARK, ed. 3,000, numbered only, 16″ x 20″, pub WII	22.50	—
☐ BUFFLEHEAD DUCK, ed. 3,000, numbered only, 16″ x 20″, pub WII	22.50	—
BICENTENNIAL SERIES		
☐ BICENTENNIAL EAGLE, rel. 1976. ed. 776, s/n, 28″ x 42″, pub WII	350.00	650.00
☐ BICENTENNIAL TURKEYS, rel. 1977. ed. 776. s/n, 30″ x 32″, pub WII	350.00	—
LIBERTY SERIES		
☐ BLUE WINGED TEAL, rel. 1977. ed. 500, s/n, 17″ x 24″, pub WII	75.00	450.00
☐ GREEN WINGED TEAL, rel. 1978. ed. 500, s/n, 17″ x 24″, pub WII	75.00	400.00
COASTAL SERIES		
☐ BROWN PELICAN, rel. 1977. ed. 500, s/n, 29″ x 27″, pub WII	125.00	250.00
☐ WILSON'S PLOVER, rel. 1978. ed. 500, s/n, 16″ x 15″, pub WII	75.00	—
HOMESTEAD SERIES		
☐ SCREECH OWL, rel. 1977. ed. 950, s/n, 12″ x 12″, pub WII	50.00	325.00
☐ CHICKADEE, rel. 1978. ed. 950, s/n, 12″ x 12″, pub WII	50.00	275.00
☐ CALIFORNIA VALLEY QUAIL, rel. 1979. ed. 950, s/n, 11″ x 11″, pub WII	50.00	—
INTERNATIONAL SERIES		
☐ BATELEUR EAGLE, rel. 1978. ed. 750, s/n, 24″ x 34″, pub WII	110.00	—
AMERICAN INDIAN SERIES		
☐ CHIPPEWA BRAVE, rel. 1978. ed. 950, s/n, 21″ x 18″, pub WII	50.00	—

	ISSUE PRICE	CURRENT PRICE
ARCTIC SERIES		
☐ ARCTIC FOX, rel. 1977. ed. 950, s/n, 33″ x 25″, pub WII	150.00	475.00
☐ TIMBER WOLF, rel. 1978. ed. 950, s/n, 25″ x 33″, pub WII	150.00	—
GAME BIRD SERIES		
☐ AMERICAN WIDGEON, rel. 1978. ed. 950, s/n, 16″ x 19½″, pub WII	65.00	—
☐ PHEASANT, rel. 1980. ed. 950, s/n, 16″ x 20″, pub WII	75.00	—
SONGBIRD SERIES		
☐ CARDINAL, rel. 1978. ed. 950, s/n, 17″ x 21″, pub WII	75.00	450.00
☐ CAROLINA WREN, rel. 1979. ed. 950, s/n, 13″ x 17″, pub WII	50.00	—
SPORTING DOG SERIES		
☐ DUSTY (Golden Retriever), rel. 1979. ed. 950, s/n, 21″ x 24″, pub WII	125.00	600.00
☐ RUMMY, rel. 1980. ed. 950, s/n, 21″ x 24″, pub WII	150.00	500.00
☐ DUSTY, rel. 1981. ed. 950, s/n, 21″ x 24″, pub WII	150.00	550.00
☐ SCARLET, rel. 1982. ed. 950, s/n, 21″ x 24″, pub WII	150.00	—
WINTER SERIES		
☐ CEDAR WAXWING, rel. 1978. ed. 950, s/n, 15″ x 15″, pub WII	50.00	100.00
☐ SAW-WHET OWL, rel. 1979. ed. 950, s/n, 11″ x 11″, pub WII	50.00	—
WOODLAND SERIES		
☐ RED FOX (in the snow),rel. 1979. ed. 950, s/n, 26″ x 33″, pub WII	150.00	500.00
☐ GRAY FOX, rel. 1981. ed. 1,500, s/n, 23″ x 30″, pub WII	150.00	—
HUMMINGBIRDS OF NORTH AMERICA		
☐ RUBY-THROATED, rel. 1977. ed. 750, s/n, 14″ x 17″, pub WII	75.00	—
☐ ALLEN'S, rel. 1977. ed. 750, s/n, 14″ x 17″, pub WII	75.00	—
☐ RUFOUS, rel. 1977. ed. 750, s/n, 14″ x 17″, pub WII	75.00	—
☐ ANNA'S, rel. 1978. ed. 750, s/n, 14″ x 17″, pub WII	75.00	—
☐ RIVOLI'S/BLUE THROATED, rel. 1978. ed. 750, s/n, 14″ x 17″, pub WII	75.00	—
☐ BROAD-BILLED, rel. 1978. ed. 750, s/n, 14″ x 17″, pub WII	75.00	—
OWL FAMILY SERIES		
☐ SAW-WHET OWLS, rel. 1982. ed. 1,500, s/n, 14″ x 17″, pub WII	75.00	—
☐ GREAT HORNED OWLS, rel. 1982. ed. 1,500, s/n, 14″ x 17″, pub WII	75.00	—
☐ SNOWY OWLS, rel. 1983. ed. 1,500, s/n, 14″ x 17″, pub WII	75.00	—
☐ BARRED OWLS, rel. 1983. ed. 1,500, s/n, 14″ x 17″, pub WII	75.00	—
MISCELLANEOUS, not part of a Series		
☐ WINGS IN THE WIND (Blue Goose/Snow Goose), rel. 1982. ed. 750, s/n, 25″ x 33″, pub WII	200.00	—
☐ SAND HILL CRANES, rel. 1982. ed. 950, s/n, 26″ x 21″, pub WII	150.00	—
☐ OSPREY, rel. 1981. ed. 750, s/n, 25″ x 34″, pub WII	175.00	—
☐ MALLARD, rel. 1981. ed. 500, s/n, 16″ x 21½″, pub WII	75.00	—
☐ CARDINAL, rel. 1981. ed. 950, s/n, 16″ x 20″, pub WII	75.00	200.00
☐ BALD EAGLE, rel. 1982. ed. 350, s/n, 19½″ x 45″, pub WII	350.00	—
☐ KESTREL & MOUSE, rel. 1982. ed. 950, s/n, 16½″ x 40″, pub WII	150.00	—
☐ KINGLETS, rel. 1982. ed. 950, s/n, 16″ x 20″, pub WII	75.00	—
☐ NUTHATCH, rel. 1982. ed. 950, s/n, 16″ x 20″, pub WII	75.00	—
☐ TOWHEES, rel. 1982. ed. 950, s/n, 16″ x 20″, pub WII	75.00	—
☐ WINSTON, rel. 1982. ed. 950, s/n, 21″ x 25″, pub WII	150.00	—
☐ FRIENDS, rel. 1983. ed. 500, s/n, 16″ x 20″, pub WII	75.00	—
☐ GOLDFINCH, rel. 1983. ed. 950, s/n, 16″ x 20″, pub WII	75.00	—
☐ PAPAW BANDIT, rel. 1983. ed. 600, s/n, 16½″ x 22½″, pub WII	125.00	250.00
☐ PILEATED WOODPECKERS, rel. 1983. ed. 350, s/n, 15″ x 39″, pub WII	350.00	—
☐ AUTUMN ON THE AU SABLE, 25th Anniversary print for Trout Unlimited. ed. 1,000, s/n, size not available, pub WII	125.00	—
☐ CANVASBACKS, Ducks Unlimited Print. ed. 150, s/n, size not available, pub WII	425.00	600.00
☐ SPRING FLOWERS, ed. 600, s/n, size not available, pub WII	125.00	—
☐ SIPPING WELL, ed. 750, s/n, size not available, pub WII	75.00	—

TOM RYAN

THEMES: Contemporary Western art

AWARDS: Gold medal from the Cowboy Artists of America; Gold medal from the National Academy of Western Art

MUSEUMS/COLLECTIONS: His work is included in every significant institutional and private collections of contemporary Western art

GALLERY/DISTRIBUTOR: Mill Pond Press, Inc.

	ISSUE PRICE	CURRENT PRICE
☐ **MONDAY MORNING BLUES,** rel. 1984. ed. 950, 24½″ x 19½″, pub MPPI	95.00	—

MORNING WATCH by Billy Saathoff

BILLY SAATHOFF

THEMES: Landscape and wildlife art

STYLE: Realism

GALLERY/DISTRIBUTOR: Arts Limited, Inc.

	ISSUE PRICE	CURRENT PRICE
☐ MORNING WATCH, rel. 1981. ed. 1,500, s/n, 23″ x 29½″, pub ALI	60.00	—

MANABU SAITO

THEMES: Flowers

BOOKS: The artist illustrated *The Boy Who Drew Cats; The Golden Guide on Cacti; What Is a Tree?; Collier's Encyclopedia Yearbook; From One Seed*

EDUCATION: Pratt Institute

GALLERY/DISTRIBUTOR: Frame House Gallery, Inc.

	ISSUE PRICE	CURRENT PRICE
☐ SPRING FLOWERS, rel. 1972. ed. 750, s/n, 21″ x 27″, pub FHG	35.00	125.00
☐ SUMMER FLOWERS, rel. 1973. ed. 1,500, s/n, 21″ x 27″, pub FHG	45.00	75.00
☐ AUTUMN FLOWERS, rel. 1974. ed. 1,500, s/n, 21″ x 27″, pub FHG	45.00	90.00
☐ CACTI, rel. 1974. ed. 1,500, s/n, 187⁄8″ x 24¼″, pub FHG	50.00	75.00
☐ PEONIES, rel. 1974. ed. 1,500, s/n, 23″ x 32″, pub FHG	45.00	75.00
☐ APPLE, rel. 1975. ed. 2,250, s/n, 6½″ x 9½″, pub FHG	7.00	20.00
☐ CINNAMON FERN, rel. 1975. ed. 1,000, s/n, 22″ x 29″, pub FHG	50.00	125.00
☐ ROSE, rel. 1975. ed. 1,500, s/n, 16″ x 20″, pub FHG	25.00	40.00
☐ SUNFLOWER, rel. 1975. ed. 1,000, s/n, 28″ x 20″, pub FHG	50.00	Sold Out
☐ TULIP/DAFFODIL, pair, rel. 1975. ed. 1,500, s/n, 16″ x 20″, pub FHG	40.00	100.00
☐ SOUTHERN MAGNOLIA, rel. 1976. ed. 900, s/n, 24″ x 28″, pub FHG	50.00	90.00
☐ BANSHU, rel. 1977. ed. 750, s/n, 28″ x 22″, pub FHG	50.00	80.00
☐ MAIDENHEAD FERN, rel. 1977. ed. 750, s/n, 29″ x 24″, pub FHG	50.00	120.00
☐ NIGHT-BLOOMING CACTI, rel. 1977. ed. 750, s/n, 27″ x 22″, pub FHG	50.00	—
☐ ORIENTAL POPPY, rel. 1977. ed. 750, s/n, 30″ x 23″, pub FHG	50.00	210.00
☐ FUJI, rel. 1978. ed. 500, s/n, 33½″ x 18¾″, pub FHG	100.00	Sold Out
☐ NEW MOON, rel. 1978. ed. 750, s/n, 15½″ x 13″, pub FHG	25.00	35.00
☐ RISQUE, rel. 1978. ed. 750, s/n, 15½″ x 13″, pub FHG	25.00	—
☐ SAKURA, rel. 1978. ed. 500, s/n, 33½″ x 18¾″, pub FHG	100.00	200.00
☐ CHRISTMAS FERN, rel. 1979. ed. 750, s/n, 23″ x 30″, pub FHG	60.00	—
☐ BANKA IN STILLWATER, rel. 1979. ed. 750, s/n, 29½″ x 21″, pub FHG	60.00	—
☐ MATSU, rel. 1979. ed. 500, s/n, 33½″ x 18¾″, pub FHG	100.00	—
☐ MOMIJI, rel. 1979. ed. 500, s/n, 33½″ x 18¼″, pub FHG	100.00	—
☐ OYSTER PLANT, rel. 1979. ed. 5,000, s/o, 15″ x 12″, pub FHG	10.00	—
☐ TULIP, rel. 1979. ed. 5,000, s/o, 14″ x 14″, pub FHG	20.00	—
☐ MAI, rel. 1980. ed. 375, s/n, 16¾″ x 29½″, pub FHG	125.00	—
☐ SPRING BOUQUET, rel. 1980. ed. 600, s/n, 30″ x 24″, pub FHG	75.00	—
☐ SUMMER BOUQUET, rel. 1980. ed. 355, s/n, 30″ x 24″, pub FHG	75.00	—
ed. 245, s/n, remarqued	90.00	—
☐ RED EMPEROR, rel. 1981. ed. 1,000, s/n, 20″ x 16″, pub FHG	40.00	—

TOM SANDER

THEMES: Wildlife art

EDUCATION: University of Oregon

GALLERY/DISTRIBUTOR: Frame House Gallery, Inc.

FOGHAND by Tom Sander

	ISSUE PRICE	CURRENT PRICE
☐ FROM COVER, rel. 1977. ed. 500, s/n, 24″ x 30″, pub FHG	40.00	115.00
☐ BLACK LABRADOR AND MALLARD, rel. 1977. ed. 500, s/n, 18″ x 26″, pub FHG ..	40.00	300.00
☐ HONORED POINT, rel. 1977. ed. 750, s/n, 24″ x 30″, pub FHG	50.00	125.00
☐ ENGLISH SETTERS AND RUFFED GROUSE, rel. 1978. ed. 750, s/n, 22″ x 29″, pub FHG	50.00	100.00
☐ FINAL APPROACH, rel. 1978. ed. 750, s/n, 21″ x 30″, pub FHG	75.00	125.00
☐ WINTER SUN, rel. 1978. ed. 750, s/n, 21″ x 30″, pub FHG	75.00	125.00
☐ BLACK LAB, rel. 1979. ed. 850, s/n, 18½″ x 26″, pub FHG	60.00	120.00
☐ GOLDEN RETRIEVER, rel. 1979. ed. 850, s/n, 21″ x 30, pub FHG	65.00	—
☐ IRISH SETTERS, rel. 1979. ed. 850, s/n, 20″ x 30″, pub FHG	65.00	125.00
☐ OCTOBER'S JOURNEY, rel. 1979. ed. 750, s/n, 21″ x 30″, pub FHG	75.00	125.00
☐ PHEASANT/BOBWHITE, pair, rel. 1979. ed. 950, s/n, 17½″ x 14½″, pub FHG	50.00	125.00
☐ DAWN PATROL, rel. 1980. ed. 750, s/n, 16½″ x 30″, pub FHG	75.00	250.00
☐ FALL (WHITE-TAIL DEER), rel. 1980. ed. 750, s/n, 20″ x 11½″, pub FHG	50.00	—
☐ SPRING (RED FOX), rel. 1980. ed. 750, s/n, 20″ x 11½″, pub FHG	50.00	—
☐ SUMMER - WOOD DUCKS, rel. 1980. ed. 750, s/n, 20″ x 11½″, pub FHG	50.00	—
☐ WINTER - CANADA GEESE, rel. 1980. ed. 750, s/n, 20″ x 11½″, pub FHG	50.00	—
☐ COLD DUCK, rel. 1981. ed. 850, s/n, 15½″ x 26″, pub SCG	85.00	—
☐ RUFFED GROUSE/GAMBEL'S QUAIL, pair, rel. 1981. ed. 950, s/n, 18½″ x 15″, pub FHG	65.00	125.00

	ISSUE PRICE	CURRENT PRICE
☐ SUMMER PONDERING, rel. 1981. ed. 750, s/n, 19″ x 30″, pub FHG	75.00	—
☐ SUNNING FOXES, rel. 1981. ed. 750, s/n, 18″ x 24″, pub FHG	65.00	—
☐ AUTUMN RETREAT, rel. 1982. ed. 975, s/n, 21″ x 28″, pub FHG	75.00	—
☐ GLACIAL VALLEY, rel. 1982. ed. 975, s/n, 24″ x 36″, pub FHG	75.00	—
☐ SPRING SNOW, rel. 1982. ed. 975, s/n, 21½″ x 30″, pub FHG	75.00	—
☐ THE SENTRIES, rel. 1982. ed. 975, s/n, 17″ x 30″, pub FHG	75.00	—
☐ THE APPRENTICE, rel. 1983. ed. 975, s/n, 21½″ x 30″, pub FHG	80.00	—
☐ THE FOG BANK, rel. 1983. ed. 975, s/n, 22″ x 28″, pub FHG	80.00	—

CAROLYN SANDERS-TURNER

THEMES: Varied

MEDIUM: Watercolor

EDUCATION: Chicago Art Institute; Sullins College

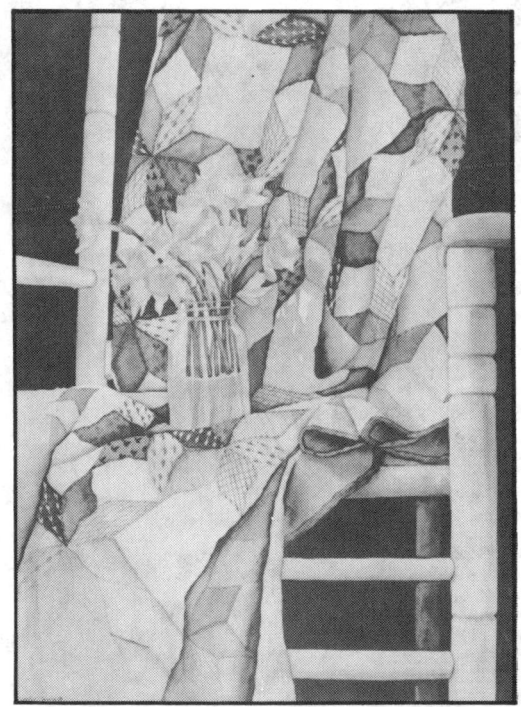

JONQUILS AND EIGHT POINT STAR *by Carolyn Sanders-Turner*

AWARDS: She has won over 50 awards

GALLERY/DISTRIBUTOR: Watermark Press

	ISSUE PRICE	CURRENT PRICE
☐ **FORGOTTEN TREASURES,** rel. 1982. ed. 750, s/n, 18⅛" x 24½", pub WP	45.00	—
☐ **WEDDING RINGS,** rel. 1982. ed. 750, s/n, 18¼" x 24½", pub WP	50.00	—
☐ **JONQUILS AND EIGHT POINT STAR,** rel. 1983. ed. 750, s/n, 18⅛" x 24⅞", pub WP	60.00	—

ROBERT SAUBER

THEMES: Varied

EDUCATION: Art Center College of Design

GALLERY/DISTRIBUTOR: Vague Shadows, Ltd.

	ISSUE PRICE	CURRENT PRICE
☐ **BUTTERFLY,** rel. 1982. ed. 3,000, s/n, 24" x 20", pub VSL	45.00	—

SAM SAVITT

THEMES: Horses

STYLE: Realism

BOOKS: He has written over 14 books and illustrated more than 100. His authoritative works have been used by the Smithsonian and encyclopedias

EDUCATION: Pratt Institute; Art Students League

AWARDS: Official artist for the United States Equestrian Team

GALLERY/DISTRIBUTOR: Mill Pond Press, Inc.

COMMENTS: Savitt states: "The horse is beauty, strength, rhythm, and action. To really know and understand him, to capture his magnificence with pencil or brush, will to me be forever challenging"

	ISSUE PRICE	CURRENT PRICE
☐ **SUMMERTIME,** rel. 1978. ed. 950, s/n, 20" x 23", pub MPPI	65.00	—
☐ **GOING HOME,** rel. 1978. ed. 950, s/n, 20" x 25", pub MPPI	75.00	—
☐ **THE DROP JUMP,** rel. 1979. ed. 950, s/n, 20" x 25", pub MPPI	75.00	—
☐ **THE LAST DAY OF THE RACE,** rel. 1980. ed. 950, s/n, 20" x 25", pub MPPI	65.00	—
☐ **THE STEEPLE CHASER,** rel. 1980. ed. 950, s/n, 18" x 25", pub MPPI	65.00	—
☐ **A DESPERATE TRY,** rel. 1984. ed. 950, s/n, 15½" x 12¼", pub MPPI	40.00	—
☐ **A GAME PONY,** rel. 1984. ed. 950, s/n, 15½" x 12¼", pub MPPI	40.00	—
☐ **A HARD BUMP,** rel. 1984. ed. 950, s/n, 15½" x 12¼", pub MPPI	40.00	—
☐ **TAKING THE MAN FIRST,** rel. 1984. ed. 950, pub MPPI	40.00	40.00

SUMMERTIME *by Sam Savitt*

PAUL SAWYIER
American Impressionist (1865-1917)

THEMES: Landscapes, portraiture

MEDIUM: Watercolor

STYLE: Impressionism

EDUCATION: Cincinnati Art Academy, Art Student's League

GALLERY/DISTRIBUTOR: Paul Sawyier Galleries, Inc.

COMMENTS: During his lifetime, it is estimated that he did over 2,000 paintings, mostly watercolor landscapes, but fewer than 100 portraits. Less than 500 of his works can be accounted for to date.

	ISSUE PRICE	CURRENT PRICE
☐ **ELKHORN CREEK SCENE,** rel. 1965. ed. 1,000, n/o, pub PSGI	15.00	45.00
☐ **KENTUCKY ARSENAL,** rel. 1965. ed. 1,000, n/o, pub PSGI	20.00	275.00
☐ **MOONLIGHT ON THE KENTUCKY,** rel. 1965. ed. 1,000, n/o, pub PSGI	20.00	175.00

CAMP NELSON PALISADES *by Paul Sawyier*

	ISSUE PRICE	CURRENT PRICE
☐ A RAINY DAY IN FRANKFORT, rel. 1965. ed. 1,000, n/o, pub PSGI	20.00	850.00
☐ BARGES ON THE KENTUCKY, rel. 1970. ed. 1,000, n/o, pub PSGI	20.00	65.00
☐ BRIDGE STREET, rel. 1970. ed. 2,000, n/o, pub PSGI	20.00	135.00
☐ THE FISHERMAN, rel. 1970. ed. 2,000, n/o, pub PSGI	20.00	150.00
☐ KENTUCKY RIVER, rel. 1970. ed. 1,000, n/o, pub PSGI	20.00	175.00
☐ NEW YORK HARBOR, rel. 1970. ed. 2,000, n/o, 14⅜" x 20", pub PSGI	20.00	—
☐ THE OLD CAPITOL, rel. 1970. ed. 1,000, n/o, pub PSGI	20.00	365.00
☐ OLD COVERED BRIDGE, rel. 1970. ed. 1,000, n/o, pub PSGI	5.00	25.00
☐ SOUTH END OF OLD COVERED BRIDGE, rel. 1970. ed. 2,000, n/o, pub PSGI	20.00	55.00
☐ SOUTH FORK ELKHORN CREEK, rel. 1970. ed. 2,000, n/o, pub PSGI	10.00	25.00
☐ WAPPING STREET FOUNTAIN, rel. 1970. ed. 1,000, n/o, pub PSGI	20.00	270.00
☐ WINTER IN KENTUCKY, rel. 1970. ed. 1,000, n/o, pub PSGI	20.00	435.00
☐ PEAK'S MILL BEND, rel. 1971. ed. 2,000, n/o, pub PSGI	5.00	20.00
☐ A RAINY DAY AT THE BRIDGE, rel. 1971. ed. 500, n/o, pub PSGI	50.00	260.00
☐ SHAKERTOWN ROAD, rel. 1971. ed. 500, n/o, pub PSGI	50.00	470.00
☐ BIG EDDY, rel. 1972. ed. 2,000, n/o, 13" x 15", pub PSGI	20.00	—
☐ DIX RIVER, rel. 1972. ed. 500, n/o, pub PSGI	50.00	240.00
☐ GOING TO SPRING, rel. 1972. ed. 2,000, n/o, pub PSGI	20.00	55.00
☐ PALISADES, rel. 1972. ed. 500, n/o, pub PSGI	50.00	225.00
☐ THE ROCK BREAKER, rel. 1972. ed. 1,000, n/o, pub PSGI	40.00	—
☐ SHAKERTOWN FERRY, rel. 1972. ed. 2,000, n/o, 17¾" x 31", pub PSGI	30.00	85.00
☐ SPRINGTIME, rel. 1972. ed. 2,000, n/o, pub PSGI	20.00	285.00
☐ THE SUTER HOUSE, rel. 1972. ed. 6,000, n/o, 5½" x 6¼", pub PSGI	5.00	—
☐ THE FOUNTAIN, rel. 1973. ed. 4,000, n/o, pub PSGI	10.00	45.00
☐ GOOD OLD DAYS, rel. 1973. ed. 2,000, n/o, 14" x 19½", pub PSGI	20.00	50.00
☐ LANDMARKS, rel. 1973. ed. 2,000, n/o, 16" x 18½", pub PSGI	20.00	30.00
☐ THE LOWER POOL, rel. 1973. ed. 8,000, n/o, 6¼" x 9½", pub PSGI	5.00	—
☐ MISTY EVENING, rel. 1973. ed. 2,000, n/o, 15" x 19", pub PSGI	20.00	30.00
☐ REFLECTIONS ON ELKHORN CREEK, rel. 1973. ed. 3,000, n/o, pub PSGI	10.00	25.00
☐ A RIVER VIEW OF FRANKFORT, rel. 1973. ed. 3,000, n/o, pub PSGI	15.00	—
☐ A SHADY LANE, rel. 1973. ed. 3,000, n/o, pub PSGI	20.00	—

	ISSUE PRICE	CURRENT PRICE
☐ SUNRISE, rel. 1973. ed. 2,000, n/o, pub PSGI	10.00	—
☐ BRAKING HEMP, rel. 1974. ed. 2,000, n/o, pub PSGI	30.00	—
☐ BEND IN THE RIVER, rel. 1974. ed. 2,000, n/o, pub PSGI	15.00	—
☐ BOYHOOD MEMORIES, rel. 1974. ed. 3,000, n/o, pub PSGI	20.00	90.00
☐ THE CHANNEL'S FORD, rel. 1974. ed. 2,000, n/o, pub PSGI	20.00	45.00
☐ COVERED BRIDGE IN AUTUMN, rel. 1974. ed. 2,000, n/o, pub PSGI	20.00	160.00
☐ KENTUCKY RIVER SCENE, rel. 1974. ed. 8,000, n/o, pub PSGI	5.00	—
☐ LOUISVILLE ROAD, rel. 1974. ed. 2,000, n/o, pub PSGI	20.00	—
☐ MACY'S KENTUCKY RIVER, rel. 1984. ed. 2,000, n/o, pub PSGI	20.00	—
☐ MORNING MOON, rel. 1974. ed. 2,000, n/o, pub PSGI	20.00	—
☐ NORTH FRANKFORT, rel. 1974. ed. 2,000, n/o, pub PSGI	10.00	—
☐ RIVER LOGGING, rel. 1974. ed. 2,000, n/o, pub PSGI	15.00	—
☐ RIVER VALLEY, rel. 1974. ed. 6,000, n/o, pub PSGI	5.00	10.00
☐ SUMMERTIME, rel. 1974. ed. 2,000, n/o, pub PSGI	20.00	30.00
☐ THE WALLED CITY, rel. 1974. ed. 2,000, n/o, pub PSGI	20.00	—
☐ COVERED BRIDGE IN SUMMER, rel. 1975. ed. 3,000, n/o, pub PSGI	20.00	45.00
☐ THE COVERED POND, rel. 1975. ed. 3,000, n/o, pub PSGI	20.00	85.00
☐ FISHERMAN'S CATCH, rel. 1975. ed. 3,000, n/o, pub PSGI	20.00	—
☐ FORKS OF ELKHORN TURNPIKE, rel. 1975. ed. 6,000, n/o, pub PSGI	3.00	—
☐ KENTUCKY RIVER AT CANOE CREEK, rel. 1975. ed. 3,000, n/o, pub PSGI	20.00	—
☐ KNOB HILL ROAD, rel. 1975. ed. 6,000, n/o, pub PSGI	5.00	—
☐ LOUISVILLE PIKE, rel. 1975. ed. 3,000, n/o, pub PSGI	20.00	85.00
☐ MILL POND FISHERMAN, rel. 1975. ed. 6,000, n/o, pub PSGI	3.00	—
☐ OLD RIVER ROAD, rel. 1975. ed. 6,000, n/o, pub PSGI	5.00	—
☐ THE SCENIC KENTUCKY, rel. 1975. ed. 6,000, n/o, pub PSGI	5.00	—
☐ SWITZER COVERED BRIDGE, rel. 1975. ed. 3,000, n/o, pub PSGI	20.00	—
☐ TURKEY RUN, rel. 1975. ed. 3,000, n/o, pub PSGI	20.00	85.00
☐ LOVER'S LEAP, rel. 1976. ed. 1,250, n/o, pub PSGI	50.00	310.00
☐ SHADOWS OF SPRINGTIME, rel. 1976. ed. 2,500, n/o, pub PSGI	10.00	25.00
☐ SNOWY SENTINEL, rel. 1976. ed. 2,000, n/o, pub PSGI	20.00	—
☐ WINTER SOLITUDE, rel. 1976. ed. 3,000, n/o, pub PSGI	15.00	40.00
☐ BURLEY RIDE, rel. 1977. ed. 2,000, n/o, pub PSGI	20.00	—
☐ ELKHORN CREEK DAM, rel. 1977. ed. 2,500, n/o, pub PSGI	15.00	—
☐ EVENING REFLECTIONS, rel. 1977. ed. 2,500, n/o, pub PSGI	20.00	—
☐ OLD ELK'S CLUB, rel. 1977. ed. 2,500, n/o, pub PSGI	30.00	105.00
☐ HIGH BRIDGE, rel. 1978. ed. 2,500, n/o, pub PSGI	25.00	85.00
☐ MAYME ON THE ELKHORN, rel. 1978. ed. 2,500, n/o, pub PSGI	25.00	70.00
☐ THE ROAD TO TOWN, rel. 1978. ed. 2,000, n/o, pub PSGI	25.00	130.00
☐ RIVER CLIFFS, rel. 1978. ed. 1,250, n/o, pub PSGI	65.00	215.00
☐ CAPITOL IN WITNER, rel. 1979. ed. 3,000, n/o, pub PSGI	30.00	175.00
☐ FIRST TRAP, rel. 1979. ed. 1,450, n/o, pub PSGI	65.00	250.00
☐ RIVER FRIENDS, rel. 1979. ed. 2,500, n/o, pub PSGI	20.00	45.00
☐ RIVER PATHWAY, rel. 1979. ed. 3,000, n/o, pub PSGI	20.00	40.00
☐ ROADSIDE SPRING, rel. 1979. ed. 3,500, n/o, pub PSGI	5.00	20.00
☐ TOLL GATE, rel. 1979. ed. 2,500, n/o, pub PSGI	20.00	60.00
☐ BRIDGE TO MEMORIES, rel. 1980. ed. 2,500, n/o, pub PSGI	15.00	—
☐ CAMP NELSON PALISADES, rel. 1980. ed. 2,500, n/o, pub PSGI	30.00	—
☐ DIX RIVER FISH TRAP, rel. 1980. ed. 3,000, n/o, pub PSGI	25.00	—
☐ AN OLD KENTUCKY HOME, rel. 1980. ed. 2,100, n/o, pub PSGI	65.00	145.00
☐ LEANING SYCAMORE, rel. 1980. ed. 2,000, n/o, pub PSGI	10.00	20.00
☐ VEST—LINDSEY HOUSE, rel. 1980. ed. 3,500, n/o, pub PSGI	20.00	} PAIR $300
☐ WAPPING STREET VIEW, rel. 1980. ed. 3,500, n/o, pub PSGI	20.00	
☐ CAPITAL HOTEL GASLIGHT, rel. 1981. ed. 3,000, n/o, pub PSGI	20.00	—
☐ CLIFFSIDE ROAD, rel. 1981. ed. 2,500, n/o, pub PSGI	25.00	—
☐ JOURNEY HOME, rel. 1981. ed. 2,500, n/o, pub PSGI	45.00	—
☐ SECLUDED BYWAY, rel. 1981. ed. 3,500, n/o, pub PSGI	10.00	—
☐ WINTER STROLL, rel. 1981. ed. 3,800, n/o, pub PSGI	30.00	50.00
☐ BEYOND THE HILL, rel. 1982. ed. 2,000, n/o, pub PSGI	4.00	—
☐ FROM THE QUARRY, rel. 1982. ed. 3,500, n/o, pub PSGI	35.00	—
☐ THE HOLIDAY, rel. 1982. ed. 2,500, n/o, pub PSGI	25.00	—
☐ INDIAN HEAD ROCK, rel. 1982. ed. 2,500, n/o, pub PSGI	45.00	—

	ISSUE PRICE	CURRENT PRICE
☐ MAIN STREET 1900, rel. 1982. ed. 3,850, n/o, pub PSGI	30.00	65.00
☐ RIVER REFLECTIONS, rel. 1982. ed. 2,000, n/o, pub PSGI	4.00	—
☐ WAPPING STREET REFLECTIONS, rel. 1982. ed. 3,500, n/o, pub PSGI	35.00	100.00
☐ KENTUCKY CLIFFS, rel. 1983. ed. 2,000, s/o, pub PSGI	25.00	—
☐ VILLAGE STREAM, rel. 1983. ed. 2,000, n/o, pub PSGI	25.00	—
☐ AUTUMN AT THE BRIDGE, rel. 1983. ed. 2,750, n/o, pub PSGI	35.00	75.00
☐ THE UPPER POOL, rel. 1983. ed. 1,000, n/o, pub PSGI	65.00	95.00
☐ MORNING RIDE, rel. 1983. ed. 2,000, n/o, pub PSGI	20.00	65.00
☐ EAST VIEW, rel. 1983. ed. 2,000, n/o, pub PSGI	5.00	—
☐ FRANKFORT REFLECTIONS, rel. 1984. ed. 2,000, n/o, pub PSGI	15.00	—
☐ KENTUCKY VALLEY, rel. 1984. ed. 2,000, n/o, pub PSGI	30.00	—
☐ STONY BROOK, rel. 1984. ed. 2,000, n/o, pub PSGI	55.00	—
☐ WINTER STREAM, rel. 1984. ed. 2,000, n/o, pub PSGI	30.00	65.00
☐ AUTUMN TWILIGHT, rel. 1985. ed. 2,000, n/o, pub PSGI	35.00	—
☐ SUMMER SUNSET, rel. 1985. ed. 2,000, n/o, pub PSGI	25.00	—
☐ THE FULLER RIFFLE, rel. 1985. ed. 2,000, n/o, pub PSGI	10.00	—
☐ PANTHER RAVINE - CAMP NELSON, rel. 1985. ed. 1,500, n/o, 18" x 27", pub PSGI	85.00	—

MANFRED SCHATZ

THEMES: Animal and hunting scenes

STYLE: He portrays wildlife as most of us see it—in quick, often shadowy glimpses

EDUCATION: School of Arts and Crafts (Stetten, East Germany); Academy of Pictorial Arts

GALLERY/DISTRIBUTOR: Russell A. Fink

	ISSUE PRICE	CURRENT PRICE
☐ BRIEF INTERLUDE, ed. 500, s/n, 15½" x 21½", pub RAF	80.00	250.00
☐ LYNX, ed. 500, s/n, 18" x 27¼", pub RAF	100.00	250.00
☐ WINGED MAJESTY, ed. 500, s/n, 16" x 22", pub RAF	80.00	350.00
☐ MALLARDS, ed. 500, s/n, 19" x 25", pub RAF	100.00	450.00
☐ OUT OF THE MIST, ed. 500, s/n, 12" x 16", pub RAF	60.00	225.00
☐ WOLF PACK, ed. 500, s/n, 17½" x 27", pub RAF	125.00	650.00
☐ WINTER FOX, ed. 500, s/n, 12" x 18⅜", pub RAF	60.00	—
☐ OUT OF THE MARSHGRASS, ed. 750, s/n, 18" x 26¼", pub RAF	125.00	250.00
☐ SNOW HARE, ed. 650, s/n, 16" x 19½", pub RAF	100.00	—
☐ SWANS, ed. 500, s/n, size not available, pub RAF	150.00	—
☐ LATE SEASON - MALLARDS, rel. 1982. ed. 500, s/n, size not available, pub RAF	125.00	—
☐ FEATHERED MAGIC, rel. 1983. ed. 750, s/n, 12" x 15", pub RAF	90.00	—
☐ LEADER OF THE PACK, rel. 1983. ed. 500, s/n, 17" x 23", pub RAF	150.00	250.00
☐ QUIET EVENING, rel. 1984. ed. 750, s/n, 12½" x 17¾", pub RAF	95.00	—
☐ COMING IN, rel. 1984. ed. 750, s/n, litho, 12" x 17¾", pub RAF	95.00	—
☐ CHALLENGED, rel. 1985. ed. 850, s/n, litho, 17" x 24¼", pub RAF	150.00	—
☐ OCTOBER MORN, rel. 1985. ed. 850, s/n, litho, 18¼" x 25", pub RAF	150.00	—

SHADOWING MEMORIES by Dennis Schmidt

DENNIS SCHMIDT

THEMES: Varied

MEDIUM: Mixed, including a challenging technique combining opaque and transparent watercolors

AWARDS: Many gold and silver awards; Popular Choice Awards, etc.

MEMBERSHIPS: Texas Association of Professional Artists

GALLERY/DISTRIBUTOR: Somerset House Limited/Dennis Schmidt

COMMENTS: The artist claims, "There's no reason why one artist, who truly loves and appreciates a wide scope of life, should not try to master every subject that stimulates him. Life is change, and adaptability is the key to survival"

	ISSUE PRICE	CURRENT PRICE
☐ **COMING IN,** rel. 1979. ed. 500, s/n, 15" x 22½", pub DS	30.00	475.00
ed. 750, s/o	20.00	185.00
☐ **GATHERING CALLERS,** rel. 1979. ed. 500, s/n, 12" x 16", pub DS	22.00	450.00
ed. 750, s/o	15.00	125.00
☐ **IN THE EARLY LIGHT,** rel. 1979. ed. 1,000, s/n, 13½" x 20", pub DS	30.00	300.00
☐ **MOURNING DOVE,** rel. 1979. ed, 1,000, s/n, 9" x 13", pub DS	20.00	200.00
☐ **COTTONTAIL,** rel. 1980. ed. 970, s/n, 10" x 14", pub DS	32.00	80.00
☐ **MISCHIEF MAKER,** rel. 1980. ed. 970, 10" x 14", pub DS	30.00	95.00
☐ **EARLY ENCOUNTER,** rel. 1980. ed. 990, s/n, 14" x 20", pub DS	30.00	275.00
☐ **SHADOWING MEMORIES,** rel. 1980. ed. 980, s/n, 12" x 24", pub DS	34.00	170.00
☐ **AFTER THE RAIN,** rel. 1981. ed. 900, s/n, 14" x 20", pub DS	45.00	125.00
☐ **CALLING A FLUSH,** rel. 1981. ed. 900, s/n, 14" x 20", pub DS	45.00	350.00
☐ **HOME SEEKER,** rel. 1981. ed. 970, s/n, 18" x 24", pub DS	60.00	365.00
ed. 1,000, s/o	35.00	165.00
☐ **BLUE HARMONY,** rel. 1982. ed. 970, s/n, 12" x 24", pub DS	65.00	170.00
☐ **RUSTIC RADIANCE,** rel. 1982. ed. 970, s/n, 12" x 16", pub DS	50.00	125.00

	ISSUE PRICE	CURRENT PRICE
☐ TURKEY ON THE ROCKS, rel. 1982. ed. 970, s/n, 17″ x 24″, pub DS	70.00	340.00
ed. 1,000, s/o	40.00	110.00
☐ YOU CAN HEAR IT IF YOU TRY, rel. 1982. ed. 970, s/n, 12″ x 24″, pub DS	65.00	110.00
☐ BREAKING THE MORNING SILENCE, rel. 1983. ed. 970, s/n, 17″ x 25½″, pub Somerset	70.00	380.00
☐ RING-NECKED PHEASANT, rel. 1983. ed. 970, s/n, 16″ x 24″, pub Somerset	70.00	150.00
☐ SPRING TRAINING, rel. 1983. ed. 970, s/n, 14″ x 20″, pub Somerset	65.00	260.00
☐ BACKWATER HAVEN, rel. 1984. ed. 970, s/n, 17″ x 25½″, pub Somerset	80.00	225.00
☐ COMPANIONS, rel. 1984. ed. 970, s/n, 18″ x 27″, pub Somerset	80.00	—
☐ MOONLIT MEMORIES, rel. 1984. ed. 970, s/n, 16″ x 24″, pub Somerset	70.00	—
☐ RENDEZVOUS, rel. 1984. ed. 970, s/n, 18″ x 24″, pub Somerset	75.00	135.00
☐ WHISPERING HAZE, rel. 1984. ed. 970, s/n, 16″ x 24″, pub Somerset	70.00	—
☐ WHISTLER'S HOLLOW, rel. 1985. ed. 970, s/n, 16½″ x 20″, pub Somerset	80.00	150.00

JAY SCHMIDT

THEMES: Indian art

GALLERY/DISTRIBUTOR: Frame House Gallery, Inc.

	ISSUE PRICE	CURRENT PRICE
☐ TOMORROW'S DREAM, rel. 1983. ed. 975, s/n, 18″ x 28″, pub FHG	80.00	—
☐ MONEY TO SPEND, rel. 1983. ed. 975, s/n, 17¾″ x 21¾″, pub FHG	80.00	—
☐ SECOND THOUGHTS, rel. 1984. ed. 975, s/n, 24″ x 29½″, pub FHG	80.00	—

MONEY TO SPEND *by Jay Schmidt*

JOHN SCHOENHERR

THEMES: Animals

BOOKS: The artist has been the illustrator for numerous books, including children's books. *The Barn* was written and illustrated by Schoenherr

EDUCATION: Pratt Institute; Art Students League

AWARDS: His book illustrations have received numerous awards and citations

MUSEUMS/COLLECTIONS: He has painted for the Air Force and private collections

GALLERY/DISTRIBUTOR: Greenwich Workshop

	ISSUE PRICE	CURRENT PRICE
☐ SAHIB, rel. 1975. ed. 850, s/n, 30″ x 20″, pub GW	65.00	185.00
☐ SPOTTED LEOPARD, rel. 1975. ed. 850, s/n, 18¼″ x 18¼″, pub GW	55.00	120.00
☐ GRIZZLY, rel. 1976. ed. 850, s/n, 30½″ x 20¾″, pub GW	65.00	—
☐ MOUNTAIN LION FAMILY, rel. 1977. ed. 1,000, s/n, 22″ x 29″, pub GW	65.00	—
☐ CLAM BAR, rel. 1978. ed. 1,000, s/n, 32″ x 22″, pub GW	65.00	—
☐ CLOSE ENOUGH, rel. 1979. ed. 1,000, s/n, 17″ x 21″, pub GW	60.00	—

THOMAS SCHULTZ

THEMES: Wildlife art

EDUCATION: University of Wisconsin

GALLERY/DISTRIBUTOR: Northwoods Craftsman

	ISSUE PRICE	CURRENT PRICE
☐ BLUE JAY, rel. 1980. ed. 400, s/n, 16″ x 20″, distr. NC	35.00	—
☐ ROSE-BREASTED GROSBEAKS, rel. 1980. ed. 400, s/n, 16″ x 20″, distr. NC	35.00	—
☐ YOUNG BIRDS - BLUE JAY, rel. 1980. ed. 400, s/n, 11″ x 14″, distr. NC	30.00	—
☐ YOUNG BIRDS - ROBIN, rel. 1980. ed. 400, s/n, 11″ x 14″, distr. NC	30.00	—

TIMOTHY C. SCHULTZ

THEMES: Wildlife art

MEDIUM: Oil

AWARDS: Wisconsin Waterfowl Stamp Contest (1981)

GALLERY/DISTRIBUTOR: Northwoods Craftsman

1981 WISCONSIN DUCK *by Timothy Schultz*

	ISSUE PRICE	CURRENT PRICE
☐ **BLUEBILLS,** rel. 1981. ed. 1,700, s/n, 14″ x 12″, pub NC	125.00	175.00
1981 Wisconsin Duck Stamp Print. ed. 300 remarqued	300.00	—
☐ **PEACEFUL PAIR - WOODIES,** rel. 1981. ed. 600, s/n, 28″ x 20½″, pub NC	75.00	—
☐ **AT CATTAILS EDGE - HOODED MERGANSERS,** rel. 1983. ed. 600, s/n, 14½″ x 25½″, pub NC	60.00	—
☐ **1984 WISCONSIN TROUT STAMP PRINT,** rel. 1983. ed. 600, s/n, 14″ x 12″, pub NC	135.00	—
ed. 100, remarqued	250.00	400.00
☐ **WINTER'S DELIGHT - BLACK CAPPED CHICKADEE,** rel. 1985. ed. 600, s/n, 9½″ x 13″, pub NC	40.00	—

KEN SCHULZ

THEMES: Wildlife art

GALLERY/DISTRIBUTOR: Swan Graphics, Ltd.

	ISSUE PRICE	CURRENT PRICE
☐ **CADES COVE,** ed. 350, s/n, 18½″ x 23″, distr. SGL	75.00	—
☐ **CHURCH IN THE GLADE,** ed. 500, s/n, 18½″ x 23″, distr. SGL	60.00	—
☐ **DOGWOOD,** ed. 500, s/n, 15″ x 19″, distr. SGL	40.00	—
☐ **GERANIUM,** ed. 500, s/n, 28″ x 23″, distr. SGL	85.00	—
☐ **GOVERNOR JOHN SEVIER'S PLACE,** ed. 500, s/n, 22″ x 26″, distr. SGL	85.00	—

		ISSUE PRICE	CURRENT PRICE
☐	GREENBRIER, ed. 500, s/n, 18½″ x 23″, distr. SGL	75.00	—
☐	JUNGLE BROOK WINTER, ed. 500, s/n, 15″ x 19″, distr. SGL	40.00	—
☐	PORTRAIT OF AUTUMN, ed. 500, s/n, 15″ x 19″, distr. SGL	40.00	—
☐	SHADOWS, ed. 500, s/n, 15″ x 19″, distr. SGL	50.00	—
☐	THE SOWERS, ed. 500, s/n, 20½″ x 26¾″, distr. SGL	85.00	—
☐	THRU THE BARN, ed. 350, s/n, 18½″ x 23″, distr. SGL	85.00	—
☐	WINTER WONDERLAND, ed. 500, s/n, 15″ x 19″, distr. SGL	40.00	—

JAMES GODWIN SCOTT

THEMES: River subjects

MEDIUM: Watercolor

STYLE: A hint of abstraction enhances his work

BACKGROUND: For over 25 years, Scott has painted along the riverbanks of America

GALLERY/DISTRIBUTOR: Mill Pond Press, Inc.

BECKY THATCHER *by James Godwin Scott*

	ISSUE PRICE	CURRENT PRICE
☐ **BECKY THATCHER,** rel. 1979. ed. 950, s/n, 20¼" x 25¼", pub MPPI	75.00	—

JOHN SCOTT

THEMES: Wildlife/Old West

BACKGROUND: For 33 years, Scott sketched and painted exclusively for *Sports Afield*

GALLERY/DISTRIBUTOR: Mill Pond Press, Inc.

	ISSUE PRICE	CURRENT PRICE
☐ **THE WATERFALL,** rel. 1981. ed. 950, s/n, 15¼" x 24½", pub MPPI	85.00	—
☐ **THE TROUT STREAM,** rel. 1982. ed. 950, s/n, 18" x 24", pub MPPI	95.00	—
☐ **YELLOWSTONE CROSSING,** rel. 1982. ed. 950, s/n, 14¾" x 24", pub MPPI	85.00	—

SIR PETER SCOTT

THEMES: Wildlife art (Wildfowl, in particular)

BOOKS: As an author and co-author, the artist has 14 books to his credit, including *The Eye of the Wind*, his autobiography written in 1962

EDUCATION: At Cambridge, Scott studied zoology. He also studied at the Munich State Academy and the Royal Academy Schools in London

AWARDS: He has been acclaimed worldwide, and made a Knight Bachelor in 1973 for his conservation efforts

MEMBERSHIPS: He founded The Wildfowl Trust; International Chairman of the World Wildlife Funds

GALLERY/DISTRIBUTOR: Mill Pond Press, Inc.

COMMENTS: In addition to being a fine artist, Sir Peter is a great naturalist, author, illustrator, ornithologist, ichthyologist, conservationist, broadcaster, lecturer, and sportsman

	ISSUE PRICE	CURRENT PRICE
☐ **CANADA GEESE ARRIVING OUT OF A MIST,** rel. 1977. ed. 950, s/n, 22½" x 31", pub MPPI	125.00	250.00
☐ **CANADA GEESE COMING TO THE MARSH,** rel. 1981. ed. 950, s/n, 22" x 26", pub MPPI	125.00	175.00

THE REFUGE - RACCOONS *by John Seerey-Lester*

JOHN SEEREY-LESTER

THEMES: Wildlife art; varied themes

EDUCATION: Salford Technical College

GALLERY/DISTRIBUTOR: Mill Pond Press, Inc.

COMMENTS: Seerey-Lester's art has aided many charities, including the World Wildlife Fund

	ISSUE PRICE	CURRENT PRICE
☐ **COOL RETREAT - LYNX,** rel. 1983. ed. 950, 19″ x 22″, pub MPPI	850.00	—
☐ **EARLY WINDFALL - GRAY SQUIRRELS,** rel. 1983. ed. 950, 17½″ x 20″, pub MPPI .	85.00	—
☐ **FIRST SNOW - GRIZZLY BEAR,** rel. 1983. ed. 950, 20″ x 24″, pub MPPI	95.00	175.00
☐ **LONE FISHERMAN - GREAT BLUE HERON,** rel. 1983. ed. 950, 21½″ x 17″, pub MPPI	85.00	150.00
☐ **RIVER WATCH - PEREGRINE FALCON,** rel. 1983. ed. 950, 21¼″ x 17½″, pub MPPI	85.00	160.00
☐ **THE REFUGE - RACCOONS,** rel. 1983. ed. 950, 15″ x 30″, pub MPPI	85.00	—
☐ **WINTER LOOKOUT - COUGAR,** rel. 1983. ed. 950, 23½″ x 18″, pub MPPI	85.00	135.00
☐ **AMONG THE CATTAILS - CANADA GEESE,** rel. 1984. ed. 950, 22″ x 27½″, pub MPPI	130.00	165.00
☐ **BREAKING COVER - BLACK BEAR,** rel. 1984. ed. 950, 22″ x 31½″, pub MPPI	130.00	—
☐ **BASKING - BROWN PELICANS,** rel. 1984. ed. 950, 21″ x 29″, pub MPPI	115.00	—
☐ **CLOSE ENCOUNTER - BOBCAT,** rel. 1984. ed. 950, 17½″ x 21″, pub MPPI	130.00	—
☐ **HIGH GROUND - WOLVES,** rel. 1984. ed. 950, 22″ x 29½″, pub MPPI	130.00	185.00
☐ **ICY OUTCROP - WHITE GYRFALCON,** rel. 1984. ed. 950, 28″ x 19½″, pub MPPI ..	115.00	—
☐ **LYING LOW - COUGAR,** rel. 1984. ed. 950, 17½″ x 21″, pub MPPI	85.00	—
☐ **MORNING MIST - SNOWY OWL,** rel. 1984. ed. 950, 19″ x 23″, pub MPPI	95.00	—
☐ **PLAINS HUNTER - PRAIRIE FALCON,** rel. 1984. ed. 950, 17½″ x 24″, pub MPPI ...	95.00	—
☐ **SPIRIT OF THE NORTH - WHITE WOLF,** rel. 1984. ed. 950, 27½″ x 22½″, pub MPPI	130.00	—

	ISSUE PRICE	CURRENT PRICE
☐ EARLY SNOW - RED FOX, rel. 1985. ed. 950, s/n, 14¾" x 24½", pub MPPI	85.00	—
☐ ISLAND SANCTUARY - MALLARDS, rel. 1985. ed. 950, s/n, 24½" x 17⅜", pub MPPI	95.00	—
☐ WINTER RENDEZVOUS - COYOTES, rel. 1985. ed. 950, s/n, 24½" x 34¼", pub MPPI	140.00	165.00

ADOLF SEHRING

THEMES: Varied

STYLE: Realism

BOOKS: *Adolf Sehring and Realism*

GALLERY/DISTRIBUTOR: Eleanor Ettinger, Inc.

	ISSUE PRICE	CURRENT PRICE
☐ END OF DAY, rel. 1980. ed. 300, s/n, litho, arches, 24½" x 29", pub EEI	450.00	—
☐ GATHERING FLOWERS, rel. 1980. ed. 300, s/n, litho, arches, 25" x 28", pub EEI ...	275.00	400.00
☐ GOLDEN HARVEST, rel. 1980. ed. 300, s/n, litho, arches, 29" x 24¼", pub EEI	350.00	500.00
☐ PRUNING, rel. 1980. ed. 300, s/n, litho, arches, 33¼" x 24", pub EEI	275.00	450.00
☐ SNOWDRIFT, rel. 1980. ed. 300, s/n, litho, arches, 34" x 22½", pub EEI	350.00	400.00
☐ SUMMER BY THE SEA, rel. 1984. ed. 300, s/n, 29" x 24", pub EEI	400.00	—
☐ SUMMER WOODS, rel. 1980. ed. 300, s/n, litho, arches, 24" x 29", pub EEI	275.00	400.00
☐ VIOLETS, rel. 1980. ed. 300, s/n, litho, arches, 25" x 29", pub EEI	275.00	500.00

OLAF C. SELTZER

MEDIUM: Oil and watercolor

GALLERY/DISTRIBUTOR: Wild Wings, Inc.

	ISSUE PRICE	CURRENT PRICE
☐ COUNCIL ABOVE THE MUSSELSHELL, rel. 1982. ed. 850, litho, 25" x 16¾", pub WWI..	125.00	—
☐ FORDING THE BREAKS, rel. 1982. ed.850, litho, 25" x 16¾", pub WWI	125.00	—
☐ SUNSET MESSENGER, rel. 1982. ed. 850, litho, 16" x 12", pub WWI	75.00	—

JOE SEME

THEMES: Still life (of varied themes)

STYLE: Trompe l'oeil

EDUCATION: Florida State University

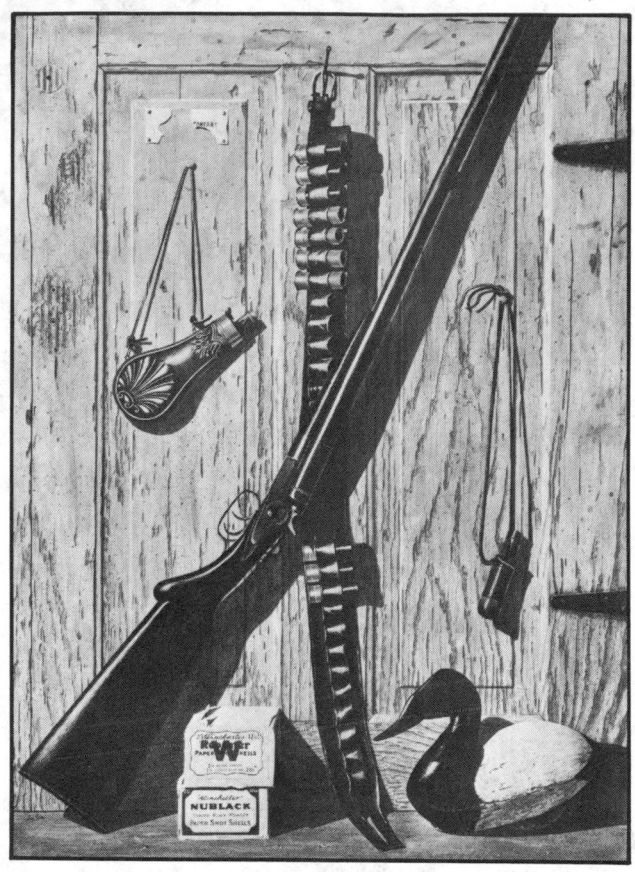

BACK BAY GUNNER *by Joe Seme*

MUSEUMS/COLLECTIONS: His work can be found in important corporate and private collections worldwide

GALLERY/DISTRIBUTOR: Mill Pond Press, Inc.

	ISSUE PRICE	CURRENT PRICE
☐ **BACK BAY GUNNER,** rel. 1981. ed. 450, s/n, 25¼″ x 20″, pub MPPI	85.00	—

KEITH SHACKLETON

THEMES: Varied

BOOKS: He is the author of five books including *Tidelines* and *A Sailor's Guide to Ocean Birds*

TIGER IN BAMBOO GRASS *by Keith Shackleton*

BACKGROUND: Shackleton was a war artist with the Army and Naval Coastal forces of Great Britain

GALLERY/DISTRIBUTOR: Mill Pond Press, Inc.

	ISSUE PRICE	CURRENT PRICE
☐ ADELIE PENGUINS, rel. 1977. ed. 950, s/n, 13″ x 9″, pub MPPI	25.00	—
☐ IN THE ISLANDS - BALD EAGLE, ed. 950, s/n, 17¾″ x 24½″, pub MPPI	95.00	—
☐ GENTOO PENGUINS, rel. 1977. ed. 450, s/n, 19½″ x 24″, pub MPPI	75.00	—
☐ M.S. LINDBALD EXPLORER, rel. 1977. ed. 950, s/n, 9″ x 12″, pub MPPI	25.00	—
☐ SKI SCENE, ed. 950, s/n, 9½″ x 16⅜″, pub MPPI	N/A	—
☐ TIGER IN BAMBOO GRASS, ed. 950, s/n, 27″ x 18″, pub MPPI	85.00	—

LEO SHANIKA

THEMES: Rural landscape art

MUSEUMS/COLLECTIONS: Harry S. Truman Center in Kansas City, Mo.

GALLERY/DISTRIBUTOR: Paul Sawyier Galleries, Inc.

	ISSUE PRICE	CURRENT PRICE
☐ **MAX CREEK ROAD,** rel. 1979. ed. 1,000, s/n, 19″ x 12⅝″, pub PSGI	20.00	—
☐ **HERSHEY'S MILL,** rel. 1979. ed. 1,000, s/n, 19″ x 16⅜″, pub PSGI	20.00	—

DAN SHORT

THEMES: Wildlife art

EDUCATION: Berea College, Kentucky

GALLERY/DISTRIBUTOR: National Wildlife Art Exchange, Inc.

	ISSUE PRICE	CURRENT PRICE
THE DECORATOR SERIES		
☐ **THE BLUE JAYS,** rel. 1976. ed. 1,500, s/n, 20″ x 16″, pub NWAEI	30.00	—
☐ **INQUISITIVE RACCOONS,** rel. 1976. ed. number unknown, s/n, 20″ x 16″, pub NWAEI	30.00	40.00

GEORGE SHUMATE

THEMES: Varied

GALLERY/DISTRIBUTOR: Frame House Gallery, Inc.

	ISSUE PRICE	CURRENT PRICE
☐ **LOOKOUT POINT,** rel. 1981. ed. 3,000, s/o, 23¾″ x 18″, pub FHG	25.00	—
☐ **NORRIS' DECOYS,** rel. 1981. ed. 975, s/n, 21¼″ x 30″, pub FHG	65.00	—
☐ **AUTUMN FROLIC,** rel. 1982. ed. 975, s/n, 20″ x 28″, pub FHG	60.00	—
☐ **ROCKY HAVEN,** rel. 1982. ed. 975, s/n, 21″ x 38″, pub FHG	65.00	—

HUBERT SHUPTRINE

THEMES: Americana

MEDIUM: Watercolor

STYLE: Realism

BOOKS: *Jericho: The South Beheld* by James Dickey and illustrated by the artist

GALLERY/DISTRIBUTOR: Highmark Press

	ISSUE PRICE	CURRENT PRICE
☐ **PLANTATION TUB,** rel. 1977. ed. 300, s/n, 30″ x 21″, pub HP	500.00	625.00
☐ **SUMMER AGAIN,** rel. 1977. ed. 300, s/n, 28″ x 40″, pub HP	500.00	625.00
ed. 750, s/o	20.00	—

MICHAEL SIEVE

THEMES: Wildlife art

MEDIUM: Oil

EDUCATION: Southern Minnesota State College

GALLERY/DISTRIBUTOR: Wild Wings, Inc.

	ISSUE PRICE	CURRENT PRICE
☐ OCTOBER SNOWFALL - WHITETAIL DEER, rel. 1980. ed. 850, s/n, size not available, pub WWI	65.00	450.00
☐ ALPINE MEADOW - ELK, rel. 1981. ed. 850, s/n, 17½" x 25", pub WWI	75.00	—
☐ EDGE OF THE FOREST - BALD EAGLE, rel. 1981. ed. 850, s/n, size not available, pub WWI	75.00	350.00
☐ FAST BREAK - WHITETAIL DEER, rel. 1981. ed. 850, s/n, size not available, pub WWI	75.00	250.00
☐ ALASKAN CLASSIC - DALL SHEEP, rel. 1982. ed. 850, s/n, 17½" x 25", pub WWI .	75.00	—
☐ DECEMBER SNOWFALL - RED FOX, rel. 1982. ed. 850, s/n, size not available, pub WWI	75.00	350.00
☐ RIVER BOTTOM BUCK - WHITETAIL DEER, rel. 1982. ed. 950, s/n, size not available, pub WWI	85.00	350.00
☐ CAUTIOUS APPROACH - WHITETAIL DEER, rel. 1983. ed. 850, s/n, litho, 16¾" x 22½", pub WWI	85.00	250.00
☐ SEASON'S END - WHITETAIL DEER, rel. 1983. ed. 850, s/n, litho, 16½" x 25", pub WWI	75.00	350.00
☐ SUMAC BUCK, rel. 1983. ed. 950, s/n, litho, 12" x 16½", pub WWI	45.00	90.00
☐ ATHABASCA RIVER CHALLENGE - ELK, rel. 1984. ed. 850, s/n, litho, 15" x 27½", pub WWI	75.00	275.00
☐ PAGODA PEAK - MULE DEER, rel. 1984. ed. 650, s/n, litho, 16½" x 25", pub WWI .	75.00	—
☐ ALASKAN CLASSIC - MOOSE, rel. 1985. ed. 650, s/n, litho, 17½" x 24", pub WWI .	75.00	—
☐ LAST GLANCE AT TRAIL'S END, rel. 1985. ed. 950, s/n, litho, 16½" x 25", pub WWI	75.00	—

ARTHUR SINGER

THEMES: Wildlife art

STYLE: Realism

BOOK: *Birds of the World*, a collaboration with Oliver L. Austin, Jr.

EDUCATION: Cooper Union

MEMBERSHIPS: American Ornithologists Union

GALLERY/DISTRIBUTOR: Frame House Gallery, Inc.

	ISSUE PRICE	CURRENT PRICE
☐ BALTIMORE ORIOLE, rel. 1973. ed. 4,000, s/o, 20" x 26", pub FHG	45.00	Sold Out
☐ PHEASANT, rel. 1973. ed. 1,000, s/n, 32½" x 24", pub FHG	75.00	100.00
ed. 2,500, s/o	60.00	Sold Out
☐ BROWN PELICAN, rel. 1974. ed. 1,000, s/n, 33½" x 24", released FHG	40.00	Sold Out
☐ CLOUDED LEOPARD, rel. 1974. ed. 4,000, s/o, 22" x 28", pub FHG	45.00	70.00
☐ ROADRUNNER, rel. 1974. ed. 3,500, s/o, 16" x 22½", pub FHG	30.00	Sold Out
☐ ROBIN, rel. 1974. ed. 4,000, s/o, 16" x 22½", pub FHG	30.00	Sold Out
☐ BELTED KINGFISHER, rel. 1975. ed. 3,000, s/o, 17" x 22", pub FHG	30.00	45.00
☐ BURROWING OWL, rel. 1975. ed. 3,000, s/o, 16" x 20", pub FHG	30.00	Sold Out

		ISSUE PRICE	CURRENT PRICE
☐ **ON THE ALERT,** rel. 1975. ed. 1,000, s/n, 30½" x 23½", pub FHG		65.00	Sold Out
ed. 1,500, s/o		50.00	Sold Out
☐ **RACCOON,** rel. 1975. ed. 2,000, s/n, 20" x 24", pub FHG		**50.00	—
**This limited edition print was released in the AMERICA'S WILDLIFE HERITAGE PORT-FOLIO, which consists of six prints in all, each by a different Frame House Gallery artist.			
☐ **GOLDEN EAGLE,** rel. 1976. ed. 1,200, s/n, 30" x 27", pub FHG		50.00	Sold Out
☐ **RED-HEADED WOODPECKER,** rel. 1976. ed. 1,000, s/o, 22½" x 16", pub FHG		30.00	Sold Out
☐ **RED-TAILED HAWK,** rel. 1976. ed. 1,500, s/o, 18" x 24", pub FHG		*30.00	90.00
*A portion of the edition reserved for The Museum of Arts and Sciences of Macon, Georgia.			
☐ **CARDINAL,** rel. 1977. ed. 1,000, s/o, 20" x 16", pub FHG		45.00	110.00
☐ **EASTERN BLUEBIRD,** rel. 1977. ed. 1,000, s/o, 20" x 16", pub FHG		45.00	Sold Out
☐ **HERON AND EGRET,** rel. 1977. ed. 500, s/n, 24" x 30", pub FHG		*75.00	125.00
*Of the edition, 100 prints were reserved for the Florida Audubon Society.			
☐ **SONGBIRD TRIO,** rel. 1977. ed. 1,500, s/o, 15" x 12", pub FHG .... set		45.00	Sold Out
☐ **JAPANESE CRANES,** rel. 1978. ed. 800, s/n, 14" x 42", pub FHG		60.00	125.00
☐ **PEREGRINE FALCON,** rel. 1978. ed. 800, s/n, 37⅞" x 18", pub FHG		60.00	115.00

ANTON SIPOS

THEMES: Varied

MUSEUMS/COLLECTIONS: He is represented in international collections

GALLERY/DISTRIBUTOR: Eleanor Ettinger, Inc.

		ISSUE PRICE	CURRENT PRICE
☐ **HANSOM CAB,** rel. 1977. ed. 250, s/n, size not available, litho, arches, pub WWI ...		100.00	—
☐ **PEOPLE,** rel. 1977. ed. 250, s/n, 21½" x 43", litho, arches, pub EEI		100.00	—

ROBERT OLIVER SKEMP

THEMES: Marine art

BACKGROUND: As an illustrator, Skemp worked for a variety of companies and publications

EDUCATION: Art Students League under the tutelage of Thomas Hart Benton, George Bridgeman, and Frank V. DuMond

AWARDS: Numerous awards, including three Gold Medals, from the Art Director's Clubs of New York and Chicago

GALLERY/DISTRIBUTOR: Mill Pond Press, Inc.

		ISSUE PRICE	CURRENT PRICE
☐ **FLYING CLOUD,** rel. 1978. ed. 950, s/n, 21" x 29", pub MPPI		125.00	150.00
☐ **HONG KONG HARBOR/NIGHTINGALE GETTING UNDER WAY,** rel. 1978. ed. 950, s/n, 23" x 29", pub MPPI		125.00	—

HONG KONG HARBOR - NIGHTINGALE GETTING UNDER WAY
by Robert Oliver Skemp

PETER SKIRKA

THEMES: Wildlife art

GALLERY/DISTRIBUTOR: Frame House Gallery, Inc.

	ISSUE PRICE	CURRENT PRICE
☐ STORM WATCH, rel. 1981. ed. 1,500, s/n, 22½″ x 38″, pub FHG	80.00	140.00
☐ BAMBOO BEARS, rel. 1982. ed. 4,000, s/o, 15″ x 12″, pub FHG	25.00	—
☐ THE HUNTER'S RETURN, rel. 1982. ed. 1,500, s/n, 20″ x 29½″, pub FHG	80.00	120.00
☐ FOREST WATCH, rel. 1982. ed. 1,500, s/n, 28″ x 22″, pub FHG	80.00	200.00
☐ BOBCAT, rel. 1983. ed. 300, s/o, 17¼″ x 14¼″, pub FHG	45.00	—
☐ LION CUBS, rel. 1983. ed. 1,500, s/n, 28″ x 16″, pub FHG	80.00	Sold Out
☐ THE PURSUIT, rel. 1983. ed. 1,500, s/n, 23″ x 30″, pub FHG	80.00	310.00
☐ THE WAIT, rel. 1983. ed. 1,500, s/n, 23¼″ x 18¾″, pub FHG	80.00	170.00
☐ COUGAR (HEAD), rel. 1984. ed. 3,000, s/n, 18″ x 15″, pub FHG	50.00	—
☐ MOONLIGHT SEARCH, rel. 1984. ed. 1,500, s/n, 28″ x 19″, pub FHG	90.00	Sold Out·
☐ ed. 250, s/n, intaglio	—	—
☐ SNOW LEOPARD (HEAD), rel. 1984. ed. 3,000, s/n, 18″ x 15″, pub FHG	50.00	—

MICHAEL SLOAN

THEMES: Landscape art

EDUCATION: Memphis Art Academy

GALLERY/DISTRIBUTOR: Cumberland Bend Publishing Co.

	ISSUE PRICE	CURRENT PRICE
☐ A MOMENTS PAUSE, ed. 4,000, i/o, pub CB	25.00	—
☐ A NEW DAWN, ed. 1,500, s/n, pub CB	65.00	—
ed. 100, remarqued	150.00	200.00
☐ A WATCHFUL EYE, ed. 1,500, s/n, pub CB	100.00	—
☐ COMPANION SET, ed. 8,000, i/o, pub CB	25.00	—
☐ COURAGE TO ENDURE, ed. 3,000, s/n, pub CB	100.00	—
☐ FOGGY MOUNTAIN MORNING, ed. 500, s/n, pub CB	40.00	400.00
ed. 2,000, s/o	25.00	125.00
☐ FOOTHILLS, ed. 1,000, s/n, pub CB	50.00	175.00
ed. 1,000, s/o	40.00	—
ed. 100, remarqued, Artist proofs	100.00	350.00
☐ LAST LIGHT, ed. 1,500, s/n, pub CB	65.00	—
ed. 100, remarqued	150.00	200.00
☐ OLD HICKORY'S CABIN, ed. 1,000, s/n, pub CB	65.00	100.00
ed. 100, remarqued	150.00	250.00
☐ OTHER AUTUMNS, ed. 500, s/n, pub CB	40.00	150.00
ed. 1,500, s/o	20.00	50.00
☐ PASSING THROUGH, ed. 1,000, s/n, pub CB	65.00	—
ed. 100, remarqued	150.00	—
☐ SNOWY MORN, ed. 5,000, i/o, pub CB	25.00	—
☐ SPRING HOUSE, ed. 1,000, s/n, pub CB	25.00	200.00
ed. 1,500, s/o	20.00	50.00
☐ STILL LIFE, ed. 1,000, s/n, pub CB	40.00	—
ed. 2,000, s/o	30.00	—
ed. 100, remarqued, Artist proofs	100.00	200.00
☐ SUMMERSET, ed. 1,000, s/n, pub CB	40.00	100.00
ed. 2,000, s/o	30.00	—
ed. 100, remarqued, Artist proofs	100.00	250.00
☐ TENNESSEE WINTER, ed. 2,500, s/n, 29½″ x 23½″, pub CB	20.00	450.00

RICHARD SLOAN

THEMES: Birds

STYLE: Realism

EDUCATION: American Academy of Art

MEMBERSHIPS: International Society of Artists; Society of Animal Artists

GALLERY/DISTRIBUTOR: Midwest Marketing

COMMENTS: "If I couldn't breathe life and warmth into a painting, my purpose would be lost, regardless of the skill the work might depict otherwise!"

SPRUCE GROUSE by Richard Sloan

	ISSUE PRICE	CURRENT PRICE
☐ **EASTERN BLUEBIRD**, rel. 1968. ed. 5,000, s/o, 22″ x 28″, pub NHI	30.00	400.00
☐ **PURPLE MARTIN**, rel. 1968. ed. 5,000, s/o, 22″ x 28″, pub NHI	**30.00	125.00
☐ **RING-NECKED PHEASANT**, rel. 1969. ed. 5,000, s/o, 22″ x 28″, pub NHI	30.00	300.00
☐ **CARDINAL**, rel. 1970. ed. 5,000, s/o, 22″ x 28″, pub NHI	30.00	150.00
☐ **CHICKADEE**, rel. 1970. ed. 5,000, s/o, 22″ x 28″, pub NHI	30.00	100.00
☐ **GREAT HORNED OWL**, rel. 1970. ed. 5,000, s/o, 22″ x 28″, pub NHI	30.00	150.00
☐ **MALLARDS**, rel. 1970. ed. 5,000, s/o, 22″ x 28″, pub NHI	30.00	225.00
☐ **MOUNTAIN BLUEBIRD**, rel. 1970. ed. 5,000, s/o, 22″ x 28″, pub NHI	30.00	150.00
☐ **ROBIN**, rel. 1970. ed. 5,000, s/o, 22″ x 28″, pub NHI	30.00	125.00
☐ **WOOD DUCK**, rel. 1970. ed. 5,000, s/o, 22″ x 28″, pub NHI	30.00	200.00
☐ **AMERICAN GOLDFINCH/WILLOW GOLDFINCH**, rel. 1971. ed. 5,000, s/o, 22″ x 28″, pub NHI...	30.00	125.00
☐ **CANADA GOOSE**, rel. 1951. ed. 5,000, s/o, 22″ x 28″, pub NHI	30.00	200.00
☐ **MOCKINGBIRD**, rel. 1971. ed. 5,000, s/o, 22″ x 28″, pub NHI	30.00	150.00
☐ **PEREGRINE FALCON**, rel. 1971. ed. 5,000, s/o, 22″ x 28″, pub NHI	30.00	125.00
☐ **PRAIRIE CHICKEN**, rel. 1971. ed. 5,000, s/o, 22″ x 28″, pub NHI	30.00	75.00
☐ **RUFFED GROUSE**, rel. 1971. ed. 5,000, s/o, 22″ x 28″, pub NHI	30.00	250.00
☐ **BALTIMORE ORIOLE**, rel. 1972. ed. 5,000, s/o, 22″ x 28″, pub NHI	30.00	100.00
☐ **BOBWHITE**, rel. 1972. ed. 5,000, s/o, 22″ x 28″, pub NHI	30.00	100.00
☐ **BROWN PELICAN**, rel. 1972. ed. 5,000, s/o, 22″ x 28″, pub NHI	30.00	125.00
☐ **ROADRUNNER**, rel. 1972. ed. 5,000, s/o, 22″ x 28″, pub NHI	30.00	100.00
☐ **YELLOW-SHAFTED FLICKER**, rel. 1972. ed. 5,000, s/o, 22″ x 28″, pub NHI	30.00	100.00
☐ **BROWN THRASHER**, rel. 1973. ed. 5,000, s/o, 22″ x 28″, pub NHI	30.00	75.00
☐ **CACTUS WREN**, rel. 1973. ed. 5,000, s/o, 22″ x 28″, pub NHI	30.00	50.00
☐ **CALIFORNIA QUAIL**, rel. 1973. ed. 5,000, s/o, 22″ x 28″, pub NHI	30.00	75.00
☐ **EASTERN MEADOWLARK/WESTERN MEADOWLARK**, rel. 1973. ed. 5,000, s/o, 22″ x 28″, pub NHI...	30.00	75.00

	ISSUE PRICE	CURRENT PRICE
☐ GREEN-WINGED TEAL, rel. 1973. ed. 5,000, s/o, 22" x 28", pub NHI	30.00	100.00
☐ RED-TAILED HAWK, rel. 1973. ed. 5,000, s/o, 22" x 28", pub NHI	30.00	125.00
☐ CALIFORNIA GULL, rel. 1974. ed. 5,000, s/o, 22" x 28", pub NHI	30.00	50.00
☐ COMMON LOON, rel. 1974. ed. 5,000, s/o, 22" x 28", pub NHI	30.00	50.00
☐ PINTAIL, rel. 1974. ed. 5,000, s/o, 22" x 28", pub NHI	30.00	75.00
☐ SCISSOR-TAILED FLYCATCHER, rel. 1974. ed. 5,000, s/o, 22" x 28", pub NHI	30.00	50.00
☐ SNOWY OWL, rel. 1974. ed. 5,000, s/o, 22" x 28", pub NHI	30.00	50.00
☐ CANVASBACK, rel. 1975. ed. 5,000, s/o, 22" x 28", pub NHI	30.00	50.00
☐ CAROLINA WREN, rel. 1975. ed. 5,000, s/o, 22" x 28", pub NHI	30.00	50.00
☐ GREAT EGRET, rel. 1975. ed. 5,000, s/o, 22" x 28", pub NHI	30.00	50.00
☐ HERMIT THRUSH, rel. 1975. ed. 5,000, s/o, 22" x 28", pub NHI	30.00	50.00
☐ PRAIRIE FALCON, rel. 1975. ed. 5,000, s/o, 22" x 28", pub NHI	30.00	50.00
☐ WILLOW PTARMIGAN, rel. 1975. ed. 5,000, s/o, 22" x 28", pub NHI	30.00	50.00
☐ BALD EAGLE, rel. 1976. ed. 650, 36" x 46"	*	
*150 of these will be used for education programs, *500 will be sold at -	*500.00	—
ed. 4,350, s/o, 22" x 28", pub NHI	30.00	125.00
☐ NENE, rel. 1976. ed. 5,000, s/o, 22" x 28", pub NHI	30.00	50.00
☐ SPRUCE GROUSE, rel. 1976. ed. 5,000, s/o, 22" x 28", pub NHI	30.00	50.00
☐ BLUE HEN, rel. 1977. ed. 5,000, s/o, 22" x 28", pub NHI	30.00	50.00
☐ BLUE JAY, rel. 1977. ed. 5,000, s/o, 22" x 28", pub NHI	30.00	50.00
☐ HUMMINGBIRD, rel. 1977. ed. 5,000, s/o, 22" x 28", pub NHI	30.00	50.00
☐ LARK BUNTING, rel. 1977. ed. 5,000, s/o, 22" x 28", pub NHI	30.00	50.00
☐ LIGHTNING THROUGH THE CYPRESS, rel. 1977. ed. 400, s/n, 18¾" x 24", pub RS	100.00	—
☐ PURPLE FINCH, rel. 1977. ed. 5,000, s/o, 22" x 28", pub NHI	30.00	50.00
☐ WHERE THE WILD AZALEAS GROW, rel. 1977. ed. 400, s/n, 20" x 24", pub RS	100.00	145.00
☐ AMBUSH, rel. 1978. ed. 600, s/n, 18" x 24", pub RS	100.00	—
☐ ICY STILLNESS, rel. 1978. ed. 600, s/n, 23⅛" x 19", pub RS	*100.00	—
*In lieu of remarques, the artist will produce 25 original pencil drawings	100.00	—
☐ LESSER SCAUP, rel. 1978. ed. 5,000, s/o, 22" x 28", pub NHI	30.00	50.00
☐ PILEATED WOODPECKER, rel. 1978. ed. 5,000, s/o, 22" x 28", pub NHI	30.00	50.00
☐ GREAT DAY IN THE MORNIN', rel. 1979. ed. 950, s/n, 23" x 18", pub RS	75.00	—
☐ ON THE BEACH, rel. 1979. ed. 600, s/n, 18¾" x 22", pub RS	100.00	—
☐ RHODE ISLAND RED HEN, rel. 1979. ed. 5,000, s/o, 22" x 28"	30.00	50.00

**Prints were sold as collection at issue price shown, providing the collector purchased each print when published. Individual purchases were $50.00 issue.

☐ CANADA GEESE PAIR, ed. 1,000, s/n, 16" x 12", distr. MM	50.00	—
☐ CANVASBACK PAIR, ed. 1,000, s/n, 16" x 12", distr. MM	50.00	—
☐ MALLARD PAIR, ed. 1,000, s/n, 16" x 12", distr. MM	50.00	—
☐ PINTAIL PAIR, ed. 1,000, s/n, 16" x 12", distr. MM	50.00	—
☐ THE ORCHARD, ed. 600, s/n, 18" x 27", distr. MM	100.00	—
☐ RAPTOR FUND PEREGRINE FALCON, Print and Stamp, rel. 1981. ed. 1,500, s/n, 6½" x 9" image, overall size 12" x 14", pub The Raptor Fund	125.00	—
☐ LOUISIANA WILD TURKEY STAMP AND PRINT, rel. 1982. ed. 1,500, s/n, 6½" x 9" image, overall size 12" x 14", pub The Louisiana Wild Turkey Federation	125.00	—
☐ FIRST NEBRASKA CONSERVATION STAMP PRINT, MOURNING DOVE, rel. 1983. ed. 650, s/n, 6½" x 9" image, overall size 12" x 14", pub Widgeon Enterprises, Inc.	100.00	—

KEN SMALLWOOD

THEMES: Wildlife art

MEDIUM: Oil

GALLERY/DISTRIBUTOR: Petersen Prints

	ISSUE PRICE	CURRENT PRICE
☐ **AUTUMN MEADOW,** ed. 800, s/n, 24″ x 18″, pub PP	75.00	—
Remarqued, s/n	165.00	—
☐ **DRIFTING IN,** ed. 800, s/n, 24″ x 18″, pub PP	75.00	—
Remarqued, s/n	165.00	—

JOE SMITH

THEMES: Still life art

MEDIUM: Acrylic

STYLE: A complex blend of "Pointillism"

EDUCATION: Ohio State University

GALLERY/DISTRIBUTOR: Wildlife Internationale, Inc.

	ISSUE PRICE	CURRENT PRICE
☐ **BITTERSWEET,** edl. 750, s/n, 18¼″ x 23″, distr. WII	75.00	—
☐ **COFFEE BIN,** ed. 750, s/n, 23″ x 18½″, distr. WII	75.00	—

FEEDING ON THE MILLER PLACE *by Tucker Smith*

TUCKER SMTIH

THEMES: Western art

MEDIUM: Oil, watercolor, dry-brush sepia

EDUCATION: University of Wyoming

AWARDS: In 1978, the artist won "Best in Show" at Electrum Festival of Arts in Montana

GALLERY/DISTRIBUTOR: Greenwich Workshop

	ISSUE PRICE	CURRENT PRICE
☐ FOAL, rel. 1977. ed. 1,000, s/n, 24" x 20", pub GW	55.00	265.00
☐ HAY SLED, rel. 1977. ed. 1,000, s/n, 24" x 20", pub GW	55.00	495.00
☐ SILL, rel. 1978. ed. 1,000, s/n, 20" x 23", pub GW	55.00	200.00
☐ SODA SPRINGS, rel. 1978. ed. 1,000, 27" x 17", pub GW	60.00	—
☐ A BREAK, rel. 1979. ed. 1,000, s/n, 28½" x 19⅝", pub GW	75.00	145.00
☐ MALAMUTE, rel. 1979. ed. 1,000, s/n, 17" x 20½", pub GW	65.00	280.00
☐ BARN CAT, rel. 1980. ed. 1,000, s/n, 21" x 15½", pub GW	80.00	—
☐ FIRST LIGHT, rel. 1980. ed. 1,000, s/n, 29" x 18½", pub GW	75.00	135.00
☐ SKIDDING LOGS, rel. 1980. ed. 1,000, s/n, 28" x 20", pub GW	80.00	—
☐ CHAUNCEY'S CORRALS, rel. 1981. ed. 1,000, s/n, 28" x 17", pub GW	95.00	—
☐ SHALLOW WATER, rel. 1981. ed. 1,000, s/n, 27½" x 22", pub GW	95.00	—
☐ FEEDING ON THE MILLER PLACE, rel. 1982. ed. 1,000, s/n, 31" x 19", pub GW	125.00	130.00
☐ McCLELLAN CREEK, rel. 1983. ed. 850, s/n, 20⅛" x 24", pub GW	125.00	—
☐ LOST CABIN CREEK, rel. 1984. ed. 650, s/n, 16⁷⁄₁₆" x 13¹⁵⁄₁₆", pub GW	75.00	—

GORDON SNIDOW

THEMES: Contemporary Western art

STYLE: It is Snidow's dramatic lighting, illuminating the past, that most often fascinates his patrons

EDUCATION: Art Center School in Lost Angeles

AWARDS: Has won nearly 20 major awards at the annual Cowboy Artists of America show

MEMBERSHIP: Cowboy Artists of America

GALLERY/DISTRIBUTOR: Greenwich Workshop

COMMENTS: "I paint real cowboys doin' real things," says Gordon Snidow

	ISSUE PRICE	CURRENT PRICE
☐ AMERICAN PAINT, rel. 1976. ed. 250, s/n, 19½" x 29½", pub FHG	100.00	—
☐ 10 A.M. AND DONE A DAY'S WORK, rel. 1976. ed. 1,000, s/n, 31" x 25½", pub FHG	100.00	—
☐ BUILDING A SMOKE, rel. 1977. ed. 250, s/n, 24" x 28", pub FHG	100.00	—
☐ THE HAPPY HOUR, rel. 1980. ed. 1,500, s/n, 21¾" x 22", pub SCG	100.00	—

	ISSUE PRICE	CURRENT PRICE
☐ THE LITTLEST STRAGGLER, rel. 1980. ed. 2,250, s/n, 15″ x 22″, pub TAP	100.00	—
☐ A REMNANT OF ANOTHER TIME, rel. 1980. ed. 1,500, s/n, 26½″ x 20″, pub SCG .	110.00	—
☐ SUNUP, rel. 1980. ed. 1,000, s/n, 21½″ x 28″, pub SCG	115.00	—
☐ BUCKAROOS, rel. 1981. ed. 2,250, s/n, 28″ x 22″, pub TAP	100.00	—
☐ LOOKING FOR THE OLD PIEBALD MARE, rel. 1981. ed. 2,250, s/n, 28″ x 18″, pub TAP	100.00	—
☐ SHIPPING THE O-6, rel. 1981. ed. 2,250, s/n, 24″ x 20″, pub TAP	100.00	—
☐ WHEN THE TRUCKS ARE LOADED, rel. 1981. ed. 1,000, s/n, 18″ x 28″, pub SCG .	115.00	—
☐ SWEET TALKIN MAN, rel. 1982. ed. 1,000, s/n, 29″ x 20⅛″, pub GW	150.00	—

BUCKAROOS *by Gordon Snidow*

EDWARD SOKOL

THEMES: Jungle scenes, seascape art

EDUCATION: Hunter College; School of Visual Arts

GALLERY/DISTRIBUTOR: Felicitie, Inc.

	ISSUE PRICE	CURRENT PRICE
☐ A VIEW OF THE METROPOLITAN MUSEUM, ed. 300, s/n, 36″ x 37″, original color silkscreen, pub FI	250.00	350.00
☐ AMSTERDAM, ed. 250, s/n, 19½″ x 27¾″, original color silkscreen, pub FI	250.00	—

	ISSUE PRICE	CURRENT PRICE
☐ APPLE ORCHARD, ed. 300, s/n, 28″ x 28″, original color silkscreen, pub Fl	150.00	175.00
☐ BACKYARDS, ed. 250, s/n, 25½″ x 25½″, original color silkscreen, pub Fl	250.00	—
☐ BLUE HOUSE, ed. 300, s/n, 24″ x 15″, original color silkscreen, pub Fl	75.00	—
☐ BLUE ROOM, ed. 375, s/n, 26⅛″ x 26⅛″, original color silkscreen, pub Fl	350.00	—
☐ CABIN IN PUNALUU, ed. 375, s/n, 20¼″ x 24″, original color silkscreen, pub Fl	250.00	—
☐ CHANGING SEASONS, ed. 250, s/n, 22″ x 26¼″, original color silkscreen, pub Fl ...	250.00	—
☐ THE CRESCENT, ed. 250, s/n, 21½″ x 26½″, original color silkscreen, pub Fl	350.00	—
☐ FIRST SNOW, ed. 300, s/n, 22″ x 26″, original color silkscreen, pub Fl	175.00	200.00
☐ FISHING PIER, ed. 300, s/n, lithograph, 30″ x 42″	200.00	—
☐ FULL SAILS, rel. in future, ed. 300, s/n, unknown as of this date, original color silkscreen, pub Fl	300.00	—
☐ GOLD JUNGLE, ed. 250, s/n, 22¼″ x 28¼″, original color silkscreen, pub Fl	200.00	—
☐ THE ICE SKATES, rel. 1980. ed. 300, s/n, 38¾″ x 27⅛″, original color silkscreen, pub Fl	300.00	—
☐ INSIDE THE CITY AND OUT, ed. 300, s/n, 36″ x 36″, original color silkscreen, pub Fl ..	250.00	400.00
☐ JUNGLE HIDEAWAY, ed. 250, s/n, 26″ x 36″, original color silkscreen, pub Fl	400.00	—
☐ JUNGLE SUNRISE, ed. 250, s/n, 28″ x 28″, original color silkscreen, pub Fl	350.00	—
☐ JUNGLE SUNSET, ed. 250, s/n, 20¼″ x 28″, original color silkscreen, pub Fl	250.00	—
☐ LONDON AT DUSK, ed. 300, s/n, 32″ x 32″, original color silkscreen, pub Fl	200.00	250.00
☐ LOOKING ACROSS AT THE CITY, ed. 250, s/n, 17″ x 33¼″, original color silkscreen, pub Fl	250.00	—
☐ MORNING HAZE, ed. 300, s/n, 26½″ x 35½″, original color silkscreen, pub Fl	200.00	—
☐ MY STUDIO, ed. 300, s/n, 28¾″ x 20¾″, original color silkscreen, pub Fl	150.00	—
☐ NASHUA, ed. 250, s/n, 20″ x 28″, original color silkscreen, pub Fl	250.00	—
☐ NIGHT JUNGLE, ed. 250, s/n, 22″ x 27¾″, original color silkscreen, pub Fl	250.00	—
☐ ON THE MANTEL, ed. 300, s/n, 28″ x 22″, original color silkscreen, pub Fl	150.00	—
☐ POPPIES, ed. 300, s/n, 21″ x 25¾″, original color silkscreen, pub Fl	150.00	200.00
☐ RED ROOM, ed. 200, s/n, 27½″ x 22″, original color silkscreen, pub Fl	350.00	—
☐ SPANISH ROOFTOPS, ed. 250, s/n, 21¼″ x 25¾″, original color silkscreen, pub Fl .	150.00	—
☐ SUMMER JUNGLE, ed. 300, s/n, 30″ x 30″, original color silkscreen, pub Fl	200.00	—
☐ SUMMER STILL LIFE, ed. 300, s/n, 24¾″ x 25½″, original color silkscreen, pub Fl ..	150.00	175.00
☐ TUG BOATS, ed. 300, s/n, 27½″ x 20″, original color silkscreen, pub Fl	150.00	175.00
☐ WEST STREET, ed. 300, s/n, 28″ x 22″, original color silkscreen, pub Fl	150.00	175.00
☐ YELLOW HOUSE, ed. 300, s/n, 24″ x 14″, original color silkscreen, pub Fl	75.00	—
☐ YELLOW TULIPS, ed. 250, s/n, 28¼″ x 22″, original color silkscreen, pub Fl	250.00	

MORTEN E. SOLBERG

THEMES: Wildlife art

MEDIUM: Watercolor

AWARDS: *Who's Who in America; Who's Who in American Art; Who's Who in the West*; three major awards from the American Watercolor Society, etc.

MEMBERSHIPS: American Watercolor Society, National Watercolor Society (past vice president)

GALLERY/DISTRIBUTOR: Greenwich Workshop

	ISSUE PRICE	CURRENT PRICE
☐ CHIPPEWA LAKE, rel. 1978. ed. 1,000, s/n, 29″ x 22″, pub GW	65.00	85.00
☐ KODIAK BEARS, rel. 1978. ed. 1,000, s/n, 29″ x 22″, pub GW	65.00	450.00
☐ POLAR BEAR, rel. 1978. ed. 1,000, s/n, 23⅛″ x 11⅛″, pub GW	55.00	485.00

	ISSUE PRICE	CURRENT PRICE
☐ WATCHING, rel. 1978. ed. 1,000, s/n, 29″ x 22″, pub GW	65.00	230.00
☐ BENGAL TIGER, rel. 1979. ed. 1,500, s/n, 14½″ x 20″, pub GW	65.00	115.00
☐ ON WINTER WINDS, rel. 1979. ed. 1,000, s/n, 19″ x 14½″, pub GW	55.00	475.00
☐ TAWNY, rel. 1979. ed. 1,500, s/n, 18¼″ x 13¾″, pub GW	55.00	135.00
☐ ARCTIC MONARCH, rel. 1980. ed. 1,500, s/n, 29″ x 22½″, pub GW	90.00	175.00
☐ AT WATER'S EDGE, rel. 1980. ed. 1,500, s/n, 20¼″ x 17″, pub GW	75.00	140.00
☐ AUTUMN REPOSE, rel. 1980. ed. 1,500, s/n, 28⅜″ x 21½″, pub GW	75.00	120.00
☐ BROWN BEAR, rel. 1980. ed. 1,500, s/n, 26″ x 16⅛″, pub GW	75.00	205.00
☐ EDGE OF YESTERDAY, rel. 1980. ed. 1,500, s/n, 29″ x 22½″, pub GW	75.00	95.00
☐ FIRST WINTER, rel. 1980. ed. 1,500, s/n, 28½″ x 21½″, pub GW	75.00	170.00
☐ TO THE VICTOR, rel. 1980. ed. 1,500, s/n, 32″ x 24″, pub GW	85.00	170.00
☐ BIRDS OF FRESH WATER MARSHES, rel. 1981. (Suite of 4). ed. 1,500, s/n, 17″ x 11″, pub GW	75.00	115.00
☐ EARLY SNOW, rel. 1981. ed. 1,500, s/n, 35½″ x 23″, pub GW	110.00	165.00
☐ FIRST REFLECTION, rel. 1981. ed. 1,500, s/n, 34½″ x 19¾″, pub GW	125.00	160.00
☐ FRESH TRACKS, rel. 1981. ed. 1,500, s/n, 28¼″ x 22¼″, pub GW	110.00	—
☐ INNOCENT, rel. 1981. ed. 1,500, s/n, 24¼″ x 13¾″, pub GW	85.00	110.00
☐ ACCEPT MY FATHER'S SPIRIT, rel. 1982. ed. 950, s/n, 30½″ x 24″, pub GW	95.00	Sold Out
☐ BEGIN THE HUNT, rel. 1982. ed. 950, s/n, 27⅜″ x 15⅞″, pub GW	125.00	—
☐ ONE WITH EARTH AND SKY, rel. 1982. ed. 950, s/n, 30½″ x 24″, pub GW	95.00	—
☐ SEA OTTERS, rel. 1982. ed. 1,250, s/n, 25″ x 18⅜″, pub GW	145.00	155.00
☐ YEAR OF THE EAGLE, rel. 1982. ed. 950, s/n, 32″ x 24½″, pub GW	150.00	225.00
☐ DARK WATERS, rel. 1983. ed. 1,000, s/n, 16½″ x 11½″, pub GW	70.00	—
☐ THE BANDITS, rel. 1983. ed. 950, s/n, 26⅜″ x 13¼″, pub GW	125.00	—
☐ WINTER'S CHILL, rel. 1983. ed. 675, s/n, 19½″ x 13⅛″, pub GW	95.00	120.00
☐ ANTELOPE RIDGE, rel. 1984. ed. 950, s/n, 28¼″ x 22″, pub GW	135.00	—
☐ BUFFALO BROTHER, rel. 1984. ed. 950, s/n, 16⅜″ x 20½″, pub GW	115.00	—
☐ INTO THE WIND, rel. 1984. ed. 950, s/n, 29″ x 23″, pub GW	125.00	305.00
☐ MORNING LIGHT, rel. 1984. ed. 950, s/n, 19⅜″ x 13⅜″, pub GW	95.00	—
☐ TOMORROW MAY BE COOLER, rel. 1984. ed. 950, s/n, 30¾″ x 14½″, pub GW	135.00	—
☐ ACROSS THE TUNDRA, rel. 1985. ed. 1,000, s/n, 30¾″ x 14⅝″, pub GW	135.00	—
☐ CHALLENGE OF THE WIND, rel. 1985. ed. 1,500, s/n, 37″ x 22½″	150.00	Sold Out

FRANK SOLTESZ

THEMES: Landscape art

MEDIUM: Watercolor

STYLE: Traditional Realism

EDUCATION: Art Students League; Huguenot School under the tutelage of Charles Kinghan

MEMBERSHIPS: American Watercolor Society

GALLERY/DISTRIBUTOR: Mill Pond Press, Inc.

	ISSUE PRICE	CURRENT PRICE
☐ SKIING ALONE, rel. 1981. ed. 950, s/n, 18″ x 24″, pub MPPI	75.00	110.00
☐ BACKYARD AT THE HARBOR, rel. 1981. ed. 475, s/n, 22¾″ x 29½″, pub MPPI	85.00	—

GARY SORRELS

THEMES: Wildlife art (big game animals of North America)

STYLE: Realism

GALLERY/DISTRIBUTOR: Wild Wings, Inc.

	ISSUE PRICE	CURRENT PRICE
☐ **WINTER RENDEZVOUS - WHITETAIL DEER,** rel. 1974. ed. 580, s/n, 16½" x 25", pub WWI	50.00	250.00
ed. 75 remarque Artist proofs	100.00	350.00
☐ **EARLY WINTER - WHITETAIL DEER,** rel. 1975. ed. 600, s/n, 14" x 21", pub WWI	40.00	550.00
ed. 75 remarque Artist proofs	75.00	650.00
☐ **PRONGHORN RANGE,** rel. 1978. ed. 600, s/n, 16½" x 25", pub WWI	60.00	75.00
ed. 75 remarque Artist proofs	130.00	160.00
☐ **INTO THE CLEARING - ELK,** rel. 1981. ed. 850, s/n, 16½" x 25", pub WWI	65.00	75.00
Remarqued	150.00	160.00

DON SPAULDING

THEMES: Old West

EDUCATION: Art Students League and studies with Norman Rockwell

MEMBERSHIPS: Founding member of The Society of American Historical Artists; The Company of Military Historians; The Order of the Indian Wars

MUSEUMS/COLLECTIONS: West Point Museum

GALLERY/DISTRIBUTOR: Swan Graphics, Ltd.

	ISSUE PRICE	CURRENT PRICE
☐ **THREE MILES TO THE FORT,** rel. 1981. ed. 750, s/n, 23½" x 16¾", pub SGL	75.00	—
☐ **FIGHTING TO SAVE THEIR HIDES,** rel. 1982. ed. 750, s/n, 26" x 17", pub SGL	75.00	—

IRENE SPENCER

THEMES: Portraiture; animals

MEDIUM: Oil

EDUCATION: Academy of Art; Chicago Art Institute

AWARDS: Silver Chalice Award (1984) for "The Capistrano Madonna"

GALLERY/DISTRIBUTOR: Irene Spencer

COMMENTS: Ms. Spencer is also a talented plate artist

THE CAPISTRANO MADONNA *by Irene Spencer*

	ISSUE PRICE	CURRENT PRICE
☐ **BEYOND THE SUN,** ed. 400, s/n, litho, pub IS, dist. Armstrong's	185.00	400.00
☐ **BITTERSWEET,** ed. 300, s/n, litho, pub IS, dist. Armstrong's	150.00	500.00
☐ **CAREFREE,** ed. 100, s/n, 10″ x 12″, etching, pub IS, dist. Armstrong's	110.00	300.00
☐ **CHRISTMAS MOURNING,** ed. 3,150, s/n, litho, pub IS, dist. Armstrong's	75.00	165.00
☐ **CONTENTMENT,** ed. 350, s/n, litho, pub IS, dist. GBS	125.00	175.00
☐ **DANNY'S TUNE,** ed. 50, s/n, 14″ x 18″, etching, pub IS, dist. Armstrong's	110.00	200.00
☐ **DEAR CHILD,** ed. 100, s/n, 10″ x 12″, etching, pub IS, dist. Armstrong's	110.00	300.00
☐ **EMPTY SADDLES,** ed. 500, s/n, litho, pub IS, dist. Armstrong's	125.00	150.00
☐ **FIRST EDITION,** ed. 550, s/n, litho, pub IS, dist. Armstrong's	135.00	550.00
ed. 25 Artist proofs		
☐ **FIRST KISS,** ed. 275, s/n, litho, pub IS	15.00	450.00
☐ **FLOWER PRINCESS,** ed. 550, s/n, litho, pub IS, dist. Armstrong's	185.00	200.00
ed. 25 Artist proofs		
☐ **HILLS OF HOME,** ed. 100, s/n, 11″ x 15″, etching, pub IS, dist. Armstrong's	110.00	400.00
☐ **HUG ME,** ed. 350, s/n, litho, pub IS, dist. Armstrong's	80.00	800.00
☐ **I LOVE LITTLE KITTY,** ed. 500, s/n, 22″ x 28″, litho, pub IS, dist. Armstrong's	95.00	150.00
☐ **I LOVE YOU,** ed. 550, s/n, litho, pub IS, dist. Armstrong's	285.00	—
ed. 25 Artist proofs		
☐ **LARMETTE,** ed. 100, s/n, 9″ x 11″, etching, pub IS, dist. Armstrong's	110.00	700.00
☐ **L'ENVOI,** ed. 500, s/n, 20″ x 30″, litho, pub IS, dist. Armstrong's	95.00	—

	ISSUE PRICE	CURRENT PRICE
☐ LONESOME MELODY, ed. 50, s/n, etching, pub IS, dist. Armstrong's	220.00	500.00
☐ LONG, LONG DAYS, ed. 100, s/n, 13" x 16", etching, pub IS, dist. Armstrong's	110.00	450.00
☐ MARK ANTHONY, ed. 350, s/n, litho, pub Plate n Pace, distr. GBS	225.00	—
☐ MIRACLE, ed. 500, s/n, litho, pub IS, dist. Armstrong's	125.00	600.00
☐ MOON GODDESS, ed. 550, s/n, litho, pub IS, dist. Armstrong's	185.00	190.00
☐ MOTHER'S HERE, ed. 500, s/n, 20¾" x 26", litho, pub IS, dist. Armstrong's	95.00	150.00
☐ MY DEVOTION, ed. 175, s/n, litho, pub IS, dist. Ira Roberts	60.00	1,000.00
☐ NO MORE TEARS, ed. 350, s/n, litho, pub IS, distr. GBS	125.00	210.00
☐ OH, MOM!, ed. 550, s/n, litho, pub IS, distr. GBS	135.00	150.00
☐ PACHAMAMA, ed. 500, s/n, litho, pub IS, dist. Armstrong's	95.00	110.00
☐ PRECIOUS MOMENT, ed. 550, s/n, litho, pub IS, dist. Armstrong's	135.00	250.00
ed. 25 Artist proof		
☐ QUEEN GUINEVERE, ed. 350, s/n, litho, pub IS, distr. GBS	185.00	200.00
☐ SANDY CLAWS, ed. 1,500, s/n, litho, pub IS, distr. GBS	85.00	—
☐ SECRETS, ed. 275, s/n, litho, pub IS, dist. Ira Roberts	60.00	1,000.00
☐ SIR LANCELOT, ed. 350, s/n, litho, pub IS, distr. GBS	185.00	200.00
☐ SLEEP LITTLE BABY, ed. 500, s/n, litho, pub IS, dist. Armstrong's	95.00	400.00
☐ SLEEP LITTLE BABY, ed. 100, s/n, 9" x 12", etching, pub IS, dist. Armstrong's	110.00	700.00
☐ SMOKE DREAMS, ed. 50, s/n, etching, pub IS, dist. Ira Roberts	55.00	2,000.00
☐ STORYTIME, ed. 500, s/n, 20" x 30", litho, pub IS, dist. Armstrong's	95.00	600.00
☐ SUMMER AFTERNOON, ed. 100, s/n, 9" x 12", etching, pub IS, dist. Armstrong's	110.00	300.00
☐ THE GREATEST GIFT, ed. 550, s/n, litho, pub IS, distr. GBS	135.00	—
☐ THE PAW THAT REFRESHES, ed. 1,500, s/n, litho, pub IS, distr. GBS	75.00	115.00
☐ THIS IS WHAT IT'S ALL ABOUT, ed. 50, s/n, 12" x 18", etching, pub IS, dist. Armstrong's	110.00	400.00
☐ YESTERDAY, TODAY & TOMORROW, ed. 100, s/n, 10" x 12", etching, pub IS, dist. Armstrong's	110.00	700.00
☐ CLEOPATRA, rel. 1982. ed. 350, s/n, 16" x 20", offset litho, pub IS	225.00	—
☐ A TAIL OF TWO KITTIES, rel. 1982. ed. 1,500, s/n, 14" x 13", original litho, pub IS	85.00	—
☐ THE CAPISTRANO MADONNA, rel. 1982. ed. 350, s/n, 16" x 21", offset litho, pub IS	225.00	—

HENRY STALLWORTH

THEMES: Hunting dogs; varied

MEDIUM: Watercolor

GALLERY/DISTRIBUTOR: Meredith Long & Company

	ISSUE PRICE	CURRENT PRICE
☐ TEN FLEW - TWO FELL, rel. 1981. ed. 600, s/n, size not available, pub MLC	95.00	—

STANLEY STEARNS

THEMES: Varied

MEDIUM: Airbrush, oil, watercolor, and other media

GALLERY/DISTRIBUTOR: Stearns & Associates

PUFFINS *by Stanley Stearns*

	ISSUE PRICE	CURRENT PRICE
☐ **COW MOOSE,** rel. 1955. ed. 6, s/n, 5″ x 8″, two color etching, pub SS	10.00	Unknown
☐ **HALF-GROWN WHITETAIL,** rel. 1957. ed. 24, s/n, 10½″ x 13″, etching, 6 states, pub SS	10.00	400.00
☐ **ALONE AT SEA,** rel. 1965. ed. 53, s/n, 14″ x 15½″, ten color woodcut, pub SS	20.00	Unknown
☐ **MARGOT'S BATH,** rel. 1965. ed. 13, s/n, 15″ x 19½″, three color woodcut, pub SS	15.00	Unknown
☐ **OPEN WATER,** rel. 1971. ed. 190, s/n, b/w, 14″ x 17″, pub SS	12.00	80.00
☐ **SPRIG,** rel. 1971. ed. 190, s/n, b/w, 14″ x 17″, pub SS	12.00	80.00
☐ **TAKING OFF,** rel. 1971. ed. 190, s/n, b/w, 14″ x 17″, pub SS	12.00	80.00
☐ **WINTER WHEAT,** rel. 1971. ed. 190, s/n, b//w, 14″ x 17″, pub SS	12.00	100.00
☐ **TOLLING IN,** rel. 1976. ed. 110, s/n, 19″ x 22½″, four color stone litho, pub Geo. C. Miller & Son, Inc.	75.00	300.00
☐ **FISHING CREEK,** rel. 1977. ed. 950, s/n, color, 21″ x 26″, pub SS	40.00	400.00
☐ **CHIAROSCURO PORTRAIT,** rel. 1980. ed. 100, s/n, 10″ x 14″, fourteen color serigraph, pub SS	80.00	300.00
☐ **PUFFINS,** rel. 1982. ed. 100, s/n, 10″ x 14″, nineteen color serigraph, pub SS	380.00	300.00
☐ **EARLY SNOW,** rel. 1983. ed. 100; s/n, 14″ x 8½″, nine colors in seven runs, pub SS	250.00	—

JOHN STEEL

	ISSUE PRICE	CURRENT PRICE
☐ **THE INTRUDER - GREAT WHITE SHARK,** rel. 1984. ed. 500, s/n, 16½″ x 25″, pub WWI	60.00	—
☐ **BALLERINAS (Seals),** rel. 1985. ed. 500, s/n, litho, 16½″ x 25″, pub WWI	60.00	—

RANDY STEFFEN

THEMES: Indian and Western art

STYLE: Realism

GALLERY/DISTRIBUTOR: Frame House Gallery, Inc.

	ISSUE PRICE	CURRENT PRICE
☐ **INDIANS OF THE PLAINS,** pair, rel. 1971. ed. 1,000, s/n, 17″ x 28″, pub FHG	50.00	150.00
☐ **INDIANS OF THE PLAINS - PORTFOLIO OF FOUR,** rel. 1971. ed. 1,500, s/n, 11″ x 14″, pub FHG	60.00	125.00
☐ **TWELVE MILES TO FORT WORTH,** ed. 1,000, s/n	25.00	—

WILLIAM JAMES STEPHENSON

THEMES: Wildlife art

STYLE: Realism

GALLERY/DISTRIBUTOR: Kalamazoo Nature Center

	ISSUE PRICE	CURRENT PRICE
☐ **RING-NECKED PHEASANT, Plate I,** ed. 500, s/n, 23″ x 35″, pub KNC	75.00	—
☐ **WOOD DUCK, Plate II,** ed. 500, s/n, 23″ x 35″, pub KNC	75.00	—
☐ **SNOWY OWL, Plate III,** ed. 500, s/n, 23″ x 35″, pub KNC	75.00	—
☐ **MALLARD, Plate IV,** ed. 500, s/n, 23″ x 35″, pub KNC	75.00	—
☐ **BOBWHITE, Plate V,** ed. 500, s/n, 23″ x 35″, pub KNC	75.00	—
☐ **RAINBOW TROUT, Plate XI,** ed. 500, s/n, 23″ x 35″, pub KNC	75.00	—
☐ **RING-NECKED PHEASANT/CORNFIELD, Plate XII,** ed. 500, s/n, 23″ x 35″, pub KNC .	75.00	—

PEGGY STEWART

THEMES: Amish people and landscapes

STYLE: Each color, based on various fabric samples, is painstakingly applied in a thin layer upon thin layer, so the finished work seems devoid of brush strokes

GALLERY/DISTRIBUTOR: Wildlife Internationale, Inc.

	ISSUE PRICE	CURRENT PRICE
☐ **AMANDA AND MAMA,** ed. 500, s/n, 18″ x 21½″, distr. WII	75.00	—
☐ **BLUE BALLOONS,** ed. 350, s/n, 16″ x 20″, distr. WII	55.00	—
☐ **PINK KITES,** ed. 350, s/n, 16″ x 20″, distr. WII	45.00	—
☐ **PUMPKIN HARVEST,** ed. 500, s/n, 18″ x 21½″, distr. WII	75.00	—

DON STIVERS

THEMES: Old West

EDUCATION: California College of Arts and Crafts

GALLERY/DISTRIBUTOR: Greenwich Workshop

	ISSUE PRICE	CURRENT PRICE
☐ **ALL WORK, NO PLAY,** rel. 1980. ed. 1,000, s/n, 32″ x 20¼″, pub GW	85.00	–
☐ **BIVOUAC,** rel. 1981. ed. 1,000, s/n, 33½″ x 20¾″, pub GW	125.00	–
☐ **THE STAFF RIDE,** rel. 1981. ed. 500, s/n, 28″ x 25, pub GW	75.00	165.00
ed. 1,000, s/n, bearing logo of the Centennial Class, U.S. Army Command and General Staff College; proceeds to the Fort Leavenworth Museum Association	75.00	Sold Out
☐ **BREAKING CAMP,** rel. 1982. ed. 1,000, s/n, 26¾″ x 22½″, pub GW	125.00	–
☐ **HURRY AND WAIT,** rel. 1982. ed. 1,000, s/n, 32″ x 19¾″, pub GW	125.00	–
☐ **PORTRAIT OF A POSSE,** rel. 1982. ed. 1,000, s/n, 21″ x 17⅜″, pub GW	85.00	–

PORTRAIT OF A POSSE *by Don Stivers*

FRED STONE

THEMES: Horseracing

AWARDS: Two N.A.L.E.D. Awards

GALLERY/DISTRIBUTOR: Graphics Buying Service, Ltd.

	ISSUE PRICE	CURRENT PRICE
☐ AFFIRMED, STEVE CAUTHEN UP, rel. 1979. ed. 750, s/n, 21″ x 23″, offset/litho, distr. GBSL	100.00	340.00
☐ MARE AND FOAL, rel. 1979. ed. 500, s/n, 17″ x 21″, offset/litho, distr. GBSL	90.00	315.00
☐ ONE, TWO, THREE, rel. 1979. ed. 500, s/n, 17″ x 23″, offset/litho, distr. GBSL	100.00	675.00
☐ PATIENCE, rel. 1979. ed. 1,000, s/n, 24″ x 18″, offset/litho, distr. GBSL	90.00	550.00
☐ THE MOMENT AFTER - LAFFIT PINCAY, rel. 1979. ed. 500, s/n, 17″ x 16″, offset/litho, distr. GBSL	90.00	225.00
☐ THE RIVALS - AFFIRMED AND ALYDAR, rel. 1979. ed. 500, s/n, 18″ x 20″, offset/litho, distr. GBSL	90.00	325.00
☐ EXCELLAR - BILL SHOEMAKER UP, rel. 1980. ed. 500, s/n, 18″ x 20″, offset/litho, distr. GBSL	90.00	645.00
☐ GENUINE RISK, rel. 1980. ed. 500, s/n, 17″ x 19″, offset/litho, distr. GBSL	100.00	490.00
☐ PASTURE PEST, rel. 1980. ed. 500, s/n, 18″ x 21, offset/litho, distr. GBSL	100.00	300.00
☐ THE BELMONT - BOLD FORBES, rel. 1980. ed. 500, s/n, 17″ x 26″, offset/litho, distr. GBSL	100.00	270.00
☐ THE KENTUCKY DERBY - SEATTLE SLEW, rel. 1980. ed. 500, s/n, 24″ x 20″, offset/litho, distr. GBSL	100.00	565.00
ed. 1,000, s/o, for Special Kentucky Derby Governor Series, State of Kentucky	100.00	550.00
☐ CONTENTMENT, rel. 1981. ed. N/A, s/n, size not available, offset/litho, distr. GBSL	115.00	305.00
☐ JOHN HENRY, rel. 1981. ed. N/A, s/n, size not available, offset/litho, distr. GBSL	160.00	700.00
☐ OFF AND RUNNING, rel. 1982. ed. N/A, s/n, size not available, offset/litho, distr. GBSL	125.00	300.00
☐ THE ARABIANS, rel. 1981. ed. N/A, s/n, size not available, offset/litho, distr. GBSL	115.00	340.00
☐ THE KIDNAPPED MARE - Fanfreluche and Secretariat Colt, Sain et Sauf, rel. 1981. ed. 750, s/n, 20″ x 21″, offset/litho, distr. GBSL	115.00	300.00
☐ THE SHOE - 8000 WINS, rel. 1981. ed. N/A, s/n, size not available, offset/litho, distr. GBSL	200.00	935.00
☐ THE THOROUGHBREDS, rel. 1981. ed. N/A, 16″ x 22″, offset/litho, distr. GBSL	115.00	275.00
☐ MAN O' WAR - THE FINAL THUNDER, rel. 1982. ed. N/A, s/n, size not available, litho, distr. GBSL	175.00	990.00
☐ THE POWER HORSES, rel. 1982. ed. N/A, s/n, size not available, litho, distr. GBSL	125.00	180.00
☐ THE WATER TROUGH, rel. 1982. ed. N/A, s/n, size not available, offset/litho, distr. GBSL	125.00	290.00
☐ FOR ONLY A MOMENT, rel. 1983. ed. N/A, s/n, size not available, litho, distr. GBSL	175.00	325.00
☐ THE ANDALUSIAN, rel. 1983. ed. N/A, s/n, size not available, litho, distr. GBSL	150.00	285.00
☐ THE DUEL, rel. 1983. ed. N/A, s/n, size not available, litho, distr. GBSL	150.00	225.00
☐ TRANQUILITY, rel. 1983. ed. N/A, s/n, size not available, litho, distr. GBSL	150.00	410.00
☐ SECRETARIAT, rel. 1984. ed. N/A, s/n, size not available, litho, distr. GBSL	175.00	410.00
☐ TURNING FOR HOME, rel. 1984. ed. N/A, s/n, size not available, litho, distr. GBSL	150.00	230.00
☐ NORTHERN DANCER, rel. 1984. ed. 950, s/n, litho, size not available, pub GBSL	175.00	235.00
☐ JOHN HENRY-McCARRON UP, rel. 1985. ed. 750, s/n, litho, size not available, pub GBSL	175.00	250.00
☐ THE LEGACY, rel. 1985. ed. 950, s/n, litho, 24½″ x 27½″, pub GBSL	175.00	—

WILLIAM F. STONE, JR.

THEMES: Varied

MEDIUM: Watercolor

STYLE: Stone calls his style, "watercolor montage"

EDUCATION: University of California at Berkeley

MEMBERSHIPS: President of the Carmel Art Association

MUSEUMS/COLLECTIONS: Monterey Peninsula Museum of Art

GALLERY/DISTRIBUTOR: Greenwich Workshop

	ISSUE PRICE	CURRENT PRICE
☐ **NEW ENGLAND BARN,** rel. 1976. ed. 1,000, s/n, 21½" x 17¾", pub GW	35.00	–
☐ **QUIET COVE,** rel. 1976. ed. 1,000, s/n, 22½" x 16", pub GW	35.00	–
☐ **WHARFSIDE,** rel. 1976. ed. 1,000, s/n, 13¾" x 15½", pub GW	50.00	–

NANCY TAYLOR STONINGTON

THEMES: Northwestern landscapes and wildflowers

MEDIUM: Watercolor

BOOKS: Her work has been featured in *The Alaska Journal; American Artist; Southwest Art; Prints*

EDUCATION: Middleburg College in Vermont, University of Colorado

GALLERY/DISTRIBUTOR: Stonington Galleries

	ISSUE PRICE	CURRENT PRICE
☐ **ALASKA FORGET-ME-NOTS,** s/o, 10" x 14", pub SG	15.00	–
☐ **ANTON LARSEN BAY,** ed. 650, s/n, 9⅝" x 13⅞", pub SG	30.00	Sold Out
☐ **ASPEN LEAVES AND CRANBERRY,** ed. 650, s/n, 9¼" x 14", pub SG	40.00	–
☐ **BAINBRIDGE ISLAND VIEW,** ed. 750, s/n, 7⅝" x 21⅝", pub SG	55.00	–
☐ **BAKER CREEK,** ed. 750, s/n, 10" x 13⅞", pub SG	40.00	–
☐ **BEACH TANGLE,** ed. 750, s/n, 12½" x 17", pub SG	55.00	–
☐ **BIRCH LIGHT,** ed. 750, s/n, 9⅜" x 14", pub SG	40.00	–
☐ **BUTTERCUPS AND SPRING BEAUTY,** s/o, 10" x 13½", pub SG	15.00	–
☐ **CHUGACH MOUNTAINS,** ed. 750, s/n, 15½" x 21½", pub SG	65.00	–
☐ **CLEARING,** ed. 750, s/n, 12½" x 19¼", pub SG	55.00	–
☐ **COMING HOME,** ed. 550, s/n, 23¾" x 15½", pub SG	50.00	–
☐ **CORMORANTS,** ed. 750, s/n, 10⅜" x 24", pub SG	70.00	–
☐ **COUPEVILLE BARNS, WHISKEY ISLAND,** ed. 650, s/n, 13¾" x 21", pub SG	50.00	–
☐ **CRIPPLE CREEK HOTEL,** ed. 650, s/n, 14¼" x 19¼", pub SG	55.00	–
☐ **DAFFODILS,** s/o, 10" x 13½", pub SG	20.00	–
☐ **DENALI,** ed. 650, s/n, 7¼" x 10¼", pub SG	30.00	Sold Out
☐ **DOGWOOD BLOSSOMS,** ed. 750, s/n, 11 15/16" x 17", pub SG	40.00	–
☐ **EAGLE BEACH,** ed. 750, s/n, 11" x 7½", pub SG	40.00	–
☐ **EAGLE WELL-HOUSE,** ed. 750, s/n, 9" x 15¼", pub SG	50.00	–
☐ **EARLY MORNING,** ed. 750, s/n, 20" x 13", pub SG	70.00	–
☐ **EUCALYPTUS AND PLUM,** ed. 550, s/n, 13¼" x 19⅜", pub SG	50.00	–
☐ **EVENING, SITKA ALASKA,** s/o, 18 11/16" x 12¾", pub SG	20.00	–
☐ **EVENING LANDSCAPE,** ed. 750, s/n, 13¾" x 20¾", pub SG	65.00	–
☐ **FELIX NECK BIRD REFUGE,** ed. 550, s/n, 18¼" x 13¼", pub SG	50.00	–
☐ **GIRDWOOD CREEK,** ed. 750, s/n, 13¼" x 20¼", pub SG	65.00	–
☐ **GOLD OREDGE NEAR CHICKEN, ALASKA,** s/o, 17¾" x 12½", pub SG	15.00	–

	ISSUE PRICE	CURRENT PRICE
☐ HANALEI BEACH, KAUAI, ed. 750, s/n, 18¼" x 13⅛", pub SG	50.00	—
☐ HAWAIIAN FLOWERS, ed. 750, s/n, 18¼" x 13½", pub SG	50.00	—
☐ IRIS AND CALENDULA, s/o, 10" x 13½", pub SG	20.00	—
☐ JUNEAU, ALASKA, s/o, 18" x 11¾", pub SG	15.00	—
☐ KETCHIKAN, ALASKA, ed. 550, s/n, 28⅜" x 18½", pub SG	65.00	—
☐ KING ISLAND, ALASKA, ed. 550, s/n, 18⁵⁄₁₆" x 13⅜", pub SG	40.00	—
☐ LADUSH, ed. 650, s/n, 8¾" x 12", pub SG	35.00	Sold Out
☐ LAST OF THE WILD ROSES, ed. 750, s/n, 13¼" x 19⅜", pub SG	60.00	—
☐ LIGHTHOUSE, ed. 750, s/n, 13¾" x 14", pub SG	45.00	—
☐ LILACS, ed. 750, s/n, 9" x 12½", pub SG	40.00	—
☐ MARTHA'S VINEYARD FARMHOUSE, ed. 650, s/n, 23¾" x 15½", pub SG	60.00	Sold Out
☐ MENDENHALL GLACIER, s/o, 18" x 12¾", pub SG	15.00	—
☐ MILKWEED PADS, s/o, 13" x 19", pub SG	20.00	—
☐ MIST OVER FOX CREEK, ed. 650, s/n, 17½" x 23¾", pub SG	65.00	—
☐ MOUNTAIN ASH AND CRANBERRY, ed. 750, s/n, 13¼" x 19⅜", pub SG	55.00	—
☐ MT. RAINIER, ed. 650, s/n, 23¾" x 15½", pub SG	60.00	Sold Out
☐ MT. SHASTA, ed. 550, s/n, 15½" x 24", pub SG	60.00	—
☐ OLD ARMY DOCK, s/o, 18" x 11¾", pub SG	15.00	—
☐ OWL CREEK, ed. 750, s/n, 13½" x 21", pub SG	70.00	—
☐ PELICAN COLD STORAGE, ed. 750, s/n, 10½" x 21⅝", pub SG	60.00	—
☐ PINEAPPLE FIELDS, MAUI, edl. 750, s/n, 18¼" x 6⅛", pub SG	40.00	—
☐ PINK POPPIES, ed. 650, s/n, 13⅜" x 20½", pub SG	50.00	Sold Out
☐ RED BARNS, ed. 650, s/n, 13½" x 18½", pub SG	50.00	—
☐ REFLECTIONS, ed. 750, s/n, 17" x 12¾", pub SG	60.00	—
☐ ROCKHOPPER PENGUINS, FALKLAND ISLANDS, ed. 500, s/n, 18¾" x 26", pub SG	60.00	—
☐ RUSSIAN RIVER, ed. 650, s/n, 13¼" x 18¼", pub SG	50.00	Sold Out
☐ SAILORS DELIGHT, ed. 750, s/n, 5" x 14½", pub SG	30.00	—
☐ S.E. ALASKA SENTINELS, s/o, 12½" x 17¾", pub SG	15.00	—
☐ SEA LION ROCK, s/o, 18" x 11½", pub SG	15.00	—
☐ SHERIDAN GLACIER, ed. 750, s/n, 9½" x 13", pub SG	40.00	—
☐ SILVER CREEK, ed. 750, s/n, 16½" x 8½", pub SG	55.00	—
☐ SPRING BLOSSOMS, ed. 750, s/n, 11" x 17", pub SG	55.00	—
☐ SPRING FLOWERS I, ed. 750, s/n, 7" x 9⅞", pub SG	35.00	—
☐ SPRING FLOWERS II, ed. 750, s/n, 7" x 9⅞", pub SG	35.00	—
☐ SNOW LIGHT, ed. 750, s/n, 20¼" x 13¼", pub SG	55.00	—
☐ SUGAR CANE FIELDS, KAUAI, ed. 750, s/n, 18½" x 6", pub SG	40.00	—
☐ SUMMER SHADOWS, ed. 750, s/n, 17½" x 7½", pub SG	45.00	—
☐ SUNFLOWER, s/o, 10" x 13½", pub SG	20.00	—
☐ SUN VALLEY VIEW OF BALDY, ed. 650, s/n, 16" x 24", pub SG	65.00	—
☐ TENAKEE SPRINGS, ed. 650, s/n, 9" x 14⅜", pub SG	45.00	—
☐ WATCHFUL, ed. 750, s/n, 11¼" x 9⅞", pub SG	45.00	—
☐ WHITE BARN, ed. 550, s/n, 13¼" x 18⅞", pub SG	50.00	—
☐ WHITE POPPIES, ed. 550, s/n, 13⅜" x 18⅜", pub SG	50.00	—
☐ WHITNEY - FIDALGO CANNERY, ed. 650, s/n, 13¾" x 20½", pub SG	55.00	—
☐ WILD SITKA ROSE, s/o, 10" x 13½", pub SG	15.00	—
☐ WILD STRAWBERRY BLOSSOMS, s/o, 10" x 13½", pub SG	20.00	—
☐ WILLOW LEAVES AND ROSE HIPS, ed. 650, s/n, 10⅛" x 14", pub SG	40.00	—
☐ WINE COUNTRY, ed. 550, s/n, 18¾" x 26½", pub SG	60.00	—

QUEENA STOVALL
(1887-1980)

THEMES: Folk art; primitivism

BACKGROUND: In 1949, when she was 62 and a great-grandmother, she began to put her memories of country life on canvas

GALLERY/DISTRIBUTOR: Voyageur Art

	ISSUE PRICE	CURRENT PRICE
☐ **CABIN ON TRIPLE OAKS FARM,** rel. 1976. ed. 600, s/o, 15″ x 20″, pub VA	30.00	185.00
☐ **END OF THE LINE,** rel. 1976. ed. 950, s/o, 16″ x 22″, pub VA	40.00	225.00
☐ **MARCH FURY,** rel. 1976. ed. 950, s/o, 16″ x 20″, pub VA	30.00	185.00
☐ **COMP'NY COMIN',** rel. 1977. ed. 275, s/o, 20″ x 24″, pub VA	60.00	275.00
☐ **HEREFORDS IN THE SNOW,** rel. 1977. ed. 275, s/o, 19″ x 24″, pub VA	60.00	275.00
☐ **FAMILY PRAYERS,** rel. 1978. ed. 300, s/o, 18″ x 24″, pub VA	60.00	250.00
☐ **FIRESIDE IN VIRGINIA,** rel. 1978. ed. 300, s/o, 18″ x 24″, pub VA	60.00	250.00
☐ **MAKING APPLE CIDER,** rel. 1978. ed. 200, s/o, 16″ x 20″, pub VA	60.00	200.00
☐ **MAKING SORGHUM MOLASSES,** rel. 1978. ed. 200, s/o, 17″ x 22″, pub VA	60.00	250.00

VIRGINIA STROUD

THEMES: Indian (Cherokee) art

STYLE: Pictographic and "x-ray" techniques

GALLERY/DISTRIBUTOR: Native American Images

	ISSUE PRICE	CURRENT PRICE
☐ **UNDERCOVER,** rel. 1979. ed. 80, s/n, stone litho, 13″ x 20″, pub NAI	250.00	—
☐ **OVER THERE,** rel. 1980. ed. 100, s/n, stone litho, 16″ x 25″, pub NAI	300.00	—
☐ **COURTSHIP,** rel. 1980. ed. 100, s/n, stone litho, 16″ x 25″, pub NAI	300.00	—
☐ **FOR GIRLS ONLY & CATCH IT,** rel. 1982. ed. 950 sets, s/n, offset print, ea. 20″ x 16″, pub NAI .... set	100.00	—

ROBERT SUMMERS

THEMES: Western art

MEDIUM: Oil

STYLE: Realism

AWARDS: Bicentennial Artist of Texas; Gold Medal from the Franklin Mint

MEMBERSHIP: Founding Member of the Texas Association of Professional Artists

GALLERY/DISTRIBUTOR: American Masters Foundation

	ISSUE PRICE	CURRENT PRICE
☐ **BOSQUE TERRITORY,** rel. 1978. ed. 1,500, s/n, 18″ x 27″, pub AMF	35.00	170.00
☐ **FORBIDDING WILDERNESS,** rel. 1978. ed. 1,500, s/n, 18″ x 27″, pub AMF	35.00	175.00
☐ **THE MIGHTY OAK ENDURETH,** rel. 1978. ed. 1,500, s/n, 14″ x 21″, pub AMF	25.00	110.00

HIGH WATER CROSSING by Robert Summers

	ISSUE PRICE	CURRENT PRICE
☐ WHITE BUFFALO, rel. 1978. ed. 1,500, s/n, 16″ x 26½″, pub AMF	35.00	350.00
☐ COLTERS QUEST, rel. 1979. ed. 1,500, s/n, 19″ x 32″, pub AMF	50.00	260.00
☐ FOOTPRINTS IN THE SNOW, rel. 1979. ed. 1,500, s/n, 18″ x 27″, pub AMF	40.00	600.00
☐ ANOTHER DAY, rel. 1980. ed. 1,500, s/n, 17″ x 26″, pub AMF	52.00	220.00
☐ RECEDING STORM, rel. 1980. ed. 1,500, s/n, 18″ x 27″, pub AMF	50.00	275.00
☐ SLICKER TIME, rel. 1980. ed. 1,500, s/n, 18″ x 27″, pub AMF	52.00	800.00
☐ CAMP COFFEE, rel. 1981. ed. 1,500, s/n, 19″ x 31″, pub AMF	75.00	225.00
☐ COMMUNE WITH GOD, rel. 1981. ed. 1,500, s/n, 18″ x 24″, pub AMF	75.00	125.00
☐ FIRST VISIT, rel. 1981. ed. 1,500, s/n, 18″ x 27″, pub AMF	62.00	150.00
☐ LEADIN LOOSE, rel. 1981. ed. 1,500, s/n, 16″ x 24″, pub AMF	60.00	90.00
☐ COMMANCHE MOON, rel. 1982. ed. 1,500, s/n, 16″ x 23″, pub AMF	36.00	120.00
☐ COOLING OFF, rel. 1982. ed. 500, s/n, 17″ x 27″, pub AMF	80.00	110.00
☐ RENDEZVOUS, rel. 1982. ed. 1,500, s/n, 18″ x 27″, pub AMF	55.00	105.00
☐ BOOM TOWN, rel. 1982. ed. 1,950, s/n, 17″ x 26″, pub AMF	75.00	375.00
☐ FAMILY TREE, rel. 1982. ed. 1,500, s/n, 16″ x 24″, pub AMF	85.00	100.00
☐ I'D LIKE TO BE THERE, rel. 1982. ed. 1,500, s/n, 17″ x 26″, pub AMF	80.00	125.00
☐ PEACEFUL VALLEY, rel. 1982. ed. 1,500, s/n, 16″ x 26″, pub AMF	80.00	130.00
☐ TEXAS GOLD, rel. 1982. ed. 1,950, s/n, 18″ x 27″, pub AMF	90.00	135.00
☐ AGAINST THE WIND, rel. 1983. ed. 1,500, s/n, 18″ x 27″, pub AMF	90.00	110.00
☐ ALL IS CALM, rel. 1983. ed. 1,500, s/n, 18″ x 27″, pub AMF	90.00	105.00
☐ GOLDEN MORNING, rel. 1983. ed. 1,500, s/n, 17″ x 28″, pub AMF	95.00	95.00
☐ RANGE FARE, rel. 1983. ed. 1,500, s/n, 17″ x 27″, pub AMF	95.00	105.00
☐ THE PERFECT DAY, rel. 1983. ed. 1,500, s/n, 18″ x 27″, pub AMF	90.00	95.00
☐ WINTER ROUNDUP, rel. 1983. ed. 1,500, s/n, 17″ x 27″, pub AMF	85.00	100.00

GEORGE SUTTON

THEMES: Birds

STYLE: Realism

BOOKS: *High Arctic* (1971); *Oklahoma Birds* (1967); *Iceland Summer* (1961)

AWARDS: Knight Cross of the Falcon (1972)

GALLERY/DISTRIBUTOR: Frame House Gallery, Inc.

	ISSUE PRICE	CURRENT PRICE
☐ SCISSOR-TAILED FLYCATCHER, rel. 1972. ed. 1,500, s/n, 18½" x 25", pub FHG . . .	20.00	35.00

NAVAJO LITTLE ONE *by Ray Swanson*

RAY SWANSON

THEMES: Southwest Indian tribes; varied themes

MEDIUM: Oil, watercolor, and pencil

STYLE: Strong sense of sunlight, composition, and values

AWARDS: Swanson has received many awards, including a Gold Medal from the National Academy of Western Art, two Gold Medals from the Franklin Mint

GALLERY/DISTRIBUTOR: Mill Pond Press, Inc.

	ISSUE PRICE	CURRENT PRICE
☐ AUTUMN IN CANYON DE CHELLY, rel. 1979. ed. 950, s/n, 21″ x 29″, pub MPPI	95.00	115.00
☐ PLAYING WITH THE KIDS, rel. 1979. ed. 950, s/n, 21″ x 28½″, pub MPPI	125.00	—
☐ TAKING NO SHORTCUTS, rel. 1979. ed. 950, s/n, 20″ x 23¾″, pub MPPI	75.00	—
☐ PIKI BREAD MAKER, rel. 1980. ed. 950, s/n, 32″ x 24¾″, pub MPPI	135.00	—
☐ WELL, IT MUST BE LUNCHTIME, rel. 1980. ed. 950, s/n, 20″ x 23¾″, pub MPPI ...	75.00	—
☐ LITTLE SIOUX, rel. 1981. ed. 650, s/n, 20″ x 17½″, pub MPPI	135.00	225.00
☐ MEDICINE MAN, rel. 1981. ed. 950, s/n, 19⅛″ x 32¼″, pub MPPI	150.00	—
☐ THE NAVAJO DAILY WORD, rel. 1981. ed. 750, s/n, 32½″ x 24½″, pub MPPI	195.00	—
☐ THE OLD MAN AND HIS LAND, rel. 1981. ed. 450, s/n, 29″ x 24″, pub MPPI	135.00	250.00
☐ THE OLD MAN AND THE CANYON, rel. 1981. ed. 750, s/n, 32½″ x 24½″, pub MPPI	195.00	—
☐ LITTLE APACHE, rel. 1982. ed. 750, s/n, 29¾″ x 17½″, pub MPPI	135.00	—
☐ NAVAJO LITTLE ONE, ed. 950, s/n, 17½″ x 23½″, pub MPPI	—	—
☐ A DAY AT THE FAIR, rel. 1983. ed. 950, s/n, 17½″ x 10⅞″, pub MPPI	65.00	—

TOP OF THE SUMMER *by Hazel Sweeney*

HAZEL SWEENEY

THEMES: Americana

GALLERY/DISTRIBUTOR: Grey Stone Press

	ISSUE PRICE	CURRENT PRICE
☐ MORTON'S SALT, ed. 500, s/n, 23¾″ x 18¾″, pub GSP	30.00	—
ed. 2,000, s/o	20.00	—
☐ ROCK ISLAND LINE, ed. 500, s/n, 18¾″ x 22″, pub GSP	30.00	—
ed. 2,000, s/o	20.00	—

	ISSUE PRICE	CURRENT PRICE
☐ TRUE SUNSHINE, ed. 500, s/n, 21¼" x 18½", pub GSP	40.00	—
ed. 1,000, s/o	30.00	—
☐ BREAD OF LIFE, rel. 1981. ed. 1,000, s/n, 25" x 20", pub GSP	40.00	—
☐ TOP OF THE SUMMER, rel. 1983. ed. 1,000, s/n, 19" x 27½", pub GSP	50.00	—
☐ KALEIDOSCOPE, rel. 1984. ed. 2,000, s/n, 20¼" x 24¾", pub GSP	45.00	—

FRED SWENEY

THEMES: Wildlife art

GALLERY/DISTRIBUTOR: Wild Wings, Inc.

	ISSUE PRICE	CURRENT PRICE
☐ THE HEDGEHOPPERS - BOBWHITE QUAIL, rel. 1980. ed. 850, s/n, size not available, pub WWI	65.00	—
☐ THE OUTSIDER - COUGARS, rel. 1982. ed. 600, s/n, size not available, pub WWI	75.00	—

ZOLTAN SZABO

THEMES: Landscape art

MEDIUM: Watercolor

BOOKS: *Landscape Painting in Watercolor*

EDUCATION: National Academy of Industrial Art

GALLERY/DISTRIBUTOR: Grey Stone Press

	ISSUE PRICE	CURRENT PRICE
☐ RED ROSES, ed. 2,500, s/n, 9" x 16¼", pub GSP	15.00	—
☐ WHITE ROSES, ed. 2,500, s/n, 9" x 16¼", pub GSP	15.00	—
☐ ZOLTAN SZABO COMMEMORATIVE PRINT - WHITE ROSE, ed. 500, s/n, 16" x 22¾", pub GSP	30.00	Sold Out
ed. 1,500, s/o	25.00	—
This limited edition was issued to commemorate the opening of the Zoltan Szabo Gallery.		
☐ COOL DATE, rel. 1981. ed. 1,000, s/n, 18½" x 26½", pub GSP	60.00	—
☐ FOREST RENEGADE, rel. 1981. ed. 2,000, s/n, 13¾" x 20", pub GSP	25.00	—
☐ LOGAN SPRING, rel. 1981. ed. 1,000, s/n, 18½" x 26½", pub GSP	60.00	—
☐ NEW APPLES, rel. 1981. ed. 2,000, s/n, 13¾" x 20", pub GSP	25.00	—
☐ NIGHT SENTRY, rel. 1982. ed. 500, s/n, 29½" x 21½", pub GSP	100.00	—
☐ VANITY FAIR, rel. 1982. ed. 1,000, s/n, 28½" x 22½", pub GSP	60.00	—
☐ COSTUME PARTY, rel. 1985. ed. 2,000, s/o, 17¼" x 24½", pub GSP	25.00	—
☐ SPRING'S MASTHEAD, rel. 1985. ed. 2,000, s/o, 17¼" x 24½", pub GSP	25.00	—

DAVID TAMERIN

THEMES: Varied

EDUCATION: Bezalel Academy of Arts (Israel); School of Visual Art; Art Students League; Pratt Graphic Center

GALLERY/DISTRIBUTOR: Eleanor Ettinger, Inc.

	ISSUE PRICE	CURRENT PRICE
☐ **DANCERS,** rel. 1977. ed. 250, s/n, 19″ x 24″, litho, arches, pub EEI	90.00	100.00
ed. 25, japon	110.00	120.00

WILLIAM R. TAYLOR

THEMES: Wildlife art

STYLE: Realism

MEMBERSHIPS: Society of Animal Artists; the National Audubon Society, etc.

GALLERY/DISTRIBUTOR: Wild Wings, Inc.

	ISSUE PRICE	CURRENT PRICE
☐ **CAUTIOUS DESCENT - BLACK DUCKS,** ed. 580, s/n, 17″ x 23″, pub WWI	60.00	75.00
ed. 30 remarque artist proof	125.00	155.00
☐ **SAFETY OF THE BAR - CANADA GEESE,** rel. 1977. ed. 600, s/n, 24″ x 17″, pub WWI	75.00	—
Remarqued	125.00	—
☐ **PUTTIN' OUT,** rel. 1980. ed. 500, s/n, 18″ x 14″, pub WWI	60.00	—
Remarqued	110.00	—
☐ **BACK WATER - WOODIES,** rel. 1981. ed. 750, s/n, size not available, pub WWI	65.00	—

HOWARD TERPNING

THEMES: Western art

MEDIUM: Oil

EDUCATION: Chicago Academy of Fine Art; American Academy of Art

AWARDS: The artist has received numerous awards, including Tucson Festival Artist of the Year for 1985

MEMBERSHIPS: Cowboy Artists of America; National Academy of Western Art

GALLERY/DISTRIBUTOR: Greenwich Workshop

	ISSUE PRICE	CURRENT PRICE
☐ SIOUX FLAG CARRIER, rel. 1981. ed. 1,000, s/n, 19" x 21½", pub GW	125.00	165.00
☐ SMALL COMFORT, rel. 1981. ed. 1,000, s/n, 30" x 24½", pub GW	135.00	250.00
☐ STONES THAT SPEAK, rel. 1981. ed. 1,000, s/n, 32" x 25½", pub GW	150.00	305.00
☐ THE SPECTATORS, rel. 1981. ed. 1,000, s/n, 32" x 19¾", pub GW	135.00	185.00
☐ THE VICTORS, rel. 1981. ed. 1,000, s/n, 30" x 25", pub GW	150.00	240.00
☐ CHIEF JOSEPH RIDES TO SURRENDER, rel. 1982. ed. 1,000, s/n, 31½" 25½", pub GW	150.00	330.00
☐ DUST OF MANY PONY SOLDIERS, rel. 1982. ed. 1,000, s/n, 33" x 24½", pub GW*	—	—
☐ SEARCH FOR THE RENEGADES, rel. 1982. ed. 1,000, s/n, 35½" x 20¾", pub GW	150.00	185.00
☐ SHIELD OF HER HUSBAND, rel. 1982. ed. 1,000, s/n, 20⅛" x 16¼", pub GW	150.00	210.00
☐ THE WARRIOR, rel. 1982. ed. 1,000, s/n, 14⅞" x 24½", pub GW*	200.00	Sold Out
☐ CROSSING MEDICINE LODGE CREEK, rel. 1983. ed. 1,000, s/n, 22½" x 26½", pub GW	150.00	165.00
☐ PAINTS, rel. 1983. ed. 1,000, s/n, 23" x 18¼", pub GW	140.00	Sold Out
☐ SHOSHONIS, rel. 1983. ed. 1,000, s/n, 16½" x 13½", pub GW	85.00	150.00
☐ THE STAFF CARRIER, rel. 1983. ed. 1,250, s/n, 13³⁄₁₆" x 16¹⁵⁄₁₆", pub GW	90.00	165.00
☐ CROW PIPE HOLDER, rel. 1984. ed. 1,000, s/n, 22" x 17¼", pub GW	150.00	—
☐ CROW PIPE HOLDER, Special edition bearing seal of Tucson Festival Artist of the Year 1985, rel. 1984. ed. 750, s/n, 22" x 17¼", pub GW	150.00	—
☐ MEDICINE MAN OF THE CHEYENNE, rel. 1984. ed. 450, s/n, 29¾" x 35½", pub GW	325.00	495.00
☐ WOMAN OF THE SIOUX, rel. 1984. ed. 1,000, s/n, 21" x 26¼", pub GW	165.00	230.00
☐ ONE MAN'S CASTLE, rel. 1985. ed. 1,000, s/n, 27⅝" x 22", pub GW	150.00	—
☐ THE SCOUTS OF GENERAL CROOK, rel. 1985. ed. 1,000, s/n, 36" x 20", pub GW	175.00	—
☐ THE SIGNAL, rel. 1985. ed. 1,250, s/n, 16¹⁄₁₆" x 13¹⁵⁄₁₆", pub GW	90.00	—
☐ THE WARNING, rel. 1985. ed. 1,650, s/n, 31⅛" x 25¼", pub GW	175.00	

*Dust of Many Pony Soldiers and The Warrior were a set (Cowboy Artists Set) issued in 1982, edition of 1,000, issue price $200.00, current price $255.00.

VIVIAN THIERFELDER

THEMES: Floral art

MEDIUM: Watercolor

EDUCATION: University of Alberta, Canada

MEMBERSHIPS: Alberta Society of Artists; Canadian Society of Painters in Watercolour

GALLERY/DISTRIBUTOR: Victoria's Fine Arts

	ISSUE PRICE	CURRENT PRICE
☐ FILAGREE, rel. 1985. ed. 1,000, s/o, litho, 27" x 14", image 33" x 22", pub VFA	35.00	—

E. G. THOMPSON

THEMES: Indian and Western art

STYLE: Realism

EDUCATION: Beverly Hills University, CA; Northeastern State University

GALLERY/DISTRIBUTOR: Tahmels of Tahlequah

COMMENTS: Thompson believes, "Worthwhile art is never achieved by mere accident"

	ISSUE PRICE	CURRENT PRICE
☐ **ABSTRACT INDIAN,** ed. 100, s/o, 8½" x 11", pub TOT	40.00	—
ed. 400, s/n, 8½" x 11", pub TOT	80.00	—
☐ **BIG KILL,** ed. 100, s/o, 13" x 16", pub TOT	50.00	—
ed. 400, s/n, 13" x 16", pub TOT	100.00	—
☐ **BUFFALO BOUNDRY,** ed. 100, s/o, 10" x 18", pub TOT	50.00	—
ed. 400, s/n, 10" x 18", pub TOT	100.00	—
☐ **CALL OF THE WILD,** ed. 100, s/o, 8½" x 11", pub TOT	40.00	—
ed. 400, s/n, 8½" x 11", pub TOT	80.00	—
☐ **CHEROKEE BLOWGUN,** ed. 100, s/n, 11" x 16¾", pub TOT	25.00	—
ed. 400, s/n, 11" x 16¾", pub TOT	50.00	—
☐ **COME ON CHEROKEE,** ed. 100, s/o, 9" x 12", pub TOT	40.00	—
ed. 400, s/n, 9" x 12", pub TOT	80.00	—
☐ **CONNUTCHA,** ed. 100, s/o, 10" x 18", pub TOT	50.00	—
ed. 400, s/n, 10" x 18", pub TOT	100.00	—
☐ **DEADLY DISTANCE,** ed. 100, s/o, 13" x 18", pub TOT	50.00	—
ed. 400, s/n, 13" x 18", pub TOT	100.00	—
☐ **DON'T DOG,** ed. 100, s/o, 16" x 20", pub TOT	50.00	—
ed. 400, s/n, 16" x 20", pub TOT	100.00	—
☐ **FIRE OF FREEDOM,** ed. 100, s/o, 19" x 16½", pub TOT	25.00	—
ed. 400, s/n, 19" x 16½", pub TOT	50.00	—
☐ **GRANDPA'S BARN,** ed. 100, s/o, 9¼" x 17", pub TOT	30.00	—
ed. 400, s/n, 9¼" x 17", pub TOT	60.00	—
☐ **HOT AIR SPECIALIST,** ed. 100, s/o, 13" x 18", pub TOT	50.00	—
ed. 400, s/n, 13" x 18", pub TOT	100.00	—
☐ **I HEARD THE OWL CALL MY NAME,** ed. 100, s/o, 16" x 20", pub TOT	50.00	—
ed. 400, s/n, 16" x 20", pub TOT	100.00	—
☐ **MEDITATING WARRIOR,** ed. 100, s/o, 17" X 28", pub TOT	75.00	—
ed. 400, s/n, 17" x 28", pub TOT	150.00	—
☐ **MOMENTS OF MEDITATION,** ed. 100, s/o, 11" x 16¾", pub TOT	25.00	—
ed. 400, s/n, 11" x 16¾", pub TOT	50.00	—
☐ **RACE WITH THE CLOCK,** ed. 100, s/o, 9" x 12", pub TOT	40.00	—
ed. 400, s/n, 9" x 12", pub TOT	80.00	—
☐ **REMINGTON MAN,** ed. 100, s/o, 16" x 20", pub TOT	50.00	—
ed. 400, s/n, 16" x 20", pub TOT	100.00	—
☐ **RISKY RUN,** rel. 1967. ed. 100, s/o, 10" x 18", pub TOT	50.00	—
ed. 400, s/n, 10" x 18", pub TOT	100.00	—
☐ **ROUGH RIDE,** ed. 100, s/o, 18" x 24", pub TOT	50.00	—
ed. 400, s/n, 18" x 24", pub TOT	100.00	—
☐ **RUN RABBIT RUN,** ed. 100, s/o, 16" x 20", pub TOT	50.00	—
ed. 400, s/n, 16" x 20", pub TOT	100.00	—
☐ **STICK BALL PLAYER,** ed. 100, s/o, 11" x 16¾", pub TOT	25.00	—
ed. 400, s/n, 11" x 16¾", pub TOT	50.00	—
☐ **THE HOMEMAKER,** rel. 1984. ed. 100, s/o, 22½" x 29", pub TOT	80.00	—
ed. 400, s/n, 22½" x 29", pub TOT	160.00	—
☐ **THE SCENT OF MAN,** ed. 100, s/o, 10" x 15", pub TOT	40.00	—
ed. 400, s/n, 10" x 15", pub TOT	80.00	—
☐ **THE STINK OF MAN,** ed. 100, s/o, 10" x 13¾", pub TOT	40.00	—
ed. 400, s/n, 10" x 13¾", pub TOT	80.00	—

RICHARD EARL THOMPSON

THEMES: Landscape art

MEDIUM: Watercolor

STYLE: American Impressionism

BOOKS: *Richard Earl Thompson, American Impressionist: A Prophetic Odyssey in Paint*, released in 1982

BACKGROUND: Commissioned by the U.S. Government to do War Bond posters during World War II

EDUCATION: Chicago Academy of Fine Art; American Academy of Art; Chicago Art Institute

AWARDS: *Who's Who In American Art*

GALLERY/DISTRIBUTOR: Richard Thompson Gallery

	ISSUE PRICE	CURRENT PRICE
☐ DOWNWIND, rel. 1978. ed. 800, s/n, 24″ x 29″, pub RTG	100.00	150.00
☐ AUTUMN DAY, rel. 1979. ed. 350, s/n, 29″ x 23″, pub RTG	100.00	—
☐ BRUCE'S BARN, rel. 1979. ed. 1,000, s/n, 22″ x 28″, pub RTG	60.00	100.00
☐ BY THE ARBOR, rel. 1979. ed. 350, s/n, 23″ x 28″, pub RTG	100.00	—
☐ IMPRESSION IN SPRINGTIME, rel. 1979. ed. 350, s/n, 29″ x 23″, pub RTG	100.00	—
☐ IN THE SUMACS, rel. 1979. ed. 350, s/n, 29″ x 23″, pub RTG	100.00	—
☐ MOODY DAY, rel. 1979. ed. 350, s/n, 23″ x 29″, pub RTG	100.00	—
☐ SPRING SUNSET, rel. 1979. ed. 1,500, s/n, 16″ x 20″, pub RTG	40.00	75.00
☐ SUGAR MAPLE, rel. 1979. ed. 1,500, s/n, 20″ x 16″, pub RTG	40.00	—
☐ BEAVER'S HAUNT, rel. 1980. ed. 1,000, s/n, 22″ x 28″, pub RTG	60.00	Sold Out
☐ CLOUD REFLECTION, rel. 1980. ed. 1,000, s/n, 22″ x 28″, pub RTG	60.00	100.00
☐ HERON HOME, rel. 1980. ed. 1,000, s/n, 22″ x 28″, pub RTG	60.00	100.00
☐ LAZY RIVER, rel. 1980. ed. 1,000, s/n, 22″ x 28″, pub RTG	60.00	100.00
☐ NEW FALLEN SNOW, rel. 1980. ed. 1,000, s/n, 22″ x 28″, pub RTG	60.00	100.00
☐ A SIGN OF WINTER, rel. 1981. ed. 1,000, s/n, 22″ x 28″, pub RTG	60.00	100.00
☐ AUTUMN BIRCHES, rel. 1981. ed. 1,000, s/n, 22″ x 28″, pub RTG	80.00	100.00
☐ BEN'S ACRES, rel. 1981. ed. 1,000, s/n, 22″ x 28″, pub RTG	80.00	100.00
☐ CECILEY, rel. 1981. ed. 1,500, s/n, 16″ x 20″, pub RTG	50.00	75.00
☐ FROSTY MORN, rel. 1981. ed. 1,000, s/n, 22″ x 28″, pub RTG	80.00	100.00
☐ HEADING HOME, rel. 1981. ed. 1,500, s/n, 20″ x 16″, pub RTG	50.00	75.00
☐ LES CANADIANS, rel. 1981. ed. 1,000, s/n, 22″ x 28″, pub RTG	80.00	Sold Out
☐ ONLY IN AUTUMN, rel. 1981. ed. 1,000, s/n, 22″ x 28″, pub RTG	80.00	100.00
☐ SKIM ICE, rel. 1981. ed. 1,000, s/n, 22″ x 28″, pub RTG	60.00	100.00
☐ OCTOBER SERMON, rel. 1982. ed. 1,000, s/n, 22″ x 28″, pub RTG	100.00	—
☐ SIDE YARD, rel. 1982. ed. 1,000, s/n, 22″ x 28″, pub RTG	100.00	—
☐ WINDY, rel. 1982. ed. 1,000, s/n, 22″ x 29″, pub RTG	100.00	—
☐ AUTUMN MOOD, rel. 1983. ed. 1,000, s/n, 28″ x 22″, pub RTG	150.00	—
☐ BEACH STROLL, rel. 1983. ed. 1,000, s/n, 24″ x 29″, pub RTG	150.00	—
☐ WOODLAND GLEN, rel. 1983. ed. 1,000, s/n, 22″ x 29″, pub RTG	150.00	—
☐ WOODLAND POND, rel. 1983. ed. 1,000, s/n, 23″ x 28″, pub RTG	150.00	—
☐ ALONG THE FENCE, rel. 1984. ed. 1,000, s/n, 22″ x 28″, litho, pub RTG	150.00	—
☐ BROOKIE'S LAIR, rel. 1984. ed. 1,000, s/n, 22″ x 28″, pub RTG	150.00	—
☐ FLOWERING PLUM, rel. 1984. ed. 1,000, s/n, 22″ x 28″, litho, pub RTG	150.00	—
☐ NOT A SOUND, rel. 1984. ed. 1,000, s/n, 24″ x 18″, pub RTG	100.00	—
☐ SLIGHT RIPPLE, rel. 1984. ed. 1,000, s/n, 18″ x 24″, pub RTG	100.00	—
☐ SUMMER PLACE, rel. 1984. ed. 750, s/n, 27″ x 35″, litho, pub RTG	275.00	—
☐ 'TIS SPRING, rel. 1984. ed. 750. s/n. 27″ x 35″. litho. pub RTG	275.00	—

	ISSUE PRICE	CURRENT PRICE
☐ **BACK STEPS,** rel. 1985. ed. 1,500, s/n, offset litho, 19″ x 15″, pub RTG	75.00	—
☐ **COMPANIONS,** rel. 1985. ed. 1,500, s/n, offset litho, 12″ x 15″, pub RTG	50.00	—
☐ **SPRING DREAM,** rel. 1985. ed. 1,500, s/n, offset litho, 12″ x 15″, pub RTG	50.00	—
☐ **SUNLIT MEADOW,** rel. 1985. ed. 950, s/n, offset litho, 25″ x 33″, pub RTG	225.00	—
☐ **THE APPLE ORCHARD,** rel. 1985. ed. 1,000, s/n, offset litho, 22″ x 28″, pub RTG ...	150.00	—
☐ **THE ROSE GARDEN,** rel. 1985. ed. 950, s/n, offset litho, 25″ x 33″, pub RTG	225.00	—
☐ **WINTER'S MAGIC,** rel. 1985. ed. 750, s/n, offset litho, 27″ x 39″, pub RTG	300.00	—

LLOYD R. THORSTEN

THEMES: Western art

MEDIUM: Varied

MEMBERSHIPS: Past president of the Spokane Art Association

GALLERY/DISTRIBUTOR: Salt Creek Graphics

	ISSUE PRICE	CURRENT PRICE
☐ **TETON BEAVER RETREAT,** rel. 1980. ed. 1,000, s/n, 28″ x 22″, pub SCG	37.50	—
☐ **PINEY CREEK,** rel. 1981. ed. 2,250, s/n, 22½″ x 30″, pub SCG	30.00	—

JEROME TIGER

THEMES: Indian art

STYLE: Traditional

AWARDS: In 1966, he won the four major competitions for traditional Indian art held in the United States

MUSEUMS/COLLECTIONS: Gallery of the Five Civilized Tribes Museum

GALLERY/DISTRIBUTOR: Jerome Tiger Art Company

	ISSUE PRICE	CURRENT PRICE
☐ **THE COMING WEATHER,** rel. 1970. ed. 300, n/o, 12″x 14½″, pub JTAC	100.00	1,000.00
☐ **OBSERVING THE ENEMY,** rel. 1973. ed. 1,500, n/o, 18″ x 20″, pub JTAC	20.00	750.00
☐ **THE GUIDING SPIRIT,** rel. 1973. ed. 1,500, n/o, 16″ x 22″, pub JTAC	30.00	750.00
☐ **YESTERDAY, TODAY, and TOMORROW,** rel. 1973. ed. 1,500. n/o, 11″ x 15″, pub JTAC	20.00	450.00
☐ **INTERMISSION,** rel. 1974. ed. 1,500, n/o, 13″ x 22½″, pub JTAC	30.00	250.00
☐ **SEMINOLE FISHERMAN,** rel. 1974. ed. 1,500, n/o, 18″ x 22″, pub JTAC	30.00	550.00
☐ **THE MIGHTY STICKBALLER,** rel. 1974. ed. 300, n/o, 18″ x 27″, pub JTAC	100.00	1,500.00
☐ **WALK THROUGH THE GREAT MYSTERIES,** rel. 1974. ed. 1,500, n/o, 16″ x 22″, pub JTAC	30.00	250.00
☐ **TRAIL OF TEARS,** rel. 1975. ed. 750, n/o, 21″ x 28″, pub JTAC	100.00	750.00
☐ **INDIAN BURIAL,** rel. 1975. ed. 350, n/o, 17½″ x 36″, pub JTAC	100.00	750.00
☐ **NEVER GET AWAY,** rel. 1977. ed. 1,500, n/o, 13⅞″ x 18⅝″, pub JTAC	50.00	60.00

	ISSUE PRICE	CURRENT PRICE
☐ **PROTECTIVE ONES,** rel. 1977. ed. 1,500, n/o, 14⅜″ x 19⅝″, pub JTAC	50.00	250.00
☐ **STICKBALLER,** rel. 1977. ed. 650, n/o, 18″ x 27″, pub JTAC	150.00	700.00
☐ **THROUGH THE EVERGLADES,** rel. 1977. ed. 1,500, n/o, 15″ x 24¾″, pub JTAC . . .	50.00	300.00
☐ **BUFFALO HUNT,** rel. 1978. ed. 1,500, n/o, 7⁹⁄₁₈″ x 6″, pub JTAC	60.00	—
Portfolio of three miniatures. Each print same size.		
☐ **DEPARTURE,** rel. 1978. ed. 650, n/o, 23¼″ x 33¼″, pub JTAC	150.00	600.00
☐ **BEGINNING,** rel. 1979. ed. 1,500, n/o, 16″ x 19″, pub JTAC	50.00	120.00
☐ **HIS SPIRIT CALLS,** rel. 1979. ed. 650, n/o, 21″ x 26″, pub JTAC	150.00	300.00
☐ **LITTLE ARROW FIXER/INNOCENT,** rel. 1979. ed. 1,500, n/o, 5″ x 7″, pub JTAC	*60.00	60.00
*Sold as a set only		
☐ **ROUGHING IT UP,** rel. 1979. ed. 1,500, n/o, 14″ x 19″, pub JTAC	60.00	—
☐ **THE INTRUDERS,** rel. 1979. ed. 1,500, n/o, 22″ x 27″, pub JTAC	50.00	60.00
☐ **PEACE OFFERING,** rel. 1980. ed. 750, n/o, size not available, pub JTAC	150.00	300.00
☐ **AGONY,** rel. 1981. ed. 1,500, n/o, 12″ x 16″, pub JTAC	60.00	—
☐ **GETTING READY,** rel. 1981. ed. 1,500, n/o, 12½″ x 17″, pub JTAC	60.00	—
☐ **OSCEOLA DEFIANT ONE,** rel. 1981. ed. 1,500, n/o, 15″ x 20″, pub JTAC	60.00	—
☐ **SEMINOLE 1803, SEMINOLE 1903 MINIATURE SERIES,** rel. 1981. ed. 1,500, n/o, 4½″ x 6½″, pub JTAC	60.00	—
☐ **YESTERDAY THEY RODE,** rel. 1981. ed. 750, n/o, 15″ x 20″, pub JTAC	150.00	—
☐ **TANGLE AT STICKBALL,** rel. 1982. ed. 750, n/o, size not available, pub JTAC	150.00	—

JOHNNY TIGER

THEMES: Indian art

EDUCATION: Bacone College

AWARDS: Tiger has won numerous awards

GALLERY/DISTRIBUTOR: Native American Images

	ISSUE PRICE	CURRENT PRICE
☐ **DANCER'S DESIRE,** rel. 1973. ed. 1,500, s/n, 8¾″ x 11¼″, pub NWDHG	15.00	125.00
remarqued.	50.00	—
☐ **PORTFOLIO OF INDIAN LIFE (Six prints),** rel. 1975: **FIREWOOD NEEDED,** 9½″ x 5½″; **BUFFALO SCOUT,** 4½″ x 5½″; **FAREWELL,** 2½″ x 5⅛″; **WARRIOR SEARCHES,** 6″ x 6″; **NIGHT SCOUT,** 4″ x 5″; **CAMP SCENE,** 11″ x 7¼″; ed. 3,000 sets, numbered and initialed, pub NAI	30.00	120.00

BOB TIMBERLAKE

THEMES: Americana

BOOKS: *The Bob Timberlake Collection* by Charles Kuralt, *The World of Bob Timberlake* by Oxmoor House

GALLERY/DISTRIBUTOR: The Heritage Company

	ISSUE PRICE	CURRENT PRICE
☐ ELLA'S CUPBOARD, rel. 1971. ed. 250, s/n, pub BT	35.00	500.00
☐ MR. GARRISON'S SLAB PILE, rel. 1971. ed. 100, s/n, pub BT	35.00	1,500.00
☐ MY YANKEE DRUM, rel. 1972. ed. 1,500, s/n, 17″ x 25½″, pub FHG	30.00	175.00
☐ ROWBOAT, rel. 1973. ed. 750, s/n, pub THC	60.00	450.00
☐ AFTERNOON AT THE PETREA'S, rel. 1974. ed. 1,000, s/n, pub THC	75.00	350.00
☐ BALDHEAD ISLAND RESCUE STATION, rel. 1974. ed. 1,000, s/n, pub THC	**75.00	250.00
ed. 24, Artist proofs	75.00	300.00
**A special edition of 250 with an embossed seal was prepared for BaldHead Island Property owners and fewer than 50 of these prints are available	—	250.00
☐ BALDHEAD LIGHTHOUSE, rel. 1974. ed. 300, s/n, released by FKH Editions	175.00	450.00
☐ MRS. LEONARD'S MARIGOLD, rel. 1974. ed. 1,000, s/n, pub THC	60.00	350.00
☐ THE ALEXANDER LONG HOUSE, rel. 1974. ed. 300, s/n, released by FKH Editions	175.00	650.00
☐ FRONT PORCH, rel. 1975. ed. 1,000, s/n, pub THC	75.00	300.00
☐ LATE SNOW AT RIVERWOOD, rel. 1975. ed. 1,000, s/n, pub THC	150.00	700.00
☐ MAY, rel. 1975. ed. 1,000, s/n, pub THC	75.00	375.00
☐ ANOTHER WORLD, rel. 1976. ed. 300, s/n, etching, 18″ x 24″, released by Hammer Publishing	500.00	750.00
☐ DAILY SUNNING, rel. 1976. ed. 1,000, s/n, 32¾″ x 24½″, pub THC	150.00	400.00
☐ MY CIDER BARREL, rel. 1976. ed. 1,000, s/n, 18″ x 24″, pub THC	150.00	450.00
☐ SOUR PIE CHERRIES, rel. 1976. ed. 1,000, s/n, pub THC	100.00	175.00
☐ BEAN POT, rel. 1977. ed. 300, s/n, 29½″ x 22½″, etching, pub HP	600.00	—
ed. 50, Artists proofs		
☐ KNOTTS ISLAND DECOYS, rel. 1977. ed. 1,000, s/n, pub THC	150.00	300.00
☐ MORNING SUN, rel. 1977. ed. 1,000, s/n, 24″ x 33″, pub THC	150.00	350.00
☐ DAISIES, rel. 1978. ed. 1,000, s/n, 20½″ x 26½″, pub THC	*350.00	—
*All proceeds from sales will be donated to achieving the goals of Keep America Beautiful, Inc., a non-profit public service organization.		
☐ GILLEY'S HOUSE, rel. 1978. ed. 1,000, s/n, 30″ x 22¼″, pub THC	150.00	450.00
☐ JULY, rel. 1978. ed. 1,000, s/n, 19¾″ x 15¼″, pub THC	125.00	375.00
ed. 30, Artist proofs		
☐ POTTED, rel. 1978. ed. 300, s/n, 10″ x 7″, etching, pub HP	450.00	—
☐ STUDY OF HIS COAT, rel. 1978. ed. 100, s/n, 20″ x 16″, etching, pub HP	1,250.00	—
☐ IRON EYES, rel. 1979. ed. 1,000, s/n, 22½″ x 16½″, pub THC	200.00	—
*All proceeds from sales donated to Keep American Beautiful, Inc., a non-profit public service organization.		
☐ MR. ZIMMERMAN'S CORN, rel. 1979. ed. 1,000, s/n, 21″ x 27½″, pub THC	150.00	—
☐ SNOW WORLD, rel. 1979. ed. 300, s/n, 22″ x 15″, etching, pub HP	500.00	—
ed. 50, Artist proofs		
☐ SUMMER DAY, rel. 1979. ed. 1,000, s/n, 29″ x 20¾″, pub THC	150.00	600.00
☐ THE FAKES, rel. 1979. ed. 300, s/n, 9″ x 26″, etching, pub HP	400.00	550.00
ed. 50 Artist proofs		
☐ PUMPKINS IN THE SNOW, rel. 1980. ed. 1,000, s/n, pub THC	150.00	—
☐ STRAWBERRIES, rel. 1980. ed. 1,000, s/n, 22½″ x 17″, pub THC	125.00	—
☐ WATERED, rel. 1980. ed. 1,000, s/n, 29″ x 22″, pub THC	150.00	250.00
☐ FEBRUARY AT RIVERWOOD, rel. 1981. ed. 1,000, s/n, 29″ x 22″, pub THC	150.00	500.00
☐ ISLAND CRAB, rel. 1981. ed. 1,000, s/n, 12″ x 13½″, pub THC	85.00	—
☐ QUILTS, rel. 1981. ed. 1,000, s/n, 12½″ x 14¾″, pub THC	150.00	—
two prints - sold as a pair		
☐ CAPT. CHARLIE'S VIEW, rel. 1982. ed. 1,000, s/n, 18¼″ x 25¼″, pub THC	150.00	—
☐ GILLEY'S WELL, rel. 1982. ed. 1,000, s/n, 20″ x 26¾″, pub THC	150.00	350.00
☐ SNOW AT THE STUDIO, rel. 1982. ed. 1,000, s/n, 21¾″ x 26¾″, pub THC	185.00	350.00
☐ SPRING SNOW, ed. 1,000, s/n, 28¼″ x 22¾″, pub THC	185.00	300.00
☐ SOMEWHERE IN TIME, ed. 1,000, s/n, 23½″ x 29″, pub THC	185.00	450.00
☐ FEED CORN, rel. 1984. ed. 1,000, s/n, 22¼″ x 15″, pub THC	185.00	—
☐ GRUBB'S GAZEBO, rel. 1984. ed. 1,000, s/n, 27″ x 20½″, pub THC	185.00	450.00
☐ YARD FLOWERS, rel. 1984. ed. 1,000, s/n, 19″ x 16″, pub THC	185.00	—
☐ BEST FRIENDS, rel. 1984. ed. 1,000, s/n, litho, 10⅞″ x 16¼″, pub THC	150.00	—
☐ WOODLOT, rel. 1984. ed. 1,000, s/n, litho, 13⅜″ x 29″, pub THC	185.00	450.00
☐ VELVET FACES, rel. 1985. ed. 1,000, s/n, litho, 11⅜″ x 27″, pub THC	185.00	—

LARRY TOSCHIK

THEMES: Wildlife art

EDUCATION: Wisconsin Art Academy

AWARDS: Ducks Unlimited Artist of the Year (1975)

GALLERY/DISTRIBUTOR: Wild Wings, Inc.

	ISSUE PRICE	CURRENT PRICE
☐ AHEAD OF THE STORM (Mallards), ed. 800, s/n, 19″ x 25¼″, litho, pub PP	60.00	140.00
☐ BATTLE CRY OF WINTER (Canada Geese), ed. 1,500, s/n, 20″ x 28″, litho, pub AMF	40.00	—
☐ BURNISHED BRONZE (Wild Turkey), ed. 1,500, s/n, 19″ x 32″, litho, pub AMF	40.00	—
☐ CALLED IN - CANADA GEESE, ed. 800, s/n, 25″ x 17″, litho, pub PP	60.00	Sold Out
☐ CALLED IN - MALLARDS, ed. 800, s/n, 16¼″ x 25″, litho, pub PP	60.00	—
☐ CUMBERLAND SPRING, ed. 800, s/n, 16″ x 24″, litho, pub PP	60.00	—
☐ FIRST DRUMMER OF SPRING (Ruffed Grouse), ed. 1,500, s/n, 22″ x 28″, litho, pub AMF...	40.00	—
☐ PATTERN FOR THE DAY (Bobwhite Quail), ed. 1,500, s/n, 20″ x 29″, litho, pub AMF	40.00	—
☐ PLACE WHERE THEY NOW GATHER (Bald Eagles), ed. 1,500, s/n, 19″ x 28″, litho, pub AMF...	40.00	—
☐ PRESENT TENANTS (Wild Turkey), ed. 1,500, s/n, 21″ x 29″, litho, pub AMF	40.00	—
☐ SALMON CAMP ON THE LINIK TIDAL BASIN (Gulls and Old Squaws), ed. 1,500, s/n, 19″ x 28″, litho, pub AMF	40.00	—
☐ SANTEE PASS - WOOD DUCKS, ed. 800, s/n, 16″ x 24″, pub PP	75.00	—
remarqued, s/n...	165.00	—
☐ SCOUTING FOR A HAVEN (Pintail Ducks), ed. 800, s/n, 19″ x 25¾″, litho, pub PP .	60.00	—
☐ SNOWS UPON THE AUTUMN GOLD (Snow Geese), ed. 1,500, s/n, 22″ x 28″, litho, pub AMF...	40.00	—
☐ SUNDOWN BALLET - MALLARDS, rel. 1976. ed. 580, s/n, 16″ x 25½″, pub WWI ..	75.00	—
☐ TEAL MORNING (Green Wing Teals), ed. 800, s/n, 18″ x 25″, litho, pub PP	60.00	—
☐ THE BEET FIELD (Mallards Landing on Pond), ed. 750, s/n, 21½″ x 12½″, litho, pub PP	60.00	—
☐ THE MALLARD HOLE, ed. 750, s/n, 21½″ x 12½″, litho, pub PP	60.00	—
☐ UP & AWAY - GEESE, ed. 750, s/n, 27½″ x 21″, litho, pub PP	65.00	—
☐ WHISTLING IN - MALLARDS, rel. 1976. ed. 580, s/n, 22″ x 17¾″, pub WWI	70.00	—

JEAN-PIERRE TREVOR

THEMES: Landscape art

EDUCATION: Centre d'art Mediterance

GALLERY/DISTRIBUTOR: Foxfire Fine Arts, Inc.

	ISSUE PRICE	CURRENT PRICE
☐ GRAND TETONS, ed. 1,500, s/n, 24″ x 20″, pub FFFA	40.00	—
☐ SUMMER MOUNTAINS & WHITEMANTLE, ed. 1,500, s/n, 15″ x 12″, pub FFFA	45.00	—

WHITEMANTLE *by Jean-Pierre Trevor*

DON TROIANI

THEMES: Military history

MEMBERSHIPS: Charter member of the Society of American Historical Artists

GALLERY/DISTRIBUTOR: Wild Wings, Inc.

	ISSUE PRICE	CURRENT PRICE
☐ THE RECALL - TRUMPETER, rel. 1981. ed. 600, s/n, litho, 17¾" x 23½", pub WWI	95.00	—
☐ CONFEDERATE STANDARD BEARER, rel. 1982. ed. 600, s/n, litho, 20" x 16", pub WWI	75.00	300.00
☐ CORPORAL WHEAT'S - 1st BATTALION, rel. 1982. ed. 600, s/n, litho, 19" x 14", pub WWI	40.00	—
☐ SIBLEY'S TEXANS, rel. 1982. ed. 600, s/n, litho, 26" x 17¼", pub WWI	95.00	—
☐ BEFORE THE SNOW, rel. 1983. ed. 600, s/n, litho, 14" x 21", pub WWI	75.00	200.00
☐ FORWARD THE COLORS, rel. 1983. ed. 750, s/n, litho, 23¼" x 18", pub WWI	85.00	300.00
☐ UNION STANDARD BEARER, rel. 1983. ed. 600, s/n, litho, 20" x 16", pub WWI	75.00	—

MARLOWE URDAHL

THEMES: Dogs

GALLERY/DISTRIBUTOR: Wild Wings, Inc.

	ISSUE PRICE	CURRENT PRICE
☐ **PUPPY LOVE - YELLOW LAB,** rel. 1981. ed. 750, s/n, size not available, distr. WWI .	50.00	240.00
☐ **DAYDREAMER - BLACK LAB,** rel. 1983. ed. 750, s/n, 15½″ x 13½″, distr. WWI	60.00	150.00
☐ **INNOCENCE (Black Lab),** rel. 1985. ed. 850, s/n, litho, 14″ x 18″, pub WWI	65.00	—

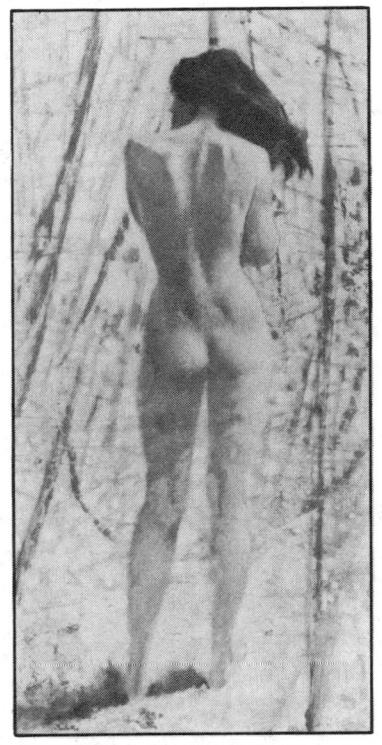

THE GREENHOUSE NUDE *by Thornton Utz*

THORNTON UTZ

THEMES: Classic nude; varied themes

MEDIUM: Watercolor

BOOKS: His credits include 50 commissions for *Saturday Evening Post* covers

EDUCATION: American Academy of Arts in Chicago

MEMBERSHIPS: Ringling School of Art Trustee; Official Artists, United States Air Force

GALLERY/DISTRIBUTOR: Mill Pond Press, Inc.

	ISSUE PRICE	CURRENT PRICE
☐ **LAVENDER LACE,** rel. 1981. ed. 950, s/n, 12⅝" x 24", pub MPPI	75.00	—
☐ **MELANIE,** rel. 1981. ed. 450, s/n, 27½" x 19¾", pub MPPI	85.00	125.00
☐ **PICNIC,** rel. 1981. ed. 550, s/n, 20" x 27½", pub MPPI	110.00	150.00
☐ **PINK LADY,** rel. 1981. ed. 450, s/n, 26" x 20¼", pub MPPI	85.00	125.00
☐ **THE GREENHOUSE NUDE,** rel. 1981. ed. 550, s/n, 35" x 19⅞", pub MPPI	95.00	125.00
☐ **THE SOFT WIND,** rel. 1982. ed. 950, s/n, 23¾" x 11¼", pub MPPI	75.00	—
☐ **INTERLUDE,** rel. 1983. ed. 950, s/n, 8¾" x 10⅝", pub MPPI	40.00	—

GEORGE CAMERON VAIL

THEMES: Varied

MEDIUM: Varied

BACKGROUND: In 1972, he founded the Vail School of Design and Illustration

MEMBERSHIPS: International Society of Marine Painters

GALLERY/DISTRIBUTOR: J. Getsinger Art

	ISSUE PRICE	CURRENT PRICE
☐ **AUTUMN WARM,** ed. 285, s/n, litho, pub JGE	60.00	85.00
☐ **BLUES,** ed. 175, s/n, 15" x 17", etching, pub JGE	25.00	35.00
☐ **CHERI,** ed. 175, s/n, 12" x 17", etching, pub JGE	25.00	35.00
☐ **CHESAPEAKE SCHOONER,** ed. 285, s/n, 25" x 30", litho, pub JGE	70.00	120.00
☐ **THE FAN,** ed. 175, s/n, 12" x 15", etching, pub JGE	25.00	30.00
☐ **FLIGHT,** ed. 175, s/n, 15" x 17", etching, pub JGE	25.00	35.00
☐ **GULLS,** ed. 175, s/n, 11" x 15", etching, pub JGE	20.00	25.00
☐ **THE HIGH SEAS,** ed. 185, s/n, 17" x 20", etching, pub JGE	50.00	70.00
☐ **MORNING SUN,** ed. 175, s/n, size N/A, etching, pub JGE	35.00	45.00
☐ **O'ER THE WAVES,** ed. 175, s/n, size N/A, etching, pub JGE	35.00	50.00
☐ **PALAVER,** ed. 285, s/n, 26" x 30", litho, pub JGE	50.00	75.00
☐ **PLEASANT MILLS,** ed. 250, s/n, 25" x 30", litho, pub JGE	50.00	65.00
☐ **RED SAILS,** ed. 225, s/n, 25" x 30", etching, pub JGE	60.00	75.00
☐ **SAILING,** ed. 185, s/n, 17" x 18", etching, pub JGE	40.00	50.00
☐ **SHOALS CLEAR,** ed. 285, s/n, 25" x 30", litho, pub JGE	70.00	145.00
☐ **SUNDOWN,** ed. 175, s/n, 14" x 18", etching, pub JGE	35.00	50.00
☐ **SHOSHONE,** ed. 175, s/n, 14" x 17", etching, pub JGE	35.00	45.00
☐ **SHOWDOWN,** ed. 285, s/n, 26" x 31", litho, pub JGE	75.00	100.00
☐ **SHOOTOUT,** ed. 225, s/n, 25" x 30", etching, pub JGE	80.00	100.00
☐ **BALLOON,** rel. 1984. ed. 60, 10" x 13", etching, pub JGE	35.00	—
☐ **MAMA-JUDA ISLAND,** rel. 1984. ed. 60, 10" x 13", etching, pub JGE	35.00	—

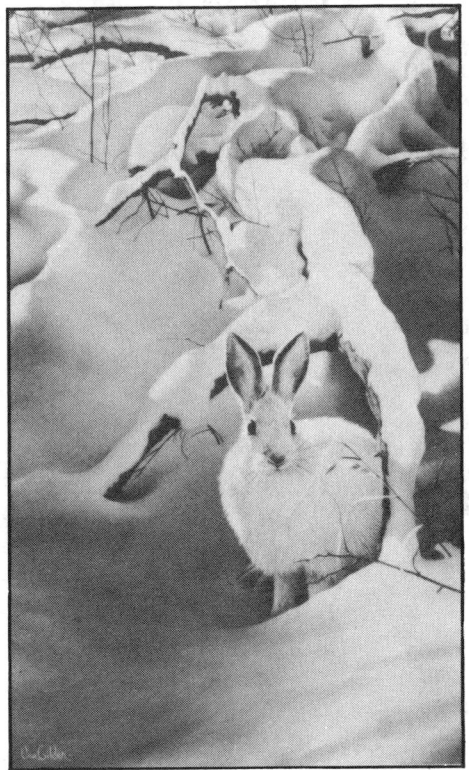

THE HIDE AWAY *by Ron Van Gilder*

RON VAN GILDER

THEMES: Wildlife art

GALLERY/DISTRIBUTOR: Voyageur Art

	ISSUE PRICE	CURRENT PRICE
☐ **AS SEASON CHANGE,** ed. 500, Artist's proofs, 15″ x 25″, pub VA	100.00	—
☐ **BROOD,** rel. 1977. ed. 580, s/n, 15″ x 25″, litho, pub VA	85.00	—
☐ **DAYBREAK,** rel. 1983. ed. 750, s/n, 15″ x 25″, litho, pub VA	85.00	—
☐ **DISTANT SHORES,** rel. 1982. ed. 375, s/n, 15″ x 25″, litho, pub VA	85.00	Sold Out
☐ **FIRST LIGHT,** rel. 1981. ed. 750, s/n, 15″ x 25″, litho, pub VA	85.00	—
☐ **HIDE AWAY, THE,** rel. 1983. ed. 750, s/n, 12½″ x 21″, litho, pub VA	85.00	—
☐ **INDIAN SUMMER BUCK,** rel. 1984. ed. 750, s/n, 20½″ x 21″, litho, pub VA	85.00	—
☐ **ON THE RISE,** rel. 1982. ed. 750, Artist's proofs, 15″ x 25″, pub VA	85.00	—
☐ **VANTAGE POINT,** rel. 1983. ed. 375, s/n, 26½″ x 21″, litho, pub VA	85.00	—
☐ **WINGING SOUTH,** rel. 1982. ed. 750, s/n, 15″ x 25″, litho, pub VA	85.00	—

DOUGLAS VAN HOWD

THEMES: Wildlife art

BACKGROUND: Official artist for the Safari Club International

GALLERY/DISTRIBUTOR: Petersen Prints

	ISSUE PRICE	CURRENT PRICE
☐ BOB WHITE FLUSHED, ed. 800, s/n, size not available, litho, pub PP	65.00	150.00
☐ COVEY BREAK, ed. 800, s/n, 16½" x 25", litho, pub PP	60.00	120.00
☐ FIRST OUTING, ed. 800, s/n, 16" x 24", litho, pub PP	60.00	120.00
☐ HIS MAJESTY - LION, ed. 800, s/n, 17" x 25½", litho, pub PP	60.00	—
☐ INDIAN SUMMER (Pintails), ed. 800, s/n, size not available, litho, pub PP	60.00	125.00
☐ PASSING PARADE, ed. 750, s/n, size not available	60.00	125.00
☐ SERENGETI EVENING, ed. 800, s/n, 18" x 24", pub PP	75.00	—
remarqued, s/n..	165.00	—
☐ THE AFRICAN BIG FIVE, ed. 3,000, s/o, set consists of Leopard, Lion, Elephant, Buffalo and Rhino, lithos, pub PP	100.00	—
☐ THE RESTING PLACE, ed. 750, s/n, 21" x 28", litho, pub PP	65.00	125.00
☐ TSAVO MONARCH, ed. 800, s/n, 16¾" x 25¼", pub PP	75.00	—
remarqued, s/n..	165.00	—
☐ TSAVO MONARCH (Elephant), ed. 800, s/n, 16¾" x 25¼", litho, pub PP	60.00	—

DONALD VANN

THEMES: Indian art

STYLE: Subtle colors and graceful lines

GALLERY/DISTRIBUTOR: Native American Images

COMMENTS: The artist states, "In our world there is an unspoken quality, a feeling, that touches and flows through everything, all of us, as well as all things of the earth"

	ISSUE PRICE	CURRENT PRICE
☐ INTO ANOTHER LIFE, rel. 1980. ed. 500, s/n, offset print, 18" x 24", pub NAI	400.00	Sold Out
☐ THE SEASONS, rel. 1980. ed. 1800 sets, s/n, offset print, 10" x 12" ea., pub NAI	80.00	—
☐ WINTER WARRIOR, rel. 1980. ed. 950, s/n, offset print, 30" x 24", pub NAI	150.00	—
☐ HIGH MT. CAMP, rel. 1981. ed. 1800, s/n, offset print, 30" x 24", pub NAI	200.00	Sold Out
☐ BERRY PICKERS, rel. 1981. ed. 1500, s/n, offset print, 20" x 24", pub NAI	75.00	Sold Out
☐ CHEROKEE HERITAGE, rel. 1981. ed. STATE I - 100, STATE II - 20, s/n, stone lithos, 30" x 22" ea., pub NAI	I 1,850.00	Sold Out
	II 1,700.00	Sold Out
☐ TRAIL OF TEARS, rel. 1981. ed. 3,500, s/n, offset print, 24" x 18", pub NAI	200.00	Sold Out
☐ WATCH OF THE OWLS, rel. 1982. STATE I- 100, STATE II - 40, s/n, stone lithos, 22" x 15" ea., pub NAI..	I 800.00	Sold Out
	II 1,400.00	Sold Out
☐ LAND OF THE SPIRITS, rel. 1982. ed. 150, s/n, stone litho, 18" x 22", pub NAI	600.00	—
☐ SOVEREIGN OF THE PAST, rel. 1982. ed. 150, s/n, stone litho, 13" x 18", pub NAI ..	500.00	Sold Out
☐ SENTINEL, rel. 1982. ed. 1,500, s/n, offset print, 18" x 24", pub NAI	75.00	—
☐ ALMOST HOME, rel. 1984. STATE I - 75, STATE II - 75, s/n, stone lithos, 18" x 27" ea., pub NAI...	I 900.00	—
	II 1,400.00	—

	ISSUE PRICE	CURRENT PRICE
☐ FRIENDLY PASSAGE, rel. 1984. ed. 150, s/n, stone litho, 20″ x 26″, pub NAI	900.00	Sold Out
☐ END OF AN ERA, rel. 1984. ed. 150, s/n, stone litho, 22″ x 30″, pub NAI	700.00	Sold Out
☐ FOLLOWING THE TRACE, rel. 1985. ed. 150, s/n, stone litho, 18″ x 26″, pub NAI ...	450.00	—

RICHARD VAN ORDER

THEMES: Wildlife art

MEDIUM: Charcoal, oil, pastel, watercolor

STYLE: Realism

GALLERY/DISTRIBUTOR: Van Order Studio

	ISSUE PRICE	CURRENT PRICE
☐ DISTURBING THE PEACE, rel. 1981. ed. 1,000, s/n, litho, 12″ x 16″, pub VOS	50.00	Sold Out
ed. 2,200, s/n, litho, 18″ x 24″, pub VOS	175.00	Sold Out
☐ HARRISON HILLS, rel. 1981. ed. 1,000, s/n, litho, 12″ x 16″, pub VOS	50.00	Sold Out
ed. 2,200, s/n, litho, 18½″ x 16″, pub VOS	200.00	Sold Out
☐ PAPOOSE LAKE, rel. 1981. ed. 1,000, s/n, litho, 12″ x 16″, pub VOS	Stock Low	11.50
ed. 1,000, s/n, litho, 14″ x 18″, pub VOS	100.00	Sold Out
☐ THE MEETING PLACE, rel. 1981. ed. 1,000, s/n, litho, 12″ x 16″, pub VOS	50.00	Sold Out
ed. 1,000, s/n, litho, 18″ x 24½″, pub VOS	150.00	Sold Out
☐ THE MILE LINE, rel. 1982. ed. 1,000, s/n, litho, 12″ x 16″, pub VOS	50.00	Sold Out
ed. 500, s/n, litho, 18″ x 24½″, pub VOS	500.00	Sold Out
☐ WINGS, rel. 1981. ed. 1,000, s/n, litho, 12″ x 16″, pub VOS	Stock Low	11.50
ed. 2,200, s/n, litho, 18″ x 24″, pub VOS	300.00	Sold Out
☐ A NORTHWOODS LEGEND, rel. 1983. ed. 300, s/n, litho, 19″ x 25″, pub VOS	100.00	Stock Low
☐ HIGH COUNTRY, rel. 1983. ed. 500, s/n, litho, 11 x 15, pub VOS	12.50	—
☐ ISLAND LAKE WOODIES, rel. 1983. ed. 350, s/n, litho, 16″ x 20″, pub VOS	45.00	Stock Low
ed. 150, s/n, litho, 23″ x 29″, pub VOS	250.00	Sold Out
☐ MANITOWISH STOPOVER, rel. 1983. ed. 250, s/n, litho, 12″ x 16″, pub VOS	100.00	Sold Out
ed. 250, s/n, litho, 19″ x 25″, pub VOS	400.00	Sold Out
☐ NORTHWOODS PRIDE, rel. 1983. ed. 500, s/n, litho, 11″ x 15″, pub VOS	12.50	—
☐ SPRING THAW, rel. 1983. ed. 150, s/n, litho, 23″ x 29″, pub VOS	300.00	Sold Out
☐ STAND GUARD, rel. 1983. ed. 250, s/n, litho, 11″ x 15″, pub VOS	100.00	Sold Out
ed. 250, s/n, litho, 19″ x 25″, pub VOS	100.00	Stock Low
☐ TENDING TO BUSINESS, rel. 1983. ed. 300, Artist proofs, s/n, litho, 23″ x 29″, pub VOS	300.00	Sold Out
☐ THE AMERICAN TRADITION - BALD EAGLE, rel. 1983. ed. 25, s/n, litho, 23″ x 29″, pub VOS	2,000.00	Sold Out
☐ GUARDIAN OF FREEDOM - BALD EAGLE, rel. 1984. ed. 350, s/n, litho, 18″ x 24″, pub VOS	45.00	Stock Low
ed. 150, s/n, litho, 24″ x 32″, pub VOS	500.00	Sold Out
☐ ALERT AT TROUT LAKE - WHITETAIL DEER, rel. 1985. ed. 480, s/n, litho, 24″ x 32″, pub VOS	100.00	Stock Low
☐ BALTIMORE ORIOLE, rel. 1985. ed. 960, s/n, litho, 11″ x 14″, pub VOS	15.00	—
☐ CARDINAL, rel. 1985. ed. 960, s/n, litho, 11″ x 14″, pub VOS	15.00	—
☐ CHICKADEE, rel. 1985. ed. 960, s/n, litho, 9″ x 12″, pub VOS	12.00	—
☐ THE CALL OF FREEDOM - BALD EAGLE, rel. 1985. Reservation Only, s/n, litho, 26″ x 36″, pub VOS	1,000.00	—
☐ THE ORPHAN FAWN DEER, rel. 1985. ed. 960, s/n, litho, 12″ x 16″, pub VOS	30.00	—

*Note: any Remarqued Print by the artist adds an additional $100.00 value to the limited edition print.

JON VAN ZYLE

THEMES: Alaskan scenes

MEDIUM: Acrylic

MUSEUMS/COLLECTIONS: Anchorage Fine Arts Museum, Nome Historical Museum

GALLERY/DISTRIBUTOR: Mill Pond Press, Inc.

	ISSUE PRICE	CURRENT PRICE
☐ **ALASKA MOONLIGHT,** rel. 1983. ed. 950, s/n, 12″ x 15½″, pub MPPI	60.00	—
☐ **FOLLOW THE LEADER,** rel. 1983. ed. 950, s/n, 17½″ x 22″, pub MPPI	95.00	—
☐ **GOOD NIGHT PATS,** rel. 1983. ed. 950, s/n, 17½″ x 22″, pub MPPI	95.00	—

JAMES VERDUGO

THEMES: Victorian Romance

STYLE: Impressionism

GALLERY/DISTRIBUTOR: Greenwich Workshop

COMMENTS: The artist regards the preparation for each painting as "a drill not unlike the pianist practicing his scales"

	ISSUE PRICE	CURRENT PRICE
☐ **HOMECOMING,** rel. 1984. ed. 850, s/n, 26⅛″ x 22″, pub GW	110.00	—
☐ **SEASIDE SERENADE,** rel. 1984. ed. 850, s/n, 26⅛″ x 22″, pub GW	110.00	—
☐ **VICTORIAN GARDEN,** rel. 1985. ed. 550, s/n, 16¹⁄₁₆″ x 13¹⁵⁄₁₆″, pub GW	90.00	—

MARY VICKERS

THEMES: Varied

STYLE: Vickers considers her work to be most influenced by the French Impressionists

EDUCATION: St. Martine School of Art; England Art Students League

GALERY/DISTRIBUTOR: Graphics Buying Service, Ltd.

	ISSUE PRICE	CURRENT PRICE
☐ **AGE OF INNOCENCE,** rel. 1970. ed. 200, s/n, litho, pub MMGI	40.00	325.00
☐ **ALICE,** rel. 1975. ed. 150, s/n, etching, pub MMGI	50.00	150.00
☐ **ALL MINE,** rel. 1977. ed. 175, s/n, etching, pub MMGI	40.00	100.00
☐ **APRIL,** rel. 1973. ed. 100, s/n, etching, pub MMGI	30.00	125.00

ALASKAN MOONLIGHT *by Jon Van Zyle*

	ISSUE PRICE	CURRENT PRICE
☐ **ATTIC TREASURES,** rel. 1978. ed. 275, s/n, litho, pub MMGI	200.00	300.00
☐ **AUTUMN,** rel. 1973. ed. 200, s/n, hand colored litho, pub MMGI	60.00	225.00
☐ **AUTUMN BOUQUET,** rel. 1973. ed. 150, s/n, etching, pub MMGI	60.00	225.00
☐ **BROTHER & SISTER,** rel. 1970. ed. 200, s/n, litho, pub MMGI	40.00	350.00
☐ **BLUE MOON,** rel. 1974. ed. 150, s/n, etching, pub MMGI	80.00	150.00
☐ **BREATH OF SPRING,** rel. 1973. ed. 100, s/n, etching, pub MMGI	50.00	250.00
☐ **CAMEO,** rel. 1975. ed. 150, s/n, etching, pub MMGI	30.00	150.00
☐ **CAROLINE,** rel. 1975. ed. 150, s/n, etching, pub MMGI	35.00	150.00
☐ **CARRIE,** rel. 1977. ed. 250, s/n, litho, pub NG	70.00	—
☐ **CLIMBING,** rel. 1974. ed. 200, s/n, litho, pub MMGI	50.00	150.00
☐ **DAWN,** rel. 1975. ed. 175, s/n, etching, pub MMGI	35.00	100.00
☐ **DRYING OFF,** rel. 1977. ed. 250, s/n, litho, pub MMGI	70.00	150.00
☐ **EMBRACE,** rel. 1975. ed. 200, s/n, litho, pub MMGI	60.00	200.00
☐ **ENGAGEMENT,** rel. 1975. ed. 150, s/n, etching, pub MMGI	90.00	250.00
☐ **FACE IN THE WINDOW,** rel. 1971. ed. 200, s/n, litho, pub MMGI	35.00	200.00
☐ **FACE TO THE WIND,** rel. 1971. ed. 200, s/n, litho, pub MMGI	40.00	250.00
☐ **FANTASY,** rel. 1976. ed. 175, s/n, etching, pub MMGI	100.00	—
☐ **FAY,** rel. 1978. ed. 175, s/n, hand colored etching, pub MMGI	50.00	75.00
☐ **FIRST DAY,** rel. 1974. ed. 150, s/n, etching, pub MMGI	20.00	75.00
☐ **FIRST GRADE,** rel. 1974. ed. 150, s/n, etching, pub MMGI	20.00	75.00
☐ **FLAPPERS,** rel. 1977. ed. 250, s/n, litho, pub MMGI	70.00	—
☐ **FLIGHT OF FANCY,** rel. 1973. ed. 200, s/n, litho, pub MMGI	50.00	200.00
☐ **FORTY-THREE MINUTES FROM BROADWAY,** rel. 1975. ed. 150, s/n, etching, pub MMGI..	100.00	150.00
☐ **GAY,** rel. 1977. ed. 175, s/n, etching, pub MMGI	38.00	125.00
☐ **GOOD TIMES,** rel. 1976. ed. 175, s/n, hand colored etching, pub MMGI	90.00	225.00
☐ **GRACE,** rel. 1975. ed. 150, s/n, etching, pub MMGI	30.00	125.00
☐ **GROWING TOGETHER,** rel. 1975. ed. 200, s/n, litho, pub MMGI	60.00	190.00

	ISSUE PRICE	CURRENT PRICE
☐ GUITAR SOLO, rel. 1971. ed. 200, s/n, litho, pub MMGI	40.00	250.00
☐ HAPPY BIRTHDAY, rel. 1977. ed. 175, s/n, hand colored etching, pub MMGI	50.00	—
☐ HIDE 'N SEEK, rel. 1975. ed. 175, s/n, etching, pub MMGI	75.00	175.00
☐ HIGHER, rel. 1974. ed. 150, s/n, hand colored etching, pub MMGI	30.00	150.00
☐ IS LUNCH READY MOM, rel. 1972. ed. 75, s/n, hand colored etching, pub MMGI	60.00	200.00
☐ JANINE, rel. 1973. ed. 150, s/n, hand colored etching, pub MMGI	70.00	200.00
☐ JEANNA, rel. 1976. ed. 250, s/n, hand colored litho, pub MMGI	100.00	235.00
☐ JOY, rel. 1974. ed. 150, s/n, etching, pub MMGI	40.00	100.00
☐ JUNE, rel. 1973. ed. 100, s/n, etching, pub MMGI	30.00	125.00
☐ KATHERINE, rel. 1978. ed. 175, s/n, etching, pub MMGI	45.00	100.00
☐ KEEPING COOL, rel. 1972. ed. 200, s/n, litho, pub MMGI	35.00	125.00
☐ LADY MARLENE, rel. 1976. ed. 175, s/n, etching, pub MMGI	35.00	100.00
☐ LETTER FROM DADDY, rel. 1977. ed. 175, s/n, etching, pub MMGI	70.00	125.00
☐ LITTLE GIRLS ARE MADE OF, rel. 1977. ed. 175, s/n, hand colored etching, pub MMGI	65.00	125.00
☐ LOVE IN BLOOM, rel. 1974. ed. 200, s/n, litho, pub MMGI	50.00	250.00
☐ LOVE STORY, rel. 1975. ed. 150, s/n, etching, pub MMGI	125.00	Sold Out
☐ LOVERS, rel. 1972. ed. 100, s/n, etching, pub MMGI	50.00	150.00
☐ MAY, rel. 1973. ed. 100, s/n, etching, pub MMGI	30.00	125.00
☐ MOTHER & CHILD, rel. 1970. ed. 150, s/n, litho, pub MMGI	40.00	300.00
☐ MY GARDEN, rel. 1974. ed. 150, s/n, etching, pub MMGI	50.00	125.00
☐ OCTOBER, rel. 1974. ed. 150, s/n, etching, pub MMGI	80.00	225.00
☐ ONE MORE GAME, rel. 1975. ed. 150, s/n, etching, pub MMGI	100.00	225.00
☐ OUR HOUSE, rel. 1976. ed. 175, s/n, etching, pub MMGI	100.00	235.00
☐ PATIENCE, rel. 1972. ed. 25, s/n, etching, pub MMGI	25.00	125.00
☐ PATIENCE, rel. 1977. ed. 250, s/n, litho, pub MMGI	70.00	150.00
☐ PIGGY BACK, rel. 1973. ed. 250, s/n, litho, pub MMGI	60.00	250.00
☐ RAG DOLL, rel. 1977. ed. 250, s/n, hand colored litho, pub MMGI	100.00	225.00
☐ RAINY DAY, rel. 1973. ed. 150, s/n, litho, pub MMGI	50.00	175.00
☐ REFLECTIONS, rel. 1974. ed. 200, s/n, litho, pub MMGI	50.00	200.00
☐ REPOSE, rel. 1975. ed. 175, s/n, etching, pub MMGI	50.00	100.00
☐ ROCKING CHAIR, rel. 1974. ed. 200, s/n, litho, pub MMGI	50.00	150.00
☐ SEATED CHILD, rel. 1970. ed. 150, s/n, litho, pub MMGI	35.00	175.00
☐ SECRET PATH, rel. 1974. ed. 150, s/n, etching, pub MMGI	50.00	100.00
☐ SECRETS, rel. 1976. ed. 175, s/n, etching, pub MMGI	65.00	160.00
☐ SEPTEMBER, rel. 1974. ed. 150, s/n, hand colored etching, pub MMGI	90.00	175.00
☐ SHARING, rel. 1971. ed. 200, s/n, litho, pub MMGI	40.00	250.00
☐ SHE LOVES ME, rel. 1975. ed. 200, s/n, litho, pub MMGI	60.00	175.00
☐ SMALL MIRACLES, rel. 1976. ed. 175, s/n, etching, pub MMGI	90.00	—
☐ SOMEDAY, rel. 1974. ed. 150, s/n, etching, pub MMGI	60.00	125.00
☐ SOUND OF MUSIC, rel. 1974. ed. 150, s/n, etching, pub MMGI	50.00	150.00
☐ SPRING, rel. 1975. ed. 175, s/n, etching, pub MMGI	50.00	125.00
☐ SPRING BONNETS, rel. 1976. ed. 250, s/n, litho, pub MMGI	50.00	150.00
☐ SPRINGTIME, rel. 1971. ed. 200, s/n, litho, pub MMGI	40.00	175.00
☐ STRING OF PEARLS, rel. 1975. ed. 200, s/n, litho, pub MMGI	60.00	200.00
☐ SUNSHINE 'N SAND, rel. 1976. ed. 250, s/n, litho, pub MMGI	60.00	200.00
☐ SUZIE, rel. 1972. ed. 150, s/n, etching, pub MMGI	60.00	150.00
☐ SWEET NOTHINGS, rel. 1976. ed. 250, s/n, litho, pub MMGI	60.00	200.00
☐ SWEET SIXTEEN, rel. 1973. ed. 100, s/n, etching, pub MMGI	30.00	100.00
☐ TATTERED HERO, rel. 1973. ed. 100, s/n, etching, pub MMGI	60.00	235.00
☐ TENDER MOMENT, rel. 1971. ed. 200, s/n, litho, pub MMGI	40.00	225.00
☐ TENDER MOMENT II, rel. 1977. ed. 250, s/n, litho, pub MMGI	70.00	125.00
☐ THREE'S A CROWD, rel. 1973. ed. 100, s/n, etching, pub MMGI	50.00	200.00
☐ THREE OF A KIND, rel. 1972. ed. 200, s/n, litho, pub MMGI	40.00	120.00
☐ TODAY'S FORECAST - SUNNY, rel. 1978. ed. 175, s/n, hand colored etching, pub MMGI	100.00	—
☐ TOGETHER, rel. 1972. ed. 200, s/n, litho, pub MMGI	40.00	120.00
☐ TOGETHER WE'RE STRONGER, rel. 1973. ed. 100, s/n, etching, pub MMGI	40.00	150.00
☐ THE LOCKET, rel. 1977. ed. 175, s/n, etching, pub MMGI	60.00	100.00
☐ TULIPS, rel. 1976. ed. 250, s/n, litho, pub MMGI	100.00	325.00
☐ TWILIGHT, rel. 1975. ed. 175, s/n, etching, pub MMGI	65.00	160.00

	ISSUE PRICE	CURRENT PRICE
☐ **TWINS,** rel. 1974. ed. 200, s/n, hand colored litho, pub MMGI	60.00	90.00
☐ **TWO CHILDREN IN FIELD,** rel. 1970. ed. 150, s/n, litho, pub MMGI	40.00	150.00
☐ **WADING,** rel. 1972. ed. 200, s/n, litho, pub MMGI	40.00	215.00
☐ **WAITING FOR DADDY,** rel. 1974. ed. 150, s/n, etching, pub MMGI	50.00	235.00
☐ **WATER BABIES,** rel. 1972. ed. 200, s/n, litho, pub MMGI	70.00	350.00
☐ **WELCOME HOME,** rel. 1976. ed. 250, s/n, litho, pub MMGI	50.00	100.00
☐ **WICKER CHAIR,** rel. 1977. ed. 250, s/n, litho, pub MMGI	70.00	—
☐ **YESTERDAY'S TOMORROW,** rel. 1974. ed. 150, s/n, handcolored etching, pub MMGI	80.00	250.00
☐ **YOUNG GARDENER,** rel. 1972. ed. 200, s/n, litho, pub MMGI	35.00	150.00
☐ **JANUARY,** rel. 1977. ed. 175, s/n, hand colored etching, pub MMGI	120.00	175.00
☐ **CLASS OF '92,** rel. 1978. ed. 175, s/n, hand colored etching, pub MMGI	150.00	—
☐ **A GIRL'S BEST FRIEND,** rel. 1979. ed. 275, s/n, litho, pub MMGI	150.00	—
☐ **CONNOISSEUR,** rel. 1979. ed. 175, s/n, etching, pub MMGI	50.00	—
☐ **GOLDEN TRESSES,** rel. 1978. ed. 275, s/n, hand colored etching, pub MMGI	150.00	250.00
☐ **WHO ME?,** rel. 1979. ed. 275, s/n, litho, pub MMGI	100.00	—
☐ **EASTERN FLOWER,** rel. 1980. ed. 275, s/n, mixed media, pub MMGI	200.00	250.00
☐ **MARY ROSE,** rel. 1980. ed. 350, litho/etch, 10" x 13½", distr. GBSL	90.00	425.00
☐ **SPRING FLOWERS,** rel. 1981. ed. 350, litho/etch, 10" x 13½", distr. GBSL	125.00	155.00
☐ **SUMMER REFLECTIONS,** rel. 1981. ed. 350, litho/etch, 10" x 13½", distr. GBSL	155.00	—
☐ **LONG AGO,** rel. 1981. ed. 350, litho/etch, 10" x 13½", distr. GBSL	125.00	—
☐ **FAR AWAY,** rel. 1981. ed. 350, litho/etch, 10" x 13½", distr. GBSL	125.00	—
☐ **MARY ELLEN,** rel. 1981. ed. 350, litho/etch, 10" x 13½", distr. GBSL	105.00	—
☐ **AUTUMN LEAVES,** rel. 1981. ed. 350, litho/etch, 10" x 13½", distr. GBSL	125.00	—
☐ **NANCY,** rel. 1981. ed. 350, litho/etch, 10" x 13½", distr. GBSL	75.00	—

RUSS VICKERS

THEMES: Old West

STYLE: His miniatures and his larger paintings reveal impeccable research and painting technique

GALLERY/DISTRIBUTOR: Mill Pond Press, Inc.

RUN FOR THE RIVER by *Russ Vickers*

	ISSUE PRICE	CURRENT PRICE
☐ **THE BEEF RATION,** rel. 1979. ed. 950, s/n, 6¾" x 14¾", pub MPPI	35.00	—
☐ **THE COMMISSIONER,** rel. 1979. ed. 950, s/n, 6¾" x 14¾", pub MPPI	35.00	—
☐ **THE SETTLEMENT,** rel. 1979. ed. 950, s/n, 6¾" x 14¾", pub MPPI	35.00	—
☐ **THE UNTAMED LAND,** rel. 1979. ed. 950, s/n, 6¾" x 14¾", pub MPPI	35.00	—
☐ **APACHE ARROW,** rel. 1980. ed. 950, s/n, 19" x 25½", pub MPPI	65.00	—
☐ **ATTACK,** rel. 1980. ed. 950, s/n, 15¾" x 19", pub MPPI	45.00	—
☐ **RETURN TO HER PEOPLE,** rel. 1980. ed. 950, s/n, 16½" x 20", pub MPPI	45.00	—
☐ **THE STORY OF THE RIFLES,** rel. 1980. ed. 950, s/n, 16½" x 19⅝", pub MPPI	45.00	—
☐ **WHEN GAME IS SCARCE,** rel. 1980. ed. 950, s/n, 16¼" x 19½", pub MPPI	45.00	—
☐ **RUN FOR THE RIVER,** rel. 1981. ed. 950, s/n, 18¾" x 32½", pub MPPI	95.00	—
☐ **RUNNING WATER LEAVES NO TRAIL,** rel. 1982. ed. 950, s/n, 18¼" x 24", pub MPPI	85.00	—
☐ **THEY LIVED WITH THE LAND,** rel. 1982. ed. 950, s/n, 15" x 24", pub MPPI	75.00	—

HAHN VIDAL

THEMES: Flowers

STYLE: Ms. Vidal uses the technique of classical painting, taught to her by noted Argentinian artist, Eduardo Couce Vidal, her husband. The results have been enchanting: romantic flowers exploding with color

MUSEUMS/COLLECTIONS: Her work is represented in museums in South America, the Orient and the United States

GALLERY/DISTRIBUTOR: Mill Pond Press, Inc.

	ISSUE PRICE	CURRENT PRICE
☐ **FLOWER MARKET PARIS,** rel. 1975. ed. 950, s/n, 29" x 30", pub MPPI	125.00	—
☐ **WATER LILIES,** rel. 1975. ed. 950, s/n, 23" x 31½", litho, pub MPPI	150.00	—
☐ **COUNTRY BOUQUET,** rel. 1977. ed. 950, s/n, 19½" x 23½", pub MPPI	75.00	100.00

JEAN VIETOR

THEMES: Wildlife art

MEDIUM: Watercolor and gouache

EDUCATION: Lindenwood College for Women

AWARDS: Since she began showing her work in 1969, she has won over 50 awards

GALLERY/DISTRIBUTOR: Frame House Gallery, Inc.

	ISSUE PRICE	CURRENT PRICE
☐ **CARDINAL,** rel. 1979. ed. 700, s/n, 23½" x 18½", pub FHG	40.00	170.00
☐ **TUFTED TITMOUSE,** rel. 1979. ed. 700, s/n, 19½" x 14½", pub FHG	35.00	190.00

WELCOME SPRING by Jean Vietor

	ISSUE PRICE	CURRENT PRICE
☐ WOOD THRUSH, rel. 1979. ed. 700, s/n, 19″ x 24″, pub FHG	40.00	Sold Out
☐ I WISH LIFE WERE A BUTTERFLY, rel. 1980. ed. 800, s/n, 18¾″ x 25½″, pub FHG	50.00	100.00
ed. 100, s/n, and remarqued	75.00	140.00
☐ RACCOONS, rel. 1980. ed. 750, s/n, 18″ x 24″, pub FHG	45.00	125.00
☐ RED SQUIRREL, rel. 1980. ed. 750, s/n, 18½″ x 23½″, pub FHG	45.00	100.00
☐ RIGHT SIDE UP . . . DOWN?, rel. 1980. ed. 750, s/n, 27″ x 21″, pub FHG	45.00	175.00
☐ SOM'BRELLA, rel. 1980. ed. s/n, 27″ x 21″, pub FHG	50.00	Sold Out
☐ A RELUCTANT FAREWELL, rel. 1981. ed. 1,000, s/n, 21½″ x 27½″, pub FHG	50.00	100.00
☐ COTTONWORLD, rel. 1981. ed. 1,000, s/n, 21½″ x 27½″, pub FHG	50.00	90.00
☐ IN MY SPIFFY RED BANDANNA, rel. 1981. ed. 1,000, s/n, 24″ x 19″, pub FHG	50.00	85.00
☐ KNOCK-KNOCK . . . WHO WHO WHO'S THERE?, rel. 1981. ed. 1,000, s/n, 19″ x 24″, pub FHG	50.00	85.00
☐ WORLD OF WONDER, rel. 1981. ed. 1,000, s/n, 19″ x 26″, pub FHG	50.00	Sold Out
☐ A TOUCH OF BLUSH, rel. 1982. ed. 1,000, s/n, 18¾″ x 23¾″, pub FHG	60.00	—
☐ DEERWATCHER, rel. 1982. ed. 1,000, s/n, 27½″ x 21½″, pub FHG	60.00	100.00
☐ FLUFF AND STUFF, rel. 1982. ed. 4,000, s/o, 13½″ x 17″, pub FHG	25.00	—
☐ OH, RED BIRD, OH, RED BIRD, rel. 1982. ed. 1,000, s/n, 19″ x 24″, pub FHG	60.00	120.00
ed. 300, exclusive, available at the World's Fair	65.00	—
☐ PARASOLS AND TABLETOPS, rel. 1982. ed. 1,000, s/n, 13½″ x 18½″, pub FHG, (Sold as a set)	50.00	Sold Out
☐ THE GOLDEN DAYS, rel. 1982. ed. 1,000, s/n, 27½″ x 21½″, pub FHG	60.00	130.00
☐ RACCOON . . . SEQUEL, rel. 1983. ed. 1,000, s/n, 19″ x 24″, pub FHG	75.00	—
☐ RENDEVOUS, rel. 1983. ed. 1,000, s/n, 19″ x 30″, pub FHG	75.00	—
☐ VINES AND FINDS, rel. 1983. ed. 1,000, s/n, 32″ x 19″, pub FHG	75.00	125.00
☐ WINTER SONG, rel. 1983. ed. 1,000, s/n, 24″ x 19″, pub FHG	75.00	—
☐ WELCOME SPRING, rel. 1983. ed. 1,000, s/n, 19″ x 24″, pub FHG	75.00	125.00
☐ HUMMMM, rel. 1984. ed. 1,000, s/n, 24″ x 19″, pub FHG	90.00	—
☐ THE HIGH TRAILS, rel. 1984. ed. 1,000, s/n, 19″ x 34″, pub FHG	75.00	—

	ISSUE PRICE	CURRENT PRICE
☐ **WITH SPRING IN MIND,** rel. 1984. ed. 1,000, s/n, 28″ x 20″, pub FHG	90.00	—
☐ **COURTSHIP,** rel. 1985. ed. 1,000, s/n, 19″ x 24″, pub FHG	75.00	—
☐ **HAPPY TIMES,** rel. 1985. ed. 1,000, s/n, 13″ x 11″, pub FHG	35.00	—
☐ **SPRING PARADE,** rel. 1985. ed. 1,000, s/n, 13″ x 19″, pub FHG	50.00	—
(this is a pair of prints)		

HAROLD VON SCHMIDT

THEMES: Western art

STYLE: Realism

AWARDS: He has received many awards over his long career, including the first Gold Medal ever awarded by The National Cowboy Hall of Fame

GALLERY/DISTRIBUTOR: Mill Pond Press, Inc.

BUFFALO BILL CODY *by Harold Von Schmidt*

	ISSUE PRICE	CURRENT PRICE
☐ **BUFFALO BILL CODY,** rel. 1982. *ed. 950, embossed and numbered, 24½" x 30½"	245.00	—
**ed. 56, Artist proofs, pub MPPI	294.00	—
**ed. 20, Publisher's proofs	294.00	—

**Fewer than half of the Artist proofs and Publisher's proofs are available for sale, as the others are donated to museums and other institutions.
*Embossed with signature seal

BRUCE VON STETINA

THEMES: Sailing ships

STYLE: Realism

GALLERY/DISTRIBUTOR: Contemplative Investments, Inc.

	ISSUE PRICE	CURRENT PRICE
☐ **ANOTHER VICTORY FOR OLD IRONSIDES,** ed. 500, s/n, 21" x 32", pub CII	95.00	—
☐ **SECOND DAY OF THE FOUR DAY BATTLE OF 1666,** ed. 500, s/n, 21" x 32", pub CII...	95.00	—
☐ **SOUTH STREET SEAPORT 1865,** rel. 1983. ed. 500, s/n, 20" x 30", pub CII	95.00	—
☐ **THE LIGHTNING,** ed. 500, s/n, 18" x 24", pub CII	85.00	—
☐ **THE RAINBOW,** ed. 500, s/n, 18" x 24", pub CII	85.00	—

DONALD VOORHEES

THEMES: Varied

AWARDS: Over 100 awards to date

MEMBERSHIPS: Past president of the New Jersey Watercolor Society; Salmagundi Club

MUSEUMS/COLLECTIONS: The artist's works are in numerous collections

GALLERY/DISTRIBUTOR: Donald Voorhees Studio

	ISSUE PRICE	CURRENT PRICE
☐ **ANTICIPATION,** rel. 1979. ed. 950, s/n, 11" x 21", pub DVS	20.00	75.00
☐ **BEACH BABE,** rel. 1977. ed. 950, s/n, 10" x 14", pub DVS	12.00	140.00
☐ **BEACHCOMBERS,** rel. 1979. ed. 950, s/n, 10" x 16", pub DVS	25.00	65.00
☐ **BEACH DAY,** rel. 1980. ed. 1,200, s/n, 14" x 21", pub DVS	35.00	—
☐ **BUDDIES,** rel. 1977. ed. 950, s/n, 10" x 14", pub DVS	12.00	140.00
☐ **CHIP SHOT,** rel. 1982. ed. 950, s/n, 19" x 27", pub DVS	100.00	—
☐ **DAD'S DAY,** rel. 1979. ed. 950, s/n, 10" x 16", pub DVS	25.00	65.00
☐ **ELEGANT WEEDS,** rel. 1978. ed. 950, s/n, 11" x 22", pub DVS	20.00	75.00
☐ **GOLFER'S PARADISE,** rel. 1985. ed. 950, s/n, 19" x 27", pub DVS	100.00	—
☐ **GOOD TO BE ALIVE,** rel. 1984. ed. 950, s/n, 11" x 15", pub DVS	40.00	—

	ISSUE PRICE	CURRENT PRICE
☐ GULL HAVEN, rel. 1978. ed. 950, s/n, 15″ x 29″, pub DVS	50.00	75.00
☐ HERITAGE, rel. 1981. ed. 950, s/n, 14″ x 27″, pub DVS	55.00	—
☐ HOLING OUT, rel. 1982. ed. 950, s/n, 19″ x 27″, pub DVS	100.00	200.00
☐ JENNIFER'S GARDEN, rel. 1980. ed. 1,200, s/n, 22″ x 30″, pub DVS	50.00	—
☐ LACE, rel. 1980. ed. 1,200, s/n, 11″ x 29″, pub DVS	25.00	—
☐ LAND'S END, rel. 1979. ed. 950, s/n, 9″ x 21″, pub DVS	25.00	40.00
☐ MISTY, rel. 1978. ed. 950, s/n, 22″ x 30″, pub DVS	40.00	120.00
☐ MISTY MORN, rel. 1984. ed. 950, s/n, 21″ x 29″, pub DVS	80.00	—
☐ NATURE'S GIFT, rel. 1977. ed. 950, s/n, 14″ x 20″, pub DVS	24.00	60.00
☐ NOT FORGOTTEN, rel. 1981. ed. 950, s/n, 14″ x 27″, pub DVS	55.00	—
☐ RUSTIC BRIDGE, rel. 1979. ed. 950, s/n, 14″ x 21″, pub DVS	30.00	—
☐ RENDEZVOUS, rel. 1982. ed. 950, s/n, 11″ x 16″, pub DVS	28.00	60.00
☐ SALTY, rel. 1982. ed. 950, s/n, 11″ x 16″, pub DVS	28.00	60.00
☐ SATIN BUDS, rel. 1984. ed. 950, s/n, 10″ x 21″, pub DVS	40.00	—
☐ SATURDAY MORN, rel. 1978. ed. 950, s/n, 14″ x 21″, pub DVS	24.00	50.00
☐ SCENT OF SPLENDOR, rel. 1982. ed. 950, s/n, 21″ x 29″, pub DVS	65.00	200.00
☐ SILK, rel. 1980. ed. 1,200, s/n, 11″ x 29″, pub DVS	25.00	—
☐ SILKEN PETALS, rel. 1984. ed. 950, s/n, 21″ x 29″, pub DVS	80.00	—
☐ SILKIN PODS, rel. 1978. ed. 950, s/n, 11″ x 22″, pub DVS	20.00	140.00
☐ SOFT BLOSSOMS, rel. 1984. ed. 950, s/n, 10″ x 21″, pub DVS	40.00	—
☐ SUMMER IMAGES, rel. 1978. ed. 300, s/n, 18″ x 25″, pub DVS	150.00	—
☐ SUNBURST, rel. 1979. ed. 950, s/n, 11″ x 22″, pub DVS	20.00	140.00
☐ SUNNY BOUQUET, rel. 1978. ed. 950, s/n, 22″ x 29″, pub DVS	40.00	—
☐ SUNSTRUCK, rel. 1981. ed. 1,200, s/n, 22″ x 29″, pub DVS	60.00	—
☐ TALL MASTS, rel. 1982. ed. 950, s/n, 17″ x 28″, pub DVS	60.00	—
☐ TEEING OFF, rel. 1985. ed. 950, s/n, 19″ x 27″, pub DVS	100.00	—
☐ THE LAST HOLE, rel. 1982. ed. 950, s/n, 19″ x 27″, pub DVS	100.00	—
☐ TWOSOME, rel. 1982. ed. 950, s/n, 19″ x 27″, pub DVS	100.00	—
☐ VELVET, rel. 1980. ed. 1,200, s/n, 11″ x 29″, pub DVS	25.00	—
☐ WHISPER, rel. 1979. ed. 950, s/n, 11″ x 21″, pub DVS	20.00	75.00
☐ WINDSWEPT, rel. 1983. ed. 950, s/n, 21″ x 29″, pub DVS	75.00	—
☐ YELLOWS OF SPRING, rel. 1978. ed. 300, s/n, 18″ x 25″, pub DVS	150.00	—

JOHN F. WAHL

THEMES: Marine life

MEDIUM: Acrylic

AWARDS: Best of Show, National Wildlife Art Exhibit 1984; Best of Show, Cincinnati Nature Interpreted; "Backwater Repast," chosen for Society of Illustrators annual publication

MEMBERSHIPS: Save the Manatee Club Committee Member

GALLERY/DISTRIBUTOR: National Wildlife Galleries

	ISSUE PRICE	CURRENT PRICE
☐ BACHELOR PARTY, rel. 1984. ed. 1,000, s/o, 8″ x 10″, pub NWGI	6.75	—
☐ BACKWATER REPAST—FLORIDA MANATEE AND CALF, rel. 1984. s/o, 14¾″ x 27½″, pub NWGI..	50.00	—
☐ ESPIRIT, rel. 1984. ed. 1,000, s/o, 8″ x 10″, pub NWGI	6.75	—
☐ MOVING OUT, rel. 1984. ed. 1,000, s/o, 8″ x 10″, pub NWGI	6.75	—
☐ SUNBATHING, rel. 1984. ed. 1,000, s/o, 8″ x 10″, pub NWGI	6.75	—

SHARON WALD

MEDIUM: Scratchboard art

GALLERY/DISTRIBUTOR: Voyageur Art

	ISSUE PRICE	CURRENT PRICE
☐ **BABY TALK,** rel. 1984. ed. open, s/n, 8″ x 8″, litho, pub VA	12.00	—
☐ **BACKYARD BUNNIES,** rel. 1984. ed. 580, s/n, 10½″ x 15½″, litho, pub VA	45.00	—
☐ **BITS OF GOLD,** rel. 1983. ed. 580, s/n, 17″ x 21″, litho, pub VA	65.00	—
☐ **BITS OF HUMOR,** rel. 1982. ed. 880, s/n, 7″ x 15″, litho, pub VA	20.00	—
☐ **DECORATOR PRINTS,** rel. 1983. ed. open, s/n, 5″ x 8″, litho, pub VA	5.00	—
☐ **GARDENS EDGE,** rel. 1984. ed. 580, s/n, 15″ x 22″, litho, pub VA	45.00	—
☐ **INDIAN SUMMER,** rel. 1983. ed. 580, s/n, 23½″ x 19″, s/n, litho, pub VA	65.00	—
☐ **MALE WOODDUCK,** rel. 1981. ed. 680, s/n, 13″ x 19″, litho, pub VA	40.00	—
☐ **NATURE PRINTS,** rel. 1983. ed. open, s/n, 8″ x 8″, litho, pub VA	8.00	—
☐ **OLD MINIS,** rel. 1981. ed. open, s/n, 6½″ x 6½″, litho, pub VA	5.00	—
☐ **ONE IN EVERY CROWD,** rel. 1984. ed. 580, s/n, 19″ x 24″, litho, pub VA	75.00	—
☐ **REST AND RELAXATION,** rel. 1984. ed. 580, s/n, 10¼″ x 15¼″, litho, pub VA	45.00	—
☐ **SMELL THE ROSES,** rel. 1984. ed. 580, s/n, 11¼″ x 11¼″, litho, pub VA	40.00	—
☐ **TEENAGE BLUES,** rel. 1984. ed. 580, s/n, 12½″ x 12½″, litho, pub VA	40.00	—

GRANDMA'S QUILT *by Wayne Waldron*

WAYNE WALDRON

THEMES: Americana

MEDIUM: Watercolor

STYLE: Interpretive realism

GALLERY/DISTRIBUTOR: Guildhall, Inc.

	ISSUE PRICE	CURRENT PRICE
☐ COUNTRY KITCHEN, ed. 1,500, s/n, 20″ x 26″, pub TWS	40.00	125.00
☐ GRANDMA'S QUILT, ed. 1,500, s/n, 20″ x 26″, pub TWS	40.00	—
☐ CLAUDE'N BETTY, rel. 1984. ed. 1,500, s/n, 26″ x 20⅜″, pub TWS	40.00	50.00
ed. 25, Artist proofs	40.00	50.00
☐ TIME FOR SUPPER, rel. 1984. ed. 1,500, s/n, 20⅜″ x 26¾″, pub TWS	60.00	75.00
ed. 25, Artist proofs	60.00	75.00

SPRING BULBS *by Maryrose Wampler*

MARY ROSE WAMPLER

THEMES: Flowers

STYLE: Realism

AWARDS: Winner of the 1974 National Flower Contest

GALLERY/DISTRIBUTOR: Nature House, Inc.

	ISSUE PRICE	CURRENT PRICE
☐ BLACK-EYED SUSAN, rel. 1974. ed. 5,000, s/o, 22″ x 28″, pub NHI	**30.00	350.00
☐ DAISY MUMS, rel. 1974. ed. 5,000, s/o, 22″ x 28″, pub NHI	30.00	75.00
☐ DOGWOOD AND VIOLETS, rel. 1974. ed. 5,000, s/o, 22″ x 28″, pub NHI	30.00	75.00
☐ IRIS AND OLD ROSES, rel. 1974. ed. 5,000, s/o, 22″ x 28″, pub NHI	30.00	75.00
☐ TRAILING ARBUTUS, rel. 1974. ed. 5,000, s/o, 22″ x 28″, pub NHI	30.00	75.00
☐ CARDINAL FLOWER AND TICKSEED, rel. 1975. ed. 5,000, s/o, 22″ x 28″, pub NHI .	30.00	50.00
☐ HIBISCUS AND ORANGE BLOSSOM, rel. 1975. ed. 5,000, s/o, 22″ x 28″, pub NHI .	30.00	50.00
☐ LILAC AND APPLE BLOSSOM, rel. 1975. ed. 5,000, s/o, 22″ x 28″, pub NHI	30.00	50.00
☐ PIEDMONT AZALEA, rel. 1975. ed. 5,000, s/o, 22″ x 28″, pub NHI	30.00	50.00
☐ RED CLOVER AND ROADSIDE FLOWERS, rel. 1975. ed. 5,000, s/o, 22″ x 28″, pub NHI...	30.00	50.00
☐ SINGLE YELLOW ROSE, rel. 1975. ed. 5,000, s/o, 22″ x 28″, pub NHI	30.00	50.00
☐ GOLDENROD, rel. 1976. ed. 5,000, s/o, 22″ x 28″, pub NHI	30.00	50.00
☐ HEPATICA, rel. 1976. ed. 5,000, s/o, 22″ x 28″, pub NHI	30.00	50.00
☐ PEACE ROSE AND PEONY, rel. 1976. ed. 5,000, s/o, 22″ x 28″, pub NHI	30.00	50.00
☐ PEACH BLOSSOM, rel. 1976. ed. 5,000, s/o, 22″ x 28″, pub NHI	30.00	50.00
☐ SOUTHERN MAGNOLIA, rel. 1976. ed. 5,000, s/o, 22″ x 28″, pub NHI	30.00	50.00
☐ YELLOW JESSAMINE, rel. 1976. ed. 5,000, s/o, 22″ x 28″, pub NHI	30.00	50.00
☐ CAMELLIA, rel. 1977. ed. 5,000, s/o, 22″ x 28″, pub NHI	30.00	50.00
☐ DUNE FLOWERS, rel. 1977. ed. 5,000, s/o, 22″ x 28″, pub NHI	30.00	50.00
☐ LILLIES AND TR. VINE, rel. 1977. ed. 5,000, s/o, 22″ x 28″, pub NHI	30.00	50.00
☐ PASSION VINE, rel. 1977. ed. 5,000, s/o, 22″ x 28″, pub NHI	30.00	50.00
☐ TRILLIM, rel. 1977. ed. 5,000, s/o, 22″ x 28″, pub NHI	30.00	50.00
☐ WILD ROSE, rel. 1977. ed. 5,000, s/o, 22″ x 28″, pub NHI	30.00	50.00
☐ BUTTERFLIES (SET OF THREE), rel. 1978. ed. 2,500, i/o, 5″ x 7″, pub NHI	25.00	—
☐ COMMON SUNFLOWER, rel. 1978. ed. 5,000, s/o, 22″ x 28″, pub NHI	30.00	50.00
☐ BLUE BELLS, rel. 1979. ed. 5,000, s/o, 22″ x 28″, pub NHI	30.00	50.00
☐ INDIAN PAINTBRUSH, rel. 1979. ed. 5,000, s/o, 22″ x 28″, pub NHI	30.00	50.00
☐ SPRING BULBS, rel. 1979. ed. 5,000, s/o, 22″ x 28″, pub NHI	30.00	50.00
☐ THISTLE, rel. 1979. ed. 5,000, s/o, 22″ x 28″, pub NHI	30.00	50.00
☐ MOUNTAIN FLOWERS, rel. 1981. ed. 5,000, s/o, 22″ x 28″, pub NHI	50.00	—
☐ OLD FASHIONED ROSES, rel. 1981. ed. 1,000, s/o, 16″ x 20″, pub NHI	50.00	—
☐ RHODODENDRON, rel. 1981. ed. 5,000, s/o, 22″ x 28″, pub NHI	50.00	—

**Prints were sold as collections at issue price shown, providing the collector purchased each print when published. Individual purchases were $50.00 issue.

EDWARD WARD

THEMES: Varied

MEDIUM: Handprinted collographs, engraving, and intaglio relief prints

EDUCATION: Trenton State College

AWARDS: His work has won over 100 different awards

MEMBERSHIPS: Philadelphia Print Club; Printmaking Council of New Jersey

GALLERY/DISTRIBUTOR: Ed Ward

	ISSUE PRICE	CURRENT PRICE
☐ "A" CONVERTIBLE, rel. 1982. ed. 100, s/n, 1″ x 2″, etching, pub EW	18.00	—
☐ AMERICANA, rel. 1979. ed. 100, s/n, 21″ x 27″, collograph engraving, pub EW	50.00	75.00
☐ APOLLO XIII, rel. 1979. ed. 75, s/n, 22″ x 22″, collograph linocut, pub EW	50.00	Sold Out
☐ ARMADILLO, rel. 1982. ed. 100, s/n, 1″ x 2″, etching, pub EW	18.00	—
☐ AT & SF, rel. 1982. ed. 100, s/n, 16″ x 16″, collograph engraving, pub EW	30.00	35.00
☐ "B" CONVERTIBLE, rel. 1982. ed. 100, s/n, 2″ x 2″, etching, pub EW	18.00	—
☐ BIOSYNTHESIS, rel. 1976. ed. 75, s/n, 24″ x 20″, collograph, pub EW	60.00	Sold Out
☐ BONDED HOMAGE, rel. 1976. ed. 75, s/n, 20″ x 25″, woodcut, pub EW	30.00	Sold Out
☐ BUZZARD'S BAY, rel. 1974. ed. 75, s/n, 22″ x 28″, woodcut, pub EW	45.00	Sold Out
☐ CARIBE, rel. 1981. ed. 175, s/n, 11″ x 13″, linocut engraving, pub EW	18.00	24.00
☐ CLIPPER, rel. 1984. ed. 100, s/n, 2″ x 3″, etching, pub EW	18.00	—
☐ CUZCO I, rel. 1978. ed. 100, s/n, 21″ x 31″, intaglio relief, pub EW	60.00	75.00
☐ CUZCO II, rel. 1978. ed. 100, s/n, 23″ x 30″, intaglio relief, pub EW	60.00	95.00
☐ CUZCO III, rel. 1978. ed. 100, s/n, 25″ x 30″, collograph engraving, pub EW	60.00	75.00
☐ DANFORTHE, COOKE, rel. 1981. ed. 100, s/n, 16″ x 18″, collograph engraving, pub EW	30.00	35.00
☐ DANDYLION, rel. 1976. ed. 75, s/n, 12″ x 17″, linocut, pub EW	18.00	Sold Out
☐ DAYBREAKERS, rel. 1976. ed. 75, s/n, 17″ x 27″, collograph engraving, pub EW	24.00	Sold Out
☐ DUSK, rel. 1978. ed. 150, s/n, 18″ x 24″, collograph engraving, pub EW	30.00	45.00
☐ EDIFICATION OF MAN, rel. 1981. ed. 75, s/n, 24″ x 24″, collograph engraving, pub EW...	90.00	95.00
☐ EGRET, rel. 1978. ed. 150, s/n, 14″ x 27″, engraving, pub EW	30.00	Sold Out
☐ EHLYSUN, rel. 1980. ed. 175, s/n, 11″ x 12″, collograph, engraving, pub EW	18.00	Sold Out
☐ ELEMENTAL LANDSCAPE, rel. 1978. ed. 150, s/n, 19″ x 26″, collograph engraving, pub EW...	45.00	75.00
☐ EVENTIDE, rel. 1978. ed. 175, s/n, 24″ x 30″, collograph engraving, pub EW	50.00	95.00
☐ FAST BREAK, rel. 1978. ed. 150, s/n, 14″ x 17″, collograph engraving, pub EW	18.00	24.00
☐ GANYMEDE, rel. 1975. ed. 50, s/n, 22″ x 28″, collograph, pub EW	45.00	Sold Out
☐ GOLDFISH, rel. 1982. ed. 100, s/n, 2″ x 2″, etching, pub EW	18.00	—
☐ HANDSTAND, rel. 1984. ed. 50, s/n, 11″ x 19″, silkscreen, pub EW	45.00	—
☐ HARVEST MOON, rel. 1977. ed. 125, s/n, 22″ x 28″, collograph engraving, pub EW ..	30.00	Sold Out
☐ HUNTSMEN, rel. 1978. ed. 175, s/n, 16″ x 20″, collograph engraving, pub EW	30.00	40.00
☐ INDIANA, rel. 1975. ed. 100, s/n, 16″ x 16″, etching, pub EW	18.00	Sold Out
☐ INDIAN LAKE, rel. 1981. ed. 100, s/n, 14″ x 18″, collograph engraving, pub EW	45.00	—
☐ KANSAS LIMITED, rel. 1981. ed. 150, s/n, 11″ x 12″, collograph engraving, pub EW .	18.00	—
☐ KINDRED, rel. 1978. ed. 100, s/n, 24″ x 32″, intaglio relief, pub EW	60.00	95.00
☐ LEO, rel. 1977-78. ed. 125, s/n, 24″ x 27″, intaglio relief, pub EW	45.00	55.00
☐ LES FLEURS, rel. 1976. ed. 75, s/n, 20″ x 24″, intaglio relief, pub EW	24.00	Sold Out
☐ LO!, rel. 1977. ed. 100, s/n, 18″ x 18″, collograph, pub EW	30.00	Sold Out
☐ LUNA, rel. 1980. ed. 150, s/n, 26″ x 29″, collograph engraving, pub EW	50.00	Sold Out
☐ LORELLI, rel. 1976. ed. 50, s/n, 21″ x 27″, collograph, pub EW	18.00	Sold Out
☐ MAGONIAN MOON, rel. 1978. ed. 100, s/n, 24″ x 30″, intaglio relief, pub EW	45.00	Sold Out
☐ MEDIEVAL, rel. 1977. ed. 100, s/n, 28″ x 28″, intaglio relief, pub EW	50.00	95.00
☐ MIDDAY, rel. 1978. ed. 175, s/n, 24″ x 28″, collograph engraving, pub EW	60.00	95.00
☐ MIRAGE, rel. 1978. ed. 150, s/n, 24″ x 32″, intaglio relief, pub EW	40.00	95.00
☐ MONTEGO DUSK, rel. 1976. ed. 75, s/n, 20″ x 24″, collograph engraving, pub EW ..	24.00	45.00
☐ MOONLIT WATERS, rel. 1981. ed. 100, s/n, 14″ x 14″, engraving, pub EW	30.00	Sold Out
☐ MOON'S RISE, rel. 1978. ed. 150, s/n, 11″ x 12″, collograph engraving, pub EW	14.00	Sold Out
☐ MORNING MISTS, rel. 1979. ed. 175, s/n, 22″ x 24″, engraving, pub EW	45.00	60.00
☐ N de M, rel. 1980. ed. 100, s/n, 11″ x 14″, engraving, pub EW	18.00	—
☐ NATCHEZ, rel. 1977. ed. 100, s/n, 24″ x 30″, collograph engraving, pub EW	45.00	Sold Out
☐ NIGHTFLIGHT, rel. 1983. ed. 100, s/n, 8″ x 10″, woodcut, pub EW	28.00	—
☐ NOD, rel. 1980. ed. 100, s/n, 13″ x 14″, collograph engraving, pub EW	18.00	24.00
☐ OCCULARITY, rel. 1976. ed. 100, s/n, 24″ x 30″, intaglio relief, pub EW	30.00	Sold Out

POINT OF VIEW *by Ed Ward*

	ISSUE PRICE	CURRENT PRICE
☐ ORBIS, rel. 1977. ed. 100, s/n, 20″ x 24″, collograph, pub EW	24.00	35.00
☐ OWL, rel. 1982. ed. 100, s/n, 1″ x 1″, etching, pub EW	18.00	Sold Out
☐ PEACE ROSE, rel. 1977. ed. 100, s/n, 11″ x 13″, collograph, pub EW	18.00	35.00
☐ POINT OF VIEW, rel. 1978-82. ed. 100, s/n, 31″ x 38″, collograph engraving, pub EW	150.00	275.00
☐ QZYCAUTL, rel. 1976. ed. 100, s/n, 24″ x 26″, intaglio relief, pub EW	35.00	75.00
☐ ROSE, rel. 1976. ed. 100, s/n, 13″ x 14″, collograph, pub EW	18.00	Sold Out
☐ RUDEBECKIAS, rel. 1976. ed. 100, s/n, 20″ x 22″, collograph, pub EW	18.00	Sold Out
☐ SAIL AWAY, rel. 1981. ed. 100, s/n, 31″ x 38″, collograph engraving, stencil, pub EW .	90.00	125.00
☐ SEAFARER, rel. 1979-81. ed. 100, s/n, 31″ x 36″, collograph engraving, pub EW	90.00	125.00
☐ SEASON'S FLOW, rel. 1979. ed. 100, s/n, 21″ x 32″, collograph engraving, pub EW ..	75.00	Sold Out
☐ SIC TRANSIT, rel. 1978. ed. 100, s/n, 24″ x 32″, collograph engraving, pub EW	45.00	Sold Out
☐ SILENT REFLECTIONS, rel. 1977. ed. 100, s/n, 16″ x 20″, collograph, pub EW	24.00	75.00
☐ SNOWDRIFTING, rel. 1979. ed. 100, s/n, 16″ x 22″, engraving, pub EW	30.00	35.00
☐ SNOWFLAKES, rel. 1980. ed. 100, s/n, 13″ x 24″, engraving, pub EW	24.00	30.00
☐ SOUTHWESTERN, rel. 1980. ed. 100, s/n, 12″ x 13″, collograph engraving, pub EW .	18.00	—
☐ SPRING MOON, rel. 1978. ed. 100, s/n, 18″ x 22″, collograph engraving, pub EW ...	40.00	45.00
☐ SUMMER SOLSTICE, rel. 1976. ed. 100, s/n, 18″ x 24″, collograph engraving, pub EW..	24.00	Sold Out
☐ SUNFLOWERS, rel. 1976. ed. 100, s/n, 16″ x 20″, collograph, pub EW	24.00	Sold Out
☐ SUNSET, rel. 1978. ed. 100, s/n, 18″ x 22″, collograph engraving, pub EW	30.00	45.00
☐ SUNSET FIRES, rel. 1977. ed. 100, s/n, 24″ x 30″, collograph engraving, pub EW ...	45.00	75.00
☐ TIP-IN, rel. 1980-81. ed. 100, s/n, 23″ x 26″, collograph engraving, pub EW	50.00	75.00
☐ TITAN, rel. 1978. ed. 100, s/n, 25″ x 32″, intaglio relief, pub EW	60.00	Sold Out
☐ TWILIGHT, rel. 1978. ed. 100, s/n, 11″ x 12″, collograph engraving, pub EW	18.00	24.00

	ISSUE PRICE	CURRENT PRICE
☐ **UNION PACIFIC,** rel. 1977. ed. 100, s/n, 24″ x 30″, collograph engraving, pub EW ...	45.00	Sold Out
☐ **WANING AFTERNOON,** rel. 1979. ed. 100, s/n, 24″ x 28″, collograph engraving, pub EW	60.00	95.00
☐ **WINTER FIELDS,** rel. 1979. ed. 100, s/n, 17″ x 26″, collograph engraving, pub EW ..	30.00	45.00
☐ **WINTER SOLSTICE,** rel. 1979. ed. 100, s/n, 17″ x 19″, collograph engraving, pub EW	30.00	45.00

MELVIN C. WARREN

THEMES: Western art

EDUCATION: Texas Christian University

AWARDS: Two-time winner of the Franklin Mint award as one of the ten best Western artists

MUSEUMS/COLLECTIONS: Lyndon Johnson commissioned 20 of Melvin Warren's paintings

GALLERY/DISTRIBUTOR: Mill Pond Press, Inc.

WHEN COWBOYS GET EDGY by *Melvin Warren*

	ISSUE PRICE	CURRENT PRICE
☐ TOP HAND OF THE CONCHO, rel. 1974. ed. 700, s/n, 23″ x 31½″, pub MPPI	150.00	400.00
☐ A COLD DAY, rel. 1981. ed. 550, s/n, 24⅝″ x 38″, pub MPPI	245.00	450.00
☐ APPROACHING STORM, rel. 1981. ed. 750, s/n, 22″ x 32½″, pub MPPI	195.00	—
☐ WHEN COWBOYS GET EDGY, rel. 1981. ed. 750, s/n, 24½″ x 38″, pub MPPI	245.00	—
☐ NIGHT IN CHIMAYO, rel. 1982. ed. 950, s/n, 18¼″ x 23⅞″, pub MPPI	125.00	—

ANTOWINE WARRIOR

THEMES: Historical Indian themes

MEDIUM: Watercolor, gouache

STYLE: Traditional realism

AWARDS: Best of Class, Division & Show, Santa Fe Indian Market 1983; Wolf Robe Hunt Award, Philbrook-1977; First Place, Philbrook-1979; Smithsonian Exhibition-1982; Gold Medal, San Dimas

MEMBERSHIPS: American Indian and Cowboy Artists Association

GALLERY/DISTRIBUTOR: Native American Images

	ISSUE PRICE	CURRENT PRICE
☐ FRY BREAD - MY GRANDMOTHER'S WAY, ed. 80, s/n, 22″ x 28″, stone litho, pub NWDHG	250.00	500.00
☐ THE HISTORIAN, ed. 950, s/n, 16″ x 20″, stone litho, pub NWDHG	50.00	—
☐ SCOUT - THE WATCHFUL ONE, ed. 80, s/n, 22″ x 15″, stone litho, pub NWDHG ...	175.00	450.00
☐ WINTER CROSSING, ed. 650, s/n, 24″ x 32″, stone litho, pub NWDHG	75.00	725.00
☐ VICTORY GALLOP, ed. 1,500, s/n, 18″ x 20″, stone litho, pub NWDHG	40.00	200.00
☐ SURPRISE ATTACK, ed. 950, s/n, 24″ x 27″, stone litho, pub NWDHG	50.00	210.00
☐ MONARCH OF THE PLAINS, ed. 1,500, s/n, 22″ x 33″, stone litho, pub NAI	80.00	—

BURL WASHINGTON

THEMES: Portraiture; landscape art, etc.

MEDIUM: Watercolor

MUSEUMS/COLLECTIONS: Washington's originals are in the private collections of notable figures, such as President Jimmy Carter, Congressman Jim Wright, and the Texas Boys' Choir

GALLERY/DISTRIBUTOR: Guildhall, Inc.

	ISSUE PRICE	CURRENT PRICE
☐ BREAK TIME, ed. 500, s/n, 27″ x 19″, distr. GI	50.00	—
☐ LONE SOLDIER, ed. 650, s/n, 16″ x 24″, distr. GI	55.00	—
☐ SOLDIER OF SOLITUDE, ed. 650, s/n, 16″ x 21″, distr. GI	55.00	—

WALTER A. WEBER

THEMES: Wildlife art

BACKGROUND: Over the years, the artist has held a number of prestigious posts including staff artist and naturalist for the National Geographic Society

EDUCATION: University of Chicago; Church School of Art; the American Academy of Art and the Chicago Art Institute

AWARDS: Conservation Service Award (1967), the highest civilian honor the U.S. Department of the Interior can bestow

GALLERY/DISTRIBUTOR: Russell A. Fink

	ISSUE PRICE	CURRENT PRICE
☐ **SNOW GEESE,** ed. 550, s/n, 17″ x 22″, pub RAF	60.00	125.00

JOHN WEISS

THEMES: Animals (Dogs, in particular)

MEDIUM: Oil, primarily

GALLERY/DISTRIBUTOR: Greenwich Workshop

COCKER SPANIEL PUPPIES *by John Weiss*

	ISSUE PRICE	CURRENT PRICE
☐ **LAB PUPPIES,** rel. 1982. ed. 1,000, s/n, 19″ x 15″, pub GW	65.00	85.00
☐ **REBEL & SODA,** (matching pair), rel. 1982. ed. 1,000, s/n, 15″ x 11½″, pub GW	45.00	Sold Out
☐ **GOLDEN RETRIEVER PUPPIES,** rel. 1983. ed. 1,000, s/n, 19½″ x 13⅛″, pub GW ..	65.00	85.00
☐ **BASSET HOUND PUPPIES,** rel. 1984. ed. 1,000, s/n, 19½″ x 14⅛″, pub GW	65.00	—
☐ **COCKER SPANIEL PUPPIES,** rel. 1984. ed. 1,000, s/n, 19½″ x 14⅛″, pub GW	75.00	—
☐ **OLD ENGLISH SHEEPDOG PUPPIES,** rel. 1984. ed. 1,000, s/n, 19″ x 15½″, pub GW..	65.00	—
☐ **PERSIAN KITTEN,** rel. 1985. ed. 1,000, s/n, 12¼″ x 19½″, pub GW	65.00	—

RONNIE WELLS

THEMES: Varied

MEDIUM: Watercolor

EDUCATION: Louisiana Tech University

GALLERY/DISTRIBUTOR: Arts Limited, Inc.

	ISSUE PRICE	CURRENT PRICE
☐ **A MOMENT IN MARCH,** ed. 1,000, s/n, 29½″ x 20½″	50.00	—
☐ **COOLING SHED,** rel. 1976. ed. 850, s/n, 33″ x 35, pub ALI	50.00	—
☐ **RURAL SETTING,** rel. 1976. ed. 850, s/n, 33″ x 25″, pub ALI	40.00	—

JAMES D. WERLINE

THEMES: Varied

MEDIUM: Watercolor

EDUCATION: Morehead State University

GALLERY/DISTRIBUTOR: Wildlife Internationale, Inc.

	ISSUE PRICE	CURRENT PRICE
☐ **COUNTRY WINTER,** ed. 750, s/n, 18½″ x 24″, distr. WII	30.00	—
☐ **COUNTRY MEMORIES,** ed. 750, s/n, 24″ x 18″, distr. WII	45.00	—
☐ **COUNTRY SUMMER,** ed. 750, s/n, 24″ x 18″, distr. WII	45.00	—
☐ **GEORGETOWN COMMERCIAL ROW,** ed. 500, s/b, 15″ x 18″, distr. WII	50.00	—
☐ **STONY HOLLOW,** ed. 500, s/n, 20″ x 26″, distr. WII	75.00	—

RED TAIL HAWK *by Bill Wesling*

BILL WESLING

THEMES: Wildlife art

EDUCATION: Art Institute of Pittsburgh

MEMBERSHIPS: Florida Audubon Society; National Wildlife Federation; National Wild Turkey Federation, etc.

MUSEUMS/COLLECTIONS: Hundreds of collections worldwide

GALLERY/DISTRIBUTOR: Salt Springs Wildlife Art Studios, Inc.

COMMENTS: In May, 1985, the artist was honored in the Florida State Senate and met with Bob Graham, Florida's governor, in recognition of his conservation efforts

	ISSUE PRICE	CURRENT PRICE
☐ A PAIR OF WOODIES, ed. 500, s/n, sealed, 16″ x 20″, pub SSWASI	50.00	Sold Out
☐ AMERICAN BALD EAGLE, ed. 500, s/n, sealed, 22″ x 28″, pub SSWASI	40.00	75.00
☐ AUTUMN IN ALL IT'S GLORY, ed. 500, s/n, sealed, 22″ x 24″, pub SSWASI	75.00	75.00

	ISSUE PRICE	CURRENT PRICE
☐ BARRED OWL, ed. 500, s/n, sealed, 22″ x 28″, pub SSWASI	50.00	75.00
☐ BLUE SENTINELS, ed. 500, s/n, sealed, 22″ x 28″, pub SSWASI	100.00	450.00
☐ BOB WHITE QUAIL, ed. 500, s/n, sealed, pub SSWASI	40.00	2,500.00
☐ DRUMMER GOES A COURTIN', ed. 500, s/n, sealed, 21″ x 26½″, pub SSWASI	100.00	125.00
☐ EIGHT IS ENOUGH, ed. 500, s/n, sealed, 16″ x 20″, pub SSWASI	75.00	75.00
☐ FOREST NURSERY, ed. 500, s/n, sealed, 16″ x 20″, pub SSWASI	75.00	75.00
☐ GRAY SQUIRRELS, ed. 500, s/n, sealed, 16″ x 20″, pub SSWASI	40.00	350.00
☐ GREAT BLUE HERON, ed. 750, s/n, sealed, pub SSWASI	75.00	350.00
☐ GREAT HORNED OWL, ed. 500, s/n, sealed, 23″ x 29″, pub SSWASI	40.00	450.00
☐ IN THE EYES OF THE BEHOLDER, ed. 500, s/n, sealed, 22″ x 28″, pub SSWASI	75.00	75.00
☐ INTERRUPTED INTERLUDE, ed. 500, s/n, sealed, 22″ x 24″, pub SSWASI	75.00	75.00
☐ IT'S RUDE TO POINT, ed. 500, s/n, sealed, 20″ x 24″, pub SSWASI	100.00	Sold Out
☐ JUST A PAIR OF HOODS, ed. 500, s/n, sealed, 16″ x 20″, pub SSWASI	50.00	50.00
☐ LIKE FATHER-LIKE SON, ed. 500, s/n, sealed, 22″ x 28″, pub SSWASI	100.00	500.00
☐ OSPREY, ed. 500, s/n, sealed, 22″ x 28″, pub SSWASI	50.00	75.00
☐ PAIR OF GREAT HORNED OWLS, ed. 500, s/n, sealed, 20″ x 24″, pub SSWASI	75.00	450.00
☐ PARTNERS FOR LIFE, ed. 500, s/n, sealed, 16″ x 20″, pub SSWASI	50.00	50.00
☐ DEVELOPING FOR RIVALRY, ed. 500, s/n, sealed, 16″ x 20″, pub SSWASI	50.00	50.00
☐ RACCOON FAMILY, ed. 500, s/n, sealed, 23″ x 29″, pub SSWASI	50.00	450.00
☐ RED SHOULDER HAWK, ed. 975, s/n, sealed, 22″ x 28″, pub SSWASI	50.00	75.00
☐ RED TAIL HAWK, ed. 975, s/n, sealed, 22″ x 28″, pub SSWASI	50.00	75.00
☐ RING NECK PHEASANTS, ed. 500, s/n, sealed, 22″ x 28″, pub SSWASI	40.00	650.00
☐ THE LITTLEST PUDDLE JUMPER, ed. 500, s/n, sealed, 16″ x 20″, pub SSWASI	50.00	50.00
☐ THE TRANQUIL PAIR, ed. 500, s/n, sealed, 16″ x 20″, pub SSWASI	50.00	50.00
☐ WINNER AND STILL CHAMPION, ed. 500, s/n, sealed, 16″ x 20″, pub SSWASI	50.00	50.00
☐ WHITE TAIL DEER AND JAYS, ed. 500, s/n, sealed, 23″ x 29″, pub SSWASI	40.00	400.00
☐ WOOD DUCK DRAKE, ed. 500, s/n, sealed, pub SSWASI	40.00	1,400.00
☐ GOLDEN SLIPPERS, ed. 500, s/n, sealed, 26″ x 19″, pub SSWASI	100.00	125.00
☐ PILEATED WOODPECKERS, ed. 500, s/n, sealed, 20″ x 24″, pub SSWASI	75.00	100.00
☐ CONFRONTATION, ed. 500, s/n, sealed, 24″ x 18″, pub SSWASI	100.00	100.00
☐ INTRUDER 1776, ed. 975, s/n, 22″ x 28″, sealed, pub SSWASI	50.00	75.00
*Additional 500 ed. for NWTF fund raising.		
☐ CHEETAHS, ed. 75, s/n, sealed, pub SSWASI	50.00	—
☐ CHIMPANZEES, ed. 750, s/n, sealed, pub SSWASI	50.00	—
☐ SIBERIAN TIGER, ed. 750, s/n, sealed, pub SSWASI	50.00	—
☐ SONGBIRDS PORTFOLIO, ed. 2,500, s/n, sealed, 12″ x 13″, set of three, pub SSWASI	30.00	30.00
☐ BASS PRINTS, ed. 2,500, s/n, sealed, 16″ x 20″, pub SSWASI	20.00	30.00
☐ DESIGNS OF NATURE 15TH ANNIVERSARY PORTFOLIO, rel. 1984. ed. 250, s/n, sealed, 14″ x 16″, pub SSWASI	300.00	—
☐ RACCOONS & BOX TURTLE, rel. 1984. ed. 250, s/n, sealed, 14″ x 16″, pub SSWASI	40.00	—
☐ COTTON-TAIL RABBITS, rel. 1984. ed. 250, s/n, sealed, 14″ x 16″, pub SSWASI	40.00	—
☐ BROWN PELICANS, rel. 1984. ed. 250, s/n, sealed, 14″ x 16″, pub SSWASI	40.00	—
☐ COMMON LOON, rel. 1984. ed. 250, s/n, sealed, 14″ x 16″, pub SSWASI	40.00	—
☐ PEREGRINE FALCON, rel. 1984. ed. 250, s/n, sealed, 14″ x 16″, pub SSWASI	40.00	—
☐ YELLOW-SHAFTED FLICKERS, rel. 1984. ed. 250, s/n, sealed, 14″ x 16″, pub SSWASI	40.00	—
☐ A QUESTION OF SURVIVAL, ed. 1985. ed. 500, s/n, sealed, 16½″ x 20½″, pub SSWASI	100.00	—
☐ ST. JOHNS RENDEZVOUS, rel. 1985. ed. 500, s/n, sealed, 19″ x 23″, pub SSWASI	100.00	—

E. GORDON WEST

THEMES: Wildlife art

GALLERY/DISTRIBUTOR: Arts Limited, Inc.

	ISSUE PRICE	CURRENT PRICE
☐ BARRED OWL, ed. 1,000, s/n, 16″ x 20″, pub ALI	30.00	—
☐ BUSHY TAIL, rel. 1973. ed. 1,500, s/n, 20″ x 16, pub ALI	20.00	—
☐ CHATTER BOX, rel. 1973. ed. 1,500, s/n, 16″ x 20″, pub ALI	20.00	—
☐ CORKY, rel. 1974. ed. 1,500, s/n, 16″ x 20″, pub ALI	20.00	—
☐ CORN PATCH RASCAL, rel. 1973. ed. 1,500, s/n, 20″ x 26″, pub ALI	20.00	30.00
☐ PORCUPINE, ed. 1,000, s/n, 16″ x 20″, pub ALI	30.00	—
☐ SCREECH OWLS, ed. 1,000, s/n, 20″ x 16″, pub ALI	30.00	—

WILLIAM WHITAKER

THEMES: Western art; Varied themes

EDUCATION: University of Utah, Otis Art Institute

JENNY *by William Whitaker*

AWARDS: Winner of many awards from the National Academy of Western Art

MEMBERSHIPS: National Academy of Western Art

GALLERY/DISTRIBUTOR: Mill Pond Press, Inc.

	ISSUE PRICE	CURRENT PRICE
☐ **JENNY,** rel. 1983. ed. 950, 23⅝" x 19", pub MPPI	95.00	—

GARY WHITE DEER

THEMES: Indian art

STYLE: His paintings have an unusual depth that creates striking effects of mood and movement

EDUCATION: Institute of American Indian Arts; Haskell Indian College

GALLERY/DISTRIBUTOR: Native American Images

	ISSUE PRICE	CURRENT PRICE
☐ **SEARCH FOR THE EAGLE'S WAY,** ed. 1,500, s/n, 14" x 21", pub NWDHG	30.00	75.00
☐ **PEYOTE EAGLE SONG,** ed. 20, orginal litho, pub NAI	250.00	1,000.00

OLAF WIEGHORST

THEMES: Western art

STYLE: Realism

AWARDS: Trustees Gold Medal from a joint organization that included the National Cowboy Hall of Fame; Eisenhower Library and others

MUSEUMS/COLLECTIONS: Wieghorst paintings hang in the private collections of such notable figures as J.P. Morgan; Barry Goldwater; Leonard Firestone and countless others

GALLERY/DISTRIBUTOR: The Wooden Bird

COMMENTS: Wieghorst has said that he makes a point of leaving his paintings "unfinished" in the sense that he encourages viewers to complete them in their imaginations

	ISSUE PRICE	CURRENT PRICE
☐ **NAVAJO MADONNA,** rel. 1972. ed. 1,500, s/n, 20⅛" x 22", pub FGH	40.00	6,000.00
☐ **BOYS IN THE BUNKHOUSE,** ed. 1,000, s/n, 26" x 32", distr. Armstrong's	150.00	—
☐ **BUFFALO SCOUT,** ed. 1,000, s/n, 26" x 32", distr. Armstrong's	100.00	700.00
☐ **CALIFORNIA WRANGLER,** ed. 1,000, s/n, 26" x 32", distr. Armstrong's	100.00	150.00

	ISSUE PRICE	CURRENT PRICE
☐ CORRALLING THE CAVVY, ed. 1,000, s/n, 26″ x 32″, distr. Armstrong's	100.00	400.00
☐ MISSING IN THE ROUNDUP, ed. 1,000, s/n, 26″ x 32″, distr. Armstrong's	100.00	200.00
☐ NAVAJO PORTRAIT, ed. 1,000, s/n, 26″ x 32″, distr. Armstrong's	75.00	300.00
☐ PACKING IN, ed. 1,000, s/n, 26″ x 32, distr. Armstrong's	100.00	200.00
☐ APACHE RENEGADE, rel. 1978. ed. 500, s/n, 24″ x 22″, pub ALL	125.00	250.00
ed. 50, Artist proofs	125.00	300.00
☐ DRIFTING, rel. 1978. ed. 500, s/n, 24½″ x 22½″, pub ALL	125.00	250.00
ed. 50, Artist proofs	125.00	300.00
☐ HORSE WRANGLERS, rel. 1978. ed. 500, s/n, 24½″ x 22″, pub ALL	125.00	250.00
ed. 50, Artist proofs	125.00	300.00
☐ MOGOLLON TRAIL, rel. 1978. ed. 500, s/n, sealed, 22″ x 26½″, pub ALL	125.00	250.00
ed. 50, Artist proofs	125.00	300.00
☐ TALKING SIGN, rel. 1978. ed. 500, s/n, sealed, 24″ x 22″, pub ALL	125.00	300.00
ed. 50, Artist proofs	125.00	350.00
☐ THE LOST TRAIL, rel. 1978. ed. 500, s/n, 24″ x 22″, pub ALL	125.00	250.00
ed. 50, Artist proofs	125.00	300.00
☐ ARIZONA RANGE, rel. 1979. ed. 500, s/n, 22½″ x 25½″, pub ALL	125.00	250.00
ed. 50, Artist proofs	125.00	300.00
☐ COW COUNTRY, rel. 1979. ed. 500, s/n, 15″ x 20¼″, pub ALL	125.00	250.00
ed. 50, Artist proofs	125.00	300.00
☐ INDIAN SCOUT, rel. 1979. ed. 500, s/n, 26½″ x 22″, pub ALL	125.00	1,500.00
ed. 50, Artist proofs	125.00	—
☐ INDIAN TRAIL, rel. 1979. ed. 500, s/n, 22″ x 25″, pub ALL	125.00	250.00
ed. 50, Artist proofs	125.00	300.00
☐ PLEASANT CREEK, rel. 1979. ed. 500, s/n, 15″ x 20″, pub ALL	125.00	400.00
ed. 50, Artist proofs	125.00	450.00
☐ RANGE CHUCK, rel. 1979. ed. 500, s/n, 15″ x 20½″, pub ALL	125.00	400.00
ed. 50, Artist proofs	125.00	450.00
☐ RANGE PONIES, rel. 1979. ed. 500, s/n, 15″ x 20¼″, pub ALL	125.00	400.00
ed. 50, Artist proofs	125.00	450.00
☐ WATER AHEAD, rel. 1979. ed. 500, s/n, 22″ x 25″, pub ALL	125.00	650.00
ed. 50, Artist proofs	125.00	700.00
☐ CHIEF SIOUX HUMP, rel. 1980. ed. 900, s/n, litho, 26½″ x 22″, pub ALL	150.00	200.00
☐ DEAD COTTONWOOD, rel. 1980. ed. 900, s/n, litho, 25″ x 30″, pub ALL	150.00	200.00
☐ LOS CHARROS, rel. 1980. ed. 999, s/n, litho, 25″ x 30″, pub ALL	150.00	200.00
☐ NIGHTHAWK, rel. 1980. ed. 999, s/n, litho, 25″ x 29″, pub ALL	150.00	200.00
☐ TIRED, rel. 1980. ed. 900, s/n, litho, 24″ x 31″, pub ALL	150.00	200.00
☐ WAGON AND REMUDA, rel. 1980. ed. 1,000, s/n, litho, 25½″ x 33½″, pub ALL	150.00	200.00
☐ CANYON TRAIL, rel. 1982. ed. 900, s/n, 21″ x 27¾″, pub WB	150.00	300.00
ed. 90, Artist proofs	150.00	350.00
☐ MOONLIGHT AND SHADOWS, rel. 1982. ed. 900, s/n, 21″ x 27¼″, pub WB	150.00	300.00
ed. 90, Artist proofs	150.00	350.00
☐ NAVAJO AT CASTLE CREEK, rel. 1982. ed. 900, s/n, 21″ x 28½″, pub WB	150.00	300.00
ed. 90, Artist proofs	150.00	350.00
☐ ROCKY MOUNTAIN TRAIL, rel. 1982. ed. 900, s/n, 21″ x 25½″, pub WB	150.00	300.00
ed. 90, Artist proofs	150.00	350.00
☐ SALT RIVER CANYON, rel. 1982. ed. 900, s/n, 21″ x 35″, pub WB	150.00	300.00
ed. 90, Artist proofs	150.00	350.00
☐ WATERING THE REMUDA, rel. 1982. ed. 900, s/n, 21″ x 28¼″, pub WB	150.00	300.00
ed. 90, Artist proofs	150.00	350.00
☐ COLD CONFERENCE, rel. 1982. ed. 900, s/n, size N/A, pub WB	150.00	300.00
☐ OPENING OF CHEROKEE STRIP, rel. 1982. ed. 900, s/n, size N/A, pub WB	150.00	—
☐ APPALOOSA, rel. 1983. ed. 950, s/n, 18½″ x 22″, pub WB	200.00	—
☐ INDIAN COUNTRY, rel. 1983. ed. 950, s/n, 19½″ x 24¾″, pub WB	200.00	—
☐ NEZ PERCE ON APPALOOSA, rel. 1983. ed. 950, s/n, 19½″ x 23¾″, pub WB	200.00	400.00
☐ RANGE BOSS, rel. 1983. ed. 950, s/n, 18½″ x 28″, pub WB	200.00	—
☐ RANGE HORSES, rel. 1983. ed. 950, s/n, 18½″ x 22½″, pub WB	200.00	—
☐ THE NAVAJO, rel. 1983. ed. 950, s/n, size N/A, pub WB	500.00	1,000.00
ed. 90, Artist proofs	1,250.00	—
☐ TRACKING THE STRAYS, rel. 1983. ed. 950, sn, 18½″ x 22″, pub WB	200.00	—
☐ WILD ONES, rel. 1983. ed. 950, s/n, size N/A, pub WB	225.00	—

	ISSUE PRICE	CURRENT PRICE
☐ **PARTNERS,** rel. 1984. ed. 950, s/n, size N/A	225.00	450.00
☐ **RANGE HORSES,** rel. 1984. ed. 950, size N/A	200.00	400.00
☐ **NOMADS OF THE PLAINS,** rel. 1984. ed. 1,500, s/n, size N/A, pub WB	500.00	—
☐ **WHEN SHELTER IS SCARCE,** rel. 1985. ed. 1,500, s/n, size N/A, pub HH	250.00	—

LESLIE A. WILCOX

THEMES: Marine art

BOOKS: Mr. Wilcox has written and illustrated numerous books about ships

MEMBERSHIPS: Royal Society of Marine Artists (a 30-year member)

MUSEUMS/COLLECTIONS: Paintings by the artist hang in collections in the U.S. and Europe

GALLERY/DISTRIBUTOR: Mill Pond Press, Inc.

	ISSUE PRICE	CURRENT PRICE
☐ **SOVEREIGN OF THE SEAS,** rel. 1978. ed. 950, s/n, 21" x 28", pub MPPI	95.00	110.00

SOVEREIGN OF THE SEAS *by Leslie A. Wilcox*

JASON WILLIAMSON

THEMES: Southwestern scenes

MEDIUM: Watercolor

EDUCATION: Vesper George School of Art

AWARDS: He has received many awards in prestigious competitions, some of which include the AWS, the NWS, and the Rocky Mountain National

MEMBERSHIPS: American Watercolor Society; National Watercolor Society; co-founder of the Tennessee Watercolor Society; the Southern Watercolor Society; and the 22 x 30 Painters of Arizona

GALLERY/DISTRIBUTOR: Grey Stone Press

	ISSUE PRICE	CURRENT PRICE
☐ **BURNT WATER,** ed. 500, s/n, 27″ x 22½″, pub GSP	100.00	—
☐ **GRIST,** ed. 1,500, s/n, 27″ x 21″, pub GSP	30.00	60.00
☐ **PATCHWORK,** ed. 1,500, s/n, 27″ x 21″, pub GSP	20.00	—
☐ **PEGGY'S PATCH,** ed. 1,500, s/n, 27″ x 21″, pub GSP	20.00	—
☐ **THE DREAMER,** ed. 500, s/n, 29½″ x 19½″, pub GSP	100.00	—
☐ **THE PROVIDER,** ed. 500, s/n, 22″ x 29½″, pub GSP	100.00	—
☐ **THUNDER GOD,** ed. 500, s/n, 29½″ x 20″, pub GSP	100.00	—
☐ **TUMBLEWEED,** ed. 500, s/n, 29½″ x 22½″, pub GSP	100.00	—
☐ **WATER SPRITE,** ed. 500, s/n, 21½″ x 29¾″, pub GSP	100.00	—
☐ **WATER BRIDGE,** rel. 1981. ed. 500, s/n, 29½″ x 21½″, pub GSP	100.00	150.00
☐ **MISSION VISIT,** rel. 1981. ed. 500, s/n, 22½″ x 24¾″, pub GSP	100.00	—
☐ **ACT II,** rel. 1982. ed. 500, s/n, 29″ x 24¾″, pub GSP	100.00	—
☐ **LIQUID GOLD,** rel. 1984. ed. 500, s/n, 29″ x 23½″, pub GSP	100.00	—
☐ **THE SAND HILL,** rel. 1984. ed. 500, s/n, 28½″ x 21⅜″, pub GSP	100.00	—

JAN WILLS

THEMES: Landscape art

EDUCATION: Art Institute of Chicago

AWARDS: The Chicago Municipal Art League Award; Illinois State Award

GALLERY/DISTRIBUTOR: Connoisseur's Gallery of Art, Ltd.

	ISSUE PRICE	CURRENT PRICE
☐ **A PAIL OF CLAMS,** ed. 950, s/n, 24½″ x 16½″, pub CGAL	131.00	150.00
ed. 12, Artist Accented/signed	375.00	420.00
☐ **AN EIGHTY ACRE PLACE,** ed. 950, s/n, 24½″ x 16″, pub CGAL	131.00	150.00
ed. 12, Artist Accented/signed	375.00	420.00
☐ **BAILEY'S TRAWLER,** ed. 950, s/n, 15½″ x 23″, pub CGAL	131.00	150.00
ed. 12, Artist Accented/signed	375.00	420.00
☐ **CORNERS POSTS,** ed. 950, s/n, 16″ x 24½″, pub CGAL	131.00	150.00
ed. 12, Artist Accented/signed	375.00	420.00

	ISSUE PRICE	CURRENT PRICE
☐ END OF THE LANE, ed. 300, s/n, 24½″ x 16½″, pub CGAL	300.00	330.00
ed. 38, s/o, Artist proofs	300.00	330.00
ed. 12, Artist Accented/signed	375.00	420.00
ed. 600, General print	75.00	90.00
☐ HUNTING THE HEDGEROWS, ed. 950, s/n, 25½″ x 17″, pub CGAL	131.00	150.00
ed. 12, Artist Accented/signed	375.00	420.00
☐ LIGHT IN THE KITCHEN, ed. 950, s/n, 25½″ x 17″, pub CGAL	131.00	150.00
ed. 12, Artist Accented/signed	375.00	420.00
☐ MENDING CHORES, ed. 950, s/n, 24½″ x 16″, pub CGAL	131.00	150.00
ed. 12, Artist Accented/signed	375.00	420.00
☐ MOVING ON, ed. 950, s/n, 17″ x 25″, pub CGAL	131.00	150.00
ed. 12, Artist Accented/signed	375.00	420.00
☐ OFF THE HARD ROAD, ed. 950, s/n, 24″ x 17½″, pub CGAL	150.00	–
ed. 12, Artist Accented/signed	420.00	–
☐ ON THE GRADE, ed. 950, s/n, 16½″ x 24″, pub CGAL	131.00	150.00
ed. 12, Artist Accented/signed	375.00	420.00
☐ OUT OF NANTUCKET, ed. 950, s/n, 17″ x 24½″, pub CGAL	131.00	150.00
ed. 12, Artist Accented/signed	375.00	420.00
☐ OVERSHOT WHEEL, ed. 950, s/n, 16″ x 24½″, pub CGAL	131.00	150.00
ed. 12, Artist Accented/signed	375.00	420.00
☐ PRAIRIE FARM, ed. 950, s/n, 15″ x 24½″, pub CGAL	131.00	150.00
ed. 12, Artist Accented/signed	375.00	420.00
☐ SEPARATOR, ed. 950, s/n, 24½″ x 16″, pub CGAL	131.00	150.00
ed. 12, Artist Accented/signed	375.00	420.00
☐ SETTING IN, ed. 300, s/n, 17″ x 25½″, pub CGAL	300.00	330.00
ed. 38, s/o, Artist proofs	300.00	330.00
ed. 12, Artist Accented/signed	375.00	420.00
ed. 600 General print	75.00	90.00
☐ SOUTHWEST HACIENDA, ed. 950, s/n, 24½″ x 16½″, pub CGAL	131.00	150.00
ed. 12, Artist Accented/signed	375.00	420.00

CHARLES BANKS WILSON

THEMES: Oklahoma scenes

BOOKS: Author and editor of a standard work on the Indian Tribes of Eastern Oklahoma, he is also the illustrator of 22 books

AWARDS: Governor's Art Award, etc.

MEMBERSHIPS: Oklahoma Hall of Fame; Western Heritage Trustee's Award from the National Cowboy Hall of Fame

MUSEUMS/COLLECTIONS: New York's Metropolitan Museum of Art; the Smithsonian, etc.

GALLERY/DISTRIBUTOR: Charles Banks Wilson

	ISSUE PRICE	CURRENT PRICE
☐ CHEROKEE FARMER, rel. 1938. ed. 10, 10¾″ x 13¾″, original litho, pub CBW	3.50	500.00
☐ TRIBAL HONOR, rel. 1939. ed. 10, 15¼″ x 9¾″, original litho, pub CBW	5.00	400.00
☐ NEW RICH, rel. 1939. ed. 20, 13″ x 10⅜″, original litho, pub CBW	5.00	400.00
☐ TRIBAL BAND, rel. 1939. ed. 10, 13¾″ x 9¾″, original litho, pub CBW	N/A	400.00

	ISSUE PRICE	CURRENT PRICE
☐ DANCE DRUM, rel. 1939. ed. 10, 12¾" x 8⅛", original litho, pub CBW	5.00	300.00
☐ OKLAHOMA, rel. 1939. ed. 15, 15⅝" x 13½", original litho, pub CBW	5.00	500.00
☐ WHITETREE, rel. 1939. ed. 10, 12¼" x 5⅛", original litho, pub CBW	N/A	300.00
☐ PETE BUCK, rel. 1939. ed. 22, 12¾" x 8¾", original litho, pub CBW	10.00	400.00
☐ MAN WITH A PLOW, rel. 1939. ed. 26, 12" x 7½", original litho, pub CBW	10.00	600.00
☐ AFTERNOON DANCE, rel. 1939. ed. 16, 13⅜" x 10¼", original litho, pub CBW	10.00	500.00
☐ SAVAGE, rel. 1939. ed. 12, 9⅞" x 4⅜", original litho, pub CBW	7.50	750.00
☐ STORY TELLER, rel. 1939. ed. 23, 12⅞" x 10", original litho, pub CBW	10.00	500.00
☐ KIOWA DANCER, rel. 1940. ed. 19, 12" x 7¾", original litho, pub CBW	12.00	750.00
☐ INDIAN SMOKE, rel. 1940. ed. 10, 9⅜" x 5⅜", original litho, pub CBW	7.50	300.00
☐ MEAL TIME AT A QUAPAW POW WOW, rel. 1940. ed. 19, 13⅜" x 9⅝", original litho, pub CBW	25.00	750.00
☐ PAINTING HER SON, rel. 1940. ed. 21, 13¼" x 9½", original litho, pub CBW	5.00	500.00
☐ OTOE EAGLE DANCE, rel. 1940. ed. 14, 12⅞" x 9½", original litho, pub CBW	12.50	750.00
☐ HENRY TURKEYFOOT, rel. 1940. ed. 25, 13⅛" x 10", original litho, pub CBW	15.00	750.00
☐ NAVAJO HORSES, rel. 1941. ed. 20, 11⅝" x 9½", original litho, pub CBW	10.00	350.00
☐ SENECA GREENCORN, rel. 1941. ed. 24, 12⅞" x 10⅜", original litho, pub CBW ...	7.50	350.00
☐ HANDGAME FEAST, rel. 1941. ed. 30, 15¼" x 9", original litho, pub CBW	12.50	750.00
☐ VISITING INDIANS, rel. 1941. ed. 20, 13" x 9⅝", original litho, pub CBW	7.50	500.00
☐ WAR DANCE FOR LITTLE INDIANS, rel. 1941. ed. 16, 13" x 14", original litho, pub CBW	5.00	350.00
☐ INDIAN PEYOTE MUSIC, rel. 1941. ed. 35, 13" x 9⅞", original litho, pub CBW ...	15.00	2,000.00
☐ OLD MEDICINE SINGER, rel. 1941. ed. 34, 13¼" x 8⅞", original litho, pub CBW ...	15.00	1,500.00
☐ QUAPAW POW WOW, rel. 1941. ed. 26, 14" x 10", original litho, pub CBW	12.00	750.00
☐ DANCERS DRESSING, rel. 1941. ed. 23, 14" x 8⅞", original litho, pub CBW	12.00	500.00
☐ THE CHIEF, rel. 1941. ed. 20, 10¾" x 7⅜", original litho, pub CBW	12.00	500.00
☐ COMANCHE PORTRAIT, rel. 1941. ed. 200, 14½" x 10¼", original litho, pub CBW ..	5.00	150.00
☐ OZARK SUMMER SWIMMIN' HOLE, rel. 1942. ed. 200, 13½" x 10", original litho, pub CBW	5.00	2,500.00
☐ OZARK SNOW, rel. 1942. ed. 25, 13¾" x 9¾", original litho, pub CBW	15.00	2,500.00
☐ JUDGE ROY BEAN, rel. 1942. ed. 25, 12⅝" x 10¼", original litho, pub CBW	25.00	2,500.00
☐ HANDGAME, rel. 1942. ed. 25, 9⅞" x 7⅞", original litho, pub CBW	25.00	500.00
☐ FREEDOM'S WARRIOR, rel. 1943. ed. 50, 13¾" x 10", original litho, pub CBW	5.00	500.00
☐ END MEN, rel. 1943. ed. 25, 14⅛" x 9⅞", original litho, pub CBW	15.00	2,500.00
☐ SHAWNEE RIBBON BETS, rel. 1947. ed. 25, 13½" x 9⅜", original litho, pub CBW ..	20.00	—
☐ HARD ROCK, rel. 1943. ed. 25, 13¾" x 9¾", original litho, pub CBW	10.00	—
☐ OLD INJUN, rel. 1950. ed. 200, 11⅞" x 8⅜", original litho, pub CBW	5.00	275.00
☐ SMALL OPERATOR, rel. 1952. ed. 10¼" x 14", original litho, pub CBW	12.50	250.00
☐ INDIAN COOKS, rel. 1953. ed. 24, 9" x 5½", original litho, pub CBW	15.00	750.00
☐ THE CHALLENGE, rel. 1961. ed. 100, 13¾" x 9⅛", original litho, pub CBW	25.00	250.00
☐ PRINCE ESQUIRE ROYAL BREED, rel. 1954. ed. 200, 14⅞" x 10⅝", original litho, pub CBW	15.00	200.00
☐ BOX HOLDER, rel. 1954. ed. 43, 13" x 8¾", original litho, pub CBW	20.00	200.00
☐ PIGEONS, rel. 1954. ed. 50, 12" x 6¼", original litho, pub CBW	20.00	250.00
☐ EDGE OF TOWN, rel. 1956. ed. 50, 15" x 7¾", original litho, pub CBW	25.00	300.00
☐ THE OKLAHOMAN, rel. 1956. ed. 25, 13¾" x 9⅝", original litho, pub CBW	25.00	375.00
☐ ROADSIDE WILLOWS, rel. 1956. ed. 14, 14½" x 11⅛", original litho, pub CBW	45.00	200.00
☐ INDIOS ARAPHO MAN, rel. 1958. ed. 20, 9⅝" x 6⅜", original litho, pub CBW	20.00	200.00
☐ SMILING COWBOY, rel. 1961. ed. 20, 12¾" x 9½", original litho, pub CBW	30.00	150.00
☐ ADVENTURE, rel. 1961. ed. 25, 12⅛" x 9¾", original litho, pub CBW	30.00	400.00
☐ WILD AND FREE, rel. 1962. ed. 50, 14⅝" x 11¼", original litho, pub CBW	35.00	300.00
☐ RHYTHM OF THE WAR DANCE, rel. 1963. ed. 55, 16⅞" x 8", original litho, pub CBW	20.00	100.00
☐ TOM BENTON, rel. 1963. ed. 45, 9⅝" x 7", original litho, pub CBW	45.00	350.00
☐ MORNING ON THE CREEK, rel. 1967. ed. 50, 14⅛" x 9⅝", original litho, pub CBW .	25.00	250.00
☐ ANY SUMMER AFTERNOON, rel. 1967. ed. 45, 12¾" x 10¼", original litho, pub CBW	25.00	350.00
☐ TEN LITTLE INDIANS, (set), rel. 1957. ed. 50, 5" x 9", original litho, pub CBW	50.00	500.00
☐ WHITE HATS, rel. 1967. ed. 10, 7⅝" x 7⅝", original litho, pub CBW	12.00	100.00
☐ BLACKOWL, rel. 1967. ed. 30, 7¾" x 6", original litho, pub CBW	10.00	150.00
☐ BOY FISHING, rel. 1968. ed. 50, 15¾" x 10¼", original litho, pub CBW	30.00	350.00
☐ FISHING JOE'S CREEK, rel. 1969. ed. 45, 14½" x 10⅞", original litho, pub CBW ...	45.00	500.00
☐ SUGAR IN THE GOURD, rel. 1968. ed. 45, 17¼" x 12¾", original litho, pub CBW ..	45.00	500.00
☐ BOYS IN SUMMER, rel. 1968. ed. 45, 15⅞" x 12½", original litho, pub CBW	45.00	400.00

	ISSUE PRICE	CURRENT PRICE
☐ POW WOW DANCERS, rel. 1969. ed. 45, 12" x 10", original litho, pub CBW	25.00	300.00
☐ POW WOW SINGERS, rel. 1969. ed. 45, 12" x 10", original litho, pub CBW	25.00	300.00
☐ INDIAN PROFILE, rel. 1969. ed. 75, 15⅝" x 10", original litho, pub CBW	45.00	1,500.00
☐ NEW CHAMPION, rel. 1972. ed. 75, 12½" x 10¾", original litho, pub CBW	45.00	250.00
☐ TRAILS END, rel. 1973. ed. 150, 10⅞" x 9¼", original litho, pub CBW	25.00	65.00
☐ INDIAN SKETCHES, rel. 1975. ed. 25, 16¼" x 10¼", original litho, pub CBW	30.00	400.00
☐ WET WEATHER SPRING, rel. 1974. ed. 50, 15¼" x 10¼", original litho, pub CBW ..	45.00	150.00
☐ SUSANNA, rel. 1970. ed. 10, 16" x 8", original litho, pub CBW	65.00	250.00
☐ SUPERSTAR, rel. 1975. ed. 60, 10½" x 6¾", original litho, pub CBW	35.00	125.00
☐ SORGHUM TIME, rel. 1975. ed. 75, 17" x 11", original litho, pub CBW	45.00	150.00
☐ BULL RIDER, rel. 1976. ed. 200, 15" x 10¼", original litho, pub CBW	45.00	100.00
☐ YOUNG FISHERMAN, rel. 1976. ed. 45, 8⅝" x 6¼", original litho, pub CBW	25.00	75.00
☐ BOY ON THE CREEK, rel. 1976. ed. 120, 8¾" x 6⅛", original litho, pub CBW	45.00	100.00
☐ ENTER CORONADO, rel. 1976. ed. 100, 17½" x 11", original litho, pub CBW	65.00	250.00
☐ OSAGE TRADE, rel. 1977. ed. 250, 16¼" x 13", original litho, pub CBW	65.00	300.00
☐ THE RACE, rel. 1976. ed. 200, 14½" x 10⅝", original litho, pub CBW	65.00	300.00
☐ PLAINS MADONNA, rel. 1977. ed. 300, 17" x 11½", original litho, pub SRS	50.00	800.00
☐ PLAINS MADONNA, rel. 1982. ed. 1,500, s/n, 18" x 23½", original litho, pub CBW ..	—	—
☐ THE YOUNG CHIEF, rel. 1983. ed. 1,500, 17¾" x 23⅛", original litho, pub SRS	150.00	—

JOHN WILSON

THEMES: Wildlife art

AWARDS: South Dakota Pheasant Restoration Stamp Competition (1979, 1981); Federal Duck Stamp Competition (1981)

GALLERY/DISTRIBUTOR: Wild Wings, Inc.

	ISSUE PRICE	CURRENT PRICE
☐ EARLY AUTUMN—WHITETAIL DEER, rel. 1981. ed. 850, s/n, size N/A, pub WWI ..	65.00	—
☐ FIRST SNOW—PHEASANTS, rel. 1981. ed. 850, s/n, size N/A, pub WWI	75.00	—
☐ CANADAS IN SPRING, rel. 1982. ed. 850, s/n, size N/A, pub WWI	75.00	—
☐ FALL PLUMAGE—WOOD DUCKS, rel. 1982. ed. 850, s/n, litho, 13¼" x 17½", pub WWI..	45.00	200.00
☐ AUTUMN ENCOUNTER - WHITETAILS, rel. 1983. ed. 1,500, s/n, 16½" x 25", pub WWI...	65.00	—
☐ BLUE WING TEAL, rel. 1983. ed. 850, s/n, 16½" x 22", pub WWI	65.00	—
☐ FALL PLUMAGE—PHEASANTS, rel. 1983. ed. 850, s/n, 13¾" x 17½", pub WWI ..	45.00	—
☐ WALLEYE, rel. 1983. ed. 850, s/n, 13¼" x 17½", pub WWI	45.00	—
☐ SURPRISE PARTY, rel. 1984. ed. 680, s/n, litho, 15" x 20", pub WWI	55.00	—
☐ NORTHERN RETREAT - LOON, rel. 1985. ed. 750, s/n, litho, 15" x 20", pub WWI ...	65.00	—

NICK WILSON

THEMES: North American mammals

BOOKS: His work has been reproduced widely in numerous publications

MUSEUMS/COLLECTIONS: Paintings by the artist hang in personal, public, and art museum collections nationwide

GALLERY/DISTRIBUTOR: Mill Pond Press, Inc.

	ISSUE PRICE	CURRENT PRICE
☐ BIGHORN SHEEP, rel. 1977. ed. 950, sn, 18½" x 18½", pub MPPI	60.00	—
☐ ELEPHANTS AND BAOBOB TREE, rel. 1977. ed. 260, sn, 23" x 18", stone litho, pub MPPI	100.00	—
☐ JAGUAR, rel. 1977. ed. 950, s/n, 17" x 24", pub MPPI	75.00	125.00
☐ KIT FOX, rel. 1977. ed. 950, s/n, 18½" x 18½", pub MPPI	60.00	—
☐ MOUNTAIN LION, rel. 1977. ed. 950, s/n, 17" x 24", pub MPPI	75.00	—
☐ OCELOT, rel. 1977. ed. 950, s/n, 26" x 18½", pub MPPI	75.00	—
☐ PRONGHORN ANTELOPE, rel. 1977. ed. 950, s/n, 24" x 17", pub MPPI	60.00	—
☐ TIMBER WOLF, rel. 1977. ed. 950, s/n, 18½" x 18½", pub MPPI	60.00	—
☐ TWILIGHT - GREAT HORNED OWL, rel. 1978. ed. 260, s/n, 20" x 16½", pub MPPI .	100.00	—
☐ BEAR CUB, rel. 1979. ed. 260, s/n, 14¾" x 13¾", pub MPPI	50.00	—
☐ BOBCAT, rel. 1979. ed. 950, s/n, 20" x 16", pub MPPI	60.00	—
☐ BURROWING OWL, rel. 1979. ed. 260, s/n, 14¾" x 13¾", stone litho, pub MPPI . . .	50.00	—
☐ COTTONTAIL RABBITS, rel. 1979. ed. 260, s/n, 13¾" x 14¾", stone litho, pub MPPI	50.00	—
☐ RACCOON, rel. 1979. ed. 260, s/n, 13¾" x 14¾", stone litho, pub MPPI	50.00	75.00
☐ REMNANTS, rel. 1980. ed. 200, s/n, 21¾" x 35", pub MPPI	200.00	Sold Out
☐ HOT AFTERNOON—MOUNTAIN LION, rel. 1981. ed. 950, s/n, 18" x 24¼", pub MPPI	75.00	—
☐ SNOW BUNNY—COTTONTAIL RABBIT, rel. 1981. ed. 950, s/n, 21⅜" x 18¼", pub MPPI	75.00	—

DALHART WINDBERG

THEMES: Landscape art

MEDIUM: Oils

STYLE: Contemporary American rendered in traditional European style

BOOKS: *Dalhart Windberg . . . In the Path of the Masters*

AWARDS: Texas Artist of the Year (1979-80)

GALLERY/DISTRIBUTOR: Windberg Enterprises, Inc.

	ISSUE PRICE	CURRENT PRICE
☐ AUTUMN'S GOLD, rel. 1973. ed. 1,567-TIME-LIMITED, s/dated, 18" x 24", pub AMFI	30.00	220.00
☐ AUTUMN MEMORIES, rel. 1973. ed. 1,000, /sn, 18" x 24", pub AMFI	40.00	800.00
ed. 2,000, s/o	30.00	650.00
☐ BLUE SPRINGTIME, rel. 1974. ed. 1,000, s/n, 18" x 24", pub AMFI	50.00	295.00
ed. 2,000, s/o	30.00	190.00
☐ OLD HOME PLACE, rel. 1974. ed. 750, s/n, 12" x 24", pub AMFI	50.00	400.00
ed. 2,250,s/o	30.00	200.00
☐ SECLUSION, rel. 1974. ed. 1,000-TIME-LIMITED, s/n, 18" x 24", pub AMFI	50.00	600.00
☐ SUNDAY OUTING, rel. 1974. ed. 1,428-TIME-LIMITED, s/dated, 12" x 16", pub AMFI	30.00	250.00
☐ AUTUMN'S WAY, rel. 1975. ed. 1,000-TIME-LIMITED, s/n, 16" x 16", pub AMFI	40.00	400.00
☐ GOIN' COURTIN', rel. 1975. ed. 1,000, s/n, 12" x 16", pub AMFI	35.00	800.00
ed. 1,000, s/o	25.00	400.00
☐ HILL COUNTRY, rel. 1975. ed. 1,000, s/n, 18" x 27", pub AMFI	50.00	275.00
ed. 1,000, s/o	30.00	200.00

A REFRESHING PAUSE *by Dalhart Windberg*

	ISSUE PRICE	CURRENT PRICE
☐ **LOVE'S REFLECTIONS/GLOW OF LOVE,** rel. 1975. ed. 1,000, s/o, 12″ x 24″, pub AMFI	*60.00	1,050.00
*Sold as a set		
☐ **MORNING MIST,** rel. 1975. ed. 1,000, s/n, 12″ x 16″, pub AMFI	35.00	550.00
ed. 1,000, s/o	25.00	400.00
☐ **SAFE PASSAGE,** rel. 1975. ed. 1,000, s/n, 16″ x 20″, pub AMFI	50.00	300.00
ed. 2,000, s/o	30.00	200.00
☐ **SECLUDED FALLS,** rel. 1975. ed. 1,000, s/n, 12″ x 24″, pub AMFI	60.00	400.00
☐ **SPRING'S WAY,** rel. 1975. ed. 1,000-TIME-LIMITED, s/n, 16″ x 16″, pub AMFI	50.00	350.00
☐ **SUMMER'S WAY,** rel. 1975. ed. 1,000-TIME-LIMITED, s/n, 16″ x 16″, pub AMFI	50.00	300.00
ed. 1,000-TIME-LIMITED, s/o	35.00	200.00
☐ **UNDISTURBED,** rel. 1975. ed. 1,000, s/n, 18″ x 27″, pub AMFI	50.00	500.00
☐ **WINTRY PASTORAL,** rel. 1975. ed. 1,000, s/n, 18″ x 24″, pub AMFI	40.00	250.00
ed. 2,000, s/o	30.00	200.00
☐ **WINTER'S WAY,** rel. 1975. ed. 1,000-TIME-LIMITED, s/n, 16″ x 16″, pub AMFI	50.00	300.00
ed. 1,000-TIME-LIMITED, s/o	35.00	200.00
☐ **CONTENTMENT,** rel. 1976. ed. 1,000, s/n, 12″ x 38″, pub AMFI	80.00	800.00
☐ **FLEETING SPLENDOR,** rel. 1976. ed. 1,000, s/n, 18″ x 24″, pub AMFI	60.00	210.00
ed. 1,250, s/o	36.00	200.00
☐ **FOUR FACES OF AMERICA,** rel. 1976. ed. 1,000, s/n, 16″ x 16″, pub AMFI	*200.00	800.00
ed. 1,000, s/o	*150.00	600.00
*This folio consists of four prints.		
☐ **LOVE'S REFLECTIONS/GLOW OF LOVE,** rel. 1976. ed. 1,000, s/n, 12″ x 24″, pub AMFI	*100.00	1,500.00
*Sold as a set		
☐ **NATURE'S INNER GLOW,** rel. 1976. ed. 1,000, s/n, 12″ x 24″, pub AMFI	50.00	350.00
ed. 1,250, s/o	35.00	200.00

	ISSUE PRICE	CURRENT PRICE
☐ PELICAN'S WHARF, rel. 1976. ed. 1,000, s/n, 12″ x 16″, pub AMFI	40.00	450.00
ed. 1,000, s/o	30.00	225.00
☐ TRANQUIL TIMES, rel. 1976. ed. 1,000, s/n, 12″ x 24″, pub AMFI	80.00	800.00
☐ EVENING RADIANCE, rel. 1977. ed. 1,000-TIME-LIMITED, s/n, pub AMFI	65.00	325.00
ed. 3,000-TIME-LIMITED, s/o	45.00	175.00
☐ GLADSTONE SOLITUDE, rel. 1977. ed. 1,000, s/n, 14″ x 28″, pub AMFI	60.00	320.00
ed. 2,000, s/o	50.00	200.00
☐ HARMONY IN THE HIGHLAND, rel. 1977. ed. 1,000, s/n, 12″ x 24″, pub AMFI	55.00	250.00
ed. 3,000, s/o	45.00	175.00
☐ LAST STAND, rel. 1977. ed. 1,000, s/n, 20″ x 30″, pub AMFI	70.00	1,350.00
☐ NIGHTLONG SENTINELS, rel. 1977. ed. 1,000, s/n, 18″ x 24″, pub AMFI	60.00	300.00
ed. 2,500, s/o	45.00	200.00
☐ REFLECTIVE ELEGANCE, rel. 1977. ed. 1,000-TIME-LIMITED, s/n, pub AMFI	80.00	300.00
ed. 3,000-TIME-LIMITED, s/o	50.00	175.00
☐ SNOW CLAD RELICS, rel. 1977. ed. 1,000, s/n, 18″ x 24″, pub AMFI	60.00	800.00
ed. 1,250, s/o	45.00	600.00
☐ IN SEASONAL ATTIRE, rel. 1978. ed. 1,000, s/n, 18″ x 24″, pub AMFI	65.00	250.00
ed. 3,100, s/o	50.00	150.00
☐ ROSEATE-SHORELINE, rel. 1978. ed. 1,000, s/n, 12″ x 24″, pub AMFI	65.00	120.00
ed. 3,100, s/o	45.00	80.00
☐ PERPETUAL HAVEN, rel. 1978. ed. 1,000, s/n, 18″ x 24″, pub AMFI	90.00	275.00
ed. 3,100, s/o	60.00	170.00
☐ SPANNING THE STREAM OF TIME, rel. 1978. ed. 9,109-TIME-LIMITED, 18″ x 24″, pub AMFI	30.00	100.00
☐ NOCTURNAL HARMONY, rel. 1979. ed. 1,000, s/n, 18″ x 24″, pub WEI	80.00	275.00
ed. 3,500, s/o	60.00	200.00
☐ SEASON OF RENEWAL, rel. 1979. ed. 1,000, s/n, 18″ x 24″, pub WEI	80.00	300.00
ed. 3,500, s/o	60.00	200.00
☐ SNOW CROWNED SILENCE, rel. 1979. ed. 1,000, s/n, 18″ x 24″, pub WEI	90.00	450.00
ed. 3,500, s/o	70.00	250.00
☐ GIFT OF LOVE, rel. 1980. ed. 1,000, s/n, 29″ x 11½″, pub WEI	120.00	250.00
ed. 3,500, s/o	80.00	100.00
☐ MOTHER EARTH, FATHER SKY, rel. 1980. ed. 1,000, s/n, 18″ x 24″, pub WEI	90.00	300.00
ed. 3,500, s/o	70.00	200.00
☐ TIME WORN SHELTER, rel. 1980. ed. 1,000, s/n, 18″ x 24″, pub WEI	90.00	260.00
ed. 3,500, s/o	70.00	175.00
☐ DELIGHTFUL RETREAT, rel. 1981. ed. 1,000, s/n, 30″ x 20″, pub WEI	120.00	200.00
ed. 3,500, s/o	80.00	85.00
☐ ENDURING REFUGE, rel. 1981. ed. 1,000, s/n, 18″ x 24″, pub WEI	120.00	Sold Out
ed. 3,500, s/o	80.00	Sold Out
☐ SLUMBROUS INTERLUDE, rel. 1981. ed. 1,000, s/n, 18″ x 24″, pub WEI	120.00	250.00
ed. 3,500, s/o	80.00	100.00
☐ TRANQUIL CROSSING, rel. 1982. ed. 1,000, s/n, 18″ x 24″, pub WEI	120.00	250.00
ed. 3,500, s/o	80.00	190.00
☐ A REFRESHING PAUSE, rel. 1982. ed. 1,000, s/n, 18″ x 24″, pub WEI	120.00	250.00
ed. 3,500, s/o	80.00	180.00
☐ WINTER'S VELVET MANTLE, rel. 1982. ed. 1,000, s/n, 12″ x 36″, pub WEI	150.00	250.00
ed. 2,500, s/o	90.00	180.00
☐ OLD FRIENDS, rel. 1983. ed. 1,000, s/n, 12″ x 16″, pub WEI	150.00	150.00
ed. 2,250, s/o	90.00	100.00
☐ SPRING VELVET, rel. 1983. ed. 1,000, s/n, 12″ x 16″, pub WEI	150.00	150.00
ed. 2,000, s/o	90.00	90.00
☐ 1984 DAWNLIGHT, rel. 1984. ed. 1,000, s/n, 18″ x 24″, pub WEI	150.00	—
ed. 2,000, s/o	90.00	—
☐ 1984 SUMMER OF INNOCENCE, rel. 1984. ed. 1,000, s/n, 30″ x 12″, pub WEI	300.00	—

JONATHAN WINTERS

THEMES: Varied

BACKGROUND: Jonathan Winters is known mostly for his work as a comedian

GALLERY/DISTRIBUTOR: Contemplative Investments, Inc.

	ISSUE PRICE	CURRENT PRICE
☐ A LIGHT IN THE ATTIC, ed. 475, s/n, 25″ x 19″, litho, pub DPC	150.00	—
☐ THE THOUGHTS OF A MATADOR, ed. 475, s/n, 25″ x 19″, litho, pub DPC	150.00	—
☐ THE UMBRELLA DANCERS, ed. 475, s/n, 25″ x 19″, litho, pub DPC	150.00	—
☐ THOUGHTS OF A HOLLYWOOD ACTOR WHILE DROWNING IN HIS POOL, ed. 475, s/n, 25″ x 19″, litho, pub CII	150.00	—

FRANZ WOLF

THEMES: European scenes

MEDIUM: Mixed; color etchings

EDUCATION: Academy of Fine Arts in Vienna; Art Academy in Munich

GALLERY/DISTRIBUTOR: Graphics International

	ISSUE PRICE	CURRENT PRICE
☐ AMBOISE, 13¾″ x 11½″, pub GI	—	140.00
☐ BOATS AT ANCHOR, 19¾″ x 15½″, pub GI	—	130.00
☐ CHARTRES, CATHEDRAL - INTERIOR, 17″ x 11″, pub GI	—	140.00
☐ CHARTRES, CITY GATE, 12¾″ x 11½″, pub GI	—	140.00
☐ CHARTRES, CITY GATE MINI, 4¾″ x 6″, pub GI	—	46.00
☐ CHARTRES, RIVER RURE, 11⅞″ x 10¼″, pub GI	—	140.00
☐ CHARTRES, RIVER RURE, MINI, 6⅛″ x 4¾″, pub GI	—	46.00
☐ DUERNSTEIN ON THE DANUBE, 14″ x 10¾″, pub GI	—	140.00
☐ ESTERELLE, HORIZONTAL, 9⅝″ x 12⅜″, pub GI	—	100.00
☐ ESTERELLE, VERTICAL, 10⅝″ x 7¼″, pub GI	—	90.00
☐ GRAZ, 16⅜″ x 13¼″, pub GI	—	160.00
☐ HALLSTAFF, 16¼″ x 13¼″, pub GI	—	160.00
☐ HAMBURG, HARBOR, 10¼″ x 11¾″, pub GI	—	110.00
☐ HEIDELBERG CASTLE #2, 12⅝″ x 9⅞″, pub GI	—	130.00
☐ INNSBRUCK, GOLDEN ROOF, 11⅝″ x 8⅛″, pub GI	—	100.00
☐ INNSBRUCK, LARGE, 16½″ x 12¾″, pub GI	—	160.00
☐ INNSBRUCK, SMALL, 11″ x 7⅝″, pub GI	—	100.00
☐ KITZBUEHEL, SUMMER, 11½″ x 9¼″, pub GI	—	110.00
☐ KITZBUEHEL, WINTER, 12⅜″ x 13⅜″, pub GI	—	140.00
☐ PARIS, BIRD MARKET, 11¾″ x 14½″, pub GI	—	130.00
☐ PARIS, BOOKSTALLS WITH DOG, 14½″ x 12″, pub GI	—	150.00
☐ PARIS, BOOKSTALLS #2, 9⅞″ x 11¾″, pub GI	—	130.00
☐ PARIS, JUSTIC PALACE, 12⅜″ x 9⅞″, pub GI	—	130.00
☐ PARIS, NOTRE DAME AND BOOKSTALLS, 11″ x 13″, pub GI	—	140.00
☐ PARIS, NOTRE DAME IN RAG, 10¾″ x 8″, pub GI	—	90.00
☐ PARIS, PORTE ST. DENIS, 15¼″ x 11½″, pub GI	—	140.00
☐ PARIS, RUE CALENDE, GREENGROCER, 12⅜″ x 9¾″, pub GI	—	130.00

	ISSUE PRICE	CURRENT PRICE
☐ PARIS, SACRE COEUR, 11½" x 6", pub GI	—	90.00
☐ PARIS, TUILLERIEN, 12⅝" x 10⅞", pub GI	—	140.00
☐ ROUEN, 10¾" x 7¼", pub GI	—	100.00
☐ ROUEN, OLD TOWN, 13¼" x 10", pub GI	—	140.00
☐ ST. WOLFGANG, 16¾" x 13¼", pub GI	—	160.00
☐ SALZBURG, FRANCISIAN CHURCH, 12¼" x 9¾", pub GI	—	140.00
☐ SALZBURG, MURABELL GARDENS, 7½" x 7½", pub GI	—	44.00
☐ SALZBURG, RESIDENZ SQUARE, LARGE, 13½" x 16⅜", pub GI	—	150.00
☐ SALZBURG, RESIDENZ SQUARE, SMALL, 9⅞" x 16⅜", pub GI	—	130.00
☐ TOURS, ST. JAQUES, 11⅝" x 8¼", pub GI	—	130.00
☐ VENICE, CA D'ORO, 12⅝" x 16¼", pub GI	—	150.00
☐ VENICE, CA D'ORO, SMALL, 8⅛" x 11¾", pub GI	—	130.00
☐ VENICE, CANAL & GONDOLAS, 10" x 12¾", pub GI	—	140.00
☐ VENICE, FISH MARKET, 11" x 15¾", pub GI	—	140.00
☐ VENICE GRAND CANAL, 14¾" x 17¼", pub GI	—	190.00
☐ VENICE GRAND CANAL #2, 11⅝" x 12⅝", pub GI	—	140.00
☐ VENICE, MARIA DELLA SALUTE, 12½" x 14¼", pub GI	—	140.00
☐ VENICE, RIALTO BRIDGE, 16¼" x 19", pub GI	—	190.00
☐ VENICE, SAILBOATS, 13¼" x 16½", pub GI	—	160.00
☐ VENICE, TWO SAILBOATS, HORIZONTAL, 7" x 10¼", pub GI	—	80.00
☐ VIENNA, GRABEN, 15⅜" x 12¾", pub GI	—	160.00
☐ VIENNA, HOHER MARKET, 14" x 10¾", pub GI	—	140.00
☐ VIENNA, KARL'S CHURCH, 14" x 11¾", pub GI	—	140.00
☐ VIENNA, MARIA AM GESTADE CHURCH, 11½" x 7½", pub GI	—	90.00
☐ VIENNA, OPERA HOUSE, 11¾" x 15¾", pub GI	—	140.00
☐ VIENNA, STEPHAN'S SQUARE, 15⅜" x 12¾", pub GI	—	160.00

WALTER WOLFE

THEMES: Wildlife art

EDUCATION: Art Instruction, Incorporated; California College of Arts and Crafts

AWARDS: California Duck Stamp Design (1979); National Wild Turkey Stamp Competition (1980)

GALLERY/DISTRIBUTOR: Wild Wings, Inc.

	ISSUE PRICE	CURRENT PRICE
☐ A LITTLE SPICE - CINNAMON TEAL, rel. 1981. ed. 600, s/n, size N/A, pub WWI	65.00	—

SCOTT WOOLEVER

THEMES: Wildlife art

EDUCATION: Washington College, the Maryland Institute of Art; University of Delaware

MEMBERSHIPS: Society of American Artists

GALLERY/DISTRIBUTOR: Sportsman's Edge, Ltd.

	ISSUE PRICE	CURRENT PRICE
☐ WATER'S EDGE - GEESE, ed. 750, s/n, 18⅛" x 27¼", pub SEL	120.00	—

KNIGHTS OF THE SKY, by Frank Wootton

FRANK WOOTTON

THEMES: Aviation art

STYLE: Mr. Wootton portrays land and sky with the hand of a fine landscape artist

GALLERY/DISTRIBUTOR: Greenwich Workshop

	ISSUE PRICE	CURRENT PRICE
☐ KNIGHTS OF THE SKY, rel. 1982. ed. 850, s/n, 34½" x 23", pub GW	165.00	—
☐ THE BATTLE OF BRITAIN, rel. 1983. ed. 850, s/n, 29½" x 23¾", pub GW	150.00	—
☐ HUNTSMEN AND HOUNDS, rel. 1985. ed. 650, s/n, 22⅝" x 16⅝", pub GW	115.00	—

REAGAN WORD

THEMES: Wildlife art

GALLERY/DISTRIBUTOR: Grey Stone Press

	ISSUE PRICE	CURRENT PRICE
☐ **AFRICAN LION,** ed. 2,500, s/n, 26½″ x 20½″, litho, pub GSP	30.00	—
☐ **BORN FREE,** ed. 1,000, s/n, 28″ x 21½″, litho, pub GSP	75.00	—
ed. 100, Artist proofs, remarqued, pub GSP	125.00	—
☐ **DANDELION,** ed. 850, s/n, 20″ x 16″, litho, pub GSP	30.00	—
☐ **POLAR BEARS,** rel. 1982. ed. 1,000, s/n, 28½″ x 21¼″, pub GSP	75.00	—
☐ **RACCOON,** rel. 1982. ed. 1,000, s/n, 27″ x 22″, pub GSP	75.00	—
☐ **SIBERIAN TIGER,** ed. 2,500, s/n, 26¾″ x 20½″, litho, pub GSP	30.00	—
☐ **SNOWY OWL,** ed. 2,500, s/n, 18″ x 22″, litho, pub GSP	30.00	—
☐ **THE CHIPMUNK & THE ANT,** ed. 1,000, s/n, 23½″ x 17⅞″, future release, pub GSP	50.00	—
☐ **THE HIGH COUNTRY,** ed. 1,000, s/n, 27″ x 22½″, pub GSP	75.00	—
☐ **THE WATER HOLE,** rel. 1981. ed. 1,000, s/n, 24¼″ x 18¾″, pub GSP	55.00	—
☐ **WINTER'S SONG,** ed. 1,000, s/n, 18¾″ x 23½″, pub GSP	45.00	—
ed. 1,000, s/o, pub GSP	35.00	—

SACAJAWEA *by David Wright*

DAVID WRIGHT

THEMES: Varied

MEDIUM: Watercolor, tempera, and pencil

GALLERY/DISTRIBUTOR: Grey Stone Press

SACAJAWEA by David Wright

	ISSUE PRICE	CURRENT PRICE
☐ A WAY OF LIFE, ed. 1,500, s/n, 18¾" x 25", litho, pub GSP	40.00	80.00
☐ BRIAR SCYTHE, ed. 700, s/n, 24¾" x 19", litho, pub GSP	30.00	50.00
☐ COLORADO CROSSING, rel. 1981. ed. 1,000, s/n, 22½" x 29", pub GSP	75.00	200.00
ed. 100, Artist proofs, remarqued	125.00	300.00
☐ FRIEND OR FOE, ed. 1,000, s/n, 29" x 21", pub GSP	75.00	100.00
Artist proof, remarqued	125.00	—
☐ GOLDEN-MOUNTAIN MAN, rel. 1983. s/n, ed. N/A, size N/A, pub GSP	75.00	250.00
Artist proof	125.00	500.00
☐ GREEN RIVER TRAPPER, rel. 1980. ed. 1,000, s/n, size N/A, pub GSP	60.00	200.00
ed. 100, Artist proofs remarqued	100.00	175.00
☐ NO TIME TO LINGER, ed. 1,100, s/n, 26¼" x 21", pub GSP	75.00	—
Artist proof, remarqued	150.00	—
☐ SACAJAWEA, ed. 1,100, s/n, 15½" x 24", pub GSP	75.00	—
Artist proof, remarqued	150.00	—
☐ STARTLED FLIGHT, ed. 500, s/n, 29½" x 19", litho, pub GSP	40.00	125.00
ed. 1,500, s/o, pub GSP	25.00	—
☐ SYCAMORES AT DUSK, ed. 1,000, s/n, 23¾" x 18½", litho, pub GSP	25.00	450.00
ed. 1,500, s/o, pub GSP	20.00	175.00
☐ THE BUCKSKINNER, ed. 1,000, s/n, 18¼" x 24", pub GSP	75.00	150.00
Artist proof, remarqued	125.00	200.00
☐ THE CONTINENTAL SOLDIER*, ed. 1,000, s/n and dated 1976, 12" x 15", pub GSP	10.00	—
☐ THE FRONTIERSMAN, rel. 1979. ed. 1,500, s/n, size N/A, pub GSP	40.00	—
☐ THE HUNTER, rel. 1981. ed. 1,000, s/n, 22½" x 29", pub GSP	75.00	200.00
ed. 100, Artist proofs remarqued	125.00	200.00
☐ THE MINUTEMAN*, ed. 1,000, s/n and dated 1976, 12" x 15", pub GSP	10.00	—
☐ THE PRINCESS, rel. 1985. ed. 1,200, s/n, 24" x 34", pub GSP	80.00	Sold Out
Artist proof, remarqued	160.00	—
☐ THE TURKEY HUNTER, ed. 2,000, s/n, 20" x 16½", pub GSP	45.00	—
Artist proof, remarqued	125.00	—
☐ WAGON AT CADES COVE, ed. 2,500, s/n, 29½" x 23½", litho, pub GSP	20.00	—
☐ WIND RIVER MAN, ed. 1,000, s/n, 21" x 29"	50.00	300.00
ed. 100, Artist proofs, remarqued, pub GSP	100.00	250.00
☐ WINTER MEMORIES, ed. 500, s/n, 23" x 29¼", litho, pub GSP	40.00	125.00

*These prints were commissioned by American Advertisers for special promotional distribution by them. In order to make this edition available to collectors 1,000 sets were signed and dated by the artist.

CHARLES WYSOCKI

THEMES: Americana

EDUCATION: Art Center School of Design in Los Angeles

GALLERY/DISTRIBUTOR: Greenwich Workshop

STORIN' UP *by Charles Wysocki*

COMMENTS: "I consider myself a painter of Early American life," he says. "The people in my pictures are country folk, simple in manner and happy in their activities. If some naivete appears in my work, it is because it was planned that way and is, undoubtedly, a desire to live that way myself"

	ISSUE PRICE	CURRENT PRICE
☐ **BUTTERNUT FARMS,** rel. 1979. ed. 1,000, s/n, 30" x 26", pub GW	75.00	405.00
☐ **FAIRHAVEN BY THE SEA,** rel. 1979. ed. 1,000, s/n, 31" x 17", pub GW	75.00	265.00
☐ **FOX RUN,** rel. 1979. ed. 1,000, s/n, 30" x 26", pub GW	75.00	605.00
☐ **SHALL WE?,** rel. 1979. ed. 1,000, s/n, 22" x 26¾", pub GW	75.00	140.00
☐ **CALEB'S BUGGY BARN,** rel. 1980. ed. 1,000, s/n, 25" x 20", pub GW	80.00	105.00
☐ **DERBY SQUARE,** rel. 1980. ed. 1,000, s/n, 36" x 28¼", pub GW	90.00	255.00
☐ **JOLLY HILL ARMS,** rel. 1980. ed. 1,000, s/n, 22½" x 25½", pub GW	75.00	250.00
☐ **YANKEE WINK HOLLOW,** rel. 1980. ed. 1,000, s/n, 30½" x 24", pub GW	95.00	235.00
☐ **CARVER COGGINGS,** rel. 1981. ed. 1,000, s/n, 30" x 21½", pub GW	145.00	220.00
☐ **OLDE AMERICA,** rel. 1981. ed. 1,500, s/n, 30" x 23½", pub GW	125.00	165.00
☐ **PAGE'S BAKE SHOPPE,** rel. 1981. ed. 1,000, s/n, 25" x 20", pub GW	115.00	190.00
☐ **PRAIRIE WIND FLOWERS,** rel. 1981. ed. 1,000, s/n, 25" x 20", pub GW	125.00	225.00
☐ **NANTUCKET,** rel. 1982. ed. 1,000, s/n, 24⅜" x 22", pub GW	145.00	—
☐ **SLEEPY TOWN WEST,** rel. 1982. ed. 1,500, s/n, 26½" x 23¾", pub GW	150.00	—
☐ **SUNSET HILLS TEXAS, WILDCATTERS,** rel. 1982. ed. 1,000, s/n, 23¾" x 24¼", pub GW	125.00	—
☐ **THE 1982 GREENWICH WORKSHOP, CHRISTMAS PRINT,** rel. 1982. ed. 2,000, s/n, 18" x 18½", pub GW	80.00	435.00
☐ **AMISH NEIGHBORS,** rel. 1983. ed. 1,000, s/n, 22½" x 23", pub GW	150.00	160.00
☐ **APPLE BUTTER MAKERS,** rel. 1983. ed. 1,000, s/n, 21½" x 22", pub GW	135.00	160.00
☐ **COUNTRY RACE,** rel. 1983. ed. 1,000, s/n, 31" x 22⅛", pub GW	150.00	170.00
☐ **PLUM ISLAND SOUND (Poster),** rel. 1983. ed. 1,000, s/n, 32" x 21", pub GW	55.00	Sold Out
☐ **TEA BY THE SEA,** rel. 1983. ed. 1,000, s/n, 30" x 17", pub GW	145.00	225.00
☐ **1983 COMMEMORATIVE PRINT,** rel. 1983. ed. 2,000, s/n, 13¾" x 14¼", pub GW	55.00	—
☐ **CAPE COD COLD FISH PARTY,** rel. 1984. ed. 1,000, s/n, 27½" x 20", pub GW	150.00	Sold Out
☐ **COTTON COUNTRY,** rel. 1984. ed. 1,000, s/n, 18½" x 21⅜", pub GW	150.00	—
☐ **STORIN' UP,** rel. 1984. ed. 450, s/n, 46" x 21¼", pub GW	325.00	Sold Out
☐ **SWEETHEART CHESSMATE,** rel. 1984. ed. 1,000, s/n, 15⁵⁄₁₆" x 16", pub GW	95.00	105.00
☐ **THE BIRDHOUSE,** rel. 1984. ed. 1,000, s/n, 16½" x 13¾"	85.00	95.00
☐ **THE FOXY FOX OUTFOXES THE FOX HUNTERS,** rel. 1984. ed. 1,500, s/n, litho, 32" x 24½", pub GW	150.00	Sold Out
☐ **BIRDS OF A FEATHER,** rel. 1985. ed. 1,250, s/n, 24¾" x 20⅝", pub GW	145.00	—
☐ **CLAMMERS AT HODGE'S HORN,** rel. 1985. ed. 1,000, s/n, 30¾" x 22", pub GW	150.00	Sold Out
☐ **1985 COMMEMORATIVE PRINT,** rel. 1985. ed. 2,000, s/n, 13¹¹⁄₁₆" x 13¹¹⁄₁₆", pub GW	55.00	—
☐ **SALTY WITCH BAY,** rel. 1985. ed. 475, s/n, 45¾" x 21⅛", pub GW	350.00	Sold Out

RICHARD EVANS YOUNGER

THEMES: Wildlife art

MEDIUM: Watercolor

BOOKS: The artist collaborated on *Field Guide to Fresh Water Fish of North America; Exotic Plants* and others

EDUCATION: Kansas City Art Institute; Missouri Valley College

GALLERY/DISTRIBUTOR: Frame House Gallery, Inc.

	ISSUE PRICE	CURRENT PRICE
☐ **BALD EAGLE,** rel. 1978. ed. 1,500, s/n, 22″ x 30″, pub FHG	50.00	Sold Out
☐ **BEECH PEEPS,** rel. 1974. ed. 3,000, s/n, 30½″ x 22″, pub WHI, distr. FHG	35.00	50.00
☐ **BENGAL TIGER,** rel. 1975. ed. 3,000, s/o, 20″ x 16″, pub FHG	30.00	Sold Out
☐ **BLUE AND GOLD MACAW,** rel. 1972. ed. 2,896, x/o, 17″ x 30″, pub WHI, distr. FHG	35.00	115.00
ed. 104, s/n	35.00	Sold Out
☐ **BOBCAT (ON GROUND),** rel. 1972. ed. 2,000, s/o, 25¾″ x 17″, pub FHG	20.00	50.00
☐ **BOBCAT (ON ROCK),** rel. 1976. ed. 1,200, x/n, 18″ x 24″, pub FHG	60.00	—
☐ **BOBWHITE,** rel. 1974. ed. 4,000, s/o, 37½″ x 17″, pub FHG	40.00	Sold Out
☐ **BROWN PELICAN,** rel. 1977. ed. 3,000, s/n, 15½″ x 17½″, pub WHI, released FHG	25.00	75.00
☐ **CANADA GOOSE (IN FLIGHT),** rel. 1976. ed. 1,500, s/n, 18″ x 25″, pub FHG	40.00	50.00
☐ **CANADA GOOSE (IN WATER),** rel. 1976. ed. 1,500, x/o, 14″ x 18″, pub FHG	35.00	—
☐ **CHEETAH,** rel. 1973. ed. 1,000, s/n, 40″ x 20″, pub FHG	75.00	50.00
ed. 4,000, s/o	60.00	50.00
☐ **CHIMPANZEE,** rel. 1975. ed. 2,000, s/o, 20″ x 16″, pub FHG	25.00	60.00
☐ **EASTERN COUGAR FAMILY,** rel. 1978. ed. 1,400, s/n, 20″ x 20″, pub FHG	75.00	—
ed. 100, s/n were sold in conjunction with a membership in North Carolina Zoological Society embossed with the North Carolina state seal and signed by the Governor	1,000.00	Sold Out
☐ **EASTERN TIMBER WOLF,** rel. 1974. ed. 1,000, s/n, 33″ x 20″, pub FHG	65.00	Sold Out
ed. 3,000, s/o	50.00	Sold Out
☐ **ELK,** rel. 1977. ed. 1,500, s/n, 22″ x 28″, pub FHG	50.00	—
☐ **GOING TO ROOST (Wild Turkeys),** rel. 1979. ed. 950, s/n, 21″ x 27″, pub TCG	125.00	—
☐ **GREAT HORNED OWL,** rel. 1975. ed. 2,500, s/o, 19″ x 24″, pub FHG	40.00	60.00
☐ **JAGUAR,** rel. 1974. ed. 5,000, s/o, 16″ x 20″, pub FHG	30.00	Sold Out
☐ **MALLARD,** rel. 1976. ed. 1,500, s/n, 18″ x 25″, pub FHG	40.00	—
☐ **MOCKINGBIRD,** rel. 1974. ed. 5,000, s/o, 20″ x 24″, pub FHG	*50.00	Sold Out
*A portion of the edition donated to Florida Audubon Society for 1974 membership campaign.		
☐ **MOURNING DOVE,** rel. 1975. ed. 1,500, s/o, 16″ x 20″, pub FHG	25.00	35.00
☐ **OCELOT,** rel. 1975. ed. 3,000, s/o, 16″ x 20″, pub FHG	30.00	—
☐ **OCTOBER MORNING,** rel. 1979. ed. 950, s/n, 20″ x 24″, pub TCG	150.00	—
☐ **RACCOON,** rel. 1977. ed. 1,500, s/n, 20″ x 24″, pub FHG	50.00	50.00
☐ **RING-NECKED PHEASANT,** rel. 1978. ed. 1,000, s/n, 20″ x 26″, pub FHG	50.00	50.00
☐ **RUDDY DUCK,** rel. 1977. ed. 1,500, s/n, 15½″ x 21½″, pub FHG	50.00	—
☐ **RUFOUS-THIGHED FALCONETS,** rel. 1973. ed. 3,500, s/o, 16″ x 20″, pub FHG	20.00	80.00
☐ **SCARLET MACAW,** rel. 1979. ed. 950, s/n, 17″ x 30″, pub TCG	95.00	—
☐ **SCRUB JAY,** rel. 1973. ed. 5,000, s/o, 16″ x 20″, pub FHG	30.00	Sold Out
☐ **SERVAL,** rel. 1974. ed. 5,000, s/o, 22″ x 22½″, pub FHG	35.00	80.00
☐ **SMALL ANIMAL FOLIO,** rel. 1974. ed. 1,000, s/n, pub WHI, released FHG	100.00	Sold Out
Folio consists of - Four prints - **COTTONTAIL RABBIT,** 29″ x 12¼″, **EASTERN GRAY SQUIRREL,** 13¼″ x 30″, **RACCOON,** 13¼″ x 30″, **STRIPED SKUNK,** 29″ x 12¼″.		
☐ **SNOW GOOSE AND BLUE GOOSE,** rel. 1976. ed. 1,500, s/n, 18″ x 25″, pub FHG	50.00	—
☐ **SNOWY OWL,** rel. 1977. ed. 1,500, s/n, 20″ x 30″, pub FHG	50.00	—
☐ **THE VANISHING SPECIES SERIES,** rel. 1973. The Vanishing Species Series was published by Caribbean Gardens, Naples, Florida (1969) in an edition of 1,000, 21½″ x 35¼″, reproductions of each subject, of which 300 were signed and numbered. The prints remaining unsold by Caribbean Gardens were acquired by Frame House Gallery in 1972 and released in February, 1973. Complete portfolio of eight prints, signed and numbered	400.00	Sold Out
Portfolio consists of the following:		

	ISSUE PRICE	CURRENT PRICE
☐ AMERICAN EAGLE, s/n	50.00	150.00
s/o	35.00	125.00
☐ CANADA GOOSE, s/n	50.00	Sold Out
s/o	35.00	Sold Out
☐ EVERGLADE KITE, s/n	50.00	Sold Out
s/o	35.00	—
☐ LAYSAN DUCK, s/n	50.00	Sold Out
s/o	35.00	—
☐ NENE GOOSE, s/n	50.00	Sold Out
s/o	35.00	Sold Out
☐ SANDHILL CRANE, s/n	50.00	Sold Out
s/o	35.00	—
☐ TULE GOOSE, s/n	50.00	Sold Out
s/o	35.00	Sold Out
☐ WHOOPING CRANE, s/n	50.00	Sold Out
s/o	35.00	Sold Out
☐ WHITE-TAILED DEER, rel. 1975. ed. 2,000, s/n, 20″ x 24″, pub FHG	50.00	—

This limited edition print was released in the AMERICA'S WILDLIFE HERITAGE PORT-FOLIO, which consists of six prints in all, each by a different Frame House Gallery Artist.

	ISSUE PRICE	CURRENT PRICE
☐ WILD TURKEYS, rel. 1973. ed. 500, s/n, 40″ x 30″, distr. FHG	225.00	—
☐ WOOD DUCK, rel. 1973. ed. 1,000, s/n, 30″ x 23½″, pub FHG	45.00	Sold Out
ed. 4,000, s/o	45.00	Sold Out
☐ WOOD DUCK (ON FENCE), rel. 1976. ed. 1,500, s/n, 17″ x 23½″, pub FHG	50.00	—

SURFWIND *by Bill Zaner*

BILL ZANER

THEMES: Landscape art

GALLERY/DISTRIBUTOR: Arts Limited, Inc.

	ISSUE PRICE	CURRENT PRICE
☐ **6 A.M. GULF BEACH,** rel. 1981. ed. 1,500, s/n, 30″ x 25″, pub ALI	60.00	—
☐ **SURFWIND,** rel. 1981. ed. 1,500, s/n, 27″ x 19¼″, pub ALI	60.00	—

THEY'LL BE SORRY WHEN WE'RE GONE *by Jessica Zemsky*

JESSICA ZEMSKY

THEMES: Varied

MEDIUM: Watercolor

BACKGROUND: Advertising and book illustration occupied an earlier part of Ms. Zemsky's career as an artist

MEMBERSHIPS: Former official artist for the New York City Opera Company

GALLERY/DISTRIBUTOR: Mill Pond Press, Inc.

	ISSUE PRICE	CURRENT PRICE
☐ WHEN THE THEN AND NOW HOLD HANDS, rel. 1979. ed. 950, s/n, 18″ x 24½″, pub MPPI	65.00	185.00
☐ JORDAN'S DOLLY, rel. 1979. ed. 950, s/n, 24½″ x 19½″, pub MPPI	65.00	—
☐ LOVE AT FIRST SIGHT, rel. 1979. ed. 950, s/n, 18″ x 27½″, pub MPPI	75.00	—
☐ COME SEE THE NEW COLT, rel. 1979. ed. 950, s/n, 18″ x 23½″, pub MPPI	65.00	—
☐ JORDAN AT THE WEDDING, rel. 1979. ed. 950, s/n, 24¾″ x 20″, pub MPPI	65.00	125.00
☐ JORDAN'S SPRING, rel. 1979. ed. 950, s/n, 25¼″ x 19¾″, pub MPPI	65.00	—

WILLIAM ZIMMERMAN

THEMES: Wildlife art

BOOKS: *Waterfowl of North America*

EDUCATION: Cincinnati Art Academy

AWARDS: Ducks Unlimited Award of Merit, among other numerous honors

MEMBERSHIPS: Society of Animal Artists

GALLERY/DISTRIBUTOR: Northwoods Craftsman

	ISSUE PRICE	CURRENT PRICE
☐ EASTERN BLUEBIRD, rel. 1973. ed. 3,500, s/o, 16″ x 20″, pub FHG	20.00	50.00
☐ SWALLOW-TAILED KITE, rel. 1973. ed. 1,000, s/n, 30″ x 25¼″, pub FHG	50.00	Sold Out
ed. 1,500, s/o	35.00	Sold Out
ed. 1,500 signed and bearing embossed seal, benefit Columbia, S.C. Zoological Park	50.00	—
☐ BOBWHITE, rel. 1977. ed. 1,750, s/n, 16″ x 20″, pub SG	35.00	—
☐ MOURNING DOVE, rel. 1977. ed. 1,000, s/n, 16″ x 20″, pub SG	40.00	—
☐ MALLARD, rel. 1978. ed. 950, s/n, 20″ x 24″, pub SG	75.00	125.00
☐ WOOD DUCK, rel. 1978. ed. 950, s/n, 20″ x 24″, pub SG	75.00	125.00
☐ NESTING GROUND, rel. 1979. ed. 600, s/n, 22″ x 28″, pub FHG	55.00	—
300 Exlusive for Ducks Unlimited		
☐ OPEN WATER, rel. 1979. ed. 400, s/n, 24″ x 30″	75.00	175.00
ed. 100, s/n, remarqued, pub FHG	125.00	200.00
☐ OUTFOXED, rel. 1979. ed. 600, s/n, 23″ x 30″, pub FHG	80.00	—
ed. 100, s/n, remarqued	130.00	Sold Out
☐ SOARING AMERICAN EAGLE, rel. 1979. ed. 5,000, s/o, 24″ x 20″, pub FHG	25.00	—
☐ THE EAGLES, rel. 1979. ed. 5,000, s/o, 14″ x 11″, pub FHG	20.00	—
☐ WATERFOWL OF NORTH AMERICA, rel. 1979. ed. 1,000, s/n	1,000.00	Sold Out
single deluxe volume, 42 elephant folio size color plates, 27¾″ x 22″, pub FHG. Included w/book were two color plates of identical size, not bound into book, signed & numbered by the artist.		
☐ HARVEST MOON, rel. 1980. ed. 750, s/n, 22″ x 28″, pub FHG	50.00	85.00
ed. 100, s/n, remarqued	130.00	Sold Out
☐ SILENT WINGS, rel. 1980. ed. 600, s/n, 30″ x 21″, pub FHG	75.00	—
☐ DARK WATER MUSKY, rel. 1984. ed. 600, s/n, 25″ x 16½″, pub NC	75.00	—
☐ REFLECTIONS OF THE NORTH, rel. 1984. ed. 600, s/n, 26″ x 15″, pub NC	85.00	—

REFLECTIONS OF THE NORTH-LOON *by Scott Zoellick*

SCOTT ZOELLICK

THEMES: Wildlife art

BOOKS: Zoellick has illustrated numerous books for Raintree Publishing Company and Willow Creek Press

EDUCATION: Milwaukee Institute of Art and Design; University of Wisconsin

AWARDS: Trilene Outdoor Illustration Award (1981); Wisconsin Inland Trout Stamp Design (1983)

GALLERY/DISTRIBUTOR: Northwoods Craftsman

	ISSUE PRICE	CURRENT PRICE
☐ WISCONSIN TROUT STAMP PRINT, rel. 1982. ed. 500, s/n, 14″ x 12″, pub NC	125.00	—
ed. 100 remarqued	125.00	—
☐ STEELHEAD, rel. 1982. ed. 400, s/n, 14″ x 12″, pub NC	45.00	—
☐ TIP-UP, rel. 1982. ed. 450, s/n, 24″ x 17½″, pub NC	50.00	—
☐ AUTUMN MIST-RUFFED GROUSE, rel. 1983. ed. 600, s/n, 28¼″ x 20¼″, pub NC ..	95.00	—
☐ LAST RUN MUSKIE, rel. 1983. ed. 500, s/n, 21½″ x 29″, pub NC	60.00	150.00
☐ 1983 WISCONSIN TROUT STAMP PRINT, rel. 1983. ed. 600, s/n, 14″ x 12″, pub NC	125.00	—
ed. 100, remarqued	250.00	400.00
☐ DARK WATER MUSKIE, rel. 1984. ed. 600, s/n, 25″ x 16½″, pub NC	75.00	150.00
☐ REFLECTIONS OF THE NORTH-LOON, rel. 1984. ed. 600, s/n, 26″ x 15″, pub NC ..	85.00	—
☐ BAD RIVER BUCK, rel. 1985. ed. 600, s/n, 9½″ x 13″, pub NC	40.00	—
☐ CHICKADEE, rel. 1985. ed. 600, s/n, 12″ x 16″, pub NC	60.00	—
☐ GUARD DUTY-LOON, rel. 1985. ed. 600, s/n, 25″ x 18½″, pub NC	95.00	—
☐ WALLEYE, rel. 1985. ed. 600, s/n, 13″ x 9″, pub NC	40.00	—

DONALD ZOLAN

THEMES: Early childhood

MEDIUM: Oil

AWARDS: *Plate Artist of the Year, 1985* (Plate World Magazine); "Sabina in the Grass" was the 1979 Plate of the Year

GALLERY/DISTRIBUTOR: Pemberton & Oakes, Ltd.

COMMENTS: Donald Zolan is one of the best-liked American limited-edition collector plate artists and is known primarily for his works depicting the wonder and joy of early childhood. A soft spoken artist and father of two children, Zolan lives and works in South Barrington, Illinois

	ISSUE PRICE	CURRENT PRICE
☐ **ERIK AND DANDELION,** rel. 1982. ed. 880, s/n, litho, 22″ x 20″, pub P&OL	98.00	178.00
☐ **BY MYSELF,** rel. 1983. ed. 880, s/n, litho, 22″ x 20, pub P&OL	98.00	125.00
☐ **SABINA IN THE GRASS,** rel. 1984. ed. 880, s/n, litho, 22″ x 20″, pub P&OL	98.00	154.00

STAMPS

THE FEDERAL DUCK STAMP

For sometime in the early years of this century there was a great concern for some type of program which would help the United States preserve their wetlands and their waterfowl. Early in the 1930s an idea was presented to the government by J. N. "Ding" Darling who at that time was Chief of the U.S. Bureau of Biological Survey, for a Federal Duck Stamp program and the proceeds to be used for this purpose. In 1934 President Roosevelt signed the Migratory Bird Hunting Stamp Act. At the time few sportsmen, conservationists, and others realized how significant its passing was.

This law was probably the single most important step toward the conservation of waterfowl in United States history. A little known fact is that 90 cents of every dollar collected on the sale of Duck stamps goes toward the purchase and maintenance of waterfowl refuges throughout the United States.

The designer of the first stamp in 1934 was J. H. "Ding" Darling. Then the U.S. Bureau of Biological Survey and the U.S. Bureau of Sport Fisheries and Wildlife, Department of Interior, began a program of stamp design selection through a national contest. The artist is allowed to market prints (original or reproductive) in limited or unlimited editions in order to obtain remunerative benefit from the singular honor of his painting having been selected for the design.

The prints have been issued every year since Mr. Darling's first one in various media and varying editions. Because the second winning design was issued in an edition of only 100 it follows that there can be only 100 complete collections in existence; however, there are many other collections partially complete and naturally many who may own just one print. The companion duck stamp print, signed by the artist and framed along with the duck stamp, has become a very desirable collectible. This makes the print much more meaningful and enjoyable.

The original Duck Stamp sold for $1.00 and the print for $15.00. Over the years the price for the print remained much lower than comparable prints on the market until 1966 when the year's winner, Stanley Stearns, raised the price to $40 to equal the market. The Duck Stamp now costs $7.50.

All of the prints have risen in value since original issuance, many substantially. A few have been printed in second editions. They are available from several dealers throughout the country. A few of these are Russell A. Fink, Wild Wings, Inc., Sportsman's Edge, Ltd., and Midwest Marketing. Please refer to the pages listing Publishers and Distributors for the addresses of these companies.

There are several good sources of additional information about Duck Stamps and prints. Available from the U.S. Government Printing Office, Bureau of Sport Fisheries and Wildlife, Washington, D.C. 20402 are DUCK STAMP DATA, price $10.00 Domestic, $12.50 Foreign; BUY A DUCK STAMP: THE MONEY FROM DUCK STAMP SALES BUYS MORE WETLANDS, price $5.00 Domestic, $6.25, Foreign; DUCK STAMP STORY, which is a small folder, price $1.75 Domestic, $2.20 Foreign; DUCK STAMP PRINTS, third edition, compiled by Jean Pride Stearns and revised by Russell A. Fink, available through Mr. Fink at P.O. Box 250, Lorton, Virginia 22079. It contains much information very useful and valuable to anyone interested in collecting these prints and is updated annually with an inexpensive addition.

FEDERAL DUCK STAMP PRINTS

YEAR	PRINT DESIGN	ARTIST	MEDIUM	EDITION	CURRENT RETAIL PRICE
1934	MALLARDS	"Ding" Darling	Etching	300*	4,400.00
1935	CANVASBACKS	Frank W. Benson	Etching	100	6,800.00
1936	CANADA GEESE	Richard E. Bishop	Etching	unlimited	1,000.00
1937	GREATER SCAUP	J. D. Knap	Gravure	260	3,000.00
1938	PINTAILS	Roland Clark	Etching	300	3,700.00
1939	GREEN WING TEAL	Lynn Bogue Hunt	Stone litho	1st ed. 100*	6,200.00
				2nd ed. 100*	5,700.00
1940	BLACK DUCKS	Francis L. Jacques	Stone litho	1st ed. 30	7,000.00
				2nd ed. 30	6,000.00
				3rd ed. 200	3,500.00
1941	RUDDY DUCKS	E. R. Kalmback	Gravure (rev.)	100-110	3,600.00
			(reg.)	unknown	1,300.00
1942	WIGEON	A. Lassell Ripley	Etching	unlimited	1,200.00
		(signed by Mrs. Ripley)			600.00
1943	WOOD DUCKS	Walter E. Bohl	Etching	unlimited	1,000.00
				2nd ed.	500.00
1944	WHITE FRONT GEESE	Walter A. Weber	Stone litho (rev.)	100	4,500.00
				2nd ed. 200	2,500.00
				3rd ed. 90.00	850.00
1945	SHOVELERS	Owen J. Gromme	Gravure	250	6,200.00
1946	REDHEADS	Robert W. Hines	Stone litho	1st ed. 300*	2,000.00
				2nd ed. 380	150.00
1947	SNOW GEESE	Jack Murray	Gravure	300	2,400.00
1948	BUFFLEHEADS	Maynard Reece	Stone litho	200	1,200.00
				150	1,000.00
				400	600.00
1949	GOLDEN EYES	Roger E. Preuss	Stone litho	250	3,200.00
1950	TRUMPETERS	Walter A. Weber	Gravure	1st ed. 250*	1,500.00
				2nd ed. 300	400.00
1951	GADWALL	Maynard Reece	Stone litho	1st ed. 250	1,500.00
				2nd ed. 400	750.00
1952	HARLEQUINS	John H. Dick	Stone litho	250*	1,100.00
1953	BLUE WING TEAL	Clayton B. Seagears	Stone litho	250*	1,100.00
1954	RING NECKS	Harvey D. Sandstrom	Stone litho	275	1,100.00
1955	BLUE GEESE	Stanley Stears	Etching	1st ed. 1st pr. 250	1,100.00
				1st ed. 2nd pr. 53	1,100.00
				2nd ed. 100	600.00
1956	MERGANSERS	Edward J. Bierly	Etching	1st ed. 325	1,000.00
				2nd pr. 125	800.00
1957	EIDERS	Jackson Miles Abbot	Stone litho	1st ed. 253	1,100.00
				500	300.00

YEAR	PRINT DESIGN	ARTIST	MEDIUM	EDITION	CURRENT RETAIL PRICE
☐ 1958	CANADA GEESE	Leslie C. Kouba	Stone litho	1st ed. 250	1,100.00
				2nd ed. 250	1,000.00
☐ 1959	LABRADOR DOG	Maynard Reece	Stone litho	1st ed. 400	2,700.00
				2nd ed. 300	1,600.00
				3rd ed. 400	900.00
☐ 1960	REDHEADS	John A. Ruthven	Litho	1st ed. 400	1,000.00
				2nd ed. 400	600.00
☐ 1961	MALLARDS	Edward A. Morris	Etching	275	1,100.00
☐ 1962	PINTAILS	Edward A. Morris	Etching	275	1,100.00
☐ 1963	BRANT	Edward J. Bierly	Etching	1st ed. 550	1,000.00
				2nd pr. 125	800.00
☐ 1964	NENE GEESE	Stanley Stearns	Stone litho	1st ed. 300	1,100.00
				2nd ed. 300	700.00
☐ 1965	CANVASBACKS	Ron Jenkins	Stone litho	1st ed. 700	750.00
				2nd ed. 100	600.00
				3rd ed. 250	200.00
☐ 1966	WHISTLING SWANS	Stanley Stearns	Stone litho	1st ed. 300	1,100.00
				2nd ed. 300	500.00
☐ 1967	OLD SQUAWS	Leslie C. Kouba	Etching	275	900.00
☐ 1968	MERGANSERS	Claremont G. Pritchard	Stone litho	750	1,100.00
☐ 1969	SCOTERS	Maynard Reece	Stone litho	750	1,000.00
☐ 1970	ROSS GEESE	Edward J. Bierly	Photo litho-rem.	1,000	3,200.00
			-reg.	total	2,500.00
				2nd ed. 2,150	150.00
☐ 1971	CINNAMON TEAL	Maynard Reece	Stone litho	950	5,200.00
☐ 1972	EMPEROR GEESE	Arthur M. Cook	Photo litho-rem.	950	4,000.00
			-reg.	total	2,800.00
☐ 1973	STELLER'S EIDERS	Lee LeBlanc	Photo litho-rem.	1,000	2,100.00
			-reg.	total	1,900.00
☐ 1974	WOOD DUCKS	David A. Maass	Photo litho	unknown	1,100.00
☐ 1975	CANVASBACK DECOY	James Fisher	Photo litho-rem.	3,150	1,100.00
			-reg.	total	950.00
☐ 1976	CANADA GEESE	Alderson Magee	Photo litho with companion pc.	1,000	2,100.00
			without companion pc.	3,600	1,000.00
☐ 1977	ROSS' GEESE	Martin Murk	Photo litho-rem.	5,800	750.00
			-reg.	total	600.00
☐ 1978	HOODED MERGANSER	Albert Earl Gilbert	Photo litho-rem.	5,800	1,100.00
			-reg.	total	550.00
☐ 1979	GREEN WING TEAL	Ken Michaelson	Photo litho with etching		600.00
			-reg.	total	450.00
☐ 1980	MALLARDS	Richard Plasschaert	Photo litho	12,950	600.00
☐ 1981	RUDDY DUCKS	John Wilson	Photo litho	16,000	300.00
☐ 1982	CANVASBACK	David Maass	Photo litho	22,250	300.00
☐ 1983	PINTAILS	Phil Scholer	Photo litho	17,000	
☐ 1983	PINTAILS	Phil Scholer	Photo litho w/medallion-	17,000 7,000	
			-rem.		1,000.00
			-reg.		450.00
☐ 1984	WIDGEON	William C. Morris	Photo litho	20,400	200.00
			w/medallion	7,800	400.00
☐ 1985	CINNAMON TEAL	Gerald Mobley	Photo litho	N/A	135.00
			w/medallion		250.00

STATE DUCK STAMP PRINTS

Within the last few years a number of states have been issuing Duck Stamp prints also, and below you will find listed the information we have been able to assemble for this edition.

YEAR	ARTIST	MEDIUM	EDITION	CURRENT RETAIL PRICE
ALABAMA				
☐ 1979	Barbara Keel			400.00
☐ 1980	Wayne Spradley			100.00
☐ 1981	Jack Deloney			105.00
☐ 1982	Joe Michalet			105.00
☐ 1983	John P. Lee			105.00
☐ 1984	William C. Morris	s/n	850	125.00
☐ 1985	Larry K. Martin	s/n	1,280	110.00
ALASKA				
☐ 1985	Dan Smith		N/A	140.00
ARKANSAS				
☐ 1981	Lee LeBlanc			
☐ 1982	Maynard Reece			600.00
		-rem.		250.00
☐ 1983	David Maas	s/n w/stamp		175.00
		-rem. w/silver medallion w/stamp		275.00
		-rem. w/gold medallion w/stamp		1,505.50
☐ 1984	Larry Hayden	s/n	7,200	200.00
☐ 1985	Ken Carlson	s/n	7,200	125.00
CALIFORNIA				
☐ 1971	Paul Johnson		500 & 150	700.00
☐ 1972	Paul Johnson		500 & 150	1,800.00
☐ 1973	Paul Johnson		500 & 150	300.00
☐ 1974	Paul Johnson		500 & 150	300.00
☐ 1975	Paul Johnson		500 & 150	300.00
☐ 1976	Paul Johnson		500 & 150	300.00
☐ 1977	Paul Johnson		500 & 150	300.00
☐ 1978	Ken Michaelson		500 & 150	900.00
☐ 1979	Walter Wolfe		500 & 150	850.00
☐ 1980	Walter Wolfe		500 & 150	300.00
☐ 1981	Robert Steiner		1,150 & 300	200.00
☐ 1982	Robert Rickert		950 & 300	175.00
☐ 1983	Charles Allen		750 & 250	125.00
☐ 1984	Robert Montanucci		950	135.00
DELAWARE				
☐ 1980	Ned Mayne		1,980	500.00
☐ 1981	Charles Rowe		1,981	125.00
☐ 1982	Lois Butler		1,982	125.00
☐ 1983	John Green		1,982	125.00
☐ 1984	Nolan Hann		1,980	125.00
FLORIDA				
☐ 1979	Robert Binks	-reg.	1,250	700.00
		-rem.		850.00
☐ 1980	Ernest C. Simmons	-reg.	1,000	100.00
		-rem.		175.00
☐ 1981	Clark Sullivan	-reg.	1,000	100.00
		-rem.		175.00
☐ 1982	Lee Cable	-reg.	1,250	125.00
☐ 1983	Heiner C. Hertling	-reg.	1,000	125.00
		-rem.		200.00
☐ 1984	John Taylor	-reg.	1,000	125.00
		-rem.		200.00

YEAR	ARTIST	MEDIUM	EDITION	CURRENT RETAIL PRICE
☐ 1985	Robert Binks	-reg.	1,000	135.00
		-rem.		235.00
GEORGIA				
☐ 1985 "First of State"				135.00
ILLINOIS				
☐ 1975	Robert F. Eschenfeldt		500	1,400.00
☐ 1976	Robert Larson		500	500.00
☐ 1977	Robert Lynch		500	400.00
☐ 1978	Everett Staffeldt		500	300.00
☐ 1979	John Eggert		500	250.00
☐ 1980	Bart Kassabaum		500	250.00
☐ 1981	Jim Trandell		500	900.00
☐ 1982	Art Sinden		600	150.00
☐ 1983	Bart Kassabaum		600	135.00
☐ 1984	George Kieffer		600	135.00
INDIANA (Discontinued)				
☐ 1976	Sonny Bashore		500	350.00
IOWA				
☐ 1972	Maynard Reece	-reg.	500	4,500.00
		-rem.		5,000.00
☐ 1973	Tom Murphy		500	700.00
☐ 1974	Jim Landenberger		500	1,300.00
☐ 1975	Mark Reece		900	200.00
☐ 1976	Nick Klepinger		600	200.00
☐ 1977	Maynard Reece		900	650.00
☐ 1978	Nick Klepinger		600	200.00
☐ 1979	Andy Peters		800	600.00
☐ 1980	Paul Bridgeford		850	150.00
☐ 1981	Brad Reece		900	150.00
☐ 1982	Tom Walker		600	125.00
☐ 1983	Paul Bridgeford		600	125.00
☐ 1984	Larry Zach		600	135.00
KENTUCKY				
☐ 1985	Ray Harm	-reg.	N/A	140.25
		pencil -rem.		405.25
		color -rem.		555.25
MAINE				
☐ 1984	David Maass			300.00
☐ 1985	David Maass			135.00
MARYLAND				
☐ 1974	John Taylor		500	2,000.00
☐ 1975	Stanley Stearns		650	1,500.00
			2nd ed. 300	550.00
☐ 1976	Louis Frisino		700	900.00
☐ 1977	Jack Schroeder		850	700.00
☐ 1978	Stanley Stearns	-reg.	1,200	200.00
		-rem.		300.00
☐ 1979	John Taylor		1,050	200.00
☐ 1980	Jack Schroeder		1,175	400.00
☐ 1981	Art Eakin		1,250	125.00
☐ 1982	Roger Bucklin		1,575	125.00
☐ 1983	Roger Lent		1,200	125.00
☐ 1984	Carla Huber		1,400	130.00
MASSACHUSETTS				
☐ 1975	Tom Hennessey		500	700.00
☐ 1976	William Tyner		500	150.00
☐ 1977	William Tyner		145	1,400.00
☐ 1978	William Tyner		275	500.00
☐ 1979	Randy Julius		300	450.00
☐ 1980	John Eggert		600	200.00
☐ 1981	Randy Julius		250	250.00
☐ 1982	John Eggert		400	125.00

YEAR	ARTIST	MEDIUM	EDITION	CURRENT RETAIL PRICE
☐ 1983	Randy Julius		250	125.00
☐ 1984	Joseph Cibula		480	150.00
MICHIGAN				
☐ 1976	Oscar Warbach		600	700.00
☐ 1977	Larry Hayden		650	1,200.00
☐ 1978	Richard Timm		700	300.00
☐ 1979	Andrew Kurzman		700	125.00
☐ 1980	Larry Hayden		900	900.00
☐ 1981	Dietmar Krumrey	-reg.	1,200	115.00
		-rem.		210.00
☐ 1982	G. Frankenhuyzen	-reg.	1,200	120.00
		-rem.		220.00
☐ 1983	Rod Lawrence		950	700.00
MINNESOTA				
☐ 1977	David Maass		unknown	1,200.00
☐ 1978	Les Kouba		3,500	700.00
☐ 1979	David Maass		3,800	500.00
☐ 1980	Jim Meger		3,500	600.00
☐ 1981	Terry Redlin		7,800	150.00
☐ 1982	Phil Scholar		6,500	125.00
☐ 1983	Gary Moss		5,000	125.00
☐ 1984	Tom Gross		4,200	135.00
☐ 1985	Terry Redlin			135.00
MISSISSIPPI				
☐ 1976	Kirtley Perkins		500	800.00
☐ 1977	Allen Hughes		500	750.00
☐ 1978	John Reimers		500	450.00
☐ 1979	Carole Hardy		500	400.00
☐ 1980	Robert Thompkins		500	300.00
☐ 1981	John Reimers		500	275.00
☐ 1982	Jerry Johnson		500	250.00
☐ 1983	Gerri Glaster		500	175.00
☐ 1984	Tommy Goodman		500	145.00
MISSOURI				
☐ 1979	Charles W. Schwartz		2,000	400.00
☐ 1980	David Plant	-reg.	1,250	100.00
		-rem.		175.00
☐ 1981	Tom Crane	-reg.	1,000	110.00
		-rem.		180.00
☐ 1982	Gary Lucy	-reg.	1,800	125.00
		-rem.		225.00
☐ 1983	Doug Ross	-reg.	1,000	130.00
		-rem.		230.00
☐ 1984	Glenn Chambers	-reg.	1,000	130.00
		-rem.		230.00
MONTANA				
☐ 1978	Marlowe Urdahl		1,300	300.00
☐ 1979	John Marion		750	150.00
☐ 1980	Ron Jenkins		300	100.00
NEVADA				
☐ 1979	Larry Hayden		2,490	900.00
☐ 1980	Dick McRill		1,990	250.00
☐ 1981	Phil Scholer		2,000	250.00
☐ 1982	Richard Timm		2,200	125.00
☐ 1983	Charles Allen		1,990	125.00
☐ 1984	Robert Steiner		1,990	135.00
NEW HAMPSHIRE				
☐ 1983	Richard Plasschaert		12,000	300.00
☐ 1984	Phillip Crowe		5,507	135.00

YEAR	ARTIST	MEDIUM	EDITION	CURRENT RETAIL PRICE
NEW JERSEY				
☐ 1984	Tom Hirata	-reg.		135.00
		w/medallion		350.00
NEW YORK				
☐ 1985 "First of State"	Larry Barton			135.00
NORTH DAKOTA				
☐ 1982	Richard Plasschaert		9,939	300.00
☐ 1983	Terry Redlin		5,000	135.00
☐ 1984	David Maass			135.00
NORTH CAROLINA				
☐ 1983	Richard Plasschaert			500.00
☐ 1984	James Killen			200.00
☐ 1985	Tom Hirata			135.00
OHIO				
☐ 1982	John Ruthven		9,830	300.00
☐ 1983	Harry Antis		1,350	125.00
☐ 1984	Harold Roe		2,000	125.00
☐ 1985	Ron Lougue	-reg.	2,000	135.00
		pencil rem.		200.00
		color rem.		350.00
OKLAHOMA				
☐ 1980	Pat Sawyer		1,980	500.00
☐ 1981	Hoyt Smith		1,980	125.00
☐ 1982	Jeffrey Frey		1,980	125.00
☐ 1983	Gerald Mobley		1,980	125.00
☐ 1984	Hoyt Smith		1,980	125.00
☐ 1985	Gerald Mobley		1,980	125.00
OREGON				
☐ 1984	Michael Sieve			250.00
PENNSYLVANIA				
☐ 1983	Ned Smith	-reg.	N/A	300.00
		rem. w/medallion		600.00
☐ 1984	James Killen		7,380	135.00
☐ 1985	Ned Smith	-reg.	7,380	135.00
		w/medallion		300.00
SOUTH CAROLINA				
☐ 1981	Lee LeBlanc		3,500	900.00
☐ 1982	Bob Binks	-reg.	4,000	200.00
		-rem.		450.00
☐ 1983	James Killen	-reg.		130.00
		-rem.		250.00
☐ 1984	Al Dornisch		4,000	125.00
SOUTH DAKOTA (Discontinued)				
☐ 1976	Robert Kusserow		500	1,000.00
☐ 1977	Richard Steinbeck		300	800.00
☐ 1978	John Moisan		300	300.00
TENNESSEE				
☐ 1979	Dick Elliott		1,979	500.00
☐ 1980	Philip Crowe		1,250	250.00
☐ 1981	Robert Gillespie		1,200	110.00
☐ 1982	Ken Schultz		1,250	125.00
☐ 1983	Philip Crowe		1,250	125.00
☐ 1984	Allen Hughes		1,250	125.00
☐ 1985	Jimmy Stewart	s/n	1,000	141.50
		-rem.		256.50
TEXAS				
☐ 1981	Larry Hayden		16,500	600.00
☐ 1982	Ken Carlson		9,500	200.00
☐ 1983	Maynard Reece		9,000	450.00
☐ 1984	David Maass		9,000	500.00
☐ 1985	John Cowan	s/n		125.00

YEAR	ARTIST	MEDIUM	EDITION	CURRENT RETAIL PRICE
WISCONSIN				
☐ 1978	Owen Gromme		5,800	300.00
☐ 1979	Rockne Knuth		1,700	350.00
☐ 1980	Martin Murk	-reg.	1,550	800.00
		-rem.		900.00
☐ 1981	Tim Schultz	-reg.	1,700	175.00
		-rem.	300	250.00
☐ 1982	William Koelpin	-reg.	2,300	135.00
	First Day of Issue dating		70	175.00
☐ 1983	Rockne Knuth	-reg.	1,550	175.00
	First Day of Issue dating		50	225.00
☐ 1984	Michael Riddett	reg.	1,500	135.00
	First Day of Issue dating		50	175.00
		pencil -rem.		250.00
		color -rem.		350.00
☐ 1985	Greg Alexander			135.00
		pencil -rem.	100	250.00
		color -rem.	50	350.00
WYOMING				
☐ 1985 "First of State"	Robert Kusserow	-reg.		135.00
		w/medallion		300.00

WILD TURKEY STAMP PRINTS

YEAR	ARTIST	MEDIUM	EDITION	PRICE
NATIONAL FEDERATION				
☐ 1976	Russ Smiley			2,200.00
☐ 1977	Chuck Ripper			250.00
☐ 1978	Richard Amundsen			200.00
☐ 1979	Kenneth Carlson			150.00
☐ 1980	Walter Wolfe			150.00
☐ 1981	David Maass			125.00
☐ 1982	Robert Abbett			125.00
☐ 1983	Lee LeBlanc			125.00
☐ 1984	Richard Plasschaert			125.00
ALABAMA				
☐ 1983	Bill Sanders	-reg.		130.00
		-rem. pencil		200.00
		-rem. color		275.00
LOUISIANA				
☐ 1981	Don Edwards	-reg.		400.00
		-rem. pencil		500.00
		-rem. color		600.00
☐ 1982	Richard Sloan	-reg.		125.00
		-rem. pencil		250.00
		-rem. color		375.00
☐ 1983	Richard Plasschaert	-reg.		130.00
		-rem.		none
MISSOURI				
☐ 1983	Maynard Reece			130.00
NEW YORK				
☐ 1982	Peter Corbin			130.00
NORTH DAKOTA				
☐ 1983	Susan Pederson			100.00
PENNSYLVANIA				
☐ 1981	Ned Smith			275.00
☐ 1982	Larry Toschick			130.00

CONSERVATION STAMP PRINTS

YEAR	ARTIST	MEDIUM	EDITION	CURRENT RETAIL PRICE
DEER UNLIMITED				
☐ 1980	Ralph McDonald		1,000	**450.00**
☐ 1981	Lee LeBlanc		2,000	**200.00**
☐ 1982	Ed Bierly		1,500	**125.00**
☐ 1983	Dalhart Windberg			**125.00**
IOWA HABITAT				
☐ 1979	Pat Costello		1,300	**500.00**
☐ 1980	Andy Peters		600	**500.00**
☐ 1981	Maynard Reece		950	**600.00**
☐ 1982	Tom Walker		650	**400.00**
☐ 1983	Paul Bridgeford		600	**125.00**
☐ 1984	Ken Wind		600	**110.00**
IOWA TROUT				
☐ 1974	Craig Ritland		380	**225.00**
☐ 1975	Jim Landenberger		380	**250.00**
☐ 1976	Ken Prestley		425	**175.00**
☐ 1977	John Bald		425	**175.00**
☐ 1978	Robert Alsbury		650	**150.00**
☐ 1979	Jim Landenberger		380	**250.00**
☐ 1980	Paul Bridgeford		380	**200.00**
☐ 1981	Nick Klepinger		350	**100.00**
☐ 1982	Maynard Reece		950	**250.00**
☐ 1983	Paul Bridgeford			**125.00**
☐ 1984	Tom Carter			**125.00**
MARYLAND TROUT				
☐ 1977	Louis Frisino		500	**300.00**
☐ 1978	Louis Frisino		500	**200.00**
☐ 1979	Louis Frisino		700	**150.00**
☐ 1980	Louis Frisino		700	**75.00**
RUFFED GROUSE SOCIETY				
☐ 1979	Jim Foote		980	**1,800.00**
☐ 1980	David Maass		1,380	**400.00**
☐ 1981	David Hagerbaumer		1,780	**250.00**
☐ 1982	Robert Abbett		1,780	**175.00**
☐ 1983	Maynard Reece		1,800	**175.00**
☐ 1984	Gary Moss		1,800	**125.00**
SOUTH DAKOTA PHEASANT				
☐ 1977	Richard Sloan		Unlimited	**450.00**
☐ 1978	Robert Kusserow		300	**300.00**
☐ 1979	John Wilson		300	**600.00**
☐ 1980	John Moisan		300	**200.00**
☐ 1981	John Wilson		600	**500.00**
☐ 1982	Robert Kusserow		500	**110.00**
☐ 1983	Rosemary Mallete		500	**110.00**
☐ 1984	Robert Kusserow		500	**110.00**
☐ 1985	Rosemary Mallete		500	**115.00**
WILD SHEEP FOUNDATION				
☐ 1980	Gary Swanson		1,300	**450.00**
☐ 1981	Robert Kuhn		1,500	**200.00**
☐ 1982	Ken Carlson		1,300	**150.00**
☐ 1983	Robert Bateman		1,300	**300.00**
WISCONSIN GREAT LAKES SALMON and TROUT				
☐ 1982	Martin Murk		850	**275.00**
	First Day of Issue dating		200	**350.00**
		-rem.	125	**550.00**
☐ 1983	Chuck Mitchell		650	**135.00**
	First Day of Issue dating		35	**175.00**
			750	**125.00**

YEAR	ARTIST	MEDIUM	EDITION	CURRENT RETAIL PRICE
☐ 1984	Rockne Knuth		750	125.00
	First Day of Issue dating		75	175.00
		-rem.	100	250.00
☐ 1985	Sam Timm		600	135.00
		-rem. pencil	100	250.00
		-rem. color	50	350.00
WISCONSIN TROUT				
☐ 1978	Tom Rost	-reg.	600	250.00
		-rem.		450.00
☐ 1979	Martin Murk	-reg.	600	500.00
		-rem.		900.00
☐ 1980	Robert Frankowiak	-reg.	600	350.00
		-rem.		600.00
☐ 1981	Tom Rost	-reg.	600	250.00
		-rem.		400.00
☐ 1982	Nick Pitt	-reg.	600	125.00
		-rem.		250.00
☐ 1983	Scott Zoellick	-reg.	500	125.00
		-rem.		250.00
☐ 1984	Tim Schultz	-reg.	500	135.00
		-rem.		275.00
☐ 1985	Sam Timm	-reg.	500	135.00
		-rem.		275.00

READER SURVEY

The House of Collectibles continually seeks to improve, expand, and update the material in *The Offical Price Guide Series*. The assistance and cooperation of numerous collectors and dealers have added immeasurably to the success of the books in this series. Please take a few seconds and give us your help so we can provide you with information needed to become a successful collector.

Name _____ Phone (___) _____

Address _____

City _____ State _____ Zip _____

Age Group: ☐ under 18 ☐ 18-24 ☐ 25-34 ☐ 35-44 ☐ 45-54 ☐ 55 & over

Title of book purchased _____

Date of purchase _____

Name & address of bookshop _____

_____

Reason for purchase: ☐ I was looking for a book about this subject.
☐ I had the previous edition.   ☐ I saw it advertised.
☐ I saw it in a public library.   ☐ It was recommended to me.

Do you plan to buy the new revised
edition of this book when it's published?   ☐ Definitely   ☐ Probably   ☐ No

Did you have difficulty locating a bookshop
that carries The House of Collectibles titles?   ☐ Yes   ☐ No

Is this the first House of Collectibles book that you've purchased?   ☐ Yes   ☐ No

Is there any way you feel this book could be improved? _____

_____

How do you feel this book compares with other books about the same subject?

_____

Check the publisher's catalogue at the back of this book, then tell us:
are there any titles you'd like to see added to our series? _____

_____

Would you consider yourself primarily a:
☐ Collector   ☐ Dealer   ☐ Investor   ☐ Home Decorator   ☐ General Reader

Do you have any information not included
in the book but which you think should be?   ☐ Yes   ☐ No

If you do, would you be interested
in becoming a contributor to a future edition?   ☐ Yes   ☐ No
(If your answer is yes, we'll be contacting you will full details on how you can become an "Official Member" of the world's largest hobby publishing team!)

THE OFFICIAL PRICE GUIDES TO:	
☐ 465-8 **American Silver & Silver Plate** 4th Ed.	10.95
☐ 482-8 **Antique Clocks** 3rd Ed.	10.95
☐ 283-3 **Antique & Modern Dolls** 3rd Ed.	10.95
☐ 287-6 **Antique & Modern Firearms** 6th Ed.	11.95
☐ 271-X **Antiques & Other Collectibles** 6th Ed.	9.95
☐ 289-2 **Antique Jewelry** 5th Ed.	11.95
☐ 270-1 **Beer Cans & Collectibles,** 3rd Ed.	7.95
☐ 262-0 **Bottles Old & New** 9th Ed.	10.95
☐ 255-8 **Carnival Glass** 1st Ed.	10.95
☐ 453-4 **Collectible Cameras** 2nd Ed.	10.95
☐ 277-9 **Collectibles of the Third Reich** 2nd Ed.	10.95
☐ 281-7 **Collectible Toys** 3rd Ed.	10.95
☐ 490-9 **Collector Cars** 6th Ed.	11.95
☐ 267-1 **Collector Handguns** 3rd Ed.	11.95
☐ 290-6 **Collector Knives** 8th Ed.	11.95
☐ 266-3 **Collector Plates** 4th Ed.	11.95
☐ 476-3 **Collector Prints** 6th Ed.	11.95
☐ 489-5 **Comic Books & Collectibles** 8th Ed.	9.95
☐ 433-X **Depression Glass** 1st Ed.	9.95
☐ 472-0 **Glassware** 2nd Ed.	10.95
☐ 492-5 **Hummel Figurines & Plates** 5th Ed.	9.95
☐ 451-8 **Kitchen Collectibles** 2nd Ed.	10.95
☐ 291-4 **Military Collectibles** 5th Ed.	11.95
☐ 268-X **Music Collectibles** 5th Ed.	11.95
☐ 491-7 **Old Books & Autographs** 6th Ed.	10.95
☐ 298-1 **Oriental Collectibles** 3rd Ed.	11.95
☐ 297-3 **Paper Collectibles** 5th Ed.	10.95
☐ 276-0 **Pottery & Porcelain** 5th Ed.	11.95
☐ 263-9 **Radio, T.V. & Movie Memorabilia** 2nd Ed.	11.95
☐ 288-4 **Records** 7th Ed.	10.95
☐ 485-2 **Royal Doulton** 4th Ed.	10.95
☐ 280-4 **Science Fiction & Fantasy Collectibles** 2nd Ed.	10.95
☐ 477-1 **Wicker** 3rd Ed.	10.95
THE OFFICIAL:	
☐ 445-3 **Collector's Journal** 1st Ed.	4.95
☐ 365-1 **Encyclopedia of Antiques** 1st Ed.	9.95
☐ 369-4 **Guide to Buying & Selling Antiques** 1st Ed.	9.95
☐ 414-3 **Identification Guide to Early American Furniture** 1st Ed.	9.95
☐ 413-5 **Identification Guide to Glassware** 1st Ed.	9.95
☐ 448-8 **Identification Guide to Gunmarks** 2nd Ed.	9.95
☐ 412-7 **Identification Guide to Pottery & Porcelain** 1st Ed.	9.95
☐ 415-1 **Identification Guide to Victorian Furniture** 1st Ed.	9.95

THE OFFICIAL (POCKET SIZE) PRICE GUIDES TO:	
☐ 473-9 **Antiques & Flea Markets** 3rd Ed.	3.95
☐ 442-9 **Antique Jewelry** 2nd Ed.	3.95
☐ 264-7 **Baseball Cards** 5th Ed.	4.95
☐ 488-7 **Bottles** 2nd Ed.	4.95
☐ 468-2 **Cars & Trucks** 2nd Ed.	4.95
☐ 260-4 **Collectible Americana** 1st Ed.	4.95
☐ 294-9 **Collectible Records** 3rd Ed.	4.95
☐ 469-0 **Collector Guns** 2nd Ed.	4.95
☐ 474-7 **Comic Books** 3rd Ed.	3.95
☐ 486-0 **Dolls** 3rd Ed.	4.95
☐ 292-2 **Football Cards** 5th Ed.	4.95
☐ 258-2 **Glassware** 2nd Ed.	4.95
☐ 487-9 **Hummels** 3rd Ed.	4.95
☐ 441-0 **Military Collectibles** 2nd Ed.	3.95
☐ 480-1 **Paperbacks & Magazines** 3rd Ed.	4.95
☐ 443-7 **Pocket Knives** 2nd Ed.	3.95
☐ 479-8 **Scouting Collectibles** 3rd Ed.	4.95
☐ 439-9 **Sports Collectibles** 2nd Ed.	3.95
☐ 494-1 **Star Trek/Star Wars Collectibles** 3rd Ed.	3.95
☐ 493-3 **Toys** 3rd Ed.	4.95
THE OFFICIAL BLACKBOOK PRICE GUIDES TO:	
☐ 284-1 **U.S. Coins** 24th Ed.	3.95
☐ 286-8 **U.S. Paper Money** 18th Ed.	3.95
☐ 285-X **U.S. Postage Stamps** 8th Ed.	3.95
THE OFFICIAL INVESTORS GUIDE TO BUYING & SELLING:	
☐ 496-8 **Gold, Silver and Diamonds** 2nd Ed.	9.95
☐ 497-6 **Gold Coins** 2nd Ed.	9.95
☐ 498-4 **Silver Coins** 2nd Ed.	9.95
☐ 499-2 **Silver Dollars** 2nd Ed.	9.95
THE OFFICIAL NUMISMATIC GUIDE SERIES:	
☐ 481-X **Coin Collecting** 3rd Ed.	9.95
☐ 254-X **The Official Guide to Detecting Counterfeit Money** 2nd Ed.	7.95
☐ 257-3 **The Official Guide to Mint Errors** 4th Ed.	7.95
☐ 256-6 **The Official Hewitt-Donlon Price Guide to Small Size Paper Money** 15th Ed.	7.95
☐ 162-4 **Variety & Oddity Guide of U.S. Coins** 8th Ed.	4.95
SPECIAL INTEREST SERIES:	
☐ 506-9 **From Hearth to Cookstove** 3rd Ed.	17.95
☐ 370-8 **Lucky Number Lottery Guide** 1st Ed.	3.50
☐ 504-2 **On Method Acting** 8th Printing	6.95
TOTAL	

FOR IMMEDIATE DELIVERY

VISA & MASTER CARD CUSTOMERS

ORDER TOLL FREE!
1-800-638-6460

This number is for orders only; it is not tied into the customer service or business office. Customers not using charge cards must use mail for ordering since payment is required with the order—sorry no C.O.D.'s.

OR SEND ORDERS TO ▮ ▮ ▮ ▮ ▮ ▮

THE HOUSE OF COLLECTIBLES, *P.O. Box 149 Westminster, MD 21157 (301) 583-6959*

┌─── POSTAGE & HANDLING RATE CHART ───┐

TOTAL ORDER/POSTAGE	TOTAL ORDER/POSTAGE	
0 to $10.00 - **$1.25**	$20.01 to $30.00 - **$2.00**	$50.01 & Over -
$10.01 to $20.00 - **$1.50**	$30.01 to $40.00 - **$2.75**	**Add 10% of your total order**
	$40.01 to $50.00 - **$3.50**	(Ex. $75.00 x .10 = $7.50)

Total from columns on reverse side. Quantity _____ $_____

☐ Check or money order enclosed $_____ (include postage and handling)

☐ Please charge $_____ to my: ☐ MASTERCARD ☐ VISA

Charge Card Customers Not Using Our Toll Free Number Please Fill Out The Information Below.

Account No. (All Digits) _____ Expiration Date _____

Signature _____

Name (please print) _____ PHONE _____

ADDRESS _____ APT. # _____ (10)

CITY _____ STATE _____ ZIP _____